Alexis Lichine's
New
Encyclopedia of
WINES
&Spirits

FIFTH EDITION
Revised

Alexis Lichine's New Encyclopedia of Wines & Spirits

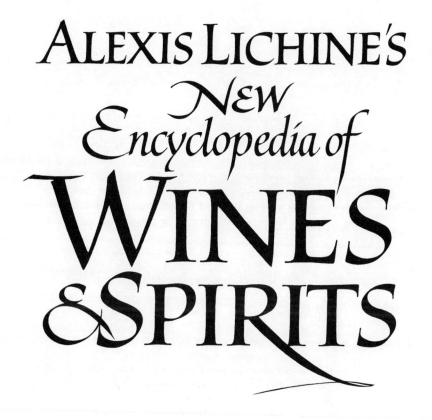

IN COLLABORATION WITH

William Fifield

AND WITH THE ASSISTANCE OF

Jonathan Bartlett, Jane Stockwood, John Laird,
Samuel Perkins, and Katie Philson

NEW YORK   *Alfred A. Knopf*   1987

THIS IS A BORZOI BOOK
PUBLISHED BY ALFRED A. KNOPF, INC.

Copyright © 1967, 1974, 1981, 1982, 1984, 1985, 1987 by Alexis Lichine

Library of Congress Cataloging-in-Publication Data
Lichine, Alexis.
Alexis Lichine's new encyclopedia of wines & spirits.

Bibliography: p.
Includes index.
1. Wine and wine making—Dictionaries. I. Title.
II. Title: New encyclopedia of wines & spirits.
III. Title: New encyclopedia of wines and spirits.
TP546.L5   1987   641.2'22'0321   85–2590
ISBN 0–394–56262–3

Manufactured in the United States of America

First Edition published November 6, 1967
Reprinted seven times
Second Edition, completely revised, enlarged, and reset, October 1974
Second Printing, corrected and updated, August 1976
Third Printing, corrected and updated, November 1977
Fourth Printing, corrected and updated, November 1978
Fifth Printing, corrected and updated, November 1979
Third Edition, fully revised and with a new appendix, published April 1981
Reprinted twice
Second Printing, corrected and updated March 1982
Third Printing, corrected and updated, April 1984
Fourth Edition, revised, published August 1985
Reprinted twice
Fifth Edition, fully revised, published October 1987

To Sacha and Sandra,

raised in the vineyards of France

and now grown to be my companions

in the enjoyment of wine

Contents

Preface

This book is written for the consumer and those in the trade whose function it is to relate the taste, traditions, and knowledge of wine, the subtle changes between one vineyard and another, and the inescapable limitations of fine wines produced from limited acreage. Such knowledge adds immeasurably to the real enjoyment of a good bottle. Also, it helps to blow away the cobwebs from a subject which, for too long, has been shrouded in mystery. Some of the people who approach wine with awe are not even sure that it is made from grapes. That is why so much attention has been given in this book to the sciences of viticulture and wine-making. Detailed information on these matters—as well as on the history, value, and serving of wine—will be found in the chapters which precede the alphabetical entries.

It has been impossible, because of restrictions of space, to give every topic its own entry, and some subjects will be found included under an entry of greater importance. No hard and fast rules have been laid down, however. Wine is a subject of infinite flexibility, and every aspect is treated according to its individual merits and placed where it seems to fit best. It should therefore be stressed that full use must be made of the index, which in cases of doubt will quickly pinpoint all references to a particular aspect of any subject. The appendixes supply complete documentation of such matters as cooperage and bottle sizes, useful conversion tables, lists of worthy but non-classified châteaux of the Bordeaux region, and complete lists of the register of German vineyards. Any production figure quoted in the text is a mean average unless a specific figure is given as representing a typical year. These figures are naturally subject to the fluctuations of season from year to year. Any regulations quoted in the encyclopedia are in force at the time of going to press, but some are liable to annual amendment.

In order to make quite clear when reference is being made to the genuine wine and when to an imitation of it, an initial capital letter is given to such wines as Sherry, Port, Burgundy, etc. only when they are legally restricted wines coming from Spain, Portugal, France, etc.

My first book, *Wines of France* (since completely rewritten and published as a new book, *Alexis Lichine's Guide to the Wines and Vineyards of France*), was so well received and widely bought that I decided to embark, in somewhat the same manner, on a general survey of the wines and spirits of the world. This volume would not, however, have been possible without the particular collaboration of the following persons:

The late Herr Karl Ress, not only a great taster, but one whose sincere dedication to his beloved Rheingau was an invaluable source of information for that and other important German wine regions. His son Joachim has admirably followed in his late father's footsteps, generously contributing to all revised editions.

Dr. Franz Werner Michel of the Stabilisierungsfonds für Wein in Mainz, who has been especially helpful in seeing that all the German entries are up to date, reflecting the changes of the West German wine laws.

Mr. Peter M. F. Sichel of New York, the final member of this faithful trio, each of whom has done so much to assure the completeness of the new German entries.

Dr. Maynard Amerine, the leading oenologist of the United States, whose technical assistance has been sought by governments throughout the world. His books, reflecting his knowledge of the science of modern wine-making, are respected by such authorities as Dr. Peynaud and Dr. Ribéreau-Gayon of France; and he is a wine-lover who realizes that wine is not only a science, but also one of the civilizing graces.

Monsieur Patrick Leon, formerly of Alexis Lichine & Co. and now with the Baronnie of Philippe de Rothschild, who spent long hours and many late nights checking the small vineyards of France and their production, with the result that no other book published, even in France, can approach this one in the wide range of statistics surveyed.

Monsieur Claude Taittinger, who has given of his time and knowledge to ensure that the Champagne entry is as complete and authoritative as it can possibly be.

The late Monsieur François Hine, Cognac-shipper of Jarnac, whose jovial nature was as internationally esteemed as his product.

Messieurs Protin and Friedas of the Office International du Vin, Paris, who kindly offered important statistical information on the wine-producing countries around the world, and so generously supplied some of the many maps, once intended for publication as a separate wine atlas.

The late Prof. Georges Portmann of Bordeaux, who, as the successor to Louis Pasteur, contributed willingly to the chapter on wine and health.

Monsieur Pierre Perromat, wine-grower and former president of the I.N.A.O., whose kindness is reflected on many pages of this book.

Monsieur Pierre Bréjoux, former inspector-general of the I.N.A.O., who personally checked the entries on his native Anjou and gave freely of his time for the preparation of entries on the recent Appellations Contrôlées.

The late Dr. Philippe Dufaye, who abandoned medicine to become a wine-grower in Châteauneuf-du-Pape, feeling that he could find a fuller and happier life dealing with the nature of the soil than with human nature.

Monsieur Georges Duboeuf, a dedicated broker who started off as a grower, and who today, with his qualifications for selecting wines and working toward the unity of Beaujolais growers, has become the outstanding personality of his famous wine region. His colleague, Monsieur Michel Brun, also provided great assistance.

The more than fifty brokers, shippers, owners, and knowledgeable friends who helped with the revision of the Bordeaux wine classification appearing on pages 127–129. Once the pressures of politics and bias are removed, reasonable men are capable of ranking with constructive good will the red wines of the Gironde. The frank opinions of these advisers have been kept privileged as promised, so as not to hinder their daily work in the Bordeaux marketplace.

Mr. Len Evans, whose great knowledge of Australian wines, and of their ever-increasing importance throughout the world, has been most valuable.

Dr. Bruno Roncarati of London, who made an effective beginning in the sorting out of the vast array of D.O.C. Italian wines.

Miss Jane Stockwood, who has worked diligently with me over the past twenty years, who shared my frustration when 20 per cent of the manuscript was inadvertently destroyed by a typist, and gave me a helping hand in getting the missing sections into order again. If it had not been for her, this book would never have reached the publishers.

Mr. John Laird, an able student of wines, who gave yeoman service during the year-long revision of this book in 1974.

Mr. Sam Perkins and Mr. Martin Sinkoff, who in 1978 and 1979 assisted with its further updating; Miss Katie Philson, who efficiently continued her work in 1980, 1981, 1983 and 1986; Anne Gay in 1986, who dedicated months in helping to update this fifth edition; and finally, thanks to the thorough efforts of Kerry Stewart, the German entries have been updated to reflect the latest changes up to and including 1987.

The chapter describing the wines of the United States has been totally revised and updated in this edition. Among others, I owe many thanks to Craig Goldwyn, whose assistance and knowledge of eastern wines—not least the wines and vineyards of New York State—have been invaluable to me.

All those who were close to me in the original thirteen years starting in 1954, when I optimistically believed this book would be finished in 1959 and not 1967. And the many friends who worked patiently through the massive 1974 and 1987 revisions, which both began as an updating, but ended as expansions of most of the book.

Others, too many to name here, have given me considerable help, and these are listed on pages 725–729.

ALEXIS LICHINE

Nota Bene: The author began work on this volume in 1954, and it was first published in 1967. Over the course of subsequent editions or reprintings, the work has undergone eleven major revisions to keep pace with the ongoing developments, major and minor, in the world of wines and spirits. In the interests of continuing to keep the book up to date, the author would greatly appreciate hearing from readers of this 1987 edition concerning any changes they are aware of, so that these may be incorporated into future editions.

Alexis Lichine
Château Prieuré-Lichine
33 460 Margaux-en-Médoc

Introduction

I can truthfully say that since I reached the age of discretion I have consistently drunk more than most people would say was good for me. Nor do I regret it. Wine has been to me a firm friend and a wise counsellor. Often wine has shown me matters in their true perspective, and has, as though by the touch of a magic wand, reduced great disasters to small inconveniences.

Wine has lit up for me the pages of literature, and revealed in life romance lurking in the commonplace.

Wine has made me bold but not foolish; has induced me to say silly things but not to do them.

Under its influence words have often come too easily which had better not have been spoken, and letters have been written which had better not have been sent.

But if such small indiscretions standing in the debit column of wine's account were added up, they would amount to nothing in comparison with the vast accumulation on the credit side.

Duff Cooper: OLD MEN FORGET

Wine as a business is of international importance, an affair of vast ramifications. It provides a livelihood for some 35 million people throughout the world. More than 10 million hectares (nearly 25 million acres) of the earth's surface are planted in vines. Each year the world's harvest is some 300 million hectoliters (7.94 billion U.S. gallons, 6.6 billion imp.), or roughly the equivalent of 3.5 billion cases of wine. And more than one-quarter of this great quantity comes from the Common Market countries. If all the vineyards were laid low by a sudden plague, millions of people would be thrown out of work or ruined, many others would be hard-hit, and an unmanageable economic crisis would follow.

As the world becomes increasingly industrialized and standards more materialistic, as automation brings more leisure, people everywhere expect a share in the good things of life—the pleasures of civilized eating and drinking among them. It is harder now to find young men prepared to give the necessary time and devotion to the cultivation of the vine. Yet, in the cities, interest in wine, far from declining, is growing all the time.

Since the publication of the first edition of this book in 1967, interest in wines all over the world—and especially in the United States—has grown as never before. There are still those for whom drinking wine

revolves around the First Classified Growths of the Médoc, which have become the most expensive red wines in the world; but for the more broad-minded recent convert, with perhaps less money to spend, this new edition gives thorough attention to the less well-known growths from nearly every wine-producing country on the globe. Though the wines of Bordeaux and some of Burgundy have fluctuated in price, the importance of the many other different wines can only continue to increase, as each nation recognizes the value of its own wines; the tremendous expansion of viticulture in California (and the increase in price for premium California wines) is but one example of this increasing awareness. The new West German, Italian, Spanish, and South African wine laws are another result. After having suffered the record prices of the first years of the world wine boom, the consumer can look forward to greatly improved average-quality wines achieved through the application of oenological know-how.

A bursting desire for a way of life closer to nature has impelled Australians and Americans from coast to coast to turn to vine-growing and wine-making, especially in California. New vineyards and wineries popped up in increasing numbers in newly found areas during the seventies and eighties. In this fifth edition I have tried to reflect these changes.

Thus wine, one of the first and now one of the most passionate interests of civilized man, is at once a major industry and a major pleasure of life. The figures comparing yearly *per capita* consumption in different countries vary greatly and make interesting reading. In the lead is Portugal, whose inhabitants annually consume some 85 liters (about 22.4 U.S. gallons, 18.7 imp.) *per capita*. France and Italy seesaw back and forth between second and third place, each with an average consumption of around 82 liters. Argentina, with 66 liters, ranks fourth, and in fifth place is Spain, with some 57 liters downed annually per person. In the course of a year, an average American will drink scarcely nine liters (somewhat over two gallons), a little more than an Englishman, but one-fifth the consumption of a Greek, Swiss, Chilean, Austrian, or Luxembourgeois. A Russian, who used to consume very little wine, has lately seen his country's vineyards and imports expand by more than 60 percent, and now drinks rather more wine than does the American; but the wine itself is considerably inferior in quality to that which the Australian or the American puts in his glass.

As more and more people travel and acquire a taste for good wine, the civilized custom of having a bottle on the table gains ground. Will demand outrun supply? In the past half dozen years, it indeed has for some superior wines in certain parts of the world; hence the price spiral of the early eighties. Though some regions can still increase their vineyard acreage, Burgundy, for example, has reached its maximum; and some fine and famous areas are extraordinarily small: 2,000 hectares (5,000 acres) for the whole Chablis district. (Compare this figure with the thousands of bottles labeled "Chablis" to be found on restaurant tables all over the world and draw your own conclusions.)

The present cry is for more of everything, turned out faster and more cheaply. If there is one thing which does not respond to this call, it is great wine. It can be made expensively but still will not increase in quantity. It can be made in bulk but will not then be a fine wine. The best wines have always been those from comparatively nonproductive grapevines—which are pruned short in order to reduce output and channel the plant's energy into the production of superior fruit. Because the grower cannot at the same time obtain both quantity and quality, enlightened laws have been set up to limit production. That is why the statistics of this book represent the amount the soil can produce—not the amount to which an unscrupulous merchant may, accordion-like, stretch his merchandise, while his labels claim for it the geographical limitations of a vineyard, a district, or even a region to which it has no right. In these malpractices many countries have been at fault.

At this time there is an oversupply of bulk wines coming from many parts of the world, especially Spain, Australia, and certain regions of southern France. Since 1982 there has been an increase of 20 per cent in world production, to about 400 million hectoliters per year (10.56 billion U.S. gallons, 8.79 imp.), which can be accounted for by the overproduction of ordinary wines. This trend can only be cut back by more judicious matching of better grape varieties to the soil and greater care in finding the proper microclimates. California is pulling ahead in this regard. Until a decade ago, 50 per cent of its production was appropriate only for use as table grapes or raisins, but the state now grows more of the better *Vinifera* varieties. In the interest of the consumer and the top producers of California wine, the B.A.T.F. or the Bureau of Alcohol, Tobacco and Firearms of the U.S. government and the state of California are taking a well-advised hard look at the philosophy of the Appellation Contrôlée laws enacted in France and of similar laws in other Common Market countries; and a number of well-considered appellations or place-names have been legally established in the United States. But stricter control of place-names is still needed in California, where many of the mediocre wines of the central valley and southern parts of the state seek refuge under the umbrella of quality wines produced by the best wineries in the northern counties.

There have been other recent changes throughout the world regarding the sale and distribution of bulk wine. These include huge imports of Algerian wine by the Soviet Union. Prior to the independence of Algeria, most of this country's production was used for blending with the *vin du Midi* or *vin ordinaire* of France, and for bolstering certain Burgundies. Now the Soviet Union is trying to fight vodka alcoholism with the promotion of Algerian wines, and currently the French are bringing in Italian wines, high in alcoholic content, to replace the Algerian. This has become profitable since the devaluation of the lira, and since these wines can be imported duty-free as a result of the Common Market.

In this book I have set out to represent wine in terms of today. By stressing the small production of the great vineyards, I hope to be able to guide the consumer through the mazes of nomenclature and of impermissible—as against permissible and honest—blending. For the contemporary trend toward a standard product is one which creates difficulty for the wine-maker. His harvest will be different in different years. He may honestly blend them toward uniformity —but no blending vat in the world is capable of turning out a standard wine of the highest quality. Fine wines will survive if the consumer insists on higher and more regular standards. That is what this book is dedicated to.

Clearly, the average wine-drinker cannot expect to enjoy the greatest wines every day. Even if he could afford to, there would soon not be enough to go around. But the supply of sound, honest wines is fortunately not short. Bordeaux is one region which has been able to increase the size of some of its classified vineyards by as much as 30 per cent; and the American customer, who once believed he must always aim as high as Château Lafite, has learned to extend his knowledge not only to the other Classified Growths offering great quality but also to the unclassified ones and the many sound regional wines. He will be quite content if he—and the shippers—will get used to honest labeling, and if he does not expect a true Pommard for the price of an ordinary red Burgundy. Conversely, experience will teach him that for the price of a commercial Liebfraumilch (even with the 1971 West German Wine Law, and despite the 1982 EEC regulations, it is a rather meaningless name unless backed by a good shipper), he can find a wine from a good vineyard and double his enjoyment.

As Ernest Hemingway wrote in *Death in the Afternoon*, "A person with increasing knowledge and sensory education may derive infinite enjoyment from wine."

I have tried, in what follows, to help the reader distinguish the small wine from the great, and by comparing one with the other, to educate his palate and develop his taste and his pleasure. To quote again from Hemingway: "Wine is one of the most civilized things in the world, and one of the material things of the world that has been brought to the greatest perfection and which offers a greater range of enjoyment and appreciating than, possibly, any other purely sensory thing which may be purchased."

1 History of Wine

The history of wine is inextricably interwoven with the history of man. It has been said that civilization grew out of agriculture: when the first nomads planted seeds and waited for the crop to grow, their wandering ceased. It might be as true to say that it was with wine that civilization began, for the vine takes longer to mature than any other crop, and does not produce grapes for the *vendange* until its fourth year—after four years in one place, a nomad tribe would be well settled and already practiced in domestic arts.

We do not know when men first had wine, but it was accepted as a gift from the gods: the Egyptians attributed it to Osiris, the Greeks to Dionysos; the Armenians maintained that Noah planted the first vineyard near Erivan. Since grape seeds have been found in prehistoric caves, it is conceivable that wine is older than history—although it is unlikely that the cavemen knew how to ferment their grapes. That discovery, when it came, was probably accidental. According to one legend, a Persian king who was very fond of grapes stored some away in a great jar marked *Poison*. Some time afterward, one of the neglected beauties of his harem, tired of life, drank from the jar—and the poison was by then so delicious that, much revived, she took a cup to the king, who drank from it, took the lady back into favor, and ordained that thereafter the grapes should be allowed to ferment. However they discovered it, the Persians evidently loved wine: according to Herodotus, all important matters were discussed twice in the councils of state—once when they were drinking, and again when they were sober.

Mesopotamia and the Caucasian slopes were no doubt early sources of wine: the Libation Scene in the "Standard" panel from Ur (now in the British Museum) dates from the first half of the third millennium before Christ. In Egypt, vineyards were being planted for funerary wines soon after 3000 B.C., and legendary tales of wine-drinking in China date from much the same period. In any case, it is believed that Greece, the first European country to make wine, received the art from the East, and also, no doubt, from Egypt.

The earliest records of wine in Egypt are the sealing inscriptions on the stoppers of amphorae found in pre-Dynastic tombs. In early days, the king had his own vineyard, from which the funeral wines came, and (according to H. F. Lutz) a domestic vine-plot to provide his table wine. Vineyards belonging to important persons were given names: Rameses III (1198–1166

B.C.) developed the famous Ka-n-komet, as well as new plantations in oases. Another, more long-winded name was King Zoser's "Praised be Horus, who is in the front of Heaven"—the wine from there was sometimes more succinctly described as "Beverage of Horus." Wine labels, on the other hand, could be models of clarity: "In the year xxx Good wine of the large irrigated terrain of the Temple of Rameses II in Per-Amon. The chief of the wine-dressers, Tutmes." Would that all labels were as honest, explicit, and simply expressed.

In the unchanging climate of Africa, vintage years were not very important. But soil matters vitally to the vine, wherever it grows, so the Egyptians were concerned about the sites of their vineyards. The vines grew best near the Delta, where they were irrigated by the annual flooding of the Nile—but since marsh is not the land for them, the walled vineyards were planted on artificially raised plots.

The reliefs and wall-paintings in the tombs, in which so clear a picture of Egyptian life is preserved, show workers harvesting the vine with curved knives like the hand-sickles still occasionally in use, the grapes being picked by women and dropped into wicker baskets to be carried on the men's backs—or balanced on shoulder yokes—to the press. The Egyptians used fermenting vats of acacia wood, in which they trod the grapes in a compulsive rhythm, sung and clapped out by hand—this is a sight familiar to everyone who has watched the vintage on the Douro or in Spain. Nor does the parallel with modern times end there: a certain Bilgai, "Overseer of the Fortress of the Sea," shamelessly recorded, on a stele, that he had assessed the people 23,568 measures of wine in excess of his due as tax-collector. Moreover, the Code of Hammurabi (Babylon, *c.* 2000 B.C.) stipulated the conditions under which wine could be bought, and a seller who gave short measure was thrown into the water—then, as now, there was fraud in the business.

We know little about the wine of the common people because they lacked the means to have themselves buried in great tombs or to have their thoughts and histories carved out in stone—probably they drank the wines made from palms and dates, and the barley beer. The wine of the royal and the rich was mainly white. The most celebrated kinds were as follows. Mareotic: grown near what was to be the city of Alexandria—a white wine, sweet and light, long-lasting, and with a fragrant bouquet. Centuries later, it was known in Rome: Horace wrote that this was the wine which fired Cleopatra. Taeniotic: Athenaeus (c. A.D. 200) declared that this was even better than the Mareotic—an unctuous, greenish-white wine, sweet and aromatic, and of a slightly astringent character. (He went on to say that the wine-loving Egyptians often ate boiled cabbage before a feast, and took cabbage-water to cure a hangover.) Sebennyticum: described by Pliny as being the product of three different grapes, the Thasian, the soot grape, and the pitch-pine. Egyptian wines were sealed up in amphorae of the Greek pattern—and since they were not sufficient for the people of the country, many more came in from Greece, from Phoenicia, and from Syria.

It has been reckoned that wine is mentioned 155 times in the Old Testament and 10 times in the New. In the Book of Numbers it says that, at the time of the Exodus, the Hebrews regretted leaving behind the wines of Egypt; but they need not have feared, for the land of the Philistines and the Plain of Sharon were green with the vine, and Palestine came to be rich in vineyards. Indeed, vines flourished prolifically in the eastern Mediterranean countries and around the Caspian and Black seas. In Ezekiel, Chapter 27, we read about Damascus, that great center of the wine trade: "thy merchant . . . in the wine of Helbon." The wine of Byblos was celebrated too. The Syrians and the Phoenicians sent their wine by the old caravan routes to Arabia and Egypt, to India, and as far as China; and their famous Chalybon went to the Persian kings. Vines were planted in Arabia too, and large quantities of wine—mostly red—were made there.

There are also many references to wine in the Babylonian Talmud, and in Babylonian art and inscriptions. The southern parts of the country were not very suitable to the vine, and here, as in the Nile Delta, plots had to be raised by human labor. But in the north, soil and climate were favorable, and at one time Babylonian wines were much esteemed, and traveled as far as Arabia. Wine was blessed and offered to Abraham by King Melchizedek (Genesis, Chapter 14): libations were made with daily burnt offerings at the Feast of the Tabernacles; and so a link is made with King Nebuchadnezzar, dedicating wines with strange names to the pagan god Marduk, and with Assurbanipal in Nineveh, making libations freely—pouring wine on cornerstones, on sacred objects, on lions killed in the hunt, or on beheaded enemies. In the voodoo ceremonies of Haiti, libations are still offered to the gods; nor is there anything surprising about this custom, since primitive gods are largely anthropomorphic—and what more natural than to offer wine to an honored guest?

The ancient Greeks also poured libations to their gods, and from Homeric times and earlier they were a wine-drinking people. Vines decorated the shield of Achilles, the gold cup of Nestor is still famous, and Odysseus and his men washed down "abundant flesh with sweet wine." The Greeks liked their wines old and watered down. These sweet wines, trodden in stone vats and matured in earthenware crocks, may have borne some resemblance to Malmsey. Hesiod, the Boeotian farmer-poet, who was writing his *Works and Days* in about 700 B.C., pruned and planted his vines in the ways that were to be followed by countless generations (*see* Classical wines). The Pramnian and pure Maronean first described in Homer are still discussed—and regretted: some writers are of the opinion that the well-matured vintages of ancient Greece were the quintessence of fine wine. Nobody alive is in a position to dispute this view. Yet the pitched vessels in which much of the Greek wine was stored, the mixture, with some of it, of sea water, and the addition of perfumes must have combined to produce flavors not much to our taste.

Some of the grapes which yielded the Greek wines were almost certainly transplanted to the Greek colonies in Sicily and southern Italy, and the wine would surely have been made there in the same way. Up on the mainland, the Etruscans (migrants, it has been said, from Asia Minor) were already a wine-drinking people, loving luxury and splendid banquets in which their women took a prominent part. The Etruscans' wine god was called Fufluns. In the same province of Tuscany some of the best Italian wines are made today.

Viniculture, therefore, would have been a natural heritage of the Romans. Like the Greeks, they made red, white, and amber wines; and they too could drink them "pitched and pickled," sometimes mixed with sea water or exposed in a smoky room (*fumarium*). In old age some of them would be, as Tovey said, "reduced to a syrup and rendered so muddy and thick they had to be strained through cloths and dissolved in hot water." But the *fumarium* was intended to mellow the wine by heat rather than by smoke—the principle was not unlike that of maturing Madeira near ovens—and the jars were protected by a thick coat of plaster or pitch. The Romans themselves complained of "smoky wines" when they returned from Marseilles—settled about 600 B.C. by Greeks from Phocaea, and surely the first place in Gaul to have made real wine. The wines most prized in Rome were luscious, less in need of acrid preservatives—they probably resembled the Lágrima of today (*see* Classical wines). Wine traveled in earthenware amphorae, and fragments of these jars have been found in riverbeds and along roads. Wrecked ships loaded with amphorae have been retrieved from the Mediterranean—the jars, still corked, contain a liquid that, in the years before Christ, was new wine.

Where the Romans went, conquering and colonizing, the culture of the vine went with them. Using the waters of the Rhône to make their way northward in what is now France, they are said to have planted the Picatum, a hardy grape with a slight taste of pitch. On an old wine cup found in the region, the legend reads, "Give us Aminean, not Picatum." At the end of the first century, Martial tells that this wine was being exported to Rome. When in A.D. 92 the Emperor

Domitian issued an edict calling for the uprooting of many vines throughout the Empire, no doubt protecting Italian wines was one of his motives (along with encouraging agriculture and controlling surplus wine production). But it is not to be supposed that all of the vines were destroyed—the French character being what it is, orders are not much regarded; still, however halfheartedly the growers carried out the order, their descendants must have been relieved when in 280 the Emperor Probus repealed it.

When the vines were openly planted again, they spread beyond the old vineyard regions of Marseilles, the Rhône Valley, and the Iberian peninsula to the northern and western regions of France and Germany, and to Britain. When Ausonius, the Bordelais professor, poet, and consul, accompanied the Emperor Valentinian to the Moselle, he compared the well-kept vines and broad rivers of France and Germany and was charmed by both. In Germany, as in France, viticulture was encouraged by Charlemagne; soon, in an age when most wine was only fit to drink when young, the Germans, storing theirs in huge casks, promoted a taste for "old Rhenish." In Alsace, grapes were planted and casks of wine taken to Colmar and Strasbourg for shipment to Germany. The wine also came to England, where it was known as Osey or Aussey, and much appreciated. It is mentioned in Langland's *Piers Plowman* in the mid-fourteenth century.

With the spread of Christianity, monasteries sprang up, and royal or noble patrons endowed them with vineyards, particularly in Burgundy, where several wines, such as those of Beaune, had been known in Rome. Charlemagne himself (*c.* 800) had vines at Corton (hence the great vineyard name, Corton-Charlemagne); about 1100 the Cistercians made Clos de Vougeot and produced wine in Chablis as well. All through the early Middle Ages the Church was the principal producer. Because of their learning and their industry, the monks took the lead in viticulture: the pure wine of the grape was needed both for sacrament and for sustenance. Cluny, in Burgundy, was the great monastic center. When life there became too luxurious, the ascetic Cistercians broke away, disseminating the Gospel and the culture of the vine wherever they went, inside France and across her frontiers.

In early medieval times vines were grown in England mostly by monks in the southern counties. But wine was also imported from the Rhine and the north of France. In spite of the marriage of Henry II and Eleanor of Aquitaine (*see* Bordeaux), it was not until the beginning of the thirteenth century that Bordeaux (Gascon) wines began to come in any quantity to England, Flanders, and the Hanseatic ports. A record of wines imported for King John lists only those from places farther north—Gaillac, Auxerre, and the Rhine; there is no mention of any from Gascony.

Yet within a few years, the king was drinking Gascon wines and granting favors and tax cuts to the burghers of Bordeaux. English merchants went over at harvest time to spend some weeks bargaining with the Bordelais. The Gascon wine was soon much loved in England, where it was known as claret. By the early fourteenth century, the people were also able to enjoy table wines from Spain and Portugal, as well as the sweet wines of Crete and Cyprus. Malvasia, or Malmsey, came originally from Greece; but when the Turks occupied the mainland, the wine was shipped from Candia (Crete) and other islands, often in the vessels of the powerful Venetians, who, in the reign of Richard III, were bringing the legendary Helbon of Damascus to Western Europe. To England, they were obliged to bring with each cask ten Levantine yews to be made into bows. Inside the country also, there were strict controls. Officials boarded the merchant ships to supervise the cargoes and test the quality of the wine, and the king took his *prise* from every load. Although the wine was cheap, the common people did not drink very freely. Each town was allowed only a specified number of taverns; and no man except a peer or one with a considerable income and household was permitted to keep more than ten gallons of wine at home. Yet an Archbishop of York bought and dispensed one hundred tuns at his enthronement—wine was not, however, as strong then as it is now.

In the meantime, the wine which had come so early to the Middle East had been forbidden to the followers of Mohammed—yet the prohibition must not have been taken too seriously, since certain Turks are known to have been devoted to drink. But as the power of the Moslems spread, so did the rule of abstinence; and when the practical monks of Carbonnieux wanted to sell their wine to the Turks, they labeled it "Mineral Water of Carbonnieux." The Crusaders, however, are said to have found new vines in the lands of the Saracen and to have brought back with them sweet Muscat grapes, which they planted at the foot of the Pyrenees, and which produced Muscat de Frontignan, Lunel, and Rivesaltes. It was from the abstemious Saracens that Europe learned the art of distilling spirits.

Since in the Middle Ages all wine was drunk young, some of it must have been very acid and crude; this, especially at banquets, was made palatable by admixtures of honey and spices known as *piments*, which combined "the strength of wine, the sweetness of honey, and the perfume of aromatics." Of these liqueur-like drinks, the most celebrated were hippocras, about which poets rhapsodized, and clarry—the basis for claret.

Because Burgundy was far inland and served by bad roads, its wines were little known in England and the northern capitals, but their fame grew in their own region, where the dukes and princes were often at war with the French kings. In 1395, Philip the Bold of Burgundy made laws to maintain the quality of the wines, banishing the inferior Gamay grape and trying to keep out the wines of other districts which might have been used to stretch the Burgundy. Having possessions in Belgium, he moved his court—and some of his wine—to Brussels. Burgundy was also appreciated by the popes during their exile at Avignon. In 1443, Nicolas Rolin, chancellor of Philip the Fair, founded the Hôtel Dieu, or Hospice, at Beaune.

The vineyards of Champagne, planted by the Romans, yielded, in the Middle Ages and for some two hundred years afterward, still red wines which were at first lumped in with those of the Île de France and sold abroad earlier than were the Gascon growths. Saint Remi, who baptized Clovis at Rheims in 496, was a vineyard owner and patron of wine in the district. Henry VIII of England and Cardinal Wolsey bought some of the wine, which was enjoyed by the Valois kings, one of whom, Henri IV, was the first to give the name *Champagne* to the products of Rheims and Épernay.

In England, by Elizabeth I's reign, although the gentry still drank a lot of wine, the price of French wines had risen and the common people drank less of it—and more beer; Sack and Sherry were already well established (the name *sack* was applied to wines from the Canaries and other places besides Jerez). James I loved his claret; Oliver Cromwell, who hated fun and destroyed beauty, was yet human enough to approve of good wine. Osey remained popular; but when, in 1618, the Thirty Years' War broke out, the vineyards were largely destroyed, and the trade did not flourish again for two centuries.

Charles II brought back from France a new taste for Champagne, which was fostered also by the French philospher and wit Saint-Evremond, who was in exile in England. The wines of Rheims and Épernay were now sometimes white, or *vins gris* with a faint, evanescent foam. It was not until the last years of the century that the cellarer-monk Dom Pérignon was credited with the discovery of Champagne more or less as we know it. King Louis XIV was known to favor the red wine of Burgundy, and a keen competition developed between the growers of that district and of Champagne: doctors were asked to debate the qualities of the rival products. Under the Regency and in the reign of Louis XV, Champagne had a great success at court; and some of the big *négociants* were already becoming established, starting with Ruinart in 1729. About a century later, the sparkling wine was perfected by the addition of a sweet *liqueur de tirage* and the evolution of *dégorgement* to rid the bottles of their sediment (*see* Champagne).

Under William of Orange and his German successors, crippling duties were put on French wine; and the Methuen Treaty of 1703 gave overwhelming preference to Port—not then the fortified drink we know, but simply Portuguese table wine which was, as Englishmen complained, much inferior to Bordeaux. Many of them refused it and turned to "Florence" wine instead. The poorer people turned, regrettably and excessively, to gin. Rhenish, also, was to be had, and some Spanish table wine, as well as Sherry—by the early eighteenth century, Sack was seldom heard of. Claret, of course, was smuggled in, and the rich got

their share. But gradually people took to Port—perhaps the first "brandying" (which started, probably, about 1715) had something to do with it. In time, the shippers of Oporto learned to fortify and mature the wine as they do now, and by the end of the century Port was first in popularity, although Hermitage, Champagne, and Madeira were doing well. During these years, wine bottles, which had formerly been nothing more than squat jugs for holding wine taken fresh from the barrel, developed more or less the form they have now, and so, in 1781, the first Clairet to be stored in a well-rounded bottle was laid down in the cellars of Château Lafite.

When the French Revolution broke out, the vineyards were taken from the nobles and the Church and given to the people. A few years later, Napoleon secularized the vineyards of Germany—almost as great a revolution, from the point of view of the German growers. In France, ever since, the Burgundian holdings have mostly been divided into small parcels, although in Bordeaux the big estates were soon reestablished. Talleyrand became the owner of Château Haut-Brion, and some sharp wits attributed his diplomatic successes at the Congress of Vienna to the talents of his cook. At delicious dinners he would ply his guests with fine wines, and then play them off against one another. The chief opponent of Talleyrand was Metternich, later proud possessor of the great German vineyard Schloss Johannisberg.

By the middle of the nineteenth century, new vineyards were established in new countries: in South Africa and Australia and, most importantly, in America. When Leif Ericson crossed the Atlantic, he found a country green with wild vines and called it "Vineland." Later settlers made many experiments with transplanted European vines; finally, they discovered that, while the *Vitis vinifera* would grow in California, it was better to stick to the native species in the eastern states (*see* United States).

It was never guessed that the American vine, living independently, was developing an immunity to certain vine pests and diseases, themselves strengthened continually in the competition. But when American vines were brought to Europe a hundred years ago, the pests struck, and in the second half of the century nearly all the vineyards of Europe were decimated by the burrowing plant louse phylloxera. Indeed, the plague swept over the world, and wine as we know it might have vanished. Luckily, the growth that brought disaster also contained the cure. American roots became immune to phylloxera, and it was found that the European varieties would grow on American rootstocks. What the final result will be, in terms of quality, of grafting onto American stocks cannot yet be determined. Some people say that the wines are better than "before phylloxera"; others deny this. The long adjustments of the vine to soil and weather, changes very gradual in all wine history, must be given their own time.

In addition to this effect of the American vine on

Europe is the story of wine in America itself. At first, in the Colonies, European wines were drunk. How discriminating were the drinkers, and of what kinds the wines, can be judged from records of the time. The writer Washington Irving was a famous lover of wine, and we have many of his letters and receipts for orders of hogsheads from France and Spain. There were a great number of others, but we will cite excerpts from two letters of Thomas Jefferson, a true expert, the first written in 1792 to Henry Sheaff, a Philadelphia merchant, and the second in 1817 to President James Monroe at the White House.

Burgundy. the best wines of Burgundy are Montrachet, a white wine. it is made but by two persons, to wit, Mons' de Clermont, & Monsieur de Sassnet. the latter rents to Mons' de la Tour. this costs 48 sous the bottle, new, and 3 livres when fit for drinking.

Meursault, a white wine. the best quality of it is called Goutte d'Or. it costs 6 sous the bottle new. I do not believe this will bear transportation. but the Montrachet will in a proper season.

Chambertin, Vougeau, Beaune, are red wines, of the first quality, and are the only red wines of Burgundy which will bear transportation and even these require to be moved in the best season, & not to be exposed to great heat or great cold. These cost 48 sous the bottle, new & 3 livres old. I think it next to impossible to have any of the Burgundy wines brought here in a sound state.

Champagne. the Mousseux or sparkling Champagne is never brought to a good table in France, the still, or non-mousseux is alone drunk by connoisseurs.

Bordeaux red wines. There are four crops of them more famous than all the rest. These are Chateau-Margau, Tour de Segur, Hautbrion, & De La Fite. they cost 3 livres a bottle, old: but are so engaged beforehand that is it impossible to get them. the merchants, if you desire it, will send you a wine by any of those names, & make you pay 3 livres a bottle: but I will venture to affirm that there never was a bottle of those wines sent to America by a merchant, nor is it worthwhile to seek for them; for I will defy any person to distinguish them from the wines of the next quality, to wit.

Rohan-Margau, which is made by Madame de Rohan this is what I import for myself & consider as equal to any of the four crops.

There are also the wines of Dabbadie, la Rose, Quirouen & Durfort which are reckoned as good as Madame de Rohan's. yet I have preferred hers. these wines cost 40 sous the bottle, when of the proper age for drinking.

Bordeaux white wines.

Grave. the best is called Pontac, & is made by Mons' de Lamont. it costs 18 sous a bottle.

Sauterne. this is the best white wine of France (except Champagne and Hermitage). the best of it is made by Mons' de Lur-Salur and costs at 4 years old (when fit to drink) from 20 to 24 sous the bottle. there are two other white wines made in the same neighborhood called Prignac & Barsac, esteemed by some. but the Sauterne is that preferred at Paris, & much the best in my judgment. they cost the same. a great advantage of the Sauterne is that it becomes higher flavored the day the bottle has been opened, than it is at first.

Mr Fenwick, Consul of the U.S. at Bordeaux, is well informed on the subject of these wines, and has supplied the President and myself with them genuine & good. he would be a proper person to endeavor to get from the South of France some of the wines made there which are most excellent & very cheap, say 10 or 12 sous the bottle. those of Rousillon are the best . . .

. . .

I promised you, when I should have received and tried the wines I had ordered from France and Italy, to give you a note of the kinds which I should think worthy of your procurement. They are the following:

Vin blanc liquoreux d'Hermitage de M. Jourdan à Tains. this costs about .82 a bottle put on shipboard. . . .

There is still another wine to be named to you, which is the wine of Florence called Montepulciano, with which Appleton can best furnish you. There is a particular very best crop of it known to him, and which he has usually sent to me. He knows too from experience how to have it so bottled and packed as to ensure its bearing the passage, which in the ordinary way it does not. I have imported it through him annually 10 or 12 years and do not think I have lost 1 bottle in 100.

By the middle of the nineteenth century, tariffs between England and France had been so much lowered that the English bourgeoisie became claret-drinking people again—although Cyrus Redding, a few years earlier, had written that the English palate, coarsened by a long diet of brandied wines imported under the Methuen Treaty, could not appreciate a great growth of Bordeaux in its pure natural state, and so, especially for the English market, fine clarets were "sophisticated" with Cahors, Hermitage, Benicarlo, and even brandy. The Premiers Crus, even of the "year of the comet" (1811), were subjected to this treatment; and when Nathaniel Johnston—one of a number of foreigners who had settled into the Bordeaux wine trade—wanted to drink some of the excellent 1798 unblended, he ordered bottles of "neat Lafitte" to be kept apart for him.

But Burgundy, Redding believed, could not be successfully adulterated—because its exquisite delicacy and bouquet were inimitable. (That he should have supposed blended and over-chaptalized imitations to be unacceptable seems odd today.) Burgundy was also held by the eighteenth-century writer Barry to be too delicate a wine to travel, and it was not in fact widely known in England in his time.

It must be added that, even if Mr. Redding's strictures on the clarets prepared for England were deserved, a race of keen connoisseurs was to spring up in the second half of the century, whose rhapsodies over the great pre-phylloxera vintages of the 1860s and '70s are still quoted today. By that time, Englishmen must have earned the right to buy their claret pure.

Also about mid-century came the first disastrous

vine disease—the oïdium mildew, considered the greatest of plagues until it was followed by phylloxera.

The other momentous event was the Official Bordeaux Classification (based on earlier unofficial ratings) of the great growths of the Médoc in 1855. The age of jurisprudence in the organization of the wine trade was beginning. It was clearly necessary that place-names should be controlled in a way which would make it difficult if not impossible for an inferior wine to masquerade as a great one. The campaign, which began on the Douro to protect the good name of Port, was carried on in France through the early years of this century until, in 1936, the laws of Appellation Contrôlée were passed—models of their kind, which the other vine-growing countries of the world

have only recently begun to imitate (*see* Appellation d'Origine).

Wine is getting more expensive, but the demand for it is greater than ever and, in spite of bad summers in Europe, production flourishes. The Office International du Vin, a working group of wine-growers and legislators, has assessed the production of forty-four member countries; it now amounts to nearly 300 million hectoliters (7.95 billion U.S. gallons, 6.6 billion imp.). In this age of mechanization, man has returned as never before to the wine of the soil, the drink of civilization.

NOTE: *See* Classical wines, for additional history. Also regional entries (United States, Bordeaux, Burgundy, etc.) for local history.

2 History of Spirits and Distillation

In the Middle Ages spirit was known as *aqua vitae*, a term which survives today in Swedish and Norwegian aquavit and Danish akvavit. This was symptomatic, because the name means "water of life."

In ancient Greece, Aristotle wrote: "Sea water can be rendered potable by distillation. After it has been converted into humid vapors it returns to liquid." A Greek is said to have discovered this simply by noticing how steam condensed on the inner lid of a dish.

The principal remedies of the ancients were, as we know, wine and herbs. From the time of the Egyptians great use was made of flowers, plants, and spices, cooked, macerated, or infused for pharmaceutical or culinary purposes. With wine or water, the healing perfumed liquid was preserved in airtight jars. The science of distillation, if not continuously practiced, crops up again and again in history. The distillates, as far as we know, were water and scents. The discovery of the distillation of alcohol was made by the Arabs in the early Middle Ages. The philosopher Avicenna in the tenth century produced a complete description of the alembic, but did not mention alcohol—although it must have been discovered about that time. Like alchemy, the word *alcohol* derives from the Arabic. A certain black powder was liquefied, converted to vapor, allowed to solidify again, and then used as eye-paint by the harem beauties. This was *kohl*, which is in use throughout the Arab world today. And when the spirit of wine began to be distilled, the Arabic name for this powder—*Al Koh'l*—was adopted, because of the similarity of the process.

In fact, we inherited the Arabian science of distillation by way of alchemy, which played a large part in the medieval world. The earliest name of genuine importance in distillation is that of Arnáu of Vilanova (d. 1313), a Catalan professor at the University of Montpellier. He was probably the first to write of alcohol, and his treatise on wine and spirits was a handbook of the time. His pupil Raimundo Lulio (or Raymond Lull) was a philosopher and chemist who carried on with the experiments.

Eau-de-vie, Lulio wrote, is "an emanation of the divinity, an element newly revealed to men but hid from antiquity, because the human race was then too young to need this beverage destined to revive the energies of modern decreptitude." Arnáu had been more ecstatic. To him, the liquor was the long-sought panacea, the elixir of life itself, the dream of the alchemists. Although they never found what they were looking for—the secret of transmuting base metal into gold, or the elixir of everlasting life—the alchemists discovered a great many other things by the way. They developed the science of chemistry; and while they did not discover *aqua vitae*, they used it extensively and bequeathed its uses to us.

To the general public *aqua vitae* was a medicine and tasted like one. Another name for it was *aqua ardens*—firewater. The fruit and herbs with which the spirit was doctored helped to hide the taste as well as to heal the patients. When, later on, people began to think of brandies and liqueurs primarily as drinks, there was much experimenting with different plants to improve the flavor; and except in such favored regions as Cognac, Frenchmen were still tackling the same problem at the end of the eighteenth century. Then, in 1800, Adam invented the process of rectification or rectifying—that is, a redistillation which removed the *mauvais goût*. Unfortunately, it removed all taste, good as well as bad, and the French, who had been adding herbs and fruit concoctions to hide the nasty taste, had to restore them again to give flavor to the neutral spirit.

Aqua vitae was on sale in Italy in the Middle Ages; at about the same time, or a little earlier, it appeared in Ireland, gaelicized into *uisge beatha* and distilled from a barley beer. Variants of this name for "the water of life" persisted throughout the centuries, but in the end it was unquestionably whisky.

Scotch whisky originated in the Highlands. By the fifteenth century, it was a familiar drink there and was purely malt whisky. Gradually it seeped through to the Lowlands and the Scottish court.

The English at first preferred the fine French Cognac brandies miraculously distilled from the thin sharp wines of Charente. In early days, ships from the north used to put in at La Rochelle, principally to pick up salt. Then the inhabitants began to sell their wine as well; and afterward, to save space in the ships—and perhaps to avoid taxes—they began to boil down the wine, which traveled much better when it was thus metamorphosed. At first the idea was to restore the wine by adding water when it reached land again; but it was soon discovered to taste better as it was. A gentleman called Croix-Maron, who is supposed to have had a lot to do with the boiling down of the wine, is said to have remarked: "In cooking my wines, I have discovered their soul."

A report from 1688 says that very little wine of the

7

Charente region could be sold abroad, but "when the white wines are converted to *eau-de-vie*, which is the customary thing, then the English and Danish fleets come to the ports of the Charente in search of it." So, by that date, the brandy of Cognac was established. The name *brandy* may well have come from the Germanic *Branntwein*—burnt wine. There are mentions of "brand wine" in English in 1622 and 1650.

It is interesting that much of the early distilling was done in the house, and the politest ladies were proficient in this domestic art, as common as cooking. Scotch whisky was at first almost entirely made at home: the best was for the Highland chiefs; the crofters mashed their surplus grain into whisky. When, in that mountainous and inaccessible country, the domestic stills were banned by the Hanoverian kings, and heavy taxes and duties began to be placed on the spirit, the distillers quite naturally took to the hills.

It is estimated that of the roughly half a million gallons of Scotch whisky being made annually in 1800, the amount made legally was approximately nil. Some 300,000 illegal gallons are said to have eluded the excise men and flowed down over the border into England year after year. At one time there were two hundred illicit stills in the famous glen of Glenlivet, where perhaps the finest unblended whisky in the world is made today.

The Scottish distillers were defiant men who brewed their illegal potions quite openly. All that was necessary was to choose a defendable glen, and then go about armed to the teeth. In 1823, the English government lowered the duty on whisky in order to encourage the open and legal distillation of good spirit. Yet the illicit stills were so well established that when a daredevil named George Smith came to Glenlivet itself and set up a legal distillery, he was considered to have shown great effrontery. His memoirs tell nothing of how he made his whisky, but they do tell the secret of his success. He hired the toughest men he could find, and by standing watch in turn with them around the clock he saved his still from being burned out, the fate that befell the few others as bold as himself. Smith's foothold in Glenlivet was the beginning of the end. The sad decline in illegal distilling can be read in the statistics of illicit stills detected in Scotland: in 1834, 692; in 1835, 177; in 1854, 73; in 1864, 19; in 1874, 6. Whisky-runners were a dying race, like the romantic highwaymen of the previous century.

American whiskey (the word is spelled "whisky" in Canada, England, and Scotland, "whiskey" in the United States and Ireland) began to be made in the eighteenth century. Distilling of rye and barley grains had become so strong a habit by the year 1794 that such interferences as taxation and control were resented to the point of armed revolt—this was the year of the Whiskey Rebellion in Pennsylvania. The distillers, losing the fight, moved west in large numbers, preferring the Indians to revenue men. A few years before, in Bourbon County, Kentucky, they had started making corn whiskey; with the arrival of the refugees from the east, the trade prospered. At first corn whiskey was made to reduce the carrier's load: the packhorses winding down the narrow mountain trails of Kentucky could carry only 4 bushels of corn each; when the corn was distilled to whiskey, they could carry the equivalent of 24 bushels. This corn whiskey took the name *Bourbon* from Bourbon County.

There was another incentive for home distilling, and that was the whiskey price in Kentucky. In 1782, about the time when the first Bourbon stills were set up, the price fixed by the court in Jefferson County, Kentucky, was 15 dollars a half-pint and 240 dollars a gallon. The Indians had already set the example, making a corn spirit they called Nohelick (the Apaches, farther west in undiscovered territory, were brewing their Teeswin from boiled corn), and the settlers pitched in. The first may have been Elijah Craig. At any rate, that intrepid Baptist preacher "considered it as honorable a business as any. Even preachers did not deem it derogatory to their high calling to lend their countenance to its manufacture and engage in it themselves, or drink a little for the stomach's sake."

Adam's process of rectification eventually set off a complete revolution in the manufacture of spirits. Even Cognac (which even now is never rectified, but is pot-distilled by the ancient method derived from the alembic) changed its manner of exportation some three-quarters of a century ago as a consequence of the growing competition from rectified spirits. Traditionally shipped in barrel, it began to be exported in bottle, so that the distillers and shippers could be sure of having full control over the liquid they were selling—sent abroad in cask, it was increasingly likely that it would be stretched and adulterated at the end of its journey. One important consequence was that the brandy began to be called after the little rivertown from which it was shipped, and for the first time it was known as Cognac.

Rum—the sugarcane spirit of the West Indies—had a riotous history in those islands. It was the traditional drink of the fighting men along the sea lanes of the empire-builders—and if the sailors did not get their issue of rum, there was danger of mutiny. The blazing cane-juice brew was also the drink of the western American Colonies and, in one sense, fired them to revolt and form an independent United States—for England's taxing of rum was resented at least as bitterly as her taxing of tea. Even more romantic was the connection of rum with the pirates of the Spanish Main. In the coves of Barbados, Jamaica, and the other islands, the privateers hove to for concealment—and a fresh load of rum.

We drink—by and large—rather tamed rum today. Once again it is rectification that has brought about the revolution. By repeated redistilling, all by-products can be eliminated from any base liquid—in many a light modern rectified rum little of the lustiness of the pungent cane is left. These light rums are the Puerto Rican and Cuban—different from the pungent, sweeter liquors of Demerara and Jamaica, and more to the modern taste.

It is in the vast popularity of gin and vodka that the true effects of rectification appear. Both are, fundamentally, spirits made neutral by rectification, then—in the case of gin—reflavored. The persisting predilection for gin may be called "the vogue of the Martini." During Prohibition, complex mixtures of alcohol appeared all over North America and spread their influence over the world. These mixtures were known as cocktails. Evolving perhaps from cold punches or mint juleps, they certainly developed and multiplied as they did because illicit synthetic "bath-tub" gins needed to be well disguised by other, less disgusting flavors. Nowadays the cocktail—once so complex—grows simpler and simpler. The overwhelming preference is for the Martini—simply gin with a touch of vermouth, a concoction which is only possible when the basic ingredients are good.

Vodka is the latest craze. Originally a Russian, Polish, Balkan, Lithuanian and Estonian spirit, it is now made from grain in the United States and in England, France, and elsewhere in Europe. The Smirnoff vodka formula bought by an American firm in 1939 from a White Russian refugee started this postwar fashion.

3 Wine and Food

Matchmaking, always a diverting occupation, becomes a positive pleasure when its object is a marriage between food and wine: once complementary flavors are brought together, the two combine in a gastronomic treat infinitely more delicious than either could provide alone. A fine meal, cooked well and served so that it is as seductive to the eye as to the appetite, is a delight in itself; add a glass of wine—gleaming red or a translucent greenish-gold—and delectation will be doubled. The flavor and aroma of wine enormously enhance the taste of food; moreover, the combination induces a sense of well-being—euphoria—and stimulates the imagination. That is why, since the days of Socrates, a dinner table has been the traditional setting for good conversation.

The tradition was, indeed, broken by the contemporary habit of sitting over cocktails before dinner, and hurrying out of the dining room afterward to look at television; but fortunately there is, all over the world, a reviving interest in wine, and people who plan their dinner parties with care and round out the meal with several good bottles usually see to it that the aperitifs are Sherry, dry Champagne, or dry vermouth well chilled. It is a waste of time to achieve felicitous matches between the wine and food unless the drinks also complement each other: wine should be preceded (and followed) by the products of the grape, not of the grain—wine and spirits, excellent apart, do not go well together.

That wine and food *do* go well together was discovered by our remotest ancestors. In the old days, vast meals would be washed down by jugs of new wine fresh from the wood. Then, in the eighteenth century, wine began to be matured in glass bottles, and by 1800 it was no longer a refreshing drink to be gulped down: the country gentleman still ate hugely and sometimes downed his three bottles a day; but in the renaissance of fine French cuisine, in the time of Carême and the other great cooks, dinners began to be planned with finesse, and the carefully selected wines were appreciatively sniffed and sipped. Even then, and until late in the nineteenth century, meals were, by our standards, enormous and endless, with a formidable array of glasses beside each plate.

In comparison with the vigorous Victorians, we eat and even entertain sparingly; yet at a special dinner where three or more wines are served (each course planned so that the accompanying bottle may be greater than the one before) it is still possible to play the classic music of the wines: instead of draining your glass, leave a little in it to taste against the wine which comes with the next course, until the best bottle arrives with the cheese.

The meal may start with a dry white wine, go on to a red one, and then an older or finer red—for instance, a Chablis, a Claret, and an older or greater Claret; or, depending on the dishes served, there may be three red wines, beginning with the youngest and ascending to the finest, often the oldest. In France, the cheese always comes before the pudding, and the red wine is finished with this course. Then, if the host has a luscious dessert wine to offer, it will make its own counterpoint of sweetness with the sweet. Champagne (semi-sweet) and Vouvray are good with fruit; Sauternes or Barsac with desserts, tarts, and sweet fruits.

To offer wine is the most charming gesture of hospitality, and a host brings out for his guests the finest he has. Whether there are four wines or one, the gesture is the same. A single wine, chosen for the main dish, will be more of a success if it goes with the first course too; if, for instance, it is a Bordeaux, the meal might start with a cheese soufflé. It is worth considering, however, that a bottle of white wine and a bottle of red may be just as easy to produce as two of red. In France, where almost everybody drinks wine every day, most households content themselves on ordinary occasions with a single modest wine. A Frenchman's dinner table always shows if it is Sunday, a holiday, or a christening, because then a special bottle of good wine appears. And there will be chicken, fish, or meat for dinner according to which will best show off the qualities of that wine.

COMBINATIONS OF FOOD AND WINE

Traditionally, certain wines accompany certain dishes—Chablis and oysters go together like bread and butter—and wine-bores (of whom, unfortunately, there are plenty, since on no subject is a little learning such a tedious thing) tend to be extremely didactic about it. Most of the rules are sound, however, since they are the result of experiment over the centuries: dry white wines taste best before red ones, the great ones taste better when they follow lesser ones of a similar type; sweet wines are not at all good with meat—all this was discovered long ago. Moreover, many wine and food partners are near relations: with the famous sausages of Lyon, no wine is so good as a fruity young Beaujolais grown in the region; and in the Loire Valley they wash down the *rillettes de Tours* with local Sancerre, Vouvray, or Pouilly-Fumé.

The man who likes to make up his own mind would be wise, then, not to reject the rules—even if they are laid down for him by wine-snobs—but to prove them for himself and to test them in his own experiments. In choosing the wine for his meal, the important consideration is, after all, that it should please *him*. He should remember, though, when he makes his experiments, that time and place must be taken into account: the light rosé which goes so well with a midday sandwich will be out of place with a fine dish at dinnertime. The author remembers drinking, on a torrid night in the Caribbean, a fine Bordeaux, followed by a great red Burgundy; and although the food suited them, the temperature did not. (Rules are only useful to those who know how to break them; and in the tropics, chilled pink or white wines are most agreeable, whatever the menu.) Conversely, the cool rosé one enjoyed on a warm day in the south of France would not do with a big steak on a cold winter's night.

Some foods clash resoundingly with some wines: a hot curry will kill a Claret; but a white wine with a distinctive flavor (a Gewürztraminer, for example) can hold its own against the spicy taste. As for such things as anchovies, kippers, and vinegary salad dressings—they are deadly to all wines and should not be served with them.

TYPES OF WINE

Some wines are good to drink alone or with a biscuit; these are usually the very sweet Sauternes, Barsacs, and the German Beerenauslesen, Trockenbeerenauslesen, Auslesen, Vin Santo, Moscato, and late harvest wines, or the fortified wines—Sherry, Port, Madeira. Natural still wines cannot be truly appreciated without the harmonious taste of food. A great dish needs wine to set it off; and a fine bottle is wasted when it is accompanied by a discordant series of food flavors.

TABLE WINES

These are the still beverage wines we drink with meals. They are light—from 9 percent to 14 percent in alcohol—and may be red, pink, or white; dry or sweet; light or heavy.

Dry white wines are traditionally associated with seafood. Chablis, as we have said before, is perfect with oysters—but so are Champagne, Muscadet, Riesling, and other dry wines; and white Burgundy is also excellent with shrimp or lobster, and with ham, veal, or chicken cooked in a white wine sauce. With poached sole, a Montrachet is magnificent; and a dry white Hermitage is so distinctive in taste that it can balance curry and other highly spiced dishes. As a general rule, it should be remembered that dry white wines are light and delicate in flavor, and so they should be accompanied by food in the same category. Rich heavy dishes will usually overpower them.

Sweet white wines, we know, are delicious with sweet fruits and puddings. At the start of a meal, the sugary content kills the taste buds and spoils the appetite; whereas at the end these same characteristics are precisely what is needed to induce a feeling of satisfaction and content. Yet in the early years of the century, Sauternes was constantly served with the fish; and even today some Frenchmen in the Bordeaux country consider this the wine that goes best with a rich fish such as salmon. Sauternes also complements a good *foie gras*.

Red wines are almost exclusively dry. (Some sweet red wines do exist, but they fall into much the same category as red sparkling wines—pleasant if you like that sort of thing, but not generally distinguished; and their sweetness renders them incompatible with food.) Everywhere in the world, more red wine than white is consumed; in Western Europe, *vin ordinaire* is the workingman's staple beverage.

The outstanding characteristic of red wines is their variety: white wines are either dry or sweet, still or sparkling; dry red wines range from lightness to full-bodied robustness, each with its own distinctive taste and complexities derived from differences in soil and grape variety. Clearly, the heavier the food, the heavier the wine you will want to drink with it. Fowl, veal, and other light meats are excellent with red wines—as with white; but full-blooded meats need heartier company, and game and pasta with meat sauce usually demand the sturdiest of wines. The best accompaniment for red wine is cheese; but it must not be too strong, especially if the wine is old and delicate. Because of this affinity, the finest wine always comes on with the cheese—which is always mild.

SPARKLING WINES

Most fully sparkling wines are white, but a very few are red, and they range from dry to sweet—sometimes too sweet. Sweet red sparkling wines are generally shunned by experienced wine-drinkers because many are quite mediocre, and even the best lack the distinction of their fine white counterparts. Moreover, they do not go well with food. On the other hand, the Italians, among others, have been making them for centuries and seem to enjoy them.

Champagne, of course, is far and away the best sparkling white wine. Many others have borrowed this famous place-name; but only the French wine made by the true Champagne process in the region of Champagne is entitled to bear it. And it is usually easy enough to distinguish the original from the imitations at the first sip. Yet many white sparkling wines are very agreeable, and, like Champagne itself, these may be dry, semi-sweet, or sweet. There are people who consider Champagne to be the only drink; and certainly it is delicious late in the evening: before meals, if it is dry; with fruit or dessert at the end of a meal, if it is fairly sweet. By its devotees, it is sometimes drunk all through dinner; this is not to be recommended, yet there is no valid reason why you should not do so, as long as you do not continue a Champagne *brut* into the sweet course—and once you have tried other wines and decided that you really enjoy the Champagne most. The general opinion is, however, that when it comes to balancing the wine against the food, Champagne has too little body and too many bubbles. But there is no doubt that for launching ships, for toasting the New Year or the new bride, this bubbly wine is superlative.

FORTIFIED WINES

These may be white or red, dry or sweet. Dry Sherry (Fino or Manzanilla) is generally considered the perfect aperitif, particularly before a meal at which fine wines are to be served. After dinner, Port is held by many to be incomparable; yet some people prefer sweet Sherries or Madeiras. There is also a variety of lesser fortified wines, esteemed, as a rule, in their own country—the Italian Moscato, for instance, and the *vin doux naturel* of Banyuls. It is as well to know, however, that in certain parts of the world, outside Europe, fortified wines of a kind are made, cloyingly sweet and excessively alcoholic—really nothing but a substitute for cheap spirits. Naturally, nobody would think of drinking fortified wines with meals—except, perhaps, for a dry Sherry with the soup.

A FEW SIMPLE RULES

It is possible to make endless permutations and combinations of food and wines—and everyone can discover new ones for himself. He will not, however, waste good wine on unnecessary mistakes if he observes these simple rules.

Dry white wines taste best before red; and red wines are better when they are served after others of the same type but lesser quality. In the second instance, it is an elegant—and most enjoyable—practice to serve more than one red wine with a fine meal. In this case, it is a good idea to stick to the wine of one region, offering, for example, Bordeaux after Bordeaux, and Burgundy after Burgundy, rather than mixing the two. And it is advisable to serve the wines in reverse order of age—the youngest first. With wines of the same age, the lesser should come first.

Certain foods and flavors simply do not harmonize with wine. Vinegar has been mentioned; and such pungent things as onions, garlic, and fishy *hors d'oeuvres* spoil the palate for wine. Spices, curry, and mustard also have a regrettable effect, unless the wine itself has a taste so pronounced that it can prevail over the others.

Once these obvious pitfalls have been avoided, it is as well not to worry too much (unless you are planning a dinner party) about what to drink with what. Wine and food have a natural affinity, and in more cases than anyone would think possible, they unite with felicitous results.

4 Serving Wine

White wines are served chilled, red ones at room temperature—but a good deal of care must be expended on them before they ever reach the table.

HALVES AND MAGNUMS

Half-bottles are good buys when you want to try out a wine, or if you are in the habit of using a small quantity at a time; but only young or average wines should be bought in this way, since great wines age prematurely in small bottles and are, indeed, happier in magnums. In extra-big bottles wine matures more slowly, and this, in a great wine, is a guarantee that it will eventually achieve real quality—a quickly matured wine will never attain great heights.

IN THE CELLAR

To begin with, if you have bought an old red wine which will probably have formed a sediment, let the bottle stand upright for a day or two before laying it down in the bin; in this way, the deposit stirred up on the journey will not come up into the neck. Afterward, lay the bottle flat in the rack, label upward, to be read at a glance (this applies, of course, to all table wines, red or white). Again before bringing an old red wine out of the cellar to the table, it should be stood upright for some hours so that the sediment may sink.

AGE AND TEMPERATURE

White wines should mostly be drunk young: the chances are that after five years many of them will lose their freshness and start oxidizing. Yet a good white Burgundy may live some years longer. (What is a young wine? In Bordeaux of good vintage, less than four years old; in red Burgundy, less than two-and-a-half years.)

White wines need to be chilled—the sweeter, the colder; but it is a mistake to freeze wines too much, since this kills the taste and destroys the character. Rather drink a fine white Burgundy under- than over-chilled. Most people now put their wine in the refrigerator. One or two hours is sufficient, as 40° to 50°F. (5° to 10°C.) is the ideal temperature for dry white wines, although an ice bucket is said to be a better cooler, because less time is required, twenty minutes being sufficient. Naturally, the time for chilling a wine largely depends on the temperature of the bottle before chilling. If you have no ice bucket, lay the bottle in a big salad bowl full of crushed ice or ice cubes with some water. Just before you are ready to serve it, take the bottle from the cooler and pull the cork.

Pink wines, as well as white, are served chilled.

Red wines which are young and full-bodied (great young Médocs, for instance) should be uncorked several hours before dinner; a very young one may even benefit from being opened the night before—this extra time for breathing will help it to achieve some maturity and softness. In Beaujolais, extreme youth is an advantage: nine months to under three years is its age cycle; treat it like white wine, and uncork it immediately before serving. Although it need not be chilled in a cold climate, Beaujolais is better chilled in a very hot one. A Claret between five and fifteen years old should be opened about two hours before drinking; but a very old wine needs less breathing space—if it is really old and delicate, decant it at dinner: even then, it may have faded and died a little by the time you pour the second glass, whereas a younger red wine will expand and develop in the glass.

DECANTING

Wine which contains sediment less than a quarter of an inch thick should be taken up very gently, held steady in the position in which you first grasp it, and poured in one continuous movement into a clean crystal decanter, until the deposit begins to rise to the neck of the bottle—then stop at once. So that you may keep an eye on the sediment, hold the bottle in front of the light. Since the process of decanting enables the wine to breathe, there is no need to leave the stopper out. Here again, the age of the wine will determine how long it should be exposed to air before drinking. However, all red wines should be brought into the dining room a couple of hours before the meal, so that they may come up to room temperature (or become *chambrés*): to warm them suddenly before a fire or in hot water is injurious. They should be drunk at about 63° to 65°F. (17° to 18°C.) in temperature. The purpose of a wine basket is to hold steady a bottle which may contain sediment; since in restaurants many waiters pour the wine in jerks and wave these baskets about, they are usually superfluous adjuncts to the often meaningless ritual which has grown up about wine.

OPENING

When you open a bottle of wine, cut the capsule and tinfoil below the tip with a knife; use a clean cloth to remove the mold which usually forms under the capsule; draw the cork and then carefully clean the lip of the bottle inside.

Don't choose fancy corkscrews with all kinds of levering gadgets. These are all right for young wines but not for old ones, where the cork is apt to break or crumble into powder. The best is the old-fashioned T-screw: look for one with a long stem (great wines have long corks) which is rounded—not sharp enough to cut the cork. If the cork *should* break or turn out to be old and powdery, it can be got out by leverage: insert the screw delicately, slightly sideways; set the bottle on its side, so that the pressure of the wine is against the inside face of the cork, then turn the screw gently, using some leverage to lift the bottom of the cork toward the upper side of the bottle. One occasionally finds a defect in even the finest of corks—sometimes an invisible vein which, with age, is liable to deteriorate and turn moldy (this is not the fault of the winemaker or merchant and may happen to the best of wines). The wine will then have an unpleasant corky taste and smell—and the cork will smell of itself and not of the wine. In a restaurant, the waiter should smell the cork and then bring it to you; and the reason why a little wine is poured first into the host's glass is so that he may make sure the wine is not corked, before it is offered to his guests. Sometimes the infection is so slight that only the first glassful is spoiled; therefore, when you open the wine at home, it is worth putting the bottle aside to see if it will afterward be fit for you yourself to drink. In a restaurant it must, of course, be sent back at once.

SERVING

At a small dinner for four or five people, given in a private house, the bottle of wine is set on the table in front of the host, who will pour it; if the party is larger, a second bottle should be given to the hostess to pass around at her end of the table. When the wine is brought around by a servant, he serves the ladies first, starting on the right side of the host and moving, clockwise, to the lady on his left; then the men, beginning with the one sitting on the right of the hostess. Never make the mistake of leaving the wine until after the food has been served. At his own table, a host does not taste the wine first, because, having opened it himself, he knows that it is not corked.

For the order in which wines should be brought on, *see* A Few Simple Rules, p. 12.

GLASSES

Choose plain crystal to display the sparkle of the wine itself. Great wines can be ruined in small glasses; there should be room for the wine to be swirled around and for it to breathe and reveal its bouquet. The best glass is large and tulip-shaped, clear and thin, without markings, the bowl the size of an apple or orange. Different shapes exist for different wines, but this tulip glass serves equally well for all, including Champagne—in the shallow "Champagne glass" the carefully manufactured bubbles will be dissipated and the flavor lost. (Incidentally, the swizzlestick is a negative instrument, designed as it is deliberately to destroy the sparkle which is the distinctive characteristic of Champagne and the result of years of labor. People who do not care for bubbles would do better to order a still Champagne.)

BRANDY

That served with the coffee should be poured, not into a small liqueur glass but into one big enough to be warmed in the palm of the hand and to allow the brandy (serve good Cognac, Armagnac, or marc) to be rolled around in it. For *eau-de-vie* or white spirits (such as framboise, mirabelle, quetsch, or kirsch) chill the glass first by swirling a piece of ice in it: this mellows the taste of the very alcoholic drink.

PORT

It is the custom, particularly in England, to serve Port at the end of dinner and before or with the coffee. Very often the ladies leave the dining room and the men remain to enjoy their wine alone. The decanter is passed clockwise.

SMOKING

In England, it is bad form to smoke with good wine. The French are less strict in some ways, and many growers smoke when they are drinking wine—between meals. The French fortunately have never adopted the American custom of smoking between courses.

5   Value and Wine

Wine is good value when you find the right bottle for the right purpose, and at the right price. A bogus Burgundy at fifteen dollars is expensive; a genuine Richebourg is reasonable at fifty dollars. A regional wine, or a shipper's wine with a brand name, blended for consistent year-after-year quality and character by a shipper whose own name is its guarantee, may be the same price as a château-bottled Bordeaux growth; but even though the shipper's blend is a reliable one, the first is a bad buy—whereas if it were to be sold for less it would be a good one. In every case, personal choice must be considered: no wine, however honest, can be good value unless it pleases you and goes well with the food you are going to eat.

The obvious way for an amateur in wine to find out what he likes best and to learn which wines best accompany which dishes is to consult a wine merchant who knows his business and who is a man of integrity and taste as well. In England more than anywhere else, and in America, in a number of old-established houses, sound traditions of selling wine flourish—and one of their lists alone is a store of information and advice. In France, they hardly exist; people buy direct from the grower—or from the grocer; and it is not always easy, in one part of the country, to find wine from elsewhere. A village shop in Burgundy will stock the local wine, but is unlikely to supply you with Bordeaux. In France, however, wine-drinking, chauvinistic as it may be, is part of a way of life; in America, it is not. Yet well-informed wine merchants do exist in the United States, and the increasing number of tourists who return from Europe or California with a new appreciation of wine is encouraging them to expand their business. The number of serious wine merchants is increasing all over the U.S.

WINE FOR THE HOUSE

Wine is bought either to be drunk within the next month or two or to be laid down for future use. In the old days, when life was stable and people lived in houses with large cellars, it was customary to buy wines of a fine vintage, as soon as possible and at a good price, and lay them away to mature. By the time they had reached their peak, the retail price would have risen considerably and the early purchaser (or the son who succeeded him) could congratulate himself on his foresight. Nowadays, when the tendency is to live in the present rather than plan for the future— and to live also in apartments where storage space is limited—there is less laying down of wine. The small quantity that can be fitted into a modern cupboard should be chosen with extra care: for suggestions on cellarage conditions, *see* Chapter Six.

INEXPENSIVE WINES

Many of the wines bought for immediate consumption will probably be unpretentious regional types: but there is every reason why these should still be sound and palatable, honestly living up to the statements on the bottle label—and some labels offer a better guarantee of validity than others. On French wines, look for the words Appellation Contrôlée; on Spanish, Denominación de Origen; on Italian, Denominazione di Origine Controllata. The better bottles from the vineyards of South Africa, Australia, and California will, at a moderate price, be good value; but they will be better value if you avoid those bearing such meaningless generic names as "South African Claret" and "California Burgundy" (for neither Claret nor Burgundy could come from anywhere outside the Bordeaux and Burgundy regions of France) and look instead for "varietal wines"—that is, wines named for the dominant grape variety, such as Riesling, Cabernet Sauvignon, or Pinot Noir. If the specific place of origin is also named, the wine will probably be above average in quality.

Some South American wines—notably, those from Chile—are good bargains and very agreeable to drink—as are many from Italy, Spain, and Portugal. Pleasant wines can also be found from Yugoslavia and Hungary: the best are those bearing a state seal. With red wines, look for the vintage on the label, for the date will give an indication of how much ageing the wine has undergone; and, if possible, choose any of these wines when it is from three to five years old.

In France and Germany, the choice becomes infinitely expanded and the price range wider; and the first question to ask yourself about such wines is simply: "Is this what it pretends to be—is it authentic?"

FRENCH WINES

French wines sold abroad often, though not always, bear the words "Produce of France" and *Appellation Contrôlée*, signifying that it has been made in accordance with the strict laws of place-name (*see* Appellation d'Origine) and that it conforms to certain minimum standards. Since France produces about 10 million hectoliters (256 million U.S. gallons, 220 million imp.) of wine of Appellation Contrôlée in an average year, even bottles carrying this legend will vary considerably. In buying fine wines, the rule is: the more specific the place, the better the wine will be (i.e., Médoc should be better than simply Bordeaux; Margaux will be better than Médoc). The exception is the wine of Alsace, where grape variety takes precedence over place, the better bottles selling as Alsatian Riesling, Alsatian Gewürztraminer, and so on—and in rare cases bearing the vineyard as well as the grape name. Clearly, then, some detailed knowledge of geography will be invaluable in selecting wines. With French wines, for example, it is impossible to choose the bottle from the more specific place unless you know whether Saint-Julien, say, is in the Haut-Médoc (as it is) or the Haut-Médoc in Saint-Julien (which it isn't).

FINE FRENCH WINES

Apart from Champagne, the great wines of France are those from Bordeaux and Burgundy, and the finest examples carry the name of the vineyard where the grapes were grown. If you are prepared to spend the large sum demanded for some of these great wines, the surest indication that you are getting your money's worth is the guarantee on the label that the wine (if it is a Bordeaux) was bottled at the château where it was made: the French words are *Mis en Bouteilles au Château*. Burgundies bottled by the growers are rarer, since the Burgundian estates are so small (*see* Burgundy); but domaine bottling is done more than ever, due to the growing demand for wines sold directly from the estates. Failing one of these, look for the label of a reliable shipper such as Bouchard Père et Fils, Louis Jadot, Joseph Drouhin, and Louis Latour.

The system for labeling wines from other districts is much the same—except that individual vineyard names do not occur so frequently. Champagne is usually a blend of wines from that region, made by one of the big firms whose names are famous. The best carry vintage years. (Other sparkling wines are poorer value than Champagne, since few of them can compare with it, and yet taxes on sparkle put them in the same high price range.) Wines from other regions are often blended, although some come from specific vineyards; and one such from Châteauneuf-du-Pape, Hermitage, Côtes du Rhône, or Tavel in the Rhône Valley, or from Anjou, Vouvray, or Pouilly-sur-Loire in the Loire Valley, can be not only pleasant but admirable.

GERMAN WINES

There is no cheap way to make fine wine, particularly in Germany, where growing conditions are so difficult and production costs are high. It is physically and economically impossible for Germany to compete with her large neighbors to the west and south in producing large quantities of inexpensive, pleasant table wine. At best, no more than 5-10% of an average annual German harvest (approx. 10 million hectoliters, compared to 70 million hectoliters in France) yields table wine, which is called *Deutscher Tafelwein* or *Deutscher Landwein* (vin de pays). It is consumed primarily with meals or as quaffing wine in local wine pubs, usually not far from where it is produced. This is not to say that decent, everyday German wine is scarce or quite expensive. On the contrary, Germany does produce many moderately priced *Qualitätsweine* (quality wines) which offer good value. They show regional character and often bear the names of some of the most popular villages (e.g., Piesporter Michelsberg, Niersteiner Gutes Domtal, etc.) or districts, called Bereiche in German, which themselves usually take their name from the best-known villages of the area (e.g., Bereich Bernkastel, Bereich Johannisberg, etc.). Liebfraumilch (known for centuries) and Moseltaler (new, as of 1986) are popular, everyday regional wines without complicated nomenclature on the label (no village or vineyard names, no grape varieties), and their production is precisely defined by law (i.e. which varieties may be used in the cuvée, permissible levels of residual sugar, etc.). The key to finding good value in these regional wines lies in the name of the producer or shipper printed on the label. The final cuvée can only offer quality (and thus value) if the components were selected on the basis of quality rather than the cheapest price. Many of the cooperatives (*Winzergenossenschaft* or *Zentralkellerei*) offer good value, as do reliable shippers, such as Sichel, Deinhard, Valckenberg, or St. Ursula, to name but a few.

In the fine wine sector, many consider that Germany's white wines are second to none. The *Qualitätsweine* mit Prädikat (quality wines with a special attribute indicating the ripeness of the grapes at harvest) range from light, delicate, elegant Kabinett wines (usually the driest of the Prädikats), to riper, late-harvested Spätlese wines (in the trocken, or dry, and halbtrocken, or medium-dry, styles outstanding with meals), to the rich and luscious Auslese-style wines made from very ripe or overripe grapes, often with their concentration of aroma and flavor. The finest of these wines will usually bear the name of a village, followed by a vineyard name and the name of the grape variety. The name of the producer or shipper must also be stated on the label, and if the wine is estate-bottled (*Erzeugerabfüllung = Mis en Bouteilles au Château*), this, too, will be indicated on the label. In the 19th century, it was still common to find top German wines labeled with only the name of the village of origin (e.g. Hochheimer, Bernkasteler, Oppenheimer) and it was assumed that a white wine was Riesling, a red wine was Spätburgunder (Pinot Noir). It is a very rewarding experience indeed to take the time to discover the subtle nuances which distinguish villages, vineyards, and varieties of Germany's finest white wines.

THE GREATEST WINES

Sooner or later every amateur of wine will be tempted to taste one of the world's great growths. First, let him educate his own palate, starting with lesser wines, learning to recognize a good bottle when one comes his way, before he sits down to savor the best. A great wine must be sufficiently aged if its true excellence is to be appreciated—and it is axiomatic that it will not be cheap, especially if (as now is so often the case) it must be bought fully aged from a wine merchant. Whether it is bought young, for laying down, or later, for immediate use, it is wise to take no risks in planning such a treat, but to decide on one of the illustrious names among the acknowledged elite (Château Margaux, Chambertin, Château d'Yquem, Montrachet) and from a great year. Vintage charts, as we have said elsewhere, are not as infallible as they seem; but a great vineyard is unlikely to produce a poor wine, however bad the summer may have been, and a Chambertin or a Château Prieuré-Lichine of an off year may be very good and less expensive than usual, and the fully matured fine wine of a great year will be an incomparable experience. Look for these supreme names in the First, Second, Third, Fourth, or Fifth Growths (*Premiers, Seconds, Troisièmes, Quatrièmes, Cinquièmes Crus*) of Bordeaux (*see* Médoc and Bordeaux classifications), among the Burgundian *grands vins* (*see* Burgundy), or the fine German wines (*see* Germany).

The best California wines come from the Napa and Sonoma valleys and other parts of the North Coast vineyard district. (*See* United States: California for names of reliable wineries.)

WINE IN THE RESTAURANT

Getting value for your money in a restaurant is rather different from doing the same thing in a shop. In many restaurants in France, diners-out discard the list of mediocre wines at inflated prices and order the carafe Beaujolais or rosé instead—and these, incidentally, are often quite good value. This is the easier way out, but it is not the answer; constructive criticism would be much more effective. Complain, complain, complain—but make allowances for the fact that the management must make a fair percentage on the bottle. A number of restaurants keep good cellars and present excellent wine lists; it is easy to find out which these are, since their reputations will be generally known; at other places, the manager may really know

very little about wine, and, tactfully handled, might be willing to learn and to change his source of supply to one of the more reliable shippers or merchants. It cannot be repeated too insistently that in a restaurant the regular customer gets the wine he deserves.

VINTAGE CHARTS

As for the great years, read the vintage charts but do not let yourself be hypnotized by them: in the small space of one of these printed lists, only the broadest generalities can be included. The vintage notes in the catalogue of the first-class wine merchant will be fuller and therefore more reliable—but even those cannot possibly cite the many exceptions to every rule.

The men who devote their lives to making wine are agreed on one point: wine is a living, constantly changing complex. In any given year, it will start out "green," generally fruity, often harsh, and will mature, first in barrel and then in bottle, until it is soft and mellow. Then (it may be years after bottling) the wine is at its peak—a state of excellence which endures for varying lengths of time. Those wines which, in the opinion of the experts, will slowly mature to greatness and hold it are given high marks on vintage charts; if a wine is marked low, it may be not unpleasant but one which should be drunk when it is young. What the marking system cannot take into account is the fact that individual wines are full of surprises. Wines from adjoining vineyards, all made by experienced and devoted men, may yet vary enormously. In Burgundy, 1953 was a good year, yet many growers made poor white wines because their grapes were too high in sugar and volatile acidity; 1945 was a good vintage—but not in Chablis, where the vineyards were spoiled by hail.

Once its limitations are realized, however, a chart is useful. Some notes on recent vintages follow.

RECENT VINTAGES

The factors determining quality are the soil, the climate, the grape variety, and the man who makes the wines, taking for granted that the grape varieties will be suited to the vineyards in which they are planted. When all these elements are perfectly married, the buyer will be justified in expecting value in a bottle of wine. Vintage years are important; yet overemphasis on vintage charts will not solve all the buyer's problems.

Provided the possibilities of fraud have been set aside, the expert can select in any given year the best wines from the château-bottlings of Bordeaux and the estate-bottlings of Burgundy, eliminating the failures of both nature and man. Some great vintage years will produce some disappointing wines through premature picking or faulty wine-making. Nature does not bless a large area with a uniform balance of sunshine and rain when needed.

Vintage charts at best can only generalize. In lesser years, often condemned categorically as "poor," the wine-buyer can find well-selected, good, enjoyable values, and occasionally he will find an absolute delight. This especially applies to red wines. A minimum amount of sunshine is required for white wines; otherwise, excessive acidity will throw them out of balance. In a perfect vintage, a red wine will have a higher degree of alcohol, plus an abundance of tannin. This will make for a slow-maturing wine, one which often disappoints the early drinker and requires ageing to carry it to a high level of quality where well-matured velvet will replace the harsh bitterness of tannin.

A great vintage in a red Bordeaux is one which, thanks to the abundance of sunshine, will have a high sugar content that is transformed into a high degree of alcohol. To some great years, like 1961, 1970, 1975, 1978, 1982, 1983, 1985, and 1986, vintage chart makers will, perhaps sincerely, give the highest possible rating; but they will be rating in terms of the "high" the wine will reach once it is fully matured. Sometimes such memorable vintages have an overabundance of tannin. This tannin acts like a corset, to hold the wine together over a period of years until it reaches its apex. This may only be attained at the end of some fifteen or twenty years. To drink the 1961 in 1965 might have been a disappointing experience. If you had waited until the 1970s that wine—from a great vineyard—would have been one of the most memorable experiences available to living man in the enjoyment of wines.

If one must generalize, one can say that vintage charts are much more important in white wines than in reds, since in the poor years the high acidity caused by lack of maturity is expressed in a certain greenness, and the defects of the wine are more apparent. In red wines, one must consider the district, whether its wines are generally fast or slow in maturing. Another generalization is that the greater the wine, the more slowly it matures. Bearing these facts in mind, here are the generalities, always remembering that they may be upset by the storage and the climate in which the wines will be drunk, for warm storage ages the wines prematurely and perfect cool storage will allow the wines to reach their potentials naturally.

BORDEAUX

1955—A very great year for red wines. Magnificently balanced.

In white wines this was a perfect year for those who find Sauternes over-sweet.

1957—Good vintage for red wines. A tendency to hardness (until the early '70s) made the wines relatively slow-maturing and harsh. Enjoyable in the '80s.

1958—Light, fast-maturing. Expect faded bottles.

1959—A very good vintage, though, contrary to expectations at the time, not the very greatest. The red wines were full, harmonious, and slow-maturing. For those who like Barsacs and Sauternes, 1959 is the year.

1960—Good red wine in the Médoc, which is now fading.

1961—One of the smallest years remembered in the Médoc. The flowering during the cold and rainy month of May resulted in a diminution in production of 40 to 50 percent. Then a hot summer, followed by a superb September, gave us the greatest red wine vintage since 1945.

This was a good vintage for the sweet wines of Sauternes and Barsac.

1962—These very good red wines were ready long before those of 1961. Will be delightful through the '90s.

1963—A year to forget.

1964—A very plentiful year for red wines. A magnificent summer was followed by an excellent September. Certain châteaux in the Médoc waited to harvest late, but unfortunately it rained incessantly from October 8 onward. Very successful in Saint-Émilion and Pomerol, where the harvest finished before the rain started. Fair for sweet white wines.

1965—The summer was rainy. Fair wines.

1966—Uniformly a great vintage. A very dark deep color with perfect balance made these round wines outstanding. The best since 1961. Slow-maturing, they are now starting to be ready and will last for some time.

Barsac and Sauternes—One-third very good. The remainder disappointing.

1967—Softer than the '66s, hence faster-maturing—a good vintage requiring selectivity—abundant in quantity. Will not last over 25 years. The Sauternes are superb.

1968—Owing to a rainy summer—some rot during the harvest—the wines were disappointing.

1969—Fairly good, rather unbalanced in the Médoc; disappointing in Saint-Émilion and Pomerol. July and August had abundant sun followed by freakish rains in September.

The sweet Barsacs and Sauternes are only fair.

1970—A great vintage. Unquestionably the best since 1961, with an abundance not seen since the beginning of the century. The wines have matured at different ages, with some wines to be drunk early, and some put away for drinking in the late 1980s or in the '90s.

1971—A very good vintage, lighter and faster-maturing than the '70s. The reds are light but round. Some growers preferred the '71s to the '70s because of the elegance, breed, and perfect balance of the former.

The white wines are generally good, with some very exceptional highs in Sauternes, which will be delightful until the year 2000.

1972—After a disastrously rainy summer, the vintage was somewhat saved by hot sunny weather from late September through the October harvest. The reds showed too much acidity when young, and even when mature they will be pleasant at best. These wines were originally sold in Bordeaux at ridiculously high prices.

Forget the light dry wines of '72; those of Barsac and Sauternes did not approach the quality of the '71s.

1973—The reds are round, though lacking the tannin that would give them longevity. They are light and pleasant drinking in the 1980s. Wines from the Médoc were more successful than those from Graves, Saint-Émilion, and Pomerol. Some of the better red wines resemble those from 1967.

Sweet white wines were barely average. Hail destroyed the Sauternes vineyards several times.

1974—For red wines, a fair to good vintage. The large harvest and the fact that these wines will eventually surpass the '73s make this vintage a good value. The harvest in Sauternes was a disaster.

1975—A very great vintage for red wines; rich, harmonious, slow-maturing—the best since 1961. Only a small quantity was produced (50 percent less than in 1974).

Superb sweet Barsac and Sauternes due to the prevailing good weather in late October and early November.

1976—The better '76s were enjoyable before the slow-maturing '75s from the great vineyards. The '76s compare to the '75s as the '71s did to the somewhat harder '70s. Some '76s show a tendency to decline.

Sauternes and Barsac were spotty owing to the October rains. Rot set in before the *Botrytis cinerea* could exercise its "noble rot" process.

1977—After a rainy summer, the 1977 growing cycle performed something of a miracle. At the end of a cool August, a warm, dry, sunny period began, lasting until the completion of the late harvest, which took place under very good conditions at the end of October. This late hot spell produced wines dark in color, fruity, and slightly on the hard side, which have, however, matured fairly rapidly. Selectivity required.

Of the sweet wines of Barsac and Sauternes, only a minute quantity was produced; a few of them acceptable.

1978—A great vintage. Relatively even in quality, with some reds superior to many '70s, 1978 will unquestionably be one of the memorable years of the past few decades. Very long-lasting on the palate, the '78s have beautiful color, depth of character, and good harmony and balance.

Small quantities of good Barsacs and Sauternes were made, requiring careful selection.

1979—An exceptionally abundant harvest, especially for red wines. The wines are of generally very good quality. The wines are deep-colored, and despite their fullness they have a tendency to be soft and round. They will mature relatively quickly. They are characterized by the softer Merlot grape, which rip-

ened more completely than the harder Cabernet Sauvignon. Many top châteaux claim that the 1979 vintage is better than the 1978.

The Sauternes are fine without achieving the concentration of the '71s or the '67s.

1980—A pleasant vintage, round and fast-maturing wines. The very late 1980 harvest reached satisfactory maturity. Some wines show good tannins and aromas—this despite some rain during the harvest in mid-October

In the Médoc the wines are round and soft—with a tendency toward quick development. Results were less favorable in Saint-Émilion and Pomerol.

The good October and November were especially beneficial to the sweet wines of Sauternes and Barsac, which produced an excellent vintage. At Château d'Yquem, for instance, 80 percent of the harvest will be sold under its label, as opposed to 40 percent in 1979.

1981—A very good vintage. A few intermittent rains toward the end of the harvest (in mid-October) helped to eliminate any hardness the wines might have had.

The sweet Barsacs and Sauternes (picked after the end of the harvest of the reds), are of exceptional quality.

1982—This year will be remembered for its superb red wines—round, perfumed, and long on the palate, with great potential for the coming years. This is particularly so for the *Grands Crus Classés* which started their harvest in mid-September and were very selective in the choice of their vats. Experts predict great affinity to the wines of 1947, of 1955, and of 1959, but whichever it may be, a great vintage is assured.

Excellent dry whites. The Barsacs and Sauternes were partly ruined by the late October rains, but there were some good sweet whites produced nonetheless.

1983—The miraculous, record-beating hot weather starting in mid-September and continuing to the very end of the harvest, without a drop of rain, unexpectedly gave birth to a vintage which many growers may well consider better than 1982. Harder and more tannic, it may be slower-maturing than its superb predecessor. The intense, dark color and high density are promising signs of a great classic vintage, one that will be superior to 1978.

In Sauternes and Barsac, Châteaux d'Yquem, Guiraud, Coutet, and other vineyards—by patiently waiting to pick late—produced another superb vintage. One of the greatest since the war.

1984—After a record, rainy May which resulted in poor flowering of the Merlot grape variety, reducing the quantities by 50 to 80 percent, the summer and early autumn weather which followed was sunny and faultless except for an eighteen-day period of intermittent rain from September 16 to October 5. This prompted many irresponsible forecasters in the press to confuse quality and quantity. They did not wait to see the good results in many vineyards that started harvesting on Monday, October 8, under sunny, dry conditions and achieved good results which in some instances in the Médoc are comparable to the 1981 vintage. These pleasant wines promise to be a cross between 1980 and 1981. In Sauternes and Barsac the *Botrytis* developed well, and some very good small quantities were produced.

1985—A great vintage. After a long, hot drought a small harvest of fairly hard wines was predicted. Because of the considerable amount of grapes, and contrary to expectations, a large harvest of this great vintage was produced. The quantity helped to dilute the hardness, and the agreeable, subtle tannins may, at this early stage, make this vintage resemble a cross between 1982 and 1983.

Although the success was very marked in the Merlots in the Médoc, this was less evident in Saint-Émilion and Pomerol. In Sauternes there was good maturity. Finally, in November the needed mist slowly helped the development of *Botrytis*. The picking went on into December, and Sauternes enjoyed a fair vintage having some ups and downs.

1986—For the Médoc an exceptionally great vintage. A shade harder than 1985. Some mistakenly find resemblances with 1961. Generally better than 1975 and 1970. Although high in tannins, they are not as harsh as in 1975 and 1970. 1986 is a Cabernet Sauvignon vintage; hence, Saint-Émilion and Pomerol, which produced fine wines, will not be up to the exceptional quality of the Médocs.

Sauternes has produced a great vintage. Some compare it with 1966, but it is a relatively fast-maturing vintage.

BURGUNDY

1961—A very great year for red Burgundies. Rich, tannic, and well-balanced wines with a beautiful color.

A high degree of alcohol counterbalanced by acidity gave the white Burgundies an excellent, well-deserved reputation. This is now a matter of the past.

1962—Very fine, light, and well-balanced red Burgundies with a tendency toward early maturity. They were ready before the '61s.

1963—Red Burgundies were disastrous.

1964—In some instances the red Burgundies were better than the red Bordeaux. These well-rounded wines could be drunk fairly early, as was the case with the '62s.

Though the white Burgundies were well balanced, they tended to lack acidity and matured quickly.

1965—The floods, which spoiled many vineyards, and the lack of maturity made the red wines a disaster.

1966—Burgundies from the Côte d'Or were similar to '64, being full, round, and fast-maturing.

1967—Good vintage lacking the body of the '66s.

1968—Light, disappointing wines.

1969—Great vintage in the Côte d'Or with a deep color—round, full, with lasting character. The white wines lacked the required acidity and have now faded.

1970—A good vintage, not in the same league as the '69s.

1971—The red wines were full-bodied with good color, though not equal to the '69s.

1972—In spite of the good weather during the late harvest in October, the Pinot Noirs lacked maturity. Some reds have good color and balance, but on the whole are only average.

The white wines were generally disappointing.

1973—The quality was less than could have been hoped for. Not worthy of any consideration today.

Whites better than reds, but with a tendency to fade.

1974—A rather good vintage, at the same level as the '71s.

Good white wines, to be consumed rather rapidly.

1975—Very disappointing vintage, with too little color because of abundant rain.

The fair white wines have little longevity.

1976—A great vintage for Burgundy, which had suffered from a lack of good vintages. Many of the wines were full, round, deep in color and character.

The whites were full-bodied, though lacking in the acidity needed to give them freshness.

Beaujolais enjoyed its best vintage since 1961.

1977—Small in quality and large in quantity, these wines were too light, thin, and short. A few exceptional wines may be found acceptable.

1978—A very good year. The reds are soft and not overly tannic.

The whites also turned out well. Excellent Chablis.

1979—Quality is uneven, although good on the average. The wines are fruity and well-colored, but they lack depth and body.

Abundant quantities of Beaujolais were produced. Here, too, quality was uneven: 20 percent good, 20 percent acceptable, 60 percent poor.

White Burgundies were light-bodied, well-balanced, and fruity. Although not wines for laying down, they are better than the reds.

1980—The red wines had a fairly good vintage. They will be fast-maturing. Meursault, Puligny, and Chassagne made well-balanced whites on the fruity side—a good vintage, but no more than that.

In the Beaujolais, 1980 produced a fair "typical" light vintage. They should be drunk quickly.

1981—The deep color of the reds is pleasing, but there is a certain lack of depth of character in the taste. Some sparse rains during the harvest lowered the potentially very good quality. Nevertheless, the wines are pleasant. The quality was evenly good in the Beaujolais.

The whites are better than the reds, fruity and elegant. They can stand up well.

1982—A good year for the red wines. The quality was uniform, with good deep color and tannin content. An exceptionally large harvest for Beaujolais, but with great unevenness in quality, requiring skillful selection.

The white Burgundies were supple, elegant, low in acidity, and superior to those of 1981.

1983—The hot, sunny weather in late September and during the harvest produced a very good, rather tannic, hard vintage in red wines, which Burgundy has needed since 1976—this despite the hail which destroyed some of the flag-bearers in Vosne-Romanée, the heart of the Côte de Nuits. Top reds can be found.

The richness of the 1983 white wines makes the 1982 more appealing if one is seeking fruit and freshness. The whites were flat.

In the Beaujolais, 1983 was a prized vintage for those who were willing to sacrifice lightness and fruit for the staying power needed for wines exported to distant shores.

1984—Despite having a good color, the red wines are on the light side and of average quality. In the Beaujolais the quality was good. Some growers compared it to 1973 and 1982. The white Burgundies are good. They have been criticized for a lack of fullness and depth.

1985—A good vintage, good fruit and color. They are better than the '82s and '84s. Some liken them to the '78s and '79s. They could have had more subtlety, which would have given them more character. A very large quantity of wines was produced, if somewhat diluted as regards the whites in Puligny and Chassagne. A few exceptional highs could be found.

1986—An average vintage. The red Côte de Beaune were generally on the light side. The whites were better than the reds.

RHÔNE

1960—The only region in France that produced good-quality wines this year.

1961—Like other regions in France, the Rhône Valley produced a great vintage, especially in the northern Rhône, from the Côte Rôtie to Hermitage.

1962—A small vintage; many decent wines.

1963—A small vintage. Very clearly inferior to the '62s.

1964—An average vintage.

1965—A fair vintage. The Côtes du Rhône region, unlike other parts of France, did not lack sunshine. The harvest weather was nearly ideal.

1966—A top vintage. The best since the great 1960, which was exceptional in the Rhône. Some growers claim that the great '66s even surpassed that.

1967—Blessed with more good vintages than any other wine district in France, the Rhône outdid itself again.

1968—A few pleasant wines were produced.

1969—Small in quantity and short in quality—disappointing color. The main exceptions were in the Côte Rôtie, where excellent wines were produced.

1970—A very good vintage, in quantity and quality.

1971—Fair to good.

1972—Most of the Rhône wines were disappointing, but a few were good.

1973—Quality was only average, since the wines lacked both acidity and fruit. Many mediocre wines.

1974—A good vintage in general, with, unfortunately, many exceptions. Good color, good fruit, and character, in some cases an excellent lasting ability.

1975—Average quality at best, with a few highs and lows, more of the latter than the former. Châteauneuf-du-Pape was particularly disappointing.

1976—Rather good. Thirty percent of the wine, generally from Condrieu, Côte Rôtie, and Hermitage, was of very good quality. Twenty-five percent or so was very acceptable, and the remaining forty-five percent—those of Châteauneuf-du-Pape and other southern Côtes du Rhône—were mediocre. Late summer rains lasted through the harvest in the south, swelling the grapes and producing weak wines.

1977—The Côtes du Rhône was unquestionably one of the most favored regions in France in 1977. The sun and warm weather prevailed, producing an abundant crop of full, round, well-balanced wines which will be long-lasting both on the palate and in the cellar.

1978—An exceptionally excellent vintage.

1979—Good quality. On the whole, the wines were well structured and had good color.

1980—A good vintage.

1981—Good quality. Good, full-bodied wines were produced. In Châteauneuf, the wines were sturdy and hard. In the Côtes du Rhône, the quality was evenly good.

1982—Generally, 1982 was far better than 1981. The Côtes du Rhône-Villages were good. The Northern Rhône produced particularly outstanding wines in the Côte Rôtie and Hermitage vineyards.

1983—The brokers and growers were categorical that the Côtes du Rhônes were bigger, better, and darker wines than the 1982s. There was more good, harder wine available with finer, delicate aromas. This also applies to the Tavel and the Châteauneuf-du-Pape.

However, the northern districts—including Hermitage, Crozes, and the Côte Rôtie—are claimed to be of an exceptional quality rarely seen since World War II.

1984—Some brokers consider certain 1984 wines to be even superior to those of 1983 and 1982.

1985—A very great vintage according to the Rhône's best authorities. "Very exceptional" describes the high quality.

1986—Some very good wines; however, in the lower Côtes du Rhône the huge quantity diluted the quality.

LOIRE

1970—A fairly good vintage for the Loire in general.

1971—Good, with excellent Muscadet, now faded.

1972—Not a good vintage. The wines were light and without character. They are now a thing of the past.

1973—Fair for most of the wines; but the Muscadet was quite fine, if not perfect.

1974—Fruity, well-balanced wines were produced. These wines were fine when drunk very young.

1975—Very good vintage. Many excellent Muscadets were produced, but some were harvested a bit too late and the grapes were thus overripe, lacking their characteristic greenness.

An exceptionally good vintage in the Anjou, Vouvray, and Pouilly-Fumé and Sancerre.

1976—Very good in Muscadet. France's drought brought about a premature ripening, which for these wines meant a lack of acidity. In other parts of the Loire such as Vouvray, Sancerre, and Pouilly-Fumé, the quantities and quality in general were good, especially for the Vouvray.

1977—Good, some pleasant wines were produced.

1978—A vintage which produced wines of a very good quality.

1979—Quality was good. Well balanced: the wines had good fruit without excessive acidity.

The Anjou harvest took place during the rain, and, in general, the wines were thin and disappointing. The Cabernet Franc made the best wines.

In Vouvray the quality was poor. Fortunately, most of the wines were processed as sparkling wines.

1980—Muscadets lacked ripeness and maturity and were therefore slightly acid; not equal to 1979. However, in Anjou and Vouvray, 1980 was better than 1979.

1981—The Muscadets produced a good vintage, considerably better than the 1980 and 1979: perfumed, lighter but fruity, without the predominant acidity of the previous vintages. The problem here, as in the other white-wine-producing sections of France, was quantity: only 300,000 hectoliters (7,950,000 gallons)—or 40 percent less than in 1980—was produced.

Unlike the 1979 and 1980 vintages, 1981 was a quality vintage of well-balanced wines. Very little sweet Vouvray was produced, because late rains prevented the development of *Botrytis*, the "noble rot." Contrary to 1979, sparkling Vouvray was produced only in small quantities, as most of the wine was made into good dry wines.

1982—The abundant Muscadet crop produced some very good wines, eminently drinkable, well balanced and harmonious, even though of unusually low acidity.

In Anjou and Saumur, the abundant harvest resulted in wine of varying quality, as was also the case in Touraine. The crop for sweet white wines was vastly reduced by late rains, while the reds had a successful year, producing fruity, elegant wines.

The dry Vouvrays were generally good, but the late rains prevented any production of sweet botrytized wines.

Sancerre and Pouilly produced fine, balanced wines with a rich bouquet, far superior to those of previous years.

1983—Growers making dry wines at both ends of the Loire—from Muscadet at one end to Pouilly-Fumé and Sancerre at the other—were elated. Some feel that the 1983 vintage may be superior to 1982.

In Anjou and Vouvray, the dry wines will be good but the producers made very little, if any, sweet wines, as *Botrytis* did not develop.

1984—Muscadet was the most favored area of the Loire. The wines were in excellent balance and enjoyed more character than the overly soft 1983s. In Vouvray the quality was fair, and again, as in 1979, a large amount had to be made into sparkling wine. As to the other areas, one could rate them as fair to good.

1985—From one end of the Loire to the other, the growers were happy. Muscadet was round, full, and pleasant. *Botrytis* developed, to make marvelous sweet wines in the Coteaux du Layon, which had not been produced for a few years.

1986—Good, fruity, light Muscadet with good acidity. The Loire throughout was good, but cool. With the exception of Anjou, rainy weather prevented *Botrytis* from developing to make sweet wines.

ALSACE

1971—Fair to good. Many small producers successful in their endeavors will look back at '71 as a highly prestigious vintage.

1972—Though pleasant and typically Alsatian, most of the wines lacked depth and were slightly acid.

1973—Most wines showed a certain lack of acidity, and should have been drunk young. By now they have faded.

1974—Well balanced, fresh despite rains throughout harvest, these should have been drunk when very young.

1975—A good vintage; fruity and harmonious.

1976—Both the quantity and the quality were high.

1977—Fair, drinkable, fruity wines, a bit hard.

1978—A very good vintage.

1979—A good abundant vintage. The wines are well-balanced.

1980—A fairly good vintage, though lacking in quantity, especially the Gewürztraminers.

1981—The quality was excellent (superior to the '79s). Those Rieslings that were not prematurely harvested were excellent.

1982—A very good vintage for both quality and quantity; the wines had great personality and bold aroma.

1983—An excellent vintage. Alsatian wines are generally fairly good from year to year. The Riesling and Gewürztraminer growers were overjoyed with the hot harvest weather of 1983, which produced late-harvest, sweet wines not seen since 1976 or 1921.

1984—After the great 1983s, 1984 was a big disappointment. A few fair dry wines will be found.

1985—A great vintage. Some growers claim it was better than the great '83s. The Gewürztraminers had more character than the preceding vintages, and the "late harvest" wines produced beautiful results.

1986—A good vintage proving that Alsace can produce high-quality wines. Furthermore, the good producers have learned to make a very careful selection of their vats.

To be appreciated at their best, these wines should ideally be consumed within their first five years in order to catch the freshness and youth so characteristic of Alsatian wines; left to mature too long, they tend to maderize.

CHAMPAGNE

Only when of a superior quality is the vintage indicated on a bottle of Champagne; hence the expression "a vintage year," meaning one of quality.

Like all white wines, sparkling or not, Champagne should be drunk fairly young, say at the most within ten to fifteen years after the harvest.

1966—Magnificent wines. Excellent bouquet.

1967—Rains between the fifth and twenty-first of September, just one week before the harvest, diminished the potential quality down to a non-vintage.

1968—Disastrous vintage.

1969—A good vintage, well-balanced and full-bodied.

1970—The quality was good to fair.

1971—Good vintage.

1972—Not a vintage year.

1973—A good and very plentiful vintage year.

1974—Fairly good vintage; wines without too much depth of character.

1975—A vintage year. Wines of a good quality, with a tendency toward lack of acidity.

1976—The 1976 vintage was one of significant quantity and good quality. A vintage year.

1977—Some Champagne winemakers were moderately well pleased and had a vintage year.

1978—A good-quality harvest, though bad weather at the beginning of the summer limited production.

1979—An abundant quantity of good quality. Some firms will produce vintage wines.

1980—Fair to good quality, disastrously small quantity, ridiculously high prices. Not a vintage year.

1981—Quality was good, but owing to late spring frosts, quantity was disastrously low: only 350,000 barrels were produced (compared with an insufficient 420,000 in 1980, and 800,000 in 1979). The quality, with less acidity than 1980, was in good balance, making 1981 a good average year in this respect.

1982—The Champagne region was one of the most prosperous this year, producing a fine vintage in suffi-

cient quantities (300 million bottles) to counterbalance the short harvests of 1980 and 1981.

1983—Once again, as in 1982, a tremendously large quantity of over 300 million bottles was produced. However, unlike 1982, the quality was not as good; hence, it was not a vintage year.

1984—Poor summer and autumn weather. At best it made a fair nonvintage.

1985—"Extraordinary" is the word applied by many to this harmoniously well-balanced vintage. But, though high in quality, it suffered from a lack of quantity. 120 million bottles were produced, which did not replace the 190 million bottles sold by the shippers in 1985. The shortfall in quantity was due to the January freezing weather, which hit Champagne more than any other region of France and resulted in a loss of some 30–40 million vines.

1986—Good wines; however, not a vintage. The quantity was satisfactory, and it will replace the annual sales depletion.

RHINE AND MOSEL

1959—A very great year, comparable to 1949 and 1953. High in alcohol, rich in sugar. The rare sweeter wines made history.

1960—A very large crop but below average in quality.

1961—The Mosel was good. Along the Rhine there were some disappointments.

1962—The Rheingau was favored, the Mosel was not.

1963—Large quantity but small in quality.

1964—Good vintage with many very high peaks.

1965—Uninteresting.

1966—Good, especially in the big estates, where they started picking on October 28.

1967—Mixed quality: one-third was a good vintage, of which some was great; the other two-thirds was average or downright disappointing. The difference in quality was caused by poor weather during the harvest.

1968—Light, mediocre wines.

1969—Better than 1966 and 1967, yet not great. A good elegant vintage.

1970—Great expectations, but, unfortunately, cool rainy weather in early October prevented the grapes from maturing properly. The larger estates waited to harvest, and in some cases the grapes were picked as late as Christmas. The delay was fortuitous, resulting in wine of great quality.

1971—One of the greatest vintages of the century, by far.

The wines had the miraculous balance of sugar and acidity that makes good German white wines among the world's very best. They will last long. In the Rheingau an astonishing 95 percent of the harvest was *Qualitätswein mit Prädikat*, the new legal phrase first applied in this year, for Kabinett, Spätlese, Auslese, etc. wines.

1972—After a rather cold summer the wines were poor, since the grapes failed to ripen completely.

1973—The hot and sunny summer made good quality likely, but two opposite problems made the wines less than very good. The lack of snow and rain during the previous winter damaged the vines in some areas; and then just before the picking was to commence in the fall of 1973, rain fell steadily for several days. A few cold days in December froze many grapes still on the vines at some of the Rheingau estates, and a few growers were able to make Eiswein.

1974—Small in quality. A few agreeable wines to be rapidly drunk were the result. No Spätlesen or Auslesen were produced.

1975—A great year, not approaching the '71s but with a good quantity of outstanding wines. The Rheingau produced Qualitätswein in 50 percent of the harvest. The Mosel-Saar-Ruwer was very lucky, with 45 percent Spätlesen and 15 percent Auslesen. The Palatinate and Rheinhessen areas produced 50 percent Qualitätswein, 15 percent Spätlesen.

1976—A very great year. The exceptionally hot weather had an especially positive effect in the Rheingau and the Mosel. The sugar content of the grapes was so high during the harvest, most notably in the Rheingau, that the Rieslings gave very little wine below the Spätlesen standard. In fact, one of the largest quantities of Auslesen wines, including the usually rare Beerenauslesen and Trockenbeerenauslesen, was produced—perhaps more than the market could absorb. Only half the normal crop was harvested in the Mosel, where the quality of the sweet wines was just as high as in the Rheingau. Sweet, perfectly balanced wines earmark this vintage, and good dry wines were hard to find.

1977—Of fairly low quality. For a vintage to be rated great in Germany, much sun is required, which 1977 notably lacked. For those who enjoy dry German wines, many pleasant bottles could be found.

1978—An extremely cold and wet summer created unfavorable growing conditions. The quality and quantity of the harvest were low. In the Rheingau, Rheinhessen, and Rheinpfalz, quantities were reduced, in some cases, by two-thirds. Surprisingly, the wines have turned out to be very drinkable, in some instances more so than the '77s.

1979—Extreme winter frosts hampered wine production; the total German harvest was below average with 8.5 million hectoliters (224.4 million U.S. gallons, 187 million imp.). The quality was generally good, with no real highs or lows. Young vines suffered, especially in the Rheinhessen and the Palatinate, but the small crops yielded wines of very good, although not excellent, quality. The Rheingau crop was high in both quality and quantity.

1980—In the Rheingau, as in the rest of Germany, the good harvest weather was not enough to make up for the wet and cold summer that preceded. Production was less than 50 percent of the normal crop, and quality was poor. This was also the case in the Mosel. In the Saar-Ruwer, winemakers produced only 10 percent of their normal harvest, and the quality was poor.

In the Rheinhessen and Palatinate, the harvest was down by half. The quality was fair, owing to the many new *vinifera* grape varieties planted, which managed to resist the cold, wet summer weather.

1981—The year went well until mid-September. Both quantity and quality were spoiled by the incessant rains from that time until the end of October. Do not look for Spätlesen, Auslesen, or better.

1982—Despite the long, hot summer, which allowed perfect maturity of the grapes, the general quality of the 1982 vintage was fair—at best—and little top-class wine was produced. This was due to the heavy, prolonged rains which occurred at the beginning of the harvest. The new grape varieties produced some very disappointing wines because of their low acidity caused by the dry summer. However, the Kabinett and traditional Riesling wines were better, being fruity and elegant. A fair vintage in the Rhine, a little better along the Mosel.

1983—Generally a very good vintage, with a good balance of acidity and sugar, with a high proportion of Prädikat wines among the late-ripening varieties, such as Riesling. A large quantity of Eiswein was produced.

1984—A cold and rainy summer followed by a dry spell during the harvest produced wines from poor to fair. Many pleasant, drinkable bottles will nevertheless be available.

1985—A wonderful three-month period of dry and sunny weather starting in late August brought the Rhine river to the lowest level ever. The traditional Riesling areas along the Rhine and Moselle rivers benefited from this weather; however, wide areas of new grape varieties in the Rheinhessen, the Palatinate, and elsewhere suffered from the drought, and the yield was fair in quality, producing clean and typical wines. In the Moselle some Beerenauslese was made.

Severe frost in mid-November helped make this an excellent year for making Eiswein in all areas.

This was a vintage for good Kabinett and Spätlese-type wines; however, there were hardly any top wines.

1986—What potentially appeared exceptionally promising in quality dwindled with a four-week spell of cold and rain prior to the harvest. As a whole, the quality was fair.

6   Starting a Cellar

Until I was nearly forty such liquids as I possessed had to endure very inferior accommodations.

NOTES ON A CELLAR-BOOK
George Saintsbury

A wine cellar conjures up a picture of a more spacious age when men laid down their crusted Port and pre-phylloxera Claret—or when their fathers were drinking their three bottles a day and suffering from gout. A country house with ample cellars is an undeniable asset; but even the owner of a modern 2½-room apartment can emulate Professor Saintsbury's "very inferior accommodations," if he exercises some ingenuity.

The ideal wine cellar should be roomy, airy, and dry, away from light, free from vibration, and maintaining a constant temperature of about 55°F. (13°C.). Obviously this ideal is not very often attainable, and even in France only a few cellars approach it. The next best thing is to contrive a storeplace which satisfies as many of these conditions as possible. An understanding of why these conditions are ideal and how they affect the wine is a great help.

A roomy, airy, dry place. Lack of room, of course, means simply that you will be cramped for storage space, and so you lay down less wine. Proper ventilation will ensure that the air doesn't get stale and musty, creating an atmosphere which will eventually permeate through the corks, slowly imparting a moldy taste to the wine. A certain amount of humidity is to be sought for. This prevents the corks from drying up prematurely. A good "flooring" is to cover the ground with an inch of small gravel, sprinkling a little water over it periodically. The gravel will contain the humidity. Excessive humidity is injurious to the labels but rarely to the wine. For the fortunate one owning a large cellar, it would be wise to have the bottles re-corked every fifty to sixty years. This is the maximum expected life span of a good cork.

Away from light and free from vibration. Some of the diseases that afflict wine—such as protein casse, a precipitate formed by the presence of excess protein—react only in the presence of light. Strong light may also "bake" your wine, maderizing or oxidizing it—i.e., turning it prematurely flat, musty, and brown like Madeira in color. Vibration agitates wines and also ages them prematurely: a house near a railway is therefore a bad place for a wine cellar, although if the

disturbance is not too great and the wine is placed close to the ground there may be no ill effects.

A constant temperature of about 55°F. This is almost certainly the biggest bugbear of the would-be wine-keeper. Yet wines will not be ruined by temperatures rising as high as 75°F. (24°C.), provided that the rise is gradual, although they will age faster; old wines in particular are fragile and will not keep very long above 60°F. (16°C.). Between 50° and 57°F. (10° to 14°C.) wines age normally, and although they can generally adapt themselves to an almost imperceptibly rising temperature, sudden changes will soon injure them. To keep them near hot pipes is particularly harmful; and any house where the temperature rises during the day and drops suddenly during the night is a bad wine-store. In general, red wines are less susceptible to heat than are white ones; and white wines are best kept closest to the floor in the coolest part of the cellar.

It will be perfectly obvious that a "wine cellar" need not necessarily be in the cellar. With a little ingenuity, it is often possible to convert some corner into a store for wines that are to be consumed reasonably soon. It will not then be possible to buy great wines very young—when prices are most advantageous—and keep them until they are old and mature; yet a variety of good wines can be kept on hand at all times. A hall cupboard, for instance, would do—or the space under the stairs; then you can start planning what you will put into it.

To begin with, all natural wines—that is, wines not fortified with brandy—should be stored lying on their sides, so that the wine wets the cork, keeping it from shrinking and letting air into the bottle, ruining the wine. Sherry, Port, spirits, and liqueurs can be stored standing up since the higher alcoholic content will preserve them; but since—with the exception of Vintage Port and Madeira—these do not improve in bottle, there is little point in keeping a great store on hand. As you will probably want to keep both wines and spirits in your cellar, you will need shelves on which to stand the spirits, and bins and racks in which to lay the wines.

Many wine shops have metal and wooden racks at fairly reasonable prices, and they make excellent containers for wines. As a substitute, a whiskey carton, laid on its side, is a simple and effective arrangement. Special bins can also be made; these should be of stout wood, preferably in the shape of a honeycomb or lozenge to keep the bottles from rolling when one of them is removed. Clay pipes, fifteen inches around, may also be used; these provide a protective cover for the bottles and insulate them from sudden changes in temperature. The bins need not be large—one a foot and a half square will hold almost a case of wine—but unless you plan to keep large quantities of the same wine on hand, they should not be too deep either. Wines keep best when they are not disturbed, and scrambling through them to find a bottle at the bottom of the pile is restful neither for the wine nor for the searcher.

Once you have your racks or bins installed, the cellar needs very little extra equipment: the main things are a thermometer, some tags, and a cellar-book.

Of these, the thermometer is the most important, since it shows at once if the temperature of your store-place is proper for the normal ageing of wines. Tags come in handy for identifying bottles which are laid on their sides and in helping you to find the one you want without upsetting all the others. Finally, the cellar-book. While it may seem pretentious to keep a book if you only have half a dozen bottles or at most a case of wines on hand, the book will nevertheless be useful—and a pleasure to look back on later.

Whatever book you choose, your entries in it will run true to form: the wine, its name and year; the amount purchased, from whom, and on what date; the name of the shipper, and the price paid. On the other side of the page you will want space to enter the date of drinking and your comments. It is a good idea to devote one full page to a wine, particularly if you have bought a number of bottles.

Cellars provide the most enjoyment if the selection is a balanced one with a variety from which to choose. This variety may include wines of different types, qualities, and prices. If you are planning a large and elaborate cellar, it is best to call in an expert wine merchant who will be familiar with the market and can secure the best values.

WHICH WINES?

In previous editions of this encyclopedia I had an arbitrary list of a small selection for a basic 36-bottle cellar. As consumers have become more sophisticated throughout the world and the world is now producing, in most countries, better wines than before and as selections differ according to the market and the country, consumers should lean more on the advice of one's accessible wine merchant and the adventure of finding wines to suit one's own palate.

7 Wine and Health

Wine can be considered with good reason as the most healthful and the most hygienic of all beverages.
Louis Pasteur

Wine is one of the noblest cordials in nature.
John Wesley, founder of Methodism

Wine is a food.

Oliver Wendell Holmes

The magic of wine is intrinsic and complete. It induces confidence, a sense of well-being, and euphoria, thus conditioning a moderate wine-drinking man to be happy and healthy—for good wine is a tonic in convalescence. It disposes him to relax and encourages his appetite—a process well understood in this age of psychological study, but one which can only partially be demonstrated scientifically. A laboratory rat cannot show how wine will influence a tired or debilitated man, nor would a man feel the same after a hypodermic injection of wine as he does when he holds a sparkling glassful up to the light, sniffs the bouquet, and rolls the first sip around on his tongue. The secret is not in the alcoholic content alone, for wine has virtues which other alcoholic beverages do not share. In the chemical compound wine, which awaits final analysis, there are infinitesimal esters, contributing largely to the smell, taste, and character of the whole, but too subtle to have been trapped by the chemist so far. Its main ingredients have nevertheless been long established. The astonishing thing about modern scientific research is the way it proves that wine-making traditions dating from the earliest times are, according to our lights, perfectly logical and sane. Practices which might, at first glance, seem to be dictated by superstition have taken on a new authority in the cold light of science.

The study of wine is necessarily the study both of the particular and of the general effect—of the component and the composite. In France it is held that men who drink wine are happy, men who drink beer are heavy and often slower-witted, and men who drink spirits may be hectic and are often ugly-tempered. Professor Arnozan has said:

"Wine taken every day in moderation gently excites the intellectual faculties of him who absorbs it. It ends by giving him certain special characteristics: sharpens his wits, animates, renders more amiable, confers a great facility of assimilation, producing a sort of self-confidence—such are the traits of the man who every day makes use of wine."

It is worth remembering that not only were the Greeks and Romans wine-drinking people, not only are the French, Spanish, and Italians today, but the English, during their most vivid and adventurous period, the Elizabethan Age, were wine-drinkers too.

WINE AS FOOD

Depending on its richness in sugar and alcohol, a liter of wine is equal to 600–1,000 calories. More than one hundred chemical ingredients have been isolated in wine. It contains vitamins A, B, and C; and all thirteen of the minerals established by E. J. Underwood in 1940 as necessary to human life are also present. These are: calcium, phosphorus, magnesium, sodium, potassium, chlorine, sulfur, iron, copper, manganese, zinc, iodine, and cobalt.

Vitamin B is significantly present in wine. Red wine is richer than white in many food elements because it is obtained by maceration or steeping with the skins during fermentation; this is not the case with white wine, yet studies at the University of California College of Agriculture have established that in vitamin B content there is no difference between red and white wine, nor between dry and fortified wine. In riboflavin, white wines tend to lead, some of them having two-thirds the value of fresh milk. The vitamin B complex in wines remains stable and does not deteriorate as they age; but the freezing or pasteurizing necessary to preserve unfermented grape juice destroys vitamin B, including riboflavin, the content of which may reach 120 micrograms in 100 grams, with 50 micrograms of thiamine and other elements.

Besides these vitamins and minerals, which help to maintain the body and its metabolism, are the nutritive components in the grape sugars (dextrose is valuable here), polyphenols, proteins, and alcohol. ("It has been demonstrated that natural grape sugars in wine are readily absorbed by the human system and are desirable in the diet, that the alcohol in wine is a quick source of caloric energy, that wine has a definite blood-building iron content."—*Encyclopaedia Britannica.*) Ninety-five per cent of the energy in alcohol is converted for immediate use—so Neumann said in Germany at the beginning of the century, and it has been confirmed by Atwater and Benedict. "Ethylic alcohol is absorbed directly and progressively unless the stomach is empty." (Starling.) "Carried by the blood to every part of the system, it is burned up in the tissues." (Duroy, Perrin, and Lallemand.) The nutritive value of wine has been recognized in Spain, where it is placed under the same price controls as bread. Because of the nourishing quality of the other ingredients in wine the alcoholic content is taken into the body more slowly and utilized more efficiently than when it is absorbed in a higher percentage from more potent drinks. Research by Professor Georges Portmann of Bordeaux, president of the International Committee for the Scientific Study of Wine, and by Max Eylaud has revealed that while a small amount of alcohol can increase the vigor of the human machine by 15 per cent, a double and triple dose does not have a proportionately greater effect, and it has been found independently that in larger quantities of alcohol there is an inhibition which actually decreases its utility. The approximate 11 per cent of alcohol in natural wine is believed to be the most effective proportion. Even more surprising is the claim that alcohol as an internal disinfectant seems to be most powerful in solution in wine and even in wine-and-water. The increase of prophylactic effect with the *decrease* of proportion of alcohol remained totally baffling until very recently, when it was discovered that certain elements of wine, other than alcohol, prevent or impede the growth of the germs of certain diseases in the human body.

WINE IN WEIGHT REDUCTION

Various investigations and experiments have established in graphable figures the predictable effects of wine on the human system. Taken in dilution of about 10 to 11 per cent—the saturation of natural wine—the body oxidizes approximately half a gram of alcohol per pound of body-weight in twenty-four hours, provided that the drinks are taken at well-spaced intervals. This quantity completely disappers in the vital processes, leaving no residue in the blood, urine, or other analyzable media. It is excess alcohol, not this assimilable amount, which causes inebriation. The ideal intake, therefore, totally used by the system in restoration and in generating energy, with nothing left over, is the number of pounds of body-weight multiplied by half a gram of alcohol.

In a man of average size this comes to a rough 500 calories per day, a gram of alcohol providing 7 calories. (150 pounds of body-weight multiplied by half a gram of alcohol=75 grams; 75 × 7 calories=525 calories.) The average daily caloric expenditure under normal conditions is 3,000 calories; wine therefore can supply 17 per cent of the calories needed in daily life. In fact, in a great part of the world, it does—here is a laboratory experiment verified on a gigantic scale in many lands and over thousands of years, where wine has always been a chief element of diet. This vast human experiment was confirmed under closely controlled conditions by W. O. Atwater and others of the American Academy of Science. Three healthy men between the ages of twenty-five and thirty-three and conditioned by different environments, a Swede, an American, and a Canadian, one an individual accustomed to drink wine and two teetotalers, were observed in a calorimetric chamber. They were given a diet which included 72 grams of alcohol a day. The heat production and by-products of their bodies were studied. The alcohol provided 20 per cent of total calories during rest and 14 per cent during work, and was found to be capable of replacing proteins, carbohydrates, and fats, and of protecting proteins and other tissue substances ingested from other sources. The weight of all three men remained constant throughout the experiment.

The significance of wine in diet has been summarized as follows by Georges Portmann, professor of medicine, who is one of Europe's outstanding authorities on wine and health: "Wine can be used to replace 500 calories of fat or sugar intake in the daily diet. These calories will be completely consumed and will not add an ounce of body-weight. So employed, wine is very useful in reducing—it being understood that the food intake will be reduced by the 500 calories replaced by the wine."

Experiments in the United States and Italy have shown that wine not only replaces carbohydrate calories but in doing so reduces carbohydrate hunger, making it easier to do without the weight-producing sugar foods. Although there may be disagreement on the subject, it was shown that in lessening the type of intake and thus the food mass, alcohol has been demonstrated to lighten proportionately the work of the digestive glands.

The standard bottle of wine (three-quarters of a liter), if it is at 10 per cent of alcohol, provides 525 alcoholic calories. Considered as food alone, a bottle of natural wine a day is the desirable average for a person of normal size, although for one not engaged in manual labor, a little less wine (say half a liter) may be sufficient. While providing about one-sixth of required nourishment, it cannot add weight.

WINE IN ANOREXIA (LACK OF APPETITE)

While it has been found to reduce carbohydrate hunger, wine—dry white wine and especially red wine—excites the olfactory nerves and the taste buds, and so sharpens sluggish appetite.

Taken in the heavy-artillery concentration of the before-dinner cocktail or highball, alcohol *inhibits* appetite.

Alcohol in the dilution in which it is found in natural wine (in combination with sugars, acidity, and vitamin B_2) prompts the flow of saliva, hydrochloric acid, and gastric secretions—as, to some extent, does fruit juice. In other words, wine starts hunger and appetite into action. S. P. Lucia, professor of medicine in the University of California School of Medicine, describes what happens when too brutal a dose is taken. "If, however, the concentration of alcohol surpasses the optimum, then the albumin-coagulating action of the alcohol, the changes in osmotic pressure, and other physico-chemical alterations will induce a suppression of secretion" (*Wine as Food and Medicine*).

Tartaric and acetic acids and the tannins in dry wine, white or red, stimulate appetite quite apart from the influence of the alcohol. In order to investigate this, the acids alone in non-alcoholic solutions were fed to twenty-one men and women between twenty-two and fifty-three years of age in an experiment conducted in 1953 by the Institute of Medical Research in Oakland, California. The individuals engaged in their regular clerical work, and on certain test days took the wine-derived acids with their meals, or even, in a few cases, in place of their meals.

After the normality of the subject's nasal passages had been established by making him breathe on a polished metal surface (which would show cloudy patches of equal size and consistency), a nose-piece was fitted on, attached by pure gum rubber tubes to a bottle from which air could be injected into his nostrils under completely controlled conditions. By this method, the exact amount of any given odor projected to the subject could be known. The odor selected for the entire experiment was a standard brand of coffee.

It was found that after a normal meal olfactory sensitivity always decreased. This was graphed. When the acids accompanied the meal, olfactory sensitivity remained constant, the graph line cutting straight through the sharp zag which indicated the individual's usual loss of capacity to respond to the smell of an appetite-provoking substance. This corresponded more or less exactly with the capacity of the acids to remove the sensation of satiety usual after a large meal.

Independently, in the 1950s, an appetite-stimulating ingredient, apart from the acids and still incompletely understood, was isolated in red wine.

WINE AS MEDICINE

Wine serves as medicine, either as a general tonic, or as a specific in the cure of a large number of diseases. Its greatest value is probably in the way it can stimulate energy and give moral support, preparing the ground for recovery. It is an alkaline agent.

From very early times, the therapeutic and antiseptic properties of wine were known and valued. Medical papyri of ancient Egypt have preserved prescriptions in which wine played an essential part. Xenophon, in his *Anabasis*, recorded Cyrus's orders to his troops to take wine with them and, while it lasted, mix it with unaccustomed water of foreign lands; and in the nineteenth century wine was still recommended to be mixed with the impure water that caused cholera.

From Homeric days until a few centuries ago, wine was used for the cleansing and poulticing of wounds: Hippocrates advised it also as a diuretic and for cooling fevers; Galen made a list of wines and their different healing virtues. During the Middle Ages and after, the various theriacs and pharmaceutical compounds of herbs, spices, and magic animal ingredients were mixed in wine; and right up to the last century wines were employed in great quantity in hospitals and in private practice: white wines as diuretics, red Burgundy for dyspepsia, red Bordeaux for stomach trouble and diarrhea, German wines for nerves, Champagne for nausea and catarrh, Port and Sherry in convalescence. Even now a base of wine is not unknown in medical prescriptions. Its fall from favor in many of these instances was due in the first place to American agitation against intoxicants and, secondly, to the discovery of new drugs.

Some specific curative effects of pure unadulterated wine in cardiology, neurology, geriatrics, etc., are as follows:

(1) In France the general opinion is that by their richness in tartrates, certain wines add to the intestinal secretion, although red wines with high tannin content decrease it. Such red wines have long been well known for relieving diarrhea, particularly through the influence of the tannin in red wine on the large intestine. (But this is only true of good wine, especially Bordeaux; it is not suggested that a wine which has been adulterated with coarser blends will have the same beneficial effect.) Wine is beneficial also in cases of colitis and hemorrhoids.

(2) It is indispensable in low-sodium diets: a glass of wine contains from 1.3 to 9.9 milligrams of sodium, whereas an egg contains 40 milligrams; a glass of milk, 120 milligrams; an ounce of Cheddar cheese, 210 milligrams; a slice of white bread, 215 milligrams.

(3) Regular wine-drinkers are less apt than others to develop gallstones.

(4) "It is the safest of all sedatives" (according to Haggard and Jellinek).

(5) Wine that is rich in iron counteracts iron deficiency in anemia.

WINE AS A GERM-KILLER

Wine and alcohol have always been known as germ-killers both inside and outside the body. Curiosity about the effectiveness of wine prophylactics dating back to the Romans caused a student at the University of California College of Pharmacy, John Gardner, to track down an ingredient in red wine—not the alcohol—capable of killing *Staphylococcus aureus* and other bacteria. Numbers of germs, including that of typhus, had long been known to succumb to alcohols and certain of the acids in wine. Ordinary wine is equally capable of killing the dysentery bacillus, and even in great dilution red wine has been effectively utilized in purifying polluted water. The universal use of red wine in drinking-water in the past, and throughout much of the world today, has contributed immeasurably to the preservation of human life. Even in countries where the water supply is pure, this bactericidal action is useful. Wine taken with the meal functions in the system against such germs as may have been eaten on leafy vegetables or fruit, or derived from infectious organisms present in uncooked shellfish and other foods.

A wine of nine per cent or more alcohol has been shown to delay or prevent digestive liberation of trichinosis (J. B. McNaught and G. N. Pierce, Jr.: *The Protective Action of Alcohol in Experimental Trichinosis*, American Journal of Clinical Pathology, 1939). "I should be sorry to give up the use of wine in severe forms of enteric and pneumonic fever"—so said Sir William Osler, the distinguished Canadian physician. And wine is well known in the treatment of bronchitis and influenza.

WINE IS NOT ALL ALCOHOL, AND ALCOHOL DOES NOT NECESSARILY LEAD TO ALCOHOLISM

It is now certain that small quantities of wine stimulate and large amounts of alcohol stun. Cocktails are depressants, only appearing to be otherwise because they release the inhibitions. But natural wine is generally only one-tenth alcohol, whereas a cocktail will be 40 per cent or over. Another difference is the presence in wine of the many elements other than alcohol which have their effect. A big dose of alcohol will inhibit the flow of bile; a 10 per cent dose in natural wine will cause the flow to increase. Professor Georges Portmann once said: "Wine is a total complex—balanced, living, and in existence nowhere else. Do you know anything about food and life and think that balance and vitality count for nothing? It is the only thing man consumes that comes to him direct from the earth and alive."

Excess, not habit, in wine as in spirits may lead to harm. In wine, where the amount of alcohol is less, the danger is less. Old theories regarding the diseases caused by alcohol are now mostly exploded; these were often caused by vitamin and food deficiencies. Bright's disease, or inflammation of the kidneys, supposed in 1827 by Bright to have been sometimes caused by alcohol, has been established as having no connection with alcohol, which actually helps the kidneys to function. If the drinker eats properly, it is only with some difficulty that heavy consumption of alcohol can cause cirrhosis of the liver. There is at present no known ailment caused by natural wine, provided it is not consumed in great excess.

8 The Vine

Grapevines belong to the botanical family *Ampelidaceae*, a family which includes such other assorted plants as the Virginia creeper (*Ampelidaceae, Parthenocissus quinquefolia*) and other climbing berry-bearing growths, but not common ivy (*Hedera helix*). Of the ten genera of the family, only one—the genus *Vitis*—is important to the wine-maker, although others are capable of producing grapes. (Wine has been attempted from grapes of the genus *Ampelocissus,* but the result was light and sour and the experiment should not be repeated.) The genus *Vitis* suffices, however, for its vines are found virtually everywhere in the temperate world, growing wild generally between 35° south latitude and 50° north latitude and cultivated between 38° south and 53° north. The genus embraces two subgenera (*Euvites* and *Muscadiniae*) and numerous species. The varieties within the species proliferate enormously.

Genus *Vitis* (subgenus *Euvites*) species *vinifera* is responsible for all the world's great wines. Thought to have originated in Transcaucasia, *Vitis vinifera* found its most successful home in the warm Mediterranean basin where early civilization domesticated it; and from there it has been transplanted to California, Australia, North and South Africa, and South America. It has rivals as far as wine-making is concerned—but none serious—in species native to western Asia and America. None of the eastern species is of particular note for the viticultor, although a few are planted in Japan and some wines of *Vitis coignetiae* were imported into France at the height of the phylloxera influx. (Even with *Vitis vinifera* stock grafted onto them they bore an attractive distinctive fruit, which fermented into something nearer to a sweet liqueur than a wine.) Nor are the American species of vines of much importance in the development of wine, although they are used extensively in the eastern United States and Canada. Otherwise, they are useful in France and other places as rootstocks, resistant to phylloxera, onto which *Vitis vinifera* species are grafted.

The classification of the species of genus *Vitis* is open to considerable debate; botanical classifications are arbitrary things at best and scientists often disagree about them. Perhaps the most widely accepted—especially in Europe and academic American circles—is that used by Professor Branas (perhaps the world's foremost ampelographer) in his classes at the École Nationale d' Agriculture at Montpellier, in southern France. This classification divides the species as follows:

I—Sub-Genus *EUVITES*

A American Species

(1) TEMPERATE REGIONS

(EASTERN ZONE)

Vitis labrusca	Vitis aestivalis
Vitis lincecunici	Vitis bicolor

(CENTRAL ZONE)

Vitis riparia	Vitis rupestris
Vitis rubra	Vitis monticola
Vitis berlandieri	Vitis cordifolia
Vitis candicans	Vitis cinerea

(WESTERN ZONE)

Vitis Californica	Vitis Arizonica

(2) TORRID REGIONS

(FLORIDA AND THE BAHAMAS)

Vitis coriacea	Vitis gigas

(TROPICAL AND EQUATORIAL ZONES)

Vitis Bourgoeana	Vitis Cariboea

B Eastern Asian Species (incomplete)

(1) TEMPERATE REGIONS

Vitis amurensis	(Japan, Mongolia, Sakhalin Is.)
Vitis coignetiae	(Japan, Sakhalin Is., Korea)
Vitis Thunbergii	(Japan, Korea, Formosa, Southwest China)
Vitis flexuosa	(Korea, Japan, India, Nepal, Cochin-China)
Vitis Romaneti	(China)
Vitis Piasezkii	(China)
Vitis armata	(China)
Vitis Wilsonae	(China)
Vitis rutilans	(China)
Vitis Pagnucii	(China)
Vitis pentagona	(China)
Vitis Romanetia	(China)
Vitis Davidii	(China)

(2) SUB-TROPICAL REGIONS

Vitis Retordi	(Tonkin)
Vitis Balansaeana	(Tonkin)
Vitis lanata	(India, Nepal, Dekkan, Southern China, Burma)
Vitis pedicellata	(Himalayan Mountains)

C European and East and Central Asian Species

Vitis vinifera

II—Sub-Genus *MUSCADINIAE*

A North American Species
> *Vitis rotundifolia*
> *Vitis Munsoniana*
> *Vitis Popenoei*

On the American side of the Atlantic, most practicing viticulturists have adopted the classification of the American scientist Bailey. Considered by Europeans to be technically less accurate—but extremely effective from a practical standpoint—the Bailey classification includes several variations in nomenclature and some slightly different divisions. The notable changes are in nomenclature: *Vitis riparia* becomes *Vitis vulpina*, *Vitis bicolor* is *Vitis argentifolia*. Bailey also divides *Vitis Cariboea*, recognizing two distinct species (*Vitis tilioefolia* and *Vitis sola*) where Europeans see mutations of the same one.

HYBRIDIZATION

A distinct difficulty in the classification of vines is that they can be interbred, and the result may be a new vine with some characteristics from both parents, but all the characteristics of neither; and such a hybrid may seem to be a new species altogether. In the United States, artificial hybridization has been practiced to a large degree and many of the better wines of the eastern part of the country—where for various reasons *Vitis vinifera* simply will not grow—result from efforts made over the past century and a half.

Americans are not the only people interested in hybrids. Practically every wine-growing country in the world has its viticultural stations, and the French in particular have experimented widely. The French hybrids—crosses between *Vitis vinifera* and American species or *Vitis vinifera* and hybrids—are named after the men who developed them, and some of the achievements of Baco, Seibel, and Couderc are known to vineyard owners the world over. Hybrids of varying sorts occupy large areas of vineyards in the eastern United States and Canada, in southern France, in Italy and Spain; and while they produce more than do *Vitis vinifera*, and are more resistant to disease, they give wine which is sound and reasonably priced but nothing more. Yet the search for a better hybrid continues. Throughout the world, researchers strive to perfect the cross which will combine vigor, resistance to disease, and productivity with fruit of the quality of *Vitis vinifera*. The world's great wines continue, however, to come exclusively from *Vitis vinifera*. Moreover, they continue to come, as they have for the past several centuries, from the same handful of vineyards.

FACTORS THAT DETERMINE QUALITY

Oenologists, or wine scientists, maintain that four factors determine the quality of any wine: soil, climate, vine-type, and man. Other minor factors, such as the prevailing yeasts, may enter the equation as subheadings, but these are the essentials. In order to arrive at a great wine, they must all be linked together, each one supporting and complementing the others, each adding its indispensable qualities. In this combination the vine is of paramount importance; and next, the soil in which it grows.

Soil. The elements that make soil "noble" for wine are many and difficult to analyze. The outstanding attribute of the soil of fine wine vineyards is its obvious poverty, for vines often do their best in land where nothing else will grow. The oolitic debris of Burgundy prompted the Burgundian paradox: "If our soil weren't the richest in the world it would be the poorest"; and the scarcely fertile chalk of Champagne, the sandy gravel of Bordeaux, and the slate of sections of the German Mosel Valley nourish plants whose grapes yield some of the world's greatest wines. By the same token, such rich and fertile soils as those of France's Mediterranean coastline and Italy's Po Valley produce little more than a good *vin ordinaire*.

Together with the poverty of the soil must go a certain type of richness: a richness in trace elements. One of wine's greatest glories resides in the nuances of taste and aroma, and these come—at least in part—from the action and interaction of the elements that nourished the vine.

These elements, broadly speaking, are present in rock or soil in relatively small quantities. Among them may be such minerals as boron, cobalt, copper, iodine, manganese, molybdenum, nickel, selenium, vanadium, and zinc. These, if they are too concentrated, can be harmful to plant life; but they are often essential in small quantities. While tests have not been extensively performed on vines, the effects of trace elements on plant life have been dramatically demonstrated in orchards and vineyards in the United States, where even a small increase in the boron content of the soil has eliminated a defect in the flesh of apples. Similar results with other elements have been obtained in other parts of the world, such as Germany and Australia.

It is thought that trace elements affect wines by controlling the rate of growth and the processes of the vine and by modifying the enzyme complex of the growth. The soil elements that nourish the vine affect taste and aroma. The type and number of fermentation-causing yeasts can have considerable effect upon wine (*see also* Chapter Nine).

Very small transformations in soil may affect wine made from grapes grown in it, but obviously the basic essentials must be present before these trace elements can assume any importance. Vines produce their finest fruit generally in quartz, calcareous, or slate soil, and where soil composition is large-grained and consequently well-drained. This leads to riper grapes. Nitrogenous and humus materials prompt the vine to produce luxuriant foliage, but the quality of the fruit suffers. Small amounts of iron are to be found in most fine vineyards; but if there is too much the wine may be difficult to clarify and stabilize (although some experts maintain that it is the iron in the wine-making equipment rather than in the soil which causes this trouble). A plenitude of elements will be present in one degree or another, and the components and the interplay between them dictate the quality of the fruit. The result is that a prospective vineyard-owner can tell with little difficulty where the vine will grow well; to tell where it will produce with grandeur is a matter of time, trial, and a large measure of luck.

Climate. Heat and rainfall are the direct climatic influences on vines. Moderately cold rainy winters and fairly long hot summers with some—but not much—rain are the most desirable. The first cold of the late autumn or early winter encourages the vine to become dormant and allows the wood to toughen and mature; but severe cold during the winter will kill it. Sufficient summer heat is necessary to mature the fruit; and later summer sunshine, in particular, will soon mature the grape internally. Therefore, growers in cool temperate regions must harvest as late as possible, taking advantage of any late summer sun they may get. The quality of a marginal harvest may not be decided until the final week or so of the summer when a sudden burst of sunshine may produce a very pleasant wine, whereas the result of rain will be mediocre wine at best. Most of the rain a vine gets should come during the winter and early spring, for the diseases that afflict vines are most active in hot humid weather, and in very wet years the fruit is apt to rot on the vine. Moreover, the lack of sunshine will mean that grapes do not mature so well as they would in a sunny year.

Among the indirect climatic influences are the frequency and severity of frosts, hail, and wind. A late frost, occurring in May, just before or during the flowering of the vine, may destroy the entire year's crop; and late summer hail or a very strong wind can easily remove the grapes before the harvest. Other important factors are the proximity of water—for lakes and rivers have a tempering effect upon heat and cold—and the situation of the vineyard on the slope. For proper drainage and exposure to the sun most great vineyards are on slopes, ranging from the gently rolling near-plains of Bordeaux to the swift-plunging cliffs of the German Rhine and Mosel valleys.

Vine-type. For any specific conditions of soil and climate the right vine type—of the thousands that exist—must be found. An example of the importance of grape variety is Burgundy, where the noble red vine is the Pinot Noir along the Côte d'Or, and the Gamay some thirty miles to the south in the Beaujolais. Even in so small a distance as this, the difference is markedly great: Gamay, on the Côte d'Or, gives ordinary wine; Pinot Noir, in the Beaujolais, produces flat and insipid wines; yet put the two where they belong, and the results may be superlative.

Man. The last major factor is man. Human error is always to be considered in human endeavor, and only when man is most skillful and nature most bountiful will great wine be made. Much of the skill will be needed after the harvest; but unless the grapes are brought to proper maturity, the harvest will hardly be worth the effort. Tending these grapes is arduous and exacting work, and the conscientious grower finds little time for other pursuits.

VINEYARD PREPARATION

The preparation of a new vineyard requires the greatest care and backbreaking labor. In some sections of the world—such as the steep Rhine Valley in Germany or Portugal's River Douro—the grower may have to blast rock, build terraces, and even carry earth to his high site simply to get enough soil to nourish his vine. In parts of Europe, "trenching" is a necessity. This may be a very deep plow, but it can be more—depending upon the needs of the specific soil. The ground may be plowed so that topsoil and subsoil both benefit without the two being mixed; or both may be mixed together; or topsoil may be turned under and subsoil over, each taking the place of the other; or subsoil may be plowed without disturbing the topsoil too much. This process is often desperately complicated, because so many European vineyards are planted on slopes which cannot always be worked by tractor and sometimes not even by horses, so that man has to plod away alone. After this plowing, a cover crop is usually planted, and in one or two years the vineyard is ready for its vines. These, when they are set out, are sometimes one, more often two years old.

In California and other newer grape areas where land in most cases can be leveled, or the lower slope levels (workable by tractor) are available, it is customary to clear, plow, and plant the vines within a few days. Most soils are virgin and quite fertile, so that cover crops to enrich the soil are not necessary. Mechanization of the work allows many acres to be planted in a day by very few men. In California first, and now all over the world, the land must be fumigated to kill off oak fungus or other diseases.

PROPAGATION OF THE VINE

There are various ways in which vines can be made to reproduce, not all of them useful to the viticulturist. The original purpose of the grape was to carry seeds, and vines will reproduce by seedlings, but this is perhaps the most impracticable method for the vineyard-owner. In order that they may reproduce, vines must be pollinated; and they may or may not be pollinated by plants of the same variety. If not, the seedlings will not be of the same variety as the parent, they will be hybrids. Since the vineyard-owner is looking for an exact replica of his bearing vine, and since seedlings require such expensive extras as greenhouses and potting sheds, he leaves this to the nurseryman and hybridist.

Layering or *marcottage* was once the traditional way of propagating vines, but has been much less used since the phylloxera outbreak of the last century. It allows vine-shoots to establish roots of their own before being cut from the parent vine—which permits a shoot to draw nourishment from the old vine until its own roots are strong enough to support it. The usual practice was to lead one shoot—still attached to the vine—down, into the ground, then out again. The nodes along the buried section of the shoot sent forth roots while the exposed end developed foliage. When the new roots were considered fully developed, the shoot was cut from the parent. *Provignage* was a variation by which an old vine was buried with one single shoot coming forth from the ground. This shoot developed roots but also drew nourishment from the old ones as long as they lived, and the fruit had characteristics of the old vines. Neither of these methods is widespread today, because of phylloxera. In most cases, modern vines are made up of *Vitis vinifera* tops grafted onto American or hybrid roots. If either *marcottage* or *provignage* were used, it would mean establishing a vine with *Vitis vinifera* roots, and these would probably be open to attack by phylloxera—although *marcottage* has been extensively used in a part of Château Prieuré-Lichine vineyard since 1958, with no visible ill effects. In California, however, where soil and climate are not conducive to the growth of phylloxera, 65 per cent of the vines are planted on their own roots. Similar conditions prevail in Turkey, Cyprus, and some parts of Germany.

The only practical means of allowing vines to reproduce today is by cuttings. Vine canes—cut in the autumn or winter from the dormant vine and kept until the spring in sawdust or sand—are placed in fertile ground until the roots develop. At the end of a year or so, these roots are strong enough to support transplantation. The rooted portions, of course, are normally of American or hybrid stock and the *Vitis vinifera*-bearing wood is grafted onto them.

Bench-grafting and field-budding or -grafting are the two methods usually found in vineyards. In bench-grafting, the two sections—scion (top of the vine—*Vitis vinifera*) and stock (root)—are joined at a nursery, and only after the graft has healed is the new vine placed in soil to develop roots. In field-budding, the stock forms the roots and is placed in its proper spot in the vineyard; the top is cut off when the bud has become established, and the scion is grafted or budded on in its place.

In California in recent years, owing to the extreme demand for grapevine rootings—which has resulted from a rapid expansion in vineyard planting—a quick method of propagation has been developed and is widely used. Mature canes are cut into one-bud pieces and grown in 85°-chambers under an intermittent fine mist of water. After the buds have sprouted and grown leaves, the shoots are cut into one-bud-plus-one-leaf pieces, dipped in a growth hormone, and rooted in the mist chamber. By this method, called mist propaga-

tion, a single five-year-old vine can produce thousands of new rootings in a single year.

Whichever of these methods is chosen, the result is the same—a new vine is in existence. Four years after the vine has been planted it will start producing fruit worthy of being made into wine, although many varieties produce grapes of sorts after three years.

CARE OF THE VINE

Although this is an oversimplification, it might be said that during the first year of the vine's life the major preoccupation of the grower is to make sure that his vine develops good roots; during the second year, strong and well-placed branches; in the third year (and thereafter) that the fruit be of the best possible quality. All of these considerations will be concurrent throughout the life span of the vine, but in the early years they take on extra significance. The above-ground portions of the vine can be divided into the following parts:

The TRUNK—the body of the vine. From it come:

ARMS—or branches. These in turn, support:
1. SHOOTS—the current season's growth, including
   (a) new foliage
   (b) tendrils (slender winding shoots that twine around trellises and other supports)
   (c) watersprouts (shoots growing on wood more than one year old)
   (d) suckers (shoots which appear below the ground)
2. CANES—one-year-old matured shoots. The most important are fruit canes (or canes that will bear the current year's crop)
3. SPURS—short canes, divided into
   (a) fruit spurs (intended to bear fruit)
   (b) renewal spurs (intended to bear the next season's canes)
   (c) replacement spurs (used to replace existing branches)

Pruning and training—two technically separate but interrelated practices—are the methods the vine-grower uses to keep the vegetative parts of his vine in order and to ensure a fairly—and consistently—large quantity of good fruit. Pruning is the removal of excess portions of the vine's growth; training, the directing of the vine into conformations that will make it easy to handle and convenient to work.

Pruning. The purpose of pruning is to achieve an optimal balance between vine growth and the amount of crop. If allowed to grow without pruning, the vine will produce more grapes than it is capable of ripening, while overly severe pruning will excessively limit the overall growth of the vine. Ideally one wishes to achieve the largest amount of leaf area which will be able to ripen the largest amount of fruit to the optimum condition.

The amount of pruning performed will depend upon the fertility of the soil, the vigor of vine, the warmth of the climate, and the amount of available water. When the weather is hot, the soil fertile, and the vine vigorous, long pruning—leaving four or more buds or "eyes" on each cane—may be used, for the vine has the energy to support large crops and plenty of foliage. Alternatively, a greater number of normal-sized spurs may be retained to allow for the extra growth. The number, length, and placement of spurs are determined by the type of training system used. In California, the espalier system (*see* below) is being used increasingly for premium-wine grape production even though an expensive trellis is required, so several canes each with fifteen to twenty eyes may be left on each vine. In regions where the weather is rather cold—such as Germany and northern France—the vine will be feebler, and gobelet training (*see* below) with short spur pruning is often adopted.

In practice, once the vine is mature and the desired shape established, one determines the amount to prune by the performance of the vine in the last season. If the crop was well balanced, one leaves the same total number of eyes on the vine as there were canes the previous year, while if the vine overproduced one year, the number of canes (and hence the amount of crop) should be reduced.

Training. The method of pruning chosen, and the conditions which dictated the pruning, will also have an effect upon the way the vine is trained. The three major methods of training are: (1) *cordon*, (2) *gobelet* or head, and (3) *espalier*.

(1) A *cordon*-trained vine has the trunk extended in a single direction, be it vertical, horizontal, or oblique.

There are numerous variations of cordon training, but the most frequently encountered consists of a trunk coming out of the ground, bent sideways to run parallel with the ground and usually supported by a wire or style. The quantity of spurs that grow up and down from this trunk may be regulated as well as the number of eyes on each spur, and the method—although requiring some skill to establish—rewards the skillful with large harvest. It is not applicable to all vine varieties and cannot normally be used for the finer—and less fruitful—types. Perhaps the most important of the cordon styles is the Guyot—one of the most widespread in the world of fine wines—which consists usually of a trunk and one arm. Canes coming forth from that arm are trained along wires. It is particularly effective for vines with infertile basal nodes and those that form small and compact bunches of grapes.

In California, the most common form of cordon is in the shape of a T, with the trunk branching to form two horizontal branches.

(2) *Gobelet* (or head) training leaves a single vertical trunk terminating in several arms rising in approximately the shape of a vase or goblet (French *gobelet*). It has the particular virtue that no support is needed for the vine, and it is simple to establish and maintain. However, if the basal buds of the vine are infertile it cannot be used, and in some cases very vigorous vines tend to set their fruit badly.

(3) *Espalier* training leaves a trunk terminating in one or two arms and several canes, most often all trained in the same plane. Like the cordon-trained vine, it must have a trellis or wire for support. There are a number of variations on this system, including the decorative trellis-trained vine, so often found in formal gardens.

CYCLE OF THE VINE

The growth-cycle of the vine starts in the spring when the dormant winter stage has passed and sap begins to flow. Five to six weeks after the rising of the sap, the vine begins to produce foliage and the buds along the canes swell, bursting out of the brown scaly wood which has covered and protected them during the winter and revealing a small woolly bud. Tiny delicate leaves form, and from this point until the vine flowers—for unlike many fruits the vine does not put forth fruit and leaves at the same time—it is budding out, a time of growth before floral parts develop (French *débourrement*). The time this occurs depends mainly on the warmth of the soil, but also to a certain extent on the time chosen for pruning.

If a vine is pruned during the winter season—as most are—budding will occur naturally; but if it is pruned after the sap has begun to flow, budding will be delayed by as much as two weeks. Late pruning involves loss of a considerable amount of sap and although this sap has practically no nutrient value, growers usually feel that such a loss could only be detrimental to the vine, and so they tend to avoid late pruning. In areas where late frosts prevail, however, it can be valuable, retarding budding until the danger of frost has abated. "Green" or "summer" pruning implies the removal of succulent growth.

A variation of this used in California is called "double pruning"; the vines are pruned in the normal manner in the fall or mid-winter except that long spurs are left, four to eight buds instead of two to four buds. The apical buds are allowed to push, and the spurs are immediately cut to normal length before excessive starch reserves are used up. Using this method, second pruning may be done at leisure with no worry that growth will commence before pruning is complete, and yet the bud-push is delayed five to fourteen days.

The young shoots of the vine put forth leaves and, later, flower clusters. On each cluster is a group of tiny blossoms in the form the grape bunch will eventually take. At first each flower in the cluster is covered by a cap—which slips away, revealing the flowering parts of the vine.

In most vines, the flower consists of a conelike female pistil and five male stamens, equally vigorous. The pistil has an ovary, style, and stigma, and the stamens are composed of filaments carrying anthers, tiny sacs of pollen. When the sacs open, pollen is discharged and the grains are trapped by the stigma, where the pollen germinates. The pollen tube grows down the style and into the ovary, where fertilization takes place.

Most *Vitis vinifera* vines are hermaphroditic, and

both male and female organs of the same vine are equally developed. In some other vines one set of organs may be stunted, and the vineyard-owner will need both female (to bear fruit) and male (to fertilize the female) vines. Hermaphroditic vines usually fertilize themselves—the pollen falling from the male to the female portions—but unisexual vines *must* be cross-pollinated. It is a curious fact that cross-pollination has little or no effect whatsoever upon fruit. The grape will always run true to the bearing vine, and changes will take place only in the seeds, which are of no interest to the vinicultor.

The vine flowers for a period of about two weeks. During this time the weather is of the utmost importance, for on it depends the fruit the wine will yield. Failure to flower properly or completely is the condition known as *coulure* (see Vine Pathology *below*) and, if serious, this may mean that the plant will develop no grapes at all. At the end of a normal flowering a tiny green berry will form, growing and maturing into the grape.

The flowering (*floraison*) is followed by the slow preliminary maturing of the fruit. The grapes, green with chlorophyll, assimilate carbon in exactly the same manner as the leaves; they grow in bulk, and chemically they show very little change beyond a slight rise in acidity. The next state, usually starting in August, is the *véraison*, when the grape changes color, turning from early green to its final red-purplish hue, or translucent greenish-white, after which the final maturing will occur. The approximate duration of these various operations is:

Putting forth leaves	72– 75 days	
Flowering	10– 20 days	
Developing grape	40– 45 days	
Maturing grape	48– 50 days	
Total	170–190 days	

This chart is only valid for grapes of "first epoch," because different varieties of grape mature their fruit at different intervals. The most widely accepted classification of *time* of maturing is that of the Frenchmen Pulliat, devised toward the end of the last century. pulliat took the Chasselas Doré grape as a "standard," and from its cycle built up the following table.

Designation		*Time of Maturing*
		Before or after
		Chasselas Doré
"Precocious"	Very early	10 days before
First epoch	Early	about same time
Second epoch	Early mid-season	12 days after
Third epoch	Mid-season	24 days after
Fourth epoch	Late	36 days after

The system of Pulliat is not the best guide to predict the days to maturity, since it does not account for environmental influences. It does allow comparison of the relative *rate* of maturation of different varieties. A more precise determination of the time to mature is the method of Winkler and Amerine, based on the total heat summation required to mature a given variety. With knowledge of the required heat summation and weather records, the number of days to mature a given variety in a given area may be predicted.

After the *véraison* the grape starts its significant change. It has already achieved its acid; and from this point on, acidity will decrease and sugar content increase. The bulk also increases, and the reaction speeds its pace as the grape approaches maturity. Full maturity is attained when no more sugar is generated, and the grapes are then ready for picking or for the second stage of going into the noble rot. In some cases there will be an increase in *apparent* sugar content after final maturation, but this is due to evaporation of water rather than to increase in sugar. (In certain parts of the world, as in the Barsac-Sauternes districts of Bordeaux and, to a much smaller extent, the Mosel and Rhine districts of Germany, the mold *Botrytis cinerea*, the noble rot, forms on the grapes, hastening the process and resulting in an extremely sweet wine.) During the ripening period of the fruit a waxy "bloom" forms on the outside, protecting the grape from sunburn and trapping the yeasts that will cause the fermentation (see Botrytis cinerea).

While the vine is preparing itself and producing its fruit, there are a number of maladies to which it may succumb. The most crippling of these thrive in wet weather, since they multiply faster under humid conditions and since rain washes off the chemical sprays used by the grower in an attempt to counteract or control them. Some of the more important diseases—and their antidotes—are outlined below.

VINE PATHOLOGY

The ills to which the vine is prone fall into two major categories: (1) accidents and non-parasitic maladies and (2) maladies of parasitic origin. The first group embraces afflictions caused by climate, soil, vine, and man, and the second those caused by viruses, bacteria, cryptogams, and animal parasites.

1. Accidents and Non-Parasitic Maladies

(a) *Climate*

Frost is the most important climatic danger. Although most vineyards are so situated that frosts will have a minimal effect, those that do occur can be devastating. The severe winter of 1956 in Bordeaux caused a decrease in production of as much as 90 per cent in some districts; but it is partly because such winters are so rare (1956 was the second-worst winter in the region since 1709) that growers are unprepared to cope with them. In general, winter temperatures below 5°F. (-15°C.) are dangerous for vines, and in the spring when the vine has started to leaf, temperatures even a few degrees below freezing (25°F. or -4°C.) are equally critical. Many American vine-types are more resistant to cold than are *Vitis vinifera*, and the Beta grape—a crossing of *Vitis labrusca* and *Vitis riparia* found in the northern United States and Canada—can withstand temperatures as low as -4°F. (-20°C.), while *Vitis amurensis* can live at fantastically low temperatures. (Up to now, unfortunately, *Vitis amurensis* has not given useful grapes.) In exceptionally cold vineyard areas, vines may be protected from winter cold by covering them completely with soil, a practice occasionally followed in Russia, Hungary, Bulgaria, Asia Minor, and Canada. Late spring frosts are also a great hazard, but late pruning will sometimes retard flowering until the danger has passed.

In many parts of California, early spring frosts are common and can destroy the larger part of a crop by killing the young shoots. In the past, growers employed oil or butane heaters in the vineyards in an attempt to prevent frost, or installed motor-driven propellers called wind machines to circulate the higher warmer air. Today the most effective method of preventing spring frost where water is available is to install overhead sprinkler systems. During a cold period, the sprinklers are turned on to maintain a constant coating of water on the vines, protecting them from freezing by the heat released when the water freezes to ice. This method, though expensive, is so effective that it is allowing vineyards to be successfully planted in areas previously unplantable due to the severity of spring or autumn frosts.

Heat, if excessive, may damage vines, although temperatures must rise above about 110°F. (43°C.) before the critical limit is reached. This kind of heat is unusual in vineyards elsewhere than in North Africa, where the hot, dry, dehydrating, sustained winds of the sirocco sometimes wreak enormous damage.

Hail scars leaves and branches and may remove vegetation, weakening the vine. Late summer hailstorms are called "harvesters" by vine-growers and may destroy or remove the entire crop. Rockets fired into hail clouds sometimes cause them to burst before they come over the vineyards, but it is not easy to do this successfully because of the height of the clouds and the speed with which they form.

Wind breaks off and cracks shoots, fruit, and vegetation; and salt winds blowing in from the sea, as sometimes happens in the Médoc—even as far as fifty miles inland—can wither the leaves.

(b) *Soil*

Drought causes vine leaves to turn yellow, and unless some manner of irrigation is installed the plant eventually degenerates or dies.

Excess moisture may drown the plant, but only after some time. If the vine is flooded for less than ten weeks, it is able to survive. This has led to flooding as a counter-measure to phylloxera; the water drowns the pest and is then drained off before the vines are affected.

Chlorosis is a yellowing of the leaves caused by a lack of chlorophyll. In Europe it is often due to an excess of calcium in the soil, which results in iron deficiency. Vines differ in degrees of resistance to it, and most *Vitis vinifera* varieties are practically unaffected. Treatment is with ferrous sulfate, on the theory that a comparative excess of calcium impedes the vine from assimilating iron, thus causing the disease. *Vitis berlandieri* is somewhat resistant and is thus used as rootstock.

Soil deficiencies are principally caused by lack of boron, potassium, or zinc. Zinc deficiency is fairly common in California and Australia, and the vine is treated with zinc; the more widespread boron deficiency is treated in various ways, either by increasing the soil's boron content or by injecting boron into the vine.

Soil toxicity comes mainly from an excess of salt. Selection of rootstock may overcome it (hybrids, particularly those from *Vitis candicans*, whose native habitat is the swamps of Mississippi, are highly resistant); or the land may be "washed" by flooding for a short period with clear water. Micronutrients, especially boron, are occasionally present in toxic amounts.

(c) *Vine*

Coulure is the dropping of flowers, flower clusters, or of the tiny berries during the period of their initial development; or it is their failure to develop. Its most important cause is bad weather, for proper flowering can only take place under rainless, warm, sunny skies. Too rapid a growth can also cause *coulure*, in which case the vines would be better grafted onto rootstock more appropriate to their vigor.

Shot berries (*millerandage*) is the name given to grape clusters with grapes of varying sizes. If the flowering has not been complete, some or all of the grapes may remain small, green, and hard, resembling buckshot. It is an aftermath of *coulure*.

Leaf reddening (*rougeau*), if not caused by a virus, is due to a wound which interrupts the flow of sap to the roots, The wound may be on the above-ground portion of the vine—in which case the afflicted part will be removed, if possible. If it is due to wounds on the roots, potassium fertilizers sometimes have a restorative effect by translocating more potassium, especially when the root growth is restricted.

(d) *Man*

Browning (*brunissure*) is a result of overproduction, of not pruning the vine sufficiently. Brown stains appear on the leaf, which drops off; the quality of the fruit suffers, and eventually the vine may lose some of its reserves of strength and die. Decreasing the number of grape bunches may combat the malady in its early stages; but if the disease exhausts the vine too much, there is no cure.

The Vine

Burning of leaves by insecticides, chemical fertilizers, or even in some instances, by smoke from nearby factories may do damage to the vine, whether caused by carelessness of man, or by unfavorable vineyard sites.

2. Maladies of Parasitic Origin

(a) *Viruses and Rickettsiae*

Infectious degeneration or *fan leaf (court noué)* is a virus disease that apparently appears only in the wake of phylloxera. Fan leaf is spread in the soil by the vector *Xiphema index*. The leaf turns yellow along its veins and in patches between them; leaves grow misshapen, shoots bifurcate and multiply laterally, and flowers form double clusters. The malady forms in "stains" or patches throughout the vineyard and spreads slowly. Its insidious character is threefold: it progressively shortens the life of the vine; it lives in the soil; there is no known treatment. It is spread and intensified by plowing, and the only present solution is to pull up affected vines and plow lightly, if at all. The progressive action means that, while a pre-phylloxera vine might have lived a hundred years, the first generation thereafter may survive only for forty years and the second for fifteen. When this life span gets down to four years there will be no more wine from that vineyard. The infected soil may be cleaned up by removing vines from infected areas, allowing the land to lie fallow until all the old roots rot, and fumigating with D.D. (dichloropropane dichloropropylene).

Pierce's disease is found in California. The leaves yellow along the veins, the edges burn, the vine puts out dwarf shoots, fruit wilts and colors prematurely, and the vine dies in from one to five years. The disease is caused by the same *rickettsiae* which cause alfalfa dwarf, and it is spread by insects, i.e., sharpshooters. Treatment: pulling up the affected vines is useless; the insect-carriers of the disease must be attacked with powerful insecticides. Other widespread virus diseases which cause considerable damage are *corky bark, yellow vein, leaf roll,* and the *mosaic complex.*

(b) *Bacteria*

Oleron's disease or *bacterial blight of vines* causes stains on leaves and flower clusters and destroys intercellular walls. European in origin, it is of little importance today outside the vineyards of South Africa. It is thought that widespread use of copper sprays and sterilization of pruning instruments have led to its disappearance in Europe.

(c) *Cryptogams or fungus diseases*

Downy (or *false*) *mildew* (in Europe known as mildew) is the most crippling fungus disease of the vine. American in origin, it is caused by *Plasmospora viticola* and attacks the green portions of the vine, but only before the *véraison*—the changing of color in the grape. On leaves, an oily stain later turning to white forms on the undersides and spreads. It also appears on shoots just below the buds, and it can attack flowers and fruit. Downy mildew needs high humidity and heat to generate, and since it is partly spread by wind, it can be devastating once it gets started. (Most American vine-types are resistant to downy mildew and American vineyards are not treated for it. The fungus is thus allowed to run rampant and this has been one of the major factors in keeping *vinifera* vines out of eastern America, although the primary problem with *vinifera* in the eastern United States is winter cold—and black rot, if not controlled, is a menace.) Treatment is by copper sulfate ($CuSO_4$), 80,000 tons of which are used annually in France to combat mildew. It is usually applied in the Bordeaux mixture, made up of varying amounts of copper sulfate, chalk, and water.

Powdery (or *true*) *mildew* (in Europe known as oïdium) also attacks only green organs. Introduced into Europe from America, it caused widespread damage in 1854, reducing the crop in France by 20 per cent. Powdery mildew limits growth, attacks leaves, and splits berries, and if untreated will kill the vine—especially the susceptible *vinifera*—in a few years. Wines made from grapes affected by this disease will have a disagreeable taste and smell, a poor color, and a low degree of alcohol. Even when only the leaves of a plant have been attacked, the ensuing wine will be tainted. Finely ground sulfur—75,000 tons of which are used annually in France—combats it.

Black rot is also of American origin. It forms stains speckled with black on green organs, and the fruit shrivels and turns brown. It is most virulent when the temperature is about 70°F. (21°C.) and when humidity is high. The treatment, which is copper sulfate, is the same as for downy mildew, and since this has little or no effect in the eastern United States, black rot is most vicious there.

Anthracnose is the only important vine disease of European origin. It forms small polygonal stains on leaves, fruit, and shoots. It develops under the same conditions as black rot, and treatment is the same as for downy mildew.

Excoriose is exceedingly rare and attacks mainly branches. Treatment is to spray with a concentrated Bordeaux mixture.

Gray rot (pourriture grise) is caused by the same fungus that is the noble rot responsible for the sweet white wines of Sauternes, Germany, and Hungary—*Botrytis cinerea*. At an optimum temperature of about 77°F. (25°C.), in moist weather, and often after other diseases have weakened the vine, gray rot forms, causing stains on the leaves and alterations within the fruit. Only under certain conditions—i.e., high humidity followed by hot weather—can it become *pourriture noble* (noble rot), and in most areas and under most conditions it is simply a hazard (*see* Botrytis cinerea).

White rot (rot blanc) forms on ripening berries, splitting them. Prompt treatment with copper or sodium bisulfite counters it.

Brenner is a browning between the veins on basal leaves, caused by a fungus. Early sulfate treatment will counter it, and it only occurs where winters are cold and dry—the conditions of life for the fungus. It is most prevalent in Germany.

"Apoplexy" (Esca) gets its name from the spectacular way the vine dies in the hottest part of the summer. It is a disease found in all plants in all parts of the world and is caused by a cryptogamic growth entering the wood and liberating an enzyme that kills the wood ahead of it. Sodium arsenite seems to combat it, although the reasons are as yet unknown.

Armillaria root-rot (pourridié) develops on shoots, trunk, and roots, with the result that the upper roots develop at the expense of the lower and more useful ones, which remain weak. It is especially virulent in sandy soils and is often found near streams. There is no effective treatment short of pulling up the vine, disinfecting the soil, and letting it rest until all traces of the causative fungi—*Armillaria mellea* and *Rosellinia necatrix* or *Dermatophora necatrix*—have been killed.

(d) Animal parasites

Animal parasites differ widely from one place to another, and those found in France will not necessarily be the same as those in South Africa or California, or even in Spain. However, some of the most important are:

Phylloxera, found the world over (with the exception of the vineyards of Chile and a few isolated sections elsewhere). A burrowing vine louse native to America, phylloxera caused the greatest single viticultural disaster since the Flood, necessitated significant changes in viticulture, and started off the Great Debate among connoisseurs: is post-phylloxera wine equal to that of pre-phylloxera days? Phylloxera and the questions and problems it raised are all discussed in the encyclopedic section of this book (*see* Phylloxera).

Grape berry moths (Eudemis, Cochylis, and *Polychrosis viteana)* produce larvae which feed on grape bunches, leaving those not completely ruined open to attack from other quarters. Treatment is by arsenic or D.D.T.

Meal-moth (Pyralis) feeds on foliage and fruit. Arsenic and D.D.T. are the most effective insecticides.

Altise, a type of beetle, feeds on leaves, reducing them to the aspect of very fine lace. Killed with insecticides.

Cochineal (cochnilles) bugs, of varying sorts, attack vines—and other plants—feeding on sap and weakening the vine until it dies. Various emulsions of oil, applied both during winter and summer, are used to combat them.

Acariose, a species of mite, feeds on fruit and foliage. Destroyed by copper sprays.

Erinose (Phytoptus vitis or *Eriophyes vitis)* is a microscopically small mite which causes blisters on leaves, grapes, and flower clusters. Most vines are resistant to it; and those that are not are treated with the same solution as is normally used against powdery mildew.

Eelworms (anguillules) are nematodes, or threadlike parasitic worms, which puncture roots and form nodosities resembling those of phylloxera. *Vitis vinifera* vines are particularly susceptible, but proper choice of rootstock on which the *Vitis vinifera* will be grafted obviates much of the danger. Sterilization of the soil by D.D. is necessary if the nematodes become too numerous. Next to phylloxera this is by far the most important animal parasite.

Japanese beetles are a considerable menace in the eastern United States, but have not as yet appeared in California or in Europe. D.D.T. and arsenic compounds are used to fight them.

A VINEYARD CALENDAR

In addition to the combating of diseases, there is a considerable amount of work to be done in a vineyard. The details of the labor and the time chosen for each chore will vary according to the situation of the vineyard and the traditional practice of the area. The following calendar represents a part of the seasonal division of labor at the author's Château Prieuré-Lichine in the town of Margaux in the Bordeaux region of France. Usual practice elsewhere will be very similar to that represented here, although there are slight variations even among the other vineyards in Margaux.

Autumn. In late September or October the harvest, which lasts for more than two weeks, is followed by a general cleaning-up of ditches and the turn-around spaces in the vineyard. Autumn plowing aerates the soil and covers and protects the sensitive graft zone of the plants against the cold.

Winter. Pruning continues throughout the winter. Pickets and support wires are replaced and repaired as needed and the trunks and branches attached to them.

Spring. A second plowing, for the same reasons as before; and women follow with special rakes to draw out the soil from between the plants where it cannot be reached by the plow. During budding, excess buds are removed from the vines, and "suckers" growing below the graft are removed. A third plowing is done and any necessary planting of vines (April-May).

Summer. Weeds are removed and in June shoots are attached with reeds to the supporting wires. The ends of the shoots are trimmed—to curb excessive growth—and the spraying treatments against vine maladies started (there may be anything from three to eight during the course of the summer). A fourth plowing does away with summer weeds and the grapes are left to ripen.

Autumn. When the grapes reach maturity, the harvest starts. After this the cycle recommences with the cleaning-up.

9 Wine: What It Is, How It Is Made

Wine comes from the fermentation of grape sugar. Dandelions, parsnips, and elderberries can be made to yield a kind of "homemade wine," but properly wine comes from grapes and nothing else—and it is the natural product of grapes which have been gathered, carted to the wine shed, pressed (for whites), and left in vats until the grape sugar has fermented into alcohol. The biochemical reactions of wine fermentation are due to yeast. These microscopic plants grow in the rich natural medium of the fresh juice and produce enzymes which convert the sugar, through an intricate series of biochemical reactions, to alcohol, carbon dioxide, and other fermentation products.

The result of such a haphazard process as natural fermentation would undoubtedly be a poor vinegar, although the first wine known to man must have been just that, the historic consequence of a felicitous accident. But fine wine comes from good management rather than good luck, and over the centuries men have been learning, first by trial and error and later by scientific experiment, how to improve the technique of making it. The discoveries of Louis Pasteur (1822–1895) shed new light on the scientific theories of earlier wine-makers and provided a logical explanation for many time-honored practices, some of them dating from ancient Greece and Rome. The scientists did not, in fact, add very much that was new to the practical art of wine-making, but they did show contemporary vintners *why* certain things should be done and encouraged them to use the wisest methods. And they cut out the "lows" of the poor vintage years by teaching growers how to salvage a harvest that might have been a disaster fifty years before.

THE GRAPE

The basic ingredient of wine is clearly the grape. At perfect maturity it will have certain specific characteristics, although fruit from differnt vine varieties will differ considerably. Skins, pulp, and—with some exceptions—seeds all donate certain qualities to the wine.

Grape skins give mainly tannins and coloring matter. The color and tannin are generally conceded to be bound in the internal portions of the skin cells. Until these cells are killed it is very difficult to remove the pigments. Several methods are available to cause cell death and cell wall collapse—heat, alcohol, or physical disintegration. The second method is usually used, in which the juice and skins are allowed to ferment together until sufficient alcohol is produced to cause the cell walls to become permeable and the color to be released. The extraction of color rises to its peak after a few days, then diminishes; but duration of vatting time is the most important factor in coloring wines. Rosés, which are separated quickly from the skins, are vatted for a shorter time than reds, while white wines are made from grapes that have been separated from the skins at the outset. Some minor grape varieties keep the pigment in the inner layers of the skin and yield tinted juice, while a very few have colored flesh and give deep red juice. The tannins also pass from skin and pulp to juice during vatting—the essential difference between red and white wines lies more in tannin content than in color.

In some cases the skin contributes another element—an odorant which may be either agreeable or disagreeable. In many *Vitis vinifera* varieties this odorant imparts a fresh light perfume—a whiff of the grape. This is most apparent when the wine is young but tends to disappear as it ages and bouquet develops. In some eastern American vines—notably *Vitis labrusca*—the odorant gives a "foxy" scent and taste, strange and sometimes disagreeable to those brought up on European wines, and the variety is not allowed in France. Many eastern American and Canadian wine-makers keep the vatting period of their wines as short as possible to prevent this characteristic from developing.

The bulk of the grape is pulp, comprising from 80 to 90 per cent of its weight. While composition of a ripe grape varies, an approximate breakdown has been given by the French scientist Jules Ventre in his *Traité de vinification pratique et rationnelle*:

COMPOSITION OF A RIPE GRAPE

Constituent	Range (per cent)	Remarks
Water	70-80	
Extract	15-30	
Carbohydrates		
Sugars	12-27	Dextrose and levulose
Pectins	0.1-1.0	Includes gums, etc.
Pentosans	0.1-0.5	Also small amounts of pentoses

COMPOSITION OF A RIPE GRAPE

Constituent	Range (per cent)	Remarks
Inositol	traces	
Acids, total		
Malic	0.1-0.5	Varies with region, variety, and season
Tartaric	0.2-0.8	Mainly potassium bitartrate
Citric	traces	
Tannin	0.0-0.2	
Nitrogen	0.01-0.20	Mostly proteins, amino acids, ammonia
Ash	0.2-0.6	

The skin and pulp of the grape are the important elements for the wine-maker. Seeds contain tannin and an oily resinous material that would render the wine unpalatable if released, and so care must be taken not to break the seeds in the pressing.

Another element that may figure in the constitution of wine is the stalk or stem of the grape bunches. Rich in tannin, it will be included in the materials vatted in areas giving soft wines. In most cases, however, stems are taken out before grapes and juice go to the fermenting vats, removed either by hand in the very small European wineries or by a device called a stemmer or *égrappoir*. In white wines seeds are definitely obnoxious, because of an enzyme (oenoxidase) which may impart to the unfermented grape juice (must)—and later to the wine—a brown stain, like an apple bitten into and exposed to air. This stain may take as little as an hour to develop.

HARVEST

The time chosen for the harvest (or *vendange*) has an important effect upon the quality of the wine. In the fine wine districts, the grapes are tested for maturity with great care and are picked only at the latest possible moment in the cooler regions where it is extremely difficult to obtain maturity. In the warmer areas the grapes are harvested when the sugar and acid have the proper balance to make the desired wine. Once the red grapes are picked, they are destemmed immediately and run off into the fermenting vats. A delay, even of little more than twelve hours, could result in serious difficulties: (1) the elements that naturally form the bouquet might oxidize in the presence of too much air, giving the wine an unpleasant aroma; (2) undesirable or unwanted bacteria or tiny sugar-flies might begin to attack the sugar, spoiling the wine.

FERMENTATION

Alcoholic fermentation is defined by Yves Renouil and Paul de Traversay as the biochemical phenomenon which causes sugar to be transformed into ethyl alcohol and carbon dioxide.

Before the experiments of Pasteur (c. 1857) fermentation was largely a mystery, and only in comparatively recent times have the processes of fermentation been studied at all. The list opposite shows the elements present in must and wine.

(For an up-to-date summary of the approximate amounts of these materials present in wine *see* Ribéreau-Gayon and Peynaud's *Traité d'oenologie*.)

Most of the constituents found in the must remain to some degree in the wine. The sugars are greatly depleted and usually are found only in small amounts in dry wines. However, many new products appear

Must	Wine
Water	Water
Sugars:	Sugars:
glucose	glucose
fructose	fructose
pentoses	pentoses
sucrose	
	Alcohols:
	ethanol
	glycerol
	2, 3-butanediol
	acetoin
	isoamyl
	active amyl
	isobutyl
	n-propyl
	Esters:
	ethyl acetate
	ethyl succinate
	ethyl lactate
	other esters
Acids:	Acids:
tartaric	tartaric
malic	malic
citric	citric
ascorbic	succinic
	lactic
	acetic
Minerals:	Minerals:
sodium	sodium
potassium	potassium
calcium	calcium
iron	iron
phosphorus	phosphorus
sulfur	sulfur
	copper
Nitrogenous substances:	Nitrogenous substances:
ammonia	ammonia
amino acids	amino acids
proteins	proteins
	Acetaldehyde
Phenolic substances	Phenolic substances
Color pigments	Color pigments
Vitamins	Vitamins

during the fermentation and it is these that make wine different from solutions of water, acid, and alcohol.

In plain language, the process is essentially the changing of hexose sugars—dextrose and levulose—into alcohol and carbon dioxide gas through the action of yeasts. The classic chemical expression is that of Gay-Lussac:

$$\underset{\text{(hexose sugar)}}{C_6H_{12}O_6} \rightarrow \underset{\text{(ethyl alcohol)}}{2C_2H_6O} + \underset{\text{(carbon dioxide)}}{2CO_2}$$

While this formula remains the basic statement of the beginning and end of fermentation, it is only 90 per cent valid—10 per cent of the sugar is fermented into by-products such as glycerin, butylene glycol, aldehydes, etc.—and is actually a simplified statement of a complicated series of chemical reactions. According to Amerine and Joslyn (*Table Wines: The Technology of their Production in California*), the dextrose molecule alone passes through twelve stable intermediary stages before forming alcohol. Actually decarboxylation takes place all along the way and CO_2 is given off at several places. In addition, there are thirty-odd organic and inorganic substances which must be present if the process is to succeed. The Amerine-Joslyn definition of fermentation is: "Essentially a process of a series of reversible inter- and intra-molecular oxidation reductions, phosphorylations, and an irreversible decarboxylation."

YEASTS

The yeasts are responsible for the fermentation of wine sugars into ethanol in wines. A number of microorganisms are capable of accomplishing fermentation, but not all are useful to the wine-maker. Yeasts differ according to genus, species, and variety, and the combination of varieties found in one place will never be exactly the same as that found in any other.

The yeast strain *Saccharomyces cereviseae* is the workhorse of the wine-maker. (It should be noted that yeasts are classified according to morphological and physiological traits. They are broadly divided into more than twenty genera of yeasts, which are subsequently subdivided into many thousands of individual species and strains with slightly different characteristics.) Occurring in numerous mutations and variants, this strain is valued for its ability to ferment sugar more completely than can any of the others. But it is not the only yeast to contribute to fermentation; others help to develop bouquet and flavor, and it is thought that the number and type of yeasts active in fermentation have a considerable effect upon the wine. Not even the finest yeasts will make a good wine of mediocre grapes, but in providing the last nuance of quality subsidiary yeasts may play an important part. In the traditional fine-wine regions, the yeasts used are those trapped by the waxy "bloom" on the outside of ripe grapes and are thus completely natural to the region.

Centuries of wine-making in Western Europe have established such large populations of desirable wine yeasts that the danger of "bad" fermentation from unwanted spoilage yeasts has been greatly reduced. In newer wine regions such as California and Australia, however, there is such a great risk of spoilage by undesirable native wild yeasts that sulfur dioxide is added immediately to inhibit them and the must is inoculated with a pure culture of a desirable yeast, often imported from European wine-growing districts.

Yeast variations contribute minor amounts of "nuances" of flavors, but the climate and the choice of varieties have greatly overriding effects. The final touch of glory on a superlative wine might be the slight increase in esters caused by an ester-forming wild yeast. However, the same wine could be ruined by the same yeast if it produced too much ester. Common sense and scientific knowledge demand that in order to obtain the greatest degree of continued success yeast cultures of pure yeast of known quality should be used. The study of these organisms is not so far advanced that laboratory-procured mixed cultures can always be used with complete assurance.

To the uninitiated the rapid wine fermentation appears to be a seething cauldron and may sound like a hive of angry bees. However, this type of fermentation is rapidly disappearing. As the technical skills and mechanical equipment become available, musts are being fermented at lower temperatures, sometimes in closed tanks, and the wines may take weeks instead of days to complete their fermentations.

The yeasts multiply very rapidly in fresh must and the usual number of live yeast cells in one milliliter of must after initial yeast growth will be above 100 million. This amount will vary with temperature and the nutrient qualities of the must.

If no yeast culture is added, then sulfur dioxide in minor amounts can be added, since wild yeast is easily inhibited by the sulfur dioxide. But if pure yeast cultures are employed then a little sulfur dioxide may be used to inhibit the growth of wild yeast. The pure culture can be acclimatized to the sulfur dioxide and will grow vigorously in its presence without delay.

Wine yeasts ferment effectively over a wide temperature range of 50° to 90°F. (10° to 32°C.). However, white wines are usually of the best quality if fermented at the lower temperatures. Red wines are improved in quality by fermenting on the skins at slightly warmer temperatures, i.e., 65° to 85°F. (18° to 29°C.). If the temperature exceeds 100°F. (38°C.), the yeast cells may be killed, resulting in a "stuck" fermentation. This situation is carefully avoided by competent wine-makers, since quality is greatly decreased, and the fermentation is very difficult to restart.

Wines with incomplete fermentations are a big problem in some areas. The reasons for this are not always apparent, but may be the use of yeast with low tolerance for alcohol, or low nutritional value of the grapes, or too high or low a fermentation temperature.

RED WINES

For red wines, grapes are fermented with their skins for varying lengths of time, depending on the type of wine, the specific characteristics of the vintage, and the traditions of the region. In Bordeaux, the old style—followed decreasingly by a very few vineyards—was to leave the wines in the fermenting vats for from four to six weeks. The modern method is to vat from nine to twenty days, with the result that the wines are lighter, more supple, and ready to drink sooner, since they do not pick up so much tannin from the skins. (But some of the younger growers in Bordeaux are returning to the longer vatting time of three weeks.) In Burgundy the practice was for a long time totally different. From the end of the First World War until the last few years, wines were vatted for the shortest possible time, and five to seven days was considered optimum, eight to nine days extreme. Recently, however, it has become the practice to prolong vatting to fifteen days.

During fermentation, the pulp and mass of color- and tannin-imparting skins float on top of the juice, forming the *chapeau*, or "hat"; in a large vat, this may attain a thickness of two or three feet. Various methods exist for diffusing the elements contained in the *chapeau* throughout the wine: (1) the *chapeau* may be punched down two or three times a day; (2) a sort of chimney may be inserted into the vat, through which the wine rises and spills over to water the "hat"; (3) a false top may be put on, forcing the *chapeau* down into the seething grape juice. Pumping the wine through a thick hose affixed to the lower spigot in the vat and up over the *chapeau* on top of the vat is the method most commonly used in France.

When fermentation is over, the wine is drained off and the *chapeau* falls to the bottom of the vat. This residue is then pressed for whatever wine it still contains. The first lots of the "press wine" may be kept separate or added to the free-run juice, and the later ones will be vinified separately into ordinary wine for the workers. When drained off after vatting, the wine is put into oak barrels to age.

Wine is aged in the wood to allow it to clarify and throw off its "gross lees," and to permit it to complete any remaining physical and biochemical changes—continuation of fermentation, precipitation of various compounds, etc.—before bottling. Many of the reactions that must take place need the presence of oxygen—which comes through the pores of the wood and through the bung—of which the wine will be deprived in bottle.

In his *Etudes sur le vin*, Pasteur observed that, without oxygen, wine could not mature or outlive its early sharpness. The wine, on ageing in a wooden cask or barrel, will usually change in alcohol concentration. If the humidity is low the water will evaporate at a greater rate than the alcohol, but if the humidity is high then the alcohol will evaporate more quickly than the water. The evaporation will slightly increase the concentration of the non-volatile constituents but not enough to be noticeable in most dry wines. But oxidation of the sulfurous salt ($SO_2 + O_2 \rightarrow SO_4$) will increase the wine's acidity, as will concentration of the liquid (10 to 15 per cent) and the action of bacteria.

Initial ageing and racking

For the first year of ageing of a red wine, it is kept in a lightly bunged barrel—one that can always be kept filled. In most *chais* (wine sheds or cellars), twice weekly in winter and three times in summer, a worker will "top" the barrel to compensate for evaporation. (This is called *ouillage*, ullage.) If the level were allowed to go down there would be an air space in which undesirable bacteria could set to work creating excessive volatile acidity. As the months go by, the wine, losing some of the astringency of its tannin, becomes gradually less harsh to the taste—malolactic fermentation (*see below, under* Secondary Fermentation in Red or White Wines) mitigates the bitterness. The color, growing less vivid, will by the end of the year have achieved its deepest red; the hue may be affected by variations in the wine's sulfurous acid content.

During the early phase, the wine is in repose and any particles left over from fermentation slowly settle to the bottom; after this wine is "racked"—racking is the draining or pumping of wine from one barrel into a clean sterile one, leaving the lees or sediment behind.

The ideal time for racking wine is when the moon is full, the wind in the north, and the weather clear—science supports these superstitions. Such conditions imply high atmospheric pressure, conditions in which the wine will be at its least active. (When atmospheric pressure is low, the dissolved gases coming out of solution are apt to stir up the lighter lees, which will then be less liable to stay behind in the old barrel.) However, few vineyards of any size can afford the luxury of waiting on nature to this extent. The changes due to atmospheric variations are extremely small and can be neglected with little penalty. Since most of the harmful bacteria collect in the lees, racking helps to free the wine from infection. These lees are then gathered together and, by further settling, give a small amount of wine, one of inferior quality, usually for the staff. Racking is generally done about four times during the first year—and if the wine is a small one, it is bottled at the end of that year or is sold to be served straight from the barrel. A fine wine requires more care.

Quality wines, to be barrel-aged further, are kept in the barrels usually for another year and rarely longer. During this second year of ageing the barrels are tightly bunged and put on their sides so that the bung will stay wet and seal well. Oxidation still proceeds, as the barrels allow a certain amount of air-transfer through the wood. The wine may be racked twice or three times during this period. When it is removed from the barrel it is usually fined and filtered and may be stabilized by certain treatments, depending on the standard practices of the area. Oxidation is replaced by reduction, and the bouquet begins to develop. During the second year, changes in the wine are not so noticeable. It goes on deepening in color and flavor, deriving character and mellowness from contact with the wood. There will still be some precipitation.

The wine rests in this way for another year—longer in some cases—during which time the rackings will continue; just before being bottled or shipped the wine undergoes a "fining."

Fining

Fining, or *collage*, ensures that a wine will be perfectly clear and free from any suspended particles and also helps stabilize the wine against precipitation of certain protein, color, or polyphenolic material, depending on the type of fining material used. Colloidal matter is added to the cask; it coagulates, attracting to itself any minute particles which may be floating in the wine, and the whole mass settles to the bottom. The recommended colloidals for red wines are gelatine, white of egg, blood, etc. These organic agents perform a chemical action—or one which is at once chemical and physical. Inorganic clarifiers, such as Spanish clay, with its active ingredient kaolin, and the special clay of Wyoming (bentonite), are also used, especially in California. When the sediment has settled, the wine is racked once more and bottled or shipped in barrel.

For satisfactory results, clarification should be effected at least six months after vintage, when both fermentation and malolactic fermentation (*see below, under* Secondary Fermentation in Red or White Wines) are complete. At the same time, the wine must be inert, so that there shall be no agitation of the sediment; it follows that the wine must have been adequately racked. The task will be more easily accomplished on a day when the temperature is stable.

Where wines need sulfite treatment, this should be given the day before the fining. The tiny additions of sulfurous acid temporarily inhibit the active microorganisms in the wine.

In some modern French plants outside the fine wine regions fining is an almost obsolete practice, and filtration has taken its place. Filters differ in type and design, but the object is to clear the wine with the least possible exposure to the air. In other large wineries centrifuges are used to clarify rapidly the wine which is to be sold as quickly as possible (within several months of fermentation), and the procedure in these plants is to rack and centrifuge the new wine several times, put it into a cold tank (39°F., 4°C.) for a week or two, centrifuge, filter, and bottle.

Filtration in itself does no harm to a wine if the necessary competent help and the proper filters are available. Filtering is used in most modern wineries after each racking or fining and certainly before bottling. As long as the filter is made of suitable materials and the pumps used are of a non-aerating type the wines profit by this treatment.

Fining is not replaced by filtration. Fining does more than clarify a wine; it also makes a wine of improved flavor and balance and one which will remain clear in the bottle for a longer period.

WHITE WINES

It should be made clear at the outset that the methods of making dry and sweet white wines are not the same. And special cases such as Sherry, which is a fortified wine, are discussed separately in this book and are not considered here (*see* Sherry).

White wines are sweet, semi-sweet, or dry, depending on how complete is the conversion of sugar into alcohol. Sweet wines result from the fact that sugar will not normally ferment after 15 to 16 per cent of alcohol has been generated. In practice dry wines are allowed to proceed until all the sugar is fully fermented.

Sweet white wines

Sweet wines are made by four methods: (1) by using grapes so rich in sugar that all will not be converted, (2) by stopping the fermentation artificially, usually by chemical means, (3) by racking several times during fermentation, and (4) by fortifying the wine either before or during fermentation with brandy or wine alcohol. (An alternative to (4) is the addition of sugar to wine, but the results are poor and the practice is generally frowned upon.)

(1) Grapes rich enough in sugar to stop fermentation are rare. They are found mainly in the Sauternes district of France, in the German Rhine and Mosel valleys, and in a part of Hungary. In all these cases, the grapes are left on the vine until the special mold *Botrytis cinerea*—known to the French as *pourriture noble* and to the Germans as *Edelfäule*, both meaning "noble rot"—has formed, to cause certain chemical changes. These grapes, in fact, contain not an abnormal amount of sugar—merely less water. Another way of getting the same result is to dry grapes—as is done in sections of France, Italy, and Spain; but drying can never, as does *Botrytis*, proportionately decrease acidity as well as water.

(2) The commonest way of stopping fermentation artificially is by the addition of sulfur dioxide. This invaluable chemical has the ability to kill yeasts and microorganisms, but has a lesser and later effect upon the desirable ones than on the undesirable. If it is added in large quantities, the good as well as the bad microbes will be killed and fermentation will cease altogether, leaving any remaining sugar unresolved. The danger is that too much SO_2 might stay in the wine, and impart to it the unpleasant flavor and aroma of sulfur—a fault of many mediocre sweet and semi-

sweet white wines. Alternative methods are pasteurization or severe and sterilizing filtration. In all cases the ferments will be killed or removed before all sugar has been resolved.

(3) Whatever the method used, the wines must be chilled to a temperature close to 32°F. (0°C.) or lower for the treatments to be effective.

(4) Alcohol added before or during fermentation prevents or stops it, and guards all or part of the unresolved sugar. Many of the world's sweet fortified wines are made on this principle. An alternative method is also used by wine-makers, both for red and white wines. Starting with a base of grape juice, the maker adds sugar and alcohol, a concoction which some people feel should not be allowed the name of wine.

Semi-sweet wines

Of increasing popularity, especially in California and in Germany, are white table wines with 1 to 3 per cent residual sugar. These wines are low in alcohol, and are most commonly made in California by fermenting the juice dry, then sweetening with concentrate of unfermented grape juice and stabilizing either chemically or by sterile filtration.

Pressing the grapes

The significant practice in the making of all white wines is the removal of the grape juice from the skins at the earliest possible moment: grapes are crushed and pressed immediately upon arrival at the vatting shed and the juice collected in tanks or barrels to ferment. Fine white wines are made only from the "free-run" juice and that of the earliest pressings, for as pressure increases, quality decreases.

Clarification of the must

To make the highest quality of white wine in California, it is important that the juice be as free as possible from suspended solids before fermentation. The traditional practice has been to allow the solids to settle overnight, then to rack the clear juice from the sediment. In recent years, centrifuges have become increasingly popular as the most satisfactory method of white must clarification.

Fermentation and racking

White wines are fermented either in large vats (bulk method) or small barrels of about 60 U.S. gallons (50 imp.) maximum (quality French method). The exception is Germany, where great wines are fermented in large barrels. The secret of a fine white wine is in a slow, controlled fermentation at a low temperature. Oxygen plays a less important role in the maturing in wood of white wines than it does with a red, nor is oxygen necessary for the improvement of white wine.

Vats are only partially filled, for the must expands and quantities of foam and grape particles rise to the top: if the containers were filled, the must would overflow and be wasted.

However, white wine fermentation that takes place in barrels is probably of a lesser quality than that in a 1,000-gallon tank if starting with the same juice. The *only* reason for the French using barrels in their vineyards is that formerly it was all they had. It has become a tradition and it allows some, but not much, temperature control. White wines to be at their best must be protected from oxygen, and a half-full 60-gallon barrel is poor protection.

When the first tumultuous fermentation has ended, the lees begin to settle, and afterward a light racking is done—a more thorough racking would remove active as well as spent yeasts, and any further fermentation that might remain could become "stuck." In many wine regions, this first racking is extremely light, for removal of all the particles would hinder the secondary or malolactic fermentation (*see* below) which diminishes acidity. In hot areas (parts of California, for example) the contrary is true, for in making their low-acid wines great care is taken to ensure that malolactic fermentation does not start.

In addition to the periodic light rackings, fermentation is also controlled by temperature. Most growers consider that a fermentation temperature of 60° to 70°F. (16° to 21°C.) is optimum, but some prefer an even lower one. A slow, cool fermentation extracts the fruity quality of the grape and results in a wine with greater finesse than is possible if fermentation is fast.

In warmer countries where the addition of acid is permitted, malolactic fermentation is sometimes encouraged, and the wine acidity is adjusted with tartaric or citric acid to an optimum amount after the malolactic fermentation is completed. It is desirable that such fermentation be controlled, since it can occur many times during the initial fermentation or within a month afterward. There is no sure way to control it, but judicious use of sulfur dioxide and the raising of the acidity, as well as thorough rackings and early clarifications, do help. The fermentation at lower temperatures will also reduce the likelihood of a malolactic fermentation.

The fermentation temperature is usually kept as low as the vineyard can manage with its facilities. Some well-equipped California wineries ferment all their white wines at less than 60°F. (16°C.) and at an average temperature of slightly above 50°F. (10°C.). Racking can be used to reduce fermentation rates, but the danger of "sticking" the wine is always present.

Initial ageing of white wines

White wines are conserved at lower temperatures than reds. Tartrates and other dissolved substances—more noticeable in white wine than in red—precipitate best at low temperatures, and nowadays most people like their wines perfectly clear. In spite of every precaution, suspended particles of potassium bitartrate sometimes show, forming white flecks like snow and, though generally tasteless, detract from the appearance of the wine. If the wine is kept at the proper low temperature and is not bottled too early—before the particles have had a chance to precipitate—these flecks will not generally appear.

Fining and bottling

Dry white wines are bottled young—younger than sweet white wines. A year or eighteen months in the barrel often suffices for clarification, and the wines are fined, racked, and either bottled or sold in barrel. Most fine white wines of California, with the exception of Chardonnay, remain in stainless steel tanks blanketed with carbon dioxide to prevent oxidation and are stabilized and bottled as soon as possible. The fining of white wines, like the fining of reds, should be done only if taste and chemical or physical tests deem it necessary. The most common problem is the formation of a white protein cloud, a stituation which is best prevented by fining with bentonite.

Unless they are kept in very new wood and have picked up a lot of wood tannin, the use of organic fining agents is questionable. There are also some new agents in use—nylon powder and very occasionally P.V.P. (polyvinylpyrrolidone). These substances help stabilize the wines against changes to brown color. Sweet white wines are now often fined with bentonite, which removes protein matter from them, helping to establish proper stabilization. Bottle-ageing is similar in principle for white and red wines: less time for dry, longer for sweet wines. In general it is the fresh, early scent of the grape that is appreciated in dry white wines, while the sweet varieties develop bouquet after several years in glass and keep far longer; some of the great ones have been known to hold their excellence for a half-century or even longer.

SECONDARY FERMENTATION IN RED OR WHITE WINES

Many wines undergo a secondary fermentation sometimes concurrent with, often after, the first. Not a sugar-alcohol process, it is called malolactic fermentation and is caused by bacteria attacking the malic acid and turning it into much weaker lactic acid and carbon dioxide gas. It is *not* responsible for Champagne and other sparkling wines. These are produced by a second sugar-alcohol fermentation, generally induced artificially, either in the bottle—Champagne process—or in enclosed tanks or vats—Charmat process (*see* Champagne *and* Charmat).

If secondary fermentation occurs before bottling, the gas will escape and the result will simply be a wine with reduced acid strength. An extra racking will often be a good thing. In the normally high-acid wines of Switzerland, malolactic fermentation is considered of enormous importance; and the Bordeaux oenologists hold it responsible for much of the excellence of the wines of the region, both red and white. In the case of red wines, it is a good thing to have the secondary

fermentation completed soon after the first. If this does not occur, it may take place six or nine months—or even a year or more—later. There is no known process for bringing about this biological deacidification at a given time. Once begun, however, it can be helped by the use of big butts: the reason is that a large volume of liquid will retain the heat generated by the alcoholic fermentation longer than will a small quantity. If secondary fermentation starts or continues in the bottle, the gas is confined and the wine becomes turgid and gassy, frequently unpleasant. If the bubble is a slight one, it can sometimes be eliminated by airing the wine—either by swirling it around in the glass or by pouring it from one glass to another; but if such a wine is served in a restaurant, it is best to send it back.

Recently, scientific knowledge has increased to the point where specific malolactic bacteria can be cultured in the laboratory and added to must prior to fermentation, thus inducing the malolactic fermentation to proceed along with the primary fermentation. Occasionally a bad strain of malolactic bacteria would occur in the wine, spoiling it by off-aromas and -flavor. This can sometimes be avoided now by the controlled use of a known strain—which allows the wines to be brought to maturity sooner and avoids the occurrence of secondary fermentation in the bottles.

AGEING OF WINES

Not all wines improve with age. Some—notably the dry whites—are at their best when young. Most fine wines improve, both in barrel and in bottle, but eventually pass their prime, decline, and finally fall apart altogether. What happens to wine while it is ageing? Salts precipitate, acidity decreases, and alcohols, acids, and other components are transformed into innumerable complex compounds—esters, aldehydes, acetals, and the like. Professor E. Peynaud of the Bordeaux Oenological Station recognizes two sharp divisions in wines: (1) those such as Port, Sherry, and the sweet fortified wines in general, whose excellence comes from a process of oxidation and the formation of aldehydes, notably acetaldehyde (other oxidative changes occurring at the same time, as well as the components picked up from the barrels, give this wine an aged character); and (2) those wines which can only develop their best characteristics in the absence of air. In the case of wines of the second category, the characteristics come from the grape used; for example, Bordeaux mainly comes from the Cabernet grape, and Burgundy from the Pinot Noir. Bouquet is an important product of ageing, and this can only come about, in wines of the second category, when there is an odorant supplied by the grape, when the wine is effectively sealed from air, and when good reducing conditions are provided.

Barrel-ageing is important in hastening the clarification and stability of wines and in imparting certain characteristics donated by wood—for, once bottled, the wines can no longer be treated and cared for—but the amount of oxygen that enters the wine, and its importance, is disputed and perhaps overestimated. Bottle-ageing of fine wines is very incompletely understood, but the scientists differ from the wine-makers, maintaining that the amount of air which enters a bottle through the cork plays a very small role, if any. Professor J. Ribéreau-Gayon, of the University of Bordeaux, states in the impressive *Traité d'oenologie:* "The quantity of oxygen that normally penetrates into bottles is infinitesimal if not nil; it is improbable that an important role could be attributed to it." He supports his statement with the observation that wines age as well in hermetically sealed tubes as in corked bottles. With these matters so incompletely understood, it seems unlikely that artificial ageing, a process which has received a good deal of attention, will very soon become practical.

What is generally overlooked by the non-scientist is that there is some air in the wine when it is bottled, and this can play a role in the changes which occur. Actually 8 to 10 milliliters of air are present in the average bottle of wine. If the cork is kept wet little or no air transfer would be expected to occur, but the air already there would cause certain variations to take place. Extreme care should be taken to reduce the amount of air at the time of bottling so that bottle oxidative changes are at a minimum and reductive changes can proceed. Bottle age bouquets can be developed by artificial treatments and do show some promise for certain common wines.

EXCEPTIONAL PRACTICES

The wine-maker must always reckon with the possibility of unfavorable weather during the growing season of the vine and thus with the prospect of immature or badly matured grapes. In earlier times this spelled disaster, but today there are ways of bringing the wine up to standard. Some of these methods are:

Chaptalisation. Named after its French inventor, Dr. Chaptal, who proposed the idea around the turn of the nineteenth century, it is also called in Germany *Gallization* (after Dr. Gall) and *Anreicherung* (meaning "enrichment"). *Chaptalisation* is the addition of sugar to sugar-deficient musts—but never wines—to make certain that the wine will have an alcoholic content commensurate with its other qualities. Regular sugar (sucrose) hydrolyzes into hexose sugars (dextrose and levulose) when added to the must and ferments normally. Used discreetly, *chaptalisation* may bring the alcohol into better balance with the other constituents of the wine; but abused—as it unfortunately is in some areas—it results in "wine" being made from grape skins, sugar,

and acids. *Chaptalisation* is widespread in Germany and Burgundy, and may sometimes be found as far to the south as Bordeaux—but only when specifically authorized by the government. In Burgundy, where unfortunately it is a yearly practice, some of the great wines are now allowed to be overabundantly sugared. In regions where the sun is hot enough to generate the requisite amount of sugar in the grapes, it is not necessary. In their *Dictionnaire du vin*, Messieurs Renouil and de Traversay say that *chaptalisation* could with advantage increase the alcoholic content, since the fermentation of sugar gives rise not only to alcohol but also to by-products (such as glycerol, succinic acid, etc.) which exert a considerable influence on the flavor of wine. The operation also decreases the excessive tartness of certain wines by precipitating the cream of tartar.

Chaptalisation is not legal in California.

De-acidification. When the weather is really bad, the grapes may be too high in acid as well as deficient in sugar. The common way of handling this is to blend the wine with low-acid wines, a perfectly proper procedure, providing the wine is not then sold under an *appellation*, or place-name, to which it has no right. A rarer method is to add calcium carbonate. This reacts with the acids and mainly precipitates out, but calls for very careful handling and usually gives poor results.

Acidification. After an exceptionally hot summer, grapes may have too little acid, resulting in a flat and tasteless wine. This may be corrected quite legally by adding to the must either a small amount of tartaric acid (which does not improve the quality of fine wines) or the less mature—and therefore more acid—grapes from a late flowering of the vine; or by blending with high-acid wines.

De-coloration. If a white wine is tinged with red—or a pink wine is too deeply colored—fining with charcoal will remove as much of the color as desired. Unfortunately it also removes any character the wine might otherwise have had.

Concentration. Sugar deficiency may be corrected by adding concentrated must, from which some of the water has been boiled off. Alcohol-deficient wines may similarly be treated by adding wine from which some of the water has been removed by freezing. In either case, the sugar or alcohol of the must or wine will be proportionately raised. The drawbacks are that in some countries these practices are illegal, and while they increase sugar or alcohol, they also increase acidity, sometimes to the detriment of the wine.

Pasteurization. The applicability of the method of sterilization by heat is still disputed. Many experts feel that heat kills wine, although the Bordeaux oenologist Professor Ribéreau-Gayon says that this is true only under certain conditions. Pasteurization, or heating wine quickly up to a temperature of 130°F. (54°C.), effectively sterilizes wines in barrel, destroying all bacteria—but it is impracticable, if not impossible, for wines already bottled. It is also a cumbersome

BASIC RULES OF WINE-MAKING

Recommendations to follow

1. Cleanliness is essential. See that all equipment coming into contact with the wine is kept clean. Avoid iron utensils or copper-containing metals—certain plastics, glass, and stainless steel or wood are recommended for tools, tanks, pipes, etc., where the wine is contacted.

2. Gather the grapes in as sound a condition as the year permits, and in a suitable state of ripeness.
Bring them whole to the presses, and free of soil.

3. Pressing must be done rapidly for white musts, nor should the grapes be overpressed.
Avoid oxidation of the musts by maceration of the crushed grapes in the open air.

4. Cleanse the must—and so the wine—by the addition of a small but adequate dose of sulfurous acid. Remove the suspended solids of a white must before fermentation, either by settling, filtration, or centrifugation.

5. Control fermentations at suitable temperatures, as low as possible but not too low, otherwise the fermentation may be arrested.
With red wines, time the fermentation periods very carefully.
Beware of deterioration which may be caused by the exposure to air of the top crusts.

6. As soon as fermentation is complete, the wines should be ullaged (i.e., the barrels topped up). Never leave a broached wine in contact with air.

7. Red, rosé, and dry white wines must not retain the slightest trace of reducing sugars. (Yet in many places small amounts of residual sugars in dry white and rosé wine are tolerated or even encouraged—without excessive alcohol. It is quite possible to preserve such wines successfully by use of sorbic acid and sulfur dioxide. Many German wines have residual sugar, and this is thought of as a necessity for quality in some instances.)

Faults to be avoided

Unpleasant taste or smell.
Metallic casse (or breakdown) of the wine; deterioration, and microbial cloudiness.

Unpleasant taste of mold.
Turning sour (for mildewed wines).
Excessive, or insufficient, acidity.
Depreciation and microbial cloud, breakdown due to metal content.

Lack of freshness and fruitiness.
Excessive tannin. Colloidal cloud.
Excess of proteids.
Oxidasic breakdown, molding.

Deterioration and microbial cloud, oxidasic casse.
Excessive hydrogen sulfide formation, poor clarification.

Excess of reducing sugars, moldiness.
Scouring or excessive volatile acidity and ropiness (if the temperature is too high).

Fungoid growth, deteriorations, and microbial cloud.

Lactic acid moldiness.
Mannitic fermentation.

---

procedure, partly because the mechanics of it have never been satisfactorily worked out. In certain circumstances it can be very useful; but in the fine wine districts it is best avoided, since wines so treated tend to become inert. However, in sweet or semi-sweet table wines of many countries it is routine to pasteurize before bottling or during bottling. The common wines are heated to 180°F. (82°C.) for one minute or may be bottled at 130° to 140°F. (54° to 60°C.) and then cooked slowly. Some large wineries selling competitive wines have the systems so perfected that not one bottle will spoil from yeast or bacteria out of the thousands bottled every hour unless a defective closure or something unforeseen oc-

curs. The mechanical conditions for wine pasteurization are well understood. Recent research shows that the more rapidly the wine is heated and cooled, the less it is decreased in quality. Very rapid-flash pasteurizers are being developed, but the process is costly and still plagued with the problem of recontamination of the wine during bottling.

THE COMPOSITION OF WINE

Wine is an extraordinarily intricate and inconstant complex of different ingredients. It is because of its ability to change in many ways from the time the grape

Recommendations to follow	*Faults to be avoided*
The high alcoholic content of the great sweet and mellow white wines helps to preserve them without much sulfur dioxide.	Secondary fermentation.
Conversely, the lesser white wines, sweet and mellow, are difficult to keep.	
To avoid giving the wines large doses of sulfur dioxide they may be sterilized before bottling.	Development and depositing of yeast.

8. Carry out rackings at the right time, and sufficiently often, either with aeration or away from air, as the case may be. Do not forget that malolactic fermentation to a certain extent may either be achieved or avoided according to the amount of acidity which the wine should retain. This operation calls, however, for constant care, particularly as regards white wines. Other factors besides acidity determine whether or not there will be malolactic fermentation. Fornachon points out that it depends on nutrients, aeration, pH, and sulfur dioxide. It is a very complex system and interactions exist, making it impossible to predict with assurance if a wine will naturally undergo a malolactic fermentation.
   Filtering will assist the maturing of all wines.

   Excess or deficiency of acidity.
   Ropiness.

9. The wine will attain physical maturity during the first winter by means of precipitation of the various tartars. The ordinary wines, drunk a few months after the harvest, may be treated with metatartaric acid or, preferably, they may be refrigerated. Filtering will assist the maturing of all wines.
   Clarification, without excessive use of fining agents, will help the maturation of wines.

   Crystalline precipitations.

   Colloidal cloudiness.

   Over-fining, making a thin wine lacking in character.
   Coagulation of the proteins.

10. The blending of wines can only be recommended when it is possible to marry qualities which complement each other. It is better to lower the classification of an inferior wine if these inferior qualities can only be diluted, rather than improve it by blending in a better wine and giving it the somewhat misleading classification of the superior component.

    No character.

11. In order that the maker may guarantee his product, it is essential for the wine to be delivered in bottle to the consumer, and bearing a label with the bottler's guarantee, as is the case with mineral waters, soda-waters, beers, etc.

    Deterioration and microbial cloud.
    Poor keeping qualities.
    A loss of authenticity.

12. Put the bottles up for sale in such a way as not to mislead the consumer.

    Reprehensible labeling. (Regulatory action by the enforcing agency of the country.)

---

is picked until the wine is poured that wine is said to "live"—as indeed it does.

Alcohol

The most obvious but not the most important element of wine, alcohol, derived from the fermentation of the non-alcoholic grape juice, comprises from 7 to 24 per cent of the contents by volume; most is ethyl alcohol, but some—less than 0.15 per cent—is methyl alcohol, present in wine in quantities varying between 36 and 350 milligrams per liter. In addition, there are varying amounts of such higher alcohols as amyl, isoamyl, n-propyl, isopropyl, n-butyl, sec-butyl, isobutyl,

a-terpineol, and perhaps n-hexyl, n-heptyl, and sec-nonyl.

Ethyl alcohol (ethanol). The degree of this essential component is decided by the amount of sugar in the must. It varies, according to the maturity of the grape, between 7 and 16 per cent of the volume (higher when extra alcohol has been added). In fine wines, the amount, which influences both quality and longevity, is of vital importance. As the acids in the wine gradually combine with alcohol to produce esters, so the elements that compose the bouquet develop. The antiseptic properties of the ethyl alcohol help to inhibit the growth of the various bacteria and yeast disorders to which wine is prone.

Wine: What It Is, How It Is Made

Acids

Acids give freshness and tartness to the taste. An acid-deficient wine is flat; a too-acid wine undrinkable. The organic acids (malic, tartaric, etc.) are those which impart the characteristic flavor, sharp on the tip of the tongue—a sensation caused by the presence of hydrogen ions. A wine vinified from unripe grapes will have a total acidity and a low pH. In brandy, a high degree of acid is a fault, although a moderate content gives it body.

Acidity, by preventing or slowing down the development of such harmful bacteria as the mannitic (which turns wine sour), helps to preserve the wine. It affects also stability and color—the higher the acid content, the more brilliant the hue. The total acidity of a young healthy wine averages four to five grams a liter, expressed in sulfuric acid. This will be less, by about 25 per cent, than the acidity of the original must.

Three of the major acids in wine are naturally present in the grape (tartaric, malic, and citric; it is interesting that the grape is the only temperate fruit in which there is tartaric acid), and the rest are the result of fermentation. Most of the acid content is tartaric, and about 10 to 40 per cent is malic, so called because it is present in apples and supposedly responsible for the "fruitiness" of many wines. Citric acid is found in very small amounts, as are succinic, lactic, and acetic acids; there are minute traces of butyric, capric, caproic, caprylic, formic, lauric, propionic, and, in sparkling wines, carbonic. Acetic, butyric, carbonic, formic, and propionic acids are the "volatile" acids, and chemists consider volatile acidity in wines to be of the same order as temperature in man: it is always present, but when it deviates from normal there is somthing wrong. The others are the "fixed" organic acids. The sum of the fixed and volatile acidity makes up the "total acidity" of the wine; that is, the titratable acidity expressed usually as grams of tartaric acid.

Tartaric acid. This is the most important of the fixed acids in wine and the one particularly associated with the grape; it is rarely found elsewhere in nature. The quantity of the acid present in the grape is decreased by respiratory combustion, during the periods of high temperature. The addition of tartaric acid to the must is allowed in cases of low acidity. At too high a concentration, however, it will impart to the wine a certain astringency, even harshness.

Malic acid. The principal acid in many fruits and vegetables. The quantity present in grapes at the *vendange* is of considerable importance in winemaking. While the fruit is ripening, cellular respiration causes the malic acid concentration to be lowered. Under the influence of bacteria, it undergoes lactic fermentation. The tartness of wines made after a cold summer and the sharpness of young wines are due to the malic acid which determines almost by itself the state of ripeness of the grape.

Citric acid. This occurs in all varieties of grapes, both ripe and unripe—and to a greater extent where *Botrytis*

cinerea has developed. Wines made from grapes in a state of noble rot may contain as much as a gram of citric acid. Normal quantities (usually increasing somewhat during fermentation) vary between 1 and 10 grams and tend to be much lower in red wines than in white. The bacteria which cause malolactic fermentation may ferment the citric acid and produce volatile acidity. Wines vary in the amount of citric acid naturally present, and this may affect a casse formation. Amounts which may be added to vine vary from country to country.

Carbonic acid. Carbonic acid is formed by the reaction of carbon dioxide and water ($CO_2 + H_2O = H_2CO_3$). The amount of carbonic acid in wine depends upon the amount of dissolved carbon dioxide, which in still wines is usually less than 0.5 grams per liter. Carbon dioxide is produced during the decomposition of sugar in alcoholic fermentation, by the decomposition of malic acid in malolactic fermentation, and during respiration of any yeast or bacteria in the wine. It is the continual production of carbon dioxide during fermentation that limits the amount of oxygen available in the wine, inhibiting acetic acid-forming bacteria and causing the yeast to produce ethanol rather than to completely break down the sugar to carbon dioxide and water. Carbon dioxide is purposefully trapped in the bottle for Champagne production by adding extra fermentable sugar to dry wine and sealing the bottle.

Sulfurous acid. Sulfur dioxide (SO_2) gas, when added to wine, reacts with water to form sulfurous acid H_2SO_3. A chemical equilibrium is established between the sulfur dioxide and its hydrated forms as follows:
$$SO_2 + H_2O \leftrightarrow H_2SO_3 \leftrightarrow H^+ + HSO_3^- \leftrightarrow 2H^+ + SO_3^=$$
Sulfur dioxide is used for preserving casks of wood and, being antiseptic, is carefully added to wine, which it protects against deterioration. Sulfurous acid and sorbic acid are at present the only two antiseptics allowed under French law. The former, an anti-oxidant, is also a reducing agent.

Among the useful properties of this acid are its antiseptic qualities, effective against those microbial diseases caused by harmful yeasts and bacteria. Sulfite treatment is used to subdue overly violent fermentation. Sulfurous acid has its drawbacks, however. Because it is solvent in contact with various metals and minerals, it is apt to cause ferric casse, both blue and white, and, in white wines, cuprous casse (see Wine Disorders *below*). It is likewise well known that wines which have been overdosed with it retain a disagreeable smell and taste of sulfur.

In the French vineyards, when a wine is to receive sulfite treatment, it (or the must) is poured into a cask in which a stick of sulfur has been burned. This old-fashioned method is not precise, since unburned sulfur is liable to remain at the bottom of the barrel and sulfur dioxide may escape through the bung. The theory that 10 grams of sulfur will produce, when burned, 20 grams of sulfur dioxide is incorrect—under favorable conditions the sulfur may make 15 grams, which will only be completely effective if put in through the bung of the cask. Barely half a stick (about 20 grams) can be burned in a cask of 225 liters: it can be estimated, therefore, that the sulfur burned introduces into the wine the equivalent of its own weight in sulfur dioxide.

An ordinary water solution of sulfur dioxide is saturated at about 5–6 per cent sulfur dioxide and cannot be further concentrated. Of course, a solution of sodium sulfite or sodium bisulfite or metabisulfite can be made more concentrated. The 5–6 per cent solution is extremely corrosive to metal.

Bisulfites or metabisulfites should be used in the form of pellets or crystals. In all wine-making countries, sulfite treatment is restricted in terms of free and total sulfurous acid content. Total sulfur dioxide is the aggregate of free sulfur dioxide and compound sulfur dioxide. The amount of free sulfur dioxide decreases steadily to an equilibrium level because part is combined with aldehydes, color pigments, sugars, etc. Some sulfur dioxide is oxidized to the sulfate by the oxygen in solution. The amount of free sulfur is proportionate to the amount of the total once an equilibrium is reached with the combining materials (generally about two weeks). After this there is a slow loss by chemical change, but the relative amounts of the total and free sulfur dioxide stay the same.

Usually sulfur dioxide is added at the time of bottling as a protection against oxidation and to combine an inactivated acetaldehyde. Over a period of years the total sulfur dioxide will become greatly reduced. However, if the wine is well made and in the bottle, little will happen because of this loss.

Volatile acidity. The primary source of volatile acidity in most wines is acetic acid. However, other acids—such as formic or sulfurous acid, or any other steam-distillable acid—do contribute. The actual smell of "acetic" wine can be attributed to ethyl acetate in many instances. The presence of these chemicals is normal, and only when they are in excess do they become objectionable. In France, volatile acidity in wine is expressed in sulfuric acid, averaging between 0.3 and 0.7 gram per liter. When this figure is exceeded, the wine is affected. In France there have from time to time been strict regulations about the degree permissible in wine to be sold: the current law lays down that a wine is spoiled at 0.9 gram per liter at the wholesale, and 1.2 grams at the retail stages. In California, the legal limits for volatile acidity are 1.10 grams per liter for white wines and 1.20 grams per liter for red wines, expressed as acetic acid.

Sugar and glycerin

In a sugar-alcohol fermentation, the most important by-product is glycerin (or glycerol). This donates some of the sweetness and smoothness to a wine and was once erroneously thought to be responsible for the "legs"—the streaks that run down the side of a glass in which wine has been swirled. (Legs are now

TABLE OF WINE ACIDS

(according to J. Ribéreau-Gayon and E. Peynaud)

Name of Wine Acid	Remarks
Fixed organic	
Tartaric	
Malic	These acids come from the grape.
Citric	
Succinic	
Lactic	Produced by fermentation.
Gluconic	
Glycuronic	Eudemized grapes.
Dioxymalic	
Dioxytartaric	Oxidation of the tartaric acid.
Glycolic	
Glyoxylic	
Glyceric	Not yet studied thoroughly in wines.
Saccharic	
High fatty	
Volatile organic	
Formic	Acetic alone is always present in
Acetic	wine.
Mineral	
Hydrochloric	
Sulfuric	
Sulfurous	Authorized antiseptics.
Orthophosphoric	
Carbonic	Produced by fermentation.

Acidification Procedures Permitted in Various Wine-producing Countries

Algeria: Musts: tartaric acid, without restriction (during fermentation); citric acid: 50 grams per hectoliter maximum (after fermentation). Wines: tartaric acid forbidden; citric acid: maximum 50 grams per hectoliter, providing the original must has not been acidified at this dose.

Austria: Forbidden in principle to increase the acid content.

West Germany: Same as Austria.

Bulgaria: Tartaric and citric acid only for the sparkling wines.

Spain: Pure citric acid, maximum 1 gram per liter; tartaric acid only in musts or wines of low acidity, but not for other usages.

U.S.: Tartaric, malic, and citric acids—within specified limits.

France: Musts: tartaric acid. Wines: citric acid, maximum 0.50 gram per liter.

known to be a result of ethyl alcohol.) Compounds related to glycerin and found in very small quantities are 2,3-butylene glycol, acetylmethylcarbinol, and diacetyl. Sugar will also be present—even in a completely "dry" wine. (Less than 0.2 per cent sugar is about standard for dry wines; this amount cannot be tasted, nor will it ferment further.) Some of this is hexose sugar—dextrose and levulose, of which levulose is the sweeter—and some are pentose sugars, mostly arabinose and some xylose. There are also related compounds such as rhamnose, pentosans, methyl pentosans, dihydroxymaleic acid, and pectins.

Aldehydes and esters

Adehydes are a halfway step between alcohols and acids and are formed by the oxidation of alcohols; esters are the result of a combination of acid and alcohol. Both play an important part in wines, particularly in bouquet.

The most important wine aldehyde is acetaldehyde. In addition there are traces of formaldehyde, propionaldehyde, cinnamaldehyde, cenanthaldehyde, vanillin, methyl ethylketone, acetal, capraldehyde, and benzaldehyde—and probably furfural and acrolein, although these two have not been sufficiently established for chemists to be quite sure. In certain sweet wines—those that have been heated, such as Madeira and some imitation "sherries"—there is also a trace of hydroxymethylfurfural.

Esters fall into two groups: (1) volatile odoriferous esters usually formed from acetic acid, and (2) the neutral and acid esters of the fixed acids, mostly tartaric and malic. Ethyl acetate is by far the most prevalent ester, but others, formed from all the acids mentioned above plus those of valeric, caproic, and pelargonic acids, will be present to a greater or lesser degree.

Dry extract and ash

When wine is placed in a test tube and carefully heated, the liquid boils away, leaving salts which, when heated to high temperatures, form the ash, useful to the wine chemist in determining what is present and in what quantity. The salts include chlorides, phosphates, silicates, and sulfates; and the minerals include potassium, calcium, magnesium, sodium, iron, copper, and small amounts of boron, iodine, manganese, molybdenum, titanium, vanadium, and zinc. The type and amount of minerals present will largely depend upon the soil in which the grapes were grown, what minerals nourished the vine, and the elements which came into contact with the wine.

Nitrogen and vitamins

The most important nitrogen by-products are the amino acids, some of which disappear during fermentation or are used by yeasts to form the higher alcohols. Other amino acids are formed by the yeast. Common amino acids are alanine, arginine, aspartic acid, cystine, glutamic acid, glycine, histidine, isoleucine, leucine, lysine, methionine, proline, serine, threonine, tryptophan, tyrosine, valine, and phenylalanine. Vitamins include vitamin A, ascorbic acid, thiamin, riboflavin, pyridoxin, nicotinic acid, pantothenic acid, p-aminobenzoic acid, biotin, and inositol.

Phenolic substances and tannin

The phenolic constituents of wine are a complex group which includes the tannins, anthocyanins, catechins, and other flavonoids, cinnamates, etc. Tannins occur primarily in the seeds and stems and contribute an astringent flavor to wines. They have antiseptic qualities, helping to inhibit noxious bacteria, and serve as anti-oxidants to protect the wine during ageing. The longer a red wine has fermented on the skins, the greater will be the tannin content and consequently the longer the wine will be able to age. During ageing, the tannins undergo complicated oxidative reactions and polymerizations with aldehydes, pigments, and other constituents, so that the harshness of the young wine is gradually reduced as the tannins combine and precipitate. These changes contribute greatly to the character and appearance of a fine aged wine.

The anthocyanins are the primary red pigments of grapes, located in the cells of the skin and released during fermentation as the skins are degraded by alcohol. Grape varieties differ as to quantity and types of anthocyanins, and therefore as to the stability of the pigment in the finished wine. During ageing, the anthocyanins complex and precipitate out, so that a very old wine may have a sediment of pigment at the bottom of the bottle and an orange-brown color, due mainly to the remaining tannin complexes.

White wines generally contain less than 350 milligrams per liter of phenols expressed as gallic acid, while red wines may contain as much as 3,000 milligrams per liter.

WINE DISORDERS

Young wine is a living thing in the sense that biochemical processes are taking place continuously. It is subject to diseases and disorders of various sorts. These may be divided into maladies caused by biological disorders and those caused by the physical environment.

(1) Biological disorders

Bacterial or yeast spoilage can take place under either aerobic or anaerobic conditions. In many cases it is extremely difficult to pinpoint the organism causing the trouble; the same bacteria may cause apparently different diseases under different conditions. Over the years the nomenclature of the various diseases also changes. The most common bacteria are the lactobacilli, which will ferment malic acid and also citric acid under certain conditions. These are only dangerous if the strain metabolizes undesired substances or gives off odor or flavors, or the wine is so low in acid as to become flat and unbalanced after the secondary fermentation. Some widely recognized diseases are:

Flowers of wine (flor). "Flowers of wine" is the name given to a particular film-forming yeast which will grow on the surface of young wines if they are exposed to air. This is not a disorder when used to produce the distinctive character of Spanish Sherry or the *vin jaune* of the French Jura. This yeast growth generally has to be encouraged and can easily be prevented by keeping the wine container full.

Mycoderma (fleur). This is a fairly harmless microbe which grows rapidly on the surface of young wine, forming a film. It is often mistaken for *flor*, but under microscopic observation the difference is easily determined. This disease can also be prevented by limiting the exposure of the wine surface to the air.

Acescence (piqûre) or *acetification.* Like *fleur*, acescence is marked by the formation of a film on the surface of the wine—but of a translucent gray rather than white in many instances. *Acetobacter* causes a rapid decrease in alcohol and sugar and produces varying amounts of acetic acid and ethyl acetate which give the wine a disagreeable vinegary taste, thus ruining it. Again, this disease can be easily prevented if the wine is not subject to excess aeration by exposure of the partly full container to air and by good cellar practice.

Tourne. The wine becomes gassy—with a thoroughly disagreeable aroma and taste resembling that of acescence—hazes, and loses its color. *Tourne* is caused by bacteria attacking tartaric acid and chemically shows a loss of tartrates, an increase of volatile acidity, and a decrease of fixed acidity and acid strength (as shown by a rise in pH value).

Graisse (fatty degeneration). The wine becomes turgid and viscous and flows like oil. There is a decrease in sugar, an increase in both total and volatile acidity, and a gummy deposit. The disease is often found in Champagne, where it affects the *rebêche* (the low-quality last run of the winepress), which is vinified and given to the workers.

Amertume (bitterness). The wine throws a deposit and becomes bitter and very acid. It is caused by bacteria attacking glycerin and chemically shows a decrease in glycerin and an increase in total and volatile acidity.

These last three diseases are generally considered to be caused by either lactobacilli, leuconostoc, or bacilli.

Mannitic fermentation. When the temperature of the fermenting vat becomes excessive, the useful yeasts die and other bacteria take over, attacking the sugar. The resultant wine is cloudy and has a curious bittersweet, sometimes "mousy" taste. Instead of converting grape sugar to ethyl alcohol and carbon dioxide, these bacteria convert it to acetic acid, lactic acid, carbon dioxide, and mannite, a non-fermentable sugary substance. Mannitic fermentation is a particular menace in hot countries.

(2) *Chemical disorders (casses)*

There are four types of casse: oxidasic, protein, ferric, and cuprous.

Oxidasic casse. Caused by an enzyme (polyphenoloxidase), it makes wine cloud on exposure to air and change color—red wines turn brown and white wines yellow, and, after a time, form a deposit. It is often present in wines made from slightly overripe or moldy grapes. Wines containing a fairly high proportion of alcohol or acid, and especially of tannin, are best qualified to resist this breakdown. Preventive treatments for the condition are judicious use of sulfur dioxide; the addition of ascorbic acid (which in its natural state increases browning) at 100 to 200 milligrams per liter; heating of the musts (to 158° to 167°F., 70° to 75°C.) in a pasteurizer, by the addition of bentonite and yeast.

Protein casse. There is always a certain amount of protein matter in white wines and, if present in too great a degree, it reacts with the tannins to coagulate, first turning the wine hazy, later forming a precipitate. Once troublesome to makers of sweet white wines, protein casse has been reduced in importance by the practice of fining with bentonite, which removes protein matter, so that wines need no longer be aged until enough tannin has been absorbed to cause the reaction.

Ferric casse. In primitive times, nothing but bare feet and wood touched grapes. In installing labor-saving devices, wine-makers found that iron and copper often contaminated wines, imparting off-tastes and cloudiness. Ferric (iron) casse is caused by a high iron content (reacting with phosphates in the presence of air and causing blue or black clouding and precipitation) in a wine which may also be rich in tannin but of low acidity. Sometimes the casse is allowed to run its course, and then the wine is clarified. Many red wines, young and older, will become cloudy as a result of oxygen dissolving or exposure to the air. White wines also are subject to a form of phosphatoferric casse when they are rich in iron or phosphoric acid and are exposed to the air in the course of racking, bottling, or, especially, filtering. The deposit, which forms slowly, is grayish in color; the cloudiness will sometimes disappear when the wine is kept airtight and away from the light. One remedy is to add to the wine a solution of sodium bisulfite—not more than one gram per liter. In this case too, the best preventive measure is to keep the wine away from metal utensils. Ferric, like cuprous casse, can be prevented by "blue fining"—precipitating the metal with minute amounts of potassium ferrocyanide. Officially forbidden in many countries, including France, "blue fining" is, in some places such as Germany, allowed under rigid governmental control.

Two forms of iron compounds can form precipitates in wine. One, called white casse, is due to ferric phosphate and the other, called blue casse, is due to ferric tannate. The first forms if the pH of the wine is below 3.60 and sufficient iron (above five milligrams per liter) is present. If conditions are favorable then the compound will usually form, since there are sufficient phosphates present normally. The iron must be oxidized to the ferric state. The most obvious preventive measure is to have no iron in contact with the wines. However, this is not always practicable. Therefore, wines are either aerated and the casses allowed to form or, better, the metals are removed by the proper fining. This is accomplished by treating the wines with ferrocyanide, in countries where this is allowed, and with safer compounds (such as Cufex in the United States) if the use of ferrocyanide is forbidden. As a help against formation of these casses, citric acid can be added, and it will chelate the iron and prevent casse formation.

Cuprous (or copper) casse. Copper casse is usually considered as cupric sulfide. It will not form in the absence of protein but will quickly flocculate in its presence. Sulfur dioxide, or hydrogen sulfide, must be present, and if one is not then a copper-protein precipitate will form slowly. Aeration will hinder formation of these compounds, as will organic acids to a small extent. Cold treatments, metal removal, filtration, and the usual methods of control will save the wine.

Cuprous casse may occur in white wines containing even a few tenths of a milligram per liter of protein and copper, when these wines have been kept for some time away from air and in a warm light place. The condition can be remedied by aerating the wine, by adding a few drops of hydrogen peroxide, or by clarification with bentonite to remove the protein matter. Since cuprous casse requires light to develop, vulnerable wines are often put into dark green bottles. Like ferric casse, this form of breakdown responds to "blue fining" with potassium ferrocyanide, in the few countries where its use is not forbidden.

Copper, exposed simultaneously to light and air, becomes oxidized—and so does the wine. Preventive measures can therefore be taken before introducing the wine into copper pipes or containers by washing them out with a solution of tartaric acid at a concentration of five grams per liter and then rinsing with clear water. Better still, the wine or the must should not be allowed to come in contact with copper at all.

3. Accidents

Most accidental off-tastes in wines are caused by carelessness on the part of the maker. Extraneous odors affect wines to a far greater extent than is generally realized, and wines may be spoiled by being stored in places where they come into contact with such strong-smelling things as gasoline, insecticides, tobacco, or even scent.

The odor caused by moldy barrels and unclean hoses or tools is dangerous because it may help to impart an off-taste to wine. The so-called romantic cellars shown with pride by their European owners all contribute to the creation of this problem.

Off-odors and -flavors can also be caused by the addition of excessive chemicals such as sorbic acid, sulfur dioxide, and diethylpyrocarbonate.

STEPS TO BE TAKEN AGAINST WINE DISORDERS

Sterilizing of utensils. Cobwebs clustering on the walls of the wine sheds harbor harmful bacteria. They must be cleared away, and the dirty walls sprayed with whitewash solution mixed with 1 per cent of copper sulfate. Moldy walls should be rubbed over with carbonate of soda—about 2 pounds to 10 liters (2.6 U.S. gallons, 2.2 imp.) of boiling water. After rinsing with clear water, the walls may be brushed over a tepid solution of 1 per cent potassium permanganate. The floor, when it has been scrubbed, can be treated with calcium chloride (1 per cent solution) and then rinsed with water.

Fermenting vats must be descaled, from time to time; and wine presses and wooden vats (which should always be well scrubbed and rinsed) ought, when they accumulate a layer of gray mold, to be washed first in a 10 per cent solution of carbonate of soda, then with clear water.

WINE: THE SUM TOTAL

If in wine, as in geometry, the whole is the sum of its parts, it is at least theoretically possible to duplicate wine in the laboratory. The overwhelming complexity of such a job can be seen from the foregoing list of some of the ingredients and components of wine. At present, according to Professors Ribéreau-Gayon and Peynaud of Bordeaux, the scientist has successfully isolated and measured over one hundred different compounds, comprising about 97 to 98 per cent of the composition of wine. Of the nature of its all-important remaining 2 to 3 per cent, we have little or no idea, nor how many separate compounds they represent. More important still, if we take the known ingredients and mix them together in their proper proportions, we obtain nothing resembling wine. With this in mind, there can be no wonder that leading wine chemists admit that the final judgment of a wine must not be in the test tube but in the wineglass.

10 Spirit-Making

Potable spirits are beverages of high alcoholic content obtained by distillation—that is, the separation, by heating, of ethyl alcohol from wine or other spirituous liquids. Alcohol vaporizes at a lower temperature than water, and the process of distillation makes use of the differences in their volatility. Under normal atmospheric pressure, water boils at 212°F. (100°C.) and alcohol at 173.5°F. (78.4°C.). When heat is applied to a diluted mixture of water and alcohol between these temperatures, the alcohol will be converted to vapor; and if it is then drawn off through a tube and condensed by cooling, it will become separated from the original liquid—which may be wine or the fermented product (mash) of grain, from which whisky and many vodkas are made; or of molasses, the basis of rum; or potatoes, for some vodka; or of apples, for applejack. These various liquids will evaporate at different temperatures, depending on the percentage of alcohol each contains—the smaller the amount of alcohol in the mixture, the greater proportionately will be the quantity of alcohol in the distillate.

APPARATUS

The apparatus in which the liquid is distilled is called a still, and the simplest form, known as a "pot still," consists of a pot where the mixture can be heated, a head, or alembic, through which the vapors pass, and a condenser in which the vapor is cooled and transformed into liquid again. The pot is heated either by direct firing or by steam, the heat being introduced by means of a heating jacket or a coil. To obtain a purer distillate, the mixture may undergo this process a second or third time, until spirit of the desired purity and strength is obtained (this is the disadvantage of the pot still; its advantage is that a finer flavor is preserved). In the first distillation, the wine or mash is brought to the boil and yields a spirit of some 25 per cent alcohol by volume or about 45° British proof or 50° U.S. proof. When it is distilled again, the first and last of the steam—the head and tail—are discarded and only the middle distillate, called the heart, is kept. This finishes at between 60 and 70 per cent alcohol by volume, 105° U.S. to 122° British proof.

The ancient pot still is used today in the distillation of Cognac and native Scotch and Irish malt whiskies; but most spirits are now made by a continuous process in patent stills derived from the one invented by Coffey about 1830. Basically, this consists of two columns, long and rectilinear, known as the rectifier and the analyzer. Each of these contains several compartments divided horizontally by perforated copper plates and communicating with each other by means of a drop-pipe—while the columns themselves are connected by two pipes, one of which carries vapor from the top of the analyzer to the bottom of the rectifier while the other, in reverse, takes the wash from the bottom of the rectifier to the top of the analyzer. Steam enters the still at the bottom of the analyzer (the left-hand column), and the cold wash comes in near the top of the rectifier (on the right), passes through a zigzag tube to the bottom of the column and up the connecting pipe to the top of the analyzer. As it enters this left-hand column, the now-heated wash meets the ascending vapors; and while it drips down step by step, onto the successive plates, the steam heats it and carries off its content of alcohol, so that in the final stage the spent wash falls as waste to the bottom of the analyzer and is drawn off—while the alcohol is carried up with the steam, which passes out of the column and is conducted by the vapor pipe to the bottom of the rectifier. Here again, the alcoholic vapor rises to the top, warming, as it goes, the zigzag pipe, which is introducing the new wash and, in consequence, growing cooler as the wash rises. Near the upper part of the rectifier, the vapors reach the "spirit plate," where they condense. This plate is fitted with a pipe which leads the alcohol to a cooler. Finally, it is collected in a spirits receiver. By means of strategically placed condensing coils, the alcohol is separated from certain aldehydes and volatile substances, particularly fusel oil.

Where a pot still can distill only one lot of wash at a time, the continuous still, which does not need to be emptied and recharged, is more economical and also enables the operator to exercise greater control over the product.

RAW MATERIALS

Wine is the foremost of the alcoholic liquids used to produce spirits, in the sense that it is itself already an alcoholic liquid; but sugary substances are also fermented into alcohol and then distilled, or the starch of cereals is converted into fermentable sugar, which in turn is fermented to obtain alcohol. (For a fuller description of the processes by which ingredients for different spirits are fermented and distilled *see* Gin; Rum; Cognac; Whisky, Scotch; etc.)

BY-PRODUCTS

The principal component of all spirits is ethyl alcohol, diluted with water and various secondary and tertiary ingredients to give the spirit its essential characteristics. The raw material incorporates a quantity of substances which are carried throughout the fermentation and the distillation and enter into the ageing process. The various processes influence the conditions and the proportion of the secondary ingredients that will be present in the final alcoholic spirit. Such brandies as Cognac and Armagnac contain after fermentation substances coming from wine—mineral salts, fixed acids, tannin, and organic substances—which are not desirable in the distillation procedures. The distiller of brandies is concerned with the volatiles—alcohols (butyl, amyl, propyl, caproic, etc.), aldehydes, esters (for the bouquet of the finished product), and acids. These volatiles pass from fermentation into the distillation and distribute their value. Aldehydes, extremely volatile, pass into the distillate, and a proportion of them may combine with alcohol to form certain acetals. Acetification and esterification action, which develop in the later stages, contribute to the flavor and aroma of the brandy; but the complexity of the aldehydes, if not properly managed, may impart a certain bitterness to the brandy—and so an excess of aldehydes is undesirable.

The secondary substances of spirits can be classified as follows:

(1) *Higher alcohols*—fatty alcohols higher in acid than ethanol. The makeup of the higher alcohols depends on the raw material of the spirit. Post-still whiskies produce a higher alcohol mixtue composed of isoamyl and isobutyl ingredients as well as propyl alcohol. Patent-still whiskies, of higher proof and rectified, while containing a smaller amount of total higher alcohols than pot-still whisky, have a greater proportion of propyl and isobutyl and a low proportion of isoamyl ingredients. Neutral grain spirit for gin contains no appreciable amount of higher alcohols. Potato spirits produce isobutyl.

(2) *Esters*. These are formed during the fermentation period and are a result of the intermixture of alcohol and acids. Some of the esters arise from the fatty acids combining with a small amount of ethyl or amyl alcohols; e.g., ethyl acetate (the principal ester, known as ascetic ester), ethyl valerate, butyrate, etc.

(3) *Acids*. Acetic acid forms the greater percentage, although acidity will vary according to the spirit. Butyric, tartaric, and succinic acids are among the best known.

(4) Aldehydes result from the oxidation of the ethyl alcohol. Furfural or pyromucic aldehyde is formed at the beginning of distillation and diminishes as the spirit develops in the casks.

(5) Other substances such as essential oils, terpenes, and minor volatile ingredients are called tertiary constituents and add to the character of the spirits.

AGEING

The time the spirit spends in the wood (the maturation stage) depends on its character. Brandy is all the better for ten or twenty years' ageing; gin, a highly refined spirit, need not be very much aged and would not benefit from maturation of more than one year. Generally, all the secondary ingredients—total acids, aldehydes, esters, etc.—tend to increase with age. Furfural increases in whiskies, but in some spirits it diminishes with ageing. The type of cask and the condition of storage are of major importance in this process. Limousin oak is the special wood used to heighten the quality of Cognac during the long time of maturation; charred white oak imparts flavoring and tanning substances to whiskies—especially American whiskies. Water usually evaporates through the wood as time goes on, and the percentage of alcohol increases in proportion to the loss of liquid: after one year in barrel, an American whiskey will have an average proof of 116.5; after six years this will increase to 122.7, and at eight years, the whiskey will be 124.9 proof. The evaporation of liquid through the barrels will be greater in a dry cellar than a damp one; and the temperature of a cellar in which spirits are stored is generally constant.

See separate entries for Brandy, Cognac, Gin, Rum, Vodka, *and* Whiskey (Whisky).

Alphabetical Entries

A

Abboccato

Term for semi-dry or semi-sweet wine in Italy.

Abocado

Spanish term for wine which is of delicate bouquet and medium sweet.

Abricotine

French apricot liqueur made by steeping apricots in brandy. It is tawny in color and tastes of apricots, with a slight hint of almonds from the apricot stones.

Abruzzi (Abruzzo)

Red and white wines.
District: East-central Italy. On the Adriatic

A mountainous agricultural region which makes a few agreeable wines. Montepulciano and Cerasuolo d'Abruzzo are light and robust red wines. The Montepulciano, produced in huge quantities (2 million cases), is named for the grape variety but is sometimes vinified with a little Sangiovese; the wine is ruby-red, robust, with occasionally a sweetish aftertaste. It is grown around Canosa, Sannita, Casoli, and several other villages, and bears the D.O.C. (Denominazione di Origine Controllata). Cerasuolo, also a D.O.C., is a clear cherry-pink, and like the Montepulciano comprises 12° alcohol. The straw-colored Trebbiano d'Abruzzo is dry and neutral; its name, too, comes from the grape variety, either Trebbiano d'Abruzzo or Trebbiano Toscano. The wine can come from anywhere in the region and still bear the D.O.C.
See Italy.

Absinthe

A light-green extremely potent liquor of spirits infused with herbs, chiefly anise and wormwood (*Artemisia absinthium*). Because of its potency and the harmful effect it is considered to have on the nerves, its sale has been banned in most Western countries. This is not so in Spain, where the dangers of absinthe are hotly denounced over full glasses of the cloudy liquid.

Absinthe was invented in Couvet, Switzerland, by Dr. Ordinaire, a Frenchman who sold the recipe to a M. Pernod in 1797. It enjoyed great popularity throughout Europe until it was banned, and many substitutes, similar in taste but without the dubious wormwood, have taken its place. Of these, anis and pastis (*qq.v.*) are the favorites, particularly in the south of France, and two of the best-known proprietary brands are Pernod and Ricard. The firm of Pernod used to manufacture absinthe in its Spanish distillery.

Acariose

A species of mite which feeds on the fruit and foliage of vines.
see Chapter Eight, p. 39.

Acariosis

A vine disorder resulting in stunted young shoots, its causes vary from country to country. Growth may be slowed or stopped either by the grape rust mite (*Calepitrimerus vitis, Phyllocoptes vitis*) or by the grape bud mite (a form of *Eriophyes vitis*).

Acescence

The formation in wine of an excessive quantity of acetic acid, often caused by prolonged exposure to air and apparent in the formation of a translucent gray film caused by the *Acetobacter* microbe. The result is a wine which is vinegary, or *piqué* (pricked).
See Chapter Nine, p. 53.

Acetic acid

An acid (CH_3COOH) always present in wine in very small quantities and the principal acid of vinegar. This is one of the volatile acids; if it is allowed to form freely, it will "acetify" the wine, turning it vinegary, or *piqué* (pricked).
see Chapter Nine, p. 51.

Acetification

See Acescence.

Achaea

A province of Greece on the Peloponnesus along the southern shore of the Gulf of Corinth. Especially around the town of Patras, the area produces a rather large quantity of red and white wine.
see Greece.

Acid

The generic term applies to substances that may exchange one or more hydrogen atoms for a metal or its basic radical. Acids, which give freshness and tang, are essential constituents of wine. An acid is known as monoacid, bi-acid, or tri-acid, according to whether it contains one, two, or three exchangeable hydrogen atoms.

Hydracids are combinations of hydrogen and certain metalloids. The term *hydro* or *hydric* appears in their names (e.g., hydrochloric acid, sulfhydric acid). Oxyacids derive from the action of an anhydride on water; generally speaking, their names end in -ic (e.g., nitric, sulfuric), but certain simple substances form different oxyacids according to valencies. They can be distinguished in order of decreasing valency as follows:

per——ic	persulfuric acid	$H_2S_2O_8$
——ic	sulfuric acid	H_2SO_4
——ous	sulfurous acid	H_2SO_3
hypo——ous	hyposulfurous acid	$H_2S_2O_4$

(Yves Renouil and Paul de Traversay: *Dictionnaire du vin.*)

Acidity

Acids, which give freshness, tang, and protection from most bacterial spoilage, are essential constituents of wine. Without acidity, it would be insipid; with too much, sharp or vinegary. But when the proper balance is reached, the wine is flavorsome and fresh. Some acids are natural in grapes, some the result of fermentation; but the type and quantity in any wine will depend upon the grape variety, the soil of the vineyards, the climate during the growing season, the yeasts and other microorganisms, and the additions made to the wine during vinification.

Among the acids desirable in wine are tartaric and malic. The most undesirable is acetic. Citric acid is one of several found in very small quantities; and in sparkling wines some carbonic acid is present.

The expert recognizes three types of acidity: volatile, fixed, and total. Acetic is the predominant volatile acid, although the insignificant amounts of butyric, formic, and propionic acids which may be present are also in this category. Volatile acids in small quantities are indispensable to the stability and bouquet of wine, yet can be most unpleasant if they are present in excess, giving the wine a vinegary character. Of the fixed, or stable acids, the most important are tartaric, malic, and citric. Together, the two types make up total acidity.

See Chapter Nine, p. 50.

Aconcagua Valley

Red wines.
District: Central Chile.

One of the best vine regions of Chile, specializing in Cabernet and Malbec wines and producing wines which are strong in finesse, well balanced, and long-lasting.

See Chile.

Acquavite

Italian spelling of *aqua vitae,* or brandy (*qq.v.*).

Acquit

More exactly, *acquit-à-caution;* an official French document that accompanies all shipments of wines and spirits on which internal taxes have not been paid. (For tax-paid shipments, the *congé* is used.) The *acquit* is employed for exports—exempt from taxation—and for shipments made in bond. The color of the paper changes with the type of wine or spirit to facilitate identification. *Papier bulle,* whitish-brown paper, is used for ordinary wines; green signifies table wines of controlled place of origin; yellow-gold is for Cognac and Armagnac; orange for sweet fortified wines of controlled place of origin; etc. If importing countries were to demand that these papers, which usually stop at the French border, accompany each shipment and be subject to strict controls, the amount of fraudulent wine now going out of France would be considerably curtailed.

A copy of the *acquit* must accompany the wines into the United States.

Adega

The Portuguese name for a *bodega* (*q.v.*).

Adom Atic

Leading red wine of Israel.
See Israel.

Advocaat

A beverage resembling eggnog, usually made of brandy and egg yolks, and bottled. In the Netherlands it has a rather low alcoholic content of 15% to 18% and is so thick that it is often taken with a spoon.

Agave

This, known also as the century plant, is the source of tequila, pulque, and mescal.
See Tequila.

Aglianico del Vulture (D.O.C.)

A deep-red sturdy warm wine from Aglianico grapes in the vineyards of Monte Vulture in southern Italy.
See Basilicata.

Agrafe (agraffe)

A clamp used to hold the cork prior to *dégorgement* and final corking of Champagne.

Aguardiente

The name for spirits in Spanish-speaking countries. Specifically, a spirit distilled from grapes in grape-growing countries and from molasses or sugarcane in cane-growing countries.

Ahr

German State of Rheinland-Pfalz
Vineyard area: approx. 426 hectares (1,000 acres)
70% red wines; 30% white wines

Location: The Ahr is the northernmost and one of the smallest of Germany's eleven wine-growing regions. It takes its name from a river, the Ahr, which flows into the Rhine just south of Bonn. Bad Neuenahr is the main town and a popular spa. All of the region's vineyards are within one district, Bereich Walporzheim-Ahrtal, which consists of one collective vineyard site (*Grosslage*), Klosterberg.
Grape Varieties: Spätburgunder (Pinot Noir) (37%); Portugieser, a red variety (26%); Riesling (15%); Müller-Thurgau (12%).
Wine: Spicy, velvety Spätburgunder; light, mild, fruity Portugieser which are slow in character; steely, lively white wines.
The vineyards are extremely labor-intensive, planted mostly on steep, terraced cliffs of slate and volcanic soils. Thanks to the soil, which heats up quickly and retains heat, and the beneficial micro-climate created by the river, vines survive here. The Ahr Valley is sheltered by the Eifel mountain range.
The majority of the Ahr's 740 growers are part-time vintners with an average holding of .64 hectare (1.6 acres). About 90% deliver their grapes or must to the trade or one of the region's five cooperatives. The first German cooperative winery was founded here, in Mayschoss, in 1868. Nearly all of the region's wine is consumed locally or taken home by tourists.
Historically, viticulture on the Ahr dates back to Roman times, and here, as elsewhere, the Church fostered the planting of vines during the Middle Ages. Today, Kloster Marienthal, an Augustinian convent from the 12th to 19th centuries and now owned by the state, is one of the region's most prestigious estates (Staatliche Weinbaudomäne Marienthal, with the stylized black eagle on the label). Although red vines were not planted here until 1680, the wine became so popular that for the next two and a half centuries, Ahr wines were almost exclusively red.
See Appendix B, p. 672.

Aiguebelle

French liqueur produced near Valence. It is said to be made according to an ancient formula discovered in a Trappist monastery, and its taste derives from a blend of some fifty herbs. There are two varieties—green and yellow—of which the green is the stronger.

Aiven

Tartar spirit made from fermented milk.

Aix-en-Provence

Red, white, and rosé wines.
District: South of France.

In and around Aix, the ancient capital of Provence, in vineyards that stretch from the rocky inland slopes down to the Riviera itself, some pleasant wines are made. They are usually heady and sturdy and are perfect to drink in their own district, slightly chilled, in the summer. Red, white, and rosé are made, but the rosés are generally the best.
See Provence; Coteaux d'Aix, Coteaux des Baux.

Akevit

See Aquavit.

Akvavit

Danish spelling for aquavit *(q.v.)*.

Alambrado

The Spanish term for a bottle of wine enclosed in a light open wire netting called an *alambre*. Wines of better than average quality are often packaged this way.

Alasch

A variant spelling of allasch *(q.v.)*.

Alavesa

One of the best types of Spanish Rioja wine, it is frequently identified on the label. It is somewhat like a Rhône wine.
See Rioja.

Alba Flora

A white wine of Majorca, Spain.

Albana di Romagna

The principal white wine of the Emilia-Romagna region of Italy. This D.O.C. may be dry or sweet and sparkling, and in the good years it has a noticeably velvety quality.
See Italy.

Albariza

The typical chalky-white soil of the region around Jerez in the Spanish Sherry country, producing the best Finos and Manzanillas.

Alcamo (D.O.C.)

Red or white wine from Sicily *(q.v.)*.

Alcohol

One of the principal components in wine. During fermentation the enzymes created by yeast cells convert the sugar in the grape juice into alcohol as well as into carbon dioxide gas. In fermented grape juice, alcohols combine with acids to produce esters. In general, alcohol (as defined by Yves Renouil and Paul de Traversay) is "the derivative resulting from the substitution of a hydroxyl radical for an atom of hydrogen in a hydrocarbon." Pure alcohol is colorless and will ignite at temperatures ranging between 10.4°F. (−12°C.) (absolute alcohol) and 51.8°F. (11°C.) (95% alcohol). It is antiseptic—admirably so in wine. A rectified alcohol is one that has been distilled.

See Chapters 9 *and* 10 *and* Rectification.

Alcoholic content (by volume)

The proportion of alcohol contained in a wine, or the alcohometric strength of that wine, is always expressed in France in terms of its volumetric alcohol content at 59°F. (15°C.), determined in accordance with the Gay-Lussac principle: pure alcohol has a strength equal to 100 degrees, and the alcohol content is equal to the number of liters of ethyl alcohol contained in 100 liters of wine, both these volumes being measured at a temperature of 59°F. (15°C.). One degree of alcohol then corresponds to 1 c.c. of pure alcohol contained in 100 c.c. of wine. The amount of alcohol can be expressed in grams per liter at 68°F. (20°C.). (Renouil and de Traversay: *Dictionnaire du vin*.)

The British evaluation is based on the "proof gallon" and on "proof spirit."

The proof gallon is a unit of volume and alcoholic content corresponding to 4.5459631 liters of standard proof spirit.

Proof spirit is a standard alcohol which at a temperature of 51°F. (11°C.), weighs exactly twelve-thirteenths of an equal quantity by volume of distilled water. It is in fact a mixture of water and alcohol containing 49.-28% by weight and 57.1% by volume of alcohol at 60°F. (15.6°C.).

For the calculation of alcoholic content, the graduation by Sikes degrees is used. Since "proof" corresponds to 57.1 degrees by Gay-Lussac, a higher alcoholic content is expressed in degrees Sikes O.P. (over proof) and 100 degrees Gay-Lussac is represented by 75.09 degrees Sikes O.P. Conversely, a lower alcoholic content is expressed in degrees Sikes U.P. (under proof) and in this case 100 degrees Sikes U.P. corresponds to 0 degrees Gay-Lussac. In the United States, alcoholic content of wine is expressed as per cent by volume at 60 degrees F.

See Appendix D, p. 707.

Aldehyde

A volatile fluid obtained by the oxidation of alcohol; a large class of compounds intermediate between alcohol and acids. These play an important part in wines, particularly in bouquet.

See Chapter Nine, p. 52.

Ale

An alcoholic barley malt beverage.
See Beer.

Aleatico

A grape of the Muscat family which produces a sweet aromatic wine. Used in various parts of Italy for red wine.

Aleatico di Portoferraio

Sweet red dessert wine from Elba (15–16% alcohol).
See Tuscany.

Aleatico di Puglia

Deep-colored, red D.O.C. Italian dessert wine, sweet and strong.
See Apulia.

Alella

Principally dry white wine produced north of Barcelona in the Catalonian village of that name. Some red is made.
See Spain.

Aleyor

A red wine of Majorca, Spain.
See Spain.

Algeria

Once among the leading wine-producers of the world, Algeria has cut production and begun a general reorganization of her wine and grape industries. While still a French *département* in 1961, Algeria made almost 16 million hectoliters of wine (413 million U.S. gallons, 344 million imp.) from nearly 360,000 hectares (900,000 acres) of vines. Algeria's rank among the wine-making nations is now nineteenth, after many years of being sixth in total volume. Most of the wine is red.

The indigenous population of the country consumed little of all this wine, since, although 35 to 40% of the working population was employed in wine-making, most Algerians are Moslems for whom the drinking of wines or any sort of alcoholic beverage is forbidden.

A great deal of it went abroad anonymously to be blended with the wines of France (particularly those of the Midi); and of the rest, millions of gallons went to

France and other places abroad under its own labels as useful ordinary wine for washing down everyday meals. But with the declaration of Algerian independence in the summer of 1962, quality began to fall off: the Moslem workers missed the guidance of their French supervisors. There was also a large drop in exports to France; the growers of the Midi and other bulk-producing areas protested Algerian independence by putting pressure on the French government to reduce the quantity.

As the quantity of wine sent to France and the other Common Market countries trickled to virtually nothing, as a result of the Evian agreements, the Algerian government redirected the wine industry. The 1.3 million hectoliters of Algerian wine (87 million U.S. gallons, 72 million imp.) which previously went each year to France now goes partially to the Soviet Union, Scandinavia, and Eastern Europe. With this change of trading partners have come steps to tear out old vine stocks and replace some of them with young table grape plants. The program aims to shift Algerian agriculture toward cereals, to improve the land under cultivation, and simply to plant healthy vines in the place of less fruitful ones. The area in wine grapes is being reduced to 85,000 hectares (212,500 acres) and production stabilized near the present level of 2 million hectoliters per year.

In the past, there was a tendency for Algerian wines to be produced in huge quantities for use as *vins médecins* for the Midi, Burgundy, and other areas needing high-alcoholic wines. Today, despite the Koranic taboo on alcoholic beverages, the Algerian government is moving away from *vins ordinaires* and has set up seven *vins d'appellation d'origine garantie* (V.A.O.G.), many of them achieving quality which was unknown prior to the setting up of these districts in 1970 as a result of independence. Overall, the production, which is 60% red, 30% rosé and 10% white, is divided into: ordinary bulk red and rosé wine of a higher alcoholic content, much of which is exported in tank ships; *vins fins* red and rosé, of which there are ten commercial brands; and the V.A.O.G. (see the listing of these on p. 64). Algeria does not export any white wine, as most of it possesses a color which gives the impression that it has oxidized, and until the government can correct this flaw, one will not see white Algerian wine outside of the country.

Throughout the vast domains modern machinery is found, and the grapes are brought to the enormous wine sheds where they are processed on a production-line basis in huge cement vats, where they ferment. So that the vats will be ready for the next batch of grapes coming in from the vineyards, selected yeasts are added to the grape must to ensure a quick and sound fermentation. When the fermentation is over, the wines are stored in other enormous vats and are later sold by the barrel, truckload, or tank car, the price depending on alcoholic content. Until recently, the vines planted have been the lesser varieties—Carignan, Cinsault (or Cinsaut), Grenache, Alicante-Bous-chet, Aramon, Morrastel, and Mourvèdre for red wines; Clairette, Listan, Ugni Blanc, Faranah, Maccabéo, and Merseguéra for whites.

Algerian red wines, which make up 60% of the country's total production, are generally heavy, dark in color, and run in alcohol from 11% up. It is not unusual to find some which are naturally of 15% with very low acidity—an alcoholic content that would be extremely rare in cooler countries, where the summer sun is not sufficiently hot to generate so much sugar in the grapes. Since the wines of the French Midi may be light in acid and low in alcohol (sometimes no more than 9%), these Algerian wines were often used to "correct" them, adding color, body, and alcoholic content. The wines of Mascara were notorious as the base for many a shipper's "Burgundy."

WINE HISTORY

Grape-growing in Algeria started in ancient times, and the wines—or some of them—were known to have been transported to Rome for the delight of the rulers of the Mediterranean world. The arrival of the Moslem faith did not spell the end of all the vineyards, despite the interdiction of alcohol in any form, for table grapes and raisins have always been appreciated there. It is probable, as has been suggested, that the Muscat types exist solely because of the Moslem prohibition of alcohol and the resulting search for table grapes of quality, which could not keep many of the vineyards alive.

In about 1830 the French colonized Algeria, eventually making it a part of metropolitan France rather than a colony (until its independence in 1962), and under French rule viticulture revived. The first vineyards appeared in 1865. Later in the century, as the phylloxera, the devastating plant louse, took its toll of the French vineyards, various growers gave up their ruined fields and moved to Algeria; and in many cases the vines they planted were those they were accustomed to use at home. Colonists from Lyons imported the Gamay and Pinot vines; Burgundians leaned toward the same plants; Bordelais colonists put in Cabernets; former inhabitants of the Midi planted Aramon; and refugees from Alsace and Lorraine (some of them fleeing German occupation of their homeland as well as the phylloxera) nurtured Chasselas and Pinot Gris. Throughout, also, were found Mourvèdre, Morrastel, and Grenache. When the phylloxera finally hit Algeria too, many of these vines were abandoned and the vineyards were replanted mostly in Carignan, with some Cinsault and Alicante-Bouschet, all of them grafted onto American roots. In the case of white wines, the vines used are mostly Clairette, Merseguéra, Maccabéo, and Ugni Blanc.

Today the know-how comes from workers employed by French growers prior to independence, from students who studied oenology in France, in

Bordeaux as well as Burgundy, and from a few agricultural engineers who have been trained in Algerian viticultural technical schools.

VINE-GROWING REGIONS

The vineyards of Algeria are spread throughout the regions of Oran and Alger and yield the great bulk of the nation's wines. But the departments of Oran and Alger have between them some 60,000 hectares (150,000 acres) of vines planted along the slopes which produce wines that had been granted A.O.G. (Appellation d'Origine Garantie) status by the Algerian authorities. The better Algerian wines are often of very pleasant quality, softer and more alcoholic than those of the Midi, and with more fatness. These wines are made from the Cinsault, Carignan, Grenache, and Morrastel vines; some other varieties are allowed in certain cases. The whites come from Clairette and Muscat grapes. On the slopes, some vines of the Cabernet, Grenache, Mourvèdre, Pinot, and Syrah varieties are also cultivated.

The following wines are those which were established by the Algerian authorities in 1970.

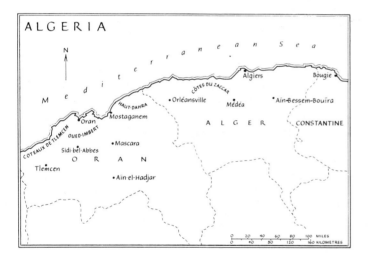

District of Alger

Aïn-Bessem-Bouïra: red and rosé wines. A small area. The vineyards are planted at an elevation of 500 to 700 meters. South of the city of Algiers.

Médéa: red, rosé and white wines. To the west of Aïn-Bessem, south of the city of Algiers. This area, planted at an altitude of 1,300 meters with its cool winters and dry, hot summers, produces good, sturdy reds with some Cabernet and Pinot Noir plantings.

Coteaux du Zaccar: red and white wines. Around the town of Miliala, the hillsides of Zaccar produce some noteworthy reds from the Pinot Noir and the Syrah.

District of Oran

Dahra: red and rosé wines. The Dahra region, east of the town of Oran, includes the following areas: Taoughrite, ex-Paul Robert; Ain Merane, ex-Rabelais; Mazouna, ex-Renault; Khadra Achaacha, ex-Picard. They produce strong, highly alcoholic wines including some formerly known as Mostaganem.

Coteaux de Mascara: red and rosé wines. Perhaps the best of the Algerian wines, from the slopes around Mascara, on the plateau of Ghriss. This is an area which produces vividly colored wines, formerly known as *vin teinturier,* capable of producing some surprising wines, from Cabernet Sauvignon, Syrah, and other grape varieties found in Algeria.

Monts du Tessalah: red and rosé. Deeply colored reds are produced from these hillsides, especially around Sidi-bel-Abbès, which, prior to Algerian independence, was the headquarters of the French Foreign Legion.

Coteaux de Tlemcen: red, rosé, and white. Southwest of Oran. Again, very full-bodied mountain wines are produced here.

Alicante

Red Spanish wine, known in Shakespeare's time as Tent.
See Spain.

Alicante-Bouschet

Extremely productive red-wine grape developed in the nineteenth century by the French hybridizers L. and M. Bouschet. It is grown throughout the French Midi, Algeria, and California, but everywhere gives the same inferior characterless wine with low acidity and intense but quickly fading color.

Aligoté

Burgundian white grape which gives pleasant but unexceptional wines; these are at their best when young, as they tend to oxidize within three years.

Alkermes

A red cordial once made from the kermes insect of the Cochineal genus, long supposed (because invariably found on the tree) to be the berry of the Mediterranean kermes oak.

Allasch (alasch)

A type of kümmel favored in England, Poland, and Russia. The liqueur draws its name from Allasch near Riga (U.S.S.R.), a place famous for its caraway seeds, which are the essential flavoring agents of kümmel.

Aloxe-Corton (Appellation Contrôlée)

Burgundy red and white wines.
District: Côte de Beaune, France.

The commune is at the northern end of the Côte de Beaune, but its finest white wines rank with those from the unofficial "Côte de Meursault"—the great white wine-giving southern end of this famous slope—and its reds are the finest of the Côte de Beaune, among the finest of all Burgundy. But in order to get what you want, you must know what to ask for.

Some of the wines are sold as Aloxe-Corton. These are communal wines—pleasant and enjoyable, sometimes distinguished, seldom great. Others have, as well, the full communal name, such as Aloxe-Corton Les Maréchaudes, signifying that they come from one selected excellent vineyard and that the wine has attained higher than minimum standards. The best wines do *not* bear the name Aloxe; they are either Corton alone or Corton followed by some other, more specific designation. The three greatest names are:

Corton: more red wines than white, sometimes further defined to determine the exact portion of the vineyard from which they come (e.g., Corton-Bressandes, Corton-Renardes, etc.).

Corton-Charlemagne: the superb full-bodied white wine of Aloxe.

Charlemagne: applicable to certain outstanding white wines but rarely used, since these wines have equal right to the preferred Corton-Charlemagne.

See each under separate heading.

The vines grow on a prominent hill known as La Montagne, which stands back from the main road, its gentle slopes crowned with the Bois de Corton, a quiet peaceful woodland. The vineyard strip fronting these woods is Corton, but farther down are the even more outstanding sections of the same vineyard: Bressandes, Renardes, and the Clos du Roi. On a level with Corton is Charlemagne, and both Charlemagne and the upper portion of Corton are planted in Chardonnay. Local growers say that the upper sections are best for white wines, the middle and lower parts for red. The soil itself is the clue. At the top it is light and dry, with a whitish tinge from the chalky subsoil; farther down, it becomes ferruginous and reddish.

Aloxe is one of the oldest of the wine-growing communes along the ancient Slope of Beaune. Charlemagne, Henry II, and Charles the Bold (the Burgundian duke who lost both his life and his lands to Louis XI) were growers, and Voltaire was one of the most celebrated admirers of the wines. In the famous letter to Monsieur Le Bault—who built the commune's Château Corton-Grancey—he said: "Your wine has become a necessity for me. I give a very good Beaujolais to my friends from Geneva but in secret I drink your Corton." Le Bault's reaction was a note scribbled in the margin: "This man is a *villain*," implying Voltaire was at the very least a miser and a scoundrel. The château has been renovated a number of times since its construction in 1749, and today—thoroughly modernized—it is in the hands of the good shipping firm of Louis Latour.

Whether red wine or white comes first in Aloxe is a matter of choice, and most wine-lovers are willing to settle for both. The reds are powerful, full, and big, tending toward harshness when young but maturing beautifully and taking on a great balance. They have a magnificent aroma, with sometimes a hint of violets. Corton, of all Côte de Beaune wines, is the one to lay down, for it develops slowly and holds its majesty for years. The best Corton whites are sometimes in the same class as Montrachet—the wine from the south of the Côte de Beaune which many experts consider the greatest dry white wine in the world. These wines have a firmness that borders on a touch of steel and an almost overwhelming perfume of the grape, especially when young. Some connoisseurs maintain that they can also detect a scent of cinnamon in the bouquet; and the wines have exceptional breed and a lingering aftertaste with an enormous range of sensations.

The area on which the vines are grown is not large. The total for Aloxe-Corton is about 240 hectares (600 acres), and the best vineyards cover considerably less ground (some of these, entitled to the Appellation Contrôlée of Aloxe-Corton, are partly in the neighboring Pernand-Vergelesses and Ladoix-Serrigny villages). Production in an average year for quantity may amount to 5,250 hectoliters (139,125 U.S. gallons, 115,500 imp.) of red wine, and less than 25 hectoliters (662 U.S. gallons, 550 imp.) of white. These statistics do not include the production of the vineyards Corton and Corton-Charlemagne (*qq.v.*). Those vineyards which may produce wines that will carry both commune and vineyard name—the First Growths (*Premiers Crus*)—have only tentatively been established and the list is provisional—the acreage has not, at the time of writing, been fixed.

The minimum degree of alcohol allowed for these wines is: red, 11½ percent; white, 12 percent. Maximum production must not exceed 30 hectoliters per hectare (320.7 U.S. gallons, 267 imp. per acre). The *appellation* Charlemagne is seldom used, since most of the land is entitled also to the name Corton or Corton-Charlemagne.

Climats SOLD AS CORTON

In Aloxe-Corton: (red and white wine)

Le Corton	Voirosses
Clos du Roi	Les Fietres
Les Bressandes	Les Perrières
Les Renardes	La Vigne-au-Saint
Les Languettes (*in part*)	Les Grèves
Les Chaumes (*in part*)	Les Meix (*in part*)
Les Maréchaudes (*in part*)	Les Combes (*in part*)
En Pauland (*in part*)	Le Charlemagne (*in part*)
Les Meix-Lallemant (*in part*)	Les Pougets (*in part*)

In Ladoix-Serrigny: (red and white wine)

Les Vergennes	Le Rouget-Corton (*in part*)
Le Bois de Vergennes	Ladoix-Serrigny (red only)
Les Carrières	

In Pernand-Vergelesses: (white wine)

Le Charlemagne (*in part*)

FIRST GROWTHS (*Premiers Crus*)

La Maréchaude	Les Fournières
La Coutière	Les Vercots
Les Petites-Lolières	Les Meix (*in part*)
La Toppe-au-Vert	Les Maréchaudes (*in part*)
Les Grandes-Lolières	En Pauland (*in part*)
Les Chaillots	Les Valozières (*in part*)
Les Guérets	

The following vineyards in Ladoix-Serrigny, bordering on Aloxe-Corton, are allowed the place-names of Corton and Corton-Charlemagne:

Les Vergennes-Corton
Le Rognet-Corton
Clos de Corton

Alsace

Rhine wines of France.
District: Northeast France.

Alsace makes the Rhine wines of France: dry and fresh, some spicy, some lively and light, with the faint prickle they call the *pointe de fraîcheur*. The vineyards are planted along the sheltered slopes of the Vosges; from high on the hills, one can look eastward over the wide river to Germany. The wine region, officially divided into Haut-Rhin and Bas-Rhin, is one of the most attractive in France. On the lower ground, orchards flourish as well as vines, providing some of the fruit for the superb white *eaux-de-vie:* kirsch, fraise, framboise, poire. Although pressing machines and the whole process of winemaking are extremely up to date, there is an unhurried rural atmosphere in the countryside where tractors rumble along to the *vendange,* and some of the villages, with their half-timbered houses, storks' nests, and flowery balconies, look like pictures from German fairy tales.

The vines stretch between the Rhine and the mountains for more than 75 miles (120 kilometers), from Thann in the south (Haut-Rhine) to Marlenheim in the north (Bas-Rhin), covering more than 12,000 hectares (30,000 acres) divided into many properties, often quite small, and worked by some ten thousand growers and their families. The wines are named from the grapes: only in Alsace is the Appellation d'Origine given for the vine type instead of the place of origin. The wines which may be described as Vins d'Alsace come from the following grapes, which are classified as: *Standard Variety*—Chasselas; *Fine Variety*—Sylvaner and Pinot Blanc (or Clevner); *Noble Variety*—Riesling, Gewürztraminer,

Muscat, and Tokay d'Alsace (or Pinot Gris). Vineyard names are not generally important here, although there are exceptions—such as Rangen at Thann, Sonnenglanz at Beblenheim, Les Sorcières at Riquewihr, and others attached to the towns listed below, under "The Famous Wine Towns," p. 68.

WINE HISTORY

From Roman times Alsace has made wine. Already in the eighth century the lower slopes of the Vosges were green with vines. In the Middle Ages, the Rhine as its waterway, Alsatian wine flowed downriver to Cologne, to be shipped to Scandinavia and England. Alsace was then called Aussay—spelled in various ways—and the wines of "Osoy" are mentioned by Shakespeare. But the Thirty Years' War caused terrible destruction in Alsace and much of the vineland was laid waste. It was the first of many crushing blows to the wine industry of the contested Rhineland. At that time (1635–48) France participated with Sweden in the final stages of the war—their common enemy being the troops of the Holy Roman Emperor and of southern Germany. Under the Treaty of Westphalia (1648) France received sovereignty over the landgraviate of Upper and Lower Alsace, and the government of ten imperial cities in Alsace.

In the eighteenth century, Alsatian wines were popular in Austria and Switzerland. Quality controls very much like the French wine laws of today, although in primitive form, had already been put into force, and shipments were rigorously inspected by the *magistrats de la vigne,* forerunners of I.N.A.O. (Institut National des Appellations d'Origine) inspectors and of our modern wine brokers, still known in Alsace as *gourmets.* Place of origin of the wine and conditions of production were carefully inscribed on the invoices. Vine control laws also prohibited the planting of a larger proportion of quantity-producing vines than of quality producers.

The French Revolution brought drastic changes, breaking up all the large holdings and establishing the pattern of small ownership still in effect today. Yet by 1870 the vineyards were flourishing again and the wines, known as Vins d'Alsace du Rhin Français, were good. But in that year war broke out between France and Germany and in 1871 Alsace became German. To protect their own Rhine wines the Germans forbade the Alsatians to call theirs Vins du Rhins; and so the name was cut down to Vins d'Alsace. The economics of German wine production also put Alsace into a position where every incentive was given to the producer of *vin courant.* This attempt to lower the quality of Alsatian wine remained in force until 1918, when France liberated Alsace.

With the return to France in 1918, there was a disheartening collapse of the market. It looked as if liberation carried a fatal sting for the Alsatian wine-growers. In Germany, where the wines produced along the Rhine and Moselle are fine but not plentiful, there had been an enormous demand for cheap table wines. But in France, the largest producer in the world of every kind and quality of wine, this need did not exist. Cheap Alsatian wines, produced on a mass scale, had nowhere to go.

The decision taken was courageous—and it proved to be right. In the 1920s, Alsace returned to making the best possible wines and is still doing so today. Success came from the fact that, many as her wines were, France had lacked native wines of the Rhine type. The light pleasant growths of Alsace, designed for drinking rather than sipping, filled a necessary need for the French.

Alsace experienced another tragedy in 1944–45, when the battle for the liberation of the province caused wide devastation. Yet travelers driving up now from Lorraine into the peaceful mountains would never guess how many of the towns were leveled and the vineyards destroyed; and Orbey, which lies waiting in the valley, is placid-looking and rich with good living—*foie gras* and trout, sausages and succulent ham, and piles of whipped cream. The people were quick to rebuild their towns, to reconstruct their cellars, and to replant their vines; and the wine business is brisker than ever.

The wines have gained a world market. Annually, some 300,000 hectoliters (7.95 million U.S. gallons, 6.6 million imp.) are exported, the leading customers being (in this order): Germany, Belgium and Luxembourg, the United Kingdom, Switzerland, the United States, Canada, the Netherlands, Italy, Scandinavia, Mexico, and Africa; Common Market countries buy three-quarters of the wine shipped.

In spite of the checkered history of the vineyards there has been continuity of a kind in the history of the *vignerons*: among the well-known firms today are those of families who have been making wine in the same Alsatian villages for four hundred years—although now such firms will probably market wines not only from their own grapes but from small growers in the area. An Alsatian vineyard provides wines of different character and quality—Zwicker, perhaps, and one or more of Riesling, Gewürztraminer, Pinot, or Muscat. So the large grower-shippers, who not only produce *grands vins* but also store and blend the various wines to obtain a consistent character, play an important part in the Alsatian trade. In recent years a second branch of this trade has grown up: that of the cooperatives. After the last war some small proprietors decided that by pooling their resources they could more easily rehabilitate their vineyards and regain their sales. Now merged into the Union Vinicole pour la Diffusion des Vins d'Alsace, these cooperatives control 15% of the market. Trading on equal terms with such old-established family firms as Hugel, Dopff & Irion, Lorentz, and Willm, whose preeminence they do not challenge, they are instrumental in stabilizing prices and in supplying the chain-store trade.

In the cellars of the great family firms one is shown enormous wooden vats, carved with escutcheons, with mermaids and dolphins. Huge vats are still in use, although some of the wine is stored in glass-lined concrete containers. To preserve its freshness the wine is disturbed as little as possible, racked only once—in the January after the harvest—filtered, and bottled when it is from seven to twelve months old. The average Alsace wine should be drinkable at once, although it will improve for a few years in bottle. But some late-gathered (*vendange tardive*) wines will mature to a greater age.

WINE LAWS AND LABELS

In all fine French wines except Alsatian, the place of origin is the thing to look for on the label. If the soil is worthy, it pays the grower to produce the best wines he can. The laws of Appellation Contrôlée, based on soil and location of vineyards, guarantee that the quality he achieves will be recognized.

Alsace used to be the only important still-wine zone in France which had no Appellation Contrôlée. If you asked the reason, you were told that control in this one French province was by grape variety and that the statute of November 2, 1945, served as a wine control.

(Statute of November 2, 1945, governing the wines of Alsace: *The designations* Grand Vin *and* Grand Cru, *indicating superior quality, may be used only for wines from noble grape varieties having at least 11% of alcohol. Such wines, if sold in bottle, may be sold only in the type of bottle designated* Alsatian Wine Bottle. . . .)

Alsatian wine-makers considered the regulation concerning the type of bottle unfair, since it obliged them to use this bottle but did not protect them from the competition of other growers in other regions copying the shape; so they began a fight in the French wine jurisdiction, which ended in the winning of the decree of May 21, 1955. By this decree, the typical tall, slender, tapering bottle was limited almost entirely to Alsatian wines.

November of 1945 was also when the Comité Régional d'Experts des Vins d'Alsace was set up as guardian of quality wines. Its twenty-seven members, appointed by the minister of agriculture, must include eighteen growers and/or shippers and nine technical or administrative advisers. This body decides the limitation of vineyard acreage for wines allowed the Appellation d'Origine Vins d'Alsace and the grape varieties from which they may be made. It is largely due to the work of this committee that the practice of late picking has been introduced for some grapes, resulting in fuller, more lasting wines; and that in 1962 the quality and purity of vine species used was recognized in the award of the A.O.C. (Appellation d'Origine Contrôlée) to the Vins d'Alsace. The A.O.C. laws are tighter than those passed in 1945. This form of control specifies that, in addition to other rules about maximum alcoholic content and minimum vineyard size, only wines from certain kinds of vines (already specified on page 66) may be called Alsatian Vins d'Origine. And in accordance with another law passed in 1972, all A.O.C. wines must be bottled in the region of production; that is, in the departments of Haut-Rhin or Bas-Rhin.

In 1963 the Comité Interprofessionel du Vin d'Alsace was founded as a semi-public body, in order to provide growers with technical and practical assistance, to act as liaison between growers and shippers, and to develop public relations with consumers. The committee is aided in its work by the oenological experiments of the Oberlin Wine Institute at Colmar, which has been in existence since 1893.

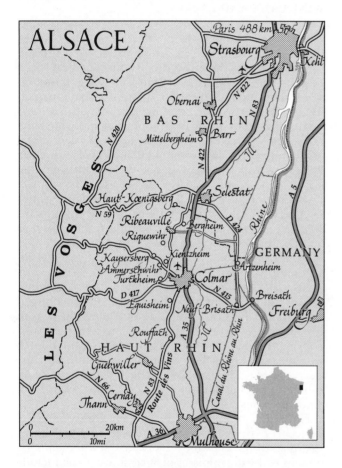

Another committee—or rather an ancient brotherhood invested with scarlet capes and black tricornes—exercises, through its voluntary ritual rules, a beneficial surveillance over the finest Alsatian wines. The Confrérie Saint-Étienne, founded in the fourteenth century at Ammerschwihr, was known originally as Herrenstubengesellschaft (Guild of Burgesses). The founder-members were local magistrates and their friends, who each year elected a grandmaster from among their number. It was he who arranged the tastings at which the new wines were judged, and the annual banquet on the Feast of

St. Stephen (though the patron saint of the Society is St. Diacre). Having lapsed during the dark days of Alsatian viticulture, the Confrérie was revived in 1947 as a grand council for the whole wine region of Alsace. Its *raison d'être* is the organization of tastings, at which the fine wines of the last harvest are judged and graded. A dozen each of the best of the *grands crus* are laid down as collectors' items, setting a standard of quality for member-growers. Those with the highest qualifications may be granted the seal of the Confrérie, which is attached to each bottle with a gold ribbon. Every year at the Colmar Wine Fair the society selects (by examination and blind tastings) new candidates for admission to its ranks. Established members also entertain important visitors from abroad, who come to enjoy the fair and sample the wines on display in the different booths.

THE FAMOUS WINE TOWNS

The band of vineyard is one continuous strip stretching north-south along the eastern fringe of the Vosges Mountains, where the range touches the Rhine plain. The most important areas are the section between Riquewihr and Ribeauvillé, and the clusters around the villages of Barr to the north and Guebwiller to the south.

Most visitors to Alsace drive along the splendid Route du vin. If they set out from Strasbourg they will see perhaps fifty of the more than one hundred communes allowed the *appellation* for the Vins d'Alsace. They might stop on the way at Colmar, a city which retains some of its old narrow streets, a few beautiful houses, and—in the museum which was once a convent—the extraordinary Isenheim Altarpiece painted by Matthias Grünewald in the early sixteenth century. It is at Colmar that the big Wine Fair is held every year. There is a special link between the town and the United States: Bartholdi, sculptor of Colmar's Lion de Belfort, created the Statue of Liberty. In the flatter agricultural land of this region lies the cabbage-growing center for sauerkraut, that most famous of Alsatian dishes, which goes much better with the local beer than with the wines.

Obernai

Sheltered by the Mont Sainte-Odile, this Bas-Rhin town, with its fountains and statues of the saint and its charming market square, prepares the traveler for the prettiness of the Route du Vin.

Barr

This, in the Bas-Rhin, is a thriving little place, with a fine town hall. Its wine is mostly Sylvaner, although some good Riesling is made. The town lies near the mouth of a valley descending from the highest peaks in that part of the Vosges.

Bergheim

Bergheim, just inside the Haut-Rhin, has a high reputation for its wines, especially the Gewürztraminers, and more especially those from the Kanzleberg site. It is a charming walled village, approached through an archway on which the date, 1300, is carved. In some of the old streets the splashing gutters are so wide they have to be bridged. The center of the town is a shady square with a handsome town hall on one side and a parish church—which has a tower called La Tour des Sorciers, because here alleged witches of the sixteenth century were tried and condemned.

Ribeauvillé

Ribeauvillé is slightly less important than Riquewihr, farther along the route. Three castles look down from the mountains on this village, which preserves its historic tradition as the town where the pipers of France are protected. Each year the old winding streets of Ribeauvillé resound with the Festival of the Pipers (who themselves have long disappeared), and there is much wetting of whistles with Alsatian wines.

Riquewihr

Circled by its city walls and untouched by war, Riquewihr is lovelier than any wine town in France, except Saint-Émilion and perhaps Sancerre. The cobbled streets, lined with houses of the sixteenth and seventeenth centuries, bright with painted shop signs and flowering window boxes, are cooled by splashing fountains. A vine-trellised courtyard of one of the old inns is the best place in the world to taste the fresh Alsatian wines, green-gold in a green-stemmed glass.

Riesling, Gewürztraminer, Muscat, and Pinot all flourish here. The chalky mixture in the soil suits the Riesling, which develops a very fine bouquet. Sporen and Schoenenber are the favored slopes.

Kaysersberg

Testing the wines in a cave such as that of Salzmann in Kaysersberg is a great experience. The courtyard is Gothic and unspoiled, a relic of the Middle Ages, overshadowed by the ruin of the old castle on a crag across the river. This charming village, with its reputation for fine wines, is the birthplace of Dr. Schweitzer.

Ammerschwihr

The ancient vineyards surrounding this village on the mountainward side are in some places scored by the ridges, moats, and battlements of vanished castles and fortresses. The town itself is utterly clean, mod-ern, and completely new—for ancient Ammerschwihr disappeared almost to the last stick and stone in the bombardments of December and January 1944–45.

Reconstructed with the original stones, Ammerschwihr is as functional as a fine machine. M. Gaertner's Aux Armes de France is one of the best regional restaurants in France, proudly serving with *foie gras* or *choucroute* the wines from Ammerschwihr's great vineyards, of which the Kaefferkopf is perhaps the most famous. In this town, in the fourteenth century, was founded the Confrérie Saint-Étienne.

Turckheim

Slightly to the northeast of Colmar, Turckheim is a picturesque town with an old fortified wall pierced by three great gates. Its important vineyard is Brand.

Éguisheim

An ancient village, built in a circle. Visiting the Beyers, one of the family firms which, in a fashion not uncommon in Alsace, has descended from father to son since the sixteenth century, one might be entertained with Kougelhoff, the traditional Alsatian cake, accompanied by a fragrant Gewürztraminer, and a sip of the rosy Pinot Noir, a minor but agreeable local wine.

Guebwiller

Very good wines, mainly Rieslings, are produced with painstaking care at the terraced vineyards to the north and south of the town. Vines grow so high on slopes so steep that tractors work all year round to bring back the soil (which keeps sliding downhill), and masons follow to mend the walls. The best vineyard is Wannen.

THE GRAPE VARIETIES

Riesling and Gewürztraminer are the finest wines, the crown perhaps going to the Rieslings. There is much argument among non-Alsatian lovers of Alsace wine as to which of these ought to stand first, but no knowledgeable drinker would claim first place for any other than the Riesling. Alsatians themselves say firmly that the Riesling is the king of wines. The bulk of the common wines of the better type are Chasselas and Knipperlé.

Gewürztraminer

The confusion as to whether or not there is any actual difference between the Gewürztraminer (spicy Traminer) and the Traminer need no longer trouble the amateurs of wine, since it has been decided that only the term of Gewürztraminer shall be used, and that the vine is a selected strain of the old species, Traminer. This wine (from a small reddish grape with a musky flavor) can be slightly sweetish in the biggest years but is generally fairly dry. It has a high alcoholic content for an Alsatian wine, reaching nearly 14% in the supreme year of 1976, with unresolved sugar remaining in the wine. It just lacks the breed, distinction, and steeliness of a really fine Riesling, and its pronounced taste and bouquet may be too unsubtle for some tastes. Gewürztraminer is the most individual-tasting white wine in France. It is the second most planted grape in Alsace, and new plantings are forbidden by the I.N.A.O. A delicious fruity wine when good and an excellent accompaniment to such strong-tasting, spicy dishes as curry, it is also served with meat and with local cheeses.

Riesling

This grape, the oldest species in Alsace, produces the great German Rhines and Moselles. Alsatian Riesling can be a splendid wine with oysters, fish, and all seafood, and with meat. It has less body than the Alsatian Tokay, and it is less individual than a Gewürztraminer, but unquestionably it has more breed than either. Riesling is dry, fruity, and fresh, and can achieve great elegance. The vine thrives in a soil with a fair proportion of chalk; the great Riesling slopes are found near Riquewihr, Kellenberg, Ribeauvillé, and Dambach.

Tokay d'Alsace or *Pinot Gris*

Many people consider this next in quality after the Rieslings and Gewürztraminers. A very full-bodied golden wine, either dry or slightly sweet, it improves in bottle. There is a theory that it is called Tokay because the grape variety may have been imported three hundred years ago from the Tokaj district of Hungary. The wine has no other connection with the Hungarian Tokay, which comes from the Furmint, and there is some opposition to this misleading name; the *Dictionnaire du vin* simply states that the name Tokay is generally used for wines made from the Pinot Gris. It usually accompanies *foie gras* and meats.

Muscat d'Alsace

A very dry fruity Muscatel, often with a fine bouquet. This is another old species. A popular aperitif in Alsace.

Sylvaner

Intermediate in quality between the more common wines and the finer wines. A pleasant light luncheon wine, sometimes refreshingly prickling (with a *pointe de fraîcheur*) and comparable with Sylvaners of the same

class from the German Palatinate. The wine has a pale green-gold color, fruitiness, and a discreet bouquet, and is the most popular of noble Alsatian wines. It should be drunk young. Sometimes qualifies as a *Grand Vin*.

Pinot Blanc

This has more body generally than the Sylvaner, which it resembles slightly, but is not among the most distinguished wines—though at its best it is well balanced, with a delicate bouquet. It may sometimes be slightly prickling. The wine may be served with *foie gras* or meat.

Chasselas

The largest producer of carafe wines, light and agreeable, with the alcoholic content of average Alsatian wines (about 9% to 10%). It is seldom bottled and so is rarely, if ever, exported. Much Chasselas forms the basis of many shippers' wines.

Müller-Thurgau

This crossing of Riesling and Sylvaner, gaining headway in Germany, is quite rare. At one time in Alsace it produced a wine somewhat like, but not as good as, the Chasselas.

Knipperlé

Another of the common wines of Alsace, not quite as good as the Chasselas. New plantings of Knipperlé are now forbidden by the I.N.A.O.

Zwicker

Not a grape variety but, on a bottle label, it indicates that the wine is a blend of both noble and common varieties. Most Alsatian wines bearing the invented name given by a shipper or grower are zwickers.

Edelzwicker

A blend exclusively of noble grape varieties. *Edel* is the German word for "noble."

Vins Gris

Famous—except in Alsace—as the Alsatian *vin rosé* or pink wine, but more apt to be a blend of red and white wines than a true rosé. Important Alsatian wine authorities, such as the late René Kuehn of Ammerschwihr—former member of the French Chamber of Deputies, and former delegate to the United Nations—state that the best pink wine of Alsace is Rosé d'Alsace, which must come from the Pinot Noir grape and be made at the two or three vineyards only in each of the three or four communes throughout Alsace which produce true rosé. *Vins gris* are made on a considerable scale in Lorraine.

SPIRITS

The *eaux-de-vie* of Alsace are many and famous: these fruit brandies are called *alcools blancs* because they are aged not in wood but in crockery. Vineyards alternate with orchards along the east slope of the Vosges Mountains skirting the Rhine plain. The blue-plum trees producing quetsch fan out onto the plain; in the forest are the wild strawberries, raspberries, and holly.

Kirsch

The most important of all the *eaux-de-vie*, it is distilled from cherries, including their stones. Some 60 pounds of fruit render about eleven bottles at 50% of alcohol. The best section for the wild-cherry tree that produces kirsch is along the middle height of the Vosges slope between valley and summit, around Trois-Épis, Ammerschwihr, Haut-Koenigsbourg, and Sainte-Odile.

Fraise

Distilled from both wild and cultivated strawberries. The genuine *eau-de-vie* is very good and very expensive.

Framboise

Since a brandy distilled directly and exclusively from raspberries would be too concentrated to be palatable, *eau-de-vie de framboise* is made in a unique fashion by macerating the fruit in neutral spirits protected from exposure to oxygen. The liquid is then distilled to create the *eau-de-vie*. One liter of spirit with the desired percentage of alcohol is made from 8 or 9 pounds of fruit, as compared to the costly 60 pounds needed if the brandy were made in the usual way.

Mirabelle

Made from yellow plums of a size that can be enclosed in the hand. The finest mirabelle comes from neighboring Lorraine.
See Mirabelle de Lorraine.

Quetsch

This brandy comes from blue plums, of a tree more common and hardy than that of the mirabelle, producing successfully on the broad plain.

Houx or Holly Spirit

This extraordinary beverage distilled in the mountains above Ammerschwihr is one of the rarest and probably one of the most expensive in the world. Less than five hundred bottles of it are produced a year, by fermenting together holly berries and sugar, then distilling.

Enzian

This spirit is distilled from the astonishingly long roots of the yellow gentian.

Reine-Claude

This variety of plum (the greengage), named, in French, after the daughter of Louis XII, is infrequently distilled, but it gives a spirit with an almost overwhelming bouquet.
Other spirits are made from apricots, peaches, rowan or sorb-apples *(alises)*, bilberries *(myrtilles)*, and blackberries *(mûres)*.

Altar wine

Wine used for sacramental purposes. It must be pure, unadulterated, natural wine.

Altise

A beetle that feeds on vine leaves.
see Chapter Eight, p. 39.

Amber dry

Name under which Clairette du Languedoc *(q.v.)* is sometimes sold in Great Britain.

Ambonnay

Village of the Mountain of Reims district, producing a First Growth Champagne *(q.v.)*.

Amelioration

Any treatment of, or addition (such as sulfur or sugar) to grape juice or new wine for the purpose of improving the quality.

Amer Picon

A proprietary French bitters used as an aperitif, made with a wine and brandy base to which has been added quinine (to impart a bitter taste), orange peel, and innumerable herbs. It is drunk with ice, diluted with water, and usually sweetened with grenadine or Cassis.

America

See United States.

Amertume

Bitterness in wine that has thrown a deposit and turned acid.
See Chapter Nine, p. 53.

Aminaean wine

One of the most lasting and famous of the Augustan Era, to which "even the royal Phanaean" paid homage. (Virgil: *Georgics II.*)
See Classical wines.

Ammerschwihr

Wine town in Alsace *(q.v.)*.

Amontillado

A kind of Spanish Sherry, not so pale in color as the Finos and with more bouquet. It is naturally dry; but for the Anglo-Saxon trade sweeter wine, made from the Pedro Ximénez grape, is often added.
See Sherry.

Amoroso

Sweetened Oloroso Sherry prepared for the British market. Unknown in Spain.
See Sherry.

Ampelidaceae

Botanical family to which the grapevine belongs. Of the ten genera of the family only one, the genus *Vitis*, is important in wine-making, although others are capable of producing grapes. *Vitis* embraces two subgenera, *Euvites* and *Muscadinia*, and numerous species. Of these, *vinifera* is the most important, for it yields the great wines of the world. Native to Europe, it has been transplanted to other continents.
See Chapter Eight, p. 31.

Ampelography

(1) The descriptive study, identification, and classification of vines.
(2) A book or document describing the structural characteristics of a vine. The written information is often accompanied by a detailed drawing or photograph of a leaf of each plant covered in the book.

Ampelotherapy

Treatment of human or animal ills with grapes which possess therapeutic properties.

Amphora

A two-handled vessel—pitcher or jar—used in ancient times for holding wine or oil.
See Classical wines.

Angelica

(1) A sweet yellow liqueur, somewhat similar to Chartreuse, made in the Basque country.
(2) A very sweet Californian mixture of partially fermented grape juice and brandy.

Château l'Angélus

Bordeaux red wine.
District and Commune: Saint-Émilion, France.

One of the many Grands Crus, according to the 1955 Saint-Émilion Classification. The property has been owned by the Boüard family since 1924, and its wine is made by very up-to-date methods in a modern *chai*.
Vineyard area: 25 hectares (63 acres).
Average production: 150 *tonneaux* (13,000 cases).

Château d'Angludet

Bordeaux red wine.
District: Haut-Médoc, France.
Commune: Cantenac-Margaux.

Rated an Exceptional Growth (*Cru Exceptionnel*), just below Fifth Growth (*Cinquième Cru*), in 1855, the vineyard went through a bad period in the thirties and forties. In earlier times it had always been considered the equal of a Fourth Growth (*Quatrième Cru*). Formerly owned and run by the son-in-law of the owners of Château Coutet, the estate is now the property of Peter Sichel, the managing director of Sichel and Co.; he has done much to restore the vineyard, which deserves a higher classification. He is also part-owner of Château Palmer.
Characteristics. A well-made wine from good soil. The vineyard certainly should be a classified one.
Vineyard area: 30 hectares (75 acres).
Average production: 120 *tonneaux* (12,000 cases).

Angola wine

Palm sap fermented in West Africa.

Angostura

Rum-based bitters made in Trinidad from a formula still the secret of the Siegert family, heirs of the inventor. Dr. Siegert was a German who became surgeon-general to Simón Bolívar during the liberation of South America. He developed his bitters from various herbs and plants to counteract the enervating effects of the tropical climate. The product proved so popular that in the early nineteenth century he founded the firm which still manufactures it.

Anis

Popular French and Spanish liqueur and aperitif. The dominant taste derives from the seeds of the star anise plant (an important ingredient of absinthe), whose pods resemble starfish. Anis was developed as a substitute for absinthe *(q.v.)* and, like absinthe, can be drunk diluted with water, turning cloudy with a pale greenish tinge when the water is added. A similar drink is pastis *(q.v.)*. The difference between the two is that licorice replaces aniseed as the principal flavoring ingredient of pastis. One of the best-known brands of anis is that of the firm of Pernod, known as Pernod 45, although Ricard has now become the best-selling French aperitif of this type. The anis liqueur is the most popular of all the cordials in Spain.

Anisette

Liqueur of aniseed flavor. A well-known formula is said to have been confided by a West Indian traveler to Marie Brizard of Bordeaux.

Anjou-Saumur

White, rosé, and red wines.
District: Loire Valley, France.

There are over 12,000 wine-producers in the historic province of Anjou (now the department of Maine-et-Loire), which embraces a large vineyard area on the slopes west of Touraine and rising from the left bank of the Loire. Anjou and Touraine are alike in many ways: the hills around Saumur are made of the same chalky limestone deposit as those at Vouvray, and in both districts the wine is aged in caves dug deep into the hillside. In Anjou, west and south of Angers, however, the shallow soil covering a bed of hard rock resembles that of Brittany. The château country proper is within Touraine, but in Anjou also the wide River Loire flows through a peaceful green countryside, past old manors and castles, relics of the days when the Plantagenet Kings of England were also Counts of Anjou. In the thirteenth century the wines were very popular in England. Later on, when the English were importing mainly Bordeaux, the people of the Netherlands were the biggest buyers, sailing up the river as far as Rochefort and Saumur to collect the barrels. In those days, the best wines were saved for the foreign trade and the lesser ones sent to Paris.

Today these wines are most popular in Belgium, Holland, Germany, and the United States. Like those from other parts of the Loire Valley, the Anjou wines are fresh and sprightly; even the lesser growths are often charming, though seldom seen outside their native region. Best known abroad now are the Muscadet and the Anjou rosé.

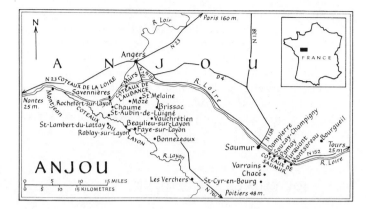

One-third of the 650,000 hectoliters (17.3 million U.S. gallons, 14.3 million imp.) of wine produced annually in Anjou is white, and rosé makes up most of the remaining quantity, although a small amount of relatively minor red wines is produced also. The best Angevin white wines are sweet, as were the vast majority at one time; but changes in taste have converted many growers to vinifying their wines at least comparatively dry, and this trend is healthy for Anjou. Those vineyards capable of producing natural sweet wines continue to do so; others—where doses of sugar once had to be added to impart the requisite sweetness—have turned to drier and better wines. A percentage of the annual output is made into sparkling wine, especially in and around Saumur, but the finest Angevin remains non-sparkling.

SOIL AND VINES

It has already been stated that the region divides into two basic types of soil: chalky clay around Saumur and along the slopes of the little Loir River; and elsewhere, a hard schist covered with a layer of flinty clay, so thin that growers are often forced to use dynamite to loosen the earth in which to plant their vines—or, if dynamite is not used, they must spend many weary hours with a pickaxe.

The only grape allowed for fine white wine is Chenin Blanc, a standard in Anjou since the ninth century. Red wines—made principally in Saumur in the communes of Souzay-Champigny, Chacé, Dampierre, and Varrains, as well as in Saint-Cyr-en-Bourg, Brézé, and Brain-sur-Allones—come from Cabernet Franc grapes with some Cabernet Sauvignon and ever-decreasing amounts of Pineau d'Aunis, which is giving way to the Cabernets. Two kinds of rosé are produced: Rosé d'Anjou from Groslot, Gamay, Cot, Noble, and Pineau d'Aunis grapes; and Rosé de Cabernet, entirely from Cabernet grapes. The latter is the better—fruitier, fresher, cleaner-tasting, and with a more appealing color. It also tends to be higher in alcohol, the legal minimum being 10%. Of the former, it should be noted that the Gamays from California are closer to

Beaujolais and better. Some of the Anjou rosés are dry, others are sweet. There is a growing tendency for the ordinary consumer in the region to ask for a sweeter pink wine.

Only about a third of the wine is labeled Anjou. The rest (including the best) bears the name of one of the subdistricts with the Appellation Contrôlée, and these names are more likely to be found on bottles sent abroad.

ANJOU-SAUMUR SUB-DISTRICTS

Coteaux de la Loire (Appellation Contrôlée)

This area, on both banks of the river, is one of the best and most well known in Anjou. In soils of varying consistency and quality, it grows Chenin Blanc grapes which give way, west of Montjean, to the Muscadet. The wines, therefore, also vary; sweet, yet in general drier than those of the Layon district, they are lively and well made. A few, rather sharp when young, take some time to come around. Others will be mature after years in bottle.

Savennières. An attractive village, Savennières has its own Appellation Contrôlée. The wines from the Chenin Blanc grape incline to dryness, and are slow to mature. The leading vineyards are La Coulée-de-Serrant, La Roche-aux-Moines (both of which make fine, very elegant wines), Château de Savennières, Château d'Epiré, Château de la Bizolière, Clos du Papillon, and Clos de la Bergerie.

Other communes worth noting are Bouchemaine, La Possonnière, Saint-Georges-sur-Loire, Champtocé and Ingrandes, Montjean, La Pommeraye, and part of Chalonnes.

Coteaux du Layon (Appellation Contrôlée)

This is the other leading district of the region. Thirty miles of vineyard are scattered along the banks of the little stream, the Layon, which descends from the hills near Les Verchers to meander through a string of wine-growing villages until, just above Chalonnes, it enters the Loire. The wines are high in alcohol, and some of the best vineyards are picked only after the *pourriture noble* has set in. These sweet wines are probably the finest of all the sweet wines of Anjou, but dry white wines are also made in the area. The sweet whites are fuller in body and longer-lasting than any from the Coteaux de la Loire. In the seventeenth century they were very popular with the Dutch, but now are chiefly drunk in the north of France and Belgium.

Bonnezeaux. This Great Growth of the region has its own Appellation Contrôlée and ranks almost as a subdistrict on its own. The vineyards, in the commune of Thouarcé, sprawl down the slopes toward the riverbank, and a solitary windmill stands guard above—

once there were three. They produce a limited quantity of sweet white wine, soft and fruity.

Quarts de Chaume. Almost equally distinguished (indeed, some say it is really the best of the Layon slopes) is the sweet wine from this vineyard, near the village of Chaume in the commune of Rochefort. It resembles a sweet Vouvray and is more flowery than a Sauternes. In lightness and bouquet it is unique, and yet in most years its alcoholic content is between 13% and 16%. At one time the vineyard belonged to a single proprietor who rented it out in return for a quarter-share of each vintage. He reserved the right to choose which section of the vineyard his quarter should come from, and so it came to be called Quarts de Chaume.

Six more communes in this area add their names to the Appellation Contrôlée of Coteaux du Layon. These are Beaulieu-sur-Layon, Faye d'Anjou, Rablay-sur-Layon, Rochefort-sur-Layon, Saint-Aubin-de-Luigné, and Saint-Lambert-du-Lattay.

From the middle reaches of the Layon comes a quite considerable quantity of white wine permitted the more general Appellation Anjou, although this is predominantly a district for *vin rosé*.

Coteaux de l'Aubance (Appellation Contrôlée)

The wines of this small district north of the Coteaux du Layon are better known in their own part of the country than elsewhere. Yet they are pleasant, typical Anjou wines. Most of them are white, but rosé is produced as well. The whites have not all the rich mellowness of a wine from the slopes of the Loire or the Layon but are often outstanding—especially the medium-dry, which have character and an agreeable bouquet. The leading communes are Brissac (making mainly good pink wines from Cabernet and Groslot grapes), Vauchrétien (good white wines), Saint-Jean-des-Mauvrets, Juigné-sur-Loire, Saint-Melaine, Soulaines, Mozé, Mûrs, and Denée, which is near Rochefort and makes very similar wines.

Coteaux du Loir

Now an Appelation Contrôlée in the department of the Sarthe, this former sub-district on a small tributary of the River Loire produces wines that are white and pleasant, red and indifferent, rosé and charming.

Saumur, Coteaux de Saumur, and Saumur-Champigny (A.O.C.)

The old town of Saumur is dominated by a rambling castle which has been turned into an equestrian museum—this is where the cavalry school of the French army is stationed. The riverside bluffs are tunneled with vast caves, perfect for ageing, and the sweeter white growths make a sparkling wine. A good deal of the wine, however, is dry or semi-dry, with 10% to 13% of alcohol, and sometimes it is slightly *crémeux*.

The sparkling Loire wines preserve their own flavor; they are different from Champagne, and Saumur is overpriced if it costs the same—the producers suffer from the fact that it is usually taxed as much. Made of two-thirds Chenin Blanc and one-third Cabernet, it is fuller and heavier than sparkling Vouvray.

Thirty-seven communes share the Appellation Saumur in the department of Vienne. They include Pouançay, Berrie, Saint-Leger-de-Montbrillais, Ternay, and Ranton.

The Coteaux de Saumur is still being defined by the I.N.A.O. In principle, the vineyards follow the slopes along the Loire. Dampierre is the leading commune, with a good production of two-thirds white wine, one-third red and rosé. Souzay-Champigny, Parnay, and Turquant make fresh fruity wines; the white wine of Montsoreau has a definite character. Located on the Thouel River, Varrains and Chacé are better known for their rosé and red wines than for their smaller harvest of white; Saint-Cyr-en-Bourg makes more white; Brézé, Epieds, and Saix do quite well with their red wines, but the white have the greater reputation.

Saumur-Champigny, the good red wines from Champigny, the wine village just south of Saumur, is also made in many of the surrounding villages, mentioned as part of the Coteaux de Saumur. Saumur-Champigny, as a Cabernet-Franc-based red wine, is, with the Borgueuils and Chinons, the best red wine of the Loire.

(See also under individual headings.)

Anthracnose

A vine disease of European origin.
See Chapter Eight, p. 38.

Aperitif

A broad term for nearly any drink taken before a meal to tease the palate and stimulate the appetite. Diverse flavored and fortified wines generally sold under some proprietary label such as Byrrh, Lillet, and Dubonnet are popular; so are stronger spirits and bitters usually served with soda or water. Among this second group are Campari, Amer Picon, and pastis. Perhaps the very best aperitif is either dry Champagne or Sherry.

Apoplexy

A spectacular vine malady.
See Chapter Eight, p. 39.

Appellation d'Origine

Guaranteed place-name for a French wine. Champagne, for example, is a name which can properly be applied only to the products of certain approved vineyards and wine-making processes inside that region; no other sparkling wine (even when made by the authentic champagne process) has a right to the name. In France this rule is enforced by the laws of Appellation d'Origine. For an account of the events and legislation which led to the formulation of these laws, and of further controls over the viticultural and vinicultural standards essential for the production of fine wines, *see* Appellation d'Origine Contrôlée, below.

Appellation d'Origine Contrôlée (*or* A.O.C.) (control laws)

Literally "controlled place of origin"; on a bottle of French wine the guarantee not only of place of origin but of the quality standards traditionally associated with wines from that place. These control laws represent the most flexible, most enlightened, and most effective body of legislation existing at present for the protection of fine wines.

HOW THE LAWS WORK

Fine wines always bear the stamp of the place where the grapes were grown and—given the conditions necessary for producing fine wines—the more restricted the place, the better the wine. Recognizing this fact, the Frenchman drew his control laws as a series of large and small circles: the smaller the circle, the more elite the terrain and the stiffer the wine's minimum requirements. The result: the more specific the name or *appellation*, the higher the guarantee of quality.

A typical example is the large Bordeaux wine region in southwest France. Imagine a great circle drawn around the city of Bordeaux and the land surrounding it. Everything within this circle (excepting land obviously unfit for the purpose) has the right to grow grapes for Bordeaux. Just northwest of the city—but within the circle—is the district of the Haut-Médoc; to the southeast are Graves, Barsac, and Sauternes; to the east, Saint-Émilion and Pomerol. These are all districts represented by smaller circles within Bordeaux, and although their wines have the right to bear the more general name, they will always take the more restricted if they can qualify for it. Within these smaller circles, the terrain is finer, the requirements higher, and the wines better. The contraction of the circles does not end there. Within, for example, the Haut-Médoc, yet smaller circles represent specific towns or communes, the best of which are Margaux, Saint-Julien, Pauillac, and Saint-Estéphe. Again, growers always choose the most restricted name for which their vines qualify, and again the quality of the wines is raised and the characteristics more specifically determined. The system reaches its logical conclusion in Burgundy, where certain superb vineyards (one—La Romanée—a mere 2.1 acres) have special separate *appellations* and highly stringent requirements for their magnificent wines.

The system has the confidence of both grower and consumer, and thus prices for wines with specific names are higher than for those with general names, and the more specific, the higher. It is to the credit of French lawmakers that such wines are almost invariably worth the increased price.

WHAT IS CONTROLLED

These laws control every factor that contributes to the wine, every process that may affect it—in fact, every detail literally from the ground up is regulated until the bottle of wine is sold to the consumer or leaves the boundaries of France. An easy and harmonious working relationship between the technical and administrative experts of the Institut National des Appellations d'Origine in Paris and technical experts in each wine region makes this complex and seemingly cumbersome system workable. The Institut National des Appellations d'Origine (it is usually referred to as the I.N.A.O.) sets down the broad outline of the controls, the local people contribute the specific points, the Minister of Agriculture makes it law, and the fraud inspectors see that the law is enforced. While each control law will be adapted to its specific area, all will contain the following broad general points:

(1) *Area of Production.* The geological composition of the soil deemed fit for the production of the wine in question is outlined. The land is then studied and marked out by experts in the region, and only vineyards within the delimited area are permitted to use the name. The boundaries are reflected on the property land maps or *cadastre* kept in each town hall of a village with Appellation Contrôée vineyards.

(2) *Permissible Grapevine(s).* In different soils and under different skies, the same vine will produce grapes of different characteristics. Selection of varieties follows the best traditional practices of each area.

(3) *Minimum Alcoholic Content.* Alcohol helps to give wine its staying power—its ability to live long enough to develop into greatness. If vines are allowed to overproduce, the grapes may develop so little sugar that the wine will end up unbalanced, with too little alcohol to match its other characteristics. Stipulation of alcoholic content before enrichment of the wine is thus an assurance of quality.

(4) *Viticultural Practices.* Pruning, fertilizing, and the general handling of the vine show in the quality of the wine. Viticultural practices are closely regulated, hence the type of pruning is specified for each area, with special emphasis on outlawing methods which produce huge crops but mediocre fruit.

(5) *Permissible Harvest.* Since quality is inversely proportional to quantity, the amount of permissible harvest is specified. This is expressed in hectoliters/hectare (which may be converted into gallons/acre) and usually drops sharply as names get more specific.

(6) *Vinicultural Practices.* The traditional wine-making procedures of any region are largely responsible for the reputation of each of the great wines, instilling much of the wine's distinctive character. These have thus been codified into law. Tasting panels have become more frequent, especially in the Bordeaux region.

(7) *Distilling.* The I.N.A.O. also controls the *eaux-de-vie* of France. The traditional distillation procedures that made the fame of these spirits are also formalized into law.

THE EVOLUTION OF THE LAWS

The outlook for French wines at the turn of the century was bleak and unpromising. Phylloxera had invaded France in the middle of the nineteenth century, reducing vast areas of vineyard to rows of bare wooden stumps—resembling huge graveyards. Growers replanted prolific grape varieties in the southern plains once reserved for the cultivation of cereals, which, more often than not, yielded wine which was common and harsh and of inferior quality. A not uncommon practice, despite strict laws forbidding it, was to add sugar and water to grape pomace, or pulp, let the concoction ferment, and then sell it as wine. Fine wines had been hit as badly as ordinary ones, and in many cases there was no connection between bottle contents and label. Into this chaos stepped the French legislature, with the law of August 1, 1905, creating statutes for eliminating fraud. This step saved the table wines from a major crisis. The laws were excellent; they became the pattern for all agricultural controls of place-names, and were often imitated abroad, though never equaled. Where fine wines were concerned, the law was completed in 1908 in order to anticipate governmental restrictions and amendments. This is known as the administrative phase of appellation law.

The trouble was that the laws did not take into account that fine wines are produced not only by the place and the soil where they are grown, but also by the grapes planted and the manner in which they are cultivated. In controlling the geographical place of origin without either exacting certain traditional practices of cultivation or imposing tests of tasting or analysis, they opened the way to two abuses: (1) that wines of great name would be made without the care to which they owed their superlative characteristics, and (2) that some proprietors would take advantage of the geographical guarantee regardless of the grape variety, thus producing quantities of inferior wine which, under the letter of the law, were entitled to bear the label of a prestigious name.

The legislation of 1908 codified for wines the more general legislation of 1905. Thus were fixed the geographic zones of Bordeaux, Banyuls, Clairette de Die, Cognac, and Armagnac. But the government was unable to make any satisfactory decision regarding Champagne.

The region of Champagne extends over several French departments; growers in the Marne disputed the right to the great wine name "Champagne" with the growers of the Aube. The administration's delimitation was a compromise, intended to please both factions. Like so many decisions of the sort, it pleased neither. There was little outcry, however, before 1910. In that year severe frosts ushered in one of the most disastrous harvests in Champagne history, and the growers erupted. They said that, had the limits of the region been more tightly drawn, and had the shippers respected the limits, the normal price of grapes would have been higher and the growers would have been able to save enough to tide them over a poor year. It should be pointed out that at this time the merchants in Champagne could produce simple sparkling wines without an A.O.C. but with an address in Champagne using grapes grown well outside the limits of Champagne. As it was, riots broke out in January 1911, and troops had to be sent to restore order. In June, the limits of the region were amended—and again there were riots. Thus, later in the year, the legislature declared the law unworkable and set it aside, without offering anything to replace it.

In 1911, a sensible modification of the previous laws was prepared and discussed in the Chamber of Deputies. The opponents' argument, however, was: "Can you contest the right of a cultivator to make what use he pleases of the name of his property and the fruits of his soil?" The result was that no reforms were made. Trying again in 1914, Deputy Jenouvrier pointed out the collective character of the Appellation d'Origine: "The reputation attached to these products is the result of the sustained effort of successive generations; the fruit of their combined labor became famous, and the proprietorial right was thus established for the whole commune or region."

When, after the war, a new law was passed in 1919, M. Jenouvrier's modification was incorporated; but there was still no clause controlling varieties of grapevine, methods of cultivation, delimitation by soil type, and other guarantees of quality. The results of this law, therefore, were disastrous. Almost anyone who claimed that an Appellation d'Origine was contrary to his interests and rights or to customs locaux, loyaux, et constants (local, loyal, and constant) could go to law to demand an interdiction, causing a great deal of senseless litigation.

Called to clarify its understanding of the law of 1919, the court chose a strict geographical interpretation, thinking that such was the intention of the legislators. This precipitated a movement to create new and inferior vineyards in delimited areas. Deputy Capus, in his account of the long struggle to obtain the control law as we now know it, recalls the effect of the 1919 act on his native Barsac, a district of Bordeaux. The sweet, rich, justly famous white wines of Barsac traditionally stem from Sauvignon and Sémillon grapes grown on the hilly sections of the commune. In the valleys and along the palus—the moist lowland near the River Garonne—the traditional vines had been for red wine, none of it Barsac, all of it ordinary.

In the litigation following the law, the courts authorized the producers who grew vines in the palus of Barsac to sell their wines under the label of the famous white wine, overlooking the fact that legal right could not endow the land with the proper geological conditions. A few growers balked, since the law of 1919 said nothing about vines, but most accepted the ruling and did the legal but improper thing. As Capus said: "Bad laws make bad citizens." The vines in the palus were rooted out, those for bulk production of white wine were planted or grafted with hybrids, and for the first time Barsac was grown in the palus. A further result was that the small-bearing noble vines of the slope could not match the productivity of the newcomers, and in some vineyards they were replaced by bulk varieties, often hybrids. So, great seas of wines ranging from mediocre to frightful went to market emblazoned with the famous name. Prices, of course, dropped. So did the reputation of Barsac, and the situation could have occurred elsewhere.

This state of things was bad for the grower as well as for the consumer; the honest man who spent money on his vineyard and worked hard to produce a small quantity of great wine found himself under siege by less scrupulous competitors, turning out far more and far worse wine which bore the same label of authenticity. Soon buyers from abroad began to complain that their customers were refusing to pay the prices asked for such inferior stuff; and when the agitators for a stronger law increased their activity, it became clear that public opinion was changing. Monsieur Cheron, the Minister of Agriculture, had been shocked, when he paid a visit to the Gironde, by the number of vines in the Great Growths (Grands Crus) which were being uprooted to make room for the more prolific hybrids; and a commission was set up to inquire into the affair.

In all these years, the troubles in Champagne had never been settled, and now the two parties appealed to Monsieur Édouard Barthe, president of the Groupe Viticole, to mediate for them. He drew up a plan which both resolved satisfactorily the question of delimitation and established every necessary condition for the production of fine Champagne. This plan, since it had the approval of all the associations of viticulture concerned, was able to be incorporated intact into the new Law of 1927, which added to the regulations of 1919 amendments (1) restricting the place of origin to "the surface areas comprising communes or parts of communes for the production of wine of the appellation"; and (2) forbidding the right of appellation to wines produced from hybrids or from any vines other than those traditionally bearing the great wines. This was known as the Appellation Simple. The consequence was that the palus and other unsuitable lands dropped back to inferior status and the noble vines returned—in those regions which observed the law. For one of the law's weaknesses was that it was optional. Some districts did observe it—in the region of Châteauneuf-du-Pape, the Baron Le Roy, a proprietor himself, went further and persuaded the other growers to endorse guidelines related to quality. He then had these guidelines confirmed legally in court. Other regions followed this example, and some one hundred appellations were created.

The Law of 1927, although a great improvement on its predecessors, was still imperfect—because, except in the separate clause dealing with Champagne, it ignored all guarantees of quality except those of soil and place-name: that is, it overlooked the extent of permissible harvest and the minimum alcoholic content of the wine, as well as the necessary standard of vine-tending and winemaking practices.

In spite of the imperfections of the Appellation Simple, it was significant that for the first time the French legislature admitted that the name of a wine embraced something other than geography. The way to the present stricter controls was not to be smooth; but from that point it had been marked out and paved. In 1935 these stricter controls began going into operation, and the fine French wines became the province of a committee, now the Institut National des Appellations d'Origine des Vins et Eaux-de-Vie (the National Institute of Place-names of Wines and Spirits), whose capable hands guide the fortunes of French wines both in France and in some instances abroad.

THE EFFECT OF THE LAWS

In the case of every Appellation Contrôlée that has gone into effect, the result has been an immediate and marked increase in quality. Passage of a control law cut out the lesser wines, and the grower—conscious that his efforts would be reimbursed—strove for high quality. The existence of an Appellation Contrôlée is of itself immediate evidence that the wine is fine, and the gain is twofold: the grower gets more money for his wine, and the consumer gets better wine for his money. It is only unfortunate that other wine-producing countries have not followed that example more closely. It is as well to understand that it is the place-name which is controlled and not always the wine—i.e., Pommard Appellation Contrôlée means that geographical boundaries and minimum standards have been set up for Pommard. But the controlling of the wine in the bottle is much more difficult, with a limited "police force." Therefore, there are still loopholes in the enforcement of wine authenticity.

Appellation Simple

"Simple name of origin"; a predecessor of the system of Appellation Contrôlée, which at present protects the quality and origin of fine French wines. Before the creation of the *Appellation d'Origine Contrôlée* in 1935, appellations were said to be *simple*. As pointed out, the creation of these laws went through administrative and judicial phases. These first laws of 1905,

1908, 1919, and 1927 were insufficient. They were repealed.

See Appellation d'Origine Contrôlée.

Apple brandy

Brandy made from apples; distilled cider. The best French apple brandy is Calvados; the American variety is applejack.

See Calvados; Applejack.

Applejack

Applejack, strictly speaking, is the American name for apple brandy. Americans do not always speak strictly about applejack, however, since the name applies both to apple brandy—which is a spirit made by the distillation of fermented apple juice—and to a rougher spirit made by a more primitive process. In the early days, both methods were used; but now the second method is confined to a few backcountry areas, where the cider is still fermented completely and then frozen. Since water freezes at a higher temperature than alcohol, the ice which forms and is skimmed off is almost pure water, and the unfrozen liquid left behind is almost pure alcohol. This potent and slightly oily spirit is applejack.

Applejack was for a long time one of the most popular spirits in America—partly, perhaps, because at that time the common drink was cider. This was comparatively low in alcohol (about 6% by volume) and, if contemporary reports are to be believed, the early American liked his liquor as potent as it was plentiful.

Actually, neither cider nor applejack was popular, nor even available, when the first settlers came to America, for the simple reason that there were no apple trees. The English and the Dutch brought beer with them; and the English set about planting hops and barley in New England—where they did not thrive. Then they planted fruit trees, which flourished exceedingly and began to bear fruit (so it was said) much sooner than they would have in England, where cider was already being drunk in the sixteenth century, and probably earlier. The word, spelled "sider" in earlier times, comes from the Hebrew *shekar*; at first it may have meant any strong drink, although by the sixteenth century it was specifically the strong drink made from apple juice.

Since New England had proved to be a poor place for the growing of hops, the taste for beer changed to a liking for cider, for rum—imported from the West Indies and later made in New England from West Indian molasses—and for applejack, which was soon being carried inland by travelers and Indians. As time went on, the Dutch and German settlers in Pennsylvania began brewing beer with great success, and the Scots and the Irish, who arrived early in the eighteenth century, started the whiskey industry; but for a long time after this, the common drink in rural areas was still applejack.

The economic factors which encouraged the Pennsylvania grain-growers to start making whiskey in quantity worked in the same way upon the New England apple-growers. Since roads were universally poor, it was risky to try to transport heavy or bulky cargoes, and so both grain and fruit were fermented or distilled. The lighter loads of liquor, much easier to carry, commanded better markets too. In the cider industry, New England, with Connecticut outstanding, led other producers. The ingenious Connecticut Yankee, in addition to making himself famous by selling wooden nutmegs, proved his adaptability in the field of spirituous beverages. By taking cider, coloring it with Indian corn, and letting it age for three months, he got fairly strong liquor quite like Madeira in color, and sold it as such to gullible Europeans. How much of this went on is not known, but the practice could not have been extensive, for cider was too much in demand at home to be wasted on others.

One of the strongest beliefs held by the American of Revolutionary times was that the drinking of strong spirits was necessary to health—and, with great gusto, he set about taking care of his health, not infrequently starting with cider or applejack for breakfast and then carrying the jug out to the fields with him. Social events of all kinds, from weddings to funerals, and from church suppers to political rallies, were well supplied with rum, cider (or applejack), or some kind of strong punch—and sometimes with all three at once. At one church function in New England, thirty bowls of punch were drunk before the morning meeting by eighty Christians—and a great deal more of a formidable mixture of drinks that same evening. As stills became easier to buy, many farms set up their own, thus raising applejack to the level of a distilled spirit, although much of the primitive frozen type was made too. That the product was powerful is proved by the way it was referred to in the local taverns, where customers would ask for a "slug of blue fish-hooks," "essence of lockjaw," or, after the center of the trade had moved to New Jersey, "Jersey lightning."

For the making of applejack only the cider from sound, firm, well-matured apples is chosen. For commercial applejack the product is distilled. The kind of still used in the old days (and often, but not always, found today) was the pot still. In modern applejack-making, the fluid is distilled twice, the first time coming through at about 60° of proof, and the second time at anywhere from 110° to 130° of proof. (In America, a spirit that contains 50% alcohol by volume is said to be at 100° of proof.) Today, after distillation, the applejack is cut with water and grain neutral spirits to bring it down to 85° or 100° proof as the distiller desires—since apples are more expensive than grain, a pure applejack would cost the customer too much. In the more robust frontier days, applejack was often put on sale raw and fiery, straight from the still. It is

placed in oak casks today and kept in bonded warehouses to age—anywhere from one to five years.

In other times, a rougher and inferior spirit was sometimes obtained by the slapdash method of distilling the pomace without pressing it first. Alternatively, the pomace from which all the juice had been pressed out was sometimes taken and soaked in water. The water was then fermented and became a weak spirit known as ciderkin which, in colonial days, was considered fit for children.

Among the terms for applejack are: apple brandy, cider brandy, cider spirits, cider whiskey, and sometimes just plain "apple." Although the name applejack is strictly an American one, apple brandy is made in various parts of the world, the most famous being that from the Calvados area in the province of Normandy in France.

See Calvados.

Apricot brandy

A dry unsweetened brandy made from the distilled juice of apricots. The original, and most famous, apricot brandy was Barack Pálinka, made in Hungary (*q.v.*).

Apricot liqueur

A beverage, not to be confused with apricot brandy, made of mashed apricots and sweetened brandy.

Apry

Tawny-colored liqueur made from apricots soaked in sweetened brandy. It is produced by the firm of Marie Brizard et Roger in Bordeaux, France.

Apulia (Puglia)

Red and white wines.
District: Southeast Italy. On the Adriatic.

Apulia, the largest wine-producing region in the country, juts down into the Mediterranean to form the "heel" of the Italian "boot." The sun-drenched, shadeless, wheat-bearing plain changes farther south into a vast rolling sea of vines and gnarled olive trees, the two often rubbing branches in the same field. The soil is as heavy as the sun is hot, but the vine adapts itself so prolifically that Apulian grapes are crushed into 11 million hectoliters (291 million U.S. gallons, 242 million imp.) of wine annually—mostly red and mostly run from fermenting vat to tank or barrel to be sold throughout the country as the indispensable ordinary table wine. Some of it is used for blending—because of its rough body and high alcoholic content—and much floods into the vermouth plants or is concocted into the various wine-based aperitifs Latin countries consume in such abundance. As in the

French Midi, one pretends that these bulk wines are fine. There are, nevertheless, some delightful exceptions.

San Severo is a D.O.C. that applies to white, red, and rosé wines produced within the communes of San Severo and seven others in the province of Foggia. The white is a pale (straw-colored), dry, light, and eminently drinkable wine from the northern end of Apulia's *tavoliere*, the "chessboard" or plateau extending around Foggia. The wine is of medium strength and from Bombino grapes. Some experts consider it among the finest white wines of Apulia. Other offerings from the "chessboard" are Locorontondo, Martina Franca, Castel del Monte, and Matino, all D.O.C.

Locorontondo and *Martina Franca* are both white wines produced from different proportions of Verdeca and Bianco di Alessano grapes grown in neighboring areas southeast of Bari. Both have a delicate bouquet, a dry taste, pale green color, and about 12% alcohol.

Castel del Monte is the D.O.C. for white and red wines made respectively from Pampanuto and Uva de Troia in the area around Bari. White Castel del Monte is a dry fresh wine of good character, but not so good as the red, which improves quite well with ageing and may be given the cachet *riserva* after three years. It is excellent, with a good balance of tannin and acidity.

Matino comes from farther south, around the town of Lecce, famous for its baroque architecture; the wine takes its name from another small town called Matino. The reds and rosés bearing this name may contain up to 30% Malvasia and Sangiovese, and the Negro Amaro grape gives the wines their characteristic slightly burnt taste.

Moscato di Trani is a D.O.C. for the naturally sweet wines made from the Moscato Bianco grapes grown around Bari. The name is also given a *liquoroso* wine from the same area, but with a higher degree of alcohol.

Among other D.O.C.s are Aleatico di Puglia (sweet-red), the dry-white Ostuni, the semi-sweet Gravina, and the reds: Alezio, Brindisi, Cacc'e Mmitte di Lucera, Copertino, Orta Nova, Primitivo di Manduria (slightly sweet), Rosso Canosa, Rosso di Cerignola, and Salice Salentino. For the red wines, the main grape varieties are: Malvasia Nera di Brindisi, Sussumaniello, Montepulciano, Sangiovese, Trebbiano Toscano, and Uva di Troia. For the whites: Malvasia del Chianti, Greco di Tufo, and Bianco d'Alessano. Bari and Brandisi are the largest cities and the main ports of Apulia on the Adriatic, leading to Greece and Taranto on the Ionian Sea.

The lesser D.O.C. wines include Rosso Barletta and Squinzano. They derive their names from the towns near which they are made, and are produced in enormous quantity. They are distinctly minor wines.

Aqua vitae

The early name for brandy, from the Latin, meaning "water of life." The Italians claim, however, that the original name was not *aqua vitae* but *aqua vite*, or *acqua di vite*, the Italian for "water of the vine," referring to the colorless fluid which has been distilled from wine. Later, they say, either because of the power of liquor to stimulate and revive, or through a simple mistake in spelling, the more familiar term came into use.

Aquavit (akvavit, akevit)

A spirit, found generally in the Scandinavian countries, distilled from grain or rectified potato spirit and flavored with certain aromatic seeds and spices—caraway seeds in particular. Aquavit is drunk chilled and traditionally accompanies Scandinavian smörgåsbord. The name, a contraction of the Latin *aqua vitae*, meaning "water of life," was coined during the thirteenth century in Italy to designate the first distilled liquor produced from wine.

Today, Sweden is generally considered the world's foremost producer of aquavit, or "snaps," as it is often called in that country. The first license to sell aquavit in Stockholm was granted in 1498. During the next century, the liquor was produced merely by distilling wine, and as the requisite grapes are not grown in Sweden, the wine had to be imported from abroad, which made aquavit so expensive that it was used mainly for medicinal purposes. Not until Swedish soldiers learned to produce the spirit from grain did it become more common. During bad harvest years, however, the authorities had to prohibit all distilling of aquavit, and so the search for substitutes continued. Experiments were made with roots and berries; but in the eighteenth century the potato was found to be so suitable for the purpose that it has been the main source of aquavit ever since.

Most of the potato distilleries in Sweden today are situated in the southern province of Skåne. The clean potatoes are first boiled in steam under pressure, and the resultant starch mass is then mixed with crushed malt (made from barley or mixed grains) to convert the starch into sugar. Yeast culture is added to the mash, and in the ensuing fermentation the sugar is converted into alcohol. The spirit is rectified again (to remove the taste of potato) before it is used as an ingredient in the finished product.

A high-quality aquavit cannot be obtained merely by diluting such alcohol with water, for it would have no flavor. For this reason the diluted spirit is allowed to come into contact with birch charcoal made active through the effect of steam at high temperature. This not only increases the aldehyde content of the alcohol but also forms small quantities of taste elements called esters. A few selected spices are generally accepted as especially suited to flavor aquavit, the most popular of which are caraway seed, aniseed, fennel seed, and bitter orange.

There is a general misconception that aquavit must be strictly an unsweetened spirit. In fact, "aquavit" has been adopted as a general term both for the spiced and sweetened liquor—specifically known in Sweden as aquavit—and for Brännvin, which is usually (but not always) unspiced and unsweetened.

At present there are some twenty aquavit brands in Sweden. The O. P. Anderson Aquavit is a leading export brand made with caraway seed, aniseed, and fennel seed. Another well-known brand is Ödakra Taffel Aquavit, which was brought into the market in 1899: it is lightly spiced and comparatively dry. Överste Brännvin has a stronger spice aroma than O. P. Anderson and contains somewhat more sugar; while Skåne Aquavit very much resembles the O. P. Anderson, although it is less spicy.

Second to Sweden in the production of aquavit is Denmark, where this beverage, usually known as schnapps, is looked on as the national drink—it accounts for 70% of Danish spirit consumption. Schnapps is generally a nonsweetened, colorless beverage.

The Danish Distilleries were founded in 1881, and up to 1914 aquavit could be purchased for about the equivalent of fifteen cents (sevenpence) a bottle. Today there is one distillery only, owned by Danish Distilleries, which since 1923 has enjoyed the sole right of producing alcohol and yeast in Denmark. The Danes sometimes use potatoes and grain. The latter is invariably used for export.

Aalborg Taffel Akvavit, which was first produced in 1846 and is the best-known brand in Denmark and abroad, is seasoned with caraway seeds and contains 43% alcohol by volume. Other brands worthy of mention are Brøndum Kummenaqvavit, a caraway seed aquavit with cinnamon; Aalborg Export Akvavit, which has a slight taste of Madeira; Harald Jensen Taffel Akvavit; and Perikum-Snaps.

Norway produces less of the spirit than either Sweden or Denmark, and its best-known brands are: Lys-

EQUIVALENCE TABLE OF THE DENSITY OF A WINE AND THE WEIGHT OF SUGAR IT CONTAINS

Specific Gravity of Dry Wine at Equal Strength	Sugar to be Added to Achieve Specific Gravity of 1,000 (in grams per liter)	Specific Gravity of the Same Wine after Adding Sugar per liter					
		9g	18g	27g	36g	45g	54g
990	25	994	998	0°1	0°6	1°1	1°6
991	22	995	998	0°3	0°8	1°3	1°8
992	20	996	1,000	0°4	0°9	1°4	1°9
993	17	997	0°2	0°6	1°1	1°6	2°1
994	15	998	0°2	0°7	1°2	1°7	2°2
995	12	999	0°4	0°9	1°4	1°9	2°4
996	10	1,000	0°5	1°0	1°5	2°0	2°5
997	7		0°1	0°6	1°1	1°6	2°1	2°6
998	5		0°2	0°8	1°3	1°8	2°3	2°8
999	2		0°4	0°9	1°4	1°9	2°4	2°9

EQUIVALENCE TABLE FOR BAUMÉ DEGREES, POTENTIAL ALCOHOL DEGREES AND SPECIFIC GRAVITY
(AT A TEMPERATURE OF 59°F. [15°C.])

Baumé Degrees	Alcohol Content Potential Coeff. 17	Corresponding Specific Gravity	Baumé Degrees	Alcohol Content Potential Coeff. 17	Corresponding Specific Gravity
6	5	1043	24	29.5	1199
7	6.2	1051	25	31	1209
8	7.4	1058	26	32.6	1219
9	8.6	1066	27	34.3	1230
10	9.9	1074	28	35.9	1240
11	11.1	1082	29	37.6	1251
12	12.4	1090	30	39.3	1262
13	13.7	1099	31	41.1	1273
14	15	1107	32	42.9	1284
15	16.4	1116	33	44.7	1296
16	17.7	1124	34	46.5	1308
17	19.1	1133	35	48.4	1320
18	20.5	1142	36	50.3	1332
19	22	1151	37	52.3	1344
20	23.4	1160	38	54.2	1357
21	24.9	1170	39	56.3	1370
22	26.4	1179	40	58.5	1383
23	27.9	1189			

EQUIVALENCE TABLE FOR BAUMÉ DEGREES, OECHSLE DEGREES AND SPECIFIC GRAVITIES
(AT TEMPERATURE OF 59°F. [15°C.])

Baumé Degrees	Oechsle Degrees	Corresponding Specific Gravity	Baumé Degrees	Oechsle Degrees	Corresponding Specific Gravity
0	0	1000.0	2.1	14.7	1014.7
0.1	0.7	1000.7	2.2	15.4	1015.4
0.2	1.4	1001.4	2.3	16.1	1016.1
0.3	2.1	1002.1	2.4	16.8	1016.8
0.4	2.8	1002.8	2.5	17.5	1017.5
0.5	3.5	1003.5	3.0	21.2	1021.2
0.6	4.2	1004.2	4.0	28.5	1028.5
0.7	4.9	1004.9	5	35.9	1035.9
0.8	5.6	1005.6	6	43.4	1043.5
0.9	6.3	1006.3	7	51.0	1051.0
1.0	7.0	1007.0	8	58.7	1058.7
1.1	7.7	1007.7	9	66.5	1066.5
1.2	8.4	1008.4	10	74.5	1074.5
1.3	9.1	1009.1	11	82.5	1082.5
1.4	9.8	1009.8	12	90.7	1090.7
1.5	10.5	1010.5	13	99.0	1099.0
1.6	11.2	1011.2	14	107.4	1107.4
1.7	11.9	1011.9	15	116.0	1116.0
1.8	12.6	1012.6	16	124.7	1124.7
1.9	13.3	1013.3	17	133.5	1133.5
2.0	14.0	1014.0	18	142.5	1142.5

holm Aquavit, a light, elegant, and rather delicate type matured in newly empty Sherry casks; Løiten Aquavit, a full-bodied, more robust type; and Linie Aquavit, a rather interesting type, the name of which refers to a "crossing of the Line" (i.e., the equator). This is in keeping with the old tradition that the liquor improves with a sea voyage—and today it is sent to Australia and back on the Wilhelmsen cargo liners.

Aramon

An enormously productive grape variety, giving ordinary wines, and cultivated principally in southern France and in California.

Arbois (Appellation Contrôlée)

White, red, and rosé wines.
District: Southeast France.

The best-known wine district of the Jura. White and red wines are made here, and rosés which are among the better wines in France.
See Jura.

Château d'Arche

Bordeaux white wine.
District and Commune: Sauternes, France.

Located on a hill near the village of Sauternes, this Second-classed Growth in the 1855 Classification makes a well-balanced wine. The property is one of the oldest in the district and is owned by M. Bastit-St. Martin.
Vineyard area: 42 hectares (105 acres).
Average production: 80 *tonneaux* (7,500 cases).

Ardine

Apricot brandy made by the French firm of Bardinet.

Areometer

Device for measuring specific gravity—a form of densimeter *(q.v.)* with arbitrary graduations. There are different versions of the instrument: the Oechsle, for one, and, of particular interest here, the Baumé.

This areometer (French: *mustimètre*) has always been used since the time of Chaptal (*see* Chapter Nine, p. 47) to check the density of the grape must, since luck would have it that the graduation so obtained represents approximately the proportion of alcohol which wine will contain after fermenting—so that 1° Baumé corresponds nearly enough to the density of 17.18 grams of sugar in a liter of water.

The instrument shows 0° in distilled water, 15° in a solution of 15 parts (by weight) sea salt in 85 parts water.
See tables on previous page and above.

Argentina

Argentina, with more than 300,000 hectares (750,000 U.S. acres) of wine-producing vines, makes more wine than any other country in the Western Hemisphere, and ranks fifth in world production after Italy, France, the U.S.S.R., and Spain. An average annual output of 20 million hectoliters (528 million U.S. gallons, 440 million imp.) puts Argentina just ahead of the United States in wine production. Of this huge quantity, only a small amount has reached the world market, owing to several factors. The Argentine is himself a wine-drinking man: the population of 30 million consumes nearly 66 liters (17.4 U.S. gallons, 14.5 imp.) per capita every year—the world's fourth-highest level of consumption. Moreover, the country's traditional wine-making practices have produced a product which, while suited to domestic tastes, has had little appeal for the discriminating export markets. The past ten years, it is true, have seen some notable progress—important technological improvements, a modernization of methods, and the importation of European equipment and yeast cultures, thus enabling the major Argentine producers to compete more aggressively in today's sophisticated world markets. Even so, about 70% of the country's wine is still *vin ordinaire*.

WINE HISTORY

In 1556 a Jesuit priest named Father Cedron planted the first vineyard in the Cuyo region. Five closely related descendants of those original plantings brought to Argentina four hundred years ago survive today as the Criolla grape variety. The Criolla Grande is still a leading producer of indifferent light red, rosé, and whites.

About a century ago, Italian and French immigrants recognized the great vinicultural potential of what was then the unpromising desert of Mendoza, a province that abuts the mile-high mountain boundary with Chile. They used water from the Andes mountains for irrigation, and these Andean waters worked the same miracle in Argentina that had been brought about by irrigation in Algeria and California: a new vineland was born.

VINE-GROWING REGIONS

Mendoza province, about 600 miles (1,000 kilometers) west of Buenos Aires, produces 80% of the wine of Argentina, and 40% of the entire cultivated acreage is devoted to the vine. Wine-making is the only important industry in the region. The total number of vine-growers is about 40,000, but as much as 20% of the

output is produced by nine large firms, each of which maintains its own vineyards, bottling plants, and sales organizations throughout Argentina. Red wines represent 38% of total production, whites 15%, rosés 30%, and table grapes 17%. As might be expected in a new flat wine area under Italian influence, the methods are chiefly the modern ones of mass production. Yet, too, the land and climate encourage a tremendous quantity of reasonable wine.

Mendoza and the neighboring province of San Juan are gigantic flat platters of green vines stretching like an ocean, with islandlike wineries containing some of the highest fermentation vats anywhere in the world. The positive and unsubtle qualities of the wines stem from the mass vinification methods. Wine fermented and matured in lots exceeding 10,000 hectoliters is not uncommon. In such conditions, individual care is impossible. One winery in the town of Mendoza processes a staggering total of one million hectoliters a year. Of course, not all of the two hundred *bodegas* in the town are so huge, but Mendoza is still a virtual honeycomb of cellars and storage sheds. Altogether, 220,000 hectares (550,000 acres) are in vineyard in Mendoza province.

The northern zone of the province contains more than half of this total area. In the eastern section of north Mendoza, Criollas, Malbec, and the incorrectly

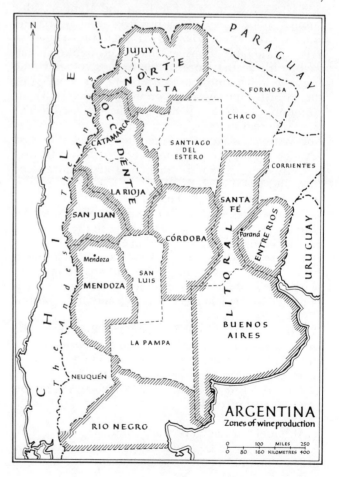

ARGENTINA
Zones of wine production

named Pedro Ximénez varieties are irrigated with water from the Tunuyán and Mendoza rivers and with water from wells. In the saline soils of the northwestern part of the province, the same varieties predominate. The southwestern zone of northern Mendoza makes Argentina's very best wines. There the Malbec is widely planted and produces a better wine than its more famous brother, the Cabernet Sauvignon. The wine is by no means fabulous, but is some of the best Argentina can offer.

The Uco River Valley is the central vineyard zone in Mendoza. Here the Malbec, Tempranilla, and Sémillon are the most important varieties. In the southern sector of the province several stocks yield some quite good wines. These include the Criollas, again the Malbec, Muscatel Rosé, and Chenin, all of which grow on land irrigated with water from the Atuel and Diamante rivers.

Directly north of Mendoza, in San Juan, also lying against the continental spine of the Andes, a heavier, richer wine is made. The vineyard area is about 60,000 hectares (150,000 acres). This is, of course, nearer the equator and the climate is therefore hotter, resulting in the heavier wine. San Juan produces 20% of Argentine wine, mostly in the Zonda, Ullun, and Tulun valleys. The grape varieties are generally the same as those grown in Mendoza. Since irrigation is essential in both San Juan and Mendoza, the familiar slope wines of European vineyards are unknown, and water coursing through the irrigation veins of the table-flat vineyards has brought death as well as life to the vines. While in most other countries the lethal vine louse phylloxera has traveled in the air or been transported on infected vine stalks, in Argentina the parasites may also have been flushed from one region to the next in the ducts of the irrigation system. Conversely, Argentines have in the past (though no longer) used irrigation to fight phylloxera. Attacked areas were flooded or kept underwater for a short period so that the pest was drowned and the vineyards made phylloxera-free.

South of Mendoza, in Rio Negro, about 5% of the country's total output is grown. Here in the Southern Hemisphere the pattern found in European countries is reversed and the lighter wines are found to the south, while pleasant dry white and sparkling white wines are produced in the colder, more rigorous climate. These are often considered some of the best of the country's wines.

Along with Mendoza, San Juan, and Rio Negro, the other important areas of wine-production in the republic of Argentina are Litoral (adjoining the provinces of Buenos Aires and Santa Fe), Córdoba, Occidente (La Rioja and Catamarca), Norte (Salta and Jujuy), and Entre Ríos.

Although virtually every *vinifera* variety of Western Europe is now to be found in Argentina, the varietal grape name has often been absent from the label, as the Argentines have tended to favor proprietary labels for their *vinos finos*. Of late, however, the variety *has* been increasingly cited on the label.

Throughout the country, the Malbec grape produces two-thirds of the premium red wine—often in blends—but the better reds now include Cabernet Sauvignon, Merlot, Pinot Noir, Syrah, Barbera, and Sangiovese. Notably, Syrah is the true Syrah of the Rhône, and Argentine growers make good wine from it. The predominant whites include Chardonnay, Sémillon, Sylvaner, Ugni Blanc, and Chenin Blanc.

Confusion surrounding names and origins of wines and grapes is prevalent, and some liberties are taken with appellations. The Argentine "Riesling," for example, while among the very best of the whites, may actually be made of the Sylvaner. Along with the Chardonnays, it tends to be fairly low in alcohol, at about 11 to 12%, and may more accurately resemble the French Mâcons. The Chenin Blanc (sometimes—wrongly—labeled Pinot Blanc) has a unique taste, quite unlike what one might ordinarily expect from this grape variety. In addition, two distinct varieties of Cabernet Sauvignon exist under the same name: one reminiscent of a Médoc, the other much coarser, and similar to a vin du Midi.

Until recently, white wines were poorly vinified in wood and then kept too long before drinking, so that the wine lost its freshness and tasted of the cask. Many of the reds, too, were aged longer than they should be. With the introduction of modern vinification methods, growers eager to improve their opportunities in the export market are becoming increasingly sophisticated in their techniques, creating improved wines especially for foreign tastes.

It should be noted that the Argentines are very imaginative in creating blends and mixtures. A common and popular example is that of the so-called Rieslings and Chardonnays, resulting in a wine sometimes unbalanced, with no beginning, no middle, and a flat or oxidized finish. One of the country's best-selling reds is made of Barbera, Syrah, and Malbec. Condensed must is exported.

The largest exporter of Argentine wines to the United States is the Mendozan firm of Penaflor, S.A., marketed in the U.S. under the labels "Andean Vineyards" and "Bodegas Trapiche." Lopez and Toso are two other major exporters of quality wines. Lopez is known for their Cabernet, Malbec, and Merlot; Toso, for Cabernet Sauvignon. Other producers offering strong competition include Weiner, San Telmo, and Calvet. Sparkling wines are now being produced by Castel Chandon (Moët et Chandon of France) and Crillon (Seagrams).

Arjan

Another name for koumiss, or fermented sour mare's milk, made by the Tartars.

Arkansas

Small wine-producing region of the United States. The vineyards are centered around the northern sector, in the Ozark Mountains.

See United States: Arkansas.

Armagnac

Brandy.
District: Southwest France.

Armagnac comes from the land of d'Artagnan, a land of vines, geese, and horses; of the bland cream-colored cattle of the Pyrenees and swarthy hot-blooded people, some of them descended from the Goths, Visigoths, and Basques who settled in the wide spaces of Gascony. They say that witches are still to be found in Armagnac, to bring luck to their friends and put curses on their enemies; but here, in the country of Henry IV, there are many good Protestants, their farms marked by cypress trees as a sign of their faith. The landscape is blackened with short, knotty oak and pine; in winter, a cold wind howls down from the Pyrenees, and in summer the rolling plain, veined with streams, is burned brown by a searing sun. Armagnac brandy, matching the extreme climate in which it is nurtured and the determined character of the people who make it, is full-bodied, pungent, and strong. Much of it goes to market in a flat, fat, long-necked flagon, known as a *basquaise* and labeled, usually, Armagnac or Bas-Armagnac. Ténarèze and Haut-Armagnac also are permitted place-names but are seldom seen, since they are the lesser designations of the region. The words *bas* (lower) and *haut* (higher) are used in France simply in the geographical sense and are no indication of quality.

DELIMITATION

In 1909, in order to establish the name and capture a market after the example of Cognac, the region of Armagnac brandy was marked out. It is mostly in the department of Gers, although a little of the best corner juts into Les Landes, south of Bordeaux. The chief centers are Condom, for Ténarèze; Auch, for Haut-Armagnac; and Eauze, in Bas-Armagnac, scene of the Thursday market in Armagnacs, when the narrow streets bulge with men buying and selling the brandy, testing the quality by rubbing a drop between their hands and sniffing it.

About 11,000 hectares (27,500 acres) of vines are cultivated for distilling into Armagnac. Bas-Armagnac, to the west, flattening into the pine forest which extends to the dunes along the Atlantic, gives brandy of the greatest finesse, from mixed clay and sand. This brandy, if it is to carry the choice name of Bas-Armagnac, Ténarèze, or Haut-Armagnac, must not only be 100% of the original appellation but must also have been blended in a separate warehouse, apart from any other types which might be handled by the same shipper. The brandies from the south part of Ténarèze, where the soil is clay and chalk, are lighter and develop more quickly. Haut-Armagnac, to the east, is predominantly chalky—and although it is chalk content which determines the finest Cognacs, here the brandy is of a ruder type and never appears on the market, except as a basis for liqueurs, an important part of the Armagnac business.

VINTAGE

Armagnac age and vintage, though officially regulated, are still a matter of some dispute. The Armagnac producers and the Bureau National d'Armagnac use the same system to date their brandies as is used in Cognac. In late September or October the wine is made and distilled almost immediately; its age is then designated as *compte* 00. On the thirtieth of April, all distillation must stop and all brandy be distilled; the harvest becomes *compte* 0. Every year on April 1, all of the brandies officially gain another year, although in fact they may be a number of months older. The minimum age at which Armagnac may be sold as Armagnac is *compte* 1; for Three-Star or its equivalent, *compte* 2; for V.S.O.P., *compte* 4; and for *Extra* or *Hors d'Age*, at least *compte* 5. Unlike Cognac, Armagnacs are still permitted to indicate specific vintage years and specific vintages (except when imported into the United States). Armagnac labeled as "ten years old" may be a blend of Armagnacs from different years, but the youngest Armagnac may be no younger than ten years old.

Since certain growers consider that vintage brandy is better than a blend (although, as in Port or Champagne, only in certain years), some firms produce an occasional vintage Armagnac, putting the other years into blends. Exceptionally, a producer will deal exclusively in vintage Armagnac. In the *chai* of one such grower, which is connected to his house beneath one long-sloped Basque roof in Bas-Armagnac, barrels of Armagnac are ranged on their scantlings into two tiers, each dated in chalk with the vintage. The proprietor, in sabots, Basque beret peaked forward over his eyes, will tell how the greater number of his customers come in person, from various parts of France and even from abroad, to taste the brandies of the different years and make their choice. A large shipper-grower a few miles away has the only glass-lined storage tanks in Armagnac. This might be thought a sad departure from tradition, an infiltration from the French Midi or Algeria—until the magic 1904, 1891, 1888, and other old vintage Armagnacs are drawn one by one with the little silver spigots and nosed and tasted. After about fifty years, Armagnac will no longer improve in the wood but will begin to go down; when in glass, like every other spirit, it does not change. That is why the Bas-Armagnac shipper-grower has captured his old brandies at their height and put them into glass. Nearly black from age in oak, smoldering with a fresh fire that seems to burn inside velvet, and with such an aroma that the perfume sometimes lingers for over a week in the emptied glass, these vintage Armagnacs are indeed supreme.

To bear a date on the lable an Armagnac need not be from a single year; brandy blended down through the years will sometimes be dated, but in this case the date is required by law to be the year of the youngest brandy included.

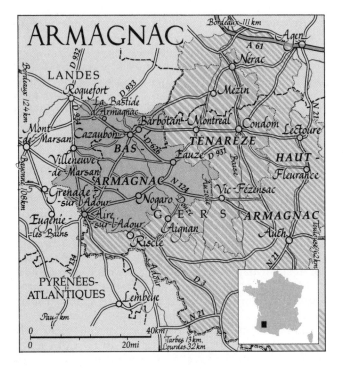

AUTHORIZED VINES

For the white wines of the Gers from which Armagnac is made, Picpoule, Saint-Émilion, Jurançon, and Plant de Grèce (called Baco) are the chief vines. Blanquette, Mauzac, Clairette, and Meslier are also authorized but are seldom seen. Folle Blanche, which used to be the leading variety, is steadily giving way to the Saint-Émilion and other sturdier plants.

In recent years, the hybrid vine Baco 22A, a cross of the Folle Blanche and the American Noah, has been included among the authorized vines, but only in the sandy terrains of Bas-Armagnac. Its merits are hotly debated in Armagnac. A basic rule of French viticulture is that hybrid vines produce grapes inferior in quality, and in every vineyard with a controlled placename for wine they must be rooted out. In the sandy vineyards of Bas-Armagnac, the Baco seems, so far, to produce a wine which can be distilled into a brandy as

fine as that from the Picpoule or Folle Blanche. It is early, however, to judge the ingredients of a product which must mature for forty years to reach its best.

COMPARISON WITH COGNAC

Armagnac differs basically from Cognac in several ways. The best of it comes from a sandy soil, while the fine Cognac is from the area richest in chalk. The climate is different, for in Cognac it is maritime, mellow, and misty; in a more primitive region, Armagnac is closer to its origins than Cognac, not so smoothed out by blending, a natural product to which no sugar need be added.

Many Frenchmen besides the Gascons prefer Armagnac, at its best, to Cognac—but unfortunately, it is not always at its best. Cheap Armagnacs are too prevalent, and some people who are in the habit of buying these are unacquainted with the finer types. In the United States no good was done to the name by false claims to great age; ninety-nine years was a frequent boast until the 1951 law stamped out this practic. Now, an Armagnac label may state (if true) that the brandy is "at least ten years old," but no greater claim can be made.

Different also in Armagnac and Cognac are the methods of ageing and distilling—a difference deliberately emphasized.

In the brandy cooperative at Réans, on the edge of Eauze, new distillations of Bas-Armagnac wine, all from the same still and all 1952, were put into a row of barrels, half of which were of the native oak of Armagnac and half of the Limousin oak in which Cognac is aged. The bung of every barrel was wax-sealed and officially taped. Tasted in 1956, the brandy in the Armagnac oak barrels was good, but the Limousin oak barrels contained something which was neither Armagnac nor Cognac. There was a practical reason for the experiment: Armagnac oak is slowly running out and is consequently soaring in price; yet again it had been proved that Armagnac must be made in Armagnac oak and nothing else.

Distillation of Armagnac in Cognac stills has often been tried. The result is indicated by the fact that since 1936 a law has decreed that Armagnac must be made in the native continuous still. Cognac is double-distilled, the final issue being around 70% alcohol. Armagnac cannot exceed 63% and is usually 10% less. This means more non-alcoholic grape products in the brandy and more native taste. Originally, the Armagnac still resembled the one used in Cognac—but by the nineteenth century the present continuous still was becoming common. Fundamentally, it is a pot still in which the vapors are refined by the wine itself (*see* Chapter 10, p. 55), and it is designed to distill wine of 9% to 10% alcohol—a more highly alcoholic wine is not desirable, as the aim is to pass over as much as possible of the non-alcoholic taste and aroma-giving quality. The result is that Armagnac, retaining many of the original elements of flavor and scent, has an astonishing perfume, even when it is less than a year old and is too fiery to drink. This young brandy is often taken in coffee, to which it gives a heady burst of fragrance. Armagnac is now promoting Floc, an aperitif consisting of sweet, unfermented wine with an Armagnac base.

One hundred fifty or so of the smaller growers share the twenty perambulating stills. This alembic is one of the traditional sights of the countryside: like an ancient black locomotive drawn backward, it moves slowly across the Armagnac landscape. It halts in the night, its mouth gushing fire as the sticks of oak are thrust in. From peasant to peasant it goes—and thus the product of those without an alembic of their own is distilled. Leading firms are studying a new type of alembic which will produce an equally pure *eau-de-vie* while eliminating certain ethers. This will cut short the period of ageing.

Some Armagnac was bad because of the lack of tradition among shippers; and Armagnac is still exported in smaller quantities than Cognac because the growers did not know how to advertise their brandy. These matters have now been taken in hand by some of the better shippers and the more important growers. At the head of these was the late Marquis de Montesquiou, Duc de Fézensac, a parliamentary deputy who worked his estate, the Château de Marsan, as a model farm and experimental station, and who made strenuous efforts to maintain the highest standards of Armagnac and to protect the small peasant grower from the sharp practice of certain shippers who would try to buy their brandy for the lowest price and then sell it at the highest. A visitor to the Château de Marsan would dine off the traditional Gascon dish, Henry IV's favorite, *poule au pot*, followed at the end of dinner by a fine old Armagnac. And in his bedroom, the visitor would find more Armagnac in a small decanter—another tradition in which the host believed.

Because this is the country of the famous companion of the Three Musketeers, most firms have their Réserve d'Artagnan: the one who is entitled to this splendid name is the Marquis de Montesquiou. He is a descendant of the hero, who really lived at the Château de Castelmore, near Lupiac, although his name was not d'Artagnan. The plaque over the gate of the neglected seventeenth-century building bears these words: *Ici naquit vers 1615 d'Artagnan, de son vrai nom Charles de Batz* (Here d'Artagnan was born, about 1615, under his real name, Charles de Batz).

Since 1951, Armagnac has had a brandy fraternity comparable with the wine orders of the Chevaliers du Tastevin in Burgundy and the Commanderie du Bontemps in the Médoc. These fraternities provide a good deal of dressing-up, oath-swearing, and other amusement for the members, and excellent means, also, of attracting attention to the brandy of the region. In Gascony, the Company of the Musketeers dress up in high boots, plumed hats, and magnificent mustaches;

Cardinal Richelieu and the King of France appear, too. The hilltop city of Auch is crowned by a cathedral begun in the fourteenth century and finished by Louis XIV. It contains a choir-seat decorated with hundreds of wooden figures marvelously carved by a pupil of Michelangelo and approached by a fine flight of steps. Up these steps sweep the modern Musketeers; and halfway up stands d'Artagnan, in stone—a surprisingly young and girlish figure, looking out over the land whose character he personifies.

Armillaria root-rot

A fungus disease of the vine.
See Chapter Eight, p. 39.

Aroma

The impression that a young wine makes on the nose—to be distinguished from bouquet. The aroma of a young wine relates directly to the smell of the fresh fruit from which it was made, and not to any esters which have a chance to develop when the wine is older. Aroma is most pronounced in those wines which, rather than being extremely dry, have retained some of the original grape sugar—as is the case with easily identifiable Gewürztraminers.

Arrack (arraki, arack, arak, raki, etc.)

The name derives from the Arabic for "juice" or "sweat" and generally designates "native spirits," so there are probably as many types of arrack as there are of native spirits in the Orient and in Eastern Europe. Arrack has been distilled in the East Indies from fermented palm sap and from rice, from grain spirits in Greece, and from dates in the Middle East and Egypt; and Batavia arrack is a highly aromatic rum distilled in Java. The number and type of herbs and spices which have been used as flavorings are probably as wide as the human imagination. In any case arrack is a coarse drink made for tough palates. A French proverb states that "He who has once tasted arrack never forgets the taste."

Arroba

Spanish wine measure of 11.5 kilograms (25.36 pounds), approximately equal to one basket of grapes. Sixty *arrobas* theoretically give one butt of 516 liters (136.3 U.S. gallons, 113.5 imp.) of wine. The liquid *arroba* equals 16.0 to 16.5 liters (4.23 to 4.36 U.S. gallons, 3.52 to 3.63 imp.).

Artichoke brandy

Spirit distilled in France from the Jerusalem artichoke. In Italy there is an aperitif called Cynar which is made from artichokes.

Artisan (Cru Artisan)

The minor class of Bordeaux growths ranking below a Cru Bourgeois and above a Cru Paysan. These wines are the *vins ordinaires* of Bordeaux, usually blended and not château-bottled, and hardly ever showing a vineyard name. Yet in the present market, more and more of these wines are being bottled and sold under their proprietary labels.

Asali

An East African beverage fermented from honey.

Asciutto

Italian term for dry wine.

Assmannshausen

A good red-wine-growing village in the Rheingau, known especially for its elegant, fine, fruity Spätburgunder (Pinot Noir) wines. The vines flourish on the extremely steep, southern slopes of quartzite and slate. Best site: Höllenberg.
See Rheingau.

Asti

Italian town celebrated for its sparkling white wine, Asti Spumante or Asti D.O.C. (which is sometimes dry, more often sweet, and always bubbly) and, to a lesser extent, for its Moscato d'Asti D.O.C.
See Piedmont.

Astringency

With reference to wine, this means sharpness from acid content and tanning and sometimes indicates that the wine will be long-lived.

Asztali bor

Hungarian term for common wine. *Bor* means wine.

Athol Brose

Scottish drink based on whisky, mixed with honey and/or oatmeal.

Attemperators

Spiral-shaped metal coils which are immersed in fermenting vats, and through which hot or cold water is run to regulate the temperature of the fermenting must or grape juice.

Aubance

See Coteaux de l'Aubance; Anjou.

Aube

French department in the less important southern section of the Champagne region, with about 4,000 hectares (10,000 acres) of vines.
See Champagne.

Aude

Red and some white wines.
District: Southern France.

Quantitatively, one of the three most important wine-producing departments of France; the other two are Hérault and Gard. All three make up the bulk wine area known as the Midi. The Aude vineyards in the Roussillon region, near the Franco-Spanish border, produce very large quantities of undistinguished wines, mostly red; also a very limited quantity of fair white and rosé wines, more particularly those of Limoux, Corbières, and Minervois.

Aurum

A proprietary Italian liqueur, pale gold in color and with an orange flavor.

Auslese

A German term meaning wine made from selected bunches of very ripe grapes. Beerenauslese is the selection of individual grapes from the bunches, Trockenbeerenauslese the selection of overripe individual grapes.
See Germany.

Château Ausone

Bordeaux red wine.
District and Commune: Saint-Émilion, France.

Traditionally first among the wines of Saint-Émilion, Ausone is now sometimes thought to have fallen behind Cheval-Blanc—and is considered by some to be below Figeac, although Ausone still commands fabulous prices. When Saint-Émilion wines were officially classified in 1955, however, Ausone and Cheval-Blanc were placed in their traditional position at the head of the First Great Growths (*Premiers Grands Crus*), the others following alphabetically, although they were not ranked in a class apart.

Ausone is believed by some to stand on the site of the villa of the fourth-century Roman poet Ausonius—and, if what Ausonius wrote is true, the wine was a favorite of Julius Caesar. In any case, the vineyard is magnificently placed on the western edge of the eleventh-century hilltop village of Saint-Émilion; the château looks over its terraced and sloped vines, all facing southeast. Because of its high situation, Ausone escaped the terrible frost of February 1956, in which so many other vineyards, including Cheval-Blanc, were frozen—they not only lost their 1956, 1957, and some later vintages, but were still feeling the effects into the sixties. The Ausone cellar is a deep rocky cave hewn centuries ago out of the soft stone upon which Saint-Émilion stands. The neighboring Château Bel-Air wine (the vineyards adjoin) was, until 1974, aged in the Ausone cave. Both châteaux were owned by the late M. Dubois-Challon, who was the leading figure in the Saint-Émilion wine society—the Jurade. Madame Jean Dubois-Challon, his widow, and the family of Madame Cecile Vauthier, his sister, now own Château Ausone.

Characteristics. Less robust than many of the Saint-Émilions; nevertheless, a full wine of considerable distinction.

Vineyard area: 7 hectares (17.5 acres).

Average production: 30 *tonneaux* (2,500 cases).

Australia

The Australian wine industry became two hundred years old in 1988 and, outside of the United States, it is a country which has seen the greatest amount of change and growth. Wine is made in all the Australian states, even in the Northern Territories. In 1987 over half of Australia's production, which amounted to 350 million liters or the equivalent of 39 million cases of twelve bottles each, came from South Australia, regarded as the wine state of this continent. The popularity of wine has grown to an annual consumption of 21 liters per capita. Vineyard plantings total approximately 65,000 hectares (162,500 acres). Wine regions have multiplied. While climatic conditions in most of the continent are generally too hot, too arid or too wet for successful winegrape viticulture, quite intensive cultivation has expanded across the relatively cooler southernly quarter. Within a boomerang-shaped, 6500-kilometer arc Australia now has over 600 wineries and 7000 vineyards in 33 distinct wine regions, covering more than 80 sub-districts and encompassing a range of microclimates and soil types of proven suitability. More districts are slowly being established.

One of the apocryphal notions of Australian viticulture is that "every year is a good year" and that an evenness of climate results in an evenness of wine quality. Though this does apply, to some extent, to the large irrigated areas of vineyard and to some "dry" areas, there is, in fact, considerable vintage variation in those regions that produce fine wine. Soil conditions vary enormously, too, from rich-black alluvial soil through basalt to mixtures of sand, light loam, and gravel. One small area may have several different soil types as well as different drainage conditions. Various diseases, insects, and fungi have varying effects, dependent on conditions and control. Australia is a vast continent, and new areas are being exploited continually.

With one of the stablest economies in the world, Australia provides her wine industry with a healthy environment. In fact, the demand for high-quality domestic table wine in Australia itself was until recently so strong that only small quantities of her finest wines left the continent. But now production has increased.

WINE HISTORY

The vine in Australia is as old as the settlement itself. When Captain Arthur Phillip set sail from the Thames with his fleet of eleven ships, he included in the cargo "plants for the settlement," among which were the first vines to enter Australia. He landed in Sydney on January 26, 1788, and planted vines on the site where the Botanical Gardens now stand. It was soon found that this location was far from ideal for the propagation of the vine, since the humid conditions on the waterfront encouraged the development of a fungoid disease later identified as anthracnose—more familiarly known as "black spot."

The first man to make any serious attempt to produce wine on a commercial scale was Captain John McArthur, who was given a grant of land some 30 miles from Sydney. This he named Camden Park. Rootlings of all procurable varieties were obtained from the official collection, and afterward a certain number of seedlings were planted with a fair measure of success. Later, Captain McArthur was joined by his two sons—James, born in 1798, and William, born in 1800. The feud between McArthur and Governor Bligh is common knowledge, and it was even carried into the ordinary procedure of wine-making: when, in 1807, McArthur imported two stills for making brandy from some of his wine, Bligh had these confiscated, repacked, and returned to England. At the same time, he had McArthur tried in the criminal court, holding that the stills were illegally imported to produce rum—the currency of the N.S.W. Corps. The McArthur family nevertheless continued to thrive and to play an important part not only in Australian viticulture but in the public affairs of the state.

Another important individual in the early history of Australian wine was Gregory Blaxland, who was the first grower in Australia to export his wine to London. Certainly the quantity involved was not great, being only a quarter-pipe of red wine, but it can be cited as the forerunner of the subsequent very considerable trade in export "burgundy." Five years later, Blaxland exported from the same Parramatta vineyard three half-pipes of wine. He achieved further fame when, with Wentworth and Lawson, he crossed the formidable barrier of the Blue Mountains and explored the fertile plains beyond—a venture which was to mean much to the development of agriculture in New South Wales.

In 1824 a remarkable young man arrived in Sydney. His name was James Busby and he was then twenty-four years old. While still in Scotland, with only the viticultural background of a few months spent in the best wine districts of France, he was imbued with the belief that there was a great future for the vine in

Australia. Shortly after his arrival he wrote his first book, *A Treatise on the Cultivation of the Vine and the Art of Making Wine*. On May 8, 1824, a grant of 2,000 acres of land in the Hunter River district was made to him. He named it Kirkton, afterward well known for its wine.

At this time Busby arranged with McArthur, Blaxland, and others who had established vineyards, for their surplus cuttings to be distributed among intending planters. Busby's crowning work, however, was his voyage of viticultural research into southern European wine regions and the introduction into Australia of his great vine collection, which included nearly all the best varieties grown in France and southern Spain at that time. The vines reached Sydney in good condition, and Busby offered them to the government for the formation of an experimental nursery there, "to prove their different qualities and propagate, for general distribution, those which may appear most suitable to the climate." The vines were planted in the Botanical Gardens, and of 678 varieties, 362 were successfully struck. This collection has been the basis of the vine population of Australian vineyards since 1833.

Right up until 1925, nearly all the wine exported from Australia was of the export burgundy-type. In 1854, consignments were only of a token nature, and it was not until 1872, when the firm of P.B. Burgoyne & Company started operations, that the wine trade showed any important development. It grew, was maintained at around 900,000 U.S. gallons (750,000 imp.), and was distributed throughout the United Kingdom by such firms as Burgoyne's, with Harvest and Tintara; as Gilbey's, with Rubicon; as Stephen Smith, with Keystone; and Pownall's with Emu. Then, at the end of the First World War, it became the responsibility of the Bruce-Page government to absorb the returning soldiers into sound occupations. At that time, as established growers on the Murray were gathering crops of Gordo Blanco grapes at the rate of about 10 tons (11 short tons) to the acre, at A£12 per ton, grape-growing appeared to be the ideal occupation for the repatriated men. Despite warnings from the industry itself that only limited settlement was possible, the government went ahead with the greatest vigor, so that when the vines bore fruit, there was an inevitable glut of grapes, accompanied by an economic crisis of the worst kind. The government was impotent to solve this problem, which was flung back upon the industry itself. The federal Viticultural Council advised that the only possible remedy was to establish new markets by the granting of an export bounty, which would have the effect of creating a demand for fortifying spirit in this new market, and thus absorb the glut of Doradillo grapes—which were the distilling variety. Having no better plan, the government announced a bounty of 2s. 9d. a gallon and gave a drawback of excise on the fortifying spirit used, which was considered equivalent to 1s. 3d. a gallon, making a total remission of 4s. a gallon on all the sweet

wine exported. Within a few years these measures had proved successful. The export of fortified wine sustained a great impetus, and in 1927 the total export of wines rose to 4,553,000 U.S. gallons (3,773,000 imp.).

Australia, with its innovative dedication to making fine wines, is forced to consume most of its production and only approximately 5% is likely to be exported. The major exporters are Thomas Hardy and Sons/ Emu, Lindemans, Orlando, Penfolds/Kaiser, Stuhl/ Wynns, Consolidated Cooperative Wineries (Berri/ Renmano), Mlldara/Hamilton, McWilliams, Seppelts and S. Smith and Son (Yalumba/Hill Smith Estate).

Improvements are visible everywhere in the vineyards and wines. Production has increased by more than nine times since 1936. Australia is now a major table wine producer, no longer just specializing in great quantities of bulk fortified wines and bulk reds for the British trade.

In spite of this increased activity, it is most unlikely that the amount of wine exported will ever again seriously contend, in volume terms, with the amount of wine consumed locally. Until the sixties there was little table wine consumed by the general public. Then dry reds became popular, followed by a boom in white wine sales during the seventies. The most dramatic increases in wine consumption at this time took place in sales in containers other than bottles (*i.e.*, in flagons, in bulk and in "bag-in-box" containers). By the mid-1980s over 60% of all sales were in other than bottle form, with "bag-in-box" sales alone being over 50% of the total. These container wines are generally sound and, of "vins ordinaires" intended for local consumption, rank among the best in the world.

WINE REGIONS

New South Wales

As the oldest state in the Commonwealth, New South Wales was also the earliest wine producer. The major wine districts are the Hunter Valley (north of Sydney), the Murrumbidgee Irrigation Area (M.I.A.), centered around Griffith-Leeton (the nation's second-largest wine district, producing alone about 18 per cent of Australia's wine), Mudgee, and Forbes and Cowra.

The Hunter Valley remains one of the most famous wine districts of them all. Much of the fine white wine produced by its forty wineries is made or blended from the Sémillon grape. Among the leading and older-established firms are: Tyrrell's, Lindeman, McWilliams, Tulloch, Drayton and the Wyndham Estate. Tyrrell's pioneered the use of Chardonnay in the district, leading to another boom, with all sorts of styles emanating from the variety. The Chardonnays are often matured in small new wood from France and the United States, as local woods are unsuitable. Re-

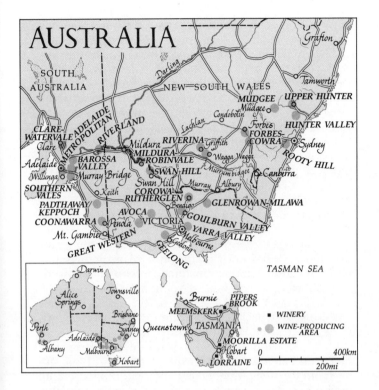

ial conditions there attracted a number of settlers to the cultivation of the vine, so that by 1900 there were over 1,200 separate vineyards, in almost every part of the state. Victoria was by far the biggest wine-producer at that time, with 1889–90 production as follows:

	Hectoliters	U.S. Gallons	Imp. Gallons
South Australia	23,231	613,294	510,674
New South Wales	31,329	827,076	688,685
Victoria	71,811	1,895,808	1,578,590

Unfortunately for Victoria, the dread scourge of phylloxera began to appear, first in Geelong, then in Bendigo, and later in the vineyards of the northeast, with the ultimate result that the main areas devoted to viticulture were devastated. In many cases, the costly process of reconstitution with phylloxera-resistant vines from America proved too frightening and the land concerned was turned to more stable forms of agriculture. By the mid-fifties, production was limited to the irrigated areas of Mildura and Swan Hill, plus pockets of fine wine from Great Western near Ararat, Chateau Tahbilk in Central Victoria, and the North Eastern districts (including Rutherglen, Wangaratta, Glenrowan, and Milawa), known for the justly celebrated Muscats and Tokays (actually from the Muscadelle grape variety), which are matured in wood for up to 30 to 50 years. In addition, some hearty dry reds are made in these districts. At Milawa, which has a cooler microclimate, the Brown Brothers produce a stunning range of dry white and red varietals, as well as some interesting late-picked sweet wines.

Since the much-proclaimed "rebirth" of its wine industry began in the mid-1960s, Victoria, partly forgotten for over a hundred years, is now very much in the foreground. It has more than 120 wineries in the following 11 recognised regions: Mildura-Robinvale (Sunraysia), which in size ranks third in Australia, producing about 10 per cent of the national output; Rutherglen, Milawa-Glenrowan-King Valley; Great Western; Murray Valley; Goulburn Valley; Bendigo-Central Highlands; the Victorian Pyrenees; Yarra Valley; Geelong; and Mornington Peninsula.

Of the many small and acclaimed new makers, leaders are Balgownie, the French-operated Taltarni, Tisdall, Yellowglen, Idyll, Le Amon, Redbank, Château Yarrinya, Lilydale and St Huberts. Old champions and larger makers with reputations include Brown Brothers, Château Tahbilk, Morris of Rutherglen, Baileys of Glenrowan, Bullers, Best's, Stanton and Killeen, Campbells, All Saints, Mildara, Mitchelton and Château Remy, operated by Remy of France. Another French company, Moët, has made a substantial investment in a new, sole-owned vineyard operation in Central Victoria. Some wonderful wines have come from all of them, mostly Cabernet Sauvignon, Pinot Noir, Chardonnay, Sauvignon Blanc, and Riesling, but also Marsanne and Shiraz. These find a ready market in

cently new, mostly small, family-operated wineries have opened, their production fair to good in quality. Some of the wine varietals which have achieved world recognition were Sémillon and Chardonnay. Quality performers among the newcomers include Allandale, Lake's Folly, Robson, Brokenwood, Peterson's, Terrace Yale, Rothbury Estate, Sutherlands, Rosemount, Hunter Estate, Saxonvale, Hungerford Hill and Arrowfield, the last five being enterprises of substantial size.

The Shiraz, (also called Hermitage), Cabernet Sauvignon, and lately Pinot Noir have been successfully grown.

The huge, irrigated vineyards of Griffith-Leeton, way in the interior of the M.I.A., are the bulk-wine-producing areas supplying much of the "bag-in-box" wines, some of them making sparkling wines as well as "ports," "sherries," muscats, and vermouths. There are twenty-one wineries. The bigger ones are McWilliam's, Orlando, De Bortoli, San Bernadino and the smaller Lillypilly Estate, Scenic Hill and The College.

The Mudgee district is still a new and developing wine region and its relatively cooler high altitude has attracted sixteen interesting wineries. The largest is the Italian-owned Montrose Company. Some of the best wines have come from Huntington Estate, Botobolar, and Miramar.

Victoria

The first record of a vineyard in Victoria was that planted at Yering in Lilydale in 1838.

Although vine culture in Victoria started later than in New South Wales and South Australia, the congen-

Victoria and are not often exported, even to other Australian states. However, among them are some of the most exciting new wine styles in Australia today. The boom of the mid-sixties attracted all sorts of non-wine professionals—doctors, dentists, pharmacists and lawyers. Many have since disappeared from the scene, but some fine wines from the above wineries have resulted: Cabernet Sauvignon, Pinot Noir, Chardonnay, Sauvignon Blanc, and Riesling.

Victoria has a promising future as a maker of good commercial wines in limited production, and of high-quality "boutique" wines for which there will always be an enthusiastic demand despite the higher prices.

South Australia

The Murray River's irrigated Riverland region is by far the most prolific in Australia, producing about 40 per cent of the nation's wine. Much of it comes from large cooperatives owned by local grape-growers in the Renmark, Berri, Loxton and Waikerie districts. The three largest winery operations are the family-connected Angove's, the giant Berri-Renmano amalgamation trading as Consolidated Cooperative Wineries Ltd, and Loxton Cooperative Ltd.

The reality today is that most wine consumed by most Australians is the skillfully made product of irrigation areas. Many of the well-regarded and biggest-selling table wines marketed by national producers are based extensively, if not exclusively, on wines from hot, irrigated vineyards. For instance, recently, some remarkable Chardonnay has been produced. The Riverland's 15 wineries, most of them large by Australian standards, can today produce a wider spectrum of wine styles at extremely competitive prices.

The "dry" vineyard areas of the state, however, produce most of the fine table wines. These range from Clare, over one hundred kilometers to the north of Adelaide, to Coonawarra, four hundred kilometers to the south of it. The most famous of them is the Barossa Valley, settled by Germans in the middle of the last century. The Germanic influence is still very strong, with a local dialect, Barossa Valley Deutsch, still in existence among the older people and signs abounding in old German lettering at every turn. Barossa, north-east of Adelaide, is the most concentrated vineyard area in Australia, claiming 35 wineries. The great and small wineries, several of them picturesque (particularly Yalumba and Seppeltsfield, dynastic seats of generations of the Hill Smith and Seppelt families) are the centerpieces of what has become one of Australia's principal tourism districts. Among other drawcard names are those of Wolf Blass, Penfold, Kaiser Stuhl, Orlando, Henschke, Krondorf, Masterson Barossa and Tollana who have had very satisfactory results with Cabernet Sauvignon, Shiraz, or blends of the two.

The best dry whites come from the Riesling variety, notably from fruit from the higher hill ranges, and here Orlando, Burings, and Yalumba dominate, the latter with grapes from their Pewsey Vale and Heggies developments.

The Adelaide metropolitan district, which until recent years boasted some famous vineyards virtually within sight of the city's downtown business area, is now all but defunct as a wine producer in its own right. Driven out by the relentless rise in suburban land values, vineyards have spread back into the Adelaide Hills—where a small number of noteworthy wineries (among them Petaluma, in which Bollinger of France has a 20 per cent partnership), have taken advantage of the cooler elevated conditions to produce wine of high quality—and out on to the Adelaide Plains. The plains are hot and dry, but winemakers there have developed vineyard techniques and winery skills which have gone a long way toward overcoming those problems. Best-known of the new plainsmen is Joe Grilli of Primo Estate, a small maker who in a remarkably short time has built a reputation for wines of unusual quality and character—particularly a Beerenauslese style from Riesling grapes which have undergone induced botrytisation after picking.

Only 45 minutes from Adelaide's centre, the McLaren Yale district opens spectacularly with the superb old Reynella winery complex, restored to perfection soon after Thomas Hardy and Sons bought the handsome but run-down estate in 1982 and moved corporate headquarters there—a $9 million (Australian) exercise which saw the family owned firm at last return to it founder's winemaking origins of the 1840s. McLaren Vale's 50 wineries are mostly small and located in attractive, rolling hill country where vineyards are bordered by groves of flowering almond trees. The quite warm climate is favourably modified by sea breezes off the neighbouring Gulf of St Vincent, but the district achieves quite high yields while latterly making considerable advances in quality. Previously known almost exclusively for its excellent vintage port wines and powerful reds made for the British trade and for blending, the district is earning attention as a producer of elegant, flavorsome red and white varietals. Among the old established producers and extremely promising newcomers are Hardy's, including the firm's Raynella and Tintara operations, Seaview, Pirramimma, Wirra Wirra, Woodstock, Hazelmere, Kay Brothers, d'Arenberg and Coriole. Unhappily, the sturdy independents of McLaren Yale have yet to resolve the newest and perhaps most threatening problem that confronts them: Adelaide's urban sprawl is steadily approaching the vineyards, and must inevitably begin to encroach unless action is taken to preserve the district's precincts for the future.

The most celebrated of South Australia's premium wine districts (some would argue the most celebrated anywhere in the nation) is Coonawarra, a small area which has the unchallenged distinction of being Australia's only wine district which can be exactly defined in area. It occupies the whole of a meandering, closely charted "terra rossa" belt—an island of rich, red loam about 14.4 kilometers long and varying from only 200 meters to 1.5 kilometers wide. Underlying its lime-stone base is an unusually high water table, a combination providing excellent natural irrigation and drainage. Coonawarra's reputation has in no way diminished since it lost the mantle of Australia's coolest and latest vintage to the more recently developed vineyards of Victoria's Geelong, Western Australia's Mount Barker-Frankland and the island state of Tasmania. Cabernet Sauvignon is the main variety and reds from it have some similarity, at their best, to those of Bordeaux, possessing great finesse and breeding. Latterly, after a new developmental period in the 1970s, during which Coonawarra was classed by some as a disappointing area for quality white varieties, the district has furthered its standing by producing some very good white wines indeed, particularly Riesling and Sauvignon Blanc. Plantings of Chardonnay, which have come into production more recently, are considered to be showing even greater promise.

Many of Australia's top wine producers own vineyards in Coonawarra or take Coonawarra grapes. Established in the district are the big companies of Lindemans, Wynns, Mildara and Penfolds; among the locally based makers well-known in their own right are the relatively small Redman, Leconfield, Kidman, Brand's Laira and Hollick, all with solid records and devotees. Companies which have missed out on Coonawarra land, or have been unable to acquire more, are successfully developing the neighbouring districts of Keppoch and Padthaway, which share the natural advantages of cooler summers and good water and drainage. Thomas Hardy and Sons is among those producing fine wines from vineyards there.

The Clare Valley/Watervale wine district is perhaps more typically "Australian" in appearance than any other, and may also lay claim to being the most picturesque. Hot and dry, with a still and timeless air about its burnished slate country, it is a place of many surprising wines and engaging eccentrics. Some of South Australia's oldest vineyards are located here, among them the Sevenhill estate which has been operated since 1848 by the Brothers of the Jesuit College of St Aloysius, and which is a major supplier of sacramental wines to countries throughout the Pacific basin. Sited on low, rolling limestone hills, the vineyards are generally unirrigated and characteristically produce wines which are big and long-lived. Most of the district's 16 wineries are smaller, notable exceptions being those of the Stanley Wine Company, Quelltaler (owned by

Remy of France) and Taylor's Château Clare, all of which produce particularly aromatic, flowery, dry white wines from the extensively grown Riesling.

Western Australia

Wine production of this state was centered on the Swan Valley, outside Perth, with Houghtons and Sandalford being the two main producers. Though these companies are still important, it is felt that the future of quality wine in Western Australia will depend on cooler areas of the state. The Swan Valley produces fortified wines, large, soft reds and huge-flavored soft whites, but those from the Margaret and Frankland River areas in the Southwest and from Mount Barker, farther south, are the ones that provide the awakened interest today. Small wineries, owned often by professionals from other than the wine trades, continue to proliferate, and wines from Evans and Tate, Leeuwin, Cape Mentelle, Moss Wood, Vasse Felix, Cullens, Plantagenet, and many others, are worthy of investigation in this, one of the "new" wine areas of the world.

Tasmania

The island of Tasmania and some of its cool areas have attracted some quality producers: Mo Estate, Heemskerk, Marion's and the new joint venture of Louis Roederer of France with Pipers Brook.

Queensland

The Stanthorpe "Granite Belt" area, cooler than the rest of the state, provides hope of future wine quality, and a few Queenslanders are pursuing it.

Austria

The spectacular western provinces, like Vorarlberg, produce little wine and all of it is consumed locally. The 58,000 hectares (145,000 acres) planted in vine lie mainly, in order of size, in Lower Austria, Burgenland, Styria, and in the neighborhood of Vienna. The vineyards, where over 42,000 growers have been making wines for generations, are mostly cut up into parcels of less than 20 hectares (50 acres), and the annual production of wine averages nearly 3 million hectoliters (79.5 million U.S. gallons, 66 million imp.)—83% white and 17% red. Most of the harvest is stored by the growers in their own vaults, but in abundant years some of it is taken over by the wine trade and the growers' associations. They combine voluntarily in these cooperatives, surrendering their crops for storage and sale on a trust basis. The societies have a reputation for good-quality wines. Consumption of wine per capita is about 36 liters, a relatively small average for a European country—although this is more than Austria produces, so much of the wine (most of it red) is imported from Spain, Italy, France,

PRODUCTION FIGURES FOR A TYPICAL YEAR

	Hectoliters	U.S. Gallons	Imp. Gallons
South Australia	2,000,000	53,000,000	44,000,000
New South Wales	700,000	19,550,000	15,400,000
Victoria	350,000	9,775,000	7,700,000
West Australia	50,000	1,325,000	1,100,000
Queensland	1,500	39,750	33,000
	3,101,500	83,689,750	68,233,000

and increasingly from Hungary, Yugoslavia, and the Balkan states. The annual importations are now around 250,000 hectoliters (6,600,000 U.S. gallons, 5,500,000 imp.)

Until a few years ago, the demand for wine meant that most of the native harvest was consumed at home. The situation has now changed and Austrian wines are seen abroad—from Schluck, perhaps made from Grüner Veltliner grapes, to luscious Spätlese and estate-bottled Auslese. The annual total is about 420,-000 hectoliters (11 million U.S. gallons, 9 million imp.). Historically, the principal buyer has been Germany, but sales in other markets, particularly in Great Britain, are steadily increasing. A wine institute, established in 1968, has begun to regulate the export industry.

In 1985, very strict wine laws were passed in order to remedy embarrassing, previous frauds. The labels carry either the name of the village or district of origin—or, less often, of the individual vineyard; or they may state the name of the grape variety, as in Alsace. Occasionally, both will be found. (For example, Wachauer 1984—i.e., wine of the 1984 vintage from the important Wachau region of Lower Austria; Grüner Veltliner 1984—i.e., wine of the 1984 vintage of the Grüner Veltliner grape; Steiner Veltliner 1984—i.e., wine of the 1984 vintage from Stein in the Wachau region and from the Grüner Veltliner grape.) Schluck is a light dry wine that asks to be swallowed. Among the better bottles, Riesling and Traminer will be found, and also some Spätlese wine from late-picked grapes; and ice-wines, such as the Nicholas wine from Krems. Among important place-names are Krems, Klosterneuburg, Gumpoldskirchen, Retz, Vöslau, Nussdorf, Grinzing, Oggau, and Rust—they will usually appear with the possessive.

WINE HISTORY

In A.D. 955 Otto I ordained the replanting of the Austrian vineyards for the first time since the departure of the Romans. The vines were to be tended principally by monks, in the monasteries of Bavaria and Salzburg.

All producers were allowed to sell their own wine (*Eigenbauwein*) free of tax. This law still causes trouble at the *Heurigen*, the popular Viennese wine-gardens.

When a grower wished to announce that stocks of his new wine were on sale, he hung up branches outside his house. The German verb "to hang out" is *aushängen*; hence, the name of these wines became *Hengelweine*.

No writing about Austrian viticulture is complete without some mention of Dr. Lenz-Moser. The importance of his work on *vinifera* hybrids and, above all, the revolutionary "high culture" method of growing vines that bears his name, are now recognized in all wine-

growing countries. More than 90% of vines in Austria are grown on the Lenz-Moser system.

WINE REGIONS

Lower Austria

This eastern province, with over 34,000 hectares (85,000 acres) of vineyard, watered by the Danube, is the granary of Austria—a country of cornfields, market gardens, and vines; a country, also, of churches, baroque monasteries, and romantic castles. It is the only district in Europe which actually produces oil in a vineyard region. The wine-producing regions are Wachau, Kamptal-Donauland, Donauland-Carnuntum, Weinviertel and, south of Vienna, the Thermenregion. The principal varieties for white wines are Grüner Veltliner (a native vine that accounts for 44% of all Austrian production), Müller-Thurgau, Wälschriesling, Neuberger (another native vine), Rheinriesling, and Zierfander (Spätrot), which with Rotgipfler makes one of Austria's best-known wines—Gumpoldskirchner. The Muskat-Ottonel and the Pinot Blanc (called either Weisser Burgunder or Klevner) are also fairly important. For the very small production of red wines, the most common are Blau Portugieser and Blaufränkisch.

The Danube section begins west of Willendorf with the Wachau, a lovely stretch of country between there and Krems-Stein, where the vines climb up steep terraces of gneiss and mica schist. At Stein, the district of Krems begins. This belongs to the Wachau with its loess terraces, but the center is Krems itself, a historic wine town with big vaults for bulk storage, a school of viniculture, and a fascinating wine museum. Last harvesting in Strass bei Krems has been completed as late as December 10. In addition to those places already mentioned, Spitz, Dürnstein (lying picturesquely at the foot of a ruined castle), Weissenkirchen, and Loiben are worth noting. In the Kamptal-Donauland and the Wachau districts, the Riesling produces increasingly popular wines with a fine bouquet.

On the right bank of the Danube, the vineyards follow the river from Oberarmsdorf to Traismauer. The Kamp Valley, on the left bank of the Danube, is an important wine-growing area in which the most important place is Langenlois. East of the Kamp Valley is the district known as Am Wagram, its vines planted along a terraced ridge of hills very like those at Krems. Downstream, on the right bank of the river, the valley widens into the fertile Tullnerfeld until, at Greifenstein, the mountains close in again, and the vines climb their slopes. Close to Vienna lies Klosterneuburg, a town which is celebrated for fine wines. It contains an experimental school of viticulture, a wine museum, and the enormous vault of the Chorherrenstift, three stories deep.

The principal place-names besides those cited above are Zöbing (distinguished for its excellent Riesling), Strass, and Schönberg; and, in the Klosterneuburg area, Kahlenberg.

Northward, on the left bank of the Danube, good wines grow on the slopes of the Bisamberg. Below Vienna, on the right bank, is the Hainburg and Bruck district.

The *Weinviertel* lies north of the Danube and consists of the countryside around Retz and south to the Eggenburg, Hollabrunn, and Ravelsbach districts. It includes also the "Brünnerstrasse" district, on both sides of the old main road between Vienna and Brünn, which is one of the most productive areas in the country. Light palatable wines come from this fertile country, although in the southwest the Veltliner produces spiced and fruity growths, and Matzen has some good red wines.

The principal place-names in the Weinviertel are Retz, Pulkau, Haugsdorf, and Mailberg; Eggenburg, Hollabrunn, and Ravelsbach; Poysdorf, Zistersdorf ("Steinberg"), Matzen, Wolkersdorf, and Falkenstein.

The Thermenregion district. Some excellent vineyards are planted on the hill slopes of the Vienna Woods. Gumpoldskirchen, at the foot of the Annigen Mountain, is the best-known wine town. From Baden and Traiskirchen come fiery, spicy wines; and in Vöslau a red wine (Vöslauer Rotwein) is made mostly from the Blauer Portugieser.

Burgenland

Until 1919, this southeastern province was part of Hungary, and even now some of the villages are entirely Magyar or Croat. The landscape here is different too; its dominant feature, set in the midst of *Puszta*, a kind of steppe, is the Neusiedlersee, a great lake rimmed with reeds—and exotic birds nesting on its marshy shores. The country, rich in orchards and vegetable gardens, also bears vines—nearly 21,000 hectares (52,500 acres) in four different areas, the Neusiedlersee, Neusiedlersee-Hügelland and Mattersburg districts, and South Burgenland.

Here the main varieties are Muscat-Ottonel, Pinot Blanc, Wälschriesling, Neuberger, Grüner Veltliner, Traminer, Bouvier (a native vine), Riesling and Muller-Thurgau—all for white wines. Blaufränkisch (Gamay) and Blauburgunder (Pinot Noir) go into the red wines.

The lake district is the most important for wine, with vineyards bordering the Neusiedlersee on three sides. The vines are protected by the Leitha Mountains, and the glassy surface of the vast lake retains and reflects the warmth of the sun's rays. Excellent white wines are made here from Welschriesling and Muscat-Ottonel, and some pleasant red ones from Blaufränkisch. At the end of a good summer there will be some fine Ruster Ausbruch from late-picked grapes, notably the Furmint. On the sandy soil of the Seewinkel the origi-

nal vines escaped the phylloxera plague, and this is one of the very few places in Europe where wine is still made from ungrafted vines. The principal place-names are Oggau, Mörbisch, St. Margarethen, and Rust.

The Eisenstadt district. The great center is Gols. Close to the lake, vines planted in sandy soil, immune from phylloxera, produce Sandweine. The principal place-names are Gross-Höflein, Klein-Höflein, St. Georgen, Podersdorf, Illmitz, and Apetlon.

The Mattersburg district. South of Eisenstadt, in the foothills of the Rosalien Mountains, the vineyards produce mainly red wines—one of them Blaufränkisch. The principal place-names are Pöttelsdorf, Trausdorf, Neckenmarkt, Deutsch-Kreutz, and Lutzmannsburg.

South Burgenland. The wine-growing districts here center around Eisenberg and Rechnitz, where pleasant soft red wines are made from Blaufränkisch and Blau Portugieser.

Styria

Lying between the lovely lakes of the Salzkammergut (where St. Wolfgand and the White Horse Inn are to be found) and Yugoslavia, Styria is the green province, a country of meadows and woodlands, of fat cattle and plodding cart-horses, of rolling hills and rivers well stocked with fish. Its capital, Graz, is the second-largest town in Austria. Once it was the peaceful resort of retired officers; now it is a busy industrial city. The *Steirergewand*—the gray loden suit with green facings—worn all over Austria, originated in Styria (Steiermark in German), where it is the national dress. The province has about 2,000 hectares (5,000 acres) of vineyard scattered over three districts: Süd-Oststeiermark (Southern Styria), Weststeiermark (Western Styria), and Klöch-Oststeiermark (Klöch-Eastern Styria).

For white wines the important grape varieties are Wälschriesling, Ruländer (Pinot Gris), Pinot Blanc, Traminer, Muscat-Sylvaner hybrids, and Rheinriesling. Blauer Wildbacher (a native vine) goes into the West Styrian Schilcherwein; for the small red wine, the varieties are Blau Portugieser, Blaufränkisch and St. Laurent.

Western Styria. The wines of Weststeiermark are divided into two subdistricts: Schilcher and Sausal-Leibnitz. The Schilcher wines extend from Graz to Eibiswald on the southern frontier. In Stainz, a light red wine is made, and in Deutschlandsberg, a dark red one—fresh, spicy, digestible: this is the Schilcherwein. Other names to remember are Hitzendorf and Ligist.

The Sausal-Leibnitz district is a stretch of country lying east of the Schilcher district between two streams, the Lassnitz and the Sulm, the latter the home of the world's finest capons. Its highest point is Demmerkogel, where the vineyards are planted at nearly 1,920 feet (600 meters).

Southern Styria. Southern Styria's wine district is cen-

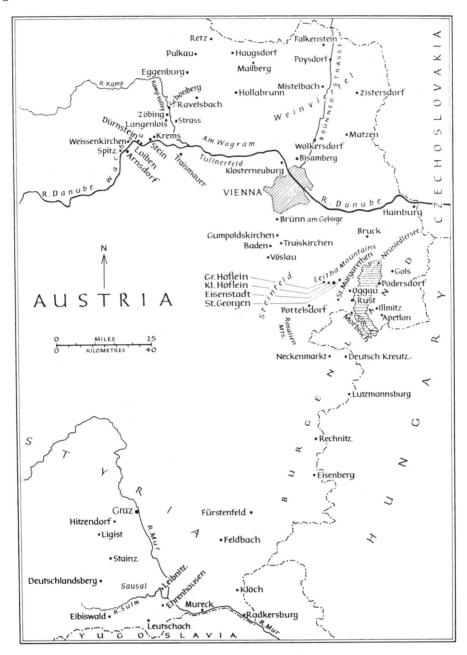

tered on the towns of Leutschach and Ehrenhausen. Extending to the northern slopes of the Windische Bühel, this is similar in soil and grape varieties (Wälschriesling, Sylvaner, Weissburgunder, and Traminer) to the Sausal-Leibnitz vineyards, but the wines are stronger and fuller.

Southeastern Styria. The vineyards of Süd-Oststeiermark border Yugoslavia and are concentrated around the town of Klöch. These wines are of good quality, some of them sparkling, with a charming bouquet. They are particularly agreeable when young. The principal place-names are Radkersburg and Mureck.

The rest of eastern Styria is not greatly cultivated in vines. Wines are made, however, and the vineyards struggle up the slopes of hills as high as 2,000 feet (615 meters). The best-known places are Hartberg, Fürstenfeld, and Feldbach.

Vienna

The beautiful city is almost encircled by trees and meadows—the Vienna Woods, on the slopes of which the vines grow—nearly 700 hectares (1,750 acres) of them. From two of the hills, Kahlenberg and Leopoldsberg, the Turks were driven back from Western Europe—but their Oriental languor is said to persist in the leisurely café life. The wine villages of Grinzing, Sievering, and Nussdorf are now within the suburbs, and the stinging new *heurige* wine served in their wine-garden is, for the tourists who flock there, the essence of Viennese gaiety. Outside the little vine-covered houses, green boughs are hung out when the wine of the year is ready. Some may actually come from the proprietor's vine plot, but he will need more than he is likely to make to satisfy all the customers who come to the long wooden tables in his garden and sing to the music of zithers and guitars. There is a law permitting them only to sell wine which has been produced in their own vineyards, and to sell wine from other vineyards they must get a special permit.

Prevailing grape varieties: Grüner Veltliner, Neuburger, and some native vines.

Auxerrois

Grape grown in the Lorraine district for the light pink *vin gris*.

Auxey–Duresses and Auxey-Duresses-Côte de Beaune (Appellation Contrôlée)

Burgundy red and white wines.
District: Côte de Beaune, France.

Auxey is one of the poor relations of the Côte de Beaune. Its wines are about 80% red and, while they are considered sound enough in body, fragrance, and color, they are rarely, if ever, distinguished otherwise. Yet, because of the difference in price between these and others from the famous slope, they are often good value.

The vineyards are set back in the hills, slightly too high to be first-rate. They cover about 170 hectares (420 acres) and wines from grapes grown in about 100 hectares (250 acres) within this area may add the term Côte de Beaune to the commune name. Such wines may occasionally be slightly superior to the communal ones. In an average year Auxey produces 1,100 hectoliters (29,150 U.S. gallons, 24,200 imp.) of white and 3,200 hectoliters (84,800 U.S. gallons, 70,400 imp.) of red. Wines from the best vineyards may add vineyard name to commune name, and although the final list of these First Growths (*Premiers Crus*) has not yet been drawn up, the following vineyards are considered the best.

FIRST GROWTHS (*Premiers Crus*)

Vineyard	Acres	Hectares
Les Duresses	26.6	10.6
Les Bas-des-Duresses	5.9	2.39
Reugne	7.8	3.16
Les Grands-Champs	12.0	4.86
Climat-du-Val (or Clos du Val)	23.0	9.31
Les Écusseaux	15.9	6.43
Les Bretterins	5.0	2.02

Avelsbach

German commune in the triangle between the Mosel and Ruwer. The wines are classed sometimes with one group, sometimes with another. The best-known vineyards are: Altenberg, Dom Avelsbach, and Dom Herrenberg.

See Mosel-Saar-Ruwer.

Avize

Village in Champagne which produces one of the finest wines of the Côte des Blancs.

See Champagne.

Ay

Town in the Marne Valley near Épernay, whose cellars lie underneath the fine Champagne red-wine vineyards of that region.

See Champagne.

B

Bacardi

A well-known brand of Cuban rum, now produced in Puerto Rico, Brazil, Mexico, and the Bahamas. Also a cocktail based on the rum.

See Rum, Puerto Rican.

Bacchus

(1) From the Greek *Bacchos*—an alternative name for their wine god, better known as Dionysos. The Romans adopted him as Bacchus, identifying him with their own wine deity, Liber.

(2) An American hybrid grape, small and black, which at best produces wines with body and of fair quality.

See Classical wines; Dionysos.

Baco

French hybridizer Maurice Baco, whose grapes are grown in France and America. Many Baco vines have become especially important in several parts of the United States. Baco 1 is widespread but produces better wine in New York State than in France; Baco 22A is legally allowed in the sandy soils of France's Bas-Armagnac to be used in making the region's fine brandy, but its merits are still disputed.

Bacterium (pl. bacteria)

Microscopic unicellular organism which lacks rigid cell walls or a well-defined nucleus.

Bad Dürkheim (Dürkheim)

See Dürkheim; Palatinate.

Bad Kreuznach

Wine town and region in the Nahe (*q.v.*).

Badacsonyi Kéknyelü

The best-known of the Badacsonyi wines—a dry greenish-white dessert wine. Both red and white wines are grown in this region.

For this and other Badacsonyi fine wines, *see* Hungary.

Baden

German State of Baden-Württemburg
Vineyard area: approx. 15,000 hectares (37,000 acres)
77% white, 23% red

Location: The Baden vineyard, like an edging worked in vine and grape motif, borders the extreme southwest corner of Germany. It begins along the south shore of Lake Constance (or Bodensee, as it is called in German), skirts the thickly wooded slopes of the Black Forest on the fringes of Switzerland and France, and then marches parallel with Alsace on the other side of the Rhine, past Strasbourg on the Alsace side and Baden-Baden on the German side, until it reaches the Heidelberg region.

The wines are not the most important in Germany, but as a wine-growing region (third largest), Baden has managed a spectacular comeback during the last three decades and wine quality has improved dramatically. In the 1860s, Baden was the largest German vineyard, but shortly afterward the phylloxera plague struck, reducing the plantation by almost half. A second catastrophe for local production—although good was expected to come out of it—was a law which required the uprooting of hybrid vines. The Baden vine area then shrank another 20%; but the replanting with varieties such as Pinot Noir (Spätburgunder), Pinot Gris (Ruländer), Pinot Blanc (Weissburgunder), as well as Müller-Thurgau, Silvaner, Traminer and some Riesling generally improved the wines as the vineyards aged. The Müller-Thurgau crossing of Riesling and Silvaner has gained rapidly in this district, as it has elsewhere.

The region, now larger than the Mosel area, has undergone much improvement with the coming of the great cooperatives. These giant organizations, which manage as much as 90% of the vineyard acreage in Baden, have shaped new vineyards suitable for modern machine cultivation. Under the impulse of the cooperative movement, the image of Baden has improved as well, thanks to an array of self-imposed quality standards and controls. By strictly applying these rules, Baden has earned recognition for outstanding quality at national competitions. These qualities fetch generally higher prices than comparable wines of better-known regions. The Central Cellars of Baden Cooperatives: Zentralkellerei Badischer Winzergenossenschaften (ZBW) in Breisach is acknowledged as Europe's largest and most modern individual winery. This organization produces wines with over 400 appellations annually. They are well-made and typical of their origin and variety.

Grape Varieties: Much of the good wine comes from the Müller-Thurgau grape; and better quality red wines are made from Spätburgunder, the variety brought originally from Burgundy, where it is called Pinot Noir—this is the standard grape for such good red wines as are found in Germany. In Baden, Spätburgunder is also used to produce a rosé wine called Weissherbst. Another local speciality, also a rosé wine, is Badisch Rotgold, made from a blend of the two Burgundy grapes, Spätburgunder and Grauerburgunder (Ruländer). Light in color, it is however surprisingly hearty and full-bodied.

Gutedel, a grape variety brought from Vevey on Lake Geneva in 1780, produces the Markgräfler wines grown below Freiburg in the southwest corner of Germany. It is also found in considerable quantities in Switzerland, where it is known as Fendant, and in France, under the name of Chasselas.

The Ruländer grape variety is actually the French Pinot Gris. Its German name derives from the fact that the grape was brought from France to Germany by one Ruländ. It gives a golden wine which can be very rich and fruity and in the big years quite full-bodied.

Riesling has some significance in Baden. There is some on the south face of the Kaiserstuhl and in the Ortenau, the areas producing the best Baden wines.

Statistics: Müller-Thurgau (37%); Spätburgunder (22%); Ruländer (a.k.a Grauerburgunder or Pinot Gris), (12%); Gutedel (a.k.a Fendant or Chasselas), (8%) and Riesling (7%).

Annual production, based on a ten-year average (1976–85): 1,200,000 hectoliters (32.4 million U.S. gallons, 26.4 million imp.).

THE DISTRICTS (BEREICHE)

The long hook-shape of Baden, following the Rhine from Lake Constance to Heidelberg, includes several distinct vineyard areas with their own characteristics of soil and climate, and therefore of wines.

For a complete list of districts (Bereiche), collective vineyard sites (Grosslagen) and individual vineyard sites (Einzellagen), see Appendix B, p. 672.

Bereich Bodensee

The wines are known as the *Seeweine*, or Lake Wines. The name refers to the influence on them of the large lozenge-shaped lake along which they lie. Even more influential than the mild climate of the lake is the *Föhn*, a warm wind peculiar to the surrounding alpine area in Germany, Austria, and Switzerland. While it has such a disturbing effect on plants, men, and animals that it commonly causes insects to swarm and milk to turn sour, and has been taken into account by the Austrian penal laws covering crimes of violence, its hot breath brings the grapes quickly to ripeness. The better types are Spätburgunder, Ruländer, and Gewürztraminer. Each little lake port has its vineyard, but nearly all the wine of consequence grows around Meersburg, cultivated by the Baden State and called Domäne Meersburg. None of the Bodensee wine escapes the tourists. The little lake steamer glides along from port to port, first in Switzerland and then in Germany, where snowy peaks tower in the distance. Meersburg itself is a medieval jewel set in vines; it has a castle which is thirteen hundred years old and still carefully preserved. In the lantern-hung outdoor restaurants on the shore of the lake, the wines accompanying the characteristic Bodensee blue trout taste better than they really are.

Bereich Markgräflerland

The name comes from Markgraf, a German title approximately equivalent to marquis. Markgraf Karl Friedrich planted vines in this extreme southwest tip of Germany in the late eighteenth century. It was during this period that the Gutedel, the dominant variety, was brought from Vevey in Switzerland; other varieties worth mentioning are Müller-Thurgau and Gewürztraminer.

Bereich Kaiserstuhl-Tuniberg

Crossing the little bridge over the Rhine in the vicinity of Colmar in Alsace and going toward Freiburg, you see on your left a low cone-shaped hill ringed with vine. The Kaiserstuhl is of volcanic origin; and the mingled clay and volcanic soil gives rich red wines and darkish white wines with an amber tinge—all of which are definitely full-bodied, ripe and vinous. One-third of the Kaiserstuhl is planted with Müller-Thurgau; Spätburgunder and Ruländer account for another 25% each. The best Ruländers thrive on the south and southwestern slopes where they yield relatively fiery wines with concentrated flavor and depth. The same is true of the Spätburgunders and Traminers. Riesling and Silvaner are limited to a few isolated sites in the northern and southern sections of the Kaiserstuhl. Among the best villages are Ihringen, Achkarren, Bickensohl, Oberrotweil, Schelingen, Leiselheim, Merdingen and Bahlingen.

Bereich Breisgau

The small area just north of Kaiserstuhl and Markgräflerland produces wines that are lighter, with less complexity, but quite pleasant. The town of Freiburg, with its great cathedral (the tower is among the highest stone structures in Europe), is at the southern end; Lahr is in the north. The *Weissherbst* from the Glotter Valley near Freiburg is one of the best Baden wines.

Bereich Ortenau

After the very circumscribed area of the Kaiserstuhl, the best Baden wines come from the region called the Ortenau. It stretches along the thin plantable zone from the Rhine to the forested mountains, from the town of Offenburg up to Baden-Baden. The soil is mainly crumbled granite. Riesling and Traminer are the best white wines; Spätburgunder is the best red.

Bagaceira

Among the best villages (which usually grow both white and red varieties): Durbach, Ortenburg and Neuweier. Here, too, the wines are permitted to be bottled in the Bocksbeutel (flagon-shaped bottle, traditional in Franken). Red wine specialties are from Durbach, Sasbachwalden (Alde Gott), Kappelrodeck (Hex von Dasenstein) and Waldulm (Pfarrberg). Affenthaler is a popular light red wine with a distinctive bottle molded to feature a monkey clutching the side of it.

Bereich Bergstrasse-Kraichgau

This is the region lying between the Ortenau and the section just below Heidelberg where the Bergstrasse begins. Today the vineyards are planted with Müller-Thurgau (50%), Riesling, Weissburgunder and Ruländer.

Bereich Badisches Frankenland

The northernmost of the Baden *Bereiche* and somewhat separated from the main viticultural sections. Most of the vines grow around Tauberbischofsheim and in the valley of the River Jagst, a tributary of the Neckar.

Bagaceira

Portuguese spirit made from grape skins.

Balance

The degree of harmony achieved by the different parts of a wine when they are considered as a whole. Simply, a well-balanced wine has all of its aspects in control, with none too prominent and none obviously deficient. A well-balanced wine may not be great, but a great wine is always well-balanced.

Balaton, Lake

Center of one of the principal wine regions of Hungary.
See Hungary.

Château Balestard-la-Tonnelle

Bordeaux red wine.
District and Commune: Saint-Émilion, France.

Among the oldest growths in the district, the property is particularly famous because of a reference in a poem by François Villon (1431–1463): *ce divin nectar/ Qui porte le nom de Balestard* (this divine nectar, which bears the name of Balestard). The energetic Capdemourlin family, some of the most dedicated promoters of Saint-Émilion wines, owns this *Grand Cru* of the 1955 Classification.
Vineyard area: 8 hectares (20 acres).
Average production: 40 *tonneaux* (3,700 cases).

Balling or Brix

A hydrometer scale used to measure the approximate sugar content of grape juice, sweet wines, and sugar solutions. The scale is calibrated to indicate percentage by weight of sucrose when it is immersed in sucrose solutions. The Brix hydrometer is usually calibrated at 17.5°C. or 20°C. and the Balling at 60°F.

Balthazar, balthasar

A bottle—notably in Champagne—more suitable for display purposes than for holding wine or spirits. No longer used, it had a capacity of sixteen normal bottles.

Banadry

French banana liqueur made by Bardinet of Bordeaux.

Bandol

Controlled place-name for certain wines of Provence, France.
See Provence.

Banyuls (Appellation Contrôlée)

Sweet wine.
District: Roussillon.

Area on the Mediterranean border between France and Spain. Banyuls produces a sweet fortified wine known as *vin de liqueur*, of little interest in countries where Sherry and Port can be had. Banyuls is a sweet natural wine, often drunk before meals by those French who like sweet aperitifs; it is taken also as a dessert wine.
See Sweet fortified wines of France.

Barbados Rum

See Rum, West Indies.

Barbados Water

One of the earliest names for rum. From Barbados, a formerly British island in the West Indies, now an independent country, where rum originated.

Barbaresco

A red wine from Piedmont. One of the better red wines of Italy—big, strong, slow-ageing, with considerable depth and pungency. Awarded D.O.C.G. status in 1981.
See Piedmont.

Barbera

Italian red-wine grape, used especially in Piedmont (*q.v.*).

Barbera Amabile

Sweet, slightly sparkling red Italian wine from the Barbera grape, grown widely in northern Italy.

Bardolino (D.O.C.)

Red wine grown in the vineyards between Verona and Lake Garda, Italy.
See Veneto.

Bärentrank

A beverage from East Prussia, distilled from potatoes and flavored with honey. The name in German means "bear's drink."

Barolo

A red wine from Piedmont. One of the best red wines of Italy—robust, heavy, and slow-maturing, with a pungent aftertaste. Awarded D.O.C.G. status in 1980.
See Piedmont.

Barossa Valley

Vine-growing district near Adelaide, South Australia.

Barr

Wine town in Alsace, France.
See Alsace.

Barrel

Standard container. In America, a barrel contains 31.5 U.S. gallons; in England, 36 gallons imp. For table of capacities of barrels, casks, and containers of various nations, *see* Appendix C, p. 703.

Barrica

Spanish for the Bordeaux *barrique* or barrel, found in Spain.
See Barrique.

Barrique

French barrel or hogshead, especially the *barrique bordelaise*, or Bordeaux hogshead, containing 225 liters (59.4 U.S. gallons, 49.5 imp.) A *barrique* contains the equivalent of 300 bottles, or 25 cases of 12 bottles each. In Bordeaux, four *barriques* make up a *tonneau* (*q.v.*).
See Appendix C, p. 703.

Barriquot

Old French for small barrel or keg.

Barsac (Appellation Contrôlée)

Sweet white wine.
District: Bordeaux, France.

Even in the minds of people who are knowledgeable about wine, there is apt to be some confusion between Barsac and Sauternes—is Barsac a Sauternes or is it a place-name on its own? In fact, it is both.

The natural sweet white wine district of Barsac surrounds the town of that name in the northern stretch of the official Sauternes region, about 25 miles southeast of Bordeaux. Sauternes is composed of five communes, of which Barsac and Sauternes itself are two. (*See* map on p. 460.) All were once separate, and each was known in its own right; but the production of the commune of Sauternes was small, and some considerable time ago it was decided to include in the *appellation* the similar wines grown in neighboring villages, in order to have a large enough production to make the wine known in the world market. But Barsac, although it was brought into the Sauternes communes, was considered too famous to give up its own name. Consequently, the French wine-law authorities decided that Barsac wines (grown in the vineyard region of Sauternes as now constituted and having all the characteristics of the wines of Sauternes, yet remaining in the traditional district of Barsac) were entitled to both place-names, both Barsac and Sauternes. In practice, some are called Sauternes, some Barsac. Either is correct; the greatest are likely to keep the *appellation* Barsac.

Of the thirteen Second Growths (*Seconds Crus*) classified in Sauternes, eight are in Barsac which, however, possesses only two of the eleven First Growths (*Premiers Crus*). Château d'Yquem, the single First Great Growth (*Premier Grand Cru*), classed above all the others, is in the south of Sauternes. Yet Barsac can boast of Château Coutet and Château Climens, the two First Growths which deserve to be placed immediately after Château d'Yquem. The most aristocratic of the five Sauternes communes is Bommes, with one-third of its vineyards classified as First Growths. In general, quality is spread quite evenly over the region of Sauternes, Barsac, and Preignac, where the soil is intermediate between that of the other two areas. The wines from the stonier, hillier southern section are slightly more unctuous and richer in sugar; the Barsacs tend to be lighter and more fruity and to develop more quickly. Differences, however, are very subtle, and grape varieties, methods of production, and general characteristics are identical.

The Barsac section is flat—in contrast to the rest of Sauternes, which is hilly—and its boundary is roughly parallel to a brook called the Ciron, which runs diagonally across the region and empties into the Garonne. It was tragic, in the summer of 1956, to drive along the Circuit du Sauternais, a road marked with golden directional arrows which winds among the greatest vineyards, and to pass one blighted vineyard of Barsac after another, the leafless stumps of vine like scorched arms. The February frost in that year was most devastating in the lowlying areas. On the slope vineyards of Sauternes, losses were not nearly as heavy as they were in Barsac, which lost most of its wine for the 1956 and 1957 vintages and was able to produce little during the recuperative replantation period which followed. The soil of Barsac is less stony and more chalky than that across the Ciron—hence the difference, slight though it is, between Sauternes and Barsac wine.

CLASSIFIED GROWTHS (1855 CLASSIFICATION)
OF SAUTERNES SITUATED IN BARSAC

FIRST GROWTHS (*Premiers Crus*)

Château Coutet	Château Climens

SECOND GROWTHS (*Seconds Crus*)

Château de Myrat	Château Broustet
Château Doisy-Dubroca	Château Nairac
Château Doisy-Daëne	Château Caillou
Château Doisy-Védrines	Château Suau

See Château Climens; Château Coutet; Sauternes.

Bartzch

A spirit made from fermented hogweed in northern Asia. Hogweed is a general name covering various coarse plants such as ragweed and sow thistle.

Basi

A Philippine Islands spirit of fermented sugar-cane.

Basilicata

Red and white wines.
District: Southern Italy. South of Campania, North of Calabria

In this region, once known as Lucania, Aglianico del Vulture is the D.O.C. wine of note; a garnet-red, sturdy, warm wine from the vineyards of Monte Vulture, and one which is often very agreeable. Indeed, it is one of the very best red wines of southern Italy, capable of some improvement in the bottle. After three years of ageing, including two in wood, it may be called *vecchio* (old); after five years, *riserva* (special reserve). Southern Italian wines tend to pick up a tang from the volcanic soil, strange and rather unpleasant at first tasting; but the soil of Monte Vulture does not

impart too strong a flavor and consequently its Aglianico is more immediately appreciated by outsiders.

Muscat and Malvasia vines abound here, as they do throughout Italy. Both are most at home in hot climates, and both lend themselves well to *passito* treatment—that is, letting the grapes dry before vinifying them, in order to obtain a stronger, sweeter wine. Both normal and *passito* styles are made in Basilicata and may be either red or white. Normal wines run to about 12% of alcohol, *passito* up to 15%, but neither is in the class of Aglianico.

Basler Kirschwasser

A Swiss kirsch.
See Kirsch.

Bas-Médoc (the Appellation Contrôlée is "Médoc")

The 3,400-hectare (8,500-acre) northern end of the famous district of Bordeaux. Here the terrain is flatter and the rocky soil has less gravel and so is less good for vines than the soil of the Haut-Médoc (*q.v.*). There are no classified growths in the Bas-Médoc, and most of the wine originating here is sold simply as Médoc or under the names of any of the hundreds of châteaux in the area.

Bastardo

Important grape in the making of Port (*q.v.*).

Château Batailley

Bordeaux red wine.
District: Haut-Médoc, France.
Commune: Pauillac.

Situated a mile back from the River Gironde on high land just south of Pauillac, the vineyard overlooks Châteaux Pichon-Longueville and Latour. From 1942 until his death, the late M. Marcel Borie of the wine firm Borie-Manoux owned the estate. He was also proprietor of Château Trottevieille, the fine Saint-Émilion vineyard. A Fifth Growth (*Cinquième Cru*) of the Médoc, according to the 1855 Classification, Batailley is now owned by M. Borie's widow and other heirs. Château Grand-Saint-Julien is a secondary vineyard of the same property. The wine enjoys a limited reputation.

Characteristics: Fairly robust, but not one of the leaders.
Vineyard area: 55 hectares (137.5 acres).
Average production: 220 *tonneaux* (20,000 cases).

Bâtard-Montrachet (Appellation Contrôlée)

Burgundy white wine.
District: Côte de Beaune, France.

Beaujolais

Commune: Puligny-Montrachet (and in part Chassagne-Montrachet).
Official Classification: Great Growth (Grand Cru).

This is one of the magnificent Montrachets which are the greatest of all white Burgundies and consequently among the most superb white wines in the world. Bâtard ranks next to Chevalier-Montrachet, which is second only to the great Montrachet itself. The vineyard, some 29 acres in size, is walled in from the road behind the village of Puligny. It is on the left, with Bienvenue-Bâtard-Montrachet beside it, and across the road, approached through stone archways, is Le Montrachet, backed by Chevalier and the vineyard once known as Les Demoiselles, now discreetly renamed Le Cailleret. Nearby is the remaining vineyard of the Bâtard trio—Criots-Bâtard-Montrachet, a small property of 1.6 hectares (3 to 4 acres) which falls entirely in the commune of Chassagne-Montrachet. Bienvenue-Bâtard, not a great deal larger with 3.6 hectares (9 acres), is, like Montrachet itself, partly in Puligny, partly in Chassagne. The average yield for Bâtard-Montrachet is about 325 hectoliters (8,581 U.S. gallons, 7,145 imp.), not a great deal for a delicious wine which is in demand all over the world; so it is not surprising that much spurious Montrachet is sold. This is why it is so important to get to know the names of shippers and of those growers who bottle their own good wines at the domaine. In its characteristics, Bâtard resembles the greater Le Montrachet: it is dry yet rounded, with great elegance and breed and a seductive bouquet. Often this wine is better made than Montrachet itself.

See Montrachet; Puligny-Montrachet.

Batavia arrack

See Arrack.

Batzi

A Swiss apple brandy. The French equivalent is known as Calvados, and the American as applejack.

Baumé

A hydrometer scale widely used for measuring the density of musts and sweet wines. One degree Baumé is approximately equal to 1.8 degrees Brix.

See Areometer; Balling.

Béarn (Appellation Contrôlée)

An old French province which is today most of the Basses-Pyrénées department. The best-known wine is the sweet white Jurançon (*q.v.*). A new place-name, Vin de Béarn, is for reds and rosés. All of the wines, however, must take second place to the gastronomic triumph of the province—shallots, vinegar, and tarragon-flavored *sauce béarnaise.*

Beaujolais

Red wine.
District: Southern Burgundy, France.

Beaujolais is now one of the most widely drunk red wines in the world. Like a blooming country girl whose freshness is her charm, it has been captivating the capitals of the world, and whether the quality of the wine will survive the inordinate demand remains to be seen.

Above all, Beaujolais is a wine to be taken young and to be drunk, not sipped. Nowadays it is fermented very quickly, depending on the maturity achieved on the vine in the particular summer, and this is why it is light, fruity, and flowery. Such a quintessential Beaujolais as Fleurie will be more characteristic than the bigger wines, the Morgon and Moulin-à-Vent. Tasters sometimes say they detect the taste or scent of peach, of apricot, or of rose in the wine: but whatever the individual may find, it will always be the flower and fruit and freshness that will give distinction and beauty. This is the reason for drinking Beaujolais young—although to some degree, exception may be made for the Morgon and Moulin-à-Vent. Obviously such a wine is in danger of being ruined by success, and both the *vin nouveau* which fills the carafes in Paris cafés, and the more consequential Beaujolais which goes abroad are increasingly apt to be stretched with the lesser wines of more prolific regions.

Beaujolais, lying in the Saône-Rhône Valley, which cuts France in two, has always been on a highway traveled by man. Plentiful relics remain from the Stone Age. Julius Caesar conquered the tribes of Beaujolais, and his name and vestiges of Roman occupation remain in ruined walls and chapels, especially in the north, or the border of the Mâconnais, and in the names of such regions and villages as Juliénas and Romanèche-Thorins. At the time of the Crusades, the River Saône was the eastern frontier of France, and even in very recent times it was still the habit of the river pilots on that broad stream to call out "Turn to the Kingdom!" if they wanted the helmsman to steer toward the Beaujolais side or "Turn to the Empire!" if they meant the other.

Yet the wine of Beaujolais is comparatively modern, and its wide success is quite new. In the eighteenth century, a certain amount of Beaujolais began to be carried over to the nearby Loire—the land route through Burgundy was then all but impassable—and ferried in boatloads down to Paris. Until lately, the young Beaujolais was strictly a child of Lyon, which lies just to the south. The saying is: "Three rivers flow into Lyon—the Rhône, the Saône, and the Beaujolais." Even today, a Lyonnais calls for his Beaujolais by the *pot*, not the bottle. A *pot* is now actually larger than a half-bottle, containing 50 centiliters or 17 fl. oz., but not long ago it was a gray mug with blue trimming. These mugs sat in rows in the cafés of Lyon, and down the throats of the men of Lyon was poured practically all the Beaujolais that existed.

Beaujolais stands on the parallel which divides the north of France from the Mediterranean south. Above this region roofs are pointed, below they tend to be flat. The accent changes, and the game of bowls (*boules*), becomes the rage. All Beaujolais takes the pitching and knocking together of the balls with deadly seriousness: there are clubs, leagues, and whole newspapers devoted solely to the sport. Every village café has its court of *boules*, its row of *pots*, and usually the "Fanny," an impudent figure of a young girl to be kissed by the losers.

Out of this country backwater existence, Beaujolais wine has emerged suddenly into the great world. The people themselves show the change. Beaujolais was at least as peasant and country-mannered as any other wine area of France; but now the peasants have begun to be arrogant and difficult, because they are sought-after and successful. The wine shows the change: it is not called Burgundy any longer, which it may be, if it conforms to certain conditions—for instance, the wine must come from the Pinot grape instead of the now all but universal Gamay. But "*Beaujolais suis . . .,*" they say—(Beaujolais I am).

A wine which is drunk very young and is sometimes very light in alcohol does not travel well. Ideally, a Chiroubles, for example, should be drunk from the barrel and only rarely bottled. Yet such wines may be exported to the far corners of the globe. Moreover, high alcoholic content is taken by too many people to indicate value. This has its effect in Beaujolais, where they shudder to hear their wine spoken of condescendingly as a "nice little wine." Many growers are trying, in fact, to make it "bigger"—that is, more alcoholic—and this means longer vatting, which is likely to ruin its freshness. Others begin to talk of the *goût parisien*; they are afraid that too much Beaujolais is going to conform to the Parisian taste, which seems to be for higher alcohol content at the expense of freshness.

In recent years something of a fad has developed in the United States and other countries abroad for drinking the very young wine, Beaujolais *nouveau*. Though touted as wine just as the Parisian and Burgundians are drinking around the end of the vintage year, *Beaujolais nouveau* as it is exported is far from that. To prepare the wine for bottling—for it is shipped in bottles, not casks—it must be racked and re-racked both to remove the sediment that would normally have time to settle out naturally and to prevent a malolactic fermentation. In the process of this premature preparation, the very heart of the wine is poured away.

RESTRICTIONS, PRODUCTION, AND GEOGRAPHICAL LIMITS

Most Beaujolais is red wine, but not all the wine made in the Beaujolais region is red. Some Pinot Chardonnay white wine growing on the boundary line of Beaujolais and Mâconnais is known as Mâcon or Saint-Véran—except for a small quantity known as Beaujolais Blanc. The latter, superior to the Mâcon, is of a quality equal to that of Pouilly-Fuissé but does not come from communes entitled to that name.

The red wines from the important place-name districts may be labeled Burgundy. They are Burgundies, but nowadays the tendency is to use the popular name of Beaujolais. The production is in Gamay grape, which makes a delightful wine here, although it produces a common wine further north on the Côte d'Or.

From the viticultural standpoint the region is divided into two sections: Haut-Beaujolais and Bas- (or sometimes Bâtard-) Beaujolais. The geographical division is the little stream of the Nizerand, which cuts across the region at Villefranche-sur-Saône; Haut-Beaujolais extends north to the border of Mâconnais, and Bas-Beaujolais stretches south. But the reason for the division is a distinct difference of soils. With the Gamay grape, the climate balanced between the sharp north and soft south, and the short fermentation period, the soil characteristic accounts for the nature of the wines. Since the soil of the lesser Beaujolais is more chalky, the best wines come from Haut-Beaujolais, where the soil is characteristically granitic, with a good deal of manganese in the subsoil—near Moulin-à-Vent and Fleurie is the site of a manganese mine which was worked from the time of the French Revolution until the First World War.

The Beaujolais vineyard begins about 5 miles south of the city of Mâcon and extends at a width of never more than 9 or 10 miles for a distance of about 45 miles to the outskirts of Lyon. The zone is very carefully marked out by the French wine authorities and technically is delimited by the Turdine on the south, by the natural termination of vineyards at an altitude of about 1,500 feet on the slopes of the Monts du Lyonnais to the west, by the national Paris-Riviera route and the Saône on the east, and by a boundary line with the Mâconnais to the north just above a stream called the Arlais. Except for a little bulge at Saint-Symphorien-d'Ancelles in front of Moulin-à-Vent, the vineyard never crosses the highway, for the good reason that the rest of the distance to the river is a flat plain which could never produce wine worthy of the name Beaujolais.

Within this expanse are four grades of wine: Beaujolais, Beaujolais Supérieur, Beaujolais-Villages, and the nine Growths (*Crus*)—Saint-Amour, Juliénas, Chénas, Moulin-à-Vent, Fleurie, Chiroubles, Morgon, Brouilly, and Côte de Brouilly.

Beaujolais, with less than 10% of alcohol (9° for red and rosé, 9.5° for white), is the wine of fifty-nine communes not entitled to a higher classification. Except for narrow strips on both the mountain and river sides of the greater areas in Haut-Beaujolais, the wine is almost entirely made in Bas-Beaujolais, and nearly all is bought in barrels by shippers for their blends. The product, if called Beaujolais, must be 85% Gamay. Beaujolais Supérieur is wine from the same communes which surpasses 10% of alcohol. The yield of Beaujolais may not exceed 50 hectoliters per hectare (535 U.S. gallons, 445 imp. per acre), that of Beaujolais Supérieur 45 hectoliters per hectare (481 U.S. gallons, 400 imp. per acre). If it does, the wine must be called simply Vin Rouge.

The 21,600-odd hectares (54,000 acres) of vineyard making up all Beaujolais produce some 1,200,000 hectoliters (31.7 million U.S. gallons, 26.3 million imp.) yearly, a little more than half of which is Beaujolais. The nine Growths account for approximately two-thirds of the rest, with approximately 300,000 hectoliters (7.9 million U.S. gallons, 6.5 million imp.) a year; and there are also about 350,000 hectoliters (9.2 million U.S. gallons, 7.6 million imp.) of Beaujolais-Villages and Beaujolais Supérieur.

There are two ways of pruning the vine in Beaujolais. That method called Guyot is for the more ordinary wines, and the plant is trained on wires. The gobelet method calls for very close pruning, and the vines, not trained on wires, are most often hardly a foot high. The gobelet is the system for obtaining quality and is obligatory for wines entitled to be called either Beaujolais-Villages or listed among the nine Growths.

HAUT-BEAUJOLAIS

The wines of the nine Growths must not exceed 40 hectoliters per hectare (428 U.S. gallons, 356 imp. per acre) or they drop to the simple class of Beaujolais, although in certain great years the French wine authorities may allow the classification for wines surpassing the maximum if they are satisfactory in quality.

The nine select areas of the Growths lie islanded within the section of Beaujolais-Villages and Beaujolais Supérieur, all of which are in Haut-Beaujolais above Ville-franche and comprise the heart and nearly the whole bulk of the zone. The wines not in the Growth area but entitled to the classification Beaujolais-Villages, an official place-name, may be called by their commune name, if the name Beaujolais is attached.

BAS-BEAUJOLAIS

The wines, not having the advantage of the granite soil, lack distinction and are generally less complete and lighter than Haut-Beaujolais wines. Although lighter, they are a little like the wines in the Mâconnais, as if the same general characteristic established themselves on both sides of the true Beaujolais area.

Topographically, the region is a vast bowl dotted with small farmhouses, and from certain points dozens of village steeples may be seen. The slopes are rolling rather than sheer, but the peasants consider their domain wild and rough. It must once have been so, in manners if not in landscape, if we are to believe the stories told in the town of Anse. There, if a girl tosses her head at men and looks hard to handle they say: "She's walked in front of the oven at Anse." Apparently, in Napoleon's day, the women of Anse ran the men like horses, and if the men balked they were tortured in front of the oven. When a village priest tried to stop the women, they popped him into the oven.

BEAUJOLAIS-VILLAGES

The following communes are entitled to the official place-name or Appellation Contrôlée Beaujolais-Villages, or they may couple their names with Beaujolais:

Leynes, Pruzilly, Chânes, Saint-Amour-de-Bellevue, Saint-Véran (which also have white wine called Mâconnais Blanc), and

Arbuissonnaz	Odenas
Les Ardillats	Le Perréon
Beaujeu	Quincié
Blacé	Régnié
Cercié	Rivolet
La Chapelle-de-Guinchay	Romanèche-Thorins
Charentay	Saint-Étienne-des-Ouillières
Denice	Saint-Étienne-la-Varenne
Durette	Saint-Julien-en-Montmélas
Emeringes	Saint-Lager
Jullié	Saint-Symphorien-d'Ancelles
Lancié	Salles
Lantigné	Vaux-en-Beaujolais
Marchampt	Vauxrenard
Montmélas-Saint-Sorlin	Villié-Morgon

GROWTHS (Crus)
(Ranged from the fullest to the most delicate)

Moulin-à-Vent (Appellation Contrôlée)

Known as the king of Beaujolais wines, it is generally considered first among the noble growths—with the possible exception of Fleurie.

The bigness and fatness of a Moulin-à-Vent give it its character, but even this monarch of Beaujolais usually loses some of its fruitiness and freshness when it is bottled for more than two years.

The windmill itself, which has given its name to the wine and terrain, is a three-hundred-year-old stone cone standing up like a lighthouse in a rolling sea of vines. Far newer-looking is the stretch of the Paris-Riviera road passing a mile or so toward the Saône; neon signs flash on and off, several saying *Moulin-à-Vent*: yet it is the best place to taste the real Moulin-à-Vent.

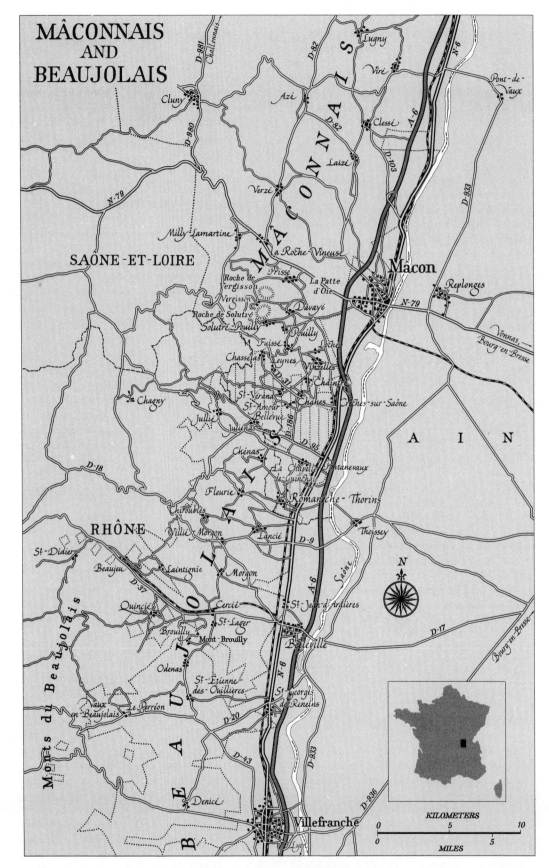

MÂCONNAIS
AND
BEAUJOLAIS

Cluny

D-981

Challonnais

D-82

Lugny

Viré

Pont-de-Vaux

Azé

M
Â
C
O
N
N
A
I
S

Clessé

A-6

N-6

D-82

D-103

Laizé

N-79

D-933

Verzé

Milly-Lamartine

SAÔNE-ET-LOIRE

la Roche-Vineuse

Prisse

Roche de Vergisson

Vergisson

Roche de Solutré

Solutré-Pouilly

Chasselas

Davayé

La Patte d'Oie

Mâcon

Replonges

N-79

Vonnas

Bourg-en-Bresse

Fuissé

Pouilly

Loché

Leynes

Vinzelles

D-31

Chaintré

St-Vérand

St-Amour-Bellevue

Chanes

Crèches-sur-Saône

A I N

Chagny

Jullié

Juliénas

D-186

D-95

Chénas

D-18

La Chapelle-de-Guinchay

Fontanevaux

Fleurie

Romanèche-Thorins

Chiroubles

Villié-Morgon

Lancié

D-9

Thoissey

N

St-Didier

Beaujeu

Laintignie

Morgon

Saône

A-6

St-Jean-d'Ardières

Bourg-en-Bresse

Quincié

Cercié

D-37

Brouilly

St-Lager

Mont-Brouilly

Belleville

D-17

M
o
n
t
s
　
d
u
　
B
e
a
u
j
o
l
a
i
s

Odenas

St-Étienne-des-Ouillières

N-6

St-Georges-de-Reneins

Vaux-en-Beaujolais

Le Perréon

D-20

D-43

D-833

B
E
A
U
J
O
L
A
I
S

RHÔNE

Denicé

Villefranche

Lyon

D-936

KILOMETERS

0　　　　5　　　　10

0　　　　　　5

MILES

Chénas is a place-name itself. Nevertheless, the best part of the commune of Chénas, about 475 hectares (1,200 acres), is within the zone of the place-name Moulin-à-Vent, and the wines are sold under this, the more famous name of the two. Three-quarters of the commune of Romanèche-Thorins, 600 hectares (1,500 acres) is in Moulin-à-Vent. Thorins and Moulin-à-Vent wines, always famous in the past, frequently compared for their very similar qualities and now joined as Moulin-à-Vent, grow on a very shallow soil of decomposed granite. The vine roots drive right down into the rock, so that it crumbles even more. Manganese, strong in the subsoil here, undoubtedly contributes to the breed of the wines.

Juliénas (Appellation Contrôlée)

The wines sometimes preserve the pleasant fruitiness of their youth into a lusty age—for these wines and the Morgons are the longest-lasting of the Beaujolais.

An average 30,000 hectoliters (792,540 U.S. gallons, 659,940 imp.) is made from some 445 hectares (1,100 acres). Château Juliénas is one of the best vineyards. Bessay and Château Les Capitans are well-known names.

Morgon (Appellation Contrôlée)

This, the hardest of Beaujolais wines and very full-bodied, is unlike the others in that it is not so delightful when young, but improves with some ageing; a "true Morgon" is not bottled until seven or nine months after the harvest and needs a year in the bottle. The heaviest of the Morgons stands on the dividing line of characteristics between a more typical Beaujolais and a Burgundy; and in fact a considerable amount of it is used by shippers for its strength in blending and never reaches the consumer in its true state. The area entitled to the name Morgon, with its 910 hectares (2,275 acres), is one of the largest of the Growths, but there really is no typical Morgon wine because the soil varies greatly. The part in Morgon is called "true Morgon," and that in Villié-Morgon produces a generally lighter wine. Not all Villié-Morgon can call itself Morgon, the remainder being Beaujolais-Villages. The best parcels of all lie on a ridge called the Côte de Py, where the brownish decomposed slate soil may be seen on the surface—the "rotted soil," as the peasants inelegantly put it, that gives the special goût de terroir often present in a Morgon. Until recently, these were robust, fat wines which repaid laying down. The tendency now, however, is to make lighter wines in Morgon. Their relative lightness or heaviness will still vary from vintage to vintage: in 1985, for instance, the wines were all harder and longer-lived than usual and will be an exception to the trend.

Chénas (Appellation Contrôlée)

Most of Chénas lies within Moulin-à-Vent. A small slice of the commune, however, caps Moulin-à-Vent on the north, and its wine is sold as Chénas. The production is not large and the wines are not quite as good as Moulin-à-Vent, yet often they closely approach it in character and they are likely to be excellent value.

Fleurie (Appellation Contrôlée)

If Moulin-à-Vent is the king of Beaujolais wines, Fleurie is the queen, best of all the fine Growths if the standard is the most typically Beaujolais. Before the strict place-name laws were drawn up—between the world wars—most of the wine was sold as Moulin-à-Vent, which adjoins Fleurie on the south side. The result is that the name was not until recently as well known as Moulin-à-Vent today. Fleurie is the only one of the best Growths entirely within one commune, that of Fleurie, but not quite all the wine is entitled to the place-name. A little produced to the west and south must be sold as Beaujolais.

The characteristic of the wine is its exceeding fruitiness, and while it is among the heavier Beaujolais, it does not seem as heavy as a Moulin-à-Vent, or, in their different ways, a Morgon or a Chénas.

Roughly 42,000 hectoliters (1,108,800 U.S. gallons, 919,800 imp.) are made each year on 688 hectares (1,700 acres), about a quarter of this coming from the Cave Coopérative, excellently run by the successor of Mme. Chabert. The best vineyards are Clos de la Roilette; Grand Cour; La Madone; Les Moriers; Augarant. There are approximately four hundred vineyard owners.

Saint-Amour (Appellation Contrôlée)

This is the farthest north of the Growths, nearly touching the domain of Pouilly-Fuissé in the Mâconnais. About 600 hectoliters (15,000 U.S. gallons, 12,500 imp.) of white wine are made, and 15,000 hectoliters (414,000 U.S. gallons, 345,000 imp.) of red. The white wine, sold as Saint-Véran, Mâcon Blanc or Beaujolais Blanc, bears a considerable likeness to the Pouilly-Fuissés and is definitely fruity and to be drunk young. This is equally true of the red, which carries the *cru* designation Saint-Amour and is one of the lightest of all fine-growth Beaujolais.

The wine grows on a granite and slate soil pebbled with stones sometimes as large as eggs. Most of the slopes face east and southeast on the mountain of Bessay, bordering Juliénas, and a smaller hill called l'Église.

Côte de Brouilly (Appellation Contrôlée)

The center of Brouilly. The wines from these 255 hectares (637 acres) have more character and longer

Beaujolais-Villages (Appellation Contrôlée)

life and are more full-bodied than those simply labeled Brouilly.

In the exact middle, in vine only halfway to the summit, is the Mont de Brouilly. At the top of the hill, on the bush-covered crown, is Notre-Dame du Raisin (Our Lady of the Grape). Built a hundred years ago by penitents seeking to exorcise the vine plague of oïdium, it is the goal of a yearly pilgrimage on September 8, preceding the harvest. The friends of the wine wind up the long climb, acquiring a proper thirst. At the top there is a religious ceremony in which protection is asked for the coming crop. And then thirsts are slaked under the September sun, welcoming the Côte-de-Brouilly Beaujolais.

Brouilly (Appellation Contrôlée)

This, the southernmost of the Growths, gives a fine wine. The 875 hectares (2,162 acres) are in the communes of Saint-Lager, Cercié, Odenas, Charentay, and a small segment of a little over 40 hectares (100 acres) in Quincié. The center and best part of Brouilly has the separate *appellation* Côte de Brouilly.

Château de la Chaize, built by the nephew of the confessor to Louis XIV, makes a fine Brouilly in its vast cellars. With its dignified, rather frigid rooms, preserved exactly in the style and spirit of the period, it is the tourist haven of the area.

Chiroubles (Appellation Contrôlée)

The wine is usually as elegant as a Fleurie and less hard than a Morgon. The vineyards adjoin both districts on the west.

This is a wine to be taken very young, and ideally it should never be drunk in bottle but only from the barrel. Although until recently it was the least known, it is now becoming the Growth best liked in France as a fast-maturing light Beaujolais.

The alcoholic content is actually fairly high but does not show in the wine, which is soft, light, exceedingly fruity, and, when very young, a fresh and typical Beaujolais. It can be drunk as early as two months after the harvest, and generally ought to be. Production averages 19,000 hectoliters (501,942 U.S. gallons, 417,962 imp.).

In the square of the village of Chiroubles itself, facing the church, is what must be one of the most appropriate statues in any wine town of France. Neither Napoleon nor Joan of Arc is commemorated here, but one Pulliat, the man who planted the first grafted vine in Beaujolais during the crisis of the phylloxera vine louse. The best wines from this area come from the Domaine de Raousset and from the growers Jean Desvigne and Marcel Dufoux.

Beaujolais-Villages (Appellation Contrôlée)

Name applied to the wines of thirty-six communes or townships in the French Beaujolais. After the fine-

growth Beaujolais such as Fleurie, Moulin-à-Vent, Morgon, and others, the Beaujolais-Villages are the best of these pleasant fresh red wines now the rage in France and growing popular everywhere.

See Beaujolais.

Beaulieu-sur-Layon

Commune with the right to an Appellation Contrôlée in the Coteaux du Layon district of Anjou, France.

See Anjou: Coteaux du Layon.

Beaumes-de-Venise (A.O.C.)

Vin doux naturel and *vin de liqueur* are made in this area of Vaucluse, south of Gigondas and east of Châteauneuf-du-Pape, from the Muscat grape. The successful vinification of this wine justifies an anticipation of great popularity in the United States which is going to overflow into the other markets.

See Sweet fortified wines of France.

Beaune (Appellation Contrôlée)

Burgundy red and white wines.
District: Côte de Beaune, France.

The ancient city of the same name is the largest and most important of the Côte de Beaune and is called—not without reason—the "Capital of Burgundian Wines." Beaune's long history has been one of storm and terror, for many ambitious nobles converged there as they struggled for supremacy. Walls have been built and razed, castles constructed and toppled, and the city archives hold more stories of intrigue and violence than do those of many a Hollywood producer. Lying between the once-powerful strongholds of Autun and Besançon, Beaune is strategically placed, and its wines added to its desirability. Characteristic of the change that has come over the city is that the one remaining medieval fort now houses the offices and cellars of the Maison Bouchard Père & Fils. The pillars—all that remain of the stout walls which once girdled Beaune—are used today to house wine instead of broadswords.

The great change in the life of the place occurred in the seventeenth century, when the citizens beat their swords into pruning knives and turned their attention to wine. Beaune's undisputed place as the center of the Burgundian wine trade and its aura of bustling commerce and prosperity date from that era. As a result of its energy and enterprise, the economy not only of the Côte de Beaune but of the entire Côte d'Or is based on the cellars of Beaune, and the city lives for its wines. Cellars tunnel and wind beneath the twisting streets, wine slogans adorn walls of buildings and restaurants, and billboards lure passing tourists and wine-buyers from all over the world into the storerooms of the great firms. Finding these firms is no trouble, but discovering the difference between them sometimes is. The Beaune telephone directory carries a couple of dozen under a single number; names of established and reliable firms are imitated by fly-by-nights to within an inch of a lawsuit, and merchants abound who will agree to sell any wine in any quantity, sometimes in excess of its production. Yet behind it all lies a genuine love of Burgundian wines, a conviction that there are no others in the world to rival them, and an enthusiasm unequaled in any region of the world.

There is more to Beaune than the winding streets, the clatter of great tank-trucks carrying wine, and the hum and buzz of conversations about vintages, comparative tastings, and prices. Outside the city, but still within the limits of the commune of Beaune, are more vineyards planted in fine vines than can be found in any other commune of the Côte d'Or, although both Pommard and Meursault generally make more wine each year. The wines from these vineyards—both red and white—are sold as Beaune or may have the vineyard name following that of the commune. Sometimes they are sold as Côte de Beaune, which means simply that they come from any vineyard allowed to use the name Beaune, and from several others as well. (When blended with wines from specified other communes of the slope they may also be sold as Côte de Beaune-Villages.)

The outstanding vineyards of Beaune today are substantially the same as those which received top rating when the vineyards of the Côte d'Or were classified in 1860. At that time, there were eight Outstanding Vineyards (*Têtes de Cuvées*) and all but one of them are still considered outstanding. The French authorities included all eight in their list of the thirty-four First Growths (*Premiers Crus*)—superior vineyards whose wines have the legal right to carry both commune and vineyard name on the label—established in 1936. The best Growth is generally considered that from the vineyard of Grèves and particularly from the section called L'Enfant Jésus. The name is said to have been bestowed by early monks and comes from the expression: "It goes down the throat as easily as the little Jesus in velvet trousers." Since the monks did not consider this irreverent, no one in Burgundy does either. Grèves is one of the fullest wines of Beaune and one of the suavest. Les Clos des Mouches is another wine noted for its body (considerable for a Beaune) and for its elegance. Slightly behind these is Fèves, a smaller vineyard and thus one with far less output, its wines noted for their fineness and delicate yet pronounced aroma. Beaune Bressandes—not to be confused with Corton-Bressandes in nearby Aloxe-Corton—and Marconnets, Champimonts, and Cras are also highly reputed, and the wines are light but firm with a distinctive bouquet. Finesse, delicacy, and an expressive and often remarkable bouquet are the characteristics which excel in all Beaune wines.

In the past, Beaunes were considered at their best immediately after harvest. During the seventeenth century, wines were generally drawn straight from the

FIRST GROWTHS (*Premiers Crus*)

Vineyard	Hectares	Acres
Les Marconnets	8.81	22.03
Les Fèves	4.40	11.00
Les Bressandes	21.80	54.50
Les Grèves	31.68	79.20
Les Clos des Mouches	25.13	62.83
Clos du Roi (*in part*)	8.44	21.10
Sur-les-Grèves	4.02	10.05
Aux (or Les Cras)	5.02	12.55
Le Clos de la Mousse	3.36	8.40
Les Teurons	21.52	53.80
Champimonts (or Champ Pimont)	18.07	45.18
Aux Coucherias (*in part*)	9.27	23.18
En l'Orme	2.02	5.05
En Genêt	4.32	10.80
Les Perrières	3.18	7.95
À l'Écu	5.00	12.50
Les Cent Vignes	23.50	58.75
Les Toussaints	6.43	16.08
Les Chouacheux	5.04	12.60
Les Boucherottes	8.60	21.50
Les Vignes Franches	8.56	21.40
Les Aigrots	22.00	55.00
Pertuisots	5.16	12.90
Tiélandry	1.98	4.95
Les Sizies	8.50	21.25
Les Avaux	13.40	33.50
Les Reversées	4.97	12.43
Le Bas des Teurons	7.32	18.30
Les Seurey	1.23	3.08
La Mignotte	2.41	6.03
Les Montrevenots (*in part*)	8.28	20.70
Les Blanches Fleurs (*in part*)	1.16	2.90
Les Epenottes (*in part*)	8.06	20.15
Les Tuvilains	8.73	21.83
Bélissaud	4.88	12.20

barrel instead of being bottled and were vinified to be very light, very fast-maturing, and for immediate drinking. Beaunes are still reasonably light and reasonably fast-maturing, but the drinking is nowhere near so immediate as it once was, and a couple of years in the bottle will aid the wines considerably. Some of the better wines will hold for a number of years, but they are the exception to the rule; five years in glass will usually suffice. After this the wines tend to fade.

The great event in Beaune each year is the annual auction sale at the impressive Hospices de Beaune, the charity hospital which has been in continuous operation since the fifteenth century and which gains some of its revenue from the sale at auction of wines coming from vineyards donated by philanthropic Burgundians. The sale, usually held in mid-November, gathers swarms of buyers, mostly from France and Belgium, and the prices determine the value of the harvest throughout the Côte d'Or. The Hospices has holdings all over the Côte de Beaune; it vinifies its own wines and also distills a Marc de Bourgogne which is sold at the same times as the wine (*see also* Hospices de Beaune).

Within the limits of the commune there are 537 hectares (1,329 acres) of vineyard allowed for grapes going into Beaune, and this and twenty-two more for wines labeled Côte de Beaune. In an average-quantity year Beaune produces 8,700 hectoliters (230,000 U.S. gallons, 191,500 imp.) of red wine and about 200 hectoliters (5,300 U.S. gallons, 4,400 imp.) of white. The white is rarely in the class of the red, but some may be delicate and perfumed, and it is often excellent wine. Beaune is sold mostly in France, but large quantities go to the Low Countries and not only because of geographical proximity. The historical links forged when the Burgundian ducal family held court in the Netherlands were strengthened by the Huguenot refugees from Beaune in the sixteenth century, many of whom settled in Belgium and Holland and retained, as do their descendants today, their traditional drinking preferences. England, Switzerland, the United States, and Austria are also big buyers.

See Côtes de Beaune.

Château Beauregard

Bordeaux red wine.
District and Commune: Pomerol, France.

This property owned by the Clauzel family faces south on the plateau of Pomerol and makes one of the soundest wines in the district.

Vineyard area: 13 hectares (32 acres).
Average production: 51 *tonneaux* (4,500 cases).

Château Beau-Séjour-Bécot

Bordeaux red wine.
District and Commune: Saint-Émilion, France.

Formerly owned by Dr. Jean Fagouët and now by M. Bécot. The vineyard was justifiably ranked as a First Great Growth (*Premier Grand Cru*) in the Saint-Émilion classification, until 1986.
Characteristics. Fine wine, with a fine bouquet in a good vintage year.
Vineyard area: 16 hectares (40 acres).
Average production: 85 *tonneaux* (6,500 cases).

Château Beauséjour-Duffau-Lagarosse

Bordeaux red wine.
District and Commune: Saint-Émilion, France.

Placed on a little hill outside the walls of Saint-Émilion, with a view over the lazy curve of the Dordogne, the two Beauséjour vineyards were a single property until 1869, when they were divided between two branches of the Ducarpe family. Mademoiselle Ducarpe had become Madame Duffau-Lagarosse by marriage, and it is in her line that the original château and the immediately surrounding part of the vineyard have descended. Both Beauséjour-Duffau-Lagarosse

and **Beau-Séjour-Bécot**, which adjoins it, were ranked First Great Growths (*Premiers Grands Crus*) of Saint-Émilion in the official Classification of 1955. Care must be taken not to confuse them, since in both cases the words "Château Beauséjour" will generally be found on the labels printed in large letters, with the proprietor's name in smaller print.
Characteristics. Both vineyards are well placed between Canon and Fourtet, and they yield an agreeable wine. In the '60s, this vineyard was not as good as Beau-Séjour-Bécot In the late '70s and '80s, this trend has been reversed.
Vineyard area: 6 hectares (17 acres).
Average production: 25 *tonneaux* (2,000 cases).

Beer

The origins of beer go almost as far back as those of wine; beer has been made by virtually all people in all stages of civilization. African tribes produce it from millet, the Japanese from rice; Europeans, Americans of both continents, Australians and countless others make theirs mainly from barley. It is consumed the world over—most of all in Belgium, whose citizens manage to down an impressive 134 liters (35.5 U.S. gallons, 29.5 imp.) per capita yearly.

Beer is the general term for all classes of beers—draft, bottled and canned, pale ales, lagers, and stouts. It is brewed from malt, sugar, hops, and water and is fermented with yeast. Beer quality is largely dependent on the suitability of these main raw materials for the type of beer being produced.

Malt begins its life as barley. Special types are grown and carefully ripened. In the malting, barley is dampened with water and allowed to germinate under controlled conditions in order to convert the insoluble starch to soluble sugar: it is then dried and cured, to a pale color for pale beers and to a richer color for dark beers.

Sugars used in brewing are manufactured from cane sugar which is treated in different ways to give various flavors and sweetness.

Hops are specially grown for brewing and give beer its bitter flavor. Only the flower, a cone of golden petals carrying resin and oils, is used.

The water used in brewing is usually specially treated with mineral salts for the particular type of beer being processed. Before the days of water analysis, famous brewing centers emerged because the local water was particularly suitable for the brewing of certain types of beer. For example, Pilsener, the famous beer of Pilsen in Czechoslovakia, is brewed with natural water and is recognized as one of the finest beers in the world.

Yeast, a living organism, is the agent which ferments the beer.

The brewing process is not very complicated. The malt passes through a mill and is crushed, after which it is mixed with water at a carefully controlled temperature. The sugar solution from the mixture is drawn off from the vessel. Rotating water sprinklers spray the grain to ensure that all the malt extract is used, leaving only husks, which are usually sold as cattle food.

The solution (wort) is pumped to the boiling coppers, where hops and sugar are added. The resultant mixture is boiled for an hour or two and in the process the aroma and distinct bitterness of hops combine with the sweetness and flavor derived from the wort and sugar. After boiling, the hops are removed by straining, and the wort is cooled and collected in a vessel where yeast is added, splitting the sugars into alcohol and carbon dioxide gas: the gas is usually collected for later use in carbonating bottled and canned beers.

Fermentation takes several days, at the end of which the bulk of the yeast, in lager, settles on the bottom of the fermenting vessel; in ale, it rises to the top of the beer; in both it is collected. The yeast produced during fermentation is several times the original quantity and is used for subsequent fermentations, the surplus forming a very valuable by-product, since it is a source of vitamins for humans or animals.

In most beer-consuming countries the beer is stored in large cold tanks near the freezing point to improve its stability and ensure long and satisfactory quality, after which it is filtered, carbonated, and filled into a cask, bottle, or can for dispatch to the consumer. Most beers are now pasteurized (heated to 140°F., 60°C.) to ensure that any minute quantities of yeast which may be left in the beer after filtration do not ferment and multiply and in so doing turn the beer cloudy.

Draft beer, which is drawn from a cask, now usually metal, is still very popular in most beer-drinking countries. All containers are washed and sterilized before being filled with beer. Bottles and cans are filled, labeled, and packaged on high-speed machines which can work at the rate of up to six hundred bottles a minute.

The quality of beers varies widely, depending upon the skill, plant, and management of the manufacturer. One of the most famous is the Tuborg plant in Copenhagen, which produces a product known throughout the beer-drinking world. Other countries and cities have become famous for their beers: Pilsen of Czechoslovakia, Carlsberg of Denmark, Heineken of Holland, the Munchener beer of Munich. England and Ireland are renowned for their heavier ales and stouts. The beers of Mexico, the U.S.A., Australia, Cuba, and Canada are also very good.

MAJOR TYPES OF BEER

Lager

Light highly carbonated beer. The name comes from the German *lagern* (to store), and lager beer is one that is allowed to rest until all sediment of the fermentation has cleared and is then carbonated and bottled. Most American beers—unless the labels bear a statement to the contrary—are lager beers, although the term itself is seldom used.

Ale

A kind of beer, formerly made without hops and drunk fresh. Today there is little difference in Great Britain between this and other beers. In the U.S.A., ale is usually fermented at a higher temperature than beer and different yeast strains are used.

Stout

A dark heavy ale, often slightly sweet, with a pronounced taste of malt, usually heavily flavored with hops. Great Britain and Ireland are most famous for their stouts, which include the famous names of Guinness and Oyster Stout.

Porter

Similar to stout but not so strong, usually with a heavy creamy foam. The name is said to derive from the fact that it was the favorite drink of the London porters.

Bock

Special heavy beer made in the United States in the spring, purportedly from sediment taken out of the fermenting vats in their annual cleaning. The bock beer season usually lasts for about six weeks. In France, however, bock is the term for a mugful of light beer.

Beerenauslese

German wine term for the selection of individual grapes from bunches.
See Germany.

Beeswing

A light thin crust—resembling the transparent wing of a bee—which forms on some old bottled Ports.

Château Bélair

Bordeaux red wine.
District and Commune: Saint-Émilion, France.

Owned by Madame Jean Dubois-Challon—widow of the former leader of the Jurade (Saint-Émilion's wine society), and part-owner of the neighboring Château Ausone—Bélair matured in the Ausone cellars until 1974. Many people feel that the distinction between Bélair wine and the much more famous Ausone is not very real. Others maintain that Bélair closely resembles Ausone but in most years is less generous and less fine. While Roman origins are often claimed for the vineyard, it is certain that in the fourteenth century it was the property of the Englishman Robert Knolles, when he was governor of Guyenne. Until 1916 the estate belonged to the French family Cannolle—French descendants of Knolles. Bélair was named a First Great Growth (*Premier Grand Cru*) in the Saint-Émilion Classification of 1955.

Characteristics. A subtle, very agreeable wine.
Vineyard area: 13 hectares (32 acres).
Average production: 50 *tonneaux* (5,000 cases).

Château Bélair-Marquis d'Aligre

Bordeaux red wine.
District: Haut-Médoc.
Commune: Soussans-Margaux.

One of the best wines of the tiny commune of Soussans, whose production is entitled to the place-name Margaux. A Cru Exceptionnel according to the 1855 Classification, many of its vines neighbor those of Château Margaux. The soil of the vineyard is gravelly and the subsoil flinty.

Vineyard area: 17 hectares (42 acres).
Average production: 50 *tonneaux* (5,000 cases).

Château Belgrave

Bordeaux red wine.
District: Haut-Médoc, France.
Commune: Saint-Laurent.
(Saint-Laurent is not a place-name and the wine has the place-name of Haut-Médoc.)

Classified a Fifth Growth (*Cinquième Cru*) in 1855 and on the boundary line of Saint-Julien, the estate was known by varying names in the past. The name Belgrave, which it shares with a few other Bordeaux vineyards, is claimed to be the inspiration for the naming of Belgrave Square in London. This wine should not be confused with a lesser wine called Château Bellegrave.
Characteristics. Frequent changes in proprietors have made for a certain amount of variation in this wine, which is usually fairly full.
Vineyard area: 80 hectares (200 acres).
Average production: 250 *tonneaux* (25,000 cases).

Bellegarde

A commune on the great Languedoc plain of southern France in the confines of which Clairette grapes are planted for making a small white wine.
See Clairette de Bellegarde.

Bellet

Controlled place-name near Nice in the south of France. This is one of the best vineyard districts planted along the Riviera.
See Provence.

Ben Ean

Important vineyard in New South Wales.
See Australia.

Bench Grafting

For a description of this method of grafting vines, *see* Chapter Eight, p. 34.

Benedictine D.O.M.

A famous and very popular liqueur supposed to have been first compounded about 1510 at the Benedictine monastery in Fécamp, France, by Dom Bernardo Vincelli, to fortify and restore the weary monks. The liqueur is said to have found royal favor in 1534, when Francis I passed through the region and tasted it; but at the time of the French Revolution the monastery was destroyed, the order dispersed, and manufacture of Benedictine halted. Some seventy years or so later, the formula came into the hands of M. Alexandre Le Grand, who established the present secular concern which produces the liqueur. It no longer has any connection with Benedictines or any other religious order. Every true bottle of Benedictine (numerous unsuccessful attempts have been made to counterfeit it) still carries the ecclesiastical inscription D.O.M., which means not "Dominican order of Monks," as it has sometimes been construed, but *Deo Optimo Maximo* (to God, most good, most great).

The liqueur is greenish-yellow and flavored with a variety of herbs, plants, and peels on a base of brandy; and it is claimed that no more than three people at any given time know its exact formula. When the firm realized that great numbers of people were ordering their Benedictine mixed half-and-half with brandy in order to reduce sweetness slightly, they put on the market an official "B & B" (Benedictine and Brandy).

Benicarlo

Muscular red wine from the region of Castellón de la Plana in Valencia, Spain.

Benin Wine

Nigerian palm "wine," or fermented palm sap.

Bentonite

A kind of clay, bentonite is an excellent clarifying agent for white wines, one which prevents protein precipitation and discoloration from copper. Its use is allowed by law.

The bentonite (a hydrated silicate of aluminum, composed mainly of montmorillonite) swells in water to form a gelatinous paste. After dilution, it should be stirred briskly into the wine to be treated. The most satisfactory dose is usually about 100 grams per hectoliter, diluted in at least two liters of water.

See Chapter Nine, p. 44, Fining.

Bercy

A section of Paris along the Seine known as the Quai de Bercy, where most of the city's everyday table wine is received and distributed.

Bereich

The German word for "district," especially subdivisions of the eleven main German wine-producing areas.

Bergerac (Appellation Contrôlée)

Red and white wines.
District: Southwest France.

Bergerac's proximity (100 kilometers; 62 miles) to Bordeaux and the similarity of their wines, vines, and viticultural practices lead to widespread and—for Bergerac—unfortunate comparisons. Some Bergerac wines, however, have improved considerably of late, one such being Domaine de la Jaubertie.

The city itself is dull and quiet—hardly worth visiting were it not for the castles and strongholds which guard the beautiful wide valley of the Dordogne above it. Many battles of the Hundred Years' War were fought along these hills, and it is easy to imagine the mounted knights emerging from the ancient fortresses in full battle array.

The vines are planted along the hills that girdle the city, especially on the right bank of th river, called the Côte Nord. The soil ranges from sandy gravel to flinty clay and ends in a chalky clay with traces of iron. Bordeaux varieties are the most common grapes: Cabernet Sauvignon, Cabernet Franc, Merlot, and Malbec for red wines; Sémillon, Sauvignon, Muscadelle, Ondenc, and Chenin Blanc, for whites. For red wines benefiting from the most general place-name—Bergerac—the Fer and Perigord vines are permitted.

PLACE-NAMES

Monbazillac (Appellation Contrôlée)

The most important. Sometimes known as the "poor man's Sauternes," it will, in good years, have much of the full sweet richness of Sauternes but generally fails in its full finesse, tending to be too obvious. In recent years the quality of Monbazillac has diminished as growers have abandoned the traditional methods of selective harvesting. It is grown in the parishes of Monbazillac, Pomport, Rouffignac, Colombier, and a part of Saint-Laurent-des-Vignes.

The vineyards extend on the south side of the Dordogne and face north, an exception to the general rule that southerly facings are best for vines. The soil is the chalky clay, with occasional veins of gritty sandstone. As in Sauternes, the grapes stay on the vines until late in the autumn, when the noble rot mold *Botrytis cinerea* attacks them, drying up much of the water. The vineyards cover some 2,500 hectares (6,250 acres), and production averages slightly more than 40,000 hectoliters (1 million U.S. gallons, 880,000 imp.).

Pécharmant (Appellation Contrôlée)

The best of the red Bergeracs. Light and vivacious, and sometimes bearing a resemblance to wines made in the lesser areas around Saint-Émilion—the closest of the Bordeaux districts—it is made in four communes to the north and east of Bergerac: Creysse, Mouleydier, Saint-Sauveur, and Lembras. The slopes closest to the city are thought to be the best. The 220 hectares seldom produce more than 10,000 hectoliters (264,000 U.S. gallons, 220,000 imp.) annually.

Rosette (Appellation Contrôlée)

Only applicable to white wines. Semi-sweet and rarely distinguished, the wine comes from six communes, three of which have title to the name Pécharmant for red wines. The small amount of 800 hectoliters (21,134 U.S. gallons, 17,598 imp.) is produced in a very good year.

Montravel (Appellation Contrôlée)

Includes Haut-Montravel and the Côtes de Montravel. Grown in fifteen communes downstream—almost due west at this point—from the town of Bergerac, the vines are all on the north side of the river. Like Rosette, the wine is semi-sweet. Montravel makes about 30,000 hectoliters (795,000 U.S. gallons, 630,000 imp.) every year, while Haut-Montravel and the Côtes de Montravel annually produce approximately 6,000 hectoliters (160,000 U.S. gallons, 130,000 imp.) each.

Bergerac and the Côtes de Bergerac (Appellation Contrôlée)

Together, these two produce about 250,000 hectoliters (6.5 million U.S. gallons, 5.5 million imp.) of wine annually, two-thirds of which is white. They make up the most general place-names in the region, and thus the wine is less good than that carrying more specific names.

Bergheim

Beautiful old wine village in Alsace (*q.v.*).

Bergstrasse (Hessische Bergstrasse)

German State of Hesse
Vineyard area: approx. 390 hectares (975 acres)
98% white wines; 2% red wines
Location: Germany's smallest wine-growing region lies along the ancient "Strata montana" (literally, mountain road) between Darmstadt and Heidelberg, bordered by the Rhine on the west and the protective Oden forest on the east. The Bergstrasse as such extends south of Heidelberg, but this wine section belongs to the German State of Baden-Württemberg (Baden's Bereich Badische Bergstrasse). The northern district, near Darmstadt, is Bereich Umstadt, a tiny area, planted mainly with Müller-Thurgau. The heart of the region lies within Bereich Starkenburg and includes the towns of Bensheim and Heppenheim. Riesling is the predominant variety here.
Grape Varieties: Riesling (53%); Müller-Thurgau (19%); Ruländer (Pinot Gris) (8%); Silvaner (7.7%).
Wine: hearty, rich and refreshing, thanks to a pronounced acidity; often compared to lesser Rheingau wines, but said to be fuller-bodied.

Most of the vineyards are very steep and hilly (labor-intensive), with a southern or southwestern exposure. The soil is deep, sandy loam-loess, granite and around Heppenheim, weathered colored sandstone. The climate is mild—in fact, fruit trees blossom earlier here than anywhere else in Germany.

The region's 740 growers are mostly part-time or hobby vintners (and members of cooperatives), individually owning less than half a hectare (about one acre) of vineyards. As an average, some 75% of the wine produced in Bereich Starkenburg is handled by the regional Bergstrasse cooperative in Heppenheim. The region's other large cooperative is in Gross-Umstadt. Bensheim is known for its own estate, as well as the prestigious State Wine Domain. Other producers in Bensheim: Josef Mohr and Tobias Georg Seitz; in Heppenheim: Heinrich Freiberger and Hans Strauch. Hessische Bergstrasse is a small but beautiful and hospitable region. Most of the wine is consumed locally—a good reason to attend one of the local wine festivals in the medieval town of Heppenheim (June) or Bensheim (September).
See Appendix B, p. 677.

Bernkasteler Doctor (Doktor)

The site of Doctor, among the best-known of great Mosel wines, seems to bring out the best of Riesling grown on slate in a particularly favorable micro-climate. With proper aging, the Doctor's balance of rich ripeness and fruity acidity makes it a prime exemplar of Germany's fine white wines.

The Doctor is, however, a source of controversy: Is its quality commensurate with its reputation (and very high price)? Will its ultimate size and ownership ever be agreed upon?
See Mosel-Saar-Ruwer.

Château Beychevelle

Bordeaux red wine.
District: Haut-Médoc, France.
Commune: Saint-Julien.

The château, long and low, with a great wing, is one of the most beautiful and imposing in the Médoc. It stands on the site of earlier feudal fortresses and was reconstructed in its present style in 1757 by the Marquis de Brassier. An enormous belvedere, nearly 50 meters (about 160 feet) long, commands a vista of the lawns, which run down to the River Gironde for more than a kilometer. The prospect is not unlike some of those at Versailles, but on a smaller scale.

In 1984 two-thirds of the shares of this Fourth Growth *(Quatrième Cru)* of 1855 owned by the Achille-Fould family were sold to a pension fund. In 1986 Mme Achille-Fould took over the presidency after the sudden death of Aymar, her very popular husband who was a deputy of the Médoc and a former cabinet minister. She is aided in this task by M. Foureau, who manages the estate.

M. Armand Achille-Fould, former Minister of Agriculture and father of the previous owner, used to tell the amusing story of how Beychevelle came into the family: his father went to the United States and married an American; while on a tour of France, he was pleased to hear his wife say at Beychevelle, "This is where I would like best to live"—whereupon he bought the estate.

The name comes from *baissez les voiles* (strike sail), the salute once given by ships passing on the river to the Duke of Epernon, Grand Admiral of France, when he was lord of the domain in feudal times. The Grand Admiral also knew the secondary wine, Clos de l'Amiral, which is still produced.

Beychevelle is very well known in England and the United States.
Characteristics. Great finesse. This vineyard has a following, and some of its vintages are definitely remarkable; others may be rather disappointing.
Vineyard area: 70 hectares (175 acres).
Average production: 280 *tonneaux* (26,000 cases).

Bhang, Bang

A "wine" made in India from hemp leaves and twigs infused in water.

Bianchello del Metauro (D.O.C.)

Italian white wine from the Marches *(q.v.)*.

Bianco

White. Italian term for white wine.

Bienvenue-Bâtard-Montrachet (A.O.C.)

Burgundy white wine.
District: Côte de Beaune, France.

Commune: Puligny-Montrachet (and in part Chassagne-Montrachet).
Official Classification: Great Growth (Grand Cru).

One of the memorable Montrachets, which are the greatest of the great white Burgundies. The vineyard, covering only about nine acres, is beside that of Bâtard-Montrachet. In character and quality the wines are similar. It is only in the past thirty years that a distinction has been made between Bienvenue, Criots, and Bâtard. Before that, all three wines were sold under the last name. Average yearly production of Bienvenue is about 125 hectoliters (3,310 U.S. gallons, 2,750 imp.).
See Bâtard-Montrachet; Puligny-Montrachet.

Big

A wine that may be called big has more than the average amount of flavor, body, and alcohol. Not necessarily a term of distinction, since a wine that is too big tends to be coarse and heavy.

Bin

English term for the place in which bottles of wines are stored in a cellar—or cupboard, if it is in a flat. When a merchant sells wine "in bin" (or "ex-bin"), it means that the customer must pay the cost of packing and delivery.

Binger Rochusberg

An outstanding wine of Bingen on the German Rhine. It has great character and is from slate-quartz soil.
See Rheinhessen.

Bishop

Mulled Port. The Port wine is heated up with sugar, orange, and cloves and set alight before being poured. Some authors give Claret, not Port, as the wine in a Bishop, but others say that Claret is used in an Archbishop.

Bitters

Spirits of varying alcoholic content flavored with roots, barks, and herbs, having in common only their bitterness and their claims to medicinal powers. Originally they were elixirs, and some are still so called. Bitters are either used as flavoring for mixed drinks or taken as aperitifs, liqueurs, or digestives. Some of the better-known ones are: Amer Picon (France) *(q.v.)*, Angostura (Trinidad, West Indies) *(q.v.)*, Boonekamp's (Holland), Campari (Italy) *(q.v.)*, Abbot's Aged Bitters (U.S.A.), Fernet Branca (Italy) *(q.v.)*, Law's Peach Bitters (England), Orange Bitters (England), Pommeranzen (Holland and Germany), Secrestat (France), Toni Kola (France), Unicum (Hungary), and Welling's (Holland).

Black Death

Popular name for the aquavit—and the national drink—of Iceland. This spirit is flavored with caraway seeds.
See Aquavit.

Black rot

A vine disease of American origin.
See Chapter Eight, p. 38.

Black Velvet

A mixture of stout and Champagne, popular in England in Edwardian days and still in existence. Usually associated with oysters.

Blackberry liqueur

A cordial made by steeping blackberries in sweetened brandy.

Blagny (Appellation Contrôlée)

The only Burgundian communal place-name that has no accompanying commune. Blagny is a hamlet, divided between Meursault and Puligny-Montrachet on the Côte de Beaune. Its wines are similar in almost all respects to those of Meursault. Meursault-Blagny denotes the wines from the best part of Blagny, adjoining Meursault.
See Meursault.

Blanc

White. French term for white wine.

Blanc de Blancs

Champagne made from the Chardonnay grape only. It is easily distinguishable by its light color from the golden wines made from red grapes. Blanc de Blancs is also becoming a widespread term for the white wines made from white grapes in many of France's lesser-known wine districts.
See Champagne.

Blanc Fumé de Pouilly (Appellation Contrôlée)

Dry white Loire Valley wine usually called Pouilly-Fumé.
See Pouilly-sur-Loire.

Blanc de Noirs

White wine from red grapes.
See Champagne.

Blanco

Spanish term for white wine.

Blanquette de Limoux and Vin de Blanquette (Appellation Contrôlée)

Sparkling, and some still, wines.
District: Southwest France.

Limoux, a small town near Carcassone, makes two types of wine, both from the same grape. That called Blanquette de Limoux or Limoux Nature is a sparkling wine, and the Vin de Blanquette is the still variety. Made from grapes of the Mauzac (at least 70%), Chardonnay (about 20%), and Clairette Blanche (no more than 10%), the wines come from a delimited area of forty-two communes of which Limoux is the center.

The sparkling Blanquette de Limoux has won some small renown. The wines contain at least 10% alcohol and have been made sparkling by the Champagne process, that of secondary fermentation in the bottle. Recently, the efforts of trained oenologists have considerably improved the quality of this sparkling wine.

The amount of the wine that is not rendered sparkling is always a small proportion. It too must have at least 10% alcohol, and it usually has a slight sparkle to it. Together, the wines are produced on some 2,000 hectares (5,000 acres) with an average yearly output of 50,000 hectoliters (1,325,000 U.S. gallons, 1,100,000 imp.).

Blauer Portugieser

A grapevine producing red wines and grown in the Vöslau region of Austria and in several regions of Germany.

See Austria.

Blaufrankische

A red-wine grape cultivated in Austria, Hungary, and elsewhere.

Blaye, Premières Côtes de Blaye, Côtes de Blaye

Red and white wines.
District: Bordeaux, France.

White and red wines lacking distinction and produced in a large and ancient vineland on the Gironde in southwest France. The three distinct place-names or Appellations Contrôlées apply to the same area, circling the historic river-town of Blaye, and indicate gradations of quality. Blaye (or Blayais) and Côtes de Blaye both make white wines, neither of great distinction. Premières Côtes de Blaye, 15% white and the remainder red, alone merits consideration for certain bottles, and alone is restricted to noble grape varieties (except that, in red wine, Prolongeau, Cahors, and Béquignol are varieties permitted up to 10%).

The white wines are dry, or, if they are labeled sweet, will be found to be semi-sweet. The red wines are lighter than those from the adjoining region of Bourg, and if tasted together with red Bourgs in the Blaye-Bourg House of Wine opened in Blaye in 1955 they will be found to be less distinguished, if smoother and suppler.

Separated from the Médoc by the considerable width of the river Gironde, Blaye is a romantic-looking region of rolling hills, its chief landmark a huge starfish-shaped fortress, originally built in the eleventh and twelfth centuries, rebuilt by General Vauban, strategist of Louis XIV, and now largely in ruins. From thimble-topped watchtowers in the corners of its walls, the view over the Gironde includes Pauillac, in the distance on the opposite shore, and in the wide river a trio of large islands given over to vineyard. From the river in the vicinity of Blaye comes the only true caviar produced outside Russia, Rumania, or Iran.

Bleichert

German term for rosé wine.

Blending

The practice of mixing together or "marrying" wines or spirits to obtain uniform quality from year to year, or to obtain a product better than any one of the components taken individually. In some cases, blending is a practical way of increasing quantity—but not quality; for if the original wine or spirit has been a fine one, quality is lowered and all individuality or distinction lost.

All Sherry is blended, as is most Champagne, Cognac, and whisky. In these instances the practice often enhances the product.

Blue Fining

Fining or clearing wines of copper casse with crystals of potassium ferrocyanide. This is effective in stabilizing white wines, but the results of an overdose are so dangerous that those countries which permit it do so only under very strict regulations. Blue fining is allowed in Germany but forbidden in France and the United States. In the United States a similar but safer commercial product called Cufex may be used to remove copper.

See Fining: Chapter Nine, p. 44.

Bõa Vista

One of the best known *quintas* of the Alto Douro in Portugal, for many years the property of the Forrester family.

Boal, Bual

A type of Madeira: full, sweet, rich in color, and with an extraordinary bouquet.
See Madeira.

Boca (D.O.C.)

Italian red wine from Piedmont *(q.v.)*.

Bock

See Beer.

Bocksbeutel, Boxbeutel

The flat flask-shaped wine bottle of Franconia (Germany) and Styria (Austria), rarely used except for these wines—although Undurraga in Chile has a somewhat similar bottle for Riesling, and some Australian wines and some Portuguese rosés are now being marketed in flasks of this type. While a variety of Franconian wines appear in the Bocksbeutel inside Germany, it is principally the green-gold Steinwein which is found abroad.

The origin of the flask is accounted for in several ways. Obviously, it resembles the once common leather wineskin. A Bocksbeutel carryall favored by old-fashioned German women is also cited as a possible pattern—and so is an organ of the goat, which takes much the same shape. In any case, the Bocksbeutel has been in use for some time: in 1728, the Burgerspital wines of Würzburg began to be bottled in these flasks.
See Franconia.

Bocoy

Chestnut barrel used for shipping Spanish wines, holding usually 650 to 700 liters (172 to 185 U.S. gallons, 143 to 154 imp.). There is also a Media Bocoy, or half-bocoy, containing generally 350 liters (92 U.S. gallons, 77 imp.). The two measures are the same in content as the Germand Halbstück (half-"piece") and Viertelstück (quarter-"piece").

Bodega

In Spain a place for storing wine, not a cellar usually, but above ground; and, colloquially, a wine shop. The term is often used in England for a wine-bar.

Body

A wine with stubstance or body fills the mouth. Alcohol and tannin give the characteristic. Many great white wines, such as Moselles, can be light, lacking body, but all great red wines will have it. When young, a great wine often has excessive body. With age, if the wine succeeds, this modifies and becomes part of the full roundness. The French term is *corsé*.

Bois Ordinaires

See Cognac.

Bolivia

Not one of the more important of the South American wine-producing countries, Bolivia has about 1,600 hectares (4,000 acres) planted in wine-producing vines. In addition, there are about 4,000 more acres producing table grapes. The wine made amounts to a negligible 20,000 hectoliters (530,000 U.S. gallons, 440,000 imp.) or so a year; there is also an almost equal amount of brandy. Bolivian brandy is usually Pisco brandy, as in Peru and Chile.
See Pisco brandy.

Bombom Crema

A honey-flavored Cuban liqueur.

Bonarda

Grape used for dark red wine made principally around Asti in Italy. The wine is sometimes sparkling.
See Piedmont.

Bonde

French term for a barrel stopper, or bung *(q.v.)*.

Bonded spirits or wines

Spirits or wines held in store by Customs and Excise until duty is paid by the purchaser. In the United States, a bonded whiskey must remain a minimum of four years in bond before it can be called Bonded Rye or Bourbon. Until 1958, these whiskeys could be aged for eight years only. After that, Internal Revenue taxes had to be paid.

Bonnes Mares (Appellation Contrôlée)

Burgundy red wine.
District: Côte de Nuits, France.
Communes: Chambolle-Musigny and Morey-Saint-Denis.
Official Classification: Great Growth (Grand Cru).

The origin of the name is obscure, but no one has seriously put forth the theory that it has anything to do with stagnant pools (the French word *mare*), good or otherwise.

A large vineyard by Burgundian standards, 11 hectares (37.8 acres), Bonnes Mares is split with 1.8 hectares (4.6 acres) in Morey-Saint-Denis and the rest in Chambolle. It borders Morey's Clos de Tart and the twisting vineyard road (on the uphill side). Although it lies in two communes, the name of neither will normally appear on bottle labels. Bonnes Mares is a Great Growth (*Grand Cru*), one of only thirty-one so designated among the hundreds of Burgundian vineyards, and is put on sale with no further indication of source than the vineyard name. The information on labels should include vineyard, year, grower, and/or shipper and his address—anything else is superfluous.

Like most Burgundian vineyards, Bonnes Mares is divided among a number of growers (who at one time included the author of this book) who all tend their own sections; but for some reason the very great wine they make is not very well known abroad. The peer of most red wines of the Côte de Nuits, and finer than most on the Côte de Beaune—with the exception of Corton—it is overshadowed nonetheless by many lesser but more widely recognized growths. Perhaps it has been eclipsed by the fabulous Musigny—on the opposite side of Chambolle—or bypassed by wine-lovers speeding north toward the fine wines of Gevrey-Chambertin.

As is true of all the great Côte d'Or reds, the grape used is the Pinot Noir. In the soil of Bonnes Mares, it produces wines which are generally softer than most of the great Moreys, with much of the elegance and delicacy of Musigny. Richer in tannins than most Burgundies, they have a firm strength which permits them to age and to round out beautifully, and they keep longer than many other red Burgundies.

No great quantity is made. In an average-quantity year, production is some 300 hectoliters (7,950 U.S. gallons, 6,600 imp.), or 3,100 cases.

Bonnezeaux

A small choice section of the Coteaux du Layon district of Anjou, France, with the right to an Appellation Contrôlée.

See Anjou.

Bons Bois

See Cognac.

Bor

Hungarian term for wine.

Bordeaux

Red, white, and rosé wines.
District: Southwest France.

Bordeaux is the most important wine region of France. About half of the fine wines of the world come from France, and about half of these from Bordeaux, which has a long and troubled history.

When the Romans arrived in 56 B.C. to occupy what was then Burdigala, it was already a port (although not yet the most important of the Gironde) doing some trade with Britain and other northern ports; and it was connected by road and river with the earlier colony of Narbonne in the south. According to the Bordeaux writer Gaston Marchou, Roman rule was lenient in Burdigala and the native Bituriges were easily and happily Latinized. The city flourished and so did the surrounding vineyards—Pliny mentions the wines that were being made here in the first century A.D.; and in the fourth century, Ausonius was writing from his agreeable villa on an estate outside the town. This good life lasted through his time. Afterward, the Visigoths came and a dark age set in for the vineyards as well as for the city. Luckily Christianity had arrived first, and here, as elsewhere, it was the Church that preserved a vestige of the old learning and saved the culture of the vine—but with many setbacks, over several hundred years.

In 1152, Eleanor of Aquitaine married Henry Plantagenet, Count of Anjou and King of England, bringing Guyenne (Gascony) and Bordeaux as her dowry. At first the Bordelais resented their new rulers. Richard Coeur de Lion spent some time in the city and seems to have charmed them. Yet, in an edict of his successor, King John, on the French wines selling in England in about 1200, no mention was made of any from Bordeaux. Very soon, however, this same king was drinking the Gascon wines and granting favors to the Bordelais. By the end of the reign of Henry III (1216–72), the Bordeaux merchants had gained many privileges: their taxes were eased, and they were given the right to sell in English markets, to set up a council (the Jurade) in their own city, and to elect their mayor. Then, as at the present time, the products of Bourg and Blaye were also in demand. Although ships still sailed from Soulac and other harbors, the crescent-shaped port of Bordeaux (*le port de la lune*) was now first in importance, bristling with the masts of merchant ships. The wines of Graves became the fashion in England (as late as the sixteenth century, the Médoc was described as a savage district, and its wines were little known for another hundred years); the bourgeoisie began to build new houses. By the fourteenth century, the Jurade was very powerful. No one was allowed to sell his wines until the big burghers had made all the sales they wanted—even aristocratic families with estates outside the city were asking to be accepted as bourgeois. As for the wines of other towns (Libourne, Poitiers, and Gaillac), these could not be brought in for sale to foreign buyers until the very end of the autumn wine fair—in those days, wines were drunk from the wood in their first year, and the English ships had to be home with the new vintage before Christmas, by which time the fragile wine would spoil. The underprivileged barrels were kept apart on the Quai des Chartrons, which was afterward to become the preserve of the great Bordeaux merchants themselves. When the Hundred Years' War (1337–1453) began, the Bordelais, quite happy under a rule so beneficial to them commercially, took the English side. In 1356, after the battle of Poitiers, the Black Prince held the French King John II prisoner and brought him into Bordeaux. "It cannot be recorded," said the chronicler Froissart, "the great feast and cheer that they of the city, with the clergy, made to the Prince." The French king also seems to have had a fair share of the good time before he was taken off to England. Next year came the Black Death, but as soon as the plague had died down the war revived. In his last years the Black Prince, spent, ill, and sadly changed from the magnificent conqueror of Poitiers, carried out senseless destructive raids in the country beyond Bordeaux, and what he did not destroy was ravaged afterward by the French armies in the struggle to recapture the whole of Gascony. For a long time, the Bordeaux vineyards remained untouched, and overseas trade went on. Even when the helpless Henry VI became king of England, Bordeaux and the famous Archbishop Pey Berland believed the English could defend them still. They asked for help. Little came. A small force under the eighty-year-old John Talbot, Earl of Shrewsbury, brave but outnumbered, was defeated at Castillon. Talbot was killed in 1453 (his name survives at Château Talbot in the Médoc) and Bordeaux was French again. At first the burghers were not pleased. The city lost its privileges, and the foreign trade on which, in those days of bad roads to Paris, they depended, was almost at a stop. But the French king Louis XI, when he succeeded Charles VII, realized the value of a flourishing wine trade and restored many of the privileges, even at the expense of some of the upriver towns which had been loyal to the French kings. He allowed the Bordelais to elect their own parliament and the English to return for their wine.

In the next century, the troubles were religious. Calvinism spread in the district. There were religious persecutions, uprisings, and in 1572 Bordeaux had its own version of the Massacre of Saint Bartholomew. Henry IV, with his Edict of Nantes, recognized the Protestants (or Huguenots) and things began to look up again. By the seventeenth century, Bordeaux wine was known in Paris and at court. When Cardinal Richelieu planted a new vineyard in the Loire region, he sent for vines from Bordeaux. Mme de Sévigné said Bordeaux would soon go out of fashion "like coffee and Racine," but time has proved her wrong. Louis XIV is said to have washed down big helpings of meat with Saint-Émilion and Chambertin. But his rule was oppressive to the *grands bourgeois* of Bordeaux, who found all their power transferred to the king's intendant, while the king's wars were bad for trade. His unfriendly relations with England (and the change there to Dutch and German kings) led to the Methuen Treaty, which announced new customs duties, favorable to Iberian wines, taxing French ones almost out of the market. Yet the English upper classes wanted their Claret, and smugglers brought it in.

The middle of the eighteenth century was the *belle époque* in Bordeaux—in spite of the fact that at one time the intendant ordered growers to root up their vines and grow corn instead. Orders like that have never been universally obeyed, and one who defied this one was the writer and grower, Montesquieu. The wine trade was always first, but other industries (distilling, ship-building, glass-blowing, sugar refining) were started. Now Bordeaux had an important new customer in North America. The town grew rich, and elegant houses and public buildings appeared: the Place de la Bourse, the Allées de Tourny, and the splendid theater of Victor Louis—all these are still to be seen. When, in 1758, the Duke de Richelieu followed Tourny as intendant, he brought down troupes to act in the theater and invited actresses to supper. He was frivolous, to say the least, and quite unlike the rich bourgeoisie of Bordeaux, some of them Protestants, who lived well but rather austerely. During this period many of the foreigners whose names have become local in Bordeaux—Barton, Lawton, Johnston—first settled in; their descendants are there today.

The first Claret to be put down for ageing, in one of the first bottles sufficiently well rounded to be laid on its side, was the Château Lafite 1797. A dusty old bottle of that vintage is even now on show in the cellars of the château.

The Revolution and the Napoleonic Wars brought particularly bad times for Bordeaux. Cut off from English, American, and Colonial trade, some of the merchants were reduced to selling prunes instead of wine. By 1808, there was no life in the port. Napoleon paid a visit and promised a subsidy, but nothing came of it—except the warm support of Bordeaux for the Restoration. When the wars were over, trade naturally picked up. England lowered taxes in the eighteen-twenties and -thirties. In the fifties came the terrible mildew epidemic, but in spite of it the Classification of 1855, based on earlier classifications and on then current prices for the different wines, was drawn up so that the best wines of Bordeaux could be recognized when they were shown at the Paris Exhibition of that year. In 1860, Gladstone's government lowered the duties on wines coming into England and allowed grocers to sell them. The result was lower prices, bigger trade, and a boom in the import of Claret. The twenty pre-phylloxera years, from 1858 to 1878, produced some memorable vintages—ten good years, of which the greatest were 1858, 1864, 1865, 1870, and 1875. When this book was first published, connoisseurs then alive had tasted these wines and maintained that nothing like them would ever be seen again. Even if we do not agree that the great days are over, it must be allowed that today's fine wines are to some extent different, because they are produced from vines grafted onto American root-stocks, whereas the earlier vines were purely *Vitis vinifera*. Moreover, in those leisurely times, vatting and barrel-ageing lasted longer than is now required for quality. Nevertheless,

1893, 1899, and 1900 are agreed to have been excellent years in Bordeaux, as were 1904, 1906, and 1914. Wines from these years and even earlier often still appear at auction, principally in London. The post-First World War vintages of 1924, 1928, 1929, 1934, and 1937 are everywhere remembered. People who bought these wines to lay down before World War II were lucky: claret was unprecedentedly cheap in the nineteen-thirties. We know from Professor Saintsbury's *Notes on a Cellar-Book* that château-bottled wines were being sold for much the same figure in the 1860s, when money was worth more.

BORDEAUX PLACE-NAMES

In 1911, after long litigation and dispute, the boundaries of the zone of Bordeaux were fixed as those of the department of the Gironde—except for the strip of dune soil along the Atlantic coast, which is not accepted.

The Gironde, largest of the French departments, produces 5.6 million hectoliters (147 million U.S. gallons, 123 million imp.) of wine each year on more than 100,000 hectares (250,000 acres) of vineyard which comprise one-tenth of its entire land surface. The name is derived from the French *hirondelle* (a swallow). The two rivers Dordogne and Garonne meet a little above Bordeaux and flow into the broad tidal Gironde, which descends another 50 miles into the Atlantic. The graceful confluence of the two tributaries sketches a swallow's tail; and around the *hirondelle* and the wider estuary, with Bordeaux at its center, the departmental boundaries of the Gironde are flung. The wines are mostly river wines—all the great ones, except the Saint-Émilions and the Pomerols, grow within sight of flowing water.

Within the region, at least three dozen place-names, or Appellations Contrôlées, designate different wines. All these are Bordeaux, although the wines carrying the looser designation Bordeaux are less distinguished than those with a more specific place-name. Yet, not all wine grown in the district is labeled Bordeaux, because, to be entitled to the *appellation*, minimum standards of viticulture and viniculture must be met (*see* Appellation d'Origine Contrôlée). The more restricted regional *appellations*—Haut-Médoc, Saint-Julien, etc.—will nearly always have been bought from different vineyards within the given region by a Bordeaux shipper and blended by him. His reputation will be the additional—and usually soundest—indication of the value of the wine. The Monopole Bordeaux of the various shipping houses are wines of this class, on which the shipper means to stake his name. Nearly all these regional wines are blends. If the vintage year appears on the bottle, it is a blend within the stated year; when the vintage date does not appear, the blend may be from different vineyards and different years. The best shippers blend with the intention of producing a consistently good wine, a "type" which can be reproduced year after year and which can therefore "follow itself"—a basic principle in the making of all the better blended wines and spirits. This means, nevertheless, that year-to-year conformity brings the standard down to a common denominator which can never be very high.

Bordeaux Rouge, Bordeaux Blanc, regional bottlings, and Château bottlings are the types to be found on the market. The last are wines from individual vineyards or blends from several lesser vineyards or even from small châteaux, as Bordeaux vineyards are nearly always called—even when they do not possess a "castle" or big house; for, compared with the châteaux of the Loire, many of these are modest country houses, some of them merely villas. Château wine is never blended with wines from outside the limits of the château itself and is always marked with the vintage year—thus, it is the wine of one vineyard and one harvest. With weather and other viticultural conditions fluctuating as they do, these wines will never have the year-to-year consistency of regional bottlings; but they will touch the highest peaks in the finest years. They are bottled at the château itself and carry on the label the words *Mis en Bouteilles au Château*, or some slight variant of this phrase—the owner's guarantee that the wine is authentic, a guarantee that he could not make with assurance if it had left his premises unbottled.

About 200 of the more than 3,000 châteaux of Bordeaux have been officially classified at various times, beginning in the 16th century. Three of these lists—the Médoc and Sauternes Classification of 1855, the Graves Classifications of 1953 and 1959, and the Saint-Émilion Classifications of 1955, 1969 and 1986—are extant today (*see* Médoc, Sauternes, Graves, Saint-Émilion). All châteaux classified as outstanding are treated individually (*see* Château Lafite, Château Latour, Château d'Yquem, Château Cheval Blanc, *etc.*). The important sub-regional and communal names or Appellations Contrôlées are as follows:

APPELLATIONS CONTRÔLÉES OF BORDEAUX

	Wine	Hectares	Acres
Sauternes	Sweet white	1,450	3,625
Barsac	Sweet white	560	1,400
Médoc	Red	3,400	8,500
Haut-Médoc	Red	3,200	8,000
Saint-Estèphe	Red	1,100	2,750
Pauillac	Red	1,000	2,500
Saint-Julien	Red	800	2,000
Margaux	Red	1,100	2,750
Listrac	Red	500	1,250
Moulis	Red	350	875
Pomerol	Red	835	2,007
Saint-Émilion	Red	5,000	12,500
St.-Émilion: Satellites	Red	3,500	8,750
Graves	White	1,450	3,625
Graves	Red	2,120	5,300

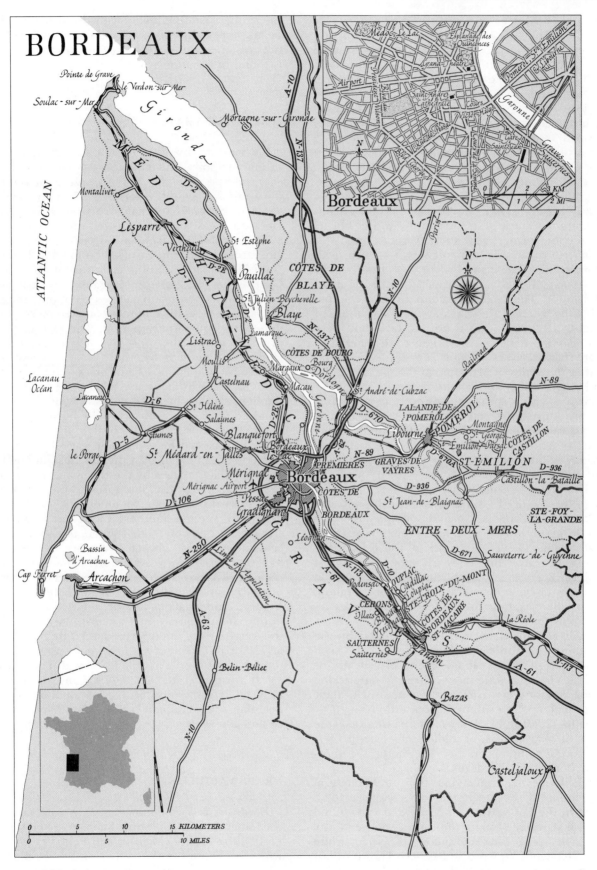

BORDEAUX

CHARACTERISTICS

It is evident, from the multiplicity of names, that the range of Bordeaux wines is the greatest anywhere. Roughly, it may be said that red wines are made north of the city and white wines to the south, with the Graves district, in which the actual town is set, forming an intermediate zone where both white and red wines are grown, frequently in a single vineyard. The white wines, with some exceptions, change gradually from dry to sweet through the vineyards in Graves on the edge of Bordeaux to Sauternes at the southern extreme of the region.

Red Bordeaux is, in its own delicate yet firm, feminine style, the finest of its kind in the world; but its characteristic softness and subtlety come only with age. In a Bordeaux the tannin content—which, with alcohol, decides the "heaviness" or "lightness" of any wine—is actually higher than in an authentic and natural Burgundy. This might be said to disprove the theory that the wines of Bordeaux are light and those of Burgundy are heavy. This is not the case, but there are, in fact, a number of exceptions to the rule. The delicate characteristics of "light" Bordeaux are exemplified in the wines of Margaux, in the middle of the Haut-Médoc, which are definite in taste but mild in texture. Generally speaking, however, natural Bordeaux are sturdy when young, but they mature beautifully and attain softness with age; the greater the Bordeaux, the greater will be the recompense of patience, especially in the case of the wines grown around the village of Pauillac, and of the very sturdy wines of Saint-Estèphe, where the softening qualities of age are most necessary. Red Graves also is earthy and full when young and attains a magnificent splendor later on. In Burgundy, on the other hand, young wines tend to mature much faster; and some of those from the Beaujolais region of Burgundy are among the lightest red wines of France, if not of the world. A Côte de Nuits may well be more delicate than a Saint-Émilion, which usually has great fullness and is sometimes referred to as the "Burgundy" of Bordeaux.

Certain generic characteristics are shared by the great gamut of Bordeaux wine. Uniquely, for such volume, it is perfectly natural. White or red, dry or sweet, the châteaux wines never have anything added to them; and for this reason, and also because of their iron content, they are wonderfully health-giving. (Occasionally—1980 and 1984 are modern instances—the process of *chaptalisation*, or adding sugar before fermentation, a common practice elsewhere, is authorized in Bordeaux.) Bordeaux are characterized, too, by their longevity, tremendous for purely natural wines. Some of the greatest Médocs will live for a century in the bottle (the stubborn 1870 vintage did not fulfill its early promise until it was between fifty and seventy years old); and among the sweet white wines, Château d'Yquem also has been known to last a hundred years. In spite of the huge multiplicity and range, there is something peculiar to the scent of Bordeaux, especially the aged reds—a woodland freshness or an earthy smell of low-growing violets which is found in no other wine.

SOIL AND CLIMATE

Such a diversity of wines indicates an equal variety of vineyard soils. The most characteristic soil element, very widespread, is the presence on the surface and in the subsoil of pebbles, forming either the gravel or *graves* which gives the name to several of the finest vineyard areas, or the egg-sized and even fist-sized *cailloux* (pebbles) figuring proudly in the names of such vineyards as Château Beaucaillou in Saint-Julien and contributing largely to the character of, for example, Château Latour, Château Margaux, and Château Prieuré-Lichine. With only a few exceptions, the finest wines come from the vineyards planted on soil deposited in the Quaternary period. The extreme of this principle is that the most recent river soils are excluded as vineyards for wines accorded any of the Bordeaux Appellations Contrôlées. The late alluvial strips and marshy areas are called *palus*; an interesting sidelight on the changing tastes in wine is that a few hundred years ago these were the most sought-after areas in the four categories of land then established.

All Bordeaux wines—though not all to the same degree—are influenced by the mildness and humidity of the climate created by the rivers and the nearness of the sea, and by the pine forests which blanket the land toward the ocean. Summer heat rarely fails to generate a sudden thundershower, and long parched stretches are uncommon. Winters are short and are seldom very cold. The chief menace to the vines is hail, which in recent years has struck most often in the regions of Barsac-Sauternes, more than once destroying the crops of Château d'Yquem, Château de Rayne-Vigneau, and adjacent vineyards. Frosts are a danger, but are less frequent than in most fine vineland. For this very reason, the unprecedented freeze of February 1956 killed hundreds of acres of vineyard; vines unprepared to resist frost failed to withstand the coldest Bordeaux winter since 1709, and the crop was reduced by some 50%, with a loss of about a million hectoliters (26.4 million U.S. gallons, 22 million imp.) of unmade wine.

GRAPE VARIETIES

Bordeaux red wine must be made from varieties of the Cabernet vine (Cabernet Sauvignon and Cabernet Franc), the Merlot, Malbec, and Petit-Verdot. White wines are limited to the grapes of the Sémillon, Sauvignon, and Muscadelle. Only very rare instances exist of a wine made from a single variety, and practically all are blends of the permitted grapes, varying somewhat in proportion according to the theories of the different growers, but tending to follow the rough formula which time has proved best suited to that particular section. Until 1953 a number of other, less noble vines were tolerated, up to a maximum of 10% of the wine; but in the decade beginning in March 1953 these all have been systematically uprooted. The writings of Montesquieu indicate a very different situation in his time. In 1785, according to him, no less than twenty-seven varieties of red and twenty-two varieties of white vine contributed to the wines.

VINTAGES

Vintage is very much overemphasized in Bordeaux wines. From 1795 to 1870, 40% of the years were poor or mediocre and 60% were good or better. Since 1870, the proportion has been 80% good or excellent, and 20% mediocre: thus the number of poor years before 1870 was proportionately double the number today. Modern science has eliminated the conditions which gave rise to emphasis on vintage by helping to cut out the "lows."

This does not mean that vintages do not differ—they only fail to differ in commonplace wine zones—but it does mean that the terms used to describe vintages no longer conform to the real case, especially in the highly abbreviated and therefore misleading and sometimes biased vintage charts. On these lists, the opposite of a "great" year is always a "poor," or perhaps a "small" one. In fact, small years occur in quantity, but never in terms of wine character or quality, and it is a distinct misnomer to refer to a light wine as "small." A "great" red Bordeaux is simply a Bordeaux which has been produced in a "big" year—when continuous sunshine has destined a wine to develop slowly and to last a long time. A "small" year is merely one when there is less sun, and the wines of this year will mature relatively quickly. Deluded by vintage charts, too many people suppose that they must buy the wines only of the big years, usually indicated by outsized ciphers on the vintage chart; in doing so, they are buying essentially what ought properly to be called long-lasting wine, and too often they drink it before it has come to its proper bottle-age. Had they chosen instead the wine of lighter year, they would have paid less and had a better bottle *at the time they drank it.*

Yet it would not be correct to say that the big vintages are overvalued; properly laid down and waited for, they will finally achieve the highest peaks. It is true, however, that the lighter years, having less tannin, are undervalued, for the wines of those years, ready to be drunk much earlier, are not always inferior but develop and provide pleasure more quickly and fade sooner.

HARVESTING

Bordeaux is usually harvested at the end of September, sometimes in early October, and very rarely in August or November. As a general rule, the hotter the summer, the earlier the harvest. In the last century and a half, the number of vintages starting in the effective month were as follows: August (1822 and 1893), 2; September, 129; October, 60; November (in 1816), 1. Red wines and most white wines are picked straight over the vineyard, but the extra-sweet Barsacs and Sauternes are selectively picked, bunch by bunch and almost grape by grape as the individual berries reach super-ripeness. Therefore, Barsac and Sauternes harvests take about three times as long as they do elsewhere, often ending in November. The following chart depicts the cycle of the vine in certain significant years.

RIPENING OF THE VINE AT CHÂTEAU MOUTON-ROTHSCHILD (GREAT VINTAGES ONLY)

| | Flowering | | Beginning of reddening of | |
Year	Beginning	End	the grape	Start of harvest
1979	June 12	June 28	Aug. 6	Oct. 1
1978	June 10	June 26	Aug. 10	Oct. 10
1976	May 30	June 12	July 4	Sept. 15
1975	June 3	June 21	July 21	Sept. 23
1970	June 5	June 19	July 22	Sept. 28
1966	May 25	June 15	July 25	Sept. 26
1961	May 15	June 5	July 25	Oct. 2
1952	May 19	June 5	July 8	Sept. 18
1947	May 26	June 15	July 15	Sept. 17
1945	May 11	June 1	July 2	Sept. 7
1929	May 24	June 25	July 22	Sept. 21
1921	May 19	June 13	July 18	Sept. 10
1900	May 29	June 14	July 26	Sept. 25

MATURING

Wines of Bordeaux previously stored in jars, or amphorae, began to be kept in cask at the suggestion of Charlemagne. Centuries later—not long before the French Revolution—a greater integrity was established by the enforced use of the *barrique bordelaise*, the barrel which survives today and which was at that time forbidden to all other wines. It is an ideal size—225 liters—for maturing red Bordeaux, although in white Bordeaux some experiments are being made to see if a larger barrel, slowing the development of the wine and keeping it fresher and fruitier, will not better accord with the taste for ever younger white wines. The cost of the barrel itself, in Bordeaux as elsewhere, has risen sensationally and become a factor in the price of the wine. The hand-made oak barrels at the time of writing cost 1,900 francs (approximately 290 dollars, or 190 pounds) per barrel. Oak used to be imported from Poland, Sweden, and the United States; but since the Second World War some of it has come from Yugoslavia, most from the Limoges forest (where the wood is shared with makers of Cognac), the Allier and Nevers. A certain amount of poorer-quality wood from Alsace is used to make up the deficit.

White wines are both fermented and matured in cask; red wines are matured in cask, but are fermented in large vats, formerly in oak, today at most vineyards they are now made of cement or stainless steel. Controversy rages between traditionalists and modernists in Bordeaux over the use of concrete vats, but no one has been able to prove that the modern method of fermenting in concrete, easier to clean, is less efficient or entails loss of quality, and it is fast gaining adherents. There are a few vineyards which began cautious experiments maturing red Bordeaux in the oak barrels in which it is fermented, an innovation which, if successful, would both reduce cost by eliminating expensive casks and produce a lighter wine which could be drunk sooner. The great red Bordeaux will never be made by this method, because part of the tannin which gives it longevity is absorbed from the new oak of the barrels, renewed for each vintage; but perhaps there will be room also for the lighter, younger wine. It is, however, understandable that since the Second World War there has been a laudable tendency in Bordeaux to advance the bottling by additional rackings (four per year), which hastens the development of the wine. Forty years ago, red Bordeaux was always kept for a minimum of three years in the wood. Nowadays, all the châteaux are bottling at anything from eighteen to thirty months.

BORDEAUX BOTTLES

The characteristic Bordeaux bottle has shoulders to retain the sediment and a neck very suited by its straight length to the long corks which distinguish and preserve the finest wines. Half-bottles, called in Bordeaux *fillettes* (little girls), are often used, especially for dry white wines, which ought to be drunk very young. A wine will mature more quickly in a half-bottle than in a bottle, because its ripening is partly caused by oxygen coming through the cork, relatively greater in proportion to the lesser quantity of wine in the small bottle. For this reason, a young wine may be good from the half-bottle, but old wines from the half-bottle will be "gone." The ideal bottle for great old Bordeaux is the magnum, with double the content of the standard bottle, in which the wine matures more slowly. The double magnum and the six-bottle jeroboam are rare; and the imperial, with the content of eight normal bottles, has not often been seen since the Second World War. Some experts contend that the old red Bordeaux are better in the sizes greater than

the magnum, on the same law of ever lesser cork dimensions in relation to wine mass; while others believe the magnum is the optimum size. This is an argument limited almost entirely to the Bordelais and almost impossible to settle, since it concerns wines more than thirty years old, bottled long ago and subject to dozens of subtly influential conditions.

EXPORT

Export in 1985 of Bordeaux-controlled place-name wines amounted to approximately 1.6 million hectoliters (42 million U.S. gallons, 35 million imp.). This figure represents an increase of 33% from the amount exported in 1982. Of the total, Bordeaux exported 251,000 hectoliters (about 6.65 million U.S. gallons, 5.50 million imp.) to the United States alone.

BORDEAUX GROWTHS: CLASSIFICATION

In 1855 there was a great Exhibition in Paris; the organizers sent to Bordeaux for samples of its best wines, and this set off the local notables on a classification of their finest growths. Only two districts were dealt with—the Médoc and Sauternes. At that time Graves, which had once been the leading district, had fallen behind, and these two regions produced the recognized quality wines of Bordeaux, whose wine merchants discriminated (partly out of snobbery) against the merchants of Libourne and its adjoining vineyards in Saint-Émilion and Pomerol. Hence Château Pétrus of Pomerol, Château Cheval-Blanc and Château Ausone (celebrated as the oldest fine vineyard of the region) in Saint-Émilion were omitted from the 1855 Classification of the Wines of the Gironde and had to wait until 1955 to be officially rated. The grading was done by the Bordeaux brokers (or *courtiers*) who sell the product of the various vineyards to the shippers and are therefore considered to know the wines better than anybody else. The brokers based their judgments on soil, prestige, and prices.

That this was a sensible decision has been proved by the long life of the 1855 Classification. Climate, soil, and surface-exposure of vineyards do not change, and these elements have exercised the same beneficial influence since 1855 as they did before; but owners change, some tend their vines and make their wine better than others do—and there is no doubt that this century-old assessment is now, in some parts, obsolescent. There are few important châteaux which have not changed their holdings. Patches of vineyard are continually being bought and sold. The classification is still, however, completely valid for the First Growths (*Premiers Crus*)—the three great Médoc châteaux, Lafite, Margaux, and Latour—and Haut-Brion, which has always been on the list. Although it is actually in

Graves, Haut-Brion wine was too good to be left out and so, defying geography, was classed in with the Médocs. Château Mouton-Rothschild, which in 1973 was justifiably decreed a First Growth, was in the 1855 Classification listed as first among the Second Growths (*Seconds Crus*).

In considering the 1855 Classification, it should be emphasized that a Second, Third (*Troisième*), Fourth (*Quatrième*), or Fifth Growth (*Cinquième Cru*) is not a second-, third-, fourth-, or fifth-rate wine. Actually, only 62 among about 3,000 vineyards were considered worthy of being listed Great Growths (*Grands Crus*)—whether First or Fifth—and they are the absolute cream of the vineyards which, as a group, are probably the world's finest in red wine. To be second after only Lafite, Latour, Margaux, and Haut-Brion is very far from being second-rate. Moreover, it is only on average that the first are the best; in certain years, others equal and even surpass them. Anyone can be sure of a superb bottle when he buys the best years of the famous vineyards (at a price); but there is adventure—and economy—in seeking out other years and other vineyards from the splendid list of Bordeaux wines.

Exceptional Growths (*Crus Exceptionnels*) are *not* classed higher than the Great Growths, but are those classified in 1855 after the 62 great vineyards—and were themselves followed by the Bourgeois and Artisan classes (*Crus Bourgeois* and *Crus Artisans*). Among these are some fine wines which now deserve to be elevated to greater recognition.

In fact, the old classification no longer tells the whole truth; and opinions expressed in the press and elsewhere have proved that even in Bordeaux uneasiness has, in certain quarters, been steadily increasing—although the general view was that, while the ruling of 1855 had its faults, it was impossible to improve upon it. And this in spite of the fact that some of the vineyards then listed are no longer in existence.

In 1959, a committee was formed to decide what was to be done about reclassifying the work of 1855. Two alternatives were discussed: should the 1855 Classification be amended to reflect the changes of today; or should the Classification of 1855 remain untouched and a new one be drawn up? The author, feeling that many alterations are needed, was a member of one of the original committees, which consisted of leading Bordeaux growers, shippers, and brokers, and he published in 1959 a private classification of all the red wines of Bordeaux, on the lines of the recent official ratings for Saint-Émilion and Graves—Pomerol has not even yet been classified. Revised several times, the most recent classification was prepared in 1986. Each expert was interviewed privately and "off the record," therefore, no one person's views are quoted: but it was soon evident that on certain points there was no difference of opinion. Investigation of land records in the various communes revealed that some of the châteaux no longer occupied the same terrain they did in 1855; in many cases changes were insignificant, but in others important transfers of par-

cels of land had been made—and therefore even the essential qualification of first-rate soil cannot, in these instances, go unchallenged. Other classified châteaux, including some Second and Third Growths, no longer make any wine; the names stand for Great Growths of 1855 as a Roman ruin may persist as a reminder of a vanished monument of classical times. This absurdity does harm to the Bordeaux wine trade; and the reverse case, of a vineyard classed as a Fifth or even a Bourgeois Growth, when it deserves to be sold as a Second or Third Growth, deprives both grower and customer of a satisfactory transaction.

It was generally agreed that if the 1855 standards were applied today, they would have to rate as a First Growth Château Pétrus—still unclassified in the as yet unclassified district of Pomerol; would have to advance Château Mouton-Rothschild from Second to First Growth which was done in 1973, and elevate Cheval-Blanc from a First of Saint-Émilion to a Bordeaux Great Growth. Indeed, so many vineyards of Saint-Émilion, Graves, and Pomerol clamored for their rightful place that it became obvious that any workable classification should include all Bordeaux wines. In fact, the system of 1855 should not now be used, for if a guide is no longer completely reliable, the public loses confidence. This is now happening.

As to the form a new classification should take, opinions were almost unanimous that the error of grading vineyards First, Second, and so on must not be repeated. In an age of publicity and competitive salesmanship, any wine listed as a Second, Third, or Fourth would be unfairly handicapped; the newer classifications for Saint-Émilion and Graves do not follow this pattern, and grade their wines First Growths, Great Growths, and Other Principal Growths (*see* Appendix A). In his suggested revision of the Classification, the author has adapted and expanded these as follows: Outstanding Growths (*Crus Hors Classe*), Exceptional Growths (*Crus Exceptionnels*), Great Growths (*Grands Crus*), Superior Growths (*Crus Supérieurs*), and Good Growths (*Bons Crus*).

Finally, most of the experts consulted were of the opinion that, in assessing the position of the vineyards, price, value, quality and prestige could still be (as they were in 1855) indications, and it was on this basis that the following classification was prepared. The fact that a great soil, given proper management, will produce great wines was taken into account: certain vineyards have not been downgraded as much as their present management warrants, because the soil is intact and, under new management, these vineyards may rise again.

A classification should not be planned for a shorter span than 25 to 50 years. The present condition of the 1855 list proves that no such ruling can remain valid indefinitely; but, conversely, too frequent change would cause confusion and loss of confidence among buyers.

In 1960, after the committee had made a formal request for a revision of the 1855 Classification, the

THE APPELLATIONS CONTRÔLÉES OF THE BORDEAUX REGION

Figures can vary by at least double, from year to year.   Maximum Yield   *Average Production*

Place-name	Date Established	HECTO- LITERS/ HECTARES	GALLONS PER ACRE U.S.	Imp.	WHITE Hectoliters	U.S. Gallons	Imp. Gallons	RED Hectoliters	U.S. Gallons	Imp. Gallons
Barsac	Sept 11, 1936	25	267.25	222.5	13,000	343,000	286,000			
Blaye or Blayais	Sept 11, 1936 white	45	481	400.5	26,000	687,000	572,000			
	Sept 11, 1936 red	60	639	532.2						
Bordeaux Blanc	Nov 14, 1936	65	692.5	576.5	600,000	15,851,000	13,199,000			
Bordeaux Rouge	Nov 14, 1936	55	586	488				790,000	20,870,000	17,378,000
Bordeaux Côtes de Francs Blanc	May 26, 1967	50	534.5	445						
Bordeaux Côtes de Francs Rouge	May 26, 1967	50	534.5	445				10,000	265,000	220,000
Bordeaux Côtes de Castillon	July 15, 1955	50	534.5	445				120,000	3,170,000	2,640,000
Bordeaux Sec	Dec 14, 1977	65	692.5	576.5						
Bordeaux Clairet or Rosé	Sept 13, 1951	55	586	488				9,500	251,000	209,000
Bordeaux Supérieur Blanc	Oct 14, 1943	65	692.5	576.5	15,000	396,000	330,000			
Bordeaux Rouge Supérieur	Oct 14, 1943	50	534.5	445				300,000	7,925,000	6,599,000
Bordeaux Mousseux (sparkling)	Mar 16, 1943		Figures not available							
Cadillac	Mar 13, 1969	40	427.6	356	2,300	61,000	50,600			
Canon Fronsac	July 1, 1949	47	500.7	417				10,500	277,000	231,000
Cérons	Sept 11, 1936	40	427.6	356	30,000	793,000	660,000			
Côtes de Blaye	Sept 11, 1936	60	639	532.2	11,000	291,000	242,000			
Côtes de Bordeaux Saint-Macaire	July 31, 1937	50	534.5	445	3,700	98,000	81,000			
Côtes de Bourg	May 14, 1941 white	60	639	532.2	5,000	132,000	110,000			
Bourg or Bourgeais	Sept 11, 1936 red	50	534.5	445				140,000	3,700,000	3,000,000
Entre-Deux-Mers	July 31, 1937	60	639	532.2	120,000	3,170,000	2,640,000			
Fronsac	Mar 14, 1938	47	500.7	417				27,000	713,000	594,000
Graves Blanc	Mar 4, 1937	50	534.5	445	43,000	1,136,000	946,000			
Graves Rouge	Mar 4, 1937	50	534.5	445				67,000	1,770,000	1,474,000
Graves Supérieures	Mar 4, 1937	40	427.6	356	19,000	502,000	418,000			
Graves de Vayres	July 31, 1937 white	60	639	532.2	12,000	317,000	264,000			
	red	50	534.5	445				6,600	174,000	145,000
Haut-Médoc	Nov 14, 1936	48	511.30	425.8				105,000	2,774,000	2,310,000
Lalande de Pomerol and Néac	Dec 8, 1936	42	447.4	372.5				37,000	977,500	814,000
Listrac	June 8, 1957	45	481	400.5				20,000	528,400	440,000
Loupiac	Sept 11, 1936	40	427.6	356	10,500	277,400	231,000			
Lussac-Saint-Émilion	Nov 14, 1936	45	481	400.5				39,000	1,030,000	858,000
Margaux	Aug 10, 1954	45	481	400.5				34,000	898,000	748,000
Médoc	Nov 14, 1936	50	534.5	445				110,000	2,906,000	2,420,000
Montagne-Saint-Émilion	Nov 14, 1936	45	481	400.5				65,000	1,717,000	1,430,000
Moulis	May 14, 1938	45	481	400.5				12,500	330,000	275,000
Pauillac	Nov 14, 1936	45	481	400.5				42,000	1,110,000	924,000
Pomerol	Dec 8, 1936	42	447.4	372.5				24,000	634,032	528,000
Premières Côtes de Blaye	Sept 11, 1936 white	60	639	532.2						
	red	50	534.5	445				150,000	3,963,000	3,300,000
Premières Côtes de Bordeaux	July 31, 1937 white	50	534.5	445	30,000	800,000	660,000			
	red	50	534.5	445				50,000	1,320,000	1,100,000
Puisseguin-Saint-Émilion	Nov 14, 1936	45	481	400.5				23,500	620,000	517,000
Sainte-Croix-du-Mont	Sept 11, 1936	40	427.6	356	15,000	400,000	300,000			
Saint-Émilion	Nov 14, 1936	45	481	400.5				246,000	6,500,000	5,412,000
Saint-Émilion Grand Cru	Oct 7, 1954	40	427.6	356				170,000	4,492,000	3,740,000
Saint-Estèphe	Nov 14, 1936	45	481	400.5				56,000	1,500,000	1,200,000
Sainte-Foy-Bordeaux	July 31, 1937 white	55	586	488	6,500	172,000	143,000			
	red	50	534.5	445						
Saint-Georges-Saint Émilion	Nov 14, 1936	45	481	400.5				6,000	158,000	132,000
Saint-Julien	Nov 14, 1936	45	481	400.5				26,000	687,000	572,000
Sauternes	Sept 30, 1936	25	267.25	222.5	29,000	770,000	640,000			

Institut National des Appellations d'Origine was called in to arbitrate. Two years later, however, it was decided in Bordeaux that the jurisdiction of this body was too limited for it to resolve a matter so complex and so controversial. The Bordeaux Chamber of Commerce and the Académie des Vins de Bordeaux then took up the question of the proposed reforms. At the time of writing, there is insufficient courage and leadership in Bordeaux to push through the necessary changes in the obsolete 1855 Classification.

More and more the problems of the 1855 Classification are recognized. In 1973 Mouton-Rothschild was named a First Growth by decree of the Minister of Agriculture. The 1855 ranking is the exclusive property of the Comité des Grands Crus Classés and can never be officially altered. The following, revised as of 1986, is the only classification that "dares" combine the best red wines of the four important Bordeaux regions.

PERSONAL CLASSIFICATION OF BORDEAUX

Crus Hors Classe (Outstanding Growths)

HAUT-MÉDOC

Château Lafite-Rothschild (Pauillac)
Château Latour (Pauillac)
Château Margaux (Margaux)
Château Mouton-Rothschild (Pauillac)

GRAVES

Château Haut-Brion (Pessac, Graves)

SAINT-ÉMILION

Château Ausone
Château Cheval-Blanc

POMEROL

Château Pétrus

Crus Exceptionnels (Exceptional Growths)

HAUT-MÉDOC

Château Brane-Cantenac (Cantenac-Margaux)
Château Cos d'Estournel (Saint-Estèphe)
Château Ducru-Beaucaillou (Saint-Julien)
Château Gruaud-Larose (Saint-Julien)
Château Lascombes (Margaux)
Château Léoville-Barton (Saint-Julien)
Château Léoville-Las-Cases (Saint-Julien)
Château Léoville Poyferré (Saint-Julien)
Château Lynch-Bages (Pauillac)
Château Montrose (Saint-Estèphe)
Château Palmer (Cantenac-Margaux)
Château Pichon Longueville, Comtesse de Lalande (Pauillac)
Château Pichon-Longueville-Baron (Pauillac)

GRAVES

Domaine de Chevalier (Léognan)
Château La Mission-Haut-Brion (Talence)
Château Pape-Clément (Pessac)

SAINT-ÉMILION

Château Figeac
Château Magdelaine

POMEROL

Château La Conseillante
Château l'Évangile
Château Lafleur
Château La Fleur-Pétrus
Château Trotanoy

Grands Crus (Great Growths)

HAUT-MÉDOC

Château Beychevelle (Saint-Julien)
Château Boyd-Cantenac (Cantenac-Margaux)
Château Branaire-Ducru (Saint-Julien)
Château Calon-Ségur (Saint-Estèphe)
Château Cantermerle (Haut-Médoc)
Château Cantenac-Brown (Cantenac-Margaux)
*Château Giscours (Labarde-Margaux)
Château d'Issan (Cantenac-Margaux)
Château La Lagune (Haut-Médoc)
Château Malescot-Saint-Exupéry (Margaux)
Château Mouton-Baronne-Philippe (Pauillac)
*Château Prieuré-Lichine (Cantenac-Margaux)
Château Rausan-Ségla (Margaux)
Château Talbot (Saint-Julien)

GRAVES

Château Haut-Bailly (Léognan)

SAINT-ÉMILION

Château Beau-Séjour-Bécot
Château Bélair
*Château Canon
Clos Fourtet
Château La Gaffelière
Château Pavie
Château Trottevieille

POMEROL

Château Gazin
Château Latour-Pomerol
*Château Petit-Village
*Vieux-Château-Certan
Château Nénin

Crus Supérieurs (Superior Growths)

HAUT-MÉDOC

Château Batailley (Pauillac)
Château Chasse-Spleen (Moulis)

*These wines are considered better than their peers in this classification.

Château Clerc-Milon-Rothschild (*Pauillac*)
Château Duhart-Milon-Rothschild (*Pauillac*)
Château Durfort-Vivens (*Cantenac-Margaux*)
Château Gloria (*Saint-Julien*)
Château Grand-Puy-Lacoste (*Pauillac*)
Château Haut-Batailley (*Pauillac*)
Château Kirwan (*Cantenac-Margaux*)
Château Lagrange (*Saint-Julien*)
Château Langoa-Barton (*Saint-Julien*)
Château Marquis d'Alesme-Becker (*Margaux*)
Château Marquis de Terme (*Margaux*)
Château Pontet-Canet (*Pauillac*)
Château Rauzan-Gassies (*Margaux*)
Château La Tour-Carnet (*Haut-Médoc*)

GRAVES

Château Carbonnieux (*Léognan*)
Château de Fieuzal (*Léognan*)
Château La Louvière (*Léognan*)
*Château Malartic-Lagravière (*Léognan*)
Château Smith Haut-Lafitte (*Martillac*)

SAINT ÉMILION

Château l'Angélus
Château Balestard-la-Tonnelle
Château Beauséjour-Duffau-Lagarosse
Château Cadet-Piola
Château Canon-la-Gaffelière
Château La Clotte
Château Croque-Michotte
Château Curé-Bon-la-Madeleine
Château La Dominique
Château Larcis-Ducasse
Château Larmande
Château Soutard
Château Troplong-Mondot
Château Villemaurine

POMEROL

Château Beauregard
Château Certan-Giraud
*Château Certan-de-May
Clos de l'Église
Clos de l'Église-Clinet
Château Le Gay
Château Lagrange
Château La Pointe

Bons Crus (Good Growths)

HAUT-MÉDOC

Château d'Agassac (*Haut-Médoc*)
*Château Angludet (*Cantenac-Margaux*)
Château Beau-Site (*Saint-Estèphe*)
Château Beau-Site Haut-Vignoble (*Saint-Estèphe*)
Château Bélair-Marquis d'Aligre
 (*Soussans-Margaux*)
Château Belgrave (*Saint-Laurent*)

These wines are considered better than their peers in this classification.

*Château de Camensac (*Haut-Médoc*)
Château Citran (*Haut-Médoc*)
Château Cos-Labory (*Saint-Estèphe*)
*Château Croizet-Bages (*Pauillac*)
Château Dauzac (*Margaux*)
Château Ferrière (*Margaux*)
Château Fourcas-Dupré (*Listrac*)
Château Fourcas-Hosten (*Listrac*)
Château Grand-Puy-Ducasse (*Pauillac*)
Château Gressier-Grand-Poujeaux (*Moulis*)
Château Hanteillan (*Haut-Médoc*)
Château Haut-Bages-Libéral (*Pauillac*)
Château Haut-Marbuzet (*Saint-Estèphe*)
Château Labégorce (*Margaux*)
Château Labégorce-Zedé (*Margaux*)
Château Lafon-Rochet (*Saint-Estèphe*)
Château Lamarque (*Haut-Médoc*)
Château Lanessan (*Haut-Médoc*)
Château Lynch-Moussas (*Pauillac*)
Château Marbuzet (*Saint-Estèphe*)
Château Maucaillou (*Moulis*)
*Château Les Ormes-de-Pez (*Saint-Estèphe*)
Château Pédesclaux (*Pauillac*)
*Château de Pez (*Saint-Estèphe*)
Château Phélan-Ségur (*Saint-Estèphe*)
Château Pouget (*Cantenac-Margaux*)
Château Poujeaux (*Moulis*)
*Château Saint-Pierre (*Saint-Julien*)
Château Siran (*Labarde-Margaux*)
Château du Tertre (*Arsac-Margaux*)
Château La Tour-de-Mons (*Soussans-Margaux*)
Château Villegeorge (*Haut-Médoc*)

GRAVES

Château Bouscaut (*Cadaujac*)
Château Larrivet-Haut-Brion (*Léognan*)
Château La Tour-Haut-Brion (*Talence*)
Château La Tour-Martillac (*Martillac*)

SAINT ÉMILION

Château l'Arrosée
Château Bellevue
Château Berliquet
Château Cap-de-Mourlin
Domaine du Châtelet
Clos des Jacobins
Château Corbin (*Giraud*)
Château Corbin (*Manuel*)
Château Corbin-Michotte
Château Coutet
Château Dassault
Couvent-des-Jacobins
Château La Fleur-Pourret
Château Franc-Mayne
Château Grâce-Dieu-Les-Menuts
Château Grand-Barrail-Lamarzelle-Figeac
Château Grand-Corbin
Château Grand-Corbin-Despagne
Château Grand-Mayne
Château Grand Pontet

Château Guadet-St. Julien
Château Laroque
Château Moulin-du-Cadet
Château Pavie-Decesse
Château Pavie-Macquin
Château Saint-Georges-Côte-Pavie
Château Tertre-Daugay
Château La Tour-Figeac
Château La Tour-du-Pin-Figeac
Château Trimoulet
Château Yon-Figeac

POMEROL

Château Bourgneuf-Vayron
Château La Cabanne
Château Le Caillou
*Château Clinet
Clos du Clocher
Château La Croix
Château La Croix-de-Gay
Clos de l'Église
Château l'Enclos
Château Gombaude-Guillot
Château La Grave-Trignant-de-Boisset
Château Guillot
Château Moulinet
Château Rouget
*Clos René
Château de Sales
Château du Tailhas
Château Taillefer
Château Vraye-Croix-de-Gay

Note: All Saint-Émilion and Pomerol châteaux classified above bear the strict commune designations of Saint-Émilion and Pomerol respectively

Bordeaux: Mousseux, Supérieur

Mildly sparkling wines with Appellations Contrôlées in the Bordeaux region.
See Bordeaux.

Bordeaux mixture

A mixture of copper sulfate and slaked lime used as a fungicide spray in many parts of Europe. Applied in the summer months to fight mildew and oïdium, the spray gives French and German vineyards a characteristic blue-green tinge.
See Chapter Eight.

Borderies

Lesser region of Cognac, producing brandies with considerable taste and finesse.
See Cognac.

These wines are considered better than their peers in this classification.

Bosa

Malvasia di Bosa (D.O.C.) is a richly-colored red wine of Sardinia *(q.v.)*.

Bota

(1) Wine bag; the modern conventional Spanish wine bag is of untanned goatskin, holding about a liter. It has a bone or wooden nozzle out of which the wine may be squirted by squeezing the bag. It is thus possible for several different persons in turn to drink from the *bota* without touching the nozzle with their lips.
(2) Spanish wine barrel of 500 liters (132 U.S. gallons, 110 imp.) widely used for storing and ageing wines. A Sherry butt. There is also a *media bota*, or half-*bota*, with a capacity of 250 liters (66 U.S. gallons, 55 imp.)

Botrytis cinerea

A parasitic fungus or mold that attacks grapes; in certain climates the grapes then develop gray rot and spoil while in others the *Botrytis cinerea* produces some of the greatest sweet white wines of the world. Called *pourriture noble* by the French (literally, noble rot), it is carefully cultivated in Sauternes, Monbazillac, Anjou, and Touraine—as well as in Germany, where it is known as *Edelfäule* and is responsible for the Auslese, Beerenauslese, and Trockenbeerenauslese wines of the Rhine and Mosel. It also produces Tokay in Hungary. In no other area has it so far proved possible to make those late-gathered sweet wines from overripe grapes, since the climate must be exactly right for them. (The proper weather conditions have reportedly been found in the New York State Finger Lakes district and in California, but few wines have been made.)
The fungus penetrates the skin of the fruit without breaking it, and thus without exposing the pulp to air. If all is in order, the grape begins to wither and become desiccated, and there is a corresponding concentration of the juice. In the shrinking of the fruit, loss of acidity is greater than loss of sugar. Consequently the percentage of soluble solids becomes greater, sugar and glycerin mounting faster than acidity. When vinified, the wines become smooth and almost oily in texture, very sweet and high in alcohol. The climatic conditions must be such that as the grapes mature moisture must be present in the air to allow the fungus to grow, alternating with periods of dry weather to cause the water in the grapes to evaporate and so keep the mold from growing too fast. Yet if the temperature rises too high, the fungus will be killed. At the end of this uncertain and difficult culture, the juice that remains in the grape makes only a small amount of wine, which is thus extremely expensive.
See Chapter Nine, p. 44.

Botticino (D.O.C.)

An Italian red wine, good to drink young.
See Lombardy.

Bottle sickness

A temporary indisposition to which wine is sometimes subject when it is first bottled.

Bouché

French term for a wine-bottle stoppered with a cork; not to be confused with *bouchonné* (spoiled by the cork).

Bouchet

One of the grape varieties of the Saint-Émilion and Pomerol districts of Bordeaux; synonymous with Cabernet Franc and Cabernet Sauvignon.

Bouchon

French term for cork.

Bouchonné

A bottle of wine spoiled by a bad cork. Corky.

Bouquet

Volatile acidity is responsible for the bouquet of a wine. It should be clean, with no trace of moldiness. The scent is produced by the vaporization of esters and ethers, those elusive chemical components which the wine contains. When a wine is cold or when a bottle is first opened, the bouquet is faint and hard to identify. (The first perfume is the bouquet; the later, more lingering odor, is the aroma.)

Bourbon

A type of American whiskey.
See Whiskey, Bourbon.

Bourg, Bourgeais, Côtes de Bourg (Appellation Contrôlée)

Red and white wines.
District: Bordeaux, France.

Official French wine place-names, all applying to the red and white wines made in nearly equal quantity on the hills of Bourg fringing the River Garonne and the River Dordogne as they enter the Gironde, and all but enclosed within the larger Blaye wine region. The two ancient fortified towns of Bourg and Blaye are less than half a dozen miles apart, and the wines can be considered together. Red Bourg is fuller-bodied than red Blaye, and, all in all, is superior. Some of the white

Premières Côtes de Blaye are the best white wines of the linked regions.

Bourgogne: Aligoté, Mousseux, Passetoutgrains

Wines with Appellations Contrôlées in Burgundy (*q.v.*).

Bourgueil and Saint-Nicolas-de-Bourgueil (Appellation Contrôlée)

Loire Valley red and rosé wines.
District: Touraine, France.

These growing areas are separate and distinct but are adjacent; and the wines are so alike that they are invariably classed together. They have also in common the fact that they are the only Loire vineyards where the place-name is restricted to red and rosé wines; white can be called only Touraine.

The wines are light, soft, and delicate, with a pronounced fruitiness and a strong bouquet which calls to mind raspberries, or perhaps violets. Wine labeled Saint-Nicolas-de-Bourgueil comes from grapes grown only there and is generally better than Bourgueil, for which the grapes may be grown in seven parishes. Soil throughout is a gravelly sand enriched with limestone and clay, and the only permissible grape is Cabernet Franc. Wines must have a minimum alcoholic content of 9.5%. About 45,000 hectoliters (1,188,000 U.S. gallons, 990,000 imp.) are made annually.

Château Bouscaut

Bordeaux red and white wines.
District: Graves, France.
Commune: Cadaujac.

Classed in 1953 among the five top Graves vineyards making white wine and the eleven top Graves vineyards making red wine, Château Bouscaut is the first important estate on the Graves-Sauternes road leading to Toulouse. The rebuilt house is a handsome mixture of medieval and modern, with its tapestries, swimming pool, and huge walled park. The *chais* are divided in two—for the making of red wines (which are fermented in huge oak vats) and white wines, which are crushed in electric presses, contained in a reservoir the first day, and are then tapped off directly into barrels in the *chai*, where both red and white ferment and age. Once in barrel, red and white wines age side by side.

In October 1968 a small group of American wine-lovers led by Charles Wohlstetter, chairman of the board of Continental Telephone, and Howard Sloane purchased the vineyard. Lucien Lurton, proprietor of Château Brane-Cantenac and Château Durfort, as well as Château Climens in Barsac, bought the property in 1979.

The red wine is made from 45% Merlot, 40% Cabernet Sauvignon, 10% Cabernet Franc, and 5% Malbec. The white is 60% Sémillon and 40% Sauvignon Blanc.

Characteristics. Strong and full. In 1970 a better wine was made than before. The vineyard bears watching for great improvement.

Vineyard area: Red—39 hectares (97 acres); white—5 hectares (12.5 acres).

Average production: Red—120 *tonneaux* (10,000 cases); white—18 *tonneaux* (1,500 cases).

Bouzy

Village of the Mountain of Reims district, producing red grapes for a First Growth Champagne, and a red still wine.

See Champagne.

Boxbeutel

A flat flask-shaped wine bottle.
See Bocksbeutel.

Château Boyd-Cantenac

Bordeaux red wine.
District: Haut-Médoc, France.
Commune: Cantenac-Margaux.

There is no château, but the vineyard itself, owned by M.P. Guillemet, is a Third Growth (*Troisième Cru*) of the Médoc, according to the 1855 Classification. The wine is made at Guillemet's Château Pouget. Until 1961 the vineyard did not deserve its high classification but it has improved considerably and is again making wine worthy of the 1855 rank, thanks to the enormous efforts of M. Guillemet. The breakdown of vines planted in this now well-tended vineyard is 70% Cabernet Sauvignon, 20% Merlot, 6% Cabernet Franc, and 4% Petit Verdot. The vinification is supervised by Dr. Peynaud, former professor of oenology at the University of Bordeaux.

Characteristics. Light, round, and elegant.
Vineyard area: 18 hectares (45 acres).
Average production: 80 *tonneaux* (7,000 cases).

Brachetto

Red wine grape of Italy, which produces a wine of strong color and agreeable flavor.
See Piedmont.

Brachetto d'Acqui (D.O.C.)

A semi-sparkling red wine from the Italian Piedmont (*q.v.*).

Château Branaire-Ducru

Bordeaux red wine.
District: Haut-Médoc, France.
Commune: Saint-Julien.

Facing Château Beychevelle across the vineyard road as it winds north into Saint-Julien, Château Branaire, Fourth Growth (*Quatrième Cru*) by the 1855 Classification, is now owned by M. Tapie, the son of an enterprising Algerian wine-grower who in the early fifties acquired the vineyard. For some years it was known simply as Château Branaire, after the elder M. Tapie deleted (in 1969) the name of a former owner, a M. Ducru; but that name has since been restored. The vineyard is well placed on the flattish top of rising ground, and there is an excellent large *chai* for old wines, sunk two-thirds underground to achieve a beneficial dampness. Mme Tari, wife of the owner of Château Giscours, and her able son own a major share in the vineyard.

Characteristics. Sturdy, big wines, sometimes quite hard at the outset; but among the best of Saint-Julien.

Vineyard area: 49 hectares (123 acres).
Average production: 200 *tonneaux* (19,000 cases).

Brandy

The word alone means distilled wine. It has been appropriated to refer to distillates from other fruits—apples, pears, cherries, etc.—but in such cases will always be qualified by the source. Brandy, when it stands alone, is a product of the grape and is distilled throughout the world.

The best brandies are the French Cognac and Armagnac. A fact too often overlooked is that Cognac is not brandy, but *a* brandy. It is perhaps, at its best, the world's most exquisite example of spirits of this type; Armagnac can be almost as perfect. Brandies are made in most wine-growing countries, sometimes of extraordinarily good quality, sometimes not. The secret of a fine brandy is partly in the wine distilled, partly in the distilling process (the best is made in pot stills), but also in the age and the wood in which it is aged. Cognac, for instance, matures best in Limousin oak. It should be remembered that once brandy is bottled, it ceases to improve and may even deteriorate after a certain time. Such labels as "Napoleon Brandy" thus become meaningless or worse, as any brandy kept in barrel since the days of Napoleon would have evaporated, and any kept in bottle would be the same, or perhaps not so good as when it was placed in glass. In any case, there would be none left.

Fruit brandy is made from all kinds of fruit.
Other leading brandies of the world are:
Calvados: the apple brandy of France.
Marc: distilled from grape pomace.
Grappa: another name for marc.
Applejack: American apple brandy.
See under separate headings.

Château Brane-Cantenac

Bordeaux red wine.
District: Haut-Médoc, France.
Commune: Cantenac-Margaux.

Once famous as Château Gorce, this, the largest vineyard with the largest production of any Classified Growth in the Haut-Médoc, was acquired early in the nineteenth century by the "Napoleon of the Vines," Baron de Brane. In 1820 he gave it his name, a bold gesture for the day. "Gorce is widely known," he wrote to the press, "but I have faith in the name of Brane." Acquiring a vineyard in Pauillac named Château Pouyallet, he named it Brane-Mouton—now famous as Mouton-Rothschild. In those days, Brane-Cantenac was considered the superior vineyard, and the Baron disposed of the present Mouton-Rothschild in order to devote all of his attention to it. Lucien Lurton is now the owner of this huge Second Growth (*Second Cru*) as well as Durfort-Vivens in Margaux, Château Climens in Barsac, and Château Bouscaut in Graves.

Brane long lingered in a twilight zone of quality. Some rather mediocre wines were made in this very great vineyard which disappointed many Médoc admirers. Several recent vintages have helped to re-establish its waning reputation. To hold the huge production, Lurton has built large storage tanks resembling the silo-like vats one finds in California.

Characteristics. The wine has the delicacy and suppleness of a typical Margaux, yet it is often surpassed by its neighbors.

Vineyard area: 115 hectares (288 acres).
Average production: 375 *tonneaux* (35,000 cases).

Brännvin

An alternate name for aquavit *(q.v.)*.

Brauneberger Falkenberg

One of the best elegant wines in the village of Brauneberg on the German Mosel.
See Mosel-Saar-Ruwer.

Brauneberger Juffer and Juffer-Sonnenruhr

The more famous of the best wines in the Brauneberg vineyard section , one of the top-quality regions of the German Mosel. Flowery, elegant and fine wines.
See Mosel-Saar-Ruwer.

Brazil

Brazil's 3,287,203 square miles make it the largest of the South American countries. Roughly 60,000 hectares (150,000 acres) of the country are cultivated in vines. Of late years there has been considerable development in wine production, and a greater demand for wine inside the country. Growers have introduced modern fertilizers and more efficient methods of processing and purifying, and so quality has been improving.

Brazil was colonized by wine-drinking Portuguese, yet vine-tending was not one of their early occupations. Few vines were brought into the country until the turn of this century, and most of them were planted after the First World War by settlers from Italy.

The principal wine region is the southern state of Rio Grande do Sul with 40,000 hectares (100,000 acres). It lies in the southern temperate zone and is the part of the country where the climate is most favorable to the vine. Other centers are São Paulo (9,000 hectares, or 22,500 acres), Paraná (2,000 hectares, or 5,000 acres) and Minas Gerais (700 hectares, or 1,750 acres) at an altitude of between 2,300 and 6,000 feet. Santa Catarina (6,000 hectares, or 15,000 acres) also is expanding its vineyards and shipping the harvest to São Paulo to be fermented into wine. Pernambuco covers 700 hectares (1,750 acres).

Seventy per cent of the vines planted in Brazil are hybrids of the species *Vitis labrusca* and only thirty per cent, unfortunately, are *Vitis vinifera*. The *labrusca* bears the hot damp climate better than does *Vitis vinifera*. Other grapes are: Duchesse (also known as Riesling de Caldas), Niagara, Folha de Figo (Fig Leaf), Black July, Seibel, Two 10096, 6905, several of the Couderc types, Delaware, Jacques Gaillard, and different kinds of Bertille-Seyve. In Santa Catarina, Concord, Cintiana, Herbemont, Gothe, Trebbiano, Poverella, and several of the Moscatelle type are planted too. For quality wines, some distinguished European stocks are cultivated.

The leading types of Brazilian wine are:
Cheaper Table Wines. Reds of the "burgundy" and "claret" types, rosés, and white wines—dry, semi-dry, sweet, and sparkling.
Good Table Wines. Reds from the Barbera, Bonarda, Cabernet, Merlot, and other fine vines. White wines from Trebbiano, Poverella, Malvasia, Riesling, and Sémillon.
Expensive Wines. Espumante (fermented in bottle and in vat), Moscatels, Malvasias.

One of Brazil's best wines is made by the firm Indústria, Comércio e Navegacáo, Sociedade Vinícola Rio Grandense, Ltda., which distributes its wines under the label Granja União. These are both red and white. Some of the reds come from Merlot, Cabernet, and Gamay grapes. The white are Trebbiano, Chardonnay, Gewürztraminer, Pinot Blanc and Riesling. Trebbiano is the Italian name for the Ugni Blanc. Much of the recent development of the Brazilian wine industry can also be attributed to the Central Vinícola do Sul (Vinosul S/A).

Most Brazilian wines are sold inside Brazil. São Paulo and Rio de Janeiro are the heaviest consumers. Wines are imported, also: from Europe, and from South American neighbors, particularly Chile. Brazilians are not used to drinking wine. A decrease in duties would encourage imports, which would be helpful in creating a market for domestic wines. Among the sixty-odd wine firms in Brazil, the most important, after the ones already cited, are: Luiz Antunes & Cia., Luiz Michielon S.A., Sociedade Vinhos Unico, Ltda.,

Carlos Dreher Neto, E. Mosele S.A., Sociedade Brasileira de Vinhos, Ltda, and Almadén Vineyards.
Distilled Liqueurs. Conhaques, and liqueurs of various types.

Breathing

A wine breathes or oxidizes when it comes in contact with air. In general, red wines need more airing than whites, and young red, with high tannin content, requires most of all. To enjoy the bouquet of a wine at its best, uncork the bottle and let the wine breathe for an hour or two—the best way of letting it show to its best advantage.
See Chapter Four, p. 13.

Château de la Brède

Bordeaux white wine.
District: Graves, France.
Commune: La Brède.

La Brède, the home of Montesquieu at the end of the seventeenth and the beginning of the eighteenth century, was the estate not only of a great writer, but also of a great wine-grower. Montesquieu's vineyard was much larger than the La Brède of today, spreading over miles of Graves and including many of the vineyards now famous under other names. The great author plied his vines as actively as his pen and pushed the sale of his wines with energy in both France and England. Today La Brède is only of historical interest, although the château remains Bordeaux's most beautiful castle. The small quantity of wine made is undistinguished; the quality of the wine does not match the beauty of the château. The vineyard was not included in the 1959 Graves Classification.
Vineyard area: 6 hectares (15 acres).
Average production: 10 tonneaux (900 cases).

Breed

Delicacy and discretion are the attributes of breed in wine. This undisputed superiority comes from the soil (*terroir*). The French words for it are *race* and *finesse*.

Breganze (D.O.C.)

Italian red or white wines.
see Veneto.

Brenner

A fungus disease of vines found notably in Germany.
See Chapter Eight, p. 39.

Breton

The Cabernet Franc grape is so called in the Touraine region of France.
See Cabernet.

Bristol Cream

Sweetened old Oloroso Sherry bottled in Bristol, England.

British Compounds

British excise term for redistilled, rectified, or flavored spirits.

British Wines

Of dubious quality. These wines are made from grape must, imported from another country.
See English Wines and United Kingdom.

Brizard

Firm of Marie Brizard & Roger, liqueur-makers in Bordeaux, France.

Brolio

An excellent classical chianti; the best is sold, not in the popular *fiasco*, but in bottle.
See Tuscany.

Brouilly

See Beaujolais; Côte de Brouilly.

Château Broustet

Bordeaux white wine.
District: Sauternes, France.
Commune: Barsac.

The property makes a typically sweet wine, classed among the Second Growths of Sauternes in 1855.
Vineyard area: 16 hectares (40 acres).
Average production: 30 tonneaux (2,700 cases).

Brown Sherry

Sweet, dark Oloroso Sherry.
See Sherry.

Brunello di Montalcino

One of the best, longest-lived red D.O.C.G. wines of Italy.
See Tuscany.

Brunissure (browning)

Vine disease. Brown skins appear on the leaf, which drops off—the result of overproduction and insufficient pruning of the vine.
See Chapter Eight, p. 37.

Brut

This word on the label of a bottle of Champagne indicates that the wine is very dry, and is, in fact, drier than that labeled Extra Sec—or Extra Dry.
See Champagne.

Bual, Boal

A full, sweet Madeira wine.

Bucelas

A golden Portuguese wine, once world-famous but now little seen abroad.
See Portugal.

Buchu

A South African liqueur virtually unknown elsewhere. The reason for this may be inferred from C. de Boscari's account of buchu in his *Wines of the Cape*, where he describes it as: "The herb with which savage Africa cured all its ills, from stomach-ache to snakebite, from housemaid's knee to witch-doctor's spell, for centuries before the White Man appeared. Grafted on to the European pharmacopoeia, buchu is today cultivated as a farm crop round Paarl: its extract is used externally as an embrocation and internally, mixed with brandy, for disorders of the digestive tract. It is credited with miraculous powers of healing, and it certainly tastes noxious enough to possess them."

Bulgaria

Few countries can claim older traditions of wine-making than Bulgaria: the commercial organization of viticulture and the marketing of wine are believed to have started in ancient Thrace, part of which is now within her borders.

As with all the Balkan lands, frontiers have advanced and receded over the centuries, and today the country is bounded to the north by the Danube, her Rumanian frontier; to the east, there are 150 kilometers (94 miles) of coastline on the Black Sea and to the south and west, frontiers with Turkey, Greece, and the Yugoslavian states of Serbia and Macedonia. Nearly half the land surface is mountain range: the Balkan Mountains to the west, and the Rhodope Mountains to the south; but the fertile lands of the Danube and Meritza valleys endow Bulgaria well for the agriculture which is the basis of the economy. A geographical location on about the same latitude as northern Spain and the Tuscan and Umbrian regions of Italy means that the land is well situated for growing grapes and making wine.

HISTORY

Bulgarian viticulture was brought almost to a standstill under five centuries of Turkish Moslem rule, yet it survived here as elsewhere in the Ottoman Empire. The country did not become completely independent of Turkish influence until the end of the First World War; but from that time the area of vineyards and the annual total of wine production increased until, in 1940, it reached about 2 million hectoliters (53 million U.S. gallons, 44 million imp.), of which about 300,000 hectoliters were exported, mainly to Germany. The Second World War and the disturbed times that followed caused the virtual collapse of Bulgarian viticulture. In 1948, the "Vinprom" State Enterprise was formed to revive and take charge of all wine production and marketing, and today Bulgaria is perhaps the most interesting and successful example of modern commercial production methods applied to a basis of ancient traditions of peasant cultivation—the common pattern now in all Balkan states. The 450,000 peasant growers already had a well-established experience of cooperatives, which gave a foundation for the "collectivization" of existing production. In addition, vast new vineyards have been established by "Vinprom," and Bulgaria's annual production of wine is now well over 4 million hectoliters (105 million U.S. gallons, 88 million imp.). Plans to double this figure over the next ten years or so may seem ambitious, but Bulgaria is successful as an exporter of wine, mainly to Russia—where there is an apparently insatiable demand—and to West Germany, her oldest export customer, but also, and increasingly, to wine-importing countries all over the world. The Bulgarians claim now that 60% of their production is exported, and half of this goes to the Soviet Union. They also claim to be the world's biggest exporters of bottled wine—surprising, but difficult to disprove. Experts from the West, mainly Germany, were called in to advise in the vast post-war reorganization, and the nationwide network of wineries and cellars is equipped with the latest German, French, and Italian machinery.

Bulgaria makes no fine wines, and never has, but she now has the capacity to produce enormous quantities of good wines to supply an ever-increasing world demand. The production is equally divided into 50% white wine and 50% red, the latter being the better of the two. Bulgarian wines fall into four categories: the ordinary one; those called "superior"; the better ones are the geographic wines and finally the controlled ones similar to the *appellation contrôlée*. Such wines are not liked in general by Western Europeans, but under the new organization—and undoubtedly as a result of German expertise—Bulgaria is now also making surprisingly good, light, acidic white wines to meet the ever-growing demand for drier wines. The Bulgarians drink 22 liters of wine per capita annually (not a big total for this part of Europe), but they also like beer, and, of course, the plum brandy which is distilled in all parts of southeastern Europe.

GRAPE VARIETIES AND TYPES OF WINE

White Wines. The most widely grown native vine was the Dimiat, used both for wine-making and as a table grape. Dimiat is the same as the Serbian Smederevka and is probably closely related to Chasselas. The wine made from it is of no distinction. A much more interesting wine comes from the red Misket, one of the big Muscat family, with the distinctive flavor and aroma of that grape. It flourishes in the region of Karlovo in central Bulgaria in the Sangulare Valley near the Black Sea, and in the northern part of the country generally. Although there are more than twenty vine-growing districts of varying importance in most parts of the country, place-names are of minor importance in considering Bulgarian wines, which are increasingly described by grape names only, especially those for export. The huge wineries, where most wine is made, draw from wide areas. This is particularly true of the wines produced from vines planted in the big state vineyards: Rhine and Wälschriesling, Sylvaner and Chardonnay from Western Europe, Furmint from Hungary, and the Georgian Rczaziteli from the Soviet Union. They have some well-established brand names, however: "Hemus," a sweet Misket from Karlovo; "Rosenthaler Riesling," from a blend of both types of Riesling, grown near the Valley of the Roses, again in the Karlovo district, "Euxinograd," a blend of Dimiat, Misket, and Wälschriesling; and "Sonnenküste," a Dimiat. The last two are made in the Black Sea area near Varna. Wines made from Chardonnay and Sylvaner imported into Great Britain are pleasant, dryish, surprisingly light wines. The Bulgarians also have a large and old-established production of sparkling wine (*champanski*) sold under the brand name "Iskra." production is centered on the town of Ljaskovec in the north of the country, and both the Champagne and Russian tank methods of manufacture are employed, as much as 15% of the total still being made by the *méthode champenoise.*

Red Wines. Many Bulgarian red wines are good, Gamza—a vine similar to the Balkan Kadarka—being the most widely grown, making wine that is best drunk when young, like a Beaujolais. The best native vine is Mavrud (meaning "black"), which gives a wine deep in color and flavor, needing time to become drinkable, and improving with age. The best of it is made in Asenovgrad near Plovidiv, Bulgaria's second-largest city. In the south, they grow Pamid (the same as the Serbian Plovdina grape, which is used to make a *Siller* wine for local consumption) and also the Russian

Saperavi. But again, as with the white wines, the Bulgarians have been very successful with new plantings of Western European vines, notably Cabernet Franc and Cabernet Sauvignon, from which they make wine with more than a touch of Bordeaux quality.

SPIRITS

Good brandy is distilled at Preslav in the Balkan Mountains from Dimiat wine, the best being bottled mainly for export under the trade name of "Pliska." As in all Balkan countries, a strong spirit is made from the blue plum, Slivova. They also produce a version of the Greek Mastika, something like the French pastis. A Bulgarian specialty is Rosa, a sweet liqueur from the petals of the damascene rose, from which they have made attar of roses for centuries.

Bulk gallon

A gallon (128 U.S. fl. oz., 160 imp.) of wine or spirits irrespective of proof or alcoholic strength; a wine gallon.
See Proof gallon.

Bumper

A cup or glass filled to the brim. To "drink a bumper" is an old English expression specially used for a toast.

Bung

The cork for a wine cask. It may be made of wood, earthenware, glass or rubber. The last two types are generally used as light stoppers for barrels of new wine, in which secondary fermentation may occur. Some contain a device to facilitate the escape of carbonic gas. In the second year of ageing, the racked wine is sealed into its barrel with a wooden cork, often bound in linen; or with a patent unbroachable stopper, such as the *Bonde Bordelaise de Sûreté.* The barrel is then set on its side, or *couché.*
See Chapter Nine.

Burdin

A French hybridizer who has developed a red-wine grape, Burdin 4503, out of a white-wine grape, comparable with the Sylvaner, and known as Burdin 5201.

Burgenland

White and red wines.
District: Southeast Austria.

Wine region of Austria. The principal vineyard towns are Rust, Oggau, Saint-Margarethen, and Mörbisch. Burgenland touches the Hungarian border, and

Burgunder

one of the principal grape varieties is the Furmint, which also goes into Tokay.

See Austria.

Burgunder

The Pinot grape of Burgundy transplanted to German-speaking countries, where vines of this variety are known as Spätburgunder, Frühburgunder, Weissburgunder (white), or Grauerburgunder (gray). The more usual name for the Pinot Gris, however, is Ruländer.

Burgundy

Red and white wines.
District: Central Eastern France.

The ancient realm of the Dukes of Burgundy is neither the largest nor the financially most important wine region in the world, but it is one of the very greatest. Nowhere else is wine so much a part of daily life and conversation, and nowhere is there such honest love of wine and such pride in its perfection, except in Bordeaux.

For more than two thousand years Burgundians have been making and drinking magnificent wines and shipping them all over the world. From father to son the tradition has been passed, from nobleman to priest to peasant. Over the centuries, the finest vineyard sites have been carefully tended, the best vines for the soil planted. However, the criticism of this great wine region today is that between pruning for greater quantity and planting new vines, Burgundy has lost considerably in quality. Unfortunately, in the late 1960s as well as in the 1970s and 1980s production has tended to be inconsistent.

It is true, unfortunately, that one man's Burgundy is another man's *ordinaire*, for no other name is so persistently misapplied. In large areas of the world "Burgundy" has become almost synonymous with a heavy, dark red wine, sometimes too rough, sometimes oversweetened; and the buyer (if not the seller) is often unaware that many Burgundies are light, subtle wines—and that some of the greatest Burgundies are white.

The red wines of the Burgundian district of the Beaujolais, for example, are at their best light and fresh and fruity; and the red wines of the Côte d'Or vineyards of the communes of Volnay, Pommard, and Beaune can be exquisitely fine and delicate. The misconception is encouraged by sellers the world over who do not hesitate to put the name Burgundy on red wines, no matter where they originated. In fact, the only wines with any historical, geographical, moral, or (in the Common Market) legal right to the name, are those from certain clearly defined sections of the French departments of the Côte d'Or, Yonne, Saône-et-Loire, and the *arrondissement* of Villefranche-sur-Saône in the department of the Rhône. As is the case

with all French wines of Appellation Contrôlée, the permissible vines are legally controlled, the amount of harvest is legally controlled, and the methods of pruning, growing, and fertilizing, as well as of vinifying and ageing, are all legally controlled—and if the resultant wine does not meet the minimum standards it is not Burgundy. (These controls are applied not in Burgundy alone, but to all French wines of Appellation Contrôlée.) This means that bottles labeled California burgundy, South African burgundy, or Chilean burgundy may all have their merits but will *not* be Burgundy (*see* Appellation d'Origine Contrôlée). Burgundian vineyards cover only 40,000 hectares (100,000 acres).

HISTORY

It is not known who first introduced the vine into Burgundy. The Romans found vines when they made their conquest, and under their influence the vineyards certainly increased and prospered. It is probable that the barbarians who followed destroyed the plantations, and the Burgondes began to reconstitute them at the end of the fourth century. In the fifth century A.D. Pliny told of Gauls drinking wine at Auxerre.

In the year 581, Gontran, King of Burgundy, gave the vineyards of Dijon to the Abbey of Saint Bénigne, a move that was to have far-reaching consequences. The monks were happy to receive the gift, which assured a steady source of pure wine for their religious services. In the centuries that followed, Burgundy changed from a kingdom to a duchy and various nobles, following Gontran's example, gave to different religious orders such vineyards as those of Aloxe, Fixey, Fixin, Santenay, Auxey, Comblanchien, Chassagne, Savigny, Pommard, and Meursault.

To the medieval world wine was wealth, and, overwhelmed by the sudden influx, some of the clergy began to forget the strict monastic rules and live too well. By the twelfth century the great reformer Saint Bernard of Clairvaux was denouncing this luxuriousness and greed. He came, in 1112, to the Cistercian monastery at Cîteaux and transformed it. With the Benedictine monastery of Cluny, Saint Bernard was at complete odds. Cluny had been the most powerful arm of the Church in France and its vineyard holdings were substantial. Adopting the motto *Cruce et Aratro* (By Cross and Plough) the Cistercians began cultivating sections of the desolate countryside. In Burgundy, nothing else thrives so well as the vine, and viticulture became one of the main occupations of the order. Their greatest accomplishment was the founding of the Clos de Vougeot, built up slowly from grants given by land-owners who were impressed by the sanctity and industry of the monks. Their sister order founded the Clos des Dames de Tart, later shortened to the Clos de Tart.

As the Middle Ages wore on, the vines flourished and increased—too much in variety if not in quantity. In 1395, Philip the Bold, Duke of Burgundy, banned from Burgundian vineyards the grape he refers to as the "disloyal Gaamez," which gives wine in abundance but wine full of "very great and horrible harshness." The introduction into fine wine regions of inferior grapes which produce quantity rather then quality is a recurrent evil. The Gamay vine mentioned by the Duke is not unknown in Burgundy today; one of its varieties is responsible for the excellent wines of Beaujolais, but on the Côte d'Or it gives a wine similar to that described by Duke Philip more than five centuries ago. Another ducal edict of the Middle Ages attempted to ban the storage of wines coming from any other district.

The wines of Burgundy, of Beaune especially, appealed to the kings of France. Philip Augustus, faced by the Imperial army, is said to have called for a barrel of Beaune; during the coronation of Philip VI, at Reims, the wine flowed from the nostrils of a bronze stag set up outside the cathedral. Louis XI was extremely fond of Volnay, and he had the happiness in his reign of adding the rebellious Dukedom of Burgundy to the French crown.

At peace at last from ducal wars, Burgundy was to be trampled in the wars of religion—and again in the Thirty Years' War (1618–48). Here, as in Bordeaux, there were sporadic orders to root up vines and plant more corn, but this does not seem to have seriously prevented the sale of wine. As late as the seventeenth and early eighteenth centuries, Burgundy came back into favor. A gigantic peasant named Brosse trundled some casks of his Mâcon safely over the bad roads to Paris, attracted the attention of Louis XIV by his great stature, and successfully sold his wine. Fagon, the king's physician, now credited with killing off most of the heirs to the throne, did a better thing when he recommended to his master the good wine of Burgundy. It was not yet the wine we know: it was very much lighter, and sometimes white grapes were mixed with the red to produce the pinkish, partridge-eye color then preferred. Foreign customers—particularly Germans and Dutch—are said to have wanted a heavier drink and for them, before the days of *chaptalisation*, sugar was sometimes introduced when the vintage was not big enough. Stories about Napoleon and various wines of Burgundy have been too often told to be repeated here—it seems certain that a heavy luggage of casks followed some of his marshals around the battlefields of Europe. Chambertin was the growth of which Talleyrand is quoted as saying: "Sir, when one is served such a wine, one takes the glass respectfully, looks at it, inhales it, then, having put it down, one discusses it." And of the same wine Dumas said: "Nothing inspires such a rosy view of the future."

When the French Revolution erupted, a great part of the Burgundy vineyard was in the hands of the Church. So the established pattern of Burgundian viticulture was completely disrupted by the wave of anti-clericalism that swept France in the 1790s and through the First Empire. The vineyards were seized by the state, and afterward sold to the people. The most important consequence was the setting up of the pattern of small ownership that still prevails in this region: the system has been maintained as a primitive kind of insurance. A grower who has all his grapes in one vineyard might be ruined if hail should hit that vineyard; whereas, if he owns only part of that one and part of another some miles away, he is likely to salvage something from the storm. The result was—and is—that the great vineyards continue to exist as entities, but each one is divided between a number of owners, each with his own parcel of land. Thus, two bottles of wine coming from the same vineyard, in the same years, may be quite different from each other, their characteristics depending to some extent upon the wine-maker's industry and talent. The Bordeaux system of large estates—unified under one ownership—is today practically unknown in Burgundy; with a very few exceptions, there are no Burgundian châteaux in the Bordeaux sense of the word, and a domain may inlcude bits and pieces of a number of widely scattered vineyards unified only in the ownership of one man. In Burgundy, there are more than a hundred separate place-names; at first glance the system appears complicated and confusing. Actually it is neither.

BURGUNDIAN PLACE-NAMES

There is a large number of different controlled place-names in Burgundy simply because there is an equivalent number of separate and distinct wines. The names run from the general to the particular, and—as is true with all French wines of Appellation Contrôlée—the more specific the name, the better the wine. The vineyard of Chambertin provides an example of how the system works.

Chambertin is one of the greatest of Burgundian vineyards and its wines, when well made and from a good year, are unsurpassed. The 13-hectare (32-acre) vineyard is legally rated a Great Growth (*Grand Cru*)—one of only thirty-one of the hundreds of Burgundian vineyards to receive this distinction. Its wine can take the name Chambertin, the commune name of Gevrey-Chambertin, the district name of Côte de Nuits, or the general name of Burgundy (Bourgogne); yet it will always be labeled with the famous name of Chambertin if the wine meets the high minimum standards demanded. The name is more specific, the minimum standards are higher, the wine is finer, and the system is strong enough to guarantee the grower a higher price for the better wine as reflected by the name. Vineyard name—commune name—district name—regional name. Chambertin—Gevrey-Chambertin—Côte de Nuits—Burgundy. The formula is repeated over and over again in each commune along the fa-

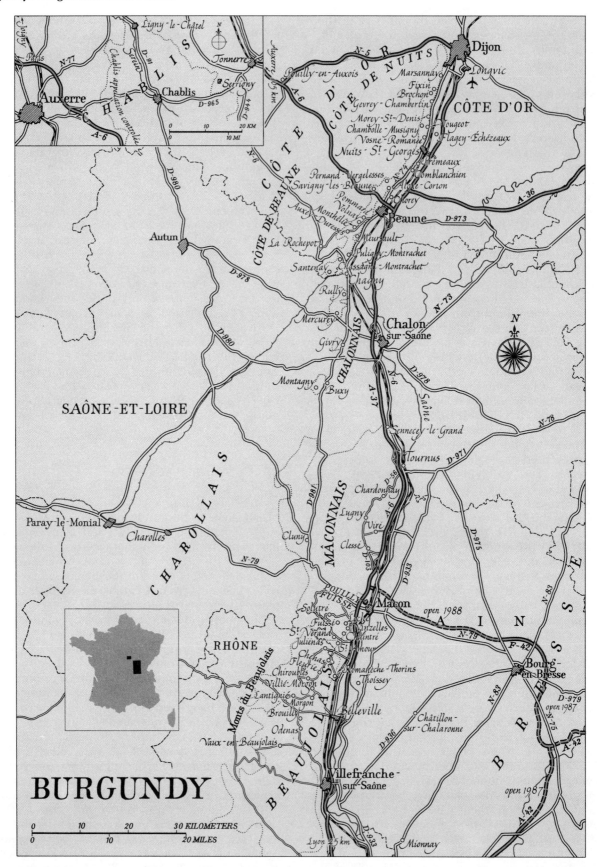

BURGUNDY

mous Côte d'Or (Slope of Gold), and through the other sections of Burgundy (although here and there may be minor exceptions to the rule).

The fact that there will be a number of growers in even so small a vineyard as Chambertin has given rise to a special way of handling the wines and putting them on sale—a method that was worked out to decrease the inherent confusion. Under this system, the shipper (*négociant*) buys wines from various growers in, for example, Chambertin, blends them together and sells them labeled as Chambertin from his own particular firm. The wines will be blended so that they will be reasonably the same year after year. The system has this advantage: that a number of growers will not be putting out different wines under the same name, and the customer can learn the name of the wine and the firm he prefers and feel comfortably sure that he can buy the wine year after year and it will always be very similar. The disadvantages are that, in spite of the shipper's care, the wine will not be identical, and that when wine from a talented wine-maker is blended with that from an inept one, the quality of the finer wine is inevitably dragged down.

Burgundy is not large and the 2 million hectoliters (52 million U.S. gallons, 44 million imp.) of wine—80% red, 20% white—made each year does not, for example, compare with the annual 5 million hectoliters (132 million U.S. gallons, 110 million imp.) that come out of Bordeaux. Furthermore, authentic Burgundy is not cheap, nor can it be. The weather is too often unfavorable for growers to count on a good harvest every year, and the proceeds from good years must tide them over the others. When quantity is lowest, the revenue to the grower is correspondingly small—although he must still eat, and the vines must receive the usual expensive care, to keep them healthy. This does nothing to reduce prices. Since these prices are rather high, and variations in the wines considerable, it is more important to know what you are buying from Burgundy than from any other fine wine region, for get-rich-quick shippers have for centuries found it expedient to buy wines other (and cheaper) than the great Burgundies and use them to stretch the supply when it runs low, so that they can sell more wine at lower prices and make a higher profit on each sale. The great epoch of fraud occurred shortly after the First World War and was flourishing in the 1930s when some enlightened Frenchmen banded together to amend and perfect the laws of Appellation d'Origine, which gave wide powers to the inspectors of fraud. The laws have not completely done away with deceit, but they have made it much more difficult. And some of the growers themselves are adopting a system (modeled on the château-bottling of Bordeaux) which makes fraud practically impossible. This is known as estate or domain bottling. An estate-bottled wine is simply a wine that has been grown, made, and bottled by the same man, usually a small peasant grower with anything from two to ten acres of vines. In such a case, the label will tell the name of the wine, the year, the name of the grower, and the fact that the wine is *Mis au Domaine* (bottled at the domain). Alternative phrases are *Mise du Domaine* or *Mis en Bouteilles par le Propriétaire*, or else *Mis en Bouteilles à la Propriété*.

The greatest wines come from the golden slopes of the Côte d'Or, a low range of hills topped by brush and scrub and rolling along the western edge of the Burgundian plain. Geographically, it begins at Dijon (in days gone by, there was a Côte de Dijon, too, and an effort has been made to bring it back into currency, particularly with the rosés of Marsannay) and ends just south of Santenay. It is divided into two sections: the Côte de Nuits, to the north, making the regal reds, Chambertin, Musigny, Romanée—the first great vineyard the motorist sees is Clos de Vougeot; and, to the south, the Côte de Beaune with its more delicate red wines (Beaune, Pommard, Volnay) and the magnificent whites of Meursault and Montrachet.

Of the great number of Burgundian place-names there are several that will seldom or never appear on bottles outside Burgundy. These most general names are applied to wines which often make very pleasant drinking if caught young and near the place where they were made, but which neither age nor travel well. Among them may be such names as are listed on page 140.

BURGUNDIAN VINES

Vines for Red Wines

Pinot Noir. The noblest vine of them all. Head of a distinguished family (although the other members do not generally come up to the excellence of the Noiren, as it is sometimes called), it adapts itself in the varying soils of the Côte d'Or to produce grapes giving some of the world's most magnificent wines. Oddly enough, in the granite of the Beaujolais it can give no better than flat and undistinguished wine and is replaced by the Gamay.

Gamay. Except in the Beaujolais—where it gives a fruity, light, and eminently delightful wine—Burgundian Gamay wine tends to be common, acid, and harsh. Much was once planted on the Côte d'Or, but this practice is passing and most of the Gamay today is maintained by the workers for their own consumption. However, a very small amount of Passetoutgrains (a vatting together of Gamay and Pinot Noir) is still put on the market.

Pinot Liebault. Indistinguishable, to all intents and purposes, from the Pinot Noir, except to a specialist.

Pinot Gris. No wine is made exclusively from the Pinot Gris in burgundy, as it is, for example, in Alsace. Some plants may be found, however, and growers claim that the addition of some of this to Pinot Noir results in a wine with more elegance, finesse, and delicacy.

| Place-name | Date Established | | *Maximum Yield* | | |
			HECTO-LITERS/ HECTARE	GALLONS PER ACRE U.S.	Imp.
Bourgogne	July 31, 1937	rouge, rosé, clairet	55	1,452.9	1,209.8
Vin Fins des Hautes Côtes					

The most general name of all. It is allowed to any blanc — 60 — 1,585 — 1,319.8
wine coming from the specified area of Burgundy—
red wines to be made from the Pinot Noir grape
(with allowances for the Pinot Liebault and Pinot
Beurot, for the César and Tressot in the Yonne, for
Gamay in certain parts of southern Burgundy);
white wines from the Chardonnay. The wines must
have a minimum alcoholic content of 10% if red,
10.5% if white.

Bourgogne-Passetoutgrains	July 31, 1937		55	1,452.9	1,209.8

Once made in enormous quantity, this is a mixing
or vatting together of grapes of Pinot Noir and
Gamay—at least one-third Pinot. The wine must
have an alcoholic content of 9.5% and can often be
pleasant on the spot but does not travel or keep
well.

Bourgogne Aligoté	July 31, 1937		60	1,585	1,319.8

White wines exclusively, from the Aligoté grape.
Chardonnay may also be used, but in practice it is
not. Alcoholic content of 9.5%.

Bourgogne Ordinaire	July 31, 1937				
Bourgogne Grand Ordinaire	July 31, 1937	rouge, rosé, clairet	55	1,452.9	1,209.8

Only in France could a wine be "great" and "ordi-
nary" at the same time. These two place-names blanc — 60 — 1,585 — 1,319.8
cover red, white, and rosé made from Pinot and
Gamay grapes (and Tressot in the Yonne) and
white from Pinot Blanc, Chardonnay, Aligoté, Melon de Bourgogne, and, in the Yonne, Sacy. At least
9% of alcohol for red and rosé, 9.5% for white.

Crémant de Bourgogne or					
Sparkling Burgundy	March 16, 1943	7,500 kilos per hectare			

Sparkling Burgundy may often be pleasant enough,
but too often is mediocre or worse. It is vinified from
any red or white wine that has the right to a general Burgundy *appellation* but rarely from those with
any merit or distinction. Since taxes are as high in
Great Britain and the United States on this as on
Champagne, the latter is almost inevitably much
better value.

Listed below are the districts of Burgundy, followed by the place-names of the Appellations Contrôlées, making wines more distinguished than the foregoing:

Côte d'Or	red and white wines	Mâconnais	red and white wines
Chablis	white wine	Chalonnais	red and white wines
Beaujolais	red (and very few white) wines		

See under individual headings.

THE APPELLATIONS CONTRÔLÉES OF THE BURGUNDY REGION

Vineyards benefiting from special, controlled place-names are indented under pertinent commune.

Place-name	Date Established	HECTO-LITERS/ HECTARE	GALLONS PER ACRE U.S.	Imp.	Hectoliters	WHITE U.S. Gallons	Imp. Gallons	Hectoliters	RED U.S. Gallons	Imp. Gallons
I—CÔTE D'OR—*best communes marked with an asterisk* (*).										
*Aloxe-Corton	March 11, 1938	35	374.1	311.5	25	662	550	5,250	139,125	115,500
Corton	July 31, 1937	30	320.7	267	25	662	550	3,250	86,125	71,500
Corton-Charlemagne	July 31, 1937	30	320.7	267	1,100	29,150	24,200			
Auxey-Duresses	July 31, 1937	35	374.1	311.5	1,150	30,475	25,300	3,200	84,800	70,400
*Beaune	Sept. 11, 1936	35	374.1	311.5	600	15,900	13,200	15,000	397,500	330,000
Blagny	July 31, 1937	35	374.1	311.5				225	5,960	4,950
*Chambolle-Musigny	Sept. 11, 1936	35	374.1	311.5				6,500	172,250	143,000
Bonnes Mares	Dec. 8, 1936	30	320.7	267				500	13,250	11,000
Musigny	Sept. 11, 1936	30	320.7	267	10	265	220	300	7,950	6,600
*Chassagne-Montrachet	July 31, 1937	35	374.1	311.5	3,750	99,375	82,500	6,200	164,300	136,400
Bâtard-Montrachet	July 31, 1937	30	320.7	267	450	11,925	9,900			
Chevalier-Montrachet	July 31, 1937	30	320.7	267	160	4,240	3,520			
Criots-Bâtard-Montrachet	June 13, 1939	30	320.7	267	50	1,325	1,100			
Montrachet	July 31, 1937	30	320.7	267	275	7,285	6,050			
Cheilly-les-Maranges	July 31, 1937	35	374.1	311.5				400	10,600	8,800
Chorey-les-Beaune	July 31, 1937	35	374.1	311.5	7	185	154	4,000	106,000	88,000
Côte de Beaune	July 31, 1937	35	374.1	311.5	15	395	330	450	11,925	9,900
Côte de Beaune-Villages	July 31, 1937	35	374.1	311.5				6,800	180,200	149,600
Côtes de Nuits-Villages	Aug. 20, 1964	35	374.1	311.5	5	130	110	6,500	172,250	143,000
Dezize-les-Maranges	July 31, 1937	35	374.1	311.5						
*Fixin	Dec. 8, 1936	35	374.1	311.5				1,000	23,850	19,800
*Gevrey-Chambertin	Sept. 11, 1936	35	374.1	311.5				15,500	410,750	341,000
Chambertin	July 31, 1937	30	320.7	267				500	13,250	11,000
Chambertin-Clos de Bèze	July 31, 1937	30	320.7	267				500	13,250	11,000
Chapelle-Chambertin	July 31, 1937	32	342	284.8				210	5,565	4,620
Charmes-Chambertin	July 31, 1937	32	342	284.8				1,000	26,500	22,000
Griotte-Chambertin	July 31, 1937	32	342	284.8				85	2,250	1,870
Latricières-Chambertin	July 31, 1937	32	342	284.8				250	6,625	5,500
Mazis-Chambertin	July 31, 1937	32	342	284.8				350	9,275	7,700
Mazoyères-Chambertin	(same as Charmes-Chambertin)									
Ruchottes-Chambertin	July 31, 1937	32	342	284.8				130	3,445	2,860
Bourgogne Hautes-Côtes-de-Beaune	Aug. 4, 1961	50	534.5	445	150	3,975	3,300	8,500	225,250	187,000
Bourgogne Hautes-Côtes-de-Nuits	Aug. 4, 1961	50	534.5	445	150	3,975	3,300	1,750	46,375	38,500
Ladoix	July 31, 1937	35	374.1	311.5	125	3,310	2,750	2,200	58,300	48,400
Bourgogne Marsannay-la-Côte	June 3, 1965	50	534.5	445				1,500	39,750	33,000
*Meursault	July 31, 1937	35	374.1	311.5	12,500	331,000	275,000	800	21,200	17,600
Monthélie	July 31, 1937	35	374.1	311.5	50	1,325	1,100	3,000	79,500	66,000
*Morey-Saint-Denis	Dec. 8, 1936	35	374.1	311.5	40	1,060	880	2,600	68,900	57,200
Bonnes Mares	(see under Chambolle-Musigny)									
Clos de la Roche	July 3, 1944	30	320.7	267				500	13,250	11,000
Clos Saint-Denis	July 3, 1944	30	320.7	267				200	5,300	4,400
Clos de Tart	Jan. 4, 1939	30	320.7	267				275	7,285	6,050
*Nuits-Saint-Georges	Sept. 11, 1936	35	374.1	311.5	50	1,325	1,100	12,500	331,000	275,000
Pernand-Vergelesses	Dec. 8, 1936	35	374.1	311.5	400	10,600	8,800	2,600	68,900	57,200
*Pommard	Sept. 11, 1936	35	374.1	311.5				13,250	351,125	291,500
*Puligny-Montrachet	July 31, 1937	35	374.1	311.5	7,000	185,500	154,000	300	7,950	6,600
Bâtard-Montrachet	(see Chassagne-Montrachet)									
Bienvenue-Bâtard-Montrachet	June 13, 1939	30	320.7	267	125	3,310	2,750			
Montrachet	(see Chassagne-Montrachet)									

THE APPELLATIONS CONTRÔLÉES OF THE BURGUNDY REGION
(continued)

Vineyards benefiting from special, controlled place-names are indented under pertinent commune.

		Maximum Yield				Average Production				
		HECTO-	GALLONS PER			WHITE			RED	
		LITERS/	ACRE			U.S.	Imp.		U.S.	Imp.
Place-name	Date Established	HECTARE	U.S.	Imp.	Hectoliters	Gallons	Gallons	Hectoliters	Gallons	Gallons
Saint-Aubin	July 31, 1937	35	374.1	311.5	800	21,200	17,600	2,000	53,000	44,000
Saint-Romain	Oct. 14, 1947	35	374.1	311.5	1,100	29,150	24,200	750	19,875	16,500
Sampigny-les-Maranges	July 31, 1937	35	374.1	311.5	150	3,975	3,300	100	2,650	2,200
Santenay	Dec. 8, 1936	35	374.1	311.5				10,000	265,000	220,000
Savigny-les-Beaune	Dec. 8, 1936	35	374.1	311.5	400	10,600	8,800	11,000	291,500	242,000
*Volnay	Sept. 9, 1937	35	374.1	311.5				9,000	238,500	198,000
*Vosne-Romanée	Sept. 11, 1936	35	374.1	311.5				6,500	172,250	143,000
Échezeaux	July 31, 1937	30	320.7	267				1,100	29,150	24,200
Grands-Échezeaux	July 31, 1937	30	320.7	267				350	9,275	7,700
La Tâche	Sept. 11, 1936	30	320.7	267				250	6,625	5,500
Richebourg	Sept. 11, 1936	30	320.7	267				300	7,950	6,600
Romanée-Saint-Vivant	Sept. 11, 1936	30	320.7	267				300	7,950	6,600
La Romanée-Conti	Sept. 11, 1936	30	320.7	267				75	1,985	1,650
La Romanée	Sept. 11, 1936	30	320.7	267				35	925	770
*Vougeot	Dec. 8, 1936	35	374.1	311.5	75	1,985	1,650	650	17,225	14,300
Clos de Vougeot	July 31, 1937	30	320.7	267				2,100	55,650	46,200
II—CHABLIS										
Chablis	Jan. 13, 1938	40	427.6	356	30,000	530,000	440,000			
Chablis Grand Cru	Jan. 13, 1938	35	374.1	311.5	4,000	66,250	55,000			
Petit Chablis	Jan. 5, 1944	40	427.6	356	6,000	159,000	132,000			
Chablis Premier Cru	Jan. 13, 1938	40	427.6	356	15,000	331,000	275,000			
III—BEAUJOLAIS										
Beaujolais	Sept. 12, 1937	50	534.5	445	5,000	132,500	110,000	500,000	9,937,500	8,250,000
Beaujolais-Supérieur	Sept. 12, 1937	45	448.9	373.8				20,000	662,500	550,000
Beaujolais-Villages	Sept. 12, 1937	45	448.9	373.8	300	7,950	6,600	320,000	5,300,000	4,400,000
Brouilly	Oct. 19, 1938	40	427.6	356				50,000	728,750	605,000
Chénas	Sept. 11, 1936	40	427.6	356				10,000	265,000	220,000
Chiroubles	Sept. 11, 1936	40	427.6	356				15,000	291,500	242,000
Côte de Brouilly	Oct. 19, 1938	40	427.6	356				15,000	397,500	330,000
Fleurie	Sept. 11, 1936	40	427.6	356				35,000	728,750	605,000
Juliénas	March 11, 1938	40	427.6	356				25,000	583,000	484,000
Morgon	Sept. 11, 1936	40	427.6	356				45,000	927,500	770,000
Moulin-à-Vent	Sept. 11, 1936	40	427.6	356				30,000	795,000	660,000
Saint-Amour	Feb. 8, 1946	40	427.6	356				15,000	397,500	330,000
IV—MÂCONNAIS										
Mâcon	July 31, 1937	50	534.5	445	15,000	79,500	66,000	2,500	66,250	55,000
Mâcon-Supérieur	July 31, 1937	50	534.5	445	35,000	2,120,000	1,760,000	47,000	1,590,000	1,320,000
Mâcon-Villages	July 31, 1937	50	534.5	445	60,000	662,500	550,000			
Pouilly-Fuissé	Sept. 11, 1936	45	448.9	373.8	40,000	954,000	792,000			
Pouilly-Loché	April 27, 1940	45	448.9	373.8	1,500	39,750	33,000			
Pouilly-Vinzelles	April 27, 1940	45	448.9	373.8	2,200	58,300	48,400			
Saint-Véran	June 1, 1971	45	448.9	373.8	12,000	318,000	264,000			
V—CHALONNAIS										
Givry	Feb. 8, 1946	40	427.6	356	350	9,275	7,700	3,500	92,750	77,000
Mercurey	Sept. 11, 1936	35	374.1	311.5	1,000	26,500	22,000	20,000	530,000	440,000
Montagny	Sept. 11, 1936	40	427.6	356	3,000	66,250	55,000			
Rully	June 13, 1939	40	427.6	356	1,500	52,000	44,000	1,500	58,300	48,400

César. Only allowed in the Yonne for wines taking the most general of place-names.

Tressot. Only allowed in the Yonne for wines taking the most general of place-names.

Vines for White Wines

Chardonnay (also called Aubaine, Beaunois). Once erroneously thought to be a member of the Pinot family (and called Pinot Chardonnay), this vine is responsible for all the great white wines of Burgundy. In chalky soil—as on the Côte d'Or, Chablis, and the Mâconnais—it gives wines that vary with local conditions, but tend at their best to be rather full yet delicate, imbued with the scent of the grape, beautifully balanced and with enormous finesse.

Pinot Blanc. The white grape of the Pinot family. It is added to the Chardonnay in the making of the better white wines.

Aligoté. The grape that makes the common secondary white wine of Burgundy. The wine rarely has much breed and does not travel well, but when young and drunk on the spot it can be extremely pleasant; it is sometimes made to be slightly sparkling (*pétillant*).

Sacy. Only allowed in the Yonne for wines taking the most general of place-names.

Melon de Bourgogne. Allowed throughout Burgundy, but only for wines taking the most general of place-names.

BURGUNDIAN VINICULTURE

After the harvest—which starts in the middle of September in good years, but not until the first weeks of October in bad—Burgundian red wines are not long-vatted. Here, as elsewhere, they are fermented in their skins, while the white are pressed from their skins and fermented apart; but in Burgundy, red wines only stay in contact with the skins for from six to twelve days—the optimum is about ten. This contrasts markedly with Bordeaux—where wines are vatted for twelve to twenty-five days—and the results are apparent.

Long-vatted Bordeaux reds pick up more tannin—from the skins and seeds—than do Burgundies. This makes them harder at the outset and allows them to reach a greater "high" with longevity; only with age do the great reds of Bordeaux achieve their full glory. Red Burgundies, not having so much tannin, will be ready to drink far sooner, often from two to five years after harvest. Furthermore, the Cabernet Sauvignon grape of Bordeaux produces wines that are bigger and fuller than those produced by the Pinot Noir of Burgundy. Thus, a natural Burgundy may, by its lightness, confound the traditional notion that all Burgundies are full-bodied and all Bordeaux light.

Apart from the duration of vatting time, wine-making in Burgundy does not differ significantly from standard practice as outlined in Chapter Nine (*q.v.*). The only major modification is the widespread use of *chaptalisation* (adding sugar to sugar-deficient musts), for in most years the Burgundian summer sun does not generate enough sugar in the grapes to make a perfectly balanced wine. The additional sugar—added under strict control by the government—ferments with the natural grape sugar and results in a wine with a higher alcoholic content than it would otherwise have had, and sometimes with more force and body as well. Yet the present regrettable tendency is to over-chaptalise fine wines.

Burgundian wines are aged, from eighteen to twenty-four months, in containers of varying sizes. Wines for current consumption are kept in large vats, but finer wines need small cooperage. The standard barrel size is the *pièce*, holding 228 liters (60 U.S. gallons, 50 imp.). Very occasionally reference is made to the old measure *queue*, which is simply two *pièces*; there is no actual barrel of this size. Half-barrels are called *feuillettes* and quarter-barrels *quartauts*, and they each hold exactly what one would expect. In Chablis, however, there is another *feuillette* holding 132 liters (34.9 U.S. gallons, 29 imp.); the traditional *pièce* of the Mâconnais holds 215 liters (56.8 U.S. gallons, 47.3 imp.); and that of the Beaujolais 216 liters (57.1 U.S. gallons, 47.5 imp.). Fortunately these odd sizes are being replaced by the more standard Burgundian *pièce*.

White wines in Burgundy are given less ageing than was once customary: twelve to twenty months is now standard practice. This results in a cleaner, fresher, fruitier wine, and experts feel that the change is thoroughly justified. When bottled, Burgundian wines are always put in the typical, squat, slope-shouldered Burgundian bottle.

Although many a Burgundy will be ready to drink any time from a few months to a few years after being put into bottle, others will sometimes hold their excellence as long as a half-century or perhaps more. Unfortunately these old bottles are becoming exceedingly rare. Burgundies are not made in the same way as they used to be. Before the First World War the wine was long-vatted and the extra tannin it picked up naturally from the contact with the skins and the wood gave it longevity. Tannin occasionally added to young wine by some shippers does not have the same effect but serves instead to deform the taste of the wine. Another deformation suffered by a great deal of the Burgundy in the cellars of shippers (*négociants*) is caused by the practice of giving the wine a so-called Burgundy character by blending it with heavy wines from other regions. The past hundred years have seen the supply of honest Burgundy running so far short of the demand that cheap heavy wine from the Rhône valley or Roussillon has been brought in to stretch the precious supply. As the contents of Burgundian bottles grew further and further away from the characteristics of real Burgundy wine, a mar-

Butt

ket was built up among inexperienced wine-drinkers who were taught to believe that if a wine did *not* have the thick or oversugared consistency they had come to associate with Burgundy, it lacked the true characteristics. This puts them in the paradoxical position, when they manage to obtain a bottle of estate-bottled wine or one put out by an honest shipper, of finding fault with it, because it is utterly different from any "Burgundy" they have ever drunk. To those who judge wine by taste rather than by labels, it is often a revelation.

See Côte de Beaune; Côte de Nuits; Côte d'Or.

Butt

Standard British cask. A butt of ale, Sherry, or Málaga contains 491 liters (129.6 U.S. gallons, 108 imp.); of any other wine, 573 liters (151.3 U.S. gallons, 126 imp.). In general use, a synonym for a cask or barrel to hold wine, beer, or rainwater.

Buza

Alcoholic beverage of Egypt distilled from fermented dates.

See Egypt.

Buzet (A.O.C.) (until 1986 called Côtes de Buzet)

This Appellation Contrôlée comprises approximately 1,200 hectares (3,000 acres), 80% of which are planted in the red varieties of Merlot, Cabernet Sauvignon and Cabernet Franc, and the remainder in Sauvignon, Sémillon and Muscadelle for the white. The production amounts to approximately 80,000 cases and most of this is produced by a cooperative.

See Côtes de Buzet.

Buzz

British university term for a glass of Port from the bottom of the decanter.

Bybline

A sweet Phoenician wine mentioned in classical writings. Native to Byblos, it was probably grown afterwards in Thrace also.

See Classical wines.

Byrrh

Very popular French proprietary aperitif based on wine, flavored with quinine, and fortified with brandy. It is made at Thuir on the Mediterranean coast near the Spanish border.

C

Cabernet

The outstanding grape variety used for the finest clarets of the Médoc district of Bordeaux, for Superior wines in California, Chile, Australia and elsewhere. The finest and most widespread is Cabernet Sauvignon; Cabernet Franc is grown in the Médoc, in Graves, in Saint-Émilion, and the Loire Valley and is spreading slowly; Ruby Cabernet is an American hybrid that combines Cabernet Sauvignon and Carignane.

Cabinet wine, Kabinettwein

A term, applying chiefly to many German Rhine wines, which originally was used to identify the special reserve of the vineyard owner. It may have originated at Kloster Eberbach on the Rhine, where the finest Steinbergers were kept in a special small cellar called Das Kabinett, which may be seen today. The importance of Cabinet wines was and is based on the fact that fine German wines are not only harvested and barreled individually from the different parts of the vineyard, but also on different days of the harvest. In most vineyards, the designation "Cabinet" was applied to a wine and put on the label if the barrel had surpassed a certain price when sold. Today, the term "Kabinett" can be applied when the wine reaches a certain level of quality, and these wines do not have the right to be sugared.

See Germany.

Cachiri

Guiana liqueur from the cassava plant, from which tapioca is also obtained.

Cadillac

Bordeaux white wine.
District: Southwest France.

On the right bank of the River Garonne, facing Graves and Sauternes, the vineyards of this recent Appellation Contrôlée are planted with Sémillon and Sauvignon Blanc. The wines are similar to those of neighboring Sainte-Croix-du-Mont.

Cahors

(1) Red grape, not a noble variety, permitted in limited quantities in, for example, the district of Bordeaux. Known also as Malbec and Cot.
(2) *Red wine.*

District: Southwest France.

As it flows to meet the Garonne, the River Lot cuts through the great Causse plateau, a limestone high-land which produces more truffles than Périgord. On either side of the Lot for 50 kilometers (30 miles), between Cahors and Soturac, lie the vineyards of the Cahors Appellation Contrôlée. The delimited region of nearly 40,000 hectares (100,000 acres) is 160 kilometers (100 miles) east of Bordeaux and 100 kilometers (62 miles) north of Toulouse. Most of this acreage does not produce wine. The annual production of 180,000 hectoliters (4.7 million U.S. gallons, 3.9 million imp.) comes from small plots scattered along the riverbank which total only 3,200 hectares (8,000 acres). The best vineyards face south and southeast.

The Cahors grape is the Malbec or Cot, known locally as the Auxerrois. Alone it makes a rather inky-looking, dark, hard wine, so Merlot and Jurançon as well as some Tannat and Syrah are also planted. The wines, however, are still 70% Cot. The vines grow in the old alluvial soils which have formed terraces and little hills inside the steeply banked bends of the River Lot. About one-third of the grapes are cultivated along the edge of the Causse plateau, where the soil consists primarily of Kimmerridge clay, the well-known limestone of Chablis. Throughout Cahors limestone pebbles cover the fine red earth, so that the vines in many places seem to grow only in broken stones. What little soil exists is very shallow, but the fissured subsoil allows for very deep roots; thus, vigorous stems and vines with an almost unlimited life span.

The wines of Cahors have often been described as "black." Here the Malbec makes a very heavy and dark wine, one that was commonly used in centuries past to color and flavor lighter Bordeaux wines. Since the devastation of the vineyards by phylloxera, the wines have not been so terribly high in alcohol or tannin but still require long ageing in the barrel and in the bottle. When the wine is properly matured, it can be soft-scented and smooth, and it is always dark in color. In recognition of the wine's quality, the district was granted an Appellation d'Origine Contrôlée in 1971.

At Parnac, near the center of the delimited area, the large cooperative Les Caves d'Olt handles almost half of the region's production. George Vigouroux's Château Haute-Serre and Jean Jouffreau's Château du Cayrou are two of the better estate-bottled Cahors.

Château Caillou

Bordeaux white wine.
District: Sauternes, France.
Commune: Barsac.

Château Caillou, classified a Second Growth in 1855, adjoins the two Barsac First Growths, Château Climens and Château Coutet. *Caillou* is French for "pebble," and pebbles are thick in the vineyard soil which gives so much to the quality of the Bordeaux

Cairanne

wines. M. Bravo, the proprietor, also owns the Barsac vineyards, Château Baulac and Château Petit-Mayne.

Characteristics. Small and pleasant, yet high in alcohol.

Vineyard area: 17 hectares (42.5 acres).

Average production: 40 *tonneaux* (3,700 cases).

Cairanne

One of the best communes of the Côtes-du-Rhône, producing red, white, and rosé wines.

See Rhône.

Cajuada

A West African beverage made from fermented cashew nuts.

Calabria

White and red wines.
District: Southern Italy.

Calabria is the "toe" of the Italian "boot." The land is hot, mountainous, and poverty-stricken, except for a strip along the coast cooled by the sea and fruitful with orange and lemon trees. The soil is for the most part volcanic, and vines do as well as anything here, where they have been grown since the time of the Greek settlers. Most Calabrian wines, however, are not of the first order.

Cirò is a D.O.C. applicable to red, white, and rosé wines from Cirò, Cirò Marina, and parts of the communes of Crucoli and Melissa, due east of Cosenza. The white is made of Greco Bianco with some Trebbiano Toscano, the red and rosé of Gaglioppo and a bit of Greco and Trebbiano. White Cirò is straw-colored; the red and rosé are full-bodied and warm.

Greco di Bianco is a D.O.C. sweet yellow wine very high in alcohol (17%). It is produced in small quantities around Gerace in the Calabrian Apennines and apparently was held in high esteem in classical Rome.

Savuto (D.O.C.) is a frequently encountered red wine from the Gaglioppo and Greco Nero grapes. In spite of the dissimilarity of the grapes used, it shares certain characteristics with Cirò *rosso*, notably pungent strength and headiness. It comes from Arvino, Pecorello, Greco, and some Malvasia. Lacrima di Castrovillari and Moscato di Cosenza (sometimes Moscato di Calabria) complete the list of the better-known wines. The first is a red table wine obviously from around Castrovillari; the second, the inevitable Muscat, is sometimes made from dried grapes and is not one of Italy's more distinguished examples of that wine. Donnici, Lamezia, Melissa, Pollino and Sant'Anna di Isola Capo Rizzuto are all D.O.C. wines.

Caldaro (Lago di) (D.O.C.)

An almond-flavored red wine from North Italy.
See Trentino-Alto Adige.

Caledon

Wine-growing district of the Cape province, South Africa.
See South Africa.

California

See United States: California.

Calisaya

A Spanish liqueur with the bitter taste of quinine.

Château Calon-Ségur

Bordeaux red wine.
District: Haut-Médoc, France.
Commune: Saint-Estèphe.

The vineyard is a classified Great Growth. Here, as at Château Latour, the vines are allowed to achieve their maximum age and are not uprooted by sections; individually removed and replaced, some live for ninety years and more. Quality at the expense of quantity is the consequence of this method: the vine produces better and better wine all its life, but there is less and less of it after the fifteenth or twentieth year. Yet, since the vineyards are large, there is no shortage of the wine.

In early times, Calon-Ségur was one of only three vineyards in Saint-Estèphe. It is ironical to consider that while in 1855 Calon-Ségur was classed a Third Growth (*Troisième Cru*) and Château Montrose a Second Growth (*Second Cru*), in 1825 Montrose had been a forestland parcel of the Calon-Ségur estate. Today Calon-Ségur could be classed as a Second Growth. It is one of the best of the Thirds and better than many Seconds.

The name Calon comes from a little river skiff used in the Middle Ages to ferry timber across the Gironde; eventually the name spread to the whole district of Saint-Estèphe, which was known as the Calones or Saint-Estèphe-de-Calon, until the eighteenth century. At that time the property had passed, by marriage, into the hands of the Président de Ségur—Marquis de Ségur-Calon. He was the proprietor at the same time of the great Châteaux Lafite and Latour, but Calon was his favorite, apparently, for he said: "I make wine at Lafite and Latour, but my heart is at Calon"—and this motto is still inscribed on an archway in the courtyard. This charming legend has been disclaimed, but there are those who say that the word "calon" in Welsh means "heart"; hence the presence of the heart on the label.

The soil is of three types: sandy gravel, giving finesse and nose to the wines; fatty gravel, or a limy and heavy soil, which, if it were not blended with the other, would give common but full-bodied wines; thinnish gravel which alone could produce wines with breed but with considerable harshness. The late proprietor, Édouard Gasqueton, played the scale of these soils to produce his outstanding wine. Since his death in 1962, the vineyard has been owned by Philippe Gasqueton, his nephew.

Characteristics. Body is the foremost characteristic, although this robustness is held in the traces of a certain suppleness. The wines of Saint-Estèphe are the heaviest and most masculine of the Médocs, and generally Calon-Ségur produces one of the most powerful and longest-lived wines of the Saint-Estèphes.

Vineyard area: 50 hectares (125 acres).

Average production: 200 *tonneaux* (20,000 cases).

Caluso (D.O.C.)

A sweet white wine of different types made near Turin.

See Piedmont.

Calvados

Apple brandy, the finest in the world. It is distilled from cider, in Normandy: the name is taken from the department of Calvados, and the best comes from the Vallée d'Auge, its greatest cider-making district. When old, Calvados can be a magnificent brandy, but fine ones can rarely be found outside the cellars of Normandy. While cider is being produced, a distillation is made from the residue of apple pressings, and this is usually called Eau-de-vie de Marc de Cidre.

Château Camensac

Bordeaux red wine.
District: Haut-Médoc, France.
Commune: Saint-Laurent.

(*Saint-Laurent is not a place-name and the wine has the* appellation *Haut-Médoc.*)

A little-known and almost-forgotten Fifth Growth (*Cinquième Cru*) as classified in 1855. In recent years new plantings have increased the size of the vineyard, which yields a relatively small production.

Characteristics. A marked improvement in quality.

Vineyard area: 62 hectares (155 acres).

Average production: 260 *tonneaux* (25,000 cases).

Campania

Red and white wines.
District: Southwest Italy.

Campanian wines are the very essences of the sunny province which produces them. Nowhere else is life so exuberant and carefree as it is in Naples, Campania's capital, but without its wines even Naples might lose some of its gaiety. The city is surrounded by beaches and islands—Sorrento, Capri, Ischia—of such legendary beauty that ever since classical times they have been resorts of pleasure.

The entire coast of the Bay of Naples might be Paradise on earth—and this, according to Neapolitan mythology, is precisely the case.

MAJOR WINES

Lacrima (or *Lacryma*) *Christi (D.O.C.).* The "tear of Christ" is a dryish pale golden wine, made from grapes grown along the southern slope of Mount Vesuvius. The story they tell about it may well have been established to rival that of Latium's Est! Est!! Est!!!, but the Neapolitans swear that it is true. They say that when Lucifer fell from grace, he and his retinue landed with such a crash that the land beneath them collapsed, to form the Bay of Naples. Lucifer soon realized that he was in the place nearest to his lost Paradise, and so he populated Naples and its surrounding areas with his demons—with the result that Naples soon became a citadel of wickedness. The Savior, looking down one day, grieved to see the terrestrial paradise so steeped in sin and He wept, His tear falling on Mount Vesuvius. From the tear a vine sprang up, and it multiplied into a vineyard, and every year the tear is reproduced in the wine vat as a reminder of the glory which awaits the honest winemaker. This all happened, of course, a very long time ago, and Greco and Fiano have been planted to replace the original vines, but the story still lives on, retold with each glass. The wine, incidentally, has nothing in common with the Spanish Lágrima Christi (*see* Málaga) except that Italian and Spaniard each claim the original inspiration for the name.

Falerno is another wine with a long history. In Roman times it was known as Falernum and seems to have been considered almost as one of the wonders of the ancient world, but unfortunately we do not know from what grapes it was made and have only an imperfect idea of how it tasted. Modern Falerno is made in Campi Flegrei, Capua, Sessa Aurunca, and Mondragone and the wine today, from Falanghino grapes, is generally golden-yellow, semi-dry, and low in quality. Much of it is exported. Red Falerno is made also, mainly from Aglianico grapes, and is a pleasant local table wine provided that the price is reasonable.

Capri (D.O.C.). These white wines are more typical of Campania than the more famous Lacrima Christi and Falerno. The better of the two is Capri, from Greco and Falanghino grapes grown on the island, and vinified into a heady, sprightly, dry (or sometimes semi-sweet) white wine which is perfect with seafood fresh from the Bay, with a sandwich or a meal, or as an aperitif sipped on a vine-shaded terrace. This is a delightful wine and one almost never found outside Capri, for it is made in such small quantities that it could never satisfy the thirst even of Capri itself—and so rather similar wines are imported to masquerade under Capri labels. (The same is true of the wine of the neighboring island of Ischia—some of which is sold as Arturi.) Some red and rosé Capris are also made, but there is even less of them than there is of the white.

Ischia. Now a Controlled Denomination of Origin for white (Ischia Bianco) and red (Ischia Rosso) wines produced entirely on the island. White Ischia is from Forastera and Biancolella grapes; it has a straw color, inclining to gold, with a delicate bouquet and a pleasant enough taste. Some of the white grown in one of the better sections of the island may be called Ischia Bianco Superiore. The red wine of Ischia may come from anywhere on the island and is produced from Guarnaccia, Piedirosso, and Barbera grapes. The taste is dry and slightly tannic.

Greco di Tufo. A D.O.C. white wine from the area about the town of Avellino. Greco di Tufo and Coda di Volpe grapes go into the wine, which is dry and has a good golden yellow color. The name may also be rightfully given the sparkling wine made in the same region.

Taurasi (D.O.C.). Vigorous and strong red wine made from Aglianico grapes, and some Piedirosso, Barbera, and Sangiovese. Since the wine is often too harsh when young, it can be sold only after four years of ageing.

LESSER WINES

Conca. Made from Sangiovese, Canaiolo, Malvasia, and Aglianico grapes grown on slopes overlooking the Bay of Sorrento.

The wine is red, sometimes slightly coarse, generally high in alcohol. It is typically Italian and like so many Italian wines is excellent with pasta and other Italian dishes, but usually disappointing with more subtle fare.

Fiano di Avellino (D.O.C.). Light, white, flowery wine grown from Fiano grapes about 30 miles east of Naples.

Gragnano. The least of the Campanian red wines, made inland from Amalfi on the peninsula which juts out between Naples and Sorrento. It has a rich, deep hue but a light texture, and its outstanding charms are its freshness and a bouquet recalling violets or fresh strawberries. These, of course, are characteristics of young wines, and it follows that Gragnano should be taken fairly young. Jaculillo, Piede di Palumbo, and Aglianico grapes are the traditional components, and the wine is now and again brought out *frizzante*, or slightly sparkling, but whether by accident or design it is difficult to say.

Ravello. Red, white, and rosé wines are made in (and named for) this flower-filled resort on the Amalfi coast; the rosé, or Rosato, is the most appealing. Greco and Fiano grapes produce the white; the others are from Aglianico, the best on the Amalfi coast.

Solopaca (D.O.C.). Red and white wines from the small city in northern Campania from which they take their name. The white is made from Trebbiano and Malvasia grapes, the red from Sangiovese and Piedirosso.

Vesuvio (D.O.C.). Lacryma Christi del Vesuvio is the superior Vesuvio. Red and rosé wines from Aglianico, Piedirosso and Olivella, and also white from the Colpa di Volpe grape, are all grown along the slopes of Mount Vesuvius. It is said that Vesuvio is used to augment the production of red Capri, at a distinct mark-up in price.

Campari

Reddish-brown Italian bitters flavored with herbs and orange peel, made by Fratelli Campari of Milan. It is used in the Americano and Negroni cocktails or drunk straight with a twist of lemon peel and a dash of soda as an aperitif.

Campbeltown

One of the two chief centers for Western Highland malt whisky: the other is the nearby island of Islay. Campbeltown is on the sea-girt peninsula of Kintyre, which extends southward down the Firth of Clyde. Until two centuries ago Kintyre was always considered a detached island of the Inner Hebrides.

See Whisky, Scotch.

Canada

The vineyards of Canada are mainly in the Niagara peninsula of southern Ontario (by far the more important region) and in the Okanagan Valley of British Columbia.

WINE HISTORY

It is told in the Norse sagas that Leif Ericson first discovered North America and named the country Vineland because of the profusion of wild vines there, which in reality were probably blueberries. The first wines were probably made by French missionaries for sacramental purposes, for in LeJeune's *Relation of the Jesuits for 1636* it is stated: "In some places there are many wild vines loaded with grapes. Some have made wine of them through curiosity. I tasted it, and it seemed to me very good." While this is the first record of wine-making in Canada, it was not until much later that viticulture assumed commercial importance, and then it was due to German, not to French, influence. In 1811, John Schiller, an ex-corporal of the German army, settled in Cooksville near Toronto, Ontario, and established a vineyard and a small winery. Canadians accept this date as the beginning of their wine industry. By the year 1890, grape-growing had become established principally in the Niagara peninsula with about 2,000 hectares (5,000 acres) planted. These have increased through the years to approximately 11,000 hectares (27,500 acres). Another 6,000 hectares of vineyards lie in the Okanagan Valley, in the central interior region of British Columbia, where vines were planted in the 1920s by a Hungarian wine-maker named Eugene Rittich. The western wineries prospered not with their local grapes, but with fruit trucked in from California. Until the 1960s, nearly all of British Columbia's "Canadian" wine was made from California grapes. At that time quotas were established to specify the percentage of Okanagan grapes that must be present in wines carrying the local label. The quota is now 80%. Wine production of the two major regions is 815,000 hectoliters (22 million U.S. gallons, 18 million imp.), but several more regrettable thousand gallons are made from grape juice concentrates by wineries in the eastern Atlantic provinces, fortunately this practice is declining.

A major portion of the vineyards were planted with North American varieties. These became the backbone of the industry but are gradually being augmented with European hybrids and certain varieties of *Vitis vinifera*. In Ontario the *vinifera* and hybrid grapes now represent 45% of grape production and are increasing annually as producers respond to changes in consumer demands. In British Columbia, all the grape production is of *vinifera* or hybrid grapes. At first, it was thought that *Vitis vinifera* could not be grown in Canada, but research and experimentation indicate that it is possible. Vineyards of this variety are not yet extensive, but they are being expanded. The focal point of Canadian viticultural research is the Ontario Department of Agriculture Experimental Station at Vineland, Ontario, where more than three hundred varieties of vines have been under test for wine-making qualities. Many of the wineries and particularly the newer small wineries are expanding the research into viticulture of *Vitis vinifera* grapes and vinification techniques. While in the past most of the wine produced in Canada was of this sweet dessert fortified type, demand for table wines has grown considerably, with production of them now about 90% of the total. With the exception of the table varieties, most of the wines are blends of different years and different vineyards. They are aged in wood. Contrary to European practice, the wines must be marketed by the winery producing them. In all provinces, except Ontario, wineries may sell only to the Alcohol Control Boards, which sell retail through their stores to consumers and to hotel and restaurant establishments. In Ontario, wineries sell to the Alcohol Control Board, which operates 600 retail stores, and to consumers through a limited number of winery-operated retail stores.

Eight of the Dominion's provinces voted for prohibition of alcoholic beverages in 1916, but in Ontario, which did not ban liquor, wineries flourished. Quebec province held out against prohibition until 1919 and even then only banned spirits.

VINE-GROWING REGIONS

About 85% of the grapes grown in Canada come from the fertile alluvial soils of the Niagara peninsula, bordered by Lake Ontario, Lake Erie, and the Niagara River. The principal vineyard area is west of Niagara Falls and across Lake Ontario from Toronto. Most of the vines are planted below the 100-meter (328-foot) Niagara escarpment, but recently many vineyards have been moved to the top of the cliff as land grows scarce. Although the climate of the country is generally supposed to be cold and harsh, the Niagara region has an average growing season of 173 days. Because it is near these large bodies of water, the district actually has more frost-free days than do many areas 200 to 300 miles south. The winters are mild, and the average temperature during the dormant season is about 25° to 30°F. (–4° to –1°C.). Adequate rainfall, hot summers, and long autumns provide good conditions for growth and harvesting.

Nearly three-fourths of the nation's wine is produced on the peninsula by eight of the sixty wineries in Canada. Niagara peninsula grape production is second only to apples as Canada's largest fruit crop. Labrusca grapes such as Concord, Niagara, and Elvira with their foxy taste predominate. These Labrusca varietals are progressively being replaced by French hybrids and *Vitis vinifera* varietals such as Seyval Blanc, Marechal Foch, de Chaussac, Riesling and Chardonnay. This progress is being accelerated by market demand which provides growers of hybrids such as Seyval Blanc with twice the price of Labrusca grapes and more than three times for *Vitis vinifera* varietals. Outside of the city of Niagara Falls, at T. G. Bright and Co., Canada's largest wine-maker, the case for *Vitis vinifera* and hybrid vines was made after the Second World War by a French chemist named Adhemar de Chaunac (hence the grape variety of the same name) who imported such plants to eastern North America. Bright's vineyard includes Pinot Noir and Pinot Chardonnay from which a sparkling white wine has been made since the late 1950s. The firm has also had good success with a Gewürztraminer. Other important wineries on the peninsula are Château-Gai at Niagara Falls, which buys its grapes from local producers, and the Andres firm in Winona. Also of interest is the Jordan Winery and its adjoining wine museum at Twenty Mile Creek. Several newly established wineries are specializing very successfully in the production of *Vitis vinifera* grapes as well as French hybrids. Such wineries as Inniskillin and Château des Charmes have made successful wines from Chardonnay and Riesling grapes. Some experiments have included the making of Botrytis-infected "ice wines" from Vidal grapes. Although the vineyards are concentrated on the Niagara peninsula, some grapes are grown south of Toronto, where Château Cartier, Turner, Charal and Pelee Island Vineyards make wines, and as far west as Windsor, across the river from Detroit.

Canadian whisky

Twenty-five hundred kilometers (more than fifteen hundred miles) west of the Ontario vineyards lies the Okanagan Valley grape-growing region of British Columbia. Situated between the Trepanier Plateau and the Monashee Mountains east of Vancouver, the 100-kilometer-long (over 150-mile) valley extends south from the head of Okanagan Lake. As in the east, the lake waters moderate the climate, and the growing season is as long as 185 days. Irrigation with water from the lake and the upland streams supplements the meager rainfall of 20 to 30 centimeters (8 to 12 inches) per year. Many Okanagan growers have planted French hybrids and *Vitis vinifera* varietals so that currently Riesling, Chardonnay, Seyval Blanc and Gewürztraminer grapes predominate. Wine experiments include the successful making of late harvested wines.

Canada's wine industry has reached the point where it has turned away from making so much sweet fortified dessert wine and has begun to concentrate on higher quality table wines. Production of table wines now amounts to 95% of total sales.

See also Whisky, Canadian.

Canadian whisky

See Whisky, Canadian.

Canaiolo

One of the red grapes used in making Chianti.
See Tuscany.

Canary

See Spain.

Candia

Crete. This name is sometimes found on the labels of Cretan wines.
See Greece.

Cane

A mature shoot of the vine.

Cannelle

Cinnamon-flavored liqueur.

Cannonau di Sardegna (D.O.C.)

Red or rosé wine from Sardinia *(q.v.)*.

Château Canon

Bordeaux red wine.
District and Commune: Saint-Émilion, France.

Classed a First Great Growth *(Premier Grand Cru)* in 1955, the vineyard is planted right over some of the ancient quarries out of which the building stone of the medieval town of Saint-Émilion was dredged. The "château" is an unprepossessing farmhouse. The 1982 is outstanding even among the great bottles of that year. Canon has always been one of the top Saint-Émilions, its recognition antedating by generations the recent official classification.

Characteristics. A supple, generous wine with considerable finesse.

Vineyard area: 18 hectares (45 acres).

Average production: 75 *tonneaux* (6,500 cases).

Canteiro

A rather rare type of Madeira: the designation means that the wine was matured in the heat of the sun.

Château Cantemerle

Bordeaux red wine.
District: Haut-Médoc, France.
Commune: Macau.

(Macau is not a place-name and the wine has the appellation *Haut-Médoc.)*

Classified a Fifth Growth *(Cinquième Cru)* in 1855, Cantemerle is now universally considered to be very much superior to its official classification. Actually it deserves to be reclassed as a Second or Third Growth *(Second or Troisième Cru).* The second great Médoc vineyard north of Bordeaux (the first is La Lagune), Cantemerle lies about two miles south of the first cluster of famous growths within the grouped communes entitled to the place-name Marguax. The château is surrounded by one of the largest and most beautiful parks in Médoc, and the vines planted at either side of the woodland produce an excellent wine.

Cantemerle existed long before many of today's famous vineyards were established. In the Middle Ages it was the site of a fortress called Sauves, and it played its part in the turbulent history of that time as a portion of the Barony of Cantemerle. Acquired in 1579 by the family of Jehan de Villeneuve, it remained in their hands until 1892, when it was bought by the father of the late M. Pierre J. Dubos; after Pierre Dubos' passing, the vineyard was run by his son-in-law, the highly regarded Henri Binaud. The property was sold to an insurance group in October 1980.

The present high reputation of the wines was achieved largely through the efforts of old M. Dubos, a twinkling little man with his sturdy legs wrapped in field puttees, still remembering the English he learned to speak in England decades ago, and revered as one of the most dedicated wine men of Médoc. His Vintage Book was a legend in Bordeaux, recording unfailingly every morning, afternoon, and evening, for more than sixty-five years, wind direction, temperature, and barometer readings, with, alongside, the behavior of the vine, its flowering, ripening, etc. When the vintage arrived, each day was graphed by M. Dubos—section harvested, yielding how many tubs, put to ferment in which vat.

Since 1981 the vineyard has expanded considerably; 34 hectares of new vines have been planted under the supervision of the Domaines Cordier, who are now running the vineyard.

During the decade of the eighties, it is to be hoped, a judicious selection of the vats will be made during the "assemblage," with each vintage to set aside some of the wines from the young vines, so that they are not incorporated into the final blend to the detriment of this fine classified growth.

Characteristics. Beautiful, fine, supple, fast-maturing wines with remarkable finesse. Another example of how obsolete the 1855 Classification is, since Cantemerle, a Fifth Growth, has come up with many a superb bottle.

Vineyard area: 55 hectares (137 acres).

Average production: 280 *tonneaux* (25,000 cases).

Cantenac

Sometimes Cantenac-Margaux. A village of the Haut-Médoc district of the Bordeaux wine region in southwest France. The wines are sold under the controlled place-name of the adjoining commune, Margaux. There is no appreciable difference in quality or style between the wines of the two communes. Eight vineyards of Cantenac were classified in 1855: Château Brane-Cantenac, a Second Growth (*Second Cru*); Château Kirwan, d'Issan, Palmer, Boyd-Cantenac, and Cantenac-Brown, all Third Growths (*Troisièmes Crus*); and Châteaux Prieuré-Lichine and Pouget, Fourth Growths (*Quatrièmes Crus*).

See under individual headings.

Château Cantenac-Brown

Bordeaux red wine.
District: Haut-Médoc, France.
Commune: Cantenac-Margaux.

Accorded the right in 1955 to the place-name Margaux with the other vineyards of Cantenac, Brown faces the village of Margaux from a distance of about one kilometer. The huge red brick château with its many chimneys looks like a Tudor English boarding school.

The vineyard, a Third Growth (*Troisième Cru*), as classified in 1855, was established by a M. John Lewis Brown, a Bordeaux merchant, who sold it in 1860 to the owner of Léoville-Poyferré, M. Armand Lalande. At that time the vineyard was more than double its present size. The du Vivier family, who formerly owned the de Luze shipping firm in Bordeaux, bought the property in 1969 from Jean Lawton, the jovial chief of another shipper, Lalande. A few years after acquiring the vineyard, the du Viviers purchased the château itself from M. André de Wilde. In 1987 the du Viviers sold the property to a French insurance group.

Characteristics. Big full wines, made from the typical Médoc varieties: Cabernet Sauvignon, Merlot, Cabernet Franc. Rather heavier than the wines of the neighboring châteaux. The new owners need to improve both the quality and the reputation of the wine.

Vineyard area: 42 hectares (105 acres).

Average production: 150 *tonneaux* (13,000 cases).

Cap Corse

French wine-based aperitif made with the heady wines of the Cap Corse (northernmost) peninsula of Corsica and flavored with quinine and herbs.

Château Capbern

Bordeaux red wine.
District: Haut-Médoc, France.
Commune: Saint-Estèphe.

The property of 150 acres, approximately half of it in vine, is set on high gravelly land at the edge of the village of Saint-Estèphe and overlooking the River Gironde. Directly across the town is Château Calon-Ségur, which nowadays produces one of the finest red Bordeaux; both châteaux are owned and worked by the Gasqueton family. Capbern wines are as well cared for by these expert vinicultors as the famous Calon-Ségur and deserve elevation to classification among the Great Growths (*Grands Crus*). Various parts of the production are sold as Château Capbern, Château Grand-Village-Capbern, and Château La-Rose-Capbern.

Characteristics. A full-bodied, round wine combining a certain amount of hardness and finesse. Better made than many Classified Growths.

Vineyard Area: 36 hectares (90 acres).

Average production: 100 *tonneaux* (9,000 cases).

Cape Smoke

South Africa's cheapest and worst brandy. A wise policy of favorable taxes on high-quality brandy and high taxes on the poorer examples is causing it to disappear.

Cape wines

See South Africa.

Caperitif

South African aperitif, deep gold in color, based on wine, blended with spirit, and flavored with herbs. It is bitter but reminiscent of vermouth.

Capri (D.O.C.)

Mainly a dry white wine from the island of Capri. Some of this is made in Capri itself, some in Ischia and

Carafe

other neighboring places. A small quantity of red and rosé wine is also made.
See Campania.

Carafe

In French, a decanter or glass bottle for serving wines. In French restaurants the ordinary wine is usually drawn from a cask and brought to the table either in a carafe or a *carafon*, a small carafe.

Caramel

Burnt sugar added to spirits as coloring matter. All spirits emerge pale and colorless from the still, and unless color is absorbed from the wooden barrels during ageing, caramel—tasteless and practically odorless—must be used.

Carbon dioxide

CO_2, produced in approximately equal weight with alcohol when sugar is fermented by the action of yeast. Normally it escapes, but it is trapped in the fluid in the production of sparkling wine, beer, and cider. In French, *gaz carbonique*.

Carbonated wines

Wines in which an unnatural sparkle has been induced by gasifying with carbon dioxide.
See Sparkling wines.

Château Carbonnieux

Bordeaux red and white wines.
District: Graves, France.
Commune: Léognan.

With the charming wine goes a charming story. To sell their wines in Turkey (which meant getting round the Islamic interdiction on wine) the fathers of the Abbey of Sainte-Croix of Bordeaux, then owners of the vineyard, sent off bottles of Carbonnieux labeled as mineral water. The sultan tasted it and said: "If the French mineral water is so good, why do they take the trouble to make wine?"

Set in the ancient vineyard, the beautiful château dates from the fourteenth century. In 1959 both red and white Carbonnieux wines were classified as among the leading Graves growths. The Perrin family makes a good, full-bodied red wine but, excellent and consistent as this is, it is the dry, brilliant white wine that has made the vineyard famous.

Characteristics. A wine with both lightness and finesse. The preponderance of Sauvignon Blanc grapes, especially in the white, gives it a particularly agreeable flavor. The white is dry, clean, and well known.

Vineyard area: red—40 hectares (100 acres); white —40 hectares (100 acres).

Average production: red—150 *tonneaux* (14,000 cases); white—150 *tonneaux* (14,000 cases).

Carboy

A large bottle of glass, or occasionally earthenware, with a wicker or wooden frame. The name is derived from the Persian *garabana* (large flagon); a demijohn.

Carema (D.O.C.)

A fresh wine of Nebbiolo grapes from the area of Turin.
See Piedmont.

Carignan

Grape grown mostly in southern France and similar hot climates for robust, heady table wines and dessert wines. It has also been transplanted to America, where it is spelled Carignane.

Cariñena

Best-known wines of Aragón, both red and white.
See Spain.

Carmel

Some of the wines of Israel bear this name, followed by a grape variety or wine type—e.g., Carmel muscat, Carmel port.
See Israel.

Carpano

The oldest maker of Italian vermouth, now producing in Turin two kinds, the regular and a special bittersweet one called Punt e Mes.

Carta Blanca (White Label)

A light-bodied Puerto Rican or Cuban rum, a little lighter, paler, and less sweet than Carta Oro.
See Rum: Cuban, Puerto Rican.

Carta Oro (Gold Label)

A light-bodied Puerto Rican or Cuban rum which, owing to the addition of caramel coloring, is slightly darker than Carta Blanca. It is usually a little heavier and sweeter, too.
See Rum: Cuban, Puerto Rican.

Case

A case of wine contains twelve 750-milliliter or 24- to 26-oz. bottles, or twenty-four such half-bottles; or forty-eight splits, six magnums, or three jeroboams of Champagne. The cases used to be made only of wood, but today so many wines are being shipped in cardboard cartons that these are also called cases.

Casein

This useful protein is employed in the ageing of white wines, both as a clarifier and as a remedy against maderization. The substance, which contains phosphorus, is generally extracted from milk, where it is present as a calcic salt. When it has been washed, dried, ground and sieved, it can be used, in doses of from 5 to 20 grams per hectoliter, for clearing wines; or from 25 to 30 grams per hectoliter as a preventive and curative treatment for oxidation, or maderization.

Cask

A wine barrel, usually of wood and bound with hoops. Sizes and capacity vary widely, following traditional customs of particular localities (for standard casks and containers, *see* Appendix C, pp. 704–706). Casks are used for maturing, storing, and transporting wines, spirits, and beers. In Europe ordinary wine is always sold in cask, the wine being drawn off as needed.

Casse

Clouding and precipitation, with an off-taste, caused in wine by the presence of too much air, protein, iron, or copper.
See Chapter Nine, p. 40.

Cassis (Appellation Contrôlée)

(1) Controlled place-name in the wines of Provence, France. The vineyards are planted on the hillsides behind the picturesque fishing village of Cassis, some 20-odd kilometers (15 miles) east of Marseille.
See Provence.
(2) Sweet, dark red liqueur made from black currants. The most notable Cassis is that of Dijon, in northeast France, although it is also made elsewhere. Around Dijon, Cassis is used as a popular aperitif: a little is put in a glass that is then filled with a fairly neutral dry white wine. The local and somewhat inelegant name for this is *rince cochon* (pig rinse). Also called kir.

Castel del Monte (D.O.C.)

Fresh Italian red and white wines from Apulia *(q.v.)*.

Castelli di Jesi (Marches)

A D.O.C. white wine.
See Verdicchio dei Castelli di Jesi.

Castelli Romani

Inexpensive wines very popular in the restaurants of Rome.
See Latium.

Catalonia

The northern provinces of Spain where Catalan is spoken—Barcelona, Gerona, Lérida, and Tarragon—produce a wide variety of usually inexpensive wines, ranging from heavy and sweet Priorato to light and pale Penedès—a sparkling wine made by the champagne process. Many sound and some great table wines come from the region as well. *See* Spain.

Catawba

Pink American grape of uncertain origin, said to draw its name from the River Catawba in western North Carolina. Its juice is white, dry, and heavy-flavored, and was widely used in the nineteenth century, particularly for sparkling wine. "Sparkling Catawba," the most famous of which was made by the Longworth Vineyards of Cincinnati, Ohio, was extremely popular.

Cava (Méthode Champenoise)

A term for superior Spanish wines which are fermented in bottles in Catalonia.

Cave

French term for cellar.

Cavistes

French term for cellarmen.

Cellar

Place for storing wine.
See Chapter Six, p. 25.

Centerbe

Italian liqueur said to be made from a hundred different herbs, with mint outstanding. It is also called Silvestro, from the reputed originator, Fra San Silvestro, an Italian monk.

Central Valley

Californian wine region. The major district is Escalon-Modesto, in San Joaquin County. The area comprises also part of Stanislaus and Merced counties.
See United States: California.

Cépage

French term for grape variety—e.g., Chardonnay, Pinot Noir, Cabernet Sauvignon, or Riesling.

Cerasella

Dark, red, sweet Italian liqueur made from and flavored with cherries, although the taste is enriched by the addition of a number of herbs.

Cerasuolo d'Abruzzo (Montepulciano) (D.O.C.)

Italian light red wine.
See Abruzzo.

Ceres

Wine-growing district of Cape province, South Africa.
See South Africa.

Cerise d'Alsace

White *eau-de-vie* made with cherries.
See Alsace.

Cérons (Appellation Contrôlée)

White wines.
District: Bordeaux, France.

The vineyard road goes down the left bank of the River Garonne, past the great châteaux of Graves, and eventually in among the hills of Sauternes, winding through a flat country of neatly kept vines as solid as a carpet. The highway is beaded with gaudy stands, some in the shape of wine bottles or clapboard castles, into which the public is urged to step and taste the wine. The district is Cérons, and while it is a continuation of Graves, its wines are neither as dry as the white Graves nor as sweet as Sauternes. They are produced by impeccable wine-making methods from the same grapes as Sauternes—Sémillon, Sauvignon, and some Muscadelle—and according to the Sauternes system of letting the grapes achieve a sugar-rich overripeness, in which condition they are selectively picked. Finally, as indicated by the many stands along the road, Cérons' white wine is far more popular in France than might be imagined from its small fame abroad.

(In Bordeaux it is assumed that Cérons has failed to make a definite impression in the world market, where there are so many names to choose from, because it is an in-between style, neither sweet nor dry.)

A considerable amount of dry Cérons is being made now, however, in response to present market conditions. But the typical Cérons is a little less sweet than a Barsac, which region it touches and of which it once was a part, just as a Barsac will be a little less sweet than a Sauternes. Cérons makes about 4,000 hectoliters (105,700 U.S. gallons, 88,000 imp.), as com-

pared with 14,000 hectoliters from neighboring Barsac and 30,000 hectoliters from Sauternes.

Château Certan-de-May

Bordeaux red wine.
District and Commune: Pomerol, France.

Once a part of the Barreau family property that also included Vieux-Château-Certan, the château makes a typical Pomerol wine, but one that has failed to show in recent vintages some of its earlier success.
Vineyard area: 4 hectares (10 acres).
Average production: 18 *tonneaux* (1,500 cases).

Certosa

Red Italian liqueur resembling Chartreuse.

Cesanese

Grape variety found in Italy.

Cesanese del Piglio (D.O.C.)

The outstanding red wine of Latium, made from Cesanese grapes.
See Latium.

Chablis

White wine.
District: Burgundy, near Auxerre, Central France.

Chablis is one of the most famous wine names in the world but, used correctly, it refers to one of the world's rarest great wines—to the steadily decreasing quantity of magnificent flinty-dry white wines which are made from grapes grown on hilly acres in and around the Burgundian town of Chablis, about 183 kilometers (114 miles) southeast of Paris.

The village lies in a small valley in the department of Yonne, surrounded by gently rolling hills on which the vines are grown—but not in any great numbers. The bare hills overlooking the town are astonishingly empty, and it is sometimes said that if present trends continue, the wines of Chablis may cease to exist within a few generations.

The soil is hard and hard to work. Easily exhausted, the vineyards must rest as much as twenty years at a time, and at present about half of the land is resting. The topsoil is thin and in many spots the white, marly, calcium-rich subsoil (a formation known as Kimmeridge clay) shows through. The thin top layer is easily washed down the slopes by the rains and must be carried up again on the backs of the workers, for only at mid-slope can the greatest wines be produced.

A further hazard is the inclemency of the climate, for Chablis is more to the north than any other fine-wine district of France except Champagne and Alsace. When the vine is planted that far north it must expend a great part of its vigor simply struggling to survive the hard winters, the uncertain summers, and the often disastrous frosts—the month of May is by far the most critical, for a May frost can ruin the prospects for the entire year. The best vineyards, often those more susceptible to frost, are now using *Chaufferettes* or fuel heaters in the vineyards to heat the freezing air. Alternatively, there are spray or "aspersion" systems where the vines are sprayed so that a protective covering of ice forms round the young buds. Such practices have completely transformed the economy of Chablis.

The Burgundian *vigneron* is passionately attached not only to his land but to his wine. For the older growers no sacrifice is too great if the result may, in very favorable years, be great wine. The younger men, however, are not inspired with this ideal of perfection, and many are leaving to find occupation elsewhere. In regions as unrewarding as Chablis, the exodus is greater than in more favored spots.

The greatest Chablis vineyards are on one hill visible from the main square of the town; they cover a mere 100 hectares (247 acres) of which only half is usually in production, and are generally sold with the name of the vineyard or the words *Grand Cru* (*see* Grands Crus *below in this entry*). Another 450 hectares (1,125 acres), half of which are in production, are divided into vineyards designated First Growth (*Premier Cru*), which form the second-rank vineyards, producing excellent wines that only occasionally reach the high level of the Great Growths. Chablis and Petit Chablis are the minor wines—but minor only in comparison with their splendid cellarmates. The I.N.A.O. authorized a doubling of the vineyard size in 1978.

All of the vineyards now encompass an oblong area of only 2,000 hectares (5,000 acres). They fall in the communes of Chablis, Chichée, Chemilly-sur-Serein, Poilly-sur-Serein, Préhy, Fyé, Rameau, Courgis, Beines, Poinchy, Maligny, Milly, Béru, La Chapelle-Vaupelteigne, Villy, Lignorelles, Ligny-le-Châtel, Fontenay, and Viviers, but the name of the town will rarely be found on the labels. The single permissible grape is Chardonnay, known in the district as Beaunois, Burgundy's only noble white-wine vine. At one time Sacy, Melon, and Aligoté vines were fairly prevalent, but these have been rooted out and their grapes forbidden. The present vines are grown low to the ground—to allow the brown and white chalky soil to deflect the sun's rays onto them and so hasten the maturing of the fruit—and they are severely pruned, with the result that the amount of fruit they give is small, even in the finest years.

Chablis growers normally have a number of small and often widely separated vineyard plots, the total acreage of each grower amounting to anything between 1 and 8 hectares (2 and 20 acres). Though small, each of the famous vineyards is divided into as many as half a dozen sections, each section owned and worked by a different man; for this reason, the wine shippers adopted the general Burgundian practice of blending wine from different growers in any given

vineyard and selling it under the firm's label. Many growers, however, have started estate-bottling their wines—harvesting the grapes, making the wine, caring for it themselves, and bottling it under their own labels.

The low-lying vines are planted in rows running up and down the slopes—in contrast to the planting of earlier days, when they followed the ridge lines. Both cultivation and drainage are enhanced by this method.

Harvest time in Chablis generally falls in the first two weeks of October and the weather is often chilly. As soon as the grapes are ripe they are picked and taken, the same day, to be pressed. If they were left overnight, fermentation might start by itself, bringing trouble for the vintner.

The great heaps of grapes are brought and taken off the stems to prevent the bitter tannin in the stems from imparting harshness to the eventual wine. The grapes are then crushed lightly in presses and the juice run off into barrels: the Chablis barrel is traditionally the *feuillette*, containing 132 liters or about 35 U.S. gallons (29 imp.). Many growers are abandoning this slightly odd-sized container and adopting the more widespread Burgundian *pièce* of 228 liters (60 U.S. gallons, 50 imp.) or the larger *fûts* of 400 liters (105.7 U.S. gallons, 88 imp.). Once the juice is in the barrel, fermetation begins.

In all the cellars and *chais* of Chablis, just after harvest time, there is a pungent sweetness mixed with the unpleasant smell of gases rising from the fermenting grapes. During the first tumultuous days of fermentation wine-makers are careful not to remain too long in the cellars, for the gas is powerful and could overcome them. Cellars are small and dark, usually with rows of barrels stacked two or three high down both sides and sometimes with another row down the center. In one corner is a small stove, for the weather gets cold quickly and unheated cellars might become too cold for the yeast to work and the wine to ferment.

In most years the summer sun does not instill enough sugar into the grapes to produce the amount of alcohol essential for great wine, so the vintner has to resort to *chaptalisation*, the addition of sugar. In many years this is necessary; in some years it is advised; occasionally it is unnecessary. *Chaptalisation* has the full sanction of the French law and is carried out under government control.

When the grape must has fermented, the wine is ready for its first clearing or racking—normally done in the February after the harvest. The slow, careful pumping from one barrel to another—leaving behind the deposit and a small amount of wine, which together form the lees—both airs the wine and clarifies it. Some of the very minor wines (such as Petit Chablis) are bottled in the summer following the harvest, but the great ones are left to sleep longer in wood. Bottling for them will not usually occur until fourteen to twenty months after the harvest. The smallest wines are never bottled at all but are sold to restaurants and served directly from the barrel or vat.

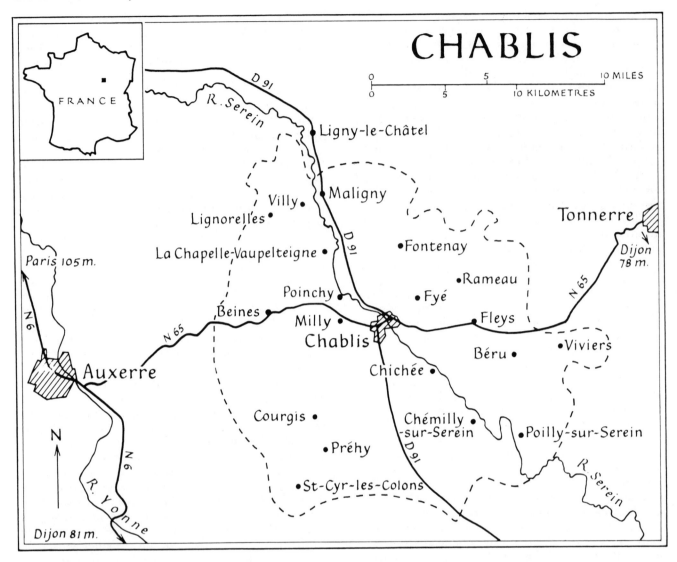

WINE HISTORY

The fame of Chablis goes back to ancient times. It is one wine which has kept its reputation and renown while others once equally well known have been forgotten. The department of the Yonne once produced two-thirds of all Burgundies, but now Chablis is the only significant area remaining. (Minor red wines are still grown in the villages of Irancy, Saint-Bris-le-Vineus, Chitry and Joigny, but production is small and the wines command neither great acclaim nor high prices.)

No one knows when the first vines were planted in Chablis. It is certain that, whether or not Julius Caesar found vines in the region when he arrived in Gaul, they were there when the Romans departed. The decline of the Roman Empire was accompanied by a decline of the vineyards, but in the twelfth century they revived under the care of the monks. The Cistercian Abbey at Pontigny, ten miles from Chablis, had extensive holdings throughout the vineyards and it is

thought that the Chardonnay vine was introduced then. Most of the monks came from the Côte d'Or, where the Chardonnay rules the slope for white wines, and the Chablis word *Beaunois* (plant of Beaune), for the Chardonnay, supports the theory. Other orders had portions of the Chablis vineyards too: the Church of Saint Martin at Tours, for example, whose vineyards were donated to one of the abbots by his brother, Charles the Bald, in the ninth century. The association between Tours and Chablis lasted until 1790, when the revolutionary state confiscated all church property.

One factor in the decline of Chablis is the lack of adequate compensation for the amount of labor required, another was the onset of phylloxera.

This lethal vine louse came to Chablis about 1893. Previously discovered in other French vineyard regions, it had caused little trouble in Chablis until an extremely hot summer gave it the conditions in which it thrived. By this time, the French growers had discovered that grafting French *vinifera* vines onto hybrids or

American rootstock was an effective way of combating the scourge, and many Chablis vineyards were quickly reconstituted in vines grafted onto roots with such numerical tags as 161–49, 3.309, 41–B, and B.31. But, because of the expense of reconstitution, some growers took this opportunity to find different employment.

In the 1930s, Chablis was again in production, but again in trouble. Fame had brought the wines into great demand and much wine was supplied which was white and dry but otherwise had nothing in common with Chablis. The French control laws, beginning in 1936, have taken the matter in hand, and today the amount of fraudulent Chablis found on the market is nothing compared to what it was.

GREAT GROWTHS (Grands Crus)

Seven vineyards, totaling 100 hectares (250 acres), comprise the Great Growths of Chablis. They are adjoining vineyards halfway up the southwesterly slope and with one exception (Blanchots, in neighboring Fyé) are all within the limits of the town of Chablis. The wines are almost always sold with vineyard names on the labels: Blanchots, Les Clos, Valmur, Grenouilles, Vaudésir, Les Preuses, and Bourgros.

Another vineyard which might have been included is La Moutonne, but it has never received official recognition, although such action was considered. Its somewhat hazy status began with the French Revolution, when the vineyard was taken over by the state and sold to a local grower. The document accompanying the sale seems to have been extremely vague and the location of the vineyard not well established, although people in Chablis can point it out with no trouble. (It takes in about five acres between Vaudésir and Les Preuses.) In 1951, the French wine authorities recommended to the Minister of Agriculture that the vineyard be recognized as a Great Growth of Chablis, but, as the quality was disappointing, the request was never followed up and the edict died a quiet bureaucratic death.

Just what makes these vineyards clearly superior to the others—and even to those close by—is impossible to define. The interplay of soil, sunlight, and whatever other mysterious elements combine to produce just exactly the right grapes for making a specific wine is too complex for analysis. The differences between them will, however, be abundantly clear in the wines themselves.

Wines from these Great Growth vineyards are Chablis, but they are Chablis with a difference. All Chablis has a certain green-tinged yellow-gold color, an impeccable dryness, and a delicate light perfume. The greater the wine, the more varied and richer it will be, and the more it will have that indescribable quality known as elegance or breed. Since the wines from these specific vineyards are consistently superior, they alone are rated Great Growths. In addition to their source in a Great Growth vineyard, these wines must have a minimum of 11% alcohol. Wines of a good year may be expected to hold their greatness as long as ten years—a considerable life span for a dry white wine. In most cases, however, the rewards for keeping them more than five are not great enough, since only about 100,000 hectoliters (2.6 million U.S. gallons, 2.2 million imp.) are made annually—the equivalent of some 20,000 cases—and the greater part is exported to the United States.

FIRST GROWTHS (Premiers Crus)

Thirty-odd vineyards in various towns around Chablis on both sides of the River Serein have the right to the name. The wines stand just below the Great Growths but are often so similar that even the most accomplished wine-taster finds it difficult to differentiate between them. They are usually sold with the name Chablis and that of the vineyard (e.g., Chablis-Montée de Tonnerre).

The wine must have an alcoholic content of 10.5% or forfeit the right to the designation. An average 25,000 hectoliters (660,000 U.S. gallons, 547,500 imp.)—about 270,000 cases—is made each year.

The vineyards, and the towns from which they come, are as follows:

RIGHT BANK OF THE SEREIN

Vineyard	Commune
Chapelot	Fyé
Côte de Fontenay	Fontenay
Vaupulent	Fontenay (part), La Chapelle-Vaupelteigne (part)
Fourchaume	La Chapelle-Vaupelteigne
Mont de Milieu	Fyé and Fleys
Montée de Tonnerre	Fyé
Pied d'Aloup	Fyé
Vaucoupin	Chichée
Vaulorent	Poinchy

LEFT BANK OF THE SEREIN

Vineyard	Commune
Beauroy	Poinchy
Beugnon	Chablis
Butteaux	Chablis
Châtain	Chablis
Côte de Léchet	Milly
Les Forêts or Forests	Chablis
Les Lys	Chablis
Mélinots	Chablis
Montmain	Chablis
Séchet	Chablis
Troesme	Beines
Vaillon and Côte de Vaillon	Chablis
Vosgros or Vogiras	Chichée

CHABLIS (Appellation Contrôlée)

On a wine label, Chablis, without any further qualification, means a wine from one of the slopes in the district, but not one of the outstanding ones. About 60,000 hectoliters (1,584,000 U.S. gallons, 1,314,000 imp.) of this wine, which must contain at least 9.5% of alcohol, are made annually. Much of it is sold in barrel, but some is bottled.

PETIT CHABLIS (Appellation Contrôlée)

The least of the wines made mostly from grapes grown in the Chablisian hinterlands. The towns in which the vineyards lie are Lignorelles, Ligny-le-Châtel, and any allowed the place-name Chablis. The wines are mainly sold in barrel, mostly in France or the Low Countries. However, much of the better wines are shipped in bottle to the U.S. Annual output averages about 6,000 hectoliters (158,400 U.S. gallons, 131,400 imp.).

Chai

A wine shed, or place above ground where wine is stored in cask. In Bordeaux wine properties, where virtually all wine is kept in such sheds, there is one *Chai* for *vin nouveau* (wine of the year) and another for *vin vieux* (wine of the previous year not yet bottled).

Chalonnais

Red and white wines.
District: South Burgundy, France.

The slope is almost an extension of the Côte de Beaune and there is a distinct resemblance between the wines of the two districts. The Chalonnais are lesser wines, indeed, only rarely attaining the same level of excellence, but they are well known, produced in considerable quantity, relatively inexpensive, and often very good.

The name derives from Chalon-sur-Saône, a small quiet town about five miles west of the vineyards. Vines are grown between these vineyards and the city, but the output is not, oddly enough, Chalonnais. To benefit from the name the grapes must be grown along specified hillsides in the four communes of Givry, Mercurey, Montagny, and Rully. Anything else in the vicinity cannot hope for a place-name more specific than Burgundy.

The favored slopes generally face east, although some look southeast and a very few face directly south. The soil is virtually the same as that of the Côte de Beaune but more fertile.

The standards ordained for these wines these wines do not differ markedly from those in other sections of Burgundy. Red wines must be made from Pinot Noir (with allowance for the almost identical Pinot Liebault and Pinot Beurot) grapes, and the white are restricted to Pinot Blanc and Chardonnay; the permissible amount of harvest is 55 hectoliters per hectare (1,453 U.S. gallons, 1,210 imp. per acre) for Mercurey, and the same amount of hectoliters for the other three communes (all subject to modification in abnormal years). Red wines must have a minimum alcoholic content of 10.5%, white of 11%; no rosé is made.

Chalonnais red wines are usually lighter than Côte d'Or Burgundies, often have considerable perfume, and do not hold for any length of time. A bottle which is more than five to eight years old could conceivably be excellent, but the odds are against it. White wines are pleasant enough as a rule, but only a few are worth exporting. As for sparkling Burgundy—vast quantities of which are made in the Chalonnais—this is a drink which has its followers, but it is not to be taken seriously.

PLACE-NAMES

Rully (Appellation Contrôlée)

Most of the output is sparkling. Rully, northernmost of the Chalonnais wine communes, has been a center for sparkling Burgundy since 1830 and for a considerable period it supported itself almost entirely on the sales of these wines, which are not made from top Burgundies.

At the end of the First World War, once-prosperous wine-growers of France found themselves in serious difficulty. No provision had been made to protect the names of fine wines, and in the chaotic aftermath of the war many members of the trade found more incentive in fast profits, so the market was flooded with cheap bulk wine sold under famous names. Simultaneously, agitation for workable controls was gaining strength. The growers of Rully found themselves in trouble. The wines were—and are—above the average; but Rully had been selling them under the name of neighboring Mercurey, whose growers were not entirely pleased with this practice. When they drew up their controls, they excluded the wines of Rully from the place-name Mercurey.

Three courses were open to the vintners of Rully: to press Mercurey to readmit their wines; to establish a control of their own; or to sell their wines simply as Burgundy, at a considerable reduction in price. Rather than try to establish Rully as a name in its own right—which might have taken a considerable time—the growers chose the first course; but, fortunately for them, the town had its sparkling Burgundy trade to support it, for the French wine authorities proved as stubborn as the Mercurey growers. In 1939 the fight was given up and Rully, benefiting from its own controls, has become a producer of still as well as sparkling wines. Rully produces 7,500 hectoliters (198,000

U.S. gallons, 164,250 imp.) annually, 50% of which is white, 50% red.

Though the red is not so good as Mercurey, the white shows more quality—and in fact is considered one of the better offerings of southern Burgundy, just below the whites of the Mâconnais. Rully's still white is marked by a pronounced bouquet and a winy flavor described as "vinosity," but, like most dry white wines, it should be consumed young. Wine stemming from the better vineyards is elevated to the rank of First Growth (*Premier Cru*)—assuming that it attains a half-degree of alcohol more than the normal minimum. These vineyards, some of which produce red as well as white wines, are:

Vauvry	Raboursay
Mont-Palais	Ecloseaux
Meix-Caillet	Marisson
Les Pierres	La Fosse
La Bressande	Chapître
Champ-Clou	Préau
La Renarde	Moulesne
Pillot	Margoty
Cloux	Grésigny
Raclot	

Mercurey (Appellation Contrôlée)

The best-known and the best wines of the Chalonnais. The grapes are grown in the communes of Mercurey, Saint-Martin-sous-Montaigus and Bourgneuf-Val d'Or and, although the law permits growing grapes for both red and white wines, those of Mercurey are about 95% red.

The wines are often very like those of the Côte de Beaune, light but sometimes surprisingly rich, and while not generally as fine, they come astonishingly close in good years. These are definitely wines to be consumed when young—from two to five years old. They are sound and pleasant but rarely stamped with greatness. One of the best organizations of the commune is the Cave Coopérative, run in a more than usually enlightened manner, respectful of the wines of each one of its members, and used as a source of supply rather than as a blending mill. Each member has his own wines, his own tools, and his own equipment, and the great advantage is that he can procure his supplies more cheaply since the organization buys in bulk and at wholesale prices.

The fame of Mercurey is so widespread that it is one of the few communes which did not go through the periods of recession after the two world wars. The renown of the wines, coupled with the fact that they are generally less expensive than comparable wines from the Côte de Beaune, was the dominant contributing factor to Mercurey's continued prosperity. The grapes are mostly Pinot Noir, and the amount of wine grown is about 20,000 hectoliters (520,500 U.S. gallons, 400,000 imp.) per year.

Here, as elsewhere, certain vineyards have the right (if their wines attain half a degree of alcohol higher than the standard minimum limit) to add the words First Growth to the label, or to be sold as Mercurey, followed by the name of the vineyard. These vineyards are:

Clos-du-Roi	Clos-des-Fourneaux
Les Voyens	Clos-des-Montaigus
Clos Marcilly	

Givry (Appellation Contrôlée)

The wines are predominantly red, although some white is grown. Tradition claims that Givry was one of the favorites of Henry IV of France, a monarch who seems to have had a colossal thirst and a penchant for almost every wine in France. The red wines of Givry are slightly lighter and generally coarser than those of Mercurey, although very often wines of the finer vineyards (Clos-Saint-Pierre, Clos-Saint-Paul, Cellier-aux-Moines, and Clos-Salomon) stand on a fairly equal footing with them. One of the more important owners is the Baron Thénard family which has holdings in numerous vineyards, including Givry's Cellier-aux-Moines and the famous Montrachet on the Côte de Beaune. Their cellars in Givry house wines from their holdings. They consist of caves dug deep below the town—huge ornate chambers which look like the set for a Hollywood costume-piece.

About 4,000 hectoliters (104,000 U.S. gallons, 80,-000 imp.) of wine are made each year, most of which is sold as Givry and 80% of which is red. Provision has been left in the decree of 1954 for certain vineyards to be designated First Growths, but the French authorities have not yet drawn up a definite list of those that may add vineyard name to that of the commune.

Montagny (Appellation Contrôlée)

The only name of the Côte Chalonnaise which applies to white wines exclusively. The vineyards are in the towns of Montagny, Buxy, Saint-Vallerin, and Jully-les-Buxy, but only in those portions selected by experts as fit and proper for growing Montagny wines. The permitted area totals just over 300 hectares (750 acres).

After Mercurey, Montagny is the largest producer of the district but little of the wine is of the first quality. *Pleasant* is the word most frequently used to describe it and is particularly apt if the wines are caught young. The dominant grape is the Chardonnay, and about 6,000 hectoliters (158,500 U.S. gallons, 132,000 imp.) of wine are made annually.

A surprising number of vineyards have been selected as superior, their wines allowed to be sold with the designation First Growth, the vineyard name following that of the commune. Although bottles carrying these indications are rare, the vineyards are:

Chambertin (Appellation Contrôlée)

Sous-les-Roches	Les Bouchots
Les Combes	Les Vignes-sur-le-Clou
Les Saint-Catages	Les Vignes-Couland
Les Vignes-Saint-Pierre	Les Trouffières
Les Charmelottes	Les Vignes-du-Soleil
Les Champs-Toizeau	Les Marais
(or Chantoiseau)	Les Perrières
Les Garchères	Le Pallye
Les Chacolets	Le Varignus
Les Clouseaux	Les Thilles
Les Carlins	La Vigne-Devant
Le Breuil	La Corvée
Les Champs-de-Coignée	Les Vignes-Dessous
Les Burnins	Les Marcques
Les Montcuchots	La Thi
Les Crets	Les Mâles
Les Beaux-Champs	La Condemine
Les Pandars	Les Vignes-Longues
Les Jardins	Les Vignes-Blanches
Les Saint-Morille	Cornevent
Le Clou	Le Mont-Laurent
Les Vignes-Derrière	Les Bonnevaux
Les Resses	Les Bassets
Le Perthuis	La Mouillère
Les Gouresses	Les Pasquiers
Les Bordes	Les Coères
Les Las	Les Thillonnés
Clos-Chaudron	Les Chandits
La Grande Pièce	Les Chazelles
Les Pidans	Le Vieux-Château
	Les Vignes-du-Puits

Chambertin (Appellation Contrôlée)

Burgundy red wine.
District: Côte de Nuits, France.
Commune: Gevrey-Chambertin.
Official Classification: Great Growth (Grand Cru).

Chambertin is the *Grand Seigneur* of Burgundy, partly because of the unquestionable magnificence and nobility of the wine, and partly in deference to Napoleon, who preferred it to all others. It is not surprising that the commune of Gevrey chose to add this name to its own, becoming Gevrey-Chambertin—although this does tend to confuse inexperienced buyers.

When buying Chambertin, make sure the label says simply Chambertin. If it says Gevrey-Chambertin, the wine is regional, could come from any vineyard in the commune, and will be a lesser wine (albeit lesser only in respect to its great neighbor). It hardly needs to be pointed out that a bottle of Chambertin should always carry the vintage year.

The vineyard lies on the gently sloping midsection of the hill to the south of the village, next to the Route des Grands Crus (Route of the Great Growths), which leads to Morey-Saint-Denis. It directly adjoins the vineyard Clos de Bèze—the only other which has the right to produce wines to be called Chambertin. Since the Clos de Bèze is less well known—but no less outstanding—than its neighbor, this right was inserted as

a clause in the law. In practice, some of its wine is sold as Chambertin-Clos de Bèze and the rest simply as Chambertin. But Chambertin has no right to the name Clos de Bèze.

Together, the two vineyards comprise some 28 hectares (70 acres)—13 as Chambertin and 15 as Clos de Bèze. Within this area are more than two dozen growers. Each tends his own vines, harvests his own grapes, makes his own wines, and sells to whom he pleases and, for this reason, there is always a certain amount of variation among bottles. The scrupulous care of one grower contrasted with the more casual methods of another creates shades of difference even in wines from the same small vineyard and the same year. Yet there will also be a strong family resemblance between Chambertins from different growers in the same year, and between wines from Chambertin and from the Clos de Bèze. Some local experts maintain that the wines from the two vineyards are so similar that it is impossible to tell them apart.

At its finest, Chambertin is big and sturdy with a deep, strong color—the color or *robe* is one of the wine's most distinctive characteristics—and a pronounced, lingering, and glorious aftertaste. It is a wine with a tremendous "nose" (for the wine-taster often transfers the perceptive organ to the wine itself). The nose is so outspoken that bouquet—the usual term—fades into insignificance beside it. In a well-made and distinctive Chambertin of a good year, all the characteristics are welded together into a balanced unity, and the wine improves with age, developing the wonderful austere masculinity which causes experts to exclaim "Chambertin," and novices, "Great wine!"

The quantity made is not great, yet it is perhaps greater than might be expected from the size of the vineyard because of the amount of Clos de Bèze which assumes the name; but in an average year for quantity only 490 hectoliters (12,985 U.S. gallons, 10,780 imp.) were made. This is the equivalent of about 5,000 cases and obviously not enough to satisfy the clamorous demand for Chambertin all over the world.

Chambertin-Clos de Bèze (A.O.C.)

Burgundy red wine.
District: Côte de Nuits, France.
Commune: Gevrey-Chambertin.
Official Classification: Great Growth (Grand Cru).

In A.D. 630, Almagaire, Duke of Lower Burgundy, founded the Abbey of Bèze near Dijon, endowing it with nearby lands and fields from which to draw support. One such holding was a wooded lot of 15 hectares (37 acres) in what is today the commune of Gevrey-Chambertin. The monks cleared the land, planted vines, and established the vineyard of Clos de Bèze. They tended it until the thirteenth century, when it passed into the hands of another order; but the vineyard did not really become exceptional until the eighteenth century, when a man named Jobert—secretary to the king's legal representative and reputedly a very clever businessman—took over both Chambertin and the Clos de Bèze and proceeded to make them famous. The vineyard was so good that its reputation lasted, and when the French wine authorities classified Burgundian vineyards in 1937, it was recognized as a Great Growth (*Grand Cru*)—one of only thirty-one outstandingly great vineyards of Burgundy.

The Clos de Bèze stands just to the south of Gevrey-Chambertin on the twisting, winding vineyard road. On the side away from the village, and adjoining it, is Chambertin, and the two vineyards are the commune's finest, although there are others near them. Wines from both may legally be sold as Chambertin; and although the Clos de Bèze is considered slightly the superior of the two, many growers take advantage of this rule, feeling that the shorter and simpler name is the better known and the easier to sell.

The official name—that which will be found on bottle labels—is Chambertin-Clos de Bèze, and not very much is made in any year. The figure in an average year for quantity amounts to a little more than 510 hectoliters (13,515 U.S. gallons, 11,220 imp.) or the equivalent of about 6,000 cases, not including the amount sold as Chambertin. The characteristics of the two wines are virtually the same and are discussed under Chambertin (*q.v.*).

Chambéry

An old city of Savoy in France, famous for the extra-dry vermouths produced there.

Chambolle-Musigny (Appellation Contrôlée)

Burgundy red and some white wines.
District: Côte de Nuits, France.
Commune: Chambolle.

The red wines are delicate, elegant, entrancingly perfumed, and have the fragile yet resolute charm of "feminine" wines. The whites—made in very small quantities—share this same charm but tend to lack some of the finesse of their great counterparts.

The wines have been famous for centuries and they succeeded for a long time in overshadowing those of neighboring Morey-Saint-Denis, with which in fact they have little in common. Morey's wines tend to be big, hard, assertive—the reverse in every way of the Chambolles. Yet much of the production of Morey once went to market under Chambolle place-names until the laws of Appellation d'Origine outlawed the practice and established Morey as a place-name in its own right. One outstanding vineyard—Bonnes Mares—is shared by the two communes; the wines are more like the Chambolles than the Moreys.

Bonnes Mares and Musigny (*qq.v.*), lying on opposite sides of the town, are Chambolle's greatest vineyards. Both are legally rated Great Growths (*Grands Crus*) and the wines are labeled only with the name of the vineyard, signifying outstanding excellence. Other superb wines are included among the First Growths (*Premiers Crus*)—wines that have stature and breeding but generally fall just below the topmost two, and this status is signified by labels bearing both communal and vineyard name. The best is Les Amoureuses, directly below the vineyard of Musigny and lying on the imaginary dividing line which separates Chambolle-Musigny and Vougeot. "Women in Love" is the meaning of the name, and Burgundians consider it highly appropriate. The wines are slightly less distinctive than those of Musigny, and in a good year are delicate and feminine, with a warming bouquet.

Nineteen other vineyards are considered in the same category as Les Amoureuses, and while their output seldom attains the same extraordinary quality, they too may often be perfectly made and beautiful wines. The wines which do not stem from one of these, or from other vineyards classified but not tested here (and do not otherwise meet the elevated minimum standards demanded for these ratings), are sold as Chambolle-Musigny and have many of the same characteristics.

Chambolle-Musigny has about 175 hectares (437 acres) of vines and annually produces some 6,500 hectoliters (172,250 U.S. gallons, 143,000 imp.) of red wine.

GREAT GROWTHS (*Grands Crus*)

Vineyard	Hectares	Acres
Les Musigny	10.7	26.5
Les Bonnes Mares (*in part*)	13.7	33.9

(*See* under individual headings.)

FIRST GROWTHS (*Premiers Crus*)

Vineyard	Hectares	Acres
Les Amoureuses	5.25	13
Les Charmes	5.8	14.4
Les Cras	4.5	10.4
Les Borniques	1.5	3.6
Les Baudes	3.5	8.8
Les Plantes	2.6	6.3
Les Hauts-Doix	1.75	4.3

FIRST GROWTHS (*Premiers Crus*) (continued)

Vineyard	Hectares	Acres
La Combe d'Orveau	5	12.5
Les Chatelots	2.6	6.3
Les Gruenchers	3	7.3
Les Groseilles	1.5	3.7
Les Fuées	6.2	15.3
Les Lavrottes	1	2.5
Derrière-la-Grange	0.73	1.8
Les Noirots	2.9	7.1
Les Sentiers	4.8	12.2
Les Fousselottes	4	10
Aux Beaux-Bruns	2.4	6
Les Combottes	0.65	1.6
Aux Combottes	2.27	5.6
Les Carrières	0.7	1.7
Les Chabriots	1.5	3.6
Combe d'Orveau (*in part*)	2.3	5.7
Aux Échanges	1.0	2.5
Les Grands Murs	0.9	2.3

Chambrer

French term for bringing a red wine slowly to the temperature of a room (*chambre*), the best temperature for most red wines. Warming the wine by plunging the bottle in hot water or putting it before a fire is not to be recommended: such sudden shocks are apt to change the chemical equilibrium of a wine, with the result that its excellence is impaired or destroyed. A wine that is too cold can be warmed by the heat of the hands on the glass, but one that has been heated too quickly is ruined.

Champagne (Appellation Contrôlée)

Principally white sparkling wine; some still white and a small quantity of red and rosé
District: Northeast France.

The deliciously sparkling wines of Champagne are the most famous in the world. There are indeed some people who feel that Champagne should be reserved for launching ships and debutantes, and others who would like to drink it with meals, before meals, after meals, in the middle of the morning, or in the middle of the night. But most everyone experiences a thrill of pleasure as the cork slowly pops out of the bottle, the whiff of smoke curls up into the air, and the pale-gold wine foams into the tall glasses. Champagne is unique—a fact which, outside France, is too often ignored.

The only wine with any right to the name Champagne is that made from certain legally specified grapes grown in limited and well-defined sections of the province of France called Champagne—vines tended and vinified according to a body of strict local rules. Soil, climate, vines, labor, and tradition all make Champagne what it is. Sparkling wines produced in other parts of the world may be good, but none will ever be Champagne—although some of them masquerade under the name. What is not universally known is that several wines of Champagne are not sparkling. Still wines are also made in the province and gaining in popularity. For the sale of the still Champagne, the name Coteaux Champenois is now required.

The region of Champagne begins some 55 kilometers (90 miles) to the east and slightly to the north of Paris. It is a vast chalky plain, carefully cultivated, broken only now and again by an occasional river and dominated by the Mountain of Reims. Between the city of Épernay, on the Marne, and Reims on the Vesle, a deformed hunch rises from the sturdy back of Champagne; an outcropping of chalk which, when viewed from above, resembles a huge question mark superimposed on the plain. This Mountain of Reims could only be a mountain in a flat country, since its average height is 200 meters (600 feet), with a maximum of about 300 meters (900 feet) in a few places. The stem of the question mark extends beyond Reims,

moving north to the section known as the Petite Montagne—the "Little Mountain"—and the arc curls round toward Épernay to the south, terminating in the section known as the Côte de Bouzy, after the principal town. At Épernay, the region of the Great Growths splits, one part following the Marne toward Château-Thierry, and the other heading due south to form the famous Côte des Blancs, where the Pinot Noir gives way to the white-grape Chardonnay vines. These sections are not all of Champagne, but they are the best. All are in the department of the Marne, but the limits of Champagne extend slightly beyond these borders. Four-fifths of Champagne comes from the Marne, the rest from the adjoining departments of Aube, Aisne, and Seine-et-Marne. Of the 195 million bottles shipped in an average year from Champagne, 73 million are exported out of France, with the U.S. and the U.K. each importing 15 million, Germany 8 million, Italy 6 million, and Belgium nearly 5 million bottles.

HISTORY

The vines in Champagne are among the oldest in Europe; there is adequate fossil evidence that vines were there during the Tertiary era, which geologists set at from 1 to 60 million years ago. The use of the vine for the making of wine may have been established before the Romans, although there are no records, but the Romans increased the planting of the vine throughout Champagne, as they did throughout France. The wines were originally still, however, and provided strong competition for Burgundy. A bitter rivalry broke out between these two districts, eventually coming to a head over the question of which was better for the health. The point was finally decided when the court physicians of Louis XIV cast their votes in favor of Burgundy.

Sparkling wines did not make any headway in Champagne until the seventeenth century, when, it is said, the discoveries of a Benedictine monk, Dom Pérignon, drastically changed the methods of wine-making. Sparkling wines had certainly been known over the centuries. All the growers of the world must have noticed that certain wines refermented in the spring and, if enclosed, became sparkling, usually breaking the container in which they were kept. Such wines were often referred to as *saute bouchon* (cork popper) or as *vin diable* (devil wine). Dom Pérignon (or some of his contemporaries) realized that the pressure built up was due to carbon dioxide and recommended that stronger bottles be used. Until this time, stoppers had not usually been made of cork but of cotton wadding soaked in oil. Now they began to make thicker ones and tied them down with a string. Dom Pérignon is also credited with being one of the pioneers in blending the wines of Champagne—most of which need the additional qualities only blending can give.

He was cellar-master at the Benedictine Abbey of Hautvillers for forty-seven years until his death in 1715, and his name is still honored in Champagne. Once each year there is a wine festival in Hautvillers celebrating the achievements attributed to him.

Alongside the work of Dom Pérignon, that of another seventeenth-century Champagne monk should be noted. Frère Jean Oudart ran the cellars at the Abbey of Pierry and did much to improve the techniques of bottling the sparkling wine. Frère Jean was among the first to use stoppers made of Spanish cork rather than the old ones of wood and oakum. It is conceivable that the two monks knew each other and compared their wine experiments.

CLASSIFICATION AND RATING

The small towns of Champagne and the vineyards lying within them are classified according to a complicated percentage scale, and the rating given the town will determine the price for the grapes in any given year. Each autumn the growers meet with the shippers who will be buying their harvests and haggle over the prices to be paid. Seldom do the growers in Champagne vinify their own grapes, and price must be decided in advance: once the harvest is started, there can be no delay if the grapes are not to suffer. The price decided on is for the very best growths, officially rated at 100%; that for the produce of other places will be proportionate to the town's percentage rating. In lesser districts, premiums may also be paid for certain types of grapes, encouraging the growers to plant the vines which give better fruit but less of it. Since 1966, the base price of grapes per kilogram has been augmented by various premiums paid to the growers. In 1986 the base price was 19.80 francs, plus 0.80 franc for white Chardonnay grapes, plus 1.20 franc for grapes from a 100%-rated commune. On top of this total an 8% premium is paid to those growers willing to sign a supply contract for several years, making an approximate total of 21 francs (more than $3) per kilo (about 2¼ pounds) for Chardonnay grapes from the best vineyards. The premium paid for the Chardonnay reflects the demand for lighter Champagne.

The Mountain of Reims boasts five growths rated at 100%: Beaumont-sur-Vesle, Mailly, Sillery (at one time the most renowned wine-name in England), Puisieulx, and Verzenay. Moving south toward the Marne Valley, off the Mountain and into the Côte de Bouzy, the best growths are Ambonnay, Ay-Champagne, Bouzy, Louvois, and Tours-sur-Marne, and, on the Côte des Blancs, Avize and Cramant. In towns where there are both red and white grapes grown, the percentage will be different for each, and except in the Côte des Blancs, the higher rating nearly always goes to the red, plants giving white grapes being more or less curiosities in other sections.

GROWTHS (*Crus*)

ARRONDISSEMENT DE REIMS

Canton d'Ay	%
Ambonnay	100
Avenay	93
Ay-Champagne	100
Bisseuil	95
Bouzy	100
Champillon	93
Cormoyeux	85
Cumières	93
Dizy	95
Hautvillers	90
Louvois	100
Mareuil-sur-Ay	99
Mutigny	93
Romery	85
Tauxières	99
Tours-sur-Marne red	100
Tours-sur-Marne white	90
Canton de Beine	
Berru	84
Cernay-les-Reims	85
Nogent-l'Abbesse	87
Canton de Bourgogne	
Brimont	83
Cauroy-les-Hermonville	83
Cormicy	83
Merfy	84
Pouillon	84
Saint-Thierry—basses vignes	87
Thil	84
Villers-Franqueux	84
Canton de Reims	
Ormes	85
Reims (lot Brisset)	88
Taissy	94
Trois-Puits	94
Canton de Verzy	
Beaumont-sur-Vesle	100
Chamery	90
Chigny-les-Roses	94
Ludes	94
Mailly-Champagne	100
Montbré	94
Puisieulx	100
Rilly-la-Montagne	94
Sermiers	89
Sillery	100
Trépail	95
Verzenay	100
Verzy	100
Villers-Allerand	90
Villers-Marmery	95

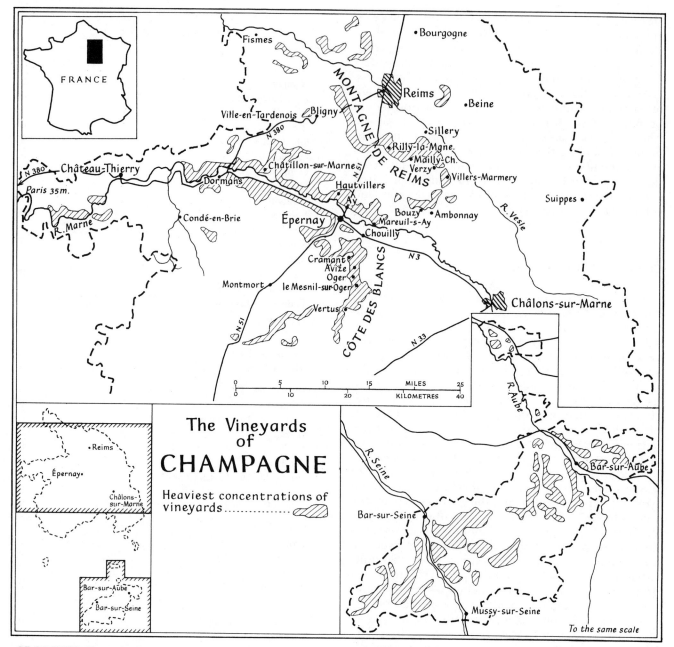

The Vineyards of **CHAMPAGNE**

Heaviest concentrations of vineyards ....

To the same scale

GROWTHS *(Crus) (continued)*

Canton de Châtillon-sur-Marne	%
Baslieux	84
Belval-sous-Châtillon	84
Binson-Orquigny	86
Champlat-Boujacourt	83
Châtillon-sur-Marne	86
Courtagnon	82
Cuchery	84
Cuisles	86
Jonquery	84
Montigny-sous-Châtillon	86
La Neuville-aux-Larris	84
Olizy-Violaine	84
Passy-Grigny	84
Pourcy	84

	%
Reuil	86
Sainte-Gemme	84
Vandières	86
Villers-sous-Châtillon	86
Canton de Fismes	
Châlons-sur-Vesle	84
Chenay	84
Crugny	86
Hermonville	84
Hourges	86
Pévy	84
Prouilly	84
Trigny	84
Unchair	86
Vandeuil	86

Canton de Ville-en-Tardenois

Bligny		83
Bouilly		86
Bouleuse		82
Branscourt		86
Brouillet		86
Chambrecy		83
Chaumuzy		83
Coulommes-la-Montagne		89
Courcelles-Sapicourt		83
Courmas		87
Écueil		90
Faverolles		86
Germigny		85
Gueux		85
Janvry		85
Jouy-les-Reims		90
Lagery		86
Les Mesneux		90
Marfaux		84
Paigny-les-Reims		90
Poilly		83
Rosnay		83
Sacy		90
Sainte-Euphraise		86
Sarcy		83
Savigny-sur-Ardre		86
Serzy-et-Prin		86
Tramery		86
Treslon		86
Villedommange		90
Ville-en-Tardenois		82
Vrigny		89

ARRONDISSEMENT D'ÉPERNAY

Canton d'Avize

Avize		100
Brugny-Vaudancourt		86
Chavot-Courcourt	red	88
	white	88
Cramant		100
Cuis	red	90
	white	95
Grauves	red	90
	white	95
Le Mesnil-sur-Oger		100
Mancy	red	88
	white	88
Monthelon		88
Morangis		84
Moslins		84
Oger		100
Oiry		100

Canton de Dormans

Boursault		84
Champvoisy		84
Comblizy		83
Courthiézy		83
Dormans (Try, Vassy, Vassieux, Chavenay)		83

Festigny		84
Le Breuil		83
Le Mesnil-le-Hutier		84
Leuvrigny		84
Mareuil-le-Port		84
Nesle-le-Repons		84
Oeuilly		84
Port à Binson		84
Soilly		83
Troissy		84
Verneuil		86
Vincelles		86

Canton d'Épernay

Chouilly	red	95
	white	100
Damery		89
Épernay		88
Fleury-la-Rivière		85
Mardeuil		84
Moussy		88
Pierry		90
Saint-Martin-d'Ablois		84
Vauciennes		89
Venteuil		87
Vinay		86

Canton d'Esternay

Bethon	red	85
	white	87
Chantemerle	red	85
	white	87

Canton de Montmort

Baye		85
Beaunay		85
Broyes		85
Coizard-Joches		85
Congy		85
Courjeonnet		85
Étoges		85
Fèrebrianges		85
Oyes		85
Talus-Saint-Prix		85
Villevenard		85

Canton de Sézanne

Barbonne Fayel	red	85
	white	87
Fontaine Denis Nuisy	red	85
	white	87
Saudoy	red	85
	white	87
Sézanne	red	85
	white	87
Vindey	red	85
	white	87

ARRONDISSEMENT DE CHÂLONS

Canton de Vertus

Bergères-les-Vertus	red	90
	white	95

ARRONDISSEMENT DE CHÂLONS (continued)		%
Coligny		87
Etrechy	red	87
	white	90
Givry-les-Loisy		85
Loisy-en-Brie		85
Soulières		85
Vert-Toulon		85
"		85
Vertus		95
Villeneuve-Renneville		95
Canton de Suippes		
Billy-le-Grand		95
Marne (crus non côtés)		80
Vaudemanges		95

ARRONDISSEMENT DE SOISSONS

Canton de Braine	
Cerseuil	84

ARRONDISSEMENT DE CHÂTEAU THIERRY

Canton de Condé-en-Brie	
Barzy-sur-Marne	85
"	85
Passy-sur-Marne	85
Trelou-sur-Marne	85
Aisne (less the communes of the Canton de Condé-en-Brie listed above)	80
Canton de l'Aube	
Villenauxe-La-Grande	
black grapes	85
mainly Pinot Noir and Pinot Meunier	
white grape	87
only Chardonnay	
Other Growths of Aube	80

Most of the sparkling wines of Champagne are made from a blend of red and white grapes. Some are Blancs de Noirs, or white wines made from black grapes; and a few are Blancs de Blancs, or white wines made from white grapes—the latter are almost entirely confined to the Côte des Blancs south of Épernay. (Most Champagnes do not carry any designations, although it is fairly common practice to use them on labels for still Vin Nature de la Champagne.) Some Champagne makers say that white grapes tend to improve the final blend. The present vogue is toward the Blancs de Blancs. Thus, whether for blending with red grapes or not, the increased demand for Chardonnay has made them more expensive than the Pinot Noirs. A certain small amount of pink, or rosé, Champagne is also made, as well as various still wines known correctly as Coteaux Champenois, or commonly as Champagne Nature, Bouzy Rouge, and Rosé de Riceys. But the name Champagne, with no other qualification, always refers to the sparkling variety.

The total area of Champagne planted in fine vines amounts to about 24,000 hectares (60,000 acres). Of this, 20,000 hectares (49,400 acres) are in the Marne, with the remaining vineyards divided among the Aube, Aisne, and Seine-et-Marne. Rather less than a century ago, the area planted came to about 15,000 hectares (40,000 acres), but the rapacity of the vine louse phylloxera, which arrived in Champagne about 1890, and the ravages of the First World War (throughout the war, from 1914 until 1918, the countryside was cut up with trenches) combined to decrease the vineyard area. However, each year over 1 million hectoliters (20 million U.S. gallons, 16 million imp.) of wine are taken to the cellars to be made sparkling. The amount of still wine varies considerably. No matter how abundant the crop, the grapes for sparkling wine cannot be harvested in excess of 7,500 kilograms per hectare (about 3 tons per acre), and everything else must be vinified into Coteaux Champenois. In some years there may be as little as 20 hectoliters (528 U.S. gallons, 438 imp.) and in others as much as 700 hectoliters (18,840 U.S. gallons, 15,330 imp.). The still Bouzy Rouge (red Bouzy) hardly ever exceeds 1,000 hectoliters (24,000 U.S. gallons, 20,000 imp.); and Rosé de Riceys is made virtually every year but in negligible amounts.

Almost all Champagne is made sparkling in the cellars of the big shipping firms, most of which are in Reims and Épernay. Deep below the cities the chalk subsoil has been cut out into vast caves and cellars. One firm has 11 miles of underground cellars so deep that the visitor must descend 116 steps to reach them. Most of these cellars are laid out in broad alleyways, named after the principal cities of the world where Champagne is sold. Statues carved into the chalk walls give them a certain resemblance to art galleries. These cellars were used during the war as underground shelters, but they provide a better home for wine than for refugees. Holding their temperature of about 50° F. (10°C.) the year round, they are fresh and clean and require no attention to keep them fit for the storage of wine.

Épernay and Reims, in whose splendid cathedral the kings of France were once crowned, are the two main headquarters for the shipping firms, many of which maintain offices in both. Some of the more important firms with their main headquarters in Reims are: Veuve Clicquot-Ponsardin, Heidsieck Monopole, Charles Heidsieck, Mumm, Piper-Heidsieck, Pommery and Greno, Louis Roederer, Ruinart, and Taittinger. Those with their main offices in Épernay include Mercier, Moët et Chandon, Perrier-Jouët, Castellane, and Pol Roger. In addition to these, there are a few firms in the small city of Ay overlooking the Marne, among them Ayala, Besserat de Bellefon, and Bollinger.

CLIMATE, SOIL, AND VINES

The vineyards of Champagne are the farthest north of any producing French wines of Appellation Contrôlée. When a vineyard is so critically close to the northern limit, every care must be taken to protect the vine from the unfavorable climatic conditions—not only because of the natural hazards which afflict it, but also because the vitality of a plant is lowered while struggling for existence, and such a plant is less fitted than one grown in more favorable climates to combat the dangers of frost and disease. Yet it is this northerly climate which is responsible for the exquisite delicacy of Champagnes. The situation and exposure of the vineyards is important, and most of the vines look to the south and southeast. The exceptions are those of the Côte des Blancs, which look east, and of the town of Verzenay (rated 100%), which actually faces the north. Southern exposure means that the hills will provide a shield against harsh winter winds and the vines will get the full benefit of the summer sun. The frosts and cold waves of the winter have a tendency to settle in the valleys and depressions and therefore the vines are mostly planted along the midsection of the hills, where they are relatively unaffected, although disastrous frosts have been known. Humidity is not excessive—an important factor, since most fungus diseases which attack vines thrive on moisture. The important Chardonnay vine is also subject to the *pourriture grise*, a type of rot which is at its worst in humid climates.

Climate is only one factor which contributes to making Champagne what it is. Another is the exceptional soil from which the vines draw their nourishment and whose qualities are reflected in the grapes and in the wines. Chalk is the major element, but there are others. Silicon and clay give the soil a workable consistency, and various trace elements add to the mixture. Most of the chalk in Champagne is Kimmeridge clay and is the same formation found in the soil of Chablis (*q.v.*) and in the village of Kimmeridge in southern England, where it was first studied and identified. The coarse-grained composition of this soil throws off excess moisture but holds at the same time enough to nourish the vine. The white pebbles absorb the heat of the sunshine, reflecting and radiating it evenly onto the ripening fruit and holding it well after the sun has disappeared below the horizon. Without this extra source of heat, the grapes, in some years, would never ripen at all.

The vines which may be planted in Champagne are closely controlled; predominating is the Pinot Noir, a vine which gives red grapes for making wines of the purest gold. Pinot Noir is by far the major vine, but also important are Pinot Meunier and Chardonnay (sometimes called Pinot Chardonnay, although modern research has established that it is not a member of the Pinot family); and a very little of Meslier and Arbanne is also planted. In the department of Aube

there were still some plantations of Gamay after the war, and the result was not particularly happy. Originally, all the Gamay vines were to have been rooted out by 1942, but because of the war the date was postponed until 1962. The firms which buy the grapes generally pay a slight premium over the fixed price to any grower who brings in grapes from the permissible vines but not for Gamay, which lately has gone only into the cheapest Champagnes.

The vines are generally planted in rows some three feet apart, the plants about 30 inches from each other and trained along wires which run the length of the rows. There are generally two or three rows of wires along which the vine tendrils grow, bending their bunches of fruit toward the ground. Pruning is controlled by law, and the only permissible methods are Chablis, Royat Cordon, guyot, and gobelet—all measures to ensure that the vines will give a moderate production of high-quality grapes year after year.

The grapes are usually small and quite acid. The comparatively cold climate of Champagne matures them slowly and in some years incompletely. Acidity drops as the summer wears on and the sugar content rises, but never gets so high as it does in warmer regions. Yet in some years these acid-high grapes are capable of producing 12% of alcohol; in exceptionally hot years the wine-maker may even be forced to add acid; and in most years the grapes are vinified into a delicate sparkling wine with the subtlest combinations of color, aroma, and taste.

Champagnes, like all great wines, are dependent on the weather, and like all great wines they will, in some years, be superb. Some of the better years for Champagne have been: *1928*, 1929, 1934, 1937, 1945, *1947*, 1949, *1952*, *1953*, 1955, *1959*, 1961, 1962, *1964*, *1966*, 1967, 1969, *1970*, *1971*, 1973, 1975, *1976*, *1978*, 1979, 1981, 1982 and 1985 (greatest years indicated in italics).

WINE-MAKING IN CHAMPAGNE

As is the case with any wine, the making of Champagne begins in the vineyards at the harvest. In ancient times the date of the harvest was set by law, and anyone who started too early was brought before the regional officials for punishment. The Ban de Vendange, the official proclamation, still exists, although now as a formality rather than a legal requirement. The deciding factor today is the grape, which must be ripe but not overripe. Harvests are fairly late in the autumn, usually beginning during the second and third weeks in October; the minimum amount of sugar in the grapes and the minimum alcoholic content to be formed by this sugar in fermentation are decided each year by the Comité Interprofessionel du Vin de Champagne (Interprofessional Committee for the Wine of Champagne)—the semi-official body in Épernay which governs all Champagne activity, including promotion.

When the harvest starts, the women and children go out into the vineyards, their heads protected by characteristic faded blue sunbonnets, and cut the heavy ripe bunches of grapes. The younger men patrol the rows with baskets and carry the grapes to the ends of the rows, where they are inspected. The overripe or defective ones are discarded and the others placed in *caques or mannequins*—deep wide baskets holding about 60 to 80 kilograms (150 to 175 pounds) of grapes. The baskets are loaded onto trucks and are rushed to the *vendangeoir*, or press-house.

Only in a few isolated cases does the grower in Champagne vinify his own grapes—they are nearly always sold to one of the shipping firms, sometimes before the harvest has started, and the firm makes the wine and carries it through the extensive series of operations which will result in Champagne. Most of these shipping firms have their own holdings in the vineyards to ensure at least a part of each year's harvest, and an estimated 3,000 to 3,400 of the 22,000 hectares (7,500 to 8,500 of the 55,000 acres) are owned by them. They maintain *vendangeoirs* in all the important towns, and the grapes are pressed on the spot. Here and there, however, cooperative cellars can be found where the growers themselves make the wine. Such is the case in the 100%-rated town of Mailly. During the Depression, the big wine firms refused to buy grapes from the growers, who banded together and built a cooperative in their spare time, starting with no capital and doing all the work themselves after they had finished in the fields. Today, the cooperative has some seventy members; it makes both pink and white vintage Champagnes and ships them all over the world.

Throughout the harvest, the roads are packed with the laden carts on their way to the press-houses, and pressing starts as soon as they arrive. Most of the grapes in Champagne are red, and if the juice is left in contact with the color-imparting skins, an undesirable tinge may discolor the wines. This tinge can be removed by passing the juice through charcoal, but the wine-makers prefer to press their grapes immediately, before the color has had time to form. Pink (or rosé) Champagne is sometimes made by adding some red wine to the white, a practice held in the lowest esteem except in Champagne alone, where the results seem to justify the practice. However, the usual way is by short-vatting red grapes, ensuring only a small amount of coloration. Either way, at least some Champagne makers consider the pink variety something of an oddity and not in the same class as the rest.

The oak presses are round and wide and built close to the ground with a trough around them to collect the juice as it runs out. The size and shape of the presses are such that they take exactly four tons of grapes, evenly distributed in a thin layer. The first pressings, called first, second, and third *serre*, give the high-quality wine, and the last (*rebêche*) produces common wine

to be given to the workers. The first *serre* gives the top-quality wine, the *vin de cuvée*, amounting to 2,000 liters (528 U.S. gallons, 440 imp.) or the equivalent of ten *pièces*, or barrels. The second gives from one and a half to two barrels of wine, called *première taille*, and the third, another one and a half of *deuxième taille*, both of which go into the secondary wine of the makers. Between each *serre* the mass of grapes is spaded over with wooden spades (in none of the fine-wine districts does metal ever touch the grapes) to ensure that the pressure, which is greatest in the middle of the press, is equally applied to all the grapes. Before the marc, or pomace, is pressed for the *rebêche*, it is moistened slightly and again spaded over.

The wine which flows from the presses usually goes into huge vats and then into barrels, to be sent to the cellars of the firms in Ay, Épernay, and Reims. The pressing takes place in the vineyards, but everything else is done by the firms, and the newly extracted juice is usually given a light dose of sulfur to stop fermentation before the wine-maker is prepared for it. Once in the cellars, it is tested to determine its consistency. In Champagne, in many years, sugar must be added, a practice known as *chaptalisation*, which is widespread in Burgundy and is even found in a very few vintage years as far south as Bordeaux. The aim in Champagne is to make a wine which will have from 10% to 12% of alcohol and a moderate acidity. Depending on the year, the wine-maker may add sugar, or he may de-acidify his must, or unfermented grape juice. Sometimes citric or tartaric acid has to be added. Apart from sugar, which is added fairly frequently, these measures are exceptional and undesirable except in difficult years.

After the additions are made, the wine begins to ferment. For eight to ten days, it boils ferociously in the barrels, sounding like a hive of angry bees. After this preliminary action, it calms down considerably and for another ten to twenty days bubbles serenely and quietly. During this fermentation, the sugar is converted by the action of yeasts into alcohol and carbon dioxide gas, and the gas is allowed to pass off into the air through the bung-hole of the barrel. When the fermentation is finished, the wine is allowed to rest and clarify.

By the December after the harvest, the wine will have settled and all the grape particles left from the pressing as well as the spent yeasts will have fallen to the bottom of the barrel. The wine is ready for its first racking, in which it is carefully drawn off from the barrels, and the lees (or impurities) are left behind. After the first racking, the *assemblage* of wines from different vineyards, which have fermented separately in the same cellar, takes place. This is the blending of wines from a single town, and when it has been completed, all those from Ay or from Sillery or Verzenay will be uniform and consistent throughout. After a second racking at the end of January and a third just before the wine is bottled, the wines are ready for the second fermentation, which will make them full-blown

Champagnes. Those which are to remain non-sparkling undergo the racking, but their development stops there and they are sold as Vin Nature de la Champagne.

THE CHAMPAGNE PROCESS

The Champagne process is the name for the traditional method of making a wine sparkle by allowing it to ferment a second time in the bottle. The preparations for it usually start after the second (January) racking, when the *assemblage*, or blending, is done. Some firms specialize in *vins de cru*, or wines which come from one town only, but most Champagnes are blends. The wines from a single town are almost certain to be from one of the Côte des Blancs, usually Cramant or Avize. Most of the rest are blended, and the top quality wine of any firm is referred to as the *vine de cuvée*. Sometimes only wines from 100%-rated towns are used and may be sold as Champagne Grand Cru.

The delicate blending process starts with samples taken from the various wine barrels in the firm's cellars. These samples are taken up to special tasting rooms—spotlessly clean, airy, and hygienic, free from any extraneous odors or anything which might divert the taster's attention from the wine. These measures are of great importance, since the man is working with raw wines and must be able to detect any flaws or possible impurities before they develop. The desired result is a Champagne which will resemble the product the firm has put out in the past. When the proportions have been decided, the chosen wines are blended together and the lesser ones kept aside to be bottled under another label as the second quality of the firm.

After the wine has been made and racked and blended, it is ready to be bottled and to undergo the secondary fermentation which will impart the sparkle. Bottling usually starts about April and lasts until July. The first step is the addition of the *liqueur de tirage*, usually a solution of cane sugar dissolved in wine, very occasionally with a little citric acid added. (The acid speeds up the splitting of cane sugar into the fermentable grape sugars.) The amount of sugar added is usually calculated at 20 to 26 grams per liter of wine to be treated (equivalent to about 1.5 pounds for each 10 gallons). Sometimes less liqueur is added, and the result is a Champagne which is *crémant*, or only lightly sparkling. The word *crémant* (literally, "creaming") should not be confused with the town of Cramant, one of the leading or 100%-rated towns of the Côte des Blancs.

The sugar added as *liqueur de tirage* ferments to make the wines sparkling. It ferments under the action of yeasts which may already be present in the wine or which may be added from special strains. The fermentation is the exact replica of the first, forming alcohol (the alcoholic content of the wine will be raised by about 1%) and carbon dioxide gas. This time, however, the wine is not lying free in an open barrel, but is confined in a stout bottle and capped with an extra-heavy cork wired in place.

In the spring, as the sap begins to rise in the vines, the wine mysteriously starts its second fermentation, as though there were some mystic bond between the two. The cellars are cool and prevent temperature from speeding the action of the yeasts, since experience has shown that a better wine will result if the fermentation is allowed to proceed slowly. The bottled wine is laid in great stacks in the cellars, and every six months or so the stacks are moved and the bottles are given a hearty shake to free any sediment which may have formed. Marks painted on the bottoms of the bottles indicate which way they were lying, and they are always put back in the same position. As they are restacked, those which were in the middle of the pile are placed on the outside and vice versa, since the warmth generated in the middle will be greater than at the sides.

As fermentation continues, the carbon dioxide generated builds up pressure. Eventually, this pressure will amount to some five to six times that of the atmosphere, and it is for this reason that the bottles and corks are of such heavy construction. Occasionally during this process a bottle will break, because the mounting pressure exceeds it in strength, and each time the bottles are moved from place to place these broken ones must be abstracted. The fermentation itself will only take about three months, but the wines are left in these cellars for a period of years to "ripen," during which time the bottles are shaken occasionally to keep the sediment from forming permanently. At the end of this ripening period, the wines are ready for the *remuage* and *dégorgement*, the long series of operations to remove the sediment from the bottle.

Remuage means "shaking," and bottles of Champagne must be shaken in a particular manner. The first step is the gradual *mise sur pointe*, turning them upside down. This is done in special racks or *pupitres*—hinged, sloping boards, much like artists' easels. Holes are cut on both sides of the *pupitre* in such a way that they will hold a bottle firmly when it is inserted neck first in any position between the horizontal and the vertical. The bottles are put in at a very slight angle—usually about thirty degrees—and over a period of time are slowly changed until they are literally upside down. Each day a trained man, a *remueur*, goes through and carefully shakes each bottle, putting it back at a slightly more elevated angle, and turning it about a quarter turn each time. This slightly shakes the sediment, and slowly, as the bottle is raised, it slides down to the neck, where it rests against the cork. The *remueur* is a highly expert man, one who works at top speed, using both hands; and he is capable of turning 32,000 bottles a day. To ensure that the bottles are absolutely sound, he is given a bonus for any defective ones he finds. When he has finished, the bottles are standing on their heads in the racks, the sediment is next to the cork, and the wine is ready for the next step—the *dégorgement* which will shoot out the sediment. Today, machines have replaced the shaking by hand.

Dégorgement is another ticklish procedure, particularly if it is done in the old traditional manner. The bottles are taken, the cork slowly pried off, and the sediment is allowed to shoot out, propelled by the pressure in the bottle. The trick is to lose as little wine as possible but not leave any sediment. The high degree of skill and practice necessary for this job has been modified by the more modern method of freezing the necks of the bottles. The sediment and a small amount of the wine become frozen, and again the pressure that has been built up shoots it out in a solid lump. The wine is then brought back to its original level with a little of the same wine from another bottle and is ready for *dosage* and the final cork.

The *dosage* of a Champagne depends on the potential clientele. Sophisticated customers usually prefer their Champagne *brut*—that is, as dry as possible, except when it is to be served with sweets or fruit, when a Champagne of one of the varying degrees of sweetness should be chosen. The wine is sweetened by the addition of sugar dissolved in some *vin de reserve*. Generally only the best-quality wines are used for *brut* Champagne, since any defects, which in the others will be masked by the added sugar, will here be apparent.

The sweetening is referred to as *liqueur d'expédition* and consists of a small amount of sugar mixed up with a little of the same Champagne to be dosed and a little brandy. The amounts generally added are:

French Names	Percentage	English Name
Brut	0 to 2	Brut
Extra-Sec	2 to 3	Extra Dry
Sec	3 to 6	Dry
Demi-Sec	6 to 8	Semi-dry
Doux	8 to 10	Sweet

After the *liqueur d'expédition*, the bottles are ready for their final corking. Although the cork changes, the wine remains in the same bottle throughout its development, except when it is to be transferred into larger bottles. Champagne is always re-fermented in the regular Champagne bottle of 26 ounces, in magnums of 52 ounces, or in half-bottles of 13 ounces. As 2% to 3% of the bottles break each year, it is too risky to use the larger sizes, into which the wine is poured only at the time of *dégorgement*. The corks, however, change. The best come from Spain or Portugal, from special cork trees from twelve to fifteen years old. However, many firms are now using plastic corks until the final bottling, and some Champagnes are retailed with plastic stoppers.

All corks used finally, according to French law, must have the word *Champagne* printed on them. If the word does not appear, the wine is not Champagne. These corks are soaked in water to soften them and are driven into bottles which are then returned to the

cellars for another period of checking and ageing. Watched fairly closely, to ensure that the *liqueur d'expédition* has mixed well into the wine, and to see that no unwanted third fermentation will start, they remain there sometimes for as much as two years. In total, the finer Champagnes may be six to seven years developing before they are ready for the consumer, and a bottle may be handled from 150 to 200 times before it leaves the cellar.

Name		Metric		fl. oz.
Split *(quart)*		20 centiliters		6
Pint *(demi-bouteille)*		37.5	"	12.7
Quart *(bouteille)*		75	"	25.4
Magnum *(2 bouteilles)*		1.5 liters		50.7
Jeroboam *(double magnum)*		3	"	101.4
* Rehoboam *(6 bouteilles)*		4.5	"	152.1
* Methuselah *(8 bouteilles)*		6	"	202.8
(Methusalem)				
Salmanasar *(12 bouteilles)*		9	"	304.2
* Balthazar *(16 bouteilles)*		12	"	405.6
*Nebuchadnezzar *(20 bouteilles)*		15	"	507.1

*These bottles are no longer being used.

SERVING CHAMPAGNE

It is usually considered that Champagne is at its best served chilled—not iced. The makers generally take a slightly more tolerant view about opening the bottle than do some drinkers, suggesting that the cork should come out in your hand rather than being encouraged to careen across the room to the accompaniment of popping noises and spilled Champagne. Letting the cork come out too fast, they say, allows too much pressure to escape, and with it some of the bubbles which have been so carefully developed over the years. Swirling Champagne with swizzle-sticks has the same effect. That and dropping ice cubes into the wine are looked upon with horror by connoisseurs.

Some Champagne growers also suggest that tall flute-shaped glasses be used rather then the wide shallow ones; an eight-ounce tulip-shaped glass is even better. The bubbles disappear too quickly in the open-bowled glasses; and it is the bubbles which make Champagne. As the columnist Art Buchwald put it: "I like Champagne, because it always tastes as though my foot's asleep."

Chantepleure

In Vouvray, a *pipette* or tube for removing wine from a cask or other bulk container.

Chapeau

A "hat" or thick layer of solids, consisting of pulp and skins, which forms on top of the must in the vats during fermentation.
See Chapter Nine, p. 43.

Chapelle-Chambertin (Appellation Contrôlée)

Burgundy red wine.
District: Côte de Nuits, France.
Commune: Gevrey-Chambertin.
Official Classification: Great Growth (Grand Cru).

Chapelle is one of the more delicate of the wines of this northerly commune of the Côte de Nuits. Generally, the wines of Gevrey are full-bodied and robust, assertive and strictly masculine; and while those from Chapelle share these qualities, they have a lightness, a fruitiness sometimes, and a certain finesse which tends to set them apart.

All of the nine vineyards which make up the family of Chambertin are clustered around the nucleus of Le Chambertin and Chambertin-Clos de Bèze and either adjoin or are visible from the little road which runs through the vineyard joining Gevrey and Morey-Saint-Denis. Leaving Gevrey by this road, Chapelle is the first of the important vineyards on the left, though there is little chance that the newcomer will notice it unless a local inhabitant points it out. Throughout these renowned wine communes there is little to distinguish one great vineyard from another, the significant differences becoming apparent only in the wines themselves.

The vineyard of Chapelle has been rated as Great Growth (*Grand Cru*) and covers some 5.37 hectares (13.3 acres). The amount of wine made by the several growers who own sections of it comes to 150 hectoliters (3,975 U.S. gallons, 3,300 imp.) in an average year for quantity. This is the equivalent of about 1,800 cases.

Chaptalisation

The addition of sugar to the fermenting wine must, in order to build up the alcoholic content.
See Chapter Nine, p. 47.

Charbono

A wine grape which probably came from Italy but which is now cultivated extensively in California, especially in the Napa Valley, where it produces a full-bodied, pleasant, but somewhat rough red wine.

Chardonnay

Excellent white grape grown, notably, in Burgundy. It resembles the Pinot Noir but is not a true Pinot, although it was once thought to have been a white variant of that grape and therefore was often called Pinot Chardonnay. Other local names include Arnoison, Aubaine, Beaunois, Melon Blanc. It yields rich well-balanced wine with a distinctive aroma and a superb, lingering aftertaste. It has been particularly successful in California.

Charente wines

Principally, the light, thin, tart white wines which are distilled into Cognac brandy, although this district also produces some red wine (from which Cognac is never made) and some white wine which is not made into Cognac.
See Cognac.

Charlemagne (Appellation Contrôlée)

Burgundy white wine.
District: Côte de Beaune.
Commune: Aloxe-Corton.
Official Classification: Great Growth (Grand Cru).

The vineyard area is about 35 hectares (88 acres), and the white wines are excellent; but the name Charlemagne is rarely used alone, since growers are entitled to the preferred Corton-Charlemagne. The Emperor Charlemagne once owned the vineyards that bear his name and which he afterward gave to the Church, in the person of the Abbot of Saulieu. In the sixteenth century the lands were leased to an innkeeper of Beaune, appropriately named Charles; by the seventeenth century the holdings had been carved up, and some of them became the property of the Hospices de Beaune (*q.v.*).

Charmat

In 1910 the French wine-scientist Eugene Charmat developed a process for making sparkling wines in bulk which is still, with modifications, used today.

The original Charmat process required four tanks—three for wine and the other for yeasts. Still wine is run into the first tank and artificially aged by being heated for twelve to sixteen hours, then cooled. Pumped into the next tank, it has yeast and sugar added and ferments for ten to fifteen days; then it is pumped into the third tank, where it is clarified by refrigeration; and finally it is filtered and sent to the bottling machine. The entire process is interconnected, and the wine never loses the pressure built up during fermentation.

Although no replacement for the Champagne process of second fermentation in the bottle, the Charmat system allows the wine-maker to produce a continuous flow of cheap sparkling wine of sound but uninspiring quality.

Charmes-Chambertin (Appellation Contrôlée)

Burgundy red wine.
District: Côte de Nuits, France.
Commune: Gevrey-Chambertin.
Official Classification. Great Growth (Grand Cru).

Charmes-Chambertin and Mozoyères-Chambertin form a partnership with Mazoyères—the silent senior partner. The ruling is that wine from either Charmes or Mazoyères may be sold as Charmes but that

Charmes may not be sold as Mazoyères. In practice it is all Charmes.

The two vineyards form an unbroken expanse to the left of the vineyard road as you move south toward Morey-Saint-Denis, with the smaller Charmes coming up first, directly opposite Le Chambertin, and Mazoyères following, opposite Latricières-Chambertin. Together they compose some 31.61 hectares (79.02 acres). The wines are considered by local growers to be almost identical; Charmes has slightly more body and Mazoyères more finesse. Mazoyères, they say, would be the superior growth except that it is sold as Charmes, with the result that there is no way of telling between them.

Whichever vineyard it comes from, wine sold as Charmes is remarkably light and delicate for this commune where the emphasis generally is on austere masculinity. Classified in 1937 as a Great Growth (*Grand Cru*), the highest rating given to Burgundian wines by the Institut National des Appellations d'Origine des Vins et Eaux-de-Vie (National Institute of Place-Names of Wines and Spirits), the wines must live up to the rigid standards demanded by both law and tradition (for standards, *see* Côte de Nuits). The vineyard is reasonably divided up among several growers. The average amount of wine grown in the two vineyards comes to about 1,000 hectoliters (26,400 U.S. gallons, 22,000 imp.), a fairly representative figure, which is roughly the equivalent of 11,500 cases.

Charnu

French term for full in body; literally, "fleshy."

Chartreuse

The famous liqueur made in Tarragona, Spain, and Voiron, France, by monks of the Carthusian (Charterhouse) order. The Spanish distillery was established in 1903 when the order was expelled from France for the second time (the first was from the Revolution until 1815), and they have continued to operate it since their return in 1932. In the early part of the present century there was considerable confusion because the goods of the order were seized and sold at the time of their expulsion; the trademark went, but not the formula. The "Chartreuse" thus sold in France was no more than a pallid imitation of the real liqueur, and the monks were forbidden to use the name and resorted to the inscription *Liqueur fabriquée à Tarragone par les Pères Chartreux*. This has, of course, been changed since the return, and the name now belongs exclusively to the rightful owners.

Chartreuse is made on a base of brandy, with extracts of a considerable number of herbs and plants to provide the flavoring. The still-secret formula is said to have been given to the order in 1605 and perfected some time thereafter by Father Jérôme Maubec; but it was not sent outside the monastic walls until 1848, when a group of French army officers tasted it and

were so impressed that they undertook to make it known everywhere. The original liqueur was the Elixir, white and stronger than it is now, but its manufacture has been discontinued. Chartreuse is either green or yellow, the green the stronger and the yellow less alcoholic and sweeter.

Chassagne-Montrachet and Chassagne-Montrachet-Côte de Beaune (A.O.C.)

Burgundy red and white wines.
District: Côte de Beaune, France.
Commune: Chassagne-Montrachet

At the southern end of the Côte de Beaune is the Côte des Blancs, where the finest white wines of the Côte d'Or are produced. The greatest by far is wine from the vineyard of Montrachet—shared in almost equal parts by Chassagne-Montrachet and Puligny-Montrachet—but those just a shade below it are still magnificent. Chassagne also makes some very good red wines which, because they are little known and are slightly eclipsed by the celebrated whites, are often comparatively inexpensive and sometimes exceptional value. This has not always been the case.

During the eighteenth century Chassagne was famous for red wines. It is reported that red wine from the vineyard of Morgeot was so highly thought of that the rate of exchange was two bottles of Montrachet for one of Morgeot. The tables are so far turned today that Morgeot no longer makes red but, although they do not merit the ancient exchange rate, its whites are among the finest in the commune.

Chassagne, whose wines are often exceptional, is the last of the important communes of the Côte de Beaune. To the south is Santenay, where the wines are often good, seldom extraordinary; and after Santenay the slope tails off eventually to merge with the Côte Chalonnaise.

The leading vineyard is, of course, the incomparable Montrachet, but Bâtard-Montrachet and Criots-Bâtard-Montrachet are others of topmost rank (*see each under individual heading*). These are all Great Growths (*Grands Crus*) as rated by the French government and are thus on a level with the handful of the finest wines of Burgundy. Slightly behind them in the legal hierarchy—but often their equal in quality—are such vineyards as Morgeot, Ruchottes, and Caillerets. Chassagne's whites share many of the characteristics of Puligny—the dry, firm but never hard, full, flowery richness and lingering aftertaste. Montrachet itself has astonishing stamina for a dry white wine, but the others tend to maderize reasonably quickly. After ten years they will usually be significantly diminished, and they are generally at their best when from two to five years old.

The reds of Chassagne are generally finer than those of Puligny and often finer than the better-known Santenays. They are hardish, well-rounded wines, with a *goût de terroir* which is characteristic, and they form a transition between the other reds of the Côte d'Or and those of the southern Burgundian wine districts. Boudriottes is the most masculine at the outset, but it matures into a mellow and not over-assertive richness; while Clos Saint-Jean reaches its peak rather faster, has more finesse, and develops its bouquet considerably earlier. In general, the red wines of Chassagne are at their peak after about five years.

Chassagne has about 348 hectares (860 acres) planted in vines. The wine—when it meets the legal minimum standards—is allowed to use the commune name. It may add the designation Côte de Beaune if it comes from a 332-hectare (820-acre) section of this greater whole.

The better vineyards are the First Growths (*Premiers Crus*), which are entitled to be labeled with vineyard name and commune name, and the finest are the Great Growths (*Grands Crus*), which carry the vineyard name only. Average production in Chassagne is about 6,200 hectoliters (164,300 U.S. gallons, 136,400 imp.) of red wine, 7,000 hectoliters (184,800 U.S. gallons, 153,300 imp.) of white.

GREAT GROWTHS (*Grands Crus*)
WHITE WINES

Vineyard	Hectares	Acres
Montrachet (*in part*)	3.56	8.8
Bâtard-Montrachet (*in part*)	5.82	14.4
Criots-Bâtard-Montrachet	1.42	3.5

(*See* Puligny-Montrachet.)

FIRST GROWTHS (*Premiers Crus*)
WHITE AND RED WINES

Vineyard		Hectares	Acres
Les Grandes Ruchottes	(*white wines only*)	0.64	1.59
Les Ruchottes	(*white wines only*)	1.73	4.26
Morgeot		3.94	9.75
Les Caillerets		5.49	13.6
Clos Saint-Jean		14.36	35.5
Clos de la Boudriotte		2.02	5
Les Boudriottes		17.81	44.3
La Maltroie		8.9	22.8
Champgain		28.35	70.7
La Romanée		3.16	7.86
Les Brussanes		17.72	43.8
Les Chaumées		10.12	25.1
Les Vergers		9.54	23.6
Les Macherelles		8.01	19.8
L'Abbaye de Morgeot		10.92	26.99
La Grande Montagne		8.18	20.22
Les Champs-Cain		4.24	10.48
Bois de Chassagne		8.79	21.73

Chasselas

This is one of the good European table grapes, but it is used only for small light wines: although these have a delicate bouquet, they are low in acid and do not keep well. Varieties of this family are the Gutedel (Germany), the Fendant (Switzerland), and the Chasselas Doré (California).

Château Chasse-Spleen

Bordeaux red wine.
District: Haut-Médoc, France.
Commune: Moulis.

Moulis is an official place-name in its own right, and the commune lies a little to the north and to the west of Margaux. Its best wine is Chasse-Spleen, classified Exceptional Growth (*Cru Exceptionnel*) in 1855. A reclassification of Médoc wines today would find this vineyard rated higher, among the great Classified Growths. Served frequently in recent years at banquets of the Médoc wine fraternity, the Commanderie du Bontemps, it has held its own among Médocs of high classification and worldwide reputation. M. Jacques Merlot is the co-proprietor of the château.

Characteristics. One of the best of its class, round and full. Very good breed.
Vineyard area: 23 hectares (57 acres).
Average production: 60 *tonneaux* (5,000 cases).

Château

In the wine world this means not a great castle, like a château of the Loire, but a wine estate (especially in the region of Bordeaux) where vineyards and wine sheds are controlled as a rule from the country house which is the center of the estate. This may look like a small castle; it may just as well be an average villa. The wine made and bottled on the estate is the fine château-bottled wine always more prized than regional wines, which may be blends.

For the names of the wine châteaux of Bordeaux (e.g., Château Haut-Brion, Château Prieuré-Lichine) *see* under individual names.

Château-bottled

Wine bottled at the château where it was grown and made: a guarantee that it is untampered with and authentic. At most leading vineyards the legend *Mis en Bouteilles au Château* is also a guarantee of quality. If the vintage of any year does not come up to standard, it will be disposed of to shippers and sold as regional wine.

Château-Chalon (Appellation Contrôlée)

A *vin jaune* of the French Jura. Yellow-colored, this wine is akin to Sherry and can last up to sixty or seventy years.
See Jura.

Châteauneuf-du-Pape (Appellation Contrôlée)

Rhône Valley red, and some white, wines.
District: Rhône Valley, France.

Midway between Avignon and Orange, on the left bank of the Rhône, Châteauneuf has about 3,000 hectares (7,500 acres) of vines, producing one of the Côtes du Rhône's finest red wines, and boasts the most stringent wine controls in the world. Were it not for Châteauneuf and its most distinguished grower—the Baron le Roy de Boiseaumarié—there would probably be fewer controls in France today, for in 1936 the authorities followed the rules which had already been established by the Baron and others in Châteauneuf since 1923 and applied them to other fine French wines. The late Philippe Dufaye, who abandoned medicine for viticulture, was a moving spirit in the commune.

Legislation in Châteauneuf came about through necessity, for after the First World War a bottle was apt to contain something quite other than its label claimed, and anything but good wine. Since 1923, however, the picture has changed drastically, and fraud, while not completely rooted out, has been given an almost mortal blow.

Most Côtes du Rhône wines are the product of one grape, but in Châteauneuf there are thirteen varieties. Because of this there will be differences between wines coming from different growers, all of whom maintain that each type of grape adds certain characteristics and that only by playing the scale of the varieties can a Châteauneuf-du-Pape be achieved.

Grenache gives mellowness and alcohol; Mourvèdre, Syrah, Muscardin, and Vaccarese add body, color, and firmness; Counoise, Picpoule, and Cinsault give vinosity, bouquet, and freshness; Clairette and Bourboulenc, finesse and warmth. Terret Noir, Picardan, and Roussanne are also allowed. The vines grow far apart, with often as much as 1.5 meters (5 feet) between rows, in soil covered with flattish stones the size of small coconuts. The bunches of grapes mature, caught between the scorching heat of the sun and the reflected heat from the stones. As a result of this roasting and of new, shorter vatting methods, the wines usually surpass the required 12.5% of alcohol (a legal minimum matched by few French wines and exceeded by none) and often reach 13% or even 14%. The wine is characteristically deep in color and full-bodied, but softer than either a Hermitage or a Côte Rôtie, and is much quicker to mature than are most Côtes du Rhônes. It is often ready after three or four years. The wine has a good bouquet (though not so intense as in the Côte Rôtie) and a special winy taste termed "vinosity."

Some very pleasant white wines are made and, while conserving the same distinctive taste, they are less well known—almost curiosities compared with the reds.

The name Châteauneuf-du-Pape comes from the crumbling ruins of an old castle built in the time known as the Babylonian Captivity (1305–1377), when successive popes were French, and Avignon, not Rome, was the seat of the Papacy. The "New Castle" was to be their summer headquarters and was started by Clément V, a lover of wine and former Bishop of Bordeaux—in which region Château Pape-Clément still stands in tribute to him. The building of the castle was finished by Pope Clément VI, although the vines were probably established by an intervening pontiff, John XXII. The holdings were attacked during the religious wars and the castle burned in 1552. Most of the remaining donjon was destroyed in the Second World War.

It is probable that wine from the district was not called Châteauneuf-du-Pape much before the nineteenth century; in earlier times it was known as "Wine of Avignon." Today a varying amount is made each year, for in areas as dry as this the grapes sometimes remain small from lack of water; but in a good year there will be about 108,000 hectoliters (2.85 million U.S. gallons, 2.37 million imp.), nearly all of it red. A little very good white is produced.

The word "Châteauneuf," with its associations with châteaux and Bordeaux, is attractive to the public. In the last year or two, some of these wines have been bottled within twelve months of the harvest and are thus lighter than the traditional Châteauneuf-du-Pape, and comparable with the best growths of Beaujolais.

Some important Châteauneuf-du-Pape vineyards are:

Vineyards	Hectares	Acres
Domaine des Fines Roches	47.35	117
Domaine de la Nerthe	46.54	115
Clos Saint-Jean	44.49	109.9
Domaine de Nalys	46.54	115
Château de Vaudieu	29.70	73.04
(about 40% of this is actually in production, although the whole rates an Appellation Contrôlée)		
La Gardine	24.44	60.5
Château Fortia	25.86	63.9
Domaine des Sénéchaux	23.59	58.3
Clos-des-Papes	13.51	33.4
Domaine de Saint-Préfert	14.16	35

Châtillon-en-Diois (Appellation Contrôlée)

French red, white, or rosé wine from the Drôme department.

Chauché Gris

This grape is grown in the Livermore and Santa Cruz regions of California. The wine it makes is sold as "Gray Riesling" or "Rhine Wine" (although the grape is not a Riesling) or even as a "Chablis."

Chaume

See Quarts de Chaume.

Chautauqua

Wine-growing district in New York State.
See United States: New York.

Cheilly-les-Maranges and Cheilly-les-Maranges-Côte de Beaune (A.O.C.)

Burgundy red and white wines.
District: Côte Beaune, France.

Cheilly and its neighbors (Sampigny and Dezize)—all of which have added the name of the vineyard they jointly share to their own—make up the southernmost communes of the Côte de Beaune. Cheilly's wines are usually blended with those from other communes along this famous slope and sold as Côte de Beaune-Villages, but may occasionaly be found over some 125 hectares (310 acres), and grapes grown on 43 hectares (106 acres) enclosed within the larger area may be made into wine that has the right to add Côte de Beaune to the communal name. The vineyards Les Maranges, Plantes-de-Maranges, and La Boutière are the commune's best, and wines from these three may—although they almost never do—carry both commune name and vineyard name on the bottle label.

Chénas (Appellation Contrôlée)

Wines of Beaujolais, France, grown in small quantity, generally inside the famous district of Moulin-à-Vent; not quite of that excellence, they are nevertheless first-rate and, being much cheaper, are outstanding value.
See Beaujolais.

Chenin Blanc

The dominant white grape of the lower Loire Valley, going into Vouvray and other wines of the Touraine, and into most of the white wines of Anjou. Sometimes known as Pineau de la Loire, Blanc d'Anjou, etc. It is also used in California.
See Anjou; California; Touraine.

Cherry brandy

Technically a brandy distilled from fermented cherry juice, but in practice a liqueur derived from it, containing a proportion of crushed cherry stones to impart a bitter-almond taste.

Cherry Heering

This cherry liqueur made by the firm of Peter Heering of Copenhagen has made its name throughout the world. Having a true cherry flavor and made according to Heering's special formula, it is not over-sweet, on account of the proportion of cherry stones used in the distillation. This is one of the most popular cordials sold in the United States.

Cherry liqueur

Cherry cordial made by steeping cherries in sweetened brandy. Cherry Rocher is famous in France. An English variety is produced by Thomas Grant & Sons.
See Cherry Heering; Maraschino.

Château Cheval-Blanc

Bordeaux red wine.
District and Commune: Saint-Émilion, France.

Generally considered the best Saint-Émilion wine today, Cheval-Blanc is one of the twelve vineyards officially classified First Great Growth (*Premier Grand Cru*) of Saint-Émilion in 1955 and is privileged to stand with Château Ausone at the head of the list, the others following alphabetically. The vineyard is predominantly gravelly, although it covers various soils, and lies on flat land on the northeast borders of Saint-Émilion, on the edge of Pomerol. As a building the château is not distinguished.

The geographical position, otherwise excellent, proved disastrous in the freeze of February 1956. The Pomerol area was the hardest hit; and since the frost lay on the lower, flatter land and spared the hills, of all the great Saint-Émilion vineyards Cheval-Blanc suffered most. The late owner, M. Fourcaud-Laussac, in whose family the property has been for a little more than a hundred years (and whose heirs still own it), afterward made an average of about eight barrels of wine in each of the vintages of 1956, 1957, and 1958 (the usual yield is 600 barrels), because the cold killed the productive shoots and branches, which cannot be renewed under three or four years. Approximately a quarter of the plantation was actually destroyed, so that the vineyard was unable to return to normal production until the early 1960s.

Characteristics. Undoubtedly one of the greatest red vineyards of Bordeaux, on a par with the First Growths of the Médoc. Its reputation has grown tremendously in recent years, and three qualities may be said to have contributed to its success. The wine is one-third Pomerol, for the vineyard touches the Pomerol boundary, it is one-third Graves, since the soil is gravelly, and the remaining one-third is a typical Saint-Émilion. The result is a strong, supple, excellent wine.

Vineyard area: 35 hectares (87 acres).
Average production: 160 *tonneaux* (14,000 cases).

Domaine de Chevalier

Bordeaux red and white wines.
District: Graves, France.
Commune: Léognan.

Chevalier-Montrachet (Appellation Contrôlée)

Placed among the top eleven red-wine vineyards of Graves in 1959 and among the top five white wine vineyards for its lesser quantity of white wine. After almost a century of ownership and because of the numerous Ricard heirs, the domaine was sold to the Bernard group in 1983, with a proviso that Claude Ricard would continue to run the vineyard. The red is not quite what it was at the turn of the century, but Chevalier is still an outstanding Graves, with quality often compared to that of La Mission Haut-Brion. The white is something of a connoisseur's favorite.

Characteristics. A very fine wine with great vigor, even in the lesser years. Among the best of the red Graves. The white is excellent.

Vineyard area: red—13 hectares (32.5 acres); white—3 hectares (7.5 acres).

Average production: red—50 *tonneaux* (4,500 cases); white—10 *tonneaux* (950 cases).

Chevalier-Montrachet (Appellation Contrôlée)

Burgundy white wines.
District: Côte de Beaune, France.
Commune: Puligny-Montrachet.
Official Classification: Great Growth (Grand Cru).

These wines are the closest to the great Montrachet itself. They have the same enveloping richness with no trace of sweetness, and the same overwhelming perfume and magnificence. This is not really surprising, since the vineyards are contiguous. Chevalier is lighter and not as powerful a wine as Montrachet, but, depending upon the skill of the grower, it can sometimes be as great or even greater. Superb finesse is the attractive characteristic of this beautiful white wine.

The Chevalier is directly above Montrachet in the commune of Puligny-Montrachet. On one side of it is Cailleret—good, but not in the same class as the other two—and on the other two sides no vineyards at all.

Chevalier, not much more than 5 hectares (12 acres), is split among several owners. Mme Boillereault de Chauvigné is one; and much of the rest is in the hands of Bouchard Père et Fils, Jadot and Latour (joint ownership), and Chartron. The average production of the vineyard is 160 hectoliters (4,240 U.S. gallons, 3,520 imp.).

Cheverny

Facing Blois across the Loire in the heart of Touraine is the village of Cour-Cheverny with its fine château. In the surrounding district lie the vineyards of the V.D.Q.S. wines called Cheverny. White wines are made mostly from the Chenin Blanc and Pineau de la Loire grapes, reds from the Gamay Noir and Cabernet Franc; some rosé is produced from the same grapes used for red. The V.D.Q.S. name—which was recently shortened from Mont-près-Chambord-Cour-Cheverny—also applies to the *vin blanc mousseux* of the region.

Chian wine

A Greek wine famous in antiquity.
See Classical wines.

Chianti (D.O.C.G.)

Chianti is one of the most abused names in the world of wine. Almost every wine-growing country has taken the name and applied it to almost any red wine as long as it is sold in straw-covered flasks. Real Chianti is made in a small district in the region of Tuscany in central Italy, and it may come in a flask (*fiasco*) or in a bottle. In either case, some Chianti Classicos will have on the neck of the bottle or flask a seal depicting a black cockerel on a gold background; and other permissible Chianti from a wider area in Tuscany will show a white cherub on the seal. The nine Chianti associations, called consorzios, each have their own seal.
See Tuscany: Chianti.

Chiaretto

An Italian rosé from Lake Garda.
See Italy.

Chica

South American drink, brewed from maize by the Indians.

Chicken

General name covering various types of native American grapes, some of which can be used by the wine-maker.

Chile

Chile makes the best wines in South America, and in quantity produced is counted eighth among the wine-producing countries of the world. Soil and climate helped by irrigation are favorable to viticulture; the French *vignerons* who planted the better vineyards have left behind them a high tradition of wine-making—although the Spaniards have been growing vines in Chile ever since they conquered it; and finally, the Chilean government takes a progressive and enlightened interest in wine and the vine.

From its roughly 130,000 hectares of vineyards (325,000 acres) Chile makes annually about 9 million hectoliters (237,760,000 U.S. gallons, 198,000,000 imp.) of wine. Only about 72,000 hectoliters, 0.8% of the total, is exported, mainly to other South American countries, a few European ones, and the United States. Before the 1973 coup, much wine went to Cuba. It is everywhere appreciated, for although not great wine, it is good—and usually a very good buy for the price. The amount of wine consumed each year inside Chile has been limited to 40 liters (10.5 U.S. gallons, 8.7 imp.) per inhabitant, and average consumption is well below the limit. The restriction was placed some years ago as the government attempted to control alcoholism. Two percent of all arable land in the country is planted in vines, and about 35,000 workers are constantly employed in the wine industry, about four times the number working the big copper mines.

Three types are produced: fortified wines in the north, good table wines in Central Chile, and ordinary table wines in the south. Those of the central section often bear a close resemblance to the lesser Bordeaux wines. This is not really surprising, for the soil and climate in the two regions are very similar and the vines and viticultural practices are direct imports. Chilean wines might not, of course, match a top château-bottled Claret of a good year, but they often equal or surpass some of the regional bottlings—and they have the advantage of being much cheaper. In addition to the wines of the Bordeaux-type from Cabernet grapes, there are some Burgundy types from Pinot Noir, but the former is by far the more successful. Though the wines can be good values, not all Chilean wine-makers have the skill to produce sound, clean wines.

One of the best Chilean white wines is the Riesling, but its production is reduced, not because of the quality of the wines but because the growers find the results too expensive. Chilean white wines are now made from the Pinot Blanc, Sauvignon, and Sémillon vines, for the most part. The red *vin ordinaire* grown in the southern section of the country comes both from grapes of French stock and from the País, a vine of Spanish origin which has been in Chile long enough to be considered a native. The País is very much like the prolific Mission variety common in California. In Chile it accounts for 70% of all vines.

TERRAIN AND CLIMATE

Chile is so fortunately situated that the country has so far escaped the devastation of mildew—the most crippling fungus disease of the vine—and of phylloxera, although this vine louse has taken its toll in vineyards of Argentina to the east and Peru to the north. Chileans say that the Andes, which lie between Chile and Argentina, have prevented the influx of the pest from that side; that the desolate Atacama Desert has obstructed its entry from Peru; and that the prevailing winds blowing in from the sea guarantee that it will not make its entrance by air. The result is that in Chile even the most tender of European vine-types need not be grafted onto American roots; yet experiments have been made, and this could be done with a minimum of confusion should phylloxera ever get into the country, though precautions taken at Chilean border stations make this improbable.

As there are three types of wine, so there are three zones of grape production:

The northern zone, from the Atacama Desert to the River Choapa, consists of vineyards planted mostly in Muscat and produces the country's best table grapes. Irrigation is a vital necessity since as a rule the rainfall is negligible; what there is, however, is closely connected with the cold Humboldt Current off the coast and when—as sometimes happens—this current is displaced by warmer water, catastrophic rains result, ruining the vineyards and everything else in the region. The vines are mostly cultivated in the transversal valleys, and irrigation is based on the occasional rivers which flow down from the mountains. The wines are strong and high in alcohol, and some are fortified to resemble Sherry, Port, or Madeira.

The central zone, the most important vine-growing region in terms of quality, runs from the Aconcagua River to the River Maule. Here the influence is almost entirely Bordelais, both in viticultural practices and in vine planting. The most important vines are Cabernet Franc, Cabernet Sauvignon, Merlot, Malbec (here spelled Malbeck), and Petit Verdot for red wines, and Sémillon and Sauvignon for whites. All these come from the Bordeaux area. Other important vines are Pinot Noir, Pinot Blanc, and, of lesser importance, Riesling and País. The vines are tended and cared for according to traditional Bordeaux methods, with the single important exception that they are virtually all irrigated and therefore give more output than those which are watered naturally. This factor is not prejudicial to the quality of the wine. Since all the best vineyards of Chile are irrigated, it cannot at this point be decided whether or not the wine would improve under different conditions. In irrigated vineyards, the Cabernet Sauvignon may yield as much as 200 hectoliters per hectare, or nearly 12 tons to the acre. The most important grape for white wine, the Sémillon, will produce almost as much in similar situations.

The two best sections of the central region (and thus the best of Chile) are the Aconcagua Valley and the valley of the River Maipo. Both specialize to a large extent in Cabernet vines, and the wines have finesse, are well balanced, and tend to hold their excellence longer than most other Chilean growths. The Maipo Valley, in the section southeast of the Chilean capital city of Santiago, is the top vineyard district. The soil has more limestone than elsewhere (there is generally a higher percentage of sand and slate), and the Cabernet Franc and Cabernet Sauvignon produce wines which are strong and stable, deep in color and rich in perfume. There is a good yield per acre in this district, although this claim can be attributed partly to irrigation.

The southern zone; this section of Chile runs between the rivers Maule and Bio-Bio. With a few exceptions in the extreme north, the vineyards are not irrigated. The subsoil is hard and the topsoil is made up of slate and mud, sometimes rich in iron, with occasional outcroppings of lime. These wines are

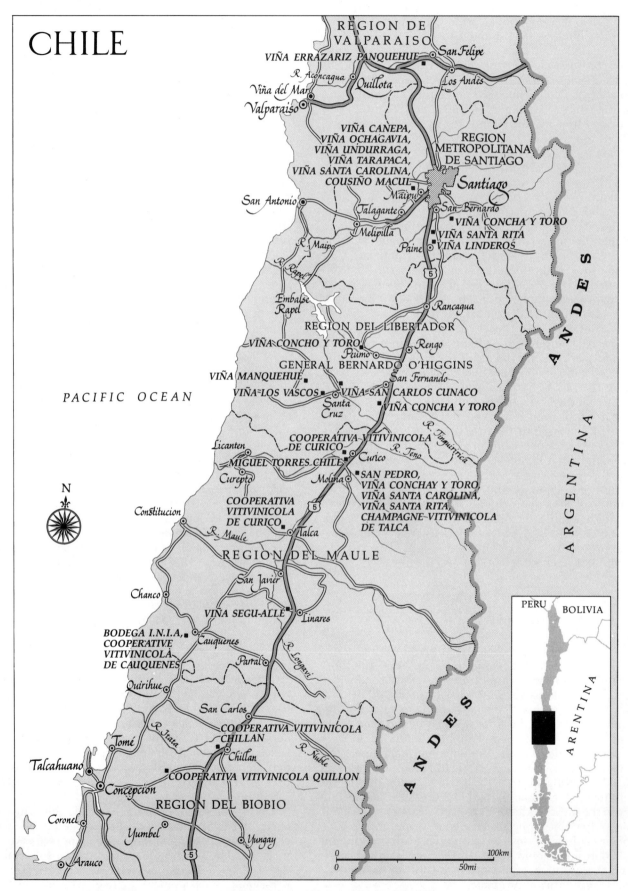

CHILE

REGION DE
VALPARAISO

VIÑA ERRAZARIZ PANQUEHUE ☐ San Felipe

R. Aconcagua Quillota Los Andes

Viña del Mar

Valparaiso

VIÑA CANEPA,
VIÑA OCHAGAVIA,
VIÑA UNDURRAGA,
VIÑA TARAPACA,
VIÑA SANTA CAROLINA,
COUSIÑO MACUL

REGION
METROPOLITANA
DE SANTIAGO

Santiago

San Antonio

Maipu

Talagante

San Bernardo

VIÑA CONCHA Y TORO

Melipilla

VIÑA SANTA RITA
VIÑA LINDEROS

R. Maipo

Paine

R. Rapel

Embalse
Rapel

Rancagua

REGION DEL LIBERTADOR

VIÑA CONCHO Y TORO

Peumo Rengo

PACIFIC OCEAN

GENERAL BERNARDO O'HIGGINS

VIÑA MANQUEHUE

San Fernando

VIÑA LOS VASCOS *VIÑA SAN CARLOS CUNACO*

Santa
Cruz

VIÑA CONCHA Y TORO

N

R. Tinguiririca

COOPERATIVA VITIVINICOLA
DE CURICO

R. Teno

Licanten

Curico

MIGUEL TORRES CHILE

Curepto

Molina

SAN PEDRO,
VIÑA CONCHAY Y TORO,
VIÑA SANTA CAROLINA,
VIÑA SANTA RITA,
CHAMPAGNE-VITIVINICOLA
DE TALCA

COOPERATIVA
VITIVINICOLA
DE CURICO

Constitucion

Talca

R. Maule

REGION DEL MAULE

San Javier

Chanco

VIÑA SEGU-ALLE Linares

BODEGA I.N.I.A,
COOPERATIVE
VITIVINICOLA
DE CAUQUENES

Cauquenes

R. Longavi

Parral

Quirihue

San Carlos

COOPERATIVA VITIVINICOLA
CHILLAN

Tomé

R. Itata

Chillan

R. Ñuble

COOPERATIVA VITIVINICOLA QUILLON

Talcahuano

Concepción

REGION DEL BIOBIO

Coronel

Yumbel

Yungay

Arauco

ANDES

ARGENTINA

ANDES

| PERU | BOLIVIA |

ARGENTINA

0   100km
0   50mi

distinctly less interesting than those farther to the north, and while there are some vines of French origin (Cabernet, Malbec, Sémillon) and a little Riesling, much of the area is in the bulk-giving País. A certain amount of blending is done with these wines and the rest make up the everyday wine of the Chilean. Though the product is perhaps inferior to wines made farther north, viticulture is important in this part of Chile as the livelihood of some 13,000 small vineyard owners. South of the Bio-Bio River, the climate becomes too harsh for the successful cultivation of wine grapes.

WINE HISTORY

Despite the fact that they were conquered and settled by wine-drinking Latin people, most of the countries of South America had to await the influx of Italians after the First World War before they had substantial vineyards of their own. But both Chile and Peru have had vines for just about as long as they have had Spaniards.

Vines were brought into these countries by the missionaries who followed the Conquistadores and were established as a source for altar wine. It is thought that the first vines were carried into Chile by either Francisco de Carabantes or Bartolomé de Terrazas. One of these two—it is not known definitely which—took part in the expedition into Chile of Diego de Almagro, somewhere between 1535 and 1537. The vine they brought with them is recorded as giving grapes which were small and red and extremely tasty.

Culture of the vine received its first impetus about 1556, in the neighborhood of Santiago, whence it spread to what is today Argentina. The important vines of this era were Muscats, in particular the Muscat of Alexandria. Another useful variety was one that Chileans, for lack of a better name, call the País; it is known to have come from Spain, but otherwise its origins are shrouded in mystery. The wines were mostly altar wines or were modeled on Spanish types, and the real upsurge in the industry had to wait until the middle of the nineteenth century.

In 1851, the "Father of Chilean viticulture," Silvestre Ochagavia, realized that the country had the potential of becoming one of the best vineyard regions of the American continent. Acting on his conviction, he imported from France a number of viticultural experts. In addition, he imported a variety of cuttings from the better French vines, which were mostly planted in the central valley of Chile, where the better vineyards are still to be found. As his experiment became an almost unqualified success, the Chilean government stepped in and had more French vines imported, and the new industry was well launched.

Today, the typical vineyard of Chile is a small one indeed. Of the 32,000-odd vineyards, more than 26,-000 are of 5 hectares (12.5 acres) or less. This raises various problems of cultivation; problems which have a direct bearing on the quality of the wine. A small Chilean grower who has neither the capital nor the proper equipment cannot hope to produce a really fine wine and stay in business. But the Chilean government has established a fund to provide loans for the building of cooperative cellars. This eliminates the necessity for each grower to buy all the expensive machinery he would otherwise need and provides a central place for a technical expert to advise growers on the latest and best methods. There are now only about a dozen cooperatives, making some 1 % of all Chilean wine.

The Maipo River Valley, as an area with some of the best vineyards, is the location of some of the best wineries in Chile. Concha y Toro owns 1,500 hectares (5,625 acres) of vines in Pirque, Torconal, Maipo, Chachapoal, and San Juan de Peteroa; its two wineries are in San Miguel and Pirque. There, good wine is made, especially from Merlot, Cabernet Sauvignon, Sauvignon Blanc, Sémillon, and Riesling grapes. Bulk process "champagne" is produced at the Pirque winery from a blend of Pinot Blanc, Pinot Gris, Riesling, and Chardonnay.

The Canepa winery at Valparaiso makes wine from grapes grown in the Maipo Basin southwest of the capital. Most of the vineyards, planted with Cabernet Sauvignon and Riesling, are along the sand and gravel banks of the Puangue River where the geography is not unlike that of Bordeaux.

West of Santiago in Santa Ana is Viña Undurraga, whose founder, in 1912, was the first to export Chilean wines to the United States, and whose vines now thrive in a moderate climate on land irrigated with river water. Most of the good *Vitis vinifera* varieties common in Chile are grown, along with the Pinot Noir, and sparkling wine is produced.

Also south of Santiago in the Llano del Maipo—the Maipo Basin—is Viña Santa Rita, and farther to the east, Viña Cusiño-Macul. At Cusiño-Macul, as in other good Chilean vineyards, vine cuttings were brought from the great vineyards of France, in this case from Pauillac in the Haut-Médoc and Martillac in Graves. More than half of the 260 hectares (650 acres) produce grapes for red wine, mostly Cabernet Sauvignon. Sémillon accounts for most of the white wine. Here, and at Undurraga, among other *viñas*, the better wines age in American oak barrels.

Two other important wineries lie south of the Maipo district. In Talca Province at Molina is Viña San Pedro, founded in 1865, with 400 hectares (1,000 acres) of vineyards. In Curicó, since 1979, the Torres family from Spain has developed 150 hectares (375 acres) of vineyards and a large, well-equipped bodega using modern technology to produce new oak barrels from the U.S. and France to age their Santa Digna Cabernet Sauvignon. The two main Chilean cooperatives are in this same area: Curicó and Talca.

GOVERNMENT CONTROLS

The Chilean wine industry is one of the best regulated in the world. Perhaps the main reason for this is the effort to control alcoholism; but the outcome is that the wine which is encouraged is of high quality.

Chilean growers have a production figure they may not exceed—and if by any chance they do exceed it, they must get rid of their surplus, the two most popular methods being the attempt to export and distillation to industrial alcohol. In any year, each grower must declare to the government how much wine he has made. If the total comes to more than the legal maximum for the country, he must dispose of a certain amount, depending on the national total and the percentage of the wine he has made in proportion to his acreage. He must also declare to the government how much wine he eventually disposes of, and the way in which he has done it. The dumping of poor wine on the export market is prevented by restrictions imposed by the National Council of External Commerce. These rules decree that, for export, white wines must have at least 12% alcohol, red wines 11.5%; and that the wines must be clear, healthy, and at least one year old.

The final control placed on Chilean wines by the government refers to age. There are four classes of export wines: Courant refers to wines one year old, Special to two-year-olds, Reserve to four-year-olds, and Gran Vino applies to wines six years old or more. In many cases the Reserve wines may be Chile's best.

SPIRITS

Much of the production of fine Muscat wine made in the northern zone is used for the distillation of fine brandy native to Chile and to some other South American countries.

See Pisco Brandy.

China

From very early times, wines have been made sporadically in China. Today, wild vines grow in the south. There are some experimental stations for viticulture, and a small number of cooperative vineyards. Some European grapes (such as Pinot and Riesling) have been introduced, and American-type vines, descended from *Vitis labrusca*, as well as native Asian stock, have been planted. Some of the vines are cultivated in irrigated land, on a curious system by which the plants are supported on a fan-shaped trellis-work of wires; in other, non-irrigated vineyards, the pergola method of training was seen.

Wine is, however, apparently a drink for special occasions; lemonade or beer seems to be the common accompaniment for everyday meals. But wine has a place in plans for the future. Wineries have been rebuilt and more are planned. Officials confirm that grape, fruit, and rice wines, plus a variety of distilled beverages are now produced.

WINE HISTORY

Chinese history has it that wine-making started as early as 2500 B.C., when the wine was called Li or Chang, instead of Chiu, its present name. According to legends and written history, the originator of sweet wines was one I Ti (who was perhaps a woman), a contemporary of the Emperor Yu (2205–2197 B.C.). The product did not find imperial favor, and a prohibition of alcoholic drink seems to have followed. Chinese spirits—often called "wine"—may have been invented soon after the unfortunate debut of fermented wine. Shao K'ang is credited with distilling Kaoliang from sorghum, and variations of his original formula are still made today, with alcoholic strengths ranging from 50 to 100 proof.

None of these earliest concoctions was wine by the Western definition of wine as a drink fermented from grapes, for grapes did not arrive in China until the late second century B.C. The first vines came from the Arabs in Turkestan, and even today many of the best Chinese grapes come from around Turfan in the section of old Turkestan along the main route to Central Asia. Having introduced the Chinese to vines, the Arabs might also have taught them the art of making wine from grapes.

Even though vines—and probably wine, too—had for years traveled to China from the Mediterranean and Persia on the long, slow relays of caravans which brought silk westward, it was not until the seventh century A.D.—when the Chinese dominated all of Central Asia—that viniculture spread more widely. It was not a drink for the masses, but poets and mandarins loved it. In the resplendent period of the T'ang Dynasty, art and poetry flourished, and the drink of the courtiers and the artists was wine. The poet Li Po, a sort of innocent Villon who wandered about, writing and reciting his poems and always praising wine, was most poetically drowned: being drunk, and wanting to clasp the reflection of the moon in his arms, he plunged into the river.

Today, red and white wines, dry, sweet, and sparkling—and some which could be called rosé—are being made from grapes. The Chinese name for grape wine is *p'u t'ao chiu*. Present acreage is presumed to be approximately 85,000 (34,000 hectares). The principal grape varieties, or "ancient Chinese grapes," can be greatly improved. They are the Longyon (Dragon's Eye), the Niunai (Cow's Nipple), and the Wuhebai (Thompson Seedless).

Vines are grown in the northwest, primarily in Sinkiang province north of the Yangtze, and in central and eastern China, north and south of the Great Wall and near the River Liao. Production is especially heavy in Sinkiang, Shanxi, Hebei, Henan, Shandong, and Jiangsu provinces. Those wines likely to be encountered outside of the mainland are the sweet red and white Chefoo, dry Tsingtao red and white, and the sparkling wine called Ta-hsiang-pin-chiu. The red Chefoo is rather like a light Port, the white is strong and aromatic. The Tsingtao wines are closer to the Western conception of table wine. Some wine may even be seen from the famous Lung Yen vineyard at Peking, where wine popular with the Ming Emperors was grown.

In the 1970s, the Rémy-Martin Cognac group pioneered a joint venture with the Chinese government outside of Tientsin to make a wine called "Dynasty" of Muscat de Hambourg table grapes. 15,000 to 18,-000 cases are made annually. The other wine found in China is called "The Great Wall." The increase is approximately 5% per annum, which seems promising to the Remy Martin, Pernod Ricard and Martini Soprex groups who entered the initial venture. The Chinese government is now attempting to increase wine production from the present 80,000 tons.

RICE WINE

This traditional Chinese drink is made by sweetening and fermenting glutinous rice or millet. Called Shaohsing, from the town in Chekiang Province where the wine was first made during the period of the Warring States (403–221 B.C.), the wines have a golden color. Alcoholic content ranges from 11% to 15%, and the sugar content may be as high as 20%. Though rice wine is consumed throughout China, it seems to be especially popular in the provinces along the Yangtze. The best-known brands are Yen Hung, Shan Niang, Chia Fan, Hsiang Hsueh, and Hua Tiao. Other rice wines are Fukien Loh Chiu and Mi Lao Chiu, made from yellow rice in Shantung Province.

SPIRITS

Brandy is made from wine, but it is not the most typical distilled Chinese drink. Spirits made from grain are the most popular alcoholic products in China. Called *pai chiu*, these gained great attention during the Yuan Dynasty (1280–1368); they are made from cereals which have undergone various processes of yeasting, sweetening, and fermenting. By far the most famous is the fiery Mao-t'ai, from the town of that name in Kweichow Province in southwest China. It is distilled from fine millet and wheat and is generally aged for a considerable time before being consumed. A drink for special occasions, Mao-t'ai has an alcoholic content of 53 proof or more.

The other famous *pai chiu* is Fen Chiu, from Sing Hua Village in the Shansi Province town of Fen. Distilled from millet, wheat, and beans, it is quite fragrant, with a clear, crisp taste.

Ta Chu from Szechwan, Si Fen from Shensi, and Wu Liang Yu, also from Szechuan, are other well-known Chinese spirits.

Chinchon

Spanish anis-flavored spirit diluted with water and drunk in a tall glass.

Chinon (Appellation Contrôlée)

Loire Valley red, white, and rosé wines; still, semi-sparkling, and sparkling.
District: Touraine, France.

The ruined medieval fortress of Chinon rising above the quiet River Vienne stands on the top of a steep hill, to the slopes of which cling the picturesque buildings of the old town. Chinon, a wine center for a considerable period, claims as its most exuberant admirer the writer Rabelais, who once tended a nearby vineyard—La Devinière—and made there what he described as "taffeta wines," soft and velvety. The description has lived on in Chinon and is still apt.

Red, rosé, and white wines are made, the red being the most interesting. White Chinon is almost invariably overshadowed by Vouvray or Montlouis and the rosé by Anjou; but the reds are apt to be soft, flowery, and have a bouquet often compared with raspberries. To be good, Chinon requires the maturity of great vintage years, and such vintages only fall about twice in a decade. Red and rosé—a fresh and clean-tasting if unexceptional wine—are made from Cabernet Franc grapes grown in flinty clay soil, white from Chenin Blanc grapes grown in chalky soil. All wines must have at least 9.5% of alcohol. About 30,000 hectoliters (795,000 U.S. gallons, 660,000 imp.) are made each year, nearly all of which is red.

Chiroubles (Appellation Contrôlée)

A village in the Beaujolais producing an excellent light red wine now becoming the most popular of all red Beaujolais wines in Paris and throughout France.
See Beaujolais.

Chlorosis

A vine disease caused by an excess of calcium in the soil which prevents the vine from assimilating iron. It is treated by adding iron to the soil, by injecting iron into the vine, or replanting with vines grafted onto calcium-resistant root-stock.
See Chapter Eight, p. 37.

Chopine

French pint.

Chorey-les-Beaunes (Appellation Contrôlée)

Burgundy red and white wines.
District: Côte de Beaune, France.

A Burgundian wine village where there is more village than wine. Like so many of her sister communes, Chorey has the option of selling her wines either as Chorey or, after blending with those from other specified communes, as Côte de Beaune-Villages (*q.v.*). The result is that one year may see 750 hectoliters (20,000 U.S. gallons, 16,500 imp.) and another only 4,000 hectoliters (104,000 U.S. gallons, 88,000 imp.).

Chorey is on the right side of the railway but the wrong side of the road. Throughout the Côte d'Or the hills descend gently to a plain, the start of which is marked by Route Nationale (National Highway) No. 74. As you drive south, you will see vines on both sides of the road; but only on the hilly right are the vineyards really good. To the left, on the plain which extends to the railway, they are distinctly minor—and most of Chorey is on the left. A small pocket, amounting to 167 hectares (412 acres), crosses the road but does not climb far enough up the hill to make a great deal of difference; and none of the vineyards is classified First Growth (*Premier Cru*). Both red and white wines could be made, but in practice all are red.

Chromatography

A process of analysis by selective absorption of a mixture of substances on a porous material. In winemaking, paper is generally used. Chromatography has been found to be effective in assessment of certain organic acids as well as in the differentiation between *Vitis vinifera* and hybrids.

Chusclan

One of the best communes of the Côte du Rhône, producing rosé wines.
See Rhône.

Cider

Fermented juice of sweet apples, commonly made in England, France, and other parts of Europe. English settlers introduced it into North America.

The apples were first reduced to a pulp known as "pomace." At first this was done by beating the apples in a stone or wooden trough with wooden paddles; but the earlier practice was supplanted by the cider "mill," consisting of a large wheel that revolved on its side in a circular trough filled with apples and reduced the fruit to a jelly. (the modern method is to place the apples between two cylinders equipped with sharp knives which, when revolved at high speed, perform the same operation much more quickly.) The pomace was then made into a "cheese" to be pressed. This "cheese" was produced by putting on a bed of straw enough of the pomace to make a pile several inches high, followed by another layer of straw at a different

angle from the first, and then more pomace. Care was taken that the straw was not only on the top and bottom of the "cheese" but could fold over the sides as well to keep it in shape and act as a filter during pressing. When the "cheese" was about three feet high, it was taken to a press and then squeezed until all the juice had been taken out of it. Today, the substitution of collapsible forms which mold the "cheese" and are removed before pressing, using cloths instead of straw, brings the procedure up to date without changing any of the essentials. Now, however, the dry pomace is no longer fed to the pigs, as it often was in earlier times. Once the juice of the pomace has been expressed, it is put into vats or barrels to ferment until it is quite dry.

On some of the Somerset and Normandy farms, it will then be aged for a year or more and will be unexpectedly strong. Commercially manufactured cider will sometimes have cultivated yeasts added to the natural fermentation. Sweet cider is filtered before all the sugar has fermented out; the champagne type continues to ferment in the bottle; the cheaper sparkling ciders are carbonated.

Cinqueterre (D.O.C.)

White Italian wine made from Vernaccia grapes.
See Liguria.

Cinsault (or Cinsaut)

Grape used in the wines of southwest France, the Midi, the Rhône Valley, and Algeria. It is known also as Picardan Noir, Espagne, Malaga, and by other local names. In combination with Grenache, this grape produces warmth and fullness in the wine.

Cirò (D.O.C.)

One of the best-known red wines of Calabria, Italy.
See Calabria.

Citric Acid

Though abundant in citrus fruits and at least present in most others, this acid is found only in very small amounts in grapes, and hence very little of it is found in wine. The formula for citric acid is $COOH \cdot CH_2 \cdot C(OH)(COOH) \cdot CH_2 \cdot COOH$.

Clairet

In French, formerly a light blend of red and white wine or sometimes simply a very light red one. From the word was derived the English claret, applied to the red wines of Bordeaux.

Nowadays, a Clairet is not a rosé but a light red wine, supple and fruity but lacking in tannin—one that can be drunk cool and young. A good Clairet is the product of grape varieties which tend to give a delicate wine of this nature, and which, because of low acidity, have been allowed to achieve full maturity. The skins of the fruit are not left in the fermenting vat for more than a day or two. So that malolactic fermentation may not be hindered, the wine is lightly treated with sulfur. Once alcohol and malolactic fermentation have been fully achieved, the wine is stabilized by fining or by treatment with sulfur.

Clairette de Bellegarde

White wine.
District: Southern France.

The commune of Bellegarde, about ten miles from Nîmes, southern France, makes a small, light, yellow wine from the Clairette grape variety. Grown on a mass of pebbles washed down by an arm of the River Rhône, it is one of the few white wines of the Languedoc area enjoying an Appellation Contrôlée, or legal place-name. Subject to the usual restrictions of geographical area and pruning, and required to attain 11.5% of alcohol, the wine must also—and this is not universal under French wine law—submit to a committee of tasters and receive their seal of approval, which will go on the bottle. Otherwise, it cannot be called Clairette de Bellegarde. The commune produces an average of 6,000 hectoliters (159,000 U.S. gallons, 132,000 imp.) of Clairette each year.

See Languedoc.

Clairette de Die (Appellation Contrôlée)

White wine.
District: Southern France.

A semi-sparkling, yellowish-gold wine and a still wine made in 25 parishes around the village of Die on the River Drôme—a tributary of the Rhône—in southeast France. Produced from grapes of the Clairette and Muscat de Frontignan, Clairette de Die dates back to Roman times, when it was the wine of Dea Augusta.

In making the wine, the growers must use a minimum of 50% of Clairette and may vinify by either one of two methods. The modern way is the Champagne process of secondary fermentation in the bottle. The other is the more traditional "rural" way. Following this method, the marker allows his wine to ferment slowly, filtering frequently and adding sulfur in small quantities to slow down the yeasts. The sulfur has a cleansing effect, killing all the harmful bacteria. When the wine has finished its first fermentation, the vintner closes it up tightly in the barrel and allows any unresolved sugar to re-ferment. He puts it throught a pressure filter and effectively stops all action, purifying his wine but allowing the carbon dioxide gas which has been generated to remain in it. This is the more usual process at present.

The result is a more or less sparkling wine with a pronounced flavor of Muscat and an alcoholic content of at least 10.5%. The average yearly output is 40,000 hectoliters (1,060,000 U.S. gallons, 880,000 imp.), most of which is produced by the Cave Cooperative de Die. Appreciation of this wine is an acquired taste.

Clairette du Languedoc

White wines.
District: Southern France.

The great plain of Languedoc in southern France stretches from Arles, near the River Rhône, toward the Spanish border and produces almost half of the wines of France. Very few of these, however, are more than the most ordinary of *vins ordinaires*. Scattered here and there are small holdings of vineyards whose product has been considered good enough to be controlled by French law as wines of Appellation d'Origine Contrôlée. Clairette du Languedoc is one example.

The wine is grown principally in the seven communes of Adissan, Aspiran, Paulhan, Fontès, Cabrières, Péret, and Ceyras, somewhat to the west of Montpellier in the department of Hérault. Two types of wine are made along the sun-scorched slopes, both coming only from grapes of the Clairette vine, with some Picpoule and Terret. The first is that wine carrying on its label simply Clairette de Languedoc, with or without the name of the commune of origin. This is a dry, heavy, white wine of at least 13% of alcohol. The other has the qualification *rancio (q.v.)* added to it. To earn the name of *rancio*, this unpleasant wine must come from grapes which have been left on the vine until well after they are ripe. The wine must have an alcoholic content of at least 14%, must be allowed to maderize and age for at least three years before it is put on sale, and must have the taste characteristics associated with a rancio (or oxydized wine).

The vineyards growing the Clairette du Languedoc comprise about 1,130 hectares (2,800 acres) and average production is less than 11,200 hectoliters (297,-000 U.S. gallons, 265,000 imp.).

See Languedoc.

Claret

In Great Britain especially, and frequently in the United States, red Bordeaux is known as claret.

From the first days of the wine trade with the Bordelais (which began to flourish early in the thirteenth century), the pinkish light wine became a favorite in England and has remained so. The French called it Clairet; the blunter English tongue clubbed it into claret—but the wine was not claret as we know it now. At the time of the Roman occupation, wines were aged; but not again, until almost modern times, was Bordeaux anything but "wine of the year," drunk sometimes as early as two weeks after its harvesting —or the time it took the fleet of wine ships to return to England. It was a wine very briefly fermented. The practice was for a listener to stand posted with ear to the vat, and soon after the boiling of fermentation was heard, the wine was run off.

Today, too, some wine is made after a short fermen-

Château Clarke (Cru Bourgeois)

tation of less than four days. With the new taste for young light wine, Clairet is again being produced in Bordeaux, and it is so called to distinguish it from claret, now the term for the old red wine of Bordeaux. It is also called rosé; and recently this rosé from Bordeaux has become very popular and many excellent examples are made.

Bordeaux Clairet—or rosé—is not red and white wine blended together, though in the past the light claret sometimes was *vinum claratum* (clarified wine), often confused with *vinum clarum* (wine light and clear by its nature). Clarified wine was common white wine added traditionally to red wines which were too murky.

Château Clarke (Cru Bourgeois)

Bordeaux red wine.
District: Haut-Médoc, France.
Commune: Listrac.

Vineyard acquired in 1970 and planted by the dedicated Baron Edmond de Rothschild in 1973. The new winery is a showplace between Moulis and Listrac.

Characteristics: rather hard, well-made, full-bodied.
Vineyard area: 131 hectares (327.5 acres).
Average production: 500 *tonneaux* (50,000 cases).

Classical Wines

A great deal is known about wine and the vine in ancient Greece and Rome. In viticulture, in particular, methods have not changed radically since about 700 B.C., when Hesiod wrote of the planting and pruning of the vines on his Boeotian farm. What we cannot learn from books is exactly how the wines tasted, and so modern specialists have pursued their own fancies. One says that the liquors would have been disgusting to us, boiled down to a muddy sediment, smoked, cloyed with honey, ruined with resin or salt water. Another maintains that those Greek wines kept to a ripe age actually were what the primitive heroes believed them to be—the most divine drink ever enjoyed by man. A few shipwrecked amphorae dredged up from the bottom of the Mediterranean are still in existence and still sealed. The date and the name of shipper or grower are decipherable; but if the jars were opened, the tantalizing liquid inside—brackish and half-evaporated—would not taste like wine. It was the opinion of the nineteenth-century wine historian Cyrus Redding that the better growths probably tasted like Malvasia, or the sweet wines of Cyprus, which (in his day as sometimes in ours) were made by the traditional methods.

GREECE

Vines grew from earliest times in Greece and the Greek islands, and the inhabitants were naturally wine-drinking people. In the adventures of Odysseus wine played an important part. Nausicaä, when she found Odysseus by the stream, revived him with food and the wine she had brought in a goatskin bottle. Later on, in the king's palace, he ate and drank with Alcinous and the chieftains; and afterward the king said: " 'Mix the bowl and serve out the wine to all in the hall, that we may pour forth before Zeus' . . . and Pontonius mixed the honey-hearted wine and served it out to all when he had poured for libation into each cup in turn." (A custom that might be compared with the loyal toast.)

Sweet Wines. Generally, the wine seems to have been sweet. That with which Odysseus made the Cyclops drunk was given to him by Maron—"sweet wine, unmingled, a draught for the Gods." When Maron broached this best vintage—"that red wine, honey sweet"—he would mix it in the silver bowl with twenty parts to one of water, "and a marvellous sweet smell went up from the mixing bowl." Hesiod's wine would have been sweet too—he spread the grapes in the sun for ten days after picking. Just so, Mago of Carthage, about 550 B.C., and Columella, repeating six hundred years later his instructions for making *passum optimum* (the best luscious wine), said that the sun-dried grapes should be laid out on a raised frame and covered with reeds until they were sufficiently shriveled; they were then kept in a jar of good must for six days, before pressing. The practice is near enough to that followed in making straw wines today. Sweet wines have never lost their appeal for the people of southern Italy, of Cyprus and the Aegean. Clearly the ancient Greeks liked them, and they also preferred old wine to new—even now, the rich Commandaria of Cyprus may live to a great age. The best wines are said to have been made from a blend of red and white grapes; and the famous Pramnian must have been an essence like Tokay.

Mixing of Wines. Not all Greek wines, however, were pure and unmingled. Sometimes honey was put in the wine jars. Pliny was later to describe the Greek habit of invigorating wine with potter's earth, powdered marble, and salt water. And, although the use of resin in ancient Greece is not unanimously accepted, it is improbable that the pitch-pine so common in early Roman viniculture and surviving in the peasant wine-making of modern Greece was really avoided in Classical Greece. The mixing of sea water in the must was not quite as crude as it sounds. The water (taken from a calm sea) was boiled down to a third of its original volume (with spices for flavoring), strained, and kept for several years before use. One wine would be improved by blending with another; great growths which had been kept until they were sticky and thick as honey were often fit for nothing else, and many well-matured sweet vintages had to be strained before drinking. These would be mixed with water—indeed, the Greeks usually drank their wine well diluted. Sometimes, as a finishing touch, they added perfumes.

Wine-jars and Pots. At an Athenian dinner-party, while the guests (all men usually) reclined on sofas, slaves would mix wine and water in bowls, take the mixture around in jugs, and pour it into each cup. First a libation would be offered; then the host or leader of the feast would decide how much wine was to be taken, and how strong it should be. In summer, the wine would be cooled with snow brought down from the mountains. Many of the pots and jars for the keeping and serving of wine have been preserved. *Pithoi* (Latin: *dolia*) were the fermenting jars. For the better conservation of lighter wines, these would be smeared with pitch and sunk in the ground. Amphorae were the tall two-handled jars in which the wine was aged and brought from the storeroom; the squatter *hydria* was the covered water pot which was taken out to be filled at the fountain; the *krater* was a wide bowl for mixing wine and water; the *kantharos* a ladling cup with two handles; the *kylix* a shallow goblet, somewhat like a Champagne glass—when the wine was drained, a surprising picture would sometimes be discovered at the bottom. In classical Greece, where there was no paper and little papyrus, talented artists and topical illustrators used wine jars as their canvases. On these we can see the Greeks at their banquets, and expensive flute-players and dancing-girls who sometimes came to entertain them, or the young men aiming their heel-taps into a raised saucer in the game of *kottabos*, said to have been invented in Sicily. As he flung the dregs, a youth would often invoke a girl's name.

Women and Wine. Women, apart from *hetairai* and flute-girls, seldom came to these parties, but some of the courtesans had strong heads, and from Nausicaä onward, Greek women generally drank wine—which is only to be expected in a country where it is the normal drink. A lot has been written by old writers about almost legendary times in Greece and the austere early days in Rome, when women drank nothing but innocuous *sapa* (unfermented wine); but the women of a more sophisticated Rome drank with the men and sometimes got very drunk. As for the Greek rites of Dionysos, a fever which broke out originally in Thrace, women were the more numerous of the worshippers and the more violent—and even when the worship of the wine god had sobered down to a ritual without Maenad dances and destruction, women, as Mr. Charles Seltman has pointed out, still made Bacchic pilgrimages to Delphi.

ROME

Wild vines flourished in the temperate zones that border the Mediterranean, and no doubt the primitive people who lived there made a weak kind of wine. But the Greeks, the Phoenicians—wine-makers also—and ultimately the Romans, taught the natives to prune their vines and make a wine that would keep. The Greeks were early and adventurous navigators, and

their first Italian settlement is believed to have been made by Euboeans at Cumae, on the coast of Campania, probably in the eighth century B.C. By the end of the seventh century B.C. there were Greek cities along the east coast of Sicily and around the Tarantine Gulf, as well as on the mainland. Whether or not it is true that the Greeks found the Etruscans already making good wine from cultivated vines, it is accepted as fact that these people were fond of luxury and feasts, in which the women took part and drank their share. In general, it is assumed the Romans learned viticulture and viniculture from the Greeks and passed on the knowledge to most of the people they conquered. The first true wine was precious and used sparingly: a victorious general vowed only a single cup to Jupiter. At a time when small cultivators were being persuaded to take vine-tending seriously, Numa Pompilius (715–673 B.C.) is said to have forbidden the people to make libations with wine from unpruned vines.

Roman Viticulture. The earliest first-hand account in Latin of Roman vines and wines comes down to us from Cato the Censor (234–149 B.C.). From *De Agri Cultura*, his book on farming (referred to with admiration by Pliny two hundred years later), from Pliny the Elder himself, and from Columella (roughly contemporary with him), we get the most connected account of vine-growing—how to plant and graft, when to prune—and of wine-making in the first century A.D. and earlier. Pliny relates that even in his day some of the vines, particularly in Campania, were allowed to grow as tall as houses and to twine around treetops, so that a man hired to prune them had to ask for danger money. But "here our vines are kept short by pruning," he wrote, "in order that their strength may be concentrated in the shoots." Grape varieties in Greece he believed to be uncountable, and in Italy he knew of eighty sound wines, the best of which were from the Aminean grape (dividing into five varieties), the Nomentane vines with red-tinged stalks, and the Muscatel, which flourished greatly in Tuscany. All these were indigenous. Among others transplanted from Greece and the islands, he picked out the Graecula (rivaling the Aminean), and the Eugenia, successfully imported from Taormina to the Alban district. The Rhaetian and the pine-flavored Allobrogian from Gaul would not produce quality wines on Italian soil, but they made up for it in quantity.

How the Wine Was Made. The natural flavor of pitch (or resin) in the Allobrogian grape was considered desirable, since the Romans smeared the insides as well as the outsides of their wine jars with this piny gum. In the twelfth book of his *Res Rustica*, in which he outlines the innumerable duties of a steward's wife, Columella gives clear instructions for doing this. Then he describes various ways of preserving the must: with liquid resin mixed with vineash, with salt water and sweet herbs and spices. So that they might age more quickly, the wine jars were kept in a loft above the *fumarium*, or smoke-room, where wood was seasoned. In the city, those not in need of smoking would be kept in public cellars (or in private ones) and treated much as wines are today. Even the apparently superstitious rule that wine should never be racked except in a north wind becomes reasonable when one realizes that the opposing wind in parts of Italy is apt to be the sirocco, maddening men and turning milk sour. Pliny considered that, within reason, smoking improved the flavor of wine; but he had hard things to say of the forced ageing by smoke of wines imported from Narbonne, some of which might also be adulterated with obnoxious herbs and drugs. The only Gallic wine he seems to have found passable was that from Marseille. The Spanish he liked better, rating the growths of Tarragona, Lauron, and the Balearics as high as the best Italian.

The Prized Wines. Imported Greek wines, of course, were held in high esteem, although not so rich and rare in Pliny's lifetime as they had been two generations earlier, when guests at a dinner party would not be offered more than one glass. In the first century A.D., the Greek was rivaled by the Falernian. The Greek islands (Lesbos, Chios, Thasos) which shipped the favorite wines knew the value of publicity: they had their coinage stamped with clusters of grapes or with the head of Dionysos. All these expensive growths, Greek and Italian, must have gone untasted by the common people, who no doubt washed down their meals with drafts as new and as ordinary as our *vin ordinaire.*

The Romans made black (very dark red) wines, clear red, amber, and white ones; those they laid down for ageing were as concentrated as the old vintages of Greece. In the *Satyricon* of Petronius, the newly rich tycoon Trimalchio produces at his supper party (overloaded, pretentious, but not well conducted) a little glass amphora labeled *Opimian Muscadine, a Century old.* "Alas," he says, "that wine should live longer than man. We'll try if it has held good ever since the consulship of Lucius Opimius." This wine of a vintage year (121 B.C.), as celebrated as the Comet Year of 1811, was one of the longest-lived in history. When Pliny tasted it, it was so dried and thick that it had to be scraped off the sides of the amphora and mixed with a younger wine. Trimalchio also offered his guests a *vino cotto* "boiled off a third part and kept underground to preserve its strength." Before the meal, there had been *antepasti*—a honey-sweet aperitif and the olives and hot sausages that would appear at a cocktail party today, and dormice covered with honey and poppy-seed, which would not.

SOME LITERARY SOURCES OF CLASSICAL WINE LORE

Greek

Homer. From references throughout the *Iliad* and the *Odyssey*, a few of which have been quoted above, we know that the heroes of epic times—and their women—habitually drank wine. We know they liked it sweet and diluted with water; and how they served it and poured libations, in princely gatherings, between the eleventh and the eighth centuries B.C.

Hesiod. The first plain if limited account of viticulture in Europe is to be found in Hesiod's *Works and Days.* The Boeotian farmer-poet, writing in about 700 B.C., reckoned his calendar by the stars, but he pruned and planted his vines much as small-holders do to this day. It is clear that he had to work hard on his land, and he complained of the oppressions of the local princes.

Alcaeus. The lyric poet of Mytilene, who flourished a hundred years after Hesiod, was himself one of the nobles of Lesbos. Island tyrants rose and fell and his love-songs and verses in praise of wine ("Hurry, my boy, and pour me out a cup of luscious lesbian wine") were interspersed with patriotic odes. His "Let us drink and dance, since Myrsilus is dead" is the model for Horace's ode on the death of Cleopatra, which begins *Nunc est bibendum.* Alcaeus was banished for his political behavior, and Sappho may have been exiled at the same time.

Anacreon. A generation or so later, Anacreon of Teos came to Athens. He was another lyric poet and boon companion, singing of wine and garlands. He referred to the game of *kottabos*—"heel-taps flying from the Teian cup."

Plato, Xenophon, Aristophanes. In the great classical age of Athens, they described the drinking customs of their time: Aristophanes by topical references in his comedies; Plato and Xenophon each by a *Symposium* in which Socrates took part, giving a valuable account of a Greek supper party.

Dioscorides. For sixteen hundred years from the time when it was written (in the first century A.D.), his *Materia Medica* remained the authority on every vegetable substance used in medicine and on natural, medicinal, and doctored wines, both Greek and Roman.

Galen. This great physician, born in Asia Minor, court doctor to Marcus Aurelius, was also a connoisseur of wines. Searching in the Palatine cellars for the best Falernian for his master, he would only consider that which had reached twenty years of age. Athenaeus referred to his surpassing output in philosophical and medical writings, and to his *Treatise on Wines*—but these were lost.

Athenaeus. the author of the long-winded *Deipnosophists* (learned, indeed pedantic, banqueters) is an unrivaled source of gossip and information, accurate or not. In long dialogues and discussions on fish, riddles, wine-making, cheesecakes, and the use of words he inserts quotations from almost every author of his day (c. A.D. 230) and earlier. His accounts of different kinds of wine are valuable; his preservation of fragments of lost writings even more so. Athenaeus himself was born at Naucratis in Egypt. As his work proves, he was a great reader and amasser of encyclopedic knowledge. The *Deipnosophists* is a description of a banquet at the house of Laurentinus, a Roman noble. Galen was one of the guests.

Latin

Cato. The first practical account, written in Latin, of Roman wine-growing appeared in *De Agri Cultura* by Cato the Censor, a hard-headed old Roman born on a farm in 234 B.C. Pliny, writing two hundred years later, quoted some of his precepts with approval.

Marcus Varro. This "learned historian," who lived in the time of Julius Caesar and Augustus Caesar, wrote a handbook on farming, *De Re Rustica*, always considered one of the best of its kind and not begun until his eightieth year. He gives lucid instructions on vine-tending and wine-making, and cites in his work the maxims of earlier Greek writers—and of Mago of Carthage.

Virgil. Because of his supremacy as a poet, Virgil's second *Georgic* is one of the (if not *the*) best-known works on the vine. Yet he was not an experienced cultivator (although his father was a farmer), and Varro was said to be his authority. Pliny remarked that, gracious poet though he was, Virgil only mentioned fifteen varieties of grape.

Pliny the Elder (A.D. 23–79). Book XIV of his *Naturalis Historia* is devoted to vines and different kinds of wines with recipes for making them. He referred in his work to most of the important wine writing then extant. Always keen in pursuit of scientific knowledge, he died investigating an eruption of Vesuvius.

Horace. He knew wine (and grew it), and famous vintages are mentioned in the *Odes* and *Satires*—Chian, Lesbian, Caecuban, and Falernian. The Lesbian, he said, was harmless, leaving no headache. Calenian, produced near the Falernian vineyards, was one of the wines he liked, and he offered it to his patron Maecenas in place of the Falernian he could not afford.

Juvenal and *Martial.* Both were writers of satire, flourishing about A.D. 100. Each wrote of wines and of customs fashionable at the time. Martial especially has a lot to tell—of old wives' tales about wine, about faked wines from Marseille, etc.

Petronius. Very little is known about him. He may have been the same Titus Petronius who was known as a lazy, dissipated fellow, who yet managed to be a consul. His account of Trimalchio's feast in the *Satyricon* has already been mentioned.

Columella. Of this writer, also, little is known. From internal evidence he seems to have been born about the beginning of the first century at Cadiz. He had an uncle, also Columella, a farmer in Spain, whom he sometimes quoted. He wrote a book about trees and twelve books of *Res Rustica*, a remarkably clear and complete treatise on Roman farming and viniculture. In Books III and IV are detailed directions for planting and dressing a vineyard; in Book XII (the responsibilities of the steward's wife) instructions on preparing the vintage, making wine, correcting the must, and so on.

Ausonius. The Bordeaux professor who became tutor to the future Emperor Gratian (son of Valentinian), and afterward governor of the province of Gaul and a consul, retired in old age to his villa and his vineyards—he had one at Pauillac, another small property on the Dordogne, and later, a property in the Charente district. It is by no means certain that he ever lived on the site of Château Ausone. During his travels with the Emperor Valentinian he visited the Mosel Valley, which delighted him because it reminded him of the Bordeaux vineyards. In his writings, however, he had more to say about food than about wine.

SOME ANCIENT WINES

Descriptions of the following wines whose names have not been forgotten are collected from the writers listed above, who sometimes contradicted each other. Some of them would grow lyrical about rose and violet in the bouquet of a wine, as writers on wine do now.

Greek

Maronean. This, already referred to as the wine that Odysseus gave to Polyphemus, was described by Pliny as the most ancient of all—grown near the Thracian shore, dark in color, and generally mixed with eight parts of water to one of wine. According to Pliny, the Maronean retained in his day all its strength and vigor.

Pramnian. This most glorious wine of antiquity was said by Homer to be Nestor's favorite, and the wine—"very strong and nutritious"—which he gave to the wounded Machaon with relishes of goat cheese and raw onions. It was the base of Circe's magic potion and still known in Athens when Aristophanes was writing—he did not care for it. It was the opinion of Dioscorides that the grapes pressed out the must by their own weight (thus producing a rich essence); but Athenaeus reported that it was neither a sweet nor a thick wine, but dry and hard and extraordinarily strong.

Chian. According to more than one writer this was the best of Greek wines, "faultless, never causing a headache," and the island's first growths appear to have been Phanean and the wine of Arisium. Horace got in amphorae of Chian for a party and gave orders that half of it should be mixed for the temperate guests, nine cups of water to three of wine; the rest for the hard drinkers, nine cups of wine to three of water. The Chians, who were great gourmets, had a legend that the son of Dionysos first taught them to make the dark red wine. Evidently it was sweet and rather thick.

Lesbian. This was a sweet wine. "How sweet the Pramnian Lesbian wine," said one of the characters quoted by Athenaeus (thus, Pramnian must have been a type, not a place-name). Some declared it the nicest of all but, in the opinion of Athenaeus, it was less astringent, more diuretic than the Chian, and not so pleasant. No sea water was mixed with it, he said.

Thasian. A "rich and rosy" wine, said to have been a noble growth when mellowed by age. Theophrastus told that it was "wonderfully delicious and well flavored; they knead dough with honey and put that in the jars, so that the wine receives sweetness from the honey and fragrance from itself." It was a wine that had to be strained.

Coan. The wine of the island of Cos, where Hippocrates wrote his famous treatise on medicine, was heavily mixed with sea water and white in color. Cato gives a recipe for faking it with Italian wine and salt. It has been described as headachy.

Bybline. Originally the famous wine of ancient Byblos in northern Syria. Vines were probably transplanted to Thrace afterward. It must have been sweet and fragrant. Hesiod wrote, "In weary summer, when the goats are fattest and the wine is at its best, then let me have the shadow of a rock and some Bybline wine."

Helbon, or *Chalybon.* A celebrated sweet wine of Syria, made near Damascus and mentioned in the Bible. It was a favorite of the Persian kings.

Roman

Falernian. The most famous of all the Roman wines was often praised by Horace, although Pliny classified it among the second growths, while admitting that it ranked high at that time. He added that it was the only wine which would take fire when lighted, and that it came in three styles: light and dry, yellow, sweet and dark. Trimalchio's Opimian wine was a Falernian. Galen's view was that the wine (of other years than the Opimian, presumably) was not fit to drink until it was ten years old, at its best between fifteen and twenty, and liable to give one a headache after that. Redding, describing the Falernian that grew in volcanic Campania near Naples, where Massic was also produced—rough, dark, and strong until it grew mellow—guessed that it would have resembled Lacrima Christi.

Setine. The favorite of Augustus Caesar, diplomatically placed in the first class by Pliny. Athenaeus also recorded that it was first-class, "like Falernian," but lighter and not so apt to make one drunk. It was produced at Setia on the Appian Way.

Caecuban. Another of Pliny's "firsts." Athenaeus said it was a wine of breed, generous and heady, not reaching its peak for many years. Horace knew it; but the vineyards disappeared when Nero started to make a canal from Lake Baiae to Ostia.

Alban. The wine of Alba, referred to by various writers, seems to have been of two kinds, sweet and dry. Pliny classified it a "third," and it was said to be good for the stomach.

Sorrentine. Opinions differed about this. Galen considered it was no good until it was twenty-five years old. Doctors recommended it for the health, but Tiberius called it "generous vinegar." Pliny said it was made from Aminean grapes, grown low on props.

Mamertine. The wine was produced near Messina, in Calabria. Galen found it light, well balanced, and pleasing. Julius Caesar brought it into fashion when, to celebrate his third Consulship in 46 B.C., he dispensed not two wines but four: Falernian, Chian, Lesbian, and Mamertine. A wine of that name, pale in color, high in alcohol, is still made in the same district.

Classification of 1855

See Bordeaux.

Clean

A clean wine is one that is refreshing and agreeable, without any definite off-taste.

Château Clerc-Milon-Rothschild

Bordeaux red wine.
District: Haut-Médoc, France.
Commune: Pauillac.

Adjoining Châteaux Lafite and Mouton-Rothschild, the vineyard is a Fifth Growth (*Cinquième Cru*) of the Médoc as classified in 1855. The property was purchased by Baron Philippe de Rothschild in 1970, joining his other two Pauillac growths, Mouton-Rothschild and Mouton-Baronne-Philippe.

Characteristics. Well-made wines with typical Pauillac traits: hard at the outset, full-bodied, and quite rich.
Vineyard area: 25 hectares (62.5 acres).
Average production: 125 *tonneaux* (9,000 cases).

Climat

Burgundian term for a vineyard, equivalent of Growth (*Cru*) in Bordeaux.

Château Climens

Bordeaux white wine.
District: Sauternes, France.
Commune: Barsac.

One of the two best vineyards in Barsac—the other is Château Coutet, an eighth of a mile away—Climens stands in a winding country lane running between old stone walls and marked at turnings with golden arrows to direct visitors along the Route de Sauternes. Entitled to either of the place-names, Barsac or Sauternes, the wine often uses Barsac-Sauternes. (In the past Barsac was a celebrated district; but since 1936 the wines of the commune have been allowed to take the name of Sauternes, which has become more famous. Barsac wines are legitimate Sauternes, slightly lighter and drier.)

In 1855, the year Climens was classified a First Growth (*Premier Cru*) of Sauternes, M. Henri Gounouilhou acquired the property, and his heirs sold it in 1971 to Lucien Lurton of Brane-Cantenac and Durfort in Margaux, and Bouscaut in Graves. The unpretentious low wooden château is not lived in by the proprietors; but the *chais* across the gravel courtyard from it are large and impressive. The vineyard is four-fifths in Sémillon vine and one-fifth in Sauvignon and Muscadelle, and in the summer after the February 1956 freeze it presented a tragic picture. Most of the vines were blackened stubs, with hardly a sprout of green, and Climens vintages of 1956 and 1957 were nonexistent. Afterward, the vines began to bear again, except in those patches so badly struck they had to be replanted. All the flat-lying Sauternes vineyards were in the same plight.

Characteristics. A wine which is much better when young. It reaches the height of finesse in great years. For sheer delicacy in sweetness, the beautiful 1929s, 1947s, 1949s, and 1971s were classics. In such years, Climens possibly excels Château d'Yquem—it is lighter, with less vinosity and body, yet miraculously subtle.

Vineyard area: 30 hectares (75 acres).
Average production: 65 *tonneaux* (6,000 cases).

Château Clinet

Brodeaux red wine.
District and Commune: Pomerol, France.

Traditionally one of the best growths of Pomerol, the château is now owned by Georges Audy and makes a sound but unremarkable wine.

Vineyard area: 9 hectares (22.5 acres).
Average production: 36 *tonneaux* (3,500 cases).

Clinton

Productive American vine giving small, black, spicy grapes yielding wines suitable for blending but little else. The vine is mostly cultivated for rootstock for other vines rather than for its fruit.

Clone

A group of individual plants propagated asexually from one single source.

Clos

A walled vineyard—or a vineyard which was once enclosed by a wall. These occur mainly in Burgundy. Some of their wines are sufficiently important to be entered under individual headings. Other well-known vineyards are as follows: Le Clos (Pouilly-Fuissé); Les Clos (Chablis); Les Clos (Côte Rôtie); Clos des Arlots (Nuits-Saint-Georges-Prémeaux); Clos Blanc (Pommard); Clos de la Boudriotte (Chassagne); Clos du Chapitre (Fixin); Clos de la Commaraine (Pommard); Clos des Corvées (Nuits-Saint-Georges-Prémeaux); Clos des Ducs (Volnay); Clos des Forêts-Saint-Georges (Nuits-Saint-Georges-Prémeaux); Clos des Lambrays (Morey); Clos de la Maréchale (Nuits-Saint-Georges-Prémeaux); Clos des Mouches (Beaune); Clos du Papillon (Savennières-Loire); Clos des Perrières (Meursault); Clos des Porrets-Saint-Georges (Nuits); Clos des Réas (Vosne); Clos du Roi (Aloxe-Corton); Clos du Roi (Beaune); Clos Saint-Jacques (Gevrey); Clos Saint-Jean (Chassagne); Clos Saint-Paul (Givry); Clos Saint-Pierre (Givry).

Clos de Bèze

See Chambertin-Clos de Bèze.

Clos Fourtet

See Fourtet, Clos.

Clos Haut-Peraguey

See Haut-Peraguey.

Cloudy

Cloudiness in wine is caused by tiny particles in suspension and often clears spontaneously. This condition is sometimes brought on by a rapid and excessive change in temperature.

Coarse

Cheap California "burgundies" or most French, Italian, and Spanish *vins ordinaires* are basically coarse wines. They both have plenty of body but are completely without character or finesse.

Cobblers

In America, long iced drinks concocted with fruit juice, wine, or spirits and decorated with pieces of fruit or berries.

Cochineal

Grubs of various sorts which attack the vines (*see* Chapter Eight, p. 39).

Cochylis moth

The Cochylis pest, attacking by laying eggs on the grapes and eventually smothering them in cocoons, was formerly one of the most dangerous enemies of the vine. It was fought ineffectively by nicotine and arsenic. Now, however, the Swiss chemicals Nirosan and Gesarol, sprayed individually or used in combination with the Bordeaux mixture (copper-sulfate and chalk solution), are successful in eradicating the pest. *See* Chapter Eight, p. 39.

Cocktail

A mixed aperitif, containing spirits and served iced in small glasses. The best-known examples are the

Cocuy

Manhattan (two parts rye whisky to one of Italian vermouth, and a dash of bitters) and the Dry Martini (four parts gin or vodka and one part French vermouth—which in the United States is sometimes sprinkled in with an atomizer).

Cocuy

Venezuelan liquor from the desert plant sabila.

Coffey still

The Coffey (or patent) still, developed by the Irish inspector-general of excise whose name it bears, made possible the rapid and therefore large-scale production of grain whisky. Other patent stills, such as the Barbet and Ilye, are now also in use.

Cognac

Brandy.
District: Western France.

In 1860 a French geologist named Coquand made a trip to the Charente district of France on the Bay of Biscay, an often misty seaboard region irradiated with a strange quality of ultraviolet light. With him he took an odd companion for a scientific excursion—a professional taster of brandies and wines. From farm to farm the pair went, from one brandy warehouse to another, each pursuing his own science. Coquand, the geologist, went into the vineyard and analyzed the soil; the taster merely stayed inside and sniffed and sipped the brandy. At the end of the trip the two compared notes on the qualities and characteristics of each of the Cognac brandies—one as he had deduced them from the soil, the other as he discovered them in the grape. And their notes tallied in every single case.

Coquand had proved his theory on the relationship of the soil and the Cognac, and this changing relationship accounts completely for the division of the region into six zones—Grande Champagne, Petite Champagne, Borderies, Fins Bois, Bons Bois, and Bois Ordinaires—but it does not quite account for Cognac.

It is interesting to speculate upon the unique excellence of Cognac and its causes. To begin with, there is the chalk in the soil—the exact degree decreasing from Grande Champagne down the range of officially marked-out areas to Bois Ordinaires, the value and the quality of the brandy decreasing with it. But chalk does not create a fine wine beverage in Cognac only—it produces Champagne and Sherry too. Chalk-lime is a mother-bed for exceptional vines.

Cognac wine (or, correctly, Charente wine—the name of the town had not then overspread the district) was always sourish, it seems; but in early days it was not distilled, and the acidity had not become a virtue. English and Norse seamen used to come to the Charente not for the wine but for the salt in the region; but once they were there they bought wines as well. In the

centuries that followed, the vineyards were encouraged to overproduce. The next significant development was that the wines were boiled down—to save space in the ships which carried them away, to strengthen them before the North Sea voyage, and finally to avoid taxation, which was then on bulk. The idea was to reduce them and later on to restore them with water. Nobody could have imagined what a miraculous essence would be distilled from the hard Charente wines.

When Cognac was first distilled, sometime after 1600, other brandies were already being made in France: but where Charente wine gave a drinkable natural brandy, all other spirits—until the invention of multiple distillation a century later—had to be doctored by herb and fruit flavors to hide the bad taste. The final contributing factor to the unique perfection of Cognac was the barrel in which it was aged.

Immediately to the east above the Charente area, in the first rises of the Massif Central, where the River Charente has its source, is a forested district around Limoges, the land of Limousin oak.

When the distillation of Cognac was an art almost two hundred years old, the makers began to age the brandy in barrels of Limousin oak which happened to be at hand. The result was Cognac as we know it now. Prices these days are high, and the oak forests of the world have been combed for another wood that would do for the brandy what the Limousin oak does. But there is no substitute. "It's hard to say which is more important, the wood or the wine," they tell you in Cognac. In one hectoliter (26.4 U.S. gallons, 22 imp.) of the brandy aged twenty-five years in the oak there will be one pound of wood extract, an immense factor in the bouquet and taste of old Cognac. The oak from the forest of Tronçais in the Allier was used extensively because of its fine grain. It gave excellent results, though aging took place a little more slowly than in the Limousin oak. Tronçais oak is used less and less, since its prices are extremely high.

Until 1860 Charente brandy was not shipped in bottle, and it probably was not called Cognac. Old-timers in the industry opposed shipping in bottle, saying that since brandy ages only in wood it should travel in the barrel. True though this was, bottling the brandy for the first time gave the makers control over what would be in the bottle when it reached the consumer. This is an example of a fundamental law in wine: the surest bottle is the one that passes through the hands of middlemen with its cork in. Moreover, the name of the label of the place the brandy came from became famous, until finally the brandy was known as Cognac.

Today there may be Coñacs and Koniaks (a Greek imitation now suppressed)—but there is only one Cognac by law in France, and in many other countries. It is specifically a brandy distilled from the wine of certain varieties of grapes grown in delimited areas of the Charente and Charente-Maritime departments of France (and to a very small extent in two others) and which has been twice distilled in a pot still—never in the more common continuous still—and has then been aged.

Roughly a century ago the whole vineyard was wiped out by the vine pest phylloxera, and the industry had to be restarted. The makers, while they were doing this, realized that the many neutral spirits then being developed by multiple distillation were competing in their own market; and since, because of the growing tendency to sell in bottle, the spirit could no longer be aged abroad, the Cognac firms themselves undertook the ageing of the brandies. The financial load may be assessed when it is considered that the sale of Cognac now touches 6 billion new francs (or nearly 1 billion dollars) a year, and that a man selling five-year-old Cognac must, of course, have the full supplies for five different years in stock. If his sales were exclusively for forty-year Cognac he would demand an astronomical capital sum and warehouses of a size to cover half the Charente. With proportionately small stocks of older brandy, two firms today each hold about 52,000 barrels of old and new Cognac.

TYPES OF COGNAC

Nowadays most firms concentrate on two types of Cognac. The first is Three-Star, which amounts to about 65% of the Cognac sold. Various legends account for the star device; it began to be used about a century ago, when the blending of Cognacs to type was coming into fashion—it is said in Cognac that the first Three-Star was made and shipped for the Australian market. It is important to know that this sign does not mean that the brandy is three years old. It does, however, indicate a Cognac usually older than those designed for mixing with soda, and one always younger than a V.S.O.P. Generally, with many important firms the Three-Star has several years of barrel-age (spirits do not age in glass as wine does, so that an 1860 Cognac bottled in 1900 and a 1900 Cognac bottle in 1940 are exactly the same age).

Then there is V.S.O.P.: the letters stand for Very Superior Old Pale—somewhat contradictorily, because the longer a Cognac is left in the barrel to age the more of the darkening tannin it absorbs from the oak. It begins as a colorless liquid; tannin tans it. Very Superior Old Dark would be a more logical name.

As with Three-Star, V.S.O.P. is really a style of brandy, not a brandy of any specified age—the oldest V.S.O.P. put out by many firms may be called a Reserve, Extra, X.O., or Cordon Bleu, or one may find in rare cases a straight vintage brandy. All of these are produced in relatively small quantities.

A V.S.O.P. put out by one of the better houses may vary between five and ten years of barrel-age. It is essential to understand, however, that V.S.O.P. refers to a type; Cognac, except in the "Straight Cognacs," which are seldom made commercially now, is always a blend of brandies from different areas and different years. Each firm establishes its V.S.O.P.—the process is exactly the same for its Three-Star—and continues by skillful blending to copy the original model and so to repeat the same bottle over and over again. Master samples are kept, and with great care and art—by "sniffers," so called because they smell the Cognacs rather than taste them—diverse brandies are mixed to reproduce the sample, always from year to year in differing proportions to equalize the difference of the years. A so-called "ten-year-old" brandy is likely to contain Cognacs both older and much younger than ten years.

V.S.O.P. describes what the brandy is—i.e., a particular firm's interpretation of V.S.O.P. style. V.S.E.P. (E for Extra), formerly seen, is now disappearing from the U.S. market.

It is worth mentioning that the buyer gets greater value for his V.S.O.P. or the other older Cognacs than for Three-Star. Duty, casing, bottling, etc., are the same, and the extra cost for a much finer Cognac is often comparatively little, whereas enjoyment will be doubled.

VINTAGE AND AGE

Age is considered the great virtue in Cognac, and at present there are four age indications for the British-American market based on facts that can be checked. They are:

(1) In England, Cognac must be at least three years old by British law.

(2) In the United States, Cognac must be at least two years old by American law.

(3) V.S.O.P., by French law, must be at least four years old to be exported from France.

(4) British Bonded—Cognac shipped in cask to England and matured in the warehouses of London docks—is aged in bond, and a record of the years is kept. This record is generally authentic, and at the present time a British Bonded may be seen not only in England but also in the United States, because it bears the only age indication beyond the American legal minimum, and the Cognac can be sold at a premium which makes transhipment worth the trouble. In the trade, British Bonded is also known as "Old Landed" because it is landed before it is bottled. The style, matured in the London climate, very different from that of Cognac, has a somewhat clean, melted taste (which some people like and some do not); and it may be expected to have lost strength, as brandies do when they age in damp places. Yet some of the greatest Cognacs available today are London bottlings which have never been blended but are straight vintage brandies. Delicate with age, they often become the prototypes of great Cognac. Since the Second World War, shipment in cask to England has dwindled greatly.

The young Cognac fresh from the still is as raw and harsh as the wine was thin and acid. Its official age is designated *compte* 00. On April 1st after the distillation officially ends, only a couple of months later, the age becomes *compte* 0, and thereafter it changes every year at April 1. As of now the minimum age of three-star Cognac or its equivalent is *compte* 2, for V.S.O.P. or its equivalent it is *compte* 4, and for old Cognacs the minimum is *compte* 6. Because of the huge stocks of Cognac the producing firms have on hand, and the enormous sales volume (110–120 million bottles a year), the Bureau National du Cognac, the local regulatory agency, can keep track of Cognacs only through *compte* 6. After that, all regulation and maintenance of quality and integrity in the aging become the firm's responsibility and a matter of prestige and pride.

Cognac is aged by shippers, by farmers, and by cooperatives. There are some 175 Cognac firms, numerous cooperative distillers, and, of the approximately 50,-000 peasants and others who grow wine to make Cognac, a little over 20,000 distill and age some or all of their own product. In addition to this multiplicity of individuals, the great Cognac stores of the principal firms are spread in series of warehouses around the towns of Cognac and Jarnac and into the countryside. This is done to prevent a fire from destroying the stock; although indemnified by insurance, a firm wiped out by fire would need years to build up old brandies in order to re-establish its brands. Faced with so many owners and so many small collections of casks, Cognac authorities know that a realistic control of very old brandies is impossible. "Most of all we value public confidence and we prefer not to certify anything we can't be absolutely sure of," they rightly say.

Except for an occasional British Bonded, no Cognac can be positively identified as more than five years of age. Less and less, Cognac makers themselves like to talk about age. "We go to the impractical, enormous cost of producing a twenty-year-old Cognac," they say, "and our reward is that the public thinks it is too young because it did not travel to and from Russia with Napoleon." The brandies would be no older than the day they were bottled if they *had* been on that march to Russia; and in fact, no brandy from that time is on the commercial market. Undoubtedly, the worst deception in Cognac brandies is the fraud and fakery connected with alleged "Napoleon" brandy—though a distinction must be made between brandies pretending to derive from Napoleon's time and the Napoleon-style. The latter is an indication akin to V.S.O.P., and the Cognac will be at least six years old.

Beyond an optimum of about forty years—it depends on both the Cognac and how it is housed—barrel-ageing itself ceases to be a good thing. Cognacs from 1815 to 1850, which may still be tasted in the *paradises*—inner sanctums of the oldest casks—of firms in Jarnac and Cognac, are only echoes, although they are still useful in blends of very old Cognacs because they keep their bouquet after they have lost everything else.

The opinion in Cognac seems to be that within a dozen years V.S.O.P. brandies will not be more than ten years old and that Three-Star will dominate the output. Interest rates, duties, and taxes which double and triple the price of Cognac in most countries have made the price of a bottle so high that the makers cannot add the real cost of ageing old brandy; to do so would be to price it out of the market. A five-to-ten-year-old V.S.O.P. is already considered by many firms to be a losing proposition. The debatable question is whether small firms selling very old Cognacs to a select clientele will be able to survive. It is regrettable that Three-Star Cognacs of the smaller houses are being driven out of business as the advertising campaigns of the biggest brands gather cumulative force. Some makers believe that in a generation there will be only a half-dozen or so mammoth firms; others, while admitting that the monopolies are likely to corner Three-Star and perhaps V.S.O.P., contend that there will always be sufficient demand for brandies too old ever to be produced on a big scale, and small deluxe houses will thus be kept alive.

Vintage in Cognac brandy is a debatable point. A "straight" Cognac is the brandy of one area and one year. Blending—the nearly universal practice in Cognac—clips off the peaks to fill up the valleys. But if this were always true, all blended Cognac would be a mere compromise, a concession to marketing conditions and the demand for a stable product. But most houses in Cognac contend that no region, and seldom any year, produces by itself a fully balanced, complete, and harmonious Cognac. Granting that Grande Champagne is the best region, finest in bouquet, finesse, elegance, and charm, they point out that the Borderies sector produces Cognac known for its rapid ageing and taste of violet, and for the touch of finesse often needed in a too-princely Grande Champagne.

GRANDE CHAMPAGNE, PETITE CHAMPAGNE, FINE CHAMPAGNE, FINE MAISON, BORDERIES, AND BOIS

Vineyards as such play no role in Cognac and do not appear on labels, but the following districts are important to know and are often indicated on labels of bottles in the higher categories. The vineland of Cognac—within the boundaries of which all wine that is to become Cognac must grow—is geographically proportioned as follows:

	%
Grande Champagne	14.65
Petite Champagne	15.98
Borderies	4.53
Fins Bois	37.82
Bons Bois	22.19
Bois Ordinaires	4.83

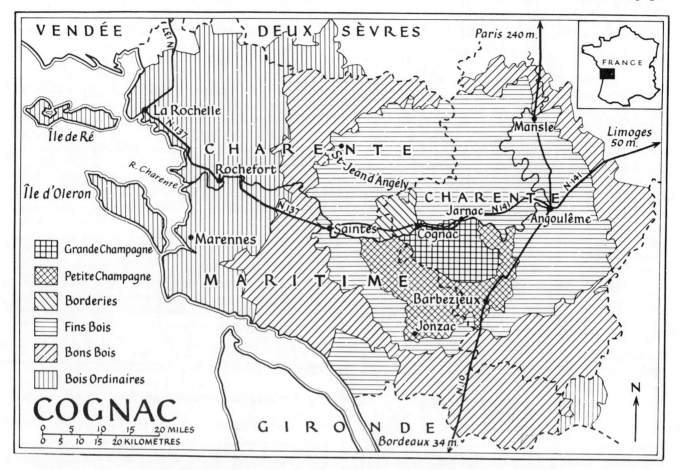

The order of quality, downward from Grande Champagne to Bois Ordinaires, is also a rough indication of the geographical order, Grande Champagne being the heart and the other zones circling it. All the districts produce some red wine (from which Cognac is never made) and some white wine which is not made into Cognac; the poorer the district the greater the proportion of these non-Cognac wines. Altogether, Cognac accounts for about half of the crude wine.

Grande Champagne (A.O.C.)

The best and the most expensive. But the difference in price is nothing like that between the wines of great vineyards and lesser ones in other famous areas. Grand Champagne has great finesse, bouquet, and elegance. But it is hard to the taste when young and must age fifteen years or longer; it has less body than Borderies but more body than Petite Champagne. It is also called Grande Fine Champagne.

Petite Champagne (A.O.C.)

Similar to Grande Champagne except that its characteristics appear in slightly lesser degree and it matures rather more quickly. The difference is due to a somewhat smaller proportion of chalk in the soil.

In France, Champagne indicates a region of chalky soil.

Fine Champagne and Fine Maison (A.O.C.)

The old blend of Cognac brandies exclusively from the Grande and Petite Champagne district. The so-called house specialty of a restaurant in France is called Fine Maison and will vary in quality, from fair to excellent, depending on the desire and ability of the restaurant to give something special.

Borderies (A.O.C.)

The district does not, as is frequently supposed, "border" the regions of Petite and Grande Champagne. It faces them—and the town of Cognac—from across the River Charente on the north. It gives the Cognacs with the greatest body.

Fins Bois (A.O.C.), Bons Bois (A.O.C.), Bois Ordinaires

The lesser zones, much larger in area but less thickly planted in vine. The Fins Bois are the finest of the three. All but a patch of the Bois Ordinaires lies along the shore, and the sea air has a tangible effect on the brandy.

OFFICIAL REGIONS OF COGNAC: COMMUNES ENTITLED TO THE MOST IMPORTANT NAMES

The zone within which Cognac may be produced is divided into six regions, of which Grande Champagne, Petite Champagne, and Borderies are the most important.

Grande Champagne (Grande Fine Champagne)

Communes: Ambleville, Angeac-Champagne, Bonneuil, Bourg-Charente (right bank of River Charente), Bouteville, Château-Bernard, Cognac (left bank of Charente), Criteuil-la-Magdeleine, Éraville, Gensac-la-Pallue, Genté, Gimeux, Gondeville, Juillac-le-Coq, Lignières-Sonneville, Mainxe, Malaville, Merpins, Salles-d'Angles, Saint-Brice (left bank of Charente), Saint-Fort-sur-le-Né, Saint-Même, Saint-Preuil, Segonzac, Touzac, Verrières, Viville.

Petite Champagne

Communes in the department of Charente: Angeac-Charente, Ars, Barbezieux, Barret, Birac, Bourg-Charente, Châteauneuf, Graves, Guimps, Jurignac, Lachaise, Ladiville, Lagarde-sur-le-Né, Montchaude, Mosnac, Nonaville, Saint-Amant-de-Graves, Saint-Bonnet, Saint-Hilaire-de-Barbezieux, Saint-Médard-de-Barbezieux, Saint-Palais-du-Né, Salles-de-Barbezieux, Vignolles.

Communes in the department of Charente-Maritime: Allas-Champagne, Archiac, Arthenac, Biron, Bougneau, Brie-sous-Archiac, Brives-sur-Charente, Celles, Chadenac, Champagnac, Cierzac, Coulonges, Clam, Échebrune, Germignac, Jarnac-Champagne, Jonzac, Lonzac, Meux, Moings, Montils, Neuillac, Neulles, Pérignac-de-Pons, Reaux, Rouffiac, Saint-Ciers-Champagne, Saint-Eugène, Saint-Germain-de-Lusignan, Saint-Germain-de-Vibrac, Saint-Lheurine, Saint-Martial-de-Coculet, Saint-Maurice-de-Vitaterne, Saint-Maurice-de-Tavernolles, Saint-Seurin-de-Palenne, Saint-Sever, Salignac-de-Pons.

Borderies

Communes: Burie, Chérac, Cherves, Cognac (right bank of River Charente), Javrezac, Louzac, Saint-André, Saint-Laurent-de-Cognac, Saint-Sulpice, Richemont.

THE VINE AND THE WINE

The vine used to be largely Saint-Émilion des Charentes or Ugni Blanc. By law, subregional Cognac—that is, entitled to one of the district names of Grande Champagne, etc.—may be distilled from wine of only the Folle Blanche, Colombard, and Saint-Émilion vines. No other grape variety is authorized by the law.

The law is very exact, and since 1955 any grower planting any part of his vineyards in unauthorized vine has had his total crop refused.

Colombard and Folle Blanche together now account for less than 6% of the total yield, nearly all of which is Saint-Émilion, a variety of Ugni Blanc. In Cognac perhaps alone, the quantity of yield does not directly affect quality; nevertheless, in order to maintain a higher standard, a maximum of 100 hectoliters per hectare (1,056 U.S. gallons, 878 imp. per acre) is imposed.

This is one indication of the peculiar relationship between the wine and the brandy. It is a local axiom that the best Cognac comes from the worst wine. Rightly understood, this is true. The wine is tart, fit only to be drunk with shellfish—or not at all, if anything better is handy. On the other hand, it must be *sound*. Distillation removes neither perfections nor imperfections—it emphasizes them; if there is a taint in the wine, the Cognac distilled from it will be undrinkable. But the virtues in wine for drinking and in wine for making Cognac are not the same. Technically the Saint-Émilion is a third-epoch vine. It is the grape called the Trebbiano in Italy and the Ugni Blanc in Algeria, in the extreme south of France, and in California. In those hotter regions—in what viticulturalists, marking off growing zones for the vine, call the Third Epoch—it is quite at home. But in Cognac, much farther north, it is not: it seldom ripens properly and gives a sourish, highly acid wine low in alcohol—which happens to be the perfect basis for the world's best brandy.

LIFE-CYCLE OF A COGNAC

The countryside, rolling and misty, infused with that special clarity of actinic sunlight said to account in part for the taste of Cognac, grows 85,000 hectares, half of which is distilled. The living unit in Cognac is not the castle but the close, a Saracen heritage. A wall encloses house, courtyard, sheds, and hen coops; it is broken only by two arched portals, which may be closed by great wooden doors.

Inside one of these domestic forts that dot the vineland, time may well seem to have stood still since the Saracens—and in a way it has. No peasant is more individual and independent than the Cognac grower. After all, he makes it his business to keep a supply of something far more stable than the fluctuating franc in his sheds.

The grapes are brought in from the vines, and the wine-making is much the same as in other regions. With the distillation, the difference—and the Cognac—begins.

The wine is heated in a massive fixed copper kettle sitting in its bed—a square brick furnace—and after a time the furious brandy elements pass up as steam into the gracefully curved "swan-throat." Condensed by cooling, the steam becomes the *brouillis*—a milky liquid with an alcoholic strength of from 27% to 28%. The process is repeated, and this time the "head," which comes over first, and the "tail," which comes last, are eliminated—and only the "heart" of the distillate is used. This is the infant Cognac, raw and unsophisticated, a white brandy of 70% alcohol per volume.

In spite of the seeming timelessness of the walled houses and the way of life, there have been changes here as everywhere else. All through the winter patient men and women must sit beside the pot stills—and the older generation was more willing to do this than the young people are. More and more shippers are finding that they must do their own distilling because the farmers' sons and daughters won't stay beside the stills.

Once distilled, Cognac goes into a Limousin oak barrel—not too full, so that the liquid may be in contact with oxygen, and in a spot which is to some extent affected by outside temperatures. In theory, the Cognac goes into a new barrel for a year, at which time it is transferred to one that still has some tannin left. Interestingly, the discarded barrel has absorbed 12 liters of Cognac. In practice, to overcome this loss, about half of the Cognac is put into new barrels and the other half straight into used barrels. In this way the brandy absorbs enough tannin from the new oak but does not stay in contact with it too long. Ideally, the cask should be made from a tree eighty to a hundred years old, which in turn has been aged for five or six years in open air to lose its harshest tannin. Only Limousin oak and that from the Tronçais forest in the Allier department may be used—and it must be weathered four or five years out-of-doors beforehand. The price for a single stave has now climbed so high that peasant-growers tend to put their brandies into old barrels to save buying new ones, and a less aged Cognac is the result. (The ability to meet the high cost of old casks is one more advantage Cognac shippers have over the growers.)

During the ageing period, various changes occur: a decrease in the volume of the brandy, a change in degree of alcohol, dissolution of tannins. At the same time there are less evident chemical changes: hydrolysis, acetylization, and the development of the rancid taste.

Blending is always done in the establishments of the shippers—some are as large and grim as prisons, others may be converted medieval castles. Barrels of different Cognacs are opened over gutters in the floor above the blending vats. The liquid streams into the vat below, where great paddles moved by machinery slowly turn and agitate it. Blending is done a stage at a time, with long halts between to let the brandies rest. Slowly they "marry."

In about half a century evaporation will reduce a new Cognac of 70% to the proper drinking and shipping strength of 40%. Because it is not economically possible to wait for this natural process, Cognac must be "reduced" before bottling. This is done by adding distilled water either directly or indirectly. Since the draft of water tends to shock the brandy, a few of the better firms reduce indirectly by means of *faible*, or weak brandy—Cognac which has been brought down by distilled water to about 27% and then given a long rest. Fit again, it is used to reduce other Cognacs—even then reduction is only 8% or 9% at a time. (The brandy is filtered and allowed to rest after each operation.) The more elaborate process and the addition of the *faible* increase the bitterness and loss by evaporation. This is the costly element in Cognac-making: the special porousness of the Limousin oak which allows the brandy to ripen also lets in air—and so it lets out the brandy. The loss by evaporation into the sky above the Charente is almost precisely the yearly figure of consumption in France and one-fourth of that throughout the world.

The Cognacs age in low, above-ground storehouses called *chais*, easily distinguishable by the blackening on the walls, which looks like soot but is a wine fungus. The casks or *tierçons* hold from 350 to 450 liters (90 to 120 U.S. gallons, 75 to 100 imp.). Some makers contend that ageing in the bigger barrel is better, others dispute this. At the end of each row of barrels is the *chanteau*—usually marked *CH*—the partly empty barrel used to replenish the others. Evaporation is encouraged, expensive as it is, for without it there would be no ageing, and the sheds are airy.

When it is ready, the brandy is put into a bottle which has been rinsed with Cognac, and a cork which has been dipped in Cognac is flogged home. It is ready to go out to the world.

EXPORT

Roughly 90% of Cognac is exported. The United States is the largest customer, and Britain the second largest. Cognac brings in the largest revenue of any French agricultural product exported.

Sales are going up in both Britain and the U.S.—annual import has passed 2,600,000 cases in the U.S. and is approaching 1,500,000 cases in Britain.

All wines and spirits in France must have a tax certificate (*acquit*), even if they are moving only from one warehouse to another. By this means, every movement can be traced. An adaptation of the domestic French *congé* is the *Acquit Jaune d'Or* which now accompanies every Cognac shipment exported. Though originally devised to expedite processes of export, the yellow-gold certificate in effect guarantees the important specifications of the brandy.

Cointreau

A famous proprietary liqueur of the Curaçao type made in Angers, France, and in the United States by the Cointreau family. Although the bottle and label are always identical, the alcoholic content varies from country to country. The original name for it was Triple Sec White Curaçao, but so many makers started using the name Triple Sec that it was changed to Cointreau.

See Curaçao.

Colares, Collares

Port wine apart, this is the most distinctive wine of Portugal. Grown on sandy vineyards overlooking the Atlantic, a forty-minute drive from Lisbon, the wine achieved prominence during the invasion of the vine pest phylloxera, which devastated world viticulture about twenty years before the end of the last century. Sand-grown wines were immune and thus sold at an enormous premium during the phylloxera wine drought. A liking for the wine itself (which was once often matured in Angola mahogany or American redwood for as long as a decade and a half) is an acquired habit, for it has an individual taste.

See Portugal.

Collage

The fining process to which wine must be subjected before it is ready to be bottled.

See Chapter Nine, p. 38; Fining.

Collar

Label on bottle neck. The French term is *collerette*.

Colli Albani (D.O.C.)

White, sometimes sparkling wines from Latium *(q.v.)*.

Colli Euganei (D.O.C.)

Light red or white wines from southern Veneto in Italy.

See Veneto.

Colli Orientali del Friuli (D.O.C.)

Red or dry white wines from northeast Italy.

See Friuli-Venezia-Giulia.

Collio (D.O.C.)

A dry, white, slightly sparkling wine from the north of Italy. Also known as Collio Goriziano.

See Friuli-Venezia-Giulia.

Collioure (A.O.C.)

Red wine.

District: Côtes de Roussillon.

The Appellation Contrôlée of Collioure is given to the "natural" red table wines of the Banyuls region, just north of the Spanish border on the Mediterranean coast. The sweet fortified aperitif or dessert wine from the same area has its own place-name—Banyuls *(q.v.)*. Grenache Noire and Carignane grapes are grown on 100 hectares (250 acres), which gives the wine the additional place-name of Collioure de Grenache. The average annual production is 2,000 hectoliters (53,-000 U.S. gallons, 44,000 imp.).

Colmar

Wine town in Alsace.

See Alsace.

Colombard

White wine grape grown in the Dauphiné region, where it is also known as Bon Blanc; in Charente as Pied-Tendre; and in Tarn-et-Garonne as Blanquette.

Colombia

There are an estimated 2,000 hectares (5,000 acres) of vineyard in Colombia, producing some 38,000 hectoliters (1 million U.S. gallons, 850,000 imp.) of wine, some sweet and the rest for brandy. These are generally called vermouth and Muscatel or miscalled "manzanilla" and "port." Some light table wines are made too, but these are also distinctly sweet.

Fruits such as apples, cherries, and blackberries provide the flavoring for most of the alcoholic beverages, and the making of spirits is a monopoly of the provincial governments. Aguardiente (with aniseed), rum, and types of vodka and gin are produced in parts of the country; but the more popular drinks are vodka among the influential classes, and Guarapo and aguardiente among the others. Anisado is a sugar-cane alcohol flavored with aniseed, while Guarapo is made from fermented sugar-cane and lemon juice. Guarapo is not commercially sold, and generally constitutes a homemade beverage for the peasants in certain regions of the country; when fresh, it has some resemblance to new apple cider.

Color in spirits

Spirits and liqueurs are by nature colorless, and the color is added after they leave the still. They may darken somewhat in the barrel, but most tawny spirits take their color from a dose of caramel; and the green color of crème-de-menthe is likewise added.

Comète, Vin de la (comet wine)

It sometimes happens that a good vintage year is glorified by the appearance of a comet. One such year was 1630, but 1811, more famous (and not so long ago), was the vintage usually referred to as the "comet year."

Commandaria

The longest-lasting wine, and one of the best wines, of Cyprus.
See Cyprus.

Commanderie du Bontemps de Médoc et de Graves (Bordeaux)

The local wine society and promotional organization of the Médoc now includes Graves and is composed of growers, shippers, and various dignitaries interested in wine. Dressed up in medieval caps and long robes, the members hold meetings, inauguration ceremonies, and luncheons.

Common Clean

The light style of Jamaican rum.
See Rum, Jamaican.

Commonwealth wines

Wines from British Commonwealth countries, notably Australia, Canada, and New Zealand *(qq.v.)*. Not of the same quality as European fine wines, they are not in the same price class either and may prove extremely enjoyable—if unexceptional—and inexpensive drinking.

Commune

In France, a parish or township. In the fine wine areas, the wines of a district clustered around one or more parishes are likely to take the name of the commune as an official place-name or Appellation Contrôlée—meaning they are legally recognized to have a certain similarity and certain standards of quality. For example, Margaux, Saint-Julien, Saint-Émilion are important commune names in Bordeaux red wine.

Coñac

Designation improperly used for Spanish brandy.
See Spain.

Concord

The most important blue-black grape of the American East Coast, hardy and productive, adaptable to an astonishing variety of soils and climates, but yielding incredibly mediocre wine—which is, however, widely sold throughout the United States, either blended with others or as kosher wine—sweet, strong, and utterly undistinguished. Concord wine is known for its pronounced foxy taste and aroma.

Condrieu (Appellation Contrôlée)

Rhône Valley white wine.
District: Rhône Valley, France.

The wines are heavily perfumed, with a distinctive taste—or *goût de terroir*—picked up from the granitic soil of the vineyards, and are practically unknown outside the district. The output is small—less than twenty-five thousand cases per year, made from the Viognier grape. Modern methods of vinification and early bottling are doubtless responsible for the fruitiness of the wines; and their rising reputation is due to the patronage of the late widow Point, owner of the great Michelin ex-three-star restaurant the Pyramide, at Vienne, south of Lyon.

Confrérie

French term for wine society.
See Wine societies.

Congé

Official French document which accompanies shipments of wines and spirits and indicates that internal taxes have been paid. It is used when wines or spirits are sent to a wholesaler, retailer, or to the consumer, inside the country—but not for export. There are about six different types of *congé*, distinguished by different initials and colors for various types of wine—e.g., the green ARB for wines of Appellation d'Origine; the gold 4B for Cognac and Armagnac. For shipments on which taxes have not been paid, the *acquit (q.v.)* is used.

Congenerics, congeners

Distilling term for the characteristics of taste and aroma retained by distilled spirits coming from the material distilled. When distillation is done at a very high proof the spirit will carry over less congenerics and will be more "neutral" than if distilled at a low proof.

Connétablie de Guyenne

Society devoted to the promotion of white sweet wines in the Bordeaux region. The members are descendants, or supposed descendants, of the *connétables* (constables) of Bordeaux who, in the Middle Ages, judged the wines passing on the river and decreed whether or not they could go to market.
See Premières Côtes de Bordeaux.

Consorzio

Italian term for a group of wine growers and shippers who have banded together to introduce some control on the use of a place-name in Italian wines. Voluntary organizations are formed in which members are bound to respect the geographical limits imposed on the wine in question and to observe certain minimum standards of quality. For this they get a seal—which differs with each *consorzio*—to put on the neck of every bottle. The seals have a distinctive design and are consecutively numbered. A brief discussion of *consorzi* can be found in the section on Italian wines, and a discussion of the workings of a typical *consorzio* appears under Tuscany.

See Italy; Tuscany.

Constantia

Celebrated Cape wines which were already being exported from South Africa by the beginning of the nineteenth century.

See South Africa.

Consumo

Portuguese term for ordinary wine.

Cooper

(1) A craftsman who makes casks.
(2) A merchant occupied with the sampling and bottling of wine.
(3) An English drink made from a mixture of stout and porter.

As a verb, "cooper" has two meanings:
(1) To make or repair casks.
(2) To stow away in casks.

Cooperage

General term for casks or the manufacture and repair of casks or barrels; the fee charged for the work done by a cooper.

See Appendix C, p. 631.

Cooperative

A jointly owned and operated winery or cellar common in Europe and the rest of the world. These arrangements usually begin as a small operation for a few producers who need expensive equipment for wine-making and marketing networks. Some always remain modest in size, but other cooperatives are among the largest wineries in the world.

Copper Sulfate

A copper salt, also called blue stone, used in fungicidal sprays. $CuSO_45H_2O$.

Corbières (Appellation Contrôlée)

The Corbières is the last vineyard region in the Languedoc Province before the beginning of the Roussillon vineyards. In the north, its 13,000 hectares (32,500 acres) of vines stretch from Narbonne nearly to the fortified *cité* of Carcassonne, and in the south to the northern border of the Roussillon. In 1986 the Corbières achieved being elevated from a V.D.Q.S. (*vins délimités de qualité supérieure*) to an *appellation d'origine contrôlée* status. About 500,000 hectoliters (13.2 million U.S. gallons, 11 million imp.) is produced annually. Ninety-five percent of the wine is red, 4% is rosé, and 1% white.

Recent developments in the Corbières region, such as *maceration carbonique*, vineyard parceling, and better vatroom techniques, have greatly improved the quality of the wines produced there.

Cordial

A beverage compounded from spirits with fruit or aromatic substances added by a variety of methods such as maceration, steeping, or simply by mixing. They are always sweetened. The word has come to be almost synonymous with liqueur.

Cordon

Method of training vines. Usually, the trunk of the plant is bent sideways to run parallel with the ground, and is supported by a wire or style. The number of canes that grow up and down from this trunk, as well as the number of buds on each cane, may be regulated.

See Chapter Eight, p. 35.

Corkage

A fee charged for opening and serving a customer's own bottle in a restaurant or hotel, or sometimes an additional charge made on any bottle that is opened and consumed on the premises.

Corkscrew

Any device used for extracting corks; in its most traditional and simplest form, only a wire spiral affixed to some sort of handle. The variations on this idea are seemingly endless, as are the modern substitutes.

More important than any of the attendant gadgetry is the screw itself. For fine wines whose bottles usually have longer than average corks, it is essential that the metal spiral be between 2¼ and 2¾ inches in length, long enough to get a good grip through all of the cork. The metal should be round like a thin wire and tapered into an open spiral, without a sharp cutting edge, which could shred the cork when it is removed. The tip is best rather sharp and fashioned so that it is not centered in the spiral.

Screws with levers and double-screw arrangements can be helpful as long as the spiral itself is well designed. Recent use of a needle to pierce the cork, injecting gas underneath it, and thus pushing the stopper out, does work if the needle is long enough to get all the way through the cork. These inventions may be a bit farfetched, but they can bring out a friable cork in one piece.

Corky or corked wine

Spoiled by a bad cork. The defect originates in the cork; it can happen to any wine if a faulty cork is used. The French term for corky is *bouchonné*.

Cornas

Rhône Valley red wine.
District: Rhône Valley, France.

The wine is never great, often good, and seldom expensive. It is red, comes from Syrah grapes, and contains the characteristics generally expected of the Rhône Valley (*see* Rhône), although not to the same exalted degree as some of its neighbors, such as Hermitage. It is usually good value, however.

As is the case throughout the Côtes du Rhône, the vines grow on terraced plots carefully built into slopes so steep they must be cultivated by hand. There are some 40 hectares (100 acres) of vineyard, and annual production averages some 1,300 hectoliters (34,000 U.S. gallons, 28,300 imp.).

Coronata

Thin, light, white Italian wine.
See Liguria.

Corowa

Vineyard region in New South Wales.
See Australia.

Corsé

French term used of a robust full-bodied wine.

Corsica

The island of Corsica, a department of France, lies to its south and to the west of Italy in the Mediterranean Sea, and the climate is almost ideal for growing vines. Climate is not the only vital factor in agriculture, however; and of the island's 850,000 hectares (2,125,000 acres), only 26,000 hectares (65,000 acres) are in vines.

The wines produced are not of any high degree of quality, with the exception of a very few grown around the principal city of Ajaccio (Domaine Péraldi) and a few more around Sartène. Most Corsican wines are rough and common, haphazardly vinified, and improperly cared for. Corsican wines were greatly improved through the immigration of hundreds of hard-working knowledgeable settlers (*pieds-noirs*) from Algeria who have now left, having been given a hard time by the local Corsicans. Corsica does not generally make enough for its own consumption; and in many years wines must be imported, the major sources being Algeria, the mainland of France, and Tunisia. Much of this wine is drunk by the tourists who flood the island for about two and a half months each year, most of them more interested in the island's savage beauty than in the wines it can offer.

Among the better wines of Corsica are those grown on the Cap Corse, the peninsula which points like a finger at the French Côte d'Azur. The best are the whites and rosés, and these, the Corsicans say, were the preferred wines of the island's most spectacular son, Napoleon Bonaparte. The peninsula is also noted for the only considerable wine export of Corsica—the fortified, wine-based aperitif Cap Corse, about 3,400 hectoliters (90,000 U.S. gallons, 75,000 imp.) of which are sent to the mainland of France each year. Other wines (mostly white) are grown around Bastia, around Corte in the center of the island (red and white), Ajaccio and Cauro (white and rosé), and the southern towns of Sartène, Santa-Lucia-di-Tallano, and Bonifacio (red and white). The best wines of Corsica are the red Domaine Péraldi (Sciacarello) and Patrimonio Rosé, grown near Bastia. Patrimonio wines are given the A.O.C., and another new Appellation Contrôlée includes the other good Corsican wines. All these wines have a distinct flavor and are higher in alcohol than the inexperienced drinker expects. Corsican wines are often compared to those of the Côtes du Rhône and the Côtes de Provence, although not as good. All supplies and equipment needed to care for vineyards and for wines must be brought in from France, and it is one of the problems of Corsica that it has little to export in return.

Most of the vines cultivated on the island are of Italian rather than French origin; they include Moscata, Aleatico, Vermentino (a variety of the Malvasia or Malvoisie), Genovesella, Sciaccarello, Biancone, Nielluco, Grenache, and Biancolella. The amount of Corsican wine made each year is almost impossible to estimate—so much of it is drunk on the spot—but it is something like 1,500,000 hectoliters (39 million U.S. gallons, 30 million imp.).

Cortaillod

The best red wine of Neuchâtel—its well-known vineyard is Cru de la Vigne du Diable.
See Switzerland.

Cortese

White-wine grape of Italy, which produces a dry light wine: Cortese dell'Alto Monferrato.
See Piedmont.

Corton

Burgundy red and white wines.
District: Côte de Beaune, France.

Corton-Charlemagne

Commune: Aloxe-Corton.
Official Classification: Great Growth (Grand Cru).

From the little town of Aloxe (pronounced Alosse), the vineyard road meanders down to Beaune. This small district produces the finest red wines of the Côte de Beaune, and the best of the Corton vineyards are Le Corton, Corton-Bressandes, and Corton-Clos du Roi. There is a great white wine also, more vigorous and perfumed than Meursault to the south, but elegant and delicate; and Corton-Charlemagne is one of the great white growths of the Côte de Beaune. Corton, like most vineyards in Burgundy, is cut up into parcels, and some of the largest slices are owned by the excellent shipper Louis Latour and by the Prince de Mérode. Wine from five parcels in Aloxe is auctioned in the Hospices de Beaune sale as Cuvée Dr. Peste and as Charlotte Dumay, after the benefactors who gave the land to the Hospices. On the label, the great name of Corton precedes that of any other fine vineyard, such as Corton-Bressandes, Corton-Clos du Roi and Corton-Charlemagne. Great wines take the name of the famous vineyard rather than that of the commune. Le Corton covers some 78 hectares (193 acres). About 30% of the production is in white wine.

Corton-Charlemagne (Appellation Contrôlée)

Burgundy white wine.
District: Côte de Beaune, France.
Commune: Aloxe-Corton.
Official Classification: Great Growth (Grand Cru).

This is one of the great white Burgundies—at its best it is in the class of the illustrious Montrachet. Since production is small, in comparison with the worldwide demand (24.7 hectares—61.5 acres), this is a rare wine, rich, with great breed, not as soft as the white Meursaults, and more steely. Corton-Charlemagne, made exclusively from the noble Chardonnay grape (at one time, the lesser sections could be planted in the coarser Aligoté, but this is no longer allowed), is big and of a golden color. The vineyard is divided into three parts: two of the principal owners are the estimable shippers Louis Latour and Louis Jadot; the rest belongs to half a dozen or so very fine growers, the most considerable of whom produces about 200 cases, the smallest only 14 cases. This splendid wine, unfortunately, is slowly shrinking in quantity, mainly because the vines planted on the steep slopes must be tended by hand, and after heavy rains the workers have to haul back the soil on their own backs, since horses and oxen cannot climb here. This is a form of hard labor which does not appeal to the younger generation of *vignerons.*

See Aloxe-Corton.

Château Cos d'Estournel

Bordeaux red wine.
District: Haut-Médoc, France.
Commune: Saint-Estèphe.

Owned by the Prats family since 1970, and before them by Pierre Ginestet, former proprietor of Château Margaux, the estate is directly across the vineyard road—which is the commune boundary between Saint-Estèphe and Pauillac—from Château Lafite. Classified a Second Growth (*Second Cru*) in 1855, Cos d'Estournel is certainly one of the greatest of the great Seconds. Typical of Saint-Estèphe, it is a big, hard wine which, under the able direction of Bruno Prats (grandson of M. Fernand Ginestet), is one of the most popular Classified Growths in the Médoc. According to the Ginestets, the name Cos was given to the vineyard by the Templar Knights returning from the Crusades, which had taken them to Rhodes and its neighboring island, Cos. M. Prats thinks the name is a phonetic distortion of "Caux," as the name appears on an eighteenth-century map. The vineyards rise comparatively high above Pauillac, and the château itself, a charming Chinese gothic fantasy unique in the Médoc, dominates the landscape. During the Second World War, the little pagodas which decorate the vineyard walls served the Germans as anti-aircraft batteries. They were destroyed but have since been restored. The present owners have compounded the exotic appearance of the château by adding to the main entrance a carved door once owned by the Sultan of Zanzibar.

Characteristics. The wines reflect the position of the vineyard—halfway between Pauillac and Saint-Estèphe. They are lighter and more supple than the other important Saint-Estèphes but are still full and rich, with a tendency to fatness, or *gras,* and have a great finesse.

Vineyard area: 60 hectares (150 acres).
Average production: 275 *tonneaux* (25,000 cases).

Château Cos-Labory

Bordeaux red wine.
District: Haut-Médoc, France.
Commune: Saint-Estèphe.

The only Fifth Growth (*Cinquième Cru*) in Saint-Estèphe as the great vineyards were classified in 1855, Cos-Labory is very well situated on the high-rising roll of hills on the boundary line of Pauillac and Saint-Estèphe. Its two neighbors are Château Lafite, just over the line in Pauillac, and Château Cos-d'Estournel. With the latter vineyard, it was once the common property of a London owner, Mr. Martyn; but it belongs now to Cécile Audoy, assisted by her son Bernard.

Characteristics. The wines are well rounded. A typical Saint-Estèphe.

Vineyard area: 15 hectares (37 acres).
Average production: 60 *tonneaux* (5,000 cases).

Cosecha

Spanish for harvest; indicates vintage year on Spanish wines—i.e., *cosecha* 1979, *cosecha* 1982.

Costières-du-Gard (Appellation Contrôlée)

Red, white, and rosé wines from the fantastically productive Hérault area of southern France. The 3,450 hectares (8,625 acres) produce 2 million cases. The wines may be made from any or all of eighteen different grape varieties and are at their best much better than a good *vin ordinaire*.

Cot

Another name for the Malbec grapevine; also known as Pied-Rouge, Cahors, etc.

Côte

French term for a slope with vineyards. When used to designate a wine—as Côtes du Rhône, Côte de Nuits, etc.—it will usually mean a wine of lesser quality than a Clos, Château, or other wine indicated by a specific vineyard name.

Côte de Beaune (Appellation Contrôlée)

Burgundy red and dry white wines.
District: Côte d'Or, France.

Although 80% of the 150,000 hectoliters (3,960,-000 U.S. gallons, 3,285,000 imp.) annually produced is red, the slope is chiefly famous for its dry white wines, the greatest of which come from the southern end, the unofficial Côte de Meursault or Côte des Blancs. In fact, however, both red and white are made throughout, and either may be superb.

The slope, the southern or lower half of the Côte d'Or, begins at Ladoix, a long stone's throw from the end of the Côte de Nuits, and runs some fifteen miles, 25 kilometers, to just below Santenay. The name derives from its major city, ancient Beaune, the "Capital of Burgundian Wines," which stands in the same relationship to wine-shippers as Chicago does to meat-packers. Beaune is simple even for the most stubbornly non-Gallic tongue, whereas many of the other Burgundian place-names look quite formidable. One apocryphal story is that a well-known London wine-merchant habitually introduced his apprentices to Burgundies with this terse advice: "There are two kinds of Burgundy: Beaune and the rest. We sell Beaune." Masssive though its output may be, however, all that is Côte de Beaune is not necessarily Beaune.

The slope is composed of nineteen separate communes, whose wines, ranging in quality from indifferent to incomparable, are sold under a variety of names. Some bottles have only the name of a single exceptional vineyard, signifying that the wine is from grapes grown only in that vineyard, that the vineyard is one which the French authorities consider among the very greatest of Burgundy (there are eight on the Côte de Beaune), and that the wine has attained the quality commensurate with the name. Slightly lower in the legal hierarchy is wine sold with the name of a commune followed by that of a vineyard. The minimum standards are rather lower than those for the greatest wines, but the difference is often impossible to detect—in many cases these wines equal or even better their own renowned cellar-mates. The lesser wines of the Côte are sold with the name of the commune of origin and nothing more. This is the skeleton of the slope's system of nomenclature, but there are always a few variations and exceptions.

Bottles will sometimes be found bearing the word "Cuvée" followed by someone's name, signifying that it is wine from Beaune's Hospices or Charity Hospital and comes from a vineyard donated by the person indicated (*see* Hospices de Beaune). By the time this wine gets to the consumer, it is usually higher in price than any of its peers—usually too high—in spite of the fact that the annual November auction sale of wines at the Hospices de Beaune traditionally sets the price standards for the entire Côte d'Or. To console him for the price he has paid, the buyer has the double pleasure of getting a good wine, provided it has not been falsified, and contributing to a worthy charity at the same time.

Another name sometimes found on bottle labels is Côte de Beaune-Villages, used to indicate a blend of wines from two or more communes along the slope. Very occasionally, labels will have the name of a commune follwed by Côte de Beaune. The appendage has little real significance and the wine may be considered the same as any other bearing simply the name of the commune concerned.

As is particularly true throughout Burgundy, it is difficult to generalize about the wine. Most red wine is reasonably light and fast-maturing, delicate, and full of perfume, but exception must be made for red Corton from the commune Aloxe-Corton, a wine which is noble and full, of a resplendent deep-red color, and one of the longest-lasting in Burgundy. White wines from the Côte de Beaune are always dry, but there is a world of difference between the great whites of Aloxe-Corton, on the northern end of the slope, and those from the Côte de Meursault to the south. Even within the Côte de Meursault, wines from Meursault itself will differ markedly from those of Puligny-Montrachet and Chassagne-Montrachet next door, the former tending to be delicate and feminine, the latter more austere. Yet all come from the same grape variety and all are vinified in much the same way, perhaps proving that if there is any justification for the abundance of wine names in Burgundy, it is simply in this very obvious truism: that two vines of the same family may be planted within less than half a mile of each other and the fruit each gives will not resemble that given by the other. If any general summary of the wines of the Côte de Beaune were to be made, it would be that, at their best, the white wines are without peer in the entire world; the reds cede top honors to their counterparts of the Côte de Nuits.

CÔTE DE BEAUNE SOIL

Geologically, the slope is composed of three types of soil, dating from different periods of the Jurassic age; but of these only two are important to the wines. Bathonian-era soil, consisting of a base of hard rock topped with a thin layer of earth and sometimes with a whitish marl, is found to some extent in the vineyards of Beaune and Pommard. The whitish marl assumes more importance in the Côte de Meursault, where it forms the best soil for grapes grown for white wines. Soil from the Oxfordian era tends to leave an iron-rich oolite at the base of the slopes, and grapes grown in it give light red wines with a pronounced bouquet. As this soil climbs the slopes, it turns grayish, its clay content increases, and the resulting grapes ferment into red wines with enormous finesse and elegance, but full and rich and beautifully balanced. Corton is the prime example. But even where this soil is at its grayest, it nevertheless preserves the iron-imparted tinge of red, with the result that the difference between vineyards giving grapes for fine red wines and those producing white is immediately apparent: the soil color is the exact indication. Perhaps nowhere else in the world is this difference so marked or so dramatic.

LEGAL WINE STANDARDS

Côte de Beaune wine must—as is the case with all French wines of Appellation Contrôlée—attain certain minimum standards before it is granted the right to any legal place-name. These standards vary according to the vineyard where the grapes were grown. Six of them have the right to carry only vineyard name and the words Great Growth (*Grand Cru*) if the wines meet the high standards required; these are asterisked on the list on this page. The other wines are communal First Growths (*Premiers Crus*) if they stem from the better vineyards, or simple communal wines. Any wine not meeting the standards for the name for which it is theoretically qualified is declassified into the highest rank for which it can qualify, but there is no advancement; no First Growth may ever be sold as a Great Growth no matter how good the wine. The standards are:

RED WINES

Great Growths (Grands Crus)

(1) Wine must be made exclusively from Pinot Noir, Pinot Liebault, and Pinot Beurot grapes. A maximum of 15% Pinot Blanc or Chardonnay grapes may be used at the discretion of the wine-maker.
(2) Production must not exceed 50 hectoliters per hectare (1,320.9 U.S. gallons, 1,099.9 imp. per acre) of vines.
(3) Each year a special extra allowance is made and is determined by the size and quality of the harvest.

First Growths (Premiers Crus)

(1) Same grape varieties as for Great Growths.
(2) Production must not exceed 35 hectoliters per hectare (374.1 U.S. gallons, 311.5 imp. per acre).
(3) Wine must contain at least 11% of alcohol.

Communal Wines

(1) Same grape varieties as for other *appellations.*
(2) Production must not exceed 50 hectoliters per hectare (528.4 U.S. gallons, 440 imp. per acre).
(3) Wine must contain at least 10.5% of alcohol.

WHITE WINES

Great Growths (Grands Crus)

(1) Only Chardonnay (also called Beaunois and Aubaine) grapes may be used.
(2) Production must not exceed 50 hectoliters per hectare (528.4 U.S. gallons, 440 imp. per acre).
(3) With the high demand for white Burgundy, the special allowance of 50 hectoliters per hectare is periodically changed.

First Growths (Premiers Crus)

(1) Only the Chardonnay vine may be used.
(2) Production must not exceed 36 hectoliters per hectare (380 U.S. gallons, 316.7 imp. per acre).
(3) Wine must contain at least 11.5% alcohol.

Communal Wines

(1) Only Chardonnay grapes may be used.
(2) Production must not exceed 50 hectoliters per hectare (528.4 U.S. gallons, 440 imp. per acre).
(3) Wine must contain 11% of alcohol.
See separately under the respective communes: Aloxe-Corton, Savigny-Les-Beaune, Beaune, Pommard, Volnay, Chassagne-Montrachet, Puligny-Montrachet, Meursault. *See also these Côte-de-Beaune communes*: Pernand-Vergelesses, Ladoix-Serrigny, Chorey-les-Beaune, Saint-Romain, Monthélie, Auxey-Duresses, Saint-Aubin, Santenay, Dezize-les-Maranges, Sampigny-les-Maranges, Cheilly-les-Maranges

Côte de Beaune-Villages (Appellation Contrôlée)

A very general name for Burgundian wines. To gain the use of it, wines must be a blend of two or more red wines of at least 10.5% of alcohol and must have title

OUTSTANDING VINEYARDS—RED WINES

Vineyard	Commune
*Le Corton	Aloxe-Corton
Le Clos du Roi	Aloxe-Corton
Les Renardes	Aloxe-Corton
Les Chaumes	Aloxe-Corton
Les Bressandes	Aloxe-Corton
Clos Saint-Jean	Chassagne-Montrachet
Clos de la Boudriotte	Chassagne-Montrachet
Clos Morgeot	Chassagne-Montrachet
Les Vergelesses	Savigny-les-Beaune
Les Marconnets	Savigny-les-Beaune
Les Santenots	Meursault
Les Fèves	Beaune
Les Grèves	Beaune
Les Marconnets	Beaune
Les Bressandes	Beaune
Les Clos des Mouches	Beaune
Aux Cras	Beaune
Les Champimonts	Beaune
Les Épenots	Pommard
Les Rugiens	Pommard
Les Jarollières	Pommard
Le Clos Blanc	Pommard
Les Pézerolles	Pommard
Clos-de-la-Commaraine	Pommard
Les Caillerets	Volnay
Les Champans	Volnay
Les Fremiets	Volnay
Les Angles	Volnay

OUTSTANDING VINEYARDS —WHITE WINES

Vineyard	Commune
*Le Montrachet (in part)	Puligny-Montrachet
*Le Montrachet (in part)	Chassagne-Montrachet
*Chevalier-Montrachet	Puligny-Montrachet
*Bâtard-Montrachet (in part)	Puligny-Montrachet
*Bâtard-Montrachet (in part)	Chassagne-Montrachet
*Bienvenue-Bâtard-Montrachet	Puligny-Montrachet
*Criots-Bâtard-Montrachet	Chassagne-Montrachet
Les Combettes	Puligny-Montrachet
Les Pucelles	Puligny-Montrachet
Les Chalumeaux	Puligny-Montrachet
Blagny-Blanc	Puligny-Montrachet
Les Ruchottes	Chassagne-Montrachet
Clos des Perrières	Meursault
Les Perrières	Meursault
Les Charmes	Meursault
Les Genevrières	Meursault
*Corton-Charlemagne	Aloxe-Corton
*Le Corton	Aloxe-Corton

to one of the place-names listed below. There will be enormous variation in the amount made in any year, following the decisions and speculations of the wine-shippers who do the blending and the amount of wine to stem from the various communes concerned. This can be anything between 5,000 and 7,000 hectoliters (132,500 to 185,000 U.S. gallons, 110,000 to 154,000 imp.). The place-names which have the right to be used for this minor Côte de Beaune wine are:

Auxey-Duresses	Meursault Blagny
Blagny	Monthélie
Chassagne-Montrachet	Pernand-Vergelesses
Cheilly-les-Maranges	Puligny-Montrachet
Chorey-les-Beaune	Saint-Aubin
Côte de Beaune	Saint-Romain
Dezize-les-Maranges	Sampigny-les-Maranges
Ladoix-Serrigny	Santenay
Meursault	Savigny-les-Beaune

Côte des Blancs

A ridge to the south of the Champagne district planted in white Pinot and Chardonnay grapes. The principal towns are Avize, Cramant, and Mesnil.
See Champagne.

Côte de Brouilly (Appellation Contrôlée)

Côte de Brouilly red wines are from the heart or best section of Brouilly in Beaujolais, Burgundy.
See Beaujolais.

Côte de Nuits

Burgundy red and dry white wines.
District: Côte d'Or, France.

The Côte de Nuits stretches for about 19 kilometers (12 miles) along the Côte d'Or, south of Fixin, and ends on the verge of a stone quarry just below Nuits-Saint-Georges, the principal town, from which it takes its name. Some of the vineyards planted on the slope are, within carefully defined limits, among the best in the world.

The natural hazards which can make wine production as uncertain as any other form of crop farming are particularly troublesome in this small area—the only district in which the Pinot Noir grape will, in favorable circumstances, give its best. Farther north, it would yield a thinner, harder wine; farther south, one which would be softer and less robust. Even in the Côte de Nuits this delicate grape is not easy to raise; and only certain sections of the slope have the soil which favors the vine. That is why the great vineyards of this region are so small, and why one will produce a fine wine while the growth from its near neighbor will be mediocre. And so the vineyards of the whole Côte d'Or are called *climats*—each "climate" varying, for better or worse, according to its exposure, soil, and drainage.

On the Côte de Nuits, all the *climats* face southeast, where the rising sun strikes the vineyards, drawing the moisture up through the vines. Farther south, the sun would be too hot and the vines would wither; farther north, it would not be hot enough. In such a region,

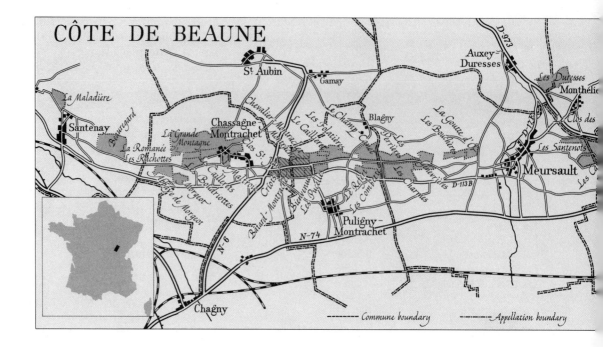

where it takes so little to spoil a vintage, wine-making is a difficult and exacting art; and each *vigneron* adds something to the character of his own wine. So, tasting one against another, anyone accustomed to wine-drinking will perceive the difference between a Côte de Nuits and a Côte de Beaune, or even between a Charmes-Chambertin and the contiguous Clos de Bèze.

The soil of the Côte de Nuits is a reddish clay full of small chalky pebbles, with varying amounts of lava, fuller's earth (a type of clay rich in the silicates of calcium and magnesium), salts of lime, potassium, and phosphorus. The subsoil, which dates from the Jurassic age, is a flinty clay with iron and chalk; but the "trenching," or deep-plowing, that vineyards go through, turns it up and mixes it all together.

The 1,500 hectares (3,750 acres) of vines are mostly Pinot Noir, but there are some Chardonnay, and a few sections are planted in Gamay, Melon, and Aligoté for wine reserved almost entirely for the workers and their families. Most of the wine is red, although a little white is grown, principally in the communes of Vougeot and Chambolle-Musigny, and the informing grape is the noble Pinot Noir. (Two other varieties may be used in wines bearing great names—Pinot Liebault and Pinot Beurot; but these vines, offshoots of the Pinot Noir they closely resemble, are planted only in small quantities.)

The wines vary in quality from the magnificent Great Growths to those bearing the names of their communes—third-grade in a classification of three. The first is Great Growth (*Grand Cru*), the intermediate First Growth (*Premier Cru*). The standards demanded by law for the wines of the Côte de Nuits are:

Great Growths (Grands Crus)

(1) The harvest must not exceed 35 hectoliters (an additional 20% is permitted) per hectare (374.1 U.S. gallons, 311.5 imp. per acre), except in the vineyards of Latricières-Chambertin, Charmes-Chambertin, Mazis-Chambertin, Ruchottes-Chambertin, Chapelle-Chambertin, and Griotte-Chambertin in the commune of Gevrey-Chambertin, where the maximum is 37 hectoliters per hectare (397 U.S. gallons, 325.6 imp. per acre).

(2) Red wines must contain 11.5% alcohol, white wines 12%. The production must not exceed 50 hectoliters per hectare (528.4 U.S. gallons, 440 imp. per acre).

(3) The only permissible grape varieties are Pinot Noir, Pinot Liebault, and Pinot Beurot for red wines and Chardonnay for white. Red wines may, at the discretion of the grower, include up to 15% Pinot Blanc or Chardonnay.

First Growths (Premiers Crus)

(1) The harvest must not exceed 40 hectoliters per hectare (422.6 U.S. gallons, 352 imp. per acre).

(2) Red wines must contain at least 11% alcohol, white wines 11.5%.

(3) The grape varieties are required to be the same as for Great Growths, listed above.

(4) These wines may be sold under the name of the commune and of the vineyard, or with commune name followed by the words "First Growth." If they fail to meet the necessary requirements, they are downgraded to communal wines.

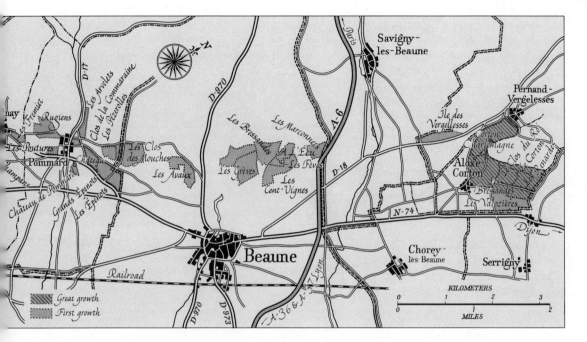

Communal Wines

(1) The harvest must not exceed 50 hectoliters per hectare (528.4 U.S. gallons, 440 imp. per acre).

(2) Red wines must contain at least 10.5% alcohol, white wines 11%.

(3) The grape varieties are required to be the same as for Great Growths.

(4) Wines that fall below these standards are declassed and sold with those of more general *appellations*, such as Bourgogne.

These regulations cover all the good wines of the slope, except those named Côte de Nuits Villages *(q.v.)*. These last are superior to the more general Burgundian *appellations*, yet do not rank among the distinguished and truly fine wines of the Côte de Nuits.

OUTSTANDING VINEYARDS—RED WINES
Listed by Commune

Fixin:
  Clos de la Perrière
  Clos du Chapitre
Gevrey-Chambertin:
  Le Chambertin
  Le Clos de Bèze
  Latricières
  Mazys (or Mazis)
  Mazoyères
  Charmes
  Ruchottes
  Griotte
  Chapelle
  Clos Saint Jacques
  Varoilles

Vosne-Romanée:
  La Romanée-Conti
  La Romanée
  La Tâche
  Les Gaudichots
  Les Richebourg
  La Romanée-Saint-Vivant
  Les Malconsorts
  Clos des Réas
  Les Suchots
  Les Beaux-Monts (also Les Beaumonts)
  La Grande Rue
Nuits-Saint-Georges:
  Les Saint-Georges

  Aux Boudots
  Les Cailles
  Les Porrets
  Les Pruliers
  Les Vaucrains
Prémeaux:
  Clos de la Maréchale
  Les Didiers
  Clos des Forêts
  Clos des Corvées
  Aux Perdrix

Morey-Saint-Denis:
  Clos de Tart
  Les Bonnes Mares
  Clos de la Roche
  Clos Saint-Denis
  Clos des Lambrays
Chambolle-Musigny:
  Les Musigny
  Les Bonnes Mares
  Les Amoureuses

Vougeot:
  Clos de Vougeot
Flagey-Échezeaux:
  Les Grands Échezeaux
  Les Échezeaux

OUTSTANDING VINEYARDS—WHITE WINES
Listed by Commune

Chambolle Musigny:
  Musigny Blanc

Vougeot:
  Clos Blanc de Vougeot

See separately under the respective communes: Fixin, Gevrey-Chambertin, Morey-Saint-Denis, Chambolle-Musigny, Vougeot, Flagey-Échezeaux, Vosne-Romanée, Nuits Saint-Georges, Nuits-Saint-Georges-Prémeaux.

Côte de Nuits Villages

This appellation today refers to Burgundies formerly known under the Vins Fins de la Côte de Nuits appellation. None of the towns producing the better

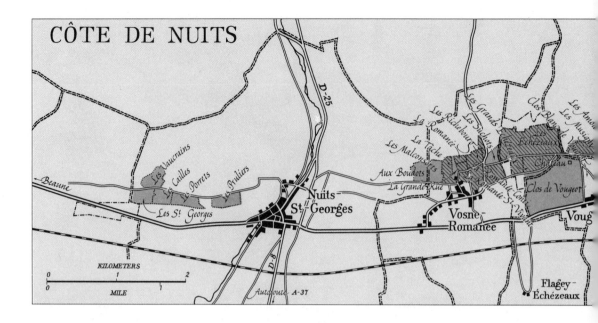

Côte de Nuits wines is entitled to the Côte de Nuits Villages appellation. Production is extremely variable: in 1985, 5,000 hectoliters (13,250 U.S. gallons, 11,000 imp.) were produced; in 1977, only 6 hectoliters (16 U.S. gallons, 13 imp.) were produced. The appellation is given to the red and white wines produced on the 320 hectares (800 acres) of these communes: Fixin, Brochon, Prissey, Comblanchien, Corgolin.

Côte d'Or

Red and dry white wines.
District: Burgundy, France.

The Côte d'Or is variously referred to as the "backbone" and as the "heart" of Burgundy, proving perhaps that the Burgundian knows his wine-making better than his anatomy. Whatever its relation to the other sections of this great region, it produces some of the most magnificent of Burgundies. Some of its reds are peerless and at least one white, Montrachet, is considered by many experts to be the most perfect of all dry white wines. In good years even the secondary Côte d'Or wines are equaled only by a handful of wines the world over. Unquestionably, the "Slope of Gold" is well named.

The slope is composed of a series of bleak, disorderly, low-lying hills stretching some 65 kilometers (40 miles) between Dijon and Santenay, and taking in twenty-four communes and one hamlet. All the vineyards are remarkable, but only those in the favored tenderloin strip—averaging 300 meters (under 1,000 feet) in width—are truly great by Burgundian standards; they alone can produce the superlative Burgundies—but in incredibly small quantities and often at fairly elevated prices. An authentic Côte d'Or Burgundy can never be cheap. Few are completely authentic, since the 7,400 hectares (18,500 acres) pro-

duce scarcely 200,000 hectoliters (5.3 million U.S. gallons, 4.4 million imp.) per year. The average holding is less than 2 hectares (5 acres).

These wines stem from two types of grapes—Pinot Noir for red and Chardonnay for white. Neither vine produces abundantly. Several close relatives of these grapes are allowed as well, but they are planted in insignificant amounts; other vines may be found on the slope, but their wines are not properly Côte d'Or, and if permitted a place-name will revert to the more general Burgundy *(q.v.)*. In addition to the relatively low yields of the noble vines, the hazards of their cultivation are considerable in so northerly a climate, where inclement weather is frequent and punishing. It is just this northerly climate, however, which is responsible for the fineness of the wines in years when they do succeed, since it exacts the maximum effort from the vine simply to bring its fruit to maturity and ensures that the hard-won grapes will be of superb quality. Not every year, of course, turns out to be an unqualified success—although here again the importance of vintage charts has been largely overestimated. Admittedly there will be more difference between the vintage years in the wines of Burgundy than there will be in those of comparatively sunny Bordeaux; yet a bottle of a Côte d'Or wine from a lesser year—if the wine is authentic and appropriately priced—may well provide a delightful experience. Often, an excellent wine is made even in the most "disastrous" of years—which proves that wine refuses to obey the rules laid down by the statisticians and chart-makers. This shows that a well-selected wine is a greater quality factor than the claim of a vintage year.

The important wines of the Côte d'Or fall into three categories: wines labeled with the name of a commune; those with the name of the commune followed by that of a vineyard—for instance, Nuits-Saint-

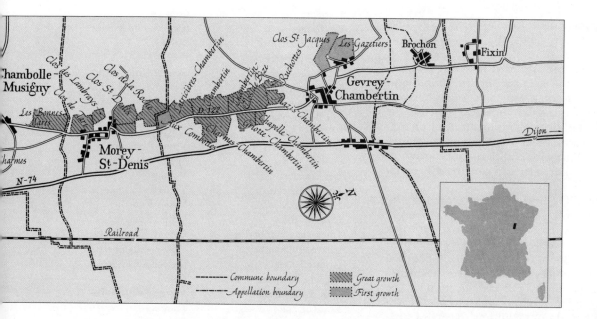

Côte d'Or

Georges Les Porets; and those with only a vineyard name (e.g., Chambertin). Wines with communal place-names only (e.g., Gevrey-Chambertin) may come from virtually any vineyard in that commune, and the standards they must attain are the lowest exacted along the slope. Such wines are often excellent, sometimes distinguished, but never great. The second group embraces wines from grapes grown only in the specific vineyard indicated, and the minimum standards are rather higher. The wines include some of the most splendid Burgundies. The third group dispenses with everything but the name of the single outstanding vineyard where the grapes are grown and makes up the class of the Great Growths (*Grands Crus*), of which there are only thirty-one on the Côte d'Or. The wines may generally be expected to be peerless, although some others which carry both vineyard and commune name equal and very occasionally better them. What is important for the buyer is an ability to distinguish commune from vineyard on the label. This not always so simple as it seems.

Many a beginner has inadvertently bought a bottle of Gevrey-Chambertin for Chambertin, or Chambolle-Musigny for Musigny. The mistake is an honest one made possible by the peculiar Burgundian custom of adding to the name of a commune that of its famous vineyard. The practice is by no means standard—Pommard, Volnay, and Beaune, for example, consider their names far more valuable than those of any vineyard the commune might possess—and to complicate matters further, several vineyards themselves have hyphenated names. Thus Gevrey-Chambertin, Charmes-Chambertin, and several others are vineyards, and outstanding ones at that. Fortunately there are only twenty-four communes on the Côte d'Or, of which about thirteen are of real importance. (A list of these communes with their leading vineyards follows at the end of this entry; and they are listed with average production under the heading *Côte d'Or* in the entry on Burgundy—*q.v.*)

The slope of the Côte d'Or itself falls neatly into two parts: the Côte de Nuits to the north and the Côte de Beaune to the south. In general it might be said that the former is responsible for the greatest red Burgundies, the latter for the whites, but there are exceptions. In bygone times there was a Côte de Dijon extending to the north of the Côte de Nuits, but the expansion of the city of Dijon and the lesser quality of the wines it produced have combined to reduce its importance almost to nothing, despite the fact that the slope was once held in considerable esteem. In the commune of Chenôve—even today the source of a few minor wines—there stands what is said to be the biggest wine press in the world. "The Duke's Wine Press" is the official name, but to the natives it is "Big Maggie," affectionately named for Marguérite, a lusty fifteenth-century Duchess who purportedly bestowed her favors on those pickers and wine-makers who did the fastest and the best jobs. Chenôve, Marsannay, and Couchey still produce wines in a minor way, but Fixin, at the beginning of the Côte de Nuits, is the first commune of any real importance.

The midsection of the hills between Fixin and Santenay has become the great vineyard region of the Côte d'Or. Determining factors are the vine, the angle of the hill and the way it is struck by the sun, the amount of rainfall, and the drainage of excess water; but perhaps most important of all is the soil—the most critical element in the production of any fine wine. The Burgundian hills date from the same time (and are part of the same formation) as the easterly Jura Mountains which give their name to the period in which they were formed, the Jurassic age, some 130 to 155 million years ago. In the intervening 129-or-so million years between their formation and the first stumbling appearance of man, the hills were alternately baked by the sun and covered with ice, drenched with water and whipped by savage winds, and the net result is the iron-rich oolitic rubble and chalky clay at present composing the soil. The Burgundian is firmly convinced that the entire scheme was preordained, that the precise combination of factors found on his hills was planned expressly for his vines and nothing else. What else could possibly grow on the Côte d'Or? And where else can you possibly equal wines such as these?

While the Côte d'Or Burgundies are among the world's handful of great wines, there are obviously some which are better than others. A classification is an ephemeral thing at best, for the men concerned have much to do with the quality of the individual wines, and men are subject to change. It is nevertheless possible to make an overall classification of the wines. The order of the following list represents a personal opinion based on the author's years of testing Burgundies and comparing them one against the other, and no wholesale agreement is anticipated. In order to give a true estimate of the quality of these vineyards, the wines should reflect the character of the soil and be estate-bottled or *Mis en Bouteilles à la Propriété*.

RED WINES

Vineyard	Commune
La Romanée-Conti	Vosne-Romanée
Chambertin-Clos de Bèze and Chambertin	Gevrey-Chambertin
La Tâche	Vosne-Romanée
Les Richebourg	Vosne-Romanée
Musigny	Chambolle-Musigny
Clos de Vougeot	Vougeot
Les Bonnes Mares	Chambolle-Musigny
Grands-Échezeaux	Flagey-Échezeaux
La Romanée-Saint-Vivant	Vosne-Romanée
Corton-Clos du Roi	Aloxe-Corton
Les Saint-Georges	Nuits-Saint-Georges
Latricières-Chambertin	Gevrey-Chambertin
Le Corton	Aloxe-Corton
Les Bressandes	Aloxe-Corton
Cuvée Nicolas Rolin	Beaune (Hospices de Beaune)
La Grande Rue	Vosne-Romanée
Les Renardes	Aloxe-Corton
Cuvée Dr. Peste	Aloxe-Corton (Hospices de Beaune)
Clos des Porrets-Saint-Georges	Nuits-Saint-Georges
Mazis-Chambertin	Gevrey-Chambertin
Les Amoureuses	Chambolle-Musigny
Clos de Tart	Morey-Saint-Denis
Les Pruliers	Nuits-Saint-Georges

Vineyard	Commune
Les Cailles	Nuits-Saint-Georges
Les Caillerets	Volnay
Clos de la Perrière	Fixin
Clos Saint-Jacques	Gevrey-Chambertin
Les Varoilles	Gevrey-Chambertin
Les Échezeaux	Flagey-Échezeaux
Les Beaux-Monts (also Beaumonts)	Vosne-Romanée
Les Malconsorts	Vosne-Romanée
Clos de la Roche	Morey-Saint-Denis
Les Fremiets	Volnay
Les Champans	Volnay
Les Suchots	Vosne-Romanée
Clos des Réas	Vosne-Romanée
Chapelle-Chambertin	Gevrey-Chambertin
Charmes-Chambertin	Gevrey-Chambertin
Griotte-Chambertin	Gevrey-Chambertin
Clos du Chapitre	Fixin
Clos des Lambrays	Morey-Saint-Denis
Les Rugiens	Pommard
Les Épenots	Pommard
Les Jarollières	Pommard
Clos de la Maréchale	Nuits-Prémeaux
Didiers-Saint-Georges	Nuits-Prémeaux
Clos des Corvées	Nuits-Prémeaux
Les Vaucrains	Nuits-Saint-Georges
Les Santenots	Meursault
Les Fèves	Beaune
Les Grèves	Beaune
Clos des Mouches	Beaune
Clos de la Boudriotte	Chassagne-Montrachet
Clos Saint-Jean	Chassagne-Montrachet
Clos Morgeot	Chassagne-Montrachet
Clos de la Commaraine	Pommard
Les Angles	Volnay
Le Clos Blanc	Pommard
Les Pézerolles	Pommard
Clos Saint-Denis	Morey-Saint-Denis

WHITE WINES

Vineyard	Commune
Le Montrachet	Chassagne and Puligny-Montrachet
Chevalier-Montrachet	Puligny-Montrachet
Clos des Perrières	Meursault
Bâtard-Montrachet	Chassagne and Puligny-Montrachet
Corton-Charlemagne	Aloxe-Corton
Les Perrières	Meursault
Les Ruchottes	Chassagne-Montrachet
Musigny Blanc	Chambolle-Musigny
Les Charmes	Meursault
Les Combottes	Puligny-Montrachet
Clos Blanc de Vougeot	Vougeot

See also Côte de Nuits; Côte de Beaune; Burgundy.

Côtes du Rhône
See Rhône

Côte Rôtie (Appellation Contrôlée)

Red wine.
District: Rhône Valley, France.

The second most celebrated of the Rhône wines, coming after Châteauneuf-du-Pape, is the red Côte Rôtie, generous, rich in color, and tasting of truffles or raspberries. The "roasted slope" is on a hillside, barely two miles long and terraced steeply with old stone walls. Here, in the exiguous parcels of vineyard, the grapes sun themselves on the vines all summer long. The Côte lies on the right bank of the River Rhône at the northern end of the Côtes du Rhône region. The vineyards are split between the communes of Ampuis and Tupin-et-Semons and face south-southeast.

The slopes is in two parts: the Côte Brune and the Côte Blonde. The difference can be seen in the soil and tasted in the wines. In the Côte Brune, the land is brownish, rich in clay, containing large amounts of iron oxide; the Côte Blonde's soil, lighter in color, is dominated by chalk and clay. The wines of the Côte Brune are the milder at the outset but become strong and vigorous with age, while their blond counterparts are sprightly and gay when young but fade considerably faster. Legend has it that the real reason for the difference between the two is that Maugiron—an early lord of Ampuis—presented these vineyards to his two daughters, one blond, the other brunette, and the slopes assumed the characteristics of their respective mistresses and have retained them ever since.

The wines of both slopes are red. Full to a point of concentrated warmth and long-lived, they have an assertive bouquet, and a suave satiny finish. To avoid an excess of vigor, the *vigneron* adds to his fermenting wine a small amount—never more than 20% of the total—of white grapes. This addition rounds it out and adds a measure of finesse. Syrah is the red grape used, Viognier the white, and the two grow side by side on the plunging cliffs.

In recent years the vineyards have been shrinking because of the steepness of the slopes where they are set out. Mechanization is impossible, and all the labor must be done by hand. Paradoxically enough, the wines have been gaining in reputation as the vineyards have been shrinking, and the obvious temptation to "stretch" the wines has not, unfortunately, always been resisted. Present official figures reveal about 65 hectares (162 acres) of vines in the Côte Rôtie, and about 2,000 hectoliters (53,000 U.S. gallons, 44,000 imp.) of wine annually.

Coteau

French for hillside (plural: *coteaux*). The word occurs in the names of certain wine districts—e.g., Coteaux de la Loire.

Coteaux d'Aix, Coteaux des Baux (Appellations Contrôlées)

Red, white, and rosé wines.
District: Provence, France.

Provençal wines harvested in and around the city of Aix-en-Provence in certain delimited areas. The wines were formerly in the category Vins Délimités de Qualité Supérieure, the secondary classification of French wines. They may be red, white, or rosé, the minimum alcoholic content of the reds and rosés being 11% and the whites 11.5%. Permissible vines are the Grenache, Carignan, Clairette, Cinsault, Ugni Blanc, Mourvèdre, Cournoise, and the Muscat vine-types.

In 1986 the Coteaux des Baux and the Coteaux d'Aix each received the distinction of becoming an Appellation Contrôlée. The 300-hectare Coteaux des Baux, producing some 10,000 hectoliters, was detached from its previous status of being part of the Coteaux d'Aix. Twelve vineyard areas having excelled in quality were responsible for this exceptional accolade.

Coteaux de l'Aubance (Appellation Contrôlée)

White and some rosé wines.
District: Anjou, France.

The small, lazy River Aubance flows northward into the Loire, joining it about 48 kilometers (30 miles) downstream from Saumur, running through gently sloping hillsides which support vineyards of a quality only slightly below those of Anjou's Coteaux de la Loire and Coteaux du Layon. The white wines made in Aubance are generally sweet, sometimes semi-sweet, and are among those Angevin wines most frequently encountered abroad. The rosés do not differ appreciably from any others made in the region. Chenin Blanc grapes only are allowed for white wines—the sweetest of which are allowed to attain the noble rot (*q.v.*) before they are picked—and Cabernet Franc is dominant for rosé. Some 2,300 hectoliters (60,750 U.S. gallons, 50,600 imp.) are produced annually.

See Anjou.

Coteaux du Languedoc (Appellation Contrôlée)

Red, white, and rosé wines.
District: Languedoc, France.
(Vins du Midi.)

Although the Hérault, Gard, and Aude departments—midway between Marseilles and Toulouse in southern France—produce the pleasant Appellation Contrôlée wines of Muscat de Frontignan and Clairette du Languedoc, their real reputation comes from the A.O.C. wines of the Coteaux du Languedoc, which are produced in far greater quantities. The Coteaux du Languedoc *appellation* was created in 1985 as a name under which a dozen smaller local A.O.C. wines could be sold. Only red and rosé wines are eligible to

Coteaux du Layon (Appellation Contrôlée)

qualify for the Coteaux du Languedoc label. Once they qualify, they may be sold with or without the commune name. Total area is about 10,000 hectares. The total amount of wine sold as Coteaux du Languedoc depends on how much is *labelisé*, varying from 100,000 to 200,000 hectoliters (265,000 to 530,000 U.S. gallons, 220,000 to 440,000 imp.) per year. The eligible wines are:

> Pic-Saint-Loup
> Cabrières
> Coteaux de la Méjanelle
> Coteaux de Saint-Christol
> Coteaux de Vérargues
> Faugères
> Saint-Chinian
> Saint-Saturnin
> Montpeyroux
> Saint-Drézéry
> Saint-Georges-d'Orques
> La Clape and Quatourze

In cases where the production is both red (or rosé) and white, only the red and rosé are eligible for the Coteaux du Languedoc label. The name Cabrières applies only to rosé wine. The reds and rosés are made mostly from a blend of Carignan, Cinsault, Grenache Noir, and Aramon. Since the soil, climate, and style of vinification are nearly the same for each of these wines, it is the blend of grapes which distinguishes one from another.

La Clape, Côtes de Cabardès et de l'Orbiel, and Quatourze lie in the neighboring Aude *département* but are considered part of the Coteaux du Languedoc.

The maximum legal yield for all the wines is 50 hectoliters per hectare, or about three tons to the acre. In this most productive of French vineyards, where the vines are those varieties which can give huge crops, the permissible yield is below the level harvested in the "premium" wine districts of California. If the French can take steps to control the quality of some of their least-known wines, certainly the growers and legislators in the United States could do the same for the most famous American ones.

See United States.

Coteaux du Layon (Appellation Contrôlée)

Loire Valley white wine.
District: Anjou, France.

Principally, the sweetest, richest, and most mellow of all the Angevin white wines, and, when successful, the best. Although less flowery than a Sauternes, they have an inimitable bouquet and a lightness that belies their alcoholic content, often as high as 15%. They are slow to mature but long-lived. Some dry white wines, also, are made in the district.

See Anjou.

Coteaux du Loir (Appellation Contrôlée)

Loire Valley red, white, and rosé wines.
District: Department of the Sarthe, France.

A small wine district north of the Loire producing red, rosé, and white wines and easily confused with Coteaux de la Loire. The River Loir is actually a tributary of the main stream.

As is true throughout the Loire, white wines tend to be better than reds. They come from Chenin Blanc grapes, must contain a minimum of 10% alcohol, and are dry wines, except when an exceptionally hot summer generates enough sugar in the grape for the making of sweet and semi-sweet wines. These, in contrast to the fast-maturing dry wines, sometimes require a certain amount of bottle-age before they are ready to drink.

Red and rosé wines come from Pineau d'Aunis (rapidly being replaced by Cabernets), from Cabernet Franc, Gamay, and Cot grapes, and Groslot (up to 25% of grapes used) is allowed for rosé. The vines are planted in soil ranging from chalky clay (which in general supports grapevines for white wines) to a mixture of clay and flint; and the wines are occasionally semi-sparkling or crackling (*pétillant* in French). Annual production is about 200 hectoliters (5,300 U.S. gallons, 4,400 imp.).

See Anjou.

Coteaux de la Loire

Loire Valley white wines.
District: Anjou, France.

Slightly harder and not quite as sweet as growths from the Coteaux du Layon across the river, these are nevertheless very agreeable dessert wines. The better ones among them have up to 12% or 13% of alcohol, and preserve a certain amount of extra sugar. The rich sweetness is achieved in the same manner as in the Sauternes region of Bordeaux—by leaving the grapes on the vine in the autumn until the noble rot (*q.v.*) sets in.

The finest dry vineyard plot in this area is Savennières, to which the French wine authority awarded a special Appellation Contrôlée in 1953.

Not all the wines grown on these slopes are sweet. The area extends into part of the Muscadet region, near Nantes, and here the wines, though the more robust of their kind, are light, pale, and dry.

See Anjou.

Coteaux de Saumur

See Saumur; Anjou.

Coteaux de Touraine and **Coteaux de Touraine-Mousseux**

See Touraine.

Coteaux du Tricastin (Appellation Contrôlée)

Rhône Valley red, white, and rosé wines.
District: Rhône Valley, France.

Motorists driving on the Paris-Riviera superhighway pass by the vineyards of this recent Appellation Contrôlée some 50 kilometers (about 31 miles) south of Valence in the department of the Drôme. The grapes grow on the slopes to the left of the road. Tricastin adjoins the much larger Côtes du Rhône region, and accordingly the grape varieties in the two districts are similar; Grenache, Mourvèdre, and Cinsaut are used to make both wines. Most of the annual 50,000 hectoliters produced (1,325,00 U.S. gallons, 1,100,000 imp.) is red wine.

Côtes d'Agly

Sweet fortified wines.
District: Roussillon, France.

Not far from the Spanish border in the eastern Pyrenees, Côtes d'Agly produces on the average about 100,000 hectoliters (2.65 million U.S. gallons, 2.2 million imp.). of strong, sweet white wine every year. A small quantity of red is also made, but it is generally inferior to the wine from nearby Corbières and seldom leaves the area.
See Sweet fortified wines of France.

Côtes de Bergerac

See Bergerac.

Côtes de Blaye

See Blaye.

Côtes de Bordeaux

See Premières Côtes de Bordeaux.

Côtes de Bordeaux Saint-Macaire (A.O.C.)

White wine district of Bordeaux making good secondary wines.

Côtes de Bourg

See Bourg.

Côtes de Buzet (Buzet)

Red and white wines.
District: Southwest France.

Between the great Bordeaux and Armagnac regions in Aquitaine lies an important fruit orchard area whose products are known throughout France. In the heart of this district, on the left bank of the River Garonne, is the Buzet Appellation Contrôlée. All of the wine—about 80,000 cases every year—is made by the cooperative run by a former manager of Château Lafite. The red wines are good and better than the white wines, and fortunately more red is produced.
See Buzet (A.O.C.).

Côtes Canon Fronsac, Côtes de Fronsac (now **Fronsac** and **Canon Fronsac**)

Red wines.
District: Bordeaux, France.

The medieval town of Fronsac, near which Charlemagne once had a castle, set in the fork of the rivers Isle and Dordogne, 24 kilometers (15 miles) east of Bordeaux, has two of the Appellations Contrôlées or official place-names in Bordeaux wines. Some white wine is made, but only red is entitled to an *appellation*. Recently the *appellation* has been shortened by the I.N.A.O., dropping the Côtes. Fronsac encloses the smaller zone of Canon Fronsac, which produces the finer wines. Canon Fronsac lies on the high rim of the Canon Hills, a great green bluff overlooking the Dordogne. The small region is proud of its name and boasts two separate Châteaux Canon, as well as eight other vineyards which include Canon in their name. These are not to be confused with *the* Château Canon of Saint-Émilion.

The wines are heavy for Bordeaux, and a delicacy formerly found only in a few of best growths is very slowly making its way downward among the wines, which in the past have not been as well made as they should. The heavy, hearty red wines find their main following in the countries bordering the English Channel and North Sea. In 1956, led by an industrialist from the north of France who has retired to his Fronsac vineyard with his American wife, the first organized attempt was made to bring the region up to date and into competition with famous neighboring places such as Saint-Émilion, Pomerol, and Médoc.

In the February 1956 freeze which destroyed or damaged one-third of the Bordeaux vineyards, Fronsac was least touched of all, because of its elevated position on high bluffs which escaped the cold; and with this fresh start the growers of the region decided both to improve their wine-making and to make the wine better known abroad. Convincing an essentially peasant and parochial-minded populace of the necessity of this has been the most difficult part of the project.

Fronsac produces about 25,000 hectoliters (6,625,000 U.S. gallons, 5,500,000 imp.) of wine each year, much of it big and fruity. Canon Fronsac makes approximately half that quantity.

Côtes de Castillon (Appellation Contrôlée)

Red wines.
District: Bordeaux, France.

Pleasant secondary wines of Bordeaux (*q.v.*). Many excellent values can be found among the well-selected

Côtes de Duras (Appellation Contrôlée)

vineyards of this district which neighbors Saint-Émilion.

Côtes de Duras (Appellation Contrôlée)

Red and white wines grown in fifteen communes around the town of Duras about 112 kilometers (70 miles) to the southeast of the city of Bordeaux, in France. The white wines are made from the Sémillon, Sauvignon, Muscadelle, and Mauzet grape varieties, and the red from the Cabernet, Merlot, and Malbec vines. The wines must have a minimum alcoholic content of 10% for red wines and 10.5% for white.

Most of the wines produced on the 1,000 hectares (2,500 acres) of vineyards are white and the total varies from about 10,000 to 50,000 hectoliters per year (265,000 to 1,325,000 U.S. gallons, 220,000 to 1,100,-000 imp.).

Côtes du Jura or Côtes du Jura-Mousseux

See Jura.

Côtes-du-Marmandais

V.D.Q.S. wines made in a small district centered around the town of Marmande, just southeast of the Bordeaux region on the River Garonne. The red and white wines are only of local interest.

Côtes de Montravel

See Bergerac.

Côtes de Provence

Since 1977 this region in the South of France has been elevated to an Appellation Contrôlée level. *See* Provence.

Côtes du Rhône (Appellation Contrôlée)

The name of a vineyard region (and its wines) bordering the River Rhône in southeast France. *See* Rhône.

Côtes du Roussillon

An Appellation Contrôlée wedged between the Pyrénées and the Mediterranean, the Roussillon vineyards produce some good dry red, rosé, and white wine and a variety of fortified sweet aperitif wines—*vins doux naturels*. *See* Roussillon.

Côtes de Toul

One of the two controlled place-names in the Lorraine area of France. The qualities are classed Vins Délimités de Qualité Supérieure (delimited wines of superior quality) and most of them are *vins gris*, the traditional light pink of Lorraine (*q.v.*).

Côtes du Ventoux

Rhône Valley red and rosé wines.
District: Southern France.

Between Provence and the Rhône Valley the dry and wind-swept Vaucluse plateau rises 40 kilometers (25 miles) east of Avignon. The Côtes du Ventoux vineyards which extend over 4,400 hectares (11,000 acres) of this plateau lie directly east of Carpentras, a town famous for its melons, and just south of Mont Ventoux.

The Grenache Noir grape, the basic variety throughout the southern Côtes-du-Rhône, is grown along with Cinsaut, Syrah, Mourvèdre, and Carignan. All these grapes do well in the poor, red Mediterranean soil, which is here a mixture of the hard limestone of the Ventoux massif itself, talus, and drift boulders. The forty-six communes in the Appellation Contrôlée, created in 1971, make about 220,000 hectoliters (5.8 million U.S. gallons, 4.8 million imp.) of predominantly red wine each year. One-fourth of the wine is solid, fruity, and tannic red, while over half of the Côtes du Ventoux production is so-called *café* or "one night's" wine. Lighter in character and in alcoholic content than the other reds, these *café* wines are de-vatted and pressed before the end of fermentation. They are by far the most popular wines of this Appellation Contrôlée.

Château Coufran

Red Wine.
District: Haut-Médoc, Bordeaux, France.

A good Cru Bourgeois having the peculiarity of being produced from a vineyard with 85% Merlot plantings. Jean Miailhe also owns nearby Château Verdignan.

Château Couhins

Bordeaux white wine.
District: Graves, France.
Commune: Villenave-d'Ornon.

Adjoining Château Carbonnieux and Château Bouscaut, Couhins and the former Château Pont de Langon (now one vineyard), until 1969 belonged to the proprietors of Château Calon-Ségur in the Médoc. Past owners of parts of the property have included a Spanish Ambassador to France and a bishop of Algiers.

The estate was purchased in 1969 by the French government for use as a center for wine experiments. André Lurton, the brother of Lucien Lurton of Château Brane-Cantenac in the Médoc, leases Couhins and makes good wine from 50% Sauvignon, 25% Muscadelle, and 25% Sémillon grapes. The wine was ranked as one of the best white Graves in 1959.

Characteristics. Light but full of character, with a charming flavor. A very well-made dry wine.

Vineyard area: red—6 hectares (15 acres); white—1 hectare (2.5 acres).

Average production: red—25 *tonneaux* (2,000 cases); white—5 *tonneaux* (400 cases).

Coulant

A wine-taster's term for wines low in tannin and alcoholic content, light, fresh, very easy to drink. In French it means "running," as applied to a stream or brook.

Coulure

Vine disease: dropping of flower-clusters or berries during the initial period of development—or simply a failure to develop the grape or to pollinate.

See Chapter Eight, p. 37.

Court noué

Another name for infectious degeneration of vines. Also called fan leaf.

See Chapter Eight, p. 38.

Courtier

French term for a wine-broker—who is known in Alsace as a *gourmet*.

Château Coutet

Bordeaux white wine.
District: Sauternes, France.
Commune: Barsac.

Château Coutet is entitled to use either of the legal French place-names Sauternes or Barsac. Barsac, an Appellation Contrôlée in its own right, is one of the five communes included in the Sauternes district. In 1855, when the wines were officially classified, Coutet, situated a mile below the town of Barsac, was made a First Growth (*Premier Cru*) of Sauternes.

A web of connections links the vineyard with Château d'Yquem. The architecture of the oldest parts of both châteaux—dating from the thirteenth century—is identical: the well in the courtyard of Coutet has its exact duplicate in the courtyard of d'Yquem, half a dozen miles away; Château Coutet belonged until 1923 to the Lur-Saluces family, which has for two centuries owned d'Yquem.

The present proprietor is M. Marcel Baly of Strasbourg, who purchased the estate from M. and Mme Edmond Rolland a few years ago. Mme Rolland's father had bought Coutet in 1925 from the syndicate which acquired it from the great-uncle of the present Count de Lur-Saluces.

The *chais* stand across the courtyard from the château. Grapes are brought in at vintage when they have achieved the sugar-rich state of overripeness standard in Sauternes and are pressed in one of the big electric Guy et Mital presses before being pitchforked into a suction funnel which carries them into a huge rolling tube. This carries away the stems, and then the pulp is pressed twice again, the juice dripping and gushing down through trapdoors into the vat below the floor. The juice must be run off every night into barrels, where it ferments and then remains for three years achieving maturity.

Believed by many to be the best of the Barsacs, the wine is the result of the most careful viniculture. When the proprietor feels that it does not come up to his standard, he sells it as anonymous Barsac, refusing to give it the name of the château.

Like all other flat-lying vineyards in Sauternes, Coutet was badly hit by the February 1956 freeze. The present label is the same as that of Château Filhot, which belongs to the Lur-Saluces family.

Characteristics. The wine is more *nerveux*, or piercing, than its Sauternes counterparts, and it is this particular quality which is said to have given the château its name. ("Coutet" comes from the French word *couteau*, or "knife"; and the wine takes its characteristics from its rocky, calcareous subsoil.) Although Barsacs have the same degree of sweetness, or *liqueur*, as the nearby Sauternes, usually varying from 3% to 6% Baumé, they are drier to the taste because of this piercing quality. This wine has great breed and holds its fruit for a long time.

Vineyard area: 32 hectares (80 acres).

Average production: 75 *tonneaux* (6,500 cases).

Cradle

A wicker or wire basket designed to hold a wine bottle in a position slightly above the horizontal and theoretically to ensure that the sediment will be stirred up as little as possible when the wine is served.

If the wine is carefully transported from cellar to table in a cradle and all of it is poured into glasses in one smooth action—which obviously requires a number of glasses—the cradle may be of some service. Otherwise the rocking back and forth of the wine in the cradle stirs up the sediment, and it is preferable to decant.

Cramant

Village in the Épernay district of Champagne which makes one of the greatest wines of the Côte des Blancs.

See Champagne.

Cream Sherry

Heavily sweetened Oloroso Sherry. Unknown in Spain, launched in England, the style is now highly popular in the United States.

See Sherry.

Crémant

A white wine made of red and white grapes and only partly sparkling. This wine is found in Champagne, but the word is not be confused with Cramant, a wine-making village of Champagne.

Crémant de Bourgogne (A.O.C.)

Formerly known as Sparkling Burgundy(*q.v.*), Crémant de Bourgogne is the sparkling wine made from any of a number of Burgundian grape varieties (Pinot Chardonnay, Pinot Noir, Gamay, César, Tressot) according to the Champagne method. In the past, the sparkling wines were red, rosé, and white; at present, however, the term "Crémant de Bourgogne" is reserved for whites and rosés alone. Annual production averages around 5,000 hectoliters (13,250 U.S. gallons, 11,000 imp.).

Crème

Literally "cream"; on a liqueur-label, the word once designated a drink that had been sweetened, to differentiate it from a dry spirit such as a brandy. In contemporary usage it still generally means a sweet liqueur. Some of the better-known Crèmes are:

Ananas (pineapple)	Mandarine (tangerine)
Banane (banana)	Menthe (peppermint)
Cacao (cocoa)	Moka (coffee)
Café (coffee)	Noyau (almond)
Cassis (blackcurrant)	Prunelle (sloe)
Chocolat (chocolate)	Roses (rose)
Cumin (caraway seeds)	Thé (tea)
Fraise (strawberry)	Vanille (vanilla)
Framboise (raspberry)	Violette (violet)

Crème Yvette

Very sweet American liqueur flavored with the Parma violet and named for Yvette Guilbert, the incomparable French diseuse who had a memorable success in the 1890s.

Crépy (Appellation Contrôlée)

Crépy is a light white wine of at least 9.5% of alcohol from the chalky slopes on the southern side of Lake Geneva in the French department of Haute-Savoie. The wines are grown on a scant 60 hectares (150 acres) and are dry and aromatic. Some of them are naturally *pétillant*, the semi-sparkling condition usually translated as "crackling." Some 4,000 hectoliters (106,000 U.S. gallons, 88,000 imp.) are made yearly from the Chasselas grape, and they are rarely, if ever, shipped.

Crescenz

Common misspelling of Kreszenz (*q.v.*), one of the German words indicating the grower.

Criollas

A *Vitis vinifera* variety descended from the vines brought by the Spanish Conquistadores to Mexico, from where it was spread by the Jesuits to Argentina. In the early eighteenth century the grape was planted in California, where it is known as Mission. Though still a leading producer, the Criollas lacks acidity and color and as a result makes only fair-quality white and rosé wines.

Criots-Bâtard-Montrachet (Appellation Contrôlée)

Burgundy white wine.
District: Côte de Beaune, France.
Commune: Chassagne-Montrachet.
Official Classification: Great Growth (Grand Cru).

Yet another of the splendid Montrachets, coming from a vineyard of about 1.4 hectares (3.5 acres). The wines of Chassagne have an unmistakable flavor: dry but not hard, inclined to be flowery, but with no sweetness in the aftertaste. The average production is about 50 hectoliters (1,325 U.S. gallons, 1,100 imp.).

See Bâtard-Montrachet; Chassagne-Montrachet.

Château Croizet-Bages

Bordeaux red wine.
District: Haut-Médoc, France.
Commune: Pauillac.

One of the several Fifth Growths (*Cinquièmes Crus*) in the 1855 Classification of great vineyards, the vineyards are planted on what was the old domain of Bages, in the hamlet now with the same name on hilly land near Pauillac. The estate is sometimes known as Château Calvé-Croizet-Bages. The proprietors, the widow and son of the late M. Paul Quié, also own the Second Growth (*Deuxième Cru*) vineyard Rauzan-Gassies in Margaux and Château Bel-Orme-Tronquoy-de-Lalande, a Bourgeois Supérieur growth near Saint-Estèphe.

Characteristics. Good but not outstanding.
Vineyard area: 25 hectares (62.5 acres).
Average production: 100 *tonneaux* (9,000 cases).

Crozes-Hermitage

French red and white wines.
See Hermitage; Rhône.

Cru

French for growth. In French usage the word denotes a vineyard of high quality, usually considered worthy of independent recognition under the laws of classification. An officially classified vineyard is a *Cru Classé*.

Crushing

The process of mashing the grapes in a mill or pounding them with a rammer to extract the juice. The French term is *broyage*.

Crust

The deposit in old Port. It is so called because it forms a crust around the inside neck of the bottle.

Crusted Port

Bigger and fuller-bodied than most Tawny Ports or Ruby Ports, the style is like that of Vintage Ports and improves in bottle. Seldom from a single vintage year and never from a great year (because in such a case a Port vintage would have been declared), it will not have quite the magnificence of a vintage-year Port. Decanting is required.
See Port.

Cruzan Rum

Of St. Croix, Virgin Islands.
See Rum, Virgin Islands.

Cryptogams

A genus of fungi, some of which cause a disease that affects vines.
See Chapter Eight, p. 31.

Culaton

This is the Piedmontese word for the bottom of the bottle, or dregs. In Piedmont, northern Italy, there is an old superstition that the dregs should be saved until the day after the bottle is opened and then given to friends. Considering the heaviness of the deposit formed by Piedmontese wines this seems an odd, unfriendly gift.

Cumin Liquidum Optimum Castelli

Generally referred to as C.L.O.C. This is a Danish liqueur, white and flavored with caraway seed. The name means "The best caraway liqueur in the castle." A form of kümmel.

Cup

A summer drink served in glass jugs and made with soda-water, with an addition of spirit or liqueur, decorated with pieces of fruit, and iced.

Curaçao

Originally a Dutch liqueur made from the skins of oranges which grow on the Dutch island of Curaçao off the coast of Venezuela. It became so popular that many distillers sell it, under different names. Cointreau and Grand Marnier are examples of proprietary types; while Triple Sec is made by many firms.

Cut

To adulterate liquor with water, or one wine with another—for example, ordinary red wines of France may be cut with Algerian.

Cuve

French term for wine vat.

Cuvée

French term for contents of wine vat; hence a vatting. The term now usually means all the wine of a vat, or all the wine made at one time and under similar conditions. In France it also means a vineyard parcel or lot. In Champagne, there are two further meanings. Vin de Cuvée is the wine of the first pressing. A *cuvée* is also a blend of Champagnes, or a special lot of wine.

Cyprus

The island of Cyprus, edged by jagged beaches, lies in the eastern-most part of the Mediterranean, about 96 kilometers (60 miles) from the Lebanon coast. Its plains are sun-baked, but snow lies on the mountain peaks from January until April, and most of the wine comes from the slopes. Viticulture is important in the island. Out of a farming population of some 64,000 families, about 30,000 are dependent to a certain extent on vine cultivation and the wine industry—which has expanded considerably in the past twenty years. The island's vineyards now cover more than 30,000 hectares (75,000 acres)—about 10% of the arable land.

These vineyards, which look so romantic to tourists, are to be found mainly in the volcanic soil of the southern foothills of the Troödos Mountains, in the districts of Limasso. Paphos, and to a lesser extent in Nicosia and the region of the Makheras Mountains. Driving from Limassol to Paphos, one sees vines planted in orderly rows—sweet table grapes twined round arches and arbors interspersed with wine grapes; young vines set out sparsely in the ash-gray soil; mature plants, tall and bushy. At harvest-time, when loads of grapes are being rushed to the big wineries in trucks, the road is slippery with red juice. On the zigzag mountain roads, the view is spectacular: a vast patchwork of vines spread over the mountain slopes, dwindling higher up into small plots around the old villages. Peasant farmers make wine for themselves—sometimes the thick, strongly concentrated dark wines of tradition—but most of the grapes are sold to the big shipping firms.

With an average harvest of over 200,000 tons of grapes, production per head of the population is relatively higher than that of various important wine-making countries in Europe. About 950,000 hectoliters of wine (25 million U.S. gallons, 21 million imp.) is made annually.

WINE HISTORY

Cyprus, island of Aphrodite, who was worshipped in the temple at Paphos, is known to have been inhabited since the Mycenean Age, and to have traded with other Aegean peoples. Both Greeks and Phoenicians founded colonies there. In the Cyprus Museum there is a beautiful amphora believed to date from about 900 B.C. Recent excavations of mosaics and other remains bear witness to the fact that wine-making flourished in ancient Cyprus; and it is known that the wines were drunk in ancient Egypt, as well as in classical Greece and Rome. Many of the local legends are connected with the cult of Aphrodite, in whose honor great feasts were held, especially on the occasion of the annual pilgrimage to her temple at Palaipaphos. Hesiod described how the Cypriot Nama was made from the sun-dried grapes. This sweet wine was renamed Commandaria by the Knights Templar, to whom, in 1191, Richard I gave the island. Because of its superb quality, the Commanders monopolized its sales, and their Commandaria has been made in Cyprus ever since. Today's Commandaria has the oldest tradition of any individually named wine. In the chronicle of Richard Coeur de Lion's journeys during the Crusades, it is recorded that on his first arrival on the island, there was a banquet at which were offered "the very best wines from the vineyards of Cyprus, which, it is reported, are unlike those of any other country." Centuries later, in 1743, Richard Pococke wrote in London of "The rich Cyprus wine which is so much esteemed in all parts of the world and is very dear and produced only about Limassol. In some places indeed they make good red wine." Cyprus wine was imported into Britain in the times of the Plantagenets. Commandaria was drunk at a great banquet given in London in 1352 by Henry Richard, Master of the Vintners' Company, in honor of King Peter I of Cyprus. There were five monarchs at the dinner: Edward III of England, David of Scotland, John of France, and Waldemar of Denmark, besides Peter I of Cyprus—and so the party came to be known as "The Feast of the Five Kings." More than two hundred years later, Queen Elizabeth I granted a profitable monopoly to Sir Walter Raleigh for the importation of Cyprus wines through Southampton, where a small colony of Cypriot merchants flourished.

There is a story that a taste for the local wine decided the Turkish Sultan Selim II to capture Cyprus in 1571. Selim, renowned for his indulgence in wine (he was nicknamed The Sot), summoned his commander-in-chief and ordered him to take the island, with the words: "Within the island there is a treasure which only the King of Kings is worthy of possessing."

Viticulture was not abolished under Turkish rule; wines were made in large quantities, but the quality was no longer that which had been eulogized by writers at the beginning of the century. It was not until 1878, when the English began to administer the island, that new life came to the vineyards. By some miracle, the phylloxera plague did not reach Cyprus, and the old vines have continued growing on their own roots.

Cyprus vines have played their part in the creation of some famous wines abroad. They were introduced into Madeira in the fifteenth century, for the famous Madeira wine. A similar origin has been attributed to Marsala and Hungarian Tokay. In the past twenty years there has been a marked improvement in the Cyprus wine trade. The foundations of the island's success in the foreign market were laid by Mr. F. Rossi of London. In 1956, he drew up a report on the Cypriot wine industry, recommending improvements and experiments. As a result, cuttings of new varieties were sent to Cyprus—where the government has since been vigorous in following up Mr. Rossi's recommendations. A wine council, representing all sides of the industry, was formed. Other investigations were carried out by such specialists as Professor J. Branas, professor of viticulture at the University of Montpelier. Consequently, the Cypriot wineries were modernized and the latest production equipment installed—including controlled fermentation units. Systematic checks and studies on viticulture, site selection, soils, and diseases were undertaken by the government agencies, and technical assistance was provided for those who needed it. Because Cyprus had never had the phylloxera, the new varieties had at first to be most carefully isolated and so were planted at a quarantine station at Ayia Irini. Gradually, these have been coming into commercial production, making an important contribution to the quality of Cyprus "sherry" and beverage wines.

The European vines have been useful in offsetting a natural tendency for white wines grown in hot climates to be a bit flat, lacking in acidity and freshness.

GRAPE VARIETIES

About 80% of the grapes are red (Mavron), 10% white (Xynisteri), about 2% to 3% Muscat, and 7% Soultana and table grapes.

The local Mavron wine is grown in most of the vineyards of Cyprus—the finest of the variety on the slopes of a hill named Afames, near the village of Platres. Some of the best red wines are made from grapes from this area.

The white Xynisteri vine is cultivated in many districts. Pitsilia and the vineyards of the Paphos area in the west are noted for this variety. This traditional white wine can also be found throughout Cyprus.

TYPES OF WINE

Red wines

These are made mainly from the local red grapes but other species are introduced to give acidity, color, and a more balanced must; notably an oval grape named Ophthalmo and the Maratheftiko, so called because it was grown originally in the Marathassa area.

The Mavron grape also is used in the production of the rosé known on the island and in Greece as Kokkineli. It is deep in color for a rosé, fresh to the palate, and usually quite dry. When iced, it can be drunk with almost any food. Among the better-known red wines are Afames and Othello, both dry, and Kykko and Olympus. It is important to remember, however, that much of the wine is made to appeal to the local taste which, in reds, is for a very full, deep-colored wine with a high tannin content. This goes well with the strongly flavored spicy foods of Cyprus.

White Wines

The finished white wines are full-bodied with a flavor entirely their own. Most of them are fairly dry: people like them so, and the local yeasts are capable of fermentation (if any free sugar is also present) in the presence of even the usual high degree of alcohol found in Cypriot wines. Among the better-known white wines are Aphrodite and Arsinöe, both dry.

Commandaria

This luscious dessert wine, the one for which Cyprus is famous, has been made for hundreds of years in the mountain villages—and especially in Kalokhorio, Zoopiyi, and Yerassa. The informing grape varieties are Mavron and Xynisteri. Now, as in ancient Greece, the growers blend white grapes with red, ad some of them still mature their wine as it was aged in Homeric days, in hugh earthenware jars, but most of it is now matured in modern cement tanks, although the grapes are first spread out in the sun as they were in Hesiod's day. Traditionally, Commandaria was developed by the Mana system, in which the oldest jar is never empty but is filled up with younger wines, as in the Sherry *solera*. The basic wines change from village to village, according to the method used and the proportion of red grapes to white. Nowadays, all the processes in the blending and maturing of commercial Commandaria are carried out by the big companies which buy the wines from the farmers; and the sweet brown product has little in common with the concentrate—so thick it can be scraped from the sides of the container with a knife—which still, sometimes, is found in the villages. Quality varies: the role of the blender is all-important. Guests of the shippers may be lucky enough to taste Commandaria a century old: dark, velvety, mellow, with the rich, toasted sweetness of the sun-baked grapes.

Sherry-types

A large range of "sherries" is made in Cyprus for the home and export markets. They vary considerably in style. Britain, the principal market abroad, has received some wines of the same alcoholic strength as Spanish Sherry, clarified and bottled in England; wines of differing alcoholic content to be blended by the importer; and a sweet wine, lower in alcohol, and least expensive of all these moderately priced sherry-types. Lately, however, the Cypriots have been concentrating on high-strength sherries, and Flor Fino. The very dry style is now exported, though not as widely as the popular sweet type. In the Keo *bodega*, the "cream sherries" are left out in their casks to mature in the sun for two or three years before they are moved into the cellars for further ageing in the wood. In making Fino, butts of American oak are almost entirely filled with a specially selected white wine, and the *flor* yeast, carefully cultivated, is placed onto the surface, converting a part of the alcohol present in the wine. Each year, about half the contents are drawn from the cask and replaced with younger wine, while the more mature is transferred to the next store for further ageing in wood.

EXPORT

Limassol, the busy port of the wine-shippers, has been described by the Cypriots as "the Bordeaux of Cyprus." It possesses spacious wineries, equipped with up-to-date installations for pressing, cooling, filtering, and testing wine. Casks are piled high in warehouses beside the sea, and in the sheds outside. At Keo, bottles are shipped in containers each holding 850 cartons, which saves freight charges. The four largest firms are Keo, Sodap, and Uc (the oldest), now combined with Etko, and Loel.

In 1985, about 400,000 hectoliters (10,600,000 U.S. gallons, 8,800,000 imp.) of table wine Commandaria, and sherry were exported, with the United Kingdom and the U.S.S.R. together taking more than half. Cyprus is, increasingly, a source of inexpensive table wines. As a result of changes in the industry, these have been improving, and more and more is being exported, especially for restaurant carafe wines.

Until Britain joined the Common Market, Cyprus enjoyed a preferential Commonwealth tariff from this largest outlet of her market. Special arrangements were made to protect Cypriot interests, at least in the early stages of the changeover. Naturally, it is hoped on the island that even as a member of the E.E.C., Britain will continue to be a major customer of the Cyprus vineyards. In fact, an agreement between Cyprus and the European Economic Community was signed and came into effect in February 1973, whereby the island was allowed to ship 200,000 hectoliters (5.3 million U.S. gallons, 4.4 million imp.) of "sherry" a year free of countervailing charges to Britain and Ireland. This annual quota continued until January 1, 1974, and was extended to include the marketing of the 1974 vintage. The government of Cyprus, for its part, undertook to adopt regulations over vines and their products corresponding to those applied inside the Community, and to bring those regulations into force from January 1, 1975.

SPIRITS

The island produces about 30,000 hectoliters (795,000 U.S. gallons, 660,000 imp.) a year of brandy, about 5% of which is exported. In proportion to the sale of wines abroad, the figure for spirits has fallen of late years. Inside Cyprus, people often drink the brandy as a long iced drink or "sour." "V.S.O.P." is made by the cognac method.

Production of brandy and other spirits on a large scale dates only from the beginning of the British administration. Filfar, rather like Curaçao, and KEO Spécialité, which resembles Cointreau, are two of the liqueurs now being made. The government generally buys up all the grape alcohol, or Zivania, of the island. Flavored with gum mastic and aniseed, it becomes Cypriot spirit in the forms of Masticha and Ouzo.

Czechoslovakia

Czechoslovakia produces wine but is mainly a wine-importing country. Its twelve viticultural regions are apportioned among Bohemia, Moravia, and Slovakia, and the total harvest now nearly meets the national demand. In these conditions, some still and sparkling wines are seen abroad.

Viticulture is an ancient craft among the Czechs but has had a more than usually turbulent history. Wine was certainly grown in Bohemia by the ninth century. In the second part of the fourteenth century, at the direction of Emperor Charles IV, Burgundian vines were imported and planted systematically. Cultivation, especially around Prague in Bohemia, was prolific in the sixteenth century, and at the beginning of the seventeenth century, before the devastations of the Thirty Years' War. A revival of viticulture was wiped out anew in both the eighteenth and nineteenth centuries, so that Czech wine-growing as it exists today dates only from the 1920s, when the whole natural viticulture was reconstructed.

Production each year is around 1,300,000 hectoliters (34.3 million U.S. gallons, 28 million imp.); more than 85% is white wine. Most of the wine is consumed in Czechoslovakia. Some still and sparkling wines are exported, mainly to the U.S.S.R. and East Germany. Even so, the Czechs must import some wine to meet the growing demand. Each person drinks 14 liters per year (3.70 U.S. gallons, 3.08 imp.). More than 46,000 hectares (1,150,000 acres) is in vineyard. The province of Slovakia produces about two-thirds of the total and Moravia makes most of the rest; little is made in Bohemia. The wine-grape growers sell most of their fruit to the state establishments for vinification; only a part of Czechoslovak wine is made by the growers themselves.

Bohemian wines inevitably have an affinity with German wines. Prague is at the same latitude as the Rheingau and the Palatinate, and the principal vines are nearly the same: Rhine Riesling, Traminer, and Sylvaner for the white wines; and Blauer Burgunder, Portugieser, and Saint-Laurent for red wines. The best quality zone is that of Litoměřice, Roudnice, and Mělník on the Elbe River not far north of Prague, and also at Velké Zernoseky.

The majority of Moravian wine comes from the southern central area of Czechoslovakia below Brno and just across the border from the Krems-Vienna wine sector in Austria. Here again are affinities which cross national frontiers. The Moravian area is bounded by Znojmo in the west, Mikulov on the Czech-Austrian border, and by Hustopeče-Hodonín to the northeast. The Veltliner grape, producing white wine along the Danube in Austria, is used in this region, as well as other varieties such as Rhine and Walsh-Italian Riesling, the latter accounting for more than 20% of all vineyard acreage. Important also are Sylvaner, Traminer, Sauvignon, Weiss Burgunder,

and a variety the Czechs call Rulandské, which may be the Ruländer-Pinot Gris. The wines around Mikulov are light and aromatic with rather high acidity.

At the eastern end of Czechoslovakia, lying to the north of Hungarian Tokaj, a "Tokay" is made from the Furmint and Lipovina grapes. Both grape varieties are widely used in Hungary. The best-known placenames in Czechoslovakia are Malá Trňa, Viničky and Streda nad Bodrogom. Throughout the rest of the Slovakian region on the borders of the Carpathian mountains much wine is made. In the west of the region is the largest vineyard area of Czechoslovakia, the regions of Little Carpathians and Nitra. The chief vines are Veltliner, Italian Riesling, Sylvaner, Müller-Thurgau, Frankovka, Saint-Laurent, Blauer Burgunder, Portugieser, Fetească Regale, Fetească Alba, Traminer, and Sauvignon. Red wine varieties make up approximately 14% of the whole crop. In Czechoslovakia 8 million bottles of sparkling wines are produced by both the "charmat" and the "méthode champenoise" process.

D

Dalwood

Important vineyard in New South Wales.
See Australia.

Dame-Jeanne

French term for a large glass bottle containing anything from one to ten gallons, usually covered with wicker and used for storing and transporting wines and spirits; the English equivalent is a demijohn. In Bordeaux, the name was also used for a bottle containing more than a magnum but less than a double magnum; the equivalent of 2½ liters.

Dampierre

Commune producing rosé and red wines in the Coteaux de Saumur district of Anjou *(q.v.).*

Damson gin

A British gin flavored with damsons—small, dark plums.

Danziger Goldwasser

White aniseed and caraway-flavored liqueur, originally plain, later with the addition of gold flakes floating in the bottle. A Silverwasser was also made in which flakes of silver replaced the gold. Both were originally made in the old port of Danzig. A number of firms put out similar liqueurs, of which the Liqueur d'Or made in France is probably the best known, though it is no longer made.

Dão

Portuguese red wines, and some white, from the vineyards south of the Douro.
See Portugal.

Château Dauzac

Bordeaux red wine.
District: Haut-Médoc, France.
Commune: Labarde-Margaux.

The vineyard, Fifth Growth *(Cinquième Cru),* lies on flat gravelly soil in Labarde and is allowed the place-name Margaux. Formerly owned by the Bordeaux wine firm of Nathaniel Johnston, then the property of H. Bernet. Previous owners, the Lynch family, emigrated from Ireland in the eighteenth century. They left their imprint on several châteaux in the Médoc and are an example of the great influence of the Irish in the area.

Mr. A. Miailhe, owner of the adjoining Château Siran, bought Dauzac in 1966. In the early seventies he planted considerable acreage, more than doubling original production; he sold the property in 1977 to Felix Chatellier, a fruit grower in Morocco for many years.

Characteristics. Excellent improvement. The new proprietor has continued the progress.

Vineyard area: 55 hectares (137.5 acres).
Average production: 220 *tonneaux* (20,000 cases).

Debrői Hárslevelű

One of the better dry white wines of Hungary. Wine made from the grape variety Hárslevelű, which also goes into Tokay.
See Hungary.

Decant

To pour wine from its bottle to another container, from which it will be served, in order to separate the wine from its deposit or to oxidate or aerate it.

Decanter

Glass vessel or container usually of attractive design used for serving old wines which have been decanted to separate them from their deposit. It is much too often used also for holding Sherries, Ports, and other wines which do deteriorate, although not rapidly, once the cork is pulled. The best decanters are made of clear crystal, to show off the color of the wine to its best advantage. When the decanter is brought to the table it is customary also to bring the cork from the wine bottle for the inspection and approval of the master of the house.

Dégorgement

French term for the removal of the deposit from bottles of Champagne and other sparkling wines.
See Champagne.

Deidesheimer Grainhübel

One of the best wines of Deidesheim in the German Palatinate, or Pfalz.
See Palatinate.

Deidesheimer Herrgottsacker

Best-known wine of Deidesheim in the German Palatinate.
See Palatinate.

Deidesheimer Leinhöhle

An outstanding wine of Deidesheim in the German Palatinate.
See Palatinate.

Delaware

One of eastern America's better white-wine grapes, found particularly in Ohio and the New York Finger Lakes district. It yields clean, fresh, spicy but "foxy" wine, much of which is made sparkling.

Délicat, Delikat

French and German terms for the subtle taste of a wine of low alcoholic content—less than 12% of alcohol by volume and sometimes, as in the case of many fine German wines, as low as 8% of alcohol by volume.

Delicatessen

Unexceptional red hybrid grape developed by T. V. Manson of Texas; said to have taken its name from the large number of different grape varieties that went into it.

Demi

Literally "half," meaning half a liter, the term to use when asking for a large glass of draft beer in France. *Demie* (the French feminine) refers to a half-bottle.

Demie-queue

Half a *queue*, Since a *queue* is an ancient Burgundian term for two *pièces* or barrels, a *demie-queue* would be one pièce. It holds 228 liters (60.2 U.S. gallons, 50.1 imp.). The term is rarely used.

Demijohn

A large glass bottle with a wicker wrapping, holding anything from one to ten gallons. It is commonly used for storing and transporting wines. The name is a corruption of the French Dame-Jeanne (literally "Lady Jane") and attempts to trace it back to Arabic or Persian have been largely discounted on the evidence that the Arabs seem to have developed their word from the Italian.

Demi-Sec

French for semi-dry. These words appearing on the label of a bottle of Champagne do not, in fact, indicate a dryish wine, but rather one which is sweetish.
See Champagne.

Denaturant

A substance added to alcohol to make it unfit for drinking, thus legally avoiding the heavy excise duty on potable alcohol. Denatured spirits are spirits so treated.

Denmark

Wine is not produced in Denmark, because of the cold climate.

There is considerable trade in "fruit wines," and most popular are the Danish berry wines such as black-currant, blackberry, and cherry. In addition, liqueurs are made. The best-known is probably Cherry Heering *(q.v.)*, and most of the cherries for this come from the beautiful little Danish island of Sealand. Another popular liqueur is Cloc Brun, a spicy drink with a slight taste of caraway seed, and 38.5% alcohol by volume.

SPIRITS

For many years the Danes have been experimenting with the production of whisky. In 1952, Cloc Whisky, the first to be distilled in Denmark, was put on the market. The manufacturers use malt barley which has been dried over a peat fire. The whisky is distilled in pot stills and seasoned in oak barrels.

The most important of the potable spirits industries in Denmark is the making of aquavit. It is often drunk with food despite its strong caraway seed taste.
See Aquavit.

Denominación de Origen

Guarantee of validity on Spanish wine labels.
See Spain.

Denominazione di Origine Controllata

The system of Italian controlled place-names, usually abbreviated D.O.C. or D.O.C.G. for the best.
See Italy.

Densimeter, Densimetry

The densimeter, used for reading the density of grape must, consists of a hollow cylindrical float with a weighted ball beneath and a graduated rod above. The instrument is based on the Archimedean law that a body displaces a quantity of water equal to its own bulk.
See Mustimeter.

Deposit

The sediment that is commonly precipitated from many red wines and some white ones during the normal course of their development in the bottle. In white

Deroldego

wines the sediment is usually a tasteless, harmless, and colorless bitter tannin and pigment and so should be left in the bottle. Fine old red wines sometimes with a considerable amount of deposit are decanted to separate the wine from the layer in the bottom of the bottle. Bottles for good red wines, such as Bordeaux or Burgundies, have indentations called punts which help hold the sediment apart from the rest of the wine.

Deroldego

Widespread grapevine in Trentino, Italy, producing red wines, especially in the districts of Mezzolombardo and Mezzocorona.

Château Desmirail

Bordeaux red wine.
District: Haut-Médoc, France.
Commune: Margaux.

Both the vineyard, classed a Third Growth (*Troisième Cru*) in the Gironde Classification of 1855, and the name have been absorbed by Château Palmer. The building, in the village of Margaux, belonged to the late M. Zuger, the former owner of Château Malescot-Saint-Exupéry, and was renamed Château Marquis-d'Alesme in 1981 by Jean-Claude, his son. This nonexistent vineyard, still included in the lists of the 1855 Classification, proves the obsolescence of this classification. M. Lurton, of Château Brane-Cantenac, bought the name from Château Palmer in 1981.

Dessert wine

Full or fortified sweet wine suitable for drinking with or after dessert. In the United States, any wine fortified with brandy or spirits. The table wines in this category are Barsac, Sauternes, sweet Vouvrays or Loire, Vin Santo of Italy, as well as Beerenauslesen and Trockenbeerenauslesen of the Rhine and Mosel, or late-harvest Californias.

Dézaley

Well-known white wine of Lavaux in the canton of Vaud.
See Switzerland.

Dezize-les-Maranges and Dezize-les-Maranges-Côte de Beaune (Appellation Contrôlée)

Burgundy red and white wines.
District: Côte de Beaune, France.

A minor wine-growing commune at the southern end of the Côte de Beaune. The wines are very light, fast-maturing, and sometimes they have a good deal of fruitiness. They are usually blended with wines from certain other communes of the slope and sold as Côte de Beaune-Villages but may occasionally be bottled

under their own names. The difference is one of geography and quality. Dezize-les-Maranges alone refers to wine which has been grown on the 60 hectares (150 acres) within the legally approved communal limits. If Côte de Beaune is added, it must come from the 30.5 hectares (75.8 acres) comprising only the best part of the larger area.

Dhroner Hofberg

Outstanding wine of Dhron on the Mosel.
See Mosel-Saar-Ruwer.

Diamond (Moore's Diamond)

An American hybrid grape—developed by Jacob Moore—once widely used as a source for white wine but better adapted to producing table grapes.

Diana

Early American hybrid grape, an attempt to improve the famous Catawba grape. It is still fairly widespread in Ohio and New York State for white wines but is not ideal, since it tends to vary considerably in quality from year to year.

Diastase

A ferment which has the power to convert starch into dextrine, and then into sugar.

Die

See Clairette de Die.

Dimyat

White-wine grape grown on the Black Sea coast of Bulgaria.
See Bulgaria.

Dionysos

Greek god of wine. Originally a nature deity of fruitfulness and wine, he probably came from Thrace. According to Greek mythology, he was the son of Zeus and Semele, a divinity with prophetic gifts, who traveled over the then known world, spreading the knowledge of vine cultivation. He also spread worship himself, with the frenetic Bacchic rites which (according to the *Bacchae* of Euripides) destroyed Pentheus, King of Thebes, who opposed them. Bacchos, another name for the wine god, was afterward adopted by the Romans as Bacchus (*q.v.*).

Dipping rod

Graduated measure for ascertaining contents of casks.

Distillation

The art or science of distilling. It is based on the fact that alcohol, being lighter than water, vaporizes at a lower temperature, with the result that when a slightly alcoholic liquid is heated to a temperature between the two boiling points, the vapors that rise can be caught and condensed back to form a liquid with a higher alcoholic content. Distilling is done either in single-shot pot stills or continuous patent stills, the quality and characteristics desired dictating the method.

Distillation is defined by J. H. Perry in the third edition of *The Engineers' Handbook* as "the separation of the constituents of a liquid mixture by partial vaporisation of the mixture and separate recovery of vapour and residue. The more volatile constituents of the original mixture are obtained in increased concentration in the vapour; the less volatile in greater concentration in the liquid residue. The completeness of separation depends upon certain properties of the components involved and upon the arrangements of the distillation process.

"In general, *distillation* is the term applied to vaporisation processes in which the vapour evolved is recovered, usually by condensation. *Evaporation* commonly refers to the removal of water from aqueous solution of non-volatile substances by vaporisation. The vapour evolved, *i.e.* the water, is discarded.

"The majority of the applications of distillation are found in the separation of one or more of the components from mixtures of organic compounds."
See Chapter Two, p. 7.

Dizy

Commune near Ay, in the Marne Valley, producing a First Growth Champagne.
See Champagne.

D.O.C. or D.O.C.G.

See Denominazione di Origine Controllata; Italy.

Château Doisy-Daëne

Bordeaux white wine.
District: Sauternes, France.
Commune: Barsac.

The château, classed Second in 1855, makes a sweet wine typical of the district and also a small amount of dry white wine, made in part from Riesling grapes, but not under the château name.
Vineyard area: 11 hectares (28 acres).
Average production: 20 *tonneaux* (1,900 cases).

Château Doisy-Védrines

Bordeaux white wine.
District: Sauternes, France.
Commune: Barsac

A Second Growth of the 1855 Classification, the property is situated between Châteaux Coutet and Climens, both First Growths according to that ranking. The wine is rich and full. Pierre Casteja—brother of Emile Casteja, vineyard owner in the Médoc—owns the property.
Vineyard area: 25 hectares (62 acres).
Average production: 60 *tonneaux* (5,700 cases).

Dolceacqua (or Rossese)

A D.O.C. wine of Rossese grapes from along the Italian Riviera.
See Liguria.

Dolcetto

Italian grape producing dry generic wines.
See Piedmont.

Dôle

Good red wine of the Valais from the Dôle or Gamay grape.
See Switzerland.

Dom

The German word for cathedral. Several cathedrals have vineyards as part of their endowment. Most notable among these is the Dom of Trier on the Mosel, which owns vineyards at Avelsbach south of the town and at Wiltingen on the Saar.

Dom Pérignon

According to legend, the father of Champagne as we know it.
See Champagne.

Domaine, Domäne

French and German terms for wine estate: *Mis en Bouteilles au Domaine* means bottled at the domain or vineyard; the former is the French term for estate-bottling.

Donnaz (D.O.C.)

Red wine from the Valle d'Aosta in North Italy.
See Piedmont and Valle d'Aosta.

Dop brandy

The South African equivalent of marc, or the distillation of grape husks after the wine is pressed out. Dop is of dubious quality, and incredibly high taxes were put on it to make its production economically impossible, with the result that it is now seldom seen.

Dosage

French term for the addition of sugar syrup to sparkling wine before final corking and shipment.
See Champagne.

Doubling

Redistilling spirits to improve strength and flavor.

Douro

One of Portugal's three important rivers.
See Port.

Dousico

Heady Greek drink flavored with aniseed.

Doux

French for sweet, as applied to wines—e.g., Sauternes, Barsac. On the label of a bottle of Champagne this word indicates a very sweet wine which is seldom sold in Great Britain or the United States.

Douzico

A Turkish spirit rather like kümmel *(q.v.)*.

Downy mildew

Also called false mildew in American and mildew in Europe, to differentiate it from powdery mildew; the most crippling fungus disease of the vine.
See Chapter Eight, p. 38.

Draff

In whisky-making, the residual solid matter after fermentation of the grain.

Draft

Beverage, notably beer, drawn from bulk, or supplied and taken directly from barrels or casks.

Drambuie

A liqueur compounded from Scotch whisky, heather honey, and herbs by a secret formula belonging to the Mackinnon family near Edinburgh. The formula is said to have been given to an early Mackinnon by Bonnie Prince Charlie, as a reward for helping him to escape to France. The derivation of the name is a corruption of the Gaelic *An Dram Buidheach*, meaning "the drink that satisfies." One of the three most popular liqueurs in the United States.

Dreimännerwein

"Three men wine," as the wine of Reutlingen in Germany is jokingly referred to. It is so called because it is said to be so bad that to make one man drink it, a second is needed to hold him fast, and a third to pour the wine into his mouth.

Dry

Opposed to sweet. A wine is dry when all the sugar in the grapes has been completely fermented into alcohol. White Burgundy, most Loire and Alsatian wines, most Graves and Champagnes, many Mosel and Rhine wines, are dry. So also are such aperitif wines as Fino and Amontillado Sherries. In American wine parlance, the term "dry wines" is mistakenly given to wines under 14% or table wines as opposed to "sweet wines," which are synonymous with fortified wines. The acid content of a wine also determines the sense of dryness, unless the latter is covered up by excessive sugar.

Dubonnet

A dark red proprietary French aperitif made of a sweetened wine base with bitter bark and quinine added to impart the characteristic taste. It is also manufactured in the United states, where a white variety, seen also in England, may be found.

Château Ducru-Beaucaillou

Bordeaux red wine.
District: Haut-Médoc, France.
Commune: Saint-Julien.

The vineyard forms an unbroken carpet with that of Château Beychevelle. The name, given by the former owner, M. Ducru, means literally "beautiful pebbles," and is very appropriate. The chief feature of the vineyard is its richness in the pebbles, or *cailloux*, which contribute to the greatness of so many of the wines of the Médoc, especially Château Latour. At Beaucaillou the gravelly soil is very deep.

The large, beautiful château itself is set away from the road on the lip of the slope over the River Gironde.

This vineyard has become one of the showplaces of the Médoc, and unquestionably produces one of its best wines. It was revived in the fifties by the efforts of its owner, Jean-Eugène Borie, and is now not only one of the best Saint-Julien vineyards but one of the best Second Growths (*Seconds Crus*) of the 1855 classification.

Characteristics. Supple yet full-bodied, a typically fine Saint-Julien. One that is definitely to be counted on for year-in-year-out quality.

Vineyard area: 50 hectares (125 acres).
Average production: 220 *tonneaux* (20,000 cases).

Château Duhart-Milon-Rothschild

Bordeaux red wine.
District: Haut-Médoc.
Commune: Pauillac.

Some of the vineyard lies alongside that of Château Lafite. Duhart-Milon-Rothschild is the only Fourth Growth (*Quatrième Cru*) of the Classification of 1855 found in Pauillac. M. Leroux, who lived in Madagascar, sold the vineyard to the Rothschilds of Château Lafite.

Characteristics. Has characteristics in common with the other Pauillac wines, but the quality has not been all that it might be. The Rothschilds have already improved the wine, and its reputation is growing fast.

Vineyard area: 58 hectares (145 acres).
Average production: 230 *tonneaux* (20,000 cases).

Dulce

Spanish for sweet, especially in terms of wine; the sweet wines added to dry Sherry to make it more appealing abroad.

Dumb

Wine slang, describing wines of quality which stubbornly remain hard for many years before reaching their peak. Usually these wines have a great deal of tannin; 1937, when young, produced such wines.

Dunder

Sugar-cane lees used to promote fermentation of rum.

Dur

French for hard; used of wine.
See Dumb.

Duras

See Côtes de Duras.

Château Durfort

Bordeaux red wine.
District: Haut-Médoc, France.
Commune: Margaux.

The vineyard, rated as a Second Growth (*Second Cru*) in the Gironde Classification of 1855, was owned by M. Pierre Ginestet. Originally the property of M. Durfort de Duras, the château was given its present name when purchased by M. de Vivens in 1924. The estate is situated at the entrance to the village of Margaux near Châteaux Margaux, Palmer, Rausan-Ségla, and Rauzan-Gassies. In 1963 the vineyard and *chai* were purchased by M. Lucien Lurton, who also owns Brane-Cantenac, has increased the vineyard area threefold from its original 10 hectares (25 acres). The château itself is now owned by Bernard Ginestet.

Vineyard area: 45 hectares (112.5 acres).
Average production: 90 *tonneaux* (8,000 cases).

Duriff

Californian grape—another name for the Petite-Sirah *(q.v.)*.

Dürkheim (Bad Dürkheim)

The *Wurstmarkt* held here in September is Germany's greatest wine festival. Dürkheim produces the best-known red wine of the Palatinate and a great deal of white.
See Palatinate.

Dutchess

American hybrid grape developed in Dutchess County, New York, during the mid-nineteenth century. It gives light dry white wines and is still cultivated to some extent in New York State.

E

East India

In the days when sailing ships went round by the Cape of Good Hope, casks of Sherry and Madeira were often put aboard as ballast: the long, rocking voyage to India and back improved and aged the wines. Some merchants still use this name for their good dessert blends, and an Amoroso (sweetened Oloroso) may be so called.

Eau-de-vie

Generic French term for brandy or spirits.

Eau-de-Vie d'Andaye

A Basque spirit from the Pyrenees near Hendaye.

Eau-de-Vie de Cidre

Calvados or apple brandy.
See Calvados; Applejack.

Eau-de-Vie de Danzig

French equivalent of Danziger Goldwasser (*q.v.*); also called Liqueur d'Or.

Eau-de-Vie de Lie

Spirit distilled from lees (wine deposit) in wine casks.

Eau-de-Vie de Marc

See Marc.

Eau-de-Vie de Vin

Spirit made from wine; brandy.

Ebullioscope

Apparatus for determining the alcoholic content of wine and spirits. It is based on the fact that at 760 millimeters of atmospheric pressure, water boils at 212°F. (100°C.), while alcohol boils at 172°F. (78°C.). The boiling point of the tested liquid will indicate its proportion of alcohol and water by its position between 172° and 212°F. (78° and 100°C.).

Échezeaux (Appellation Contrôlée)

Burgundy red wine.
District: Côte de Nuits, France.
Commune: Flagey-Échezeaux.
Official Classification: Great Growth (Grand Cru).

Échezeaux is a place-name, not a vineyard—a situation which could only happen in Burgundy. It is a place-name which takes in all or parts of eleven different vineyards (including one called Upper Échezeaux, but none called Échezeaux) and has been granted the rating Great Growth (*Grand Cru*), the highest Burgundian rating.

As though they were not satisfied with having cast their net and called everything within it Échezeaux, the French wine authorities took another step and situated their place-name in a town which has no other important vineyards (with the exception of Great Growth Grands Échezeaux). Flagey-Échezeaux is on the wrong—or east—side of the main road, between Dijon and Lyon, on the plain where no wines of note grow, and has only a small foothold on the sloping west side of the road. If wines from the vineyards of Échezeaux do not meet the high minimum standards, they are sold as Vosne-Romanée.

In fact, little wine is sold as Échezeaux, most of it going to market as Vosne-Romanée—which is next door. Another reason why little Échezeaux is sold under that name is that few people know about it and fewer have any confidence in their ability to pronounce it.

The size and diversity of the assembled vineyards means that an Échezeaux—when found under its own name—will be subject to considerable variation. Some will be beautifully rounded-out, stepping-stone wines, bridging the gap between the full, sturdy Vougeots and the light, delicate Vosne-Romanées; others will have less distinction than they should. Their lack of worldly fame, however, makes them wines of value, for there is relatively little demand for them, and they sell for lower prices than wines of similar quality but greater repute.

The vineyards from which these wines come are:

Vineyard	Hectares	Acres
Les Grands Échezeaux	9.2	22.8
Les Échezeaux	30	74.2
En Orveaux	9.7	24
Les Treux	4.9	12
Clos Saint-Denis	1.8	4.5
Les Cruots (or Vignes-Blanches)	3.3	8.1
Les Rouges-du-Bas	4	9.9
Champs-Traversins	3.6	8.8
Les Poulaillières	4.2	10.4
Les Loachausses	3.8	9.3
Les Quartiers de Nuits	2.6	6.4
Les Échezeaux-de-Dessus	3.6	8.8

Production in an average year comes to 1,100 hectoliters (29,150 U.S. gallons, 24,200 imp.), or the equivalent of 12,000 cases.

Echt

A Russian or Polish kümmel of the crystallized type. *See* Kümmel.

Edelfäule

German term for *Botrytis cinerea (q.v.)*, or noble rot.

Edelweiss

Proprietary Italian Fior d'Alpi, or liqueur flavored with extracts from alpine flowers.

Edelzwicker

On an Alsatian bottle label, Edelzwicker indicates a wine that is a blend of noble grape varieties.

Eelworm

Parasite harmful to vines.
See Chapter Eight, p. 39.

Egg nog

Hot or cold drink of egg beaten up in rum or brandy, sweetened and flavored with nutmeg.

An egg flip is a similar drink, made with hot spirits, ale, or wine.

Égrappage

French term for the separation of stalks from grapes before they are pressed or placed in the fermenting vats. This is necessary because the stalks contain oils and tannins that would render the wine bitter and harsh. The machine used is known as an *égrappoir*, or stemmer.
See Stemming.

Egri Bikavér

Probably the best-known wine of Hungary, apart from Tokay. The wine is red and the name means "Bull's Blood of Eger."
See Hungary.

Egypt

From time to time a tomb is opened and jars are found with dried traces of what, perhaps fifty centuries ago, was wine. From the remains found of ancient Egypt we know how the grapes were picked and pressed and how wine was buried in the tombs. Except for one man, that might be all. The twentieth-century adventure of the Egyptian Nestor Gianaclis is in some ways one of the most fascinating of our time. With every modern scientific help, it has been a struggle to go forward to a past lost for two thousand years.

It was well known in classical times that the wines of Egypt were very fine. Cleopatra served to Caesar Mareotic wine, which was said to come from ancient Meroë, near the fourth cataract of the Upper Nile. There were other Egyptian wines in great vogue throughout the Mediterranean world.

At the beginning of this century, Egyptian wine, so far as it existed at all, was undeniably bad. Nestor Gianaclis set out to search for the soil on which good wine could be grown. At the same time he tried to find out how good the wine of his ancestors had really been. Would not tastes have changed greatly in two thousand years? From evidence in the works of Virgil, Horace, Pliny, and others who wrote of wines in ancient Greece and Rome he came to the conclusion that if they had liked Egyptian wines, than we would like them too.

Under the sand which buried it, on the brink of the desert, he found a soil that was utterly different from the alluvial soils which came down with the river and were deposited in the delta and the valley of the Nile. Chemical analysis confirmed that the soil, chalky and free of salts, was almost identical with that of Champagne in France. This was a more than promising beginning, and the first vines were planted in 1903.

Most of the difficulty lay ahead. The ancient vine plants were barely a memory in the most weighty books on wine, hardly more than a scratch or two here and there on a pyramid or tomb. It would have been as easy to locate an ancient Egyptian as a grape of ancient Egypt.

Seventy-three known grape varieties were tried over the years, in cooperation with experts from France, Italy, Hungary, and other wine-growing countries; and twenty new types developed by Gianaclis were subjected to laboratory analysis. Great wine required the sun, the soil, the proper vine, all the right combinations. Gianaclis had to do in a few years what in other lands had taken centuries of trial and error: to match the right technique and the right vine to the climate and soil.

In 1931, after more than a quarter of a century of effort, it looked as if the battle were won. In that year, wines from the Mariout vineyard west of the Nile delta presented by Nestor Gianaclis before the Chambre Syndicale des Courtiers Gourmets of Paris were optimistically judged as worthy. Two years later, it was being said in France that the wine of the Pharaohs had been resurrected and that the world could drink again the nectar which had been praised by Virgil. Needless to say, the quality left something to be desired.

Today, some of the wines fulfill part of their promise and are drinkable. The white wines are easier to drink than the red, which could stand improvement. But a serious effort is being made to bring these rather disappointing wines from what might be called a super-Algerian climate into the world market. Samples have been sent to world fairs and, with production expanding (some 15,000 hectoliters or 395,000 U.S. gallons, 330,000 imp.) a year from about 29,000 hectares (72,500 acres), exports have increased, especially to Eastern Europe.

The Egyptian Vineyards and Distillers Company is a state-run cooperative with vineyards near Alexandria that provides several wines, including a red called Omar Khayyam which could be greatly improved.

SPIRITS

The difference in price between domestic and foreign spirits in Egypt is not great. Imported Cognac and whisky give strong competition to the domestic rum, arak and brandy, which are taxed at 55%. The rum, distilled from the molasses of Egyptian sugarcane, is of good quality. Tafia, however, a cruder spirit also from the residue of sugar-making, is produced in about twice the volume of rum and is stronger in alcohol, usually over 100° proof. Rum and tafia together, combined with a tafia-and-30%-brandy mixture made in about one-tenth the quantity of rum, account for an average 15,000 hectoliters (397,500 U.S. gallons, 330,000 imp.) annually. Brandy is made (from imported raisins or fresh grapes) in about half the volume of rum, and arak and ouzo are produced in fairly substantial amounts. A popular alcoholic beverage of Egypt is buza, distilled from fermented dates. The distillation process is usually haphazard and poorly conducted, and the dates are often half-rotten, but this keeps it affordable to the fellahin, who are the major consumers of buza.

Einzellage

The German term for individual vineyard, as defined by the 1971 German wine law.
See Germany.

Eiswein

Made from sweet frozen grapes selected in late November or December. The juice is frozen, leaving the sugar. The quality is similar to Beerenauslese.

Eitelsbacher Karthäuserhofberg

Outstanding vineyard of Eitelsbach in western Germany.
See Mosel-Saar-Ruwer.

Elbling

A quantity-producing grape which is grown in Luxembourg, Lorraine, and Germany.

Elefantenwein (Elephant wine)

Reference to a wine from Tübingen, Germany, which is said to have been made from grapes so hard that no men could have trodden them, but only elephants. The same comment was made of the Reutlinger wine of the Neckar region.

Élixir d'Anvers

Belgian liqueur made in Antwerp by F. X. de Beukelaer. It is compounded of herbs and plants on a base of brandy, is golden in color, moderately sweet, and very fragrant.

Elongated wine

British term for wine "lengthened" by addition of water to reduce strength for purposes of excise duty.

Eltviller Sonnenberg

Most elegant of the Eltville wines. The other outstanding vineyard here is Eltviller Langenstück.
See Rheingau.

Elvira

American hybrid grape developed in the late nineteenth century in Missouri and still used for white wines, usually sparkling.

Emilia-Romagna

Red and white wines.
Central Italy.

South of the River Po, running from the Apennines to the Adriatic, stretches one of the great productive plains which recur throughout the Italian peninsula. Here a mountain soars up from the flat, with the operetta republic of San Marino perched on top and vines clinging to its steep sides; but most of Emilia-Romagna is level, even ground, where the dominant activity is agriculture. Wheat and maize are cultivated and vines are not neglected, although they used to be. Solid chunks of vineyards were rare, but everywhere vines could be seen: they ran rampant over the countryside, twining around any available support, apparently without benefit of cultivation or bite of the pruning knife. This haphazard growth lent a curious charm to the scenery, but today the vineyards are neat and orderly, the vines diligently trained.

Sangiovese di Romagna

Lambrusco and Albana produce the honored fruit of Emilia-Romagna, but Sangiovese is the widespread vine. The wine it gives is variable in the extreme, sometimes slightly bitter and hard, sometimes mellow and warming. It is always, however, available, and always red and always dry—this last characteristic is enough to endear it to many visitors to the region; but in this case the D.O.C. has been granted solely through Italian enthusiasm. Sangiovese accounts for the bulk of the 1.5 million hectoliters (39 million U.S. gallons, 30 million imp.) the area produces annually.

Lambrusco

This has no connection with *Vitis labrusca*, a native North American vine species. It is the best-known example of the region's viticulture, the wine-name deriving from the grapevine. It is a red, dry or sweetish semi-sparkling wine with a bright ruby foam.

There are four D.O.C.'s for Lambrusco: Lambrusco di Sorbara, Lambrusco Grasparossa di Castevetro, Lambrusco Salamino di Santa Croce, and Lambrusco Reggiano. The first three are made near Modena, the fourth near Reggio-Emilia. Though none of the wines is especially good, particularly when too sweet and sparkling, Lambrusco is the single largest-selling wine and accounts for about half of Italian wine sales in the United States.

Albana di Romagna (D.O.C.)

A golden-yellow wine of controlled denomination of origin—which may be semi-sweet or dry (although the dry type usually retains a slight trace of sugar). Made from the Albana grapes grown on the hilly area between Bologna and Rimini. Galla Placidia, Regent of the Western Roman Empire (A.D. 435), is said to have been an early devotee of Albana. Traveling through the region, she stopped at a small town to quench her thirst at the local inn and was served with the wine, but in a coarse mug. Her reaction to the Albana was: "I must drink you in gold," and Bertinoro ("Drink-you-in-gold") has been the name of the town ever since.

Colli Piacentini

A controlled Denomination of Origin applicable to a red wine of some character produced in Ziano and six other communes in the province of Piacenza from Barbera and Bonarda grapes. It is dry, faintly sweet.

Trebbiano di Romagna

A D.O.C. wine produced from Trebbiano di Romagna grapes in a vast area that is part of the provinces of Bologna, Forli, and Ravenna. It is a straw color, with a pleasant bouquet and a dry taste. A sparkling wine is also made and is either dry, semi-sweet, or sweet.

Bianco di Scandiano (D.O.C.)

Made in the foothills of Reggio-Emilia, this is a sweetish white wine, low in alcohol, often crackling.

Colli Bolognesi (Monte San Pietro and Castelli Medioevali)

From the vineyards in the hills between Modena and Bologna, this D.O.C. covers eight types. As a regional wine, it is above average and is made from Pinot Blanc, Sauvignon Blanc, and Barbera, which are sold as varietals of Monte San Pietro.

English Wine

Made from grapes grown outdoors in an English vineyard, as opposed to a British wine made from grapes or must that are imported from another country.

See United Kingdom.

Entre-Deux-Mers (Appellation Contrôlée)

Red and white wines
District: Bordeaux, France

Light, clean, fruity red and dry white wines. The red wine made in the district is sold as Bordeaux and is not entitled to the place-name. There are no outstanding growths or vineyards. Much of the wine is made by the fifteen cooperatives, with an average production of 410,000 hectoliters (11 million U.S. gallons, 9 million imp.).

Deriving its name from its location, the region lies between the two rivers—"seas"—the Garonne and the Dordogne; and lies, also, between Bordeaux and Libourne in the zones of Pomerol and Saint-Émilion wines. The best wines have been accorded separate place-names. Loupiac, Sainte-Croix-du-Mont, Cadillac, and Premières Côtes de Bordeaux on the Garonne, and Graves de Vayres from the small gravel enclave on the Dordogne, are wines of higher quality made within the limits of Entre-Deux-Mers (A.O.C. for dry white wine only).

Enzian

Spirit distilled in the alpine and adjoining countries of Europe, from the yard-long roots of the yellow mountain gentian. It makes one of the most aristocratic forms of schnapps.

Enzymes

Large proteins produced by organisms to catalyze chemical reactions. Enzymes may be recovered and purified, then added to a solution to produce a chemical change. The enzyme pectinase is occasionally added to freshly crushed white grapes to break down the slimy pectins and thereby facilitate pressing. At present, it cannot be used to produce very good wines.

Épernay

An important center of the Champagne trade. It shares with Reims the great cellars of Champagne.

Épesses

Moët et Chandon, Pol Roger and Mercier are the best known and the most important ones. The Comité Interprofessionnel du Vin de Champagne (C.I.V.C.), the Champagne Association's headquarters, is located in Épernay.
See Champagne.

Épesses

White wine of Lavaux in the canton of Vaud, Switzerland.
See Switzerland.

Erbacher Markobrunn

See Markobrunn; Rheingau.

Erdener Treppchen

Best-known vineyard of Erden on the German Mosel and an outstanding dry wine.
See Mosel-Saar-Ruwer.

Erinose

A disease caused by a very small mite.
See Chapter Eight, p. 39.

Ermitage

See Hermitage.

Erzeugerabfüllung

A German term for estate-bottling.

Espalier

Method of training vines. The trunk terminates in one or two arms and several canes, all in the same plane and supported by a trellis or wire. There are several variations on this method, including the decorative trellis-trained vine; and the practical guyot pattern of a trunk and one arm.
See Chapter Eight, p. 35.

Espumoso

Spanish term for sparkling.
See Cava.

Est! Est!! Est!!! (D.O.C.)

The dry wine of Montefiascone, Italy.
See Latium.

Estate-bottling

The all-important practice in which individual vineyard owners bottle the unadulterated product of their own vines. The term printed on a label should always be a guarantee of authenticity and, to some extent, of superior quality. Statements that the wine is estate-bottled and comes from someone who definitely is the vineyard owner, and a clear indication that the wine was bottled by the person who made it (or at least on his premises), should appear on the main label. In France estate-bottling is virtually the same thing as château-bottling (indicated as *Mis en Bouteilles au Château*) and is most often noted with one of the following terms: *Mise du Domaine, Mise au Domaine, Mis en Bouteilles au Domaine, Mise du Propriétaire, Mis en Bouteilles par le Propriétaire,* or *Mise à la Propriété.* In Germany the phrase used to be *Original-Abfüllung,* but it has been replaced by *Auseigenem Lesegut* or *Erzeugerabfüllung.* In the United States the term can be used only on the labels of wines made from grapes grown solely by the producer himself.

Esters

An organic compound derived from the slow reaction between the acids of the wine and the alcohols.
See Chapter Nine, p. 52.

Estufades

Huge heating chambers in which wines of Madeira are "cooked."
See Madeira.

Étampé

French term for branded.

Ethers

Chemical compounds, important components of wines and spirits imparting bouquet or aroma.

Ethiopia

Though several African nations produce much wine, Ethiopia is not among them. Compared to the quantities from Algeria, South Africa, Morrocco, Tunisia, and Egypt, the average annual total was 50,000 hectoliters (1,325,000 U.S. gallons, 1,100,000 imp.), indeed small. The three principal regions for both wine and table grapes are Abadir-Dukem, Guder, and Eritrea in the north of the country. Sultana and Black Muscat predominate in the less than 500 hectares (1,250 acres) of vineyards, but a large portion of the wine is made from concentrates. Some of the wineries included the Elaberet Estate, Makanissa, Altavilla, and Alexandrakis, and most of their wines still show the strong influence dating from Mussolini's occupation.

Étiquette

French term for bottle label.

Etna (D.O.C.)

Red, white, or rosé wines from Sicily *(q.v.)*.

Étoile

One of the best white wines of the French Jura comes from this southernmost area of the region.
See Jura.

Eudemis

One of the distinctive grape-moths.
See Chapter Eight, p. 39.

Eumelan

Red-wine giving grape of the eastern United States. It is a poor producer and not outstanding for the wine-maker.

Château l'Evangile

Bordeaux red wine.
District and Commune: Pomerol, France.

Excellent wine is made by this property, a neighbor of Château Cheval-Blanc in Saint-Émilion. It is owned by the Ducasse family.
Vineyard area: 13 hectares (32 acres).
Average production: 36 *tonneaux* (3,400 cases).

Excise

Tax on home product as compared with customs.

Excoriose

A rare vine malady.
See Chapter Eight, p. 38.

Exportation of wine

Figures change, inevitably, from year to year, influenced by the season's harvest and by industrial and political fluctuations. The exports from the two largest producers, Italy and France, have been steadily increasing, but those from Algeria—which used to be the largest exporter—have been declining. Although Argentina, the United States, and the Soviet Union produce a great deal of wine, none of these three countries exports very much. The figures below are averages from the past several years, corrected to pro-

ject the trends of the next few years. In some cases, notably Great Britain and the Netherlands, statistics include wines re-exported.

WORLD WINE EXPORTS

Exporting Country	Hectoliters	U.S. Gallons	Imp. Gallons
Italy	14,800,000	391,000,000	325,500,000
France	8,800,000	232,500,000	193,600,000
Spain	5,400,000	142,600,000	118,800,000
Bulgaria	2,400,000	63,400,000	52,800,000
Hungary	2,400,000	63,400,000	52,800,000
West Germany	2,000,000	52,900,000	44,000,000
Portugal	1,600,000	42,300,000	35,200,000
Algeria	1,300,000	34,300,000	28,600,000
Yugoslavia	1,100,000	29,000,000	24,200,000
Greece	650,000	17,200,000	14,300,000
Rumania	550,000	14,500,000	12,000,000
U S S R	490,000	13,000,000	11,000,000
Cyprus	375,000	9,900,000	8,200,000
Tunisia	360,000	9,500,000	7,900,000
Austria	330,000	8,700,000	7,300,000
Morocco	300,000	7,900,000	6,600,000
Argentina	200,000	5,300,000	4,400,000
United States	175,000	4,600,000	3,800,000
Belgium	170,000	4,500,000	3,700,000
Great Britain	150,000	3,900,000	3,300,000
Albania	115,000	3,000,000	2,500,000
South Africa	85,000	2,200,000	1,900,000
Luxembourg	81,000	2,100,000	1,800,000
Australia	75,000	2,000,000	1,700,000
Chile	72,000	1,900,000	1,600,000
Netherlands	66,000	1,700,000	1,500,000
Malta	50,000	1,300,000	1,100,000
Israel	49,000	1,300,000	1,100,000
Czechoslovakia	44,000	1,200,000	970,000
Turkey	40,000	1,000,000	880,000
Egypt	25,000	660,000	550,000
Switzerland	8,000	210,000	180,000
TOTAL	40,260,000	1,168,970,000	973,780,000

Extra Sec

French for Extra Dry. These words appearing on the label of a bottle of Champagne do not, in fact, indicate an extra-dry wine, but one which is only fairly dry. A really dry Champagne will be labeled Brut.

Ezerjó

White-wine variety grown in Hungary. Also the full gold-colored wine of Mór, near Budapest.

F

Factory House

A club and club building in Oporto where the finest Ports in the world are drunk. Nowadays it is correctly called the British Association, but everyone refers to it as the Feitoria Inglesa or English Factory House. In early days the Factory system was one of British extra-territorial rights in foreign countries, which is why out of courtesy to Portugal the name of the Club has been changed. Even today, however, British Port companies have rights in Portugal accorded to no other foreigners.

Members of the Factory House comprise the most exclusive British Port circle, every one being a partner in a British Port firm in Oporto.

In the past, no British partner could join the Factory House if there was a Portuguese partner in his firm.

Falerno

The vineyards where the modern Falerno is grown are on the slopes of Monte Massico (about halfway between Rome and Naples), and the wine is generally white, semidry, and moderately strong.

Falernian was the most famous of all the ancient Roman wines, and it too came from the vineyards of Monte Massico; but we do not now know what grapes went into it, and we have only a very imperfect idea of how it tasted.

See Campania; Classical wines.

Falernum

A flavoring syrup, not very strong (6% alcohol by volume), made in Bermuda and the West Indies of syrup, lime, almonds, ginger, and spices. It is a popular flavoring for rum drinks.

Fan leaf

Another name for infectious degeneration of vines. *See* Chapter Eight, p. 39.

Fara (D.O.C.)

Red wine from the Italian Piedmont *(q.v.)*.

Fass

German for cask.

Fassle

A German drinking vessel rather similar in principle to the *porrón* of Spain, in that the liquid is spurted from a tube into the drinker's mouth. The *Fassle*, or little barrel, is a five-liter wooden cask into whose bung-hole cork a tube, the *Spitzle*, has been inserted. As with the *porrón*, the trick of drinking from the vessel entails a steady hand and a quick flick of the wrist for the drinker to avoid being doused in the stream of liquid.

Fat

A big, soft wine without the hardness to give it body and containing much natural glycerin. Typical examples are the Bordeaux Pomerols and some Saint-Émilions.

Faye d'Anjou

Commune with the right to an Appellation Contrôlée in the Coteaux du Layon district of Anjou, France.

See Anjou.

Federweisser

New wine, milky or "feather white," found in German inns after the vintage.

Fehér Bor

Hungarian term for white wine. *Bor* means wine.

Feints

Leavings of second distillation of Scotch malt whisky.

Fendant

Best white wines of Valais, Switzerland, made from the Fendant (or Chasselas) grape. In Germany known as Gutedel.

See Switzerland.

Fermé

Firm or stubborn. Usually a wine of quality; but as long as it is in this condition, it is hard and tannic and not ready to drink.

Fermentation

The decompositon of sugar chiefly into ethyl alcohol and carbon dioxide. The classic equation is given by Gay-Lussac:

$$C_6H_{12}O_6 \rightarrow 2C_2H_6O + 2CO_2$$
$$\text{(180 grams)} \quad \text{(92 grams)} \quad \text{(88 grams)}$$

Unfortunately, this is not quite accurate, careful measurement having proved that whereas the alcoholic content should be the equivalent of 51% of the sugar, in reality 47% is normal and the odd 4% forms a number of side-products, including higher alcohols, nitrogenous compounds, and glycerin. Fermentation is carried out by yeasts as their primary source of energy for growth. It can take place only when the amount of oxygen is limited, for in the presence of oxygen, the sugar would be converted completely to CO_2 and water.

Stainless steel or concrete fermentation vats are much preferable to the traditional oak ones, because they effectively keep oxygen from the fermenting musts. Although the old wooden vats are picturesque, their disappearance from Bordeaux and Burgundy will improve the quality of the wine. So that fermentation should proceed satisfactorily, temperature and aeration must be properly regulated.

See Chapter Nine.

Fernet Branca

The best-known Italian bitters. It is used as an aperitif and generally recommended to settle upset stomachs and hangovers.

See Bitters.

Château Ferrière

Bordeaux red wine.
District: Haut-Médoc, France.
Commune: Margaux.

This fair-quality vineyard, in the very heart of the village of Margaux, classed a Third Growth (*Troisième Cru*) of the Médoc in the Classification of 1855, is at present leased to Château Lascombes. Each year a limited quantity of Ferrière is made by the owners of Château Lascombes.

Fiano

The grape which makes the light, white, slightly tart wines of Avellino, near Naples.

Fiasco

Italian straw-covered glass flask holding about two liters of wine. It is associated particularly with Chianti.

Field-grafting

For a description of this method of grafting vines, see Chapter Eight, p. 34.

Château de Fieuzal

Bordeaux red and white wines.
District: Graves, France.
Commune: Léognan.

The vineyard, which once belonged to the La Rochefoucauld family, is planted on good gravelly slopes. At present, M. Gribelin runs it, and M. Negrevergne, a Bordeaux pharmaceutical manufacturer, has been the owner since 1974. The vineyard was made a Graves Classified Growth (*Cru Classé*) in 1959.

Characteristics. In quality, the wines can hold their own with almost any of the Graves. The red is generous and velvety, with a charming bouquet; the white, dry and *racé*.

Vineyard area: red—29 hectares (72.5 acres); white—3 hectares (7.5 acres).

Average production: red—100 *tonneaux* (9,000 cases); white—12 *tonneaux* (1,000 cases).

Château Figeac

Bordeaux red wine.
District and Commune: Saint-Émilion, France.

Long one of the best-known Saint-Émilions, and in 1955 classed among the First Great Growths (*Premiers Grands Crus*), Figeac must not be confused with other Saint-Émilion vineyards employing the word in various combinations of the name. Six other of these Figeac vineyards surround Château Figeac (Charles de Figeac was a nobleman of Saint-Émilion), but the unmodified name belongs to the best of the growths, one of the largest important vineyards in Saint-Émilion. Touching Cheval-Blanc, and near the Pomerol boundary, the vineyard surrounds a château and wine *chai* widely separated by the length of a broad avenue which bisects a splendid park. The owner, Thierry de Manoncourt, is an ardent and progressive wine-maker and has recently built a very fine new *chai*.

Characteristics. The wine has made a dramatic comeback over the past few years. It is a characteristic Saint-Émilion, robust and well-rounded, and one of the best wines of the district, despite its high price.

Vineyard area: 34 hectares (85 acres).
Average production: 180 *tonneaux* (17,000 cases).

Château Filhot

Bordeaux white wine.
District and Commune: Sauternes, France.

Owned by Henri de Vencelles, the vineyard produces somewhat drier wines than Yquem and is generally considered to have been unjustly classed a Second Growth (*Second Cru*) of Sauternes in 1855. If the wines were now re-rated, it might be made a First. The château, a beautiful eighteenth-century country house set in smooth lawns, looks more English than French; and as it happens, Filhot wines have always had a large following in England.

Characteristics. Was high in alcohol; one of the driest of Sauternes, but is now being made sweeter and is no longer the exception it once was.

Vineyard area: 50 hectares (125 acres).
Average production: 100 *tonneaux* (10,000 cases).

Fillette

Fillette

French slang term for a half-bottle in certain parts of France, as for instance, in Anjou. Literally, "a little girl."

Film yeast

Another name for *flor*.
See Sherry.

Filtering

The clarification of wine by passing it through special devices—or simply through a layer of filter paper—with the object of ridding it of any suspended particles. In many fine wine districts the older method of fining *(q.v.)* is used. Filtering, for all its ease and practicality, can rob a fine wine of some of its quality. It was true of the now discarded asbestos of the Seitz Filter. Too many layers or slipshod handling can filter out all distinction, leaving the wine insipid and without character.

Fine Champagne

Not a Champagne but a Cognac brandy, properly a blend from the districts of Grande Champagne and Petite Champagne.
Une fine (pronounced feen) is the popular way of calling for a Cognac in France—any Cognac—but correctly it is liqueur Cognac of the Champagne (chalky and best) Cognac district.
See Cognac.

Finesse

French term for exceptional elegance or breed *(q.v.)*.

Finger Lakes

Wine-growing region in New York State. This is the most important district in the eastern states, and some of the finest sparkling wine in America is produced here. The best vineyards are beside Lake Keuka and Lake Canadaigua; and there are others around Lake Seneca and Lake Cayuga. Some of the leading firms are established in the Pleasant Valley-Hammondsport district, and some excellent sparkling wines, as well as other types, are made here.
See United States: New York.

Fining

Fining, or *collage*, is the process by which wine is clarified of any suspended particles. This can be done either with an organic agent such as blood, casein, protein, or gelatine, which will coagulate and carry down with it the clouding particles, or with a clarifier which has a mechanical action—such as bentonite, cellulose, infusorial earth.
See Chapter Nine, p. 40.

Finish

Lingering aftertaste.

Fino

The driest type of Sherry *(q.v.)*.

Fins Bois

One of the lesser districts in the Cognac region of France.
See Cognac.

Fior d'Alpi

Literally, alpine flowers. It is a sweet Italian liqueur, yellow in color and usually containing a branch of rock-sugar crystals inside the characteristic tall narrow bottle.

Firkin

English beer barrel with a capacity of 41 liters (10.8 U.S. gallons, 9 imp.).

Fitou (Appellation Contrôlée)

Red wine.
District: Southern France.

A French wine-growing area of more historical than contemporary importance. Fitou, which adjoins Roussillon, near the Spanish border, is made up of nine communes: Fitou, Leucate, Caves-de-Treilles, Lapalme, Tuchan, Paziols, Cascastel, Villeneuve-les-Corbières, and Treilles. The hot Mediterranean sun beats down brutally on the scarcely fertile slopes, 1000 hectares (2,500 acres) of which are given over to vines.

The vine-types are mostly Carignan and Grenache, which must—singly or together—make up 75% of any wine carrying the name of Fitou. The other 25% may be made up of one or several of the following: Cinsault, Terret Noir, Malvoisie, Maccabéo, Muscat, or Picpoule. The maximum that the French authorities allow is 40 hectoliters per hectare (422 U.S. gallons, 352 imp. per acre), except in certain extraordinary years.

Fitou is one of the best wines of the Midi. It is a dark, pungent, heavy red wine, high in alcoholic content, making a good, rather common, but sound table wine. To gain the name it must be aged in the barrel for at least nine months (until 1953 the ageing period was two years in the barrel) before it is sold. The average yearly production of Fitou is less than 800,000 cases

234

and for this reason it is not often found outside its native area.

Fixed acidity

The presence of natural and desirable acids (principally tartaric), which are the cause of an agreeable tartness in wine. Fixed acids cannot be removed by steam distillation.

See Chapter Nine, p. 40.

Fixin (Appellation Contrôlée)

Burgundy red wine.
District: Côte de Nuits, France.

Fixin is the northernmost of the wine communes of the Côte de Nuits, the upper arm of Burgundy's famous Côte d'Or. Present-day Fixin includes the area that was, before 1850, that of its neighbor, Fixey. In spite of the augmentation of property, the town did not gain a great deal as far as vineyards were concerned.

Most of the wines of the town are not sold under the commune name at all but are included in the Vins Fins de la Côte de Nuits. However, rather more than 40 hectares (100 acres) within the town are allowed to be sold as Fixin, the best of which comes from the 4.8-hectare (12 acre) vineyard, Clos de la Perrière. According to the now obsolete classification of the Côte d'Or vineyards made in 1860, this vineyard was considered as an Outstanding Growth (*Tête de Cuvée*) and was the only one so honored in Fixin. The more recent classification made by the Institut National des Appellations d'Origine des Vins et Eaux-de-Vie (the National Institute of Place-names of Wines and Spirits) has, more realistically, demoted it to First Growth (*Premier Cru*) of Fixin, a status which it shares with five other vineyards. The wines from the Clos de la Perrière are generally deep, alcoholic, and slow to mature, and while they bear a strong resemblance to those from the neighboring commune of Gevrey-Chambertin, they have less breed and magnificence than do Gevrey's greatest wines. In some years, however, they can be better than many from the secondary vineyards which rank just behind the great Chambertin.

Within the confines of Fixin there are some 202 hectares (500 acres) growing wines allowed to go to market only as Vins Fins de la Côte de Nuits and about 43 hectares (105 acres) whose wines are sold as Fixin. These 43 hectares include the following Classified Growths, all of which may be sold as Fixin Premier Cru, or with the town name followed by the name of the vineyard.

FIRST GROWTHS (*Premiers Crus*)

Vineyard	Hectares	Acres
Clos de la Perrière	6.53	16.3
Clos du Chapitre	4.79	11.9
Les Hervelets	3.83	9.5

Vineyard	Hectares	Acres
Les Meix-Bas	1.88	4.7
Aux Cheusots (Clos Napoléon)	1.75	4.55
Les Arvelets	3.36	7.8

Flagey-Échezeaux

Flagey-Échezeaux in Burgundy is a town but not a place-name—in the vinous sense of the word—although the two great vineyards within its confines are place-names in their own right. The town stands to the left of the main road which runs through the Côte de Nuits, and its boundaries are so staked out that they force a small passage between Vougeot and Vosne-Romanée and fan out into a beachhead on the great slope.

The two vineyards within the town are Échezeaux and Grands-Échezeaux (*qq.v.*). Both are Great Growths (*Grands Crus*)—the highest official rating given to Burgundian vineyards—and in the years when the wine does not meet the rigorous minimum standards, they are declassed either into First Growths (*Premiers Crus*)—slightly less than Great Growth—of neighboring Vosne-Romanée, or into the more general Vosne-Romanée, with no other indication of origin.

Flagon

A large bottle usually of flattened globular shape, its capacity entirely dependent upon the wishes of its user; a squat bottle similar to the Bocksbeutel (*q.v.*) of German Franconia used for Commonwealth (and especially Australian) "burgundies."

Flat

A Champagne or other sparkling wine that has lost the sparkle—i.e., its bubbles. In the case of still wines, one that is dull, unattractive, and too low in acidity.

Fleurie (Appellation Contrôlée)

Only in recent years sold consistently under the communal name of Fleurie, these wines are not as well known as some other Beaujolais, but they are among the most typically Beaujolais of all, perfectly expressing the fresh fruity charm of this French red wine.
See Beaujolais.

Fliers

Tiny tasteless particles sometimes appearing in wine. They are caused usually by cold and disappear if the wine is warmed to normal room temperature.

Flip

A mixed drink made with wine, brandy, or both, along with shaved ice, sugar, bitters, nutmeg, and an egg.

Floc—an Armagnac Aperitif

This is to Armagnac what Pineau des Charentes is to Cognac, namely sweet, unfermented wine with an Armagnac base instead of a Cognac base.

Flor

The white skin or layer which appears uniquely on some Sherries and on certain wines of the Jura in France. When *flor* develops on Sherry, the wine becomes Fino; when it does not, the wine is Oloroso.
See Sherry; *and* Chapter Nine, p. 40.

Floraison

French term for flowering of the vines, at the ends of which very small green berries will have formed.
See Chapter Eight, p. 31.

Flowery

Taste reminiscent of flowers, found in young wines; the younger the wine, the more flowery it is apt to be. Few great wines have this quality.

Fluid ounce

In the United States, one-sixteenth of a standard U.S. pint. In Great Britain, the volume of one standard ounce weight of pure water measured at a temperature of 62°F. (17°C.) and a barometric pressure of 30 inches. The equivalents under the metric system are 2.957 centiliters to an American ounce and 2.841 centiliters to a British fluid ounce. The American is about 4% greater than the British.

Flûte

In France, the tall and thin bottle similar to that used for Alsatian and Rhine wines but made of clear glass. Many rosé wines are now shipped in flûtes. Also, the traditional and most successful glass used for sparkling wines, especially Champagne. Its slender V shape helps conserve the precious bubbles.

Folle Blanche

Once the principal grape for the thin white Charente wines which are distilled into Cognac, this has now been largely displaced by the Saint-Émilion vine, although a small percentage is still used. The Folle Blanche is now grown primarily in the area surrounding Nantes, to produce Gros Plant, the V.D.Q.S. of the Muscadet.

Forbidden Fruit

An American liqueur perhaps better known abroad than at home. It is made from the shaddock—a citrus fruit somewhat like a large grapefruit—infused in brandy. It is reddish-brown in color and is sold in a round bottle the size of a grapefruit.

Foreshots

The first crude spirit to emerge from the still in whisky-making.

Forster Jesuitengarten

Best known of the outstanding Forster wines in the German Palatinate, or Pfalz.
See Palatinate.

Forster Kirchenstück

Best of the outstanding Forster wines in the German Palatinate, or Pfalz.
See Palatinate.

Fortified wine

Wine to which brandy has been added sometimes to stop fermentation and to increase alcoholic content. Some examples are Port, Sherry, Málaga, and Madeira. In America, use of the term is illegal and such wines are usually called dessert wines.
See Port; Sherry; Madeira; Málaga; Sweet fortified wines of France.

Forzato

Italian term for wine made from overripe grapes.

Foudre

French term for large cask for maturing, storing, and transporting wine. Used to some extent in Alsace, where the word was adopted from the German *Fuder*, and for ordinary or bulk wine.

Château Fourcas-Hosten

Bordeaux red wine.
District: Haut-Médoc, France.
Commune: Listrac.

The hill of Fourcas—really not so much a hill as the culmination of the Listrac Plateau—on the north edge of the commune is shared by Fourcas-Hosten and the less well known, but pleasantly countrified, Fourcas-Dupré, just to the north. Château Fourcas-Hosten, classified *Bourgeois Exceptionel* in 1932, is perhaps rated below its true worth and might be considered a Great Growth (*Grand Cru*) of the Médoc. For many years before 1951, there were two Fourcas-Hostens, whose respective owners were cousins; the vineyard is now united under one proprietorship. In 1971, under the management of Philip Powers, Peter M. F. Sichel, and

Bertrand de Rivoyre, the property was syndicated to a group of American wine-lovers. A program of replanting and improvements has begun. In 1973, 10 hectares (25 acres) of Cabernet Sauvignon, Cabernet Franc, and Merlot were planted. In 1974–75, the planting of another 10 hectares was completed. A renovation program of the *chai* and the *cuvier* has been completed, using the most modern techniques. M. Peynaud, formerly dean of the Oenological Institute of Bordeaux, now oversees the vinification of the wine. Château Fourcas-Hosten (pronounced foor-cass) has become one of the top Listracs.

Characteristics. A full, slightly hard, and yet distinguished wine.

Vineyard area: 46 hectares (115 acres).

Average production: 200 *tonneaux* (18,000 cases).

Fourtet (Clos)

Bordeaux red wine.
District and Commune: Saint-Émilion, France.

One of the twelve First Great Growths (*Premiers Grands Crus*) of Saint-Émilion, as officially classified in 1955. The vineyard is planted along the wall of the eleventh-century village, one of the most picturesque in France. The cellars, cut in solid rock under the vines, are among the sights of the town. The estate is the property of the Lurton heirs.

Characteristics. Saint-Émilion is typified in this full-bodied fine wine. Recently, however, it has been criticized as having somewhat declined in quality.

Vineyard area: 20 hectares (50 acres).

Average production: 80 *tonneaux* (7,500 cases).

Fox-Grape

Popular name for grapes of *Vitis labrusca*, which runs wild in northeast and north-central America. It can be used for wines which have a very pronounced taste and aroma. Termed "foxy," although it has nothing in common with the scent of a fox, it is a strongly flavored grape.

Foxy

The special taste quality of the American wines—i.e., wines made from native grapes in eastern America. It is a particular characteristic of wines made from grapes of the species *Vitis labrusca*, of which type Concord is probably the best-known example.

Fraise

French *eau-de-vie*, or white alcohol, a brandy distilled from strawberries.

Framboise

French *eau-de-vie*, or white alcohol, a brandy distilled from raspberries.

Franc-de-goût

French term for clean-tasting.

France

Enjoyment of fine wines is one of the most civilized of pleasures; and the greatest wines in the world come from France, center of modern civilization, not in the fine arts only, but in the minor delightful arts of eating and drinking. Wine is a source of inspiration for her artists and the delectation of her workmen; a symbol of French *savoir-vivre* and a major French industry. The mysteries of wine-making cannot be reduced to statistics, any more than a picture can be analyzed by the size of its canvas or the time it took to paint; yet statistics are striking and important.

There are some 1.1 million hectares (2.7 million acres) of vines in France, most of which exist solely for wine—although a few produce table grapes—and their output is some 80 million hectoliters (2 billion U.S. gallons, 1.7 billion imp.) per year. Of this, by far the greatest proportion is *ordinaire* for everyday drinking, but about 10 million hectoliters (265 million U.S. gallons, 220 million imp.) are classed as Appellation Contrôlée—the fine wines of France. The vineyard area is now stabilized after having diminished by nearly 100,000 hectares (250,000 acres), in consequence of a subsidized uprooting of vines for common wine as a measure against overproduction. Some 2 million of the 50-odd million Frenchmen owe their livelihood directly to wine, including growers (about 1.2 million of them), wholesalers and shippers, regularly employed vineyard workers, manufacturers of wine-making equipment and machinery, laboratory technicians, and a host of civil servants, part of whose task is keeping track of statistics such as these. Then, carriers transport wine, among other loads; shops sell it, among other commodities; and many other Frenchmen would be living far less well than they do were it not for wine.

France exports about 11.5 million hectoliters (304 million U.S. gallons, 253 million imp.) and imports about as much, mainly from Mediterranean countries. The United States is the largest export customer, followed by England, the Benelux countries, and Germany, generally in that order. The average French family spends from 8% to 13% of its food budget on wine, and consumption is among the highest per capita in the world—82 liters (21 U.S. gallons, 18 imp.). But this amount only includes wine that has been taxed; considerably more is consumed on large and small vineyards without the interference of tax collector or official statistician. Wine is a huge industry, an incalculable economic asset, an invaluable source of foreign currency, and the means by which innumerable Frenchmen earn all or part of their livelihood. But it is more than just this. It is almost a way of life.

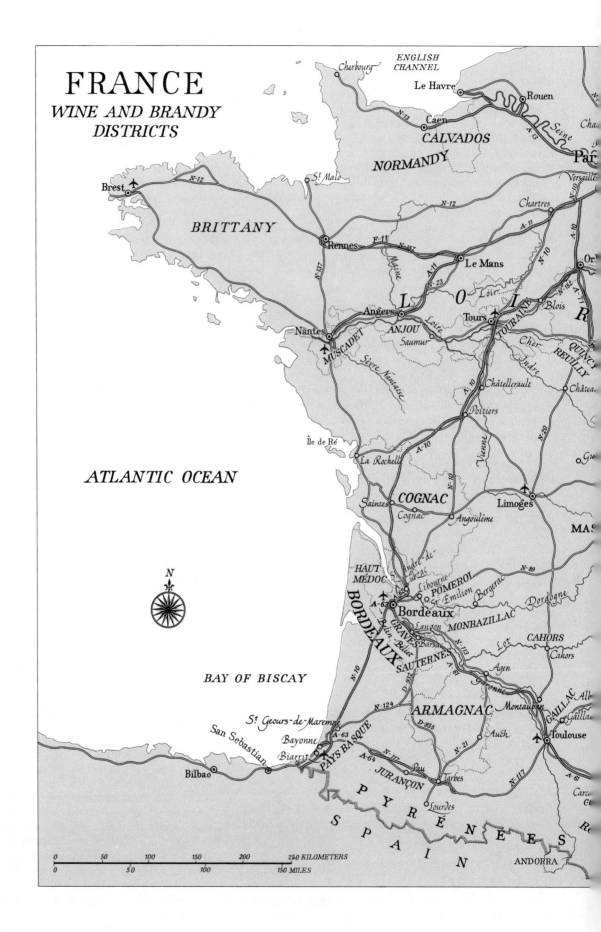

FRANCE
WINE AND BRANDY
DISTRICTS

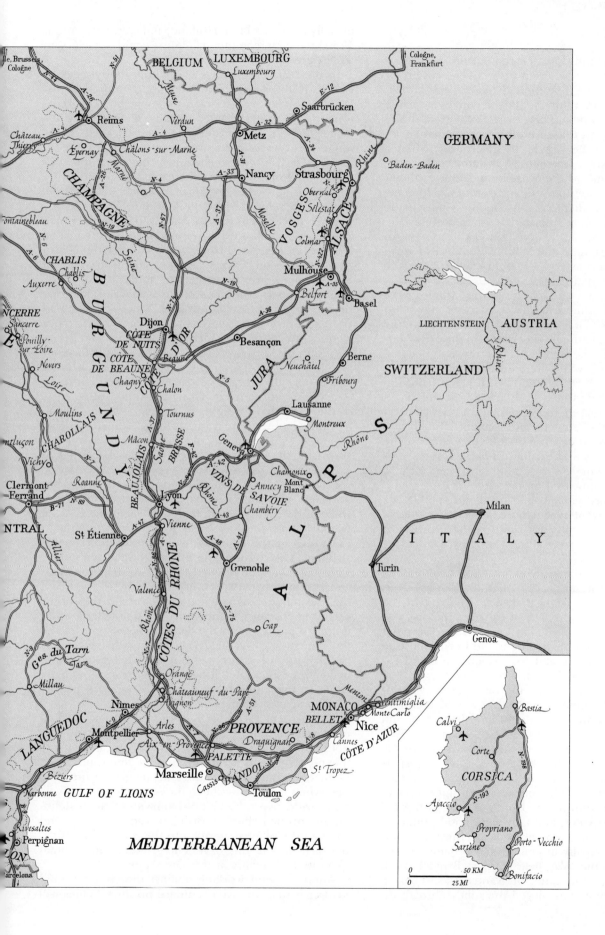

WINE HISTORY

Wine was made in Gaul before the Roman occupation, mainly, no doubt, around the Greek colony of Massilia (Marseille). The Romans spread the knowledge of wine further and taught the natives to prune and tend their vines. There were two great trade routes by river and road from the early settlement of Narbonne: from Béziers to the Garonne (whence there was already a sea route to Britain); and by the Rhône and Saône to the Moselle and Loire valleys. Goods went by water to the inland port of Chalon-sur-Saône, and from there by wagon. The Gauls made barrels, and as early as Roman times these were in use. Centuries later the saintly King Louis IX liked to make casks in his spare time and as he made his visits from monastery to monastery he would stay to taste the wine the monks had made.

Gradually, as new and hardier grape varieties were discovered, the vineyards pushed farther north: to Gaillac and the Côtes du Rhône; then as far as the Loire, Britany, and the Île-de-France. In the early Middle Ages, before the trade with Gascony had become important, Rhine wines were coming into London, along with *Vins de France*, the French wines from the districts near Paris which were greatly esteemed. As the demand increased, more supplies of wine came in from La Rochelle, Angers, and Saumur. Rouen was then a very busy port. Argenteuil, celebrated in the nineteenth century in the paintings of the Impressionists, was famous more than six hundred years earlier, when its wines appeared on the table of King Philip Augustus. Before Champagne began to sparkle, its wines probably went in with those of the Seine; toward the end of the seventeenth century, the growths of Reims, Ay, and Épernay were praised by Saint-Evremond and others.

Nor were any of the wines as strong in alcohol or as lasting as those we are accustomed to. The light red Clairet of Gascony, as it arrived in England in the fourteenth century, was drawn fresh from the cask and drunk within a year of the harvest. In 1352 this edict was issued in London: "mixing of old Bordeaux wine with young Bordeaux and passing off the blend for young Bordeaux is forbidden as an offence against the king and the people." Since the wine was kept in porous casks at the time, there was no way of ageing it, and an old wine would no doubt have been *passé* and unpleasant.

In those days, many of the vineyards of France belonged to the Church—the monks took almost as much pains to spread the vine as they did to spread the Word, and their wines became an important source of revenue. In Burgundy, the Dukes as well as the Fathers cultivated vines, and they were good publicists for their own wines. For many years Burgundy was consumed principally in France and in Flanders (the Burgundian nobles also held court at Brussels); but when, in 1685, the Edict of Nantes was revoked, fleeing Huguenots introduced Burgundy abroad, especially in Switzerland, Holland, and Germany. About 1750, the first commercial houses and travelers in wine were set up.

In Bordeaux, the wine-making bourgeoisie became rich and powerful. Throughout the Hundred Years' War and afterward, England remained the chief customer, with Holland later gaining second place for white wines. In Tudor times the English took to drinking more of both beer and Sack, and French wine did not flow so freely or so cheaply as before. But it continued to come in, even when most of it had to be smuggled, at the time of Marlborough's wars and the heavy duties imposed by the Methuen Treaty.

Wars on French soil constantly damaged French vineyards, which were patiently reconstituted. The fortunes of the vine-grower wavered over the centuries. In spite of bitter struggles and the passage of armies, monk and peasant (and noble as well) continued to care for the vines and to make wine, adapting their customs to local conditions. Vines were pruned short in Bordeaux, long in the Rhône Valley; grapes were left to rot on the vines in Sauternes; Dom Pérignon (they say) discovered the cork as a bottle fastener and how to make sparkling wines; growers in Château-Chalon put their grapes on straw mats and left them to dry in the autumn sun. Other growers in other parts of the world have developed parallel systems, but in no other country have these techniques been so richly endowed with variations of soil and climate. It is not surprising that France produces the greatest variety of great wines in the world.

Building the tradition of quality in French wines has not been without its setbacks. The attempt by the Duke of Burgundy to ban the "disloyal gaamez"—the productive grapevine Gamay which did no honor to the wines of the Côte d'Or—is one chapter in this struggle. The continual fight against fraud is another. The strict and enlightened laws of Appellation Contrôlée should provide the happy ending to the story; but the number of convictions for fraud that occur each year in France demonstrates that not all the community is motivated by the desire to strive only for the finest quality. Nevertheless, in the great wine regions the majority of growers strain all their resources to make the best possible wine year after year, though the cards in the modern era are perhaps more heavily stacked against them than ever before.

The present cry is for more of everything, turned out faster and more cheaply. If there is anything that does not respond to this call, it is wine. It can be made inexpensively, but it will not then be fine wine; it can be made in bulk, but cannot thus be great wine. The best wines have always been those from comparatively non-productive grapevines—from vines that are deliberately pruned short in order to reduce output and channel the plant's energy into the production of superior fruit, but little of it. The grower cannot obtain quantity and quality at the same time.

Another trend working against the contemporary grower is that toward a standard product. Wines will be different in different years; they can be standardized by blending, but no blending vat in the world is capable of turning out a standard wine of the highest quality. Ordinary wine from southern France, southern Italy, or Algeria can be pleasant enough with a meal; but cut with finer wines they do no justice to themselves or to the consumer.

The question is: will fine wines survive this trend? The French growers think they can continue in the traditional way; and the admirably stringent laws of Appellation d'Origine support their conviction. Many wine-drinkers, in France and abroad, support their efforts to maintain the old high standards by taking an interest such as has never before been manifested in fine wines. Others, more pessimistic, quote the rising cost of labor and equipment, which may cause the making of fine wine to become an economic impossibility, especially since even a comparatively short stretch of unfavorable weather can devastate the greatest vineyards. Fortunately for France, the high quality of her wines—admirably maintained by the laws of Appellation Contrôlée—is so firmly established throughout the world that she can charge the extra premium necessary for the protection of such standards. The extraordinarily high prices paid for the best French wines seem testimony enough that they are far from dying away in a mechanized age.

VINE-GROWING REGIONS

France is divided into ninety-five departments, and about two-thirds of these have commercial vineyards. Each wine is the result of the specific climate and soil from which it comes, the grape varieties from which it is made, and of the men and traditions behind it—factors which will differ with each wine. The history of Burgundy would not have been the same without the Cistercians and the French Revolution; the wine trade of Bordeaux was a development of her close ties with England; Champagne is inextricably linked with the discovery—whether by Dom Pérignon or another—of the champagne process; the wines of the Rhône Valley owe much of their present success to one extraordinary man—the Baron Le Roy de Boiseaumarié. But although the wines of France are numerous, the great regions are comparatively few. These are the most important (*See also under separate headings*):

Alsace

More than most other districts, Alsace is perfecting her wines. The best of them, superior to many of Germany's lesser wines, have not yet achieved the quality of rivals from the better domains in the Rheingau, the Palatinate, and the Mosel; yet some of the Alsatian wines are quite excellent.

Bordeaux

The largest of the great wine regions of France and the most productive. The reds—or clarets—of the Haut-Médoc, Graves, Saint-Émilion, and Pomerol, the sweet, rich whites of Sauternes and Barsac, and the drier whites of Graves have been imitated the world over—but rarely very successfully.

Burgundy

The wines vary so much that it is absurd to use the name to describe a single "type" of wine. Reds may be austere and aristocratic, as are Corton and Chambertin, or light and delicate as any fine wine from Chambolle should be. The whites are always dry; but the enormous variation between Chablis, Montrachet, and Meursault, for example, can only be appreciated by tasting.

Champagne

The name is so famous that many people don't know precisely what it is, but erroneously suppose it to be any "bubbly" white wine. Yet Champagne is rigidly controlled and strictly defined in France, and the name, far from applying to all sparkling wine, is only legal when applied to one that is unique and made, uniquely, in the district for which it is named.

Loire Valley

The white wines may be dry, semi-sweet, or sweet and are usually better than the reds. All are beguiling; but there is a vast difference from district to district, grower to grower, and one vintage to another.

Rhône Valley

The reds are sturdy, big, perfumed, and often magnificent. The whites also have a distinctive vigor of their own. The rosé from Tavel is probably the best known of all rosé wines.

See also Anjou; Aude; Bergerac; Corbières A.O.C.; Corsica; Côtes du Roussillon; Fitou; Gaillac; Gard; Côtes du Roussillon; Hérault; Jura; Jurançon; Languedoc; Lorraine; Midi; Minervois; Provence; Southwest France; Sweet fortified wines of France; Touraine; V.D.Q.S.; etc.

SPIRITS

As the greatest wines in the world come from France, so do the finest spirits: no brandy can compare with French Cognac, Armagnac, and Calvados; and in addition to these peerless brandies, the fertile French mind has developed countless cordials, liqueurs, and aperitifs, many strictly for the French palate, others equally appreciated outside France. The important ones, which will be found under their own headings in this book, are:

Armagnac

Wine brandy from the Gascon country, home of the boisterous musketeer d'Artagnan.

Calvados

Apple brandy from the old province of Normandy. When well made and properly aged it can be fabulous.

Cognac

Not any brandy, but a specific brandy. It is, perhaps, the most celebrated wine brandy in the world, and the one whose name is most commonly misused. True Cognac is made only in the Charente district.

Marc

Brandy from the pomace rather than the juice of the grape. Much of it too harsh and rough for consideration among fine spirits, but some, particularly an old marc of Burgundy, can be remarkable.

Brandies, or *eaux-de-vie*, are made from fruit as well as from wine; and many are called *alcools blancs* because of their white color. Quetsch is distilled from purple plums, mirabelle from yellow plums, framboise from raspberries, fraise from strawberries, and kirsch from cherry-stones. These white spirits are matured slowly in crocks and are very dry and high in alcohol. A great many of them come from Alsace and Lorraine; the Dordogne makes prune, another plum spirit.

All over France, liqueurs are made—a dazzling variety: Chartreuse (green and yellow), Benedictine, Cointreau, Crèmes (de menthe, etc.), anisette *(qq.v.)*, and aperitifs both spirituous and sickly. Among the best known of these are the dry French vermouth, Dubonnet, Amer Picon, Suze, Saint-Raphaël, Pernod, and Ricard *(qq.v.)*.

Franciacorta (D.O.C.)

Pleasant red, white, and rosé wines from Brescia. *See* Lombardy.

Franconia, Franken

German State of Bayern (Bavaria)
Vineyard area: approx. 5,200 hectares (12,800 acres)
97% white wines; 3% red wines
Location: Franken is the easternmost of the German wine-growing regions, with most of its vineyards planted on hilly and steep slopes along the W-shaped zigzag of the Main River and its tributaries. Würzburg

is the region's cultural and wine center. It is not only well-known for its splendid architecture, but also for three estates with justifiably excellent reputations: Bavarian State Cellars (Staatlicher Hofkeller), originally founded by the church in 1128, today its cellars are located in the magnificent baroque palace designed by Balthasar Neumann as the residence of the prince-bishops; and the Bürgerspital and the Juliusspital, both are charitable institutions dating back to 1319 and 1576, respectively. The Marienburg Fortress, overlooking the city, houses an interesting wine museum and an extensive collection of works by the 16th-century sculptor Riemenschneider. The region consists of three districts (Bereiche) and is administratively responsible for Bereich Bayerischer Bodensee, a tiny district on the shores of Lake Constance.

Grape Varieties: Müller-Thurgau (49%); Silvaner (20.4%); Bacchus (10%); Kerner (6%); Scheurebe (3%); Riesling (3%).

Wine: broad, full-bodied, powerful, with great depth; in terms of style, more "filling" than "enlivening" (e.g. light, racy Mosel wine); excellent with meals, thanks to their robust character and dry style (not unlike a Chablis, but with less alcohol).

That the Franconian wine-culture is the most marginal in Germany can be strikingly shown with figures. Before the Thirty Years' War (1618–48) the vineyard extended over 40,000 hectares (100,000 acres); in 1870 it was 9,000-odd hectares (about 24,000 acres); in 1900, 7,000 hectares (17,500 acres); and today about 4,000 hectares (10,000 acres). This shrinkage has been caused by war; the Thirty Years' War destroyed the whole plantation, and the Second World War was devastating, especially around Würzburg. The climate has been just as disastrous; Franconia has cold winters and hot summers, with severe frost often striking in the critical blossoming time in spring or at harvest time in October. Such conditions have driven viticulture up onto the steepest slopes where nothing else will grow, and the lower, more fertile areas have been turned over to other crops.

About 50% of Franken's 6,600 growers are members of cooperatives, with an average vineyard size of .7 hectares (1.5 acres). In addition to several local and medium-sized cooperatives, there is a very modern central regional cooperative in Kitzingen-Reppern-dorf. The wines are well made, show good regional character and are good value (although Franken wines are not inexpensive).

The western part of the region lies within Bereich Mainviereck. Except for the area near Aschaffenburg, where the soil is a mix of primitive rock and mica schist, weathered colored sandstone is predominant. Red varieties (Spätburgunder and Portugieser) do well here, although they are produced elsewhere in the region, as well. The climate is of a maritime nature.

Bereich Maindreieck is the heart of the region and includes Würzburg. Here, the shell limestone soil yields full-bodied, hearty Silvaner wines. In good years, they show elegance, with rich nuances in flavor. Scheurebe (crossing of Silvaner × Riesling), with its bouquet reminiscent of black currants and marked acidity, offers an interesting contrast. For centuries outstanding wines have been produced from Würzburg's famous site "Stein," owned jointly by the three estates mentioned above.

The famous Stein wines are the only ones known widely abroad, although all Franconian wines tend to attract attention wherever they are exported, because of the unusual shape of the flattish flask, or Bocksbeutel (q.v.), in which they are bottled.

Steinwein, or the "stone wine," is properly—and in Germany legally—the wine only of the Würzburger Stein, a steep slope above the town of Würzbur, with a southern aspect and a soil which is predominantly lime. So famous have the wines of this slope become that abroad all Franconian wines in the characteristic bottle are apt to be called Stein wines. The true Steinweine are green-gold, with an uncompromising quality that destines them for connoisseurs.

Prior to the 1971 German wine law, "Steinwein" was used as a generic term for all Franconian wines sold in the region's traditional flagon-shaped bottle, called a Bocksbeutel. Other important villages: Escherndorf, Nordheim, Randersacker, Sommerach, Sommerhausen, Thüngersheim and Volkach.

The easternmost district is sheltered by and takes its name from the Steiger forest. Very earthy, flavorful Müller-Thurgau wines are produced from the mineral-rich, gypsum and red marl soil. Bacchus, a crossing of (Silvaner × Riesling) × Müller-Thurgau, yields fruity, full-bodied wines with mild acidity. A real specialty is the Rieslaner (crossing of Silvaner × Riesling), which produces particularly elegant late-harvested and Auslese-type wines with noble fruitiness, racy acidity and rich in extract. Here, as in the central district, the climate is continental, with very cold winters (risk of frost damage) and hot summers (opportunity for the grapes to develop extra ripeness). In hot years, the total acidity is lower and this milder acidity makes it possible to produce very dry—yet harmonious—wines. In Franken, "dry" means less than 4 grams per liter residual sugar; elsewhere in Germany, the legal maximum is 9 grams/liter. Castell, Iphofen, Rödelsee and Wiesenbronn are important villages.

Producers: Fürstl. Castell'sches Domänenamt, Ernst Gebhardt, Fürst Löwenstein-Wertheim-Rosenberg, Schloss Sommerhausen-Steinmann, Dr. Hans Wirsching.

For a complete list of the districts (*Bereiche*), collective vineyard sites (*Grosslagen = GL*), and individual vineyard sites (*Einzellagen*), see Appendix B, p.

Frappé

French term for a drink, chilled or iced—or with shaved ice, as in the case of Crème de menthe frappée.

Frascati

Dry white D.O.C. wine of the Castelli Romani, Italy. *See* Latium.

Frecciarossa

A good light wine made in Lombardy (*q.v.*).

Fredonia

Prolific American red grape used for red wine, especially in New Jersey.

Free-run

Wine running freely from the residue after fermentation, or from pressed wine at the first light pressing. It is the best, and in many regions it is bottled separately.

Freisa (d'Asti, di Chieri)

Grape used in Piedmont for a sprightly red Italian wine (D.O.C.) with a delightful bouquet.

French West Indies.

See Rum, French.

Fresh

The engaging, bright charm of all rosés, most white, and some red wines exhibited only in their youth. Most of the white and all of the rosé wine made today is best drunk young, before this early pertness, one of their finest assets, is lost.

Friuli-Venezia-Giulia

Red, white and rosé wines.
District: Northeast Italy.

This small, mountainous region, in the extreme northeast corner of Italy, borders on Austria and Yugoslavia. A considerable amount of wine, about 1 million hectoliters (26.5 million U.S. gallons, 22 million imp. or approximately 11 million cases), comes from the red Merlot, Cabernet Franc or Sauvignon, Refosco, Pinot Nero, some Malbec, Schioppettino, Ribolla Nera and Tazzelenghe varieties; and from the following whites: Pinot Bianco and Chardonnay, Pinot Grigio, Riesling Renano, Sauvignon, Malvasia, Ribolla, Tocai Friulano, Traminer, Müller-Thurgau, Picolit, Verduzzo. Most of the wines whether Vino di Tavolo or D.O.C.'s are sold under the name of one of the above grape varieties.

The main D.O.C.'s are:

Aquileia, the flat zone from the Adriatic north.

Collio, Collio Goriziano, bordering on Yugoslavia near Gorizia with a suitable microclimate for whites.

Frizzante

Colli Orientali del Friuli, like other Friuli D.O.C.'s, is often sold under the name of the grape variety.

Grave del Friuli, from a section known as Grave near Udine.

Isonzo, along the Isonzo river, is most appropriate for red wines.

Latisana, the coastal plains along the Tagliamento river is also most appropriate for reds.

Frizzante

Italian term for semi-sparkling wine.

Fronsac

New appellation, no longer Côtes de Fronsac.
See Côtes Canon Fronsac.

Frontignan-Muscat (Appellation Contrôlée)

A Mediterranean district of southern France producing Muscat wines (Muscat de Frontignant). Frontignan is a term often used in France for a 75-centiliter bottle.
See Sweet fortified wines of France.

Fronton, Côtes du Frontonnais

Good, pleasant red and rosé wines made just north of Toulouse in southwestern France. They are entitled to the Appellation Contrôlée accolade.

Fruity

The springlike first expression of many wines, innocent and fresh, most pronounced to the nose. The characteristic is caused by a high volatility of the esters (flavor and perfume essences) and is likely to disappear quickly in wines not rich in sugar. The fruity dry or semi-dry wine should be drunk young, before it begins to fade. A fruity red wine will not have been fermented on the lees for a long time. It will lack tannin and will have been bottled young. Beaujolais is an example of a fruity red wine. The Mosel is known for its fruity white wines.

Fuder

German term for large cask holding 1,000 liters (264 U.S. gallons, 220 imp.) of wine.
See Foudre.

Fumarium

Roman hot room for "improving" wine by exposing it to smoke.

Fumigation

Burning of a wick of sulfur in a vat or barrel of wine to destroy bacteria or unwanted yeasts—to a considerable extent the destruction is achieved by replacing the air in the container and by bringing the wine into contact with sulfuric acid gas. Too much sulfur will spoil the taste of the wine. In Bordeaux, a quarter of a wick of sulfur to a *barrique* holding 225 liters (59.4 U.S. gallons, 49.5 imp.) is generally effective. The French term for the process is *Méchage*, from *mèche*, meaning wick.

In California, wherever oak has grown, soils must be fumigated before vines are planted.
See Sulfur dioxide; Chapter Nine.

Funchal

The port and principal town of Madeira where much of the wine is stored and aged and whence all of it is shipped.

Furfural

An aldehyde present in minute quantity in wines and spirits. An oxidation product of glucose, furfural is an important flavor component of sweet wines produced by heating, such as Marsala and Madeira.

Furmint

The fine white grape from which Hungarian Tokay is made.

Fusel oil

Term generally designating the volatile, nauseous higher alcohols removed by the rectification of spirituous liquors.

Fût

One of the French terms for a cask or barrel.

G

Gaillac (Appellation Contrôlée)

Still and sparkling white wines.
District: Southwest France.

Southeast of Bordeaux is the French department of the Tarn and the River Tarn—not a big river but one of the most beautiful in France, a sparkling trout stream cutting through rocky passes. In the hills near the city of Gaillac, the slopes are planted in vines which give the wines called Premières Côtes de Gaillac or Gaillac Mousseux.

The wine produced by the Gaillac vineyards in the Middle Ages seems to have been better than the sweetish and uninteresting whites, reds, and rosés yielded now. (Tastes have changed too.) The Plantagenet kings of England were devoted to Gaillac, as was Henry VII. In his *Mémoires de Languedoc* (1633), Catel wrote that this wine, much prized by foreign princes, left a taste of roses in the mouth.

The right conditions for the making of Gaillac wine are laid down in a series of decrees beginning in 1938. There are six grapes which may be used for white wines: Mauzac, l'En de l'El, Ondenc, Sémillon, Sauvignon, and Muscadelle. Mauzac usually accounts for 80% to 100%, varying with the vineyards. Red and rosé wines are vinified from Ouras, Gaillac, Syrah, and Negrette grapes. To qualify for the place-names under French wine law, the vines must attain 12% of alcohol for Premières Côtes de Gaillac and 10.5% for wines designated simply Gaillac. The sparkling wines must be made according to the champagne method of secondary fermentation in the bottle, or by the Gaillac method—a slight variation of this—in which the wines are bottled while they still hold unresolved sugar, causing imprisoned fermentation and often a fairly heavy bottle-sediment as well.

Galgenwein (Gallows Wine)

Humorous reference to a German wine so harsh that after it has been drunk the gallows is unnecessary.

Gallization

A term referring to the addition of liquid sugar to grape must prior to fermentation in order to increase a wine's alcohol content. Chaptalization, a similar process, involves the use of dry (cane or beet) sugar.
See Chapter Nine, p. 40.

Gallon, British imperial

The volume of ten standard pounds of distilled water weighed in air at a temperature of 62°F. (17°C.) and a barometric pressure of 30 inches; 277.274 cubic inches. It is the equivalent of 1.20095 U.S. gallons or 4.54596 liters.

Gallon, U.S.

The former British "wine gallon" of 231 cubic inches which was replaced in Great Britain in 1826 by the standard imperial gallon. It is the equivalent of approximately five-sixths of the volume of the imperial gallon (.83267), or 3.78531 liters.

Gamay

A red grape. Undistinguished in the rest of Burgundy, it yields admirable wine in Beaujolais and wine of fair quality in the Touraine. In California it is not a true Gamay. The grape called Gamay Beaujolais is a clone of Pinot Noir. The grape called Napa Gamay is also not a true Gamay.

Gambellara (Recioto, Vin Santo) (D.O.C.)

A dry white D.O.C. wine, similar to Soave.
See Veneto.

Gamza

One of the principal grape varieties in Bulgaria, producing red and some white wines.
See Bulgaria.

Gard

Quantitatively, one of the three most important wine-producing departments of France. (The other two are Aude and Hérault.) From Gard in the south of France comes a great deal of ordinary wine, as well as the robust red Costières (*see* V.D.Q.S.) and the white Clairette de Bellegarde (*q.v.*).

Garda

Name of groups of Italian wines (Chiaretto-del-Garda, Moniga-del-Garda, and the D.O.C. Riviera-del-Garda-Bresciano) grown near Lake Garda.
See Lombardy.

Garrafeira

Term on Portuguese wine labels indicating that the wine has been matured for some years in bottle before being offered for sale. It could perhaps be equated with Reserve or Special Reserve.

Gattinara (D.O.C.)

A popular full-bodied red wine of Piedmont (*q.v.*).

Gay-Lussac

French chemist who produced the classic chemical formula for the process of fermentation (*q.v.*). His work on the alcoholometer and sulfuric acid were great contributions to wine-making.

Gazéifié

French term for sparkling wine in which the sparkle comes from artificial carbonation.

Chateau Gazin

Bordeaux red wine.
District and Commune: Pomerol, France.

Owned by M. de Baillencourt and among the largest properties in the district, the château makes a wine that sometimes does not live up to its high reputation.
Vineyard area: 25 hectares (62 acres).
Average production: 80 *tonneaux* (7,500 cases).

Gean whisky, Geen whisky

A liqueur made in Scotland of whisky and black cherries.

Gebiet

The German term for region, specifically one of the eleven producing areas now defined by West German law.

Geisenheim

In this Rheingau town is the most important viticultural school in Germany. Its vineyards produce some good wines, notably Fuchsberg and Rothenberg.
See Rheingau.

Gemarkung

German town or village name of a wine. Comparable to commune name in France. Now replaced by the term "Weinbauort" according to the new West German wine laws.

Generous

A wine is generous when it has warmth and is rich in alcohol and vitality.

Geneva

The English spelling for Jenever (*q.v.*), the name used in Holland for Dutch gin.
See Gin.

Gentiane

French and Swiss liqueur distilled from the root of the gentian plant. The most popular French aperitif of this style is Suze.
See Enzian.

Gentil

Alsatian synonym for Riesling grape (*q.v.*).

Gerk

See Grk.

Germany

"The breed of the fine German wines is the result of the struggle for life at the northernmost climate in which the vine can grow. Costs are higher, cultivation is more intensive, the fight against insects and disease sterner, fertilizing more essential."

This statement by the late Professor Steinberg, director of Germany's most important viticultural school at Geisenheim of the Rhine, sums up the story of German wines. While various German vineyard areas claim to be the farthest north in the world, the fact is that more of the German wine-belt lies in a colder and less friendly climate than any other important zone. The vine accepts the challenge and, especially if it is the Riesling, produces wines of pure gold. It demands in return to be treated like a prima donna.

Viticulture is carefully controlled. To plant a vineyard, one needs a permit, obtainable from the regional authorities only after the soil, climate, etc., have been evaluated and the site has been deemed suitable for viticulture, i.e., is apt to yield grapes ripe enough to produce quality wine. Vineyards are located in the southwestern part of the country, along the Rhine and Mosel Rivers and their tributaries. There are approximately 100,000 hectares (247,000 acres) under vine, which is less than 1% of all farmland in Germany. Eighty-seven per cent of the grapes produce white wine. Annual production, based on a ten-year average, is about 8.8 million hectoliters (234 million U.S. gallons, 194 million imp.). The majority of Germany's 90,000 growers are part-time (or hobby) vintners or small farmers, with average vineyard holdings of one hectare (2.5 acres) or less. Two-thirds deliver their grapes or must to cooperatives or to the wine trade. Directly or indirectly, it is estimated that some 1 million live off the wine industry. German wine is still consumed primarily within Germany, although with domestic per capita consumption stagnant at 25 liters (an increasing portion of which is imported wine), exports account for nearly one-third of all sales. The United Kingdom and the United States are the leading markets. Others are Germany's non-wine-producing European neighbors and Japan.

WINE HISTORY

The long and tangled story of German wines, woven deeply though it is into the gothic tapestry of history along the Rhine, may be sketched fairly briefly.

It is probable that wine was being made in what is now Germany at about the beginning of the Christian era. The Romans came and left their imprint on the people, the towns, the wines, the history and customs of the Mosel and the Rhine.

After the Roman period and a later phase, in which vineyards were bandied about by medieval kings and knights, wine became the domain of the Church. The monasteries were great promoters of viticulture. The monks were shrewd merchants, as well, and their business acumen turned viticulture into an important source of income for the church. Some of the former monasteries may still be seen, their giant beam presses recalling the days when cowled men made the wines. A little anecdote told at Kloster Eberbach catches the spirit of the time. The cellar-master of this cloister above the Rhine, sampling a cask one day, detected the taste of iron. Dismayed, he ran to the cook, who, tasting in his turn, discovered not iron but a taint of leather. Both together hurried to the prior. He tasted too, to decide between them, but found them both wrong: in his opinion, the wine tasted slightly of wood. When the cask was emptied, after much sturdy drinking and disputing, a key was found at the bottom, fastened to a bit of wood by a leather strap—or so they say.

In the course of the 18th century, under the leadership of the church and aristocracy, there is evidence of a greater appreciation of quality. In some regions, notably on the Mosel and in the Rheingau, lesser vines were uprooted and replaced with the high quality Riesling vine. Wines of superior quality and from the best vintages were consciously reserved and stored separately in a special, small cellar—Cabinet Keller—from which the German Prädikat Kabinett derives its origin. The earliest mentions of a Cabinet Keller (in this context) stem from 1728 (Schloss Vollrads) and 1730 (Kloster Eberbach). In spite of the attendant reduction in quantity, the qualitative value of selective and late harvesting was recognized by better estates. After its "accidental" first late harvest (Spätlese) in 1775, Schloss Johannisberg promulgated the outstanding results and sought to have changed the existing requirement that harvesting be completed no later than October 15th—certainly a desirable step for the late-ripening Riesling. As early as 1750 and regularly as of 1775, Schloss Johannisberg began filling its best wines in bottles, and with the advent of estate bottling, came the development of a series of colored capsules to distinguish among the wines harvested at various stages of ripeness. By the end of the century wine labels were introduced, thanks to Senefelder's development of lithography in 1799.

By 1803, Napoleon secularized the German vineyards. A few great holdings remained intact, such as those held by the state and those of charitable institutions (e.g. Bischöfliches Priesterseminar or Friedrich Wilhelm Gymnasium, both in Trier). But a large portion of the properties were sold at auction. For growers who could afford to purchase, this was a unique opportunity to acquire excellent sites which until then had been owned exclusively by the church. The most significant impact of the application of Napoleon's Code, which was based on Roman law, was the fragmentation of the vineyards through inheritance. Estates were not to be passed on intact to a single heir, but were to be handed down to descendants in equal shares. As one vineyard came to have more than one owner, individuals' holdings acquired separate names—as a means of identifying each farmer's section of the vineyard. Ultimately, there were some 30,000 individually named sites. These were consolidated into about 2,600 under the German wine law of 1971.

By the end of the 19th century, advances in science and technology had led to improved methods of growing and producing wine. The state had established research and teaching institutions to foster quality and thereby help improve the economic position of viticulture. Equally important for small and part-time growers was the development of growers' cooperatives. It was also at this time that quality-oriented wine estates in the Rheingau, Pfalz and along the Mosel, Saar and Ruwer formed regional groups to market their distinctive "natural" (non-chaptalized) wines. They decided to sell at auction, which enabled them to establish producer prices on a broad market basis and which ensured a certain degree of recognition, since the outcome of the auctions was always published. In 1910, under the auspices of the Mayor of Trier, the regional groups united into one association, known today as the Verband Deutscher Prädikats- und Qualitätsweingüter, or VDP. The attribute "natural"—a prerequisite for all wines auctioned by the association—became synonymous with high quality. Its use was prohibited with the passage of the German wine law of 1971 and has been replaced with the system of Prädikats. Like their predecessors, they are never permitted to be chaptalized. Today, the 171 members of the Association of German Prädikat and Quality Wine Estates are located in nearly every region. They organize trade fairs and auctions and regularly taste-test wines of their peers to ensure that VDP membership includes only those estates which consistently produce wines superior in quality to the minimum required by their region. The high standards of the VDP have contributed significantly to the international reputation of German wine.

If not for the Gall process, small growers would probably have perished altogether: Gallization of wine is the addition of sugar, now regulated by the laws of the European Economic Community. "Sugar may be added to grape must or wines . . . provided this is done for the purpose of supplementing a natural lack of sugar or alcohol, or of counteracting a natural excess

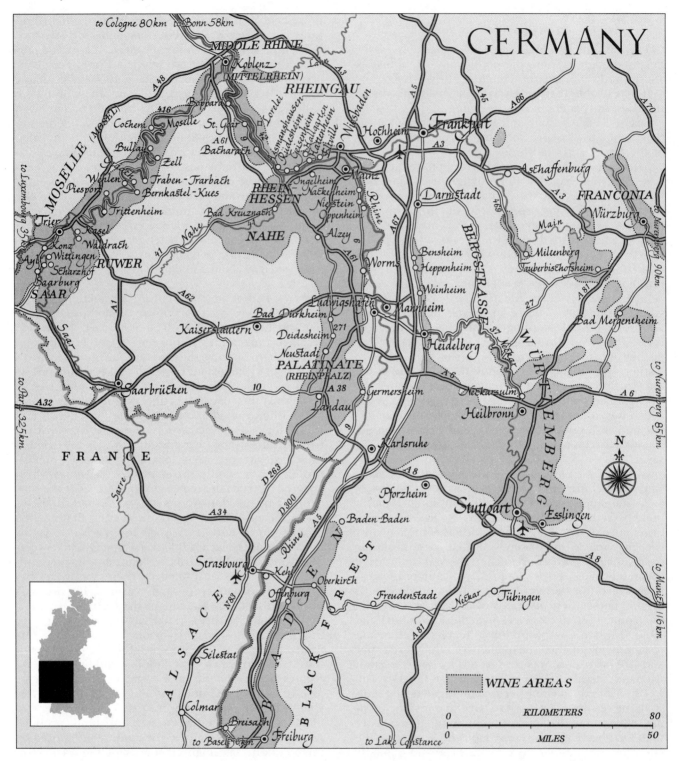

of acid, to an extent sufficient to produce in the said wines a composition equal to that of wines derived in a good year from grapes of the same kind and origin . . . and provided also that the sugar is added to the must before fermentation." This treatment, generally known by the French name, *chaptalisation*, carried small growers over the bad years, which they might not otherwise have survived. It is important to note, however, that no quality wines (*Qualitätswein mit Prädikat*) may be *angereichert* (chaptalized) except within the limits closely specified by the recent laws.

There was, in the first years after the Second World War, a pronounced trend toward sweeter wines—the result of wartime sugar-starvation in Germany. This trend has continued.

The Spätlesen wines saved the German growers at the end of the eighteenth century. The exact origin of these left-on-the-vine wines is disputed, but the Bishop of Fulda may have been the originator. One year his messenger, bearing the permission necessary to harvest the Bishop's Johannisberg estate, was captured by robbers and held for several weeks. When he finally arrived and the picking began, the grapes were nearly rotten and were thrown to the peasantry—for whom they produced a glorious elixir. This technique of letting the grapes reach noble rot (*q.v.*) late in the autumn produces the great Sauternes and the German Spätlesen and Trockenbeerenauslesen wines today, but the enormous risk of early frosts and the additional cost of labor in the individual picking of the berries are gradually forcing prices too high for the market on both Rhine and Mosel.

GRAPE VARIETIES

The grape used is of paramount importance in all vineyards of the world, as well as in Germany. Eighty-seven per cent of all German wines are white. German red wines are a specialty, very popular in Germany but not well known or appreciated abroad. They are distinguished by their fruity, rather than tannic, acidity, and—depending on the variety and the winemaker's technique—they are often lighter in color, body and intensity than red wines produced elsewhere. In any impartial assessment of the red wines of the world, German red wines cannot be considered to be in the running internationally. The following are the most important white grape varieties:

Riesling. This is the best German white-wine grape. A steely aristocracy is the outstanding characteristic of a Riesling wine, particularly when it has been grown in the slate soil of the Mosel. The grape is small and the yield not high, but the character and staying-power and the incomparable bouquet which seems to be composed of mingled fruit scents more than compensate for the lack of quantity. The vine ripens late and is resistant to cold. Once taken away from its habitat along the Rhine and Mosel (and in nearby Alsace) and planted abroad, something happens to it, and it is Riesling in name only. Nearly 20% of the German vineyard area is planted with Riesling.

Silvaner. Softer and milder than the Riesling, this variety produces full-bodied, neutral wine which reflects the character of the soil in which it is grown. Once the most widely planted vine in Germany. Usually spelled Sylvaner outside of Germany. Eight per cent of the German vineyard area is planted with Silvaner.

Müller-Thurgau. The crossing of the Riesling and Silvaner plants, named for the man who created it, produces a wine milder than the Riesling and with a taste that has something of Muscatel. It makes pleasant, everyday wines, best consumed while fresh and young. One-quarter of the German vineyard area is planted with Müller-Thurgau.

Kerner. A popular new crossing developed from Trollinger (a red variety) and Riesling (white). The wines are lesser Riesling-like. This abundant producer yields wines lacking in finesse. (7%)

Scheurebe. Very successful crossing of Silvaner × Riesling, named after its breeder, Georg Scheu (pronounced "shoy"). Lively acidity and a bouquet and taste reminiscent of black currants; nevertheless yielding common wines. (4.5%)

Bacchus. Crossing of (Silvaner × Riesling) × Müller-Thurgau. Light muscat bouquet, mild acidity, good body. (3.5%)

Burgunder (Burgundy) *varieties:* Grauburgunder, or Ruländer, (Pinot Gris), and Weissburgunder (Pinot Blanc), both grown primarily in Baden; Spätburgunder (Pinot Noir) grown in the Ahr, Baden and Rheingau; Müllerrebe, or Schwarzriesling (Pinot Meunier), grown in Württemberg and Baden. Other red varieties: Portugieser, Trollinger, Limberger.

If at least 85% of a wine is made from one grape variety, it may be named on the label. Up until the middle of this century, it was not common to indicate the variety on the label, for it was assumed that white wines were Riesling and red wines were Spätburgunder. Today, if there is no variety mentioned, one can expect a wine typical of its region and probably a *cuvée* of several varieties.

THE GERMAN WINE-GROWING REGIONS

Germany's 100,000 hectares (247,000 acres) of vineyards are located in the southwestern part of the country, between the Bodensee (Lake Constance) and Bonn. In this extreme northerly location, straddling the 50th degree of latitude (parallel to Labrador or northern Mongolia), micro-climates play an important role, for the grapes need every bit of help nature can offer to succeed in their struggle to ripen. This is why Germany's wine-growing regions follow the course of the Rhine and its tributaries—the rivers temper the climate, acting as heat reflectors which help to maintain a constant temperature day and night and provide sufficient humidity to creat mist and fog which protect the vineyards from early frost. Vineyards are usually planted on south-facing sloping hillsides of river valleys, bordered by the river and a protective forest at the summit—natural boundaries which preclude expansion.

This area is divided into eleven specified wine-growing regions (*bestimmte Anbaugebiete*), each of which produces a wine that is typical of that region (similar in taste and character) and different from wines grown elsewhere. Each region is described in more detail under its own heading, but here is a brief summary, with the regions listed according to size, not quality.

Rheinhessen

25,000 hectares (62,000 acres); 94% white wines, 6% red wines; Müller-Thurgau, Silvaner, Sheurebe.

Rheinpfalz

23,000 hectares (56,500 acres); 89% white wines, 11% red wines; Müller-Thurgau, Riesling, Kerner.

Baden

15,000 hectares (56,500 acres); 77% white wines, 23% red wines; Müller-Thurgau, Spätburgunder, Ruländer.

Mosel-Saar-Ruwer

12,800 hectares (31,600 acres); 100% white wines; Riesling, Müller-Thurgau, Elbling.

Württemberg

9,600 hectares (23,800 acres); 51% red wines, 49% white wines; Riesling, Trollinger, Müllerrebe.

Franken

5,200 hectares (12,800 acres); 97% white wines, 3% red wines; Müller-Thurgau, Silvaner, Bacchus.

Nahe

4,600 hectares (11,400 acres); 98% white wines, 2% red wines; Müller-Thurgau, Riesling, Silvaner.

Rheingau

3,000 hectares (7,300 acres); 94% white wines, 6% red wines; Riesling, Müller-Thurgau, Spätburgunder.

Mittelrhein

800 hectares (1,900 acres); 98% white wines, 2% red wines; Riesling, Müller-Thurgau, Kerner.

Ahr

426 hectares (1,000 acres); 70% white wines, 30% red wines; Spätburgunder, Portugieser, Riesling.

Bergstrasse (Hessische Bergstrasse)

390 hectares (975 acres); 98% white wines, 2% red wines; Riesling, Müller-Thurgau, Ruländer.

APPELLATION OF ORIGIN

It is mandatory for the name of the wine-growing region to be indicated on the label of a German *Qualitätswein* (quality wine). Often, there is more specific information about the wine's origin, such as the name of a district (*Bereich*) or that of a village, together with the name of a collective or individual vineyard site. The more specific (smaller) the appellation of origin, the more individual the taste and character of the wine, because of differences in soils and growing conditions.

Each region is composed of one or more districts called a *Bereich*. For Mosel-Saar-Ruwer these districts are Bernkastel, Obermosel, Saar-Ruwer, Zell and Moseltor. Immediately it is apparent where the names originated: in some cases (Saar-Ruwer) the logical geography-related name was kept for the sub-region; in others (Bernkastel) a famous town name was given an entire sub-region, with the simple bonus of adding luster and appeal to a purely regional wine label. A wine labeled Bereich Bernkastel can come from anywhere in that sizable area, but one called Bernkasteler must come from the vineyards associated with that famous town. Though the names obviously will be different, the situation is much the same in the other parts of Germany, e.g. Bereich Nierstein, Niersteiner.

Each *Bereich* is divided into one or more *Grosslagen*. The German word means "large site," but it is best to think of a *Grosslage* as a collection of similar vineyards. The process for choosing names for the *Grosslagen* was not unlike that for naming the *Bereiche*. In the Bereich Bernkastel, for example, one of the *Grosslagen* is called Badstube, a name which used to belong to one of the best vineyards of the town. A wine labeled Bernkasteler Badstube (from 1971 on) is a regional blended wine, though admittedly from a good part of the larger *Bereich*. Wines with a *Grosslage* name should be of higher quality than those with only the *Bereich* name. They will ideally have some of the same taste and characteristics of the wines from the specific vineyards within the *Grosslage* (see below) and will be less expensive.

Each *Grosslage* is composed of individual vineyards called *Einzellagen*. It was the great and confusing number (about 30,000) of these sites throughout West Germany that was one of the major reasons for passing the 1971 wine law. For a vineyard to retain its own name, it must now be a minimum size—between 5 and 10 hectares (12 and 25 acres) depending on the terrain. Those plots smaller than the legal minimum were either absorbed or grouped together in tracts large enough to bear an individual name. The move reduced the number to about 2,600, but at the same time eradicated more than a few well-respected wine names. Quality too may have suffered with this streamlining. The wine from a great vineyard may not be as fine once less good neighboring vines are appended to the original plot.

The *Einzellagen* are still associated with villages. The name of the village (+ er) precedes the name of the individual site. A town and its surrounding vineyards may fall into more than one *Grosslage*. Thus Bernkastel Kardinalsberg is part of the *Grosslage* Kurfürstlay, while Bernkastel Doctor lies in *Grosslage* Badstube. The town name will always appear on the label of a quality wine from a single vineyard.

SUMMARY OF APPELLATION OF ORIGIN

German Quality Wines
(Qualitätswein b.A.)   Example:

11 wine-growing regions   Mosel-Saar-Ruwer
(bestimmtes Anbaugebiet = b.A.)
divided into

34 districts   Bereich Bernkastel
(Bereich)
dividied into

152 collective vineyard sites   Bernkasteler Badstube
(Grosslage)
divided into

2,600 individual vineyard sites   Bernkasteler Doctor
(Einzellage).

QUALITY CATEGORY = DEGREE OF RIPENESS AT HARVEST

Under European Community wine law, there are two categories of quality:

1) table wine (*Tafelwein*), and 2) quality wine (*Qualitätswein*).

(1) Table Wine (*Deutscher Tafelwein, Landwein*). These pleasant and uncomplicated wines must be made from approved grape varieties vines in any one of the four regions: Rhein-Mosel, Bayern, Neckar, or Oberrhein. The names of the region and of the bottler (*Abfüller*) appear on the label. Brand names are permitted. The name of a grape variety may be given if 85% of the wine is from the grape variety named.

Landwein is a superior-quality *Tafelwein*. It must be dry or medium-dry. Whereas ordinary *Tafelwein* may show only the region where it was grown, e.g., Rhein

or Mosel, *Landwein* must display, in addition to the words *Deutscher Landwein*, the name of the special district (one of 15 such) from which it comes, and it may also show the *Bereich*.

(2) Quality Wine (*Qualitätswein bestimmter Anbaugebiete*). These finer, fuller wines must show the typical character of the region and the grape, as determined by a government test and local testing panel. The wines must have a minimum degree of alcohol (which varies from region to region) and must come from one of the eleven quality wine regions (*bestimmter Anbaugebiete*): Baden, Rheinpfalz, Württemberg, Franken, Rheinhessen, Hessiche Bergstrasse, Rheingau, Nahe, Mittelrhein, Mosel-Saar-Ruwer, or Ahr. (See above for a comparison of these regions to the *Tafelwein* districts.) If a wine meets these requirements, the tasting authorities record it and assign it a control number (*amtliche Prüfungsnummer*) which is printed on the label, together with the names of the region, and, if applicable, more specific information on origin—as long as 85% of the wine was made in the smallest named area. The other 15% must come from anywhere in the same region. The name of the bottler or grower will also appear. As with the *Tafelwein*, the grape name may be given if 85% of the wine was made from the variety indicated.

Quality Wine with Special Attributes (*Qualitätswein mit Prädikat*) is the highest class of German wines, produced from fully matured grapes of an approved variety in a specified *Bereich*. These wines must attain 9% of natural alcohol with no sugar added. Government officials control the grapes in the vineyard and the must in the cellar. The harvest date is set and registered by the village. Like the simple quality wines, each wine in this category is scrutinized and tasted by various panels and finally given a control number if worthy of its name. The *Prädikat*, or special attributes, are Kabinett, Spätlese, Auslese, Beerenauslese, Eiswein and Trockenbeerenauslese (see definitions on the following pages). Estate-bottled wines, formerly *Original abfüllung*, are now known as *Erzeugerabfüllung* (producer's bottling) or *aus eigenem Lesegut* (from producer's own harvest). But no wine, not even one from a famous vineyard, will be allowed a *Prädikat* if it does not exhibit the fine qualities associated with its name. This rating of the actual wine, not the vineyard, is one of the great triumphs of the new law.

Here is a description of the special attributes, or Prädikate, in ascending order of ripeness at harvest. It is important to remember that riper grapes have had more time to develop natural sugars and to absorb minerals from the soil. Wines from very ripe grapes are fuller-bodied and deeper (more golden) in color. Riper grapes yield richer wine, with a more concentrated bouquet and flavor—but richer does not necessarily mean sweet. Spätlese, for example, indicates that in the vineyard, the grapes developed at least the minimum amount of natural sugar (prescribed by law) necessary to qualify for that attribute. The naturally sweet grape juice is fermented, resulting in a dry wine, and it is at this point, in the cellar, that the winemaker decides the ultimate style of the wine. He can leave his Spätlese as it is, dry. Or, he can add some unfermented grape juice (and thus still naturally sweet) which he has reserved (called sweet reserve) to the dry Spätlese, thereby achieving a different style: medium-dry or even mildly sweet. A Spätlese, whether dry or medium-dry or sweet, will be richer, more intense, than a Kabinett. This richness was determined by nature. The style, or degree of dryness, was determined by the winemaker.

Kabinett. This was originally a Rheingau nomenclature for specially reserved wines stored in a "Cabinet" cellar; but the term was gradually stretched to include any fine growth to which a proprietor chose to give his stamp of approval, although it had a more specific meaning in some of the Rheingau vineyards. As defined by the 1971 law, a Kabinett wine (Kabinett must now only be spelled with a *k*) is made from fully matured grapes, without added sugar.

Spätlese literally means late harvest. The grapes are not permitted to be harvested for at least seven days after the normal harvest has started. The grapes are riper than those for a Kabinett.

Auslese refers to selective harvesting. Overripe bunches are selected and separated from normally ripe bunches. This requires a great deal of manual labor.

Beerenauslese is another form of selective harvest. Here, individual totally overripe berries are selected and separated from one bunch. Extremely labor-intensive.

Eiswein literally means "ice wine." Made from grapes which are harvested and crushed while frozen, Eiswein grapes must be at least as ripe as grapes which qualify for the attribute Beerenauslese. Extremely labor-intensive.

Trockenbeerenauslese refers to the selection of individual berries from a bunch, berries which have been left to shrivel on the vine almost to the condition of raisins (dried up = trocken). Extremely labor-intensive.

Qualitätsweine b.A., Kabinett and Spätlese (particularly in the dry or medium-dry styles) are excellent with meals. Auslese is a rich wine with a noble fruity sweetness. It is perfect as an apéritif (in place of sherry, for example) or with a rich pâté or with dessert.

Beeren- and Trockenbeerenauslese and Eiswein are extremely rich, lusciously sweet and quite rare. They are best enjoyed on their own (without food).

BARREL SIZES AND UNITS OF SALE

The best German wine growers sell their wines either at auction or in the cellars directly to the purchasers through commission brokers; the latter is called *Freihand* sale. Cask dimensions are not uniform, although there is an increasing trend toward a change

to the hectoliter measure, which is the standard in international usage.

Rheingau wines are sold in the *Halbstück* (half-cask), whether *Freihand* or at auction; a *Halbstück* contains 600 liters or 828 bottles. If an entire *Stück* (an oval cask of 1,200 liters) is sold, the price is nevertheless reckoned in terms of *Halbstücke*. Most wine is shipped in bottles. The finest wines are also both auctioned and sold *Freihand* in bottle.

Mosel wines are sold in the large, long barrel called the *Fuder*. It was formerly supposed to contain 960 liters, but in the last quarter of a century this has been standardized at 1,000 liters or 1,370 bottles. The finest are also sold in bottle.

Rheinhessen wines are generally sold in the *Stück* of 1,200 liters (equal to 1,656 bottles), although sometimes, and usually with the finest, the unit is 600 liters. Peak wines are also sold in bottles.

STATE WINE DOMAINS

The state is the largest vineyard owner in all Germany. Made up for the most part of former Church holdings secularized in 1803 by Napoleon, the State Wine Domains are located in nearly every region and number among the finest and most prestigious estates of Germany. The Verwaltung der Staatsweingüter, Eltville, is the largest, with 190.5 hectares (470.5 acres). It consists of six estates in the Rheingau and Hessische Bergstrasse, has three winemaking centers and administers the former Cistercian monastery Kloster Eberbach (which is also where all of the estates' wines are aged and stored). Based on the results of prices achieved at auctions, here is a ranking of some of the Domain's finest Rheingau sites: 1) Steinberger, 2) Rauenthaler Baiken, 3) Erbacher Marcobrunn, 4) Rüdesheimer Schlossberg, 5) Hochheimer Domdechaney.

WINE-GROWERS' COOPERATIVES

With the motto "We've got plenty of wine but no bread or money," the cooperative movement in winemaking began from necessity 120 years ago in Württemberg. By the turn of the century, there were 113 cooperatives. In 1930, the first national federation of cooperatives was formed, the forerunner of today's Deutscher Raiffeisenverband, the central administrative and lobbying organization for Germany's 329 cooperatives, including the six large regional central cellars (Zentralkellereien) in Breisach/Baden; Gau-Bickelheim/Rheinhessen; Bernkastel/Mosel-Saar-Ruwer; Bretzenheim/Nahe; Möglingen/Württemberg; and Kitzingen-Repperndorf/Franken. From the beginning, the cooperative movement sought to increase the low income of wine-growers. The cooperatives have been instrumental in improving the quality of small and part-time growers' crops, not least by rewarding growers with premiums for delivering quality rather than quantity. Their ability to adequately process members' grapes and long-term storage facilities have greatly contributed to price stability in the wine market. In terms of winemaking, the cooperatives' cellars are among the most modern and efficient in the world. This, together with high quality standards, explains why some 40% of all DLG (German Agricultural Society) prizes for outstanding wines at Germany's national wine competition are awarded to cooperatives. Sales fall into two broad categories: Smaller and local cooperatives usually supply local customers, including direct sales to consumers. Regional and central cellars are able to consistently supply large enough quantities of particular appellations and quality categories to service the grocery trade (where 40% of all German wine is sold) and to compete successfully in export markets. Today, cooperatives account for anywhere from 30% to 40% of German wine sales annually. In 1985, cooperative membership totaled 68,000. The approximate percentage of growers belonging to cooperatives per region: Baden and Württemberg, 85% each; Hessische Bergstrasse and Ahr, 75% each; Mittelrhein 50–60%; Mosel-Saar-Ruwer and Rheinpfalz, 30% each; Nahe and Rheingau, 20% each; Rheinhessen 12%.

Geropiga, jeropiga

Grape syrup used in Portugal for sweetening Port.

Gers

A department in southwest France whose wine is mostly unexceptional and often used for blending with other white wine. Some is distilled into Armagnac.

Gevrey-Chambertin (Appellation Contrôlée)

Burgundy red wine.
District: Côte de Nuits, France.

Gevrey-Chambertin is one of the communes of Burgundy's Côte d'Or, and more specifically of the Côte de Nuits, the northern section of the Côte d'Or. Working from north to south, it is the first of the important Côte de Nuits communes. Like almost all of the other villages along the famous strip of hills, this one has capitalized on its most famous and best vineyard and has added that name to the name of the place. Until 1847, the *appellation* was legally Gevrey, but since that time it has been Gevrey-Chambertin. The town fathers were not the only ones to be impressed by the name of their celebrated growth. At one time, practically every vineyard tried to tack Chambertin onto its own name, perhaps in hopes that some of the qualities of the wine would rub off with it. In 1936 the French authorities stepped in and decided who had the right to the name and who had not, and the matter was settled.

About 630, the Duke of Burgundy endowed the Abbey of Bèze with some land in Gevrey. The monks turned the land into a vineyard and found that they could produce an extraordinary wine. According to the stories that have come down from these ancient times, the field next to the abbey was later owned by a peasant named Bertin and was called the Champs de Bertin, or "Bertin's field." Thanks to the success of the abbey vineyards, Bertin also planted vines on his field and the name was soon shortened to Chambertin. But it was not Bertin, nor even the monks of the Abbey of Bèze, who expanded the fame of the vineyard; that was left to a man named Jobert, who owned not only Chambertin but the Clos de Bèze as well, and he made the vineyards famous. At some time, he changed his own name to Jobert-Chambertin. The vineyards are no longer united, as they were under Jobert, and are divided up into plots belonging to more than two dozen growers.

Chambertin has a great history and a great reputation, and there can be no wonder that the other vineyards of the town have wished to capitalize on it. Under the present law, the only ones which are allowed to use the name Chambertin with their own are several immediately adjoining it. Since the Clos de Bèze is considered on a par with Chambertin—and indeed can sell its wines as Chambertin if it so desires—it is allowed to place the magic name before its own, while the others must add it on after. Chambertin-Clos de Bèze is the full and proper name, and the vineyard is included in the special decree which covers Chambertin. The others fall under a different decree, the major difference being that the maximum permissible yield is raised from 30 hectoliters (780 U.S. gallons, 600 imp.) of wine per hectare to 35 hectoliters (925 U.S. gallons, 770 imp.) per hectare. The vineyards are the following: Latricières-Chambertin, Mazoyères-Chambertin, Charmes-Chambertin, Mazis- (or Mazys-) Chambertin, Rochottes-Chambertin, Griotte-Chambertin, and Chapelle-Chambertin. Altogether, they comprise the Great Growths (*Grands Crus*) of the commune, and each one is treated under its own heading.

The vineyards, most of which lie between Gevrey-Chambertin and the next town to the south, Morey-Saint-Denis, are along the midsection of the hill and they can be seen from Route Nationale (National Highway) No. 74, which runs along the plain at the foot of the slope. A repaved, winding vineyard road halfway up the slope provides a better vantage point, however. If you leave Gevrey-Chambertin by this road, the first important vineyards to come into sight will be those of Mazis (the second half of the name is usually left out in any discussion of the vineyards but should always be included on the labels) with Ruchottes just above it on the slope. Both of these are on the right, and they adjoin the Clos de Bèze with Griotte and Chapelle on the left, directly across the road from it. A small toolhouse stands in the Clos de Bèze bearing the name of Pierre Damoy, one of the better growers and the largest single owner in the place, but aside from that there is nothing to distinguish one vineyard from another. After passing the Clos de Bèze there is a large but simple sign informing the passer-by: "Here starts the vineyard of Chambertin." Almost before he has had time to digest this information, there is another sign to tell him: "Here ends the vineyard of Chambertin." The length—and it is roughly twice as long as it is wide—is barely more than 490 meters (1,500 feet). Aside from these landmarks, there is no sign in the earth or in the vines that here the soil is such that the resulting wine will be a greater or a slightly lesser one. There is no way for the newcomer to identify the various vineyards at all. For that it is necessary to go to the wines.

Like most of the villages of the Côte d'Or, Gevrey-Chambertin sits in a small defile, called a *combe*, between two hills in the range that makes up the Côte d'Or. All the Chambertins are on the slope on the southern side of the village, but there are other excellent vineyards on the north side as well. In the classification made in 1860 of the vines of the Côte d'Or, only Chambertin and the Clos de Bèze were classed as Outstanding Vineyards (*Têtes de Cuvée*), and all the others, including those which have been elevated to the modern ranks of the Great Growths (*Grands Crus*), were classed below them as First Growths (*Premiers Crus*). With these vineyards, in 1860, were several others, such as the Clos Saint-Jacques, Varoilles, Fouchère, Étournelles, and Cazetiers. Today, most of these are included among the official First Growths and are allowed to add the vineyard name to the name of the commune (selling, for example, as Gevrey-Chambertin Clos Saint-Jacques) or may add the words *Premier Cru* to the name of the commune. Many experts consider it unfortunate that the vineyards of Varoilles and Clos Saint-Jacques were not included with the finest vineyards of the commune and given Great Growth status. In many years, the excellent wines from these two vineyards compare very favorably with the others, except possibly for the wines of Chambertin and the Clos de Bèze.

The communal wines of the village, those that go to market with the words Gevrey-Chambertin and no other indication of origin, are the least of the wines of the commune, although some of them may certainly be very pleasant. Most of them are grown in Gevrey-Chambertin, but some may come from the better vineyards in the neighboring town of Brochon. The amount of wine sold as Gevrey-Chambertin or as Gevrey-Chambertin Premier Cru comes to very slightly over 15,000 hectoliters (397,500 U.S. gallons, 330,000 imp.) in an average year. The total vineyard area

for Gevrey is 205 hectares (506.5 acres). The vineyards of note in the commune are listed below. (*See also* Great Growths *under separate headings.*)

GREAT GROWTHS (*Grands Crus*)

Vineyard	Hectares	Acres
Chambertin (Outstanding Vineyard)	17.7	44
Chambertin-Clos de Bèze (Outstanding Vineyard)	15.7	39
Latricières-Chambertin	6.23	15.51
Mazoyères-Chambertin	19.18	47.75
Charmes-Chambertin	12.42	30.92
Mazys- or Mazis-Chambertin	9.47	23.58
Ruchottes-Chambertin	8.45	21.04
Griotte-Chambertin	3.18	7.91
Chapelle-Chambertin	4.06	10.10

FIRST GROWTHS (*Premiers Crus*)

Vineyard	Hectares	Acres
Varoilles	5.94	14.7
Clos Saint-Jacques	6.92	17.1
Aux Combottes	4.9	12.4
Bel-Air	3.72	9.2
Les Cazetiers	9.11	22.5
Combe-au-Moine	4.78	11.8
Étournelles	2	5
Lavaut	9.43	23.3
Poissenot	2.19	5.4
Champeaux	6.76	16.7
Les Goulots	1.82	4.5
Issarts (or Plantigone)	1.82	4.5
Les Corbeaux	3.12	7.7
Cherbaudes	2.19	5.4
La Perrière	2.47	6.1
Clos-Prieur (upper section only)	1.98	4.9
Le Fonteny	3.80	9.4
Champonnet	3.32	8.2
Au Closeau	.5	1.3
Craipillot	2.75	6.8
Champitennois (also called Petite Chapelle)	3.97	9.8
En Ergot	1.17	2.9
Clos du Chapitre	.97	2.4

Gewächs

German term meaning "growth of." Same as Kreszenz (*q.v.*).

Gewürztraminer

A type of Traminer vine, and therefore Traminer wine, said to be even more spicy than this spiciest of grape varieties in forming many Alsatian and German wines. Actually, in usage, the two names are practically interchangeable and any real difference in meaning has been lost.

For a description of Traminer and Gewürztraminer wines *see* Alsace; Germany.

Ghemme (D.O.C.)

A dry red wine from the Italian Piedmont (*q.v.*).

Gigondas (Appellation Contrôlée)

One of the best communes of the Côtes du Rhône, producing red, white, and rosé wines.
See Rhône.

Gill

Quartern, or a quarter of a British pint.

Gin

Gin is a juniper-flavored spirit obtained by the distillation and rectification of the grain spirits of malted barley and rye—or sometimes of corn or maize. Yet the definition of gin as a grain spirit is not entirely correct. Theoretically, it can be made from any rectified spirit. During the last war, gins were, in fact, distilled in England from raw molasses spirit; and some London Dry gins for domestic consumption are still based on this, although the majority of gins are now based on grain, both for home and export markets. The price of gin in the home market is the same for practically all varieties based on grain.

The two principal types of gin are British (the gin produced in the United States is made in a similar manner) and Dutch. The latter is known in the Netherlands as Jenever and in England as Hollands, or else as Schiedam, after one of the towns where it is manufactured. The English words *gin* and *geneva* are corruptions of the French *jenever* and *genièvre*, both meaning juniper—nothing to do with the Swiss city. *Genièvre* is a word seldom heard in France now: *gin* (pronounced jeen) is one of the anglicisms which have crept in since the war, and which, purists complain, are ruining the French language.

Both the Dutch and the English claim, and sometimes disclaim, the invention of gin. It is certain that in the seventeenth century gin was being made from barley, hops, and juniper berries in England; Hogarth's famous picture "Gin Lane" shows the consequences. In 1736 the Gin Act banned gin. Like most prohibitions, it did not work, and repeal followed in 1742, because illegal gin was worse than the legal kind.

Since the discovery of redistillation, or rectification, it has been possible to remove the harmful characteristics from any raw spirit, leaving practically pure alcohol. In the making of Dutch gins (as of rums and the heavier whiskies) preliminary rectification is not part of the process, which thus preserves some of the taste of the barley, malt, and grain.

Hollands is often sold in stone jars or crocks, and the Dutch usually drink it neat, out of narrow tall glasses. It is made by infusing a mash of malted barley and rye, or, occasionally, maize. When it has cooled, it is set to ferment with yeast; in two or three days, fermentation is complete and the alcoholic liquid is then distilled. The distillation is redistilled with flavoring—juniper berries and various other ingredients, according to the recipe of the maker. (In some cases, the juniper berries are mashed in with the malt.) If the process of redistillation over flavoring is repeated, the result is what is known as Double Gin. Hollands is distilled at a lower proof than British gin; and it is generally aged in bond. By law, it must contain 35% of alcohol by volume.

In the making of British or American gins, a highly rectified—or neutral—spirit, by now colorless and tasteless, is redistilled with the juniper berries and coriander or other flavorings. If this process is repeated, the product is a gin of the London Dry variety. Dry gin is so easy to make that it may fairly be classed as an art of the kitchen: since it is merely flavored neutral spirit, it must be a natural temptation to the home distiller. Some makers buy their spirit already distilled. (Inferior gins are made by adding essential oils to plain spirit and omitting distillation altogether.) Dry gins, being so highly distilled (or rectified), contain no fusel oil, and need not, therefore, be aged to remove this harmful taint. In fact, they gain nothing by ageing and are ready to drink at once.

Gins take their character from the flavoring recipe which is the secret of each maker. After the base spirit has been rectified, flavoring matter is added by one means or another. Sometimes alcohol, juniper berries, and such other ingredients as may be used are simply steeped together. Another technique is that of passing the spirit over into a flavor still, a box-like small still in which the vapors contact volatile juniper, angelica, coriander, etc. The flavors used by the various distillers, while always including juniper, are diverse. Some of the others are fennel, licorice, orange peel, anise, caraway, calamus, orris, and almond.

In addition to the variations between the different brands, there are two other distinct types of gin. Old Tom Gin is one which has been sweetened by adding sugar to the dry variety. Plymouth Gin is made in Plymouth, England, by a single firm (Coates) and is intermediate in style between the ordinary English gin and Dutch gin. (Sloe Gin [*q.v.*] utilizes gin but is not properly a gin.)

In the United States, London Dry gins may be of three kinds: gin imported from England; gin made in the U.S. under license or grant from the original British distiller; or any dry gin made in America and simply given the name as a type-name. In all cases, the general principles of preparation are the same.

Golden gin is gin which has been barrel-aged, taking its golden hue from the wood, but it is quite uncommon. The great preference in the United States is for neutral gins, because they are generally used as bases for cocktails and should harmonize with a wide

Gin Fizz

range of flavors—although most gin is drunk in Dry Martinis, in Collinses, or with tonic water.

Lemon gin, orange gin, and so on are usually artificially flavored gins, but they can be produced from the named ingredient.

Gin Fizz

A long, cool, effervescent drink composed of gin, lemon juice, a little sugar, ice, and soda-water. There are several other fizzes, variations on this recipe and based on either gin or brandy.

Ginger

Ginger Ale

A favorite English or American mineral drink, frothy and of a ginger color; it is often added to gin or whisky to make a long drink comparable with gin and tonic. The ale is carbonated water to which coloring matter has been added, drops of capsicum extract or essence of ginger, and some glucose or sugar. "Froth heading" may also be added to make the drink more foamy.

Ginger Beer

A pale frothy bottled drink popular in England. It is made by the fermentation of sugar, ginger, cream of tartar, and yeast with water, and is bottled before it has finished fermenting. The carbon dioxide thus generated produces an aerated drink.

Ginger Wine

A homely English beverage—but made commercially. The ingredients: ginger, yeast, sugar, lemon rind, raisins, and water. It is often fortified with spirits and a little capsicum.

Ginger brandy

Tawny-colored, ginger-flavored spirit made in Great Britain.

Girò di Cagliari (D.O.C.)

A Port-like wine from Sardinia (q.v.).

Girò di Sardegna

Sweet red dessert wine of Sardinia (q.v.).

Gironde

The department of Bordeaux. Also, the wide tidal estuary formed by the Dordogne and Garonne rivers, which meet north of the city.

Château Giscours

Bordeaux red wine.
District: Haut-Médoc, France.
Commune: Labarde-Margaux.

Château Giscours had fallen completely from its traditional place as one of the best of the Third Growths (*Troisièmes Crus*) of the 1855 Médoc Classification, when the present owner, M. Tari—a major winemaker in Oran, Algeria—took it over in 1954. A formerly fine growth had been debased by plantings of hybrid vines. By 1955–56, these were all ripped out by M. Tari, and the vineyard was entirely reconstituted through grafting with first-class vines. Subsequent vintages have shown a great improvement, and in the hands of M. Tari and his dedicated son, future wines can be expected to continue to do so.

The records of Giscours go back to 1552, when a Seigneur de la Bastide sold it to Pierre de l'Horme. During the Revolution, the property was confiscated from the Saint-Simon family by the state and was then sold to a M. Jacob on behalf of two Americans, John Gray and Jonathan Davis of Boston.

The present château was built by Count Pescatore, a banker in the time of Napoleon III. Eventually, in 1852, it was purchased by Édouard Cruse, in whose family it remained until 1913. The building, with its two great wings, stands at the head of one of the most magnificent parks in Bordeaux, with a lake, lily-choked canals, and at least one giant California sequoia.

The British I.D.V. group, owners of Gilbey's, became exclusive world distributor of the wine in 1973.

Characteristics. Full yet delicate, highly perfumed, and often elegant. The quality has lately made great strides, and the wine deserves its growing reputation.

Vineyard area: 78 hectares (195 acres).
Average production: 350 *tonneaux* (33,000 cases).

Givry (Appellation Contrôlée)

Commune of the Côte Chalonnaise producing mainly red wines.
See also Chalonnais.

Glen Elgin

Important vineyard in New South Wales producing red table wines and some white. The principal grape varieties are Syrah and "Riesling" (actually Sémillon).
See also Australia.

Glenloth

Vineyard in the Reynella district of South Australia.
See Australia.

Glögg

A hot wine drink spiced with brandy or aquavit, almonds and raisins, traditionally served in Sweden during cold weather.

Château Gloria

Bordeaux red wine.
District: Haut-Médoc, France.
Commune: Saint-Julien.

The vineyard contains parcels from Château Léo-ville-Poyferré and Château Gruaud-Larose (Second Growths—*Seconds Crus*), and from Château Saint-Pierre and Château Duhart-Milon (Fourth Growths—*Quatrièmes Crus*). The *chais* were originally those of Château Saint-Pierre. The owner and manager of the vineyard is M. Henri Martin, mayor of Saint-Julien and one of the leading figures both in Médoc and Bordeaux wines; in 1956 he became president of the Interprofessional Committee of Bordeaux Wines. Qualities of terrain and intelligent, energetic management have raised the wine far above its official rating. At present ranked as a Bourgeois Growth (*Bourgeois Cru*) of Médoc, it amply justifies elevation to the status of a Classified Growth.
Characteristics. Round and subtle with, at the same time, some of the best characteristics of Saint-Julien—fullness with delicacy. Usually a well-made wine.
Vineyard area: 44 hectares (110 acres).
Average production: 200 *tonneaux* (18,000 cases).

Gluco-oenometer

An instrument to test the sugar content of new musts; used in making Port.

Glycerin

A tri-hydritic alcohol formed from sugar during the fermentation of grape juice to wine. an abundance of glycerin gives wine a characteristic "fatness" and softness (a lack of body). $CH_2OH \cdot CHOH \cdot CH_2OH$.

Gobelet

Method of training vines: a single trunk terminates in several arms rising in the shape of a vase or goblet.
See Chapter Eight, p. 31.

Goblet

A drinking cup or glass with foot and stem.

Goldwasser

See Danziger Goldwasser.

Gourmet

Alsatian term for a wine-broker—who is known in the Bordeaux district as a *courtier*.

Goût américain

To the American taste. The term is a misnomer, for it refers to sweet Champagne, although this is not, in fact, shipped to the United States now.

Goût anglais

To the English taste. The term refers to dry Champagne for the English market.

Goût de pierre à fusil

French term for the gunflint taste of a very dry white wine, such as Chablis.

Goût de terroir

In French this means, literally, earthy taste; it denotes a peculiar flavor imparted by certain soils, and not the taste of the soil itself.

Graacher Himmelreich

Best of the Graach wines on the German Mosel. Josephshof is another fine wine of Graach and one of the few German wines permitted to be sold without the name of a specific vineyard site.
See Mosel-Saar-Ruwer.

Gragnano

Leading red wine of Campania, Italy.
See Campania.

Graisse

A disorder of wine; fatty degeneration, by which the wine becomes viscous and turgid.
See Chapter Nine, p. 40.

Grand Cru

French term for a great vineyard.

Grand Cru Classé

A special designation for the very best of the some 3,000 wine châteaux of the Gironde. Médoc, Sauternes, and Barsac were classified in 1855, Graves in 1953 and 1959, and Saint-Émilion in 1955 and 1986. In 1965, this designation was reserved by law exclusively for Bordeaux.

Château Grand-La-Lagune

See Château La Lagune.

Grand Marnier

An orange-flavored, brandy-based, sweet proprietary French liqueur of the Curaçao type made by the Établissements Marnier-Lapostolle in Neauphle-le-Château and Château de Bourg, in France. It is made in two types, yellow and red, of which the red is stronger and the yellow sweeter.

See Curaçao.

Château Grand-Pontet

Bordeaux red wine.
District and Commune: Saint-Émilion, France.

The château is situated on the plateau in the midst of the great vineyards of Saint-Émilion and makes one of the most reliable wines in the district. The property was owned until 1979 by Barton & Guestier, a subsidiary of Seagrams. M. Bécot became proprietor in 1981.

Vineyard area: 14 hectares (32.5 acres).
Average production: 60 *tonneaux* (5,500 cases).

Château Grand-Puy-Ducasse

Bordeaux red wine.
District: Haut-Médoc, France.
Commune: Pauillac.

A third of the vineyard is the portion of the old Château Grand Puy, the remainder of that vineyard now being Château Grand-Puy-Lacoste; another third lies near Château Batailley south of Pauillac; and a third to the north near Châteaux Pontet-Canet and Mouton-Rothschild.

Grand-Puy-Ducasse is rated Fifth Growth (*Cinquième Cru*) in the Classification of 1855, and the château itself is on the wide street bordering the river docks of Pauillac, which, until the early eighties, housed a wine museum and the headquarters of the Médoc and Graves wine fraternity, the Commanderie du Bontemps.

Characteristics. Lighter, with good breed, but less well constructed than those of Grand-Puy-Lacoste (*q.v.*).

Vineyard area: 36 hectares (90 acres).
Average production: 140 *tonneaux* (14,000 cases).

Château Grand-Puy-Lacoste

Bordeaux red wine.
District: Haut-Médoc, France.
Commune: Pauillac.

The wine is mostly exported to England, Germany and the United States. A Fifth Growth (*Cinquième Cru*) of Médoc, the vineyard lies on one of the highest parts of Pauillac. In Old French the word *puy* meant "high point," and the eminence on which the vines are planted is conserved in the name. Grand Puy, dating from at least the fifteenth century, was acquired after the French Revolution by a M. Lacoste, who tacked on his own name. Like Château Calon-Ségur and a few others, it is one of the rare Médoc vineyards to be

entirely in one section and undivided, and intact since the Classification of 1855.

Characteristics. Excellent, full-bodied wines; they mature into sturdy and extremely pleasant wines of great breed. The gastronomically minded M. Dupin, the owner during the postwar period, did much to give them the good reputation they have acquired. Today, Grand-Puy-Lacoste belongs to Jean-Eugène Borie (owner of Ducru-Beaucaillou) and deserves a better classification than the 1855 Fifth rating. Since the 1978 vintage, M. Borie's son has given Ducru-Beaucaillou a touch which has even further improved the quality of these very fine wines.

Vineyard area: 45 hectares (112.5 acres).
Average production: 180 *tonneaux* (17,000 cases).

Grand Roussillon (Côtes du Roussillon) (A.O.C.)

Red, white, and rosé wines.
District: Southern France.

Grand Roussillon is the former name for the wine district which has now become the Appellation d'Origine Contrôlée Côtes du Roussillon. The region in southern France encompasses the districts of Banyuls, Côtes d'Agly, Côtes du Roussillon, Maury, and Rivesaltes in the departments of Pyrénées-Orientales and Aude, bordering Spain and the Mediterranean. The Roussillon vineyards produce dry red, rosé, and white wines from Carignan, Cinsault, Grenache, and Mourvèdre. Within Grand Roussillon, Côtes du Roussillon is an Appellation d'Origine Contrôlée limited to dry reds, whites, and rosés. The classification Côtes du Roussillon Villages is further limited to reds and rosés made in the best villages, most located in the slate-rich hills above the Agly River. Among the best are Planèzes, Estabel, Montner, Latour-de-France, Rasiguères, Vingrau, and Caramany. Côtes du Roussillon plus the Villages produce about 270,000 hectoliters, or 3 million cases, per year.

The Roussillon also produces several *vins doux naturels* (V.D.N.): Rivesaltes, rosé and white wines from Muscat, Grenache, and Maccabéo; Muscat de Rivesaltes, made from Muscat only; Banyuls and Maury, made from Grenache Noir. Banyuls also produces a heavy, dry red wine, Collioure de Grenache. Production of V.D.N. averages 600,000 hectoliters per year.

Grand Vin

French for "great wine"; a freely used term on labels and one that is not a legally defined indication of superior quality.

Grande (Fine) Champagne (A.O.C.)

Best district of the Cognac vineyards and consequently the mark, on a Cognac label, of the finest brandy from the point of view of vineyard quality. Some say that a certain percentage of brandy derived from wine of the Borderies across the River Charente is needed to combine heartiness with the splendid finesse of Grande Champagne. Its distinction comes from the chalky soil. Similarity of sort is the only thing Grande Champagne Cognac has in common with Champagne wines.

See Cognac.

Grands-Échezeaux (Appellation Contrôlée)

Burgundy red wine.
District Côte de Nuits, France.
Commune: Flagey-Échezeaux.
Official Classification: Great Growth (Grand Cru).

(*Flagey-Échezeaux is not an* appellation, *and when the wines do not meet the required minimum standards they are declassed into communal wine of Vosne-Romanée.*)

The widely prevalent myth that all Bordeaux is light and all Burgundy heavy can easily be scotched by placing a bottle of Grands-Échezeaux next to a fine Saint-Émilion. Grands-Échezeaux lies between Vougiot and Vosne-Romanée, and the wines provide the logical half-step between the sturdy fullness of the former and the easy aristocratic elegance of the latter; they balance the body necessary for a well-rounded wine with a delicacy and a finesse which prompts the Burgundian to characterize them as *en dentelle* (like lace). Despite the fact that they are little known, they are unquestionably among the greatest of all red Burgundies.

The vineyard embraces 9.15 hectares (22.6 acres) up the hill and across a road from the Clos de Vougeot—on the southern side of the vineyard—and the entire Clos is visible from it. A number of growers own sections, including the Domaine Civile de la Romanée-Conti and such able and excellent wine-makers as the sons of René Engel and Louis Gros. Average production of the entire vineyard is about 350 hectoliters (9,275 U.S. gallons, 7,700 imp.).

Granja União

Brand name for some of the best wines of Brazil. Both red and white are sold by this company.
See Brazil.

Granjo

A natural sweet white wine of Portugal made by letting noble rot form on late-picked grapes, as is the method in Sauternes and with the Spätlese German wines.

Grape

Fruit of the vine. Wine is made from the fermented juice of the grape, of which there are many varieties.
See Chapter Eight, p. 31.

Grappa

The Italian word for marc, or spirit distilled from grape husks. The term is also used in California and in Spanish-speaking countries. Most grappa is harsh, coarse, young, and fairly mediocre.

Graves (Appellation Contrôlée)

Red and white wines.
District: Bordeaux, France.

Because they have met with only mediocre blended wines of the district, Graves, to many people outside France, was simply a sweetish white wine. In fact, the better white wines of Graves are dry, the greatest wines red. This large region—40 miles long and at some points 12 miles wide—stretching from the fringe of the Médoc to the edge of Sauternes and containing a variety of sites and soils, naturally produces wines of different types.

Graves encloses the city of Bordeaux and, as the suburbs spread, the vineyard is thrust back. Only such great estates as those of Haut-Brion and La Mission-Haut-Brion are too valuable to be given up to building, and these are now islands surrounded by houses and shops and touched by the main road. In the Middle Ages, however, when the bourgeois growers of Bordeaux used to hurry back at nightfall to the sheltering walls of the city, its closeness was a great advantage, and Graves was in both senses of the word the first district of Bordeaux. Indeed, in England, where most of the wine went, the names were synonymous. This was still the case in the seventeenth century, when Pepys wrote of the good wine of Haut-Brion; but during the next hundred years the wines of the Médoc came into fashion. For some time after the Napoleonic wars even the great vineyard of Haut-Brion sank, through mismanagement, into mediocrity. The oïdium epidemic of the early 1850s struck hard in Graves, and the growers were slower than those of other districts to reconstitute their vines. Whether for this reason or because of local politics, Graves was not included in the 1855 Classification of the Gironde wines. Yet Haut-Brion, restored to its former glory, could not be left out: so, ignoring geography, the classifiers added it to the First Growths (*Premiers Crus*) of the great vineyards of the Médoc. In fact, all the big red wines of Graves—vigorous, full-bodied, and lasting—always had their partisans. The growers pulled themselves together, and in the splendid pre-phylloxera years of 1864–65 the shippers were again doing keen business with them.

The name Graves comes from the gravelly soil in which the red grapes (Cabernet Sauvignon, Cabernet Franc, Merlot, Malbec, and Petit Verdot) flourish. The same soil occurs elsewhere, in Pomerol, Saint-Émilion, and the Médoc. The vines, also, are Médoc vines, and there is a family resemblance between the red wines of these adjoining areas. If the Médocs (especially the Margaux) are more feminine and delicate,

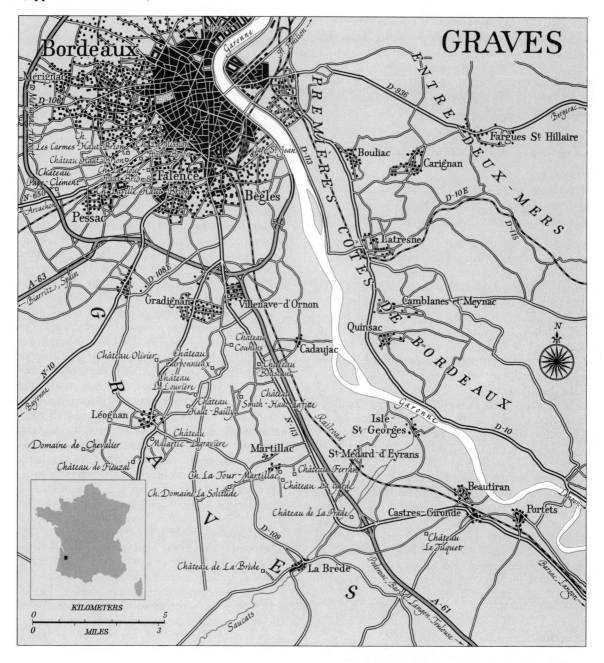

the Graves have more body, a distinct character, and a pleasing frankness.

The red Graves actually outnumber the white. In the southern part of the district toward Sauternes, and in a soil which contains a proportion of sand, white wine grapes (Sémillon, Sauvignon, and a very little Muscadelle) predominate. The same vines grow in Sauternes. These white wines are mainly dry, especially in the north of Graves (the best of all is the small production of Haut-Brion Blanc); but some, near Sauternes, are suave, soft, and *moelleux*. Down here, the land is well-wooded and crossed with little streams, the country of the most romantic Bordeaux châteaux: Olivier, mirrored in the still waters of its moat, once the hunting lodge of the Black Prince; and

the Château de la Brède, moated too, and even more beautiful. Montesquieu lived here and cultivated his vineyard. It is more famous now for its library than its wines.

In 1953, the best vineyards of Graves were classified in both red and white wines. This rating was much criticized, and was revised in 1959. Only two vineyards were added in red wines, three in white, and the revision brought little satisfaction. In each, Château Haut-Brion is classified a red wine of Graves, while remaining a First Growth of the Médoc. A glaring error in the original Graves Classification was its failure to include among the whites Château Haut-Brion Blanc, one of the finest dry white wines in the world. This error was rectified in 1960.

GRAVES 1959 OFFICIAL CLASSIFICATION

(For the individual Classified Growths, see under separate headings, and for the list of all Graves Growths, see Appendix A.)

CLASSIFIED VINEYARDS MAKING BOTH RED AND WHITE WINES

Vineyard	Commune
Château Bouscaut	Cadaujac
Château Carbonnieux	Léognan
Domaine de Chevalier	Léognan
Château Haut-Brion	Pessac
Château La Tour-Martillac	Martillac
Château Malartic-Lagravière	Léognan
Château Olivier	Léognan

CLASSIFIED VINEYARDS MAKING RED WINE

Vineyard	Commune
Château de Fieuzal	Léognan
Château Haut-Bailly	Léognan
Château Haut-Brion	Pessac
Château La Mission-Haut-Brion	Pessac
Château La Tour-Haut-Brion	Talence
Château Pape-Clément	Pessac
Château Smith-Haut-Lafitte	Martillac

CLASSIFIED VINEYARDS MAKING WHITE WINE

Vineyard	Commune
Château Couhins	Villenave-d'Ornan
Château Laville-Haut-Brion	Talence

See Bordeaux.

The I.N.A.O. in 1984 has added a discretionary breakdown for the better northern vineyards: "Graves de Pessac" and "Graves de Léognan." It may take some time before these additions appear on labels. The lesser vineyards can be expected to make use of this decree.
See Bordeaux.

Graves de Vayres (Appellation Contrôlée)

White and red wines.
District: Bordeaux, France.

Facing Libourne on the River Dordogne in southwest France, an enclave of gravel soil juts into the predominantly clay soil of the large wine region of Entre-Deux-Mers (carafe white wine). The quality on the gravel terrain is definitely superior and merits the individual wine *appellation*, Graves de Vayres. Vayres is the chief village, and *graves* is the regional term for the type of gravel. This place-name is famous beyond all reason in Germany, where the cheap Graves de Vayres are sold as the wines of Graves, although the resemblance is remote.

The red wines mature quickly and are very attractive and supple, standing comparison with all but the best of the Pomerols and Saint-Émilions from across the Dordogne, but the quantity in an average year (7,000 hectoliters) is tiny. The white wines (17,000 hectoliters; 442,000 U.S. gallons, 340,000 imp.) are suave

and mellow, distinguished by their quantity of natural fatness.

Graves Supérieures (Appellation Contrôlée)

White wines.
District: Bordeaux, France.

A former official French wine designation denoting a white wine of the delimited Graves district surrounding Bordeaux, in southwest France, which had obtained 12% or more of alcohol by natural fermentation.
See also Graves.

Gray Riesling, Gray Dutchess

A white Californian grape which is not, in fact, a Riesling at all but a descendant of the French Chauché Gris.

Gray rot

Ignoble rot, disease of the grape. When this rot forms, it causes stains on the leaves and alterations within the fruit.
See Chapter Eight, p. 31.

Greco

The grape used in Greco di Bianco, in some of the wines of Calabria and elsewhere in Italy.

Greco di Bianco (D.O.C.)

One of the best wines of Calabria, sweet and golden, with a flowery bouquet.
See Calabria.

Greco di Tufo (D.O.C.)

Dry white Italian wine from the Campania *(q.v.).*

Greece

The cultivation of the vine ranks among the first products of Greek agriculture. A grower of wine from ancient times (there are many references to it in the *Iliad* and the *Odyssey*), Greece was destined to be so by her soil and climate. The chalky soils of the Greek mainland, Crete, and other islands, and the volcanic soils of important vine-growing islands such as Santorini, are favorable to viticulture. Of the 165,000 hectares (413,000 acres) planted in vines, 90,000 hectares (225,000 acres) are devoted to wine grapes. Because the climate is so dry, the grapes grow sweet and the wines have a characteristic fresh flavor—best of all are the luscious sweet varieties. Those destined for export are made by up-to-date methods at the plants of big manufacturers. For their own use, the peasants are apt to go about their wine-making as their ancestors did in the old days when Dionysos was still worshipped.

After the First World War, refugees coming in from wine-growing regions in Asia Minor increased the vineyard area of Greece, and a great deal of wine was exported, particularly between 1926 and 1929. In the years after the Second World War, general conditions, allied to outbreaks of phylloxera and mildew, did a great deal of harm. Anti-phylloxera measures were introduced and vineyards reconstituted, so that the area in vine is now equal to the pre-war vineyards, and export figures have surpassed their pre-war status. Ranking ninth in European wine production, and fourteenth in world production, Greece now takes a comparable place in the world market. The average annual harvest is some 5,200,000 hectoliters (137,-500,000 U.S. gallons, 114,500,000 imp.), of which about 450,000 hectoliters (12 million U.S. gallons, 9 million imp.) are exported each year. Her principal customers are West Germany, Switzerland, Sweden, the Benelux countries and the United States.

Until recent years, there were few attempts to control quality or enforce the laws of appellation, and the easygoing Greek consumer made no demand upon the producer, with the result that vineyards did not maintain an even character. In general, wine has been taken for granted as something plentiful and often cheap, and most of which is not even bottled but aged in huge vats. This has meant that there has been no luxury trade to speak of, with the minimum of estate-bottling among small growers. However, legislation was set up to bring in certain controls, which were made law in the seventies, and have gradually become effective. The government began control of wine prices in 1970. Since 1976, new legislation designed to conform with the laws of the Common Market and to meet the demands of current wine-making has been in effect. Twenty-six regions of production have been defined and recognized as place-names. The Wine Institute, a branch of the Ministry of Agriculture, is responsible for maintaining quality standards. Unfortunately, a shortage of trained oenologists makes this difficult.

As it is now, the Greek wine business can be divided into three main groups: (1) the cooperatives; (2) large producers; and (3) the smaller individual producers. There are 55 cooperatives, which account for 40% of the total production, and 250 private companies. Seven of the most important concerns are Botrys; Boutari; C.A.I.R.; Kourtakis; Porto Carras; Cambas; and Achaia-Clauss—which supplies nearly 80% of all the domestic wine consumed in Greece, some 15 million bottles, and a good deal more in bulk. Per capita consumption is about 44 liters a year; and a great deal of this wine is unquestionably made by the peasant farmers themselves for almost immediate consumption.

During the last ten years, great investments have been made by the cooperatives, the wine merchants and shipping firms in order to modernize their plants and their centers of vinification. In addition, there is a growing trend toward wine in bottles (rather than bulk).

WINE REGIONS

The Peloponnese

The peninsula is the largest wine-growing district (66,000 hectares) in Greece, producing more than 1,300,000 hectoliters, or about 25% of the country's total production. One of the most important firms is the cooperative of Patras in the extreme north, across the straits from Messolonghi, where Byron died of fever. The town of Patras, reached by the lovely coast road along the shores of the Corinthian Gulf, or by the railway which runs parallel with it, nestles at the foot of a steep mountain. The vineyards, five miles wide, cover the beautiful slopes. Several wine shipping and merchant houses such as Achaia-Clauss S.A., Beso S.A., and Transetcom S.A. are located near Patras, an imporant maritime center. The principal grape varieties are Mavrodaphne, Muscat, Aghiorghitico and Phileri. There are some neat rows of trimmed vines—others grow everywhere, like bushes, basking in the

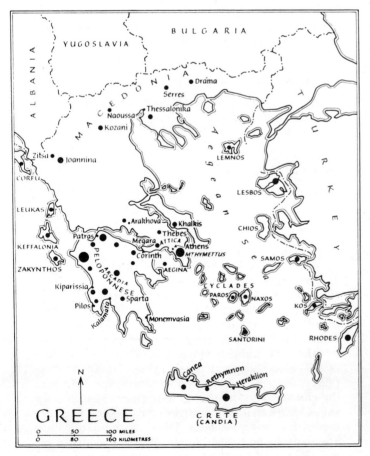

GREECE

full heat of the sun. Some of the best Greek appellations come from this district—a few red, but mainly dry white. But a sweet white Muscat is made here, too, and more important, the luscious Mavrodaphne (grown also on the island of Cephalonia); Mavrodaphne of Patras is one of the few dessert wines which seem to express themselves best when served at room temperature rather than chilled. It is an expensive, heavy, sweet red wine with 14% to 16% of alcohol by volume. Other wines of the region are the light pinkish Tegea; the supple Mantinea; and Nemea or "the blood of Hercules," dry but very dark, almost black, in color.

Attica

Attica is the second most productive region, accounting for about 15% of the wine. In this very hot country, south of Athens, bordered by splendid beaches and a well-paved coast road, the vineyards yield a great deal of the ordinary wine for domestic consumption. The white Savatiano grape, used for the best retsina, appears here; Mandilaria for red wines, and some Rhoditis for rosé. Here also the dry Hymettus is made, near Mount Hymettus, a wine that should be drunk when it is two to four years old; and Marco. One of the best white wines of Greece is from a small estate called Pallini.

Macedonia

The western and central parts of this region are particularly favorable for viticulture and have become an important red-wine production center. On the sunny southern slopes of Mount Velia the Naoussa appellation is named after the Xynomavro grape. In the 1960s, the Greek shipowning Carras family planted a vineyard near their tourist resort. The wine, called Porto Carras, was once supervised by Émile Peynaud, the eminent oenologist from Bordeaux. On the east coast, in Chalkidiki, new vines are being planted.

Island of Rhodes

This island, already civilized in Mycenean times, once famous for its Colossus, then as the stronghold of the Hospitallers, has been making wine for many centuries. The principal company is the cooperative C.A.I.R. The best-known dry white comes from the Athiri variety and the red from Amorgiano. The dry white Lindos is grown around the city of that name, where stand very famous ruins.

Island of Samos

The island, separated from Turkey by a narrow strip of the Aegean Sea, was denuded of vines when it was conquered by the Turks at the time of the fall of Con-

stantinople (1453). Yet, when the Greeks regained it in 1912, they found the vines replanted and the wines as good as ever. Laws were passed in the following twenty-five years which made Samos one of the very few guaranteed place-names in Greece. No wine not grown on the island may take the name; nor may the Samos wine be blended with any other—most Greek wines are allowed an admixture of up to 30%. In order to enforce this rule, wines from other parts of Greece are forbidden in Samos. The sweet Muscat of Samos is one of two Greek wines most often seen abroad and most liked (the other is Mavrodaphne). The white Muscat grape, planted on 2,300 hectares (5,750 acres), produces the bulk of Samos wines. The island is mountainous, and the steep slopes, often terraced, are well suited to the vine. The yellow-gold grapes flourish in the mild climate, but there is considerable variation in the times of ripening in different parts of the island: on the plain, harvesting starts in August, but it does not begin until October in the high mountain vineyards.

In addition to the natural sweet wine, dry and fortified sweet wines are made on Samos, and nearly all have the distinct, heavy flavor and bouquet of the Muscat.

Island of Santorini

Both dry and sweet wines are made from a variety of vines flourishing in the volcanic soil, and sometimes they are very pleasant. A good dry wine will always be labeled Santorini; the sweet (decreasing) may be either Santorini or Vino Santo. On the sun-perched hills of this beautiful island the grapes achieve such a high degree of sugar that the wines often run to 17% of alcohol per volume.

Island of Crete

This large island is an important center of Greek viniculture. The hilly country gets a great deal of sun, and production is fairly prolific. Among the vines planted are Romeiko, Kotsifali, Mandilari and Liatico; and the resulting table wines are big and fleshy, rich in alcohol. A serious effort is being made to protect the four appellations Sitia, Dafnès, Archanes and Peza. Some of these may be labeled Candia—or Archanes. The big cooperatives are Chania, Heraklion, Archanes, and Peza. A small area of the vineyard is owned by A. Cambas, S.A., and Achaia-Clauss, but little of what they sell comes from their own land. The 45,000 hectares produce about 1 million hectoliters of wine.

Epirus

Mountainous northwest region. The viticultural region of Zitsa near the city of Ioannina produces from the Debina semi-sparkling wines. Metsovo and Cabernet Sauvignon are its mainstay.

Other regions

The island of Cephalonia produces a white wine from Robola. Around the town of Rapsani in the center of the country, good reds from Mavroudi are made.

OTHER GREEK WINES

Retsina

This is the most popular name in Greek wines, yet it is not an individual type but a generic one. It is simply any wine which has been flavored with pine resin—and that means much of the wine made in Greece. White and rosé wines may be treated in this way, but red are not. In the southern and central parts of the country, almost everyone—especially among the peasants—prefers his wine with this piny, resinous taste. More than 80% of the Savatiano wines of Attica are treated with resin.

There are many stories of how the use of resin came about. One theory is that the ancient Greeks preserved the wine with the pine gum and, incidentally, liked to add a flavor they had soon grown accustomed to. Another suggestion is that it happened accidentally, when a shortage of oak forced growers to store their wine in barrels made of pine—this is unlikely, since discoveries in Egyptian tombs have proved that, before the days of classical Greece, the bottoms of wine jars were smeared with resin and bitumen to preserve the wine. It was considered even then that the resin improved the flavor. The ancient Romans also added pitch and other ingredients to their wine, but the use has not, in Italy, persisted into modern times. Retsina should be drunk cool. The Greeks say that the best of it comes from around Athens. The peasants who make it for their own consumption do so in the old-fashioned way and often drink it quite soon after fermentation. The usual alcoholic content of Retsina is 12.5% to 13% by volume. Unlike most wines, it does not improve with age.

Monemvasia or Malmsey

Nowadays, the name Monemvasia merely refers to wines that are more or less characteristic of the Malmsey type produced in any part of Greece. In the old days, however, Monemvasia, lying on a deep harbor in the south of Greece, was a busy port, from which this wine was exported and which gave its name to a type of wine it shipped but did not grow; the wine was produced on Naxos and others of the smaller Cycaldes—and also on the island of Crete, or Candia. Monemvasia spread through the Mediterranean world, appearing in Spain under the name Malvagia,

in Italy as Malvasia, in France as Malvoisie—while in the English-speaking countries to which it was imported, it was known as Malmsey. It was famous in England in Shakespeare's day and earlier—everyone remembers that the Duke of Clarence was drowned in a butt of Malmsey. Some confusion has been caused by a general failure to realize that Malmsey has long denoted not a place-name but a style of wine, or a wine from the Malvoisie grape variety, and that it is not restricted to Spain, Madeira, or Crete.

Other Greek wines occasionally seen abroad include Mantineia, a dry white wine from the uplands of Arcadia, at its best at around five years of age and well cooled; and Mavro Naoussis, a deeply-colored dry red wine from the Naoussa district in central Macedonia.

SPIRITS

Brandy

The better Greek brandies are made from the Savatiano and other white and red grape varieties generally grown on the mainland or on the island of Samos. They are now being produced in three styles: the youngest, supposedly five years old; the Five Star, claiming twenty-five years; the Seven Star, over forty, which is false. The color and aroma are the natural results of ageing in cask. Other brandies may be sweetened and flavored for use as aperitifs or liqueurs. Metaxa, Botrys, Cambas, and Lizas are the popular dry, light-colored brandies.

Ouzo and Mastika (or Masticha)

These are the principal aperitifs. Ouzo, an anise-flavored liquid, is usually taken cold, with water or on the rocks. It turns cloudy when water is added, and thus resembles absinthe or French pastis or Pernod. Mastika, which has a brandy base to which gun mastic is added, is made on the island of Chios, but both drinks originated on the mainland of Greece.

Raki

This is an arrack-type spirit, usually made on the east coast, from a neutral wine base with a maceration of figs and other fruits. It is clear white in color, strong and fiery in character, and usually consumed without any significant ageing period. It is a rustic drink, not one for export.

Green

A term for any wine that is too acid, raw, and harsh, thus lacking softness and maturity. The condition is not necessarily a matter of age, although young wines are more frequently green than older ones. The word is also used for the wines which come from the area of Portugal that is north of Oporto. There the grapes are prematurely picked, thus causing the wine to have that trait of acidity which is referred to as green.

Grenache

A sweet grape which gives wines high in alcohol and distinctive in bouquet. It is used for the sweet Grenache dessert wine of Banyuls in the Roussillon region and is planted elsewhere in France, where it is known as Alicante, Carignane Rousse, Tinto, etc. In Spain it appears as Alicantina or Garnacha. It is grown also in northern California, where it makes excellent rosés.

Grenadine

Sweet red syrup, usually non-alcoholic but sometimes with a very slight alcohol content, used as a sweetening agent. Originally made from pomegranates.

Grignolino

An Italian grape which in Piedmont produces a red wine—dry and rather heady or semi-sweet and *frizzante*. Cultivation of the vine is, unfortunately, on the decline in Italy. The two D.O.C.s are Grignolino d'Asti and Grignolino del Monferrato Casalese.

Château Grillet (Appellation Contrôlée)

Rhône Valley white wine.
District: Rhône Valley, France.

The estate, perched above the River Rhône, covers about 2.7 hectares (6.75 acres) of the communes of Verin and Saint-Michel-sous-Condrieu and produces some 200 to 700 cases of wine annually. The wine is dry, white, heady, well-balanced, and full, and sometimes has a slight aroma of Muscat grapes, although it is made entirely from Viognier. In good years it can be wonderful, among the best of the Rhône Valley's white wines, surpassing or ranking with white Hermitage, but its production is so small that it is rarely seen outside the district. Much of it is sold at the Restaurant de la Pyramide, in nearby Vienne, where wines must meet rigorous standards before they are admitted to the cellars. Nevertheless, the wine is renowned more for its scarcity than for its quality.

Grinzing

Wine-making slopes and suburb of Vienna. Here new *heurige* wine is drunk.
See Austria.

Griotte-Chambertin (Appellation Contrôlée)

Burgundy red wine.
District: Côte de Nuits, France.
Commune: Gevrey-Chambertin.
Official Classification: Great Growth (Grand Cru).

A full wine which can produce splendid bottles, but few of them appear under their proper names. The number of growers in the vineyard is small—for Burgundy—and the wines are generally sold to various shipping houses, some of which engage in the practice of stretching the wines of better-known place-names. Despite this regrettable habit, production of Griotte's 5.5 hectares (13.5 acres) amounts to 85 hectoliters (2,250 U.S. gallons, 1,870 imp.) of wine, or the equivalent of about 1,000 cases.

Grk, Gerk

White Dalmatian wine, dry, pale yellow in color, with an individual aftertaste.
See Yugoslavia.

Grog

Originally a diluted rum, said to be called after the nickname (Old Grog) of Admiral Vernon, who first ordered the dilution of the British navy's rum. The name is sometimes used for undiluted rum and for spirits in general, but is usually applied to hot rum, with or without lemon and spices.

Grolleau (Groslot)

Grape used in France, notably in the rosé wine of Anjou. It is known as Pineau de Saumur.

Grombalia

Region which produces 90% of Tunisian wines.

Château Gruaud-Larose

Bordeaux red wine.
District: Haut-Médoc, France.
Commune: Saint-Julien.

M. Gruaud purchased the estate, Fond-Bedeau, in 1757, and changed the name. Thirty years later, M. Larose married Gruaud's daughter and bought the lands, adding his name to that of his late father-in-law. Before 1934, labels will show Gruaud-Larose-Faure or Gruaud-Larose-Sarget. The one original vineyard was divided over one hundred years ago when the Sarget heirs, sole owners, sold the larger part to a M. Faure. In 1925, Désiré Cordier acquired the Sarget vineyard. His son Georges, the father of Jean, the present owner, reunited Gruaud-Larose-Sarget and Gruaud-Larose-Faure in 1934. (The Cordier family, who owned the shipping firm in Bordeaux, also has Château Talbot, another classified growth of Saint-Julien nearby.) M. Cordier is to be congratulated on the way he keeps his cellars. In 1982 "La Hénin," the former banking group and owners of "Listel," the sand wines in the south of France, purchased the majority shares

Grumello

of Cordier and its vineyards. Gruaud-Larose is a Second Growth (*Second Cru*) of Médoc by the Classification of 1855.

Characteristics. Big, fruity, and fast-maturing, typical of the best Saint-Juliens, with considerable finesse and a light perfume.

Vineyard area: 76 hectares (190 acres).

Average production: 250 *tonneaux* (22,000 cases).

Grumello

Red wine of Valtellina, Italy, made from the Nebbiolo grape.

See Lombardy.

Grünberg

A small isolated German wine district in Silesia, surrounding the town of Grünberg, in East Germany.

Grüner Veltliner

Chief grape variety of Lower Austria.

Guebwiller

Alsatian wine town near Colmar.

Guignolet

Black cherry liqueur brandy found mostly in France in the Anjou and Touraine districts and the department of the Vendée.

Château Guiraud

Bordeaux white wine.
District and Commune: Sauternes, France.

Château Guiraud and Château d'Yquem are the only First-classified Sauternes (Official Classification of 1855) actually in Sauternes. This is because the commune of Sauternes was considered too small to provide enough wine to earn worldwide reputation, and the designation was extended to four adjoining communes, in which all the twelve best vineyards are situated except those of d'Yquem and Guiraud. In early days, the Guiraud vineyard was known as Château Bayle. The characteristic French pepperpot turret, capped with a black conical roof, is attached not to the château but to the wine *chai*; the château is a box-like nineteenth-century-style dwelling in a nest of trees, in front of which the long, low, L-shaped *chai*, with its unexpected turret at one end, extends along the rim of a beautifully kept vineyard.

In 1981 a Canadian, Hamilton Narby, had the laudable courage to purchase the rundown Château. He has painstakingly invested some of his shares from his Montreal family's assets so that Guiraud can achieve its potential for making a great Sauternes.

Characteristics. Rather sweet, could have great breed; some remarkable vintages.

Vineyard area: 52 hectares (130 acres).

Average production: 120 *tonneaux* (11,000 cases).

Gumpoldskirchner

A delicate white wine, one of the best in Austria, made in the vineyards of Gumpoldskirchen.

See Austria.

Gunflint taste

A special taste in white wines from chalky subsoils. Chablis is the prime example of a wine with this quality.

Gutedel

German variant of the Chasselas family of grapes, found also in California.

Gutsname

German term for wine estate. The same as château or clos in Bordeaux and Burgundy.

Gutturnio dei Colli Piacentini (D.O.C.)

A good dry red wine from Italy.

See Emilia-Romagna.

Guyenne, Connétablie de

See Connétablie de Guyenne; Premières Côtes de Bordeaux.

Guyot

A variation of the espalier method of training vines. This consists of a trunk and one arm and is largely used in such fine-wine regions as the Médoc.

See Chapter Eight, p. 31.

Gyöngyös

The white sparkling wines of Gyöngyös are among the best in Hungary. Red wines are grown in this district too, and in greater quantity.

See Hungary.

H

Halbrot

Swiss term for rosé wine.

Halbstück

The cask used for ageing and storing Rheingau wines, containing 660 liters, or about 68 cases of finished wine.

Half-bottle

A bottle holding about half the contents of a standard bottle. The American half-bottle holds roughly 12.5 U.S. fluid ounces; the British, 12 British fluid ounces; 37.5 centiliters.

Half-on-half

Tawny-colored Dutch liqueur, half Curaçao and half orange bitters.

Hallgartner Schönhell

Outstanding vineyard of Hallgarten, producing one of the best Rheingau wines. Another important Hallgarten vineyard is Jungfer.
See Rheingau.

Hard

Excessive tannin in a wine gives hardness which may disappear with age. A drawback at first, it later becomes an asset, for it preserves the wine and changes with age to firmness. Usually hardness is a sign of youth and quality, but 1945 Bordeaux red wines were hard until the middle sixties.

Haro

A tiny city on the upper Ebro River in Spain which is the center of the Rioja wine trade.
See Rioja.

Harriague

Grape grown in Uruguay and elsewhere.
See Tannat.

Harsh

Hardness pushed to the most unpleasant extreme.

Hárslevelű

A Hungarian variety of grape used in making Tokay and other wines.

Hattenheimer Nussbrunnen

One of the greatest Rheingau wines.
See Rheingau.

Hattenheimer Wisselbrunnen

With Hattenheimer Nussbrunnen and with Steinberg, one of the great Rheingaus, and in the triumvirate of the greatest Hattenheimers.
See Rheingau.

Haut

French for "high"; in the feminine, *haute*. This word affixed to a regional name on a wine label is erroneously believed to imply "higher in quality." What it actually means is "higher" in the geographical sense—more northerly, upriver, etc. Example: Haut-Médoc, so named because it is above Médoc on the River Gironde. That it makes better wine is mere coincidence. As for the designation Haut-Sauternes, geographically there is no Haut-Sauternes, and from the point of view of quality, the term is meaningless.

Château Haut-Bages-Libéral

Bordeaux red wine.
District: Haut-Médoc, France.
Commune: Pauillac.

Divided into two parts, one adjoining Pontet-Canet and the other close to Château Latour, the vineyard was classed a Fifth Growth (*Cinquième Cru*) of the Médoc in 1855. The name derives from the high slopes of Bages, where it is situated, and from an early owner, a M. Libéral. The Cruse family bought the property in 1960 and incorporated part of the vineyard with its neighbor, Pontet-Canet. That move, which was entirely legal, left a small portion whose wine continues to be sold as Haut-Bages-Libéral.
Characteristics. Fairly full-bodied, but sometimes on the common side, the wines seem to have improved.
Vineyard area: 23 hectares (57.5 acres).
Average production: 100 *tonneaux* (8,000 cases).

Château Haut-Bailly

Bordeaux red wine.
District: Graves, France.
Commune: Léognan.

Unlike most of the great Graves vineyards, Haut-Bailly makes no white wine; but the red wine is among the eleven Classified Growths (1953 and 1959) of the district.
Replanted after the devastation by the vine louse phylloxera almost a century ago by Bellot des Mi-

nières, whose fame caused him to be called King of Vine Growers, the vineyard was excellent for a period, but then fell on bad times. The successor of Minières, eager to rival his predecessor, carried "improvements" in wine-making so far that the wine was being bottled only eight months after vintage, instead of the former four years, and was pasteurized. Having abandoned such "progressive" practices, Haut-Bailly has recovered its early prestige and the wines are balanced and full, distinct among Graves red wines, and rather resembling certain Médocs. The plantings at present are 70% Cabernet Sauvignon, 20% Merlot, and 10% Malbec. The present owner is Mr. Sanders.

Characteristics. A full, well-rounded wine with great finesse.

Vineyard area: 25 hectares (62.5 acres).

Average production: 100 *tonneaux* (9,000 cases).

Château Haut-Batailley

Bordeaux red wine.
District: Haut-Médoc, France.
Commune: Pauillac.

A part of Château Batailley until 1924, the vineyard shares with that estate a position of Fifth Growth (*Cinquième Cru*) of the Médoc as classified in 1855. It is now owned by Mme des Brest-Borie, the sister of Jean-Eugène Borie, who has done so much to bring Château Ducru-Beaucaillou to its present high quality. It is M. Borie who directs the vinification of this very fine vineyard.

Characteristics. Better than Château Batailley, with a certain robust strength.

Vineyard area: 22 hectares (55 acres).

Average production: 60 *tonneaux* (5,800 cases).

Château Haut-Brion

Bordeaux red and white wines.
District: Graves, France.
Commune: Pessac.

A château with a history dating back almost five hundred years, Haut-Brion is today unquestionably one of the greatest red-wine-producing vineyards in the world. It is now owned by Douglas Dillon, former Secretary of the Treasury of the United States and former United States ambassador to France, and his family. More than any other vineyard, Haut-Brion has been regarded as the quality symbol of Bordeaux and as the producer of the most traditional of all Bordeaux wines.

The spelling of the château has undergone several changes over the centuries; in the records it is given variously as d'Obrion, Daubrion, and Hault-Brion. We know that in 1509 the property was bought by Jean de Ségur and that in 1525 it passed into the possession of the Admiral Philippe de Chabot, who was with King François I when he was taken prisoner at Pavia. But Chabot did not retain the château for long. Before the

end of the sixteenth century Haut-Brion went to the Pontac family as part of the dowry of Jeanne de Bellon, and remained with the Pontacs for two hundred years, until in the eighteenth century, it became the property of the Fumel family, at one time the owners of Château Margaux.

The Pontacs had another vineyard at Blanquefort, producing white wines, but the "Pontack" wines famous in England in the seventeenth century were the red wines of Haut-Brion. In 1666 François-Auguste de Pontac acquired an interest in a London tavern known as Pontac's Head, fashionable with the nobility, where Haut-Brion was dispensed in large quantities. This, it is said, marked the first time a Bordeaux wine was referred to by name abroad, instead of being sold simply as "claret."

There was another tavern, on Lombard Street, in which a member of the Pontac family was said to have an interest, the Royal Oak, where Samuel Pepys went to drink "a sort of French wine called Ho Bryen that hath a good and most particular taste." In 1683 John Evelyn noted in his diary that he had had a talk with M. Pontac, son of the famous president of Bordeaux, owner of the excellent vineyard of Haut-Brion, whence came the greatest of the Bordeaux wines. Dryden, Swift, and Defoe also dined at the same place in their turn, and Swift found the wine dear at seven shillings a flagon. In 1677, John Locke, who had visited Haut-Brion, remarked that prices had risen "thanks to the rich English who sent orders that it was to be got for them at any price."

It was during the prosperous years of the eighteenth century that the wines of the Médoc gained in popularity on those of Graves. But Haut-Brion was never outshone. In 1770, the Comte de Fumel divided the estate in half. He kept the château and part of the vineyard; the rest, known as Chai Neuf, he sold to the Marquis de Latresne. At the time of the Revolution, the owner of the château was his fifth son, Joseph, who was the mayor of Bordeaux. In 1794, Joseph was guillotined; part of the châteaux property was seized by the government, part remained with the family, who afterward bought back the state's share—and in 1801 sold it to Talleyrand, who kept it only until 1804.

There is no record of Talleyrand having lived there, but no doubt he found a use for the wines. His success in diplomacy depended not only on his quick wit, the charm of his conversation, and the talents of his famous chef, Câreme, but also on the excellence of his wines. At the Congress of Vienna he got the better of everyone, and one of the ways in which he influenced people was by inviting them to his splendid dinner parties.

After 1804 Haut-Brion saw one of its least glorious periods under a succession of businessmen until, in 1836, M. J. E. Larrieu bought the château. Four years later he was able to buy back the "Chai Neuf," too, and so restored the property to its true state. Before long he had done the same for the wine; and when in 1855, the Classification of the Great Growths of the Gironde was made, although other leading wines of Graves were omitted, Haut-Brion was rated a First Growth (*Premier Cru*) with the three great Médocs, Lafite, Latour, and Margaux.

When the rest of the Graves were at last classified, in 1953 and again in 1959, the great red wine of Haut-Brion was, of course, listed at the head of the classification, and is now a First Classified Growth of both Graves and Médoc. The white wine is one of the most prestigious of France and certainly one of the best dry white wines of Bordeaux.

Whereas all the other First Growths have increased in production or in size, Haut-Brion has remained restricted to approximately 13,000 cases per year, its growth limited by the boundaries of the surrounding suburbs. The vineyard is situated on the outskirts of Bordeaux and is enlaced with the buildings of this city and those of the sizable township of Pessac.

Haut-Brion was the first among the great châteaus of Bordeaux to initiate fermentation vats of stainless steel, which are now preferred by all modern oenologists (from the standpoint of fermentation and temperature controls as well as cleanliness) to the old wooden vats found in the *chais* of some other Great Growths. This ambitious conversion was made in the early 1950s under the direction of Seymour Weller, who was president of Haut-Brion for nearly forty years. The château and its grounds today present a superbly dignified and well-tended picture. In the late 1960s the majestic stone entrance to Haut-Brion was restored, and a beautiful large underground cellar was built in 1973. As recently as 1974 Haut-Brion was magnificently redecorated, and its outer walls brightened to show the beauty of the original stone, by Douglas Dillon's daughter Joan, the Duchess of Mouchy, who is now the president of the corporation. She and her husband, who live in France, are regularly at Haut-Brion and run the vineyard together. Since the 1974 restoration, the château has been lived in and is not open to the public.

The soil where the white wines grow is inclined to be clayey, while the vines for the red wine flourish in the famous soil of deep *graves*—the regional word for gravel. This gravel, which has given the Graves district its name, is nowhere so prevalent as at Haut-Brion, where in places it is 50 and 60 feet deep. The porous soil, with its pebbles which reflect the sun and retain the heat, is said to be the factor that causes Haut-Brion to be good even in lesser years. The excess water drains away quickly, giving the vine the semi-aridity it likes.

Characteristics. The red wine is great and often very full, with a special taste imparted by the gravelly soil of its native Graves. It achieves great elegance, and even in the lesser years it is apt to succeed better than others of the district because, owing to its situation, the grapes mature a little earlier at Haut-Brion than in most of the other quality vineyards. Also, the recruiting of harvest workers is easier in the suburbs of Bordeaux, where large crews are available and can easily be suspended during rain. The dry white wine is one of the very best of Bordeaux.

Unlike Châteaux Lafite, Latour, Margaux, and Mouton, Haut-Brion cannot expand its vineyard acreage; and so as the other First Growths have greatly increased production in the past few years, the quantity of Haut-Brion has remained relatively small.

Vineyard area: red—40 hectares (100 acres); white—3 hectares (7.5 acres).

Average production: red—130 *tonneaux* (12,000 cases); white—8 *tonneaux* (700 cases).

Haut-Médoc

Red wine.
District: Bordeaux, France.

The finest part of the Médoc red wine region, near Bordeaux in southwest France, and an official wine place-name, or Appellation Contrôlée. The name designates the upper Médoc, in the sense that it is up-river. The famous districts of Margaux, Pauillac, Saint-Julien, and Saint-Estèphe, and all the famous Médoc châteaux, are in Haut-Médoc.

See Médoc.

Haut-Montravel

See Montravel.

Haut-Peyraguey (Clos)

Bordeaux white wine.
District: Sauternes, France.
Communes: Bommes.

The sloping vineyard surrounds a "château" that looks like a white farmhouse. The vines grow in a clayey and gravel soil. The wine was classed a First Growth (*Premier Cru*) of Sauternes in the Official Classification of 1855.

Characteristics. Carefully made, sweet, rich wine of breed and distinction.

Vineyard area: 11 hectares (27 acres).
Average production: 25 *tonneaux* (2,400 cases).

Heavy

Very full-bodied, but without much distinction or finesse. Certainly a less pejorative term than "coarse."

Hectare

Metric measure of area containing 10,000 square meters (2.471 acres).
See Appendix E, p. 710.

Hectoliter

French unit of measure equaling 100 liters (26.4179 U.S. gallons, 21.9976 imp.). All ordinary French

Heidelberg Tun

wines are sold by the hectoliter. Abbreviation: hl, or colloquially, hecto.

Heidelberg Tun

A barrel in Heidelberg Castle constructed in 1751 by the cellarmaster Jakob Engler the younger for the Elector Karl Theodor. It holds 220,000 liters (58,100 U.S. gallons, 48,400 imp.—about 300,000 bottles) but has only been filled three times and long ago sprang a leak. The pump by which wine used to be drawn out of the cask may be seen in the Königsaal, or Great Hall, of the castle.

Hérault

Quantitatively, one of the three most important wine-producing departments of France. (The other two are Aude and Gard.) The area produces 20% of all French wine. From Hérault, in the Montpellier-Béziers district of southern France, comes a great deal of ordinary wine, as well as the superior dry wine Clairette du Languedoc (q.v.) and the sweet Muscat de Lunel. The best red wine of Hérault is Minervois (A.O.C.). (See Sweet fortified wines of France; Corbières; Minervois.)

Hermitage, Ermitage (Appellation Contrôlée)

Rhône Valley red and white wines
District: Rhône Valley, France.

The big, long-lived Hermitage wines are grown on the slopes above Tain, a little town by the Rhône, 80 kilometers (50 miles) south of Lyon and 19 kilometers (12 miles) north of Valence. Small terraced vineyards, divided by stone walls into parcels known locally as *mas*, climb the hill which rises abruptly behind the town. At the summit, a local landmark is the ruined chapel of Saint-Christophe, built on the site of a Roman temple of Mercury. According to some stories, Saint Patrick planted vines here during his first sojourn in Gaul. On this hillside lived the hermit from whom the wines take their name: the knight Gaspard de Stérimberg, who turned penitent after the Crusade of 1224 against the Albigensian heretics and chose to spend in this beautiful spot the rest of a life which was to be divided between religious meditation and the cultivation of his vineyard. To the many visitors who came to see him he offered wine—all he had—and so the fame of Hermitage was spread.

The soil is meager—a thin layer of chalky limestone on a hard granite subsoil—and the whole extent of the vineyards is 220 hectares (550 acres), yielding some 40 hectoliters to the hectare (428 U.S. gallons, 356 imp. to the acre). When they are bearing, the vines are susceptible to *coulure* (q.v.). It is not surprising, therefore, that genuine Hermitage is a comparatively rare and expensive wine.

The red-wine grape is the Syrah, variously reported to be the Shiraz of Persia, brought home by Crusaders (some say by Stérimberg himself), or to have been introduced by the Romans. In any case, the vineyards here are said to be among the oldest in France. The white-wine grapes, cultivated in the center of the slope, are Marsanne and, to a small extent, Roussanne. Less than 12,000 cases is the average yield of this distinctive white wine—full, with a flinty flavor and a character so definite that it can hold its own with such highly seasoned foods as curry. This is among the longest-lasting of all dry white wines and will sometimes be good after twenty years, although it is usually at its best at between six and fifteen years of age.

Both white and red wines incline, in youth, to harshness. The red may be rough at first, but in maturity it is soft and velvety, big and generous, forming a heavy sediment. In age, it develops a rich aroma and aftertaste, a bouquet redolent of raspberries and wallflowers, and a glowing *robe* which shifts in color from deep purple to the brownish cast known as *pelure d'oignon*. In nineteenth-century England, Hermitage was much esteemed, and Professor Saintsbury described it as "the manliest of wines."

Twice as much red wine is made as white. In addition to the predominant Syrah, other grape varieties are permitted in small quantities, and these add their own qualities to the wine. The best vineyards for red are: Les Bessards, Le Méal, L'Hermitage, La Varogne, Les Diognières, Les Greffieux, and La Pierelle.

Chante-Alouette is the most celebrated of the white Hermitages, which are dry and delicate yet have body as well as bouquet. This is the name of a vineyard and also the trademark of the firm of Chapoutier, and the wine is usually a blend from the better vineyards, such as Beaumes, Les Murets, Les Rocoules, La Chapelle, Maison-Blanche—and, of course, Chante-Alouette itself. Some of the growers, aware of the value of publicity, have painted their names in whitewash on the dividing walls between the *mas*—Chapoutier and Paul Jaboulet Aîné—these are shippers as well as important growers. Production is around 3,000 hectoliters (79,000 U.S. gallons, 66,000 imp.) a year.

L'Hermitage is just below that group of vineyards which produce wines that are sold as Crozes-Hermitages—agreeable wines, but not to be compared with those permitted the distinguished name Hermitage.

Hessia

See Rheinhessen.

Heurige

New light wine served, and sometimes made, in the vine-covered houses of Grinzing on the outskirts of Vienna. The literal translation is "wine of this year," but it is more generally known as May wine.

Highball

A long, iced drink, usually whisky and soda.

Hippocras

An aromatized wine, popular in the Middle Ages. It was made, probably, from sour wine sweetened and spiced and then filtered through wool, the filter being known as Hippocrates' Sleeve.

Hochheimer-Domdechaney

This big, fruity wine is probably the best of the Hochheimers from the River Main beyond Wiesbaden, but owing to great similarity in quality, it is always classed with the Rheingau wines nearby on the Rhine. This Hochheimer contributed the name Hock used in England for Rheingaus and loosely for all Rhine wines.
See Rheingau.

Hock

British term which applies accurately to the wines from the Rheingau section of Germany and loosely to all wines of the Rhine type. The word derives from Hochheim, a town in the Rheingau.
See Rheingau.

Hogshead

A cask of varying capacity; the most commonly used container for shipping wines and spirits in bulk. The name is said to be a corruption of the Scandinavian *oxhoft*, which itself varies from 67 to 70 U.S. gallons (56 to 58 imp.). Some of the more widely used hogshead capacities are:

		GALLONS	
	LITERS	U.S.	Imp.
Burgundy and Bordeaux	225 to 228	59.4	49.5
Beer and cider	246	64.8	54
Sherry	246	64.8	54
Whisky	250	66	55
Port	259	68.4	57
Brandy	273	72	60

See Barrique.

Holland

See Netherlands.

Hollands

The style of gin usually seen in Holland, where it is called Jenever, and distinguished by the stone jar or crock in which it is frequently sold. It differs from London Dry gin, the basic British and American type, by being less thoroughly distilled. In common with Scotch whisky, Cognac, and Jamaican-style rum, it is distilled lightly enough to permit the original taste-factors to pass over into the final product. (London Dry gins are made colorless and tasteless in distillation and flavored afterward.) Hollands is not a neutral cocktail ingredient like London Dry types, but a spirit which the Dutch take neat.
See Gin.

Homeburn

In Norway, spirit distilled at home; "home-brew."

Honey brandy

A distilled mead.
See Mead.

Hops

A climbing perennial with rough lobed leaves like those of the vine. The ripened cones of the female plant are used in brewing to give flavor to the beer. Cultivated in Europe, Central Asia, and America.

Hospices de Beaune

The ancient façade of the Charity Hospital rises in the center of Beaune; and the sale of its wines each year sets the prices for those of the entire Côte d'Or, dictates the value of the harvest which is the life-blood of Beaune, and ushers in the Trois Glorieuses—the three lavish banquets at which Burgundians congregate to glorify and drink their favorite wines.

The Hospices were founded in 1443 by Nicolas Rolin, chancellor to the Duke of Burgundy, and his wife, Guigone de Salins. Beaune at that time seems to have been entirely populated by beggers (only twenty-four of its families were considered solvent), and so it was undoubtedly a wise choice as a site for the charity hospital. There were those who said that Rolin—who was, among other things, a collector of taxes—could well afford to build a hospital for the poor he had helped to grind down; but his charity has been perpetuated, and grants, often in the form of vineyards, have been coming in through the centuries.

In the high outer wall of the Hospices is an arched doorway leading into a cobbled court dotted with groups of visitors and crossed now and again by members of the Dames Hospitalières, the lay organization which, from the start, has cared for the sick. Since the Dames were members of a lay organization, the Hospices did not fall into the hands of the state during the French Revolution when anti-clerical feeling was high and Church property confiscated. Inside the court the architecture is medieval, with peaked, wood-carved dormers rising from the superb roof of multicolored tiles. Pillars hold up a balcony which runs around the court, in the middle of which is a massive stone well. There are other courts behind this one, rarely seen by visitors, and off one of the last of these the wine is made.

The auction sale of the wines of the Hospices de Beaune is one of the biggest events of the Burgundian year, and the wine merchants who come to take part are mainly French and Belgian, but others come from all over the world. The city begins to get crowded a few days before the sale—usually the third Sunday in November—and the day before, they all troop into the *chais* to taste the wine. At the end of the day, the first banquet of the Trois Glorieuses is held in the ornate hall of the Clos de Vougeot.

The actual auction of the wines takes place in one of the outer courts, or in one of the halls leading off it, and is always presided over by some public figure. Prince Bernhardt of the Netherlands and the British and American ambassadors to France have been among recent presidents. All bidding is done in true medieval manner "by the candle": three small tapers are placed in a holder, and as the auction starts one of them is lit; when it dies, the second is lit and then the third, and the last bid heard before the third has snuffed itself out takes the dubious prize. Competition is keen, because ownership of even a small amount of Hospices de Beaune wine carries considerable prestige, both for wine merchants and restaurateurs, and prices frequently soar far above value. (However, the buyer always has the consolation that he is contributing to a worthy cause.) A slight defect in the system is that all wines are carted off in barrel within a month of the sale, and buyers do not always take proper care of it. With prices so high and demand so great, the temptation to stretch these wines is strong.

The vineyards owned by the hospital are scattered throughout the Côte de Beaune, and all wines are sold under the name not of a vineyard but of the original donor. Cuvée Dr. Peste, for example, is made from grapes grown in the vineyard of Corton, in the section of Aloxe-Corton called Maréchaude; but since this parcel of land was donated by Dr. Peste, the wine is always sold under his name. The Hospices have a total of some 55 hectares (137 acres) of vines and make about 1,400 hectoliters (37,100 U.S. gallons, 30,800 imp.) of wine annually, more than three-fourths of it red.

In addition, they distill a Marc de Bourgogne, and when the wines are auctioned off, the marc of the previous year is sold with them. About 300 hectoliters (8,000 U.S. gallons, 6,650 imp.) of marc is average for any year and, as is the case with the wines, prices run slightly higher than for comparable spirits distilled elsewhere in Burgundy. At the conclusion of the auction, the second of the Trois Glorieuses—a dinner held in the cellars of the Hospices—begins. The following day the trinity is brought to a close with La Paulée, a banquet in the village of Meursault, where growers are supposed to bring a bottle of their best

and rarest wine and pass it around the table. At the end of this, everyone goes home to recover.

The results of recent sales follow. (A *pièce* is the equivalent of a barrel of 228 liters, or 24 cases of 12 bottles each.)

Pommard—Dames de la Charité, 18 *pièces*; Savigny-les-Beaune—Arthur Girard, 22 *pièces*; Beaune—Maurice Drouhin, 55 *pièces*; Beaune—Dames Hospitalières, 44 *pièces*; Volnay-Santenots—Gauvain, 28 *pièces*; Pernand-Vergelesses, 13 *pièces*; Beaune—Nicolas Rolin, 40 *pièces*; Savigny-les Beaune—Borneret, 37 *pièces*; Beaune—Clos des Avaux, 54 *pièces*; Volnay-Santenots—Jehan-de-Massol, 25 *pièces*; Corton—Docteur Peste, 33 *pièces*; Monthélie—Lebelin, 17 *pièces*; Beaune—Brunet, 32 *pièces*; Volnay—Général Muteau, 33 *pièces*; Meursault-Genevrières—Baudot, 33 *pièces*; Meursault—Humblot, 6 *pièces*; Meursault-Charmes—de Bahèzre de Lanlay, 20 *pièces*; Beaune-Guigone de Salins, 30 *pièces*; Savigny-les-Beaune—Fouquerand, 28 *pièces*; Auxey-Duresses—Boillot, 5 *pièces*; Beaune—Rousseau-Deslandes, 32 *pièces*; Pommard—Billardet, 39 *pièces*; Beaune—Hugues et Louis Bétault, 34 *pièces*; Volnay—Blondeau, 13 *pièces*; Corton—Charlotte Dumay, 31 *pièces*; Corton-Charlemagne—François de Salins, 4 *pièces*; Meursault-Charmes—Albert Grivault, 11 *pièces*; Meursault—Goureau, 11 *pièces*; Meursault—Loppin, 11 *pièces*; Meursault-Genevrières—Philippe-le-Bon, 11 *pièces*; Beaune Cryot—Chaudron, 16 *pièces*; Mazis-Chambertin—Madeleine Collignon, 23 *pièces*.

Hotte

French term for a longish back-basket for carrying grapes.

Houghton

Outstanding vineyard in Western Australia, owned by Emu Wine Company.
See Australia.

Houx

Alsatian holly spirit.
See Alsace: Spirits.

Hudson River Valley

A wine-producing region on the west bank of the Hudson, between Newburgh and Kingston, in New York State. Principal vineyards are Benmarl, High Tor, and those of the Hudson Valley Wine Company. American vines *Vitis labrusca* and hybrids are grown, of which the favorites are the Catawba and the Delaware. Red, white, and rosé wines are produced.
See United States: New York.

Huelva (The denomination is Condado de Huelva)

Province of Spain which produces strong heavy wines.

See Spain.

Hungary

The most famous Hungarian wine, the wine of kings and emperors, is Tokay (*q.v.*), and other wines of Hungary suffer the fate of younger brothers. Yet, eclipsed though they may be in fame, some of them are excellent. Hungarian wine-making standards are claimed to be among the highest of all; strict controls have been the rule, and Hungary was one of the pioneers of place-name and grape-variety regulations.

Wine has always been made in Hungary. Though three-quarters of the vines were wiped out by the vine louse phylloxera in 1875 and by the vine fungus pernospora in 1891, the industry was rebuilt on grafted American root-stocks and with the most modern methods. Over 100,000 hectares (nearly 250,000 acres) of "sand" vineyard were created, the sandy soil being practically immune to phylloxera. Production now averages about 5 million hectoliters (132.5 million U.S. gallons, 110 million imp.) per year; of this about 70% is white wine and the balance red and "Siller" wines. Hungary makes several high-quality red wines.

WINE REGIONS

Hungary falls naturally into four regions, defined by the following geographical features: The Great Plain (Alföld), Northern Transdanubia, Southern Transdanubia, and Northern Hungary.

The Great Plain (Alföld) covers nearly half the land surface east of the Danube to the Rumanian border. Transdanubia, the Roman Pannonia, is between the Danube and Drava rivers, and Lake Balaton divides the region into the Northern and Southern sections. Northern Hungary, in the Carpathian foothills east of

Budapest along the Slovakian border, is very mountainous.

Between 1948 and 1953, all Hungarian vineyards were registered and classified. About 160,000 hectares (400,000 acres) are planted in vines. The land is broken down into sixteen wine-making regions.

	The Great Plain	
1. Alföld	70,000 hectares	175,000 acres

	Northern Transdanubia	
2. Ászár-Neszmély	2,800 hectares	7,000 acres
3. Badacsony	2,500 hectares	6,250 acres
4. Balatonfüred-Csopák	2,250 hectares	5,650 acres
5. Balatonmellék	2,550 hectares	6,400 acres
6. Mór	1,300 hectares	3,250 acres
7. Somló	500 hectares	1,250 acres
8. Sopron	1,750 hectares	4,400 acres

	Southern Transdanubia	
9. Dél-Balaton	3,500 hectares	8,750 acres
10. Mecsekalja	1,500 hectares	3,750 acres
11. Szekszárd	1,850 hectares	4,650 acres
12. Villány-Siklós	1,500 hectares	3,750 acres

	Northern Hungary	
13. Bükkalja	4,000 hectares	10,000 acres
14. Eger	3,400 hectares	8,500 acres
15. Mátraalja	7,550 hectares	19,000 acres
16. Tokajhegyalja	7,000 hectares	17,500 acres

According to production and quality, the vine-growing regions can be grouped as follows:

Districts Producing White Wines of "Outstanding Quality":

Tokajhegyalja, Badacsony, Balatonfüred-Csopak, Somló.

Districts Producing Mainly White Wine of "Excellent Quality":

Ászár-Neszemély, Balatonmellék, Dél-Balaton, Bükkalja, Mátraalja, Mecsekalja, Mór.

Districts Producing Mainly Red Wine of "Excellent Qaulity":

Eger, Sopron, Szekszárd, Villány-Siklós.

The Great Plain produces the bulk of Hungary's commercial wine.

GRAPE VARIETIES

Hungary has several indigenous grape varieties, from some of which the finest wines are made.

For white wines, the most important of these are Furmint, the main ingredient of Tokay (Tokaj); Hár-

slevelű (which means "lime leaf," the characteristic shape of the leaves), the second ingredient of Tokay; Kéknyelű (meaning "blue stalk," a characteristic of the vine); and Szürkebarát ("Gray Friar"), a type of Pinot Gris. Other indigenous vines include Ezerjó ("a thousand boons"); Leányka ("young girl"); Mézesfehér ("honey white")' Juhfark ("lamb's tail"); Budai Green; and Piros Cirfandli. Varieties grown in other European wine districts include Olaszrizling (Wälschriesling, or Italian Riesling), now the most widely grown white vine in Hungary; some Rheinriesling; Sylvaner (Szilváni); Traminer; Pinot Blanc (Fehérburgundi); Sauvignon; the Austrian Grüner Veltliner, Müller-Thurgau, and Bouvier; and two Muscats, Ottonel and Sárgamuskotály ("Yellow" Muscat)—a little of the latter is used in making Tokay.

For red wines, Hungary grows mainly the Balkan Kadarka, and, from Western Europe, Pinot Noir, Kékfrankos, Merlot, Cabernet Franc, and Cabernet Sauvignon, as well as some of the Austrian Blau Portugieser and Zweigelt varieties.

Tokay, Hungary's greatest wine—indeed, one of the greatest wines in the world—is described in detail in the separate entry.

Badacsony, Balatonfüred-Csopák, and Balatonmellék, the districts numbered 3, 4, and 5 above, cover all the hill vineyards facing southeast on the northern shores of Lake Balaton. Vines have been cultivated here and wine made for over 2,000 years; in the time of the Roman occupation, the fine Balaton wines were transported to the emperors in Rome. The soil of the Badacsony district is one of heat-absorbing basaltic rock with loess topsoils; this, combined with the aspect and the Balaton micro-climate of the district, makes it a perfect site, with terraced vineyards on the hillsides producing white wines of the highest quality from Szürkebarát and Kéknyelű—and, since the replanting following the phylloxera devastation, Olaszrizling, which here makes wine of the highest quality. Often Hungarian wines are labeled with the place-name and the possessive -i added, followed by the grape variety—e.g., Badacsonyi Kéknyelű. The adjoining hills of Balantonfüred-Csopák are of a different geological structure (crystalline slate with a red sandstone topsoil), and they enjoy a particularly warm climate. The wines, softer and richer than those of Badacsony, are made chiefly from Olaszrizling, but also from Traminer, Muscat, and Sylvaner. They are of the highest quality, individual in style and, in their fashion, bear comparison with the finest white wines of France and Germany. The rest of the Balaton district makes good, very pleasant, light white wines, popular in style, from Olaszrizling, Sylvaner, Reinriesling and Traminer.

Somló is a small, vine-covered volcanic mountain, prominent in the Transdanubian plain. It has made wines of the very highest quality since the days of St. Stephen (Hungary's first king, in the 11th century), wines which are considered, next to Tokay, to be the country's finest. The production is small, the best in big dessert wines made from Furmint with some Olaszrizling, Riesling and Traminer, and, on the vineyards with less favored aspects, from indigenous vines. The wines of Somló have the reputation of possessing philoprogenitive qualities; for this reason, they were much favored by the Habsburg princes—and, perhaps not for the same reason, by Queen Victoria. Like Tokay, they need time to make and mature; the production is small, and they are always relatively expensive.

The Ászár-Neszmély and Mór districts, nos. 2 and 6 above, are, by Hungarian standards, quite recent wine-lands, the oldest part having been planted by Bavarian settlers in the mid-eighteenth century on cleared woodlands. They are of interest mainly for the Ezerjó wine, Móri Ezerjó, grown on the quartz and mica sandy soil of the Mór district. Because phylloxera cannot survive on soil of this nature, the vines are grown on their own roots. Ezerjó, producing wine of no great distinction in other parts of southeastern Europe, makes in these conditions a dry wine of excellent quality with fine bouquet and flavor.

The Mecsekalja district, no 10, is part of a pre-Roman wine complex in southern Transdanubia, formerly known as Pécs-Villány. The Mecsek hills form a white wine district around the town of Pécs and five hill villages, producing mainly excellent white wines from Olaszrizling, Furmint, and Cirfandli, pleasant, well-balanced wines, largely exported in bulk, particularly to Great Britain, where they are popular.

The large area of Mátraalja, or Mátravidék, no. 15, is, after the Great Plain, the biggest vine-growing area in Hungary. In the foothills of the Mátra mountains, it was formerly two areas, Gyöngyös-Visonta and Debrő. Most of Hungary's table grapes are grown here from Chasselas hybrids, and much good wine, white and red, is made from Olaszrizling, Leányka, Traminer, Ottonel Muscat, Szürkebarát and Kékfrankos; but Mátraalja is famous mainly for a very good sweetish, aromatic green-white wine, Debrői Hárslevelű, made from the lime-leaf Tokay vine of that name.

THE BEST RED WINE AREAS

The most famous of Hungary's good red wines is Egri Bikavér—"Bull's Blood of Eger"—grown in the country around the beautiful old baroque town of that name, district of Eger, no. 14, on a topsoil of clay on volcanic rock—good red wine land. Of course, the wine has nothing to do with bulls or blood and is now made from Kadarka, Kékfrankos, Merlot known as Médoc Noir, Oporto or Cabernet Franc grapes. At its best, it is a full, smooth, deep-colored wine, benefiting enormously from bottle-age, which it rarely gets. The legend of the name comes from a story of the sixteenth century, when strong Turkish forces attacked the town and were repulsed by the local troops, encouraged by liberal quantities of Egri Bikavér served to them by their women. It is one of the best Hun-

garian red wines. Egri Kadarka can be excellent too and equally improves from long maturing in bottle. Many good white wines are also made in this district, rich dessert wines from the Leányka and Mézesfehér, drier table wins from Olaszrizling.

Probably the best Hungarian red wine is the Kékfrankos grown in Villány and known as Villányi-Burgundi. It has many of the qualities of the Burgundy grape and, like most other red wines, develops qualities of greatness when matured for a few years in bottle. Excellent red wines are also made in the Villány-Siklós district—no. 12—from Kadarka, and rather coarse wines from the Oporto Cabernet. This is clearly a good red wine district. Szekszárd—no. 11—a little to the northwest, also makes a good full-bodied wine from Kadarka, more in the Bordeaux style. Cabernet-Franc and Kékfrankos vines are also grown here. These areas are old winelands, many of them dating back to pre-Roman times, before the Emperor Probus, who came from Pannonia and was famous for his encouragement of viticulture.

Sopron—no. 8—fourth of the Hungarian red wine districts, is in the extreme northwest, in the Hungarian Burgenland, adjoining Austria. Its wine-making dates back to the pre-Roman Celts, and it was the produce of Sopron centuries ago that first spread the fame of Hungarian wines to Western Europe. Wines of many styles, red and white, are made here, but the district's fame rests on one made from a grape closely related to the Burgundian Gamay—Soproni Kékfrankos, which is of the style of Beaujolais, and to be drunk young and fresh.

THE SANDLANDS

The Great Plain is, in general, the land of huge State Farms, on the sandlands that, over the centuries, the Magyars have tamed and made into arable land. It was, and is, an epic struggle, but vines, with their long-ranging root systems, can flourish there. This became of great importance at the time of the phylloxera scourge, since the phylloxera aphid cannot survive in soil of this nature. Most of the wine made in the Alföld is not of high quality but is useful for the large export demand (from Germany, for example), for the making of Sekt, for distillation, and to form the basis for vermouth. But there are some ancient oases in the Alföld, mainly between the Danube and the Tisza: notably at Kecskemét, an ancient vine and fruit-growing area; at Jászberény, Csengőd, Solt, Iliskörös, Kiskunhalas and Szeged in the extreme south. Olaszrizling, Eserjó, Leányka, Cirfandli, Veltliner, Hárslevelü, Kadarka, Kékfrankos Merlot, and Cabernet are the principal varieties grown, particularly in the huge new plantations, although most of the indigenous vines are found in the ancient vine areas, where some wines of high quality are made. A remarkable Cabernet is also produced at Hajós and Kadarka; Burgundi at Vaskut.

BOTTLE TYPES AND MARKINGS

Tokay Aszú and Tokay Szamorodni are marketed in special white half-liter bottles (for a description of labeling by grades, see Tokay). Most other Hungarian bottled wine, including the other styles of Tokay, is sold in the tall slender bottles usually identified with German wines. Egri Bikavér and other red wines are in the short-shouldered Bordeaux bottles.

Monimpex, the Hungarian foreign trading company in Budapest, is the only agency entitled to export wines from Hungary. Large quantities are exported in bulk for bottling by the importing country. Hungary is a large wine-drinking country, with yearly consumption at approximately 33 liters *per capita*.

SPIRITS

Hungary produces a wide range of liqueurs and brandies. The most famous is Barack Pálinka (apricot brandy), an unsweetened spirit distilled from fresh apricots which come from the orchards of Kecskemét. This is sold in the standard 70 cl. and 35 cl. bottles and in the traditional *fütyülős* (flask) of 50 cl., which has a very long neck. From the same area comes Kecskeméti Barack liqueur, a mellow apricot, rich with the fragrance of the fruit.

The best of the rest of the fruit liqueurs are the cherry brandy and the golden pear liqueur (Csázárkörte in Hungarian). Another interesting liqueur is Hubertus, based on herbs and slightly more bitter in taste.

Of the other unsweetened spirits, the most renowned are Szilva Pálinka or Szilvorium (plum brandy), vodka, Kirsch of Eger, and Casino rum. All of these are more or less known in Great Britain, Canada, the United States, and South America. The best of Szilva Pálinka comes from Szatmár County and is made from three varieties of plums.

Hunter River Valley

Wine district of New South Wales, Australia. The vineyards here are the oldest in the country and among the few that produce almost entirely table wines. They center around Pokolbin and Cessnock. *See* Australia.

Hybrid

A cross between two different vine varieties, usually one of *Vitis vinifera* stock and one from an American species. The ultimate aim of the experimental hybridizer is to develop a vine with the hardiness and resistance to disease of American vines but bearing fruit of *Vitis vinifera* quality. A number of sound hybrids exist, and a few are very good for certain localities; but the field is still uncrowded. Hybridization is carried on in the United States (in New York, Maryland, and California), in Canada, and in European countries. The vines developed by French hybridizers usually bear the name of the hybridizer and a number. Some of the better-known names are Baco, Couderc, Seibel, and Seyve-Villard. Philip Wagner in Baltimore has contributed greatly through his hybrids to the improvement of eastern American vineyards. Having found many hybrids that are indigenous to the climate and soil of the eastern states, he has reduced the "foxy" taste in the vines of this region.

See Chapter Eight, p. 31, *and* United States.

Hydromel

See Mead.

Hydrometer

An instrument used to measure the sugar content of musts, consisting of a weighted bulb with a stem containing a scale calibrated in grams of sugar per 100 grams of solution. The must is poured into a chemist's calibrated cylinder, then the hydrometer is inserted and allowed to sink to an equilibrium level, depending on the density of the solution. Since sugar accounts for most of the increase in density of the must above the density of water, the instrument can be calibrated to read the percentage of sugar directly on the stem at a specified temperature.

Hydrometer, Sikes

In Great Britain, the hydrometer is legally recognized for measuring the strength of alcoholic beverages.

For comparison with French and American measures, *see* Appendix C, p. 703.

Hymettus

Light wines, both red and white, produced near Mount Hymettus in Attica.

See Greece.

I

Illinois

Wine-growing region of very little importance, in the United States.

Immiscible liquids

Liquids which do not mix: the classic example, oil and wine. For this reason, wine was sealed by a thin film of olive oil before corks came into use.

Imperial (impériale)

An outsized bottle used for fine French Bordeaux wines put down for long keeping. The capacity of the imperial is approximately eight ordinary Bordeaux bottles, or six liters.

Importation of wine

Few generalizations can be based on the amount of wine a country imports. Some of the large producers import large quantities, others do not. Some relatively wineless countries seem to require much wine, and, even more obviously, others do not. Of note is the fact that the Soviet Union—long only an importer of average quantity—has risen to near the top of the list. Most of the wine bought by the U.S.S.R. comes from Algeria.

The figures opposite are averages over the past few years, adjusted to show the patterns which may be expected in the near future.

Incrustation

The formation of a crust in wines, specifically Ports.

India

The history of wine in India is sporadic, but it is known to have been made there two thousand years ago and was still enjoyed in the era of the Moguls—Kashmir was then a wine region. In 1628, the monarch Jahangir was pictured on a coin with a goblet of wine in his hand. There were vineyards, then, at Golconda, Kandahar, and Surat. A century ago, the wines which had survived were those of Kashmir—some were shown at the Calcutta Exhibition of 1888. But the vines, which had been imported from Bordeaux, were attacked by phylloxera and had to be grafted onto American root-stocks.

Today, there are a few vineyards near Madras. Started by French missionaries, about 1889, they have been enlarged in recent years around Kodaikanal, Dharmapuri, and Penukanda. Even so, this growing of vines is more of a hobby than a serious business. Vine-

yards besides those around Madras are located in the states of Maharashtra and Mysore, near the southern tip of the country. Vineyards near Delhi, in the north Indian state of Haryana, also produce wine grapes. Judging by a wine called Bosca, from an area south of Bombay, it is cleat that much improvement is still needed to make Indian wines palatable. While there is little demand for wine among a people who do not much care for alcoholic drinks, or are forbidden by their religion to taste them, spirits, nevertheless, are manufactured—not only fermented palm and rice drinks, but brandy, gin, rum, and whisky. In 1972 the following quantities were made:

	Hectoliters	GALLONS U.S.	Imp.
Brandy	46,000	1,219,000	912,000
Gin	40,000	1,060,000	880,000
Whisky	115,000	3,047,500	2,530,000
Rum and bitter	75,000	1,987,500	1,650,000

WORLD IMPORTS OF WINES

Importing Country	Hectoliters	U.S. Gallons	Imp Gallons
West Germany	9,450,000	249,650,000	207,880,000
U.S.S.R.	6,780,000	179,115,000	149,150,000
France	5,580,000	147,410,000	122,750,000
Great Britain	5,400,000	142,660,000	118,790,000
United States	5,185,000	137,000,000	114,100,000
Belgium	2,180,000	57,590,000	47,960,000
Netherlands	2,130,000	56,270,000	46,860,000
Switzerland	1,990,000	52,570,000	43,780,000
East Germany	1,540,000	40,680,000	33,880,000
Canada	1,475,000	38,970,000	32,450,000
Denmark	950,000	25,100,000	20,900,000
Sweden	930,000	24,570,000	20,460,000
Japan	550,000	14,530,000	12,100,000
Poland	485,000	12,800,000	10,670,000
Czechoslovakia	300,000	7,930,000	6,600,000
Hungary	265,000	7,000,000	5,830,000
Austria	200,000	5,280,000	4,400,000
Italy	165,000	4,360,000	3,630,000
Luxembourg	150,000	3,960,000	3,300,000
Finland	125,000	3,300,000	2,750,000
Ireland	110,000	2,900,000	2,420,000
Australia	85,000	2,250,000	1,870,000
Bulgaria	85,000	2,250,000	1,870,000
New Zealand	29,000	766,100	637,940
Mexico	20,000	528,360	439,960
South Africa	19,000	501,950	417,960
Spain	15,000	396,270	329,970
Rumania	12,000	317,000	263,980
Brazil	4,000	105,670	87,990
TOTAL	46,209,000	1,220,760,350	1,016,577,800

Infectious degeneration

A virus, or virus-like vine disease, also known as fan leaf and *court noué*.
See Chapter Eight, p. 31.

Inferno (D.O.C.)

Red wine of Valtellina, in Italy, made from the Nebbiolo grape.
See Lombardy.

Ingelheimer

With Assmannshauser, this is one of the best—perhaps the best—of German red wines, but certainly not among the world leaders. For even at their best, German red wines are mediocre by world standards.
See Rheinhessen.

Inspissated wine

Boiled-down must, or unfermented grape juice, used in flavoring or coloring certain wines.

Institut National des Appellations d'Origine

Commonly known as I.N.A.O.
See Appellation d'Origine Contrôlée (A.O.C.).

Iona

Native American hybrid grape, developed in New York, where it is cultivated today mostly for sparkling white wine. The fruit is sweet and dark red, and it ferments into a clean distinctive dry wine—one of several examples of white wine made from red grapes. The name comes from Iona Island, in the Hudson River near Peekskill.

Iran

The fame of Iran as a wine-making country is in the past, when it was one of the earliest lands to practice viniculture. According to one legend, wine was discovered accidentally by a shah of Persia, and Herodotus says the Persians were deep drinkers. There are many other references to the wines and to the size and prodigality of the vines in classical literature. And even after the Moslem interdiction Omar Khayyam continued to sing the praises of his native wine. Shiraz was the celebrated wine, and there was a theory that the Syrah grape, grown now in the Rhône Valley and other places, was originally brought to Western Europe from Shiraz by returning Crusaders.

Vines grew on about 135,000 hectares (337,500 acres), mainly in the foothills of the mountains and especially in the provinces of East Azerbaijan, West Azerbaijan, Khorasan, Tehran, Farse, Hamedan,

Lorestan, and Zanjan. Annual production was about 4,000 hectoliters (105,800 U.S. gallons, 88,000 imp.), nearly all of which was drunk in the country. The average Iranian drank less than half a liter of wine a year, however. One of the most widely planted grapes was the Thompson Seedless; it is good for fresh table grapes and raisins but makes poor wine. Among those cities with wineries were the capital, Tehran; Shiraz *(q.v.)*; Hamedan, 320 kilometers (200 miles) west of the capital; Malayer, near Hamedan; Shiravan in the northeast; Shahrooh in the north and Abadeh, about 160 kilometers (100 miles) north of Shiraz. As long as Khomeini's presence is felt in Iran, wine not only will be a thing of the past but will also represent the forbidden fruit.

SPIRITS

Arak was the principal spirit, and some 80,000 hectoliters (2.12 million U.S. gallons, 1.76 million imp.) were made each year. Beer was also much more popular than wine, which was sometimes reinforced with raki and sugar. *See* Arrack.

Irancy

Rather ordinary red and rosé wines produced in the department of Yonne, some 16 kilometers (10 miles) south of Chablis in northern Burgundy.

Irouléguy

Red, white, and rosé wines.
District: Southwest France.

In the extreme southwest corner of France amid the dramatic valleys of the Pyrenees are the towns of St. Jean-Pied-de-Port and St. Étienne-de-Baïgorry. Neither is far from Biarritz, famous as a resort, or from Bayonne, famous for its hams. The two villages lie in the center of the area which makes the Appellation Contrôlée wine called Irouléguy. The white wines are similar to the naturally sweet ones produced in nearby Jurançon. But better than these are the reds, which are rather light in color but with good flavor nonetheless.

Isabella

A prolific American grape, once highly thought of but now used almost exclusively for blending in the production of sparkling wine in New York State. The grape is blue, but it gives a pale, slightly "foxy" wine with no pronounced characteristics. It can also be found under the name Americano in southern Switzerland.

Ischia (D.O.C.)

Pleasant red and white wines from the island off the coast of Naples.
See Campania.

Isinglass

A whitish semi-transparent gelatinous substance obtained from the bladders of certain freshwater fishes, especially the sturgeon, and used for fining or clarifying wines and beers.
See Chapter Nine, p. 40.

Israel

Wine of almost every type is made in Israel: red and white table wine; Pearl wine; and sparkling wine for every palate—*brut*, extra-dry, semi-dry, sweet—made by the champagne method of secondary fermentation in bottle. All those designed for export are prepared under religious supervision, since for Jewish communities abroad they may be sacramental as well as beverage wines. Aperitifs are also produced, as are brandy and liqueurs.

The mainstays of Israel's production were, until recently, full-bodied, sweet red wines and white wines, golden Muscatels, and a sweet wine of the Tokay type. Now, however, dry and semi-dry table wines, both red and white, are gaining in popularity. In 1985, about 70% of the production was in table wine. In the past, appellations were often borrowed from other countries, and bottles might be labeled Carmel Málaga or Carmel Port. This practice is now abandoned, and most of these wines have new Hebrew names. Some of the most important are:

Sweet Dessert Wines

Muscatel; Partom, Porath, Porath Atic, Ashdod, Poriah, and Vered (formerly Port); Topaz, Tokeah, Tivon, and Savion (formerly Tokay); Almog, Gilon, and Nalagenia (formerly "Málaga"); Sharir ("Sherry"); Yakeneth ("Alicante"); Yashan Noshan; Yenon; Moriah; Atzmauth; Château Rishon.

Dry and Semi-dry Table Wines

Red. Adom Atic; Primor (formerly Pommard); Vin Rouge Supérieur; Château Windsor; Carmelith; Atzmon; Mont Rouge; Cabernet Sauvignon.
White. Carmel Hock; Mont Blem; Massadah; Château Montagne; Levanan; Doran; Yarden.
Red and white. Avdad; Ashkalon; Ben-Ami; Montford.

Sparkling Wines

President, Château de la Montagne, Sambation.

WINE REGIONS

Zikhron-Yaacov

As the country's largest vine-growing region, 40% of Israel's vines grow on the slopes of Mount Carmel, where they have been cultivated since the late 19th century. The specialties of the region are white and rosé wine.

Sydoon-Gezer

In the center of the country, and second in size to the Zikhron-Yaacov region, the grapes grown here have also been cultivated since the late 1800s, and produce white and especially good red wines.

Galilee

Located in the mountainous northern part of the country 600 to 1,000 meters above sea level, this new grape area with its relatively good climate has turned out some good red and white wines. Recently Gamla and Yarden have gained some international fame.

Jerusalem environs

New vineyards, planted in the last twenty-five years in this relatively small area, produce some good red and white wines.

Israel is intent on making better wines. They need additional know-how and it will take lengthy, arduous steps of trial and error to lead them to their goal in the 21st century.

WINE HISTORY

Canaan must have been among the earliest countries to enjoy wine. It is generally assumed that the first known vineyards were those of Anatolia, Persia, Mesopotamia, and Egypt, all of them growing vines over three thousand years ago. At an early date there was communication between Palestine and Egypt. A letter written about 1800 B.C. reported that Palestine was blessed with figs and with vineyards producing wine in greater quantity than water—in fact, "the children of Israel sit each beneath his vine and his fig." Another correspondent wrote that all the gardens of Canaan were full of fruit-giving vines, and the wine flowed from her cellars like waterfalls—this was about 1500 B.C.

The many references to wine in the Bible need not be repeated here. One of the first things Noah did, when the flood was over, was to begin "to be a husbandman, and he planted a vineyard and he drank of the wine." According to one theory, there actually was a flood and the approximate date was 2800 B.C. During the 18th Dynasty (1580–1450 B.C.) the Egyptians conquered Palestine, and again, about 925 B.C., Jerusalem was taken. When the Egyptian soldiers destroyed Israelite cities, they tore up the vineyards, but these were replanted and soon flourished again. As for Canaan, the land flowing with milk and honey flowed also with wine. In the Book of Numbers, Chapter xiii, the story is told of how the two men Moses sent to spy out the land came back with a great cluster of grapes which they tied to a staff and carried between them. The place where they cut it down was the brook named Eshcol.

The vintners of biblical times were knowledgeable about wine-making (as was Mago of Carthage) and many of their customs are still known and respected today. In a country where there was sometimes more wine than water, the wine was used for all kinds of things in addition to drinking and as a medicine: houses were washed out with it, clothes were dyed in it—it has been estimated that the population used as much as 3 to 4 liters a head every day.

Vines grew all over the country—on the hills, in the valleys, on the plain, even on the shores of the Dead Sea. Grapes were carefully selected for picking—the whole process was not unlike that in use in parts of Cyprus (*q.v.*). There were many different types: white; red or "pretty" wine; dark-colored "negro" wine; sultana wine; milk wine (a posset, perhaps); and asparagus wine, boiled with the vegetable. Various mixtures were prepared, also—honey and peppers with sweet wines, herbs and peppers with sharp wines. There was wine to be drunk at one year of age, at three years, or after long storage in cellars. Before big festivals, the wine was racked three times, and at the Feast of Tabernacles the booths were decorated with wine jars. Wines from Lebanon were highly thought of; and the famous Helbon, to be bought in Damascus (Ezekiel, Chapter xxvii), was a cooked white wine. It is probable that there were more white wines than red.

Wine production was at its peak in Palestine in the time of the Second Temple—destroyed in A.D. 70 in the war with the Romans. Many famous vineyards were then torn up. Some were reconstituted, but although the Jewish people continued for some time to cultivate the vine in a desultory way, production did not flourish again until modern times. Yet in the first four centuries of this era, Roman writers described various Palestine wines—Shechem, Lydda, Caesarea, Ashkelon, and Gaza—which were highly esteemed and exported to Syria, to Egypt, and even to England. After the Arab conquest (A.D. 600–1000) most of the vineyards were uprooted; so strict was the Moslem prohibition that even table grapes were destroyed lest they be pressed for wine.

In the Middle Ages, however, Crusaders found a few vineyards near the Mount Carmel Range, near Bethlehem and Nazareth, and some of them stayed long enough to cultivate vines for themselves. In 1280 it was reported that "Near Bethlehem there are still magnificent vines. The Moslems do not tend them, but the Christians make very good wine." The Christians had to pay heavy taxes for the privilege, and Moslems living near the Christian settlements made wine to sell to their neighbors.

WINE OF MODERN ISRAEL

Modern wine history in Palestine began in 1870, with the foundation of the first agricultural school. This started with a vineyard at Mikveh, bearing a few eating grapes, but mainly wine grapes, all of *Vitis vinifera*: Alicante, Bordeleau, Carignan, petit Bouchet, and others. There were at this time some Christian monastic holdings, also planted in *Vitis vinifera* but these were small. In 1880 the German Templars planted sizable areas in the Carmel district, bringing their vines from the Rhine Valley.

In 1882, at the time when the earliest Zionists were arriving in Israel, the first vineyards, under the patronage of Baron Edmond de Rothschild, were planted, again with *Vitis vinifera*. Soon there were large cellars in use, and vineyards at Shomron and in different parts of Galilee. In 1890 the area under Jewish cultivation was 2,800 hectares (7,000 acres), there was beginning to be a surplus of wine, and growers were considering problems of marketing and export when the phylloxera plague arrived, destroying many plants and putting an end to the surplus for some time. Rothschild advised the growers to replant with vines grafted onto American root-stocks.

By 1906 the industry was able to stand on its own, and Rothschild handed over to the growers the cellars at Richon-le-Zion, near Tel-Aviv, and at Zikhron-Yaacov, south of Haifa. These are still the main centers. The name given to the cooperative which was then formed was Société Coopérative Vigneronne des Grandes Caves Richon-le-Zion et Zikhron-Yaacov. It still functions to day, producing 75% of the wine of Israel. The viticultural methods were French, introduced by Baron de Rothschild.

At first, Israel's wine industry was run at a loss. Once the Jewish state was established (in 1948), with thousands of immigrants arriving, many from wine-growing countries, cultivation began to flourish. In the first five years, acreage doubled, and approximately 2,000 hectares (5,000 acres) have since been added. Today, domestic consumption of wine is some 180,000 hectoliters (4.7 million U.S. gallons, 3.9 million imp.), and there is a surplus of about 1 million U.S. gallons for export.

With so much of the land in new vine, the quality of the wine has not yet declared itself. Certain wines produced from European grape varieties growing in different regions of Israel are showing themselves to be pleasant and satisfactory; and a few of the Israel wines have lately won prizes at international competitions and exhibitions. They will undoubtedly continue to improve with the technical help and good equipment prevalent, thus making Israel a good wine-producer with regard to both quality and quantity. In 1957, the Israeli Wine Institute was established at Rehovot for the purpose of scientific and market research and for quality-testing of all wines for export.

RECENT PRODUCTION

For the past ten years average annual production of wine in Israel has been near 350,000 hectoliters (9,245,000 U.S. gallons, 7,700,000 imp.); 3,000 hectares are planted. About 60% of this figure was made by the Cooperative Society of Wine Growers, Richon-le-Zion, and Zikhron-Yaacov. Other important wineries are Hamartef, Eliaz, and Carmel Zion. About five hundred growers are today members of the Cooperative Society, which is responsible for some 75% of the export trade in wine. In 1952 the society established in the U.S. a company called Carmel Wine Co., Inc., New York, and this is their representative for wines exported anywhere in the United States or Canada. There is also a branch in Great Britain, The Carmel Wine Company, which is almost as old as modern viticulture in Israel, for it was founded in 1897, only fifteen years after the revival of the Palestine vineyards. Wines and spirits are imported partly in bottle, and partly in bulk for London bottling. Great Britain and America are Israel's principal customers, but wine is exported in smaller quantities to twenty-six other countries.

Today most wines are made from the Carignan, Alicante, Grenache, Sémillon, Muscat, and a local variety called Dabuki. In hopes of improving the quality of their wines, growers are limiting the plantations of the ubiquitous, mediocre Carignan in favor of such better grapes as the Cabernet Sauvignon, French Colombard, Chardonnay and Sauvignon Blanc. In addition, Ruby Cabernet, Emerald Riesling, and other hybrids developed in California have been planted as the Israelis continue to work toward reasonable table wines for consumption at home and export abroad.

Château d'Issan

Bordeaux red wine.
District: Haut-Médoc, France.
Commune: Cantenac-Margaux.

Before the fall of the Austro-Hungarian Empire during the First World War, Château d'Issan was the favorite wine of the Royal Court at Vienna. It is said that Emperor Franz Josef would drink no other, and everyone else followed his lead.

"For the Table of Kings and the Altar of God" is the proud motto of the vineyard and may be seen carved in the stone of the gate. The beautiful fourteenth-century château, a replacement of a fortress-castle from the thirteenth century, was near collapse when restoration was begun in 1952.

Lying across the road from Château Prieuré-Lichine on the north side of Cantenac, the château is owned by Mme Marguerite Cruse, the widow of the late Emmanuel Cruse, and her son Lionel, who headed the shipping firm of Cruse et Fils, Frères. The property is entitled to the place-name Margaux. Château d'Issan lies near Château Palmer, both Third Growths (*Troisièmes Crus*) in the Classification of 1855.

Characteristics. While the delicacy and the typical taste of a Margaux are present, the wines have a body and fleshiness slightly reminiscent of those made farther north in the Médoc—the Pauillacs, for example. Contrary to past practices, the wine is now château-bottled and has somewhat regained throughout the world the reputation lost in the sixties and seventies.

Vineyard area: 35 hectares (87 acres).
Average production: 130 *tonneaux* (11,000 cases).

Italy

Of all the large wine-producing countries in the world, Italy along with the United States has made the most revolutionary strides, from backward mediocrity to oenological highs. Since the mid '70s, the human factor, one of the four main contributors to quality, has manifested itself in region after region and traditional methods, often bad, have given way to the modern science of wine-making. This is especially true for white wines. New grape varieties, controlled fermentation, and estate-bottling have resulted in fresh, attractive wines in place of wines previously subject to oxidation.

The Italian likes his wines heady, red, and, above all, plentiful. He is the most natural wine-drinker in the world, downing his annual 82 liters (21.6 U.S. gallons, 18 imp.) a head of wine—good, bad, or indifferent—with the greatest satisfaction. The ordinary wine may be rough, incompletely fermented, thick, lacking in finesse; but it will always be a welcome accompaniment to the meal.

Italy was described as one vast vineyard—and the description was apt. Vines spilled out everywhere, climbed trees and draped their branches, ran along roads and hung festooned from fences, flourished in glorious disorder beside olive trees and fields of grain. The vine grew easily, flowering into great bunches of grapes. One did not see so many of the serried ranks of disciplined, close-trimmed vineyards here as in France and Germany. Italian viniculture was sometimes as easygoing as its viticulture. Indeed, in some vineyards it seemed that the vintner's main concern was with getting wine from fermenting vat to mouth in the shortest possible time. A drastic change has taken place. In most vineyards, vines are now beautifully tended.

Italy is the largest producer and exporter of wine in the world. The average annual production is about 77 million hectoliters (2.03 billion U.S. gallons, 1.7 billion imp.), of which 14.8 million hectoliters (nearly 20% of the total) is shipped out of the country. Italy imports wine too—some 165,000 hectoliters (4.3 million U.S. gallons, 3.6 million imp.) each year.

In fewer and fewer plots do vines still grow among other crops. Today about 700,000 hectares (1.75 million acres) are in mixed cultivation as compared with more than 2 million hectares (5 million acres) in 1964. Land devoted exclusively to intensive viticulture covers 1,400,000 hectares (3,515,000 acres). The trend of young men leaving the land to work in the cities has now reversed and there is a growing percentage of young men working on the land today. There are about two million vineyard workers registered in Italy, and peasant owners of small parcels might bring this number up to three million.

Some of the wines are excellent—among the best of them, the Barolos and Barbarescos of Piedmont, the Valpolicellas and Soaves of Veneto, Tuscany's celebrated Chianti—the Brunellos di Montalcino and the Vino Nobili di Montepulciano to mention but a few. But, unfortunately, these fine wines are not always to be found. Many of the best wines of Italy are made for their own consumption by smaller growers who sell whatever surplus they have to old-established customers, often inherited along with the vineyard—and the casual tourist is unlikely to meet with such a cultivator or his wine. What he will normally drink will be the output of the large companies—standardized wine, its quality depending entirely upon the firm which makes it.

WINE CONTROLS

Up to the late sixties, Italian wines suffered from the haphazard methods of viniculture and from an easygoing attitude to nomenclature which before the advent of the D.O.C. laws made it possible for wines which did not even deserve the name Tuscan to be sold under the label of Chianti. The root of the trouble was the government's failure to safeguard the place-names of the fine-wine regions.

The French government, afraid of having its market flooded with cheap Italian wines as the tariff barriers were constantly lowered to comply with the Common Market Agreements, urged the Italian government to set up control laws, somewhat along the lines of the Appellations d'Origine Contrôlée, which was done.

Denominazioni di Origine

In July 1963, regulations for controlling place-names, or *Denominazioni di Origine*, were made law. There are three different denominations, graded as follows:
—Simple
    e.g., Rosso Toscano, a red wine from anywhere inside Tuscany.
—Controlled
    e.g., Dolcetto d'Alba, a fine wine of Piedmont, produced 100% with Dolcetto in Alba,

Neive, Treiso, Rodello, Sinio, and all parts of Monforte d'Alba, La Morra, Verduno and Monchiero.
—Controlled and guaranteed
    e.g., a true Barolo or Barbaresco sealed and labeled with the official governmental seal.

Simple denomination (*Denominazione di Origine Semplice*) is allowed to ordinary wines made from grapes traditionally cultivated in an area. This D.O.S. has been abolished as the E.E.C. (Common Market) regulations are above those of the member states, and the wines which formerly fell into this category are now known as *Vini da tavola con indicazione geografica*, or table wines with geographic indication.

The E.E.C.'s insistence that Italy create place names accompanied by stringent laws, despite tremendous confusion, has impelled a greater respect for the individual character and identity of Italian wines. Some excellent *vino da tavola* wines which have not adhered to D.O.C. or D.O.C.G. grape requirements, among them Tignanello and Sassicaia, can be found.

Controlled denomination (*Denominazione di Origine Controllata*, usually abbreviated D.O.C.) is an appellation reserved for 11% of Italy's wines which have achieved the stipulated standards for quality. Vineyards producing such wines are inscribed in an official register.

Controlled and guaranteed denomination (*Denominazione di Origine Controllata e Garantita*, abbreviated D.O.C.G.) is awarded only to fine wines attaining qualities and prices established after the recommendation of the Ministry of Agriculture and Forestry. Such wines must be sold in containers not exceeding 5 liters (1.3 U.S. gallons, 1.1 imp.). The labels must state that the origin of the wine is controlled and guaranteed and list the net content of the bottle, the name of the grower and bottler, the place of bottling, and also the alcoholic strength. Growers who wish to have their wine classified in this top category must send in a request to the Ministry of Agriculture and Forestry for a government inspector, who will have the wine analyzed. Such applications must be backed by copious documentation as to region, average annual production, details of vine variety, characteristics of wines, etc., and an application can be put forward only if it has the support of a fair percentage of the growers concerned.

Both D.O.C. and D.O.C.G. status are formally granted by the president of the republic on the advice of the ministries concerned. Thereafter, the winemaker must adhere strictly to the following rules:

(1) Inscription of the vineyards in the appropriate register, with compulsory declaration of production and stocks.

(2) Correct labeling of bottles and flasks.

(3) Inspection by control agents appointed by the Ministry of Agriculture.

(4) Cooperation in preventive steps taken to repress

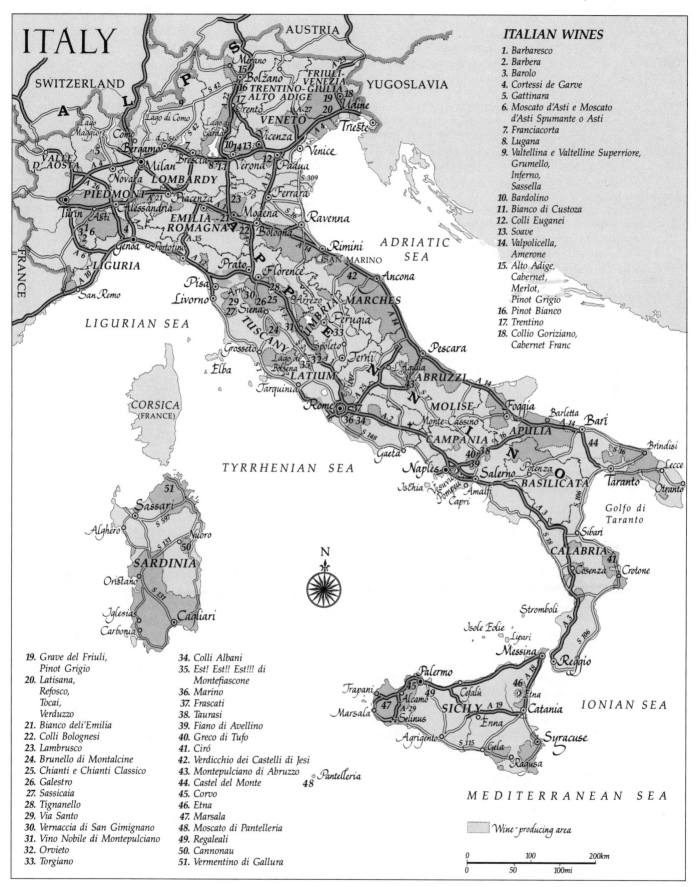

ITALY

AUSTRIA

SWITZERLAND

YUGOSLAVIA

Merano
15 Bolzano
16 TRENTINO-
FRIULI-
VENEZIA-
GIULIA
17 ALTO ADIGE
Trento 19 18 Udine
20 VENETO
Vicenza
Trieste
Venice

VALLE
D'AOSTA
Lago di Como
Lago di Garda
Lago d'Iseo
Como
Bergamo
7
Brescia
Verona
12
Padua

Turin
Novara LOMBARDY
Milan
PIEDMONT
Asti
10 14 13
8 11
Piacenza
23
Ferrara
Po

3 1 6
5
2 4
Alessandria
EMILIA-
ROMAGNA
Modena
Bologna
22
Ravenna

Genoa
Portofino
LIGURIA
Rimini
SAN MARINO
ADRIATIC
SEA

San Remo
Pisa
Prato
Florence
Arno
42
Ancona

Livorno
29 30 26 25
28
Arezzo
MARCHES

LIGURIAN SEA
27 Siena
UMBRIA
Perugia
33

24 31
Spoleto
32
Terni
Grosseto
Lago di
Bolsena
35
Aquila
Pescara
ABRUZZI

Elba
LATIUM
43
MOLISE

Tarquinia
Rome
37
36 34
Monte Cassino
Foggia
Barletta
Bari

CORSICA
(FRANCE)
CAMPANIA
40 38
39
APULIA
44
Brindisi
Lecce

TYRRHENIAN SEA
Gaeta
Naples
Salerno
Potenza
Taranto

Ischia
Amalfi
Capri
Pompeii
BASILICATA
Golfo di
Taranto

51
Sassari
Sibari
CALABRIA
41

Alghero
Nuoro
50
Cosenza
Crotone

SARDINIA
Oristano
Stromboli

N
Isole Eolie
Lipari
Messina
Reggio

Iglesias
Carbonia
Cagliari
Palermo
Etna
46
IONIAN SEA

Trapani 49 Cefalù
45
Alcamo
47 A 29
Marsala Selinus
SICILY 19 Catania
Enna

Agrigento
Gela
Syracuse
Ragusa

Pantelleria
48
MEDITERRANEAN SEA

ITALIAN WINES

1. Barbaresco
2. Barbera
3. Barolo
4. Cortessi de Garve
5. Gattinara
6. Moscato d'Asti e Moscato
   d'Asti Spumante o Asti
7. Franciacorta
8. Lugana
9. Valtellina e Valtelline Superriore,
   Grumello,
   Inferno,
   Sassella
10. Bardolino
11. Bianco di Custoza
12. Colli Euganei
13. Soave
14. Valpolicella,
    Amerone
15. Alto Adige,
    Cabernet,
    Merlot,
    Pinot Grigio
16. Pinot Bianco
17. Trentino
18. Collio Goriziano,
    Cabernet Franc

19. Grave del Friuli,
    Pinot Grigio
20. Latisana,
    Refosco,
    Tocai,
    Verduzzo
21. Bianco deli'Emilia
22. Colli Bolognesi
23. Lambrusco
24. Brunello di Montalcine
25. Chianti e Chianti Classico
26. Galestro
27. Sassicaia
28. Tignanello
29. Via Santo
30. Vernaccia di San Gimignano
31. Vino Nobile di Montepulciano
32. Orvieto
33. Torgiano

34. Colli Albani
35. Est! Est!! Est!!! di
    Montefiascone
36. Marino
37. Frascati
38. Taurasi
39. Fiano di Avellino
40. Greco di Tufo
41. Ciró
42. Verdicchio dei Castelli di Jesi
43. Montepulciano di Abruzzo
44. Castel del Monte
45. Corvo
46. Etna
47. Marsala
48. Moscato di Pantelleria
49. Regaleali
50. Cannonau
51. Vermentino di Gallura

Wine-producing area

0   100   200km
0   50   100mi

283

fraud and maintain the controls of the denomination of origin.

(5) Payment of penalties for infraction of the regulations.

Members of the National Institute for the Protection of Denomination of Origin (Istituzione del Comitato Nazionale per la Tutela delle Denominazioni di Origine) are nominated by the Ministry of Agriculture and Forestry in association with the Ministry of Industry and Commerce. The Institute is composed of a president and twenty-eight members, including one from the Italian Institute for Foreign Trade (I.C.E.), and its function is to promote and watch over the controlled and guaranteed Italian wines and to initiate research for their improvement. Membership in this class of denomination is voluntary. All the better producers are anxious to sell with this certificate for export and are ready to submit their wines for inspection and analysis.

Membership being voluntary, not all wine for export is controlled, but it is inspected. The customer should check before buying.

Following what was undoubtedly a regrettable lack of controls, these new laws are certainly to be commended. If the laws are indeed to work, everyone concerned in the Italian wine trade will have to be persuaded that quantity of production is worth sacrificing to quality. The law of July 12, 1963, amending and replacing earlier regulations which had become out of date and ineffective, requires the government to issue a decree controlling the production of musts, wines, and vinegars, and establish regulations to prevent fraud in the preparation and sale of these products.

THE CONSORZI and D.O.C.s

Inside Italy, any of the local *consorzi* may check the control of their wines to safeguard the regulations. Before the introduction of the Denomination of Origin laws, the only wine which carried any guarantee of quality was that wearing the seal of a local wine society, or *consorzio*. Where a *consorzio* exists, some firms and growers may be members, others not. Both members and non-members, unfortunately, have equal right to the local appellation, although only members are entitled to use the *consorzio* seal. The Consorzi were necessary before the D.O.C. and D.O.C.G. laws went into effect. The D.O.C. laws have helped improve the quality of Italian wines; only traditional grape varieties were specifically allowed, so despite excellent results by some progressive growers using good grape varieties such as Cabernet Sauvignon and Chardonnay, their wines were excluded from the D.O.C. distinction and were forced to be sold as *vino da tavola*, or table wine. It is hoped that the Denominazioni de Origine laws will succeed in protecting fine wines and controlling the sales.

As for the *consorzi*, the standards for each are drawn up by its members and are thus subject to wide variation. Sometimes they are so high that their wines will always be excellent; sometimes they settle for a fairly low average. They generally dictate the permitted grape varieties, the limits of the district, the minimum alcoholic content, and whether or not wines may be imported from outside the area. A universal rule is that all wine must be tasted by a select committee and approved before the seal is given—and affixed in such a way that the bottle cannot be opened without the seal being broken. Each *consorzio* has its own apparatus for enforcing rules, and in cases of gross or repeated violation the penalty may be expulsion. A degree of collaboration between the *consorzi* and the Institute for the Protection of Denomination of Origin could result in a great improvement in the overall standard of Italian wines.

WINE REGIONS

The Italian peninsula is characterized by an ever-changing landscape. The Alps give way to the Apennines, and plains and mountains alternate all the way down to the rugged hills of the "arch" and "toe" of the Italian "boot." In general, the finest wines are made in the north, but the south has several that are entrancing, particularly when drunk on the spot. The Italians have divided their nation into regions, or administrative sub-sections, and it is convenient to discuss the wines under these categories. The regions and their wines (*see the principal districts also under separate headings*) include:

Abruzzi

This region on the Adriatic seaboard gives way to central Italy. It produces some unpretentious and often pleasant wines. Red Montepulciano di Abruzzo and Cerasuolo di Abruzzo, and white Trebbiano di Abruzzo are all names for the dominant contributing grape variety; all are agreeable at home but would almost certainly lose some of this charm were they to be shipped.

Apulia (Puglia)

The great southern bulk-producing plain of Italy. The output is generally used for making vermouth, for blending, or for ordinary wines. (See p. 79.)

Basilicata (Lucania)

This southern region, once known as Lucania, is a jumble of forbidding mountains and inaccessible valleys. Some wine is made. The best-known is Aglianico del Vulture; the first part of the name is that of the vine, the second of the mountain on which it is cultivated. Fairly large amounts of Muscat and Malvasia vines are also grown. (See p. 102.)

Calabria

The extreme southern tip of Italy. Sweet white Greco di Gerace (from grapes of the same name) and deep red Cirò di Calabria (mainly from Gaglioppo grapes grown in Cirò) are the best-known wines; lovers of Muscats may also find the region to their liking. (*See* p. 146.)

Campania

The most popular wines in this region around Naples are the red Vesuvio (mainly from the Aglianico, Piedirosso, and Olivella grapes and grown on the volcanic foothills of Mount Vesuvius), and the red and white Ravello grown near the charming village of that name on the Amalfi coast. Also from this region come the white Greco di Tufo, near Avellino, and the soft white Lacrima Christi as well as the strong Taurasi. Close to Amalfi is made the red Gragnano, which is so delicious to drink on a flower-laden terrace over the Bay of Naples; and from the islands of Capri and Ischia come the gay light wines known by those names. (*See* p. 147.)

Emilia-Romagna

A vast agricultural area in central Italy, not outstanding for quality wines. Red, usually slightly sweet and sparkling, Lambrusco is the largest-selling imported wine in the U.S., and Albana accommodates those who like their wines white and not too dry. Large amounts of Sangiovese (red) and Trebbiano are also made on the hills of Romagna. (*See* p. 228.)

Friuli-Venezia-Giulia

The new up-and-coming white-producing area of Italy, in the northeast corner of Italy bordering Austria and Yugoslavia. Plantings of Tocai, Picolit, Sauvignon, Riesling, Traminer, Pinot Grigio and Pinot Bianco (some Chardonnay) have prospered in this microclimate mix of the mountain Alpine air with the winds blowing from the Adriatic.

Friuli, which produces more red than white, has gained recognition for its fair Merlot, Cabernet Sauvignon, and Franc and its native Refosco. (*See* p. 231.)

Latium (Lazio)

The wines of the Castelli Romani (Castles of Rome), among the country's best, are generally dry and white—the best known are Frascati and Marino. Many withstand the rigors of ocean travel. Est! Est!! Est!!! from Montefiascone is the white, dry, and sometimes semi-sweet wine with the best wine legend of Italy. (*See* p. 301.)

Liguria

The Italian extension of the French Riviera is not famous for wine. Dry and slightly sweet white Cin-

queterre is about the best known, although there are others, such as Dolceacqua (red). (*See* p. 305.)

Lombardy

The Valtellina reds—Sassella, Grumello, Valgella, Fracia, and Inferno—are highly prized; and the wines from the west bank of Lake Garda such as Franciacorta (D.O.C.) are delightful; they come in all three colors, but the rosés are probably the best, especially the Chiaretto. (*See* p. 311.)

The Marches

No wines of great distinction are made in this area between the Apennines and the Adriatic. The principal wines are the red Piceno and the popular white Verdicchio dei Castelli di Jesi, usually well made, often found abroad. (*See* p. 325.)

Molise

Least important wine region of Italy. The Montepulciano del Molise and Ramitello rosso are the small flag-bearers of this small, neglected wine region on the Adriatic coast.

Piedmont

The home of Italy's two finest red wines, Barolo and Barbaresco (both have achieved D.O.C.G. status), and of the dry and sweet sparkling Asti Spumanti. Other good still wines are Freisa, Barbera, Gattinara, Gignolino d'Asti, Nebbiolo d'Alba, Dolcetto, and Ghemme. The city of Turin is also the manufacturing center of Vermouth, from cheap wines and herbal extracts. (*See* p. 384.)

Sardinia

The wines from this beautiful rugged island, whether drunk on the Aga Khan's Costa Smeralda or on the mainland, are very pleasant dry whites; less attractive reds. These table wines are a welcome change from the fortified sweet wines which were the island's traditional sweet wines. (*See* p. 457.)

Sicily

One was inclined to associate Sicily with sweet fortified wines. Today, modern oenology and cooperative wine-making have transformed Sicilian wine production, and many good, popular table wines are being produced instead of Marsala, which was the island's most famous wine. Indeed, Sicily is now in the enviable position of accounting for 25% of Italian wine exports. Notable wines are white Marmertino, red Faro, the red and white wines of Etna, and especially the dry whites and full reds of Corvo. Sicilian

Marsala can be fine, although it has become difficult to find. (*See* p. 469.)

Trentino-Alto-Adige

Although bound together politically, these northerly regions of Trentino and Alto Adige (South Tyrol) are quite distinct in their German culture and language. Red wines from the area, including Cabernet, Merlot, Pinot Noir, and Santa Magdalener, go largely to Germany and Austria. White wines, including Riesling, Traminer, Pinot Grigio, and Pinot Bianco, are enjoyed both at home and abroad. Cooperative winemaking has resulted in a general improvement in quality. (*See* p. 501.)

Tuscany

The best—and most famous—wine is Chianti, a D.O.C.G. There are a number of different Chiantis, but the growers of the Chianti Classico district maintain that only they have a real right to the appellation. Under different names, some of the others would be wonderful wines, but they are not always true Chiantis. Some claim that the best wine is the overpriced Brunello di Montalcino, a powerful wine which ages for half a century; it was Italy's first D.O.C.G. wine. Vino Nobile di Montepulciano, another D.O.C.G., is also from this region. (*See* p. 506.)

Umbria

Discovering white Orvieto, Umbria's best wine, may be exciting, but exploring the artistic antiquities in the towns halfway between Rome and Florence is worth the trip. In this history-rich vineyard countryside, the red and white wines of Colli del Trasimeno are produced around the lake of the same name.

Umbria also produces Torgiano, which is made mostly from Trebbiano, and is round and strong. The red is rich and full. (*See* p. 510.)

Valle d'Aosta

Usually considered part of the Piedmont, the French-speaking Valle d'Aosta produces two quality wines, called Donnaz and Enfer d'Arvier. Both are red, the former from Nebbiolo, the latter from Petit Rouge.

Veneto

The famous wines of the Verona district are the best of this region and include dry red Valpolicella, Recioto, Bardolino, and dry white Soave.

Ives

Native American variety of grapes, hardy and vigorous but inconsistent. The red coarse-skinned grape yields a strong "foxy" red wine.

Izarra

A Basque attempt to reproduce Chartreuse, made in Bayonne in southwest France. Like its more famous prototype, it is fabricated in two styles, yellow and green, of which the green is the more highly alcoholic.

J

James

American Muscadine grape sometimes used in the south for making a strongly flavored, not very agreeable wine.

Japan

From Kyushu in the south to northernmost Hokkaido, the Japanese islands count some 30,000 hectares (75,000 acres) of vines producing both table and wine grapes. Production of all wines made from grapes is over 160,000 hectoliters (4.3 million U.S. gallons, 3.5 million imp.) per year, yet for every Japanese who picks up a glass of wine, one hundred reach for saké or beer. Consumption of beer (65%), saké, which is fermented from rice (19%), and other local grain beverages has reached such enormous proportions that the public has been warned consumption must be reduced to conserve the dwindling grain supply. Wine is being represented as a possible alternative, but alcoholic beverages imported into the country are becoming very popular among the well-to-do.

The wine-growing regions of Japan are the Yamanashi district and, to a lesser extent, those of Yamagata, Okayama, and Nagano—equally large but yielding still more mediocre wines. All are on the principal island of Honshu, and their acreage accounts for more than half of the lands planted in vines. The combination of high humidity and acid soil makes grape-growing difficult. The vines are grown on trellises to avoid humidity, particularly bad during the torrential September rains. Vines are usually planted in rows about 6 meters apart with about 400 to the hectare (150 feet).

Japan is one of the few countries in the world where the three families of vine—European, American, and Asian—are all able to flourish. Yet in Japanese soil none produces fruit for making truly good wine. Varieties of the American *Vitis labrusca* and some of the hybrid vines are about the only ones which yield adequate and occasionally agreeable wines. Delaware, Muscat Bailey and Campbell's Early are more widespread than any other vines, covering more than half of all the vineyards. European Sémillon, Chasselas, Chardonnay, and Riesling are used increasingly for white wines, and Cabernet Sauvignon, along with Merlot, accounts for 75% of the red wines produced. But in general, *Vitis vinifera* vines are particularly susceptible to such fungus diseases as mildew and oïdium, both of which run rampant in the humid climate of Japan.

Although the history of the Japanese vine goes back to the twelfth century, and vines have always been used as decoration and grapes for medicinal purposes, the story of Japanese wine is as recent as the nineteenth century, which saw the influx of Europeans and Americans. The agriculturally inquisitive and research-conscious Japanese, who had been recording their success with the Koshu *vinifera* variety since 1186, responded quickly to the new idea and sent people to France and to California to study the wine industry. The twentieth century has seen this industry grow and prosper in Japan, but it has yet to come into its own. The phenomenal growth of nearly every other sector of the Japanese economy since the Second World War has not been achieved in the wine industry.

Too many of the vineyards are small and hilly, so cultivation and harvesting are all done by hand. There are many cooperatives, but these are generally no better equipped or managed than the vineyards of individual producers. Three giant companies—Mercian, Mans Wine, and Suntory—control over 60% of the entire market. Most of these firms have plantations in the best wine district, the Kofu Valley in the Yamanashi prefecture 120 kilometers (75 miles) west of Tokyo. There the humidity and rainfall are less than in most other areas, and the warm days and cool nights help to produce better-than-average grapes. The very best wines made in the valley come from Cabernet Sauvignon, Merlot, and Sémillon, with a few pleasant ones made of the native Koshu variety. Many of these wines resemble those from the Hunter River Valley of Australia, where the temperatures, rainfall, and gravelly soil are not unlike those of the Kofu region. The best wines are light and dry; they are nearly all consumed in Kofu and in major cities, and hardly any are exported.

Japan imports annually about 200,000 hectoliters (5.2 million U.S. gallons, 4.3 million imp.) of bottled wine. Average annual per capita consumption is only 0.7 liter and despite high duties, optimists look to Japan as a vast new market for the future. In the early 1980s the taste trend was from sweet to dry whites.

A commentary on the quality of Japanese "port" has been given by a Japanese scientist in the *American Journal of Oenology*: "Natural production of Port wine by fermentation is not performed. Instead Port wine is made by blending 1–15% wine with ethyl alcohol, tap water, dye, perfume, sugar, and organic acids, and the resulting product is of unduly poor quality." Much wine is made from imported concentrates.

Japanese beetle

A parasite which attacks American vines.
See Chapter Eight, p. 31.

Jasnières (Appellation Contrôlée)

Loire Valley white wines.
District: Department of the Sarthe, France.

Jenever

A tiny Loire vineyard district in the Coteaux du Loir, north of the main stream. The wines are white dry, and *moelleaux*, or semi-sweet, and come from Chenin Blanc grapes grown in predominantly chalky soil. The vineyards are in the twin parishes of Lhomme and Ruillé-sur-Loire, and their output is not high.

Jenever

The name used in Holland for Dutch gin, which in English-speaking countries is usually called Hollands. Jenever is a combination of the French and Dutch words for juniper, on which the gin taste is based, and has no connection with the Swiss city.

Jerez de la Frontera

Andalusian town which is the center of the Sherry trade in southwestern Spain.
See Sherry.

Jeriñac

A registered name (also occasionally spelled Xereñac and Cherinac) for the brandy of Jerez de la Frontera, Spain. A little-used and unsuccessful substitute for the improper designation Coñac for Spanish brandy (because Cognac, however spelled, may correctly only be the brandy of Cognac in France).
See Spain.

Jeroboam

In Champagne it holds the equivalent of four bottles, in Bordeaux six. In England it is also normally (but not necessarily) six. Since 1981 the bottle manufacturers call it Bordelaise, containing 5 liters.

Jeropiga

See Geropiga.

Jigger

American term for shot-glass, or small measure of spirits. It equals 1.5 fluid ounces.

Johannisberg

(1) Great Growth of the Rheingau. The best-known of these wines is Schloss Johannisberger.
See Rheingau.
(2) Swiss wine from the Sylvaner grape which probably owes its renown to the fact that it shares the name of the great German Johannisberger.
See Switzerland.

Johannisberg Riesling

The name used in California for the true Riesling grape.

Johanniswein

From as early as *Minnesinger* records of the thirteenth century, St. John—who sat next to Christ at the Last Supper, and to whom legend ascribes the drinking of a goblet of poisoned wine without harm, after he made the sign of the Cross over it—has been connected in a special way with the blessing of wine in Germany. In Deidesheim, on St. John's day, December 27, the folk of the community take an especially fine bottle from their vineyards to Mass for blessing. This St. John's Wine, as it is called, is considered not only to benefit health and fertility but to bring peace as well, and it is often drunk as a loving-cup. Johanniswein is also much in demand as a wedding drink, and in many parts of Germany farewell drinks of "one for the road" are often of St. John's Wine. It is known that Martin Luther himself served these.

Jordan

Although in the distant past vineyards flourished in this part of the world and wine was regarded as a good and familiar thing, some 2,000 hectares (5,000 acres) of land now planted in vine are devoted almost entirely to table grapes.
The inhabitants of Jordan are not wine-drinking people; here, as elsewhere in the area, more arrack is made than wine.

Josephshof

Throughout the world (except in Germany, where Himmelreich is more famous) this is one of the best-known wines of Graach on the German Mosel River. Inclined, like the other Graach wines, to be long-lasting and mouth-filling, for a Mosel, this is one of the few wines permitted to be sold without the name of the specific vineyard site. Josephshof refers to the name of the (former) community, near Graach.
See Mosel-Saar-Ruwer.

Journal

An old Burgundian measure of area, about one-third of a hectare or five-sixths of an acre.

Julep

A long cold drink made with spirits (often Bourbon), sugar, mint, and crushed ice.

Juliénas (Appellation Contrôlée)

Widely known wines of the French Beaujolais. They tend to be obvious and seldom come quite up to the

Jura

reputation of the other more famous villages, Fleurie, Brouilly, or the wine of Moulin-à-Vent.

See Beaujolais.

Jura

Red, white, and rosé wines.
District: Jura Mountains, France.

From the slopes of the Jura Mountains, lying midway between the Côte d'Or of Burgundy and the Swiss border to the east, come a number of wines which make up in variety what they lack in quantity. Still and sparkling wines, red, white, and rosé wines, *vins de paille* or "straw wines," and the curious *vins jaunes*, or yellow wines, are all made under the inclusive *appellation* Côtes-du-Jura or Côtes-du-Jura Mousseux. Arbois, Château-Chalon, and L'Étoile are more specific: L'Étoile wines may only be white or *jaune*; the best white wines of the region are made at Arbois.

A landscape of sunny plains and steep cliffs, the Jura region has a wide variety of soil. Ranging from the almost pure clay of the lowlands, through the pebbly marl which has eroded the base of the cliffs, to the limestone-rich silt at the top, these slopes were once producers of wine in great quantity. The advent of phylloxera caused the vineyards to shrink drastically, and they have never been reconstituted. From about 18,400 hectares (46,000 acres) planted in 1836, the figure has dropped so far that today there are less than 1,000 hectares (2,500 acres) devoted to fine vines in the whole Jura area.

Perhaps the most characteristic wine of the Jura is *vin jaune*. Coming exclusively from the grape variety known as the Savagnin, thought to be the Alsatian Traminer, this is one of the longest-lived of white wines. Drinkable bottles aged fifty years or more are by no means rare. To obtain *vin jaune*, the grapes are harvested late and pressed in the same manner as for white wine. The juice is then sealed up in barrels and remains there for a length of time which varies from six to ten years—six years is the legal minimum. Shortly after the wine is put into the barrels, a film forms on the top, effectively sealing it off from the air. This film, which is made up of microorganisms, lives on oxygen from the air and contributes the peculiar yellow color and nutty fragrance that mark *vin jaune*. The film, or "flower," is the same as is found in the making of Sherry, where it is called *flor*. It is related to a disease of wine caused by the vinegar microbe, which combines oxygen and alcohol to make vinegar. The difference is that the vinegar microbe spoils the wine completely, whereas the microbe which appears on the wine of the Jura changes it slightly, with beneficial effect, and the wine remains the same white color as long as it is allowed to stand.

Another type of wine made in the Jura is *vin de paille*. It derives its name from the time-honored process of allowing the grapes to dry out on beds of straw before pressing, as well as from the straw color of the wine.

Actually, *vin de paille* is usually made today by hanging the grapes up in well-ventilated rooms. The long drying process, which by law must be at least two months, provides a wine of richness and longevity. Because of the difficulties of making this wine, and particularly because of the high price at which it has to be sold, the growers of the Jura are turning away from it, and there is some reason to fear that *vin de paille* may disappear from the area.

Very few of the wines of the Côtes-du-Jura are exported or shipped. Some is sold to Alsace and Switzerland, both in the vicintity of the Jura, but for the most part it is drunk in the area where it is made. One reason for this is that the wine is much appreciated by those who make it; and another is that, distinctive and unusual though they may be, the wines of the Jura are generally considered among *vins de pays*, excellent when drunk on native ground, but unable to stand comparison with the great wines of France. The wine of lesser quality, sold under the inclusive *appellation* Côtes-du-Jura, accounts for less than 25,000 hectoliters (660,000 U.S. gallons, 547,500 imp.) a year, and the balance is sold under the more exclusive names Arbois, Château-Chalon, and L'Étoile.

Arbois (Appellation Contrôlée)

Perhaps the best-known of the wines of the Jura. Made in thirteen towns in the lower foothills of the Jura Mountains, centering around the charming town of Arbois, it includes all the types described above.

The Savagnin grape variety, in addition to making *vin jaune*, also goes into the white wine to augment the Melon d'Arbois (as the Chardonnay variety is called in that area) and the Pinot Blanc *vrai*. The Poulsard, the Trousseau, and the Gros Noiren (the Pinot Noir of Burgundy) are the varieties that go into the red and rosé wines. Some of the white wines can be extremely pleasant. The red wines are not considered distinctive, but many Frenchmen, particularly around the Arbois area, maintain the Rosé d'Arbois is on a par with Tavel. Expert opinion, however, ranks it lower than this famous rosé wine of the Rhône.

The town of Arbois, besides being famous for its wines, is also known as the birthplace of Louis Pasteur, and as the place where he performed his famous experiments on wine. These experiments were made when the growers became concerned about the way their wines were spoiling on ocean voyages. The work had worldwide repercussions.

Château-Chalon (Appellation Contrôlée)

To the south and slightly to the west of the Arbois area is the small town of Château-Chalon, which gives its name to the wine grown there and in three adjoining towns. Under the Appellation d'Origine laws, only *vin jaune* is allowed to be sold under the name. This wine remains in the barrel for as long as six years—an excessive period for a white wine. At the end of this period the wine must—by law—be bottled. Less than 1,000 hectoliters (26,000 U.S. gallons, 20,000 imp.) is made each year.

The name is derived from an old castle which overlooks that area but which has nothing to do with the vineyards. (Note, therefore, that this is *not* a château wine.) Always bottled in wide, rather square bottles called *clavelins*, the only wine allowed to be put into such bottles, the *vin jaune* of Château-Chalon is considered to be the best example of this unique wine.

L'Étoile (Appellation Contrôlée)

Some of the best white wines of the Jura come from the southernmost area, that of L'Étoile, which comprises a small region of three communes. With an average production of less than 1,000 hectoliters (26,-500 U.S. gallons, 22,000 imp.), L'Étoile produces within its small area all the white wine types allowed in the Jura—white, yellow, *vin de paille*, and sparkling wines.

Jurançon (Appellation Contrôlée)

White wine.
District: Southwest France.

The vines are grown on the extremely steep hillsides in the foothills of the French Pyrenees—hillsides which are, for the most part, too steep to be cultivated by anything except the hand of man, although in some places animal and tractor power may be used. A limited amount of wine is grown along these slopes and among the foothills, the best toward the Atlantic—in the Jurançon region, near the city of Pau. The deep golden-white wines are usually sweet and have a flowery perfume uniquely their own. Only white wines are made.

At one time the vineyards of Jurançon were vast and important, but since the scourge of the phylloxera they have never reached their former productiveness. Some of the local growers are said to have shown a strong prejudice against grafting their vines onto American root-stocks—the only effective way of restoring the vineyards.

The spring frosts have a deadly effect upon the young shoots—and to combat this the vines are grown very tall. Stakes with cross-arms, making them look like fields of crosses—the unusual aspect of the region—support the vines, which are anywhere from 4 to 6 feet high. The productive parts of the vines are those trained on wires running from 3 to 4 feet from the ground, along which the vine shoots are trailed after the danger of frosts has passed.

The noble vines of the Jurançon area are the Gros Manseng, Petit Manseng, and Courbu, all of them old and all peculiar to the region. The wine made must be 85% from these vines and no more than 15% from the Carmaralet and Lauzet, the permissible secondary varieties. The vines are trimmed to carry from one to four long shoots, cut to yield from nine to fifteen cluster-producing buds or eyes. Short pruning (leaving only two or three eyes) is forbidden, and if a vine overproduces at the expense of its growth, it is regulated by leaving fewer shoots the next year. The fourth year after planting, the vines can produce grapes which may be included in the making of Jurançon wine. The maximum legal yield is 40 hectoliters per hectare (428 U.S. gallons, 356 imp. per acre).

The harvest in the Jurançon region is an extremely late one, the growers usually waiting for the *pourriture noble*, or noble rot, to form on their overripe grapes—this dries the liquid from them and leaves only a small amount of honey syrup. Sometimes the grapes are left on the vines until after Halloween. The rich, sweet wine is kept for four years in the barrel before it is bottled—and would probably be much better if it were bottled younger. Rather poor dry wine is produced—which has given this district a bad name. Less than 2,000 hectoliters is made each year—and much of it is consumed in the region of the Pyrenees, although the wine can be bought in Paris and elsewhere. About 15,000 hectoliters (400,000 U.S. gallons, 330,000 imp.) of the sweet wine is made annually.

K

Kabinettwein

German term for Cabinet wine, or a special reserve, denoting wines from the better selected barrels. This is more than just a term and can be considered a reliable line of quality demarcation, based mainly on price.
See Germany.

Kadarka

The leading red variety of grape in Hungary, known also in Rumania as Codarcă.

Kaefferkopf

Important vineyard in Ammerschwihr, Alsace.
See Alsace.

Kafir, Kefir

A Caucasian alcoholic beverage made from fermented cow's milk (*see* Koumiss). Kefir grain is added.

Kaiserstuhl

Best vineyard area in German Baden (*q.v.*).

Kallstadt

Wine town in the district of Bad Dürkheim.
See Palatinate.

Kamptal, Kamp Valley

Wine region of the River Kamp in Lower Austria. Some of the best slopes for vineyards are those of the Heiligenstein and the Gnisberg.
See Austria.

Kanyak

Turkish brandy whose name, to the suspicious, seems remarkably close to Cognac.

Karthäuserhofberg

Outstanding vineyard in the German town of Eitelsbach.
See Mosel-Saar-Ruwer.

Kasel

Most important village of German Ruwer wines. The best vineyard is Kaseler Nies'chen.
See Mosel-Saar-Ruwer.

Kava, ava-ava

A native wine of the South Sea Islands prepared from the root of the Polynesian kava shrub.

"The liquor which they make from the plant called the ava-ava is expressed from the root. The manner of preparing this liquor is as simple as it is disgusting to a European. It is thus: several people take some of the root, and chew it until it is soft and pulpy: then they spit it out into a platter or other vessel, every one into the same: when a sufficient quantity is chewed more or less, water is put to it according as it is to be strong or weak: the juice thus diluted is strained through some fibrous stuff like fine shavings: after which it is fit for drinking, and this is always done immediately. It has a pepperish taste, drinks flat, and rather insipid."—Captain Cook, 1774, at Tahiti.

Nowadays kava is usually made in a screw-type press.

Kaysersberg

Wine town in Alsace (*q.v.*).

Keg

Small wood or metal cask usually of less than 12 U.S. gallons (10 imp.) capacity.

Kéknyelű

A white wine, best-known of the Badacsony growths in Hungary (*q.v.*).

Kellerabfüllung, Kellerabzug

Formerly, a German term for bottled at the estate where the wine was grown. Literally, "bottled in the cellar."

Kintyre

A peninsula on the west coast of Scotland which, with the island of Islay, produces all West Highland malt whisky. Well into the eighteenth century, Kintyre was still considered a main island of the Inner Hebrides.
See Whisky, malt.

Kir

A popular aperitif usually made with a light white Burgundy wine and a bit of Cassis. The drink is named for the leader of French resistance in Lyon and former mayor of Dijon, Canon Félix Kir.

Kirsch, Kirschwasser

Brandy distilled from cherries complete with stones. After distillation, it is matured in paraffin-lined casks or earthenware, to prevent it taking on the color that wood would impart; true kirsch is always pure white.

Kirsch is made notably in Alsace, Germany, and Switzerland; the German kirsch often goes under the name Schwarzwalder. Much Swiss kirsch is made in the vicinity of Basle and carries the name Basler Kirschwasser.

Château Kirwan

Bordeaux red wine.
District: Haut-Médoc, France.
Commune: Cantenac-Margaux.

The vineyard lies on slightly rolling land behind Cantenac, one of the first important villages encountered on the Médoc wine road. Kirwan is between Château Brane-Cantenac, a Second Growth (*Second Cru*) vineyard, and Château Prieuré-Lichine, a Fourth Growth (*Quatrième Cru*).

Since 1955, all Cantenac vineyards have had the right to the place-name Margaux, the famous wine town a mile away which produces a very similar wine.

Kirwan was rated a Third Growth (*Troisième Cru*) in the Classification of 1855. It was then owned by a M. Godard, Mayor of Bordeaux, who left it to the city of Bordeaux upon his death. They city sold it to Daniel and Georges Guestier. Daniel's daughter married Alfred Schyler, and in 1924 his firm, Schröder & Schyler, purchased the property and has owned it ever since.

In the 1950s and early 1960s the wine was not château-bottled; the vineyard was in very poor condition and production dropped significantly. Jean-Henri Schyler, the present head of Schröder & Schyler, who owns the handsome château, went into partnership with M. Jean-Marie Moueix, cousin of Jean-Pierre Moueix, the Saint-Émilion grower and shipper. They performed an exemplary feat, revitalizing the vineyard with earthmovers in 1972 and some planting in 1973. Such expense would have been unthinkable had not Jean-Marie Moueix, the new partner, contributed the necessary investment for the vineyard. The Classified Growths reached prices in 1970 which justified the tremendous cost.

Characteristics. Fruity and distinguished, Kirwan is one of the most elegant, feminine wines of Margaux. It has become much more reliable since château-bottling became mandatory in 1970.

Vineyard area: 30 hectares (75 acres).
Average production: 150 *tonneaux* (14,000 cases).

Kislav

A Russian spirit made from watermelons.

Kloster Eberbach

Once a Cistercian monastery, now owned by the state. The vineyard, near Hattenheim, produces the fine Steinberg wine.
See Rheingau.

Knipperlé

A white-wine grape used in Alsace. Among other local names for it are Kipperlé, Kleinergelber, and Kleiner Rauschling.

Königsbacher

One of the outstanding wines in the Mittelhaardt region of the Palatinate.
See Palatinate.

Konsumwein

German term for ordinary wine.

Kontuszowka

A Polish liqueur with the flavor of oil of lavender.

Kornbranntwein

A liquor made in Germany and Holland from fermented cereal grains. Since rye is the usual ingredient, it is almost a continental equivalent of rye whiskey.

Kornschnapps

A European liquor made of fermented corn.

Kosher wine

In its strictest sense, wine made according to rabbinical law for use during Jewish religious services. The term also covers what is essentially Passover wine, which was for some time, by a considerable margin, the largest-selling wine in the United States.

Jewish ritual calls for wine at the Friday evening service, on the eve of a festival, on Holy Days, and during the Passover season. The wine must be pure, natural, unmixed, and sound, and must be made according to rigid standards of purity under the supervision of a rabbi, but otherwise it is not different from wine for everyday consumption. Kosher wine can serve both purposes. Passover wine—once homemade for the most part—differs in that it is thicker and sweeter than is usual, and it has become synonymous with Kosher wine in most of America.

In the United States, the bulk of the supply of Kosher wines comes from Concord grapes grown in the vineyards of New York State—where Concord used to command such a good price that it pushed out finer grape varieties. But substantial quantities are also imported from Israel, and, especially at Passover, limited amounts from France and other European countries.

American Kosher wine centers are New York City and Chicago, neither of which is noted for vines. As a general rule, grapes grown in upper New York State are bought by fruit-packers who freeze them and ship them as needed to the wineries, where they are thawed, allowed to ferment, dosed with cane sugar (partly to increase sweetness, partly to counteract the otherwise unpleasantly high acidity of the Concord grape), and doctored with sulfur to prevent fermentation after bottling. Wine-making is thus a year-round occupation, no longer dependent upon such old-fashioned matters as time of harvest.

Koumiss, kumiss

A Siberian or Caucasian beverage of fermented mare's, cow's, or sometimes camel's milk.

Krajina

Yugoslav wines, mainly red but some white, grown on the borders of Rumania and Bulgaria. Krajina means "borderland."
See Yugoslavia.

Krampen

A section of wineland around Cochem on the lower River Mosel in Germany, so called because of the sharp bend or cramp taken by the Mosel to accommodate itself to the increasing hardness of the slate cliffs.

The wines are not among the best of the Mosel because the soil is too hard.
See Mosel-Saar-Ruwer.

Kreszenz

Previously, one of the German words indicating the grower of a wine. Kreszenz Hans Muller on a label would mean wine from the vineyard, or parcel, of Hans Muller. This is important in Germany, where each barrel may be harvested individually and most vineyards have many owners, often handling their wines differently and getting widely different results.

Kriska

West African palm wine.

Kümmel

Both Germany and Holland claim to have invented the liqueur, but Russia, Poland, and the Baltic countries have always been among its staunchest admirers. It is distilled from grain alcohol and is flavored with caraway seeds; it is sweet and pure-white. Sugar is sometimes allowed to crystallize in the bottle, in which case it is known as Kümmel Crystallize. One of the most famous types of kümmel is Allasch Kümmel, made in Allasch near Riga, now in the U.S.S.R.
See Liqueurs.

Kvass

A refreshing Russian beer home-brewed from rye, barley, and malt and flavored with mint or cranberries.

L

La Brède (Château de la Brède)

See Château de la Brède.

Château La Conseillante

Bordeaux red wine.
District and Commune: Pomerol, France.

The vineyards of this top Pomerol château are separated from those of Château Cheval-Blanc in Saint-Émilion by only the width of a cart-path. Owned by the Nicolas family since 1871, it is one of the most highly respected vineyards of Pomerol.

Vineyard area: 11 hectares (27.5 acres).
Average production: 40 *tonneaux* (3,500 cases).

Château La Gaffelière

Bordeaux red wine.
District and Commune: Saint-Émilion, France.

Considered by some experts to be one of the better Saint-Émilion, the property is beautifully situated on the sharply curving short road which cuts from the main Bordeaux-Bergerac road up to the hillcrest town of Saint-Émilion. It is the property of Comte Malet-Roquefort, and was classed a First Great Growth (*Premier Grand Cru*) in 1955 and in 1986. The name has been shortened since 1963 by dropping Naudes and calling it simply Château La Gaffelière. This wine, for some, has been found to be unreasonably high in price.

Characteristics. Good wines, yet variable. In good years, among the best of Saint-Émilion.

Vineyard area: 22 hectares (55 acres).
Average production: 88 *tonneaux* (8,500 cases).

Château La Lagune

Bordeaux red wine.
District: Haut-Médoc, France.
Commune: Ludon.

(Ludon is not a place-name and the wine has the place-name of Haut-Médoc.)

A Third Growth (*Troisième Cru*) as classified in 1855, La Lagune is the first of the classified vineyards reached on the wine road of the Médoc going north from Bordeaux. The wines were both great and famous at the turn of the century. At that time, in order to distinguish the vineyard from others known as La Lagune, the name was changed to Grand-La-Lagune, but in the late sixties, the name reverted to La Lagune. The quality of the wine fell from its former high standard in the thirties and forties; when the severe 1956 frosts cut production to only 15 *tonneaux*, considerable replanting was necessary. The vineyard was until re-

cently the property of the Société Civile Agricole du Château Grand-La-Lagune. After the 1956 frost they embarked on the boldest planting program in the Médoc: a scheme which called for enlarging and improving the vineyard, modernizing the wine-making installations, and restoring the château to what it was when built during the reigns of Louis XIII and Louis XIV. It is now owned by the heirs of M. Chayoux of the Ayala Champagne firm.

Characteristics. A wine of great quality; as a result of the efforts now being made, it has regained and surpassed its former high position. The wine is full, with a depth of flavor, and has much of the breed found in Margaux to the north and some of the character associated with Graves to the south.

Vineyard area: 70 hectares (175 acres).
Average production: 280 *tonneaux* (24,000 cases).

Château La Magdelaine

Bordeaux red wine.
District and Commune: Saint-Émilion, France.

Particularly well known in England and Belgium, the wine was classified as a First Growth (*Premier Cru*) of Saint-Émilion in 1955. The vineyard lies alongside those of Ausone and Bel-Air on the heights of Saint-Émilion village. The vineyard is owned by Jean-Pierre Moueix.

Characteristics. The well-tended vineyards produce a pleasant wine which is full and velvety with distinctive aftertaste.

Vineyard area: 11 hectares (27 acres).
Average production: 40 *tonneaux* (3,500 cases).

Château La Mission-Haut-Brion

Bordeaux red wine.
District: Graves, France.
Commune: Talence.

The château, placed behind symmetrical vines and directly across the main road from Haut-Brion, is less than a mile out of Bordeaux on the road to the seaside resort of Arcachon. The red-wine vines surround the château and border the tracks of the Bordeaux-to-Spain railway, running in a cutting a hundred paces from the *chais*. The red wine was classified in 1953 and in 1959 among the eleven best in Graves.

The vineyard was founded in the seventeenth century by the priests of the Mission of Saint Vincent de Paul. A gem of monastic art remains to commemorate the founders: a tiny peaked chapel, on the inner roof of which the years of great vintages used to be lettered in gold—until the gold was given to the government during the war.

When the grapes are brought in, they are pitched into a sixteenth-century wooden trough; but the wines ferment in immaculate modern glass-lined vats. The previous owners, the Woltner family and Francis DeWavrin-Woltner, sold wines at a high price—fully justified, since the vineyard produces some remarkable bottles. They also owned Château La Tour-Haut-Brion and Château Laville-Haut-Brion, which produce a good red and a great white wine respectively. All three of these properties were bought by Château Haut-Brion in 1983.

Characteristics. A superb red wine. Many knowledgeable brokers classify the wine as having the same character as Château Haut-Brion across the road, but it matures more rapidly. It achieves full big roundness with considerable breed.

Vineyard area: 17 hectares (42.5 acres).
Average production: 70 *tonneaux* (6,000 cases).

Château La Pointe

Bordeaux red wine.
District and Commune: Pomerol, France.

Owned by M. d'Arfeuille, wine merchant of Libourne, this flavorful wine is, as is the estate, one of the biggest in Pomerol.

Vineyard area: 20 hectares (50 acres).
Average production: 80 *tonneaux* (7,500 cases).

La Rioja

Wine-producing province of Argentina *(q.v.)*.

La Romanée

Burgundy red wine.
District: Côte de Nuits, France.
Commune: Vosne-Romanée.
Official Classification: Great Growth (Grand Cru).

La Romanée is the smallest (less than a hectare, or about 2.1 acres) of the great vineyards of Vosne. It stands directly above La Romanée-Conti, from which it is divided by a footpath, and despite their proximity and the similarity between the names and the wines, the two are separate and distinct.

It is generally conceded in Vosne that the wines which come from this plot often lack some of the elegance and finesse of those from La Romanée-Conti; but the two are difficult to tell apart, even by the most expert tasters. La Romanée is perhaps the more robust of the two, gaining in fullness and body what it cedes in finesse.

The vineyard is now owned by the Domaine de la Romanée-Conti and annually makes but 30 hectoliters (795 U.S. gallons, 660 imp.) of wine, or the equivalent of a mere 350 cases. But as the sale and distribution of the wine are now entrusted to a shipper, the wine is never estate-bottled, and this is regrettable.

See Vosne-Romanée.

La Romanée-Conti

Burgundy red wine.
District: Côte de Nuits, France.
Commune: Vosne-Romanée.
Official Classification: Great Growth (Grand Cru).

The vineyard of the Romanée-Conti, one of the most famous in the world, is contained in a scant four and a half acres. The fabulous prices paid for the wine that trickles out are as high as any, and the wine-drinker who manages to get a bottle considers himself lucky indeed. If the wine has become overpriced, it is largely the fault of the wine snobs who order it to impress and so send up prices.

Contrary to usual Burgundian practice, *all* wine from the Romanée-Conti is estate-bottled, and every bottle carries on label and cork the seal of the Société Civile de La Romanée-Conti, owners of this vineyard and the renowned La Tâche, as well as of parts of others. The property has been in the same family since 1869, when it was bought by Monsieur Duvaut-Blochet, and that was only the ninth time it had changed hands since the thirteenth century. The vineyard has been passed down within the family and is owned today by Monsieur de Villaine, a bank manager in Moulins, and by Madame Bise-Leroy. Among previous owners have been the Government of France, which seized the vineyard during the French Revolution; and the Prince de Conti, from whom it was seized. The Prince had acquired it in 1760, in spite of the protests of Madame de Pompadour, who wanted it for herself.

Because the wine is estate-bottled, the only significant collection of older vintages of Romanée-Conti is at the Domaine, and a visit to its cellars is a mouth-watering experience. These cellars are primitive and modest, but stacked with bottles the contents of which have been described by P. Morton Shand as "a mingling of velvet and satin."

Actually, the wines fall into two distinct categories: the pre-1945 vintages, and those thereafter. Until that year the owners of the vineyard kept it planted in French vines, rather than graft their French plants onto American root-stocks as did the other growers when phylloxera first hit France. The vines had been allowed to reproduce by *provignage*—burying the old vine in the ground with only one shoot emerging to become a new one—and thus were direct descendants of the vines planted by the monks more than twelve centuries earlier. But phylloxera, the devastating vine louse, is a constant menace and the vines had to be treated with enormous care and expensive chemicals. The latter were, of course, nonexistent during the war years, manpower was desperately short, and the vines deteriorated until they were giving a meager fifty cases a year. In 1945 the owners gave up the old ways and tore up their vineyards, replanting with vines grafted onto phylloxera-resistant American root-stocks.

The result is that the quantity of Romanée-Conti

has risen sharply since 1945, but the quality is at present below that of the nectar once made.

At their best, the wines of the Romanée-Conti have perfect, rich balance combined with extraordinary breed and finesse, and local experts maintain they are the most "virile" of the wines of Vosne—meaning, perhaps, that there is an iron hand beneath the velvet glove. The wines have an aftertaste that stays in the mouth an amazingly long time. While quantity is definitely higher than it was once, it is still not considerable. An average harvest may come to only 60 hectoliters (1,590 U.S. gallons, 1,320 imp.) or 700 cases.

See Vosne-Romanée.

La Romanée-Saint-Vivant

Burgundy red wine.
District: Côte de Nuits, France.
Commune: Vosne-Romanée.
Official Classification: Great Growth (Grand Cru).

The vineyard is a Great Growth (*Grand Cru*), one of the thirty-one outstanding great vineyards of the Côte d'Or, five of which are in Vosne. Occupying 9.5 hectares, or 23.6 acres, it is the largest of the Great Growths of Vosne and takes its name from the long-since-destroyed Abbey of Saint-Vivant, its owner for a considerable period.

Romanée-Saint-Vivant is just down the hill from Romanée-Conti and Richebourg, above the village of Vosne, and despite its large size there are only four growers who share it. The wines have the qualities and characteristics of the other Great Growths of Vosne: the same velvety grace, and the expansive perfume. However, if the vines were not pruned so as to produce maximum quantity, the wines could be even better. It is also unfortunate that some unworthy vintages were bottled under the La Romanée-Saint-Vivant place-name, a practice which only harms the name. Today, the wines are vinified and managed by Domaine de la Romanée Conti. They are undoubtedly among the great wines of Burgundy. Some 300 hectoliters (7,950 U.S. gallons, 6,600 imp.) are made each year.

La Senancole

Herb-based liqueur named after the River Senancole resembling yellow Chartreuse, made originally by Cistercian monks of the Abbey of Senanque, in Provence. It is now made by a commercial distiller, but under the supervision of the monks.

La Tâche

Burgundy red wine.
District: Côte de Nuits, Vosne-Romanée, France.
Official Classification: Great Growth (Grand Cru).

La Tâche means "the task" and is associated with the concept of piecework. It is not known, however,

whether the early workers in this vineyard were paid by work accomplished rather than by the hour, or whether the name is a corruption of some other, unknown word.

The legal place-name actually embraces more than just the vineyard of La Tâche. This comprises some 3½ acres, but the name has been extended to take in 6 hectares (14.9 acres) by giving the franchise to adjoining plots such as Les Gaudichots and La Grande Rue, which stand between La Tâche and the twin Romanée and Romanée-Conti. This enlargement took place in 1936, when the laws covering Burgundy were drawn up.

La Tâche, like Romanée-Conti, is a vineyard that has but one owner: the Société Civile de la Romanée-Conti. The wines resemble those of the society's more famous growth, but are more delicate, yet they are full-bodied, with an amazing depth of flavor. In recent years, La Tâche has frequently come forth with better wines than those of Romanée-Conti, although neither is largely made. Production is the equivalent of about 1,700 cases.

Château La Tour-Blanche

Bordeuax white wine.
District: Sauternes, France.
Commune: Bommes.

The estate has slipped from the quality that caused it to be placed high among the Sauternes First Growths (*Premiers Crus*), second only to Château d'Y-quem in the Classification of 1855. On the other hand, the wine now being made, definitely lighter and less sweet than its neighbors in the Bommes-Sauternes district, has its followers. M. Daniel Osiris gave the château and vineyards to France in 1910 on the condition that it be used as a viticultural school. The Ministry of Agriculture has operated the vineyard since 1955.

Characteristics. Light and less sweet for a Sauternes, tending very slightly to be dry, and with a typical vigor.

Vineyard area: 27 hectares (68 acres).

Average production: 60 *tonneaux* (5,500 cases).

Château La Tour-Carnet

Bordeaux red wine.
District: Haut-Médoc, France.
Commune: Saint-Laurent.

(*Saint-Laurent is not a place-name and the wine carries the* appellation *Haut-Médoc.*)

Classified a Fourth Growth (*Quatrième Cru*) of the Médoc in 1855. The square tower—the donjon of a thirteenth-century castle—that gives the wine its name overlooks one of the most beautiful properties of the Médoc, and the vineyard was famous and commanded leading prices as far back as 1354. Until recently very little wine was made, and cow pastures seem to have been more important to the former owner than the vines. But since the mid-sixties, through the considerable time and effort of its present owner, M. Lipschitz, the vineyards, *chai*, and château have been vastly improved. The estate is a good example of the marginal property which has been able to regain its standing in the 1855 Classification through the very high prices paid for it in Bordeaux today.

Characteristics. Improved in recent years. Good and sound wine.

Vineyard area: 30 hectares (75 acres).

Average production: 120 *tonneaux* (11,000 cases).

Château La Tour-Haut-Brion

Bordeaux red wine.
District: Graves, France.
Commune: Talence.

La Tour-Haut-Brion is one of the three Haut-Brion suffix wine châteaux on the outskirts of Bordeaux—the others being La Mission-Haut-Brion and Laville-Haut-Brion. Like La Mission-Haut-Brion, La Tour-Haut-Brion was classed as a First Growth (*Premier Cru*) of Graves in 1953 and 1959. Both then belonged to the Woltner family, but in 1983 these châteaux, along with Château Laville-Haut-Brion, were purchased by Château Haut-Brion, the great First Growth (*Premier Cru*) belonging to the Dillon family.

Characteristics. Full, rather hard wines, similar to those of La Mission-Haut-Brion but less fine.

Vineyard area: 4 hectares (10 acres).

Average production: 20 *tonneaux* (1,500 cases).

Château La Tour-Martillac (Kressmann-La Tour)

Bordeaux red and white wine.
District: Graves, France.
Commune: Martillac.

In front of the low, long farmhouse-like château on the slope of Martillac, south of Bordeaux, is the tower which gives the wine its name. It is all that remains of a château built in the twelfth century and probably destroyed in the French Revolution.

Red and white wines are made. For many years, the white wine has been aged in big barrels the size of the German Rhine and Mosel *Halbstück*, instead of the usual Bordeaux barrel of 225 liters, to see if fruitier wines might not be obtained from the greater mass of liquid in proportion to the wood surface through which the wine breathes. A slightly larger barrel means less oxidation, so that the wine should stay young longer. This experiment has had ample time to prove itself, and the owners believe that they have improved the quality of their wine, classified with the other best whites of Graves in 1955. The red wines, too, were classified, both in 1953 and 1959.

Since 1928 La Tour-Martillac has belonged to the Kressmann family of Bordeaux. The Kressmanns, well-known shippers of good wine, bought it outright when the last owner died and they were threatened with the loss of a wine which had been a favorite of their clientele for several generations.

Characteristics. Both the red and white wines are pleasant and clean, and happily now château-bottled.

Vineyard area: red—20 hectares (50 acres); white—5 hectares (12.5 acres).

Average production: red—90 *tonneaux* (8,000 cases); white—20 *tonneaux* (2,000 cases).

Château La Tour-de-Mons

Bordeaux red wine.
District: Haut-Médoc, France.
Commune: Soussans-Margaux.

Owned, up to the early seventies, by the proprietor of Château Cantemerle, La Tour-de-Mons has for years had the benefit of the careful viticultural treatment which has raised Cantemerle far above its position as a Fifth Growth (*Cinquième Cru*). Château La Tour-de-Mons, ranked a Bourgeois Growth (*Cru Bourgeois*) in the 1855 Médoc Classification, also justifies a higher rating. The vineyard is today managed by M. Bertrand Clauzel, former mayor of Soussans. The estate has an old ruined tower tangled in vine and was founded in 1289 by Jehan Colomb of Bordeaux, one of whose Italian relatives was to discover America two centuries later. Subsidiary vineyards are Château Terrefort and Château Richeterre.

Charactertistics. A very fine round wine with all the delicacy of Margaux. Although a Bourgeois Growth, it is one of the good ones in this old-fashioned category. It deserves a better rating, since it produces wines finer than some Classified Growths. Its present good ownership guarantees that the wine will be well made.

Vineyard area: 30 hectares (75 acres).

Average production: 120 *tonneaux* (10,000 cases).

Labrusca

A species of grapevine (*Vitis labrusca*) found in North America.

See Chapter Eight, p. 31.

Lacrima (or Lacryma) Christi del Vesuvio

A soft and fairly dry D.O.C. white wine made from grapes grown along the southern slopes of Mount Vesuvius—not to be confused with the Lágrima of Málaga. A red wine is also produced.

See Campania.

Ladoix-Serrigny (Appellation Contrôlée)

Burgundy red and white wines.
District: Côte de Beaune, France.

Little wine is sold under the place-name Ladoix-Serrigny. Wines are made, but the bulk may be sold as Côte de Beaune-Villages, and the best with those of next-door Aloxe-Corton. Because of the option, the amount of Ladoix-Serrigny varies; about 2,000 hecto-liters (53,000 U.S. gallons, 44,000 imp.) is average for red wine, but only 100 hectoliters of white is generally produced.

The town is the northernmost of the Côte de Beaune and is bisected by the Route nationale (National Highway) No. 74, which runs from Dijon south to Lyon and on to the Côte d'Azur. The name comes from the Celtic *doix* (fountain); besides being a source of wine, the town has a spring. Serrigny, the other half of the commune, is an ancient hamlet which sits on the east—and, viticulturally speaking, the wrong—side of the National Highway. Throughout the Côte d'Or, wines growing on the slopes west of the highway have the right to the great place-names, while those to the east can do no better than the general name Burgundy.

The vineyards Les Vergennes and Le Rognet, bordering on Aloxe-Corton, are officially allowed the place-names of Corton and Corton-Charlemagne, and those immediately adjoining are Aloxe-Corton (for list *see* Aloxe-Corton). These wines tend to resemble their neighbors in all respects, and the lesser wines of the town are light-bodied and fast-maturing, often with an entrancing bouquet. The grapes are grown on about 136 hectares (335 acres).

Château Lafaurie-Peyraguey

Bordeaux white wine.
District: Sauternes, France.
Commune: Bommes.

Placed on a slightly lower hilltop opposite that of Château d'Yquem, the Moorish-looking walled castle, built in the thirteenth century, looks out through its fortified gates over the sloping sea of its vines. The *chai* is inside the courtyard, and there one of the most full-bodied of the Sauternes may be tasted, excellent when very young from the barrel, as fine Sauternes always are. The vineyard was classified a First Growth (*Premier Cru*) in 1855.

Characteristics. If the 1855 Classification were to be revised, these wines might be downgraded. Not as rich as many of the better Sauternes, yet distinguished wines.

Vineyard area: 18 hectares (45 acres).
Average production: 60 *tonneaux* (4,500 cases).

Château Lafite

Bordeaux red wine.
District: Haut-Médoc, France.
Commune: Pauillac.

Château Lafite, one of the best red wines of Bordeaux—which is to say, one of the most elegant wines in the world—has eight centuries of history behind it. In 1234 it was the property of Gombaud de Lafite; and a hundred years later the wines were already famous. In the eighteenth century, Mme de Pompadour served

them; and Mme Dubarry said that since Bordeaux was the king's favorite, she would drink nothing else. Lafite claims to have been in each case the chosen wine, and it may very well have been so.

The vineyard was at one time owned by the Marquis Alexandre de Ségur, proprietor also of Château Latour and Château Calon-Ségur. It became public property in 1794, after the owner (the president of the parliament of Guyenne) was guillotined in the Revolution; and afterward it was bought, first by a Dutch syndicate (in whose time the first bottles of vintage wine were laid down) and in 1821 by the English banker Sir Samuel Scott. The Rothschild family acquired Lafite when it was put up for auction in 1868. The bidding was so extraordinarily high that it was said only a Rothschild could triumph; and, indeed, the château went to Baron James de Rothschild for slightly more than $3,000,000 (£1,200,000). By an odd coincidence—or perhaps it was the association that whetted his interest—the Rothschild bank in Paris is in the rue Laffitte.

Lafite will be found on early labels spelled with two *t*'s or two *f*'s or both; and the name itself is said to derive from the old Médoc word *lahite*, which was a corruption of *la hauteur* (the height). Lafite is the highest knoll of the Pauillac area, which merges into the adjoining commune of Saint-Estèphe. The château sits high above the marshland bordering the Gironde. Great ocean-bound vessels can be seen from the windows, throwing up feathers of smoke into a clear sky, or can be heard hooting their way through the mist.

Two of the many owners of Lafite are Eric de Rothschild and Élie de Rothschild, the cousin of Philippe de Rothschild of Château Mouton-Rothschild, and between their wines—the vineyards actually touch—a kind of competition now developed. Lafite is made from the grape varieties Cabernet Sauvignon and Franc, Petit Verdot, and much Merlot, which imparts the softness for which this wine is famous. Mouton, however, having very little Merlot, is 70% Cabernet Sauvignon, and so is harder.

Lafite is proud of its great name, and no wine which is not of the first quality (the wine from young vines, for instance) is allowed to bear it. Such wine is sold instead as Moulin des Carruades. Other properties of this Rothschild branch of the family include the Château Duhart-Milon in Pauillac (*q.v.*), Clark-Malmaison in Saint-Estèphe, recently bought and autonomously run by Eric de Rothschild, and La Cardonne in the Bas-Médoc.

The estate, now run by Eric de Rothschild, consists of some 120 hectares (300 acres), three-quarters of it devoted to viticulture. There, as in other vineyards of the Médoc, the vines are planted about a meter apart and are carefully trained along two or three rows of thin sticks to keep them from damage by contact with the earth, with the plow, or even with a brisk wind. Here, as everywhere in the Médoc, the trellises are 35 centimeters from the ground and each vine runs horizontally along a wire. The owners of Lafite say that the north-south exposure of the vineyard is conducive to early ripening and that the misty atmosphere gives the grapes their thin skins, which, when they ripen, become glassily transparent. From this time nobody is allowed in the vineyard, lest the grapes be bruised.

The *chais* cluster round the château; and in the great *cuverie*, or vat-house, are twenty-four Bosnian oak vats, each holding 12,500 liters (3,300 U.S. gallons, 2,750 imp.). The château itself, set on a handsome eighteenth-century terrace, is shown on the labels. Vines grow right up to the garden walls; the house is built of pale stone, throwing into relief the green of two magnolias and an ancient cedar tree.

The old cellars of the château are heavily vaulted, their four long galleries lit by wrought-iron chandeliers, each holding six electric candles. Here is the most impressive sight in Lafite: a rank of bins, each with its wooden vintage plaque. The walls are black with mold and the bottles seem to be covered with fur. The earliest is 1797; others still have their labels 1801, 1805, and 1811, the year of the comet, said to be the best vintage of the early nineteenth century. 1870 was a famous year in the history of Lafite. Other great classical vintages were 1893, 1895, 1900, 1906, 1923, and 1926. Fine years were 1874, 1875, 1878, 1899, 1904, 1911, 1916. In 1905 the wine was light but had an exquisite flavor; in 1934 it was full-bodied and mellow. Although slow-maturing, 1945 is a classic of all time; 1949 and 1952 are excellent; while 1953 was one of the greatest of recent decades, exemplifying Lafite at its very best. Since then, the superb 1955 has been overshadowed by the fabulous 1959, 1961, 1966, 1970, and especially 1978, which reached very high prices but will nevertheless be regarded as classics. New underground cellars built in 1987 are in keeping with older ones.

Since wine ages more slowly in large bottles, there are many magnums and double magnums stocked in the Lafite cellars, as well as imperials, which hold eight bottles; the stone staircases leading to the cellars are lined with Jeroboams (five bottles). The bottles are recorked every twenty-five years. When the cork deteriorates, so that the wine begins to evaporate, the bottle is "leaky"—*couleuse*—and is then filled again; at Lafite this happens to about 5,000 bottles every year.

Characteristics. In great years, when Lafite is successful, it can be supreme. It has great finesse and a particular softness imparted by the Merlot grape. The wine tends to be firm yet delicate and supple, with an eventual lightness developed in age. Lesser vintages are still excellent wines, lighter than those of great years. In the seventies a few disappointing vintages were produced.

Vineyard area: 88 hectares (220 acres).
Average production: 250 *tonneaux* (22,000 cases).

Château Lafleur

Bordeaux red wine.
District and Commune: Pomerol, France.

On a very gravelly soil, producing a very flavorful wine, this superb small vineyard has for many years been owned by the Robin sisters, who also own Château Le Gay in Pomerol.

Vineyard area: 4 hectares (10 acres).
Average production: 14 *tonneaux* (1,200 cases).

Château Lafleur-Pétrus

Bordeaux red wine.
District and Commune: Pomerol, France.

Adjoining the very famous Château Pétrus, this reliable vineyard lives up to the connotations of its name. It is owned and excellently managed by J.-P. Moueix, one of the largest shippers of Saint-Émilion wines.

Vineyard area: 9 hectares (22 acres).
Average production: 35 *tonneaux* (3,000 cases).

Château Lafon-Rochet

Bordeaux red wine.
District: Haut-Médoc, France.
Commune: Saint-Estèphe.

The only Fourth Growth (*Quatrième Cru*) Classification of 1855 in Saint-Estèphe, Lafon-Rochet is owned by Guy Tesseron, who has recently increased the size of the vineyard and improved the wine.

Rebuilt in 1973, a good-looking château is located in the midst of the large plateau overlooking the vineyards; at the same time, considerably new cellarage was built under the château.

Characteristics. The wine has improved in the past decade. Recent vintages have achieved encouraging results.

Vineyard area: 45 hectares (113 acres).
Average production: 160 *tonneaux* (12,900 cases).

Lager

See Beer.

Château Lagrange

Bordeaux red wine.
District: Haut-Médoc, France.
Commune: Saint-Julien.

This large estate spread over the high slopes two miles back from the Gironde was purchased in 1983 by Suntory, the Japanese wine-and-spirits firm, from a Spanish family. Undoubtedly, both quality and quantity have been increased. It was classed a Third Growth (*Troisième Cru*) of Médoc in 1855. Later in the nineteenth century, the vineyard was the largest Classified Growth in the entire region, with nearly 300 hectares (750 acres) of vines.

Characteristics. Until the mid-1960s, the vineyard made poor wines which simply did not deserve the high classification of Third Growth. Within the past few years Lagrange has improved, and is now making

Château Lagrange

better wines. Suntory took over the responsibility with the 1983 vintage which is greatly improved. The cellar complex was demolished and rebuilt in 1986 with air-conditioned *chais*.

Vineyard area: 110 hectares (275 acres).
Average production: 500 *tonneaux* (40,000 cases).

Château Lagrange

Bordeaux red wine.
District and Commune: Pomerol, France.

A good wine characteristic of the district is made by this château situated on the Pomerol plateau in the midst of the best vineyards. Sometimes referred to as Lagrange-Pomerol to distinguish it from Château Lagrange in Saint-Julien.

Vineyard area: 8 hectares (20 acres).
Average production: 30 *tonneaux* (2,500 cases).

Lágrima

A sweet, fortified Málaga wine, not to be confused with the Lacrima Christi grown near Naples, although both wines are golden in color and Lágrima and Lacrima both mean "tear."

See Málaga.

Lake Erie

Important wine district in the eastern United States. Vineyards are established on the mainland, centering around Sandusky but also on the islands Kelley, North Bass, South Bass, and Middle Bass. Good American grape varieties are used, of which the favorites are the Catawba and the Delaware. Both red and white wines are produced and some interesting sparkling wines.

See United States: Ohio.

Lalande de Pomerol (Appellation Contrôlée)

Bordeaux red wine.
District: Bordeaux, France.

The commune, which now includes Néac, adjoins the famous region of Pomerol in southwest France, but the wines, although similar to Pomerols, have a distinct taste. Several of them compare well with all but the finest Pomerols. Château Bel-Air, just across the line from Pomerol, is outstanding.

See Pomerol.

Lambrusco (D.O.C.s: di Sorbara, Grasparossa, Reggiano, and Salamino)

(1) A sweetish semi-sparkling red wine of little virtue, from the Emilia-Romagna region of Italy. It has no connection with the *Vitis labrusca* of America.

(2) Grape grown in Italy for red wine, especially in Emilia-Romagna and the Alto Adige.

Château Lamothe

Bordeaux white wine.
District and Commune: Sauternes, France.

Second-classed Growth of Sauternes in the 1855 Classification, this wine is not well known outside of France.

Vineyard area: 19 hectares (47.5 acres).
Average production: 25 *tonneaux* (2,000 cases).

Château Lanessan

Bordeaux red wine.
District: Haut-Médoc, France.
Commune: Cussac.

(Cussac is not a place-name and the wine carries the place-name Haut-Médoc.).

Ranked a Bourgeois Growth (*Cru Bourgeois*) of the Médoc in 1855, the vineyard produces wine which sells well above its class and ought to be elevated to a higher position. The museum of horse-trappings, coaches, carriages, and carts draws numbers of visitors.

Characteristics. The very good wines are carefully made by the owner of Château Pichon-Longueville-Baron, M. Bouteiller. The wine is full and round, with a pleasant amount of finesse, and at the same time a delicacy which has astounded the Bordeaux merchants whenever they have tasted old bottles of this fine vineyard. This is one of the few vineyards that welcome visitors.

Vineyard area: 40 hectares (100 acres).
Average production: 220 *tonneaux* (20,000 cases).

Château Langoa-Barton

Bordeaux red wine.
District: Haut-Médoc, France.
Commune: Saint-Julien.

Glimpsed between gates a little back from the vineyard road as it prepares to wind steeply through the town of Saint-Julien, Langoa houses not only the cellars and *chais* of its own Third-Growth (*Troisième Cru*) vintages but also those of the Second-Growth (*Second Cru*) Château Léoville-Barton. The two estates adjoin. Anthony Barton, a descendant of the Hugh Barton who bought Langoa in 1821 and a third of the great Léoville vineyard in 1826, lives in Château Langoa, and makes both wines.

Characteristics. Lighter than, but very similar to, neighboring Léoville-Barton, yet not attaining quite the same degree of excellence. The wine was not bottled at the château before 1969 but in the cellars of the well-known Barton & Guestier shipping firm. All of the 1969 was château-bottled.

Vineyard area: 15 hectares (37.5 acres).
Average production: 60 *tonneaux* (6,000 cases).

Languedoc (Coteaux du Languedoc—A.O.C.)

A vast plain in southern France embracing the departments of Gard, Hérault, and Aude, where great quantities of wine are made, much of it mediocre. However, recent efforts have demonstrated that pleasing, attractive wines can be made from the hillside vineyards.

See Coteaux du Languedoc.

Château Lascombes

Bordeaux red and rosé wines.
District: Haut-Médoc, France.
Commune: Margaux.

A feudal holding of the Dukes of Duras, Lascombes may have acquired its name from the Chevalier de Lascombes who owned it early in the eighteenth century, or he may have taken his title from the estate. The local people say that the derivation was *La Côte— Lascote*—Lascombes, a corruption over the centuries of the original designation, meaning the hill, knoll, or slope. In any case, the vineyard spreads over the knoll of Margaux, the highest elevation of the commune. In 1855 the estate was classified a Second Growth (*Second Cru*) of Médoc.

By unwise selling of parcels, the vineyard had dwindled to nearly 16 hectares (40 acres) and become a patchwork when the Ginestets, former owners of Château Margaux, acquired it in the early twenties. The reconstruction and improvement of the vineyard began then and were continued by the author and a group of American friends who bought Château Lascombes in 1952; today the vineyard has been reunited in an expanse of over 100 hectares (250 acres) northeast of Margaux.

In 1971 the author and his associates sold Lascombes to Bass-Charrington, a British wines, spirits, and brewery group that had already acquired the author's shipping firm in Bordeaux several years before.

The gray stone château, on the edge of the village and the chief landmark in the village itself, was built by a nineteenth-century owner, M. Chaix d'Est-Ange, who was at the time president of the French bar—and famous for having won the case of the Suez Canal for France against Egypt. In gratitude, Napoleon III gave him a magnificent Sèvres coffee service, profusely decorated with portraits of the mistresses of Louis XIV.

In 1953 the American owners enlarged and improved the château and *chai*, and in 1973 the present British proprietors built a new *chai* and vat-rooms. Many visitors used to come to see the exhibition of paintings on the theme of Vine and Wine which was organized in 1961 by the author but discontinued ten years later. The author, since he sold Lascombes in 1971, has had no connection in any way, shape, or form with this vineyard.

Characteristics. Good finesse and has an indefinable light Margaux bouquet epitomizing the "feminine" qualities of the Médoc—a bouquet many have found reminiscent of violets. The wine matures fairly rapidly and has great staying power, so that it may be enjoyed young or old.

Vineyard area: 110 hectares (275.5 acres).
Average production: 375 *tonneaux* (35,000 cases).

Latium (Lazio)

White and red wines.
District: around Rome.

If the Castelli Romani wines ever lose their place among the eternal wonders of Rome, there is no justice in Heaven. More than 90% of Latium produces dry or semi-sweet white wines. The Alban Hills just south of the city provide the finest single means of diverting the mind from aching feet after a morning in Rome, and, judging by the amount sold, the Roman loves them as much as the visitor. The sources are the towns of Frascati, Colonna, Castel Gandolfo, Grottaferrata, Montecompatri, and Marino, although Velletri, Colli Albani, and Colli Lanuvini are names which may also be found. A unique red wine is produced close to Rome (41 km) by the Principi Boncopagni Ludovisi. The wine is called "Fiorano." It is a blend of Cabernet Sauvignon, Cabernet Franc, and Merlot. This excellent planting of top French grape varieties is most laudable and has proven, much to the joy of Roman oenophiles, that very fine red wines can be made in Latium. Undoubtedly one of the better known and most exported good wines of Latium is Frascati, which tends to be sturdier and longer-lasting than the others. Its light texture is in balance with its alcoholic content.

Colli Albani is a D.O.C. wine produced from Malvasia Rossa, Trebbiano Toscano, Malvasia del Lazio, and Bonvino grapes in the communes of Albano and Aricca and also in parts of four other villages in the immediate vicinity of Rome. The wine is straw-colored, with a pleasant, delicate bouquet and a semi-sweet taste; when it contains 12.5% of alcohol, Colli Albani may be called *superiore*. This Denomination of Origin is also given a white sparkling wine made from the same grapes. Quite similar is another D.O.C. white wine called Colli Lanuvini from the communes of Genzano and Lanuvio between Lake Nemi and Aprilia.

Cesanese di Affile (D.O.C.), often called simply Affile, comes from grapes of the same name grown around the commune called Affile, near Rome. It is red but may be dry, semi-sweet, or plainly sweet; the wine ages moderately well and is not unlike two other D.O.C. wines—Cesanese del Piglio and Cesanese di Olevano Romano.

The D.O.C. Frascati is made from Malvasia, Greco, and Trebbiano cultivated on ground especially rich in potassium and phosphorus but deficient in nitrogen

and calcium, which helps to give this wine its distinctive character. There are three types: dry, semi-sweet, and sweet—the last is known as *canellino*.

Marino is a delightful city and is rather well known for its wines: thus wrote Bacci, the physician of Pope Sixtus V, in the year 1500. Marino (D.O.C.) wines are still produced in the area between Albano Lake and Rome; they are all usually white, delicate, and fruity.

The D.O.C. Velletri covers the red wines made from Sangiovese, Montepulciano, and Cesanese and the white wines made from Trebbiano and Malvasia. White Velletri is better known and more appreciated, though the red too is likable enough.

Zagarolo, another D.O.C. white wine from Latium, takes its name from the town southeast of Rome. Typically, it is made of Malvasia and Trebbiano, is either dry or a bit sweet, and may be labeled *superiore* should the wine have at least 12.5% of alcohol.

The Castelli Romani wines come mainly from Malvasia and Trebbiano grapes; they run from about 11% to 13% of alcohol, have a yellowish tinge, and are dry, sweet, or semi-sweet. Much wine is made annually and most of this is gulped down in Rome, although a certain amount is shipped abroad. Red wines also are produced in this Roman province.

Perhaps even more famous than these Roman offerings is Est! Est!! Est!!! (*q.v.*), the D.O.C. white wine of Montefiascone near Lake Bolsena. The name is credited to the German Bishop Fugger, who made a trip to Rome in A.D. 1111. The Bishop was a discriminating drinker, and since he did not wish to risk inferior wines on his long journey, he sent a trusted servant ahead with instructions to taste those along the route and to mark on the wall of each inn and tavern *Est* (It is) where the wine was good and *Non Est* (It is not) on the

others. All went normally until the servant reached Montefiascone, where he tasted the wines, then rushed forth to scrawl the triple epithet on the wall before returning to settle comfortably into the wine cellar. The wine itself, sometimes dry, more often slightly sweet, is small and tinged with yellow, a darkness in shade which actually offers little to the cultivated palate but is certainly worth trying at its source. Other white D.O.C. are Bianco Capena, just north of Rome; Cerveteri from Trebbiano, Malvasia and Verdicchio; Cori, southeast of Rome and Montecompatri-Colonna. The red D.O.C. are Cerveteri; Cori from Montepulciano, Nero Buono di Cori and Cesanese; the three Aprilia made from Merlot, Sangiovese and Trebbiano, are found south of Rome. The good non-D.O.C. wines are the red and white Castel San Giorgio, Colle Picchioni and Torre Ercolana.

Finally, from the north of Latium comes a little-known but good wine, Aleatico di Gradoli (D.O.C.). The Aleatico grape, semi-dried, produces a sweet, rich, red dessert wine of great strength and flavor. It is usually served cold and goes especially well with fruit.

Among lesser wines are Muscats and Malvasia, a sweet white wine sometimes sold fresh out of the fermenting vat (the best comes from Grottaferrata—which also makes a dryish, fairly light wine). Terracina, a city some 120 kilometers (75 miles) south of Rome on the fabled Appian Way, is known for a Muscat which tends to be slightly lower in both alcohol and sugar content than is normally expected. It is often recommended to accompany the exquisite Roman pastries—and with good reason.

Château Latour

Bordeaux red wine.
District: Haut-Médoc, France.
Commune: Pauillac.

Château Latour, already famous, was discussed in the *Essays* by Montaigne, himself a vine-grower in Bordeaux in the sixteenth century. It was near the end of the seventeenth century that the estate passed by marriage from de Chavanas, counselor-secretary to King Louis XIV, to the Ségur family, ancestors of the recent proprietors. The second Ségur to own it was known as the Vine Prince, celebrated as the simultaneous possessor of Château Lafite, Château Latour, and Château Calon-Ségur. In the French Revolution the property was divided, and it was not until 1841 that the family succeeded in regaining the lost half. In 1842, the Société Civile de Château Latour was formed, at that time unique but since widely copied: only members of the family could belong. In 1963, the de Beaumont family sold 75% of their interest to the Pearson group of London. The firm of Harveys then bought one-fifth of this. The new president of Latour is the Honorable Alan Hare, representing the Pearson Group; Jean-Paul Gardère administered the estate. In

1986 the wine responsibility and the day-to-day administration passed to Christian Le Sommer.

The tower—La Tour—stands alone at the center of the vineyard. It was once part of a wall raised against pirates by the Médoc people of the Middle Ages. The actual stones stand as they were placed in a reconstruction, ordered by Louis XIII, from the debris of a leveled fortress. The fort itself, which stood where the *chais* are now placed, was razed during the Hundred Years' War. A legend has it that there is buried gold at Latour, and the story may not be altogether a myth, since a map found not long ago in the Tower of London affirms the presence of the gold. Corporations have been formed in England—so far unsuccessfully—to recover it.

The principal contribution to the quality of Château Latour wine is made by the soil, half of which is composed of egg-sized stones. Strain two pounds of it and a pound of stones will remain in your sieve. The plows of Latour have to be sharpened twice a day, and the soil itself has so much body that in the early sixties, before tractors were used, two oxen were required to draw a plow through it. A former Marquis de Ségur stunned the Court of Versailles with his glittering waistcoat, and King Louis XV announced: "Messieurs, here is the richest man in my kingdom. His soil produces nectar and diamonds." The gleaming stones sewn onto the Marquis de Ségur's silk waistcoat were cut and polished quartz from the vineyard of Latour.

Latour still partly employs the method of vine replacement called *jardinage*. Every vine is allowed to live to its maximum age and is then torn out and replaced individually, although in most vineyards plants are now uprooted in sections at a set retirement age—usually thirty-five or forty years. The result is that, until recently, Latour had one of the oldest average plantations, and consequently greater body, higher alcoholic content, and extra fullness in the wine. In very old vines, quality increases but quantity decreases. Latour makes about 100 cases per acre, whereas 125 to 130 is normal for some of the lesser vineyards. Seven-tenths of Latour's 59 hectares (130 acres) are in Cabernet Sauvignon grapes, the remainder in Merlot, Cabernet Franc, and Petit-Verdot.

The grape must, or fermenting juice, of Château Latour is left in the new gleaming stainless steel vats from fifteen to twenty days, depending on the characteristics of the vintage; this is almost twice the time allowed in most of the other Médoc vineyards. This method creates a harder, slower-maturing wine, which will finally achieve great heights but which must be waited for. Only the grower of an aristocratic wine commanding a very high price can afford this expensive process. Château Latour is classed a First Growth (*Premier Cru*) with Château Lafite, Château Margaux, and Château Haut-Brion.

Characteristics. Full-bodied and hard when young, Latour develops into something firm, rich, and noble. Needing long ageing to reach its peak, it is well worth

waiting for. Les Forts de Latour is the second wine, made from young vines or from lighter vats.
Vineyard area: 60 hectares (150 acres).
Average production: 250 *tonneaux* (22,000 cases).

Château Latour-Pomerol

Bordeaux red wine.
District and Commune: Pomerol, France.

This beautiful and velvety wine has been made for some time by Jean-Pierre Moueix on the estate owned by Mme Lacoste, co-owner of Château Pétrus.
Vineyard area: 9 hectares (22 acres).
Average production: 30 *tonneaux* (3,500 cases).

Latricières-Chambertin (Appellation Contrôlée)

Burgundy red wine.
District: Côte de Nuits, France.
Official Classification: Great Growth (Grand Cru).

Latricières is officially rated a Great Growth (*Grand Cru*) of the Côte d'Or (for the significance of this and the standards demanded *see* Côte de Nuits). It is in all respects the closest vineyard to Le Chambertin.

Chambertin and Latricières lie to the right of the vineyard road as you move south from Gevrey-Chambertin to Morey-Saint-Denis and only a tiny rutted track divides them. At the top of the vineyard, a tumbledown stone wall separates it from the matted and tangled undergrowth and the woodland which extend to the top of the hill, and below this stone wall is a small section of which the author was once part-owner. As is true of most great Burgundian vineyards, a number of growers own sections of Latricières.

After Chambertin and the Clos de Bèze, Latricières produces the best wines in the commune. While not generally having all the fullness and nobility of the two top Growths (*Crus*), it will share much of the same strength, the deep and virile color, and especially the breed; for its main attribute is that it excels in finesse, often to a greater degree than Chambertin and Chambertin-Clos de Bèze. The area of the vineyard is 7 hectares (17 acres), and the grapes which are grown in it are made into approximately 3,000 cases of wine.

Laudun

One of the best communes of the Côtes du Rhône, producing red, white, and rosé wines.
See Rhône.

Lavaux

Terraced vineyards in the canton of Vaud, which produces one-third of the wines of Switzerland. The white wines of Lavaux come from the Chasselas grape.
See Switzerland.

Château Laville-Haut-Brion

Bordeaux white wine.
District: Graves, France.
Commune: Talence.

This vineyard makes only white wine and is one of the five First Growths (*Premiers Crus*) among Graves white wines. Like Châteaux La Mission-Haut-Brion and La Tour-Haut-Brion, it used to belong to the Woltner family and was purchased in 1983 by Château Haut-Brion.

Characteristics. One of the best dry white wines of Bordeaux.

Vineyard area: 6 hectares (15 acres).

Average production: 20 *tonneaux* (2,000 cases).

Layon

See Coteaux du Layon; Anjou.

Lazio

Italian spelling of the region of Latium (*q.v.*).

Leaf reddening (rougeau)

See Rougeau; Chapter Eight, p. 31.

Leaker

A bottle with wine oozing from the cork, indicating that air is reaching the wine, which is likely to spoil due to premature oxidation.

Lebanon

See Syria and Lebanon.

Lees

The sediments or dregs, consisting of tartrates, left at the bottom of a wine cask. These are left after racking a wine from one barrel to another.

Château Léoville-Barton

Bordeaux red wine.
District: Haut-Médoc, France.
Commune: Saint-Julien.

Léoville-Barton, with the other two Léoville vineyards, is a Second Growth (*Second Cru*) in the Classification of 1855 and forms one-fourth of the original Léoville estate, now divided into three. Since the death of Ronald Barton, the vineyard has been run by his nephew, Anthony Barton, descendant of the Hugh Barton who bought Langoa-Barton in 1821 and Léoville-Barton five years later. Anthony Barton lives at Langoa and runs the estate very well, together with his wife, Eva, and their daughter Lillian. This beautiful château should be called Léoville, as both Langoa and Léoville are vinified and kept at the same property. The vineyard has recently been producing one of the best Saint-Juliens of all.

Characteristics. One of the best wines in the area, with excellent body and breed.

Vineyard area: 45 hectares (112.5 acres).

Average production: 180 *tonneaux* (18,000 cases).

Château Léoville-Las-Cases

Bordeaux red wine.
District: Haut-Médoc, France.
Commune: Saint-Julien.

Léoville-Las-Cases comprises roughly half the old estate of Léoville, the other half being divided between Châteaux Léoville-Barton and Léoville-Poyferré. It extends from the edge of the town of Saint-Julien to the borders of Château Latour, and in the past the combined Léoville vineyard stretched from Château Beychevelle to Château Latour. One of the most notable landmarks along the Médoc vineyard road is the Las-Cases gateway just past Saint-Julien, which appears on the wine label.

Las-Cases, with the other Léovilles, is a Second Growth (*Second Cru*) in the 1855 Classification, but one which had a temporary setback in quality during the early fifties. In 1959, 1961, and 1964, however, it was repeatedly one of the best Médoc wines. The vineyard is now run by M. Delon, but until 1900 it belonged to the Marquis de Las Cases, from which comes both the name of the principal Growth and also a secondary bottling under the label of Clos du Marquis, about one-fifth of the production.

Characteristics. At one time the wines were too light and slightly thin. There has been a marked improvement lately—the 1959 was superb, the 1961 was a classic, the 1970 and 1985 excelled. This is an example of a vineyard in which the quality of wine was improved by replanting. The young vines produced light acidic wines, but in 1959 the comparative maturity of the vines was combined with a change in the methods of vinification—brought about by Dr. E. Peynaud, professor of oenology at the University of Bordeaux—to create an overly expressive metamorphosis in this wine.

Vineyard area: 80 hectares (200 acres).

Average production: 260 *tonneaux* (25,000 cases).

Château Léoville-Poyferré

Bordeaux red wine.
District: Haut-Médoc, France.
Commune: Saint-Julien.

A Second Growth (*Second Cru*) of the Médoc as classified in 1855, Poyferré once formed a single vineyard with the two other Léoville Growths, Barton and Las-Cases. Started in the seventeenth century, it was bought and renamed by a president of the parliament of Bordeaux, a M. Léoville, who died in 1769. During the Revolution the entire Léoville property was sequestered, but eventually, in 1830, one-fourth of the vineyard was purchased by Baron Poyferré. The Cuvelier family now owns the estate.

The wine can be the best of the Léovilles, and the 1929 in particular was considered one of the finest bottles of this century in the Médoc, though it is now little more than a memory. Poyferré is now perhaps the least good of the Léovilles. A secondary mark, Château Moulin Riche-Poyferré, is popular in England.

Characteristics. Not so good as neighboring Léoville-Las-Cases, the wine is more supple and lacks the breed of the other two Léovilles. The wine has slipped sadly from what it once was, losing distinction partly because of the youth of the vines.

Vineyard area: 60 hectares (150 acres).
Average production: 220 *tonneaux* (22,000 cases).

L'Étoile

See Étoile; Jura.

Levure

French term for yeast.

Liebfrauenstift-Kirchenstueck

The vineyard site surrounding the Lieberauenkirche (Church of our Lady) in Worms and origin of the name of the generic Rhine wine Liebfraumilch.
See Rheinhessen.

Liebfraumilch

A popular German *Qualitätswein* (quality wine) from Rheinhessen, Rheinpfalz, Rheingau or the Nahe. As a quality wine, it must pass the governmental quality control tests and its production is precisely outlined by law. Made primarily from Riesling, Müeller-Thurgau, Silvaner, or Kerner grapes, it is a mild, fruity Rhine wine for everyday consumption. Quality varies according to producer or shipper, and it does not pay to shop on the basis of price alone.
See Rheinhessen.

Liechtenstein

The wine of this "postage-stamp" principality on the Swiss-Austrian border is light-red—almost rosé—and two-thirds of it comes from around Vaduz, the capital.
See Vaduzer.

Light

In red wines this will mean a small, inconsequential wine, low in alcoholic content and in tannin, though it may be very pleasant. But a light white wine such as a Mosel can be great.

Liguria

Red and white wines.
District: Italian Riviera.

Liguria forms a slim half-moon along the Mediterranean, a block of mountains rimmed with beach, its flanks formed by the Alps to the west, the Apennines to the east, with Genoa in the center. It is an extension of the French Riviera, and in keeping with the atmosphere of this lovely region, wine-making is romantic. The grapes have to be lowered down forbidding cliffs from practically inaccessible vineyards, to be carried to the press in skiffs. But however much he may enjoy watching the harvest here, the wise visitor will generally drink wines from somewhere else. Liguria makes about 400,000 hectoliters (10.6 million U.S. gallons, 8.8 million imp.) annually, but most of it is quite ordinary wine.

Dolceacqua (Rossese di Dolceacqua) (D.O.C.)

This red wine with the Controlled Denomination of Origin comes from western Liguria where flower-laden hills slope upward behind Ventimiglia and Bordighera. Most of the wine is made in the vineyards of Dolceacqua, so it has taken on that name, or that name preceded by the grape variety—Rossese. Although the Italian means "sweet water," Dolceacqua usually has enough acidity to make it an adequate table wine (the best resemble Beaujolais); it is now low in alcohol (12% to 14%). The wine was something of a favorite with Napoleon.

Cinqueterre, Cinqueterre Sciacchetra (D.O.C.)

These famous white wines are often highly praised. The name means "five lands" and the wine comes from the five towns of Vernazza, Campiglia, Riomaggiore, Monterosso, and Biassa. It is mostly dry or semi-sweet, less frequently fully sweet, is made from Vernaccia grapes, and is a sound but not inspiring wine. Nevertheless, this is by far the best-known wine of the region. The dessert or aperitif type made from semi-dried grapes is called Sciacchetra and has a minimum alcoholic content of 17%, a slightly aromatic deep bouquet, and an almost amber color.

Vermentino Ligure, Coronata, and Polcevera

Thin, light wines, similar in taste and bouquet, since each is mainly made from the Vermentino grape (although Bosco and Brachetto vines are grown too, particularly in the Coronata district). The wines should not be expensive. Vermentino Ligure may sometimes sparkle slightly.

Lillet

Semi-dry French aperitif made of 85% white wine and 15% fruit juices. Bruno Borie is president of the firm producing it, and among the backers are Jean-Eugene Borie, his father; the Bordeaux firms of Duclot and Dubos, Merlau; and Robert Drouhin of Burgundy.

Limoux (Appellation Contrôlée)

A small town near Carcassonne in southwest France, which makes a little-known, rather good, sparkling wine (Blanquette de Limoux).
See Blanquette de Limoux.

Liqueur d'expédition

French term, used in Champagne for a solution of sugar, wine, and sometimes brandy added to sparkling wine after extracting the cork just before shipment.
See Champagne.

Liqueur Jaune

Name often given to imitations of yellow Chartreuse.
See Chartreuse.

Liqueur d'Or

Pale yellow French herb liqueur with gold flakes floating in the bottle; a variation of Danziger Goldwasser.

Liqueur de tirage

French term for the solution of sugar and old wine added to Champagne and other sparkling wine to ensure a second fermentation.
See Champagne.

Liqueur Verte

Name often given to imitations of green Chartreuse.
See Chartreuse.

Liqueurs

These sweet, usually strongly alcoholic drinks which are served in very small glasses after dinner are made of sugar, syrup and spirits, flavored with plants, fruit or herbs, and are often an aid to digestion. The white fruit-brandies or *eaux-de-vie* produced in Alsace and elsewhere—framboise, quetsch, kirsch, slivovitz, etc.—sometimes referred to as liqueurs, do not really come into this category; nor do the excellent old dry Cognacs and Armagnacs, which are drunk undiluted after meals, although these are commonly known as "liqueur" brandies.

HISTORY

Although the distillation of water and aromatic liquids was known in earlier times and mentioned by Hippocrates, Galen, and Pliny, alcoholic spirits were not distilled until probably about A.D. 900 by the Arabs—unless, indeed, they were made from cereals in northern Europe somewhat earlier. Liqueurs, a still later invention, began with the mollification of crude spirits by sweet syrups and continued with the addition of sweet herbs to enhance the flavor—and also to improve the health of the drinkers. In the Middle Ages, as we know, wine (and later spirits) was the principal antiseptic for dressing wounds, while plants, roots, and herbs provided the remedies for most diseases. The monks grew these in their monastery gardens and experimented with their use; the alchemists carried their researches further. Arnáu de Vilanova, Catalan physician and chemist, born *c.* 1240, was "the inventor of modern tinctures in which the virtues of herbs are extracted by alcohol." He and his pupil, Raimundo Lulio, were the first to write about alcohol and to make known their recipes for healing liqueurs. Beginning with sweetened spirit, they were soon introducing lemon, rose, and orange-flower. Afterward, they might add particles of gold, then considered to be a universal panacea. Arnáu, whose advanced ideas brought him into trouble with the Inquisition, was protected by the Pope, whose life he had saved with potions of wine mixed with herbs and gold. When the Black Death came to Europe, liqueurs mixed with vegetable balms and tonics were treasured medicines.

By the fifteenth century the Italians had become the leading liqueur-makers, and Catherine de' Medici took some of their recipes to France with her. Montpellier was a famous center of manufacture; a liqueur that Louis XIV liked very much is said to have contained amber, aniseed, cinnamon, and musk. Other spirit bases besides wine-brandy were brought into use, including rum from the new colonies. Housewives often concocted their own liqueurs and then, as now, they were used as flavoring in the kitchen. But during the last century the industry made such progress in most of the countries of Europe and such a variety was put on sale that homemade ratafias and liqueurs began to disappear.

MANUFACTURE

One system—a simple mixing of spirits, sugar-syrup, and bottled essence of peppermint or some other flavor—would be comparatively easy to carry out in the kitchen. In a rather more complicated form, this method is sometimes used commercially. The result, in either case, is a crude liqueur.

The finest are generally those that have been distilled; but some fruits and delicate herbs which cannot be submitted to distillation will merge very satisfactorily with the spirit through the processes of maceration or infusion. The purpose of distilling liqueurs is the opposite of that achieved in the distillation of pure alcohol. There, the vegetable matter constitutes the impurity which must be separated from the spirit; whereas in the liqueur the flavoring substances must be extracted and blended with the spirit base. Of the fruit rinds, kernels, seeds, flowers, leaves, and roots which are used in the mysterious blends, a large number can be distilled. The usual process is to steep the materials in alcohol for varying lengths of time and then, when the spirit is well impregnated with the flavor, to distill it. Afterward comes the sweetening with sugar-syrup. The distilled liquid is normally colorless. Some liqueurs, such as kümmel and Cointreau, will remain so; but since many brands of liqueur are traditionally green, amber, red, or yellow, harmless coloring matter will then be added to the majority. All liqueurs, whether colored or clear, are filtered to ensure perfect clarity. In the varying intervals before bottling they repose in modern stainless steel or brass-lined vats.

Of the alternative methods, infusion is suitable for substances which are soluble in water and not very volatile. The slower cold infusion, or maceration, is resorted to when the ingredient is easily soluble in water and would be injured by heat; in such a case, the fruit or plant is steeped in spirit until this is thoroughly permeated with the taste and perfume. After maceration, the liquid may well be thick and in need of preliminary straining; and, although fruity liqueurs made without distillation often retain their natural color, the maceration of more than one substance may produce a muddy color which must be corrected. As a rule, an innocuous dye, tasteless and without scent, is added in an alcohol solution before filtration. A fine crimson, for instance, can be produced with cochineal, powdered alum, cream of tartar, water, and alcohol.

When sugar is added, the mixture gains in suavity and body as well as in sweetness. Sometimes the sweetener is simple sugar-syrup, sometimes a blend of sugar and glucose, or occasionally, honey. When one of the ingredients is the juice of a sweet fruit, the dose of sugar is, of course, proportionately smaller.

It is on the choice of flavoring substances that will blend harmoniously and easily, and on the balance of sugar and alcohol, that the success of the finished liqueur depends. Every manufacturer guards the secrets of his recipes. In some cases, the prevailing ingredients are known. Cointreau, for example, is made with orange-peel steeped in wine-brandy—but there are other, unnamed components. Aniseed, clearly, is the principal flavoring in the anis liqueurs, caraway in kümmel, peppermint in crème de menthe. The Italian mentuccia is known also as centerbe, after the hundred herbs that go into its making. The famous Benedictine, of Normandy, on the other hand, is made from a secret formula. Among the flowers, fruits, spices, and plants which have their savor extracted for liqueurs are lavender, rose, orange, lemon juniper, vanilla, angelica, thyme, fennel, mint, orris-root, camomile, cinnamon, almonds, curaçao bark, and cloves.

See also under individual headings: Benedictine, Grand Marnier, etc.

Liquor

The most widely employed word for spirit or alcoholic spirit in America; in some isolated instances, the word still retains its original meaning, "liquid."

Liquoreux

French term meaning "rich and sweet."

Lirac (Appellation Contrôlée)

Rhône Valley rosé, and some white, wines.
District: Rhône Valley, France.

Lirac lies near Tavel, and its vineyards resemble the more famous growths of its neighbor. The difference is that white wines—albeit in small quantity—are made in Lirac, only rosé in Tavel. Lirac has sandier soil than Tavel, with the result that its rosé is less full, less distinctive, but often a good value compared to the higher-priced Tavels. The white wine is enjoyable but not extraordinary.

See Rhône.

Lisbon port

A port-type wine from the Lisbon area which sought to capture some of the export market for legitimate Port before this was made illegal by Portuguese wine laws early in the century.

Listofka

A Russian aperitif flavored with black currants.

Listrac (Appellation Contrôlée)

Bordeaux red, and some white, wines.
District: Haut-Médoc, France.

Listrac is a commune of Haut-Médoc, important in wine production although none of the classified châteaux stands within its boundaries. The 500 hectares (1,250 acres) of vineyard, planted on a good stretch of gravelly soil, rising into hummocks with a favorable exposure, yield full-bodied wines—a good deal of respectable *vins fins*, and some good reds classed as Bourgeois Supérieurs and Crus Bourgeois. Among the Supérieurs are Château Fonréaud, Château Fourcas-Dupré, and Château Fourcas-Hosten. Since the late '70s Château Clarke, belonging to Baron Edmond de Rothschild, has become a contender for the best Listrac. There is also a cooperative cellar. The annual harvest is some 28,000 hectoliters (740,000 U.S. gallons, 616,000 imp.).

See Bordeaux.

Liter

Standard metric liquid measure; the volume of one kilogram of pure water measured at a temperature of 40°F. (4°C.) and an atmospheric pressure of 760 millimeters. It is equal to 1.0567 U.S. quarts, 1.9531 British pints, 33.8146 U.S. fluid ounces (35.1961 British), and 100 centiliters.

Livermore Valley

California wine region producing, notably, very good white wines in Alameda County.
See United States: California.

Ljutomer

Yugoslavian spelling of that country's best-known wine. On labels destined for English-language countries, the *j* is customarily omitted. Lutomer white wines are of several styles, identified by the grape variety and also indicated on the wine label.
See Yugoslavia.

Lobe

The division of a leaf. A typical vine leaf has five.

Locorotondo (D.O.C.)

Dry white wines from Apulia (*q.v.*).

Lodge

The word *loja* in Portuguese refers to a warehouse above the ground. However, it is the English who have made Port, in respect of its wealth, its renown, and even the wine itself, and the English tongue is notoriously unwilling to bend itself around words in other languages. *Loja* was transformed into "lodge," and the warehouses of Port wine along the River Douro in Portugal, those in Vila Nova de Gaia for example, are referred to as lodges.

Logroño

Important wine town and district in Rioja-Alta, the best wine region of Spain.
See Rioja.

Loir

A tiny French river, a tributary of the Loire, on the banks of which several pleasant wines are grown.
See Loire; Coteaux du Loir; Jasnières.

Loire, the

Red, white, and rosé wines.
District: Loire Valley, France.

The title in itself is almost a misnomer. No wine—excepting a small quantity of Muscadet de Coteaux de la Loire and Anjou, Coteaux de la Loire—is actually sold under the label Loire, and in fact a number of the vineyard areas along the river—Vouvray, Anjou, Sancerre, Pouilly, Muscadet, and Saumur—are far better known under their own appellations.

Yet, the wines are almost invariably considered as a group and as Loire wines. This nomenclature is justified by the fact that all of them share certain characteristics—all have a stamp that indelibly marks them Loire.

They can best be defined as "charming." If they lack some of the magnificent breed of the great Bordeaux and Burgundies, they have nevertheless a special style, a grace and gaiety which makes them wonderfully refreshing. All manner of wines are made—dry red and sweet white, rosé and dry white, sparkling, *pétillants*, and still, and the better ones are found abroad in fair quantity. It is usually best to drink them fairly young—red as well as white—since they tend to decline after three to five years in bottle, especially after a voyage. This does not apply to the sweet whites, for the extra increment of sugar and increased alcoholic content helps to preserve the wine and allows it to age gracefully and withstand shocks which might be fatal to one of less robust constitution. Here, more than in almost any other district of France, good vintage years are of paramount importance, for if there has not been enough sun, there can be excessive acidity that throws the wines out of balance.

The Loire comes down from the Massif Central in south-central France, flows due north, turns through a right angle, and then flows west to Nantes, where it empties into the Atlantic to finish a journey of some 1,070 kilometers (668 miles). Almost half this journey is completed before the first vineyards with controlled place-names—those of Menetou-Salon, Pouilly-sur-Loire and Sancerre—spring up on the gently sloping banks; but from this point on, vines and vineyards abound. Quincy and Reuilly are skirted (they are drained by a tributary, the Cher), but near Tours the twin districts of Anjou and Touraine stand back to back, with the Coteaux du Loir and tiny Jasnières close by on the small River Loir (*le* Loir, not to be confused with the greater *la* Loire, of which it is a tributary), and vines continue all the way to the Muscadet district, near Nantes.

WINE HISTORY

It is not clearly established whether vines existed before the Roman invasion, or whether they were introduced by Caesar's wine-drinking legions. Certainly the Romans developed and extended the vineyards of Gaul. What is well established is that the early Church was instrumental in advancing viticulture and viniculture in the Loire as elsewhere, and that the Church of

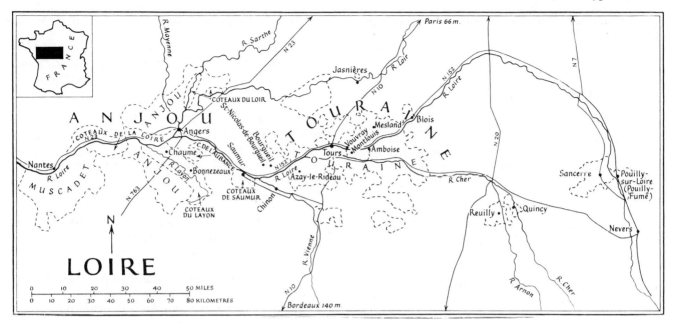

St. Martin at Tours had considerable vineyard hold-ings at various periods, some as far afield as Bur-gundy, but considerably more along the banks of the Loire. The local growers, in fact, declare that the art of pruning was discovered by that saint's donkey.

The story goes that in A.D. 345 St. Martin was mak-ing one of his periodic vineyard tours: he was an early wine enthusiast, aiding growers throughout the valley and bringing them up to date with what viticultors elsewhere were doing. Early one morning he came riding into Anjou, heading for a vineyard which be-longed to the Church. When he got there, he teth-ered his mount at the end of a row of vines. The inspection was a thorough one, St. Martin stopping here and there to ask questions or advise the monks who were tending the vines—and perhaps he went into the cellars to taste the past year's vintage. When, some time later, he returned, he was horrified to dis-cover that his donkey had been munching the leaves, and that some of the tender young shoots had been nibbled right down to the trunk of the vine. But the next year those same shoots were the ones which grew back the most abundantly and produced the best fruit. The lesson was not lost on the monks, who quickly developed a more efficient method of pruning than donkey-tethering.

During the turbulent Middle Ages the vineyards of Touraine and Anjou assumed a considerable impor-tance in Anglo-French trade, for the English Planta-genet kings were also Counts of Anjou; but before England lost all her French possessions, English taste veered toward the wines of Bordeaux. Ships from the Netherlands still sailed up the Loire to buy stocks of wine; but this trade too was curtailed when France and Holland went to war in 1672—a war in which the fa-mous song *Auprès de ma Blonde* was first sung. Having lost two of their best markets, the Loire growers were forced to start building up a trade inside France—

much more difficult than shipping wines down to the coast in those days of poor roads, high tolls, and con-stant danger from thieves and highwaymen. Yet they succeeded. And now, as then, France and Belgium remain the most important customers for Loire wines, although recent advances in viniculture have made it possible to send them overseas without damage, and they can be found in fair quantities in England, the United States, and elsewhere.

TYPES OF WINE

All the important types of still table wines are made along the Loire, as well as a substantial amount of sparkling and some semi-sparkling, or *pétillant*—a word that has become all but synonymous with Vouv-ray. The sparkle was introduced in the nineteenth cen-tury, when Champagne and other bubbly wines be-came the fashion. Most Loire sparkling wines are white and most come from Saumur and its environs, but there are others as well.

The best of the Loire wines are the still whites, both sweet and dry. The dry varieties should be consumed fairly young—nine months to five years old as a gen-eral rule—while the sweet may sometimes take as many as fifteen years to please the exacting palate of the local *vignerons*. These sweet wines are best bought young (although they must be stored until they are ready to drink), because for them, as for all good wines, the price is considerably lower when they are newly bottled. Rosé wine is something of a Loire spe-cialty, and there are two types: a light rosé, and an-other fuller in color and character and sweeter, made entirely from Cabernet Franc grapes. This Rosé de Cabernet, somewhat sweet, is the better wine of the two. Red wines are generally dry, fairly soft, fruity, and quick to mature, and when drunk young can be perfectly delightful.

VINE VARIETIES

Loire Valley wines do not always carry the name of the grape variety from which they come, as do those from Alsace, for example; but the names do guarantee that they were made from specific types of grapes. Those used are:

Cabernet Franc. The dominant grape (called Breton in Touraine) for makers of red wine, who also employ it in making vin rosé. This vine is said to have been brought to the Loire in the twelfth century. In the seventeenth the Abbé Breton planted a new vineyard for Cardinal Richelieu; hence the local synonym "Breton" for the grape. The vines came originally from the Gironde, where the grape is grown for the red wines of Bordeaux. Other local names for the grape are Véron, Bouchy Bouchet, etc.

Cabernet Sauvignon. Some Sauvignon is found, mostly in Anjou, where plantings have increased of late years. Most of the grapes are pressed for pink wine.

Chasselas. A grapevine used for about three-quarters of the production of dry white Pouilly-sur-Loire, the minor wine of the district of the same name. The best wines of Pouilly are Blanc Fumé de Pouilly, or Pouilly-Fumé, and are made with the Sauvignon Blanc, also known as Blanc Fumé.

Chenin Blanc. Despite its restriction to the districts of Anjou, Touraine, and Jasnières, this is the most widely-planted grapevine for white wines along the banks of the Loire. It is called Pineau de la Loire in Touraine. The vine is known to have grown in Anjou from very early times. It is no doubt a selection of once-wild plants. The fruit is used both for sweet and for dry white wines, the main factor being in many cases the weather—hot summers give sweet wines, chill rainy ones give dry wines. The other factor is the method of fermentation used at will by the wine-grower. The best wines made from this variety are Savennières, Coulée-de-Serrant, and Roche-aux-Moines.

Cot. A minor vine cultivated in the valley of the Cher in Touraine. The red wines it produces are uninteresting. Other names for this grape are Pied-Rouge, Malbec or Malbeck, Cahors.

Gamay. The vine of Burgundy's Beaujolais district is planted to a slight extent in the Coteaux de la Loire and in the Touraine. It is used for rosé wines rather then red, except in the Ancenis district.

Groslot. This grape is used for rosé wine in Anjou.

Gros Plant du Pays Nantais. Planted around the Muscadet district, it produces fresh white wines. Sometimes on the acid side, these wines are only consumed locally along the Atlantic coast.

Muscadet. Actually Melon de Bourgogne, but when transplanted in 1639 from its native Burgundy to the vineyards at the mouth of the Loire, the vine took on a new name. The dry white wines made from its grapes are light, fresh, slightly hard and acid, and excellent with seafood.

Noble. This is used in small quantities for red wine in the Touraine and is synonymous with Pinot.

Pineau d'Aunis. Once the important grapevine for red wines but now almost entirely replaced by Cabernet Franc. It is still found in limited amounts in Anjou, where it has been growing since the twelfth century.

Pinot Noir. This grape variety was cultivated in abundance in Sancerre up to the beginning of the twentieth century. Since then, little by little, it has been replaced by the Sauvignon. Recently, there has been a strong tendency to replant certain vineyards of Sancerre in Pinot Noir, since in good vintages it produces very good rosés. The red wines, because of their quality and because of fashion, are acquiring a noteworthy following.

Sauvignon Blanc. The white grape of Bordeaux does exceptionally well in the upper Loire, where it is used exclusively for the dry white wines of Sancerre, Quincy, Reuilly and the best wine of Pouilly-sur-Loire, the Blanc Fumé.

LOIRE WINE DISTRICTS

There are nine major districts of the Loire of which three—Anjou, Muscadet, and Touraine—are huge and contain a number of sub-districts, while the rest are small and of lesser importance. These districts are:

Anjou

Makes red and white wines (the latter both sweet and dry, of which the sweet are the better) and dry and semi-sweet rosé. It includes the sub-districts of Anjou-Coteaux de la Loire, Savennières, Bonnezeaux, Coteaux de l'Aubance, Coteaux du Layon, Quarts de Chaume, Saumur, and Coteaux de Saumur.

Coteaux du Loir

A minor and very small district taking its name from the tiny river Loir (a tributary of the greater river

Loire) and producing red, white, and rosé wines. The white are sweet, the rosé and the red sometimes not very good.

Jasnières

A small district making up the heart of the Coteaux du Loir and producing the superior wine. The wines are entirely white and are usually described *as moelleux*—slightly sweet, velvety, and rich in texture.

Menetou Salon

An appellation of white and red located in the upper Loire, south of Pouilly.

Muscadet

The 9,000 hectares (22,500 acres) of vineyards at the mouth of the Loire produce a fresh and delightful dry white wine. Muscadet is divided into three place-names. The most famous is Muscadet de Sèvre et Maine, some 16 kilometers (10 miles) south of Nantes, deriving its name from two small rivers running through the vineyard area. The second is Muscadet Coteaux de la Loire; and the third is referred to simply as Muscadet.

Pouilly-sur-Loire

A district of the upper Loire where Sauvignon Blanc grapes are pressed to make the excellent dry white Pouilly-Fumé, otherwise known as Blanc Fumé de Pouilly, and Chasselas grapes to make the similar but less distinctive Pouilly-sur-Loire.

Quincy

Although Quincy is 48 kilometers (30 miles) from the Loire and adjoins a tributary, its output is always considered as Loire wine. Dry and white, it is much like Sancerre, Pouilly-Fumé, and Reuilly, with a slightly distinctive *goût de terroir*.

Reuilly

Dry white wine—often thin, harsh, and acid—from Reuilly on the Arnon, a tributary of the Cher. It resembles the wine from nearby Quincy.

Sancerre

One of the best-known growing districts of the upper Loire, famous for its dry white wine made entirely from Sauvignon grapes. There is also a very good dry rosé and occasionally a red wine—both made from Pinot Noir.

Savennières, Coulée-de-Serrant, Roche-aux-Moines

On the right bank of the Loire, the Chenin Blanc produces these dry white wines which may be the best of the entire Loire region.

Touraine

The wines may be red, white, or rosé and the whites may either be sweet or dry. The sub-districts of the Touraine include Bourgueil and Saint-Nicolas-de-Bourgueil, Chinon, Montlouis, Touraine-Amboise, Touraine-Azay-le-Rideau, Touraine-Mesland, and the world-renowned Vouvray.

See also under separate headings.

Lombardy

Red, white, and rosé wines.
District: Northern Italy.

From the towering Alps along its northern boundary to the pleasure resorts of Lake Garda and almost to the city limits of Milan, Lombardy is a region of wines and vines. There are stretches, of course, where no vine is seen: northern reaches where the land is too forbiddingly mountainous, or central lowlands where the soggy valleys are given over to the culture of rice. In general, however, the vine is found throughout. It does best in the Valtellina section, an Alpine corner near the Swiss border, some 30 kilometers (20 miles) due south of Saint Moritz, but the wine from grapes grown near Lake Garda is also popular with the Italians. In addition, Lombardy can boast of the well-known vineyard Frecciarossa, dealing in something quite rare in Italy—estate-bottled wines.

Valtellina

In this valley centered around the town of Sondrio, the four almost identical red wines are Fracia, Sassella, Grumello, an Inferno—all from Nebbiolo grapes grown on the less steep Alpine slopes. Almost the whole production of Fracia comes from one grower, the house of Negri, based in Chivro. A similar but lesser growth is the red Valgella.

Perhaps the mountaineer is a different type from the plainsman, but wine, and even life, in the Valtellina does not seem to have changed for centuries. The peasant who pours you a glass of wine and warns you not to stay out too late (werewolves inhabiting the upper slopes are still dangerous at night) might well be from another age entirely, and it is difficult to conceive that he would ever change his wine-making techniques. Mechanization is rare and even animals often find the slopes too steep, leaving man to struggle alone to till the land. For this reason, and because the Nebbiolo is always a shy bearer, the amount of wine made is small—less than 27,000 hectoliters (700,000 U.S. gallons, 580,000 imp.) a year for the combined five wines. Once made, they seem to epitomize not only the virtues but the faults of Italy's wines. At their best they have an agreeable freshness, and occasionally, as is true throughout the country, they have a light sparkle. When these wines succeed, they are hearty and good. They are made from a minimum of 95% of Nebbiolo grapes, known locally as Chiavennasca, and grown on steep terraces, facing south, in those areas called Fracia, Sassella, Inferno, Grumello, and Valgella. The wines are in fact *Valtellina Superiore*, and bear on the label their own geographical specification added to the D.O.C. Valtellina. One of the best of these wines is Sfursat, made from partly dried grapes so that the alcoholic content reaches 14.5% or more. When aged four years, this wine may be called *riserva* and becomes a fine table wine of great character.

Lugana

This, Lombardy's leading white wine, is made from Trebbiano grapes with some Vernaccia not infrequently added. For all the fuss made about it, this is a small D.O.C. wine, generally yellowish in color, running to about 11% to 12.5% of alcohol. It is regrettable that Italian wine-makers—contrary to their general practice—usually age their white wines too long; if it were brought young out of the barrel, Lugana would probably be much better.

Frecciarossa

This estate is in the province of Pavia, bordering on Piedmont. The carefully made wines come strictly from a 28-hectare (70-acre) vineyard on a castle-topped hill near Casteggio and are of four types: Bianco (dry, white), Ambrato (semi-sweet, white), Rosso (dry, red), and Saint George (dry, rosé). The white wines are made from Riesling, the others from Pinot Noir, Bonarda di Gattinara, Barbera, and Croatina. Something under 2,000 hectoliters (50,000 U.S. gallons, 41,500 imp.) is made annually, split into almost equal parts among the four, and the wines are distrubuted widely throughout the world. Estate-bottled wines are to be found here—something very rare in Italy. Other wines of the region are the red Barbacarlo and Buttafuoco (D.O.C.).

Lombardy also makes a Muscat and a sparkling Muscat in commercially important (but fortunately not significantly large) quantities, selling them as Moscato di Casteggio and Moscato di Casteggio Spumante. The former is a typically sweet Muscat wine, the latter something like Asti Spumante (*see* Piedmont).

Several other, less well-known wines of Lombardy deserve mention here. From the southwestern shore of Lake Garda come Riviera del Garda Chiaretto and Rosso, both wines of Controlled Denomination of Origin. Both are made from Groppello and Sangiovese grapes and share something of the same marked, bitter aftertaste. The Rosso is a very deep ruby color, while the Chiaretto is a rather dark rosé.

Among the good D.O.C.s of Lombardy, from Lake Garda in the district of Brescia come the red and rosé Riviera del Garda Bresciano and the white Tocai di San Martino della Battaglia. Also, close to Milano is the red wine of San Columbano and the white and red wines of Valcalepio. A very good white from the Pinot Nero and Pinot Grigio, grown like the Frecciarossa in the Oltrepò Pavese district, is sold by Angelo Ballabio.

Another good D.O.C. red wine is Botticino, whose name comes from a small commune near Lake Garda. Barbera, Schiava, Gentile, Marzemino, and Sangiovese make up the wine which is best drunk young.

Oltrepò Pavese is the Controlled Denomination of origin for six wines from part of the province of Pavia, south of the River Po. The name is generally followed by the name of the principal grape variety used to make the wine—Barbera, Bonarda, Riesling, Cortese, Moscato, etc.—but when the name appears alone, the wine will contain mostly Croattina and Barbera.

Finally, Lombardy gives two pleasant D.O.C. wines called Franciacorta Rosso and Franciacorta Chardonnay made in twenty-one communes in the province of Brescia. The *rosso* contains Cabernet, Barbera, Nebiolo and Merlot; it is dry and even robust. The white wine named Chardonnay, after the principal grape used, is sometimes sparkling and always best consumed young.

London Dry gin

One of the two basic styles of gin—the other is Hollands. This is the gin of both the United States and England. The base spirit is distilled until neutral, and flavoring, from a number of different herbs but chiefly juniper, is added afterward. Less totally distilled, Hollands (or Dutch gin) retains flavor characteristics from the original spirit.

See Gin.

Lorraine

Red, white, and rosé wines.
District: Northeast France.

Since 1951 the wines of Lorraine, which had practically ceased to exist, have been making a small comeback. This northeastern province of France had at one time been well known for its *vin gris* (a type of rosé made from Gamay) and for its sparkling wines. Three wars, phylloxera, and the passing of rigid control laws in Champagne all but wiped Lorraine off the wine map. Two controlled place-names exist today, both established in 1951 and both of them having the right to the name of Vins Délimités de Qualité Supérieure, the secondary French classification of wines. They are the Côtes de Toul and Vins de la Moselle.

Lorraine has always been one of the more troubled parts of France. After the war of 1870 the province was split in two, half going to France and half to Germany. During this period, the wines of Lorraine probably enjoyed as much renown as they have ever had. Those grown on the German side were made into Sekt, or German sparkling wine; and those on the French side either became *vins gris* or were made sparkling and sold as Champagne; the Champagne shippers did this with Lorraine wine, until in 1908 Champagne had a disastrous year and virtually all the wine had to be brought in from Lorraine. The Champagne growers objected so violently that riots and havoc broke out in the region and a rigid delimitation law was passed in 1908, strengthened further in 1911; Lorraine wines therefore had to find another outlet.

Before the growers could get back on their feet, the First World War came. Such vineyards as survived in the battleground area fell victim to phylloxera. Hybrid vines were planted for the making of very ordinary wine to be drunk in Lorraine by the inhabitants. Only after the Second World War did the growers of Lorraine start replanting their finer vine types with any consistency.

The better wines of Lorraine are today much what one would expect from a vineyard area so cold and so far north. Low in alcohol and high in acid, the grapes are harvested late—the end of October. The red wines which result are far less pleasant than the white and rosé. High acidity in red wines is a definite defect.

Côtes de Toul

Most of the wines are *vins gris*, the traditional light rosé wine of Lorraine. They come from parts of the communes of Lucey, Bruley, Pagney-derrière-Barine, Écouvres, Dongermain, Mont-le-Vignoble, Charmes-la-Côte, Blénod-les-Toul, and Bulligny. The permitted vines are the Gamay de Toul, Gamay de Liverdun, Pinot Noir, and Pinot Meunier (all of these either separately or together must comprise at least 80% of the wine); and Aubin blanc, Blanc d'Euvézin, and Aligoté (these three comprise up to a maximum of 20%). The vines are allowed to yield no more than 60 hectoliters per hectare (634 U.S. gallons, 526 imp. per acre).

The alcoholic content of the Côtes de Toul will only run about 8.5% in an average year, but may go as high as 10% or even 11% in years that are particularly hot and acidity is markedly high. Only about 3,000 hectoliters (79,500 U.S. gallons, 66,000 imp.) are made each year. The vineyards of the Côtes de Toul are in the process of being expanded, and this figure may rise.

Vins de la Moselle

The Vins de la Moselle are made in three separate areas and each of the wines has its own characteristics. The wines from around the city of Metz are mostly light rosé wines often found under the name of Clairet de Moselle. Those which come from around Sierk are generally white. The traditional *vin gris* is made principally around Vic-sur-Seille. All must derive from the same vines, which are the Gamay (30%), Auxerrois Blanc, Auxerrois Gris, Meunier Blanc, Meunier Gris, Pinot Noir, Pinot Blanc, Sylvaner (30% maximum), Riesling, and Gewürztraminer. Like the wines of the Côtes de Toul, these tend to be extremely acidic but are often pleasantly fruity when young.

Spirits

Among the colorless *eaux-de-vie* that are made from fruits here, as elsewhere, the Mirabelle de Lorraine is the best known. It is made from small yellow plums.

Loupiac (Appellation Contrôlée)

White wine.
District: Bordeaux, France.

This is the continuation northward of Sainte-Croix-du-Mont on the right bank of the River Garonne, and facing Sauternes across the river. It produces approximately the same quantity as Sainte-Croix-du-Mont and under identical conditions, the sole difference being that these vineyards are in the commune of Loupiac. The wines may be considered with those of Sainte-Croix-du-Mont, as there are no important differences.
See Sainte-Croix-du-Mont.

Low wines

Whisky after first distillation and before redistillation.

Lugana (D.O.C.)

Principal white wine of Lombardy, made from Trebiano grapes, sometimes with an addition of Vernaccia.
See Lombardy.

Lunel, Muscat de

See Sweet fortified wines of France.

Lussac-Saint-Émilion

Commune with an Appellation Contrôlée, making red wines, in the region of Bordeaux *(q.v.)*.

Lutomer

English spelling of Yugoslavia's best-known white wine. There are different styles identified as Lutomer Riesling, Lutomer Sylvaner, etc.

See Yugoslavia; Ljutomer.

Luttenberger

The German name for the wines of Ljutomer in Yugoslavian Slovenia during the Austrian occupation before the First World War. The white wines became famous under this name, by which they are still occasionally called. They are now correctly Ljutomer wines, or Lutomer on English-language labels.

See Yugoslavia; Ljutomer; Lutomer.

Luxembourg

The white wines grown on the rolling, pretty Luxembourg bank of the Moselle are similar to their German counterparts. Light and fruity, they are stay-at-home wines for the most part, since few of them are ever seen outside the Benelux Union.

Each year the 1,000-hectare (2,500-acre) strip produces a rough average of 170,000 hectoliters (4.5 million U.S. gallons, 3.7 million imp.).

Of the wines, 55% are consumed in the Grand Duchy itself, amounting to two bottles in three of all the wine the Luxembourgers drink, the odd bottle being made up by importation, mainly from France and Italy. The per capita consumption of Luxembourg wine is twenty-seven or twenty-eight bottles per year, far down the list for a European nation. Most of the wine not used at home goes to Belgium. Holland and Germany receive a token quantity, and the amount exported to the rest of the world is a statistical drop in the bucket. To taste Luxembourg wine you must go to Luxembourg, or at least to Belgium.

WINE HISTORY

At the time of the French Revolution Luxembourg was a part of France, and the Revolution drove the monks from the vineyards they had tended. The vineland was broken up into small parcels, a condition which has survived to this day, when there are 1,000 holdings. The size of the average plot is just under half a hectare, only a few being much larger. This extreme tendency to division is counteracted by the cooperatives, one existing in each main town of the wine belt; between them they account for 65% of total production.

At the turn of the century Luxembourg wine went almost entirely into blends called vaguely Elbling—mixtures of low-quality German Palatinate and Lower Moselle wines with the Luxembourg product. When

this practice was ended by the First World War and severance from Germany, Luxembourg had no sale for the characterless bulk wine that was being produced. A long crisis extended from 1918 to 1925. Then the government Viticultural Station was founded at Remich on the Moselle. Premiums were paid for uprooting second-class vineyards. Luxembourg viticulture had accepted the principle, in force to this day, that wine is a quality—not a quantity—product. The Viticultural Station is the teacher and policeman of this movement. There is a department of analysis, free instruction and help for growers, a scientific campaign against vine disease, and supervision of the laws governing place-names on bottle labels.

Vines have grown here from the time of the Romans. Luxembourg vintage records extend as far back as 370 (when the wine was a failure). In 1866 the wine was so sour that, as a joke topical at the time, the people named it Bismarck. One of the worst setbacks occurred in 1944, when the Moselle was caught in the von Rundstedt counteroffensive, finishing with the

Battle of the Bulge; but the following year the vineyards were flourishing again.

WHAT THE WINES ARE CALLED

The Luxembourg vineland faces southeast, across the Moselle to the German bank. Wine is grown nowhere else in the tiny country. The advantage of catching the early sun on the east-facing slope is augmented by the forest protection crowning the hills, cutting off a wind which usually blows from the west all the year round. The whole gentle length of the Moselle is an alternating patchwork of vineyard and orchard. The cherry and plum trees provide the fruit for the kirsch, quetsch, and mirabelle distilled in the Grand Duchy.

Luxembourg wine labels carry, according to law, name designations of the following type:

Moselle Luxembourgeoise, Appellation Contrôlée, used in combination with the grape variety. Moselle Luxembourgeoise Riesling, Appellation Contrôlée. Locality name, with or without vineyard site, and grape variety—e.g., Wormeldange Riesling, Riesling from the Elterberg vineyard near Wormeldange.

In the categories of fine wines, labels must indicate the vintage year, the grape variety, the name of grower as well as his domicile.

Today the trend is towards quality wines and the breakdown, between 1977 and 1983, was:

—Table wine: 35%
—Marque Nationale (a wine which has undergone an analytical and organoleptic examination by twelve knowledgable members): 45%
—Vin classé: 7%
—Premier cru: 3%
—Grand premier cru: 10%

Strict regulations govern treatment and the type of vine; wines must pass official tasting tests of the Commission of the Marque Nationale.

Since its establishment by the government in 1935, the Marque Nationale has begun to appear on more and more Luxembourg wine. A small label prominently lettered Marque Nationale and indicating that the wine is from Luxembourg is affixed to the neck of the certified bottles. Marque Nationale wines are bottled under government observation and control, subjected to blind tasting tests.

GRAPE VARIETIES: BEST WINES

The best vineyards are found on the chalky marl soil of Remich and the stony chalk-and-clay soil of Grevenmacher. A chalky soil with scattered stones and a marly subsoil is considered good Riesling soil, while the peculiar clay soil varying in hue from green to red is the soil for the Pinot varieties.

The grape varieties of Luxembourg are Riesling, Traminer, Ruländer, Pinot Blanc, Auxerrois, Sylvaner, Rivaner, Elbling, and Muscat Ottonel. From these, the best wines are the following:

Rivaner. A light table wine with a slight Muscat taste. Best locality: entire Moselle. The grape is better known as the Müller-Thurgau.

Pinots. Auxerrois, Pinot Blanc and Ruländer (or Pinot Gris). Fuller, more generous and with more body than the Rivaner, though often with less bouquet. Best localities: Wellenstein, Remerschen, Schengen.

Riesling. Elegant and full of distinction, tending to be acidic in the wet years. Best localities: Wormeldange, Stadtbredimus, Wintrange, Schengen, Remich, Grevenmacher, Ehnen.

Traminer. Velvety, big, and with the typical spicy perfume and taste. Best localities: Ahn, Wellenstein, Schwebsingen, Schengen, Machtum.

SPIRITS

Kirsch, quetsch, and mirabelle are produced from the cherry and plum orchards. The number of distilleries in operation varies but is usually around 950.

Château Lynch-Bages

Bordeaux red wine.
District: Haut-Médoc, France.
Commune: Pauillac.

Classified a Fifth Growth (*Cinquième Cru*) of Médoc in 1855, Lynch-Bages actually commands prices equal to those of some Second Growths (*Seconds Crus*). It is located at Bages, hardly a quarter of a mile south of Pauillac, and is plainly seen on the left of the wine road approaching Pauillac. Originally the property of an Irishman, Mr. Lynch—who was mayor of Bordeaux—the vineyard has been, since 1933, in the Cazes family, and in recent years in the hands of the bright and energetic mayor of Pauillac, André Cazes, and his son Jean-Michel. With this capable management the growth has come rapidly into its own. In both 1955 and 1956, at blind tastings held at Château Prieuré-Lichine in Cantenac-Margaux, with leading vineyard owners, wine brokers, and Bordeaux shippers participating, Lynch-Bages took first place among the leading Médoc Classified Growths. That this fine vineyard is still classed as a Fifth Growth is one indication of the obsolescence of the 1855 Classification.

Château Lynch-Moussas

Characteristics. Can produce rich, full, round wines. It is flattering to the taste in its youth, and stands up very well as it ages.

Vineyard area: 76 hectares (190 acres).

Average production: 300 *tonneaux* (28,000 cases).

Château Lynch-Moussas

Bordeaux red wine.
District: Haut-Médoc, France.
Commune: Pauillac.

The output of this small vineyard, which was classified a Fifth Growth (*Cinquième Cru*) of the Médoc in 1855, is principally sold in Holland and Belgium. In common with its large neighbor, Château Lynch-Bages, the estate was once the property of Mr. Lynch, an Irish mayor of Bordeaux. The present owner, Jean Casteja, has replanted much of the vineyard.

Characteristics. Still to be drunk young, but the wine is improving.

Vineyard area: 40 hectares (100 acres).

Average production: 175 *tonneaux* (17,000 cases).

M

Macadam, vin de

An old Parisian term for a sweet white wine brought right out of the fermenting vat and rushed to the boulevards of Paris. Much of this wine was drunk in the open-air cafés, overlooking the macadam-paved streets and squares. The most famous of these wines came from the area around Bergerac (q.v.).

Maché

French term for a wine which tastes tired, either from racking or from travel; tastes as though it had been mashed up by chewing.

Mâcon

Market town and wine center for Lower Burgundy. *See* Mâconnais.

Mâcon Supérieur

An Appellation Contrôlée of the Mâconnais region (q.v.).

Mâconnais

White wine, some red and rosé.
District: Southern Burgundy, France.

The southern Burgundy section of the Mâconnais adjoins that of the Beaujolais. It occupies one corner of the department of Saône-et-Loire, and its southeast corner overlaps the wine district of the Beaujolais, specifically the commune of la Chapelle-de-Guinchay. The wines made in this corner are usually sold as Beaujolais if they are red and as Mâconnais if they are white—one of the rare cases where the vintner can make the best of both worlds.

The best and the most famous of the Mâconnais is the dry white Pouilly-Fuissé, a wine which has commanded a place on many good tables over the years and is still growing in popularity. It is not, however, the only Pouilly to be made. Nearby are the vineyards of Pouilly-Loché and Pouilly-Vinzelles, and in the valley of the Loire there is another dry white wine made in the town of Pouilly-sur-Loire. The Pouilly-Fumé (q.v.) from this last town is similar in color and in name, but the grapes used are different—Sauvignon Blanc—and so are the wines.

Pouilly-Fuissé is to the white wines of southern Burgundy what a cru of Beaujolais is to the red. Neither of them is ever a very great wine, either may often be an excellent wine, both are usually ex-

tremely pleasant wines. The public affection for Pouilly-Fuissé and the wines of the Mâconnais is far older than for those of Beaujolais, which has only gained its wide circle of admirers during comparatively recent times.

The Mâconnais has been sending its wines to clamoring markets since the seventeenth century, thanks, so they say, to an imaginative owner named Claude Brosse. About 1660, Brosse decided that it was high time that someone outside the region knew about the excellence of the Mâconnais wines. A man of enormous stature, and evidently fearless as well, he loaded his cart with two barrels of his finest wine and started off for Paris. Trips to Paris were rare in those days, for there were some 400 kilometers (250 miles) of muddy and nearly impassable roads, and highwaymen in waiting. But Brosse managed to arrive safely with his wine in Paris—it took him thirty-odd days. His imposing stature caught the eye of Louis XIV, who wanted to know what he was doing so far from home, and, on learning that Brosse's business was wine, desired to taste it. When the King had sipped the wine, Brosse got an immediate order for the royal cellars. What the King happened to like was also exactly what the court had always wanted, and Brosse and the wines of the Mâconnais were launched.

The present Mâconnais growers produce more than white wines. A large amount of red is also made, and the makers could add rosé, although there is comparatively little of this at present. Being next to the Beaujolais, where the noble vine is the Gamay, the growers of the Mâconnais tend to plant the same vine, but the results are less happy. The traditional red-wine vine has always been the Gamay à Jus Coloré (Gamay with colored juice), sometimes called Gamay-Teinturier. It produces large grapes in vast quantities and these, unlike those of most vines, give a dark juice. This particular vine, of all the varieties of Gamay, has come in for an enormous amount of abuse, and it has been condemned and forbidden in Burgundy over and over again. Since 1970, in fact, all Mâconnais red and rosé wine may include only 15% Gamay-Teinturier. The major part of these wines is made from Pinot Noir, with some Gamay Noir à Jus Blanc. Any replanting for these wines is done with Pinot Noir.

The reason why the Gamay vine does so much better in the neighboring Beaujolais than in the Mâconnais is the soil. Nowhere in the Mâconnais does one find the granite soil which gives Beaujolais its special appeal. By the same token, the chalky hills of the Mâconnais permit the Chardonnay vine, Burgundy's only noble white-wine vine, to produce, with delightful results. Actually there are three areas of soil, the best that of Pouilly-Fuissé, slightly to the southwest of Mâcon. Here there is a series of dips and rises where the soil is limestone mixed with slate, dating back to the Jurassic age, some 150 million years ago. To the northwest of Mâcon there is a slightly different formation, this time a long valley where the disintegration of the chalky oolite has allowed enough topsoil for the planting of vines. Both of these sections are excellent for growing grapes for white wines. Toward the northern end of the district the terrain gets more varied and confused. At one point there is a preponderance of chalk, and at another of slate, and the wines tend to follow the lead given by the soil. Some are good, some not so good, the characteristics depending upon the particular soil in which they were grown.

The soil of certain parts of the Mâconnais has always had a fascination for geologists and diggers in the earth. Not only are there several layers of rock formation underlying the district, each one dating from a different period, but the area has proved a good place for digging up relics of the distant past. Fossils dating back 6,000 years have been excavated from the vicinity of Solutré—one of the communes making Pouilly-Fuissé—and there is hardly a plowman in the region who has not at one time or another turned up some ancient bit of equipment, often dating back to Roman days. But the history of the Mâconnais is written not only in the soil. The great medieval monastery of Cluny was built at the town of that name, some 16 kilometers (10 miles) northwest of Mâcon. Its monks did a great deal to keep learning alive during the Dark Ages, and Cluny was once the most powerful arm of the Church in France. The monks also helped to forward the knowledge and practice of vine-growing and wine-making and to inspire the local peasants to increase their vineyards and care for them properly. It is not recorded whether the monks inspired the wine or whether the wine inspired the monks, but it is certain that Burgundian viniculture virtually owes its existence to the industry of the inhabitants of Cluny.

In this corner of southern Burgundy growers have their own methods of viniculture. The sun is warmer than it is farther north, on the Côte d'Or, and the warm seasons are slightly longer. The Chardonnay vine, in particular, is allowed to grow much higher here than elsewhere in Burgundy. The growers say that because of the stronger sunshine, the grapes need not be pruned close to the ground where the stony soil will reflect heat on to them. Furthermore, in the Mâconnais they can often afford to wait as much as two weeks longer than in the Côte d'Or for the grapes to ripen.

Most of the wine sold is Mâcon Supérieur, or Mâcon, followed by the name of the commune where the wine was grown. A slightly lesser amount will be sold simply as Mâcon with no other indication of source, while the best, of course, is sold under one of the three Pouilly *appellations*. As is usual with French wines, the names include more than simply place of origin.

PLACE-NAMES OF THE MÂCONNAIS

Pouilly-Fuissé (Appellation Contrôlée)

Pouilly-Fuissé is the king of the Mâconnais white wines, and the very finest rank high among white Burgundies. In general, these wines are fairly light and very dry. The better ones have a forthright round fullness that distinguishes them from the lesser light wines which are lacking in character and are over-acidic. They are less hard than the Chablis and not so fruity, with a slight *goût de terroir*, the taste imparted by the soil in which they are grown. They tend to have a very light, fine bouquet, and at their youthful best are of a pale golden color with overtones of green. They are definitely wines to be drunk when they are young, reaching their peak after about six months in bottle and holding it for from three to five years. Some of them have enough alcoholic content to last longer than that, but there will be no improvement and therefore little point in keeping them.

To be a real Pouilly-Fuissé, the wine must have been grown in one of the communes of Solutré-Pouilly, Fuissé, Chaintré, or Vergisson. It must be made only from the Chardonnay vine, the amount harvested not to exceed 45 hectoliters per hectare (481 U.S. gallons, 400 imp. per acre). The content in the must—or unfermented grape juice—should amount to 187 grams (6.5 ounces) of natural sugar per liter, and the finished wine must have a minimum alcoholic strength of 11%. The sugar is always stated to be natural, since the growers here, as elsewhere in Burgundy, are allowed to add a certain amount of extra sugar to the wine, a process known as *chaptalisation*. The purpose of this practice is to raise the sugar content in years when the sun has been too weak to instill enough natural grape-sugar into the fruit, and what is added gets converted into alcohol with the grape-sugar. *Chaptalisation* is a tricky business, for when it is practiced to excess it tends to diminish the finesse and elegance of the wine, making it fuller, heavier, and sometimes very much coarser than it should be.

Within the area of the four towns allowed the use of the name of Pouilly-Fuissé, there are about 600 hectares (1,500 acres) of vines. From these come an average of about 36,000 hectoliters (954,000 U.S. gallons, 792,000 imp.) of wine each year. The best is sold as Pouilly-Fuissé with the name of the vineyard added, and to qualify for this the sugar content of the must is elevated to a minimum of 204 grams (7.25 ounces), and the alcoholic content must be 12%. The better vineyards, and those apt to be found on a bottle label, are: (in the town of Solutré-Pouilly) Les Chailloux, Les Boutières, Les Chanrue, Les Prâs, Les Peloux, Les Rinces; (in the town of Fuissé) Château Fuissé, Le Clos, Clos de Varambond, Clos de la Chapelle, Menetrières, Versarmières, Les Vignes-Blanches, Les Châtenets, Les Perrières, Les Brûlets.

In general, the wines from Solutré-Pouilly tend to be more feminine and delicate than those from the other communes, while those from Fuissé are apt to be the strongest. The cooperative at Chaintré produces some of the best Pouilly-Fuissé, superior to that of Vergisson.

Pouilly-Loché, Pouilly-Vinzelles, and Saint-Véran (A.O.C.)

The first two are the two lesser Pouillys of the Mâconnais. Although the legal restrictions—exclusive of growing area—are identical with those of Pouilly-Fuissé, they never attain quite the same degree of excellence. As a rule, they are lighter, with less breed than the Pouilly-Fuissé, although they often have more fruitiness.

The geographical distinction is simply that Pouilly-Loché must be harvested within the town of Loché, nearest to Fuissé, and Pouilly-Vinzelles comes from Vinzelles, directly south of Loché. Together they account for about 4,000 hectoliters (106,000 U.S. gallons, 88,000 imp.) of wine per year.

Saint-Véran is a new place-name now gaining favor due to the rising prices of Pouilly-Fuissé. It does not, however, quite reach the quality of the better Pouilly-Fuissés.

Mâcon Supérieur or Mâcon

This *appellation*, followed by the name of the commune, could include red, white, and rosé wines, but in practice slightly more than half are white, and most of the rest red. The red wines are small, generally not of outstanding quality, and even in the headquarters for the area, the town of Mâcon, the red wines drunk are often from the neighboring district of the Beaujolais. The whites are perhaps less distinctive than those of Pouilly-Fuissé, but every now and then one of the better growers will come up with one which will be their equal or even better than some of the lesser Pouillys.

The wine must be grown in the delimited area that lies within the *arrondissement* of Mâcon, or within the communes of Boyer, Bresse-sur-Grosne, Champagny-sous-Uxelles, Champlieu, Etrigny, Jugy, Laives, Mancey, Montceaux-Ragny, Nanton, Sennecey-le-Grand, or Vers. It must be made from a certain selection of grapes. For red wines, only the Gamay Noir à Jus Blanc, Pinot Noir, and Pinot Gris are allowed, with up to 15% Gamay Noir à Jus Coloré and also up to 15% of Pinot Blanc or Chardonnay, the allowable vines for white wines. The normal production of any wine may not exceed 45 hectoliters per hectare (481 U.S. gallons, 400 imp. per acre). In the red there must be a minimum of 180 grams of sugar per liter and 10% of alcohol when that sugar has fermented; and for white wines there must be at least 187 grams (6.5 ounces) of sugar per liter fermenting into 11% of alcohol.

The white wines could be sold as Burgundy, if so desired, and if the reds came only from the Pinot plants, they too could be sold as Burgundy; but there is small incentive for this to be done. As it now stands,

about 150,000 hectoliters (3,975,000 U.S. gallons, 3,300,000 imp.) per year are sold as Mâcon Supérieur, a little more than half of it white.

Mâcon, Pinot-Chardonnay-Mâcon

At the bottom of the Mâconnais scale are those wines which are sold simply as Mâcon-Rouge, Mâcon-Blanc, or Pinot-Chardonnay-Mâcon (something of a misnomer, since the wines can be made from the Pinot Blanc as well as the Chardonnay, the same as the less cumbersome Mâcon-Blanc). All told, the *appellation* covers the lesser red and white wines, but mostly the red.

To earn this place-name, these wines must be harvested in a quantity not exceeding 50 hectoliters per hectare (535 U.S. gallons, 446 imp. per acre), as opposed to the 481 U.S. gallons (400 imp.) figure for the other wines of the district. It is always important to remember that quantity and quality seldom if ever coincide in wines. The same growing area is prescribed as for Mâcon Supérieur; but in the wines themselves, the differences are that red wines for this *appellation* need only have a sugar content in the grape of 162 grams (5.75 ounces) of sugar per liter, giving 9% alcohol, and the white wines must have 170 grams (6 ounces) of sugar, giving 10% of alcohol. Less wine is made today under this *appellation* than before, just over 5,000 hectoliters (132,500 U.S. gallons, 110,000 imp.), about half of it red, half white.

Madagascar

This island lying off the coast of Africa makes a certain amount of rum.
See Rum, French.

Madeira

Until the middle of the eighteenth century, Madeira was exported as an unfortified beverage wine. It is known that brandy was distilled from surplus grapes on the island of Madeira as early as 1704. However, it is not until 1753 that we have the first indication that some of the wine was being roughly fortified; at that time one Francis Newton complained that his deceitful competitors were "putting a bucket or two of brandy with every pipe." Some twenty years later, the practice was general for export wines. In those days too the custom developed of sending casks of the brandied wine on a voyage to the East Indies and back in order to mature it. Madeira then possessed its present character, a distinctive wine with its own unique excellence and the wine became most popular in Britain and the American Colonies—where the trade flourished until, in 1852, the vineyards were blighted by oïdium.

Some great Madeiras were, and still are, made, but the markets built up during the days of sailing ships and exploration have shrunk. Since the shippers united to form the Madeira Wine Association, in order to promote the wine, sales have improved. Today, approximately 500,000 cases of Madeira are produced every year. The wines used to make Madeira represent one third of all wines made on the 1,600 hectares (4,000 acres) planted in vines. The rest is consumed on the island as table wine. The shippers own very little of the vineyard land in Madeira, which is split up among the thousands of farmers, so at harvest time they buy grapes or wine at pre-arranged prices.

WINE HISTORY

The history of the island is almost the history of its wines. Madeira is politically an integral part of Portugal and geographically an island in the Atlantic 575 kilometers (360 miles) from the coast of Morocco and 850 kilometers (530 miles) from Lisbon. It is 57 kilometers (36 miles) long and 23 kilometers (14.5 miles) wide, a holiday-maker's paradise of steeply sloping, intricately terraced hillside vineyards and shady flower-filled valleys.

Madeira was known to the ancient Phoenicians, Genoese, and Portuguese as the "Enchanted Isles." But none was so audacious as to penetrate the thick woods and see what was there until Prince Henry the Navigator sent the intrepid Captain João Gonçalves (known as Zarco) to claim them for Portugal in 1419. Madeira, "Isle of Trees," was aptly named. Trees intertwined and woven together claimed the entire island and defeated all attempts to hack through them. Zarco solved the problem. He set the island on fire and sat back to wait.

According to legend he waited a long time. It is said that the fire raged for seven years . . . and when it had finally sputtered out, the trees were gone and the centuries-old humus and leaf-mold volcanic soil had been enriched into the most fertile then known.

Settlers arrived from Portugal, Spain, Holland, and Italy; sugar-cane and the Malvoisie vines were planted. The rich soil and subtropical climate made Madeira a lush garden in the midst of the Atlantic. Mariners called in at Funchal in search of fresh water, fresh food, and to replenish wine casks. Treaties between Portugal and Britain helped Madeira as well as Port wines. Englishmen who departed to establish colonies in America took their tastes with them, and Madeira began to be shipped to the New World as well as the old. As the American colonists moved toward rupture with England, Madeira became more and more the wine of America and its consumption almost a patriotic duty. In drinking Madeira, the rebellious colonist could feel he was thumbing his nose at a tyrannical king and parliament who had established a ruling that European goods going to the American Colonies could only be carried in British ships. Naturally, British shipmasters were not above charging a premium price for the exercise of this monopoly; but, geograph-

ically, Madeira is in Africa, and under the terms of the law its wines could arrive on ships bearing any flag. The idea was quickly grasped by the Americans, and Madeira was a common sight on American sideboards. In *The House of the Seven Gables*, Nathaniel Hawthorne described the glories of an old, golden Madeira. The popularity of the wine along the Eastern Seaboard lasted for the period of the clipper ships.

The English writer Captain Frederick Marryat remarked in his *Diary in America*: "Claret and other French wines do very well in America, but where the Americans beat us out of the field is in their Madeira, which certainly is of a quality which we cannot procure in England. This is owing to the extreme heat and cold of the climate, which ripens this wine; indeed, I may almost say that I never tasted good Madeira until I arrived in the United States. The price of wines, generally speaking, is very high, considering what a trifling duty is paid, but the price of good Madeira is surprising. There are certain brands which if exposed to public auction, will be certain to fetch from twelve to twenty, and I have been told, even forty dollars per bottle."

During the eighteenth and early nineteenth centuries, the fortunes of Madeira were probably at their peak. The Napoleonic Wars had cut into French wine exports, but Madeira was untouched and business boomed. Fortification had put strength into the wines, and the long sea voyage aged and ripened them. Shipments to England and America were heavy, with the ports of the southern states—Savannah and New Orleans, Charleston and Baltimore—handling the bulk of the trade.

Disaster fell on Madeira in 1852, when oïdium struck the vines. They were just recovering from the attack of this fungus blight when they were again attacked, by phylloxera in 1872. This time, weakened by the ravages of the oïdium, they succumbed to the *Phylloxera vastatrix*, which attacked their roots and killed the vines. Many of the old-established British shippers left the island, and it is to the courage, endurance, and persistence of a handful who remained that we owe the present Madeira wine. They imported American rootstocks which had become immune to the disease (phylloxera having originally spread from America to Europe). It was many years before these American vines were in full production, and when there was enough wine to ship, this was found to be coarse, although plentiful, since the American plants are prolific. The vines had to be cut down and grafted with the pre-phylloxera European vine.

WINE-MAKING

The vintage is probably as picturesque in Madeira as anywhere in the world and is certainly the longest. Starting at sea level in mid-August it continues as the grapes ripen on the slopes until October. The crushing of the grapes is still done in *lagares*, or large wooden troughs, by barefooted men, although no doubt the old custom will soon be superseded by mechanical pressing. The "dance" of the grapes is followed by a more rigorous pressing, after which the grape juice (*mosto*) is carried in goatskins to the wine sheds to be tipped into wooden casks and then carried by truck to the shippers' lodges in Funchal.

The *mosto* ferments and turns itself into wine or *vinho claro*, which is put into an *estufa* to go through a process, peculiar to Madeira, known as *estufagem* (bringing the wine up to a warm temperature either in glass jars laid out in the sun or in a sort of heating chamber). This process is a relic of the old days of the East India voyages. The rolling of the ship and the heat of the tropics obviously hastened the maturing of the wine, but during the Napoleonic Wars, when freights were difficult to obtain, the process of *estufagem* was invented.

The *estufa* today is a large store with central heating in which casks of wine are placed for six months. The temperature of the wine is gradually brought up to 104° to 114°F. (40° to 46°C.) and then allowed to drop to normal in the sixth month, thus producing much the same effect as would a voyage around the world.

The sweeter Madeiras are fortified with brandy before they go into the heating chamber; but the dry styles are allowed to ferment out, and the brandy is added after they have been in the *estufa*.

Wine which has never been *estufado* is known as *canteiro*. When the wine comes out of the *estufa*, it goes through an *estágio*, which is an eighteen-month rest to recover from the treatment. Then it is matured in a *solera* system, as used for Sherry (*q.v.*), and some wines are afterward blended before shipping.

There are no vintage Madeiras now and—since the wines were blended—the dates of old vintages serve to tell the age of the wine rather than celebrate a special year.

Madeira lives longer than any other wine; there are still some priceless old pre-phylloxera vintages in existence. Tasting them is not only a pleasure but an exciting and memorable experience.

WINE TYPES

There are four distinct types of Madeira, named after the grapes from which they are produced, ranging from dry to full-rich, with intermediate steps between. These are:

Sercial. The best of the dry Madeiras, generally taken slightly cooled, as an aperitif. Sometimes pale, sometimes golden, often slight in body, but always dry with an overwhelming nose. André Simon, the famous writer on wines, has described one of them as "a soul with a nose."

Verdelho. Sweeter and stronger than a Sercial; leaves a dry, clean taste in the mouth; excellent with soup, and is the proverbial companion to turtle soups. In Victorian days, mid-morning callers were frequently entertained with a slice of cake and a glass of this Madeira.

Bual (Boal). Fuller and sweeter than either of the preceding, russet to dark in color with a distinctive bouquet. A dessert wine.

Malmsey. From the Malvoisie grape. A rich, luscious, generous wine with considerable body, balance, and bouquet. This type of Madeira is excellent after dinner. Madeira, with its long history, has a few wines which are either scarce or extinct: Terrantez, medium-sweet, is a typical example.

Other names to be found on bottles of Madeira are:

Rainwater. A blend. Originally a trademark, it has now become almost a generic name. The wine may be dry or medium-rich but it is always pale and light, as the name implies.

Dated Soleras. Many dated *soleras* are offered for sale; the word *solera* before or after the date denotes that these wines are not only of that date but have from time to time been topped up with specially chosen younger wines of equal quality and similar characteristics. The average age of a *solera* is estimated to be some eighty years. These are always particularly fine wines.

Leading shippers in the Madeira Wine Association are Blandy's Madeiras Lda., Leacock & Co. (Wine) Lda. (whose founder arrived in Madeira in 1741), Rutherford & Miles Ltd., Cossart Gordon & Co. Ltd., T.T.C. Lomedino Lda. (a firm with a remarkable reserve of old wines), Shortridge Lawton & Co. Ltd., F.F. Ferraz Lda., Luis Gomes (Vinhos) Lda., and Freitas Martins Caldeira Lda.

Others, outside the Association, are Henriques & Henriques, H.M. Borges, Vinhos Barbeito, Marcel Gomes & Cia Lda., and Veiga Franca & Co. Ltd.

In his most explicit book, *Portuguese Wine*, Raymond Postgate also mentions Avery of Bristol who, although a merchant and not a shipper, "has a selection of Madeiras approached by no other, and taken from many sources. . . . The oldest is a Verdelho of about 1846."

Maderization

Owing to age or poor storage, white wines may lose their freshness and fruitiness and acquire a brown tinge. This browning or oxidation has been named maderization, from the Madeira taste, which is connected with the presence in the wine of ethylic aldehyde—the result either of oxidation of alcohol, or of the dissociation of aldehyde-sulfurous acid through progressive oxidation of sulfurous acid. Maderization also results from leaving white wines in the barrel too long before bottling. In the Madeiras, Marsalas, Sherry and the Château-Chalons of the French Jura, maderization adds to the greatness of the wines, producing a taste called *rancio*. In other white wines it is a flaw. It is particularly unpleasant in the Montrachets and Meursaults of the Côte de Beaune and is more unpleasant in Graves than in Sauternes (whose sweetness hides the flat, musty, brownish taste).

By combining the action of sulfur dioxide with that of casein, it is possible to protect wines against maderization, and the flat taste can be corrected with sulfurous acid.

Madiran (Appellation Contrôlée)

Red wine from the Hautes-Pyrénées district of southwest France. The wine, full in body and of a pronounced bouquet, is made from Tannat (30% to 70%), Cabernet Sauvignon, Bouchy, Cabernet Franc, and Pinenc grapes and attains 11% of alcohol. The white wine made in this area in the valley of the Adour is Pacherenc du Vic Bilh *(q.v.)*. Annual production averages 37,000 hectoliters.

Magnum

A bottle of 1.5 liters, twice the normal capacity. Since some red wines age more successfully in larger quantities, Bordeaux and Burgundies of fine years are sometimes bottled in this larger size for laying down.

Mailly

Village near Rheims producing a first-quality Champagne *(q.v.)*.

Maipo Valley

One of the best wine regions in Chile (the other is the Aconcagua Valley), specializing in Cabernet and Malbec grapes and making long-lasting wines of finesse and balance.

See Chile.

Maître de chai

French term for the man in charge of vinification and ageing of all the wine made on an estate in Bordeaux. The title, which may be shortened to *maître*, is used especially in Bordeaux, for the head cellarman at the château or at the shipper's *chais*. He is of necessity an experienced wine-maker and a good taster. In other districts, the *maître de chai* will be called a *caviste*.

Málaga

Spanish dessert wines.
District: East Andalusia.

This hottest, once sleepiest, corner of the Spanish coast, where sun-ripened grapes oozed sweetness and where the soft climate may well have induced a certain lethargy in the inhabitants, has been modernized, its capital urbanized, and its way of life transformed by the *tourismo* of Torremolinos, Marbella, and the rest of the Costa del Sol. In the past, Málaga was famous for its sweet wines, which had a great success abroad. There are many references in English literature to "Mountain" and to Málaga "Sack"; but little is seen of them in Anglo-Saxon countries today. Yet Málaga is made—some of it, produced by traditional methods, is as good as ever—and it is still exported. Germany heads the list of customers, followed by Switzerland, Scandinavia, and France. In 1975, 5,000 hectares (12,500 acres) of vineland granted the Denominación de Origen produced 55,000 hectoliters (1,457,500 U.S. gallons, 1,210,000 imp.) of wine.

The vineyards, hardly visible from the coast, are planted up the mountain slopes, with the finest plots around Archidona, Antequera, and Velez-Málaga. The Pedro-Ximénez grape, here coming into its own, is used in a ratio of 60% for blending with about 20% Lairen, 15% Moscatel, and 5% other grapes of the area, all combining to make this strong, rich, dark wine. The region has a long history. The great variety of grapes, both for wine and for eating, have been praised by ancient Greek, Roman, and Renaissance writers. The Moorish conquerors, whether or not they drank the forbidden wine, enjoyed the luscious table grapes—which are still grown, many of them to be dried into the succulent raisins of the region. Presents of wine are said to have been sent to Tamerlane the Great and Catherine the Great; the History of the Pedro Ximénez was traced in *Cosmografía de Merula*, published in Amsterdam in 1636. Columella who, in the first century, discussed the wines in his *Re Rustica*, was himself of Andalusian descent.

Málaga, unlike the dark Sherries, is a natural wine with about 16% of alcohol. It is not fortified with brandy. Formerly, the celebrated Lágrima Christi (not to be confused with the Italian Lacrima Christi, which is quite different) was made by allowing the grapes to shed their sweetness drop by drop without pressing. Such wines are not now made commercially; the name is usually given to a rather average, sweetish brown wine. From a multitude of small vineyards (some of which will produce, for the growers' own use, excellent pure "Mountains") come red wines and others; but the characteristic Málaga, the quality wine protected by the Denominación de Origen, is made by traditional methods in the big *bodegas* of the town, from wine, must, or grapes supplied by small farmers. The best are matured by the *solera* system described under Sherry *(q.v.)*.

Before pressing, the grapes are spread on straw mats to grow overripe and sugary in the sun. They ferment in large oak vats (in big *bodegas*, some of these have an enormous capacity); then the new wine is piped into oak butts to mature for two or three years, when it will either be sold to the wine shops or will take its place in the *solera* of the *bodega*'s fine wines. These, in all their nuances of sweetness and color, develop in different styles, as follows:

Málaga dulce color	Very sweet; very dark (blackish brown).
Málaga blanco dulce	Very sweet; golden yellow to topaz.
Málaga semi-dulce	Fairly sweet; both golden yellow and red.
Málaga Lágrima and Lágrima Christi	Very sweet; old gold or dark; undistinguished.
Málaga blanco seco	Only fairly dry; pale gold; agreeable aftertaste.
Málaga Moscatel	Amber color; distinct flavor of the grape.
Pedro Ximénez	Luscious-sweet; very dark with reddish glint.
Málaga Rome	Strong wines, vinified both red and golden white.
Málaga Pajarete	Strong (15% to 20%); pale and dark amber.
Tintillo de Málaga	15% to 16% alcohol; red color.

In maturity, a well-made Málaga may be a wine of considerable distinction. Describing such a one, tasted in the *bodega* Scholtz Hermanos, Mr. H. W. Yoxall wrote: "Just as a touch of something cold leaves you uncertain whether it has frozen or burnt you, so in the taste of great Málagas, the sugar is sublimated and becomes almost astringent"—adding that, in England, few Málagas are seen now, and none of the best.

Here, as elsewhere, common, cloying wines are made; others, such as Rome and Pajarete, and some of the semi-sweet types, are often mixed with *vino tinto*. The wines listed above range between 14% and 23% of alcohol.

The principal producers and exporters in Málaga are:

Hijos de A. Barceló, S.A.; Luis Barceló, S.A.; Flores Hermanos, S.A.; Felix García Gómez; José Garijo Ruiz; Carlos J. Krauel; Larios, S.A.; López Hermanos, S.A.; Compañía Mata, S.A.; Juan Mory & Cía., S.A.; Pérez Texeira, S.A.; Guillermo Rein Segura; Casa Romero, S.L.; Scholtz Hermanos, S.A.; Hijos de José Suárez Villalba; Vinícola Andalucía, S.A.; and Manuel Pacheco Morón.

Château Malartic-Lagravière

Bordeaux red and white wines.
District: Graves, France.
Commune: Léognan.

The red wine has had a good reputation for many years; it was included among the eleven best red wines of Graves in the 1953 and 1959 Classifications. The white wine was classified in 1959 and is less well known than the red.

Characteristics. The red is a big, mouth-filling wine with a distinctive taste, probably arising from the high proportion—65%—of Cabernet Sauvignon grapes. Merlot makes up the remaining 35%. The white wine is exclusively Sauvignon Blanc.

Vineyard area: red—11 hectares (27.5 acres); white—1.5 hectares (nearly 4 acres).

Average production: red—45 *tonneaux* (4,000 cases); white—6 *tonneaux* (550 cases).

Malbec

One of the lesser grapes contributing to the red wines of Bordeaux, prolific and light in character. It is grown in other places too, and is sometimes known as Cot.

Château Malescot-Saint-Exupéry

Bordeaux red wine.
District: Haut-Médoc, France.
Commune: Margaux.

The vineyard name derives from the Counts of Saint-Exupéry, who purchased the vineyard in 1827, and the château itself, a substantial gray-stone manor-house, is right in the town of Margaux. The building, nothing but a shell after being gutted by the Germans, was repaired in 1964 by Roger Zuger, the present owner.

In recent years, until 1955, the estate belonged to Seager Evans, British distillers, who sold it in that year to the late Paul Zuger—up to that time their administrator in the vineyard and one who had always been an able winemaker. Zuger was the president of the association of the official wine place-names of Margaux, which came into being in 1956.

The vineyard was classified Third Growth (*Troisième Cru*) in the Médoc Classification of 1855.

Characteristics. Quite full for a Margaux wine, very elegant and sometimes slightly hard at the outset. The wines reflect the high proportion—80%—of Cabernet Sauvignon grapes used.

Vineyard area: 32 hectares (80 acres).
Average production: 140 *tonneaux* (12,000 cases).

Malic acid

One of the most abundant acids in unripe grapes, but one that is partially destroyed as the fruit matures; $COOH \cdot CH_2 \cdot CHOH \cdot COOH$.

Château de Malle

Bordeaux white wine.
District: Sauternes, France.
Commune: Preignac.

The wine is light, fresh, and clean—every bit as pleasant as the château, beautifully maintained by the owner, Comte Pierre de Bournazel. The vineyard was placed among the Second Growths in the 1855 Classification.

Vineyard area: 20 hectares (50 acres).
Average production: 40 *tonneaux* (3,700 cases).

Malmesbury

Wine region in the coastal belt of the Cape province.
See South Africa.

Malmsey

English corruption of the name of a vine which started out as Monemvasia in Greece, became Malvasia in Italy, Malvoisie in France, and Malvagia in Spain. Malmsey is also used to refer to the wines from this vine, the most famous of which—during the present day—come from the island of Madeira (q.v.), a Portuguese possession in the Atlantic.

Malmsey was famous in the England of Shakespeare's day, and the references to it are numerous. Perhaps the best-known fact about Malmsey is that the Duke of Clarence was drowned in a butt of it. It is likely that the wine in which the unfortunate Duke found his end came from the island of Crete rather than from Madeira.

Malolactic fermentation

Secondary fermentation, caused by the conversion of malic acid into lactic acid and carbon dioxide. When this occurs while the wine is in barrel, the result is simply a reduction in acid strength; but in bottle, the malolactic fermentation causes the wine to become turgid and gassy. This happens much more frequently in Burgundy than it does in Bordeaux and may be the result of premature bottling.

The fermentation is caused by certain acid-tolerant species of *Lactobacillus* and *Leuconostoc* bacteria. The distinctiveness of different species of these malolactic bacteria endogenous to specific wineries may be an important factor in establishing the individual character of the wines produced.

See Chapter Nine, page 40.

Malta

Vines are grown mostly among the southern coastal strip of the island, but since the climate changes from torrential early rains to scorching heat, the resulting wine is generally harsh and rough; an ordinary wine, either red or white. An attempt is being made to produce sweet, rich dessert wine from Muscat grapes, principally for exportation to England. About 1,000 hectares (2,500 acres) are vineyard, especially around Burmarrad, Rabat, and Sigiewi. Gellewza, Gannaru, Nigruwa, and Dun Tumas grapes are among the better-known varieties. Production is probably about 19,-000 hectoliters (500,000 U.S. gallons, 418,000 imp.) annually.

Malvasia

Originally Monemvasia in its native Greece, the grape Malvasia has spread throughout the viticultural world, sometimes with modifications in name. In France it is Malvoisie, in Spain Malvagia, and the sweet, heavy wines it gives became famous long ago in England as Malmsey.

Mandarine

Sweet, gold-colored liqueur with the flavor of tangerines.

Manganese

This is present in almost all wines, in quantities never large but varying with the different vineyard soils. More of the mineral is found in Beaujolais than in Bordeaux, more in red wine than in white. Most of the manganese in a grape is contained in the pips.

Mannitic fermentation

When the temperature of the fermenting vat rises above 95°F. (35°C.) and when the wines are lacking in acidity, then the good yeasts die and other bacteria take over. The wine then throws a deposit and becomes cloudy, with a bitter-sweet, "mousy" taste.
See Chapter Nine, page 40.

Manzanilla

The dry fine wine, fortified and unfortified, of Sanlúcar de Barrameda, Spain, sold as a type of Sherry.
See Sherry; Montilla.

Maraschino

A liqueur made from the sour cherry Marasca, which only grew in Dalmatia. Before the Italian enclave in Dalmatia was incorporated in Yugoslavia, maraschino was not made anywhere except in Zadar (sometimes known by its former name, Zara). Maraschino, 50% proof, is sold in wicker half-liter bottles. Luxardo is the largest distiller. After the war the company moved from Trieste to Padua; to ensure their supply they planted 80 hectares (200 acres) of Marasca cherries. Drioli, a lesser firm, is the other well-known Italian maraschino distiller.

Marc, eau-de-vie de marc

Spirit distilled from the pomace which remains when the grapes have been pressed and the juice run off. It is usually distilled at a high strength and has a distinctive taste—grapey, almost leathery—when it is well aged. Most districts have their own marcs; those from Burgundy are the best known, and excellent marcs come from Romanée-Conti, Musigny, Chambertin, Nuits-Saint-Georges, Meursault, and Montrachet. Marcs from the white-wine Burgundy districts are lighter and have a little more finesse than those from the red-wine areas. The most expensive is the Marc des Hospices de Beaune; one of the lightest, and one with great finesse, comes from Champagne. Another of repute is the Marc d'Auvergne.

In Italy and California, this spirit is known as grappa.

The Marches

Red and white wines.
District: East-Central Italy.

Like the rest of the peninsula, this Italian state is steeped in history—even the name is said to date from the days when the area was a frontier province in the empire of Charlemagne. Here as elsewhere in Italy, the countryside is strewn with vines, both well-tended and ragged, which yield over 2 million hectoliters (53 million U.S. gallons, 44 million imp.) of wine annually—most of it fit solely for local drinking.

Exception should be made for the Verdicchio dei Castelli di Jesi, a good light D.O.C. wine, either dry or semi-sweet, with a pale gold or straw color. Sometimes it can be surprisingly high in alcohol—up to 14%. The wine is from Verdicchio grapes grown at Cupramontana, Monteroberto, and Castebellino in the province of Ancona and is one of the lesser wines of Italy which travel. The *classico* is a better wine from the old area, or *zona antica*. Verdicchio di Matelica is another D.O.C. wine similar to Verdicchio di Jesi but made a bit farther inland from the Adriatic coast. The annual production is about 25,000 hectoliters (662,500 U.S. gallons, 550,000 imp.), only one-fourth of the volume of di Jesi.

Rosso Piceno D.O.C. from the Sangiovese and Montepulciano varieties is often claimed to be the best red wine of the province.

Rosso Conero; Conero (red) D.O.C. derives its name from the word the Greeks gave to the marine cherry tree that still grows on the slopes of the Conero mountain. Red, dry, fairly acid, yet fruity, this is just a pleasant local wine made near Ancona from Montepulciano and Sangiovese grapes.

Bianchello del Metauro is a D.O.C. white wine made of Bianchello and some Malvasia grown on the picturesque hills of Metauro, where one of the greatest battles of antiquity was fought when the Romans defeated the Carthaginians. The wine is understandably light and dry, and the large production goes well with local fish cookery.

The Marches yield a dry and sweet red sparkling D.O.C. called Vernaccia di Serrapetrona.

Marcottage or layering

Traditional method of propagating vines.
See Chapter Eight, p. 31.

Mareotic wine

A fine wine of Ancient Egypt, very well known in classical times. Cleopatra is said to have served it to Caesar.
See Egypt.

Mareuil-sur-Ay

A village in the department of the Marne and the commune of the Champagne district, near Épernay, producing very fine wines.
See Champagne.

Margaux

Bordeaux red wines.
District: Haut-Médoc, France.

Margaux wines form a royal family. The Great Growths (*Grands Crus*) and the least among the modest vineyards all share the same characteristics. No other commune of Bordeaux and the Médoc contains such a distinct gradation of similar vineyards.

It is the summer of great sun that brings Margaux to its prime. In the best years, the greater Growths of the fine districts a little to the north, in Saint-Estèphe and Pauillac, may overreach themselves; in any case, it will be a long time before they are ready to drink. But in Margaux, the strong sun will have awakened the subtle hidden virtues which lie in the vines. In these best years, Margaux vineyards may surpass all others in the Médoc. The wines they give are the most feminine, the most delicate, the most elegant; and it is the bolder Saint-Estèphe or, characteristically, a Pauillac which will sometimes excel in the lighter years.

The name Margaux is said to derive from Marojallia, so called by Ausonius, the fourth-century Latin poet after whom the Château Ausone, in Saint-Émilion, was also named.

The village of Margaux itself lies some 25 kilometers (15 miles) northwest of Bordeaux, and it is a sleepy place. In the season of fermentation the smell of the wine is everywhere in the air, as thick as the smoke from burning leaves. Tall châteaux with steep roofs stand right in the village, and plots of vine encroach on the dwellings and shops. Beyond, everything is vine—a calm ocean, brown in winter and green in summer, but always ruffled by a breeze. An occasional château rises in the distance, with its park around it like a froth of waves.

Five villages, not one, have the right to the place-name of Margaux. A quarter of a century ago, the wine of all five was considered as one—Margaux itself, Arsac, Soussans, Cantenac, and Labarde produced similar wines and shared the same light gravelly Margaux soil. Then, the mayor of Margaux, a wine man himself, brought a suit against a certain proprietor in Soussans. This grower had a strip of land along the riverbank where the soil, a muddy alluvial deposit, is not the true soil of Margaux, and its wine had no right, therefore, to the place-name. The legal process was fought and won, but the result was hardly what had been intended. The court ruled that neither the wine from this one vineyard nor any other made in Soussans could be called Margaux.

Within a few years, similar rulings denied the Margaux name to Arsac, Labarde, and Cantenac. There was consternation, for only a single important Margaux vineyard had all its vines in Margaux, and every other overlapping into the outcast communes by even an acre now had no right to the name, since some of its wine did not come from within the permitted circle. Margaux was almost in a state of civil war—because certain rather undistinguished growers safely within the commune now had a vested interest in resisting change.

For twenty years nothing could be done. Even when the Appellation Contrôlée, or officially controlled place-name, was established, the authorities were obliged to respect the earlier rulings of the courts. Then in 1953 someone had a bright idea. If Margaux could not mean what it ought to, why have any Margaux at all? At last action could be taken; and the place-name Margaux, which could not be extended back to its rightful limits, was totally suppressed: not even Margaux wine could now call itself Margaux. Again there was consternation, and this time the sit-tight Margaux growers found that they could not sell their wines, could not get the proper documents, could not export. They demanded a decision, and the Appellation Contrôlée authorities suggested that perhaps the whole problem ought to be reconsidered.

As a result, new regulations were laid down defining Margaux wines as those from the communes of Margaux, Soussans, Arsac, Cantenac, and Labarde. The regulations also stated that the wines must be grown from soils ascertained by the experts of the Appellation Contrôlée to be typically Margaux, and that they may not yield more than 45 hectoliters to the hectare (475 U.S. gallons, 395 imp. to the acre); and in type of noble grape variety, in methods of pruning, cultivation, and wine-making, they must come up to high-quality standards and must satisfactorily pass an anonymous taste test. Some 1,000 hectares now have the right to the *appellation*—or less than 2,500 acres, producing some 4,000,000 bottles per year.

The first of the tastings for the Appellation Contrôlée Margaux took place in 1956, and the subsequent banquet and festivities were held in the great salon of Château Lascombes.

It is rare that the leading vineyard of an area epitomizes and brings to the highest perfection the district characteristics, rather than standing out for excellences more peculiarly its own, but this is the case with Château Margaux. The Margaux vineyards rated as Classified Growths (*Crus*) in the 1855 Classification are:

FIRST GROWTH (*Premier Cru*)

Château Margaux

SECOND GROWTHS (*Seconds Crus*)

Château Rausan-Ségla   Château Durfort-Vivens
Château Rauzan-Gassies   Château Brane-Cantenac
Château Lascombes

THIRD GROWTHS (*Troisièmes Crus*)

Château Kirwan   Château Cantenac-Bro\
Château d'Issan   Château Palmer
Château Giscours   Château Desmirail
Château Malescot-   Château Ferrière
  Saint-Exupéry   Château Marquis d'Alesme
Château Boyd-Cantenac

FOURTH GROWTHS (*Quatrièmes Crus*)

Château Prieuré-Lichine   Château Marquis-de-Terme
Château Pouget

FIFTH GROWTHS (*Cinquièmes Crus*)

Château Dauzac   Château du Tertre

(*For the individual Classified Growths, see individual châteaux names.*)

Château Margaux

Bordeaux red wine, some dry white.
District: Haut-Médoc, France.
Commune: Margaux.

Château Margaux, with its colonnaded portico and an interior which is pure Empire, stands in a large park beside a magnificent magnolia tree. In the fifteenth century the wine, under such names as Margou and Margous, was already known, and the site was occupied by a fortified castle known as Lamothe. It is interesting to note that one of the owners of Lamothe was the Seigneur de Durfort, whereas, until recently, the proprietor of Margaux owned the nearby Château Durfort.

The vineyard was greatly improved by M. de Fumel, also owner of Château Haut-Brion, with replantings in 1750. The present château was built at the beginning of the nineteenth century—by a pupil of Victor Louis, architect of the Bordeaux opera house. In 1836 a banker, the Vicomte d'Aguado, bought the property. His son sold it in 1879 to the Comte Pillet-Will, who introduced various vinicultural improvements. By 1925 the château had come into the possession of the Duc de la Trémoïlle, from whom a corporation (including Fernand Ginestet, then owner of the adjacent Château Lascombes) acquired it. Between the years 1935 and 1949 Ginestet bought out his partners, and became principal owner. Bernard and Pierre Ginestet owned and managed Château Margaux until 1977, when they sold it to Laura and the late André Mentzelopoulos, then the owners of the Felix Potin grocery-store chain in France. The vineyards and the château have been renovated, all to the credit of the new owners.

With Château Lafite, Latour, and Haut-Brion, Margaux has been ranked first among Médoc wines since 1855. There is also a small amount of dry white wine (approximately 3,000 cases annually), known as Pavillon Blanc de Château Margaux.

Characteristics. At its best, the most elegant and delicately feminine of the region. Perfectly balanced and quick to develop, for a Médoc. Finesse is synonymous with its name. In 1965, Pierre Ginestet instituted the controversial policy of affixing a vintage only to great vintages; the lesser years were sold as non-vintage wines, as is done in Champagne. This practice was discontinued in 1969. Since the Mentzelopoulos takeover, the wine has once again become great. In 1981, Laura Mentzelopoulos, with the help of her daughter Corinne, undertook the construction of a huge underground cellar, despite the difficulties, to achieve better storage conditions.

Vineyard area: Red—75 hectares (187.5 acres), white—12 hectares (30 acres).

Average production: Red—250 *tonneaux* (23,000 cases). Some 2,000 to 4,000 cases of white.

Marino (D.O.C.)

Usually white wines from Latium *(q.v.)*.

Markobrunn, Marcobrunn

From Erbach on the German Rhine, Markobrunn was occasionally labeled Markobrunner—but it was one of the few German wines so great in its own right as to eliminate the town or village or district name in most cases. Not perhaps the greatest of the Rheingau, although easily the best of the Erbachers, it is certainly one of the liveliest, heartiest, spiciest, and deservedly best-known Rhine wines.

See Rheingau.

Marl

The crumbly combination of calcium carbonate and clay which is often added to soils lacking lime.

Château Marquis d'Alesme-Becker

Bordeaux red wine.
District: Haut-Médoc, France.
Commune: Margaux.

Originally planted in 1616, the estate was acquired in 1803 by a M. Becker, which accounts for some confusion about the name of the wine. For a long time Becker attached his name to that of the Marquis d'Alesme, and Becker being the simpler name, the wine began to be called simply Becker in Bordeaux. Bottles labeled until a few years ago are likely to carry the name Marquis d'Alesme; but Becker has now been added again.

The small vineyard occupies one of the finest positions in Margaux, the knoll of Margaux, or La Combe. The vineyard's present owner is Jean-Claude Zuger, who inherited it from his father, Paul. Originally it shared as headquarters Château Malescot, now owned by Jean-Claude's brother Roger. Jean-Claude, however, had also inherited the château building of Château Desmirail, situated in the village of Margaux (the

building, not the Desmirail vineyard, which was sold to Château Palmer); and he has since renamed the building after d'Alesme-Becker and made it his vineyard's new headquarters. This Third Growth (*Troisième Cru*) was classified in 1855.

Characteristics. A minor and not well-known wine with the typical finesse of Margaux.

Vineyard area: 15 hectares (38 acres).

Average production: 75 *tonneaux* (7,200 cases).

Château Marquis-de-Terme

Bordeaux red wine.
District: Haut-Médoc, France.
Commune: Margaux.

This Fourth Growth (*Quatrième Cru*) of Médoc, Classification of 1855, was in the opinion of many one of the best-kept vineyards in the Médoc. In the past, the wine failed to come quite up to the expectation of the marvelously handled vines. Since 1975, judicious pruning has decreased the quantity and improved the quality of the wines. The Sénéclauze family are the present owners.

Characteristics. Relatively full for a Margaux, and although not among the top wines of this commune, despite its large production it often attains finesse and perfume. Since 1981 a new *chai*, worth visiting, has been built for the new and older stocks.

Vineyard area: 38 hectares (95 acres).

Average production: 150 *tonneaux* (14,000 cases).

Marsala

The principal dessert wine of Italy is made in northwest Sicily, where the town of that name is situated. In the late eighteenth century it was introduced into England by Mr. John Woodhouse, whose family soon built up a flourishing trade. The dark wine, which is also served as an aperitif, is a blend of an aromatic white wine, of *passito* made from grapes dried and fortified, and of grape-juice syrup. It is matured in cask for from two to five years.

Marsala all'uovo, or Marsaluovo, is a smooth, warming winter drink of Marsala combined with egg yolk and spirit—a development, perhaps, of zabaglione, the frothy sweet made from egg and Marsala.

See Sicily.

Marsannay, Marsannay-la-Côte

A town on the very northern part of the Côte de Nuits, just south of Dijon. Some pleasant white called Chardonnay de Marsannay and a small quantity of agreeable red labeled Pinot Noir de Marsannay is made, but the best wine of the town is its Rosé de Marsannay. Also made from the Pinot Noir, it is one of the most delightful and refreshing *vins rosés* in all France. The official name of the *appellation* is Marsannay or Marsannay Rosé.

Marsanne

Marsanne

White wine grape planted in Provence, Algeria, Savoy, and elsewhere.

Martina (D.O.C.)

Italian white wines from near Bari.
See Apulia.

Mascara

Important Algerian wine region, near Oran. Red, white, and rosé wines are grown here. This dark red wine was often used as a base for many of the better-known wines of France, especially in Burgundy, where it was a favorite part of a "shipper's blend."
See Algeria.

Mash

In whisky-making, grain which has been steeped in hot water. During the mashing process, the starch in the grain is converted to fermentable sugar.

Mastika (Masticha)

A favorite Greek aperitif, made on the island of Chios from a brandy base with gum mastic added.
See Greece.

Maury (Appellation Contrôlée)

Small area of the Roussillon producing fortified sweet wines.
See Sweet fortified wines of France.

Mavrodaphne

Mavrodaphne, a heavy, sweet, red dessert wine of Greece, is also the name of a grape.

Mavroud

One of the grapes widely used in Bulgaria. It produces wines of about the same acidity and alcoholic strength as those made from the Gamza, but this wine has a dark ruby color.
See Bulgaria.

Maximin Grünhäuser Abtsberg

One of the best wines of the Ruwer. Abtsberg is the top vineyard of Mertesdorf-Grünhaus.
See Mosel-Saar-Ruwer.

May wine

Traditional preparation of a light Rhine wine into which the aromatic leaves of the herb Waldmeister (woodruff) have been infused. May wine is served chilled and ladled from a bowl, usually with strawberries or other fruit floating in it. A gay and refreshing drink, it can actually be prepared almost anywhere with either a Rhine wine or any light, dry, white wine.

Mazis-Chambertin (Appellation Contrôlée)

Burgundy red wine.
District: Côte de Nuits, France.
Commune: Gevrey-Chambertin.
Official Classification: Great Growth (Grand Cru).

Mazis (sometimes Mazys) is only slightly below Latricières-Chambertin in the hierarchy of wines which add Chambertin to their names, and to achieve this place is no mean accomplishment. The two giants of the commune of Gevrey-Chambertin are Le Chambertin and Chambertin-Clos de Béze. Latricières is generally conceded to come next.

The vineyard adjoins the Clos de Bèze on the south side of Gevrey-Chambertin and its wines often have much in common with those from the ancient Clos, although they are generally lighter and with enormous finesse, perhaps lacking some of the austere strength of the Clos wines. There are 12.6 hectares (31.5 acres) planted exclusively in Pinot Noir grapevines and production in an average year for quality is the equivalent of some 2,500 cases.

Mazoyères-Chambertin (Appellation Contrôlée)

Burgundy red wine.
District: Côte de Nuits, France.
Commune: Gevrey-Chambertin.
Official Classification: Great Growth (Grand Cru).

Mazoyères is a vineyard listed as a Great Growth *(Grand Cru)* in the official classification of the wines of the Côte d'Or of Burgundy. The ruling reads Mazoyères or Charmes, and in practice it means that Mazoyères may be sold as Charmes although Charmes may not be sold as Mazoyères. Most of the growers take advantage of this ruling, feeling that Charmes is both easier to say and better known than Mazoyères.
See Charmes-Chambertin.

Mead

The drink of ancient Gauls and Anglo-Saxons, made from fermented honey. It is a clear, pale, golden liquid tasting of honey, with usually about 8% alcohol by volume. Hydromel (honey-water) was the Roman equivalent, and metheglin (from the Welsh) is a spiced mead. When mead has been distilled it is called honey brandy.

Mealie beer

A native grain beverage drunk in South Africa.

Meal-moth

The meal-moth, or *Pyralis*, feeds on the foliage and fruit of the vine.

See Chapter Eight, p. 31.

Medford rum

Name given to virtually all rum made in colonial America.

See Rum, New England.

Medicated and medicinal wines

Wines enriched with spices and/or drugs have long been used by physicians in treating diseases. Dioscorides, Galen, and others through the ages have given various recipes. Medical use of wine is mentioned in all medieval regimes for health. In modern times, cheap, red, fortified wines often have meat extract or extract of malt and other substances added, purportedly to render them more health-giving. In some instances, wines are treated with ipecacuanha or pepsin, in which case they cease to be wines and become medicines.

Médoc (Haut-Médoc)

Red wine.
District: Bordeaux, France.

The Haut-Médoc, first in importance of the great Bordeaux districts, is rated by many experts as the greatest in the world for fine red wines. Considering the bulk of good wine produced, and the incomparable vintages of some of the châteaux, this is probably a fair assessment.

A Médoc is a typical claret, possessed of a subtle bouquet in age which suggests the scent of rose or violet, or an indefinable smell of woods in springtime and clean earthiness. The wines are distinctive and delicate, compared with the fuller, heartier clarets of Saint-Émilion; they have often been described as the greatest of the world's red wines. Médocs have tremendous finesse, when properly aged; even the lesser Growths *(Crus)* respond to some ageing, and the greatest can be drunk when they have been sixty (or even more) years in bottle and still be found full of life, mellow, and magnificent.

With a few exceptions, only red wines are made in this region, and no white wine has the right to be called Médoc. The wines from the Margaux vineyards, nearest Bordeaux, are most feminine of all: heartiness increases on a gradually rising scale to the other end of the zone at Saint-Estèphe, a village about 65 kilometers (40 miles) north of Bordeaux. This is the range of Haut-Médoc (the best part of the region), a place-name in its own right which will appear on labels. Médoc is the name given, in this sense, to the wines north of the Saint-Estèphe, the point of the peninsula gradually narrowing to Soulac, where the Gironde

flows into the sea. The region beyond Saint-Estèphe produces high-quality table wines, and there are many cooperatives—one of them at Bégadan, 25 kilometers (16 miles) north of Pauillac, with a capacity of nearly 30,000 hectoliters (750,000 U.S. gallons, 625,000 imp.)—but all the famous wines are in Haut-Médoc. In addition to the two place-names, or Appellations Contrôlées, Haut-Médoc and Médoc, which will appear on labels, six communes within Haut-Médoc have official place-names of their own: Margaux, Saint-Julien, Saint-Estèphe, Pauillac, Moulis, and Listrac, of which the first four are the best known *(see under individual headings)*. The more precise the designation, the more distinguished the wine—a Margaux will generally be more individual and will have submitted to higher wine-making requirements than the wines of a broader designation, such as Haut-Médoc. All but five of the sixty-two classified vineyards are within the four communes.

This district has the advantage over all others in that vintage years, although important, mean less here than elsewhere in France because, although the wines sometimes reach great peaks, they never sink much below their normal high standard—even in the lesser years a well-made Médoc will be an agreeable wine, because the great châteaux always make good wines through vat selections. The vintages of the best years will be slow in maturing; the others will be ready to drink much sooner.

The Médoc takes its name, a corruption of the Latin *in medio aquae*, from its geographical position, almost in the middle of the water, for the 130-kilometer (80-mile) strip of peninsula, with its gravelly, sandy soil is seldom more than 25 kilometers (15 miles) in width as it stretches between the Atlantic and the Gironde. The vineyard strip is far narrower. Only lands on the Gironde side, a belt hardly 3 kilometers (2 miles) wide, produce the great wines. The rest of the Médoc westward to the giant dunes rimming the ocean is a region of pinewoods interspersed with a few fields and an occasional vineyard, and its wines are simply called Bordeaux. Along the best strip of land, the vineyards are in clusters. In the wine center in Pauillac, a map thirty feet by six feet shows in microcosm the panorama of the Médoc, with all the classified châteaux and a few others superimposed; and a glance reveals how the vineyards group thickly around Margaux, Saint-Julien, Pauillac, and Saint-Estèphe, with gaps between. The reason for this is plain: the land rises moderately at Margaux, most steeply at Pauillac and Saint-Estèphe. The moist lower land, through which the little creeks furrow to the river, is unfit for fine wine. Study of the geological chart explains the phenomenon. The ancient Quaternary land—a very gravelly, pebbly soil in modern times—appears islanded by the newer river soil which has eddied in around it in all the lower parts. The newest of all, the alluvial soil, is forbidden any of the important Médoc place-names. The Médoc's previous gravel dates from the end of the Tertiary and the beginning of the Quaternary eras. It

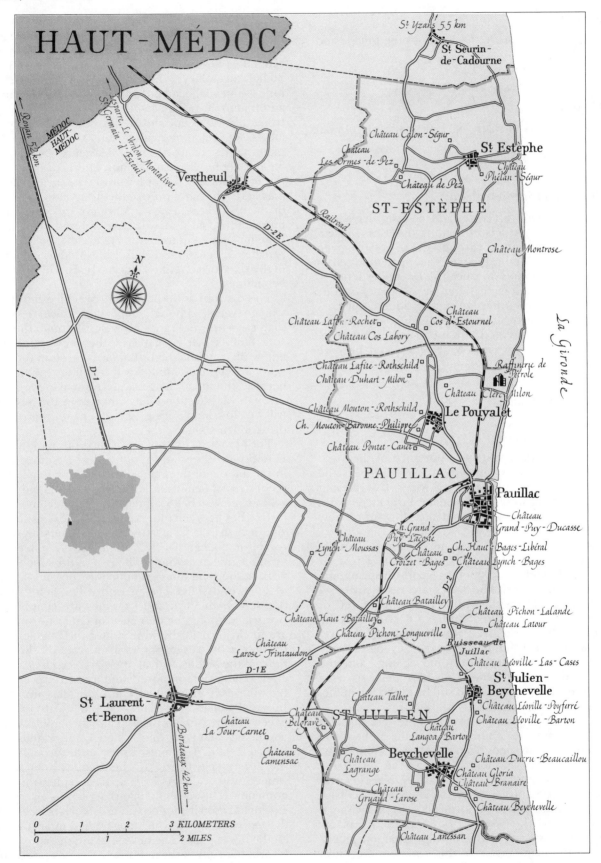

HAUT-MÉDOC

St. Yzans 5.5 km

St. Seurin-
de-Cadourne

Château Calon-Ségur

Château
Les Ormes-de-Pez

St Estèphe

Château
Phélan-Ségur

Vertheuil

Château de Pez

ST-ESTÈPHE

Railroad

D-2E

Château Montrose

N

Château Lafon-Rochet

Château
Cos d'Estournel

Château Cos Labory

Château Lafite-Rothschild

Raffinerie de
Pétrole

D-1

Château Duhart-Milon

Château Clerc-Milon

Château Mouton-Rothschild

Le Pouyalet

Ch. Mouton-Baronne-Philippe

Château Pontet-Canet

PAUILLAC

Pauillac

Château
Grand-Puy-Ducasse

Ch.Grand-
Puy-Lacoste

Château
Lynch-Moussas

Ch. Haut-Bages-Libéral

Château
Croizet-Bages

Château Lynch-Bages

D-2

Château Batailley

Château Pichon-Lalande

Château Haut-Batailley

Château Latour

Château Pichon-Longueville

Château
Larose-Trintaudon

Ruisseau de
Juillac

Château Léoville-Las-Cases

D-1E

St Julien-
Beychevelle

St. Laurent-
et-Benon

Château Talbot

Château Léoville-Poyferré

Château
Belgrave

ST-JULIEN

Château Léoville-Barton

Château
La Tour-Carnet

Château
Langoa-Barton

Château Ducru-Beaucaillou

Château
Camensac

Beychevelle

Château
Lagrange

Château Gloria
Château Branaire

Château
Gruaud-Larose

Château Beychevelle

0   1   2   3 KILOMETERS
0   1   2 MILES

Château Lanessan

La Gironde

Royan 52 km

MÉDOC
HAUT-
MÉDOC

Lesparre-Le Verdon-Montalivet
St Germain-d'Esteuil

Bordeaux 42 km

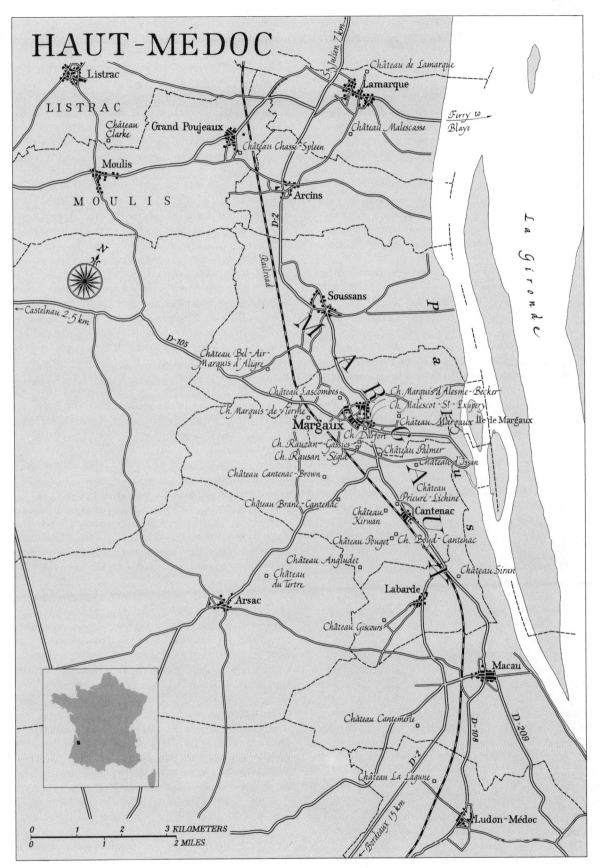

HAUT-MÉDOC

Listrac

LISTRAC

Château Clarke

Grand Poujeaux

Château Chasse-Spleen

Moulis

MOULIS

Arcins

D-2

Railroad

Château de Lamarque

Lamarque

Château Malescasse

Ferry to Blaye

La Gironde

Soussans

MAR

← Castelnau 2.5 km

D-105

Château Bel-Air-Marquis d'Aligre

Château Lascombes

Ch. Marquis-de-Terme

Margaux

Ch. Rauzan-Gassies
Ch. Rausan-Ségla

Château Cantenac-Brown

Château Brane-Cantenac

Ch. Marquis d'Alesme-Becker
Ch. Malescot St-Exupéry
Château Margaux Ile de Margaux

Ch. Durfort

Château Palmer
Château d'Issan

Château Prieuré-Lichine

Château Kirwan

Cantenac

Château Pouget Ch. Boyd-Cantenac

Château Angludet

Château du Tertre

Arsac

Labarde

Château Siran

Château Giscours

Macau

D-108

D-209

Château Cantemerle

Bordeaux 15 km

D-2

Château La Lagune

Ludon-Médoc

0   1   2   3 KILOMETERS
0   1   2 MILES

is said that glaciers, slowly moving down from the distant Pyrenees, followed the course of the nearby river, pushing back its high right bank. When the glaciers thawed, the small pebbles remained in the soil. These pebbles give the Médoc gravel its special virtue of holding the sun's heat during the day and reflecting it back to the low-pruned grapes at night.

With the qualities of the soil—the *cailloux*, or small stones, which give *race* to the wine—the elements of weather, of vine variety, viticulture, and wine-making are necessary to the formation of a characteristic Médoc. The Atlantic climate is distinctly softer and damper here than in the other Bordeaux districts. The Médoc is the closest wine zone to the sea, and the Gironde, formed by the confluence of the Dordogne and the Garonne, is as wide, when it passes Pauillac and Saint-Estèphe, as the great Mississippi.

The Cabernet Sauvignon is the characteristic grape variety, contributing different proportions to the various Médocs, but generally making up about 60% of the grapes used. Cabernet Franc, Merlot, Malbec, and Petit Verdot are used in smaller amounts, and Carménère is included infrequently and contributes a fraction. No other grapes are permitted. The wines with the most Cabernet Sauvignon will be the hardest when young but will last very long. Merlot is generally included, up to about 25%, to give a suppler balance, and these wines will be at their best in the sunnier years, the harder ones holding up better in the lighter years.

Vines are generally allowed to achieve about forty-five years, after which they are torn up and replaced by new vines. A few fine vineyards still cling to the old method of letting each vine reach its maximum age and die before replacing it individually. Most vineyards, however, use the system of rotative planting—tearing up and replanting smaller parcels at different times. Most owners try to keep their older vines for as long as possible, thus improving the wine, since the vine gives better and better quality as it ages; but it is expensive both in added labor and in lost quantity, the latter dropping sharply in the older years of the vine.

Harvesting usually starts in the last days of September; or, about one year in six, in October; and one year in eighty, in August. The hotter the summer, the earlier the harvest. Separation of the stalk from the grapes, juice, and pips is obligatory and is done by either of two methods. The new device is a revolving perforated metal sleeve: grapes and juice fall through the holes, and stems are carried off down the cone. Smaller and more old-fashioned vineyards separate by hand-scrubbing over a grid; grapes and juice fall through it, stems remain on top. In the course of great discussions, no one has ever demonstrated that either method is better than the other in producing wine of quality.

After separation from the stalks, the hulls and juice ferment together in vats, and the wine acquires its color (the pigment lies just inside the skins) and the tannin which contributes longevity. At most vineyards the wines are now vatted from twelve to twenty-five days, after which they are drawn off the skins into barrels, where they spend the twenty to twenty-eight months before they are bottled. A handful of aristocratic vineyards still vat from three weeks to a month, the traditional Médoc method, by which they achieve a wine with the maximum of tannin. Some of these same famous châteaux continue to ferment their wines in the traditional wooden vats. This practice may be good public relations, but in fact better wine is made in cement or stainless steel fermenters—of which shining examples may be seen at Châteaux Latour and Haut-Brion. Big wines of this style demand longer ageing, which they will finally repay in extra long life; the slower process is possible only for growers able to command the prices their wines will eventually cost.

In 1855, for the World's Fair in Paris, the wines of Médoc (and Sauternes) were classified by a commission of Bordeaux brokers basing their judgments principally on the verdict of the previous hundred years. The listing, from First to Fifth Growths, requires considerable overhauling, but is completely valid for the First Growths *(Premiers Crus)*. The three great First Growths of the Médoc are Château Lafite, Château Margaux, and Château Latour. To these, Château Haut-Brion was added in 1855, rightly from the standpoint of wine, if not of geography; because although geographically it is situated in Graves, its wine ranks with the great three of Médoc. Because of its quality and the high prices at which it is sold, Château Mouton-Rothschild, classified first of the Second Growths *(Seconds Crus)* in 1855, was classified in 1923 as a First Growth. And, incidentally, a Second, Third *(Troisième)*, Fourth *(Quatrième)*, or Fifth Growth *(Cinquième Cru)* is not a second-, third-, fourth-, or fifth-*rate* wine. (For a fuller treatment of this subject, *see* Bordeaux: Classification.)

Exceptional Growths *(Crus Exceptionnels)*—it is easy for English-speakers to make the mistake of supposing these to be *better* than the Great Growths *(Grands Crus)*, *which they are not*—Bourgeois Growths *(Crus Bourgeois)*, and Artisan Growths *(Crus Artisans)* were classified after the sixty-two greatest in 1855. Among these are many fine wines, and some which deserve elevation to the greater Growths. The Classification of 1855 will be found in Appendix A (p. 585). A suggested reassessment of the Bordeaux Growths, as graded by the author in 1958, 1966, 1973, and 1986, follows the general entry on the Bordeaux Growths Classification. From this it will be seen that classification of Growths no longer represents the truth in a number of cases. For the individual Classified Growths, *see* Château Lafite, Château Latour, Château Margaux, etc.

Today these wines have become the most expensive and sought-after red wines in the world. In the late 1960s prices started to climb, and soon many of the greatest Médocs were selling at five times their mid-1960s prices, reaching a peak with the 1970 vin-

CLASSIFIED GIRONDE WINES
Classification of 1855

FIRST GROWTHS (*Premiers Crus*)

	Commune
Château Lafite	Pauillac
Château Margaux	Margaux
Château Latour	Pauillac
Château Haut-Brion	Pessac (Graves)

SECOND GROWTHS (*Deuxièmes Crus*)

*Château Mouton-Rothschild	Pauillac
Château Rausan-Ségla	Margaux
Château Rauzan-Gassies	Margaux
Château Léoville-Las-Cases	Margaux
Château Léoville-Poyferré	St.-Julien
Château Léoville-Barton	St.-Julien
Château Durfort	Margaux
Château Lascombes	Margaux
Château Gruaud-Larose	St.-Julien
Château Brane-Cantenac	Cantenac-Margaux
Château Pichon-Longueville-Baron	Pauillac
Château Pichon-Longueville, Comtesse de Lalande	Pauillac
Château Ducru-Beaucaillou	St.-Julien
Château Cos-d'Estournel	St.-Estèphe
Château Montrose	St.-Estèphe

THIRD GROWTHS (*Troisièmes Crus*)

Château Giscours	Labarde-Margaux
Château Kirwan	Cantenac-Margaux
Château d'Issan	Cantenac-Margaux
Château Lagrange	St.-Julien
Château Langoa	St.-Julien
Château Malescot-Saint-Exupéry	Margaux
Château Cantenac-Brown	Cantenac-Margaux
Château Palmer	Cantenac-Margaux
Château La Lagune	Ludon (Haut-Médoc)
Château Desmirail	Margaux
Château Ferrière	Margaux
Château Calon-Ségur	St.-Estèphe
Château Marquis d'Alesme-Becker	Margaux
Château Boyd-Cantenac	Cantenac-Margaux

FOURTH GROWTHS (*Quatrièmes Crus*)

Château Saint-Pierre-Bontemps	St.-Julien
Château Saint-Pierre-Sevaistre	St.-Julien
Château Branaire	St.-Julien
Château Talbot	St.-Julien
Château Duhart-Milon-Rothschild	Pauillac
Château Pouget	Cantenac-Margaux
Château La Tour-Carnet	St.-Laurent (Haut-Médoc)
Château Lafon-Rochet	St.-Estèphe
Château Beychevelle	St.-Julien
Château Prieuré-Lichine	Cantenac-Margaux
Château Marquis-de-Terme	Margaux

*Declared a First Growth in 1973.

FIFTH GROWTHS (*Cinquièmes Crus*)

	Commune
Château Pontet-Canet	Pauillac
Château Batailley	Pauillac
Château Grand-Puy-Lacoste	Pauillac
Château Grand-Puy-Ducasse	Pauillac
Château Haut-Batailley	Pauillac
Château Lynch-Bages	Pauillac
Château Lynch-Moussas	Pauillac
Château Dauzac-Lynch	Labarde-Margaux
Château Mouton-d'Armailhacq (now called Mouton-Baronne-Philippe)	Pauillac
Château du Tertre	Arsac-Margaux
Château Haut-Bages-Libéral	Pauillac
Château Pédesclaux	Pauillac
Château Belgrave	St.-Laurent (Haut-Médoc)
Château Camensac	St.-Laurent (Haut-Médoc)
Château Cos Labory	St.-Estèphe
Château Clerc-Milon-Rothschild	Pauillac
Château Croizet-Bages	Pauillac
Château Cantemerle	Macau (Haut-Médoc)

EXCEPTIONAL GROWTHS (*Crus Exceptionnels*)

Château Villegeorge	Avensan
Château Angludet	Cantenac-Margaux
Château Chasse-Spleen	Moulis (Haut-Médoc)
Château Poujeaux-Theil	Moulis (Haut-Médoc)
Château la Couronne	Pauillac
Château Moulin-Riche	St.-Julien
Château Bel-Air-Marquis-d'Aligre	Soussans-Margaux

tage. A combination of factors obviously was responsible: general affluence and prosperity mingled with inflation and speculation, the tremendous growth of the American market, expanded demand from the Common Market countries, increased interest on the part of the French in their finest wines, and—in the case of the top five Growths—the discovery by the Japanese of the Western style of luxury. Most important was the fact that in times of inflation the prices had remained stable—until 1969. Fortunately, abundant harvests in the 1970s, such as those of '76 and '79, have made prices somewhat more reasonable. However, with the superb '82s, '83s and '85s, prices have gone up.

Meleto

A good Chianti Classico of the firm of Ricasoli. *See* Tuscany.

Mendoza

Province of Argentina producing 75% of the wine of that country. *See* Argentina.

Menetou Salon (Appellation Contrôlée)

A place name in the Upper Loire, south of Pouilly-sur-Loire, producing 340 hectares (850 acres) of white from Sauvignon Blanc grapes and a red, 53 hectares (132.5 acres) from Pinot Noir grapes.

Meranese di Collina (D.O.C.)

Wine from Trentino-Alto-Adige *(q.v.)*.

Mercurey (Appellation Contrôlée)

Burgundy red and white wines.
District: Chalonnais, France.

One of the four leading wines of the district. The Chalonnais wines bear a resemblance to those of the Côte de Beaune, perhaps because the Pinot Noir is the grape used. The best wines of the slope are the reds of Mercurey.
See Chalonnais.

Merlot

The blue-black, thick-skinned grape which imparts softness and roundness to the red wines of the Médoc district in Bordeaux. This grape is grown also in Italy, Switzerland, Chile, a little in California, and elsewhere.

Mersin

White liqueur flavored with oranges and herbs; the Turkish Curaçao.

Mescal, mezcal

One of the names for the Mexican cactus plant from which pulque and tequila are made. Also another name for tequila *(q.v.)*.

Mesnil

Village in Champagne which produces one of the best wines of the Côte des Blancs.

Metaxa

A slightly sweet deep-colored brandy made in Greece *(q.v.)*.

Metheglin

A word meaning "spiced drink," derived from the Welsh; it was generally used for mead.

Methuselah, methusalem

A giant bottle formerly used in Champagne. It had the capacity of eight standard bottles.

Meursault (Appellation Contrôlée)

Burgundy or white, and a very little red, wine.
District: Côte de Beaune, France.

Meursault is the Capital of the Slope of the Great White Wines, and although the "Côte de Meursault" does not exist in offcial terminology, it does in popular fancy, which is, in a large measure, justified. This section of the Côte de Beaune includes the communes of Meursault and Puligny-Montrachet, and the hamlet of Blagny, ranged along a cluster of hills distinct from the rest of the slope. On the north, a defile cuts it off from Auxey-Duresses and Monthélie; to the south, another separates it from Saint-Aubin; the west side terminates at the top of the slopes; and the east is set by the main road from Beaune to Chagny, which marks the beginning of the Burgundian plain and the end of the fine vineyards. A further unifying factor on the Meursault slope is the chalky, coarse-grained subsoil which predominates and provides the perfect base for the Chardonnay grapevine. Some of the Meursault vineyards fall on the wrong side of the northern divide and grow, mainly, Pinot Noir grapes; and the resulting red wines borrow the name of adjoining Volnay *(q.v.)* or are sold as Volnay-Santenots.

Meursault means "mouse-jump," and it is said the vineyards for red wines and those for white were once only a mouse-jump apart. Today it would take a pretty herculean mouse to bridge the gap in most places, although throughout the vineyards Pinot Noir vines can still be found, and the wine-makers of Meursault annually produce anywhere from 500 to 600 hectoliters (13,200 to 15,900 U.S. gallons, 11,000 to 13,200 imp.) of red.

As Côte d'Or places go, Meursault is fairly large, qualifying either as an overgrown village or a stunted town. The hills roll gently around it, rising to the hamlet of Blagny—set off in the southwest corner—where wines are sold as Blagny, Meursault-Blagny, or occasionally as Blagny-Côte de Beaune. They are both red and white; and wines having the right to the last-mentioned place-name are sometimes blended with those from certain other communes of the Côte de Beaune and sold as Côte de Beaune-Villages. Meursault itself is prosperous and has several interesting monuments. The delicate spire which rises from the rather squat church reminds Burgundians of a "beaver hat on a peasant"; and nearby is a grim, gray edifice which served as a leper colony during the Middle Ages. The Hospices de Beaune have been given several vineyards in Meursault; and as is customary with the Hospices, the wines are sold under the name of the donors: Loppin, Jehan Humblot, Baudot, Goureau, Albert Grivault, and Behèzre de Lanlay. Meursault also has a smaller Hospice of its own, older than its neighbor of Beaune, whose gate adjoins the main road leading up to the village.

Most Meursault is white, and the wines are soft, round, and feminine in texture, with a bouquet that eludes description, bordering now on the scent of violets, now on the aroma of almonds. Dry, but not so dry as the steely Chablis, they have a quiet luxuriousness and a lasting and marvelous aftertaste. They reach their peak fairly quickly, and only the best respond to ageing at all happily—the lesser ones tending to maderize fairly quickly. The finest of the Meursault whites is Perrières and those from the heart of the vineyard—the Clos de Perrières—are superb wines, often fit to challenge the incomparable Montrachet. After Perrières come Charmes and Genevrières and La Goutte d'Or, the appropriately named "drop of gold," all of which incorporate the same seductive grace and elegance but are apt to have a shade less finesse. Meursault reds are sturdy and require a certain ageing before they open up and reveal a fiery strength and excellent bouquet, but they do not quite come up to the qualities of the reds of the Côte de Nuits.

In slight contrast to the white wines of Meursault, those of tiny Blagny are long-lasting, becoming ready to drink after about two years in the bottle and holding for as long as twenty. Blagny white is, understandably enough, very close to Meursault in taste characteristics, but will be, if anything, a little firmer and slightly more assertive. The reds are much the same, and Blagny red is apt to be slightly better than Meursault red.

If you include the hamlet of Blagny, Meursault has more surface area devoted to vines than any other commune of the Côte d'Or, and it ties with Pommard and Beaune each year for first place in amount of production. The official figures for Meursault are 480 hectares (1,188 acres) of vines (wines from two hundred of which may add Côte de Beaune to the communal name), and production for an average-quantity year is 12,500 hectoliters (331,000 U.S. gallons, 275,000 imp.) in white. The best vineyards of the commune are given the designation First Growth (*Premier Cru*) and the right to produce wines that will carry both commune name and vineyard name on the label. These vineyards are:

FIRST GROWTHS (*Premiers Crus*)

In Meursault

Vineyard	Hectares	Acres
Clos des Perrières and Les Perrières	17.8	42.2
Les Charmes-dessus	15.5	38.3
Les Charmes-dessous	12.5	30.8
Les Genevrières-dessus	7.7	19.3
Les Genevrières-dessous	5.25	13.0
La Goutte d'Or	5.3	13.8
Le Porusot-Dessus	1.8	4.4
Le Porusot	1.6	4.0
Les Bouchères	4.25	10.5
Les Santenots-Blancs	2.95	7.3
Les Santenots du Milieu	7.7	19.8
Les Caillerets	1.3	3.3
Les Petures	11.0	27.0
Les Cras	4.8	11.7

In Blagny

Vineyard	Hectares	Acres
La Jennelotte	4.5	11.9
La Pièce-sous-le-Bois	11.2	27.8
Sous le Dos d'Âne	5.6	13.3

Mexico

Wine is made, mainly in the north of the country, in vineyard areas extending altogether over some 60,000 hectares (150,000 acres); a tenth of the vine-growing zones produce wines, the rest are devoted to spirits production. The zones are: northern Baja California, the Laguna district at the border of Coahuila and Durango, Parras and Saltillo in Coahuila; Aguascalientes, the San Juan del Rio region in Querétaro, Delicias in Chihuahua, and the Hermosillo district in Sonora. Grapes are also grown in San Luis Potosi, Zacatecas, Tlaxcala, and Hidalgo.

WINE HISTORY

As governor from 1521 to 1527, Hernando Cortez ordered Spanish grapevines planted on the farms of New Spain. Before the new wines bore fruit, the conquistadores made wine from wild grapes. The first vineyard was planted at Parras by a Spanish captain, Francisco de Urdiñola. His vineyard was one of the earliest cultivated in the Americas, although wild vines had been growing freely on the hillsides and in the gullies of the region. The name Parras means vine-trellises, and Parras is still a center of viticulture, with the plantation of Don Francisco, between Monterrey and Torreón, always in vine.

As the Romans had become jealous of the wine of Gaul 1,500 years before, the Spanish became envious of the viticulture in sixteenth-century Mexico. As, in A.D. 89, Domitian had ordered Burgundian vines ripped up, so in 1595 Philip II issued an edict forbidding new planting or replacement of vines in Mexico. Viceroys continued the crown's command over the following centuries, and wine remained a Spanish monopoly. In spite of the prohibition, wine-making spread from Mexico to Chile, Peru, and Argentina in the sixteenth century and to what is now the western United States in the eighteenth.

When Miguel Hidalgo began the revolution against Spain in 1810, one of his goals was to end the Spanish wine monopoly and to renew viticulture in Mexico. However, with the eventual success of the uprising, the Mexican wine industry did not immediately prosper. The Mission, or Criolla, grape brought by the conquistadores from Spain over three hundred years earlier still dominated most of Mexico's vineyards. Though a *Vitis vinifera*, Mission lacks acidity and color and yields mediocre wine. By the end of the nineteenth century the first large-scale experiments with good European vine stocks had been made. James Concannon—an Irish-American grower from Livermore, California—sent thousands of cuttings from his better French varieties throughout northern Mexico. Six years after Concannon completed his project and returned to California came the Revolution of 1910. Though a few vineyards were temporarily protected by the bandit leader and Mexican general Pancho Villa, most were neglected or destroyed during the long war. Vineyard area and wine production have expanded since the start of this century, but consumption is still very low—about a third of a pint per capita, one-fiftieth of that in the United States. Mexican wines cannot fully develop until their audience becomes more critical. Wine is a new product for most Mexicans, who drink instead much pulque (*q.v.*), beer, and soft drinks. What wine is consumed is bought by the wealthy on special occasions, for which they choose the heavily taxed wines imported from France and Spain. In order to promote wine consumption, the Vine-Growers' Association and the big marketing firms launched a campaign that resulted in improved quality and increased consumption, about 15% a year. Approximately 150,000 hectoliters (3.9 million U.S. gallons, 3.3 million imp.) of inexpensive table wines are produced annually. A large quantity of wine spirit, or *aguardiente*, is also produced.

It is to be regretted that Mexico is one of a number of countries which appropriate for some of their wines the place-names properly applicable only to specific geographical areas of the world.

VINE-GROWING REGIONS

The vineyards of Baja California are situated in the fertile valleys in the northwest corner of that forbidding, barren peninsula. Within 160 kilometers (100 miles) of the border with the United States are the five important regions: Santo Tomás, 40 kilometers (30 miles) south of Ensenada; Rancho Viejo, inland from Ensenada; Guadalupe, 100 kilometers (60 miles) south of the California border; and the districts of Valle Redondo and Tañama near the town of Tecate, just across the U.S. border. Since the rainfall ranges from only 5 to 18 inches per year, the plantings are limited by the underground water supply. Since the coast of southern California in the United States is tempered by the Pacific, these valleys are cooled by breezes and fog from the ocean.

The largest vineyards in Baja California, with an annual production of 250,000 cases, is the Bodegas de Santo Tomás, now at Ensenada. Founded by an Italian gold-miner and once owned by the president of Mexico, the *bodega* is now the property of the Elias Pando wine-importing company in Mexico City. The technical director of the vineyard was Dmitri Tchelistcheff (taught by his father, of the Beaulieu Vineyards in California's Napa Valley), who dramatically increased the quality of the wines. Tomás wines are now some of the best and best-known wines in Mexico. Half of the vineyards are in such standard vines as Mission, Rosa de Perú, and Palomino; Valdepeñas, Grenache, Carignan, and French Colombard are also grown, along with Cabernet Sauvignon, Pinot Noir, Johannisberg Riesling, Sémillon, and Chenin Blanc. Tchelistcheff has introduced sound vinicultural techniques: cold fermentation of white wines, bottle-ageing of red ones, and bottle-fermentation of sparkling wines. Many of the grapes for these wines come from private growers. Though its winery is in Ensenada, the Santo Tomás vineyards are in the valley of that name south of town and in the Guadalupe region to the northeast. Two modern wineries are also in the Guadalupe area: the Productos Vinicola makes "Terrasola" wines, and a large production-vinification facility built especially for quality wines is part of the Mexican division of Pedro Domecq, the Sherry producers from Spain. In this region, Domecq, as well as the Luis Cetto Vineyards, cultivates noble European grape varieties according to the most modern methods; their efforts have produced the best-known wines of Mexico today, the Los Reyes and Calafia.

At Saltillo, 200 kilometers (130 miles) southwest of Laredo, Texas, are the headquarters for the interests of Nazario Ortiz Garza, the most important wine- and brandy-maker in Mexico. His vineyard in Saltillo itself has been reduced to half its original size of 180 hectares (450 acres), since the expanding town must now use the land he once used for reservoirs for irrigation. Don Nazario's most important vineyard is in the state of Aguascalientes, 300 kilometers (200 miles) northwest of Mexico City. His Viñedos San Marcos covers 3,200 hectares (8,000 acres) and straddles the Inter-American Highway (CN 45) which runs between El Paso, Texas, and the capital. Other wineries include the Bodegas de San Ygnacio, owned by Filemon Alonzo; Bodegas de Monte Casino, by Victor Manuel Castelazo; Productos de Uva Aguascalientes of the Cetto family; and the Industrias de la Fermentación, owned by David Alonzo.

Fifty kilometers (30 miles) west of Saltillo is Parras de la Fuente, where Spanish vines first grew alongside the native grapes in 1593. The original winery of Mexico, the Vinícola del Marqués de Aguayo, now concentrates on good still and sparkling table wines. All that remains of the first structure built by Francisco de Urdiñola is an adobe wall in one of the modern offices. Not far from the oldest vineyard in Mexico is the second oldest, the huge Bodegas de San Lorenzo of Casa Madero, owned by cousins of the late president Madero. The family has constantly upgraded their holdings since first purchasing the Parras vineyards in 1870. Late in the nineteenth century Evaristo Madero Elonzindo brought fine grapevines and distillation equipment from Europe, and his wines won honors at the international expositions around the turn of the century. The family has replanted the vineyards after the ravages of phylloxera and the Revolution, and since 1962 has made Casa Madero one of the handsomest wineries in the world. Parras has a climate similar to that of Lodi, California, but because of its high altitude (1,600 meters—5,000 feet) the vines are often exposed to crippling frosts. Other Parras firms are the Bodegas del Delfín, owned by Aguirre Benavides; Bodegas del Rosario, by Señor Antonio Benavides and Señor Elias T. Tejada; Bodegas de Perote, the property of Señor Arturo Perez de Yarto; and Bodegas del Vesubio, which belongs to Señor Nicolás Milonás. West of Parras, at Torreón, the Mexican government established its first vineyard to supply growers with healthy stock varieties from the Oenological Department of the University of California at Davis. In this same district, but across the border in Durango, is the Vinicola del Vergel at Gómez Palacio. Vergel, built in 1943, is a combination of old European vaulted marble cellars and modern American outdoor stainless steel tanks. Although much of the Vergel vineyard is given over to table grapes and inferior vines, such fairly good stock vines as Ugni Blanc, Ruby Cabernet, and Colombard have recently been added.

One hundred and fifty kilometers (95 miles) north of Mexico City is the southernmost vineyard area in Mexico, the valley of Rio de San Juan. The valley is also the very highest vine-growing region in the country, with an altitude of nearly 2,000 meters (6,100 feet). In this high valley the Cavas de San Juan grow Cabernet Sauvignon, Pinot Noir, Gamay, and Pinot Gris, as well as lesser grapes, to make their "Hidalgo" wines. North of San Juan del Rio at Tequisquiapan, the Martell Cognac company of France produces table wine and brandy.

SPIRITS

The characteristic Mexican spirits are tequila, pulque, and mezcal (qq.v) made from the juice of the century plant. Others are obtained from sugar-cane. Among other spirits produced in Mexico are *ron* (rum), anis, and brandy. Brandy has replaced tequila and rum as the most popular distilled liquor in Mexico. The spirit's success is in part due to semantics. The Spanish word for aged brandy is *coñac*, but after the Second World War the Mexican government rightly reserved it for use only on brandies imported from the Cognac district of France. Mexican distillers then adopted the English name, even though the word "brandy" does not exist in the Spanish language. The appeal has been tremendous, and now almost 90% of the grapes grown in Mexico are made into brandy.

Michigan

Wine-growing district in the United States. The principal vineyards are situated in the southern part of the state. Sweet and sparkling wines are made there, but unfortunately they are of average quality.
See United States.

Midi

The vast stretch of land west of the mouth of the Rhône in southern France, which supplies the greatest quantity of ordinary wine in France. The Midi includes the departments of Aude, Hérault, and Gard (qq.v.).
See Grand Roussillon (Côtes du Roussillon); Languedoc; Corbières.

Mildew

The European name for downy mildew, a vine disease of American origin.
See Chapter Eight, p. 31.

Millefiori

Pale gold Italian liqueur said to have been made from the extracts of a thousand Alpine flowers. The bottles usually contain a small twig, around which sugar has crystallized. Made by Vigevanese.

Millerandage or shot berries

Vine disease; clusters with grapes of varying sizes. An aftermath of *coulure*, following unsatisfactory flowering or insemination.
See Chapter Eight, p. 31.

Millésime

French term for vintage year.

Minervois (Appellation Contrôlée)

Red wine.
District: Languedoc, France.

Minervois, just north of the Corbières wine district, is 100 kilometers (about 62 miles) southeast of Toulouse. The grapes grow on 22,000 hectares (55,000 acres) in the departments of the Aude and Hérault, northeast of Narbonne and northwest of Carcassonne, the medieval fortress-town. The land is wild and rugged, a series of giant steps where veins of shale alternate with lignite or gneiss. Most of the vineyards are on alluvial soil rich in minerals and heavy with pebbles, which improve the drainage.

The name Minervois comes from Minerve, one of the strongholds built when Rome controlled the south of France. Both Minervois and Corbières were popular in Roman days; the Tenth Legion camped in and around Narbonne, drinking much of the local wine and even importing it to Italy when they returned. Pliny the Younger and Cicero apparently liked the wine. And today some of the loyal residents are convinced that Minervois and Corbières are the wines found in the sunken wrecks of ancient galleys in the western Mediterranean.

The seacoast is only 30 kilometers (18 miles) from the heart of the vineyards; it has recently become a

Mirabelle de Lorraine

widely developed resort. The wine-making center is, however, still inland at the small town of Olonzac. There, Minervois is made from a blend of 60% Carignan, 20% Grenache Noir, and 20% Cinsault. It is strong and full-bodied and improves with a few years in the bottle. The average annual volume is 300,000 hectoliters (7.8 million U.S. gallons, 6 million imp.). Nearly all of the wine is made in forty-four cooperatives, since the small wine-maker working alone cannot make a living in this part of France from everyday inexpensive wine.

See Languedoc.

Mirabelle de Lorraine

The *eau-de-vie* or spirit distilled from the mirabelle (yellow plum) is made in both Lorraine and Alsace in the east of France, but only spirit from the plums of the region of Nancy and of Metz has the right to the place-name of Mirabelle de Lorraine. This is an official Appellation d'Origine, or controlled place-name, under French law.

Of the two, Metz plums are the better. Mirabelle Fine du Val de Metz is the designation to look for. The plums are picked in dry weather, fermented by specially selected yeasts, kept in the wood for approximately two months and then double-distilled in exactly the manner of Cognac. The liquor is afterward aged in casks.

See also Alsace.

Mis en Bouteilles au Château

French term for "château-bottled." This description on the label, with or without an "s," means that the wine has been bottled at the vineyard where it was grown and made. It guarantees the authenticity of the wine. The term is general in Bordeaux wines.

Mis en Bouteilles au Domaine

French term for "estate-bottled." Same as *Mis en Bouteilles au Château*. This term is generally used in Bordeaux; as there are few châteaux in Burgundy, where many of the vineyards are split up into small parcels. *Mis en Bouteilles au Domaine* or *Mis en Bouteilles à la Propriété* are terms for estate-bottled. It guarantees the authenticity of the wine.

Mission

The first variety of European *Vitis vinifera* planted in California.

See Criollas.

Mistelle

A fortified "wine" made by adding spirit to grape juice before it ferments. The excess of alcohol pre-

vents fermentation, and all the natural sugar is retained in the juice. It is used mainly as a base for vermouth and other wine aperitifs. Huge amounts of mistelle used to be made in, and shipped from, Algeria every year.

Mittelhaardt

Part of the Palatinate district in Germany, where the best of these wines are made.

See Palatinate.

Mittelrhein

*German States of Rheinland-Pfalz and Nordrhein-Westfalen
Vineyard area:* approx. 800 hectares (1,900 acres)
98% white wines; 2% red wines

Location: with craggy shores, crumbling castles, the racing Rhine, and its legend of the siren Lorelei, the section of the river from below Bingen down to Coblenz and beyond is the most interesting to travel by steamer, but not, unfortunately, by palate.

The Mittelrhein is one of Germany's smallest but most dramatically situated wine-growing regions, beginning just north of Bingen and stretching some 100 kilometers (60 miles) downstream on both banks of the Rhine, almost to Bonn. Bacharach, a charming medieval village, is an important wine center, with a number of fine producers. Koblenz is the modern commercial center for the wine trade. Boppard, Braubach, Oberwesel, and Steeg are noteworthy wine villages. The region is divided into three districts: Bereich Bacharach; Bereich Rheinburgengau, also includes a small number of vineyards in the Lahn River Valley; and Bereich Siebengebirge, near Bonn.

Grape Varieties: Riesling (74%); Müller-Thurgau (11%); Kerner (6%)
Wine: steely, earthy, with an austere acidity; in poor years, better suited to making Sekt.

Wine grows not only on the slopes along the Rhine, but also in the side valleys branching into the hills, where conditions are particularly unfavorable. The cold winds coming down from the Hunsrück Mountains meet the warm air rising from the Rhine and cause sudden frosts in late spring and early autumn. On the other hand, the Mittelrhein below St. Goarshausen is one of the few sections of the world's vineyards where phylloxera has not yet struck. Growing conditions on the cliffs of graywacke (a clayish slate) are enhanced by the micro-climate created by the Rhine. The best years are those with sufficient rainfall to replenish the porous soil.

None of the wine is great, and little will be encountered abroad. Half of the region's thousand growers produce their own wine. It is consumed on the spot by tourists who come to see the magnificent castle ruins and the Loreley. The remainder is sold in bulk to Sekt producers. *See* Appendix B, p. 679.

Moelleux

Literally "marrowy." A French term used of soft, sweet, fruity white wines, especially in Sauternes.

Molise

A small Italian province on the Adriatic with unimportant wines.

Monbazillac (Appellation Contrôlée)

A sweet white dessert wine from the Bergerac region in southwest France.
See Bergerac.

Monica di Sardegna (D.O.C.)

Sweet fortified wine of Sardinia *(q.v.)*.

Monimpex

The Hungarian State Export Agency for wines and spirits.

Monopole

This designation, frequently found on wine labels, literally means "an exclusive." Blank Monopole would be the proprietary brand of the wine-shipper whose name would occupy the blank. The wines are blends and are seldom if ever sold by the vintage year. The shipper attempts to produce a uniform wine year after year, sacrificing the high points which individual growths or years might achieve in order to be able to provide a consistent reliable wine.

Montagne-Saint-Émilion (A.O.C.)

A large commune in which lie some respectable vineyards of Saint-Émilion *(q.v.)* in the Bordeaux region of southwest France.

Montagny

A commune of the Chalon slope in Burgundy which is allowed the Appellation Contrôlée.
See Chalonnais.

Montagu

Wine region in the Little Karoo district.
See South Africa.

Montefiascone (D.O.C.)

White wine grown in the foothills of the Volsini Mountains, Italy. It is concerning this wine that the story about Est! Est!! Est!!! is told.
See Latium.

Montepulciano (D.O.C.G.)

Known as Vino Nobile di Montepulciano. This light red wine is grown on clay at an altitude between 300 and 600 meters.
See Tuscany.

Montepulciano di Abruzzo (D.O.C.)

Light, red Italian wine.
See Abruzzi.

Monthélie and **Monthélie-Côte de Beaune (A.O.C.)**

Burgundy red and white wines.
District: Côte de Beaune, France.

Monthélie is the *frère bâtard* of Volnay. It is one of the most picturesque wine communes of Burgundy, with steep streets and tiny houses, venerable with age. The best *premiers crus* of Monthélie, those from Champs Fulliot, Le Rougeot, La Taupine, and Le Clos Gautey, are equal to some of the best Volnay reds.

Red, white, and some sparkling wines are made, although the balance is heavily weighted toward still reds. The grapes are Pinots, as they are throughout the Côte d'Or, and are grown in soil so poor that Burgundians claim: "A chicken, in Monthélie, would starve during the harvest." Within the ancient commune—the remains of a Gallic cemetery testify to its age—are about 100 hectares (250 acres) of vines, and production in an average-quantity year is 3,000 hectoliters (79,500 U.S. gallons, 66,000 imp.), nearly all of it red. Wines may be sold indiscriminately as Monthélie or as Monthélie-Côte de Beaune-Villages. A standard, and generally accurate, rule of thumb is that Monthélie should cost about three-quarters the price of a Volnay of the same year. The best vineyards are given the rating First Growth *(Premier Cru)* and may add vineyard name to commune name on labels. Although these vineyards have not yet been finally established, interim right is granted to the following:

FIRST GROWTHS (*Premiers Crus*)

Vineyard	Hectares	Acres
Sur la Velle	6.1	15.2
Les Vignes Rondes	2.7	6.7
Le Meix-Bataille	2.4	5.9
Les Riottes	.7	1.8
La Taupine	4.3	10.7
Le Clos-Gauthey	1.4	3.5
Le Château-Gaillard	.9	2.3
Les Champs-Fulliot	8.74	21.6
Le Cas-Rougeot	.4	1.4
Duresse	10.3	25.6

Montilla-Moriles

Aperitif and table wines.
District: Southern Spain.

The wines of Montilla-Moriles (which are generally known as Montilla) resemble Sherries; but they have their own character and climate and their separate Denominación de Origen. They are the products of the province of Córdoba and are grown in the great carpet of vineyard, of sunflowers and of olive and almond trees, which stretches south of the ancient city of Córdoba, 160 kilometers (100 miles) northwest of Jerez and about 120 kilometers (73 miles) from Seville. Most of the region north of Córdoba is a great plain, with the best of the region situated in the southern part of the province, its heart a countryside of hills and plateaus rising from the olive groves and the ocher-colored soils of southern Andalusia. Plenty of good ordinary wines (vinos corrientes) are made, but fine solera wines are also produced on the slopes of the Sierra de Montilla and Moriles Alto. These are the fruit of the chalky albariza soil which, around Jerez, also nurtures the Sherry grapes. The Montilla Finos are glinting gold, with a slightly tart undercurrent; the smooth Amontillados have a faint scent of apple peel; the natural Olorosos are deep, nutty but still dry. There is also a dark, piercing-sweet wine bottled under many names, which might be compared to a Cream Sherry, but sweeter.

This ancient Córdoban province, which has a long history of occupation and conquest by Phoenicians, Romans, Moors, and the Spanish kings, has been described as the frying pan of Spain. Continental in climate, it has, on the Sierras, mild winters and blazing summers. The vines are pruned low and dug deep into the wrinkled white soil, well-mulched to hold the winter rain which will moisten the roots through the scorching months to come. The principal grape planted here is the Pedro Ximénez (plus about 20% of Lairen, Baladi, and Moscatel). P.X., as it is called in Jerez, there makes only sweet wine; but in Montilla-Moriles, where the grapes ripen quickly and are harvested early, their high sugar content is fermented right out into alcohol, with the result that the wine is strong and bone-dry. With 14½% to 15½% of alcohol in the Finos, and up to 18% to 20% in the Olorosos, it is not necessary to fortify further with brandy if the Oloroso exceeds its natural 15½%. Only for the sweet P.X. wine of the area is fermentation arrested while the sugar content of the must is still high.

Towns and villages important in the production of Montilla are Montilla, Moriles, Aguilar de la Frontera, Baena, Fernan Nuñez, Lucena, Cabra, Doña Mencia, and Puente Genil. The wine is made in much the same way as in Jerez, although there are differences: with the exception of P.X., the grapes are not laid out to dry in the sun before pressing; their long fermentation takes place not in casks but in tinajas—"Ali Baba" jars like those of Valdepeñas, except that these are even larger and made of concrete and sometimes stainless steel instead of clay. In these jars the new wine is fined with egg-white and Bentonite. When it is clear and well-filtered, it is pumped out to start its slow maturation in American oak butts inside the spacious high bodegas. By this time, the Montilla will have shown its inclination either to be an Oloroso or to develop the yeasty scum known as flor, and become a Fino. The flor forms in the spring, is reduced in summer and winter, and returns at harvest time. At the end of the first year, a third of the young wine will be sold for local drinking, in bars or at the table. The best of it will remain in the nursery (criadera) casks of the bodegas and at five years of age may go into the solera system (see Sherry). A few of the soleras contain barrels so old that the age is reckoned in centuries rather than years, and their precious liquid is dropped very sparingly into the next butt in the solera line-up. Going back further into history, amphorae from Munda (Roman name for Montilla) have lately been unearthed in Italy—the wines were praised by Columella in his Re Rustica.

At one time, before the restricting laws of Denominación de Origen were established, much of the Montilla wine went down to Jerez to reappear as Sherry—perhaps some still trickles through. But now, as always, the wine is relished for its own character, especially locally; the Finos and Amontillados are drunk as aperitifs, with prawns and tasty tapas, and even with the first course of a meal. The Amontillado is, of course, the amber wine into which some Finos deepen with age. The use of the term Amontillado in Jerez has sometimes been questioned by Montilla as a trespass on its name; in fact Amontillado is the style—perhaps first known in perfection in Jerez—for which the Amontillados of that district are named.

One variety of good wine comes from Doña Mencia, a few miles east of Montilla; and at the larger village of Rute, the making of Montilla is combined with a considerable industry in aguardientes and anisados.

Montillas are quite well distributed in England; in particular, those from the big bodegas of Alvear, Vinsur, Carbonell, and Montulia are easily found.

Latest figures for the controlled wines of Montilla-Moriles are as follows: 1,000,000 hectoliters (27 million U.S. gallons, 22 million imp.) from 18,000 hectares (45,000 acres) of vineyard. A list of export companies follows: Alvear, S.A. (Montilla); Aragón y Cía., S.A. (Lucena); Carbonell y Cía., S.A. (Córdoba); Espejo, S.A. (Montilla); Cía. Vinícola del Sur, S.A. (Montilla); Crismona, S.A. (Doña Mencia); Montisol, S.A. (Montilla); Montulia, S.A. (Montilla); Moreno, S.A. (Córdoba); Bodegas Navarro, S.A. (Montilla); Luis Ortiz Ruiz (Montilla); Pérez Barquero, S.A. (Montilla); Miguel Velasco Chacón, S.A. (Montilla); and Conde de la Cortina (Montilla).

Montilla Sierra

Like Sherry Fino. One of the two best Montillas, from Spain.
See Montilla-Moriles.

Montlouis (Appellation Contrôlée)

Loire Valley white wine; still and sparkling.
District: Touraine, France.

This is known as the unsophisticated younger brother of Vouvray, because of its resemblance to the district which faces it across the Loire and because the wines are so similar that sometimes even experts cannot distinguish between them. But while the finest Montlouis can often be classed with fine Vouvray, the bulk cannot compete. Most of the annual 18,900 hectoliters (500,000 U.S. gallons, 416,000 imp.) of Montlouis is not up to Vouvray standards.

The wine is entirely white, from Chenin Blanc grapes grown in Montlouis, Lussault, and Saint-Martin-le-Beau, and it usually remains in the twilight zone where wines are never really sweet nor really dry. A certain amount is made sparkling; but the still and semi-sparkling—or *pétillant*—are best and the most beguiling. Still wines must have 10% of alcohol; sparkling, only 9.5%.

Montrachet (Appellation Contrôlée)

Burgundy white wine.
District: Côte de Beaune, France.
Communes: Puligny-Montrachet and Chassagne-Montrachet.
Official Classification: Great Growth (Grand Cru).

Little known as late as the seventeenth century, these wines began to achieve renown in the mid- and late eighteenth century and are now considered by many connoisseurs to be the greatest of all dry white wines. "Divine," "magnificent," "formidable," "to be drunk on one's knees with head bared," "gorgeous with martial pageantry"—this and much more has been said about Montrachet, with only Professor Saintsbury demurring slightly with his "very great, but the best makes the veins swell like whipcord." It is a wine of exceptional elegance and breed, quite dry, yet it has depth and a seductive bouquet.

The vineyard stands at mid-slope, straddling the line dividing Puligny-Montrachet from Chassagne-Montrachet. At this point, nothing is to be seen but seedy wild grass and outcroppings of the meager, chalky subsoil, in direct contrast to the dense underbrush and foliage which crown the slopes in other parts of the Côte d'Or. Around it are such other famous Growths as Chevalier-Montrachet and Bâtard-Montrachet and the vineyard once called Les Demoiselles, now Caillerets. All produce exceptional wines; all are rightfully placed among the greatest of the world's dry white wines.

The vineyard of Montrachet produces a wine that is as rare as it is magnificent. The average yearly production is variable, usually under 250 hectoliters (6,625 U.S. gallons, 5,500 imp.). In the past, the harvest was often reserved for years in advance and prices were so high as to be almost meaningless. A bottle of authentic Montrachet is still a great rarity and will always be so.

In 1962 the French government paid $1,200,000 (£430,000) to preserve the 7.7 hectares (19 acres) of Montrachet—the cost of diverting the new Paris-Lyon motor road, which would otherwise have passed by Puligny and affected the vineyards.

The sad fact is that infectious degeneration (sometimes called *court noué*) has been detected in the vineyard. So little is known of this lethal disease that it is referred to as a virus or virus-like malady, of which even the cause is obscure. What is certain is that it kills vines. It also lives in the soil, and the life span of vines planted consecutively in the same spot becomes progressively shorter. Unfortunately, no cure has yet been discovered and, unless one is forthcoming (the foremost vine pathologists in many countries are working together to overcome the menace), the world's finest and most famous dry white wine may become only a memory.

Little is known of the early history of the vineyard, and nothing of the geniuses who first started making the white wines and later perfected them. Montrachet was for many years largely in the hands of the Marquis de Laguiche, and the present Marquis still has nearly a quarter of the vineyard, making about eight *pièces*, or barrels, a year. The family of the late Baron Thénard is another relatively large owner, with slightly less than the Marquis de Laguiche; and although they have other important holdings, both in vines and in outside interests, they are proudest of their rows of Montrachet.

The best section of Montrachet is that lying in the commune of Puligny-Montrachet, comprising 3.9 hectares (9.8 acres), just over half the vineyard. Perhaps it is the fact that the slope faces more to the east than in the south-exposed section which falls into Chassagne, or perhaps it is some subtle combination of imponderables that makes the wines what they are, but they have always had the finer reputation. Yet, today, a few of the well-made wines from the surrounding vineyards sometimes rival the Montrachet.

See Chassagne-Montrachet; Puligny-Montrachet.

Montravel (Appellation Contrôlée)

Dry and semi-sweet wine of Bergerac, France.
See Bergerac.

Château Montrose

Bordeaux red wine.
District: Haut-Médoc, France.
Commune: Saint-Estèphe.

Buried in the vineyard and far from the main roads, Montrose is a pleasant villa with an unusual galleried annex that looks rather like a Swiss châlet. The grounds run down to the river, past rows of small numbered houses tenanted by the workers. A peculiar touch is given by the "street names" here: rue d'Alsace, rue Mulhouse, and so on, commemorating the homesickness of a former Alsatian owner. The vineyard, classified Second Growth *(Second Cru)* in the Classification of 1855, is divided into square plantations, separated by alleys, and it is owned and worked by M.J.-L. Charmolue.

Characteristics. Hard, slow-maturing, with a bigness and fullness that characterize so many of the wines of Saint-Estèphe—although it is with Latour in neighboring Pauillac that it has sometimes been compared. Its deep fullness gives Montrose its distinctive character. In some of the recent vintages the wine has seemed lighter and less hard, but a very even quality has been maintained over the years. This full-bodied wine is very popular in England.

Vineyard area: 79 hectares (175 acres).

Average production: 320 *tonneaux* (30,000 cases).

Morey Saint-Denis (Appellation Contrôlée)

Burgundy red, and some white, wines.
District: Côte de Nuits, France.

The wines of Morey-Saint-Denis vary slightly more than those from most Côte d'Or communes. Some reflect the position of the vineyards, providing a half-step between the austere majesty of Gevrey-Chambertin and the delicate elegance of Chambolle-Musigny; others, excelling in sturdy masculine strength, are acknowledged as the most *corsés* wines of the slope. Either way, one thing is certain: the wines are little known.

In bygone days hardly any wine was sold as Morey, although a considerable quantity was made. The output of the commune was usually blended with that of its neighbors or sold outright as Gevrey-Chambertin or Chambolle-Musigny. As a result, Morey never became famous, and even today relatively few wine-lovers are familiar with the commune or its wines—which are thus seldom demanded and often exceptional value.

The village has little to offer in the way of attractions, and few visitors see more than the dusty main square through which the sloping vineyard road winds and the vineyards of both sides. Beside the square—enclosed in a great wall—is the domain of the Clos des Lambrays (one of Morey's outstanding vineyards), and next to it is the Clos de Tart. The other top vineyards are on the outskirts.

In 1860, and again in 1936, the best vineyards of Burgundy were rated. By the earlier Classification, the finest wines of Morey were considered to be Clos de Tart, Clos des Lambrays, and Bonnes Mares—although Bonnes Mares has but a small foothold in Morey, most of it falling into Chambolle-Musigny. The 1936 Classification revised this listing, designating Morey's finest wines as: Clos de Tart; Clos de la Roche; Clos Saint-Denis; and Bonnes Mares *(see under individual headings)*.

In 1981 an amendment to the Classification restored the Clos des Lambrays to this list by ranking it once again as a Great Growth *(Grand Cru)*, and it also became an Appellation Contrôlée. Many critics had long considered Lambrays' 1936 demotion a grave error, for its wines are always impeccably made, and in good years are among the greatest of the slope. At the time the Classification was drawn up, however, Lambrays' owner had not proven so adept at advancing her claims as had some others.

Lambrays and the Clos de Tart are the sturdiest of the commune's wines, followed generally by the Clos de la Roche. Bonnes Mares often verges on the delicacy of the Chambolle, yet maintains a firm strength and considerable stamina, and the Clos Saint-Denis is the lightest and most fragile. In addition to these wines are others sold each year as Morey-Saint-Denis or as that followed by the name of the vineyard. The latter come from the First Growth *(Premier Cru)* vineyards of the commune—specially selected for the superior quality of the wines they produce—and are usually excellent wines, although without the magnificence of the greatest Growths, which are identified on labels only by vineyard name. Apart from the four top-rated Growths, there are 102 hectares (251 acres) of vineyard in the commune, producing annually some 2,500 hectoliters (62,250 U.S. gallons, 55,000 imp.) of red wine and a bit of white.

GREAT GROWTHS *(Grands Crus)*

Vineyard	Hectares	Acres
Bonnes Mares	1.8	4.6
(see also Chambolle-Musigny)		
Clos de la Roche	16	40
Clos Saint-Denis	6.6	16.5
Clos de Tart	7.5	18.75
Clos des Lambrays	8.7	22

FIRST GROWTHS *(Premiers Crus)*

Vineyard	Hectares	Acres
Les Ruchots	2.6	6.5
Les Sorbet	3	7.3
Clos Sorbet	3.3	8.2
Les Millandes	4.3	10.6
Le Clos des Ormes *(in part)*	4.8	12
Meix-Rentiers	1.2	2.9
Monts-Luisants	3.2	7.7
Les Bouchots	2	5
Clos Bussière	3.1	7.4
Aux Charmes	1.2	3.1
Les Charnières	2.4	6
Côte Rôtie	.4	1.3
Calouères	1.3	3.3
Maison Brûlée	1.8	4.6
Chabiots	2.2	5.4
Les Fremières	2.4	5.8
Les Genevrières	.9	2.2
Les Chaffots	1.25	3

Vineyard	Hectares	Acres
Les Chénevery (*in part*)	3.25	8
Aux Cheseaux	2.42	6
La Riotte	2.47	6.1
Clos Baulet	.8	2.1
Les Gruenchers	.6	1.5
Les Faconnières	1.7	4.3
Les Blanchards	1.8	4.5

Morgon

Heartiest of the good Beaujolais red wines, sometimes so much so that it resembles the Burgundies grown a few miles to the north.

See Beaujolais.

Móri Ezerjó

Wine of the Ezerjó grape, made in the village of Mór.

See Hungary.

Moriles

A section of the Montilla vineyard near Córdoba in the south of Spain. The wine produced is a dry Fino.

See Montilla-Moriles.

Morocco

The wine industry of Morocco is at once very young and very old. Indigenous vines were grown in Morocco in classical times and some of them were sent to Rome. But wine-making died out under the Moslems, with their strict prohibition of alcoholic beverages, and cultivation of wine-grapes, as distinct from dessert-grapes, was only re-established after the French took control of the region in 1912, and the real expansion of Moroccan viticulture was fostered by French settlers between 1929 and 1935, an expansion that has largely resulted in the present 45,000 hectares (112,-500 acres) planted in vines.

There are no very important place-names. A few will be found on Moroccan wines as indications of superiority, but they are not to be classed with the French system of Appellation d'Origine Contrôlée. Wines, with or without these place-names, do account for one-quarter of the agricultural revenue of the country, however. Most of these are red or rosé. A smaller quantity of white wines is made too, in spite of the fact that in the hot climate these tend to maderize, or oxidize, too quickly; the makers have somewhat the same trouble with the rosés, although in this case they are more successful. *Vin gris* is produced south of Casablanca and east of Marrakech; sweet dessert wines of a deep ruby color are made and exported; and sparkling wines are produced by the champagne method.

With independence in 1956, the Moroccan ministry of agriculture inaugurated controls of vineyards, of quality of vines as well as wines, along with regulation of the wine market. All wine must be sound, healthy, and saleable, and must contain at least 11% of alcohol (not very difficult in this semitropical country) or Moroccan law, initiated by the French, will not permit it to be exported. Most of the controls of wine were formerly in the hands of French nationals, and Moslems had very little to do with the industry beyond providing most of the manual labor. In 1973, the Moroccan government nationalized all foreign-owned vineyards, most of which were French. Today, the marketing of Moroccan wines is handled by the Office of Commerce and Exports in Casablanca. Some 50% of the annual production of 400,000 hectoliters (10.5 million U.S. gallons, 8.8 million imp.) is consumed in the country. The rest of the wine is exported, especially to the Common Market countries of Europe, where Moroccan wine has filled some of the gap left when Algeria ceased sending wine to the Continent. The future of the industry in Morocco lies in supplying Europe with cheap red wine for blending.

The wines are, on the whole, rough, heady reds, much like those of Algeria and Tunisia. Just under half of them are grown in the region around Meknes, although some also come from Rabat-Rharb, Casablanca, Fez, Oujda, and Marrakech. The vines used are mostly the bulk-giving types, such as Cinsault, Carignan, Cabernet, Mourvèdre, Grenache, and Alicante-Bouschet, for red. The first two are the best, and also give a rosé which can be very pleasant when young and which is probably the most popular type inside Morocco. The principal white wine grapes are Clairette, Maccabeo, Ximénez, Plant X, and Grenache. Native grapes, still grown in the traditional vineyards, are mainly for the table, although the Rafsai white grape of the Rif mountain region is now being used in wine-making. These vines are not resistant to phylloxera, which has been ravaging the vineyards of the north.

The other ancient vineyards bearing table grapes are situated on the northern (Zerhoun) and southern (Atlas) mountain slopes. The existence of all these old vineyards, divided into small parcels and peasant-owned, is menaced by the phylloxera louse. The modern vineyards, planted in imported vines, are to be found in the flat regions of Meknes-Fez, Oujda-Taza, and Rabat-Casablanca. Cultivation is intensive here, and mechanization has largely replaced animal-drawn plows. From the northeast come the best rosés, comparable with those of west Algeria, and the muscats of Berkane. Taza, in the center, produces a red wine good for blending; red and rosé, as well as a straw-colored white, are made around Fez; one of the most important red-wine products of Morocco, a growth with color, body, and a distinctive flavor, is found at Meknes, southwest of Fez. South of the capital, Rabat, is Sidi Larbi, the other important red wine district, where a fat, soft wine is made. Red wine comes also from the Daiet or Roumi slope vineyards east of Rabat; while to the north of these, around Sidi Slimane, richly colored Dar Bel Hamri is the principal wine. The wines of the Casablanca region are not, regrettably, allowed to come to full maturity, so quickly are they consumed; and the rosés from here resemble in color the *pelure d'oignon (q.v.)*. South of Casablanca, in the old vineyards of El Jadida and Demnate, are made the dry, fruity *vins gris* which are considered very special in Morocco. At best, Moroccan wines leave something to be desired.

Moscatel de Setúbal

Fortified wine made near Lisbon.
See Portugal.

Moscato

The Italian name for the Muscat grape.

Mosel-Saar-Ruwer

German States of Rheinland-Pfalz and Saarland
Vineyard area: approx. 12,800 hectares (31,600 acres)
100% white wines
Location: Vineyards are planted along the valleys of the Mosel River and its two most important tributaries, the Saar and the Ruwer. The region is divided into five districts (Bereiche). From the confluence of the Mosel and the Rhine and Koblenz to the village of Zell, known for its "Black Cat" (Schwarze Katz) rather ordinary wine vineyards, lies Bereiche Zell/Untermosel. Continuing upstream, from Briedel to Kenn, is Bereich Bernkastel, also known as Mittelmosel, which includes some of the most famous wine-growing villages of Germany: Erdig, Ürzig, Zeltingen, Wehlen, Graach, Bernkastel, Brauneberg and Piesport. Bereich Saar-Ruwer comprises the vineyards of both rivers' valleys as well as those around the ancient Roman city of Trier. From south of Trier to the border with Luxembourg are Bereich Obermosel and Bereich Moseltor. The name of this last, southernmost district literally means "Gateway to the Mosel."
Grape varieties: Riesling (54%); Müller-Thurgau (23%); Elbling (9%); Kerner (6%). Since 1986, but only with special permission, a few growers have been allowed to plant red grape varieties.
Wine: richly fragrant, racy, piquant, elegantly fruity, delicate.

THE MOSEL: 2,000 YEARS OF WINEMAKING

The secret of Mosels can be told in two words: slate and Riesling. Like the linked syllables of a sorcerer's spell, they produce the variety that makes each wine different even from its nearest neighbor and the light delicate quality, full of incomparable bouquet, which proclaims it inimitably Mosel.

In prehistoric times, the Devonian Sea covered the area where today the deep cleft of the Mosel runs from the French Vosges Mountains down to meet the Rhine. The sea sank away, and the sea-life and the sea-flowers fossilized and became a kind of slate or shale the Germans call *Schiefer*.

Caught between the walls of slate, the River Mosel cut deeper and deeper. When the Romans arrived, bringing vines (though vines may or may not have been planted by the people who were there before them), the river canyon was already deep enough to be below the wind. The river twists like a snake, and the countless bends screen it from the wind. The wide river in the narrow valley tempers the air and reflects and intensifies the sun. The canalizing of the river, damming it between thirteen locks, has broadened the water surface and strengthened the reflected rays of the sun. The slate itself has given way slowly to the water and elements until the banks are worn and steep; where the vines are rooted the slate holds moisture and heat and reflects this heat upward when the sun is shining. These elements of the secret of the Mosel explain why for two thousand years wine has been made without interruption in the northernmost of the important vineyards of the world. The Mosel lies on a parallel a little north of Newfoundland, but frosts do not reach the protected valley until late November, when in good years and in the best (steep) sites the late-ripening Riesling grapes are still being harvested.

The people who work single-mindedly in their remote, precipitous vineyards are of mixed stock, and even today distinct types can be recognized, such as pure Celts, or Roman heads which might have been cut on ancient coins. In their isolation, they have remained conservative, religious, and hard-working, dedicated throughout the centuries to the terrific task of bringing the fruit down from the nearly perpendicular cliffs of vineyard, where the sticks which support each vine shine like steel ranks of bayonets high above the bend of the river. Mosel growers tell how no machine or animal can labor on these sheer slopes—only a man, carrying everything up and down on his back. Fortunately, a certain amount of mechanization is now developing year by year: washed-down earth, fertilizer, cylinders of spray, and even cutting plow-blades can be hauled slowly to the top by cables wound onto the drums of engines, and often suspended cable cars carry the workers up like mountaineers. Helicopters are now commonly used for much of the spraying and hauling.

Slate is half the key to the Mosel. The vineyard names frequently end in *-lay* (or *-ley*): this simply means that the soil is slaty. The Bereich Bernkastel (Middle Mosel), roughly between Longuich and Zell, is the best section. The clue again is slate, which crumbles here at just the right rate to renew the soil, keeping it constantly virgin. Below Zell, the soil and microclimate change, yielding lighter wines. In the Obermosel (Upper Mosel) the soil is not slaty but chalky, and an inferior wine results. "The slate is the *race* of the wine," they say on the Mosel. They mean that the breed of the wine comes from the peculiar and

MOSELLE

Koblenz
Winningen
Kobern
R. Moselle
Moselkern
Treis
Pommern
Klotten
Valwig
Cochem
Ellenz-Poltersdorf
Bruttig
Beilstein
Briedern
Ediger
Eller
Senheim
Bremm
Aldegund
Alf
Bullay
Zell
Reil
R. Moselle
Enkirch
Cröv
Kinheim
Wolf
Ürzig
Lösnich
Zeltingen
Erden
Traben-Trarbach
Wittlich
Wehlen
Graach
Maring
Lieser
Kues
Bernkastel
Osann
Mülheim
Kesten
Braunberg
Veldenz
Filzen
Piesport
Wintrich
Dhron
Neumagen
Frankfurt 85 m
Klüsserath
Trittenheim
Thörnich
Detzem
Leiwen
Lörsch
Mehring
Longuich
MIDDLE MOSELLE
Trier
R. Ruwer
Karlsruhe 90 m
GERMANY
R. Moselle
R. Saar
Wellen
Nittel
Wincheringen
Saarbrucken 35 m

© CASSELL & CO LTD 1967

---

beneficial working of the Riesling vine with the slate. The grape is the other half of the secret.

Riesling was not always grown on the Mosel. The Romans planted *Vitis elvenea*, a vine like the ancient variety also planted by the Romans, the Elbling, which is still cultivated on the Obermosel today. It yields light neutral white wines which, because of their high acidity, are often best used to make sparkling wine. White Burgundy grapes were prevalent in the fifteenth and sixteenth centuries; in the seventeenth century, Riesling began to appear. In 1787 Prince-Bishop Clemens Wenzeslaus of Trier made the planting of Riesling obligatory.

It is not Riesling, however, which makes it possible to track down the special characteristics and worth of almost every individual vineyard parcel. Riesling is still the primary grape variety in this region. The fourth largest German wine-growing region (after Rheinhessen, Rheinpfalz, Baden), the Mosel is the most extensive Riesling vineyard of all. About one quarter of the region, particularly the flatter sites, are planted with Müller-Thurgau (Riesling × Silvaner). The Riesling-like Kerner and the ancient variety Elbling are also cultivated, but it is the noble Riesling which is best suited to the steep slate slopes, dry and full of stones. Except in the Upper Mosel, Riesling is universal in this region. The third largest German vineyard area (after the Palatinate and Rheinhessen), the Mosel is the most extensive Riesling vineyard of all. A few small plots test out various early-ripening varieties, and there is some Müller-Thurgau (the crossing of Riesling and Sylvaner) which is gaining in most German sections but does not seem very suited to the steep slate slopes, dry and full of stones; the rest is all Riesling, with some Elbling and the quantity-giving Kerner. What does vary is the slate.

The infinity of differences among the wines, one of the things which makes the drinking of Mosels so delightful, comes from the exposure of the slope to the sun and the side of the river on which it is found. Since the character of the slate has made the character of the river, in the long run everything can be traced back to that one single factor, together with the influence of individual micro-climates.

They explain this very interestingly in the half-timbered wine taverns along the banks of the river, when they bring out a map of the Mosel and chart the individual curves. Wherever the river has encountered the hardest shale, it has had to bend; and at the same time it has silted the facing shore. The result is that the inside of the bend is steep, hardish shale or slate, and the outside is always a low promontory of heavier earth deposited by the eddy of the river. The noblest wines, with the great breed, fight for life on the sheer shale slopes. Directly opposite, a lazier, fuller wine will grow on the alluvial soil. Piesport, Bernkastel, Graach, Wehlen (the village itself is on the other shore facing the vineyards), Zeltingen, Ürzig—they are all on the inner bends of the river. By happy chance the excellent sections face a few points either east or west of south—Piesport southeast, the strip from Graach to Zeltingen southwest, and Ürzig southeast; so they get the maximum sun exposure too. The single exception to this would seem to be Bernkastel, the most famous of all. The town lies in the mouth of a small valley running back between two hills and forking out around the base of a third. The Doktorberg, on the downriver side above the town, curves in from the Mosel edge in such a way that Bernkasteler Doctor grows on a slope turned only a little west of south. This is the most costly piece of vineyard in Germany, and perhaps in the world, although its real value is not quite up to its fame.

The great events in Mosel wines have been well spaced out—the founding of the vineyards at about the beginning of the Christian era: the spreading of vine and wine by the Cistercian monks who cultivated huge areas after their arrival on the Mosel in 1134; the establishment of Riesling as the universal variety by the end of the eighteenth century; and finally the great and significant increase of production, particularly in the last fifty years. The Mosel is unique in that it still has a relatively high proportion of original (ungrafted) European vines. The Mosel's stony, gravelly soil seems to have protected the vines from destruction by the vine louse. Many feel that the exceptional quality of fine Mosel wines is related to these original vines. Both the quality and the quantity of wine produced here, as throughout Germany, have benefited from developments of scientific research and advances in technology. Yet on the Mosel, increased production is also partly the result of converting fruit orchards on flatlands into vineyards planted with varieties which ripen earlier and yield more than the Riesling. While this has enabled many growers to commercially survive the years when the Riesling barely ripens, it has not necessarily enhanced the Mosel's reputation for fine wines. Yield per hectare varies according to site, variety, and the ripeness of the crop. In an average year, such as 1986, Riesling yielded 90–130 hectoliters per hectare, which is very high, and Müller-Thurgau and Elbling at 130–150 hectoliters per hectare, which is not compatible with quality. Yield per acre varies so much that no average figure can be struck that would not be deceptive. Nevertheless, the amount of Mosel produced each year is much greater than it used to be. Improvement in growing methods, the use of commercial fertilizer, and plantings of Elbling and Kerner high-yielding vines, along with the pressure of increasing demand, account for this.

Of the some 11,000 growers in the Mosel region, most are small farmers with vineyard holdings of 1.5 hectares (3.7 acres) or less; only about 1 per cent have more than five hectares (12.4 acres). More than half of the region's wine is marketed by commercial wineries and up to a quarter is sold directly by small and large growers. The remainder is handled by wine-growers' cooperatives, most of which merged in the late sixties to form the Central Cellars of the Mosel-Saar-Ruwer (Zentralkellerei, renamed "Moselland Cooperative"

in 1986). As of early 1987, "Moselland" had nearly 5,300 members.

The traditional unit of sale is the 1,000-liter Fuder, a round-bellied oak cask which holds approximately 1,333 bottles, or just over 100 cases of wine. In spite of the widespread use of stainless steel and fiberglass tanks, which are doubtless more efficient and contribute to an overall greater consistency in quality, the Fuder is still used by many small and large estates, particularly for aging their finest wines.

It is the pleasant regional wines from villages such as Zell, Bernkastel and Piesport which have helped establish the popularity of the Mosel far beyond its borders. Yet it is for its fine late-harvested Riesling wines that the Mosel is world renowned. In this most dramatic of all wine areas—in the timbered medieval inns of Bernkastel, or in over-exploited Cochem, where the towers are like a toy-maker's fantasy—some of the most spectacular German vinicultural achievements are accomplished. The amazing golden, mouth-filling Trockenbeerenauslese is an incomparably rich concentrate of all that is the Mosel's greatest gift to the drinker. Sadly, it is a losing proposition for the grower at today's prices. Yet, weather permitting, it is produced as a matter of pride in the art and tradition of great winemaking in the Mosel-Saar-Ruwer.

THE MOSEL BEREICHE

BEREICH BERNKASTEL

The middle section of the Mosel begins below the confluence with the Ruwer and ends just before the great bend at Zell, downstream from Reil. The greatest wines, going downriver, are the Piesporters, Braunebergers, Bernkastelers, Graachers, Wehleners, Zeltingers, Ürzigers, and Erdeners. The best parts of the Middle Mosel are so valuable that parcels are valued at sixty to seventy, and in rare cases two hundred, times the price of similar parcels in the Obermosel (Upper Mosel). Bereich Bernkastel includes the following collective vineyard sites (*Grosslagen*): Vom Heissen Stein, Schwarzlay, Nacktarsch, Münzlay, Badstube, Kurfürstlay, Michelsberg, St. Michael and Probstberg.

VINEYARDS AND PLACE-NAMES

Bernkastel-Kues

Numbering 10,000 inhabitants today, Bernkastel was founded as a city in 1291, receiving city rights from Barbarossa. Nestled down between the Doktorberg and the Schlossberg, crowned by the ruin of

Landshut Castle, the town, with its medieval square, half-timbered houses and wrought-iron signs, is almost too neat and new-painted, like a film set; yet it is an authentic, if carefully preserved, old town, kept spic and span for the thousands of tourists—the greatest concentration arrives for the vintage festival on the first weekend of September, when wine stands are erected around the baroque fountains. The mixed soil of earth and shale gives the wines their special character. In some ways, the earthy terrain imparts something of the roundness and mouth-fillingness of a more southern wine, but with this, and outweighing it, is the characteristic Mosel flintiness and spicy flavor imparted by the slate. The Bernkastel slate is harder than any other—this has been proved by the oaks of Bernkastel. Oak is used for tanning shoe-leather: the Bernkastel oak for the tanning of sole-leather, the oak of Wehlen and other neighboring zones for the rest. This same influence declares itself in the *race* of the wines. Some say that Bernkastelers, especially from the Doctor site, have a slight smoky undertaste, like the wines of Bingen on the Rhine. In any case, the wines do have a distinctive flavor and the best sites, which are extremely steep and planted with Riesling, yield wines of great substance and elegance. Bernkastel vineyards make up the entire Grosslage of Badstube and part of Grosslage Kurfürstlay. The best plots are in Badstube.

Bernkastel Vineyards

Bernkasteler Doctor. The most famous Mosel wine, unquestionably first-rate, but ridiculously overpriced today. In the fourteenth century, Prince-Bishop Boemund II of Trier is said to have been cured of illness by the wine: hence the name, and countless jokes, rhymes, and poems. The slope faces south and a little west above the town, and the wines are said to profit by the sun's heat reflected from the roofs as well as from the broad surface of the river. Bernkasteler Doctor Feinste Auslese was chosen by the late Dr. Adenauer for his state gift to the late President Eisenhower—fifty bottles of what he considered to be Germany's greatest. Among the principal owners are the widow of Dr. Hugo Thanisch, Lauerburg, and Deinhard and Co. When the Deinhard share was purchased in 1902 from Herr Kunst, the mayor of Bernkastel, payment was in gold, the highest price ever paid for a vineyard up to that date.

Badstube. The Grosslage Badstube, with only 58 hectares of vines, was created in 1971 to help maintain the high reputation of the Doctor wines. In poor years, growers will sell their Doctor wine under the Badstube name. Nevertheless, the best individual vineyard sites (Einzellagen) of Bernkastel are all within the Badstube: Doctor, Lay, Graben, Bratenhöfchen and Matheisbildchen.

Parts of the Schlossberg are excellent. Lesser vineyards in Bernkastel (in the Kurfürstlay Grosslage) are Johannisbrünnchen and Stephanus Rosengärtchen.

Kues Vineyards opposite Bernkastel

Kues, across the river, became part of Bernkastel in 1905. The famous sight, where the broad bridge from Bernkastel touches shore, is the St. Nikolaus Hospital, founded in 1448. Thirty-three old, poor men were to be taken in and cared for, never more or less; and it has been done from that time to this. Kues is not as charming as Bernkastel, and the wines grown on the outer bend of the river, and therefore on a heavier soil deposited by the river eddy, are less distinguished.

Kardinalsberg is the best known of the Kues vineyards, although Weisenstein is considered by some to yield better quality because of its greater exposure to the south. The other vineyard is Rosenberg. Kues wines are fuller and less elegant than their counterparts from Bernkastel.

Brauneberg

For centuries, both the village and its majestic vineyard slope across the Mosel River, the Braune Berg (brown hill), were known as Dusemond, the Roman term for sweet mountain. In 1925, the village took the name of the famous hillside. Elegant, fragrant, with a pronounced fruitiness and rich fullness, the wines of Brauneberg are highly esteemed. In fact, when Napoleon had the vineyards of the Mosel appraised for tax purposes in 1806, those of Brauneberg were deemed to be the most valuable. Brauneberg's vineyards are within the Grosslage Kurfürstlay.

The best sites are Juffer and Juffer-Sonnenuhr. (Juffer means "virgin" and refers here to the Franciscan nuns who once owned the sites.) Other vineyard sites: Kammer, Mandelgraben and Klostergarten.

Erden

The Erden slope is called Mosel's Gold Mountain, and the tribute is justified. After the Doktorsberg, this gives the best returns of any Mosel area. The wines are particularly fruity and have great breed, coming from slate harder than usual, as is the case at Bernkastel. Along the Mosel they have a saying that the wines of Wehlen are more *Mädel* (girl) and the wines of Erden are more *Bube* (boy). They are certainly fuller than the delicate Wehleners.

Prälat is perhaps one of the best of these excellent vineyards; it is almost exclusively held by the heirs of the Berres family. Treppchen ("little staircase") ironically describes the high-terraced vineyard, the best known of Erden, producing outstanding Rieslings. Busslay and Herrenberg are the other sites. The vineyards are within the Grosslage Schwarzlay.

Graach

Graach takes its name from the Gallic term *gravos*, or gravel. The soil here is gravelly, weathered clayish slate. The clay, located under a five-meter-deep sheet of slate, gives the wines more body (much fuller than Wehleners) and a spicy flavor, and makes them age more slowly. Like Piesporters, they do best in dry years.

Its sites are all extremely steep, facing south-southwest and planted with Riesling: Himmelreich, Domprobst (altern. Dompropst = provost, or head of a cathedral), Josefshöfer and Abtsberg. Josefsjöfer, like Schloss Vollrads and Schloss Johannisberg, is one of the few appellations permitted to be sold without a vineyard name. It was originally owned by the Abbey of St. Martin in Trier and known as Martinshof. It was renamed by the commercial counselor Josef Hayn, who acquired it after the secularization of church properties in the early 1800's. He sold it to Count Kesselstatt in 1858, and today it is still owned exclusively by the Kesselstatt estate. Other leading owners of Graacher sites include estates of the Prüm and Bergweiler families as well as the Friedrich Wilhelm Gymnasium, a famous secondary school in Trier. Graacher vineyards are part of the Grosslage Münzlay. When there is no rain in September and October, Graach makes wonderful wines; in general, they are at their best in the dry years. Practically all the vineyard once belonged to the Church; today, Prüm, Thanisch, Deinhard, and Kesselstatt are the main owners, and they, not the Graach vintners, have the best parts.

Piesport

Piesport, like Bernkastel, is one of the most important wine villages of the Mosel in terms of both quality and quantity. Behind the town and on both sides, vineyards are planted on a high hill which sweeps upward and curves around like a vast bowl, facing due south and optimally situated to catch the reflected sunshine from the river. One expert describes Piesporters as "Queens of the Mosel. They are wonderfully delicate and fragrant wines, never heavy, never coarse, with an incomparable distinction of their own. In great years, they can be great Mosels." In wet years, they may be poor, for the forested summit holds too much moisture and the vineyards below cannot dry out. For marketing purposes, a considerable amount of wine is sold under the name of the Grosslage Michelsberg. But the finest wines are named after the individual vineyards of which Goldtröpfchen is the most renowned. Günterslay, Falkenberg, Grafenberg, Domherr, Schubertslay, Gärtchen and Kreuzwingert are adjacent to Goldtröpfchen. Treppchen, a large site on the opposite side of the river, is the other major vineyard of Piesport.

Ürzig

The vines, growing on a very sheltered (and in some places incredibly steep) southern exposure, have a soil structure different from that in any other part of the Mosel—a deep-strata volcanic soil of mixed slate and croppings of colored sandstone, giving a special taste. The wines, are spicier than others and have great fruitiness These vineyards, as with all the best sites on the Mosel, are planted exclusively with Riesling grapes. In hot years these wines are magnificent and, in the opinion of some experts, they are reliable even in wet years. There are two sites: Würzgarten, which literally means "spice garden" and Goldwingert. Both sites are within the Grosslage Schwarzlay.

Wehlen

An unassuming village compared to some of its neighbors, Wehlen nevertheless looks across the Mosel to what, in Germany, is commonly considered the best Mosel vineyard. Wehlener Sonnenuhr sometimes justifiably reaches the fabulous prices commanded by Bernkasteler Doctor. Many Germans say it is the better wine. The distinguishing character of the Wehleners is their extreme elegance and finesse. They are rich and full, with a uniquely delicate taste and bouquet. From its foundation in 1084 until its secularization in 1802, the Cistercian monastery Kloster Machern owned most of the present sites of Wehlen. The names of many of the vineyards reflect this: Klosterberg, Nonnenberg, Klosterhofgut, Abtei. Other sites include Hofberg and Rosenberg. Sonnenuhr is considered to be the supreme site. As in neighboring Graach, numerous estates of the Prüm and Bergweiler families are among the best-known and leading producers. Wehlen's vineyards are within the Grosslage Münzlay.

Zeltingen

Because the Zeltingen vineyard area is extensive, the quality and elegance of its wines vary among sites and producers. Vineyards in the original Himmelreich site, prior to its being enlarged through vineyard consolidation, lie on the steep, southern-facing hills behind the village and yield very fine wine. Zeltinger Himmelreich, from the newer sections of the site, further upstream and on the other side of the river, is often less distinguished. The same is true of the Deutschherrenberg site. The two best sites are Schlossberg and Sonnenuhr. The Zeltinger Sonnenuhr borders and is actually a continuation of Wehlen's famed site of the same name. Except for the difference in price, the wines are very similar, with the Zeltinger being perhaps more full-bodied than the Wehlener. The longest (about 7–8 km = 4–5 miles) uninterrupted stretch of superlative Riesling vineyards of the entire Mosel begins in Bernkastel and ends in Zeltingen. The vineyards are within the Grosslage Münzlay.

These outstanding wines have the widest range of any Mosel village, and this is not always to their advantage. In a good year, Zeltingen will produce about 2.5 million bottles of wine. No other Mosel area approaches this. As a result, many ordinary bottles of

Zeltinger are seen, obscuring the fact that some splendid ones are also made. It is hard to pin down Zeltinger as to type, for there is a considerable range, from light, flowery wines to others with as much body as is likely to be found in a Mosel. The very finest have a charming feminine quality.

OTHER POPULAR VILLAGES

Few wines outside the heart of the Middle Mosel have been really well known, except for Zeller Schwarze Katz which is average in quality at best, and one or two names along the Saar. The greatest names are great because the vineyards are held in part or entirely by the big owners and/or by outstanding producers who have earned their reputations over generations. The record-setting prices achieved at the famous auctions of Der Grosse Ring have also enhanced the reputation of many villages and sites. Yet there are many other villages whose wines are worth discovering. Because they are not as well known, they usually cost less and can offer excellent value. The villages listed below may not enjoy the international fame of those just described, but they, too, offer a wide range of reasonably priced and well-made wines for everyday enjoyment or special occasions.

Enkirch. Picturesque village with large vineyard area planted primarily with Riesling; flowery, racy and vigorous wines. *GL* Schwarzlay

Kesten. Very old village with sites once owned by the St. Paulinus Charity in Trier, now reflected in the names of its best sites, Paulinshofberger and Paulinsberg, both of which are steep Riesling slopes. *GL* Kurfürstlay

Klüsserath. Typical wine-growing village with some very steep, southern-facing Riesling slopes; delicate but racy wines; Bruderschaft is the best-known site. *GL* St. Michael

Kröv. Ancient village, once part of the Merovingian (and later, Carolingian) kingdoms; today best known for its colorful label which literally depicts the name of its site, Nacktarsch, meaning "bare bottom" . . . a little boy's bare bottom is being spanked: steep sites, planted primarily with Riesling produce fair fruity wines with average acidity. *GL* Nacktarsch

Leiwen. The vineyard area has steadily increased in size as orchards have been converted to vineyards; Laurentiuslay, however, a steep Riesling site, yields wines of good fruit and character in good years. *GL* St. Michael

Lieser. Named for the little river which flows into the Mosel; the Schlossberg site takes its name from the Von Schorlemer family's 19th-century castle (*Schloss*); Süssenberg and Niederberg-Helden are steep, Riesling sites. *GL* Kurfürstlay

Mülheim. Located just south of Bernkastel, this village produces lively Riesling wines with an elegant, fine fruitiness; in the 1920's Mülheimer Sonnenlay was popularly known as "Zeppelin" wine—light and delicate enough to travel on the famed dirigibles; one Riesling site, in particular, the Helenenkloster, often yields Eiswein. *GL* Kurfürstlay

Neumagen. Said to be the oldest wine-growing village in Germany; many Roman artifacts related to wine have been excavated here, including the tomb of a Roman wine merchant featuring a wine ship typical of that time, the Neumagener wine ship, on display in the Landesmuseum in Trier. *GL* Michelsberg

Traben-Trarbach. Two villages, straddling the Mosel, which have been an important center for the wine trade since the 16th century; popular tourist spot; dramatically steep Riesling vineyards; fair, fruity wines with pronounced acidity. *GL* Schwarzlay

Trittenheim. Known as the site of the first Riesling planting on the Mosel (1562) and birthplace of the great humanist Trithemius; vineyards are situated in a 180° loop of the river; fine, elegant, fruity wines; best-known sites are Altärchen and Apotheke. *GL* Michelsberg

Veldenz. Extremely picturesque town with a ruin-crowned little mountain, but well inland from the Mosel, in a side valley; pleasant Riesling and Müller-Thurgau wines with an appealing freshness and bouquet. *GL* Kurfürstlay

Wintrich. Some steep Riesling sites, producing good quality; flatter sites planted with Müller-Thurgau yield pleasant, fruity, light wines. *GL* Kurfürstlay

Wittlich. Historically significant site from which the Cistercian monks, arriving from an establishment in nearby Himmerode in 1134, spread viticulture over much of the Mosel and Ruwer; racy, piquant Rieslings and light, uncomplicated Müller-Thurgau wines. *GL* Schwarzlay

BEREICH ZELL-MOSEL

The lower section of the Mosel begins at Zell and ends at the confluence of the Mosel with the Rhine at Koblenz. There are many steep sites, often planted with Riesling, although a fair amount of Müller-Thurgau, Kerner, and some early-ripening varieties is planted in flatter sites. In general, the wines of this district are less elegant and distinctive than those of the middle Mosel, although most are pleasant, fruity wines with a piquant, refreshing acidity.

The district is named after the village of Zell, one of the largest wine-growing villages on the Mosel, with a high proportion of Riesling. It is known the world over for its commercial wines with the black cat (Schwarze Katz) on the label. Legend has it that a group of buyers from Aachen, unable to agree on which Fuder (cask) of wine was the best, followed the example of the vintner's cat—they chose the cask the cat selected to sleep upon. Zeller Schwarze Katz is a popular wine for everyday consumption. Vast amounts of varying quality are exported. To avoid disappointment one should look for the name of a reliable producer or shipper rather than the cheapest price.

In addition to Schwarze Katz, the district includes the following collective vineyard sites: Weinhex, which means "wine witch" and is reminiscent of the witch trials of the mid-17th century; Goldbäumchen; Rosenhang; and Grafschaft.

Here are the names of a few popular villages. Almost always picturesque, with medieval half-timbered houses and a wealth of churches, fountains and monuments of many styles (Romanesque, Gothic, Renaissance, Baroque) as well as majestic castles—these villages, along with the beautiful and dramatic landscape, provide an almost magical setting within which to enjoy the charming wines of Bereich Zell. Alf; Beilstein; Bremm, said to have the steepest vineyard in Europe; Cochem; Ediger-Ellenz; Kobern-Gondorf; Neef; Winningen, said to be home to the oldest wine festival in Germany.

BEREICH OBERMOSEL AND BEREICH MOSELTOR

The vineyards of the Mosel across the river and above Trier belong to the Upper Mosel, but they are quite different from the great Mosel Rieslings grown on slate. In these two districts, the weathered chalky soil (loamy shell limestone with patches of marl and sand) is better-suited to growing Elbling and Burgundy varieties, such Ruländer, or Pinot Gris. Elbling is the ancient variety brought to the Mosel by the Romans 2,000 years ago. The other principal grape is the Müller-Thurgau. These wines often have a particular charm of their own, but they lack the race and breed of the wines from the middle Mosel or the Saar and Ruwer. They are really linked in name only, since they lack the essential elements which go to make up true Mosel wines: slate soil and Riesling. Many Upper Mosels, good wines in their own right, are sound value, being little known and therefore not driven up in price.

Bereich Obermosel consists of two collective vineyard sites: Gipfel (formerly the name of a fine plot in Nittel) and Königsberg. Nittel is the biggest and the best known of the *Weinbauorte*. Other towns of some importance are Wellen and Wincheringen.

Bereich Moseltor (Moseltor means "gateway to the Mosel") consists of one collective vineyard site, Schloss Bübinger, named after the moated castle of Bübingen, built in 1340 by Gabriel von Remich.

BEREICH SAAR-RUWER

The district is composed of three areas brought together by the 1971 West German wine law: the Saar River Valley, the Ruwer Valley, and a large section of vineyards around the town of Trier, between the

bends where the Saar and the Ruwer join the main stream. There are nearly 2,200 hectares (5,500 acres) of vines.

The Saars can outclass the Mosels in the best years. A hot, dry summer brings great wines along this tributary that leads into the Mosel—light, spicy, unique in flavor, with a special taste like that of blackcurrants, and a bouquet resembling Muscatel. The wines are generally longer-lasting and slower to age than the Mosels. The vine is usually Riesling and the soil characteristics in the lower Saar are the same as on the Mosel—a slate which crumbles slowly and replenishes the earth. Above Saarburg there is less of this slate characteristic. From Serrig to Konz-Karthaus, where the River Saar enters the River Mosel, the banks are almost solid vineyard. Saar wines, which in the great years are in some respects almost super-Mosel in their development of the characteristic elements of *race* and steely elegance, are always classed with the Mosels.

Ockfen probably has the highest average of good wines, but the general opinion is that the best individual vineyard is the famous Scharzhofberg, lying a little farther down the river behind the village of Wiltingen.

The Ruwer wines, at their best, are the lightest of Germany—leaner than those of the Saar or of the Mosel. In the best years they have a bouquet suggesting spice, but in poorer years they may be too acidic for most tastes. In general, the nearer to the Mosel the wine grows, the better it is likely to be. Ruwer (and Saar) wines are always classed with the Mosel, and the

German wine label simply lumps them as Mosel-Saar-Ruwer. While the Saar is a substantial river, the surprising thing about the Ruwer is that it is a stream almost narrow enough to jump across. It boils down out of a narrow valley through the little town of Ruwer on the Mosel edge and enters the broad river not far below Trier. Upstream the valley widens. It is there, and in a small side valley devoted to the Avelsbach vineyards, that the Riesling vine grows and the wines are made.

The district consists of two collective vineyard sites: Römerlay (Trier and the Ruwer vineyards) and Scharzberg (Saar vineyards).

BEST VILLAGES (R = Ruwer, S = Saar)

Avelsbach (R)

Vineyards lie in the jagged triangle between the Mosel and the Ruwer. In very hot summers they bring forth excellent quality; in poorer years, they are rougher and too steely or hard for most people's taste.

Ayl (S)

The quality of the wines closely rivals the Ockfeners. Herrenberg, and Kupp (a connoisseur's wine, exquisite in a hot year, from a perpendicular vineyard) are the best sites.

Eitelsbach (R)

Karthäuserhofberg is the outstanding site. Formerly a monastery, given to the Carthusians by the ecclesiastic Balduin in the middle of the 14th century, it passed intact into the hands of the Rautenstrauch family at the time of the secularization of Church lands in 1802. Descendants of this family are the present owners. They have an unusual label: a tiny curved label affixed (only) to the neck of the bottle. The wines are labeled Eitelsbacher Karthäuserhofberg followed by the name of a site (Kronenberg, Sang, Burgberg, Orthsberg, Stirn).

Filzen (S)

Northernmost wine-growing village of the Saar, near the confluence of the Saar with the Mosel. Racy Rieslings. Pulchen, Urbelt and Herrenberg are good sites.

Kanzem (S)

Here, as in many of the villages along the Saar and Ruwer, viticulture dates back to Roman times. Vineyards are planted on a steep, south-facing hill and in good years, excellent wines with a superb fruity acidity and spicy flavor are produced.

Kasel (R)

This is the most important Ruwer *Weinbauort*, producing more wine than any other on that river. It has about double the vineyard of its peers; and the only Ruwer town equaling it in quantity—Waldrach further up the valley—makes only small wines. Probably the best is Kasseler Nies'chen, a splendidly soft, light wine in good years. Other vineyards are Kehrnagel, Hitzlay, Dominikanerberg, Kohlenberg, Paulinsberg, and Timpert.

Mertesdorf (R)

The wines of Maximin Grünhaus are always excellent Ruwer wines, particularly in dry years.It is the outstanding growth of the Weinbauort Mertesdorf and derives its name from the fact that before the secularization of Church property in Germany by Napoleon, it belonged to the St. Maximin Abbey of Trier. It is now owned by von Schubert. The wines are labeled Maximin Grünhäuser followed by the name of a site (Abtsberg, Herrenberg, Brudersberg).

Oberemmel (S)

Not far from Wiltingen, this village produces very fine wines, with great Riesling raciness.

Ockfen (S)

Among the best wines of the Saar. Bockstein is the best vineyard and rivals Scharzhofberger from Wiltingen as the finest Saar wine; it is fuller than Scharzhofberger but less elegant, and in certain years it may be the better wine. Geisberg is the other important site.

Saarburg (S)

Very picturesque town which is a very popular tourist spot and a center of the Saar wine trade. In good years, Saarburgers are very stylish and of fine quality.

Serrig (S)

Located at the extreme edge of the Saar's winegrowing area, where the climate is less dependable than in villages closer to the Mosel, Serriger wines can nevertheless be outstanding in good years.

Trier (R and S)

The largest town on the Mosel, important as a wine-trading center and home of many important, large estates with holdings in most of the best sites throughout the Mosel-Saar-Ruwer region. It is a fascinating little city whose slogan "with 2,000 steps you can experience 2,000 years of history" is well worth following. An exceptionally fine collection of Roman artifacts related to wine is displayed in the Landes-museum.

Waldrach (R)

Produces fresh wines of good quality which show more character in good years.

Wawern (S)

Herrenberg and Goldberg are the best sites. Not as distinctive as the wines of Ayl, but Rieslings grown on the steep sites are of high quality.

Wiltingen (S)

Excellent wine-growing village with wines comparable to the finest of the middle Mosel. Scharzhofberg is the finest vineyard, and in most years finest on the Saar. The wines have a superb elegance. The vineyard faces south and west on a large hill behind Wiltingen, and the story of its ownership is a curious one. It was planted 200 years ago by the monastery of St. Maria of Trier. At the beginning of the nineteenth century when Napoleon was secularizing Church property, a priest named Müller enrolled the vineyard under his name to protect it. Napoleon came and went; Müller held on to the vineyard, married a young woman, and founded a family. His descendant, affable Egon Müller, is probably the best grower on the Saar. Scharzhofberger is allowed to be sold without the name of the village. Other fine sites include Wiltinger Braune Kupp, Kupp and Braunfels.

PRINCIPAL MOSEL-SAAR-RUWER ESTATES

Here are the names of a few traditional producers, all of whom own portions of the finest, steep, southern-facing vineyards planted with Riesling vines. The wines are aged in oak casks, in the traditional manner. And the wines all benefit from bottle age—their longevity has been repeatedly confirmed by the extraordinary prices older vintages fetch at auction.

The Middle Mosel

The Prüms and the Bergweilers

From Ürzig to Brauneberg there are several fine estates with the name Prüm, Bergweiler or a double-name including one or both names. The Prüms have been wine-growers in Wehlen for centuries, but their deservedly famous reputation dates from the 19th century, with Sebastian Alois Prüm (1794–1871), who can be regarded as the founder of the estates bearing his name (S.A. Prüm Erben) today. It was his brother, Jodocus, who had the sundials in Wehlen and Zeltingen constructed in 1842, so that the vineyard workers, unable to afford watches, would be able to tell when it was time for breaks, lunch, the end of a day's work. By the turn of the century, the family estate had grown to 17 hectares (42 acres) and was one of the largest untitled private estates in the Middle Mosel. In 1911, the estate was divided among the seven children of Sebastian Alois' son, Matthias:

1) Johann Josef, the oldest son, founded the J.J. Prüm estate and acquired a large portion of his brother (3) Matthias' holdings. His son, also named Sebastian Alois, joined him in the wine business in 1920 and set about achieving outstanding quality. His success is mirrored in auction results. The tradition of high quality is carried on by his son, Dr. Manfred Prüm, the present proprietor and owner of some of the choicest parcels of the Wehlener Sonnenuhr, Graacher Himmelreich, excellent sites in Bernkastel and the Zeltinger Sonnenuhr. The estate is among the most highly respected in Germany.

2) Sebastian Alois, the second son, whose inheritance has been handed down to the estates S.A. Prüm Erben, S.A. Prüm, Wehlen (proprietor Raimund Prüm) and S.A. Prüm Erben, Christoffel-Prüm, Ürzig.

4) Peter Prüm, whose holdings have been passed on to two estates bearing his name, Peter Prüm Erben, M. Engelberting-Prüm, Wehlen, and Peter Prüm Erben, St. Studert-Prüm, Wehlen.

5) Anna Prüm, married Dr. Weins; present estates are Dr. Weins-Prüm Erben (Selbach-Weins) and Dr. Weins (Willi Weins).

6 & 7) Maria and Katharina Prüm; the latter married Zacharias Bergweiler, a very successful producer who extended his vineyard holdings considerably, recognized today under Zach. Bergweiler-Prüm Erben (divided among his five children): *Dr. Zach. Bergweiler,* Wehlen, the estate inherited by his only son (leased by Deinhard today); *Dr. Heidemanns-Bergweiler,* Bernkastel; *Dr. Adams-Bergweiler* (two estates, one bearing the name of the Loosen family of Ürzig); *Licht-Bergweiler* (Braneberg); and *Dr. Pauly-Bergweiler,* now run by his son, Dr. Peter Pauly, with excellent sites in Bernkastel, Graach, Weheln, Zeltingen and Braneberg. He married Helga Berres, of another prominent wine-growing family in the Middle Mosel, who owns the small fine estate *Peter Nicolay/C.H. Berres Erben,* Ürzig.

Original owner of the *Bernkasteler Doctor* site was Gutsverwaltung Deinhard in Bernkastel—traditional Riesling estate with 27 hectares (67 acres) of vineyards in Bernkastel, Graach, Wehlen, Lieser, Kesten (Mosel) and Kasel (Ruwer). By the end of the 19th century, so much wine was being sold under the name Bernkasteler Doctor as to raise doubts about its authenticity. To safeguard the genuine product, Deinhard bought over half of the site in 1900 at the extraordinary price of 100 Gold Marks per vine. They have the largest portion of the site. Weingut Wwe. Dr. H. Thanisch—traditional Riesling estate with some 13 hectares (32 acres) of vineyards in Bernkastel, Brauenberg, Graach and Lieser. A bottle of 1921 Bernkasteler Doctor Trockenbeerenauslese set a world record price of DM7,500 at auction in 1978; just seven years later, again at auction, the same wine fetched DM11,100. Weingut J. Lauerburg—traditional Riesling (100%) estate with 4 hectares (10 acres) of excellent vineyards in Bernkastel, Graach and Wehlen. Lauerburg is the oldest owner of a portion of the Doctor site.

Trier

Weingut Reichsgraf von Kesselstatt—largest privately held estate in the Mosel, owned by the Günther Reh family. Documents first mention the estate in 1349 and in 1377, Friedrich von Kesselstatt was appointed administrator of the royal wine cellars in Trier. The 100 hectares (247 acres) of vineyards are located near four historical estates, each of which was formerly part of a monastery: Josephshof/Graach, Domklausenhof/ Piesport; St. Irminenhof/Kasel on the Ruwer; and Abteihof/Oberemmel on the Saar. The administrative offices and cellars are housed in the baroque Kesselstatt palace in Trier, which also has a gourmet restaurant and art gallery on the grounds. In 1986, the estate initiated a "ten-year-guarantee" on their wines (valid only within Germany) in an attempt to encourage consumers to bottle-age fine Mosel Riesling wines. The estate is especially proud of its Gold Medal of Honor for excellence in winemaking, making it one of a handful of estates to have received the award.

Güterverwaltung Vereinigte Hospitien—a charitable foundation established in 1805 by Napoleon, whereby a group of Trier hospitals and social institutions were united. The wine cellars are considered to be the oldest in Germany, since the walls and foundation were once part of a Roman camp which contained the largest Roman storehouse north of the Alps. The 55 hectares (136 acres) of vineyards are in the Middle Mosel and on the Saar, primarily planted with Riesling on steep slopes. The holdings include sole ownership of Schloss Saarfelser Schlossberg in Serrig; Wiltinger Hölle; Piesporter Schubertslay; and Trierer Augenscheiner. The label depicts St. Jacob, a reminder of the St. Jacob Hospital which was originally a hospice for pilgrims en route to the grave of the Apostle Jacob in Santiago de Compostela. The Vereinigte Hospitien is a non-profit corporation which uses its revenues (10% from viticulture) to operate a hospital, 500 residences for the elderly, a children's home and center for multiple sclerosis patients.

Friedrich Wilhelm Gymnasium—estate developed through endowments to the school established by the Jesuits in 1563. Its 45 hectares (111 acres) of vineyards are on the Mosel and the Saar—steep, Riesling sites; wines are stored and aged in oak casks. The label bears the coat-of-arms of the Jesuits.

Verwaltung der Bischöflichen Weingüter—a union of three large ecclesiastical estates and numerous smaller church properties with holdings primarily on the Saar and Ruwer, with a few sites on the Mosel. The estates merged in 1966, but the wines are still sold under the traditional labels of the original estates. *Bischöfliches Priesterseminar*, a Catholic seminary whose vineyards were an endowment by the prince bishop Clemens Wenzeslaus in 1773; like all church properties in Trier, its holdings were secularized in 1794 but reinstated by special edict in 1809. Its 34 hectares (84 acres) of vineyards are located on the Mosel, Saar and Ruwer. *Bischöfliches Konvikt* is a Catholic preparatory school with some 40 hectares (99 acres) of vineyards, including part of the famed Piesporter Goldtröpfchen. *Hohe Domkirche* refers to the Cathedral of Trier. The estate consists of 22 hectares (54 acres) of vineyards on the Saar (Scharzhofberg) and Ruwer (Avelsbach).

Saar and Ruwer

Karthäuserhof—prominent estate located in Eitelsbach. Sole owners of the outstanding vineyards on the Karthäuse hofbera, overlooking the Ruwer River, and including the sites: Burgberg, Kronenberg, Sang; Orthsberg and Stirn. There are 20 hectares (49 acres) of vineyards planted mostly with Riesling on the steep hill. In the 13th century, the Karthäuserhof was the property of the electors and archbishop of Trier. From 1335–1803 it was farmed by Carthusian monks. After secularization in 1794, it was sold at auction and purchased by descendents of today's proprietors, the Rautenstrauch family. The label is unique: a neck label only . . . one of the smallest in the world, for one of the longest appellations of origin.

Maximin Grünhaus—top-ranking estate located near Mertesdorf and owned by the von Schubert family since 1882. The beautiful manor house was once the property of the St. Maximin Abbey of Trier. The 33 hectares (81 acres) of vineyards are divided into three sites: Abtsberg, Herrenberg and Brudersberg. The traditional label designed in 1900 is still in use; Prädikats are indicated on a triangular neck label.

Scharzhof—estate of international renown located near Wiltingen. Once owned by the monastery of St. Marien ad martyres of Trier; secularized in 1794; purchased at auction by Jean-Jacques Koch, the great-great-grandfather of the present proprietor, Egon Müller. The estate consists of 8.5 hectares (21 acres) in the Braunfels site of Wiltingen and in the heart of one of the most famous names in German wine, the Scharzhofberg. *Egon Müller* has the largest share of this steep hillside which still has some of its original European (non-grafted) Riesling vines. Since 1954, he has been co-owner and manager of another fine estate, *Le Gallais* (Kanzem), with 2.5 hectares (6 acres) of vineyards in Wiltingen and Wawern.
Other fine producers:

Dieter Ebert, Serrig
Robert Eymael; Ürzig
Dr. Fischer, Ockfen
Forstmeister Geltz Erben-Zilliken, Saarburg
Ferd. Haag Erben and Fritz Haag, both in Brauneberg
von Hövel, Oberemmel
Milz-Laurentiushof, Trittenheim

Moslem Prohibition

Georg Fritz von Nell, Trier
von Othegraven, Kanzem
Ökonomierat Piedmont, Konz-Filzen
Edmund Reverchon, Konz-Filzen
Max Ferd. Richter, Mülheim
Hubert Schmitz, Wiltingen
Selbach-Oster, Zeltingen
Bert Simon, Serrig
Tobias, Piesport

Moselblümchen

"Little Flower of the Mosel." A light, thirst-quenching wine for everyday consumption. A very ordinary Mosel wine and if one is looking for quality, it is not to be trusted any more than a Schwarze Katz from Traben-Trarbach.

Moseltaler

"Moseltaler" is meant to be to the Mosel what Edelzwicker is to Alsace: a typical Mosel wine with pronounced acidity and a light, fruity character. Starting with the 1986 vintage, this new regional Qualitätswein may be made from one or a blend of the white varieties Riesling, Müller-Thurgau, Elbling and Kerner grown anywhere within the Mosel-Saar-Ruwer region. Neither a grape variety nor a narrower appellation of origin may be named on the label. Residual sugar is limited to 15–30 grams per liter; total acidity must be at least 7 grams per liter.

Moslem Prohibition

The tenet of Mohammed denying the use of alcoholic drink to his followers in Islam. Aside from the decrees of early emperors in China, it is the only prohibition which has had a lasting effect. The consequence has been the almost total death of viniculture throughout the Islamic world, though isolated vineyards have held out among non-believers enclosed within Islam and among Moslems for table grapes. In modern times, Europeans, notably the French in North Africa, have restored wine-making in Moslem lands.

Mother wine

Wine concentrated by boiling, used to strengthen young wines. A mural in the tomb of Menopth in Egypt shows that this process is at least 4,000 years old.

Mou

French term for flabby.

Mouillage

French term for reduction by addition of water.

Moulin-à-Vent (Appellation Contrôlée)

Fullest in body and in some markets the best-known of the red Beaujolais wines, France.
See Beaujolais.

Moulis

Bordeaux red wine.
District: Haut-Médoc, France.

A 360-hectare (900-acre) commune of Haut-Médoc which has its own Appellation Contrôlée.

Mountain

Old English name for Málaga wine *(q.v.).*

Mourisco

Important grape in the making of Port *(q.v.).*

Mourvèdre

Red-wine grape grown in the Midi and elsewhere in France, in Algeria, and in Spain. Among its many synonyms are Négron, Espar, Mataro, Catalan, Beni Carlo, and Tinto.
See Provence.

Mousseux

This designation found on a French label means that the wine is sparkling. In France it is the term used for all sparkling wines except those grown in the geographical district of Champagne. (Only sparkling wine of that area may be called Champagne.)

Château Mouton-Baronne-Philippe

Bordeaux red wine.
District: Haut-Médoc, France.
Commune: Pauillac.

Until about two hundred years ago, Château Mouton-d'Armailhacq and the present Château Mouton-Rothschild formed one estate. In 1855 Mouton-Rothschild was classified first among the Second Growths *(Seconds Crus)* of Médoc, and Mouton d'Armailhacq was classified a Fifth Growth *(Cinquième Cru)* and is today better known than some Third *(Troisièmes)* and Fourth Growths *(Quatrièmes Crus)*. Mouton-Baronne-Philippe, as it is now known, lies between the famous vineyards of Mouton-Rothschild and Pontet-Canet to the north of Pauillac. The wines are excellent, and much of the credit must be given to Baron Philippe de Rothschild, owner of Mouton-Rothschild, who since 1930 has also been making Mouton-Baronne-Philippe and in 1951 gave this vineyard his first name—calling it Château Mouton-Baron-Philippe. He later changed the name a second time, to Château Mouton-Baronne-

Philippe, to honor his late wife, Pauline. His daughter, ex-actress Philippine, is very present at Mouton-Rothschild today.

Characteristics. A very good Pauillac, lighter than Mouton-Rothschild, but with a fine characteristic bouquet.

Vineyard area: 50 hectares (125 acres).

Average production: 170 *tonneaux* (15,000 cases).

Château Mouton-Rothschild

Bordeaux red wine.
District: Haut-Médoc, France.
Commune: Pauillac.

There are several explanations of why the vineyard is called Mouton. One suggested by the owner, Baron Philippe de Rothschild, is that in Old French the hilly land was called Mothon, meaning "mound." Moreover, the series of little rises and hills comprising the vineyard suggests the backs of a flock of sheep. The Rothschilds' predecessor, Baron de Brane, who bought Mouton in 1853, was a prominent member of the Parliament of Bordeaux. Until 1730, Mouton was all part of Château Lafite, belonging to the Prince of Ségur, and prior to that was owned by the Duke of Gloucester (1430), Jean Dunois, and Gaston de Foix. For four generations now, and more than one hundred years, the vineyard has been held by Barons de Rothschild—Nathaniel, James, Henri, and today the great-grandson, Philippe—and the quality and reputation of the wine have been constantly improving. Mouton was already highly rated in 1855 when Médoc wines were classified, and since at that time it was neither selling quite with the First Growths *(Premiers Crus)* nor with the Second Growths *(Seconds Crus)* it was placed first of the Seconds. This compromise did not please Mouton and the famous motto of the vineyard originated: *Premier ne puis, Second ne daigne, Mouton suis.* Translated as "First I cannot be, Second I do not deign to be, I am Mouton," the motto has been made into a practical reality by the Rothschilds. And in a new Classification by the Ministry of Agriculture in 1973, Mouton deservedly became a First Classified Growth—perhaps the first of many necessary amendments to an outmoded ranking.

This eminent position is due to the high quality of the wine itself and to the brilliant publicity and promotion given the name, especially since, in 1926, Philippe de Rothschild took over the administration and later the ownership. He was assisted in the running of the estate by the able late M. Marjary and now by directors Philippe Cottin, Patrick Léon, Philippe de Rothschild's daughter Philippine and soon by her son: Philippe Sereys de Rothschild. A production of an average 600 barrels is mostly in Cabernet Sauvignon grapes and is long-vatted. Pierre and Raoul Blondin, cellarmasters at Mouton, insist that great wine cannot be made except by long-vatting. The practice of leaving the grape juice in contact with the hulls and residue of the grapes in the fermentation vats for only nine to fifteen days is now almost universal throughout the Médoc. But at Mouton, juice and grape residue macerate together for a full month; that is, for twenty days or more after fermentation has ceased. This, and the high percentage (75%) of Cabernet Sauvignon used, is designed to produce a big, hard wine, which requires long bottle-ageing but matures finally into a splendid, very long-lasting wine.

The great *chai* of new wines at Mouton-Rothschild is the most spectacular in Bordeaux. Double doors are thrown open at the side of the room where the baron gives his banquets, and neatly aligned barrels stretch away for a hundred yards in five or six rows. The *chai* is at ground level; but down below, in moss-blackened cellars, tunnels store more than 100,000 bottles of Mouton at a constant temperature of 52°F. (11.1°C.). Here, too, is the fabulous wine "library" of which the showpieces are cobweb-covered bottles a hundred and more years old. Along the rear wall there is a bin of bottles made up from every vintage since the Rothschild ownership began. The sense of good taste is not restricted to the estate. Bottle labels carry each year an original illustration by a different celebrated artist—Salvador Dali, Henry Moore, Jean Cocteau, Marc Chagall, Picasso. For years Baron Philippe, expertly aided by his late wife, has been collecting paintings, goblets, tapestries, vases, and any other objects connected with wine. These were assembled in a superbly lit museum, which was opened in 1962, and form a collection for which every wine-lover should be grateful. The museum is but one achievement for which Baron Philippe de Rothschild shall always be remembered. His dedication to quality and to the artistic expression of wine is without equal.

Characteristics. Always heavy, full, and almost fleshy. It was long known for a special, almost metallic flavor that natives of Bordeaux called a *goût de capsule;* in recent vintages, however, this flavor has disappeared. The high percentage of Cabernet Sauvignon grapes makes it very slow to mature and very full-bodied.

Vineyard area: 65 hectares (162.5 acres).

Average production: 260 *tonneaux* (26,000 cases).

Mulled wine

Diluted red wine, brought to the boil, spiced and sweetened, and served very hot. It has an extraordinary ability to discourage a cold in the early stages.

Müller-Thurgau

The grape and the wine derived from the crossing of the Riesling and Sylvaner vine varieties and rapidly increasing in popularity in Germany. There is also a small amount of it in Alsace. The name is not likely to appear on bottle labels.

See Alsace; Germany.

Munson, Thomas V.

American hybridizer who developed several hybrid vines, notably Delicatessen. Munson set up his experimental vineyards in Denison, Texas, and all but revolutionized hybridization by his zealous efforts to bring in new families of grapes as "blood lines." His own work, however, is of somewhat limited importance to the winemaker, since it was oriented toward table grapes rather than wine.

Münster-bei-Bingerbruck

Better wine district of the two Münsters of the Nahe Valley, West Germany.
See Nahe.

Murray River

Vineyards on the boundary between Victoria and South Australia. They produce fortified wines and brandy and also grow Palomino and Pedro Ximénez grapes for sherry-type wines.
See Australia.

Murrumbidgee

Irrigated vineyard region on the Murrumbidgee River, New South Wales, producing both table and fortified wines.
See Australia.

Muscadel

Another name for sweet, usually fortified wine from the Muscat grape *(q.v.)*. It should not be confused with Muscadet *(q.v.)*.

Muscadelle

A white-wine grape grown in the Bordeaux region, where it contributes to both sweet Sauternes and dry Graves.

In the last century, an excellent Muscadelle was grown in South Africa, where it produced the good Cape wine called Constantia.

Muscadet (Appellation Contrôlée)

White wines.
District: Brittany, France.

The Muscadet vineyards, the only ones in Brittany to be classified, lie far down the River Loire, south of the city of Nantes. Brought to the Muscadet region by monks in the seventeenth century, the grape is the Melon de Bourgogne rechristened, though it is no longer to be found in Burgundy itself. The light, fresh wine, with a trace of musk in the bouquet, is a perfect accompaniment to seafood, and within the last few years has achieved great popularity throughout France and abroad. Muscadets should be drunk when young, the harvests there being the earliest in France, beginning September 10–20 each year and some times earlier, at the end of August, as in 1982. If the grapes are allowed to overripen, the wines will lose their characteristic freshness and acidity which are some of the main claims of Muscadet.

Good Muscadets are bottled directly from the vats where they are fermented, and the district has the only subterranean system of underground vats carved into the cool rocky earth beneath the cellar floors. A certain amount of carbon dioxide gas is in these wines (Muscadets, if racked, will oxidize and flatten) which makes them slightly crackling or *pétillant*. The term *"sur lie"* means that the wines have been drawn off the lees for bottling to retain this natural sparkle. Many of the cheaper Muscadets, however, have the sparkle added artificially and may also contain a trace of unfermented sugar, which covers the natural acid taste of the wine.

Started after the war, the Muscadet district has only recently begun to produce fine wines. There are in this area about 6,000 sharecroppers, some working vineyards as small as two hectares (five acres). The growers, for the most part, have remained unorganized, while the shippers are strong, controlling fully one-third of Muscadet's production of 9,000 hectares (22,-500 acres).

The entire region produces some 450,000 hectoliters (11.8 million U.S. gallons, 9.8 million imp.) of wine each year, of which 80% comes from the Sèvres-et-Maine, the hilly rise between the banks of these two rivers, and 10% from the rocky shores of the Coteaux de la Loire. An additional 10% is called simply "Muscadet." The problem for the enthusiast who wants to find the best-made wine of the region is that Muscadet does not classify the production of its separate communes; the individual qualities of Saint-Fiacre, La Haie-Fouassière, and Le Pallet are not distinguished in the same way, for example, that Beaujolais differentiates between the place-name of Beaujolais and Beaujolais Villages, and among the production of the better villages of Fleurie, Brouilly, and Morgon.

In Muscadet the best wines come from Sèvres-et-Maine, and a further discrimination of the nose and palate notes that the southern part of this district is superior to the northern. Noteworthy names are Vallet (unofficial capital of Muscadet), Mouzillon, Le Pallet, Saint-Fiacre, La Haie-Fouassière, Vertou, Monnières, Haute-Goulaine, and Gorges.

The V.D.Q.S. (Vins Délimités de Qualité Supérieure, a category of wines of less distinction than the Appellation Contrôlée) is Gros Plant, which tastes slightly more acid than the Muscadet from Sèvres-et-Maine and is made from the Folle Blanche, a vine formerly grown in the region of Cognac, north of Bordeaux. Abandoned as a favorite producer of Cognac brandy, the Folle Blanche now exists only in the area surrounding Nantes. Gros Plant is a larger, more common wine than Muscadet, fine for local drinking, but not considered an export wine.

Muscadine

Vines native to southern sections of North America, the best known example of which is the Scuppernong—the others are the James and the Mish.

The grape is not popular with the wine-maker, partly because of its low sugar content and high acidity and partly because of its very pronounced and unattractive aroma when vinified.

See Chapter Eight, p. 31.

Muscadinia

There are three known species within the subgenus *Vitis muscadinae,* the most important and widely planted in the United States being the *Vitis rotundifolia.* Planted in about ten southeastern states, it has its heaviest concentrations in Mississippi, Alabama, Georgia, and the Carolinas, and it is not found growing commercially anywhere else in the world except this region. It is a vigorous, late-ripening species, resistant to disease and insects, and best suited to hot climates. A single vine may cover up to an acre, with roots sometimes up to two feet in diameter. The fruit is large and varies in color depending on the variety, and it grows in clusters like cherries instead of in bunches. The mature grapes are extremely fragrant in the vineyards, and are harvested similar to cherries and olives, by spreading tarps between the rows and shaking the vines. The wines produced are generally known as Muscadine or Scuppernong, the latter derived from an old Algonquin Indian name. Some varietal names are Carlos, Creek, Hunt, Magnolia, Noble, and Southern Fox. These varieties produce a range of intensely flavorful, extremely distinctive, dry or sweet wines, red, white, or rosé, that taste peculiar to most wine drinkers. Several cross-breeding experiments are under way in an effort to produce vines that will thrive in hot climates and produce better-tasting wines.

See Chapter Eight, p. 31.

Muscat

(1) A sweet grape, usually white, subdivided into many varieties. The wines tend to be heavy, strong in scent and flavor, and are often sweet dessert wines. Muscats are also eaten as table grapes. In California, the Muscat d'Alexandrie is extensively cultivated for wine, but this is not a grape of good quality.

(2) Muscat de Beaumes-de-Venise, Muscat de Frontignan, Muscat de Lunel, Muscat de Saint-Jean-de-Minervois. (All Appellations Contrôlées.)

See Sweet fortified wines of France.

Muscat d'Alsace

A dry, fruity Muscatel of Alsace.
See Alsace.

Muscat of Samos

See Samos; Greece.

Muscatel

Wine made from Muscat grapes. These may be red or white, dessert or sparkling wines. Two of the better-known are Muscat de Frontignan and Muscat de Samos.

In California a regrettable quantity of fortified wine known as "Muscatel" used to be sold as a substitute for spirits.

Muselage

In French, literally "muzzling"; the wiring which clamps the corks on to Champagne bottles.

Musigny (Appellation Contrôlée)

Burgundy red and white wines.
District: Côte de Nuits, France.
Commune: Chambolle-Musigny.
Official Classification: Great Growth (Grand Cru).

The remark "If our slope were not the richest in the world it would be the poorest" was prompted by a view of Musigny. The vineyard lies along a small dirt road, and across it is nothing but underbrush and rubble. On one side, the land is virtually worthless. On the other, it has been known to bring up to approximately $800,000 (£550,000) per acre.

The vineyard is in three parts: Les Musigny, Les Petits Musigny, and La Combe d'Orveau. The three stretch out along the slope, with Les Petits Musigny between the other two, and on a plateau below stands the château of the Clos de Vougeot surrounded by its vineyards. Pinot Noir is the dominant vine, but there is also some Pinot Blanc and Chardonnay, not all for making white wine.

In general, the vintners who own parts of Musigny make red wine. White is produced sporadically, and rarely if ever exceeds about 7 hectoliters (200 U.S. gallons, 165 imp.). The reds, however, are noted for their delicacy, their elegance and, above all, their finesse. Burgundians claim that a slight addition of Pinot Blanc or Chardonnay grapes to the must heightens these qualities considerably. The law allows 15% of the vines to be of white variety, but the growers usually feel that 10% is sufficient.

In a good year the wines, in addition to their matchless feminine delicacy, have an incomparable bouquet reminiscent of violets or raspberries. They become ready to drink after two years or so, but a fine estate-bottled Musigny can be expected to develop for years and to profit enormously from imprisonment in the bottle.

The vineyard covers 6.5 hectares (16 acres). The amount of wine made in an average year for quantity

1. EQUIVALENT DENSITY TABLE FOR WINES AND ABNORMAL AND NORMAL GRAPE-MUSTS OF LESS THAN 10% PROSPECTIVE ALCOHOL

with their sugar and probable alcohol content and the weight of sugar to be added to raise them to 10% (according to Salleron)

Mustimeter density or degree/Oechsle*	Areometer degree Baumé	Balling/Brix %	Grams of sugar per liter of must	Alcoholic content of the wine to be made	Weight of crystallized sugar to be added to 1 liter of must to get a wine of 10% alcoholic strength in volume (in grams)
1,000	0				
1,001	0.1				
1,002	0.3				
1,003	0.4				
1,004	0.6				
1,005	0.7				
1,006	0.9				
1,007	1.0				
1,008	1.1				
1,009	1.3				
1,010	1.4				
1,011	1.6				
1,012	1.7		2	0.1	168
1,013	1.8		5	0.2	166
1,014	2.0		7	0.4	163
1,015	2.1		11	0.6	159
1,016	2.3		13	0.7	157
1,017	2.4		15	0.9	154
1,018	2.6		18	1.1	151
1,019	2.7		21	1.2	149
1,020	2.8		23	1.4	148
1,021	2.9		26	1.5	146
1,022	3.1		29	1.7	142
1,023	3.2		31	1.8	139
1,024	3.4		34	1.9	137
1,025	3.5		37	2.1	134
1,026	3.7		39	2.3	130
1,027	3.8		42	2.4	127
1,028	3.9		45	2.6	124
1,029	4.1		47	2.8	122
1,030	4.2		50	3.0	120
1,031	4.3		53	3.1	119
1,032	4.5		55	3.2	115
1,033	4.6		58	3.4	112
1,034	4.7		61	3.5	110
1,035	4.9		63	3.7	107
1,036	5.0		66	3.9	104
1,037	5.2		69	4.0	102
1,038	5.3		72	4.2	99
1,039	5.4		74	4.4	95
1,040	5.5		76	4.5	93
1,041	5.7	10,23	80	4.7	90
1,042	5.8	10,47	82	4.8	88
1,043	6.0	10,71	84	5.0	85
1,044	6.1	10,95	87	5.1	83
1,045	6.2	11,19	90	5.3	80
1,046	6.3	11,42	92	5.4	78
1,047	6.5	11,67	95	5.6	75
1,048	6.6	11,91	98	5.7	73
1,049	6.7	12,14	100	5.9	70
1,050	6.9	12,38	103	6.0	68
1,051	7.0	12,62	106	6.2	65
1,052	7.1	12,73	108	6.3	63

*For Oechsle scale read last two figures in this column.

Mustimeter density or degree/Oechsle*	Areometer degree Baumé	Balling/Brix %	Grams of sugar per liter of must	Alcoholic content of the wine to be made	Weight of crystallized sugar to be added to 1 liter of must to get a wine of 10% alcoholic strength in volume (in grams)
1,053	7.3	13,08	111	6.5	59
1,054	7.4	13,32	114	6.7	56
1,055	7.5	13,56	116	6.8	54
1,056	7.7	13,79	119	7.0	51
1,057	7.8	14,03	122	7.2	48
1,058	7.9	14,26	124	7.3	46
1,059	8.0	14,49	127	7.5	42
1,060	8.2	14,73	130	7.6	41
1,061	8.3	14,96	132	7.8	37
1,062	8.4	15,19	135	7.9	36
1,063	8.6	15,42	138	8.1	32
1,064	8.7	15,66	140	8.2	31
1,065	8.8	15,89	143	8.4	27
1,066	8.9	16,01	146	8.6	24
1,067	9.0	16,12	148	8.7	22
1,068	9.2	16,58	151	8.9	19
1,069	9.3	16,81	154	9.0	17
1,070	9.4	17,06	156	9.2	13
1,071	9.6	17,27	159	9.3	12
1,072	9.7	17,50	162	9.5	8
1,073	9.8	17,73	164	9.6	7
1,074	9.9	17,84	167	9.8	3
1,075	10.0	17,95	170	10.0	

*For Oechsle scale read last two figures in this column.

2. EQUIVALENT DENSITY TABLE FOR GRAPE MUSTS OF MORE THAN 10%

with their sugar and probable alcoholic content and the volume of water to be added to reduce them to 10% (according to Salleron)

Mustimeter density or degree/Oechsle*	Areometer degree Baumé	Balling/Brix %	Grams of sugar per liter of must	Alcoholic content of the wine to be made	Volume of water which must be added to 1 liter of must to bring it to a density in liters of 1,075
1,076	10.2	18,41	172	. 10.1	0.01
1,077	10.3	18,63	175	10.3	0.02
1,078	10.4	18,86	178	10.5	0.04
1,079	10.6	19,08	180	10.6	0.05
1,080	10.7	19,31	183	10.8	0.06
1,081	10.8	19,54	186	10.9	0.08
1,082	10.9	19,76	188	11.0	0.09
1,083	11.1	19,99	191	11.2	0.10
1,084	11.2	20,21	194	11.4	0.12
1,085	11.3	20,43	196	11.5	0.13
1,086	11.4	20,66	199	11.7	0.14
1,087	11.6	20,88	202	11.9	0.16
1,088	11.7	21,10	204	12.0	0.17
1,089	11.8	21,33	207	12.2	0.18
1,090	11.9	21,55	210	12.3	0.20
1,091	12.0	21,77	212	12.5	0.21
1,092	12.2	21,99	215	12.6	0.22
1,093	12.3	22,21	218	12.8	0.24
1,094	12.4	22,43	220	12.9	0.25
1,095	12.5	22,65	223	13.1	0.26
1,096	12.6	22,87	226	13.3	0.28
1,097	12.7	23,09	228	13.4	0.29
1,098	12.9	23,31	231	13.6	0.30
1,099	13.0	23,53	234	13.8	0.31
1,100	13.1	23,75	236	13.9	0.33
1,101	13.2	23,97	239	14.0	0.34
1,102	13.3	24,18	242	14.2	0.36
1,103	13.5	24,40	244	14.4	0.37
1,104	13.6	24,62	247	14.5	0.38
1,105	13.7	24,84	250	14.7	0.40

*For Oechsle scale read last two figures in this column.

Must

is 300 hectoliters (7,950 U.S. gallons, 6,600 imp.) or the equivalent of less than 3,600 cases.

Must

Grape before it ferments completely and becomes wine. The French word is *moût*.

Mustimeter or saccharometer

The mustimeter, or saccharometer, is defined in the *Dictionnaire du vin* as a densimeter brought into popular use by Salleron and bearing the Gay-Lussac centesimal scale; it shows the weight in grams of a liter of the liquid into which it is immersed. This instrument of paramount importance in wine-making is used in almost every vineyard in France.

The division in the center of the scale and marked 1000 represents the weight of distilled water (1,000 grams per liter); the divisions above measure lower densities and those below measure higher densities— i.e, the weight in grams of a liter of the must or liquid being tested.

To determine the density of a must, a few bunches of grapes are crushed into a container, the juice being filtered through a cloth into a test tube. The mustimeter and a thermometer are immersed one after the other in this juice and the readings re taken—e.g., 1065 on the mustimeter scale and 18°C. on the thermometer. Reference is made to the Correction Table below to see what adjustment is necessary to the mustimeter reading to arrive at what it would be if the must temperature were 15°C.

For example:

The must is tested at a temperature of 18°C.; the mustimeter shows 1065; the Correction Table shows that 0.5 must be added to the mustimeter reading, so that the weight of the must at the normal temperature of +15°C. is 1065.5. If the temperature were 12°C. instead of 18°C., the correction—0.4—would have to be deducted from 1065, the reading then being 1064.6.

Taking the corrected density of 1065.5 we refer to

CORRECTION TABLE

Temperature °C.	Correction	Temperature °C.	Correction
10°	−0.6	21°	+1.1
11°	−0.5	22°	+1.3
12°	−0.4	23°	+1.6
13°	−0.3	24°	+1.8
14°	−0.2	25°	+2.0
15°	0	26°	+2.3
16°	+0.1	27°	+2.6
17°	+0.3	28°	+2.8
18°	+0.5	29°	+3.1
19°	+0.7	30°	+3.4
20°	+0.9		

Table I (page 358) to see what is the weight of sugar contained in a liter of the must and what will be the alcohol content which the wine will have after fermentation.

In California a similar instrument is used. Called a Brix or Balling hydrometer (*q.v.*), it is calibrated in terms of grams of sugar per 100 grams of solution.

The first column of the table (pages 358–59) shows the density of the must—i.e., the mustimeter reading. The second column shows the corresponding values for the Baumé areometer (or gluco-oenometer) and of the Gay-Lussac densimeter or saccharometer. The third column gives the weight of grape sugar contained in a liter of the must. The fourth corresponds to the probable alcohol richness which the wine will have after fermentation, presuming all the sugar is fermented—which does not always occur, particularly beyond 14% to 15%. The fifth column indicates the weight of pure crystallized sugar which must be added to a liter of must for the wine to contain 10% of alcohol after fermenting. By pure crystallized sugar is meant white sugar standardized at 100°. When using less pure sugars, white or brown, the table figures would be too low; they would have to be raised proportionately to the degree of impurity of the sugar used. In Table 2 there will be found, conversely, the amount of water which each liter of must exceeding 10% will have to have added to bring it down to the normal density of 1075.

If we refer to the example given earlier we find:

(1) That a must of 1065 density corresponds to 8.8° Baumé.

(2) That it contains 143 grams of grape sugar per liter.

(3) That, after fermentation, this sugar will give 8.4% of alcohol, which means that the wine will contain 8.4 liters of alcohol per hectoliter.

(4) That 27 grams of crystallized sugar per liter must be added in order to bring the alcohol content up to 10%.

Mutage

French term for artificial interruption of fermentation. Often this is achieved by the addition of sulfur dioxide, leaving unfermented sugar in the wine; it used to be done in the Entre-Deux-Mers and other districts of Bordeaux, and elsewhere as well, producing a white wine with a very sweet finish.

Muté

Partially fermented or completely unfermented wine whose fermentation has been stopped, usually by the addition of a high-proof brandy. *Vins mutés* are often used in the production of aperitifs and in the blending of wines that need both sweetness and body.

Mycodermi aceti

Bacterium which forms vinegar, or vinegary wines. Today usually called *Acetobacter*.

Mycodermi vini

The yeast commonly believed to be responsible for the formation of a film on certain wines.
See Flor; Sherry.

Château de Myrat

Bordeaux white wine.
District: Sauternes, France.
Commune: Barsac.

The property, belonging to the de Pontac family, was included in the Second Growths of the 1855 Classification. In the early 1970s, this vineyard was ripped up as a losing proposition. The Château no longer makes wine.

N

Nackenheimer Rothenberg

Best of the Nackenheimers in the German Rhein-hessen (q.v.).

Nahe

German State of Rheinland-Pfalz
Vineyard area: approx. 4,600 hectares (11,400 acres)
98% white wines; 2% red wines
Location: The Nahe (7th largest of Germany's 11 wine-growing regions) lies between the valleys of the Mosel and the Rhine. It, too, takes its name from a river, the Nahe, which flows into the Rhine at Bingen, just opposite Rüdesheim—a point where the four regions Mittelrhein, Nahe, Rheingau and Rheinhessen come together.

Farther upstream the wines are extremely light, usually Riesling, and rather suggestive of the Saar wines (although they never attain the same finesse). This is not surprising, as a glance at the map will show. Saar and Nahe are close to each other in this section, and in earlier times it used to be customary to lump the Saar wines with those of the Upper Nahe.

The Nahe empties into the Rhine at Bingen opposite Rüdesheim. For the same reason that the wines of the Upper Nahe are Saar-like, these wines downriver from Bad Kreuznach are like Rheingaus. They come into the same climatic belt. These divisions are not to be taken as hard and fast, however; in anything as capricious and various as wine that would be impossible. In a recent tasting in the Nahe, some of the Roxheimers and Gutenbergers were lighter than Mosels.

The Nahe district includes two smaller river valleys. These are the Alsenz and the Glan, neither producing especially interesting wines.

Modernization of wine-growing methods all along the Nahe is the consequence of vine disease which destroyed whole areas. The government came to the aid of the ruined growers—otherwise viticulture on the Nahe might have ceased. Today, methods are much improved, but this has turned out to be a mixed blessing. The cost of wine-making has risen in proportion to the gain, one result of which is that only the State Domain and a relatively small number of fairly large owners can afford the risks implicit in making wine of quality. May frosts, common enough in the Nahe, may wipe out the entire crop of the year. The problem has been solved in part by the wine cooperatives, now making about one-fifth of the total annual production.

Bad Kreuznach is the region's most important town. In addition to its popularity as a health resort and spa, it is the center of the wine trade and where most of the major producers are based. The region is divided into two districts (Bereiche). Bereich Schloss Böckelheim includes the vineyards of the upper and middle Nahe Valley, located to the south and southwest of Bad Kreuznach. Bereich Kreuznach takes in the lower Nahe Valley, north of the town.

Grape Varieties: Müller-Thurgau (27%); Riesling (22%); Silvaner (14%); Kerner (8%); Scheurebe (7%); Bacchus (6%). Small plantings of the red varieties Spätburgunder (Pinot Noir) and Portugieser.

Wine: rich in nuances; piquant, racy, elegant Riesling; full-bodied Silvaner; fragrant and fruity Müller-Thurgau, Kerner, Scheurebe, Bacchus and others.

THE TASTING ROOM OF GERMANY

The Romans are credited with having brought vines to the Nahe Valley more than 2,000 years ago, as evidenced by ancient Roman viticultural tools and wine jugs which have been unearthed in and around Bad Kreuznach (on display in the local museum). Yet it is geology, far more than history, which has influenced the character of Nahe wine. The extraordinary range of soil types and mixtures found throughout this relatively small wine-growing region helps explain the great diversity of wines produced here—and hence, its nickname "the tasting room of Germany."

Strata of red sandstone—the same "Rotliegendes" to which the finest Niersteiners owe their elegance—run through the region like a broad ribbon. On the lower Nahe (closest to the Rhine) there is a good deal of quartzite and slate which yield racy wines with a fine fruitiness. In terms of style, they are often compared to Rheingau wines. Further upstream one finds weathered clay, loam, loess and marl. These soils yield broader, milder and often flowery wines. In the middle and upper parts of the valley (which many consider to be the choicest sites), the soils consists of green-gray slate and igneous rock, such as melaphyre and porphyry. The latter also provides some of the most spectacular landscape of the Nahe, culminating in the 200-meter (600-foot) porphyry precipice of the Rotenfels—which is also the steepest rock face north of the Alps. These wines, particularly the Rieslings, are among the finest of Germany. Because of their great distinction, complexity and elegance—typical of wines grown on slaty soils—they are often compared to Saar wines.

In spite of its northerly location, the climate of the Nahe is mild, thanks to the shelter of the Hunsrück mountain range which acts as a barrier against cold winds and rain. The summits are capped by the Soon forest which retains heat during the day and releases it at night, thereby maintaining an even temperature in the vineyards—important for assimilation and a steady, even ripening of the grapes.

About 55% of the Nahe's 2,300 growers also produce wine. The average size of a producer's vineyard holdings is just over 3 hectares (8 acres). Half of the region's production is sold directly by the growers; the other half is marketed through the trade and cooperatives. Annual yield, based on a ten-year average (1976–1985): 360,000 hectoliters.

IMPORTANT VILLAGES AND SITES

In Bereich Schloss Böckelheim, the village of the same name and neighboring Niederhausen are synonymous with top quality, largely due to the outstanding wines produced by the prestigious State Wine Domain (Verwaltung der Staatlichen Weinbaudomänen). The stylized black eagle on the label is reminiscent of its Prussian origins. Two sites are particularly fine: Kupfergrube (created in the early 1900's under a state employment program) and Hermannshöhle. Felsenberg and Hermannsberg are also excellent. Other villages of note: Altenbamberg (Rotenfels); Norheim (Dellchen); Roxheim (Berg, Höllenpfad); Traisen (Bastei). Meddersheim and Monzingen. Rüdesheim/Nahe not to be confused with Rüdesheim/Rheingau.

In Bereich Kreuznach, the village of the same name has excellent sites which yield very stylish, first-class wine. Finest sites include: Krötenpfuhl, Brückes, Narrenkappe, Kahlenberg and Hinkelstein. Other villages of note: Burg Layen (Schlossberg); Dorsheim (Burgberg, Goldloch); Langenlonsheim; Münster-Sarmsheim (Dautenpflänzer, Pittersberg); Wallhausen (Johannisberg, Felseneck).

PRODUCERS

The ability and dedication of men will change from one generation to another, but the following are the names of a few traditional producers. The list is by no means complete.

Weingut Paul Anheuser, Bad Kreuznach
Weingut Ökonomierat August E. Anheuser, Bad Kreuznach
Weingut Hans Crusius, Traisen
Schlossgut Diel, Burg Layen
Weingut Carl Finkenauer, Bad Kreuznach
Weingut Dr. Josef Höfer, Burg Layen
Reichsgräflich von Plettenberg'sche Verwaltung, B. Kreuznach
Prinz zu Salm-Dalberg'sches Weingut, Schloss Wallhausen
Weingut Jacob Schneider, Niederhausen
Weingut Erbhof Tesch, Langenlonsheim
Vereinigte Weingüter Schlink-Herf-Gutleuthof, B. Kreuznach

Winzergenossenschaft Rheingrafenburg, Meddersheim
Zentralkellerei der Nahe Winzer, Bretzenheim

For a complete list of districts (Bereiche), collective vineyard sites (Grosslagen = GL) and individual vineyard sites (Einzellagen), see Appendix B, p. 686.

Château Nairac

Bordeaux white wine.
District: Sauternes, France.
Commune: Barsac.

After many years of neglect, this small property near the entrance to Barsac has been revived by its new owners, Thomas Heeter, an American, and his former wife, Nicole Tari, the daughter of the owner of Château Giscours. The vineyards have been replanted and the beautiful eighteenth-century house has been restored. The wine is classified a Second Growth but it is typical of Sauternes.
Vineyard area: 14 hectares (35 acres).
Average production: 25 *tonneaux* (2,000 cases).

Napa Valley

California wine region producing some of the finest red and white table wines.
See United States: California.

Nasco di Cagliari (D.O.C.)

A dessert wine from Sardinia *(q.v.)*.

Natural wine

Wine to which nothing has been added which can influence the taste or strength.

Nature

In France *vin nature* is natural unsweetened wine. A special meaning applies in Champagne, where it denotes still wine.

Néac (Appellation Contrôlée)

Bordeaux red wine.
District: Southwest France.

Previously a very small district adjoining Pomerol, Néac ceased to exist in 1954 when it was joined to that of Lalande de Pomerol. The move was a wise one, for it did away with a place-name that served no purpose, since the two wines are similar in every respect.
See Lalande de Pomerol.

Nebbiolo

À grape used in Italian red wines; e.g., in Lombardy for Sassella, Inferno, etc.

Nebuchadnezzar

Nebuchadnezzar

An oversized Champagne bottle no longer used, containing the equivalent of twenty ordinary bottles.

Nectar

The drink of the ancient Greek gods. The name was later used for wines of special quality, and even today bottles of nectar may be found in Greece.

Negus

An old-fashioned hot drink made with Port, sugar, lemon, and spice.

Nerveux

French definition of an assertive, rigorous wine not complicated by any subtle overtones.

Netherlands spirits

In the Netherlands, the making of spirits is generally referred to as the "old national industry" and dates back to about 1500. Originally alcohol was distilled from wine, but in the second half of the sixteenth century the processing from cereals was started. It was not until the government imposed a high import duty on German brandy in 1670 and prohibited the importation of French brandy that the Netherlands distilling industry could reach its full development. In the eighteenth century, distilleries flourished, the greatest advances being made on the River Meuse, particularly at Rotterdam, Delfshaven, and Schiedam. At least forty of the 140 distilleries in the Netherlands today are established in Schiedam.

Jenever

This is the original distillation of the Netherlands. It is often supposed to be identical with gin, but in fact there are considerable differences in the taste as well as the ingredients of the two products.

The original Jenever type is made by distilling malt-wine, or a mixture of malt-wine and spirit, over juniper berries, and possibly over other aromatic vegetable ingredients, with or without the addition of sugar. Jenever is traditionally drunk neat, slightly cooled, and sipped rather than swallowed, though young Dutchmen often take it in long drinks.

Brandewijn

One of the oldest forms of brandy, it is popular in some districts of the country. The essential factors in its preparation are ripening on charcoal and the addition of certain flavors. The brandewijn is also used as the raw base for advocaat, and for putting various fruits in—cherries, plums, and the characteristic brandewijn raisins and apricots.

Bessenjenever or Blackcurrant Gin

This is another typically Dutch product, processed on a neutral alcohol base and flavored with an extract of blackcurrants.

Advocaat

This drink, so thick that it has to be taken with a spoon, is made of brandewijn, eggs, sugar, and vanilla, and it has an alcoholic content of 15% to 18%. A somewhat thinner type of advocaat is exported to England.

Raisins in Brandewijn

Sugar candy and cinnamon are added to the raisins and the spirit. The alcohol content is approximately 15%.

Liqueurs

The favorite Dutch distillations are anisette, apricot brandy, cherry brandy, Curaçao, crème de cacao, kümmel, maraschino, and persico (this last is distilled from peach stones).

Whisky

Holland manufactures a certain amount of whisky. The barley, maize, and rye are dried on peat fires, for the sake of the smoky flavor.

Elixirs (Bitters)

These are made by the infusion of herbs, seeds, and peels in alcohol, sometimes to be distilled, sometimes not. There is usually a good deal of coloring matter and very little sweetening. Elixirs are not as much in favor as they were forty or fifty years ago; the best liked are red and green Pommeranz, which have a higher alcoholic content than most—particularly important for red Pommeranz when it is used in cafés for Schilletje or Voorburg of their own making. Other elixirs or bitters are Longae Vitae, Catz bitters, Angostura, Boonekamp, and so on.

See Advocaat; Gin.

Neuberger

Grape cultivated for Austrian wines.

Neuchâtel

Swiss canton which produces, dry, light, sprightly wines, mostly white.
See Switzerland.

Neutral brandy

Brandy distilled at a very high proof. Completely neutral brandy would be distilled 200° proof, or 100% alcohol, and would lack any distinctive characteristics save those of pure alcohol. In practice, anything over 170° proof is considered neutral. The same applies to neutral spirit used as a blending agent in whiskies.

New Jersey

Wine-producing region in the United States, with Egg Harbor as its center, where the Renault Wine Company owns 72 hectares (180 acres) of native grape varieties.

New Zealand

New Zealand owes the birth and growth of its wine industry to some remarkable men—Samuel Marsden, Anglican missionary and chief chaplain to the New South Wales government, who pioneered European agricultural methods; James Busby, first British resident in New Zealand; and Bishop Pompallier, Catholic missionary from France. These were the men who introduced the early wine cuttings. Later, Romeo Bragata, first New Zealand government viticulturist, a graduate of Italy's school of oenology at Comegliano, was to put the infant industry on a proper footing and demonstrate to the settlers how good wine should be made.

The earliest written record of vine planting is contained in Samuel Marsden's journal on September 25, 1819: "I planted [at Kerikeri] about 100 grape vines of different kinds brought from Port Jackson [Sydney]. New Zealand promises to be very favourable to the vine as far as I can judge at present of the nature of the soil and climate."

The earliest written record of wine made in New Zealand is contained in the journal of the famous French explorer Dumont d'Urville of the Astrolabe, who revisited the Bay of Islands in 1840. He was offered at Busby's home at Waitangi "a light white wine very sparkling and delicious to taste. Judging from this sample I have no doubt that vines will be grown extensively all over the sandy hills of these islands."

Bishop Pompallier brought vines from France in 1838 as did French settlers at Akaroa in 1840 and Germans at Nelson in 1843.

By 1894, vines were planted in many places on the North and South Island. All the vines introduced were of the *Vitis vinifera* variety. But two cruel diseases, phyl-loxera and the rise of prohibition, inhibited the new industry. Phylloxera was to have a great effect, for many farmers went out of production altogether while others, after uprooting their *vinifera* vines, cultivated the American type of hybrid grapes which, though phylloxera-resistant, did not produce wine as good as the original *vinifera* strains. Unfortunately, too, these strains derived from *Vitis labrusca* proved prolific bearers in the humid conditions of the North and were marketable as either table or wine grapes.

By 1906 there were 220 hectares (550 acres) under vines; by 1909, when Bragata resigned from the Department of Agriculture, there were 268 hectares (668 acres). The acreage dwindled to 179 in 1923. Government apathy, the rise of prohibition, the hard work necessary to combat the diseases of phylloxera, oïdium, and bunch rot caused many settlers to give up vine cultivation and return the land to other uses. Growers narrowed to three main classes: Yugoslav immigrants and some others in the Auckland province; the occupiers of the land originally planted by the gentlemen farmers of Hawke's Bay; and the religious descendants of Bishop Pompallier, the Marist Fathers, who finally established their permanent vineyard at Greenmeadows in Hawke's Bay.

During the First World War the industry languished. Labor was not available, the prohibitionist element was strong, and more dry districts (as no-liquor-license areas were known) were established, thus depriving wine-makers of their outlets.

A new government in 1935 proved of considerable benefit. It cut the imports of wines 50% by import licensing and increased the duty on imported wines by 50%. But the greatest fillip of all was the outbreak of war in 1939. Overseas supplies were greatly reduced and New Zealand had to rely more on its own resources.

While a Cabernet Sauvignon from Hawke's Bay has been the most consistent performer at international competitions, there is a growing number of wines being accepted overseas. In 1980, at the International Wine & Spirit Festival in London, the New Zealand list of medal winners included a Chardonnay, a Rhine Riesling, and a Gewürztraminer. Growers have been encouraged by their successes and are busy planting vines as they are released from quarantine by the department of agriculture. Good Cabernet Sauvignon wine was made in New Zealand nearly 70 years ago. Other red wine grapes which have done well in the past are Pinot Noir, Pinot Meunier, Hermitage, and Pinotage.

Grape acreage approximately doubled during the war, and increased gradually in the years following. By 1973 there were some 2,000 hectares (5,000 acres), producing at least 300,000 hectoliters (7.95 million U.S. gallons, 6.6 million imp.) a year. One company has planted nearly 500 hectares (1,250 acres) of *vinifera* vines in Blenheim, in association with an American concern. This and other new vineyards have brought

New Zealand's total of land in vines to more than 4,500 hectares (11,250 acres) in 1986.

In the early days, Northland was the main center. By the end of the century, Hawke's Bay had become the most important. Later, Henderson/Auckland came into its own, and now Gisborne and Waikato have become prominent wine-growing areas. But in 1973 Blenheim in the South Island created interest by the planting of 1,200 acres and in time, because of favorable climatic conditions, this area may have as great an acreage as the rest of New Zealand put together.

For many years, almost from the turn of the century till the present, the New Zealand wine industry has suffered from a form of schizophrenia. Public demand has been for fortified wines—ports, sherries, madeira, and the like.

Experts from the beginning have testified that New Zealand's temperate climate cannot produce a natural dessert wine. "The climate is not sufficiently warm to produce grapes of a sufficiently high sugar content," said the Royal Commission on Licencing in 1946. It noted that cane sugar is added to make up the deficiency and that some sweet wines contain as much as 30% by weight of added sugar.

And this has been the wine-grower's dilemma. His climate is suited to the production of light table wines; and the demand has been for fortified wines. Under the circumstances he has coped very well, but now with a more educated interest, he is able to turn to producing table wines for which the climate and soil are most suitable. Hawke's Bay is very similar in climate to parts of Burgundy and Bordeaux. Blenheim tops the sunshine record in New Zealand and has a very low rainfall, particularly at vintage time, though it is susceptible to ground frosts at times. Contrary to some people's belief, the vine-growing areas of New Zealand do not have a cool climate similar to Germany and Switzerland. Heat summation and yearly sunshine figures are much higher.

In the white wines, Pinot Chardonnay is creating interest, as is Traminer. As yet these are available in very limited quantities, but the growers have plenty of Riesling-Sylvaner (Müller-Thurgau), which is producing some of New Zealand's most popular white wines and is readily available under the name of "Riesling." The true Riesling grape used to be planted in the pre-phylloxera days and should do as well here as it does in Australia.

In some areas New Zealand has the soil and climate to produce superb table wines in quantity. More European varieties of grapes must be grown instead of the American hybrid types which are prolific bearers but not suited for producing quality wine in the temperate climate. The last grape acreage census, taken in 1980, showed New Zealand to be the world's biggest producer of Müller-Thurgau grapes. It is believed that the planting of *vinifera* table wine varieties, both white and red, has increased since then.

During 1985–86 there were 130 grape wine license holders, of whom 120 were in production. In total, 60 million liters of wine was produced during the 1985 season.

Present wine consumption, of both local and overseas wines, has been estimated by the Viticultural Association as being 16.5 liters (3.4 U.S. gallons, 3.2 imp.) per person, whereas beer consumption is thought to be 132 liters (29 U.S. gallons, 24 imp.) per person. While up-to-date statistics are not available from government sources, it seems generally agreed in the industry that white table wine accounts for approximately 47% of the total market, rosé and red table wines 6%, bulk wine 6%, sparkling 12%, and fortified wines about 29%.

Niagara

(1) Wine-growing region in Canada and New York State. The most important vineyards are Chateau Gai, Inniskillin, and Chateau Des Charmes. The native American *(labrusca)* Niagara grape is used for table grapes and for production of a wide range of fruity, intensely foxy white wines, among the best balanced and most popular *labruscas*. The recent trend, admirably, has been to lighter, less sweet Niagaras, as well as sparkling wines. Acreage in the U.S. has increased dramatically, partially because of its popularity as a juice grape.

(2) One of the older American hybrid grapes, yielding white wine of pronounced "foxiness."

See United States: New York.

Niederhäuser Hermannshöhle

One of the best-known wines of the Nahe Valley in Germany.

See Nahe.

Niersteiner

Best Rheinhessen wines, with a good nose and elegance. All the finest are Rieslings.

See Rheinhessen.

Nip

British term for a quarter-bottle; reputed to be half a pint.

Noah

A native American *(labrusca)* hybrid first recorded in Illinois, this hardy green grape produces a white wine that is sometimes used to blend in sparkling wines. Helpful after the phylloxera disaster, new plantings of the Noah are now prohibited in France, but it is still found in other European countries.

Noble

A word usually applied to any grape variety, vineyard, or wine that shows inherent, lasting superiority when compared to other examples of its type. A noble grape will give outstanding wine in the proper setting and much better than average wine in a poor one. A noble vineyard shows at least a part of its greatness even in the worst of vintages. And a noble wine will impress even the rank beginner as remarkable.

Noble rot

A grape fungus which in sweet white-wine grapes becomes a virtue.
See Botrytis cinerea.

Noblejas

Wines of Toledo, usually sturdy reds somewhat comparable with those of the lesser Côtes du Rhône in France.
See Spain.

Noggin

A gill or a quarter of a British pint.

Norheim

Wine village of the Nahe Valley, Germany.
See Nahe.

Norton

Perhaps the best of the native American vines for red wine. It yields wines that are full, well balanced, agreeable, and not "foxy."

Norway

In the old days, lasting through the Middle Ages almost into the seventeenth century, the popular alcoholic beverages in Norway were beer and mead. Although they were, at an early stage, in contact with wine-drinking people, the Norwegians did not take much to wine until centuries later. The revolution in drinking habits came with the introduction of spirits. This was a comparatively late innovation, for not until the seventeenth century could spirits be bought on a commercial scale. Then they came very much into use. Except in the years between 1756 and 1816, every householder was allowed to make his own liquor—aquavit being the favorite. In 1830 about 11,000 stills were active.

In 1845 the change came. By then the potato had emerged as the foremost raw material for the production of spirituous drinks; and potatoes are awkward for amateur distillers to handle. In this year (1845) a law was passed to prohibit the use of stills with capacities of less than 200 liters (52.8 U.S. gallons, 44 imp.).

These two factors combined to diminish the attractions of spirit-making as a home industry.

Gradually most of the trade came into the hands of the two large firms of distillers: Jørgen B. Lysholm, Trondheim; and Løiten Braenderis Destillation, Kristiania. In 1927, however, the wine monopoly A/S Vinmonopolet took over the distilleries and still controls the sale of all potable spirits in Norway. The board of this institution and its managing directors are appointed by the king. The object of the monopoly is to control sales and thus control alcoholism. A/S Vinmonopolet is responsible for the rectification of locally produced alcohol, for the importation of wines and spirits and for their wholesale as well as retail sale. Even alcohol destined for medicinal and industrial use is controlled. The wholesale importation of beer is similarly controlled, although this is allowed to be sold in certain licensed shops. The total amount of wine sold in 1976 was more than 100,000 hectoliters (2.65 million U.S. gallons, 2.2 million imp.). There is no duty on wines and spirits, but fiscal taxes are fairly high.

In 1976 sales of spirits were more than 150,000 hectoliters (3,975,000 U.S. gallons, 3,300,000 imp.), made up as follows:
Foreign bottled spirits
A/S Vinmonopolet bottling of imported spirits
Imported spirits mixed with Norwegian alcohol
Norwegian-produced alcohol

According to the official statistics, every adult over fifteen years of age in the country consumed 6 liters (1.60 U.S. gallons, 1.32 imp.) of pure alcohol in 1982.

The Løiten and Lysholm varieties of Norwegian aquavit are exported on a large scale to most markets in the world.

Norway also produces "Linie Aquavit," which is a unique "crossed" specialty. "Linie Aquavit" is aquavit that has crossed the Line—i.e., the Equator. To uphold an ancient tradition, aquavit that has already been aged in oak is sent to Australia and then back to Norway on the Wilhelmsen cargo liners, thus crossing the line twice. During this journey the aquavit undergoes an extra maturation process influenced by the movement of the ship. The salt sea air and the changes in temperature also assist this maturation. The A/S Vinmonopolet guarantees on the label that the trip was made, when, and aboard which ship. "Linie Aquavit" is good with hors d'oeuvres and spicy foods.

Nose

The neutral term for the bouquet of a wine.

Noyau

Colorless or slightly pink sweetened liqueur with the flavor of oil of almonds, or of peach or cherry kernels.

Nu

In France, the price of wine given *nu* is the price without the cost of cask or bottle.

Nuits, Côte de

See Côte de Nuits.

Nuits-Saint-Georges (Appellation Contrôlée)

Burgundy red, and some white, wines.
District: Côte de Nuits, France.

The ancient town of Nuits, which in 1892 incorporated the name of its most cherished vineyard to become Nuits-Saint-Georges, lies close to the southern end of the slope to which it gives its name. Unlike most others of the Côte de Nuits, the official place-name covers vineyards in Nuits and in nearby Prémeaux, a little to the south, these two making up the last of the important communes before the soil changes to emerge as the Côte de Beaune. Actually, the Côte de Nuits extends slightly farther to the south, through the towns of Comblanchien and Corgoloin, but neither of these two is outstanding and their wines benefit only from the name Vins Fins de la Côte de Nuits (*q.v.*).

No vineyard in Nuits was included among the thirty-one Great Growths (*Grand Crus*)—the top-rated vineyards of the Côte d'Or, as classified by the I.N.A.O. (Institut National des Appellations d'Origine); nevertheless some very great vineyards are to be found there. Entering the town from the north, one sees the first of them on the right of the old vineyard road and on the lower slope descending from Vosne-Romanée. This slope drops gently to the River Meuzin—only a dried-up trickle most of the year—and another begins on the other side, rising steeply in a great rock-strewn bluff topped with trees and underbrush. Only the lower third of this slope is planted in vines, but along it are the best of the vineyards of Nuits: Les Pruliers, Les Porrets, Les Cailles, Les Saint-Georges, and slightly above Saint-Georges, Les Vaucrains. Les Saint-Georges lies along the town line and to its south are Didiers, Clos des Fôrets, and the Clos de la Maréchale, the best growths of Prémeaux.

Nuits, largest town on the slope named after it, is nevertheless not very big. The population is slightly less than 5,000 and virtually every man, woman, and child is engaged in the wine business in one way or another, although Nuits is also famous for its Marc de Bourgogne (*see* Marc), its cassis, a sweet blackcurrant liqueur (*q.v.*), its grape juice, and its sparkling Burgundy. Despite all these extras, the true fame of Nuits will always rest where it belongs, on its natural wines. The I.N.A.O. may not have considered any of the vineyards of the commune to be worthy of the highest rank among Burgundian vineyards, but the earlier 1860 Classification recognized no fewer than nine as Outstanding Vineyards (*Têtes de Cuvées*), the top rung of the ladder. Les Saint-Georges, Aux Boudots, Les Cailles, Aux Cras, Aux Murgers, Les Porrets, Les Pruliers, Aux Thorey, and Les Vaucrains were the nine; all of them are now offcially First Growths (*Premiers Crus*) of the commune, and all produce superb wines.

(Throughout Burgundy, First Growths are labeled with both name of vineyard and town name—e.g., Nuits-Saint-Georges Les Porrets, while the Great Growths carry *only* vineyard name—e.g., Chambertin.)

The outstanding distinction of the wines of Nuits is their firmness. Fuller in body than most Burgundies, they are apt to take years to mature. The firmest is generally Vaucrains, one of the finest of the commune and indeed of the whole Côte de Nuits; it is a wine to be laid down rather than drunk young. Bouquet is also a Nuits characteristic, and the wines are sometimes quite pungent. Les Saint-Georges will, because of its finesse, in most years take the honors in this field and in addition will be deeper in color and more "winey" than the others. Les Pruliers often starts out with a slightly metallic taste, but this passes and the wine ages wonderfully. Les Porrets, and the Clos des Porrets in particular, are the fruitiest. Clos des Porrets is a small section of the larger vineyard, and is the best part. It is owned entirely by Henri Gouges, one of the staunchest advocates of authentic Burgundian wines, and one of Burgundy's most respected growers. Gouges also makes good white wine but only in small quantities, and most of it is sold in Paris. Boudots is another good vineyard, and Cailles combines the Nuits characteristics with a special velvety quality all its own.

The vineyards Nuits-Saint-Georges total about 215 hectares (536 acres). In an average quantity year, they produce some 10,000 hectoliters (265,000 U.S. gallons, 220,000 imp.) of red wine and a very small amount of white.

In Nuits-Saint-Georges

FIRST GROWTHS (*Premiers Crus*)

Vineyard	Hectares	Acres
Les Saint-Georges	7.5	18.6
Les Vaucrains	6	15
Les Cailles	3.8	9.4
Les Porrets or Porets	7	17.5
Les Pruliers	7	17.5
Aux Boudots	6.4	15.8
Les Haut-Pruliers	4.5	11.2
Aux Murgers	5	12.5
La Richemone	2.2	5.5

The Appellation Contrôlée Nuits-Saint-Georges consists of 318.2 hectares, of which 151.2 hectares are classified as First Growths.

Vineyard	Hectares	Acres
Les Chaboeufs	3	7.2
La Perrière	3.4	8.5
La Roncière	2.1	5.3
Les Procès	1.9	4.7
Rue-de-Chaux	2.1	5.3
Aux Cras	3	7.7
Aux Chaignots	5.9	14.8
Aux Thorey	5	12.5
Aux Vignerondes	3.8	9.5
Aux Bousselots	4.2	10.5
Les Poulettes	2.1	5.3
and portions of the following vineyards		
Aux Crots	4.5	11.3
Les Vallerots	9.7	24.25
Aux Champs-Perdrix	2.1	5.3
En La Perrière-Noblet	2.2	5.5
Aux Damodes	8.5	21.3
Les Argillats		
En La Chaine-Carteau	2.6	6.6
Aux Argillats	1.9	4.8

In Prémeaux

FIRST GROWTHS (*Premiers Crus*)

Vineyard	Hectares	Acres
Clos de la Maréchale	9.5	23.6
Clos des Arlots	6.7	6.8
Clos des Corvées	7.5	18.8
Clos des Forêts	7.1	17.8
Les Didiers	2.5	6.3
Aux Perdrix	3.4	8.3
Les Corvées-Paget	1.6	3.9
Les Clos Saint-Marc	.9	2.2
Clos des Argillières	4.2	10.4
Clos des Grandes-Vignes (*in part*)	2.1	5.3

O

Oak

The only wood from which the very best barrels and casks for ageing wine are made. In a sound oak cask, new wine lacking tannin and character is sure to improve, though if left too long it may become withered *(seché)* and oaky. The most famous oak used for cooperage comes from Limousin and Nevers in France or from Yugoslavia. Tennessee white oak is most common in the United States, but some of the European species are imported for ageing fine red wines in California.

Oast house

A building containing a kiln for drying hops.

Oberemmeler

Fine wines of the Saar, in Germany. Karlsberg, Raul, Rosenberg and **Hütte** are well-known vineyards. **Scharzberg** is the collective vineyard site name.
See **Mosel-Saar-Ruwer.**

Obscuration

In brandy, the difference between actual alcoholic strength and that shown by measuring its specific gravity. The difference comes from the addition of coloring matter, changing specific gravity but not strength; its amount will sometimes, but very rarely, be noted on labels.

Ockfeiner Bockstein

Always one of the best, and in certain years *the* best, of the wines of the German Saar. Big and full-bodied for one of the Saar wines, which tend to be light.
See **Mosel-Saar-Ruwer.**

Octave

Small cask of one-eighth the capacity of a pipe. As the pipe varies considerably in capacity, so does the octave, which may range from 54.5 to 81.8 hectoliters (14 to 21 U.S. gallons, 12 to 18 imp.), but is usually given as 63.6 hectoliters (17 U.S. gallons, 14 imp.).

Oechsle

German equivalent of the Balling/Brix scale *(q.v.)* expressing the specific gravity of grape juice, which is mainly fixed by the sugar content of grapes.

Oeil de perdrix

French for "partridge eye." A term derived from the pinkish tint in a partridge's eye and applied to a pinkish tinge in white wines. It is found in some of the white Burgundies and in Champagnes. This term has been dying out since *vin rosé* began to be popular.

Oenology

The science of wine. In their *Traité d'Oenologie,* J. Ribéreau-Gayon and E. Peynaud define it also as the science which deals with the preparation and preservation of wine and its elements by the application of the rules of chemistry. The authors of the treatise have also stated that the function of oenology is to prevent wine sickness and, in general, to aid the production of the best possible wines with the minimum of waste and of unnecessary expense. There is no question of making a good wine out of a bad one: quality is governed by the soil, the weather, and the grape variety. Wine should be a natural product. But the best of wines, left to mature on its own and according to the whims of nature, would be spoiled. Man must intervene to arrange for the developing wine the conditions in which its natural characteristics and bouquet can come to perfection.

An oenologist is a technician who has gained his diploma in the science of vinification.

Oesterreicher

The Sylvaner or Franken Riesling grape.

Off-license

In England, a license permitting sale of wine, beer, and spirits to be consumed off the premises, and by extension, the shop department of the public house itself, usually referred to as an "off-license." There is a corresponding term "on-license" in the trade for public houses and wine shops, and the permit they require is an on-license. The American term is "off-premises."

Oggau

Wine town in Burgenland. This is one of the important place-names in Austria *(q.v.).*

Ohio

See: United States: Ohio.

Oïdium

Powdery mildew; a fungus disease of the vine.
See Chapter Eight, p. 31.

Okolehao (oke)

Hawaiian beverage distilled from a mixture of molasses, rice lees, and juice of baked ti-root (the root of the taro or kalo plant). It is dark and smoky, and usually bottled at 80° proof.

Old Tom gin

Gin which has been sweetened with sugar.

Oldest bottled wine in existence

The Wine Museum in Speyer, German Palatinate, boasts of the oldest bottled wine in existence. It is estimated to be approximately 1,600 years old and is tightly sealed by the hardened oil used in Roman times to provide a protective film which floats upon the wine surface. Sealed amphorae dating from Roman days have also been found in the Mediterranean.

Oleron's disease

Vine malady found to some extent in South Africa, rarely elsewhere.
See Chapter Eight, p. 31.

Château Olivier

Bordeaux red and white wines.
District: Graves, France.
Commune: Léognan.

Although both the red and white wine are rated among the top Graves Growths as classified in 1959, the dry white wine is generally the favorite. The thirteenth-century château itself, turreted and buttressed, and enclosed by a moat, is no longer concerned with wine; but *chais* and vineyard have for many years been controlled by the firm of Eschenauer in Bordeaux. The castle was the hunting lodge of the Black Prince in the fourteenth century.

Characteristics. Now château-bottled, and pleasant; wine of character; and there are some good bottles.

Vineyard area: red—18 hectares (45 acres); white—16 hectares (40 acres).

Average production: red—90 *tonneaux* (8,000 cases); white—65 *tonneaux* (6,000 cases).

Oloroso

A nutty, pungent Sherry, richer than Fino. For comparison and discussion of Oloroso and Fino, *see* Sherry.

Oltrepò Pavese (D.O.C.)

Italian red or white wine from Pavia.
See Lombardy.

Opimian wine

One of the half-dozen great wine names of antiquity and, unlike all the others—Pramnian, Falernian, etc.—not the name of a geographical place from which the wine came but the name of a vintage. During the consulship of Opimius in the year 121 B.C., the Roman summer was one of such splendor that great wines were made—chiefly Falernian and others, which were said (probably with some exaggeration) to have retained their full quality for a hundred years.

Oporto

A city at the mouth of the River Douro in northern Portugal. According to Portuguese law, any fortified wines that are to be labeled Port must be shipped from Oporto.
See Port.

Oppenheimer

In certain hot, dry years this will surpass Niersteiner as the best German Rheinhessen wine.
See Rheinhessen.

Orange

(1) Orange Bitters. Popular in England as an addition to mixed drinks. The flavoring ingredient is the peel of sharp Seville oranges. *See* Bitters.

(2) Orange Brandy. Made from brandy and oranges. The recipe, according to André Simon, is 1 gallon best brandy; the rinds of 8 Seville oranges and 2 lemons, cut very thin; 2 lbs. loaf sugar. Put it into a stone jar and cork down. Shake the bottle for a few minutes every day for twenty-one days. Strain it, bottle, and cork.

(3) Orange Wine. Made in Brazil from fermented orange juice.

Ordinaire

French term for the common wine the people drink every day.

Oregon

Wine-producing region of the United States, one of the few where *Vitis vinifera* will grow.
See United States: Oregon.

Orgeat

Flavoring syrup made originally from barley, but now from an emulsion of almonds.

Originalabfüllung

Formerly, a German term used for estate-bottled. *Erzeugerabfüllung* is now the legally accepted phrase. For full description of this and other terms of the same meaning, *see* Germany.

Originalabzug

A German term formerly used for estate-bottled. For full description of this and other terms of the same meaning, *see* Germany.

Orvieto (D.O.C.) and Orvieto Classico

Orvieto is white, and one of Italy's most consistently delightful wines, some of it semi-sweet, most of it dry. The latter is the result of the modern taste for drier wines. Orvieto was early aware of the trend; many of the growers began to vinify their wine dry, and there was a great outcry. Conservative wine-drinkers, such as Tuscany's austere Barone Ricasoli, consider sweet Orvieto one of the finest examples of Italian viniculture; vinified to be dry, it becomes a pleasant, reputable wine, but no longer Orvieto. The growers have rightly replied that the market for Orvieto *amabile* or *abboccato* (as the semi-sweet is designated) has fallen off to the point where it is no longer possible to specialize in it. "Our traditional wine is as good as it was," they maintain, "but, in addition, we are putting out a dry wine under the same name. It may have slightly different characteristics, but it is still of Orvieto quality."

Sweet Orvieto has a particular charm and special delicacy. The grapes are mainly Trebbiano, Procanico, Malvasia, Verdello, Grechetto, Drupeccio and Procanico. In the dry wine, Trebbiano is the dominant grape.

Orvieto is aged in deep cellars dug back into tufa rock cliffs resembling those found in Vouvray, and these play an important part (the growers say) in giving the wine its characteristics. Dry Orvieto is usually considerably higher in alcohol than the sweet type, in which some of the sugar has been prevented from fermenting (up to 11.5% as against 13%), but it manages to preserve the charm of its counterpart. It is rarely perfectly dry, but seems to balance a trace of residual sugar against a faintly tart aftertaste. About half of the 600,000 hectoliters (million-odd gallons) produced annually are dry, approximately 30,000 hectares (75,000 acres) are planted.

See Umbria.

Osaka

One of the main vine-growing districts of Japan (*q.v.*).

Ouillage

The topping up of wine barrels to compensate for evaporation. This is done repeatedly during the initial period of ageing.

See Chapter Nine, p. 40.

Ouvrée

An old Burgundian land measure, about one twenty-fourth of a hectare, or one-tenth of an acre.

Ouzo

A spirit with an anis base, popular in Greece, and sometimes seen in the United States, England, and elsewhere. Ouzo is a close cousin to pastis, absinthe and French Pernod. It is drunk cold with water, in which, like pastis, Pernod, and absinthe, it turns milky.

See Greece; Spirits.

Oxhoft

Scandinavian liquid measure, 254 to 264 liters (67–69 U.S. gallons, 56–58 imp.).

Oxidation

Term most generally used as a synonym for maderization—i.e., a flaw in white wine which turns it brownish in color and flat in taste, usually after too long a time in cask or bottle.

A substance is oxidized when it fixes oxygen or when it gives up hydrogen or, more basically, when it accepts electrons from another source—e.g., the oxidation of sulfurous into sulfuric acid; or of sulfuretted hydrogen, where sulfur is freed. Wine embodies such oxidizable substances as tannins, coloring matter, iron, or sulfurous acid added during ageing.

See Maderization; Chapter Nine, p. 40.

P

Paarl

River valley in Cape Province, South Africa; a region of light table wines.
See South Africa.

Pacherenc du Vic Bilh (Appellation Contrôlée)

White wine of the French Pyrenees which is made in virtually the same general area as red Madiran *(q.v.)*—that is, the valley of the Adour. The principal grapes used are Ruffiat, Mansenc, Courbu, Sémillon, and Sauvignon.

País

A grape and wine of Spanish origin which has been in Chile long enough to be considered a native.

Palatinate (Pfalz, Rheinpfalz)

German State of Rheinland-Pfalz.
Vineyard area: 23,000 hectares (56,500 acres)
89% white wines, 11% red wines.

The Palatinate, or Pfalz, is one of the most charming provinces of Germany, and the sunniest. The picturebook villages, bright with painted shop signs and flowery window boxes, are set among orchards and the "wine garden," as the people call it here. The winters are so mild and the summers so hot that figs and lemons flourish; the fruit-trees are heavy with cherries, apricots, and peaches, and the grapes ripen early to produce soft, full-bodied wines. Lying west of the Rhine and north of the French frontier and Alsace, the Pfalz is covered with great woods, rising with the fringe of the Haardt Mountains at the edge of the plain of the Rhine.

The countryside is lightly broken, flattish, and sunny, with the hills of the Haardt on the one hand and the Rhine sometimes visible at a distance on the other; the old villages are very South German, with twisting, narrow, cobbled streets and half-timbered houses, often decorated with vine motifs worked into stone—the whole Weinstrasse lives almost solely by wine and great is the rejoicing in a good year, great the sorrow in a bad one.

The province derives its name from the Latin *palatium* (palace), in German, *Palast* or *Pfalz*. The first palace of the emperors was on the Roman Palatine Hill; but afterward, every royal residence was called a "palace," and the officer in charge became the *comes palatinus* or *Pfalzgraf*—a title which was later to be handed down from one ruler of the Palatinate to another.

Location: Germany's largest wine-growing region in terms of production and second only to Rheinhessen in size, the Pfalz is bordered by Rheinhessen on the north and France on the south and west. The vineyards stretch nearly uninterrupted for 80 kilometers (50 miles) like a broad ribbon straddling the Deutsche Weinstrasse (German Wine Road) at the foot of and running parallel to the Haardt Mountains. Traditionally, the region was divided into the upper, middle and lower Haardt. Today, there are two districts (*Bereiche*): Bereich Mittelhaardt-Deutsche Weinstrasse, the northern half of the region, with Bad Dürkheim and Neustadt being the two most important centers for the wine trade; and Bereich Südliche Weinstrasse, covering the southern half of the region, with Landau as its most important commercial center.

Grape Varieties: Müller-Thurgau (24%); Riesling (15.3%); Kerner (10.7%); Silvaner (8.8%); Portugieser (7.9%); Morio-Muskat (6.9%); Scheurebe (6.2%).

Wine: elegant Riesling wines with great substance and depth of flavor; full-bodied, mild Müller-Thurgaus and Silvaners; red wines range from stylish Spätburgunder (Pinot Noir) to light, fruity Portugieser. Some 30–40% of Pfälzer wines are produced in a dry (*trocken*) style and are agreeable and harmonious, thanks to their ripe acidity and substantial body.

The warm, sunny climate of the Rheinpfalz is directly related to the Haardt Mountains, which shield the wine-growing areas against cold winds and rain. Only about three per cent of the vineyards are on very steep or terraced sites; most are planted on gently sloping (one-third) or flatter (two-thirds) sites. The soils of the vineyards to the east of the wine road are alluvial, sandy and gravelly and free of lime. Rich loess deposits are also found here. There is also a pronounced strip of chalky soil which runs through the region, from north to south, starting in Grünstadt and continuing through Herxheim, Kallstadt, Forst, Deidesheim—then reappearing further south, near Siebeldingen and Frankweiler.

Another 40–45% of the vineyard area has rich loam, loamy sand and clay soils. There are also patches of chalky marl, red marl, basalt (Forst) and red sandstone which make up about 15% of the surface area.

Of the nearly 11,500 growers in the Pfalz, 40% produce their own wine, a good portion of which they also sell directly. The average size of producers' vineyard holdings is 3.25 hectares (8 acres), whereas that of growers who deliver their grapes or must to cooperatives or the trade is just over one hectare (2.6 acres). Annual production, based on a ten-year average (1976–1985) is about 2.4 million hectoliters (63 million U.S. gallons, 52 million imp.). About 30% of the grape harvest is taken by cooperatives; 45% is sold to the trade and the rest is marketed directly by the wine-producing growers/estates. In general, growers in the

PALATINATE

southern district sell a high percentage of their crop to co-ops or the trade, who in turn supply supermarkets, large sales outlets and wholesalers, while direct sales and estate-bottled wine production are more prevalent in the northern district.

VILLAGES, VINEYARDS, PRODUCERS

Here are some of the important wine-growing villages, listed not alphabetically, but rather as they appear geographically as one would travel along the wine road from north to south, starting just below Grünstadt. The five villages which most consistently produce outstanding quality are Forst, Deidesheim, Wachenheim, Ruppertsberg and Ungstein. But it must be emphasized that very good wines are produced throughout the region, and that while the influence of climate and soil is important, it is the producer who is responsible for the ultimate quality and character of the wine. The producers mentioned below are reliable, traditional growers and cooperatives.

Herxheim, Freinsheim, Grosskarlbach and Dackenheim

Although not well known outside of the region, these villages produce high-quality white wines, mostly from the three classical varieties (Riesling, Müller-Thurgau and Silvaner) and good red wines (Spätburgunder and Portugieser). Herxheim is one of the few villages located majestically on a hill (lovely view of the valley) and Freinsheim is particularly beautiful, with its ancient town wall (still intact), Gothic church, baroque town hall and half-timbered houses.

Best sites: Herxheimer Himmelreich; Freinsheimer Goldberg and Musikantenbuckel; Grosskarlbacher Burgweg; Dackenheimer Kapellgarten. *Producers:* Herxheim: Winzergenossenschaft; Freinsheim: Lehmann-Hilgard, K. Neckerauer; Grosskarlbach: Lingenfelder; Dackenheim: Winkels-Herding. In nearby Kirchheim: Emil Hammel.

Kallstadt

The wines are usually rather full-bodied and heavy, grown on a peculiar chalk hill, the soil of which is classed as "hot". Very fine Riesling wines and exceptionally stylish Silvaner wines are produced here, as is some good red wine. The small village, with the vines sloping away below, was named prettiest on the wine road a few years ago. One of its finest sites, Saumagen (which means "sow's stomach"), gives rise to an unusual festival every spring, during which visitors can enjoy "Saumagen Twice: in the glass and on the plate." Saumagen is a very popular, hearty regional specialty made from a spicy mixture of meat and potatoes and cooked in a casing (hence the name "pig's stomach").

Best sites: Saumagen, Annaberg, Kronenberg, Steinacker. *Producers:* Stumpf-Fitz, Koehler-Ruprecht, Eduard Schuster, Henninger, Stauch and a good local cooperative.

Ungstein

"Ungsteiner awakens the dead" is the motto of Ungsteiner wine. Whether it does or not, the full-bodied white wines from the south- and east-facing slopes tend to be rich and flavorful and have great longevity. It is here that excavations unearthed a huge Roman villa and press house, complete with viticultural implements and tools as well as glass bottles and drinking vessels. Well worth visiting.

Best sites: Herrenberg, Weilberg, Nussriegel. Very good wine is also sold under the name of the *GL* Honigsäckel.
Producers: Weingut Pfeffingen-Fuhrmann.

Bad Dürkheim

Dürkheimer Feuerberg is the best-known Pfalz red wine; but about three times as much white is made as red. The Dürkheim Wurstmarkt (Sausage Market) in the second and third weeks of September has been held for more than 500 years and is Germany's greatest wine festival. A huge wine barrel on the northern outskirts of the town (it is now a restaurant) is said to be the largest in the world, holding 1,700,000 liters.

Considerable quantities of Dürkheimer wine are sold under the name of the three *collective sites:* Feuerberg, Hochmess and Schenkenböhl. *Single sites:* Michelsberg, Spielberg, Fuchsmantel, Fronhof, Abtsfronhof, Rittergarten, Hochbenn, Nonnengarten, Steinberg and Herrenmorgen. *Producers:* Fitz-Ritter, Karl Schaefer, Joh. Karst and an excellent cooperative, Winzergenossenschaft Vier Jahreszeiten.

Wachenheim

The tale they tell in Wachenheim is that generations ago the mayor of the town challenged the Abbot of Limburg to a drinking bout to the finish. Both had strong heads; but it was the mayor who was still under full sail when the abbot, overcome by good Wachenheim wine, slipped under the table. As a mark of his esteem, he freed Wachenheim from paying the tithe of one-tenth of its wealth to Kloster Limburg. Experts describe the wines as being fine, rich, fat, full-bodied, or having great substance and finesse. Much of this praise and the fine reputation of Wachenheim's wines is due to one of the great names in German wine, the late Dr. Albert Bürklin-Wolf.
Best sites: Gerümpel, Rechbächel, Goldbächel and Luginsland. *Producers:* Dr. Bürklin-Wolf, J. L. Wolf Erben and a very good cooperative, Winzergenossenschaft Wachtenburg-Luginsland. Schloss Wachenheim, founded in 1888, is well known for its excellent Riesling Sekt.

Forst

Forst is a pretty town, and its large baroque estate houses a reminder that viticulture has its prosperous side, too. A hill of volcanic basalt called the Pechstein or Basaltsteinbruch, lying to the west of the village, provides a special soil which holds the sun's heat and releases it upward onto the vines during the night. The equalization of temperature permits the grapes to ripen more completely than anywhere else in Germany, and many late-harvested wines are produced. Forst's heavier, clay soil, rich in minerals, retains water well so that in very dry (great) years, the Forster wines tend to be better than the neighboring wines of Deide-

sheim. The wines are powerful, full of flavor and rich in bouquet.
Best sites: Jesuitengarten, Kirchenstück and Ungeheuer. Much wine is also marketed under the name of the *GL* Mariengarten. *Producers:* Wilhelm Spindler, Weingut Mossbacher Hof, Acham-Magin and a good cooperative.

Deidesheim

The competition between the Forster and Deidesheimer wines is very close, but the two communities certainly lead all others in the Pfalz in most years. The soil is lighter than that of Forst, thereby producing more elegant wines, and grapes seem to ripen more quickly here, an advantage in poorer years. In very dry years, though, vines can suffer from insufficient moisture. The best sites are those located between the wine road and forested hillside.

Deidesheim itself is an old, attractive place; and Gasthaus zur Kanne, founded in 1160, is well worth a visit. Each May, in a famous wine festival, a prize goat is auctioned off at the Baroque town hall. The custom has been in force for nearly six hundred years; the little village of St. Lambrecht has had to pay this forfeit for grazing its goats on Deidesheim land ever since the fifteenth century.
Best sites: Hohenmorgen, Herrgottsacker, Leinhöhle, Kieselberg, Mäushöhle and Grainhübel. The *GL* Hofstück is used for a considerable amount of wine. Quality will depend on the producer. *Producers:* Two great names in German wine, recognized internationally as fine, traditional estates, Bassermann-Jordan and Reichsrat von Buhl; Weingut Dr. Deinhard and Gutsverwaltung Deinhard-Deidesheim; Josef Biffar; Herbert Giessen, Dr. Kern; Jul. Ferd. Kimich; Helmut Mehling; Weingut Georg Siben Erben; and a good local cooperative. Weinbau Hahnhof, the wine estate of a large catering company which runs a chain of cozy wine restaurants (Hahnhof) throughout Germany, all featuring Pfälzer specialties and wines, has its headquarters here.

Ruppertsberg

Strong fruity wines with a great deal of breed come from the best vineyards of this ancient wine town, founded before the birth of Christ, and an important junction in Roman days. It lies on the south border of Deidesheim and shares two vineyards with that village.
Best sites: Hoheburg, Linsenbusch, Reiterpfad, Nussbien and Gaisböhl. *Producers:* a good local cooperative. All of the leading estates of Deidesheim, Forst and Wachenheim have holdings in Ruppertsberg.

Gimmeldingen

On two rolling hills at the foot of the Haardt range, the sandy soils yield sound, pleasant wines. *Best site:*

Mandelgarten. Much of the wine is sold under the name of the *GL* Meerspinne. *Producers:* Kurt Mugler and a cooperative (with neighboring Mussbach).

Mussbach

New home of the region's most important viticultural institution, the State Teaching and Research Institute, which also owns the oldest estate in the Pfalz (dating back to the 8th century), the Johannitergut. Its well-preserved manor house, the Herrenhof, church and courtyard are all within an ancient stone wall. Sole owners of the site Johannitergarten.

Neustadt an der Weinstrasse

Middle point on the wine road, the southern boundary of the Mittelhaardt, and the largest wine-growing community (including neighboring villages) in the Pfalz, with more than 2,000 hectares (5,000 acres) of vineyards. In addition to a very popular wine festival every fall, Neustadt is where the German Wine Queen is crowned.
Sites: Grain, Erkenbrecht, Mönchgarten. *Producers:* Weingut Müller-Catoir (Neustadt-Haardt) and F. & G. Bergdolt.
Bereich Südliche Weinstrasse, the southern district, begins just south of Neustadt. The landscape is more dramatic as the hillsides become steeper. But because the protective shield of the Haardt Mountains is "broken" by the steeper side valleys, this part of the Pfalz has more rainfall, which, together with its very rich soils, explains the very high yields achieved here. In the past, the area was known for producing large quantities of rather common wine with a pronounced earthy taste. Today, after vineyard reorganization and thanks to the quality-oriented thinking of the cooperatives, the district produces well-made, appealing wines which show good varietal character. They are very good value.

Maikammer, St. Martin, Edenkoben, Edesheim

Very pretty villages at the foot of the Kalmit, the highest point of the Haardt Mountains.
GL: Mandelhöhe, Schloss Ludwigshöhe and Ordensgut.
Producers: Weingut Ernst Minges, Klaus Erath.

Rhodt Unter Rietburg

Very picturesque town with an ancient vineyard (300 years old) of Traminer vines. Schloss Ludwigshöhe, the former summer residence of King Ludwig I of Bavaria, overlooks the town.
GL: Ordensgut.
Producer: Very large, modern regional cooperative, Gebietswinzergenossenschaft Rietburg.

Siebeldingen and Birkweiler

The National Institute of Grape Breeding at Geilweilerhof in Siebeldingen is particularly well known for its research with essences. The new crossings Morio-Muskat, Bacchus and Optima were bred here.
GL: Königsgarten.
Producers: Weingut Ökonomierat Rebholz, Weingut Hohenberg.

Ilbesheim

Site of the other important, regional cooperative, Gebietswinzergenossenschaft Deutsches Weintor. Very well-made, sound wines which offer good value.
GL: Herrlich.

Schweigen

The last village on the German Wine Road, its huge stone gateway (Deutsches Weintor) marking the border with France. There is an interesting wine teaching trail here (Weinlehrpfad) as well as a tasting stand where wines of this district may be sampled.

Palette

Controlled place-name in the wines of Provence *(q.v.)*.

Palm wine

Spirit obtained by fermenting palm sap.

Palma

An export term for a very clean, delicate Sherry Fino.
See Sherry.

Château Palmer

Bordeaux red wine.
District: Haut-Médoc, France.
Commune: Cantenac-Margaux.

Lying between the vineyard road and Château Margaux, and directly across the road from Château Rausan-Ségla and Château Rauzan-Gassies, Palmer is one of the two or three best-known and most sought-after Third Growths *(Troisièmes Crus)* as classified in 1855. Its name, taken from General Palmer, the English general who owned it early in the nineteenth century, may contribute, by its easy pronunciation, to its fame in English-speaking countries, but the reputation is deserved. Then known as Château de Gasq, the vineyard, along with Château Lafite, was popular at the court of Versailles in the time of Louis XV.
The owners are international: French, Dutch, and British. Fifty per cent is owned by the Bordeaux firm

A LISTING OF SOME OF THE IMPORTANT WINE ESTATES

Estate	Headquarters	Hectares	Acres
Bassermann-Jordan	Deidesheim	40	100

Some of the vineyards date from before 1360; the present-day estate has been built up by the Bassermann-Jordan family since it came into their hands at the end of the eighteenth century. In the half a mile of low, black-walled cellars under Deidesheim are some of the most wonderful Pfalz wines. The historic estate, its guest book signed by celebrities—from Mendelssohn to Max Schmeling—belonged to the grand old man of Pfalz wines, the late Dr. Friedrich von Bassermann-Jordan, once president of the German wine growers. His gigantic book in three volumes is the authority in the language of the history of wine. His son, Dr. Ludwig von Bassermann-Jordan, now owns the estate.

Estate	Headquarters	Hectares	Acres
Josef Biffar	Deidesheim	11	27.5
Reichsrat von Buhl	Deidesheim	100	250

Estate	Headquarters	Hectares	Acres
Weingut Dr. Bürklin-Wolf	Wachenheim	105	262

Bürklin-Wolf properties have been in the same family since 1790. A tall, oval, carved cask of even earlier vintage stands at the bottom of steep stairs down into one of the two great cellars in Wachenheim. Within are more contemporary touches in the moist, dripping dankness; each cask is named with its vineyard parcel, and a cartoon in white paint also depicts the wine's origin; a cemented-up bomb hole gapes in one wall, Dr. Bürklin-Wolf was one of Germany's most energetic wine defenders and promoters. In 1951 he became the vice-president of the German Wine Growers' Association. His name is synonymous with the quality that he demanded and produced. His daughter Bettina and Georg Racquet, formerly with the Nahe State Domain at Niederhauser, continue the family tradition of this great estate.

Estate	Headquarters	Hectares	Acres
Weingut Dr. Deinhard and Gutsverwaltung Wegeler-Deinhard	Deidesheim	37	92.5
Weingut Dr. Kern	Deidesheim	5	13
Weingut Köhler Ruprecht	Kallstadt	8	20
Weingut Eugen Spindler	Forst	15	37.5
Weingut Stumpf-Fitz	Annaberg near Bad Dürkheim	1	2.5

Location of Holdings

- Forst: Forster Kirchenstück, Forster Jesuitengarten, Pechstein, Ungeheuer, etc.
- Deidesheim: Deidesheim Hohenmorgen / Grainhübel, Geheu, Kalkofen, Leinhöhle, etc.
- Ruppertsberg: Ruppertsberg Reiterpfad, Nussbien, Spiess, Hoheburg, etc.
- Bad Dürkheim
- Ungstein
- Deidesheim; Ruppertsberg
- Deidesheim: Deidesheimer Leinhöhle, Kieselberg, etc.
- Forst: Forster Freundstück, Kirchenstück, Pechstein, Ungeheuer, etc.
- Wachenheim: Wachenheimer, Luginsland, etc.
- Ruppertsberg: Ruppertsberger Hoheburg, Reiterpfad, etc.
- Königsbach: Königsbacher Rolandsberg, Idig, etc.
- Wachenheim: Wachenheimer Gerümpel, Goldbächel, Odinstal, Böhlig, Rechbächel (exclusive), Luginsland, etc.
- Forst: Forster Kirchenstück, Jesuitengarten, Pechstein, Ungeheuer, etc.
- Deidesheim: Deidesheimer Hohenmorgen, Kalkofen, etc.
- Ruppertsberg: Ruppertsberger Hoheburg, Gaisböhl (exclusive), Reiterpfad, Nussbien, etc.
- Bad Dürkheim
- Deidesheim: Deidesheimer Leinhöhle, Kalkofen, Kieselberg, Grainhübel, Herrgottsacker, etc.
- Forst: Forster Kirchenstück, Ungeheuer, etc.
- Ruppertsberg: Ruppertsberger Hofstück, Spiess, Nussbien, etc.
- Ruppertsberg; Deidesheim; Forst
- Deidesheim; Forst; Ruppertsberg
- Deidesheim; Ruppertsberg
- Kallstadt
- Freinsheim; Herxheim
- Deidesheim; Ruppertsberg
- Deidesheim; Ruppertsberg; Forst
- Kallstadt
- Deidesheim; Forst; Ruppertsberg
- Forst; Deidesheim; Ruppertsberg; Wachenheim
- Kallstadt; Bad Dürkheim

Palo Cortado

of Mähler-Besse. Mr. Mähler-Besse has for many years been the Dutch consul in Bordeaux. Sichel and Co., headed by the Englishman Peter Sichel, who lives at nearby Château Angludet, owns 40%. Ten percent belongs to the family of M. Bouteiller, who also own Pichon-Longueville Baron. The three owners combine to sell the wine on the markets in which they are strong; hence Palmer fetches deservedly high prices. Before the Second World War, the owners of Palmer bought Château Desmirail, another Third Classified Growth in Margaux, and did away with the name. The Palmer vineyard is planted 40% in Cabernet Sauvignon, 40% Merlot, and 10% each of Cabernet Franc and Petit Verdot.

Characteristics. Full and big, often resembled the wines of adjoining Château Rausan-Ségla, though in recent years Palmer is apt to be much finer. In the past two decades, because of its excellent qualities, it has become one of the most popular château-bottlings of the Médoc, and with Calon-Ségur one of the two most popular Third Growths.

Vineyard area: 40 hectares (100 acres).

Average production: 140 *tonneaux* (12,000 cases).

Palo Cortado

Rare Sherry wine combining the characteristics of an Oloroso and a Fino.

See Sherry.

Palomino

The dominating white grape in the making of Sherry at Jerez, Spain; used also for lesser wines in other parts of Spain. It has been planted in California, where it is used both for dry table wines and for the best of the sherry-types; it is known there as the Golden Chasselas.

Palus

Vineyard land adjacent to the rivers Dordogne, Garonne, and Gironde in the Bordeaux region of France; also the islands in the Gironde. The land is too heavy and moist for grapes to produce fine wine, but considerable quantities of *vin ordinaire* are made there, part of which becomes the everyday wine of the Bordeaux vineyard worker.

Pamid

An ancient and prolific grape variety grown in Bulgaria and used for the ordinary red wine.

Château Pape-Clément

Bordeaux red wine.
District: Graves, France.
Commune: Pessac.

Founded in 1306 by Bertrand de Goth, Archbishop of Bordeaux, the vineyard acquired its name when he became Pope Clement V. The vineyard was not ranked when the Graves Growths were classified in 1953, but the dedicated owners upgraded their vineyards and vinification techniques, so that Pape-Clément was included in the 1959 Classification. The wines have continued to improve and are now among the best red wines of Graves; they often unjustifiably fetch prices equal to those paid for the top Second Growths of the Médoc.

Characteristics. A very good wine, with the best qualities of a typical Graves. Some bottles from great vintages are outstanding.

Vineyard area: 23 hectares (57.5 acres).

Average production: 100 *tonneaux* (9,000 cases).

Parfait Amour

A very sweet spiced liqueur, either red or violet, from France and Holland.

Paris

Paris once counted her own wines among her attractions. Vineyards existed in numerous quarters of the city, the most famous in Montmartre, where there is still a street named rue de la Goutte d'Or, or "street of the drop of gold," in memory of the reputed excellence of Montmartre white. In the Passy section, warm springs once provided cures for disordered city-dwellers, and the route led to the rue des Vignes (street of the vines) for a sip of wine afterward. The heyday of Parisian viticulture was the thirteenth century, but most of the vines were afterward destroyed. Those that were not have been swallowed up by the city—with the exception of a few in Montmartre, kept for the sake of tradition. Their wines are auctioned off each year at foolishly high prices.

Parras

Center of Mexican viticulture, site of the Bodegas del Marqués de Aguayo, among others.

See Mexico.

Parsac-Saint-Émilion (Appellation Contrôlée)

Bordeaux red wine.
District: Saint-Émilion.

Commune whose vineyards, planted on chalky slopes, produced full-bodied wines of rich color. This place-name has not existed since 1975, when it was incorporated into the Montagne-Saint-Émilion place-name.

See Saint-Émilion.

Passes

French for the strip, or small label, affixed to bottles, giving subsidiary information not covered on the neck or on the main label.

Passetoutgrains (Appellation Contrôlée)

Decent red Burgundy wines made from a blend of Pinot with Gamay or other lesser grapes.
See Burgundy.

Passion fruit liqueur

Deep golden, very sweet Australian liqueur from the passion fruit.

Passito

Italian wine made from dried grapes. Usually it is a dessert wine, although such grapes are sometimes added to dry wines.

Passover wine

The wine of the great Jewish festival.
See Kosher wine.

Pasteur, Louis

The great French chemist of the Jura, eastern France, discovered pasteurization while experimenting with the local wines. Before his time (1822–1895), wine-making methods were mainly practical, owing little to scientific theory. Pasteur isolated the microorganisms which make grape juice ferment; but surprisingly, the practice of centuries has been little changed by this discovery. Quantity production of wine has definitely been influenced by Pasteur; quality production only very slightly.

Pasteurization

The process, named after Louis Pasteur, of sterilizing wine (or other liquids) by heat.

Stabilization of wine, milk, or other liquid by heating it briefly and rapidly to a temperature of, usually, 140° to 150°F. (60° to 66°C.), thus ridding it of most microorganisms. It is sometimes effective in the case of ordinary wines but is not recommended for fine wines. Not only are the bacteria destroyed but the wine also becomes dead to evolution. The process may be carried out before or after bottling.
See Chapter Nine, p. 40.

Pastis

The aperitif of Marseilles. Pastis is made on an alcohol base with herb flavorings, notably licorice. It bears a strong resemblance to anis but is slightly less distinctive in taste; and when diluted with water, it clouds and turns milky, with none of the green tinge of anis. Both pastis and anis have certain characteristics in common with absinthe. They are lower in alcohol, however, and wormwood, the ingredient which caused absinthe to be banned in most civilized countries, is omitted. Three of the better-known brands of pastis are those produced by Pernod, Ricard, and Berger in France; and a certain amount is illicitly homemade in southern France and Corsica.

Patent still

Continuous distilling apparatus. It is more economical than the older pot still in that the latter is basically a copper pot which has continually to be opened and refilled. The patent still is sometimes called the coffey still, because it is based on a patent taken out by Aeneas Coffey in 1832. Coffey's patent was an improvement on one by Robert Stein of Scotland, who patented the first design for a still of this type in 1826. Most of the finest rums and whiskies are always pot-distilled, this method allowing more of the taste and aroma to pass over with the distillate. Except for those favoring light-style liquors, pot-distilled remains synonymous with highest quality in most brandies and spirits.

Patras

Region of Greece producing good, mainly white wines. The town of Patras contains many of the large wine companies and cooperatives.
See Greece.

Patrimonio Rosé (Appellation Contrôlée)

Wine produced between Bastia and Île Rousse. This is one of the best of the Corsican wines.
See Corsica.

Patron saints of wine in Germany

The Germans have borrowed a French saint: Urban, the Bishop of Autun (between the Saône and the Loire), is one of their most honored patrons of the grape. His day, May 25, is fêted in many of the German wine districts, and a vast number of chapels and statues of St. Urban are to be found in the wine-growing areas of the country.

St. Kilian, the Frankish saint, is the patron of the vintners and their product in the wine districts of Franconia. And the vineyards bordering the Lake of Constance boast of Otmar, abbot of the monastery of St. Gallen, to whom legend ascribes a barrel which replenished its store of miraculously healing wine as quickly as its contents were drunk. Common sense should have told the vintners of Lake Constance that the potential threat of this never-ending source would in time have made their product and themselves unnecessary, yet they have chosen to commemorate the abbot as their patron.

Other saints and holy figures connected with wine in Germany include St. Cyriakus in the Palatinate, St. Genoveva and St. Magdalena, St. Walter, St. Werner, the holy Elizabeth, and even the saintly Mary—as well as St. Peter, connected with the grape through many stories and legends.

See also Saint Martin; Saint Vincent.

Pauillac (Appellation Contrôlée)

Bordeaux red wine.
District: Haut-Médoc, France.

Most important of the four great wine communes—Margaux, Saint-Julien, Pauillac, and Saint-Estèphe—of the Médoc peninsula jutting out from the mouth of the Gironde, Pauillac is paradoxically the least known. This is because the fame of the individual vineyards overshadows that of the town. Château Lafite, Château Latour, Château Mouton-Rothschild, and others are known as themselves, not as Pauillac wines, though all are in the commune. Consequently, with so much château-bottling, there is little regional wine to be sold as Pauillac.

Vineyard grading in this district is curiously uneven. Pauillac now has three First Growths (*Premiers Crus*); a single Second Growth (*Second Cru*), divided into two Pichon-Longueville vineyards; no Third Growths (*Troisièmes Crus*) at all; a well-known Fourth Growth (*Quatrième Cru*), Château Duhart-Milon-Rothschild; and then, suddenly, twelve Fifth Growths (*Cinquièmes Crus*)—out of the eighteen in the entire list of *crus classés* of the Médoc. The restricted number of Pauillac Seconds, Thirds, and Fourths illustrates the present considerable inaccuracy of the 1855 Official Classification, since several of the Fifths would be placed higher on any realistic scale drawn up now.

The wines do not possess much generic similarity, tending rather to be individual, except that all share the characteristic of being fairly full-bodied for Médocs. They are bigger than the more delicate Margaux, and, with one or two exceptions, less hearty than the Saint-Estèphes. On the other hand, no very accurate generalization can be made about wines as different as, for example, Lafite and Mouton-Rothschild, where special selection of grape variety gives the former an added finesse and the latter an advantage of stamina.

Beginning in the south at Château Latour, which touches Saint-Julien, the land is gently rolling, with vineyards placed along the soft ridge which slopes down into inferior marshy land beside the Gironde. At the old enclave of Bages, just before the town of Pauillac, there is a more pronounced rise; after Pauillac, the highest land holds Pontet-Canet, Mouton du Baron

Philippe, and Mouton-Rothschild, side by side on a plateau; and then Lafite, bordering Saint-Estèphe on the most sloping vineyard land of Pauillac. This is the only part of the first-class land in the Médoc which is almost hilly.

For centuries Pauillac itself was an important port. Even today there is a customs post, and a few ships arrive from America and Africa. But with the coming of steam and the shortening of the distance up to Bordeaux, Pauillac went to sleep. But in the middle 1960s, the town became a bustling little city—not very pretty, but perhaps the most prosperous in the whole Haut-Médoc. An unfortunate oil refinery, now closed, marred the river scenery and certainly did nothing to improve the quality of the air or the wines. Few remember that it was from Pauillac that La Fayette set sail for the American Revolution. Recently, however, the Pauillac waterfront has been renovated; the cafés that look out onto the yacht-filled harbor have been spruced up.

The Commanderie du Bontemps de Médoc et de Graves, the local promotional organization composed of growers, shippers, and various dignitaries interested in wine, has its headquarters at the Maison du Vin off the river front, and today ceremonies of the wine society are the most vivid events in the place where once river pirates met with a hot reception, and engagements of the Hundred Years' War were fought.

The Pauillac vineyards rated as Classified Growths (*Crus*) in the 1855 Classification of Médoc wines are:

FIRST GROWTHS (*Premiers Crus*)
Château Lafite-Rothschild
Château Latour
Château Mouton-Rothschild

SECOND GROWTHS (*Seconds Crus*)
Château Pichon-Longueville Baron
Château Pichon-Longueville, Comtesse de Lalande

FOURTH GROWTH (*Quatrième Cru*)
Château Duhart-Milon-Rothschild

FIFTH GROWTHS (*Cinquièmes Crus*)
Château Batailley
Château Haut-Batailley
Château Croizet-Bages
Château Clerc-Milon
Château Grand-Puy-Ducasse
Château Grand-Puy-Lacoste
Château Haut-Bages-Libéral
Château Lynch-Bages
Château Lynch-Moussas
Château Mouton-Baronne-Philippe

Château Pédesclaux
Château Pontet-Canet

See also under separate headings.

Château Pavie

Bordeaux red wine.
District and Commune: Saint-Émilion, France.

Considerably subdivided in recent years, Château Pavie is still the largest of the outstanding Saint-Émilion vineyards. It is beautifully situated on the completely vine-covered flank of hill which faces, from the south, the other flank on which Ausone and the village of Saint-Émilion stand. All the vines are south-exposed. It may be the frequent change of ownership which caused the Pavie wines to fall off for a time, but under the capable management of Mr. Valette they have returned to form, and in 1955 and 1986 Château Pavie was classified one of the eleven First Great Growths *(Premiers Grands Crus)*, while the split-off vineyards, Château Pavie-Decesse and Château Pavie-Macquin, in the lower category, were classed Great Growths *(Grands Crus)* of Saint-Émilion.

Characteristics. A big production and a good, typical Saint-Émilion—generous wine with a big nose.

Vineyard area: 35 hectares (88 acres).

Average production: 190 *tonneaux* (17,000 cases).

Pays, vins de

See Vins de pays.

Peach brandy

Properly, brandy distilled from peaches, but often used for peach liqueur, obtained by steeping peaches in sweetened brandy.

Pécharmant (Appellation Contrôlée)

The best of the red wines of Bergerac, in southwest France, bearing a resemblance to the lesser wines of Saint-Émilion.

See Bergerac.

Pecsenyebor

Quality category for Hungarian wine.

Château Pédesclaux

Bordeaux red wine.
District: Haut-Médoc, France.
Commune: Pauillac.

Classified a Fifth Growth *(Cinquième Cru)* in 1855, the small estate now belongs to M. Lucien Jugla.

Characteristics. A small uneven wine. The vinification is not always what it might be.

Vineyard area: 30 hectares (75 acres).

Average production: 130 *tonneaux* (12,000 cases).

Pedro Ximénez

A very sweet grape grown in Andalusia and elsewhere in Spain. It is used mainly in the making of sweet wines, or as a sweetener for sherries.

Pelin

Iced Rumanian wine drink with an infusion of herbs.

Pelure d'oignon

"Onion-skin." The term applies to the brownish tinge which marks some old wines. It was once used, also, for many pink wines before *rosé* became the popular term, and it is still sometimes so used.

Perlada

Just north of Figueras on the Spanish side of the Pyrenees is this tiny wine-producing town dominated by an impressive castle. Its rosé is quite popular and a good deal better than the red and white wine made there. But best known of Perlada's wines is a "Spanish champagne" sent to London, where its name was struck down by the British courts in a suit by the French Institut des Appellation d'Origine, thus confirming in Britain the exclusive right of French Champagne producers to the name Champagne.

Perlant

French term for mildly sparkling wine.
See Pétillant.

Perlwein

A sparkling wine popular in Germany, made by artificial carbonation.

Pernand-Vergelesses and Pernand-Vergelesses-Côte de Beaune (Appellations Contrôlées)

Burgundy red and white wines.
District: Côte de Beaune, France.

The village of Pernand-Vergelesses is one of the most ancient and certainly the most primitive of all the wine communes of Burgundy. It lies on the back slope of the "mountain"—the high hill that rises behind Aloxe-Corton—and is skirted by Ladoix-Serrigny and Savigny-les-Beaune. A small rutted dirt-track leads up to the tiny jumbled-together houses, and in these buildings live many of the growers of Corton-Charlemagne, one of Burgundy's greatest white-wine vine-

Pernod

yards. Few of these growers own more than a handkerchief-sized portion of the vineyard, and their annual production varies from upward of a dozen down to three or four barrels, or even less.

There are no great or famous vineyards entirely within the communal limits. Portions of vineyards allowed the place-names Corton, Corton-Charlemagne, and Charlemagne (qq.v.) fall within the commune, but this is a accident of geography and the wines are rightly considered with those of Aloxe-Corton. Wines sold under the commune name are predominantly red and are minor Côte de Beaunes. They are light, sometimes have considerable bouquet, and are often very fruity. Some Burgundians say they are wines that burn with a hot and intense flame but burn out reasonably quickly. The whites are simultaneously soft and heavy, without the breed of the great whites of Aloxe.

About 400 hectoliters (10,600 U.S. gallons, 8,800 imp.) of white wine are made annually; the amount of red varies but 2,500 hectoliters (62,500 U.S. gallons, 55,000 imp.) per year is average, even though it may be sold as Pernand-Vergelesses, Pernand-Vergelesses-Côte de Beaune (there is no difference in the wines of these two names), or, after blending with others from specified communes of the slope, as Côte de Beaune-Villages. There are about 60 hectares (150 acres) of First Growth vineyards.

The French authorities have not yet finished the task of selecting the First Growth (Premier Cru) vineyards—those that may (if the wine meets slightly higher than normal qualifications) be sold with both commune name and vineyard name on bottle labels. While this work is in progress, the following vineyards have been given this rating provisionally.

FIRST GROWTHS (Premiers Crus)

Vineyard	Hectares	Acres
Île des Vergelesses	9.3	23.1
Les Basses Vergelesses	17.5	43.3
Creux de la Net	5	12.4
Les Fichots	11	27.5
En Caradeux	20	49.8

Pernod

A popular anise-flavored aperitif made by the firm of Pernod Fils in France. Like others of this family it becomes cloudy when water is added.

See Pastis.

Perry

A kind of pear cider, either still or sparkling.

Persia

See Iran.

Peru

Peru is one of the oldest South American wine-producing countries, but is not one of the largest or most important. Vines have been grown in Peru at least since 1566, when Francesco de Carabantes planted some in the vicinity of Ica, an oasis south of the capital city of Lima.

The terrain and climate of Peru are such that it supports vines only in its suitably irrigated coastal regions. The snow-capped Andes are generally too cold and too rugged, and the northern part of the country is suitable for other types of cultivation, mining, and the rearing of livestock—especially the llama. Most of the vines are of European stock, and many wines are natural, both red and white, although some are fortified and modeled on Sherry, Port, and Madeira. One of the best grape varieties is Malbec. The table wines somewhat resemble the warm, vinous wines of Spain. 3,600 hectares (9,000 acres) of vineyard are found around Ica, where the famous Tacama Vineyard is located, 300 km south of Lima. It is a domain of 150 hectares. The wine is made by the most modern oenological methods under the supervision of Prof. Peynaud. It is entirely bottled at the vineyard. Tacama is a good example which one hopes will be followed by others.

While the Spanish population habitually drinks beer, wine is consumed on rare festive occasions. The Indians prefer chicha, brewed from corn and molasses, or one of the alcohols distilled in the country. The best of the Peruvian alcohols is the Pisco brandy (q.v.) which they distill from partially fermented Muscat wine. This brandy is the base of the Pisco sour, which is made with the white of an egg and Angostura bitters.

Pessac

Fine wine commune of the Graves district of Bordeaux. This is the village of Châteaux Haut-Brion and Pape-Clément.

See Graves.

Pétillant

French term for wine which is slightly sparkling or crackling; an alternative term is perlant. Pétillant is used only of wines which owe their sparkle simply and naturally to unfermented sugar still present in the wine when it is bottled. The maximum pressure admitted in France for pétillant types is 2 atmospheres at 68°F. (20°C.).

Petit-Chablis (Appellation Contrôlée)

Pleasant but lesser wines of Chablis produced in Lignorelles, Ligny-le-Châtel, and other places allowed the appellation Chablis.

See Chablis.

Petit Verdot

Grape grown in the Bordeaux region.
See Verdot.

Château Petit-Village

Bordeaux red wine.
District and Commune: Pomerol, France.

This expensive wine made by the Prats family contains much more Cabernet Sauvignon than the average Pomerol wine. The Prats brothers also own Cos d'Estournel at Saint-Estèphe in the Haut-Médoc.
Vineyard area: 9 hectares (23 acres).
Average production: 42 *tonneaux* (4,000 cases).

Petite Champagne

Not a Champagne, but the second best of the regions producing Cognac, which will bear its name or be called Fine Champagne.
See Cognac.

Petite-Sirah (Syrah)

A grape planted in California, yielding a fairly good red wine. It is also known as the Duriff. Some authorities say that this grape descends from the Syrah from which French Hermitage is made.

Château Pétrus

Bordeaux red wine.
District and Commune: Pomerol, France.

The outstanding wine of Pomerol and one of the top eight Bordeaux red wines, Pétrus commands prices comparable (or higher) with those of the First Growths *(Premiers Crus)* of the Médoc. On gravelly soil mixed with clay, covering a smooth rise of land higher than the surroundings but not steep enough to be called a hill, the vineyard lies about a mile from Libourne and two miles or so from Saint-Émilion on the road linking those historic vinous villages. The attractive small house in which the *chai* is to be found is decorated with the symbols and keys of St. Peter (Pétrus), and he is also the venerable gentleman carved in wood who guards the portals. Until her death in 1962, the owner was Mme Loubat, a lady of great energy and character, in her eighties and still a car driver and active *vigneronne*. The vineyard, very well run by Christian Moueix, is now the property of M. J. P. Moueix and Mme Lacoste. Along with Château Lafite, Pétrus is one of the most expensive wines of Bordeaux.
Characteristics. Superb, well-rounded, and fruity—sometimes velvety; it can be drunk before it is very old.
Vineyard area: 12 hectares (30 acres).
Average production: 40 *tonneaux* (3,800 cases).

Château de Pez

Bordeaux red wine.
District: Haut-Médoc, France.
Commune: Saint-Estèphe.

Traditionally one of the leading Bourgeois Supérieur wines of the Médoc, but actually deserving a higher classification.
Characteristics. Less full than many of its neighbors, it has the characteristic hardness and slow-maturing qualities of Saint-Estèphe. It is one of the lesser vineyards of the Médoc, consistently producing good wines.
Vineyard area: 25 hectares (62.5 acres).
Average production: 100 *tonneaux* (9,000 cases).

Pfalz

Alternative name for the Palatinate *(q.v.)* in Germany.

pH

A measure of alkalinity/acidity. A pH above 7 indicates alkalinity, a pH below 7 acidity—the lower the figure, the greater the acidity.

Phylloxera

A parasitic disease of the vine. The *Phylloxera vastatrix* is a burrowing plant louse of the Aphididae family, probably indigenous to the native vines of eastern America and certainly less harmful to them than to any other vines. In the second half of the last century, phylloxera caused considerable damage in Californian vineyards. Then, on vines sent from the United States, it was brought to Europe, where it devastated the vineyards of most of the wine-making countries. It was extremely destructive in France, where it was active in the 1870s, and elderly connoisseurs of wine are still debating the respective merits of pre-phylloxera and post-phylloxera clarets. The remedy for the disease is the grafting of *Vitis vinifera* varieties onto the native American root-stocks, which are naturally resistant to this root-eating grub. The grafting does not change the nature of the *Vitis vinifera* grape, but it does affect its longevity.

Vines no longer live as long as they once did. Old vines give quality but few grapes. Young vines give more grapes but less quality. Another consequence, not yet proven, but graver if it is a fact, is this: only since phylloxera has the vine disease fan leaf, or infectious degeneration, been found. Leading scientists have come to the conclusion that phylloxera may spread the disease.
See Chapter Eight, p. 31.

Pichet

French term for a pitcher, sometimes of wood or earthenware, for wine or cider.

Château Pichon-Longueville, Baron de Pichon

Bordeaux red wine.
District: Haut-Médoc, France.
Commune: Pauillac.

More than a century ago, the two Pichon-Longueville vineyards, now facing each other across the vineyard road, were one. The Pichon-Longueville (Baron) bottle will sometimes be found labeled simply Pichon-Longueville; the wine of the Comtesse de Lalande portion has always been labeled Pichon-Longueville-Lalande, or Pichon-Longueville, Comtesse de Lalande, and recently Pichon-Lalande. Jacques Pichon, Baron de Longueville, was the first president of the *parlement* of Bordeaux in the seventeenth century.

Pichon-Baron, built in the nineteenth century, with its "Renaissance" turrets, would be perfect for a label. Pichon is, unfortunately, another vineyard that, in 1987, was purchased by an insurance group. This series of insurance takeovers is expected to depersonalize the Médoc. The vineyard is a Second Growth *(Second Cru)* of Médoc.

Characteristics. This good wine is full-bodied and rich, although inconsistently so.

Vineyard area: 30 hectares (75 acres).

Average production: 120 *tonneaux* (11,000 cases).

Château Pichon-Longueville, Comtesse de Lalande

Bordeaux red wine.
District: Haut Médoc, France.
Commune: Pauillac.

The vineyard comprises about three-fifths of the old estate of Pichon-Longueville, separated a little more than 140 years ago, and is entirely enclosed within the semicircle of the Châteaux Latour and Pichon-Baron vineyards behind it. The wine from some parts of the estate has a character very similar to that of wines from Château Latour. A Second Growth *(Second Cru)* of the 1855 Classification, the wine was previously labeled Pichon-Longueville-Lalande, or Pichon-Longueville, Comtesse de Lalande, as it is now. Pichon-Longueville found with no qualification will mean the wine is Pichon-Longueville, Baron de Pichon *(q.v.)*. The heir of M. Miailhe, Madame de Lencquesaing, is the owner of Château Pichon-Lalande, as this *Cru* is commonly referred to today in Bordeaux and the Médoc.

Characteristics. More supple than Pichon-Longueville-Baron, the wine has gained in quality and popularity over Pichon-Baron, which in its turn was perhaps more popular thirty years ago. The quality of the 1982 and especially the 1983 and 1985 Pichon-Lalande is so good that it should still further increase in demand.

Vineyard area: 72 hectares (180 acres).

Average production: 280 *tonneaux* (26,000 cases).

Picpoule (Picpoul)

A white-wine grape grown extensively in southern France. It produces a rather thin white wine and is used also for vermouth. Catalonians call it Avillo.

Piedmont

Red and white wines.
District: Northwest Italy.

Piedmont, "foot of the mountain," is in the extreme northwest corner of Italy. Its capital is the prosperous city of Turin, center of the vermouth industry, and the region around Alba produces two of Italy's finest red wines: Barolo and Barbaresco. White, sometimes sickly sweet, sparkling Asti Spumante and the rather less popular Moscato d'Asti are also products of the province. They all have controlling organizations—or *consorzi*—to define and administrate their quality and authenticity.

Piedmont is a vast plain spreading out from the sinuous valley of the upper Po and surrounded by Alps to the north and west, the Apennines to the east and southeast, the Langhe and the Monferrato Hills to the south. In spite of the precipitous slopes of some

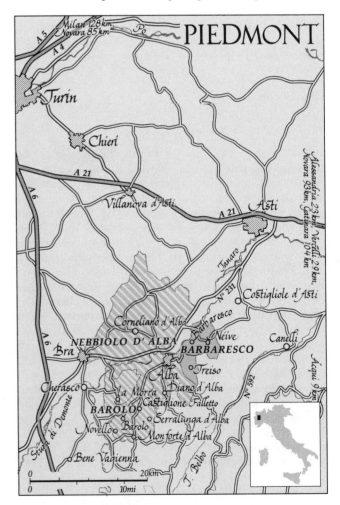

of its mountains, Piedmont is fifth—after Apulia, Sicily, Emilia-Romagna and Veneto—in wine production in Italy, making more than 5 million hectoliters (132.5 million U.S. gallons, 110 million imp.) annually, 80% of it from the southern section of the tumbled-together Monferrato Hills. These are fairly low, and incredibly steep, resembling the hills of the Beaujolais district in France. Yet in this region the tall vines used to be everywhere, sometimes sharing their plots with corn and wheat or other crops. Today, as a consequence of the D.O.C.G. wine law, intensive viticulture has for the most part replaced the haphazard planting. Vines also extend into the rest of Piedmont, but the superior wines do not match those from the Monferrato and Langhe districts. Piedmont's chief grapevine is Nebbiolo, but there are also significant numbers of Muscats and of Barbera, Bonarda, Freisa, Brachetto, Cortese, Dolcetto, Erbaluce, and Grignolino grapevines scattered from the low river valley to the austere heights of the adjoining province of Valle d'Aosta—the mountainous corner which climbs to the Swiss border.

BAROLO AND BARBARESCO

Both are good, big, strong, robust wines with powerful depth and a heavy pungency. Their fine quality has been recognized with D.O.C.G. status. Barolo is slower to mature, but Barbaresco, a little lighter, often has more finesse and as such is often preferred. Both are pungent with an uncompromisingly masculine aftertaste (so strong that in the past it was often characterized as "the aftertaste of tar"). The color of both is deep red—in a fine Barolo, almost black—fading slightly with age and assuming the brownish "onion-skin" hue around the edge.

Both wines are offspring of the Nebbiolo grapevine, whose temperament is ideally suited to the climate of beautiful Piedmont and its steep, rocky slopes. Both are fermented for fifteen to eighteen days before the juice is drawn off the must, to be run into huge oak vats to age—Barolo for two to four years, Barbaresco not so long. These vats range in size from fairly small to enormous and the best are made from time-blackened Slovenian oak from the forests of Czechoslovakia. During the long ageing process, the wines settle, rid themselves of much of their heavy deposit, and lose their harshness. Bottle-age is necessary—particularly for the finest wines—to soften them; but even after considerable ageing they will still be heavy wines which go best with red meat, pasta, or game.

The growing areas for the wines are almost adjacent to the Langhe and the Monferrato Hills—Barolo covering 1,300 hectares (3,250 acres) in the towns of Barolo, Castiglione, Falletto, Monforte d'Alba, Serralunga and La Morra; the smaller Barbaresco, 500 hectares (1,250 acres), slightly to the northeast in

Barbaresco and three other communes in the province of Cuneo. Some bottles will bear the seal of the local *consorzio* which approved the wine, and the seal bears the name of the organization (Consorzio per la Tutela del Barolo e Barbaresco): in the case of Barolo, the seal is a golden lion in a field of blue; in Barbaresco, the imprint of an ancient tower which stands in the town. Barolo's best producers are Moscarello Bartolo, Rinaldi Francesco, Renato Ratti, Cordero di Montezemolo and Giacoso. In Barbaresco, Angelo Gaja is a model of a top producer, which is reflected in his wines. More is produced by some 70 producers belonging to the cooperative Produttori Barbaresco.

GATTINARA (D.O.C.)

A full-bodied dry red wine of garnet color from Nebbiolo grapes (known locally as Spauna) and grown around the town of Gattinara, to the north of Turin. After Barolo and Barbaresco, this is one of the best wines of the Piedmont, rich in tannin and with a bouquet of roses.

ASTI SPUMANTE AND MOSCATO D'ASTI

The bottle is tilted at the proper angle, the white towel wrapped around the neck, the cork eased, but suddenly it comes out of the bottle with a vigorous "pop" and the opener will be told to "go back to Asti," no matter what the sparkling wine, nor where it is opened. For there is no doubt that Asti Spumante makes a small explosion when the cork is pulled.

When Charles Gancia brought the secrets of its manufacture back to his firm in Canelli in the late 1850s, the wine was sold as Asti champagne, Muscat champagne, or Italian champagne; but the reaction of the French combined with national pride to advocate a more original name, and Asti Spumante was finally chosen. Curiously enough, this name is now sometimes taken by growers in distant parts of the world when they wish to differentiate their sweet sparkling wine from a dryer one which is nearer to Champagne or other sparkling wines.

Asti Spumante is a dry and sweet, slightly flowery, sparkling Muscat. With its very low degree of alcohol (7% to 9%), large content of sugar, and gay bubbles, it is the perfect wine for unsophisticated festivity, and is a particular favorite in its own country. For one thing, it is cheap inside Italy—compared with sparkling wines in other parts of the world—but once import duties are added, it jumps out of its price class. Moscato d'Asti is a similar wine, but slightly lower in alcohol and made by the bulk process rather than the regular champagne process employed by the better houses for their good wines. (*See* Champagne, *particularly the section entitled* THE CHAMPAGNE PROCESS.) The wines are made in fifty-two communes near the small city of Asti in the Monferrato and Langhe Hills, entirely from Muscat grapes.

In spite of its fame, Asti Spumante is not selling as it once did. Popular taste is turning from sweet wines, and vintners are slowly overtaking the trend with dry variations on their traditional themes. In Asti, almost all the large houses are now diverting a part of their production to dry sparkling wines, mostly from Riesling and Pinot grapes but seldom from those grown in the immediate vicinity. The better firms have special vineyards where their grapes are grown and vinification is accomplished as soon after picking as possible. Some other houses are apt to import grapes from anywhere, depending on where they happen to be able to buy them in that particular year. Asti's dry sparkling wines do not usually carry the name of the city—that is reserved for the more famous sweet ones—but are usually sold as Pinot, Pinot Spumante, Gran Spumante, and a few were sent abroad labeled "Méthode Champenoise." These dry wines are generally thin, usually undistinguished, but in Italy their low cost makes them fairly good buys.

Of the sparkling wines, only Asti Spumante and Moscato d'Asti enjoy a D.O.C. protection. Bottles guaranteed by the *consorzio* as being worthy of the name they bear will carry a seal portraying San Secondo, the patron saint of Asti, on horseback, and the name of the organization: Consorzio per la Tutela dell'Moscato d'Asti e Asti Spumante.

OTHER WINES

Most of the minor wines of Piedmont are named for the grape variety from which they are made. As a rule, these wines can be considered variable in the extreme, depending largely on where they come from and the skill of the wine-maker. They have, however, certain more or less typical characteristics. Wines named after grapevines are marked with an asterisk.

Barbera*

Heavy, deep, very often harsh red wine made in quantity throughout the region and indeed all Italy, but principally in the provinces of Asti, Alessandria, and Cuneo. There are four D.O.C.s for good Barbera: Barbera del Monferrato, d'Alba, d'Asti, and dei Colli Tortonesi.

Bonarda*

Dark red wine mostly from around Asti; it is sometimes rendered sparkling.

Caluso Passito (D.O.C.) and Caluso Passito Liquoroso (D.O.C.) and Erbaluce di Caluso* (D.O.C.)

A *passito*—a wine from dried grapes—made from Erbaluce vines grown in Caluso, not too far from Turin. The wine is sweet and white and made only in very small quantities. The *liquoroso* is a fortified wine. The Erbaluce is a dry, white wine.

Carema (D.O.C.)

Medium and hard red wine from Nebbiolo grapes grown in the commune of Carema, along the banks of the Dora Baltea in the province of Turin.

Cortese di Gavi* or Gavi, Cortese dell'Alto Monferrato and Cortese Colli Tortonesi (all D.O.C.s)

Still and unexceptional dry white wine, sometimes made sparkling. It should be taken very young.

Dolcetto*

In Piedmont the wine from this grape is not sweet, as its name suggests. It is dark red in color, rather light in body. The wine has the following Denominations of Origin: Dolcetto d'Acqui, di Ovada, di Diano d'Alba, delle Langhe Monregalesi, d'Asti, Dogliani and Alba.

Freisa d'Asti and Freisa di Chieri* (D.O.C.)

Sprightly red wine with a charming fruitiness and a delightful bouquet. The best is from around Chieri (near Turin) or the Monferrato Hills. Perhaps the finest of the lesser wines of Piedmont. Some Freisas are sold as *frizzante* (with slight sparkle), which the French would call *pétillant*.

Grignolino d'Asti* (D.O.C.)

Dry, slightly bitter, pinkish-red wine lacking some of the depth and density usually found in most Piedmontese reds.

Boca (D.O.C.)

A red wine mainly from Nebbiolo, with some Vespolina and Bonarda. It is produced in Boca and four other villages in Novara. With a bouquet of violets and a bright ruby color, this wine is dry and even suggests pomegranates.

Brachetto d'Acqui* (D.O.C.)

From Acqui and several other communes in the provinces of Alessandria and Asti, this pale ruby-colored wine is delicately sweet and *frizzante*, or semi-sparkling.

Ghemme (D.O.C.)

A red wine, garnet in color, with a pleasant enough bouquet reminiscent of violets. Dry and slightly bitter, the wine ages well; it is made from Nebbiolo and a bit of Vespolina and Bonarda at Ghemme and Romagnano Sesia.

Rubino di Cantavenna (D.O.C.)

From Barbera, Grignolino, and Freisa grapes grown at Cantavenna and three other villages in Alessandria. The wine is pale-red, dry, but full in the mouth.

Sizzano (D.O.C.)

Also dry and ruby red, made at Sizzano in the province of Novara from Nebbiolo, Vespolina, and Bonarda. This wine needs to mature at least three years, two of them in cask, before it is sold.

Fara (D.O.C.)

Quite like Sizzano, except that it is made at Fara and Briona and has a finer bouquet.

Nebbiolo d'Alba* (D.O.C.) and Roero (D.O.C.)

The noble vine of Piedmont gives a light red wine with a scent of violets. Others are Lessona (D.O.C.), Bramaterra (D.O.C.) and Gabiano (D.O.C.).

VALLE D'AOSTA (D.O.C.)

In this autonomous region high above Piedmont, there are two wines worthy of mention.

Donnaz is the Controlled Denomination of Origin for a red wine made of Nebbiolo grapes (known locally as the Picoutener) in parts of Donnaz, Perloz, Bard, and Pont St. Martin. It is produced on both sides of the River Dora Baltea, just above the commune of Carema, after which another red wine is named. Donnaz is soft, with a bouquet which suggests almonds; the nut scent is most apparent when the wine has attained some degree of maturity. The color is pale garnet.

Enfer d'Arvier (D.O.C.) is good and is made on terraces around the commune of Arvier from Petit-Rouge grapes, plus some Vien du Nus, Neyret, and Dolcetto. Like Donnaz, the wine is garnet-colored and has a pleasing bitter aftertaste. Enfer d'Arvier is aged for a minimum period of one year in wooden casks holding not more than 300 liters (about 80 U.S. gallons, 66 imp.). The grapes are grown on beautiful steep terraces, which make viniculture something of a challenge.

Pierce's disease

A disease that affects vines in California.
See Chapter Eight, p. 31.

Piesporter Goldtröpfchen

Usually the best, though unfortunately overpriced, of the very great wines of Piesport, German Mosel. The Piesporter are incomparable when produced in a dry summer.
See Mosel-Saar-Ruwer.

Pimm's Cup

There are four Pimm's Cups, and it is said that they were originated by a bartender at Pimm's Restaurant in London and so delighted the customers that the staff was continually being asked to put some up for people to take home. As a result, they began to be made commercially. When bottled, each resembles a heavy cordial; but once mixed with fruit juice, cooled, garnished with borage and cucumber rind, and served in tall glasses, they become refreshing summer drinks. The four types are:

Pimm's No. 1   Gin-based
Pimm's No. 2   Whisky-based
Pimm's No. 3   Rum-based
Pimm's No. 4   Brandy-based

Pinard

French slang for wine, usually cheap and red.

Pineau d'Aunis

A grape used in rosé wines of Anjou, and in red wines of the Loire Valley, where it is gradually being replaced by Cabernet Franc.

Pineau des Charentes

Fortified wine of Cognac region, drunk as an aperitif.
See Sweet fortified wines of France.

Pineau (Pinot) de la Loire

Another name for the grape Chenin Blanc *(q.v.)*.

Pinot (Pineau)

One of the most distinguished families of wine grapes, responsible alone or in part for the greatest Burgundies and Champagnes and for many other fine wines. Pinot is a temperamental vine, however, and is not well adapted to areas outside northern France. The outstanding member of the family is Pinot Noir or Noirien, the red-wine vine of Burgundy. Pinot Lie-

Pinot Blanc

bault and Pinot Meslier contribute to Burgundian wines, but are, for all practical purposes, identical with the Noirien. Pinot Gris and Pinot Blanc, eminently noble vines, contribute to white Burgundies. All Pinots abound also in the finer Champagne vineyards. Pinot Chardonnay is actually a misnomer, for it is not a Pinot. Current usage is simply to call it Chardonnay.

Pinot Blanc

The white grape of the Pinot vine family, used in making some white wines of Burgundy and elsewhere. It should not be confused with Chardonnay. In Germany, it is known as Klevner and sometimes as Weissburgunder.

Pinot Chardonnay

See Chardonnay.

Pinot Gris

A grape of the Pinot family which yields good wine in Alsace, where it was also formerly known as Tokay d'Alsace. In other parts of France, it appears as Pinot Beurot; Fauvet; Malvoisie; and Auxerrois Gris. In Germany, it is called Ruländer.

Pinot Meunier

An inferior strain of the Pinot Noir, the grape is no longer legal in Burgundy but is used for some pleasant Loire Valley rosés. Since its leaves on the underside are powdery white, as if covered with flour, the vine was given the name *meunier*, which in French means "miller."

Pinot Noir

The Pinot Noir is one of the greatest of fine-wine grapes. It makes the fabulous red wines of Burgundy, and it is largely responsible for Champagne. The vine is difficult, only moderately prolific, but in the right soil and the right climate it produces with splendor. The Pinot Noir is planted, to a lesser extent, in other parts of Europe and in California and Oregon. Here it is sometimes confused with the Pinot Meunier, and with the Pinot St. Georges, which is not a real Pinot grape. In Germany, under the name of Spätburgunder, it produces the best of that country's red wines. Synonyms: Pineau; Savagnin; Klevner (Alsace); Clevener (east Switzerland).

Pint

Standard liquid measure, one-eighth of a gallon. The American pint contains 28.875 cubic inches, equal to 0.473 liter, or 16 U.S. fluid ounces; the British pint, 34.677 cubic inches or the equivalent of 0.568 liter or 20 British fluid ounces.

Pipe

A large cask with tapered ends and of varying capacity, used especially for Port. Some of the more widely used are:

		Gallons	
	Liters	U.S.	Imp.
Madeira	418	110.5	92
Marsala	423	111.7	93
Wine	477	126.1	105
Port and Tarragona	523	138.1	115
Lisbon	532	140.5	117

Piquant

French term, entirely derogatory, for wine which is sharp, acid, and biting on the palate.

Piqué

French term for vinegary wine.

Piquette

French term for wine made by adding water to the husks and skins of grapes, the juice of which has already been pressed out. This is low in alcohol, tart, and fresh, and has made up the wine ration of the European vineyard worker since Roman times at least. By extension, the term is used in a derogatory sense for any poor or mediocre wine.

Piqûre (acescence)

A disorder of wine which produces a gray film. *See* Chapter Nine.

Pisco brandy

Brandy distilled from Muscat wine in Peru, Chile, Argentina, and Bolivia. Originally Peruvian, the best comes from the Ica Valley, one of Peru's better wine districts, near the port of Pisco. After distillation, the brandy is placed in clay containers and is usually drunk young. This fiery brandy is still the preferred drink of Peruvian natives and has not gained popularity outside its country of origin, as Mexican tequila has in the United States.

Plastering

Addition of plaster of Paris (gypsum or calcium sulfate) to low-acid musts to induce the necessary degree of acidity. In all but a very few instances the practice is not conducive to high wine quality, but it is an accepted step in the process of Sherrymaking.

Plavac

Native Yugoslavian species of grape used extensively in red Dalmatian wines.
See Yugoslavia.

Plum brandy

A white *eau-de-vie* made from plums.
See Quetsch; Mirabelle de Lorraine; Slivovitz.

Plummer

A medium-bodied type of Jamaican rum.
See Rum, Jamaican.

Plymouth gin

Made in Plymouth, England, the style is intermediate between Dutch gin or Hollands, and London Dry gin, the type seen almost universally, in Britain and the United States.
See Gin.

Poiré

French for perry or fermented pear juice. *Eau-de-vie de poire*, made in Switzerland and some parts of France, is pear brandy, which can be superb.

Poland

Vodka, the drink associated with Poland, has been made there for hundreds of years. Indeed, the people say that vodka was originally Polish, not Russian. In the Middle Ages, the Pole made the spirit, first as a medicine, then as a drink, in monasteries and small manors all over the country. As it became popular, the word *woda* (water) achieved the affectionate diminutive and the spirit its name, wodka, or vodka. Different makers had, naturally, various recipes handed down as family secrets; and some of these formulas are still in use as bases for modern processes of manufacture.

Vodka is now seldom made from potatoes, although there is a Wodka Luksusowa, or luxury vodka, which is still obtained from potato spirits, doubly rectified and purified. Generally, the spirit comes from grain—often rye. This is filtered repeatedly, stored for a considerable time in tall steel vats, and afterward pumped out into mixing machines, diluted with a special soft distilled water, then refined by filtering. A finished product, such as the well-known Vyborova, or Wyborowa, should be neutral, mild, and crystal clear. The Polish vodka, unlike the Russian, is all bottled at home. In the last decade or so, export figures have risen by about 800%. For Western countries, there is a system of labeling according to alcoholic strength: blue for 79% British (90% U.S.) Vyborova; red label for 66% British (75.5% U.S.). Polish vodka, probably because it is expensive, is considered to be a very chic drink in France. The recommended way to drink it is freezing cold: a Pole will probably take the bottle from the ice compartment of his refrigerator and have it brought to the table in an ice bucket; and he may serve it not only at the beginning of a meal, but throughout. (For this purpose, Krakus, a high-quality vodka made according to traditional recipes, is held to be the best.)

Several types of vodka are manufactured in Poland, some of them flavored with fruit, flowers, or herbs. Among these are Zytnia, a pale spirit which retains the taste of the rye; Soplica, a dry brandy vodka to which wine distillates and matured apple spirit have imparted the aroma; Jarzçbiak, rowan vodka, its rather tart sorb apple flavor sometimes mellowed with a little sugar and softened by distillates of wine; Tarniówka, a sloe spirit. Especially characteristic of Poland and much liked abroad is the Zubrówka vodka with the bison on the label. This, when it is the genuine high-quality spirit, is flavored with the wild "holy" grass which the *zubra*, or Polish bison, love to eat in the forests of eastern Poland. This vodka, pale olive green in color, has an odd, subtle taste and scent; and in each bottle there is a blade of grass. A glass of Zubrówka is traditionally offered to returning hunters in the region of the Bialowieza Forest. The state has now taken over the monopoly of distilling all the well-known vodkas exported or drunk locally.

Liqueur Vodkas and Brandies

Starka, a very old type of vodka, is made from rye, distilled at lower proof than the Vyborova, aged in oak wine casks, and afterward blended with wine. The resulting drink is dry with a characteristic flavor and a pale brown color. Poland also produces its own brand of Śliwowica (slivovitz or plum brandy); and a Winiak Luksusowy, or brandy, from pure rectified spirit and imported wines.

Other Liqueurs and Cordials

Wiśniówka, a cordial made from black cherries, is the most popular abroad. Poland exports other fruit cordials: cherry liqueur and honey cherry brandy; a goldwasser, or Złota Woda; a strong herbal liqueur called Likier Ziołowy; and—a specialty—old Krupnik Honey Liqueur, made from rectified spirit, honey, and spices. This drink, handed down from the Middle Ages, has the peculiarity of being served hot. The legend goes that Giedymin, a Lithuanian prince of the fourteenth century, was saved from freezing to death by one of his knights who, just in time, brought him a cup of the hot liqueur.

Polcevera

Thin, light, white Italian wine.
See Liguria.

Polychrosis

Polychrosis

One of the grape-moths.
See Chapter Eight, p. 31.

Pomace

Crushed or pulped grapes or fruit after the juice has been extracted. In French, *marc*. The spirit distilled from it is also known as *marc (q.v.)*.

Pomace brandy

California *"grappa"* from pulp of grapes.

Pombo (pombe)

A beverage of the Bantu people of Africa made from millet or sorghum.

Pomerol (Appellation Contrôlée)

Red wines.
District: Bordeaux, France.

The red wines are like sturdier Médocs or Saint-Émilions with the finesse and subtlety of Médocs added. For this reason, they are often said in Bordeaux to be intermediate between the two other great red-wine types of that region. Pomerol, situated next to Saint-Émilion, uses the grape varieties which produce the Médocs, and this is sufficient to account for the transitional vines. It is true that the Pomerols on gravel soil, bordering on the Saint-Émilion vineyards on gravel soil (of which the greatest is Cheval-Blanc), greatly resemble their neighbors. Pomerol wines, however, are distinct and individual, having a velvety fatness, or *gras*, among the red Bordeaux. To liken them either to Médocs or to Saint-Émilions is to give a false impression. Intermediate in fullness of body between the other two, they nevertheless derive a special taste from the iron in the subsoil of the small Pomerol district, with the result that the wine is one of the most characteristic of the red Bordeaux.

The district of 800 hectares (2,000 acres), nearly all of it in the commune of Pomerol but a fraction in the commune of Libourne, is situated on a plateau above and behind the Dordogne river town of Libourne. Like Saint-Émilion, not half a dozen miles away, the region was important, a junction in Roman times, when most travel and transport was along the waterways.

The vine flourished in Pomerol in those days, as it did in Saint-Émilion. Templars had come to Pomerol in the twelfth century to carry forward and enlarge the viticulture of the Romans. The fighting in the Hundred Years' War destroyed some of the vineyards, but these were afterward re-established. Thereafter, the growers of Pomerol did their wines no permanent good by parading them as Saint-Émilions; and not until the nineteenth century did these begin to be

known abroad. Today, however, more and more connoisseurs are discovering the virtues of Pomerol.

The ground varies from vineyard to vineyard, and with it the wines. Soils are gravelly, clayey or sandy, sometimes all three in a single vineyard; a little clay in a gravelly soil seems to produce wines of the greatest suppleness, while those from predominantly gravel soil may be less fine. The best-known vineyards are not found in the sandy terrains.

In comparison with the manorial Médoc and such regions as Sauternes, where medieval fortresses still stand, Pomerol is almost homely. Its "châteaux" are often villas, their gardens necessarily small in a region where space is at a premium, since the great vines demand every inch. After the February 1956 freeze, which struck hardest of all in Pomerol, the area took on a blighted look, and the following summer thousands of dead vines could be seen lying in the churned soil from which they had been uprooted. It was like a battlefield.

No Pomerol 1956 and little 1957 and 1958 were seen. Where the vine was blighted but not killed, wine was made again in 1958 and 1959 vintages.

Pomerol vineyards are not classified. The best of them, and one of the eight best red Bordeaux, is Château Pétrus *(q.v.)*. Similar in type are Château La Conseillante, Château Vieux-Château-Certan, and Château Trotanoy. Château Petit-Village (belonging to the owner of Château Cos d'Estournel in the Médoc) is on an entirely gravel soil and produces very full-bodied wines with a splendid nose and the gleaming dark ruby color typical of Pomerols.

While not classified, the outstanding Pomerol vineyards are considered to be the following:

OUTSTANDING GREAT GROWTH

Château Pétrus

FIRST GREAT GROWTHS

Château l'Évangile	Château Latour-Pomerol
Château Gazin	Château Petit-Village
Château La Conseillante	Château Trotanoy
Château Lafleur	Vieux-Château-Certan
Château Lafleur-Pétrus	

Pommard (Appellation Contrôlée)

Burgundy red wine.
District: Côte de Beaune, France.

Pommard ranks second among Côte de Beaune wine communes, producing something over 10,000 hectoliters (265,000 U.S. gallons, 220,000 imp.) annually. Before the laws of Appellation d'Origine brought a measure of control into the wine business, a Burgundian writer estimated that the amount of Pommard sold throughout the world each week was more than the commune could make in ten years. Its amazing popularity still makes it one of the most abused place-names, and experts are slightly at a loss to explain it. Pommard, they maintain, even when it comes from

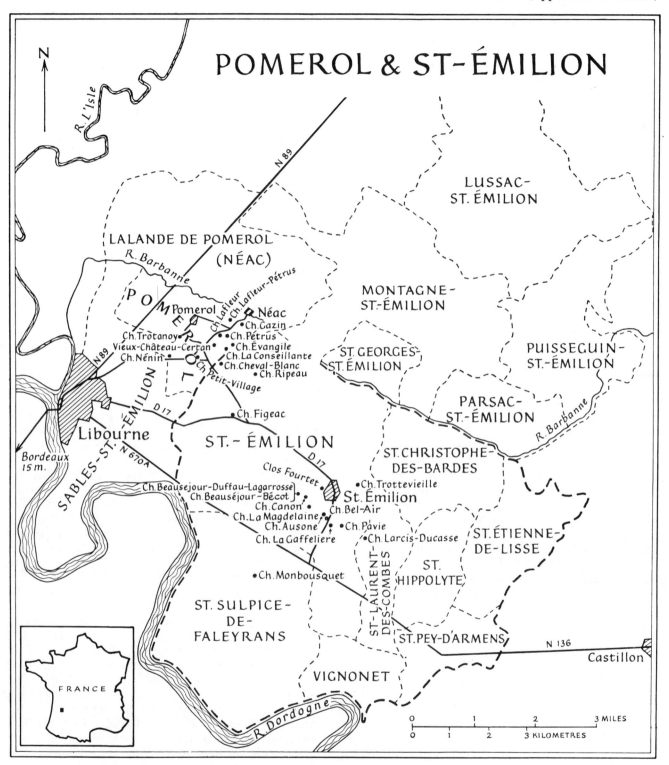

Pommard, is almost always an extraordinarily pleasant wine, but hardly ever among the greatest Burgundies.

Just south of Beaune the main highway forks, one road heading for Chagny, the other swinging into the hills past Pommard, Volnay, and Monthélie, and on to Autun. The road curves sharply, skirting the town, with vineyards on both sides of it, many of them en-closed in walls bearing the names of various shippers. If you take this road, the vineyard of Les Petits Épe-nots starts on your right at the fork, followed by Les Grand Épenots, Le Clos Blanc, and finally the town itself. Pommard is sleepy and small with a curious belfry standing in the main square, and a sluggish stream divides the town approximately in half. Almost before you have entered it, you are out again in the midst of a sea of vineyards, this time leading up the hill to Volnay.

There is less difference between wines of different vineyards in Pommard than is usual in Burgundy, although Les Épenots is generally extremely soft and round with a good bouquet. Les Rugiens the firmest, and Les Argillières the lightest. Another outstanding vineyard is Les Chaponnières. All the wines share the characteristics of firmness, fairly deep color, and bouquet. Sturdier than those of Beaune, they fill the mouth, leaving a pleasant aftertaste; but when set aside, most of the red wines of the Côte de Nuits show themselves much fuller both in body and in texture. *Chaptalisation*, or the addition of sugar to the fermenting must, will raise both body and alcoholic content; unfortunately, some shippers tend to overdo a good thing, producing a sturdier but coarser wine.

Pommard emerged better from the first of the important Côte d'Or vineyard classifications than the second. In 1860 three of the village's vineyards were ranked among the finest of the Côte d'Or, but the official list drawn up in 1936 has set them back, giving them a right only to the designation First Growth *(Premier Cru)*. In practice, this means that all the wines of Pommard will carry the town name, and the better bottles are sold with both the name of the town and the vineyard, such as Pommard-les-Épenots, or Pommard-Rugiens.

One reason why Pommard has become so well known is that the vineyards are huge and production high. There are 300 hectares (750 acres) of vines in Pommard for fine wines, considerable areas of which are owned by the large shipping houses who have kept the name well before the public.

The First Growths of Pommard have not yet been officially established. Until they are, the following vineyards have interim right to the designation:

FIRST GROWTHS *(Premiers Crus)*

Vineyard	Hectares	Acres
Les Rugiens-Bas	5.8	14.5
Les Rugiens-Hauts	7.6	18.8
Les Épenots	11	25.6
Clos des Épenots	3.64	9.1
Le Clos Blanc	4.3	10.6
Les Arvelets	8.5	20.9
Les Charmots	3.6	8.9
Les Argillières	3.64	9.0
Les Pézerolles	7.3	15.6
Les Boucherottes	1.7	4.1
Les Saussiles	3.8	9.4
Les Croix-Noires	1.2	3.1
Les Chaponnières	3.3	8.2
Les Fremiers	4.9	12.2
Les Bertins	3.7	9.1
Les Jarollières	3.2	7.9
Les Poutures	4.2	10.9
Le Clos Micot	3.9	9.8

Vineyard	Hectares	Acres
La Refène	2.5	6.1
Clos du Verger	2.55	6.2
Derrière Saint-Jean	1.2	3.0
La Platière	5.8	14.3
Les Chanlins-Bas	7.1	17.7
Les Combes-Dessus	2.8	6.9
La Chanière	10	24.7
Les Petits-Épenots	20.2	50.1
Clos de la Commaraine	4	9.8

Pommeranzen bitters

Bitters that derive their flavor from the fruit of the pommerans (a type of orange) tree. Sometimes called *Elixir Longae Vitae* (Elixir of Long Life).

Ponsigue

Venezuelan cordial flavored with the Ponsigue cherry on a base of rum.

Château Pontet-Canet

Bordeaux red wine.
District: Haut-Médoc, France.
Commune: Pauillac.

Classified a Fifth Growth *(Cinquième Cru)* in 1855, and traditionally at the head of its class, Pontet-Canet actually sells with the Seconds and Thirds. It is one of the best-known and largest of the Médoc vineyards. The wine is made principally from Cabernet Sauvignon (75%) and Merlot grapes. The huge plantation, next to the entrance of Château Mouton-Rothschild, slopes down rolling hills towards the port of Pauillac. Early in the nineteenth century, the estate was created by a M. Pontet on lands known as Canet. Many years later, in 1865, M. Pontet's heirs sold the vineyard to Hermann Cruse, head of the Bordeaux shipping form of Cruse et Fils Frères. The property is now owned by Guy Tesseron. Up to 1972 the wine was aged for nine months in the impressive underground cellars at Pauillac and then transported to the Cruse *chai* at 124 Quai des Chartrons in Bordeaux, where it was bottled.

The underground cellars at Pontet-Canet can hold 2 million bottles. Château Mouton-Rothschild, Lafite, and Beychevelle are among the few others with deep cellars, rare in the Médoc. The Pontet-Canet *chai* for first-year wines has a high roof and is uniquely airy, since the owners believe that variations in temperature during the first winter of ageing is beneficial for the wine. Guy Tesseron—owner of Château Lafon-Rochet in Saint-Éstephe and, since 1979, of Château Malescasse in Lamarque—bought Pontet-Canet from the Cruses in 1974. Alfred Tesseron, his son, is in charge at Pontet-Canet.

Characteristics. In the past sometimes very distinguished and slow to mature; some years are very common.

Vineyard area: 76 hectares (190 acres).

Average production: In previous years it was impossible to determine, since the wine was not château-bottled; but with château-bottling, as of 1972, the production is 400 *tonneaux* (40,000 cases).

Pony

Spirit measure of one fluid ounce; a small glass containing about four fluid ounces, used for brandy.

Porrón

A spouted glass drinking vessel used in Spain and derived from the leater *bota*, or Spanish wine-skin. One of the sights of Spain is the skill and good humor of the expert *porrón* drinker as he shoots a thin stream of wine through the air from spigot to mouth. This is not to be recommended to the wine-taster, however, because the wine must be gulped down to keep up with the arching stream. In Spain, the method is believed to multiply the effect of the wine.

Port (Porto)

Portuguese fortified wine.

By Portuguese law, Port is the wine of the Upper Douro (Alto Douro, Alto Corgo, and Baixo Corgo), fortified by the addition of grape brandy, and shipped from Oporto, the city at the mouth of the Douro which has given Port its name. Under British law, only the fortified wine from Portugal, and not its copies, can be designated Port.

In the United States, port-type wines are allowed the name if they carry the modification of the name of their place of origin, which generally means Californian port. Actual Port from Oporto is recognized by American laws under the name "Porto," which is the Portuguese designation of the wine, and is not referred to as "port wine," which is considered a generic category. Whatever they may be, the ports made in South Africa, Australia, California, and in North and South America are neither Port nor Porto.

What is meant when Port *tout court* is discussed, is, or ought to be, Port from Portugal, and generally red. A certain type of rock called schist is probably the factor which, in conjunction with the climate and with methods of treatment worked out carefully over a long time, gives the wine its character. The Upper Douro has only half the rainfall of Oporto, and the lowest rainfall in northern Portugal.

There are few great wine districts in the world as export-oriented as Oporto: it is still easier to get vintage Port in England than in a good Lisbon restaurant. Contrary to the past, better Ports have a larger share of the market, especially in Britain and the United States. In the United States, vintage Port is the main seller.

Originally, Port was not fortified but was harsh and raw and did not travel well. Douro wines were imported into seventeenth-century England for reasons of government policy, but were not liked (*see* Portugal). Then Port began to be treated with brandy, probably to help it travel, possibly to make it more competitive with gin. By the middle of the eighteenth century, the Port shippers were learning to make the fortified wine we know now. The brandy arrested the fermentation of the natural sugar into alcohol, retaining some of the sweetness. It is interesting to know that Port is fortified up to 20% alcohol by volume.

The history of the actual development of the Port region shows what a role the schist plays. Like the slate of the Mosel, it contributes breed, and the wine would not be the same without it. Two hundred years ago the area of the Douro was first marked out, a much smaller plot than it is today. It was gradually enlarged until it came to include the present officially delimited zone of Port wine—the region of Upper Douro, stretching about 96 kilometers (60 miles) along the river from Régua toward the Spanish frontier. This is the terrain of the schist, a soft kind of crystalline rock which easily splits and crumbles and which is set down in the midst of a tumbled, wild country otherwise almost entirely granite. These granite soils produce wine, for instance the table wines of the Lower Douro or neighboring Dão, but not Port.

Port is also a consequence of British enterprise and climate, and of the British palate too. English merchants played a leading part in the development of Port, and their wine lodges hold nearly half of the maturing wine at the mouth of the Douro today. They also own some of the biggest *quintas* (wine estates), some of which are very large. Before the Second World War, Britain bought half of all the Port produced. The postwar decline in the British market for Port, mainly due to the rise in cheaper, alternative fortified wines (but apparently also indicating a real change in taste), has by now lost the traditional Port-drinking nation its first place, a position which has gone to France. The United Kingdom is still fourth, and although cheap red Port has ceased to be a popular drink in pubs, Vintage is again in demand, and there has been some recovery in the market since the early 1960s. Inside Portugal itself there is a growing interest in Port-drinking—including the dry white aperitif-style unique to the home market, rather than the dessert wine—and figures show that sales to the Portuguese are third highest, following France and Benelux.

About 550,000 hectoliters are made in an average year (14,575,000 U.S. gallons, 12,100,000 imp.) from about 30,000 hectares (75,000 acres) of vineyards.

THE MAKING OF PORT

The vines grow on stepped or terraced levels on the sometimes very steep cliffs of the Douro. If if were not for the terracing, built up laboriously over generations, nearly the whole of the vineyard would wash into the river during the violent rains falling between December and March. The climate is hard-blazing in summer and iron-cold in winter.

The vines are planted, often by blasting, so that the roots can find their way deep enough to secure moisture during the dry summers. Before the scourge of the phylloxera the wine was made from any number of grape varieties derived from the Pinot Noir family. To a considerable extent, this is still the case. Today all vines are grafted on phylloxera-resistant American root-stocks, and while the types are not quite so various, the chief grapes still number over a dozen. It is a truly tragic sight to see the "mortórios," as they are called—the terraces left abandoned since the phylloxera, and crumbling to ruin along part of the Douro, after they were created with such enormous human effort. Often it has been considered easier to begin new and wider terraces than to try to salvage the old ones—and the tendency is to avoid the old south-facing slopes and plant on north-facing ones to escape the heat, too extreme for men to work in.

Every Port is, at least to some extent, a blend, for it is universally considered that certain plants do better in some weather conditions, some in others, and that different types contribute different qualities, no one vine being able to produce the best wine. Touriga Nacional (similar to the French Cabernet Franc), Roriz, and Barroca are very important, and four or five dark-red types are considered to give deep color. These are Sousão and the Tintas. Important among these are Tinto Cão and Touriga Francesca, the latter probably very close to the French Pinot Noir. White Ports are produced from the Verdelho, Malvasia, Rabigato, Esgana-Cão and others.

Traditionally, the bunches of grapes were cut and heaped by the picker into a tall wicker basket which he balanced at the back of his neck on a roll slung from a forehead band. In this manner the grapes were carried to the treading-troughs by a single file of men; or, if the distance was long, they were tumbled from the tipped baskets into tubs on tractors. At some *quintas*, the old custom survives. The troughs, called *lagares*, are usually made of large granite slabs. In them the fun—and the wine—begins. Barefooted men jump in, grasp one another by the arms, in a chain, to keep upright on the slippery mass, and begin to tread the grapes. While they do this, a few instruments give them a tune, and their voices rise in a chant of lament. In four-hour shifts, they trample out all the juice, which has already begun to ferment from the heat and the action. Today, however, this sight is rare, and most of the work is done by mechanized crushers. But, there is still music and dancing at the *vindima*.

At the moment when the overseer considers that fermentation has reached the proper point, and his saccharometer tells him that just the desired amount of sugar remains unconverted into alcohol, the juice, now raw wine, is let off into large containers called *toneis* or *Cubas*. Brandy is waiting, to be introduced

simultaneously in proportion of about one part to five parts of the wine. Since wine cannot ferment at over 16.5% of alcohol, fermentation stops. The sugar, which would have fermented out, remains in the wine—that is why most Ports are sweet. The degree of sweetness is determined by the point at which fermentation is checked and, of course, by the later marryings and blendings.

In the early spring of the year following the vintage, the blended wine and brandy, a young crude Port, is put into Port pipes (casks of 600 liters—159 U.S. gallons, 132 imp.) and either sent to Oporto by rail or loaded onto a tanker; the *rabelo*, a single-sailed boat like a longish scow, guided by a giant sweep, can't be used as the river is dammed. When it used to go by *rabelo*, the wine had a dizzy trip down to the mouth of the Douro; in the spring, the river was high and swift-flowing after the rains and boiled over the rapids.

It is not actually in Oporto but at Vila Nova de Gaia, just across the river, that the wine finds a home. This is where the wine lodges are located by law.

VINTAGE PORT

If it has been a great year, the maker will set the best of his wines aside to make Vintage Port. A vintage is often declared by agreement among most of the shippers, but not always. For one thing, the non-vintage Ports are blends of the wines of the various vintages; and if a shipper has a heavy demand for excellent Ports from the wood, he will be reluctant to divert his wines into a Vintage. On an average, a Vintage is declared roughly three or four times in a decade. The greatest year among Vintage Ports now obtainable is usually considered to be 1927, and it has practically disappeared. Typical of great years since are 1934, 1935, 1942, 1945, 1947, 1948, 1950, 1955, 1958, 1960, 1963, 1966, 1967, 1970, 1975, 1977, 1980, 1983, and 1985. Years still talked about over a glass of Port, but rarely a Port of the year in question, are 1878, 1896, 1908, and 1912. Of all the great vintages, 1945 and 1927 were generally considered the greatest, and of the recent years, 1963, 1970, and 1977 are the best. All of these can, in fact, still occasionally be found—even, with great difficulty, the 1878s and 1896s.

A wine selected for Vintage Port was shipped, almost invariably to England, two years, or sometimes a little longer, after its vintage, and almost immediately bottled; but since 1974, all Vintage Port must be bottled in Portugal. Vintage Port is aged in glass, the rest is aged in wood.

During the war, Vintage Ports were bottled in Portugal, but generally they were bottled at their destination and were then laid down. Port always throws a heavy deposit as it matures; when thrown in the bottle, the deposit is called the "crust." If the deposit, or crust, is disturbed, it will take some time to settle down perfectly well again, and it is advisable to stand the bottle up for at least 24 hours and to decant it before serving.

Vintage Ports usually require from ten to fifteen years to mature, and in some cases longer. Their true prime, in the great wines, lies years further on, for they improve in the bottle for a long time.

Port should be served at room temperature, which it should achieve gradually by being brought to the room several hours before use. A bottle of Vintage Port (which should be drunk after dinner) will suffer if it is open to the warm air very long, and should be kept cool for it to maintain its quality. (Some people in Vila Nova de Gaia maintain that it will keep ten days, providing the decanter is full or nearly so.) When the lighter Ports are drunk as an aperitif they may be served slightly chilled.

The small "Port glasses" do not give the wine a chance, and this is especially true of Vintage Port, which has a much bigger bouquet than any other and must have room within the glass to realize it. There is, in fact, no reason not to use the tulip-shaped clear wineglass which serves so well for most other wines, and there are good reasons for doing so. In the chimney of the tulip glass, the nose of the wine will develop fully and not be dispersed, and the color will be seen at its best through the crystal.

Vintage Port must be carefully decanted in order to bring the clear wine safely off the crust, which will have formed on the inner underside of the bottle. It is not too difficult to pour the wine without disturbing it. For some vintages, for instance 1935 as bottled by Sandeman, a granite-shotted bottle is used, because granite chips roughen the inside and anchor the deposit.

A new trend is the release of single-*quinta* Vintage Port, especially in years which are not generally declared.

CRUSTED PORT

A wine which was not necessarily that of a single vintage, but which was handled in the same way as Vintage Port and developed in the same way, was called Crusted Port—because of the sediment which forms in the bottle. A blend of a few fine wines, it was generally bottled at about four years of age and allowed to mature in bottle for some six to eight years before drinking. It had something of the quality of Vintage Port, at a lower price. It could be excellent and was more full-bodied and, in particular, had more nose than the Ports aged in wood; but it did not reach the heights of Vintage Port, simply because it was made from a slightly lesser wine. Crusted Ports have ceased to be made. The I.V.P. (the Portuguese Wine Institute) does not allow the printing of "Crusted Port" on the labels any longer.

TAWNY PORT

In the *armazens* (wine lodges) of Vila Nova de Gaia, wine from different years is blended and matured in oak. (However, this is not done with those wines selected to be bottled as Vintage Ports.) Each shipper tries to achieve a uniform wine year after year and does this by blending the vintages of various years together to reach an orchestration he considers right. This is why the Ports of this style differ from trademark to trademark but run true to type. The term often used in Vila Nova de Gaia is "bred": they breed the wines, not blend them, they say.

As the wine ages, it turns in color from purple to ruby, and then, gradually, brown-golden, the shade called tawny. Good Tawny Port takes a long time to age in the wood; years elapse before it can be bottled and sold, and therefore it is not cheap. It should be drunk soon after it has been bottled, when, if it is an old Tawny, it will have acquired a great elegance. As an after-dinner drink, it will never have the majestic power of a grand Vintage Port but can have extreme finesse. A great Vintage Port is more suited to a cold climate; a splendid, but lighter, old Tawny to a warmer climate. There is another method of producing Tawny Port which will not have the refinement of an old Tawny: Ruby and White Ports are sometimes blended together to make "Tawny." Unlike early-bottled Vintage Ports, all wood Ports are shipped ready to drink and do not improve in the bottle.

Good Tawny Port is never cheap, and if you are in one of the big *armazens* in Vila Nova de Gaia you will see why it cannot be. More than 2% of the wine evaporates each year. You glance along the three-tiered rows of casks and may see a thousand of them. Shudder then, because, from those 1,000 pipes, 15,000 bottles of good Port will vanish into the Portuguese air before you can return to the same spot a year later.

RUBY PORT

A young wood Port; rich in color, fruity, and sweet. It is a blend of the wines of several years and does not improve much in bottle. This is the wine which was used for the Port-and-lemon drink once a favorite in English pubs.

WHITE PORT

A sweet, topaz-colored fortified wine made from white grapes—it was as popular as an aperitif in France as was Ruby Port in England and is still enjoyed by some French people. In the 1950s, an effort was made to revive a flagging market by exporting a dry White Port—already doing well as an aperitif inside Portugal—made by fermenting out all the sugar before fortification. It did not, however, have much success abroad.

LATE-BOTTLED VINTAGE PORT (L.B.V.)

The wine of a good year which has been kept longer in the wood than the classic Vintage Port, usually five years or more, will by that time have deposited its crust in the cask and its ruby color will have begun to fade but not yet turn tawny. Once bottled, L.B.V. will be clear and soon ready to drink. It is a lighter wine than Vintage Port.

THE FUTURE OF PORT

The post-war drop in sales to Great Britain caused an experimental swing to dry Port. Since the amount of sweetness in any Port is determined by the residue of unfermented sugar left at whatever point fermentation is arrested, it is perfectly possible to make it less sweet. It is only necessary to let the sugar ferment out. The resultant wines are completely natural. The only question is, whether or not they are fully realized Ports; in any case, the new trend did not catch on in Britain. The Portuguese themselves enjoy the wine as an aperitif, as do the French, Oporto's biggest customer.

For the present, the long-term effort to produce the finest possible wines by rigid quality controls is being intensified. Port was the first strictly delimited wine area in the world—the original zone was marked out by the Marquês de Pombal in 1756. With a climate ideal for the ageing of wines, Vila Nova de Gaia—originally selected because the empty sheds already there have been used for centuries to store Douro wines—has always been a tightly guarded *entreposto*. Until very recently, watchmen patrolled with guns under orders to shoot on sight if anyone was found in the restricted area out of hours. The Port Wine Institute—the Instituto, as everyone refers to it in Oporto—conducts blind tastings in what must be one of the finest tasting rooms in the world. Running water effectively blots out all smells; tasters may not answer the telephone during sessions, so there can be neither disturbance nor briefing. All Ports are tasted "blind" by experts who must pass examinations and then serve as assistant tasters for four full years before acquiring a vote. Only about one-third of the approximately 250,000 pipes produced annually win the right to be called Port wine. (Most of the remainder becomes brandy for fortifying Port or table wine; some is drunk in Oporto and the district, but not as Port.)

The improvement in sales of Port has been significant over the past few decades; sales have surpassed the pre-war figure. Where the wine as wine is concerned, market considerations aside, the answer probably lies in the summary of what gives Port wine its special character, expressed by the late José Joaquim da Costa Lima, the vigorous and optimistic ex-director of the Instituto. He said Port must strive to be more "Port" than ever. It needs brandy, he said, because the greatest Port wines have the greatest body and the greatest *dis*equilibrium. Were it not for this, the wine could not assimilate 20% of brandy and would go out of balance; but a wine in *dis*equilibrium like a great Port accepts the brandy and is put *into* balance. Dry Ports have their place, but can never equal these unique and sumptuous wines.

As Raymond Postgate said, in his book *Portuguese Wines*, each shipper determines the character and quality of his Port. The history of the old companies founded in the early nineteenth centuries is fascinating and well documented. (A useful resumé can be found in *The Englishman's Wine* by Sarah Bradford.) Although some firms have now been taken over by larger interests, the distinct house style has in each case been maintained; and a sufficient number have retained their independence. The following is a list of the principal names in the Port trade:

Sandeman; Croft (including Delaforce, which was bought up not long ago); Warre; Calem; Ferreira; Offley; Taylor (including Guimaraens, a shipper of Fonseca's, taken over in 1949); Silva & Cosens (which merged with well-respected Dow's in 1877 and still ships to England under the Dow label); Cockburn & Martinez; Kopke; Barros Almeida; Real Companhia Velha; Quinta do Noval; and Ramos Pinto. The Symington family now owns Warre (founded in 1680), Silva & Cosens, Graham's, Dows, Smith-Woodhouse and Quarles Harris. The first new company to open in 50 years, and British-owned, is Churchill.

Porter

A very dark brown British beer with a bitter taste. It is brewed from malt which has dried at such a high temperature that it has become browned or charred. This is the drink to which Elizabeth Barrett Browning had such an objection.

See Beer.

Portland

A moderately productive American hybrid vine yielding both table grapes and those for wine-making. The grapes are green, the wines white.

Portugal

The wines of Portugal divide naturally into three groups: the famous fortified Port and Madeira; the table wines of Denominação de Origem from certain delimited areas, grown and produced under strict legal controls; and the ordinary wine of the country *(consumo)*.

HISTORY

It is probable that wine grapes were grown in the country before the arrival of the Romans; and the making of wine must have continued almost uninterrupted in the north, where Moorish rule did not last very long. As early as the twelfth century, Monção wine was being imported and enjoyed in England, produced evidently from the Minho area in the northwest and shipped from the port of Viana do Castelo. Edward III, in the mid-fourteenth century, encouraged the two-way trade—wool for wine—with commercial treaties and fishing rights for the Portuguese. Monção was still popular, as were the wines of Algarve and Douro, although Charneca—believed to have come from the region near Lisbon—was perhaps more in favor when, in 1580, Philip of Spain annexed Portugal and its Far Eastern possessions and interrupted the trade with England. In *Henry VI, Part II*, Shakespeare's rebels cheer each other with toasts in Sack, Charneca, and beer.

Spanish rule continued until 1640. In the interval, Dutch and British ships had been fighting the Portuguese on the high seas and interfering with Portugal's trade monopolies in India and Asia. The famous alliance between England and Portugal was restored with the marriage of Charles II and Catherine of Braganza—but not, for some time, the popularity of Portuguese wines. Compared with the French, they were rather primitive—coarse and ill-made. The fairly ineffective ban on French wines made when, in the reign of William of Orange, England and Holland went to war with France, imposed on the English a rising quantity of imports from Portugal; but very unflattering remarks were made about them. Yet the government persisted with the ban, and the Methuen Treaty of 1703 maintained the supply of cloth to Portugal and wine to Britain.

For a century at least there had been a "Factory" (factor's club) in Oporto, where English and other foreigners were establishing themselves in various trades, among them the wine trade. Port wine as we know it was not to be perfected until the second half of the eighteenth century—at much the same time as Madeira developed its character. It soon became a great success not only in Great Britain but in the newly liberated country of the United States. With the rise of these fortified wines, the table wines of Portugal lost ground and were not, outside their own country, to come to the forefront again until the wine-making industry was reorganized and new laws were passed in the 1930s and 1960s.

Portugal ranks with Italy, France, Spain, and West Germany as one of the great wine-producing countries of Western Europe. It ranks seventh in the world. The total production of table wine annually averages about 8.3 million hectoliters (219 million U.S. gallons, 182.5 million imp.). Only half of this quantity is wine with a Denomination of Origin. There is more red than white, and a great deal of rosé. Much less of the fine fortified wine is produced: 500,000 hectoliters (13,250,000 U.S. gallons, 11,000,000 imp.) of Port each year and only one-tenth that amount of Madeira. In the entire country 360,000 hectares (about 900,000 acres) are in vineyard. Three thousand of these hectares are on the island of Madeira. In Portugal itself there are more than 300,000 plots, so the average holding is just larger than 1 hectare. Well over 235,-000 people (20% of the active agricultural population) make a living from wine. Local consumption is very high—an average of 85 liters per head per year, more than nine times the U.S. rate.

The total annual exports—now about 1,600,000 hectoliters (42,300,000 U.S. gallons, 35,200,000 imp.)—of Portuguese wines decreased considerably when Portugal lost its colonies (Angola, Mozambique). Among its good customers are the United States, Great Britain, Denmark, and France. The last-named country is the largest purchaser of Port wine, but of a low quality. Strangely, Portugal exports most of its Ports and consumes very little internally.

WINE LAWS

The best Portuguese wines carry certificates of origin and are produced under controlled conditions in officially demarcated areas. Of these, Port is by far the most important. Port and Madeira apart, the wines of Denominação de Origem are Vinho Verde, Bairrada, Algarve, Dão, Colares, Dourro, Bairrada, Algarve, Bucelas, Carcavelos, and Moscatel de Setúbal. The last two are sweet wines, seldom, if ever, seen abroad. *(For* Port *and* Madeira, *see separate entries.)*

As written into the laws, controls in Portugal are now extremely thorough. And they are, now, on their way to being respected. The whole wine trade comes under one of two official bodies. The Instituto do Vinho do Porto, in Oporto, is obviously concerned with Port; the Instituto da Vinha e do Vinho, with the remaining wines. Under their aegis, supervision of wine-making is carried out at every stage from vineyard to labeling and shipping. A certificate is issued to each farmer, establishing his production and stocks of wine; another document will show that wine has reached the standard for Denomination of Origin, its quality judged by expert tasters. A later certificate of *estágio* (wine in the making) is a permit for the capsule seals of the bottles—the precise number for the exact quantity of wine contained in the vats of each grower. When the wine is taken to a warehouse, new records are made by both

PORTUGAL

SPAIN

N120

Vigo

Minho

Monção
Valença
N13

Viana do Castelo
VINHO VERDE
N103
Chaves
Bragança

Braga
TRAS-OS-MONTES

Barcelos
Guimarães
N15
Douro
Duero

Vila Real
Pinhão
Sabor

Matosinhos
Penafiel
Régua
DOURO

Vila Nova de Gaia
Porto
Douro
Lamego
N2

Pinhel
N102
MOIMENTA DA BEIRA
Viseu
Celorico
PINHEL
N620

Aveiro
Vouga
N16

Guarda
Côa

BAIRRADA
N2
Mondego
N17

to Salamanca 10 km.

ATLANTIC OCEAN

DAO
Covilhã

N

Coimbra

Zêzere
BEIRA BAIXA

Tajo

Castelo Branco

N1
Tejo

N521

Alcobaça
ALCOBAÇA
Rio de Moinhos

Peniche
Caldas da Rainha
Rib. de Sôr
Portalegre

BOMBARRAL & OBIDOS
Obidos
Tejo

Santarém
Rib. da Seda

TORRES VEDRAS
Alenquer
RIBATEJO

ARRUDA
CARTAXO

DOS VINHOS
Sorraia

COLARES
BUCELAS
Estremos
Elvas
Badajoz
Mérida

Sintra
Lisbon
N4

Estoril
Almada
SETUBAL
Redondo

CARCAVELOS
Barreiro
Evora

Setubal
ALENTEJO

Sado
Cuba
Reguengos

SPAIN

N120
Mira

Faro
N260
Guadiana

N2
N122

Sevilla

N431

ALGARVE
Ayamonte
Huelva

Portimão
Lagôa
N125

Lagos
Faro

WINE AREAS
Demarcated Regions

Non-Demarcated Regions

KILOMETERS
0 — 100

0 — 60
MILES

398

the local committee and the government organization; before shipment abroad, there will be a final inspection of quality and issue of the permit for export under the name of the wine's place of origin.

WINES WITH CERTIFICATES OF ORIGIN

Vinho Verde

The region, in northwest Portugal, lies between the rivers Minho and Douro, forming the area Entre-Douro-e-Minho, a name which the wines occasionally carry. The land presents a smiling face but a wrinkled one. In shape it is a huge bowl rising gradually away from the Atlantic. The bowl form, buttressed by higher ranges, holds the wet on-shore winds, and Minho is both warm and rainy. It is cut and furrowed by many rivers. As a result, the terrain is divided into numerous zones, six of which were declared distinct enough to become official sub-regions: Lima, Basto, Braga, Amarante, Penafiel, and Monção. Rather similar, but not the same, is Lafões, south of the Douro. There are 30,000 hectares (75,000 acres) of vines.

The greenness of the wines is in their youthfulness, not their color: pressed from grapes picked early when ripe, and drunk at about one year old, they are light, lively wines naturally rather tart, with a foamy sparkle as they are poured into the glasses and a refreshing prickle when the foam has subsided. This evanescent *pétillant* character is caused by a slight secondary fermentation in the bottle. The Minho country is delightfully green and wooded, the winters cold, the summers often wet and sometimes extremely hot. In a highly populated oasis in a largely arid country, full use must be made of the fertile land; fruit trees, vegetables, and other crops are planted and then encircled by vines which grow freely, away from scorched or waterlogged soil, climbing around trees and hedges, sometimes so high that they have to be picked from a cart. Thus sheltered from extremes of heat and moisture, the grapes produce thinner wines, with less alcohol than one would expect so far south. The whites are the most attractive: well chilled and drunk as aperitifs or with fish, they are thirst-quenching summer wines. The reds are unusual: dark in color, strong in tannin. Though interesting, they are not as easy to know as the whites. Principal Verde vines are Azal Branco, Loureiro, Trajadura, Pedernã, and Avesso for white wines; Bastardo, Alvarelhão, Azal Tinto, Espadeiro Tinto, Boaraçal, Vinhão, and Verdelho Tinto for red.

With their charm depending on freshness and youth, the Vinho Verde are among the wines which once did not travel. Under the improved conditions of shipping today, they can be enjoyed abroad—although in the United States, where the faintest sparkle is highly taxed, they arrive with their *pétillement* already stilled.

Among the best of the demarcated Vinhos Verdes are the following:

Agulha. Dry, with a faint prickle; a wine of the true character, presented in a stone bottle.

Alvarinho de Monção, Cepa Velha. Particularly good in its style; slightly stronger and with more flavor than most; a little longer-lived; in a slim brown glass bottle; from Monção.

Casa da Calçada. Very dry, not much spark, a bit tart; distinct Verde taste; from Amarante.

Casa da Seara. This white wine comes in two styles: the drier *(meio seco)*, with more savor and *pétillement*, comes in a slim green bottle; from Louro.

Casa de Vilacetinho. This has a distinct Verde flavor and comes in a slim brown bottle.

Aveleda. Made near Penafiel, this pleasant, *pétillant* white wine is now widely exported; it is perhaps the most popular of the Vinhos Verdes abroad.

Casal Mendes. A lively, agreeable wine with the true Verde character; from Aliança.

Casal Miranda. A typical wine of the region, from Louro.

Casalinho. A very light wine, not entirely dry, from Felgueiras.

Gamba. A distinct sparkle, and flavor of Verde; comes in a flask.

Gatão. A typical Vinho Verde.

Lagosta. Well-known and successful export wine, really *pétillant* and full-flavored.

Meireles. A good example of the type, refershing, with a delicate sparkle.

Mirita. Another, and slightly sweeter, wine from Aliança.

Moura Basto. A fair crackle, but less flavor than some of the others; from the Azal grape; Amarante or Basto.

Palacio da Brejoeira. The highest-priced single-*quinta* Vinho Verde.

Souto Vedro. Not for beginners; very tart and dry *pétillant* Verde; from Amarante.

Tãmega. A strong flavor, but less acid than Souto Vedro.

Tres Marias. Sweetish and not very brisk; from Vizela.

Quinta de Curvos. The special domain-bottled wine of Esposende.

Dão

The Dão wines (pronounced downg) come from the north-central area of the country, where the climate is cold and wet in winter and very hot in summer. The landscape is wild, wooded, and mountainous, and much of the vineyard is terraced—as on the Upper Douro, where Port is made. In parts of the region, granite crops to the surface and cultivation of any kind is impossible. The best vineyards lie in forest clearings in the valleys where the soil is composed of weather-crumbled granite and schist. Wine has been made around the city of Viseu for at least seven centuries; but only in this century has the Dão region been officially marked out in a triangle, the points of which are Viseu, Guarda, and Coimbra.

Several hundred times as much red wine is produced as white, and many of the white grapes suffer the fate of being thrown in with the red to make a bright ruby wine. The leading red wine grapes are the Bastardo, Alvarelhão, Tourigo, Tinta Carvalha, and Boga de Couro. A variety in wide use is called Tinta Pinheira, probably a strain of the French Pinot. The most important white varieties are the Dona Branca, Cerceal, Fernão Pires, Barcelo, and the Arinto, the last supposedly close in origin to the German Riesling. Most of the vineyard plots owned by the peasants are quite small, producing perhaps 50 hectoliters (1,325 U.S. gallons, 1,100 imp.) in an average year. In the more prosperous vineyards, Dão vines are pruned fairly low, with space between the rows; but elsewhere they grow more freely, up stakes or around bow-shaped saplings. Cultivation is very difficult, and the planting often involves blasting. The rugged nature of the countryside has enforced a continuance of primitive life. Gathered grapes are often carried to the vats in wicker or plastic baskets on women's heads, but except in rare cases the wine is no longer trodden out by the barefoot *trabalhadores*.

The chief characteristic of red Dão wines, taken as a whole, is their smoothness and suavity, a quality which shows up in chemical analysis as an unusually rich glycerin content. Yet in the coarser growths there may be a distinct *goût de terroir*. And unlike the neighboring Vinhos Verdes, these are as strong as the French Rhône wines, with an average of about 12% of alcohol. There is frequently a hint of yeast in the nose, for in this region yeasts are customarily forced. Some of the darker reds may be reminiscent of wine made from the Pinot Noir. The whites, clean on the palate, dry, and inclining to hardness, have a good distinctive taste and can be very pleasant. Though they may last up to three or four years in bottle, youth and freshness become these wines. The red wines, on the other hand, should be still good at ten years but of course do not attain the ripe age of old clarets.

The delimited area of Dão contains some sixteen communes, among which Nelas, Penalva do Castelo, Mortágua, and Oliveira do Hospital are worth remembering. But, although there may be a marked difference in the wines of these villages, they tend to be evened out by blending, though some blends naturally will be better than others. There is little domain-bottling. Both local firms and big shippers are patrolled by the Federation of Dão Wine-Growers, which has been very successful in setting up cooperatives in the region; the number of such peasant combines is increasing. Each makes its own wine but leaves the selling of it to the Union of Cooperatives and to selling concerns, which have effective regulations for checking the quality of the wine both by tasting and by chemical analysis. But their power does not, unfortunately, extend to any real control of planting in the peasant vine plots: certain grape varieties may be recommended, but there is no guarantee that the growers will accept the recommendation. Already the district produces some of the best table wines exported from Portugal; with a little extra care and control, these might be raised to the class of fine wines.

Local firms making wine inside the area are Vinícola do Vale do Dão (Viseu), Sociedade Vinícola do Dão (Viseu), J. P. Ferreira dos Santos (Povolide, Viseu), J. M. da Fonseca, União Comercial da Beira (Oliveirinha), and Vinícola de Nelas (Nelas).

Reliable shippers of Dão wine who have no cellars inside the demarcated district include Sociedade dos Vinhos do Porto Constantino, S.A.R.L.; Caves Aliancã-Vinícola de Sangalhos, S.A.R.L.; Real Companhia Vinícola do Norte de Portugal, S.A.R.L.; Caves Solar das Francesas, S.A.R.L.; Imperial Vinícola, Limitada; Sociedade dos Vinhos Vice-Rei, S.A.R.L.; Sociedade dos Vinhos Borges & Irmão; Caves do Casalinho, Limitada; João T. Barbosa, Limitada; and J. Serra & Son, Limitada.

Colares

The true wine of Colares profited by the scourge of phylloxera. When, toward the end of the last century, the vine pest was imported into Europe on American vines, it devastated practically all the plants in Continental vineyards. Behind this region, terraced on the foothills of the mountains, are inferior vineyards on firm soil (*chão rijo*). Here the phylloxera took the same course as everywhere else, and today all vines are grafted on phylloxera-resistant American root-stocks. But the Colares vineyards are planted in sand with a subsoil of clay, and, though such soil is harder to work, the phylloxera grub does not live in sand.

The result is one of the most unusual vineyards in Europe. Thirty-two kilometers (about twenty miles) from Lisbon, across the thick neck of a headland which rises to its apex in the mountain of Sintra with its woods and splashing streams, is the *chão de areia*. In this dune and seacoast vineyard, divided and sheltered by screens of reed woven together with willow and briar, the work of wine-planting is appallingly hard. A trench more than man-high must be dredged with the mattock right down to the clay, and the vine-shoot is planted deep in the hole so the root can grip in firm soil. The stem is buttressed with shoveled-back sand, but the roots themselves will not thrive in it. Because the sandy walls might cave in while the wide pit is being dug, the work is dangerous as well as back-breaking. In the years before phylloxera there was little incentive to endure this hard labor, and the area was mostly a ridge of sand and scrub pine; when the plague sliced Europe's wine production by half, it became profitable to work the arid Colares terrain. Afterward the loamy vineyards were restored with plants grafted onto American root-stocks; but the higher prices brought by the wines could not sustain prosperity in the wild region for long. Much of the true Colares is now consumed locally and only this wine is by law entitled to the Marca de Origem; some consider them the best table wines of Portugal, while others rate the red Dão more highly. As more land is given over to beach resort development, the wines grow very scarce.

These special Colares dune wines come from the Ramisco grape, a variety believed to have originally come from Bordeaux. To ease the work of planting, the vines are encouraged to propagate horizontally; as the shoot tips are buried they begin to grow new roots. The Ramisco produces a wine slow to develop, one that is sometimes left in the large casks of Angola mahogany or American redwood for as many as fourteen years. This practice is unfortunately very irregular, which accounts for the fact that a range of Colares shows great inconsistency. A successful wine should be dark red, with a big nose; but, though robust, it is unlikely to be as strong as the Rhônes, with which it might otherwise be compared. A white Colares (from the Malvasia) is made, but is of little interest.

Of all the various companies vatting in the Adega Regional de Colares, only one produces a vintage wine in the true sense. Bottles of other firms will be found to carry the designation Vindima or Coheita, followed by the year; but the wines are blends, containing only some wine of that year. It is supposed to be the informing or predominating year, but this is very dubious and vague.

Peculiar also to Portuguese wines generally, and to Colares wines in particular, is the term and usage Garrafeira, or Reserva. A bottle carrying the designation "Garrafeira" on the label is one which has been kept a certain number of years in cask and in bottle before sale. Vintage year is indicated on these wines. A Vindima will generally have been sold as soon as bottled, unless otherwise indicated.

Carcavelos

The dry and sweet wines from an old-established vineyard planted near the mouth of the Tagus on the Costa do Sol suffer, as do the wines of Bucelas, from the proximity of the vineyard to the suburbs of Lisbon and the seaside resort of Estoril, both steadily encroaching upon it. Carcavelos achieved great fame in the eighteenth century when the Marquês de Pombal, having reformed various departments in the state, turned his attention to the vineyards of his own district. In model wineries, his methods were ahead of their time, and control of quality was strict. But with the growing reputation of Carcavelos, the name was borrowed for lesser growths, and gradually the wine fell out of fashion.

In 1908, local authorities took the affair in hand, delimited the area, and introduced renewed controls. Only the Carcavelos district proper was allowed the name. Today production is confined to one vineyard only: the Quinta do Barao. Both red and white wines are made, but the whites (from the grape Galego Dourado, with some Arinto and Boal) are by far the more important. The sweet, amber wines, fortified to

about 19% of alcohol, have a nutty aroma; they improve with age up to about four or five years, when they develop in bouquet and finesse. They are used in Portugal as aperitifs and also, like Sauternes in France, as dessert wines, or to take with a biscuit at the end of the day.

Bucelas

The wine from Bucelas, from immediately north of Lisbon, used to be very well known and a century ago was widely exported, but today little of it is seen abroad. Inevitably, with the growth of the city, vineyards near Lisbon are shrinking and their output diminishing. The Bucelas wine enjoyed by the troops in the Napoleonic wars, and afterward popular in England for some time, was sweet and fortified. Yet it was sometimes known as Portuguese Hock. The addition of sugar and brandy was forbidden by law in 1911, and the wine of today is dry, with acidity, rather light and fugitive, sometimes with a certain *goût de terroir*, but very pleasant, at its best with shellfish. The name Bucelas is allowed to eleven villages, among them Charneca and Bucelas itself; the principal vineyards are in the Trancão Valley; the leading grapes are the Esgana-Cão and the Arrinto; the latter may be related to the Riesling. Annual production is around 35,000 cases.

Moscatel de Setúbal

A sweet golden dessert wine grown on untrained irregular vines which rise like black twisted arms from the earth and are seldom planted in rows. It is produced in very small quantities in a region across the bridge from Lisbon, where the vineyards rise to the slopes of the lovely Serra da Arrábida, near two villages—Palmela and Azeitão—inland from the port of Setúbal, which gives the district its name. The wine is fortified and very sweet, with a strong scent and flavor of the Muscat grapes from which it is made; fruity when young, it grows darker and softer as it improves with age. A common red wine is also grown in the area but does not bear the regional name as yet.

The Portuguese government has, for some few years now, paid serious attention to increasing its exports of wine, and the Export Promotion Board has been promoting competition among the big firms to produce new brands. At the same time, the delimitation of new areas of Denominação de Origem is being considered. The districts from which the choice is likely to be made are as follows:

Lafões. Close to the Dão region, its vines grow on granitic soil more or less in Vinho Verde country, where the grapes are trained along trellises and harvested before they are quite ripe. Leading white grapes are Arinto and Sercial; for reds, Amaral and Tourigo. Some pleasant light reds or *claretes* come from here. Among the better-known wine names are Evelita, Allegro, and Grandjo.

Águeda. The vineyards are in the north-central part

of the country, near the rivers Vouga and Águeda. Here vines grow on the edges of tilled fields, sometimes pruned low, sometimes twined high on trellises. Some wines are light, rather in the style of the Vinhos Verdes, but fuller and not so lively; others are more inclined to resemble the Dãos.

Bairrada. Situated south of Águeda and between the coast and the mountains of Caramulo and Buçaco, this is an area of big production, centered in Anadia. Some good table wines are made here—quite pleasant whites, but mostly full-bodied reds (from the Baga grape). There are rosés also, some of them carbonated for the British market; the Portuguese and the Americans take them as still wines. The good sparkling white wines of Portugal also come from this region; clean and crackly, with a flavor of their own—quite unlike that of Champagne—they are made by the *méthode champenoise.* The Bairrada district produces some 5 million cases annually.

Alcobaça. This region in central Portugal, situated near the coast, to the west of the mountain range which separates it from the Tagus basin, produces wines from a variety of soils and a variable climate. The wines, known since the twelfth century, are both red and white: the reds, bright in color, have a distinctive scent. The best of the whites come from around the beautiful walled town of Obidos.

Torres Vedras. The chief producer of ordinary wines lies to the south of Alcobaça and north of Colares. Most of the harvest is in robust, full reds, rich in tannin; among the whites, those worth noting are from Alenquer and Cadaval—strong and aromatic and flavory. Some sweet dessert wines are made also.

Ribatejo. East of Torres Vedras, the vineyards are centered around Almeirim and Cartaxo and yield earthy whites (about 8 million cases annually) and full-bodied reds (around 700,000 cases a year).

Lagoa, Portimão. From the vineyards of the Algarve (Denomination of Origin) basking in the southern sun, come more robust everyday wines, both red and dry white.

Rosados. The rosés of Portugal come under the Denominação de Origem, and can come only from specified regions, but one of them, Mateus Rosé, in its popular flagon with the pretty label, is one of the world's best-selling wines, followed fairly closely by Lancers, and prepared for the Anglo-Saxon taste with added sweetness. Lancers is a big success in the States, and Mateus throughout the world. Faisca, which has more sparkle than most and is a favorite in Portugal; and Casa de Cerca. All these wines are crackly, or *pétillant.*

SPIRITS

Portuguese brandies (known in their own country as *aguardentes*) have been distilled for centuries, ever since the time of Moorish rule. They have a character-istic flavor and smell, with little resemblance to Cognac—but most are sweetened and scented with caramel and vanilla as many brandies are.

Pot

(1) An attractive and much-needed small wine bottle in southern Burgundy, notably the Beaujolais, of about a half-liter capacity (approximately 17 ounces) into which wine is run from the cask to be served in restaurants and cafés. Larger than a half-bottle, smaller than a whole one, the *pot* Beaujolais has become very popular in France; as a result of the author's efforts it has been taken up in the United States also and is likewise to be found in England.

(2) A French wine measure, now obsolete.

Pot still

Old and simplest form of still, used in the distillation of Cognac, etc.

See Chapter Ten, p. 55.

Poteen (potheen)

Illegal Irish whiskey.

Pottle

An obsolete English wine measure equivalent to a half-gallon.

Château Pouget

Bordeaux red wine.
District: Haut-Médoc, France.
Commune: Cantenac-Margaux.

A Fourth Growth (*Quatrième Cru*) as classified in 1855, the vineyard before the Revolution belonged to the monks at Le Prieuré, a château now owned by the author. The vineyard is now worked cooperatively with Château Boyd-Cantenac, a Third Growth (*Troisième Cru*), by M. Guillemet, who owns the two estates. Both wines are made at Château Pouget and have made considerable progress since 1961.

Characteristics. Generally full and round for a Margaux.

Vineyard area: 12 hectares (30 acres).
Average production: 50 *tonneaux* (4,000 cases).

Pouilly-Fuissé (Appellation Contrôlée)

The finest dry white wine of southern Burgundy and one that has for some years received the renown which it deserves in England and the United States. Pouilly-Fuissé has made great inroads into the market once controlled by Chablis. It is made from Chardonnay grapes grown in four communes of the Mâcon slope.

See Mâconnais.

Pouilly-Fumé (Appellation Contrôlée)

Excellent dry, white, Loire Valley wine.
See Pouilly-sur-Loire.

Pouilly-Loché (Appellation Contrôlée)

A minor dry white wine from southern Burgundy's Mâcon slope bearing a considerable resemblance to the more famous and better Pouilly-Fuissé.
See Mâconnais.

Pouilly-sur-Loire (Appellation Contrôlée)

Loire Valley white wines.
District: Loire Valley, France.

At Pouilly, below Nevers in the Loire Valley, the land rises gently, almost imperceptibly, from the often sluggish river, but sufficiently for vines to grow—they are always happier on hillsides than on plains. Two types of grapevines are grown and two types of wine made, both white, both dry, but otherwise entirely different.

Pouilly-Fumé is the better wine. It comes from Sauvignon grapes and is light yet round, crisp, and eminently pleasing and refreshing. Similarities in both style and name cause it to be confused with Pouilly-Fuissé from the Mâcon district, but in truth the two are entirely different. The Loire's slightly lesser offering is marked by what is usually called a "gunflint" dryness and an indescribable flavor often compared to truffles. But although the flavor can be delightful, the wines usually lack breed.

The lesser wine is Pouilly-sur-Loire from Chasselas grapes, which are mostly grown in clay soil. The wine is almost as dry as its more impressive neighbor but has far less staying power and tends toward commonness; a respectable carafe wine in its native habitat, but of little interest elsewhere.

Some 600 hectares (1,500 acres) are devoted to Pouilly's vineyards, on which Chasselas amounts to 80 hectares (200 acres) and Pouilly Fumé predominates with 520 hectares (1300 acres). The yearly output is close to 15,000 hectoliters (397,500 U.S. gallons, 330,000 imp.) of Pouilly-Fumé, and only about one-third that much of Pouilly-sur-Loire.

Pouilly-Vinzelles (Appellation Contrôlée)

Dry white wines from the Mâcon district which, in very good years, resembles, though it never quite equals, the wine of Pouilly-Fuissé, near which it is made.
See Mâconnais.

Pourriture noble

French for "noble rot" caused by the fungus or mold *Botrytis cinerea* under favorable conditions.
See Botrytis cinerea.

Powdery mildew

Also called true mildew and oïdium—a widespread and damaging disease of the vine.
See Chapter Eight, p. 31.

Pramnian wine

Famous Greek wine of antiquity.
See Classical wines.

Precipitation

A deposit of bitartrate of potassium (cream of tartar) may appear in the form of small crystals in young wine, either red or white, which has been subjected to the cold. The remedy is to warm the wine bottles and turn them about until all the crystals have dissolved. In Europe (for cheap wines) and in California, wines are subjected to temperatures below 0°C. for three days to four weeks in order to precipitate the potassium bitartrate before bottling.

Premières Côtes de Blaye (A.O.C.)

A district of Bordeaux producing white **and red** wines. The white wines are the best of the **Blayais**.
See Blaye.

Premières Côtes de Bordeaux

White and red wines.
District: Southwest France.

The official place-name or Appellation Contrôlée accorded red and white wines from a district on the Garonne opposite Graves, Barsac, and Sauternes. Beginning just above the city of Bordeaux and running southward up the river for almost 50 kilometers (30 miles), the zone is never more than a mile or two wide. In its southern part, it encloses the good, sweet, white-wine communes of Loupiac and Sainte-Croix-du-Mont.

White wine surpasses the red in volume by six or seven times and is finer in quality. While it is not an absolute rule, red wine generally grows in the down-river half of the region nearer Bordeaux, and white wine upriver. Specified vines for red wine are the same as for Médoc: Cabernet Sauvignon and Franc, Merlot, Malbec, Petit Verdot, and Carménère—and for white wine are the same as those used in Sauternes and in Loupiac and Sainte-Croix-du-Mont: Sémillon, Sauvignon, and Muscadelle. White wines range from dry through semi-sweet to sweet. They do not quite come up to those of Loupiac and Sainte-Croix-du-Mont, but it must be remembered these compare well with all but the finest Sauternes.

The right side of the river, if a little less important in wine production, is unquestionably the prettier. The slope is steep, whereas on the Graves-Barsac-Sauternes side the land is flat. Frequent cuttings into the bluff reveal the white chalk and clay soils which contribute to the character of the Premières Côtes de Bordeaux wines. The exposure is generally south.

Cadillac, in the white-wine part of the region, houses one of Bordeaux's great wine fraternities, the Connétablie de Guyenne, devoted to the promotion of white, sweet wines. Descended from the Connétables or constables of Bordeaux who in the Middle Ages judged the wines passing on the river and decreed whether or not they could go to market, the society is housed in Cadillac's gigantic medieval château of the Dukes of Épernon.

Preuve

A small glass vessel like a test tube lowered on a chain into Cognac barrels to obtain some of the liquor, to taste or "prove" it. Called, in the local slang, a *taupette*.

Pricked wine

Sour wine with an excess of volatile acidity.

Château Prieuré-Lichine

Bordeaux red wine.
District: Haut-Médoc, France.
Commune: Cantenac-Margaux.

Originally the priory of Benedictine monks, who early spread the gospel of the vine in Bordeaux, the vineyard was bought by the author in 1951. The château is just behind the church of Cantenac, which was built partly in the seventeenth century and burned down during the Revolution, but whose façade was reconstructed in 1802. The monks were under the supervision of the Abbaye de Vertheuil, higher up in the Médoc. Over the past 35 years the property has been grouped and reconstituted on the best slightly rising ground in Cantenac, Arsac, Labarde, Soussons, and Margaux. Some of the recent vineyard acquisitions included the lands known as La Bourgade, which were owned by the La Chapelle family from the fifteenth century to 1867. In 1667 Guy de la Chapelle presented wines from his vineyard to Louis XIV. They were placed in competition with Burgundies recommended by Fagon, the king's doctor. Nevertheless, the wines from La Bourgade remained among the favorites of the Sun King for many years. Since 1952, through the exchange of two meters of land for one and the sacrifice of quantity for quality, the poorer, lower, and sandier plots have been bartered for higher, gravelly, and better-drained land. These exchanges brought into the Prieuré-Lichine vineyard portions of Châteaux Margaux (First Growth), Palmer, Ferrière, Kirwan, Giscours, d'Issan, and Boyd-Cantenac, Third Growths (*Troisièmes Crus*); and of Brane-Cantenac, Second Growth (*Second Cru*). The property was classified a Fourth Growth (*Quatrième Cru*) in the Médoc Classification of 1855, and it is the hope of the owner that by the acquisition of these excellent plots, and by extensive replanting and improvements in vinicultural methods and equipment, he is creating a wine well above its classification. A subsidiary vineyard is Château de Clairefont, a Cru Bourgeois in the village of Margaux.

Since the change in ownership, the wine has become very popular in America, and the château itself (which contains many mementos from the world's wine countries acquired by the author during the preparation of this book) was for a time, when the author founded and managed Alexis Lichine & Co. in Margaux and Bordeaux, a kind of Anglo-American club in southwest France. As visitors drive along the vineyard road to Margaux, they are welcomed to the château by elegantly lettered signs. As a vineyard situated in Cantenac, Château Prieuré-Lichine is now entitled to the place-name Margaux, a privilege accorded to Cantenac wines in 1955, because of the proximity of the famous commune of Margaux and the great similarity between wines of the two places. The vineyard was known as Château Prieuré-Cantenac until 1953, when the new name was officially recognized by the Comity of Classified Growths.

Characteristics. Soft, fast-maturing, relatively full-bodied, yet with all the delicacy for which the wines of the commune of Margaux are so justly renowned.

Vineyard area: 62 hectares (155 acres).

Average production: 260 *tonneaux* (25,000 cases).

Production of wine

It is safe to say that more than half of the total production of wine in the world is supplied by Italy, France, U.S.S.R. and Spain, although quantities vary from country to country and season to season as a result of climate changes and diseases affecting the vine—and this in spite of the modern scientific discoveries which have solved many of the old problems both of viticulture and viniculture. Wine, a natural phenomenon, is always unpredictable, so it is difficult to strike the proper figures for national productions, especially in these times of rapid expansion of vineyards in many parts of the world. The statistics below are averages for the past several years, in many cases revised upward to reflect the major plantings which will come into full production in the near future.

WORLD WINE PRODUCTION

Producing Country	Hectoliters	U.S. Gallons	Imp. Gallons
Italy	77,000,000	2,000,000,000	1,694,000,000
France	66,000,000	1,700,000,000	1,452,000,000
U.S.S.R.	34,500,000	911,500,000	759,000,000
Spain	33,400,000	882,000,000	735,000,000
Argentina	20,000,000	528,360,000	440,000,000
United States	17,900,000	472,900,000	393,800,000
West Germany	10,500,000	277,400,000	230,980,000
Chile	9,000,000	237,760,000	198,000,000

South Africa	9,000,000	237,760,000	198,000,000
Rumania	8,700,000	229,800,000	191,380,000
Portugal	8,300,000	219,270,000	182,590,000
Yugoslavia	7,400,000	195,500,000	162,790,000
Hungary	5,700,000	150,590,000	125,400,000
Greece	5,200,000	137,590,000	114,390,000
Bulgaria	4,300,000	113,600,000	94,590,000
Australia	4,000,000	105,670,000	87,990,000
Austria	3,700,000	97,750,000	81,390,000
Brazil	2,800,000	73,970,000	61,590,000
Algeria	1,800,000	47,550,000	39,600,000
Czechoslovakia	1,700,000	44,910,000	37,400,000
Switzerland	1,300,000	34,340,000	28,600,000
Cyprus	950,000	25,100,000	20,900,000
Uruguay	760,000	20,100,000	16,720,000
Tunisia	600,000	15,850,000	13,200,000
Japan	590,000	15,590,000	12,980,000
New Zealand	500,000	13,210,000	11,000,000
Canada	470,000	12,420,000	10,340,000
Morocco	400,000	10,570,000	8,800,000
Turkey	390,000	10,300,000	8,580,000
Albania	220,000	5,810,000	4,840,000
Israel	190,000	5,100,000	4,180,000
Luxembourg	170,000	4,490,000	3,740,000
Mexico	150,000	3,960,000	3,300,000
Peru	90,000	2,380,000	1,980,000
Lebanon	50,000	1,320,000	1,100,000
Madagascar	50,000	1,320,000	1,100,000
Libya	30,000	790,000	660,000
Bolivia	20,000	530,000	440,000
Malta	19,000	500,000	418,000
Egypt	15,000	395,000	330,000
Netherlands	10,000	265,000	220,000
Syria	8,000	210,000	176,000
Jordan	5,000	130,000	110,000
Iran	4,000	105,000	88,000
Belgium	2,000	53,000	44,000
Total	337,893,000	8,848,718,000	7,433,736,000

Prohibition

Prohibition of wines, spirits, and other alcoholic beverages has been tried at various times by various groups and nations. With the sole exceptions of a period in ancient China and of the successful edict prohibiting alcohol to the Moslem, no attempt has been in the slightest way a success. Probably the most spectacular one was that of the United States government between the years 1920 and 1933 with the 18th Amendment to the Constitution.

The 18th Amendment to the Constitution read, in part, that "the manufacture, sale or transportation of intoxicating liquors within, the importation thereof into or the exportation thereof from the United States and all territory subject to the jurisdiction thereof for beverages purposes is hereby prohibited." It was eventually ratified by forty-six states and it went into effect on November 16, 1920. It had been preceded slightly by the Volstead Act (October 1919), which had been passed over the veto of President Wilson and which had prohibited the manufacture, sale, or transportation of any beverage over 1% of alcohol by volume. The general result was chaos.

Throughout the nearly fourteen years of Prohibition speakeasies flourished, "bathtub gin" became the national drink (although the name was more colorful than accurate), bootleggers made fortunes, and products were sold under labels advising the purchaser that he should under no conditions add so much water to the contents or leave the solution at such and such a temperature for a certain length of time, or an illegal alcoholic beverage might result. The cellars of the country resounded with the explosions of bottles of homemade beer, and many a solid and otherwise law-abiding citizen considered it a duty to smuggle some sort of spirit home with him when he went abroad. The supreme act of illogicality was the opening in New York of a speakeasy operated by the Federal government on the theory that by breaking the laws they might better catch the lawbreakers.

The matter was resolved on December 5, 1933, when the 21st Amendment to the Constitution declared the whole dismal experiment a failure and repealed the 18th Amendment. Since that time the system of local option has prevailed whereby states are allowed to choose for themselves (Mississippi was the last dry state to vote wet in 1961), and counties, townships, and villages within states often decide for themselves. The consequences of a town's remaining dry often recall the phrase of George Bernard Shaw referring to a dry town in Ireland: "The inhabitants neither swear nor get drunk, and look as though they would very much like to do both."

Prokupac

The "national vine of Serbia," an important producer in Yugoslav wines.

Proof gallon

A gallon of spirit at proof strength; the basis for most customs and excise charges.
See Wine gallon.

Proof spirit

"I must explain for the information of Mr. Snowden that when we speak of these degrees, what we mean is degrees of proof spirit; and when we speak of degrees of proof spirit, what we mean is degrees." This was Sir Winston Churchill's clarification when asked in the House of Commons what proof spirit was. The confusion was justified. When Clark invented the hydrometer late in the eighteenth century, he knew that if he dropped his weighted float into spirituous liquor, he could determine its density and calculate the amount of alcohol by the depth to which the float sank. A certain concentration he arbitrarily named proof; anything over the mark was O.P., over proof; anything under was U.P., under proof. Thirty years later a hydrometer was developed (by Bartholomew Sikes—sometimes spelled Sykes) which has remained in use from 1816 to the present day. By Sikes's measurement, proof, in the United States, is 50% of alcohol by volume at 60°F. (16°C.). In England, proof is 49.28% of pure alcohol by weight or 52.10% by volume, at 60°F. (16°C.) Each 0.5% of alcohol over or under proof is reckoned as one degree O.P. or U.P. Alcoholic content in a spirit is usually stated as so many degrees proof: 70° proof (or, correctly, *of* proof, though it is seldom so stated) means the same as 30° under proof, in either case seventy parts of the proof being present and thirty lacking. It must always be remembered that 100% pure alcohol is not at proof, but 75.35° O.P.

Provence (Côtes de Provence) (A.O.C.)

Rosé, red, and white wines.
District: South of France.

Provence is the old province of the troubadors and the Courts of Love in southeast France, and traditionally the land of gaiety and sunshine. It faces the Mediterranean Sea, and from Marseille, which secures its western corner, it moves east through the great naval seaport of Toulon and on to Cannes and Nice. The vine grows, not far away from sun-bathing crowds, in meager soil that is rich in sand, limestone, or slate—and little else.

The first vines brought into France are said to have been planted in Provence by Phocaeans, plying their routes from Italy, Greece, and Asia Minor. Caesar is recorded to have chosen these wines to give to his

returning legions as they made their way back to Rome laden with spoils of the Gallic Wars. One village, still growing vines, is reputed to have been named by Caesar himself: this is La Gaude, which stands just above Cannes; and Caesar, tasting the local wine, is said to have smacked his lips together and proclaimed: *Gaudeamus!* (Let us rejoice!)

Officially, Provence no longer exists but is divided into the French departments of Bouches-du-Rhône, Var, Vaucluse, Basses-Alpes, and Alpes-Maritimes. To the tradition-loving French, however, and everyone else as well, it will always be Provence. With its clear, blue sea, its sun, and its Mistral—the dread wind that blows from the north always for three, six, or nine days—Provence will never change its character. And an essential part of its character is the Provençal wines.

The region produces annually almost 6 million hectoliters (159 million U.S. gallons, 132 million imp.) of wines, all of which maintain a certain Provençal character. They are wines to be taken in gulps rather than sips. While they often have a certain roughness, they manage to combine with it considerable liveliness and gaiety, and their alcoholic content is such that the drinker is apt soon to take on the same characteristics.

The greatest quantity of wine made in Provence is rosé, but white and red are produced here too—the reds sometimes resembling the wines of Italy. The rosés are among the finest of France—and the perfect accompaniment to the regional specialties, most of which are sea foods fresh from the Mediterranean. These wines should be drunk when fairly young. Some of the better red wines can be aged for a few years but rarely is any Provençal wine at its best after more than five years.

On a quantity basis, red and rosé wines outrun the whites. These white wines, rarely found outside

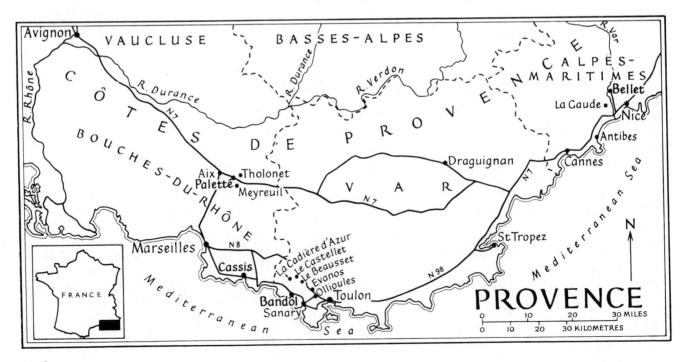

406

France, have a strength which has prompted one grower to describe them as "tarpaulin edged with lace." The rosés are fresh, clean, and heady, and the best of them (now that they are better made than once they were) have no orange cast.

PLACE-NAMES

Bandol (Appellation Contrôlée)

Some 32 kilometers (20 miles) to the east of Marseille, along the Mediterranean coast, an area of about 680 hectares (1,700 acres) has been marked off and given the right to grow wines bearing the place-name Bandol. The area falls into the communes of Bandol, Sanary, La Cadière d'Azur, Le Castellet, and several portions of the communes of Ollioules, Evenos, Saint-Cyr-sur-Mer, and Beausset, in soil that is predominantly a flinty limestone.

One of the more confusing aspects of Provence is the large number of vine-types allowed to be used for the various wines. In Bandol, there are sixteen different grapes, seven for white wines and nine for red and rosé. To complicate matters further, red and rosé are permitted to include up to 20% of their volume of grapes allowed for white wines, providing they are all vinified together. The result is then a lighter wine but not an inferior one.

Clairette and Ugni Blanc are the primary vines allowed for the whites, of which at least 50% must be Clairette; Grenache, Cinsault, Mourvèdre, and Mourvaison are the principal grapes for red and rosé. (Accessory vines are Columbeau, Frontignan, Malvoisie, Doucillon, and Sauvignon for white wines; and Carignan, Pécoui-Touar, Tibouren, Syrah, and Pinot for the others.)

For the place-name Bandol, the wine must have an alcoholic content of at least 11%. Here in the sunny south of France the limits are usually higher than the legal minimum. Wine can be sold as Bandol after an ageing period in the barrel amounting to eight months for white and rosé and a miminum of eighteen months for the red.

The name on a wine label may be either Bandol or Vin de Bandol, both meaning the same thing. Production is just about 34,000 hectoliters (897,600 U.S. gallons, 744,600 imp.) of wine annually, of which more than three-quarters is red and rosé and the remainder white. Although some export is beginning, most of the wine is sold in Provence or in the restaurants of Paris.

Bellet (Appellation Contrôlée)

Bellet, with Bandol and Cassis, is grown along the Riviera. What there is of it is usually drunk on the spot. The wine is made in a number of localities standing behind and slightly to the east of Nice, and in Nice itself.

The soil for the wines of Bellet is made up of pudding-stone, a curious formation composed of innumerable small pebbles which have been rounded and worn down by the action of wind and water. They are rich in flint, and perhaps it is this that causes the wines to be among the very best in southern France. The pudding-stone soil which falls in the district names of Les Séoules, Le Pilon, Le Grand-Bois, Golfan, Cappan, Saint-Romain-de-Bellet, La Tour, Candau, Saquier, Saint-Sauveur, Gros-Pin, Serre-Long, Crémat, Mont-Bellet, Puncia, and Lingestière has been delimited as the growing area. Here, as in the rest of Provence, a fairly large number of vines are allowed, divided into primary and accessory types.

Folle (or Fuella) and Braquet are primary for red and rosé Bellet, and the whites come from Rolle, Rousanne, Clairette, and Chardonnay. These must make up at least 60% of the grapes going into the wines. (Accessory vines are Cinsault, Carignan, Bourbolenc, and Grenache for red and rosé, and Sauvignon, Moscatelle, Sémillon, Listan, and Pignerol for whites.)

Although there are about 350 hectares (875 acres) within the Bellet appellation, only 60 hectares (150 acres) are planted. Production over the past five years has averaged around 800 hectoliters (21,000 U.S. gallons, 17,600 imp.), equally divided between the red, white, and rosé.

Cassis (Appellation Contrôlée)

One of the best Provençal rosés is that of Cassis, a little seaport town about 24 kilometers (15 miles) to the east of Marseille and one of the main supply points for the fish sent into that city. Fish and wine, in Cassis, are a perfect combination—for the sturdy dry rosé, or the full, heady white make magnificent companions for bouillabaisse, the succulent rock-fish and lobster stew which most Frenchmen rightly maintain can only be properly made in Marseille.

The vineyards growing grapes for Cassis are all in the single commune. The growers maintain that the gentle breezes from the Mediterranean are so constant that the temperature rarely changes. This, they say, explains the annual harvest, which also varies very little from year to year, amounting to some 5,000 hectoliters (132,500 U.S. gallons, 110,000 imp.). In Cassis white wines predominate over red, a situation which is not typical of Provence. The principal vines are Ugni Blanc, Sauvignon, Doucillon, Clairette, Marsanne, and Pascal Blanc for white wines; and Grenache, Carignan, Mourvèdre, Cinsault, and Barbaroux for red and rosé.

Wine must have a minimum alcoholic content of 11%. This applies equally to all Cassis wines, regardless of color.

They are often served too cold, even in Cassis—a practice that ruins their flavor—but are wonderful wines. The whites and rosés are the best. They are strong, fine, heady, and robust.

Provignage

Palette (Appellation Contrôlée)

Near the ancient city of Aix-en-Provence, the hills start rising in a steep rocky cliff leading up to the growing area of Palette. This is the only superior wine area in Provence that is not along the coastal strip. It lies in the communes of Meyreuil, Tholonet, and Aix-en-Provence. The white wines made here are among the best in Provence; the red wines are good and keep well.

Palette wines have only lately come under strict controls, and some of the practices from earlier and more haphazard days continued into the 1960s. Vine growers who had olive trees in their vineyards were ordered to uproot them. The new laws, however, permit Palette to use more vine-types than are usually found even in Provence, the total coming to twenty-five or more. For white wines, the growers are allowed to use Clairette, which must comprise at least 55% of the final mixture, and in addition any combination of the following: Grenache Blanc, White Muscats (most types), Terret-Bourret (limited to less than 20% of the total), Picpoule, Pascal, Araignan, Colombaud, and Ugni Blanc or Ugni Rosé. Red and rosé wines must be made from more than 50% of a combination of Grenache, Mourvèdre, Cinsault, and Plant d'Arles, though Mourvèdre is now particularly favored.

The Palette vineyard used to be far greater than its present 20 hectares (100 acres), but the expansion of nearby Aix has pushed the vines back. Presently there are only two properties dividing the land, the more substantial by far being the Château de Simone. Total annual production amounts to around 500 hectoliters (13,250 U.S. gallons, 11,000 imp.). Very enjoyable when drunk in the old city of Aix-en-Provence, Palette loses most of its sprightly charm and gaiety when shipped.

Côtes de Provence (Appellation Contrôlée)

In 1977 the I.N.A.O. and the French Ministry of Agriculture upgraded Côtes de Provence from V.D.Q.S. (Vins Délimités de Qualité Supérieure) to A.O.C. The vineyards of the Côtes de Provence are split into five different areas extending from Marseille inland to the city of Draguignan and on to the River Var just above Nice. Grenache, Cinsault, Carignan, Mourvèdre, Tibouren, Clairette, Ugni Blanc, and Rolle are the principal grape varieties. The resulting wines are not always of the caliber of the four Provençal wines already discussed, but they are often extraordinarily pleasant. Some of the better villages are Les Arcs, Lorgues, Pierrefeu, Cuers, and Puget-Ville. The total annual production has increased in the last decade and now averages around 700,000 hectoliters (185 million U.S. gallons, 154 million imp.).

Côtes de Provence wines are becoming known on the markets of the world, thanks to a group of owners who have formed the Syndicat de Défense des Vins des Côtes de Provence (Association for the Protection of the Wines of the Côtes de Provence). One of the many ideas the group is promoting is the use of special bottles designed to catch the eye of the Riviera tourist; now most of the companies connected with the organization are beginning to sell their wines in shapely bottles that mark a departure from tradition. This group of growers owes much of its energy to its late president, the Comte de Rohan-Chabot, the former owner of Château de Saint-Martin, now run by his daughter Madame de Casquer.

Provignage

Method of propagating vines.
See Chapter Eight, p. 31.

Prunelle

A green French liqueur made from the kernels of sloes. It is produced by the firm of Garnier.

Prunellia

A green liqueur made from the kernels of sloes by the French firm of Cusenier.

Pruning

The centuries-old viticultural art of cutting back and trimming vines to effect their life span, quality, or production. Certainly the yield from the vine is one of the most obvious factors in which pruning plays an important part: a vine's production can be multiplied by two to five times depending on the method of trimming. Since high yield does not hurt the quality of the grapes from most of the vines in the world, these plants are generally cut back for maximum production. But for the dozen or so varieties whose quality suffers with quantity, the proper pruning style is crucial for maintaining the high standards of the wine. In the great vineyards of France and Germany, the method of pruning is specified by law.

Puglia

See Apulia; Italy.

Puisseguin-Saint-Émilion (Appellation Contrôlée)

A commune of Saint-Émilion producing full-bodied red wines.
See Saint-Émilion.

Puligny-Montrachet and Puligny-Montrachet-Côte de Beaune (Appellations Contrôlées)

Burgundy red and white wines.
District: Côte de Beaune, France.

Puligny is near the southern end of the Côte de Beaune, in the unofficial sub-district locally called the Côte de Meursault—the slope that takes its name from the nearby commune of Meursault and lays claim to the greatest white wines of the world. The claim is not without justification. The wines which come from the vineyards of Puligny-Montrachet and Chassagne-Montrachet are certainly among the very greatest of the dry white wines of France, and that from one vineyard (the fabulous Montrachet) is considered by many experts as undeniably the world's greatest dry white wine.

In Puligny, everyone makes wine. The mayor himself—a powerful, heavily-set man—is a leading grower and he maintains a cordian but deep-rooted rivalry with his genial counterpart in Chassagne. The village priest is another respected grower, and between Masses is apt to be out in the vineyard, supervising work or just inspecting his vines. At harvest time, the entire village may be found in the vineyards on the slope behind the town. This slope has a slightly different appearance from the rest of the Côte de Beaune. In Puligny and Chassagne, the rolling hills are bare of trees; areas not planted in vine are covered not in the tangled underbrush found elsewhere along the slopes but in close-cropped, sickly-looking grass punctuated with rock and slabs of calcareous outcropping. The low-lying vines, however, share none of this unprepossessing appearance.

The vineyard of Montrachet is so outstanding that it is a case completely apart from the other wines of Burgundy and is treated separately under its own appellation. In addition to Montrachet, Puligny shares another Great Growth with Chassagne—Bâtard-Montrachet—and has other incomparable vineyards that it owns outright. Chevalier-Montrachet and Bienvenues-Bâtard-Montrachet are two of the greatest, and all these vineyards are ranked by the French authorities as Great Growths (Grands Crus). In theory, this means that the authorities consider the wines among the thirty-one most magnificent of the Côte d'Or of Burgundy, and in practice, that the wines—when they meet the high minimum requirements—will be labeled simply with the name of the vineyard instead of (as is the case otherwise) with commune name and vineyard name or simply with commune name. (See all Great Growths as individually entered.)

Although the Great Growths are generally accepted as the finest, some of the others are also superb and in the hands of a talented wine-maker may turn out equal to the topmost. One of them is Pucelles, just north of Bienvenues-Bâtard-Montrachet; and above Pucelles is Le Cailleret, adjoining the Chevalier. Cailleret was once called Les Demoiselles, but its position next to the Chevalier was responsible for the change in name—the jokes were too frequent and too bad. On the opposite side of town—bordering the Meursault—is the excellent Les Combettes divided by the road that forms the town line from Charmes in Meursault. Higher up the slope, toward the tiny hamlet of Blagny

—which spills over from the upper corner of Meursault to the upper corner of Puligny—is Les Chalumeaux, another exceptional vineyard.

All of Puligny's white wines share approximately the same characteristics. They are eminently dry, not so soft or so luxurious as Meursaults, and are apt to have a full, rich, flowery, or sometimes fruity, bouquet. The green-gold color takes on different highlights and hues, and the wine has a strength and a masculinity rare in white wines. It leaves the mouth fresh and full of varying sensations and the better the wine is, the more lingering will be the aftertaste.

In addition to white wines, a small amount of red is made—but not generally from grapes grown in the highest ranking vineyards—and it is seldom the equal of the reds made in neighboring Chassagne, although it often has good body and a distinctive and expressive bouquet.

Throughout the commune there are about 234 hectares (580 acres) devoted to vines. Wines that stem from 140 hectares (345 acres) within this larger area have the right to add the designation Côte de Beaune to the commune name and are often of superior quality. The best wines, of course, are those which carry simply vineyard name (Great Growths) or vineyard name and commune name (First Growths or Premiers Crus). The amount of wine produced in Puligny each year is about 7,000 hectoliters (185,000 U.S. gallons, 154,000 imp.), only a few hundred hectoliters of it red.

GREAT GROWTHS (Grands Crus)

Vineyard	Hectares	Acres
Montrachet (in part)	4	9.9
Bâtard-Montrachet (in part)	6	14.9
Chevalier-Montrachet	7.1	17.7
Bienvenues-Bâtard-Montrachet	2.3	5.8

FIRST GROWTHS (Premiers Crus)

Vineyard	Hectares	Acres
Les Combettes	6.7	16.6
Les Pucelles	6.8	16.8
Les Chalumeaux	7	17.3
Le Cailleret	5.4	13.4
Les Folatières	3.4	8.5
Clovaillon	5.5	13.7
Le Champ-Canet	4.6	11.4
Le Refert	13.2	32.6
Sous le Puits	6.9	17.1
Garenne	.4	0.9
Hameau de Blagny	4	9.9

Pulque

A Mexican brew known to the ancient Aztecs, obtained from the milky juice of the cactus variously called the agave, century plant, American aloe, maguery, and mezcal. Pulque is a fermented beverage of

Punch

4% to 6% alcohol, usually drunk when it is freshly made, and very popular among the Mexicans. Millions of gallons are sold annually on country farms and at *pulquerias* in the cities.

Punch

(1) A hot, strong winter drink made with spirits, fruit and spices and traditionally served in a bowl.

(2) Norwegian Punch: a sweetened after-dinner liqueur based on Batavia arrack and running about 26% to 27% alcohol by volume. It is made by the Norwegian state-controlled wine and spirit company, A/S Vinmonopolet.

Puncheon

A large cask of varying capacity, formerly 264 liters (70 U.S. gallons, 58 imp.), but now usually about 378 liters (100 U.S. gallons, 83 imp.). Used in the West Indies for rum.

Punsch (punch), Swedish

Swedish liquor on a base of rum. It dates from the eighteenth century, when Swedish merchants began trading with the East Indies, importing, among other things, the rice and sugar-cane spirit which is the foundation. Originally the punch was served hot, but since the nineteenth century it has generally been taken cold.

Punt (kick)

Indentation in bottle bottoms, originally to reinforce them and to hold the sediment, thus preventing it from spreading throughout the bottle.

Pupitre

French term for a hinged rack for holding sparkling wines neck down while they are prepared for the *dégorgement* or ejection of the deposit accumulated during the second fermentation.
See Champagne.

Puttonyos

Hungarian buckets for measuring quantity of specially selected grapes used in Tokay wine. Thus the collar label on every bottle of Tokaji Aszú will state: 3 Puttonos, 4 Puttonos, etc.—the export agency simplifies the spelling by removing the *y*.
See Tokay.

Pyralis

Meal-moth which feeds on the vine.
See Chapter Eight, p. 31.

Q

Quart

A quarter of a gallon, whether U.S. or imperial. An American quart equals 94.6 centiliters, a British quart 1.136 liters. (In France the term *quart* is used in restaurants and cafés for a small carafe, reputedly a quarter of a liter; also in Champagne for a small bottle used in bars for Champagne cocktails or for one glass.) The standard American quart equals 32 U.S. fluid ounces; the British quart, 40 British fluid ounces.

Quarter-cask

Originally a cask of one-fourth the capacity of a pipe *(q.v.)*. In practice, quarter-casks vary from 113 to 160 liters (30 to 42 U.S. gallons, 25 to 35 imp.).

Quarts de Chaume (Appellation Contrôlée)

Section of Coteaux du Layon, in Anjou.
See Anjou.

Quetsch

Blue plum spirit made in Alsace and in Lorraine.
See Alsace: Spirits.

Quincy (Appellation Contrôlée)

Loire Valley white wines.
District: Loire Valley, France.

Minor dry white-wine district classed with those of the Loire, although Quincy is drained by the River Cher some 48 kilometers (30 miles) away. The vineyards are in the communes of Quincy and Brinay. They are planted in a chalky soil, and the wines resemble those of neighboring Reuilly, of Sancerre and Pouilly-sur-Loire, and, like the output of these towns, come only from Sauvignon grapes. About 115 hectares (287.5 acres) are devoted to vines; output averages an annual 4,000 hectoliters (106,000 U.S. gallons, 88,000 imp.).

Quinquina

A French aperitif with a base of fortified wine and quinine added to impart a slightly bitter taste.

Quinta

The word means, literally, "agricultural estate" in Portuguese, and, by extension, has come to mean vineyard.

R

Château Rabaud-Promis

Bordeaux white wine.
District: Sauternes, France.
Commune: Bommes.

Originally the single estate of Rabaud, one of the oldest Sauternes properties; known to have been an enormously productive vineyard of more than 80 hectares (200 acres) by 1660. The present château, owned by M. Lanneluc, the mayor of Bommes, was built by Victor Louis. The holding, having come into the hands of M. de Sigalas in 1864, was sold in part to M. Promis in 1903. In the thirties, the vineyards of Rabaud-Promis and Sigalas-Rabaud were reunited, only to divide again in 1952. Since then, Sigalas-Rabaud has become the superior wine and is considered one of the best Sauternes after Yquem. When they were constituted as the single vineyard of Rabaud in 1855 the wine was classified a First Growth *(Premier Cru)* of Sauternes, and this classification extends to both Rabaud-Promis and Sigalas-Rabaud.

Characteristics. Not one of the greatest. Sweet, and a certain lack of breed.

Vineyard area: 30 hectares (75 acres).
Average production: 65 *tonneaux* (7,000 cases).

Rabigato

A grape variety used in White Ports.

Rablay-sur-Layon

Wine commune with the right to an Appellation Contrôlée in the Coteaux du Layon district of Anjou.
See Anjou; Coteaux du Layon.

Race

French word for distinction and breeding in a wine.

Racking

The draining or pumping of wine off its lees from the barrel in which it has been maturing into a new, clean one. This process is repeated several times during the ageing of wine.
See Chapter Nine, p. 40.

Rainwater

Originally a trademark, now a type denoting a light dry Madeira.

Ramisco

A grape variety which makes the dune wines of Colares in Portugal.

Rancio

This term is applied in Spain to the nutty flavor in Sherry. In California it applies to the taste brought about by cooking in sweet dessert wines. In somewhat the same sense it is used to describe a pungent taste in Madeiras, Marsalas, Málagas, and others. In France the adjective is applied particularly to the characteristic taste of the sweet dessert wines of Banyuls when they are well-aged, and also to the wine of Château-Chalon.

Raspail

French herb liqueur, yellow in color, said to be made from a formula devised by François Vincent Raspail in 1847.

Ratafia

It is claimed that the name was applied to any liqueur drunk at the ratification of a treaty or agreement. It now applies to sweetened aperitifs made from wines, such as Ratafia de Bourgogne and Ratafia de Champagne.

Rauchbier

In Germany, literally "smoke beer"—a beer made there from smoked malt.

Rauenthal

The different Rauenthalers such as Baiken and others taken together are probably the greatest of the German Rheingaus and certainly, with the exception of Schloss Johannisberg, command the highest prices. They are full-bodied fruity, spicy and very pronounced in acidity, with great potential for aging.
See Rheingau.

Château Rausan-Ségla

Bordeaux red wine.
District: Haut-Médoc, France.
Commune: Margaux.

Adjoining Rauzan-Gassies, with which it originally formed a single vineyard, Rausan-Ségla lies across the Médoc vineyard road from Château Margaux and Château Palmer on the south side of the village of

Margaux. It is classed a Second Growth (Second Cru) in the Classification of 1855.

Acquired by Pierre des Mesures de Rausan in 1661, it remained in the Rausan family for two hundred years. Thomas Jefferson wrote: ". . .Rozan-Margau, which is made by Madame de Rozan . . . this is what I import for myself. . ." In addition to the vineyard carrying their name, the Rausans—or Rozans—for a time leased Château Margaux and Château Latour, also making those wines. In 1866, Rausan-Ségla was sold to the maternal grandfather of the Cruse family, Bordeaux wine merchants, who sold it again in 1956 to M. de Mesnon, who in 1962 resold it to the British Holt group, the owners of Eschenauer, the Bordeaux wine shippers. Holt is now owned by the Lonhro group of London.

Characteristics. The wines of Rausan-Ségla had gone down in quality considerably. Since 1983 there has been an upturn in quality. In 1986 a modern new vat room and chais were constructed.

Due to the large scale replantings the potential great quality of this vineyard should not be expected before the year 2000.

Vineyard area: 23 hectares (57.5acres).

Average production: 130 *tonneaux* (12,000 cases).

Château Rauzan-Gassies

Bordeaux red wine.
District: Haut-Médoc, France.
Commune: Margaux.

Once a single vineyard with Rausan-Ségla, now adjoining it on the south of Margaux, Rauzan-Gassies was already well known in 1530. Of the many proprietors over more than four centuries, none could have been more eccentric than a Chevalier de Rauzan who, when he could not get the price he expected for his wines, put them aboard ship and sailed to London. Proclaiming that he was going to sell his wines himself from the deck of the boat, he awaited customers. Still not getting his price, he announced that he would pour one barrel into the Thames each day until he got a better offer—or had no more wine. The story goes that by the third day all London was crowding to watch this unheard-of performance; and the fame of it spread so that he was soon offered a high price for every barrel left aboard.

The vineyard is now owned by a M. Quié, owner also of Château Croizet-Bages. Rauzan-Gassies is a Second Growth (Second Cru) in the Classification of 1855. Today critics feel that the character of the wine is not equal to the quality of the vineyard as it is at present being cultivated. Hence prices paid on the Bordeaux market make Rauzan-Gassies one of the cheapest Second Growths (Seconds Crus), and its reputation has fallen accordingly.

Characteristics. In the fifties and early sixties, many Bordeaux critics remarked that Rauzan-Gassies had slipped considerably in quality. Some vintages from the 1940s and 1950s were marked by an excess of volatile acidity. Since 1973 there has been progress in the vinification, as it has been overseen by Émile Peynaud, Bordeaux's dean of oenology.

Vineyard area: 29 hectares (72.5 acres).

Average production: 120 *tonneaux* (11,000 cases).

Ravat

French grape hybridizer J. F. Ravat was a civil engineer from the Loire region who bred vines between 1929 and 1935.

Ravat Blanc

A Chardonnay cross, Ravat Blanc (Ravat 6) is an early-ripening, disease-sensitive, and difficult French-American cultivar. Because of its problems, along with its being a small producer, it is not widely grown. In recent years some Vignoles, another Ravat hybrid, has been accidentally labeled Ravat or Ravat Blanc in the eastern U.S.

Ravello

An especially beautiful little village not far from Naples and Amalfi in southern Italy which produces a moderate quantity of white and rosé wine. The wines, however, are not as memorable as the town itself.

Château de Rayne-Vigneau

Bordeaux white wine.
District: Sauternes, France.
Commune: Bommes.

Classified a First Growth (Premier Cru) of Sauternes in 1855. The vines grow in a large vineyard sloping away from the dark turreted château. The wine is not the only treasure produced by the soil. For some reason which experts have never solved, in this patch of earth alone in the whole region, precious and semiprecious stones appear. Sapphires, opals, jasper, onyx, and topaz have been found and are collected in the museums of France and many other countries. The main owners are Mestrezat-Preller, who produce cheap sparkling wines; the other owner is a shipping firm now partly owned by Pepsico.

Characteristics. This potentially great vineyard is capable of improvement.

Vineyard area: 67 hectares (167.5 acres).

Average production:150 *tonneaux* (11,000 cases).

Rebate brandy

South African trade term for brandy made under fairly rigid conditions imposed by the government and aged at least three years in wood. The measure was

Recioto di Soave (D.O.C.)

initiated to encourage distillers to increase brandy quality, the government giving a tax rebate on any brandy which contains at least 25% of "rebate." Lesser and harsher spirits, on the other hand, are very heavily taxed.

Recioto di Soave (D.O.C.)

A sometimes sweeter version of the famous Italian white wine.
See Veneto.

Recioto della Valpolicella (D.O.C.)

A fuller, interesting sort of the fine wine of Veneto (*q.v.*).

Récolte

French for wine harvest. It may mean either the harvesting or the crop, but generally *récolte* is used to refer to the crop, and *vendange* to the harvest.

Rectification (rectifying) of spirits

In distillation (the object of which is to separate or purify substances, making use of the differences in their volatility), the components of a mixture are vaporized in order of their boiling points, so that one part can be drawn off from another. If the substance is already purified or of constant composition (i.e., all components with equal boiling points), then the operation is rectification. A rectified spirit is one which has undergone purification by distillation at a licensed rectifier's premises.

The definition of rectification given by J. H. Perry in *The Engineers' Handbook* (3rd ed.) is as follows:

Rectification is a distillation carried out in such a way that the vapour rising from a still comes in contact with a condensed portion of vapour previously evolved from the same still. A transfer of material and an interchange of heat result from this contact, thereby securing a greater enrichment of the vapour in the more volatile components than could be secured with a single distillation operation using the same amount of heat. The condensed vapours, returned to accomplish this object, are termed *reflux*.

The generally used devices, in which vapours from a still on their way to a condenser can flow counter-currently to a portion of the condensate returned as reflux, are called *rectifying columns* or *towers*.
See Chapter Ten, p. 55; Gin.

Regional

Any wine whose name comes from a district or region and not from a specific vineyard. Such wines are usually inexpensive blends. Bordeaux, Provence, California, and Rioja are examples of regional names.

Rehoboam

An outsized bottle formerly used for Champagne. It held the equivalent of six normal bottles.

Reims

This ancient French cathedral city is also one of the principal centers of the Champagne trade—the other is Épernay.
See Champagne.

Remuage

Remuage (moving around) is a term used in the process of making Champagne. Bottles placed in specially built racks are turned or shaken a little every day for about four months before they are shipped, so that the sediment may move down toward the cork. Finally, sediment and cork will be removed in one skillful movement in the process of *dégorgement*.
See Champagne.

Repeal

To Americans, Repeal refers to December 5, 1933, when the 21st Amendment to the Constitution of the United States was passed, repealing the 18th (Prohibition) Amendment and allowing alcoholic beverages once again to be sold legally in the United States.
See United States; Prohibition.

Reputed pint

British half-bottle; there are twelve to the imperial gallon (1.2009 U.S.).

Reputed quart

British regular bottle for wines and spirits; about 75 centiliters; three-quarters of a U.S. quart; one-sixth of an imperial gallon.

Reserva

Indication on Rioja (Spain) wine labels that the wine has been aged; sometimes indicates quality, sometimes enfeeblement.
See Rioja.

Retsina

Greek wine, ordinary white and rosé, which has been treated with pine resin. This comprises a substantial part of the wine consumed in Greece. In the southern and central parts of the country almost everyone—especially among the peasants—prefers his wine with this piny, resinous taste.
See Greece; Other Greek Wines.

414

Reuilly (Appellation Contrôlée)

White, rosé, and red wines.
District: Loire Valley, France.

Small, little-known Loire wine district lying along the Arnon, a tributary of the River Cher, producing a small quantity of dry white wine from Sauvignon grapes. Some 90 hectares (225 acres) of Pinot Noir for red and rosé wines are also grown, but their output does not receive an Appellation Contrôlée. About 40 hectares (100 acres) of Sauvignon produce about 1,000 hectoliters (26,500 U.S. gallons, 22,000 imp.) of Reuilly annually, the wine resembling that of Sancerre and Pouilly-sur-Loire—although it is usually more acid and lighter.

Réunion Island

Rum-making island in the Indian Ocean, formerly a French colony, now one of the French *départements*.
See Rum, French.

Rhein

German spelling of Rhine.
See Palatinate; Rheingau; Rheinhessen; Mittelrhein.

Rheingau

German State of Hesse
Vineyard area: approx. 3,000 hectares (7,300 acres)
94% white wines; 6% red wines

The Rheingau wines are, if a choice must be made, the best in Germany when they are at their finest. As such they become, with their peers of the Mosel and the great white Burgundies, the finest white wines in the world for their variety in taste characteristics.

In an average or poor year, the lower Rheingau wines from around Rüdesheim and Hochheim in the upper part of the district tend to be better than the wines from the greater areas, which may be too light; but in the big years, the famous and exquisite late-harvested Riesling wines from the strip of the Rhine front between Eltville and Winkel will be incomparable. Wonderful as the loveliest Mosels may be, they will never quite touch the character and breed of the greatest Rheingaus. A few white Burgundies have the character and strength to challenge the dry Rheingaus, and it can be argued that in one sense such a wine as Château d'Yquem in Sauternes is their counterpart in sweet wines, but, owing to the milder climate in the Bordeaux district, the productivity is infinitely greater in quantity. The long-lived, late-gathered Rheingau great growths are true kings in the royalty of wines. Rich and with exquisite breed after a sunny summer and a hazy autumn, blessed with the river mist, they will last for thirty or forty years.

Location: About 30 kilometers (18 miles) west of Frankfurt, near the confluence of the Main and Rhine Rivers at Hochheim, the southern sloping vineyards begin. They stretch along the Rhine from Wiesbaden, where the river turns westward, all the way to the Hessian State border at Lorchhausen. Along this stretch, the Rhine widens up to half a mile so that it resembles a huge lake. The warmth of the sun reflected from its broad surface helps maintain a constant temperature in the vineyards throughout the day and night.

The slopes facing due south are guarded from the north wind by the heavily-treed ridge of the Taunus Hills, and further protected because the river bends enough to cut off most of the wind from east or west. The vineyards are broken and steep, rolling in green waves parallel to the river. "If the plow can go there, the vine should not," is a Mosel proverb, and in a rough way it is true for the Rheingau too. The steepness, the southern exposure, and the sheltered slopes make possible the production of the late-gathered wines, the grapes sometimes being left on the vines until the noble rot of the *Botrytis* has set in, sometimes as late as December.

Nearly all of the villages of the Rheingau enjoy an international reputation, from Hochheim—from which the term "Hock" is derived—to Rüdesheim—as renowned for its Drosselgasse lined with countless wine pubs as for its fine wine. The region lies within one district, Bereich Johannisberg, and is subdivided into ten collective vineyard sites (Grosslagen or GL)

Grape Varieties: Riesling (80%); Müller-Thurgau (6%); Spätburgunder (Pinot Noir) (5%); Ehrenfelser (3%); Kerner (2%).

The Rheingauers are extremely proud of the fact that the percentage of Riesling grown here is higher than in any other German wine-growing region. Riesling is synonymous with high quality and it is only on the basis of producing the finest-quality wines that a region this small has earned its high rank in the world of wine.

The Riesling is said to have found its origins in the Rheingau. The oldest reference to this grape variety dates back to March 13, 1435, in an invoice for the delivery of Riesling grapes from the Klaus Kleinfisch winery to the fortress in Rüsselsheim, at the gateway to the Rheingau. As estate proprietors—primarily the church and aristocracy—focused their attention on improved quality, the cultivation of Riesling in the Rheingau became mandatory. In 1672, for example, the St. Clara Monastery of Mainz ordered its tenant growers in the Rheingau to replace red varieties with higher quality Riesling vines. In 1803, the Benedictine priest and cellar-master of the Abbey of Fulda wrote: "The Riesling is now the only variety which may be planted in the whole of the Rheingau." The reputation of the Riesling flourished at this time, and with it, the excellent reputation of Rheingau wines at home and abroad. The Grape Breeding Station in Geisenheim especially deserves credit for its efforts on behalf of the Riesling in the last century. Through selection and propagation of the best strains Geisenheim's scientists have developed Riesling clones which are more resistant to frost, pests and disease. The Rheingau is the first wine-growing region in the world to exclusively cultivate virus-resistant Riesling vines. This enables Rheingau growers to practice ecologically-sound methods of viticulture. The increased longevity of these vines enhances the quality of their wines.

The other great wine grape of the region, the Spätburgunder (Pinot Noir), was brought to the Rheingau centuries ago from its home in Burgundy. In the 16th century, Lorch had more Spätburgunder vines than any other village in the Rheingau. Gradually, the center of red wine production shifted to the hillsides of neighboring Assmannshausen, where the vines were less susceptible to early frosts. Today, Assmannshausen is still well-known for its fine Spätburgunder wines, but thanks to the high quality Geisenheim clones, Spätburgunder is once again planted in Lorch and throughout the entire region.

PRODUCTION AND SALES

Although vines were cultivated here in Roman times, it was under the influence of the Archbishops of Mainz, from the 10th to the 14th centuries, that viticulture really flourished in the Rheingau. They had the forests along the Rhine cleared and replaced with vineyards. The peasants who cleared the woodlands and planted vines won their freedom. The Rheingau became known as the land of farmers with civil rights, or "he who breathes the air of the Rheingau is a free man." Both the church and the aristocracy played a vital role in the development of the wine industry in the Rheingau. Their absolute commitment to quality, together with their interest in developing new and better methods of viticulture, cellar technology and marketing, made the Rheingau famous and exemplary for many other wine-growing regions. Today's 1,940 growers demonstrate the same spirit of enterprise. The concept of private property has a long tradition here and helps explain why the Rheingauers are very independent and individualistic.

Annual production in the Rheingau, based on a ten-year average (1976–1985), is about 213,000 hectoliters. Nearly 87% of the region's vineyards are owned by the 64% of all growers who produce their own wine. The average size of a grower-producer's holdings is about two hectares (5 acres), yet there are almost 100 enterprises with holdings of five hectares (12 acres) or more.

The cooperative movement has never been as strong here as in other regions. However, the first cooperatives in the Rheingau were founded before the turn of the century and by 1904, there were 27 cooperatives with nearly 1,200 members. Their combined holdings accounted for 19% of the region's vineyards

and this figure is still accurate, although the number of cooperatives has decreased to nine local and one regional cooperative.

Most of the small and middle-sized family enterprises sell directly to their customers from charming little tasting rooms at the estate or from tasting stands operated by each village and at wine festivals. Often, growers open a small wine pub on their premises for a few weeks or months of the year; a few even have restaurants which feature their wines. Many of their customers live nearby and enjoy the personal contact with the grower—in fact, a good number of these relationships are generations old.

On the international market, the famous large estates are predominant. Here, highly qualified wine brokers have been instrumental in maintaining market stability and fostering the reputation of these estates through their networks of contacts at home and abroad. Although a broker's guild existed as long ago as the 14th century, the profession really began to flourish toward the end of the 19th century, with the introduction of auctions throughout the Rheingau. The selection of wine available had become more diverse as the names of individual sites appeared on labels—in contrast to the traditional practice of calling wines by their village names—and buying and selling wine was more efficiently handled by an agent. The estates, recognizing the brokers' expertise in wine and market conditions, gave them the exclusive right to sell their wines at auction. Even today this tradition is observed at trade fairs and auctions in the Rheingau, two of which deserve special mention.

In 1971, the State Wine Domain (Verwaltung der Staatsweingüter/Eltville) initiated a trade fair at Kloster Eberbach to provide buyers with a more efficient and economical means of purchasing its wines. It was so successful that the "Eberbacher Messe" has been repeated every April since then and has been enlarged to include the wines of four additional prestigious estates: Landgräfl. Hessisches Weingut, Johannisberg; Freiherrl. Langwerth von Simmern'sche Rentamt, Eltville; Schloss Groenesteyn, Kiedrich-Rüdesheim; and Domänenweingut Schloss Schönborn, Hattenheim. Prices set at the fair remain valid for one year, thereby ensuring price stability, and buyers are granted a generous discount calculated on a sliding scale according to quantities purchased.

Kloster Eberbach is also the site of the State Wine Domain's two annual auctions (spring/autumn) during which specialties (best barrels), rarities and selections from the Schatzkammer (cellar for especially valuable wines) come under the hammer. Auctions are no longer the forum they once were for trade sales. This is partly due to the increasing number of private (non-trade) buyers, but also because the size of an average lot today is considerably larger than the traditional 600-liter Halbstück (800 bottles or roughly 66 cases). By the way, the 1964 auction was the last at which an actual Halbstück was sold. Since then, all wines have been sold by the bottle. Nevertheless, auctions at

Eberbach are a tradition in the Rheingau, dating back to 1806. Today, the world record prices achieved at these events not only enhance the prestige of the State Wine Domain (and with it, the Rheingau)—they draw international attention to the fact that Germany's finest white wines are among the most valuable in the world, with tremendous longevity (if stored properly). In November, 1986, Dr. Hans Ambrosi, a great personality in the German wine industry and director of the State Wine Domain, welcomed over 900 guests from all over the world to the autumn auction at which a world record price was set for a single bottle of white wine: DM35,000 for an 1893*er* Neroberger Riesling Trockenbeerenauslese Cabinet. (Neroberg is the hillside site overlooking Wiesbaden.) This broke the existing record of DM22,000 set just a year earlier at an auction of the Verband Deutscher Prädikatsweingüter (Association of German Prädikat Wine Estates) of which the State Wine Domain is a member. The wine: an 1893*er* Steinberger Trockenbeerenauslese—from the State Wine Domain.

For many of the small and middle-sized estates, an important source of contacts and additional income is provided by the dozens of village wine festivals in the summer and fall, culminating in a 9-day regional fair held in Wiesbaden in mid-August, the Rheingauer Weinwoche (Rheingau Wine Week). One hundred producers from every part of the region have tasting stands where one can sample an average of fourteen different wines per stand, ranging from everyday Qualitätswein to rare specialties, such as Beeren- and Trockenbeerenauslese, Eiswein and older vintages. The wines are sold in small (0.1 liter) tasting glasses, making it physically and financially possible to enjoy the broad spectrum of Rheingau wines. In addition, each village has an outdoor community "Probierstand," or tasting stand, which features the wines of a different estate every week and is operated by the grower and his family or staff. A well-marked hiking trail (Rheingauer Riesling-Pfad) and auto route (Rheingauer Riesling-Route) make it easy to explore the beauty of the region while enjoying its wines.

THE IMPORTANT RHEINGAU TOWNS AND VINEYARDS

When looking at a flat map of the Rheingau, one misses an important dimension—elevation—which, together with soil structure and micro-climates, directly influences the character of Rheingau wines. From Hochheim and along the upper Rheingau (Wiesbaden to Hattenheim) the vineyards closest to the river are planted on rather gentle slopes which become steeper in the middle Rheingau and which are dramatically steep at Rüdesheim and around the river's bend (Assmannshausen, Lorch). At the same time, there are a number of important villages and sites located closer to the forested summit of the Taunus Hills, not always visible from the river, with very steep slopes (Rauenthal, Kiedrich, Steinberg, Hallgarten, Schloss Vollrads and Johannisberg). The steep sites yield wines often described as lean, sleek, racy—with a pronounced acidity—and piquant in character, whereas the wines grown on the gentler hillsides are fuller in body and fruitiness, with less acidity. In dry years, the sites near the moisture-retaining forests show at their best. Soil types also change from east to west. In the eastern and central part of the region, gravel, sand, loam, clay and marl form the lower strata, often covered with a layer of loess. The extreme western part of the region consists of sandstone, quartzite and above all, clayish slate. Vines on these sites do well even in cool, wet years—although in very hot years, the wines are usually not as elegant and are more alcoholic. Many experts feel the best towns and villages, in terms of quality in the great years, run from east to west and are: *first*, best vineyards of Rauenthal; *second*, best vineyards of Erbach-Hattenheim-Hallgarten; *third*, best vineyards of Johannisberg, with Schloss Vollrads and Winkler Hasensprung, in Winkel; *fourth*, best vineyards of Rüdesheim. The latter rise in medium years to the top of the list in relation to the other vineyards. In dry years, the vineyards nearest the moisture-retaining forests will make the best wine.

Geological and climatic factors "set the stage" for quality wine production, but the ultimate breed and distinction of a wine are created at the hands of skillful producers. Thanks to the highly respected research and educational institutions in Geisenheim and Eltville, Rheingau growers are well trained in contemporary methods of vineyard care and cellar technology. This, too, enhances the quality of Rheingau wines. The producers mentioned below are named under the village where the estate is located because many large, traditional estates have vineyard holdings in several villages. Interestingly, nearly all the large noble estates and the State Wine Domain have holdings in Hattenheim, in the heart of the region. For lack of space, many fine producers have had to be omitted.

Assmannshausen

Assmannshausen is often said to produce the best red wine in Germany. The red-wine vine growing in the characteristic bluish-red shale is the Spätburgunder, so called because it was brought from Burgundy by the Cistercian monks in the twelfth century. The wine it makes is mild and velvety, with a slight undertaste of almonds—something like a light Burgundy.

GL: Steil.
Best Site: Höllenberg.
Other Sites: Frankenthal, Hinterkirch.
Producers: Eulberg, Hufnagel, Schön.

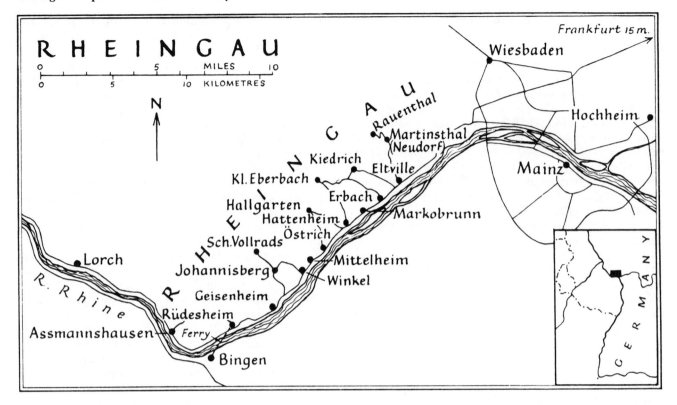

Eltville

The name of the village on the Rhine bank is of Roman origin: *alta villa*. Until the end of the fifteenth century it was the summer seat of the Prince-Electors of Mainz, and ruins and palaces of the period still stand. Johannes Gutenberg, the inventor of movable-type printing, lived and worked here in the late 15th century as well. Today, Eltville is an important center for the wine and sparkling wine (Sekt) trade in the Rheingau. The wines are of consistently good quality, somewhat softer than those of neighboring Erbach and Kiedrich.

GL: Heiligenstock, Steinmächer.

Best Sites: Sonnenberg, Langenstück, Taubenberg.

Producers: C. Belz Erben, Oek. Rat J. Fischer Erben, Freiherrl. Langwerth von Simmern, Egon Mauer, Richter-Boltendahl, and the world-renowned Verwaltung der Staatsweingüter (State Wine Domain).

Erbach

Generally full-bodied wines of masculine character, of which the best and the most famous is Markobrunn.

Markobrunn. Sometimes written Marcobrunn, sometimes Markobrunn, the wine is one of the greatest and best-known Rheingaus. It does not reach the superb elegance of a top Rauenthaler, but it has more body and is characterized by a spicy, lively quality. It was preferred to all other Rheingaus by Thomas Jefferson on his Rhine journey in 1788. The name derives from an ancient well (*Brunnen* means "spring" or "well") which may still be seen, carved out of red sandstone and bearing the name Markobrunnen, the spring of Saint Mark. The fact that this well and the famous vineyard lie on the boundary line of Erbach and Hattenheim has given rise to a story legendary along the Rhine. For generations the two villages contested the right to claim the site as theirs. Finally, ancient records were unearthed which proved that the well was on the Erbach side of the communal boundary. Great was the rejoicing among the Erbachers. But on the fourth or fifth morning they fell silent and became very glum. During the night some wit from Hattenheim had gone to the well and scrawled in huge letters:

So ist es recht und
So soll es sein,
Nach Erbach das Wasser,
Nach Hattenheim den Wein.
(All is right, all is fine,
Now Erbach has the water,
But Hattenheim has the wine.)

GL: Deutelsberg. *Other good sites:* Hohenrain, Siegelsberg, Rheinhell. *Producers:* Jakob Jung, Freiherr zu Knyphausen, Oetinger, Prinz Friedrich von Preussen (Schloss Reinhartshausen) and Tillmanns Erben.

Geisenheim

The *Weinbauort*, lying between Rüdesheim and Johannisberg, is not as well known as its wines deserve. The Schönborn castle stands in the town and has a considerable historical importance of its own.

Inside it, in 1648, an ancestor of the present count drafted the treaty which ended the Thirty Years' War.

Geisenheim is perhaps best known today for the State Research Institute for Viticulture, Horticulture, Beverage Technology and Landscaping. It consists of 14 institutes, including the famous Institute for Vine Breeding and Vine Grafting directed by Dr. Helmut Becker, recognized worldwide as an expert in his field and a leading proponent of his native Rheingau. It was here, in 1882, that Dr. Hermann Müller from Thurgau/Switzerland created the grape variety bearing his name by crossing Riesling and Silvaner. The institute is the most important supplier of resistant rootstock clones in Germany. In addition to its research facilities, nearly 30 acres of experimental vineyards and a modern winery equipped for microvinification, it is the only university-level school of oenology in Germany, with a faculty of 30 professors. Germany would not produce the quality or quantity of wine it does, were it not for the efforts of institutions like the one here. The institute's wine estate produces high-quality wines which are sold both in Germany and abroad.

Geisenheim's vineyards yield good quality even in average years. The wines have a distinctive earthy taste.

GL: Burgweg, Erntebringer. *Best sites:* Kläuserweg, Mäuerchen, Kilzberg, Klaus. *Producers:* Erbslöh'sches Weingut, Graf von Francken-Sierstorpff, Schumann-Nägler, Freiherr von Zwierlein.

Hallgarten

Many of the vineyards are extremely steep and yield particularly ripe wines, full-bodied and rich. Quality can be superb in drier years.

GL: Mehrhölzchen. *Best site:* Schönhell. Other sites: Hendelberg, Jungfer, Würzgarten. *Producers:* Karl Franz Engelmann, Fürst Löwenstein, Adam Nass. In addition, there are two important cooperatives: Winzergenossenschaft Hallgarten and Vereinigte Weingutsbesitzer Hallgarten.

Hattenheim

This very pretty village, with its half-timbered houses, has always been closely associated with the former Cistercian monastery Kloster Eberbach. It is said that in the 13th century, the earliest vines planted on the famed Steinberg were those which the clever monks had purchased from Hattenheimer growers. Hattenheim was also the home of the oldest guild of "Weinschröter" (literally barrel-rollers; the stevedores of the Middle Ages) in the Rheingau.

The wines show great finesse and delicacy. The biggest of them are typically great Rheingaus.

GL: Deutelsberg. *Best site:* Steinberg (see below).
Other sites: Mannberg, Nussbrunnen, Wisselbrunnen, Engelmannsberg. *Producers:* Hans Barth, Hans Lang, "Georg Müller Stiftung," Balthasar Ress, Domänenweingut Schloss Schönborn.

Steinberg and Kloster Eberbach

Located a few hills behind Hattenheim and adjacent to Kloster Eberbach is the Steinberg site, which, like Marcobrunn, is one of the greatest names in German wine. Cistercian monks from the Eberbach monastery planted the hillside vineyard over 700 years ago. Like Clos de Vougeot in Burgundy, it is a single parcel, enclosed by a huge stone wall. Today, the 31-hectare (77 acres) site is owned and managed exclusively by the State Wine Domain (*see also the entry* Germany). The wines are fermented at the Domain's modern facilities in Eltville, but aged in the ancient cellars of Kloster Eberbach. At their best, Steinbergers are full-bodied, with a powerful, steely acidity and a great depth of flavor. Their potential for aging is excellent (and repeatedly confirmed by the world record prices they achieve at auctions).

The monastery, nearly a thousand years old, was first established by Augustinian monks; with the changeover to the Cistercians, the first of this order in Germany, the real success began. By 1135 they were planting vines in the tract which is today the Steinberg. With their motto "Ora et Labora" (Pray and Work), and with their knowledge of wine from Burgundy, it is not surprising that they cut away the forest, put it in vines, and prospered. By the thirteenth century, their wine fleets were sailing the Rhine to Cologne, and in its greatest day Kloster Eberbach held 200 hectares (500 acres) in the Rheingau and Rheinhessen. Today, the Romanesque basilica built between 1150 and 1185 is used for magnificent concerts of classical music (the acoustics are outstanding) and other ceremonial events, such as the very beautiful Thanksgiving (Erntedankfest) service held on the first Sunday in December. The candle-lit basilica fills with the deep sounds of a brass chorus and the voices of the well over 1,000 people who attend an ecumenical service at which some 4,000 bottles of Rheingau wine are donated to a charity—the Rheingau growers' expression of thanks for the new vintage. Today, Kloster Eberbach is the cultural wine center of the Rheingau: headquarters of the German Wine Academy and Rheingau Wine Society; organizer of wine seminars and tastings; and site of important trade fairs and auctions. A museum devoted to the history of the Cistercians and wine, facilities for advanced scientific seminars and tastings, as well as guest rooms are presently under construction as part of a major renovation program begun in 1986.

The German Prädikat designation Kabinett is said to have originated in the Rheingau, possibly at Kloster Eberbach. Among the earliest recorded mentions of the word "Cabinet" in reference to a small cellar where wines of superior quality were stored separately is found in a carpenter's invoice of 1730, for work carried out at Kloster Eberbach in the "Cabernedt Keller." Monastery documents show that Eberbach's Cabinet Keller started with a select number of wines from the 1712 vintage and that between 1732 and

1782, a total of 112 casks were sold from the Cabinet Keller. The pattern had been set. Following the take-over of the monastery by the Dukes of Nassau in 1803, an edict was issued, directing the stocking of the Eberbach Cabinet-Cellar with the most exquisite wine produced by the estate, to supply the court. Today, the term Kabinett refers to a German Prädikat wine, a designation reserved for the highest quality.

Hochheim

At the far eastern edge of the Rheingau, not far from confluence of the Main with the Rhine, is the pretty town of Hochheim. Its vineyards are planted on flatter ground or gentle slopes. Thanks to an excellent micro-climate it is not unusual for wines to ripen one to two weeks earlier here than elsewhere in the Rheingau—an advantage in cool or wet years. Hochheimers are among the greatest of the Rheingau wines, with a full fruitiness and fragrance and some say a distinct earthy flavor. The name Hock, from Hochheim, has become the English name for all Rheingau and often all Rhine wines.

GL: Daubhaus. *Best sites:* Domdechaney and Kirchenstück.

Other good sites: Stein, Hölle. *Producers:* Aschrott, Domdechant Werner. Weingut Königin Viktoriaberg is the exclusive owner of the site named after Queen Victoria, who is said to have favored Hochheim wines over all others.

Johannisberg

It is said that one winter's day, from his palace in Ingelheim, Charlemagne looked across the Rhine, and upon seeing how the snow had melted on the slopes of what is now Johannisberg, ordered the first vines to be planted there. Six thousand liters of wine were harvested from the Johannisberg vineyards in 817, as documented by Charlemagne's son, Louis the Pious.

Schloss Johannisberg. Originally called the Mons Episcopi, the hill was given to the Benedictine monks by the Archbishop of Mainz at the end of the eleventh century. The Benedictines built a monastery dedicated to John the Baptist, and the hill has ever since been called Johannisberg.

After the secularization decreed by Napoleon in 1803, the vineyard was in turn the property of the Prince of Orange, of Napoleon, and the Emperor of Austria—who gave it to Metternich in 1816 for services rendered at the Congress of Vienna, and with the Metternich family it remains today.

After the Congress of Vienna the Austrian Emperor in 1816 recompensed his Chancellor for his diplomatic services. His descendent, Prince Paul von Metternich is still the owner in name, although the estate is now part of a group controlled by Rudolph Oetker, a food tycoon, and this also includes the neighboring von Mumm estate.

Schloss Johannisberg is one of the great traditional wine estates of the world, not only for its Riesling wines of great character and distinction, but also for its role in the history of German wine. A number of "firsts" are associated with it. Under the ownership of the Abbey of Fulda, the planting of Riesling was made mandatory. By 1720, Schloss Johannisberg, with some 38,500 Riesling vines, was the first Rheingau vineyard planted exclusively with the noble grape. In 1775, the courier who had been sent to procure the Abbot's permission to begin the wine harvest was delayed. By the time he had returned to Schloss Johannisberg, the grapes were rotting on the vine. Nevertheless, they were harvested and, to everyone's astonishment, yielded an unusually fine wine. Thus, Schloss Johannisberg is credited with having been the first Rheingau estate to have recognized the value of a Spätlese (literally, late harvest). That same year, in spite of the expense, the estate began to bottle some of its wines.

Schloss Johannisberg is well worth visiting. Its cellars, which date back to 1100 and 1716–21, are among the most impressive in the world and its treasure chamber, the Bibliotheca subterranea, has rarities dating from 1748. The view from the terrace is magnificent. The 50th degree of latitude runs through the vineyards facing the Rhine—as far north as Labrador or northern Mongolia—yet it is blessed by a mild climate, for not only grapes but also figs, almonds and lemons ripen in the palace gardens.

GL: Erntebringer. *Other good sites:* Hölle, Hansenberg. *Producers:* G.H. von Mumm, Landgräfl. Hessisches Weingut, Weingut Johannishof.

Kiedrich

The vineyards lie high up at the foot of the Taunus Mountains behind Erbach.

Vines have been grown here since 1131. The town is regarded as the "Gothic Gem of the Rheingau" because of its lovely Church of St. Valentine, with its elaborately-carved pews with beautiful grape motifs. Its organ is the oldest in use in Germany. The wines are highly regarded for their great style, yet they are not as well known outside of Germany as they deserve to be.

GL: Heiligenstock. *Best sites:* Gräfenberg, Sandgrube, Wasseros, Klosterberg. *Producers:* Schloss Groenesteyn and Weingut Dr. Weil.

Lorch

The vineyards are planted on extremely steep slaty slopes which require a tremendous amount of hand labor. The wines are especially lively and "spritzig"— the slate brings out the fruity acidity of the Riesling well. Best vintages are often average or poor in other parts of the Rheingau.

GL: Burgweg. *Best sites:* Bodenthal-Steinberg, Krone, Pfaffenwies, Kapellenberg and parts of

Schlossberg. *Producers:* Weingut Friedrich Altenkirch, Graf von Kanitz, Fritz Perabo.

Östrich

A huge crane from 1652 marks the site of Oestrich, one of the oldest settlements in the Rheingau. It has the largest uninterrupted expanse of vineyards in the region. The wines are full and fruity, yet not of the same class as those of neighboring Hattenheim. One exception is Schloss Reichartshausen (located midway between the two villages), a small site which yields wines with a distinctive character.

GL: Gottesthal, Mehrhölzchen. *Best sites:* Doosberg, Lenchen. *Producers:* a number of growers named Eser, Wegeler Erben (Deinhard). In neighboring Mittelheim: Hupfeld Erben, Reitz'sches Weingut Christian Reis.

Rauenthal

With Johannisberg, Steinberg, and the best parts of Hattenheim and Erbach, these wines are, in good years, some of the greatest.

The village is set back in the Taunus Hills. The vineyards are on steep, terraced slopes. In warm years, Rauenthalers are doubtlessly among the finest of Germany. They are tremendously fruity, spicy and very pronounced in acidity, with great potential for aging. Generally throughout the Rheingau the best lands are held by the big wine estates; they have the best viticultural methods and go to the most pains, and they make the finest wines. It is a special characteristic of Rauenthal that even the small growers produce excellent wines. The largest holder is the State Domain (28 hectares—70 acres), followed by Frh. Langwerth von Simmern with 3 hectares (7 acres). On an average, the Rauenthal vineyards produce about one-third less wine per acre than is grown in other districts—but they gain in quality what they lose in quantity. The greatest section has always been the Rauenthalerberg, a slope under cultivation for seven hundred years; but wines may not now be sold under that name, although Rothenberg and Gehrn are well situated on this hill.

GL: Steinmächer. *Best site:* Baiken. *Other good sites:* Gehrn, Rothenberg, Wülfen, Langenstück.

Rüdesheim

The situation of the Rüdesheimer vines on the steep slopes rising from the Rhine makes the wines quite dependable in all but the worst years and inclined to be below the general high level in the best years. The slopes have maximum sun exposure, and the benefit of reflected rays from the river; the grapes are therefore riper than elsewhere in cool summers. On the other hand, the sun burns the slopes, which drain very quickly, and in a hot summer the wines will be lacking in fragrance and roundness. While Rüdesheim is a well-known Rhine wine town in Germany, it is less

famous here than abroad, where it shares with Nierstein in the Rheinhessen the honor of being the most celebrated of all. It is a great haunt of tourists cruising along the Rhine. What is perhaps the world's best collection of drinking vessels is housed in a half-ruined castle called the Brömserburg, the oldest castle of the whole Rhine area, dating in parts from the ninth, tenth, and twelfth centuries. You may see implements used in Rheingau viniculture at the time of Christ, tiny clay cups of the Stone Age and all their descendants, as the typical high-stemmed German drinking glasses evolve before your eyes. The evolution of the German bottle is also shown, reaching its present form about 1790.

GL: Burgweg. *Best sites:* Berg Rottland, Berg Schlossberg, Berg Roseneck. *Other good sites:* Bischofsberg and Magdalenenkreuz. *Producers:* G. Breuer, Dr. Heinrich Nägler.

Walluf

The oldest mention of wine-growing in the Rheingau is found in a deed of gift of 779 in which two vineyards of Walluf were donated to Kloster Lorsch. Formerly two villages (Upper and lower Walluf), today Walluf makes very typical racy Rheingau Riesling wines as well as good Spätburgunder wines. Not well-known out of the region.

GL: Steinmächer. *Best sites:* Walkenberg, Oberberg, Berg-Bildstock. *Producers:* J.B. Becker, Arent Erben.

Winkel

A small village whose excellent reputation for fine wines is largely due to the prestigious estate Schloss Vollrads, located behind the town. The Gray House (Graues Haus) is said to be the oldest stone house in Germany. It was probably built about 850 and served as the final residence of the great scholar and Archbishop of Mainz Rhabanus Maurus. It is also the ancestral home of the Greiffenclaus (of Schloss Vollrads), who own it to this day and have had it carefully restored and developed into a comprehensive show place for all Rheingau wines. Since 1981, it has been a gourmet wine restaurant, committed to demonstrating how well Rheingau Riesling and Spätburgunder wines complement food. In the early 19th century, the Brentano home in Winkel was a favorite meeting place of the Rhine Romanticists, including Goethe, who was particularly inspired by the fabulous 1811 vintage.

Schloss Vollrads

Like its neighbors Schloss Johannisberg and Steinberg, this site is one of the greatest names in German wine. The Greiffenclaus are the family with the longest tradition of winegrowing—not only in the Rheingau, but probably in the world. The earliest documented sales of Vollrads wines date back to 1211. About 1300, the grounds of the present estate's site were cleared and the family moved from the Gray House to the moated castle tower upon its completion in 1330. The beautiful baroque palace, built toward the end of the 17th century, is the home of the current proprietor, Erwein Count Matuschka-Greiffenclau. Like his late father, Count Matuschka is a highly respected leader in the German wine industry. He is totally committed to achieving the highest quality of wine possible and to demonstrating how well Rheingau Riesling wines harmonize with food. To this end, he regularly conducts "Lucullan Wine Tastings" in the elegant reception rooms of his palace, in addition to many culinary wine tastings around the world. His promotional efforts have done much to enhance the image of German wine in overseas markets.

The wines of Schloss Vollrads are distinguished by their fruity, piquant and elegant style. They improve with bottle age. The most outstanding vintages are produced in warm, sunny years. Wines of poor years are sold in bulk—they are not permitted to bear the Schloss Vollrads name. Count Matuschka is also the proprietor of the Fürst Löwenstein estate in Hallgarten.

GL: Honigberg, Erntebringer. *Best site:* Hasensprung. *Other good sites:* Bienengarten, Dachsberg, Klaus and Jesuitengarten. *Producers:* Baron von Brentano, Geromont, Jacob Hamm, Mehrlein, Schönleber-Blümlein.

The Association of Charta Wine Estates

In the mid-1980's a group of quality-oriented Rheingau growers formed this association to promote classical Rheingau-style Riesling wines. Charta wines are bottled in the traditional, tall slim brown bottle of the Rheingau, embossed with the Charta insignia (Romanesque double arch). Only specially selected (through blind tasting by a panel of experts) Rheingau Riesling wines which have met the Association's strict criteria are permitted to be bottled in the distinctive Charta bottle. The wines must also be stored in the producer's cellars until at least October 1st of the year following the harvest.

UNION OF RHEINGAU WINE-GROWERS
(one morgen = .25 hectare, or .6 acre)

Holding	Headquarters	Morgen
Verwaltung der Staatsweingüter	Eltville	760
Freiherrl. Langwerth v.Simmern'sches Rentamt	Eltville	150
Rentmeister Egon Mauer	Eltville	15
Weingut Oek.Rat Jak.Fischer Erben	Eltville	31
Weingut C. Belz Erben	Eltville	30
Weingut Richter-Boltendahl	Eltville	51
Weingut Freiherr zu Knyphausen	Erbach	80
Weingut Dr. Weil	Kiedrich	80
Robert v.Oetinger'sches Weingut	Erbach	30
Weingut Eberhard v.Oetinger	Erbach	33

UNION OF RHEINGAU WINE-GROWERS
(one morgen = .25 hectare, or .6 acre)

Holding	Headquarters	Morgen
Gräfl.von Schönborn'sches Rentamt	Hattenheim	200
Gemeinde-Weingut "Georg Müller Stiftung"	Hattenheim	40
Weingut K.F. Engelmann	Hallgarten	16
Weingut Adam Nass	Hallgarten	16
Gutsverwaltung Geh.Rat Wegeler Erben	Östrich	400
Reitz'sches Weingut	Östrich	12
Graf Matuschka-Greiffenclau'sche-Schloss Vollrods	Winkel	188
Weingut Fürstl. Loewenstein, Schloss Vollrads	Hallgarten	80
Weingut Jakob Hamm	Winkel	18
A.v. Brentano'sche Gutsverwaltung	Winkel	35
Geromont'sche Gutsverwaltung	Winkel	16
Fürst v.Metternich	Johannisberg	160
Landgräfl.Hess. Weingut	Johannisberg	160
Weingut Freiherr v.Zwierlein	Geisenheim	98
Erbslöh'sches Weingut	Geisenheim	40
Freiherr v.Ritter zu Groenesteyn	Kiedrich	120
Gräfl.v.Kanitz'sche Weingut	Lorch	60
Domdechant Werner'sches Weingut	Hochheim	52
Geh.Rat Aschrott'sche Gutsverwaltung	Hochheim	80
Weingut Dr. H. Nägler	Rüdesheim	23
Weingut Georg Brewer	Rüdesheim	32
August Eser	Mittelheim	35
H. Hupfeld Erben	Mittelheim	42
Adm. Schloss Reinhartshausen	Erbach	270
Weingut H. Tillmann's Erben	Erbach	40
		3,487

Rheinhessen

German State of Rheinland-Pfalz
Vineyard area: 25,000 hectares (62,000 acres)
94% white wines, 6% red wines
Location: Germany's largest wine-growing region lies in a valley of rolling hills, bordered on the west by the Nahe River and to the east by the Rhine. The 'four corners' of the region and important towns for the wine trade are Mainz, Worms, Bingen and Alzey. An ancient Roman road runs diagonally through the region, from Mainz to Alzey, a reminder that vines have been cultivated here for more than 2,000 years. The region is divided into three districts (Bereiche): Bereich Wonnegau, includes the southern part of the region and the city of Worms; Bereich Bingen covers the western portion of the region, as well as the vineyard area stretching from Bingen to Mainz. The third district takes its name from its well-known village, Nierstein, and includes a succession of charming little towns adjacent to the Rhine known collectively as the Rhine Front or Rhine Terrace.

The German province of Rheinhessen, which gives its name to the wines (all produced inside the province are Rheinhessens and none grown outside may claim the name), is the Hesse which provided the Hanoverian kings of England with their Hessian troops of mercenaries, and lies in the middle of the

German wine country where the Rhine bends sharply at Mainz, and washes it on two sides.

Principal Grape Varieties: Müller-Thurgau (24%); Silvaner (13%); Scheurebe, a crossing of Silvaner × Riesling named after the grape seeder Georg Scheu (10%); Bacchus, a crossing of (Silvaner × Riesling) × Müller-Thurgau (8%); Kerner, a crossing of Trollinger × Riesling (8%); Faberrebe, a crossing of Weissburgunder, Pinot Blanc and Müller-Thurgau (7%) and Riesling (6%).

Wine: Perhaps a kind description of Rheinhessen's wines comes from Carl Zuckmayer, a writer from the village of Nackenheim (near Nierstein), who called it the "wine of laughter . . . charming and appealing." Rheinhessen provides soft wines without pronounced character, the most obvious and easy to know of all German growths. Owing probably to their intense bouquet and their straightforwardness and sweetness, the best of them have always been popular abroad. They are not wines to lay down, for they improve very little in bottle and tend to fade after eight or ten years. With the exception of the tiny quantity of specially selected Auslese and Trockenbeerenauslese, a Rheinhessen over ten years of age will seldom be interesting. Rheinhessen wines are mild, medium to full-bodied and agreeable. Riesling wines from around Bingen and along the Rhine Terrace are quite elegant and show style.

There is a saying in Rheinhessen: "If you are not a wine grower, then you're not a Rheinhessen man." For two thousand years wine has been produced in the region and today nearly all towns have vineyards. Most are tiny. Except around Nierstein, Oppenheim, and Bingen, the choicest areas, there are few large holdings, and 50% of Rheinhessen growers have no more than a hectare (2.5-acre) plot each. They live partly by wine and partly by other farm pursuits—which is a fundamental strength of the Rheinhessen economy, enabling the region to offset bad vintage years. Yet, of Rheinhessen's 11,000 growers, nearly two thirds grow grapes and produce wine, about 70% of which is sold in bulk to large wineries for bottling. The cooperative movement is not as strong in Rheinhessen as elsewhere, yet there are numerous local and one central cooperative which have contributed to market stability and generally improved conditions for growers. For the region as a whole, in terms of better methods of growing and making wine, the efforts of the viticultural experimental station in Oppenheim have been exemplary.

Under the auspices of the region's wine promotion board a new concept has been devised to stimulate a renaissance of the Silvaner grape, formerly the most widely-planted variety in Rheinhessen. Under the slogan "Rheinhessen Silvaner—the dry classic," some 100 producers have agreed to adhere to specific criteria with regard to production and sales, as well as marketing their dry Silvaner in a uniform package. Specifically, the wine must be 100% Silvaner with a maximum of 4 grams/liter residual sugar and a minimum of 5 grams/liter total acidity, and show good, above-average extract content. As a Qualitätswein it must pass the official quality control tests as prescribed by law and also pass a second test administered by the German Agricultural Society. The wines are also tested to ensure they reflect typical Silvaner character. Vintage dating is mandatory but the wine cannot be brought onto the market before March 1st of the year after the vintage. The packaging is striking—the traditional brown bottle used for Rhine wines is labeled with a simple black and yellow label highlighting Rheinhessen Silvaner Trocken (dry).

Soil, vine, weather, and man always combine to create the qualities of a wine. The climate in Rheinhessen is mild and dry, with a good deal of sunshine, and comparative freedom from the killing spring and autumn frosts which terrorize the neighboring growers, especially on the Mosel. The rule of nature being what it is, the wines lack the character they would develop in a more precarious climate where the vines would have to fight for their lives; instead, they reflect the comparative softness of Rheinhessen weather.

In addition to the three classical German white wine varieties, there are a number of new crossings planted in Rheinhessen, particularly in the hilly interior of the region. At the regional grape breeding station in Alzey quite a number of new crossings have been developed, particularly in the 'Twenties under the direction of Dr. Georg Scheu (pronounced 'shoy'). The purpose of developing new crossings is primarily to find a variety which would offer the elegance and taste of Riesling, yet which would ripen earlier. Other varieties are developed for blending purposes; they add body or bouquet or a distinctive flavor to an otherwise neutral wine or soften an unpleasantly harsh acidity in poor years.

Red wine is increasingly popular throughout Germany and Rheinhessen has long been known for its "red wine island" around Ingelheim. Spätburgunder (Pinot Noir) and Portugieser are the principal varieties, the former yielding some very elegant (but light) wines; the latter produces pleasant everyday wine. The German "philosophy" about red winemaking differs considerably from that of its more southern neighbors: fruitiness is a virtue and winemakers generally do not blend vintages to achieve a consistency in taste, year for year, but rather allow the character of each vintage to show its influence on the fruit. German red wines are low in tannic acidity and, compared with red wines produced elsewhere, they are relatively low in alcohol. They are distinguished for the most part by a fruity acidity, not unlike Germany's white wines.

The Rheinhessen soil, composed of chalk, marl, and quartz (often a chalk decking, with marl beneath), varies considerably. The facings along the Rhine around Bingen are slate, like the slate of the Mosel, while from Nackenheim to Nierstein, and a little farther on, a peculiar red sandstone is found, a deposit from the Ice Age. Its water-shedding property accounts for the fact that Niersteiners, Nackenheimers, and Schwabsburgers are likely to suffer less than most vines in very wet years.

THE IMPORTANT RHEINHESSEN VINEYARDS

The following are the most important Rheinhessen villages and vineyards, the names of growers, running into many hundreds, cannot be listed here. In the better wines, however, the grower's name or name of the wine estate appears on the label, indicated by *Weingut* or a similar term. An attempt has been made to list some of the best growers, but the list is not exhaustive.

Alsheim

Situated on a low ridge of hills just over a kilometer from the Rhine, halfway between Worms and Oppenheim. The largest producer in its area, and among the four or so largest in the entire Rheinhessen. Much Riesling wine. Part of the famous Rhine Terrace.
Vineyards: Fischerpfad, Römerberg, Sonnenberg, Frühmesse, and Goldberg.
Wine estate: Weingut Rappenhof—Dr. Muth.

Alzey

Ancient town dating back to 223 and today a country seat. In addition to its well-known grape breeding station, a governmental quality control testing station has been set up in Alzey which is responsible for testing all Rheinhessen quality wines.
Vineyards: wines are likely to be marketed under their Grosslagen (GL) or collective names, Petersberg or Sybillenstein
Wine estates: Weingut der Stadt Alzey, (owned by the town). Also home to two important wineries: Leoff and H. Sichel Söhne.

Bechtheim

Slope wines, 3 kilometers (just over 2 miles) back from low, vineless, flat land bulging into the Rhine.
Vineyards: Geyersberg, Rosengarten, and Stein.
Wine estates: Dr. Blum'sches Weingut, Ferdinand Koehler, and Weingut Wilhelm Schoeneck.

Bingen

Lying directly across the Rhine from Rüdesheim and the Rheingau, at the point where the Nahe flows into the Rhine, Bingen sprawls up a mountain famous since Roman times for its vineyards. Bingen-Kempten, on the town's outskirts, and Bingen-Büdesheim, behind it, where rolling hills fringe the Nahe, form a unit with Bingen and can be considered as such. The connection with Rüdesheim is a ferry which whirls like a feather in the powerful current when it docks at either bank. Steep, tangled Bingen qualifies for its name Wine Town, Rhine Town: surviving the plague, the Thirty Years' War, and other disasters, it had provided its six thousand citizens with 130 wine bars and 120 wine merchants by the end of the last century. Population has tripled today, and the fun goes on. When a past bishop of Mainz, addressing the Bingen clergy, asked to borrow a pencil, everyone reached under his cassock and brought out a corkscrew, which was then dubbed the "Bingen pencil," a name which has stuck. Distinctly Rheinhessen wines, though separated from the Rheingaus only by the width of the river, Bingen wines derive a liveliness from the slate soil. Those grown right along the Rhine front sometimes have a smoky taste, once said to come from the smoke of the busy railway and the river boats, but with the use of electricity and diesel fuel, it is apparent that this quality comes from the soil.
Vineyards: Bubenstück, Kapellenberg, Kirchberg, Osterberg, Pfarrgarten, Rosengarten, Schlemenstück, Schlossberg Schwätzerchen, Schwarzerberg, and Scharlachberg.
Wine estates: Villa Sachsen and Jung auf Junghof.

Bodenheim

Monastery holdings of the Middle Ages produce spicy, full wines with much bouquet, but they never reach the peaks attained by the Niersteiners and Oppenheimers a few kilometers to the south. Part of the famous Rhine Terrace.
Vineyards: Ebersberg, Burgberg, Hoch, Leidhecke, Silberberg, Westrum, Heiterbrünnchen, Kapelle, Kreuzberg, Mönchspfad, and Reichritterstift.
Wine estates: Peter Kerz III, Oberstleutnant Liebrecht'sche Weingutsverwaltung, Anton Riffel, and Weingut Kühling-Gillot.

Dalheim

Rather strong wines, quite clean-tasting.
Vineyards: Altdörr, Kranzberg, and Steinberg.

Dalsheim (-Flörsheim)

A great deal of trouble with phylloxera caused extensive replanting with American vine-stocks at a tremendous cost. Sylvaner was always the main producer, but Müller-Thurgau has been introduced and suits the clayey soil. The wines are much improved, with many made from new crossings.
Vineyards: Steig, Bürgel, Frauenberg, Hubacker, and Sauloch.
Wine estates: Dr. Becker, H. Müller, and Schales.

Dexheim

Since the Middle Ages, considered the equal of the Niersteiners and Oppenheimers, which it adjoins, but

Wiesbaden

54

R H E I N G A U

42

R. Rhine

R. Main

9

455

Rüdesheim

FERRY

Mainz

9

40

Bingen 9

Ingelheim

Büdesheim

Gau-Algesheim

Laubenheim

Ockenheim

Bodenheim

41

Dromersheim

Elsheim

Nackenheim

Gau-Bischofheim

R H E I N H E S S E N

Harxheim

Hahnheim

Nierstein

Schwabsburg

Bosenheim

Dexheim

Oppenheim

420

Wörrstadt

Friesenheim

Dienheim

Dalheim

9

Ulversheim

Ludwigshöhe

Guntersblum

Alzey

Mettenheim

40

Bechtheim

Westhofen

R. Rhine

271

Osthofen

47

Dalsheim

47

Worms

N

RHEINHESSEN

0   5   10 MILES

0   5   10 KILOMETRES

9

E 12

PALATINATE
(RHEINPFALZ)

Saarbrücken 50m

GERMANY

now it is not quite up to the peak wines of its famous neighbors.

Vineyard: Doktor.

Wine estates: Adolf Dahlheim, August Dahlheim, and Sander.

Dienheim

The village adjoins Oppenheim on the south, and the vineyards, on the Rhine front, produce first-quality wines. The "Silius Stone", evidence of Dienham's Roman past, attests that these vineyards have been producing wines for over 2,000 years.

Vineyards: Falkenberg, Herrenberg, Höhlchen, Kreuz, Siliusbrunnen, Tafelstein, Herrengarten, Paterhof, and Schloss.

Dittelsheim-Hessloch

Small village not far from Alzey at the foot of a high hill, the Kloppberg. The local growers have established a charming wine restaurant atop the hill—affording an excellent opportunity to try country cooking, enjoy the local wines, and take in a magnificent view. There is a hiking path to the top of the hill.

Vineyards: Kloppberg, Geiersberg, Leckerberg, Liebfrauenberg, Pfaffenmütze, Mönchube, Mondschein and Edle Weingarten.

Dromersheim

In a protected inner valley. One of the oldest wine areas in Rheinhessen, formerly a holding of Kloster Fulda.

Vineyards: Honigberg, Kapellenberg, Mainzweg, and Klosterweg.

Friesenheim

Vineyard area: 33 hectares (73 acres) white.

Grape varieties: Müller-Thurgau and Sylvaner.

Vineyards: Altdörr, Bergspfad, and Knopf.

Gau-Algesheim

On the Rhine front between Bingen and Ingelheim, facing the Rheingau. A famous New Wine Festival takes place during the second weekend in October in the historic marketplace, formerly the scene of one of the great annual wine markets in the Middle Ages.

Vineyards: Rothenberg, Goldberg, Johannisberg, Steinert, and St. Laurenzikapelle.

Wine estate: Avenarius'sche Gutsverwaltung.

Gau-Bickelheim

Home of the region's Central Cellars (Zentralkellerei Rheinischer Winzergenossenschaften), an extremely modern and well-run operation.

Vineyards: Bockshaut, Kapelle, Saukopf.

Gau-Bischofheim

South-facing on a hill slope just north of Nierstein.

Vineyards: Glockenberg, Herrnberg, Pfaffenweg, and Kellersberg.

Wine estate: Oberst Schultz H. Werner.

Guntersblum

Usually fruity wines. On the Rhine front; third largest producer in the Rheinhessen, with much small parceling in the shallow-slope vineyards, forming a solid stretch of vines extending about a kilometer on either side of the vineyard road. Most of the town's cellars are located along a one kilometer (two-thirds-mile) path at the foot of the vineyard slopes, known as the "Kellerweg." It is the site of one of the region's most popular wine festivals.

Vineyards: Autental, Bornpfad, Himmelthal, Eiserne Hand, Steinberg, Sankt Julianenbrunnen, Kreuzkapelle, Steig-Terrassen, Sonnenberg, and Sonnenhang.

Wine estates: Emil Schätzel, Ernst Küstner, Friedrich Frey and Schmitt-Dr. Chnacker.

Hahnheim

South-facing slope vineyards in the center of Rheinhessen.

Vineyards: Knopf and Moosberg.

Wine estate: Walter Heinz.

Harxheim

Steep-slope wines from vineyards adjoining the Nierstein area, but not approaching the quality of the wines from the Rhine front hills at Nierstein.

Vineyards: Schlossberg, Lieth, and Börnchen.

Wine estates: August Böll and Peter Lotz.

Ingelheim

Here the red wines surpass the whites, the reverse of the usual state of affairs, both in Rheinhessen and in Germany generally. The white wines are good table wines. The red wines from the Portugieser grape are pleasant, light wines, while those from Spätburgunder grapes have real quality; some experts say that the finest red growths are the best red wines of Germany and in a class with some the world's great red wines. Ingelheim, Weinheim, and half a dozen other such names of small nearby communities or parts of Ingelheim have been absorbed into the single name Ingelheim, owing to its fame; and Ingelheim wines will be from anywhere in the hilly area of the medieval town overlooking the Rhine.

Charlemagne had a fortress here, and it is said that on one winter's day, he looked across the Rhine and noticed that the snow had begun to melt on the hillside of what is today Schloss Johannisberg. He then ordered the first vines to be planted there. Ingelheim offers a magnificent panoramic view of the central Rheingau. It is also famous in May and June for its excellent asparagus.

Vineyards: Horn, Pares, and Rheinhöhe, among many others.

Wine estate: J. Neuss (reds).

Ludwigshöhe

By the time the tiny village below Oppenheim is reached, the slope has leveled to a broad plain. A good deal of Ludwigshöhe, and much wine from many of the other less well-known towns (most of which are not named here), goes in to Liebfraumilch.

Vineyards: Honigsberg and Teufelskopf.

Wine estates: Weingut Brüder Dr. Becker and Johann Graf.

Mainz

Center of the wine trade for centuries and capital of the State of Rheinland-Pfalz, Mainz is a lively university town with a charming area (behind the Cathedral) of half-timbered houses and cosy wine pubs. The Cathedral, along with its 'sister' cathedrals in Worms and Speyer, is one of the best examples of Rhenish-Romanesque architecture in Germany.

Mainz is the birthplace of Johannes Gutenberg, inventor of moveable-type printing—the Gutenberg Museum is well worth a visit. The Mainzer Weinbörse (wine trade fair) takes place here every April, sponsored by the Association of German Prädikat wine estates.

Vineyards: the wines are generally sold under the names of the two collective vineyard sites, Domherr and St. Alban.

Mettenheim

Wines grow on the edge of flat land in a wide bend of the Rhine, a little south of the excellent stretch from Bodenheim up to Guntersblum. Good average wines, without peak ones.

Mettenheim is known as the southern door to the famous Rhine Terrace. Viticulture is documented from the Carolingian period, when Kloster Lorsch was given mention.

Grape variety: Sylvaner.

Vineyards: Michelsberg, Goldberg, and Schlossberg.

Wine estate: Gerhard Koch.

Nackenheim

On the red clay-and-slate soil just above Nierstein, some really first-class white wines are grown. Nackenheimers used to be used for blending, but their high quality has become recognized. In some years Nackenheim produces the lowest quantity yield per acre in Rheinhessen, always an index of high quality. The town, dominated by a baroque church, is pushed almost into the Rhine by the steep vine-covered mountain; the moderating influence of the river on the climate aids the wines. Nackenheim has the largest wine-bottle capsule factory in Europe.

It is also the birthplace of the German author and playwright Carl Zuckmayer (*The Merry Vineyard*), who was a great promoter of the wines of this area, which he referred to as the "wines of laughter . . . charming and appealing." Nackenheim is part of the famous Rhine Terrace.

Vineyards: Engelsberg, Rothenberg (outstanding), and Schmitts-Kapelle.

Wine estates: Gunderloch-Lange and Gunderloch-Usinger.

Nierstein

The most important area, giving the best Rheinhessen wines. Everyone in Nierstein is an owner in the vineyards that have been famous for hundreds of years. Of some 550 parcels, about two dozen produce the soft, elegant, full-bodied, peak wines known around the world as Niersteiners. Look for Riesling on the label: the best Niersteiners are from the Riesling grape and are so identified. The wines have a marvelous bouquet. Nierstein derives its name from the mineral springs the Romans called Neri and from the boundary stone which once marked the division between German and Frankish territories. The town came to be called Neri am Stein, which was corrupted to Nierstein. Driving from Mainz with the Rhine on your left, you see the fairly steep *Weinberg*, solid with vine, sloping back from the road, the chief areas indicated by large white block letters spelling out HIPPING, KRANZBERG, etc. It is the largest wine *Weinbauort* on the Rhine, and much the largest in Rheinhessen.

Vineyards: Best are Glöck, Heiligenbaum, Kranzberg, Ölberg, Orbel, Hipping, Pettenthal, Bildstock, Hölle, and Paterberg. Others are Bergkirche, Schloss Schwabsburg, Zehnmorgen, Pfaffenkappe, Brudersberg, Goldene Luft, Brückchen, Kirchplatte, Klostergarten, Rosenberg, and Schloss Hohenrechen.

The collective vineyard sites Spiegelberg, Rehback and Auflangen are also well-known and wines are often shipped under these names rather than those of the individual sites.

Wine estates: Weingut Balbach Erben, Weingut J. & H. A. Strub, Emil Förster, Frh. von Heyl zu Herrnsheim, Gustav Gessert, Weingut Louis Guntrum, Georg Harth, Fritz Hasselbach, Weingut Friedrich Kehl, Franz Karl Schmitt (widow of), Hermann Franz Schmitt-Hermannshof, Geschwister Schuch, Georg Albrecht Schneider, Reinhold Senfter, and Weingut Heinrich Schlamp Jr.

The regional cooperative, Rheinfront, produces very good wine from their members' holdings in many of the best Nierstein sites. Good value.

Rheinhessen: Important Vineyards

Ockenheim

Can be very good in years with plenty of sunshine, when quite a lot of Spätlese is made on the best south-facing slopes. The Müller-Thurgau grape variety is being used more and more, owing to the public taste for the aromatic wines produced.

Vineyards: Hockenmühle, Klosterweg, Kreuz, Laberstall, St. Jakobsberg, and Schönhölle.

Wine estate: Wilhelm Merz.

Oppenheim

Generally, Oppenheimers are fuller and softer than Niersteiners, while Niersteiners have more elegance. In dry, hot years Oppenheimers are likely to surpass Niersteiners; in wet, cool years Niersteiners will be better. The Oppenheimer soil retains water, whereas the Niersteiner slope is steeper and water runs off. After two or three glasses of the splendid wine, the town may take on the virtue of its famous product. Seen coldly, it is an ugly scar of brick and dirty gray stucco along a sooty railway line. In the stark interior of St. Katherine's Church there are a few tombstones decorated with vineyard motifs from the fifteenth and sixteenth centuries. Oppenheim is also the site of the region's most important viticultural institution. A research and training center with very standards, it has done much to improve methods of wine growing and winemaking in the area. It also has 20 hectares (49 acres) of vineyards in excellent sites both here and in Nierstein. The German Viticultural Museum has an interesting collection of implements related to wine-growing.

Vineyards: Daubhaus, Herrengarten, Paterhof, Herrenberg, Kreuz, Sackträger, Schlossberg, Zuckerberg, Schloss, Schützenhütte, and Gutleuthaus.

Wine estates: Friedrick Baumann, Adam Becker, Franz Josef Gallois, Louis Guntrum, J. A. Harth & Co., Ernst Jungkenn, Karl Koch (Erben), Franz Josef Senfter, Carl Sittmann, Weingut der Stadt Oppenheim, and Dr. L. Winter.

Osthofen

Grape varieties: Müller-Thurgau, Riesling, and Sylvaner.

Vineyards: Goldberg, Hasenbiss, Kirchberg, Klosterberg, Rheinberg, Neuberg, Leckzapfen, and Liebenberg.

Schwabsburg

With its windowless tower and castle built by Frederick Barbarossa, Schwabsburg is a pretty village and vineyard lying in a little valley a mile west of Nierstein. The vineyards have south and southwest exposure, and they share the reddish slate-and-clay soil of the usually greater vineyards on the Rhine front. Schwabs-

burg vineyards have become part of the *Weinbauort* Nierstein.

Selzen

Vineyards: Osterberg, Gottesgarten, and Rheinpforte.

Wine estate: Weingut Schätzel (Erben).

Ülversheim

Wines usually strong and full-bodied, grown almost entirely on the south face of the Rhine front.

Vineyard: Schloss Aulenberg.

Westhofen

Vineyards: Brunnenhäuschen, Kirchspiel, Benn, Aulerde, Morstein, Rotenstein, and Steingrube.

Worms

An occasional tiny vineyard may be found right in among the ancient buildings and war ruins of the city known for its Cathedral, where Martin Luther was condemned as a heretic in 1521. The other church of "fame" is the Liebfrauenkirche, from which the popular regional Liebfraumilch derives its name.

Liebfraumilch and the Liebfrauenstift

On April 29, 1910, a fatal day in German wine history, the Chamber of Commerce of Worms ruled that the name Liebfraumilch could be used by any Rheinhessen wine of good quality. It was like staking out a tired old horse in the public park and saying that any child of good quality could mount it. Liebfraumilch today is a *Qualitätswein*—quality wine—and may come from the Rheinhessen, the Rheingau, the Palatinate, or Nahe. As a Qualitätswein, it must pass the governmental quality control tests (A.P.Number) and its production is precisely outlined by law. It must be made primarily from Riesling, Müller-Thurgau, Silvaner or Kerner (as of 1986) grapes, but no grape variety may be named on the label. It may not be dry (trocken) or medium-dry (halbtrocken), i.e. it must have at least 18 grams/liter residual sugar. Liebfraumilch is centuries old and remains one of the most popular German regional wines today. As with any cuvée, the final product can only be as qualitatively good as the components used in making it. Hence, it is best to look for the name of a reliable producer or shipper on the label, rather than an unrealistically low price. There are several old established brands which offer consistently good quality, such as Madonna, Crown of Crowns, Blue Nun, Hans Christof and Goldener Oktober, to name a few. The soil of the Liebfrauenstift vineyards around the tall, bleak church on the outskirts of Worms is flat river-deposit earth which gives a special taste to the wines. Nevertheless, arising in the sixteenth and seventeenth centuries, before vineyard place-names had come into being, the name Lieb-fraumilch gradually became world-famous. The production of the original vineyards around the Lieb-frauenkirche, never more than 2,000 cases in the best years, was entirely inadequate for the demand, and the name spread over other wines. Most of the parcels behind 10-foot brick walls on all sides of the church are owned by the Valckenberg and the J. Langenbach estates, though small holdings are in the hands of Eberhard, W. Mahler, and E. Rieth.

Rheinriesling

Variety of Riesling cultivated in Austria.

Rhenish

English term formerly used for Rhine wines and extended to all German wines. It has dropped out of currency in favor of Hock.

Rhine wines

General name for wines grown along the River Rhine.

See Rheingau; Rheinhessen; Mittelrhein; Palatinate.

Rhône (Côtes du Rhône)

Red, white, and rosé wines.
District: Southern France.

The Rhône is a river of wine; it drains vineyards on its broad delta plain, along the steep cliffs above Avignon, in the Cévennes and Jura mountains, and around the lake of Geneva. Yet the only wines to bear the name are those which come from the central section—the Côtes du Rhône.

Lyon, with its great gastronomic tradition, stands at the head of the Rhône Valley; east of the river is the land of the fat Bresse chickens; to the west, Périgord, rich in truffles and *foie gras*; from the south come the plentiful fruit and fish of the valley—and the great restaurants excel in *poulet en vessie*, in *quenelles Nantua*, and all the rest of the famous regional dishes and *charcuteries*. The inhabitants eat heartily and wash down their meals with the robust Rhône wine—and with Beaujolais.

The vineyards of the Côtes du Rhône extend for 220 kilometers (140 miles) from Lyon to Avignon, stretching precariously over sheer, high cliffs on both sides of the sun-baked river. Their touchstone is granite—the soil's dominant element. Drawing their character from the steep, sun-drenched granite cliffs they come from, the wines are not subtle; they are big, rough, and heady, with a strong, almost pungent perfume, and they are tamed only by long imprisonment in bottle. They compare seldom in quality, never in quantity, with the greatest clarets and Burgundies; but at their best they can be excellent. Yet it has been the

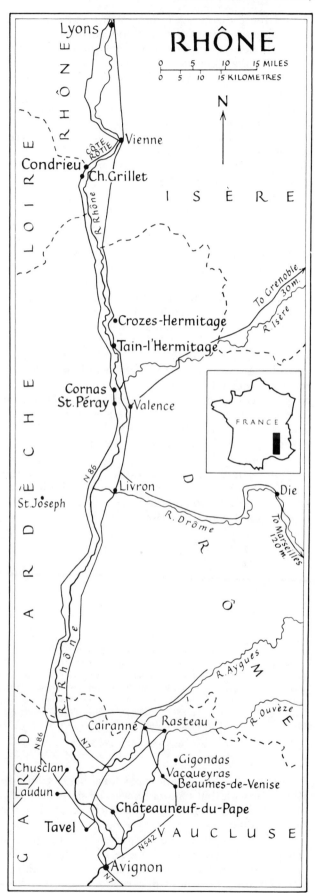

fate of these distinctive wines often to be classed as Burgundies—a practice which does justice to neither region. The reason perhaps was the proximity of the upper Rhône vineyards to those of southern Burgundy; or the sturdy Burgundy bottle in which Rhône wines also are sold.

Except for Tavel, Châteauneuf-du-Pape, and Hermitage, Rhône wines have not hitherto been well known. The situation has changed, however. As a result of the efforts of the late Baron LeRoy de Boiseaumarié the wines are often seen outside their own region. The Baron, one of the few men to have a statue erected to him during his own lifetime, was himself a grower in Châteauneuf-du-Pape and was president of the International Wine Office; he held the rank of Commandeur of the Légion d'Honneur and headed the association of growers of the Côtes du Rhône. Baron LeRoy was instrumental in formulating and obtaining the controls that brought honest wines back into Châteauneuf-du-Pape, which had been fraud-ridden, and he later extended his activities to embrace first all Rhône wines, then all of France.

The area over which the Côtes du Rhône extend is long and narrow, and the wines produced there show considerable variation. Some sections of the Côtes are more advanced than are others and are apt, therefore, to produce better wines. Overall quality has risen enormously in recent years, but it is uneven; many growers still need help, especially those in the lesser-known districts. The entire region produces more than 1.5 million hectoliters (39.7 million U.S. gallons, 33 million imp.) of wine annually, some under the name Côtes du Rhône, some—superior in both quantity and quality—under more specific headings.

The better wines include:

AVERAGE PRODUCTION

Crus	Hectoliters	U.S. Gallons	Imperial Gallons	Wines
Châteauneuf-du-Pape	100,000	2,650,000	2,200,000	red, white, rosé
Condrieu	400	10,560	8,790	white
Cornas	2,600	68,900	57,200	red, white, rosé
Côte Rôtie	4,000	105,650	88,000	red, rosé
Crozes-Hermitage	27,000	713,300	593,950	red, white, rosé
Cigondas	35,000	927,500	770,000	red, rosé
Château-Grillet	65	1,723	1,430	white
Hermitage	4,500	118,880	99,000	red, white, rosé
Lirac	20,000	530,000	440,000	red, white, rosé
Saint-Péray	2,000	53,000	44,000	white
Saint-Joseph	12,000	317,000	264,000	red, white, rosé
Tavel	30,000	795,000	660,000	red, rosé
	237,565	6,291,513	5,226,370	

The region's lesser wines are sold either as Côtes du Rhône or with that name followed by some addition. While it is generally true in French wines that the more specific name denotes the better growth, this is not strictly so along the Rhône. When the general name is followed by that of one of the better communes—Vinsobres, Vaison, Vacqueyras, Cairanne, and Laudun—the wines will have met higher than nor-

mal standards and are often delightful. If, on the other hand, the general name is followed by the name of a department—Ardèche, Drôme, Loire, Rhône—the standards are more relaxed and the wines may be inferior. One important consideration in this question of standards is the minimum required alcoholic content—always stipulated for fine French wines. Although alcoholic content is always a question of importance, it is vital to Rhône wines. Alcohol adds body and strength, two characteristics that are closely identified with these wines. If the label says simply Côtes du Rhône, the wine must have at least 10.5% alcohol by volume. If this name is followed by the name of a department (Côtes du Rhône—Drôme, for example), only 9.5% is required, sapping the wine of some of its robust strength. Those wines that come from the communes mentioned above have alcoholic contents ranging from a minimum 12% to 12.5%. Just as Beaujolais produces Beaujolais Villages, the Côtes du Rhône also produces a lesser known Appellation Contrôlée called Côtes du Rhône Villages, the best ones coming from Cairanne, Vinsobres, Chusclan, Vacqueyras, Rasteau, Laudun, and Beaumes de Venise.

Most of the finer Côtes du Rhône wines are pressed from one kind of grape, sometimes two or three—with the exception of Châteauneuf-du-Pape, where thirteen are allowed. The principal variety is the Syrah, which gives firm, robust wines of fine color and bouquet, but is sometimes inclined to be hard. The introduction of the white Viognier imparts the qualities of softness and freshness. Other leading white-wine varieties are Roussanne which, grown on a sunny slope, gives fine soft wines, and Marsanne, a sturdier and more productive grape planted more often than Roussanne. For the general name Côtes du Rhône, growers may include grapes from any or all of the following varieties: Grenache, Clairette, Syrah, Mourvèdre, Picpoule, Terret Noir, Counoise, Muscardin, Bourboulenc, Carignan, Ugni Blanc, Roussanne, Marsanne, and Viognier.

Rhône summers are long and consistently warm. As a result, there is not as much variation between the vintage years as elsewhere in France. There is, however, some difference. The best recent years were 1978, 1982, 1983, 1984, and 1985.

Characteristics of Rhône Wines

Beaumes-de-Venise. A very good sweet wine from the Muscat grape. Also produces red and rosé wines.

Châteauneuf-du-Pape. A full-bodied wine, deep in color, softer and quicker to mature than most Rhône growths. There is also a white wine, pleasant but of less importance. (Appellation Contrôlée)

Clairette de Die. A semi-sparkling white wine from the Clairette and Muscat grapes, made near the village of Die on the River Drôme. (A.O.C.)

Condrieu. White wine with a tinge of color; robust and perfumed. Both dry and semi-sweet styles are produced, and all are at their best when young and fresh.

Condrieu white wines are favorites of the Lyonnais. (A.O.C.)

Cornas. Red wine, a bit hard to begin with, of a fine garnet color. It ages well, becoming soft and velvety in maturity but never so perfumed as Hermitage. (A.O.C.)

Côte Rôtie. These robust and heady red wines stand up well. The color is rich; there is a hint of violet in the bouquet—and, some say—of raspberry in the taste. (A.O.C.)

Crozes-Hermitage. Red wine with a rather violet tinge, not so deep in color as Hermitage, nor with so much softness. It has a faint *goût de terroir.* (Appellation Contrôlée)

Château Grillet. The white wine, which shows some resemblance to Condrieu, is robust and vigorous, with perhaps a little more finesse than the latter. Since the production is very small, this wine is not much seen outside its own district. (Appellation Contrôlée)

Hermitage. The red wine is full-bodied and vigorous, with a certain delicacy and softness in maturity, and a fragrance of iris-root in the bouquet. It ages well. The white wine has a golden tinge, is dry yet fruity, with a characteristic perfume. It will last a long time without oxidizing. (Appellation Contrôlée)

Saint-Joseph. The red wines are delicate and perfumed, with less body than the Hermitage, but of a fine ruby color. They are ready after a few years in bottle. The white wines are lighter than the white Hermitage. (A.O.C.)

Saint-Péray. White, spirited wines with body, a tinge of color, and a definite bouquet. In ageing, they sometimes maderize prematurely. Some of these wines make dry or semi-sweet *mousseux.* (A.O.C.)

Tavel. One of the best rosés of France, it comes mainly from the Grenache grape. It has a clear, pink color, without any trace of orange flaw. It is light, refreshing, and at its best when chilled. (A.O.C.)

Vaucluse and Gard. The wines, planted in a variety of soils in these two departments, are of widely varying types. In general, the terraced, gravelly, clayey vineyards are planted for rosé. Lirac and Chusclan produce pink wines which are not far behind those of Tavel. Laudun makes white as well as pink and red. Gigondas, Cairanne, and Vacqueyras wines are supple and rather high in alcohol; red, white, and rosé are made. Beaumes-de-Venise and Rasteau are dessert wines—*see under* Sweet fortified wines of France.

Ribeauvillé

Wine town in Alsace *(q.v.).*

Ricard

Very popular French licorice-flavored aperitif. Because of its strong taste and reasonably high alcoholic content, it is generally diluted with water before drinking, whereupon it turns milky and cloudy. This is a commercial pastis.

Rice wine

A Japanese fermented liqueur made from rice. *See* Saké.

Riceys, Rosé de

A still, pink wine of Champagne *(q.v.).*

Richebourg

Burgundy red wine.
District: Côte de Nuits, France.
Commune: Vosne-Romanée.
Official Classification:Great Growth (Grand Cru).

Richebourg is one of the giants of its commune, partly since it is rated Great Growth *(Grand Cru)*—as high as a Burgundian vineyard can get—and partly since its 7.7 hectares or 19.8 acres (part in Richebourg, part in Les Verroilles) make it one of the largest of the great vineyards of Vosne. Only Romanée-Saint-Vivant, among the top vineyards of Vosne, is larger.

The vineyard lies well up the slope with La Romanée and La Romanée-Conti to the south of it and Romanée-Saint-Vivant just across the road and is considerably larger than its traditional size. In the 1930s, a decree of the Minister of Agriculture permitted the vineyard slightly above it on the slope, known as Verroilles or Richebourg, to be included in the controlled place-name. This made legal a practice that was actually a long-standing custom. It added, however, some 3 hectares (7.6 acres) to the *appellation* Richebourg. Unlike some of the other Great Growths of Vosne, this one is not a monopoly of any grower but is, at the time of writing, in the hands of eight different owners. Only three of these have sizable holdings: Domaine Louis Gros, Domaine de la Romanée-Conti, and Charles Noellat.

Needless to say, the fact that eight different growers make the wine means that there will be some variation between any two Richebourgs of a given year. In general terms, however, it is the "velvet wine" of Vosne. All the commune's wines have this velvety quality, but in Richebourg it is more pronounced than in the others. Beneath this veneer is a robust fullness, and the wine acquires a superb perfume with age. The amount of wine averages about 300 hectoliters (7,950 U.S. gallons, 6,600 imp.) annually or the equivalent of some 3,500 cases.

See Vosne-Romanée.

Richon-le-Zion

One of the main wine centers in Israel *(q.v.).*

Riesling

A grape variety producing the most distinctive and noble wines of Alsace, the Mosel, and the Rhine. The

Château Rieussec

fruit is small, yellowish, not very juicy; but it is one of the great grapes of the world. Alsatian Rieslings are generally sold as such and the varietal name usually, but not always, appears on the label of the great German Rhine and Mosel Rieslings. Riesling is also grown in Austria, California, Chile, and Switzerland.

Château Rieussec

Bordeaux white wine.
District: Sauternes, France.
Commune: Fargues.

After changing hands a number of times and acquiring sections which had formed adjoining small vineyards, Rieussec was consolidated in its present situation. Making a wine quite different from its neighbor, fuller-bodied but less subtle, it is contiguous with Château d'Yquem. The wine was officially classed a First Growth *(Premier Cru)* Sauternes in 1855, and the vineyard was purchased in 1971 by M. Albert Vuiller, who in August 1984 sold the majority shares to a banking group headed by Château Lafite-Rothschild. Rieussec has the considerable ripening advantage of being planted on a plateau, which gives the wines the ability to mature ahead of some of the other Sauternes. In the mid seventies, Rieussec started selling a dry wine called "R", which is made from grapes of the Sauternes section of the vineyard, as well as some of the 8 hectares which are only entitled to the appellation of Bordeaux superior.

Characteristics. Very *liquoreux* or rich in unconverted sugar, and one of the better First Growths.

Vineyard area: 61 hectares (152.5 acres).

Average production: 100 *tonneaux* (8,000 cases).

Rioja

Red, white, and rosé wines.
District: Northern Spain.

Within the last half-century the best Riojas have established themselves as some of the very best red table wines in Spain. Although a bottle from one of the better firms shows how outstanding the Riojas can be, equal to any red wine except the finest Bordeaux and Burgundies, and in spite of the fact that Riojas head Spanish wine lists and are fairly good value, they often tend to vary from very good to average wines. The trend among the large companies is to equalize quality; these companies dominate the market and comprise, with a few specified exceptions, the only firms allowed to produce those Rioja wines entitled to Certificates of Origin. On the other hand, the rise in overall quality can be expected to continue—although, unfortunately, the big firms actually making the wines which are exported are inclined to value age for its own sake, often keeping the wine too long in barrel and then selling it immediately after bottling; the result is that it loses much of the clarity, vigor, and freshness of wine allowed to mature in bottle. White

wines, sometimes subjected to the same treatment, become flat and maderized. That the wine in the bottle may yet be younger than the vintage printed on the label may be due to this same reverence for age, to a casual disregard for exactitude, and also to the semi-*solera* system of adding, from time to time, a little very old wine from the reserve *(gran reserva)*.

There are a few notable exceptions to this rule—for instance, at the *bodega* of the Marqués de Riscal at Elciego, among other better producers. Here, also, there have been new plantations of white grapes, and Dr. E. Peynaud, the Bordeaux oenologist, has been consulted about improved processes for making white wine. In general, however, Spaniards seem to feel that the weakened, over-oxidized, frail wines are more distinguished than the big, hard, more commonplace wines of the country. In any case, barrel-ageing is overdone, lasting sometimes as long as five or even ten years; when this practice is corrected—and there are signs that this is happening—the potentially splendid Rioja wines will come even more into their own.

Recently the Certificate of Origin delivered for export has increased the standard of quality of these wines. The term *crianza* requires that the wine is at least three years old and is expected to have aged at least one year in barrel. *Reservas* and *gran reservas* are meant to imply bottle-age.

Rioja did take part in the flowering of Spanish wines during the period of the discovery of the Americas and the opening of vast markets to Spanish export.

A difficulty peculiar to Rioja was the lack of any good road by which the wines could be sent to the rest of Spain and to the world. For more than half a century, beginning in 1790, the achievement of this road was the goal of a wine industry which attempted to regain the splendor of the days of Spanish power.

The success story of Rioja starts with the founding, in 1892, of the viticultural station in Haro, heart of the vineyards along the Ebro; almost simultaneously the fight was begun to eliminate all outside wine from Rioja and prevent any other Spanish wines from using the name—a fight not yet completely won. Haro is now the important center, with a wine institute and college.

History has come full circle, and it is now generally recognized that Rioja owes its unique place among Spanish table wines to its geographical position. The region divides into three zones (Rioja Alta, Rioja Alavesa, and Rioja Baja) as it goes steeply downhill into the Ebro Valley, sheltered by the Sierra Cantabria. Upper Rioja—Rioja Alta—is northerly and Atlantic in type, producing the finest wines. Those of the Alava are heavier but still good. Rioja Baja supplies mainly *vinos corrientes (vins ordinaires)*. Figures for the wines granted Denominación de Origen are 40,000 hectares (100,000 acres) of vines producing 1 million hectoliters (26.5 million U.S. gallons, 22 million imp.) of wine, red, white, and rosé *(rosado)*. It is significant that Rioja Baja produces nothing but common wines, rarely bottled and little exported.

DENOMINATIONS OF ORIGIN AND THE MAKING OF THE WINE

About sixty companies have the right to make Rioja—wine of Rioja entitled to the place-name, the Certificate of Origin, and the small, square, mill-edged stamp of authenticity, on the bottle label. The number is not officially limited, but to qualify, a producer is supposed to have 500 hogsheads in his stores—this is a big investment, and the ordinary man cannot afford the price of the wood for so many barrels. The system is admittedly hit-and-miss, not devised to keep anyone out but to permit supervision and control in a developing and improving if still imperfect situation. Already a few growers and producers, not big enough to have the 500 barrels, have been allowed in because of the excellence of their wines.

The denomination Rioja, or the place-name of one of the villages within the zone, may only be used for wines combining certain specified characteristics and standards of quality. Where wines genuinely produced in the district do not quite come up to standard, the village name may appear on the label only according to this formula: "This wine was made in the village of X, but does not have the right to be called Rioja."

The legal zone for the production of Rioja falls within the limits of the province of Logroño, and in some areas of Alava and Navarre. Wines which have been aged or "elaborated" outside the zone are not allowed to carry the name Rioja.

The making of the wines follows traditional French methods—not surprisingly, since French hands and heads did the work some three-quarters of a century ago when phylloxera had destroyed the vineyards of Bordeaux but had not yet reached Rioja.

The flood of the French into Rioja in those days has left its mark: wines are vatted and fermented in much the same way as they used to be in France, and those not sold within a year as light, common wines are matured in oak casks, some of the Bordeaux size. They are kept in cellars which, in certain *bodegas* (wine-making establishments), resemble those of France to the last detail.

One great difference is that, whereas the good wines of Bordeaux are the products of a single vineyard-owner, Riojas are blends produced in the big *bodegas* from grapes grown partly, perhaps largely, by peasant farmers in the area—as is more the case in California and, in some instances, in the Rhône. As for the lesser, regional wine, much of this is now being made very successfully by the forty cooperatives and sold as *vinos corrientes* of good quality.

RIOJA WINE TYPES: BOTTLE LABELS

The Rioja wine district, officially delimited along the two sides of the River Ebro, is almost entirely in the province of Logroño in the north of Spain, a little east of Burgos. The small part not in Logroño province bulges like a bubble into the province of Alava—where the marked difference is that the Ebro, a narrowish thin stream at this point, cuts through the land, which now begins to rise. The important difference in the wines themselves is that here in Alava the Riojas are heavier and full-blooded, while in the plain of the Ebro they are lighter, more claret-like.

The region is finely subdivided for local purposes, but in the present state of the development of the wines, three divisions are important.

Rioja Alta

Upper Rioja, the northwest end of the zone, above and including the city of Logroño. The climate is much the same here as it is around the Basque coast and the Bay of Biscay, and so not unlike that of Bordeaux. The autumns, mild and long, are favorable to harvesting, and spring is pleasant. There are hard frosts and some snow in winter but the season is not violent. Yet two dangers challenge the vines: late spring frosts, usually occurring at the end of April or the beginning of May after warmer weather has brought the sap up the plant; and the *solano*, a roasting local wind coming out of the east. Even so, in the more reliable weather of Rioja, there is not so much difference in the vintages that *chaptalisation* is ever needed.

Alavesa

Wines in Alava (8,000 hectares—20,000 acres) are listed in the high-quality group, with those of Rioja Alta. Bottle labels sometimes state that the wine is an Alavesa. Generally, it will be heartier than Rioja Alta; it is habitually compared with Burgundies but, tasted on the spot, is reminiscent rather of a good Rhône wine.

Rioja Baja

Lower Rioja. The wines are rarely bottled. As the Río Ebro drops toward the Mediterranean, below the town of Logroño, the climate changes; here, it is more like Aragón than the Bay of Biscay. Autumns and springs are violent, the weather is hotter; while Rioja Alta is moderately dry, Rioja Baja is classified as arid. Because of the greater heat, the season here is always two weeks in advance, yet in the vast stretch of vineyard along the Ebro, the grapes are harvested later than they are upriver—and, as a result of this extra maturing time, they produce a wine markedly higher in alcoholic content, reaching up to 15% or 16% as compared with 11% or 12.5% in Rioja Alta. They are dark and often rather coarse, ordinary wines.

Riojas are sold for drinking in their second year, are sold in barrel, or are matured in American oak casks either of 600 liters (*bocoyes*) or 225 liters (*barricas bor-*

delesas or Bordeaux barrels). These more mature wines are the ones which generally reach both the foreign market and the better restaurants in Spain.

Vintage wines are labeled Cosecha (harvest) followed by the year (i.e., Cosecha 1978, Cosecha 1982), or Reserva or Reserva Especial, the latter designations sometimes followed by the year and sometimes not. Reserva is a wine which has been kept longer than a Cosecha (almost invariably in wood, not in bottle), and a Reserva Especial will generally have been kept longer still. It is not always easy to choose between them: the older wines are sometimes overaged and flat from too long a life in the wood; on the other hand, the best wines of the greatest years are usually the ones set aside for this maltreatment. Vintage date, it has been said before, is to be taken as an approximation. It is considered a certain vintage if "most" of the wine in the bottle or barrel is of that vintage. The greatest years of this century in Rioja are 1904, 1920, 1922, 1924, 1925, 1928, 1934, 1935, 1942, 1948, 1953, 1954, 1957, 1962, 1964, 1966, 1970, 1976, 1978, 1981, and 1982.

White wines are sweet *(dulce)* or dry *(seco)*. The white wines cannot compete with the reds, and are too often *pasado* (maderized). Red wines are graded by age as Finos de Mesa (fine table wines) or Reservas, and by degree of color: *rosado, clarete, ojo de gallo,* and *tinto,* ranging from pale pink to deep red. *Clarete* and *tinto* are the types most often to be met with; *clarete* is an honest light red wine produced by short contact with the color-importing skin of the red grape from which it comes. *Tinto* is simply the Spanish word for red wine—which is never called *rojo,* although the literal word *blanco* is used for the white.

Here, as in California, the wines are usually known by the *bodega* names of the shippers and not by vineyards. It is freely admitted in Rioja that the various vineyards differ widely; it matters considerably whether the plot has a southern or a northern exposure; the soil naturally varies throughout the region, but on the whole, it is chalky, and this influences the wines. Nevertheless, separate vatting of musts according to vineyard is in its infancy. If a wine *does* carry the name of a vineyard—a few names, such as Viña Zaco, Viña Tondonia, and Viña Paceta have become widely known—this is largely symbolic. Certain high-grade *bodegas,* such as those of the Marqués de Riscal, Marqués de Murríeta, Compañía Vinícola del Norte de España, and Cune may use mainly grapes of their own planting, with a small quantity carefully selected from smaller growers; but most blend their wines from the harvests of numerous little vineyards.

In the past, Riojas were known as Cepa (vine variety) Sauternes, Cepa Chablis, Cepa Rhin, Cepa Barsac, Cepa Médoc, and so on; or sometimes as Estilo Sauternes, Especial Sauternes (or Graves, or Barsac), or even simply as Chablis, or Sauternes. This imitative labeling was outlawed in 1960, and by the Common Market.

VINE VARIETIES

The rolling Rioja Alta, sheltered from rough weather by high mountains—which are out of sight—has a khaki-colored, parched look, something like Arizona, or North Africa. The patchwork hills striped and quilted by the vine plots might be in Chablis.

Wine-making in the important growths is modernized. Some *bodegas* and cooperatives have installed up-to-date machinery; and even the many small growers who produce the ordinary wines sold everywhere in the north of Spain (but not entitled to the place-name Rioja) now plow the earth instead of chopping it by hand. At the same time, the backward corners of the province are primitive and picturesque. The ancient villages tucked into the hills are all off the main roads—an isolation which has safeguarded their character—and countless houses are distinguished by ornate coats-of-arms in stone. The district taking its name from a slurred-over pronunciation of one of the little rivers tributary to the Ebro, the Río Oja, is poor; much of the landscape is arid and rocky, although there are fertile and beautiful spots. The look of poverty in Rioja has comparatively little to do with the wine, all of which, from the export point of view, is at least in theory made in the flourishing big *bodegas.*

The principal wine producers in the Rioja are:

La Rioja Alta, S.A.; R. López de Heredia, Viña Tondonia, S.A.; Bodegas Martínez Lacuesta, Hnos., Ltda.; Bodegas Franco Españolas; Bodegas Ramón Bilbao; Rioja Santiago, S.A.; Campo Burgo, S.A.; Compañía Vinícola del Norte de España; Bodegas Marqués de Cáceres; Bodegas Bilbainas; Bodegas Riojanas; Bodegas Montecillo; Vinos de los Herederos del Marqués de Riscal, S.A.; Federico Paternina, S.A.; Viña Salceda; Alsavesas; Beronia; Martinez Bujanda; Campillo; Marqués de Ciria; Corral; El Coto; Domecq; Lan; Sociedad Vinícola Laserna; Laturce; Muga; José Palacios; Marqués del Puerto; La Granja Nuestra Señora de Remelluri; Carlos Serres; Velazquez; Bodegas Berberana; AGE, Bodegas Unidas, S.A.; Bodegas Gurpegui; Bodegas Lagunilla, S.A.; Bodegas Marqués de Murríeta; Bodegas Muerza, S.A.; Bodegas Olarra; Bodegas Palacio, S.A.; Bodegas Faustino Martínez; Vinícola Vizcaina, Rojas y Cía., S.R.C.; Bodegas Campo Viejo de Savin, S.A.; Bodega Coop. Del Valle de Ocón; Bodega Coop. Nuestra Señora de la Anunciación; Bodega Coop. Nuestra Señora de Valvanera de Cuzcurrita, Tirgo y Sajazarra; Bodega Coop. Nuestra Señora de Vico; Bodega Coop. San Isidro; Bodega Coop. San Miguel; Bodega Coop. San Pedro Apóstol; Bodega Coop. Santa Daria; Bodega Coop. Sonsierra; Bodega Coop. Virgen de la Vega; Bodega Coop. La Bastida.

The red wines are made principally from the grape varieties Garnacha, Tempranillo, Graciano, and Mazuelo. No Rioja vine, either red or white, is capable of making a satisfactory wine alone; all lack some essential ingredient—acidity or richness or finesse—and all the good wines are blends.

Garnacha, which resembles French Grenache, is the big common producer, weak in bouquet, and not a variety which ripens fully in the Rioja Alta, except in the hottest years. It yields the mass of wine in Rioja Baja—and in other parts of Spain, especially around Madrid, where it is generally called Aragón or Tinto Aragones, because it came originally from Aragón. Its wide use in Rioja is due mainly to its ability to resist oïdium, which, with mildew, is the great menace there.

The must of the Tempranillo, high neither in sugar nor in acid, is quite neutral, and the other elements in a blend with this grape always inform the taste. But it matures quickly—although it does not keep particularly well—and it is valued for its contribution of color. Graciano has a marked and quite individual perfume; Mazuelo, a variety close to the Carignan of the Rhône and Provence in France, would be more widely grown if it were not for its susceptibility to oïdium.

The white wines are usually a blend of Malvasia and Viura.

Château Ripeau

Bordeaux red wine.
District and Commune: Saint-Émilion, France.

Combined with Château Jean-Faure, adjoining it and long under the same ownership, Ripeau is now one of the large producers among the good Saint-Émilion vineyards. Lying next to Château Cheval-Blanc, near the boundary of Pomerol, the vineyard suffered as badly as Cheval-Blanc and the Pomerol vineyards did in the February 1956 freeze, and there was little 1956, 1957, 1958, or 1959 Château Ripeau wine. Other later vintages, however, are in the market in quantity. The property was once owned by Michel de Wilde, the son-in-law of Mme Loubat, who with her husband established both of the vineyards now combined. Today, Ripeau belongs to de Wilde's daughter and her husband, M. Janoueix, an owner and shipper in Libourne.
Characteristics. A generous wine with an individual bouquet. Typical of a good Saint-Émilion.
Vineyard area: 15 hectares (37.5 acres).
Average production: 75 *tonneaux* (6,000 cases).

Ripley

American hybrid grape developed by the New York State Agricultural Station to be used as a table grape and for wine. The wine is white and dry, but by itself tends to be flat; the grape might contribute to a very superior blend if the proper partner could be found.

Riquewihr

Wine town in Alsace *(q.v.)*.

Riviera del Garda Bresciano (D.O.C.)

Red or rosé wine from Lombardy *(q.v.)*.

Rivesaltes (Appellation Contrôlée)

Sun-baked district of Roussillon, France, famous for its Muscat wines.
See Sweet fortified wines of France.

Robertson

Wine district in the Little Karoo region of the Cape province.
See South Africa.

Clos de la Roche (Appellation Contrôlée)

Burgundy red wine.
District: Côte de Nuits, France.
Commune: Morey-Saint-Denis.
Official Classification: Great Growth (Grand Cru).

Clos de la Roche is one of the least-known wines of this section of the Côte de Nuits and is thus often good, and sometimes exceptional, value. Throughout the centuries of its existence it has been overshadowed by Bonnes Mares, by the Clos de Tart and Clos des Lambrays and neglected because the wines of Morey were more often than not sold under the name of one of the two famous adjoining communes—Gevrey-Chambertin and Chambolle-Musigny—probably more to the advantage of the two neighbors than to their loss.

The vineyard is the largest of the important Growths of Morey, covering some 15 hectares (37 acres). It stands up the hill, above the road that goes through the vineyards, along the boundary between Gevrey and Morey. Its nobility is such that it is one of the rare Great Growths *(Grands Crus)* of Burgundy, and bottles are not labeled with both vineyard name and commune name—vineyard name alone is sufficient. To earn the name, of course, the wine must meet the rigorous Great Growth standards. Like most of the wines of Morey, it is sturdy and rich, yet curiously delicate, much like a Clos de Tart. On a curve from the sturdy nobility of the great Chambertin to the elegance of Musigny, Clos de la Roche lies perhaps just beside Chambertin, lacking some of its austere majesty but adding a beguiling grace.

As is the case with most Burgundian vineyards, this one is divided among a number of growers. All together, in an average year for quantity, they produce some 500 hectoliters (13,250 U.S. gallons, 11,000 imp.)—or about 5,000 cases.

Rochefort-sur-Loire

Wine commune in the Coteaux du Layon district of Anjou *(qq.v.)*.

Romanée-Conti and Romanée-Saint-Vivant

See La Romanée-Conti and La Romanée-Saint-Vivant.

Château Romer-du-Hayot

Bordeaux white wine.
District: Sauternes, France.
Commune: Fargues.

The little-known château is situated in a wood in the commune whose wines are entitled to the place-name Sauternes. The wines tend to be heavy. Mr. du Hayot makes and sells his wines as "Château Romer-du-Hayot."

Vineyard area: 15 hectares (38 acres).
Average production: 40 *tonneaux* (3,800 cases).

Rosato

Italian term for pink wine or rosé.

Rosé

In French, pink or rose-colored wine. When properly made, it comes from red grapes fermented for two or three days on the color-imparting skins and husks, but drawn off at the delicate moment when just enough color has been absorbed to give the wine its attractive pink cast. In France, the best rosé is from Tavel near the mouth of the Rhône, but some excellent ones are now being made in Bordeaux, in Anjou, and in most wine-producing regions. In America, where rosé is popular, some good examples come from California.

Rosé de Béarn

An Appellation Contrôlée wine made in the French department of Basses-Pyrénées.

Rosé des Riceys (Appellation Contrôlée)

A still pink wine of Champagne *(q.v.)*.

Rosette

(1) White wines, semi-sweet and rarely distinguished, from Bergerac, France. (Appellation Contrôlée)
See Bergerac.
(2) Rosette (Seibel 1000) is an old French-American hybrid grape, very vigorous and winter-hardy, but a small and spotty producer. It lacks pigment, and so is often used to make a rosé.

Rosolio

A red Italian liqueur with a taste of roses. The French used to make their own version of this liqueur, which they called Rossolis.

Rossese (Dolceacqua) (D.O.C.)

Red wine from Rossese grapes, grown along the Italian Riviera.
See Liguria.

Rosso

Red in Italian. In California the word now refers to a red wine that is just slightly sweet, but the common *vini rossi* of Italy are always dry.

Rosso Conero (D.O.C.)

A fruity but rather acid red wine from the Italian Marches *(q.v.)*.

Rosso Piceno (D.O.C.)

Red Italian wine from the Piceno Hills, on the fringe of the Apennines.
See The Marches.

Rotgipfler

Grape variety cultivated in Austria.

Rouge

French term for red wine.

Rougeau (leaf reddening)

Vine disease, caused by a wound which prevents the sap from returning to the roots.
See Chapter Eight, p. 31.

Rougeon

Comparatively new French-American hybrid that is winter-hardy and a vigorous grower, but somewhat of a spotty producer. Distinctive in flavor, Rougeon (Seibel 5898) is often used in blending because of its deep red color.

Château Rouget

Bordeaux red wine.
District and Commune: Pomerol, France.

The property, owned by Jean Brochet is one of the oldest in the district and has made some very agreeable wines typical of Pomerol.
Vineyard area: 18 hectares (45 acres).
Average production: 72 *tonneaux* (6,500 cases).

Rough

A big red wine, with a considerable amount of tannin, will be rough before it has had time to mature, which in the biggest years may take well over a decade.

This roughness is not to be confused with the coarseness of wines from poor grapes and poor vineyards—a common, harsh flavor which will never disappear with age.

Round

To be round, a wine must be harmonious but also big. It will be in perfect balance, and it gives a sense of "roundness" in the way it fills the mouth.

Roussette de Savoie (A.O.C.)

The principal wine of Seyssel, in Haute-Savoie. It is white, flinty dry, and made from Roussette grapes.
See Seyssel.

Roussillon

See Grand Roussillon; Sweet fortified wines of France.

Rubino di Cantavenna (D.O.C.)

A light but full red wine from the Italian Piedmont (*q.v.*).

Ruby Port

A young, blended wood Port, rich in color, fruity and sweet.
See Port.

Ruchottes-Chambertin (A.O.C.)

Burgundy red wine.
District: Côte de Nuits, France.
Commune: Gevrey-Chambertin.
Official Classification: Great Growth (Grand Cru).

Many excellent and even outstanding bottles can be found, although this wine is one of the lesser of the Chambertin family. Some severe critics have called the wine common and lacking in breed, but while it is not generally the equal of the magnificent Chambertin, a well-made Ruchottes should be neither of these things.

The vineyard adjoins the Clos de Bèze, to the south of the village of Gevrey-Chambertin, and is fairly high on the slope for exceptionally great wines. It covers just over 3 hectares (7.9 acres), and production usually amounts to 100 or so hectoliters (2,650 U.S. gallons, 2,200 imp.), or the equivalent of about 1,100 cases.
See Gevrey-Chambertin.

Rüdesheimer Berg

The Rüdesheimerberg, or Rüdesheimer Mountain, a steep slope rising up from the Rhine, produces the best Rüdesheim wines. The label will carry the name of the village, Rüdesheimerberg, followed by the name of the actual vineyard spot such as Berg Rottland, Berg Schlossberg, or Berg Roseneck. Owing to the steepness of the clifflike vineyards, drainage is excellent, and in the wet years Rüdesheimer wines are among the best Rheingaus. The grapes roast in the sun in the hot years; hence, this popular village produces wine frequently below Rheingau average.
See Rheingau.

Rufina

A pretty, small Chianti town about 32 kilometers (20 miles) northeast of Florence in the Sieve River Valley. The wines are among the best not accorded the Classico designation.

Ruländer

Grayish-colored Burgundy grape (Pinot Gris) introduced into Germany by one Ruhland; it is also planted in Alsace and Switzerland. Also called Grauerburgunder or Tokaier.

Rully

A commune in the Chalon Slope of Burgundy which produces both red and white wines and has its own Appellation Contrôlée.
See Chalonnais.

Rum

Rum is the distillate of products of fermented sugarcane. Of all spirits, it retains the most of those natural taste factors which come to it from its product of origin. Starch-derived spirits, such as vodka from potatoes, or whisky from grain, must be cooked, or malted. In the case of rum, based on sugar, the processes by which starch is turned into sugar are not necessary: rum does not have to be distilled at very high proof, as gin and vodka do; it receives the minimum of chemical treatment and can be aged in casks which have already been used for spirit-ageing, because it does not need the tannin which such a spirit as Cognac will absorb from the oak. Rum may be flavored or adulterated by other processes than the essential reduction of its proof strength with pure water—but it need not be; and if it is a decent rum, it should not be. Its color varies from water-white, the natural hue, through amber to mahogany. The only coloring matter used is sugar caramel, which does not affect the flavor. A rum's real character will be determined by the following factors:

The Material of Which It Is Made

Rum is made principally from molasses, which is the uncrystallizable mass remaining after the formation of sugar; sometimes directly from the sugar-cane juice,

437

or from second-grade molasses and other residues. The last type is usually called tafia, not rum, and it is seldom worth exporting, or even bottling. The majority of fine rums come from molasses, but a few do not; one of the best of Haiti is made directly from cane juice; and the most famous rum of Martinique comes from cane juice concentrated into a syrup.

Changing Tastes in Rum

Full body and a distinctive richness of flavor used to be the qualities most appreciated in rum, but in the last twenty-five years tastes have been gradually changing. Many people now prefer a lighter rum, subtler in flavor and more delicate in aroma. The greater demand for the light style has led to a more general use of the continuous column patent still.

Slow or Rapid Fermentation

The rapid fermentation of *a rum of the light type* can be completed in as little as twelve hours, and a day to a day and a half is general practice. Although Jamaica and other countries are now making a good deal of this style, Puerto Rican and Cuban are the usual examples of typical light rums. Slow fermentation, reinforced by the addition of dunder (the residue left in the still after distillation), produces a heavier type; men who prefer their rum distinctive and pungent say that any other kind is like skimmed milk. Slow fermentation may take up to twelve days. The Wedderburn and Plummer types, traditional Jamaican rums of the old style, are identified with slow fermentation; and Martinique produces slowly-fermented heavy rums, of Grand Arôme. High-ester rums are made in much the same way as the Wedderburn rums, except that a much higher ester content is aimed at.

Yeast Types

The yeasts used in fermentation are cultured or natural. When they are cultured, it is said that they are likely to be bred in secret, like Derby runners, everything staked on their individuality. An important Haitian maker is convinced that the secret of his rum is in the harmony between cane and yeast, which come from the same place; whereas Puerto Rican distillers believe to a man that the taste of their product owes its every virtue (very great, they say) to the private strain of yeast they cultivate.

Pot or Patent Still

As in the making of whisky, either the pot still or the continuous-operation patent still may be used. The patent still is more suitable for the increasingly popular light rums. Pot-still spirits retain more of their natural character; the rums are heavier and not, therefore, to all tastes. The old Jamaican-style rum is the prototype for pot-distilled rums of greater body.

Proof at Which Distilled

Lighter rums are distilled at higher proof. In Jamaica, for instance, distillation strength may rise to 96° (Gay-Lussac), whereas the fuller pot-still rums will be distilled at about 86° (Gay-Lussac).

Place of Origin

A somewhat confusing question. The U.S. Federal Alcohol Administration regulation puts it this way: "Puerto Rico, Cuba, Demerara, Barbados, St. Croix, St. Thomas, Virgin Islands, Jamaica, Martinique, Trinidad, Haiti, and Santo Domingo rums are not distinctive types of rum. Such names are not generic but retain their geographical significance. They may not be applied to rum produced in any other place than the particular region indicated in the name." The fact is that each main center makes differing types of rum, but the distinct rum types *are* identified with certain areas. Jamaica is even now associated with a heavy, pungent rum, although today it is producing lighter types; and conversely, light rums are attributed to Cuba or Puerto Rico, although each island makes a certain amount of rum in other styles. Differences in the rums are the result of differing methods of preparation and of the influences of soil, climate, and especially water.

ORIGIN OF RUM

Rum is initially the essentially West Indian product of cane and water—sugar-cane perhaps brought from the Azores by Columbus on his second voyage and the pure West Indian water which tumbles down from the mountains. First records of rum are from Barbados in 1600, and here is a description of a rum punch bowl of the West Indies in the spacious days of the eighteenth century:"A marble basin, built in the middle of the garden especially for the occasion, served as the bowl. Into it were poured 1,200 bottles of rum, 1,200 bottles of Málaga wine, and 400 quarts of boiling water. Then 600 pounds of the best cane sugar and 200 powdered nutmegs were added. The juice of 2,600 lemons were squeezed into the liquor. Onto the surface was launched a handsome mahogany boat piloted by a boy of twelve, who rowed about a few moments, then coasted to the side and began to serve the assembled company of six hundred, which gradually drank up the ocean upon which he floated."

Rum was overwhelmingly popular in the American colonies before 1775; about 450,000 hectoliters (12 million U.S. gallons, 10 million imp.) a year were downed, four gallons (3 imp.) per person; whereas 2.6 gallons a year per person for all spirituous liquors combined is the best that can be done today. One historian declares that the British law of 1763, designed to make the Americans give up Spanish West Indian rums in favor of the British product, caused the

Revolution—and a revolution might just as well be fought over rum as over tea.

An apparently authentic story about Paul Revere tells that he set out on his ride in morose silence and did not begin to shout that the English were coming until he had stopped at the home of a rum distiller—one Isaac Hall, Captain of the Minute Men—for two drafts of Medford rum. (Medford was the name for all the rum along the Atlantic Coast in those days.) George Washington, at any rate, was launched on rum. He was elected to the Virginia House of Burgesses in 1758 not by campaigning but by distributing among the voters 75 gallons of rum; and it was the Virginia House of Burgesses which later sent him to the Continental Congress.

Rum was used in the slave trade, boats loaded with the spirit going to Africa to trade, and bringing back Negroes. Dead Man's Chest, a tiny West Indian island, roistered its way into history—"Fifteen men on Dead Man's Chest—yo-ho-ho, and a bottle of rum." In the 1920s, rum revived a kind of piracy, when the speed launches were running rum from Cuba to the Florida Keys.

After Prohibition, the United States developed a fad for drinking concoctions of rum mixed with slices of fruit and chunks of ice. This still goes on, although excellent brands of rum are now available.

The distillation process is approximately the same for rum as for whisky—except that rum need not be malted. (*See* Distillation; Gin; Whiskey, Scotch; Whiskey, Bourbon; etc.)

By and large, the British drink West Indian rum, from the islands that were formerly their possessions, and the French the rums of the French West Indies or Antilles. United States imports are principally from Puerto Rico, followed by the Virgin Islands, with Jamaica and Barbados a long way behind, and a still smaller amount from the French West Indies, Haiti, and other islands.

See Rum, Puerto Rican; Rum, Jamaican; Rum, West Indies; Rum, French West Indies; Rum, Haitian; Rum, Martinique, etc.

Rum, Barbados

The beautiful garden-like island of Barbados in the West Indies is composed largely of sandstone, coral, and volcanic ash deposits, a mixture which gives the soil a porous character very suitable to the cultivation of sugar-cane. Although the warm climate is ideal, the island has no rivers and all the water used for irrigation as well as for other purposes must be pumped from subterranean caverns.

Since sugar-cane is the island's major product, much rum is made; production has been increasing slowly while export has been rising more rapidly. Latest figures show a jump upward in exports of one-third to about 720,000 proof gallons annually.

Barbados rum is distilled from molasses, a by-product of sugar-cane; distillation is carried out in pot stills and patent stills. Semi-light in body and color, Barbadian rums generally have a soft, almost smoky or leathery flavor. There are five distilleries: Hanschell Inness (Cockspur Rum), West India Rum Refinery, Alleyne, Arthur & Hunt, R. L. Seale & Co. and Mt. Gay Distillers. Certain old rums of the latter company can be drunk neat, like a fine brandy.

Rum, Cuban

The light, delectable rum of Cuba is the natural drink of the Cubans, to whom the lightness of the type is all-important—and the rum is distilled and aged with that end in view, and treated with charcoal to make it even lighter.

Cane sugar, yeast, and the crystalline torrent water of the volcanic West Indian islands are the dominant ingredients of good rums. The Cuban and Puerto Rican types are generally distilled from molasses—a by-product of refined cane sugar—and fermented with cultured yeast and pure water. Cuban rum is often processed by blending or transforming newer spirits with older ones and is sand-filtered during ageing.

There are two leading styles of rum in Cuba: Carta Blanca (White Label), which was the base for Daiquiris; and Carta Oro (Gold Label), to which some caramel is added to mellow the color—this is, therefore, a little darker as well as sweeter than the Carta Blanca. The best rums came from the vicinity of Santiago, at the south end of the island. The principal producers prior to Castro's takeover were: Compañía Ron Bacardi; Alvarez Camp y. Co., Santiago; Arechabaia; Cadenas; and Matanzas. Now all exports to the Western world have ceased. Much Cuban rum goes to the Soviet Union.

Rum, Demerara

The export rum of Guyana.
See Rum, Guyana.

Rum, French

Rum is rapidly increasing in popularity in France, imported mainly from the French West Indies and to a lesser extent from Réunion Island. The rums are not very often seen outside France and, except for two or three from Martinique, cannot be considered to figure in the world market.

French West Indies or French Antilles

A considerable quantity of full-bodied rum, some of it high grade, is made in the islands of Martinique and Guadeloupe. It must be remembered that the islands are not possessions or territories of France but actual French departments, like the Gironde or Basses-Pyrénées. In this preferential situation, it is natural that the rums gravitate to metropolitan France, where they are widely sold. Of the two islands, Martinique is more important.

See Rum, Martinique.

Réunion Island

The sole spirituous product of this former French colony in the Indian Ocean off the coast of Madagascar is rum. Like Martinique and Guadeloupe, Réunion is actually a department of France. About 100,000 hectoliters (2,640,000 U.S. gallons, 2,200,000 imp.) annually are distilled showing a great recent increase. Most of this is white rum, very little aged; but a small quantity of cask-matured rum is also produced.

French Guiana

Prévot and Mirande, the two distilleries, produce annually a little less than 7,500 hectoliters (200,000 U.S. gallons, 165,000 imp.) of undistinguished white rum. No other spirit is made.

Rum, Guyana

Two types of rum are made, pot-still and continuous-still.

The distinguishing characteristic of Guyana rum is its exceedingly rapid fermentation—usually completed in from thirty-six to forty hours.

In addition to export rum, there is made for domestic consumption in this country of some 400,000 souls situated close to Venezuela a "fruit" rum made by steeping various spices and fruits in the distillation from Coffey continuous stills. The product is then lightly tinted with caramel and bottled at a strength of 24° under proof or 85.7° U.S. proof. The resulting rum is lighter-bodied than the better-known Demerara variety. Courantin, one of the "fruit" rums, is occasionally seen in England; it has a pleasant and quite noticeable scent of spices and fruit.

Demerara, named after the river along which the sugar-cane grows, is the important rum of Guyana. Most is exported. Both continuous and pot-still processes are used. Made from molasses, not directly from cane juice, the rum is fermented spontaneously in wooden vats. A trace of sulfuric acid is added to kill bacteria and a little ammonium sulfate to feed the yeast. The rum is generally quite darkly colored by the addition of caramel obtained by burning cane sugar. Demerara is not as heavy as might appear from its color. Because of the very rapid fermentation process, it is not likely to have quite the pronounced flavor of rums which are obtained by slower fermentation. Among Demeraran rums themselves, those distilled in pot stills will have up to a third more of the taste-giving esters than the Coffey-still varieties, and more than twice the amount of the higher alcohols. Demerara is exported at approximately 43° over proof, or 163.4° U.S. proof. Guyana leads the other British-influenced countries of the Caribbean in rum export.

Rum, Haitian

Although sugar-cane is grown on all parts of the island of Haiti, it is in the north, behind the small port of Cape Haitian, that the best cane for first run or raw rum-making is found. A rim of mountains runs along the north coast, and behind, in the valleys, the rainfall is not as abundant as it is elsewhere. The mountain Citadelle of the Black Emperor, Henri Christophe, who went dramatically mad and killed himself with a silver bullet, soars into the sky, high above the cane-cutting crews rhythmically swinging their machetes while the chanter calls out his rising and falling phrases to set the pace.

Almost two centuries ago Haiti revolted and freed itself from France. Nevertheless, traditions, attitudes, and customs are still predominantly French; and the French skill in making fine brandy continues to influence the making of Haitian rum—which is double-distilled in pot stills, the first run, or raw rum, being redistilled. This is the same method used in the production of Cognac brandy. First-run Haitian rum, however, is often sold as a low-priced island product, although never exported. It is completely colorless: hence its name—clairin. On the Haitian feast days, this rum is sold raw by the glass from small folding stands placed along the streets and roadways, each stand lit with a flickering lamp which gleams like a yellow star. Clairin is considered to have the special virtue of propitiating the powerful gods of Voodoo. For this reason, or perhaps only because it is cheap, it is the libation spirit poured on the ground at the Voodoo ceremonies (90% of the country still worships in the religion brought by the slaves from Africa), and the gods have their taste before the celebrants begin to drink.

The best known of Haitian rum, and one of the fine rums of the world, is Rhum Barbancourt. This is medium-bodied and has an exquisite balance. According to M. Jean Gardère, maker of Barbancourt, this is due to the fact that a certain yeast found in the area where the cane grows is used to ferment the juice. This common origin, with the same soil ingredients and conditions, has a subtle influence on both yeast and cane juice, producing the harmony which does undoubtedly exist in the rum. The juice, which is pasteurized in order to seal in the natural vitamins throughout distillation, is processed as soon as it has been crushed from the cane, and there is no secondary fermentation. The Barbancourt plant, founded in 1862, now has a capacity of 25,000 hectoliters (658,000 U.S. gallons, 547,000 imp.). Three-star, five-star, and estate reserve rums are made, the last one originally limited to Haitian sale, but all are exported.

Until Haiti's independence, France was the market for Haitian rums, import of which sometimes reached 684,000 hectoliters (18 million U.S. gallons, 15 million imp.) a year. Today, Martinique rum dominates the French market. Jean Gardère says that the persistent link between France and Haiti is the kinship of soils; the calcareous soil underlaid with lime, which yields rum in Haiti, is practically identical with that which gives two of the greatest vinous products of France—brandy in Cognac and wine in Champagne.

The following are the principal rum distillers of Haiti:

Proprietor	Name of Rum	Distillery
Jean Gardère	Rhum Barbancourt	Damiens (Port-au-Prince)
Hermann Colas	Rhum Citadelle	Cazeau (Port-au-Prince)
Max Nazon	Rhum Nazon	Port-au-Prince
Raymond Nazon	Rhum Larue	Cap-Haitien

Rum, Jamaican

No center of rum-making has been so much affected by recent changes in taste as Jamaica. Traditionally, a heavy, rich-flavored, almost pungent rum was made here—slow-fermented, strengthened with dunder, and distilled in pot stills at low proof.

Now, although Jamaican rums still tend to have a more characteristic flavor and aroma than do most others, they are definitely lighter than they used to be, and the slow-fermentation method has been abandoned. The rums made can be divided into four types: light continuous-still rum—or common clean; light and medium-bodied pot-still rum; Wedderburn and Plummer heavier types; high-ester rum.

For the first type, molasses is the raw material, and distillation is carried out in a continuous still of two or three columns—distillation strength may be as high as 96° (Gay-Lussac). Great care is taken not to remove the true rum constituents of the fermented wash.

Light and medium pot-still rums are made from a wash obtained by mixing cane juice, high-grade molasses, water, and acid. In the pot still, characteristic taste and smell are retained.

Wedderburn and Plummer rums have more body than the previous types—in these the tradition of the past is preserved, and anyone who wants to sample an old robust Jamaica rum should taste one of them. Most of the pot-still rums are distilled at around 86° (Gay-Lussac).

High-ester rums are fermented and distilled in much the same way as are Wedderburn—but the ester content must be higher.

The bulk of the Jamaican (and of other West Indian) rum is taken to London to be aged and bottled there.

Rum, London Dock

West Indian rum taken in bulk to London and aged and bottled there.

Rum, Martinique

The large production of spirits (93,000 hectoliters or 2.45 million U.S. gallons, 2.04 million imp.) is di-

vided, 55% for rum made from molasses and 45% for that made from sugar-cane juice.

There are nearly a hundred principal growers of cane sugar and about fourteen large distillers. The capital, Fort-de-France, is as much a town of rum as any other in the world. The dusty savannah with its statue of Josephine, who left the island to become in time the bride of Napoleon, is fringed all along one side by the dingy rum offices, piled up to the roofs with crates awaiting shipment. The port is at the side of the town, not along the main quay but on an inlet, where the transoceanic vessels rear over the houses, their stacks poking up incongruously along what appears to be a marine avenue, a little lazy smoke appearing as they get up steam to carry the rum out to the world. At one time, Martinique was the proud owner of a rum capital quite different from the rather tawdry and crowded town of Fort-de-France. This was St. Pierre, richest city of the Caribbean. The ruins may still be seen—handsome cobbled streets along the sides of which pure mountain water bubbles and sings. The buildings are crushed, empty skulls overgrown with wild banana, vine, and mango; in a few seconds, early in the century, a blast from the nearby volcano obliterated the town, killing forty thousand people. Despite the desolation, there are several rum companies established in the strip of St. Pierre, which is coming to life again along the coal-black volcanic beach; and one of the best-known of all the rums, Saint James, has its plantations nearby.

While about fifty proprietors make the rum, it is said in Martinique that at the head of the industry are ten families. This led, in the early fifties, to a strike probably unique in history—"the strike of the ten families." When the sugar-cane is ripe, it must be cut and treated at once. Since a Communist government was then in control of the island, the rum- and sugar-owners considered that they were being taxed out of existence. The cane ripened and the sole crop of the island was ready to be made. "Now," said the ten families to the Communist deputies, "we go on strike. We can hold out over a year of no profits. Do you think you can? Without sugar and rum there will be no crop to tax, and no income for you. Don't you think we ought to sit down and have a reasonable discussion?"

The rums made directly from cane juice are sometimes strengthened by the addition of dunder for the fermentation and sometimes not. (Dunder is the residue left in the still after distillation and is generally used in processes of slow fermentation.) When the rums are uncolored by cask-ageing and remain white they are called Grappe Blanche. Such spirits are mainly consumed on the island, forming the base for the inevitable Martinique Punch.

Punch Martiniquais, of early West Indian origin, is probably British. The recipe is: rum, cane-sugar syrup, and a slice of lemon peel. In the happy days just before inflation, the cost was 7 francs, and they gave a customer the sugar-syrup bottle, the rum bottle, a tumbler, and left him to himself. By bringing in a sugar-cane syrup usually made in Martinique, the firm of Duquesne has introduced the punch in France.

A single Martinique rum is made by the fermentation of dunder, about 60%, with concentrated cane-juice syrup. This is the well-known Rhum Saint James, sold in its squarish tall bottle. Its darkness and its aroma distinguish it from most other rums.

Rums made from molasses are fermented with dunder and colored with caramelized sugar. The premium rum of this style is called Grand Arôme, used as a heavy flavor base, and is slow fermented from eight to twelve days. The heavy, rich rums compare with the Wedderburn-type rums of Jamaica, the prototype for the style.

Many consider Rhum Clément, made both white and tawny, to be the aristocrat of Martinique rums. The distillery near the village of François is unpretentious. The canes are trundled on threading railway lines, pushed by the black workers or pulled by a tiny engine, and are then carried up into the jaws of the crushing rollers on belts like greatly enlarged tire-chains. Juice drips stickily into the vats; bled, smashed cane slides off down a chute. The juice achieved by this process is converted into several grades of rum, the finest of which, one is told by M. Charles Clément himself—small, dapper, and the most charming of men—are aged upward of a dozen years. Rhum Duquesne, another good type, is made in the south of the island. Part of the production is distilled as white rum, sold under the trademark Genippa; the rest is aged in warehouses, to be sold as Grand Case (silver label, three years old) and Val d'Or (gold label, ten years old). The whole enterprise is a family business managed by M. O. des Grottes.

Rums utilizing molasses are almost always made at distilleries connected with the large sugar refineries. There are not so many of these, the important ones being at Vive—run by Fernand Clerc, whose three hundred pounds make him in at least one sense the biggest rum man on the island—at Gallion, Rivière Salée, François, and Lareinty. The distilleries making rum direct from cane juice are much more numerous.

Several other spirituous drinks are made in Martinique, some of them based on rum. They include the native rum punch, bottled by the firm of Dogue; anisette, triple sec, crème d'orange, and other liqueurs. Orange is the most common flavoring. Maduva, messica, and maitina are all concocted with essence or juice of orange.

Rum, New England

Rum of a particularly strong, heavy, and hearty sort was among the factors which shaped New England. Blackstrap molasses came in from the West Indies to Connecticut, Rhode Island, and Massachusetts, and went out again as rum—to the taverns of the northern colonies, by ship to the southern ones to be traded for cotton and tobacco, and to Europe for the goods the New World was not yet prepared to make for itself. The most important aspect of the rum business, however, was the "triangular trade" which made the fortune of many a New England sea captain. Rum, shipped from New England to Africa, bought slaves. Slaves, carried to the islands of the West Indies, filled the ships with molasses, and the molasses was brought back to New England to make rum. The unsuccessful efforts of George III to tax molasses added as much heat to the cause of the American Revolution as did the more-renowned Stamp Tax, and "taxation without representation" was denounced over many a glass of New England rum in many a wayside tavern.

Perhaps the first of the important spirit industries of the United States, New England rum is still being made in Massachusetts, where about 7,500 hectoliters (200,000 U.S. gallons, 166,000 imp.) of it are sold each year. It is still a heavy rum, dark, pungent, and full-bodied. Distilled at no more than 160° proof, it is aged in charred oak barrels; and it is from this ageing that it takes its characteristic dark color. There are only three firms making New England rum today.

In addition to those still being made and sold, there are some superb old rums to be found in the private cellars of New Englanders—which, once tasted, stand with certain fine old American Bourbons in the same class as fine French Cognacs.

Although its population is small, the New England state of New Hampshire has the highest present per capita consumption of all rums in the United States.

Rum, Panay

See Rum, Philippine Islands.

Rum, Philippine Islands

Two leading brands of rum are made: Tanduay and Panay. These have different flavors and Tanduay is by far the better seller of the two; it is also the higher priced.

Rum, Puerto Rican

Puerto Rico is the foremost world producer of rums and its products dominate the United States market, accounting for 70% of the rum consumption there. The two main types are White Label (very light-bodied) and Gold Label (slightly less light). In the United States, White Label outsells the Gold by about three to one, while in Puerto Rico itself the proportion is reversed—although there is not such a large demand for it among the inhabitants of Puerto Rico as there is for such cheaper varieties as Palo Viejo and Ron Llave.

Cuba, the other island which is famous for its light rums, also produces White Label and Gold Label. (*See* Rum, Cuban.)

Puerto Rico has always depended on its rich and

abundant crop of sugar-cane as a vital means of support, and it is from this sugar-cane that the rum industry draws its existence. Ponce de León, who headed the first government of the island, is known to have distilled the cane, and a dispatch writer in 1526 reports that the natives were getting tipsy on sugar-cane rum. Ponce de León was a commercially-minded man, and one authority goes so far as to state that his search for the fountain of youth was nothing more than a quest for a sound distillable water.

The refining of raw sugar-cane results in fine sugar and a by-product called blackstrap molasses. Puerto Rican rums are distilled from this molasses, fermented with cultured yeast and mountain water, aged under government control, and required to be shipped in bottle. During the war years when whiskey was short, rums of every description were made, and many a bad Puerto Rican rum or purported Puerto Rican rum found its way into the United States. After the war, these could no longer be sold and they remained a glut on the market; and Puerto Rico established strict export laws to assure high-quality rums under the island imprint. The government now operates a rum pilot plant through the University of Puerto Rico—the only instance in which a project of this nature is government-sponsored.

Puerto Rican rum is a characteristic type and is usually light-bodied and dry in contrast to the thicker aromatic rums of Martinique. Generally, Puerto Rican-type rums are fermented with cultured yeast and distilled in patent stills.

Puerto Rican rums are made on widely scattered points of the island, which have sharp differences in climate, ranging from almost perpetual rainfall to almost constant drought. The soils vary too; and finally, each distiller cultivates his own yeast from a single yeast cell, producing the type which is peculiarly identified with his own brand name. Yeast is continually manufactured by every distiller in order to provide a sufficient amount for the carrying on of fermentation from day to day, and the yeast strain is never allowed to die. It is considered in Puerto Rico to be the secret of the rum. Something in these yeasts and soil and climatic conditions indelibly marks the rums, and as there are intuitive wine-tasters, so there are rum connoisseurs who boast that when they taste a glass of rum they can say exactly where it comes from.

Many of the old distillers who made rum before Prohibition were forced out of business during that period. An exception is the Puerto Rican Distilling Company, maker of Ronrico, which is generally light, although some 151° heavier-bodied rum is made. Fourteen distiller permits are at present granted in Puerto Rico. The Destilería Bacardi claims to have the largest capacity of any distillery in the world. The principal exported brands (arranged alphabetically) are: Bacardi, Boca Chica, Carioca, Don Q, Maraca, Merito, Ronrico.

Rum, Tanduay

One of the leading types made in the Philippine Islands.
See Rum, Philippine Islands.

Rum, Trinidad

The rums, which are medium-light in type, are distilled from molasses in continuous stills. Before fermentation, the molasses is diluted with water and clarified—which makes the subsequent fermentation easier to control. Yeast is added, and the quick fermentation will be over in anything from thirty-six to forty-eight hours. The resultant rums are clean, though not as distinguished as some of the other styles, and distilled at strengths varying between 83° and 96° (Gay-Lussac).

Rum, Virgin Islands

The rums tend to be medium-style, generally somewhat heavier than the light rums of Puerto Rico. Much of the product is exported in bulk.

Of the three islands, St. Thomas, St. John, and St. Croix, the last is much more suited to the growing of sugar-cane and therefore to the production of rum. St. Thomas is small, hardly more than a few mountains rearing up out of the Caribbean Sea; while St. Croix is much more extensive, with many stretches of flat land, almost the whole of its surface consisting of beautiful beaches surrounding a vast field of cane. The rums of the Virgin Islands are called Cruzan (from a former reference to St. Croix rums) and Old St. Croix. Both labels are owned by Virgin Islands Rum Industries, Ltd.

Rum, West Indies

Barbados, Jamaica, British Guiana (Guyana), and Trinidad form this group in the Caribbean; the first, second, and fourth are islands, the third a small country on the northeast coast of South America. Together they produce about 7 million proof gallons of rum annually, Barbados and Jamaica making roughly 1.5 million gallons each, while Trinidad and British Guiana make some 2 million gallons each. The leading exporter, with about 1.5 million gallons, is British Guiana, followed by Jamaica with 1 million gallons, Barbados with 700,000 gallons, and Trinidad with 300,000 gallons.

Rum is the traditional drink of the British navy. There are records of the ship's crew of Sir George Summer taking refuge from a hurricane at Bermuda in 1609 and seeking consolation in drinking rum, referred to as "comfortable waters." Hundreds of thousands of gallons of rum were included in the British supplies during the American Revolution. From the

Rumania

eighteenth century to the present day, rum has been rationed out daily to the men of the Royal Navy.

See Rum, Jamaican; Rum, Barbados; Rum, Guyana; Rum, Trinidad.

Rumania

Vines were grown in Rumania long ago; there were vineyards in Scitia Minor (today's Dobrudja) even before the Greeks founded their Black Sea colonies, early in the seventh century B.C. And on the foothills of the Carpathians there long existed such large plantations as those at Cotnari and Uricani, Huşi, Odobeşti, Panciu, Nicoreşti, Dealul-Mare, and Drăgăşani. The Greeks sent the wine in amphorae throughout the civilized world of their day. Later on, the merchants of the northern ports carried away great casks of the wine to their big fairs, which would not have been complete without the barrels of Cotnari, Odobeşti, and Drăgăşani.

Rumania now produces 8.5 million hectoliters (225 million U.S. gallons, 187 million imp.), ranking her sixth in Europe, just behind Portugal and ahead of West Germany. The vineyards have been expanding and total about 300,000 hectares (750,000 acres). Each Rumanian drinks about 28 liters of wine every year. The government has encouraged the wine industry and plans to increase the size of the vineyards over the next decade by 100,000 hectares. Even though the government plays an important role, only 20% of the grape planting belongs to the state. The bulk of the wine is made by large cooperatives, but individual plots still account for one-third of the production.

Planted recently, and now developing well, are the vineyards of Tîrnave, Sîmbureşti, and Segarcea. The extension of the vineyards over most of the country is due foremost to the fact that Rumania is situated almost entirely in the vine-growing zone (toward the northern limit), and the country has the favorable features of rolling hills. In addition to still wines there is an increasing tendency towards the production and sale of sparkling wines.

PRINCIPAL REGIONS

The Cotnari Vineyard

In northeast Rumania, near the historic town of Iassy, these vineyards cover the lower slopes of the Carpathians and enjoy splendid conditions of climate, soil, and exposure. Cotnari is one of the oldest vineyards in the country—in 1646 it was mentioned by the Jesuit monk Marcus Bandinus in a account of his sojourn in Moldavia. Old as it is, the vineyard still flourishes. Its new plantations, the result of modern scientific knowledge, promise a great development in the near future.

Grape varieties: Grasă de Cotnari, Fetească Albă, Tămîioasa Românească, Frîncuşa.

Type of wine. Cotnari is a natural dessert wine, with 13% to 15% alcohol per volume and more than 50 grams in a liter of residual sugar. It is well balanced, with a particularly fine flavor and bouquet.

The Murfatlar Vineyard

Situated close to the Black Sea, on the Murfatlar Hills, the vineyard has a character all its own: more than 17,000 hectares (42,500 acres) form an unbroken vineyard on sunny slopes fanned by a mild sea breeze, and the wine-making plants are run according to up-to-date methods by qualified technicians. There exists also, in this region, an experimental station of the Institute of Horticultural and Viticultural Research.

Grape varieties. The prevailing grape varieties here are Pinot Chardonnay and Pinot Gris. Other types, such as Muscat Ottonel, Pinot Noir, and Cabernet Sauvignon, are also grown, with satisfactory results.

Type of wine. Murfatlar is a dessert wine, with a fine bouquet in which a faint, unique nuance of orange-flower is detectable.

The Tîrnave Vineyard

Extending along the banks of the River Tîrnave, the vineyards are well known for the quality of their wines. The more important areas are: Blaj, Mediaş, Richiş, Jidvei, Seuca, Valea-Lungă, Aţel, Tigmandru—to mention only a few of the more outstanding.

Grape varieties to be found in the vineyard area are Italian Riesling, Fetească, Ruländer, Furmint, Traminer, Sauvignon, Neuburger, and Muscat Ottonel.

Type of wine. Tîrnave produces dry wines from the Fetească and Riesling grape varieties, demi-sec and sweet wines from the Traminer and Sauvignon, and a famous *vin liquoreux* from the Muscat Ottonel.

The Dealul-Mare Vineyard

Where the lower slopes of the Carpathian Hills imperceptibly meet the plain and the hillocks bask in the hot rays of the sun, the vines produce such Rumanian favorites as the wines of Valea Călugărească, Tohani, Săhăteni, Urlaţi, Istrita, and Pietroasele.

Grape varieties: Italian Riesling, Fetească Albă, Tămîioasa Românească, Muscat Ottonel, Cabernet Sauvignon, Pinot Noir, and Merlot.

Types of wine. The pride of the Valea Călugărească vineyard is the red wines from the Pinot Noir and the Cabernet Sauvignon. These are big wines of a rich, dark color, with a pleasant flavor, harmonious and velvety, yet full of character.

The Vrancea Vineyard

This is the largest stretch of vineyard in Rumania, extending over such varied country and types of soil and subject to climatic conditions so diverse that the wines produced in the region are correspondingly various. The principal types are:

Odobeşti. White table and quality wines from Galbenăçt, Fetească, Muscat Ottonel, and Aligoté grapes.

Coteşti. White and red table wines and quality wines from Riesling, Fetească, Muscat, Pinot Noir, and Cabernet Sauvignon grapes.

Panciu. White table wines, especially appreciated for their freshness.

Nicoreşti. Red table wines and quality wines from Băbească de Nicoreşti and Fetească Neagră.

The Banat Vineyard

There are two centers of production: the vineyards of the plain—Teremia, Mare, Tomnatec—which produce large quantities of pleasant table wines of a greenish-white color and of a consistent quality, and the hill vineyards, such as Buziaş, Recaş, Miniş, Ghioroc, Baratke, Pîncota, and Şiria.

Grape varieties used in the white wines of Teremia and Tomnatec are Creaţa (Riesling de Banat), Majărcă, and Steinschiller. The red wines of Miniş and Recaş are made from Kadarka and Cabernet grapes.

Type of wine. From the stony terraces of Miniş comes the famous Kadarka de Banat—a red wine appreciated for its characteristic flavor and aroma.

The Other Vineyards

The white wines of Drăgăşani (Stefaneşti, Jasi, Huşi, and Galati), the white and red wines of Segarcea (Mehedinti, Uricani, and Sîmbureşti), the semi-dry white wines of Alba Iulia, Aiud, Lechinţa, and Bistriţa, complete the wide range of wine production in Rumania.

It has been estimated that by the development of the nurseries and by the application of modern scientific methods of viticulture and viniculture Rumania's vineyards should become the most up-to-date in Eastern Europe. The present plan is to plant an additional 50,000 hectares with varieties which will ensure the basic production necessary for the big vinicultural combines which are being created in order to turn the country's great wine potential to the best account.

WINE EXPORTS

Wine has become an important export only in recent years. In 1984 nearly 550,000 hectoliters (14.5 million U.S. gallons, 12 million imp.) were sent abroad—different varieties to suit the tastes of different markets. Thus, to the German Federal Republic are exported white and red table wines from Riesling, Fetească, Kadarka, Cabernet Sauvignon, and Rotburgunder grapes. To Austria, besides ordinary white wines, Rumania sells quality wines of the Riesling, Fetească, Ruländer, Muscat Ottonel, Tămîioasa Romînească varieties, as well as red wines such as Rotburgunder and Cabernet Sauvignon. Rumanian wines are also exported to Switzerland, Belgium, Holland, Sweden, Denmark, France, the United States, and Great Britain—and, of course, in great quantities to Poland, Czechoslovakia, and East Germany.

The following are the principal varieties of wine bottled for export by the "Vinexport":

WHITE TABLE WINES

Perla de Tîrnave	Sauvignon
Fetească de Tîrnave	Aligoté
Riesling de Tîrnave	Riesling de Dealul-Mare
Grünsilvaner	Ordinary white table wine
Rulända	Superior white table wine
Furmint	

WHITE DESSERT WINES

Cotnari	Murfatler

RED WINES

Pinot Noir	Cabinet
Cabernet	Băbească de Nicoreşti
Kadarka	

Recently, Rumania entered wines for the competition organized by the French at Montpellier. According to an enthusiastic French report, these wines "were a pleasant surprise . . . a sumptuous Merlot de Nicoreşti, ruby-colored and with a delicate flavor . . . Cabinet de Ploieşti, light and with a pleasing finesse. The dry and semi-dry white wines of Coteşti remind one of our Alsatian growths, and can be classified among the best in the world. The Riesling, with its freshness, and the Fetească, with its delicate yet definite aroma, have met with unanimous approval. In the same group, the Fetească de Tîrnave lived up to its name—The Pearl of Tîrnave. . . . The thick Chardonnay de Murfatlar with its taste of honey . . . and the subtler Cotnar . . . delighted the tasters."

Rumbullion (rumbustion)

Two seventeenth-century English-West Indian terms for rum. The exact origin of the words is obscure, although it has been suggested that they come from the dialect of Devonshire.

Ruppertsberger

Good wines of Mittelhaardt in the German Palatinate. The best vineyards are Hoheburg, Gaisböhl, Linsenbusch, Nussbien.

See Palatinate.

Russia

The U.S.S.R. is the third-largest wine-producing nation in the world—after Italy and France—and both volume and vineyard size are rapidly increasing. In the ten-year period before the devastation of the Second World War, production averaged only 5 million hectoliters (132 million U.S. gallons, 110 million imp.). Now, about 34 million hectoliters (898 million U.S. gallons, 748 million imp.) are made every year, more than the amount produced in the United States.

While wine, especially on the borders of the Black Sea, has always been important in Russia, it was not until the 1930s that the government undertook a rapid expansion of viticulture in the naturally favored areas, particularly the Soviet Republics of Armenia, Azerbaijan, and Georgia (in the neck between the Black and Caspian seas) and in the Crimea. By 1948 the acreage in vine was triple the pre-Revolution figure and had passed a million acres; today there are more than 1,350,000 hectares (3,375,000 acres) of vineyards. Nearly 7 million hectoliters of wines are imported—most of it from Algeria—and more than 550,000 hectoliters (14.5 million U.S. gallons, 12 million imp.) are exported. Consumption is 13 liters per capita, and the state encourages wine-drinking to cut down on the tremendous quantities of spirits (vodka) consumed. Russians on the average drink more liquor than anyone else in the world.

Increase of production was partly due to postwar territorial acquisitions, such as the present Moldavian Soviet Socialist Republic—which decades ago was Bessarabia and a part of Rumania. Bessarabia has always produced a large quantity of wines, especially around Kishinev, the capital of the Moldavian S.S.R.; much of this wine, formerly known as Bessarabian, also comes from around the mouth of the River Dniester, in the region of what is Belgorod Dnestrovskiy, but was Akkerman—a name by which the wines were frequently known. This district is now part of the Ukraine.

Very important in the Soviet scheme of wine expansion is the making of sparkling wines. One hundred million bottles are made annually. Probably the best is Kaffia, from the Crimea. A close second, if not equal, is that made at the Abrau Dursso Collective at Krasnodar in the region of the Kuban Valley near the Sea of Azov, a section always important in Russian viticulture. The wine is the same as the white wine of Abran (sometimes wrongly attributed to the Crimea), which lies to the west.

Three-fourths of Russian wine is sweet—over 15% of sugar—with about 15% of alcohol. Oenologists at the Technical Wine Institute at Odessa and the Magarach Research Center in Yalta work with standard European varieties such as Cabernet Sauvignon and Riesling, but their experiments are not aimed at making dry table wines; they try instead to improve the quality of the sweet wines.

Russian viticulture must cope with one great problem: the winter cold, with temperatures as low as −40 °F. (−40°C.). After the harvest, the vines are pruned and taken off the training wires to be bent down and covered with dirt as insulation against the cold. Then the following spring these same vines must be uncovered and remounted before the new canes start to grow. Much emphasis has been put on mechanization, and this once time-consuming task is now performed both spring and fall by large machines. Mechanical harvesting, however, is less developed, and most of the grapes are still hand-picked. Agricultural engineers have recently developed a workable harvesting machine, though it can stand improvement.

IMPORTANT DISTRICTS

With a few mediocre exceptions, all the wine of the Soviet Union is produced in the vast arc of southern Russia, beginning at the Rumanian border on the west and stretching across the north of the Black Sea, the Causasus, the Caspian Sea, and finally the north of Iran and India to the frontiers of China and Mongolia. The whole of this huge region produces wines in larger or smaller quantities but all the important ones come from west of the Caspian Sea—from the lower River Don, from around the Sea of Azov, and especially from the Crimea. Good wines are produced in the Caucasian republics of Azerbaijan, Georgia, and Armenia.

From earliest times, vines flourished in these regions, and wines are known to have been made long before our era. Traces of viticulture have been found in the ancient kingdom of Van which, about a thousand years before Christ, extended as far as the Armenian plain and the southern part of Transcaucasia. By the time of Herodotus (*fl.* 460 B.C.), the wines of Armenia had won great renown. When, some 250 years earlier, the Assyrians descended on the cities of Van, they found and pillaged great cellars of wine. Sulfur was already in use, and some of the wine is believed to have been pressed from sun-dried grapes. The Georgians, also, learned very early to cultivate their vines. Archaeologists have discovered painted wine jars and large amphorae dating from, at latest, the second millennium B.C.; in the *Odyssey*, Homer praised the "perfumed, sprightly wines of Colchis [western Georgia], land of the golden grape." Xenophon related that the wines of the Black Sea shores were robust, pleasant, and aromatic when mixed with water.

Crimea

The sweet wines and the dessert wines, both red and white, are the most important, though dry wines and fortified wines are made, as well as sparkling wines, which include the good Kaffia. Production is not large, but the small area of the Crimean peninsula thrusting into the Black Sea is the finest wine region of Russia.

The southern and eastern sections are best, and important vineyards lie along the coasts and near the cities of Sevastopol and Simferopol. Crimean viticulture was originally developed at the beginning of the last century, under the direction of a M. Pallas, a French expert who brought many workers and managers from France to create or improve the vineyards. The chief estate, which gave its name to the most famous wine, was Massandra, the property of Prince Woronzow. Today Massandra is the name used for a combine of a number of Crimean wine collectives, and there is a red Massandra and a dry white one. But the most famous of these wines, still being made, is the rich, amber, fortified Madeira-type, sometimes considered the best wine of Russia. Other outstanding Crimean wines are the white Livadia, made from the Muscat (there is also a red Livadia from the Cabernet grape); the dry white Sémillon Oreanda (usually called Orianda outside Russia); the Saperavi or, today, the Saperavi Massandra, a dry red wine not to be confused with the great golden dessert Massandra, but a very flavorful wine on its own account; the pink dessert Alupka, and the Ay-Danil dessert wines. A number of grape varieties known in Europe are used here—for example, Riesling, Cabernet, Pinot Gris, and, most extensively, Muscat.

River Don

The lower Don, as it descends to empty into the Sea of Azov below Rostov, produces red and white wines and a relatively small quantity of sparkling wines, the best-known of which is Donski. The viticultural centers are Tsimliansk, Constantinovka, and Novocherkassk. Grape varieties are of local type: Pletchistik, Krasnotop, and Pukhliakovski, all white wine grapes.

Moldavia

Formerly Bessarabia and part of Rumania, Moldavia produces the largest quantity of wine in the U.S.S.R. Today there are also some Pinot, Aligoté, Riesling, Traminer, and other European varieties. There are 325,000 hectares (812,500 acres) of vines, of which more than 200,000 are in production. About 8% of the U.S.S.R.'s total production, or approximately 2.8 million hectoliters (74 million U.S. gallons, 61 million imp.), is from Moldavia.

Ukraine

After the scourge of the vine louse phylloxera in the last century, a great percentage of the area was replanted in hybrids. These are now being systematically replaced. Centers are Odessa, Ismalie, and Carpates. The vineyards in all parts of the Ukraine are similar in size to those of Moldavia and produce light red and white wines, low in alcohol, as well as sparkling and dessert wines.

Stavropol

Dry white wines (Riesling, Bechtau, and Sylvaner Bechtau) and Muscat-based dessert wines from the north slopes of the Caucasus Mountains.

Krasnodar

A region, and also its principal city, lying east of the Black Sea and the Sea of Azov. There are some very large cooperatives in this region. Good red and white dry wines are made along the Black Sea, near Anapa and Novorossiysk, from the Riesling and Cabernet grapes. The Kuban Valley produces large quantities of fortified and dessert wines. The Abrau-Dursso Collective, on the Black Sea, produces one of the best sparkling wines in the U.S.S.R. Two other sparkling wines that are exported from this area are Krasnodar and Isimljanskoje Ygristoje.

Georgia

With about 250,000 hectares (625,000 acres), the Georgian Republic is the largest producer among the first-quality wine districts, containing some of the oldest vineyard sites in Russia. Some Georgian wines seen abroad are white Myshako Riesling and Ghurdjurni. The Takhetia region is the best, producing the white Gourdjaani and Tsinandali; the red Mukuzani, Napuréouli, and Mzvane or Mtzvane. In this region, the must is fermented with the skins and stems in earthenware pots, and the wine has a particularly astringent taste. A good red is made from the Speravi grape, which also produces one of the finest red table wines of the Crimea. Mzvane, making the white of the same name, is also a grape variety; another local type is the Rka-Ziteli. There is also abundant production of sparkling wines and brandy.

Azerbaijan

Table wines, fortified wines, and *eaux-de-vie* are produced in Russian Azerbaijan (135,000 hectares—337,500 acres). Matrassa, a table wine named after the grape variety, is the best of the region, which has only been growing vines since the 1960s. The principal centers are Kirovabad, Kurdamirsk, Chemakhinsk, and Geokchai. Dessert wines are also made in this region.

Armenia

Wine has always been a fundamental product in the Armenian economy and the region is called "Fatherland of the Vine." Natural wines, fortified wines, and brandy are made in large quantities. The wine centers are Echmiadzin, Achtarak, Vedin, and Oktemberian (43,000 hectares or 107,500 acres of vines).

In addition to the foregoing important districts, expanding wine production by means of irrigation is underway in Turkmenistan (approximately 11,000 hectares, or 27,500 acres) where fortified wines, a so-called Tokay, and Yasman-salik and Kara-Isium are made. In Uzbekistan (around 63,000 hectares, or 157,000 acres) three-quarters of the grape culture is devoted to the locally famous Iziun table grape, but the remainder goes principally to dessert wines; in Tadzhikistan, on the north of Pakistan and Kashmir, dessert wine is now being produced from about 20,000 hectares (50,000 acres) and in the vast stretches of Kazakhstan, which reaches from the Caspian Sea to Mongolia, vine planting has been introduced in recent years (approximately 20,000 hectares, or 50,000 acres, have been planted).

The chart opposite gives the authorized Soviet wine place-names or Appellations d'Origine. These were extracted from a bulletin of the International Wine Office, to which acknowledgement is also due for some of the other material on Soviet wines. Certain wines are designated by the Soviet wine industry as port, madeira, tokay, etc. *This can never be correct*, as only a wine from the banks of the Upper Douro River in Portugal can fulfill all the conditions necessary to Port; only a wine from the island of Madeira can fulfill the conditions for a Madeira, etc. But in the situation prevailing at the time of writing, of very limited information from the Soviet Union, the terms port-type, madeira-type, etc., will be used to indicate the approximate style of the wines.

SPIRITS

The Russian national drink is traditionally vodka, which has for some time now been most popular also west of the Iron Curtain. A large quantity of brandy is also made.
See Vodka.

Russian River Valley

Californian wine district in Sonoma County on the coast 50 miles north of San Francisco.
See United States; California.

Ruster Ausbruch

A very sweet Austrian wine, made from late-picked grapes in the vineyards of Rust, Burgenland.
See Austria.

Rutherglen

Celebrated region in Victoria, Australia, producing some of the best fortified and dessert wines, and some full, red table wines as well, now, however, all in smaller quantities than formerly.
See Australia.

Ruwer

See Mosel-Saar-Ruwer.

Wine District	Type	Grape Varieties and Place-Names
Crimea (Massandra Combine)	Dry white	Sémillon Oreanda, Riesling Massandra, Aligoté Ay-Danil
	Dry red	Cabernet Livadia, Saperavi Massandra, Bordo Ay-Danil
	Sweet dessert	White Muscat Massandra, White Muscat Livadia, Pink Muscat Gourzouf
	Red dessert	Black Muscat Kuchuk-Lambat, White Muscat Kastel
	Pink dessert	Pink Muscat Alupka
	Dessert	Tokay Ay-Danil, Tokay Alouchta, Pinot Gris Ay-Danil
	Red Muscat	Aiou-Dag
	White port-type	Sou-Dag, Alupka
	Red port-type	Livadia, Kuchuk-Lambat, Alouchta, Massandra
	Madeira-type	Kuchuk-Uzen, Massandra
Ukrainian S.S.R.	White	Riesling, Aligoté
	Red	Cabernet
Krasnodar (Abrau-Dursso Combine)	Dry white	Riesling Abrau, Riesling Anapa
	Dry red	Cabernet Abrau
Georgian S.S.R.	Dry white	Tsolikohouri, Sémillon, Kahouri, Tibaani
	Red	Téliani, Mukuzani, Napuréouli
	White dessert	Ousahelohouri, Tchkhavéri, Tvichi, Psou, Tetra, Ahméta
	Red dessert	Hvantchkara, Kindzmaraouli, Ahachéni
	Brandy	Eniséli, Gremi, Vartsihé, Tbilisi
Azerbaijan S.S.R.	Red	Matrassa
	White port-type	Akastafa
	White dessert	Kara-Tachanakh
	Red dessert	Chamakha, Kurdamir
Armenian S.S.R.	White	Etchmiadzine, Voskévaz
	Red	Aréni, Norachéne
	White sherry-type	Achtaraque
	Red port-type	Aigéchate
	Red fortified	Arévchate
	Brandy	Dvine, Erévan, Arménia, Nairi
Kazakhstanian S.S.R.	Sparkling white	Ak-Kainar
	White	Issik
	Fortified, dessert	Chirine, Kazakhstane, Tselinnoe, Ak-Boulak, Muscat Violet
Kirghizian S.S.R.	White dessert	Muscat of Kirghiz, Muscat Violet
	Red	Cabernet, Kirghizstan
	Red port-type	Ala-Too
Moldavian S.S.R.	Red	Negru, Purkar, Cabernet, Sapari
Tadzhikistanian S.S.R.	Port-type	Taifi
	Red port-type	Tadzhikistan
	Red dessert	Vakche
	Dessert	Chirine, Gontchi, Guissare, Djaousse
Turkmenistanian S.S.R.	Dessert	Térbache
	Fortified	Yasman-Salik, Goulistane, Kopetdague
Uzbekistanian S.S.R.	Red	Uzbekistan
	White dessert	Aléatiko, Umalak, Bouaki
	Red port-type	Farkhad
Bessarabia Combine	White	Pinot, Aligoté
	Red	Bordo (presumably Cabernet)
Tempelhof Collective	White	Riesling, Sylvaner

449

S

Saar

See Mosel-Saar-Ruwer.

Sables-Saint-Émilion

Formerly a place-name; the wines have been incorporated into the better-known *appellation* Saint-Émilion.
See Saint-Émilion.

Saccharometer

See Mustimeter.

Saccharomyces Cereviseae

The yeast of wine, found on the skins of grapes.
See Yeasts; Chapter Nine, p. 40.

Sack

Early name for Sherry wine (see, for example, Shakespeare, *Henry IV, Part* 2, Act IV, Scene iii). It was believed at one time to come from the Spanish *seco* (dry); but because the wine at that time was probably sweet (not at all the Sherry we know) it is easy to accept Mr. H. Warner Allen's theory that the word came from the Spanish *sacar*—to take out, to export. The name of this sweet export wine was afterward attached to other, comparable wines, such as Canary Sack and Málaga Sack.

Sacramental wines

Used in the sacraments of the Christian Church. The need to keep up the supply of these wines caused the monasteries to take an active part in the viticulture of the Middle Ages. The term also applies to wines used during the Passover and other Jewish holidays.

Sacramento Valley

Californian wine region.
See United States: California.

Saint-Amour (Appellation Contrôlée)

Red wines of Beaujolais, in south Burgundy.
The vineyards are the farthest north in the region, touching the area of Pouilly-Fuissé in the Mâconnais. The red wine is one of the fullest of the Beaujolais.
See Beaujolais.

Saint-Aubin and Saint-Aubin-Côte de Beaune (Appellation Contrôlée)

Burgundy red and white wines.
District: Côte de Beaune, France.

Saint-Aubin stands back in the Côte d'Or hills behind Puligny-Montrachet and Chassagne-Montrachet, but its wines are not equal to those of its famous neighbors. For one thing, it is slightly too high above the favored strip of the slope's midsection for really first-rate wines. Because of the quality difference, the Saint-Aubins should be considerably less expensive than others of the Côte de Beaune and, if bought fairly young, can be excellent value.

Wines may be sold as Saint-Aubin, Saint-Aubin-Côte de Beaune, or, after blending with growths from other communes, as Côte de Beaune-Villages—any wine with the right to one of these names has the right to them all. Production in an average year for quantity is some 3,000 hectoliters (79,500 U.S. gallons, 66,000 imp.), about two-thirds of it white, and more is sold under the Villages name. Out of the 228 hectares (570 acres) of vineyard eligible for the name Saint-Aubin, 156 hectares (390 acres) are classified as First Growths.

FIRST GROWTHS *(Grands Crus)*

	Hectares	Acres
Champlot	8	19.8
En Remilly	2	4.9
La Chatenière	10	24.7
Les Combes	15	37.1
Les Frionnes	1	2.5
Les Murgers-des-Dents-de-Chien	3	7.4
Sur Gamay	14	34.6
Sur-le-Sentier-du-Clou	12	29.7

Saint Chinian (A.O.C)

An Appellation Contrôlée in the Coteaux du Languedoc producing red and rosé wines made from at least 50% of Carignan.

Saint-Denis

See Clos Saint-Denis; Morey-Saint-Denis.

Clos Saint-Denis (Appellation Contrôlée)

Burgundy red wine.
District: Côte de Nuits, France.
Commune: Morey-Saint-Denis.
Official Classification: Great Growth (Grand Cru).

The vineyards of the Clos Saint-Denis stand alongside the Route des Grands Crus, the road that threads through the middle of the Côte d'Or vineyards, slightly before you reach the village of Morey heading south. In 1927, the village chose to add the vineyard name to its own, although the Clos was not at that time classed among the topmost of the commune. This was remedied in 1937 when Clos Saint-Denis was ranked among the Great Growths *(Grands Crus)*—the thirty-one outstanding vineyards of the Côte d'Or.

The wine which starts its career in the vineyard of Clos Saint-Denis is among the lightest of the top-rated wines of the Côte de Nuits. In fine years, delicacy and finesse are the characteristics to look for, rather than the full robust strength of its peers, Clos de Tart, Clos de la Roche, and Clos des Lambrays. (This last is an outstanding wine which has now risen from its former classification as a First Growth [*Premier Cru*] to the Great Growth ranking it truly deserves.)

Within the 6.5 hectares (16.2 acres) of the vineyards there are a number of growers who together declare to the French government 200 hectoliters (5,300 U.S. gallons, 4,400 imp.) of wine in an average year for quantity—or about 2,200 cases.

Saint-Émilion

The vine, a variety of Ugni Blanc, which yields the greater part of the Charente wines used in making Cognac *(q.v.)*. It is grown in other districts of France, where it is also known by such names as Clairette à Grains Ronds, Clairette de Vence, Graisse, Queue de Renard, and Roussan. In Italy, this grape is called Trebbiano; in Corsica, Rossola.

Saint-Émilion (Appellation Contrôlée)

Red wine.
District: Bordeaux, France.

The wine is the fullest and heartiest of the red wines of Bordeaux. Some of the vintages require a considerable amount of time to develop; the 1970, for example, was not ready to drink before 1985. (This, however, is exceptional, and the 1970 has been very slow-maturing throughout Bordeaux.)

The vineyards can be conveniently divided into two types: those of the plain and those of the slopes. But within the groups, and across them, there is considerable variation, owing to the differences in soil and the different exposures of a terrain which, rising up into a crown around the town of Saint-Émilion itself, is very hilly, except where it flattens out on the borders of the neighboring district of Pomerol. This distinction between plain and hill played a drastic role in late February 1956, when Bordeaux viticulture experienced its second most disastrous winter since 1709. The frost settled in the lowest areas and all the vineyards of the plain, including Château Cheval-Blanc, finest of the Saint-Émilions, lost their 1956 and 1957 crops, and in many cases crops for years after,

since either the productive branches or the whole vines were frozen. (Three years later, various growers reported that vines were suddenly dying from the aftereffects of this frost.) Hill vineyards survived, and Château Ausone, probably the best of the slope wines, was, for example, unhurt.

Saint-Émilion itself is believed to be the oldest wine town in France, and certainly it is among the most picturesque. Placed on a hill of soft, easily hewn stone, it is uniquely all of a piece; the wine cellars of many of the châteaux are the old quarries from which the rock itself was cut in the Middle Ages, and blocks of the rock provide the tawny, sun-ripened stone of which the town is built. There can be no more romantic setting for drinking a great wine than in sight of the vineyard where it is grown. The terrace of the town's leading restaurant, the Hostellerie de Plaisance, is erected on the dome of a church—the gray, dim Église Monolithe, hollowed out of the solid rock underneath the inn. This ninth-century chapel is the largest in the world to be cut out of a single rock. An unforgettable sight is a ceremonial installation of the wine society, the Jurade, conducted in guttering taper light in the crypt. From the Plaisance belvedere, sipping your wine, you have a view across the mellow, red roofs of the King's Tower, built by Louis VI in 1124, of the ruined arches over the Cloister of the Cordeliers and of vineyards spilling down the Saint-Émilion slopes and spreading out·over the plain.

Ausonius, who wrote an epic poem about the Moselle, lived in a luxurious Roman villa which may or may not have been near the present site of Château Ausone. In his time, the third century, vineyards already girdled Saint-Émilion. The saint himself came in the eighth century, on his way to Santiago de Compostela in Spain, then an important goal of medieval pilgrims. If you go down into his hermitage near the church and stand by his bed and seat carved out of the stone, you will be told that he found the place a wilderness and, attracted by a miraculous spring, established a colony. It may not be irreligious to think this spring may have been Saint-Émilion wine, for the city was bustling and had already known and was forgetting the Roman grandeur. In any case, the saint lingered, and never went to Santiago de Compostela.

An Appellation Contrôlée, or legally controlled wine place-name in its own right, Saint-Émilion is also a Bordeaux, in the wine area of that name. The city of Bordeaux is about 23 miles (38 kms) to the southwest.

In addition to Saint-Émilion itself, seven surrounding communes have the right to the place-name Saint-Émilion. They are Saint-Laurent-des-Combes, Saint-Christophe-des-Bardes, Saint-Hippolyte, Saint-Étienne-de-Lisse, Saint-Pey-d'Armens, Saint-Sulpice-de-Faleyrens, and Vignonet. Lying in a semicircle on the south and west of Saint-Émilion, none produces a wine of the high level of the first-rate growths; but Château Larcis-Ducasse in Saint-Laurent-des-Combes, which is a continuation of the slope beyond

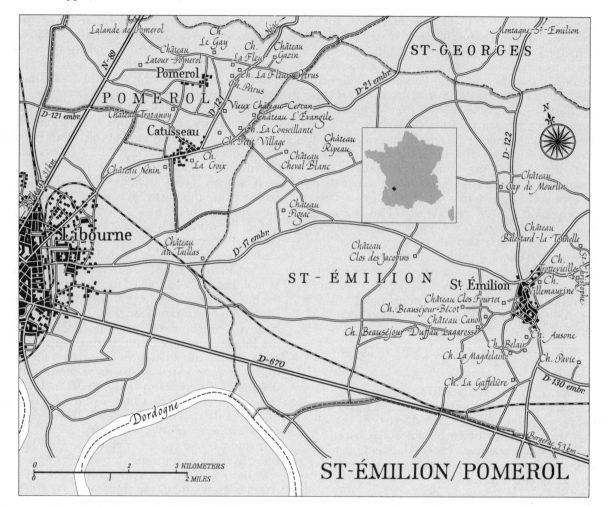

ST-ÉMILION/POMEROL

Pavie, is worthy of mention. Château Monbousquet, set back from a small country road across the Bordeaux-Bergerac road, on the flat land of Saint-Sulpice-de-Faleyrens, is an estate where wines were raised by Saint-Émilion's great promoter, Daniel Querre, certainly one of the largest growers of wine. He was a beaming man of 300 pounds, whose trumpet voice issued the call to grape harvesting from the top of a twelfth-century tower each year during the Jurade ceremony of the Ban des Vendanges. His example is now followed by his son Alain Querre.

Three communes lying to the north of Saint-Émilion and to the east of Pomerol have the right to add Saint-Émilion to their names, the Appellations Contrôlées of this district being: Saint-Georges-Saint-Émilion, Montagne-Saint-Émilion, and Puisseguin-Saint-Émilion. Since 1975 wines of Parsac and Lussac-Saint-Émilion have been sold as Montagne-Saint-Émilion. Château Saint-Georges, and to a somewhat lesser extent the other wines of Saint-Georges-Saint-Émilion, are only divided from the Saint-Émilions proper by tradition. From the quality standpoint, they have the same characteristics of longevity and splendor developing after sufficient age in bottle.

Sables-Saint-Émilion is an Appellation Contrôlée given to the wines of a small district touching Saint-Émilion on one border, but lying between Pomerol and the River Dordogne.

The wines of Saint-Émilion were officially classified in the summer of 1955 by the French Institut National des Appellations d'Origine, the body that controls wine place-names. Before that date, Château Cheval-Blanc and Château Ausone had always been considered as the leading and exceptional growths, with the others following after. In 1955 they were accorded the right to stand at the head of the First Great Growths (*Premiers Grand Crus*) but were not otherwise distinguished from ten more which were also rated Firsts and listed in alphabetical order after Ausone and Cheval-Blanc. Learning from the difficulties that had been encountered in the classification of Médoc wines exactly a century earlier, the officials who set up the Saint-Émilion Classification did not make the mistake of dividing the Classified Growths (*Crus*) into Firsts (*Premiers*), Seconds (*Seconds*), Thirds (*Troisièmes*), Fourths (*Quatrièmes*), and Fifths (*Cinquièmes*), thereby running the risk that a Third Growth might be mistaken for a third-rate wine. The vineyards of Saint-Émilion were placed in two groups only in 1955 and

1986: First Great Growths (*Premiers Grands Crus*), of which there are eleven; and Great Growths (*Grands Crus*), which total about seventy.

FIRST GREAT GROWTHS (*Premier Grands Crus*)

Château Ausone	Château La
Château Cheval-Blanc	Gaffelière
Château Beauséjour-Duffau-Lagarrosse	Château La
Château Bel-Air	Magdelaine
Château Canon	Château Pavie
Château Figeac	Château Trottevieille
Clos Fourtet	

The entire classification will be found in Appendix A, p. 631. For the individual First Great Growths, see under their names. Cheval-Blanc is unanimously elected best of all Saint-Émilions and, with Château Pétrus in Pomerol, equal to the five Médoc Greats—Lafite, Latour, Margaux, Haut-Brion (Graves), and Mouton-Rothschild. The position of Château Ausone is not so secure, but most people feel it follows Cheval-Blanc and also deserves a place in the upper hierarchy. A new classification started in 1983 came out in the winter of 1986—after many stormy disagreements.

Saint-Estèphe (Appellation Contrôlée)

Bordeaux red wine.
District: Haut-Médoc, France.

Saint-Estèphe is the northernmost and fourth in order of the great red wine communes on the famous Médoc peninsula jutting north from Bordeaux in southwest France. Of the annual 9,000,000 bottles (from 1,100 hectares; 2,775 acres) entitled to the official place-name (the largest volume of the communal wines), not all is of the very high average quality of the wines of Margaux, Pauillac, and Saint-Julien. Some of the lesser Saint-Estèphe wines are transitional between the Bas-Médocs and the more aristocratic Haut-Médocs. This is not surprising, since the village stands on the boundary of the two regions.

While the lesser wines may lack something in finesse, in Château Cos d'Estournel, Château Montrose, and Château Calon-Ségur Saint-Estèphe has three of the very distinguished Médoc vineyards. The span of the quality range is broader than in the other three famous communes, and a certain care is needed in selecting the wines.

Characteristically full and with a big nose, the wines vary within the region, and a Calon-Ségur at the northernmost extremity will be the most "Saint-Estèphe" of the Saint-Estèphes. At the opposite end of the scale from the delicate and feminine wines of Margaux, Saint-Estèphes are frequently likened in Bordeaux to Saint-Émilion wines, generally heavier than the Médocs. When young, they will be distinguished for their fruity fullness.

Saint-Estèphe has five vineyards rated as Classified Growths (*Crus*) in the 1855 Classification of Médoc wines, fewer by far than the other leading communes. They are:

SECOND GROWTHS (*Seconds Crus*)

Château Cos d'Estournel
Château Montrose

THIRD GROWTH (*Troisième Cru*)

Château Calon-Ségur

FOURTH GROWTH (*Quatrième Cru*)

Château Lafon-Rochet

FIFTH GROWTH (*Cinquième Cru*)

Château Cos-Labory

(For individual Classified Growths, *see* Château Cos d'Estournel, Château Montrose, Château Calon-Ségur, etc.)

Sainte-Foy-Bordeaux (Appellation Contrôlée)

Bordeaux white and red wine.
District: Southwest France.

Sweet white wines made according to the Sauternes method using overripe grapes with noble rot from the Sauternes varieties Sémillon, Sauvignon, and Muscadelle. The wines come from the easternmost part of the Bordeaux wine region and are more properly linked with the adjoining area of Monbazillac sweet white wines. A quantity of red wine also bears the name, but it generally amounts to about 40% of the production.

Saint Gall

Fortified French aperitif made from red wine.

Saint-Georges-Saint-Émilion

One of four communes in the north of Saint-Émilion which share the right to the Appellation Contrôlée Saint-Émilion after their place name. (*q.v.*).

Saint-Jean-de-Minervois, Muscat de

See Sweet fortified wines of France.

Saint-Joseph (Appellation Contrôlée)

Red and white wines of the French Côtes du Rhône. *See* Rhône.

Saint-Julien

Bordeaux red wine.
District: Haut-Médoc, France.

One of the four leading Médoc red wine communes in the Bordeaux region in southwest France—the others are Pauillac, Margaux, and Saint-Estèphe—Saint-Julien is smallest in production, making about 5,600,000 bottles of wine a year from some 775 hectares (1,937 acres); the wine is entitled to the official place-name or Appellation Contrôlée. As a regional wine it is probably the best-known of the four in the world market.

The wine, from vines grown in a gravelly soil marked by the presence of a considerable amount of clay, has affinities with both those of Pauillac immediately to the north, and those of Margaux, grown about 13 kilometers (8 miles) to the south, the other side of a stretch of land too low and moist for fine wines. Slightly darker in color and fuller-bodied than the typical Margaux, the wines in this respect tend to resemble the Pauillacs; but they are less full and quicker to mature than a characteristic Pauillac and have more of the finesse, delicacy, and femininity identified with Margaux.

The community, a small village lying in among the famous Léovilles, on a curve of the vineyard road running north from Bordeaux, is also known as Saint-Julien-Beychevelle, signifying the link with the ancient Beychevelle estate. After crossing pasture-land, the vineyard road suddenly climbs, and on the higher ground Saint-Julien begins, with Château Beychevelle and then Château Ducru-Beaucaillou on the river side, and Château Branaire facing them across the road. At the turning, a rather large wine bottle, an eyesore in the corner of the vineyard of Beychevelle, takes the visitor's eye. Entering the region, a large billboard announces:

PASSERS-BY!
You are now entering the ancient
and celebrated vineyard of Saint-Julien.
Bow low!

The ancient fame of Saint-Julien has been revived by its mayor, M. Henri Martin, owner of Château Gloria and Château St. Pierre, and in the middle sixties the president of the C.I.V.B., the Bordeaux wine association. Formerly head of the Commanderie du Bontemps.

In an average year, approximately sixty different wines carry the Saint-Julien place-name, to which they are entitled if grown in the delimited region, cared for according to certain quality restrictions, and approved in annual taste testings.

The Saint-Julien vineyards rated as Classified Growths (Crus) in the 1855 Classification of Médoc wines are:

SECOND GROWTHS (Seconds Crus)

Château Ducru-Beaucaillou
Château Gruaud-Larose
Château Léoville-Barton
Château Léoville-Las-Cases
Château Léoville-Poyferré

THIRD GROWTHS (Troisièmes Crus)

Château Lagrange
Château Langoa-Barton

FOURTH GROWTHS (Quatrièmes Crus)

Château Beychevelle
Château Branaire
Château Saint-Pierre
Château Talbot
Saint-Julien has neither First nor Fifth Growths.
(For individual Classified Growths, see Château Léoville-Las-Cases, Château Léoville-Poyferré, Château Léoville-Barton, etc.)

Saint-Lambert-du-Lattay

Commune making sweet white wines in the Coteaux du Layon district of Anjou (q.v.).

Saint-Laurent

Red wine grape used in Austria, Czechoslovakia, etc.

Saint Martin

Saint Martin (c. 345) was an early patron of wine in the Loire Valley, and to him is attributed the discovery that vines do better when they are pruned.
See Loire.

Saint-Nicholas-de-Bourgueil (A.O.C)

Red and rosé wines from a sub-district of the Touraine in the French Loire Valley. The total area of 14,000 hectares (35,000 acres) is planted in Cabernet Franc.
See Bourgueil; Touraine.

Saint-Péray and Saint-Péray Mousseux (A.O.C.)

Dry and sweet still wine; also sparkling wine.
District: Rhône Valley, France.

The wines were highly appreciated in France during the Second Empire (1852–70) but fell from grace shortly afterward, and are only just beginning to come back into favor. Now, as then, the full-bodied sparkling wine seems to be the more sought after.

The vines (Roussanne and Marsanne) are grown on cliffs overlooking the Rhône, on the river's right bank. Sometimes the growers will wait until the grapes are overripe and let the pourriture noble, or noble rot, form on them, drying the skin and leaving a sugar-rich grape for making an ultra-sweet wine. Generally, however, the grapes are picked at maturity and vinified into a dry wine. Much of the output is subjected to a secondary fermentation in the bottle to render the wine sparkling. About 80 hectares (200 acres) of vines exist, and production amounts to nearly 3,000 hectoliters (79,255 U.S. gallons, 65,995 imp.).

Château Saint-Pierre

Bordeaux red wine.
District: Haut-Médoc, France.
Commune: Saint-Julien.

The vineyard owes its name to a Baron St. Pierre, who bought it in 1767. In 1892 part of the vineyard was sold to M. Léon Sevaistre and named Château Saint-Pierre-Sevaistre, while the remainder of the estate became known as Château Saint-Pierre-Bontemps. The two sections were eventually reunited by the former Belgian owner, Mr. Castelein. In 1982, Henri Martin bought Château Saint-Pierre and retroceded some plots to his neighbors Château Ducru-Beaucaillou and Château Gruaud-Larose.

Characteristics. Fine, greatly improved wines are now being made.

Vineyard area: 17 hectares (42 acres).
Average production: 60 *tonneaux* (5,000 cases).

Saint-Raphaël

Delicate, red, bitter-sweet French aperitif based on fortified red wine and flavored principally with quinine. It is highly advertised throughout France, where it is very popular.

Saint-Romain (Appellation Contrôlée)

Burgundy red and white wines.
District: Côte de Beaune, France.

Lying far back in the hills, behind Meursault and Auxey-Duresses, Saint-Romain makes a little wine, of reasonably little note, although it may often represent good value compared with other growths of the famous slope. Some of it—both red and white—is sold under the communal name, and some is blended with wines of other specified communes of the Côte de Beaune and sold as Côte de Beaune-Villages. There are about 100 hectares (250 acres) allowed for the growing of the finer vines, and production in a good year for quantity is about 2,000 hectoliters (53,000 U.S. gallons, 44,000 imp.), just more than half of it white, with an unspecified further amount sold as Côte de Beaune-Villages.

Saint Véran (Appellation Contrôlée)

Burgundy white wine.
District: Maconnais, France.

Not far in fact or intent from the more famous Appellation Contrôlée of Pouilly-Fuissé, this region also makes white wine from the Chardonnay grape. Some 24,000 hectoliters (633,600 U.S. gallons, 526,600 imp.) are produced annually on the region's 240 hectares (593 acres).

Saint Vincent

Patron saint of French wine-growers. According to legend, he became thirsty in Heaven and asked permission to return to earth for a while, so that he might taste the good wines of France again. He was granted a leave of absence, and no doubt he meant to go back when his time was up. But the red wine of Graves was his undoing; he was found in the cellar of La Mission-Haut-Brion, lost to the world and to his appointment in Heaven, and as a punishment he was turned to stone.

His statue is still to be seen there, clutching a dilapidated bunch of grapes and wearing his mitred cap awry. The Saint Vincent holiday is widely celebrated in Burgundy. Processions honoring the wine saint are held in many villages of the Côte d'Or on January 22 each year.

Sainte-Croix-du-Mont (Appellation Contrôlée)

Bordeaux white wine.
District: Southwest France.

A small district south of Bordeaux and divided from Sauternes by the River Garonne. The white wines are sweet and are very reminiscent of their neighbors across the river, made from the same grape varieties—Sémillon, Sauvignon, and some Muscadelle—and produced from late-picked and overripe grapes which have achieved a concentrated sweetness, as in Sauternes. If the wines lack the very great elegance and finesse of some Sauternes, they are nevertheless the best of the white sweet wines of the right bank of the Garonne and, priced far below the famous Sauternes, are excellent buys.

The bluff or slope of Sainte-Croix-du-Mont carries solid vine like a cape over its sloping shoulders. At the top thrusts out the church of Sainte-Croix-du-Mont with its delicate spire and, a hundred yards away, the medieval fortified castle; these landmarks are illuminated in the summer and they shine for miles over the Sauternes and Graves vineyards.

Production averages around 15,000 hectoliters (397,500 U.S. gallons, 330,000 imp.), about half that of Sauternes, and to achieve the place-name the wines must attain 13% of alcohol. In fact, they frequently reach 15%. No better place for tasting them can exist than the outdoor terrace built just below the castle in 1955 and 1956. From the tables placed on the grassy ledge of the bluff, vineyard tumbles away in a rush below until it is checked by the low-lying land bordering the river. Across the river, shrouded with willows, is Sauternes, and on the horizon the outlines of Château d'Yquem can be dimly made out.

Saké

A Japanese fermented liqueur, from 12% to 16% alcohol by volume. It is made from rice which is cleansed and steamed and allowed to ferment. Toward the end of the fermentation period more rice is added, then the saké is drawn off, filtered, and put into casks for maturing.

The saké is colorless and rather sweet, with a bitter aftertaste. The Japanese serve it warm, in porcelain cups. Natives of Okinawa also make a saké, but it is harsher and usually served cold. The more than one dozen different types of the wine fall roughly into three styles: *mirin*, for cooking; *toso*, spicy and sweet, drunk for New Year's celebrations; and *seishu*, the completely refined wine known in the West.

Salmanazar

In Champagne, a large glass bottle formerly used for display purposes. When filled it contained 9 liters or 304 U.S. fluid ounces (317 British): the equivalent of twelve regular bottles.

Salta

Wine-producing province of Argentina (*q.v.*).

Saltillo

Wine-producing town in Mexico, site of the Compañía Vinícola de Saltillo.
See Mexico.

Samogon

Bootleg vodka in Russia.

Samos

The Muscat of Samos is one of the best-known wines of Greece, and the place-name is controlled.
See Greece.

Sampigny-les-Maranges and Sampigny-les-Maranges-Côte de Beaune (A.O.C.)

Burgundy red and white wines.
District: Côte de Beaune, France.

Sampigny is a minor wine commune at the southern end of the Côte de Beaune. Its wines are normally blended with those from other Côte de Beaune communes and sold as Côte de Beaune-Villages, but may also sometimes be found under their own name. The vineyards cover 44 hectares (110 acres), and wines from the 29-hectare heart may add the designation Côte de Beaune to the commune name. In exceptionally rare cases, wines may be seen with the label Sam-

pigny-les-Maranges, or Sampigny-les-Maranges-Clos du Roi, in both cases the added names being those of the better vineyards within the commune. Les Maranges and the Clos du Roi are the only two that have this right.

Samshu

The Chinese saké (*q.v.*).

San Joaquin Valley

Warm Californian region producing raisins and sweet fortified wines. The principal districts are Madera, Fresno, Kings, Tulare, and Kern counties.
See United States: California.

San Juan

Province of Argentina extensively planted in vines.
See Argentina.

San Marino (Sangiovese)

This, one of the smallest countries in the world—only 59 square kilometers (23 square miles), and half of that nearly perpendicular—produces a red table wine called Sangiovese and a sparkling sweet dessert Moscato. The total production of wine is some 20 hectoliters (530 U.S. gallons, 440 imp.) annually. Every drop of the rather hard Sangiovese, the Moscato, and a dessert liqueur named Titanium, is consumed by the approximately 1 million tourists who, every year, visit this toy state enclosed within Italy. Titanium takes its name from Monte Titano, the sheer peak that thrusts up from the Italian plain 16 kilometers (10 miles) inland from Rimini and the Adriatic. On top of this the town of San Marino is perched. The liqueur is made from the wildflowers of the mountain, as it has been for over a century. To sip it or drink the wine in an outdoor café in the spotless little stone town, looking out to the Adriatic or to the dim blue Apennines, is a bibulous experience never to be forgotten—and you are sure to hear from some native of how San Marino has kept its independence against such would-be conquerors as Cesare Borgia and Napoleon and remained a dot of freedom for 1,600 years.

Sancerre (Appellation Contrôlée)

Loire Valley white wine.
District: Loire Valley, France.

A small, well-known district of the Upper Loire producing an annual 600,000 cases of very dry white and 180,000 cases of red and rosé wine. Of a total of approximately 1,650 hectares (4,125 acres) of vines, cultivated by 500 growers, about 280 (700 acres) are of

Sauvignon. The town from which the district takes its name commands a sweeping view of the river from the top of a hill, whose slopes are planted in vines, as are the hills of twelve surrounding towns. No other grape is allowed in wine labeled Sancerre. The best vineyards are Bué, Champtin, and Chavignol.

This wine derives a special flavor from the district's limestone soil—markedly dry and apt in wet summers to have too much acidity. In warm summers, however, this acidity is balanced by sufficient alcohol and the wine has a crisp and refreshing tang. Never great, Sancerre is nevertheless one of France's very pleasant and popular white wines. The reds and rosés, made from the Pinot Noir grape, account for about 17,000 hectoliters (450,000 U.S. gallons, 380,000 imp.).

Sandweine

The "Sand wines" of Burgenland in Austria get their name from the sandy soil in which the vines grow—soil which the phylloxera louse avoids. These wines are among the few in Europe which need not be grafted onto American root-stocks. They are labeled Seewinkel followed by the informing grape variety.
See Austria.

Sangiovese

Red wine grape used in Chianti, Montepulciano, and many other Italian wines.

Sangría

A refreshing warm-weather Spanish wine punch made of red wine, citrus juice, sugar, soda or water, and sometimes garnished with berries, fruit slices, or other flavorings.

San Severo (D.O.C.)

Dry white, rosé and red; fairly ordinary Italian wine.
See Apulia.

Santa Maddalena (D.O.C.) and Classico (D.O.C.)

Red wine of Alto Adige made from the Schiava grape, sometimes referred to as Sankt Magdelener.
See Trentino-Alto Adige, Italy.

Santa Rosa

Center of Californian wine district in Sonoma County.
See United States: California.

Santarem-João Santarcm

Blue-black grape used in the hill-slope wines of Colares, Portugal *(q.v.)*.

Santenay and Santenay-Côte de Beaune (A.O.C.)

Burgundy red, and some white, wines.
District: Côte de Beaune.

Santenay is the last important wine commune of the Côte de Beaune before it tails off into the southernmost Cheilly-les-Maranges, Dezize-les-Maranges, and Sampigny-les-Maranges. The wines—which have equal right to the name of the commune or communal name with Côte de Beaune added—are predominantly red and are light, fast-maturing, sometimes extraordinarily fruity, and often very good if priced below those from some of the other Côte de Beaune wine communes. Authentic red Santenay of a good year often rivals wines from Chassagne-Montrachet or Volnay, although it never gets into a position to challenge the exceptionally great Burgundies. Some of it is blended with the output of other Côte de Beaune communes and sold as Côte de Beaune-Villages, and some is sold under the more specific commune names. Quantities go to Switzerland and the Low Countries where, being fairly low in price, the wine is highly appreciated. There are almost 400 hectares (1,000 acres) of vineyard within Santenay's boundaries, and in an average-quantity year production amounts to about 10,000 hectoliters (265,000 U.S. gallons, 220,-000 imp.) of red wine.

Santorini

A Greek wine, from the island of the same name, which may also, when it is sweet, be labeled Vino Santo.
See Greece.

Sardinia

Red, white, and rosé wines.
District: Italian island.

The mountainous island of Sardinia, in the Tyrrhenian Sea, off the coast of central Italy is, after Sicily, the largest island in the Mediterranean. It has been inhabited since prehistoric days, and it is known that even the earliest dwellers cultivated the vine. The island has a strange, wild air and is populated by a short, individualistic people to whose mysterious origins huge stone monuments may be the undeciphered clues. Giants' tombs, witches' houses, and the even more inscrutable *nuraghi*—conical stone towers which seem to have served the early Sardinians as both shelters and defenses—pepper the island. Nearly 2 million hectoliters of wine (53 million U.S. gallons, 44 million imp.) are produced annually.

Since the 1960s, Sardinian wine production has undergone an oenological revolution. New grape varieties, early harvesting to preserve acidity, temperature-controlled fermentation, and early bottling are some of the features of the modern vinification which have transformed the style and quality of Sardinian wines. The largest estate in Italy is Sella and Mosta, north of Algherro which makes a light, fragrant wine from the Spanish Torrelata grape. In place of the sweet fortified wines of yesteryear, the island now produces good, fresh, dry red and especially white wines. These light wines, with a slight pricke (CO_2), are favored by the numerous tourists who flock to Sardinia and, above all, to La Costa Smeralda, a vacationland built by the Aga Khan around Porto Cervo, Porto Rotondo, and Cala di Volpe. Costa Smeralda has become one of the best summer resorts in Europe.

Vernaccia di Oristano (D.O.C.)

Sardinia's best-known wine, made from the grape variety with the same name. Most of the vines, which were imported at the end of the fourteenth century, grow around Oristano in the Tirso River Valley, which runs from central Sardinia westward to the Gulf of Oristano, midway along the coast. The dry, sherry-like, amber-colored wine is high in alcohol and has a quick, sprightly, bitter aftertaste. Fortified Vernaccia *liquoroso* comes in two types: sweet with 16.5% and dry with 18% of alcohol by volume. If aged for four years in wood, these wines may be called Riserva.

Nuragus di Cagliari (D.O.C.)

Almost certainly the oldest wine of the island, this is also one of the better table wines, made from grapes of the same name grown around Cagliari. The straw-colored, heady wine annually amounts to about 10% of all Sardinian wine production.

Vermentino di Gallura (D.O.C.)

The wine comes from vineyards spreading south from Santa Teresa di Gallura, the northernmost town. From grapes grown on some of the most unpromising mountain slopes, about 600 hectoliters (15,900 U.S. gallons, 13,200 imp.) of wine are made annually. It is dry and amber-colored, has some 13% to 14% of alcohol, but lacks any real distinction.

Malvasia di Bosa (D.O.C.)

This is produced in very small quantities—just 150 or so hectoliters in an average year—from Malvasia and Seberu grapes grown near Bosa, on the west coast of the island, slightly to the north of center. The wine varies between 15% to 17.5% alcoholic content and has a good, nutty flavor, and compared with Vernaccia has a deeper, richer color and is somewhat less dry. Another wine from the same grape is Malvasia di Cagliari (D.O.C.), a wine with a bitter aftertaste of toasted almonds.

Oliena

The dryish, garnet-red wine is made from Cannonnau and Monica grapes grown in the district of Nuoro.

Cannonau di Sardegna (D.O.C.)

A ruby-red wine, dry or semi-sweet, made of Cannonau grapes; a rosé is also made. When fortified, the port-like Cannonau makes an excellent dessert wine or can be drunk as an aperitif (*liquoroso seco*).

Dessert Wines

Girò di Cagliari (D.O.C.) is sweet and red, slightly reminiscent of Port, and is made from Girò grapes grown in the general vicinity of Cagliari. Monica di Sardegna (D.O.C.) and Monica di Cagliari (D.O.C.) are similar but deeper in color—almost a deep purple. Nasco di Cagliari (D.O.C.) is white, or rather a deep, golden color, and is famed partly for its bouquet (said to have the perfume of orange blossoms) and partly for its slightly bitter tang. Muscats may also be found, notably Moscato di Sorso-Sennori (D.O.C.) and Moscato di Cagliari (D.O.C.), both of which are often fortified.

See Italy.

Saumur and **Coteaux de Saumur (A.O.C.)**

Still, semi-sparkling, and particularly sparkling white wines, usually dry. Some rosé and red.
District: Anjou, France.

The difference between the two names has never been clearly established and may never be, and for the moment they have substantially the same meaning. The wines are red, white, and rosé (although in actual practice few of the red wines are seen abroad) and may be either still or sparkling, the production of the latter taking up a goodly proportion of each year's harvest. Sparkling Saumur is slightly heavier and more common than sparkling Vouvray, but is no match for Champagne.

Most sparkling Saumur is vinified and aged in huge caves, which burrow back into the chalky cliffs surrounding the ancient city. French law insists that all such wines be made by the champagne process (*see* Champagne) of secondary fermentation in the bottle, and 40% of the wines must come from the juice of Chenin Blanc grapes; the rest is ordinarily made up of Groslot with some Cabernet. In recent years, the quality of the sparkling wine has improved due to the creation of a new appellation, "Crémant de Loire."

Non-sparkling white Saumur will sometimes be about the finest of its type in the region of Anjou. It is generally dry—sometimes, however, preserving a slight trace of sweetness—and often proves more robust than the dry wines from the rest of the district. Rosé (both ordinary and that made exclusively from

Cabernet grapes) is quite frequently encountered, but it does not differ markedly from good Angevin rosés. Some of the whites are *pétillants*, or semi-sparkling. About 60,000 hectoliters (1.59 million U.S. gallons, 1.32 million imp.) are made annually.

Saumur-Champigny (A.O.C.)

Red wine.
District: Anjou, France.

On the chalky slopes downstream from the confluence of the Loire and the quiet River Vienne to just east of Saumur, Cabernet Franc grapes are grown to produce a fresh, generous wine with a deep ruby color. The wine has a perfume recalling the scent of violets. Since the Appellation Contrôlée of Saumur-Champigny is nearly as far north as the Cabernet Franc can be successfully cultivated, vintage years are quite important. In very bad years part of the crop does not ripen completely and must be vinified simply as Rosé d'Anjou. The average annual production of Appellation Contrôlée red wines is 40,000 hectoliters (1,056,000 U.S. gallons, 876,000 imp.).

Saussignac, Côtes de (Appellation Contrôlée)

White wines (not very important) of the Dordogne region in southwest France. Wine-producing villages are Gageac-et-Rouillac, Monestier, and Razac-de-Saussignac. Since 1955 the name Saussignac can be replaced by Bergerac, provided the wines come from the above-mentioned communes and attain the prescribed degrees of sugar and alcohol.

Sauternes (Appellation Contrôlée)

White wine.
District: Bordeaux, France.

The suspense in the final moment of harvesting a Sauternes is worthy of a Hitchcock film. To make the entirely natural sweet wine, the grape must achieve both a state of overripeness and the famed *pourriture noble*. Failing this, the wine will lack the extra richness, sugar, and alcohol sometimes reaching 16% and even 17% with 6% of sugar; in fact, it will not even be entitled to the legal designation of Sauternes. But if, on the other hand, the beneficial overripening is allowed to go too far, the bouquet is lost in the increased suavity and richness of the wine. Add to this the fact that the overripening occurs very late in the season, when frost may strike down the vines any day, and it is easy to understand the nervous pacing of the grower in Sauternes, inspecting his vines several times a day as he decides whether to pick or not.

No other wine in the world is made on such a scale by this delicate and nerve-racking process, though a portion of the crop from certain great vineyards along the Rhine and Mosel in Germany is produced identically. *Trockenbeerenauslese,* the German word for the process and the resultant wine, perhaps best describes it. "Dried-grapes-specially-selected"—a child's Erector-set word built up with German literalness.

The Sauternes process is the only one by which a wine of such richness may be produced without human interference in the form of extra sugar, of fermentation arrested by the addition of brandy, or any of the other methods used in the production of various wines. A mold or fungus, *Botrytis cinerea*—the French picturesquely, and with botanical correctness, call it a mushroom—attacks the grapes late in the autumn, and the skins shrivel. No sugar is *added* by this process, but the proportion of sugar becomes greater as the water grows less. At the same time, the mold causes transformation within the grapes, of a nature not yet defined, that increases the glycerins and pectins and gives the wine its suavity and smoothness. The "legs" of a great Sauternes are celebrated. They are the slow streams which descend with unctuous richness down the inner side of the glass after the wine has been tipped away.

The bunch of grapes, ready for the selected picking, is dried and folded and (while it is not a pleasant comparison) has a marked resemblance to the wizened, leathery, folded-in appearance of a hanging bat. Covered over with the *pourriture noble,* it hardly gives promise of the golden nectar it is to produce. With much of the juice dried out, the quantity is reduced. To this loss of volume must be added the greatly increased cost of picking. The mold develops haphazardly over a vineyard, and the rows must be picked through as many as six to eleven times. For these reasons, true Sauternes can never be cheap.

True Sauternes. For no other wine is more widely flattered by the theft of its name. "Sauternes" is not merely a white sweet wine, but the white sweet wine of Sauternes, France. The wines to be met with in many other places in the world which call themselves "sauternes"—or even "sauterne," as if to justify bad practice by bad spelling—are not what they claim to be.

The character of a wine is determined by several factors, among which are the influences of a specific soil and climate in a given geographical place; for grapevines do not behave in the same way in different soils and climates. When the right vine or vines have been found for a certain wine-favoring area, a famous wine will result, over decades of development. Nowhere else will exactly the right combination of factors exist to produce the same wine.

The Sauternes district is composed of five communes: Sauternes, Barsac, Bommes, Preignac, and Fargues. In all sections the wine is made identically, and mainly from the Sémillon and Sauvignon grapes. Muscadelle is used in very small amounts in the blends. Because a Sauternes vineyard is not picked section by section but according to the degree of overripeness, there is a difference in quality between early-

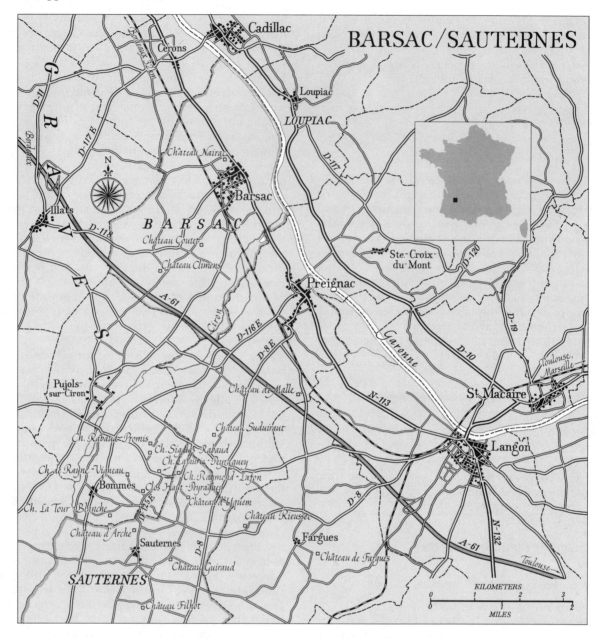

season pickings and very late pickings. When brought in, the bunches first enter a long revolving tube. This *fouloir*, or beater, extracts the first juice. Then, after destalking, the grapes are pressed three times. In the past all these different grades of juice were made into separate wines; but around the end of the last century this practice largely ceased. Today the general custom is to mix the yield. This is done in large tanks, where the day's pick remains only a few hours and is then let off into casks, where it ferments and matures. Differences in the different days' harvesting cause differences in the wine in cask, and when it becomes apparent that a wine is not up to standard, it is the practice of every fine château to exclude it from that which will be bottled under its name. Instead, it is sold to the Bordeaux shippers, to be bottled simply as Sauternes. (In such cases, shippers are strictly forbidden to let it

be known that the bottle is really from one of the Classified Growths [*Crus*], being sold at the much lower price for regional wine.)

Yielding a maximum of 3,000 bottles to the hectare (1,200 bottles to the acre), the entire region produces the equivalent of 4 million bottles a year. Sauternes tend to differ from one vineyard to another, but the only generalization to be made is that the Barsacs, which are entitled to the separate name Barsac as well as that of Sauternes, are likely to be less sweet. They come from a flatter land and a less stony, more chalky soil in the northern portion (*see* Barsac). It is Sauternes proper, the rolling, hilly region around the tiny village of Sauternes and the towns of Bommes and Fargues, which is the most picturesque. The vineyard road, hardly more than a lane, runs between old stone walls. The great vineyards clothe the slopes, the crown of which will usually display the château. Lower-lying vineyards were severely damaged in the freeze of February 1956, and from these, and to a lesser degree the slope vineyards, no 1956 or 1957 vintage was seen, and very little of vintages for several subsequent years. Hail destroyed most of the 1973 harvest; and 74s are rare.

Sauternes should be served cold, but not so iced that the taste will be numbed. It can be brought to serving temperature in an ice bucket or in the refrigerator. Some French people will serve an old Sauternes which has oxidized as an aperitif; the oxidation will have reduced some of the sweetness but not all.

Sauternes are best served at the end of the meal, when they go well with a dessert and even better with fruit; and some knowledgeable people serve a glass of sweet Sauternes *as* the dessert. Counter to all this, however, is the opinion of the owner of Château d'Yquem, who maintains the nineteenth-century tradition that Sauternes should be drunk not only with the dessert but also with certain fish, foie gras, and Roquefort.

CLASSIFIED VINEYARDS OF SAUTERNES AND BARSAC, 1855 CLASSIFICATION

FIRST GREAT GROWTH (*Premier Grand Cru*)

Château d'Yquem (Sauternes)

FIRST GROWTHS (*Premiers Crus*)

Château La Tour-Blanche (Bommes)	Château Climens (Barsac)
Château Lafaurie-Peyraguey (Bommes)	Château Guiraud (Sauternes)
Clos Haut-Peyraguey (Bommes)	Château Rieussec (Fargues)
Château de Rayne-Vigneau (Bommes)	Château Rabaud-Promis (Bommes)
Château Suduiraut (Preignac)	Château Sigalas-Rabaud (Bommes)
Château Coutet (Barsac)	

SECOND GROWTHS (*Seconds Crus*)

Château Doisy-Daëne (Barsac)	Château Caillou (Barsac)
Château Doisy-Védrines (Barsac)	Château Suau (Barsac)
Château d'Arche (Sauternes)	Château de Malle (Preignac)
Château Filhot (Sauternes)	
Château Broustet (Barsac)	Château Romer (Fargues)
Château Nairac (Barsac)	Château Lamothe (Sauternes)

Sauvignon Blanc

An exceptionally fine white grape used for some excellent white wines. With Sémillon (and some Muscadelle) it produces all of Bordeaux's finest whites, from the sweetest Sauternes to the driest Graves. Some marvelously pleasant Loire Valley white wines come solely from this grape, notably those of Sancerre, and the best wine is from Pouilly-sur-Loire, where the wine is known locally as Blanc Fumé (white smoke). In California the Sauvignon Blanc is considered among the finest grapes for white wine, especially

in the Livermore, San Benito, and Santa Clara valleys. The wine varies, of course, according to the soil and climate of the vineyard and the manner in which grapes and wine are treated; but whenever conditions are favorable, the wine will have considerable breed and distinction. Among other names for this vine are Surin, in parts of the Loire Valley, and Muskat Sylvaner in Germany.

Sauvignon (Cabernet Sauvignon)

The finest of the claret grapes grown in the Médoc; small and blue-black in color, thick-skinned, and juicy. The wine they yield is very full and slow in maturing. The other regional names for this grape include Bouchet and Vidure.

See Cabernet.

Savagnin

The dominant grape variety in the golden-white wines of Château-Châlon. Savagnin Rose is another name for the red Gewürztraminer of Alsace; Savagnin Noir is none other than the Pinot Noir.

Savatiano

One of the principal grape varieities used for Greek liqueurs and also for table wines—often those which have been doctored with resin—it is found in central Greece and in the Peloponnese.

Savennières (Anjou-Coteaux de la Loire) (A.O.C.)

One of the very best white wines from the Chenin Blanc grape. In addition, the best A.O.C.s are: Coulée-de-Serrant and Roche-aux-Moines.

See Anjou; Loire.

Savigny-les-Beaune and Savigny-les-Beaune-Côte de Beaune (Appellation Contrôlée)

Burgundy red and white wines.
District: Côte de Beaune, France.

In the early Middle Ages the vineyards were owned by Cistercians and Carmelites, but the French people and many of the nobility were not far behind in establishing their claims. A great moated castle, built in 1340, totally destroyed in 1468, and rebuilt in 1672, still stands to the side of the main square, surrounded by a rambling and slightly disheveled park. During the eighteenth century this was the home of the Duchesse de Maine. Today its opulence has declined, its windows are closed, and a few chickens scratch in what was once the main court.

Within the confines of present-day Savigny there are about 360 hectares (900 acres) of vines, and production in an average year for quantity is 12,000 hec-

Savoy (Haute-Savoie)

toliters (318,000 U.S. gallons, 264,000 imp.), all but a few hundred hectoliters red. This wine was greatly appreciated in the distant past (a Duke of Burgundy wanted to elevate one grower to the rank of a demi-god for the quality of his wine), but its reputation has diminished considerably. It is distinctly light and fragrant with considerable finesse but definitely not a wine to keep for any length of time.

The town stands between Pernand-Vergelesses and Beaune and the wines of all three are fairly similar, although those of Beaune are far and away the best. Savigny sells its wines either under the commune name or under commune name with Côte de Beaune added, but if a wine qualifies for either name it is qualified for both. Wines may also be blended with those from certain other communes along the slope and sold as Côte de Beaune-Villages. The best vineyards of the commune are rated First Growths (*Premiers Crus*)—higher minimum standards and better wines—and their wines may be sold with both commune name and vineyard name. These vineyards are Vergelesses, Marconnets, Dominode, Jarrons, and Lavières.

Savoy (Haute-Savoie)

In this region of France, four white wines are permitted Appellations Contrôlées. These are Crépy, Seyssel, Seyssel Mousseux, and the Vins de Savoie (*qq.v.*).

Scharlachberg

Excellent white wine from near Bingen on the German Rhine.
See Rheinhessen.

Scharzhofberg

Generally the finest wines of the German Saar. These wines frequently attain an incomparable elegance.

Schaumwein

A German term for sparkling wine.

Schiave

A red grape grown in Italy, particularly in the vineyards of the Alto Adige.

Schiedam

Term sometimes used for Hollands gin because Schiedam in Holland is one of the chief places of its manufacture.

Schiller wine

A pinkish wine from red and white grapes which once comprised half the wine made in the German Württemberg district.

Schloss

Literally, "castle" in German, but with regard to wine, the counterpart of the French château, encompassing the building, vineyards, cellars, etc.

Schloss Böckelheimer Kupfergrube

Good wines of the Nahe Valley in Germany, grown on the slopes of the Kupfergrube, or "Copper mine." *See* Nahe.

Schloss Johannisberg

Most expensive of the Rheingaus (German Rhine wine). The best-informed brokers and growers on the river consider it one of the finest Rheingaus consistently over the years, though not always first in any given year. (For a full explanation of the different types of capsuling, indicating the different grades and qualities of Schloss Johannisberg, *see* Rheingau: Johannisberg.)

Schloss Vollrads

Best of the wines of the Winkel section of the German Rhine, and one of the best Rhine wines, Schloss Vollrads is bottled and sold in six grades, or qualities differentiated by the colors of their capsules. For a full description of these grades and the wine, *see* Rheingau: Winkel.

Schlossabzug

Originalabfüllung and Schlossabzug were former terms to describe a natural, unsugared, estate-bottled wine; in this case, a Schloss or castle. Known today as Erzeugerabfüllung.

Schnapps

In Germany and Holland, any strong, dry spirit; in Scandinavia, usually aquavit. An aromatic schnapps is made from a base of Dutch-style gin flavored with aromatic herbs.

Schooner

A tall drinking glass most suitable for beer; usually about 15 fluid ounces.

Schwarzwalder

German name for kirsch, or cherry brandy.
See Kirsch.

Scion

A segment of a cane or shoot of one or more buds that is grafted onto a stock to make a complete plant. Scions of European *Vitis vinifera* vines were grafted onto American disease-resistant stocks after the phylloxera disaster in the late nineteenth century. When the correct rootstock is selected for the graft, it should impart none or very little of its own qualities to the fruit of the scion.

Scotch whisky

See Whisky, Scotch.

Sec

French for dry. This word appearing on the label of a bottle of Champagne does not, in fact, indicate a very dry wine, but rather one which is inclined toward sweetness.
See Champagne.

Secco

Italian term for dry wine; as French *sec.*

Séché

A term widely used in France for harsh, flat wines with an astringent aftertaste. This is usually the result of excessive oxidation.

Sediment

Lees or solid matter deposited by a wine while it is ageing. Such deposit does not necessarily affect the taste of the wine, but because of its bitter consistency and for the look of the wine, this precipitation of tartrates should be separated by decanting before serving.
See Chapter Nine.

Seeweine

Pleasant little wines of Lake Constance (or Bodensee) in the south of Germany.
See Baden.

Seewinkel

See Sandweine.

Seibel

Albert Seibel (1844–1936) from St. Julien, France, was the most important and prolific of the grape hybridizers.

Sekt

German term for sparkling wine. Ludwig Devrient, a Berlin actor famous in the nineteenth century, invented a popular joke by calling for his Sekt—cup of Sack—when he played Shakespeare's Falstaff. He began to use the same term when calling for his favorite drink, Champagne, in restaurants and the name Sekt for German champagne-type wine was established.

Sémillon

White wine grape used in the Sauternes and Graves districts of Bordeaux, and fairly widely throughout the Dordogne and southwest France. It is grown also in California.

Seppelstsfield

Famous vineyard in Barossa Valley, South Australia.
See Australia.

Sercial

A white grape variety producing one of the best Madeira wines: dry, sometimes pale, sometimes golden, with a tremendous "nose."
See Madeira.

Sève

Literally, "sappy" (from the French word for sap). The term as used in France suggests a feminine charm, elegance, and a distinction which is graceful and not assertive in a masculine way. It is employed also to describe those Sauternes which have that deep, luscious quality.

Seyssel (Appellation Contrôlée)

White still and sparkling wines.
District: Upper Rhône Valley, France.

Near the source of the Rhône is the butterfly-shaped district of Seyssel, made up of the communes of Seyssel (department of Haute-Savoie), Seyssel (department of Ain), and Corbonod. The dividing line between the twin cities of Seyssel and between the two departments is the Rhône. The wines are white, and some of them are made sparkling.

The area consists of a series of hills and depressions cut out by some ancient glacier that also left in its path the flinty clay and flinty chalk deposits which compose the present soil. These hills provide a number of southerly and southeasterly slopes, on which the vines are planted. For the still Seyssel. the only grape planted is the Roussette. Whether or not this was the vine that was grown in antiquity at Saint-Cornas and Hermitage along the lower Rhône and transported to Seyssel by boats trading in salt; whether it was imported from Cyprus; or whether or not it is the Hungarian Furmint brought in by one of the Princes of Savoy is still a matter for discussion. Whatever its origin, the vine produces a light, flinty-dry white wine that is best when drunk young and is, for that reason, usually bottled in the April following the harvest. The Roussette also goes into the sparkling Seyssel in a proportion of at least 10%, the rest being made up of Molette and Chasselas. This last vine is called, in Seyssel, Bon Blanc.

The delimited area of Seyssel has about 60 hectares (150 acres) planted in vines, and the average production is less than 2,500 hectoliters (66,250 U.S. gallons, 55,000 imp.) yearly.

Seyval Blanc

Seyval Blanc (Seyval Seyve-Villard 5276) is one of the best French-American hybrid grapes, and a popular and adaptable descendant of the Chardonnay. It matures early in tight mildew-susceptible bunches and tends to overbear, necessitating cluster-thinning in early summer. Seyval Blanc produces a good-quality white wine that ranges in style from semi-dry and fresh, similar to some German wines, to complex and oaky, similar to some Loire whites and white Burgundies. This variety is extensively planted in the eastern U.S.

Seyve-Villard

Bertille Seyve (1895–1959) was a French grape hybridizer who developed a number of hybrid vines. In 1919 he married the daughter of another hybridizer named Villard, and his crosses, most notably his whites 5276 (Seyval Blanc) and 12.375 (Villard Blanc) became known under the combined name Seyve-Villard.

Shandy (Shandygaff)

A long drink popular in England; beer mixed with ginger beer or lemonade.

Shebeen

In Ireland and Scotland, a place where taxable liquors are sold without a license; also, a low tavern or public house.

Shekar

Hebrew term for an intoxicating drink, later applied only to cider.

Sherry

Sherry, celebrated since Shakespeare's time, tends to eclipse, for most people, the fame of all other Spanish wines. It is a fortified wine, a wine to which grape brandy has been added to bring up the alcoholic content to approximately 16% for the Finos and 18% for the Olorosos. Spaniards are much more fond of Sherry than are the Portuguese of Port; but the English and Dutch drink a great deal more Sherry than do the Spaniards (though not quite as much as they once did), and exports to other European countries were until recently steadily increasing. In the early 1980's, however, a slump occurred; the better-known brands of Sherry, having gained world recognition, are managing to cope reasonably well, but the lesser firms have suffered.

The Sherry vineyards lie around the town of Jerez de la Frontera, south of Seville, in the most romantic part of Spain. Here, a great horse-fair is held each spring: just as Seville is a city of olives and bulls, Jerez (which once traded in gold and in Barbary apes) is a town of wine and horses. The great bulls and bullfighters come here, too, from Seville, and young *caballeros* in gray Córdoba hats ride with beautiful girls on horseback or drive them around in open carriages.

Only a few years ago, Jerez, in spite of the activity in the Sherry *bodegas*, looked half asleep in the midday sun: a town of dignified white houses and wrought-iron balconies, withdrawn from the invading tide of commercialization. Today, a great highway roars near the town, and everyone is wide awake. There was a real boom in the demand for Sherry; and, as exports and prices rose, some of the big firms tended to expand. Pedro Domecq, for instance, has set up a holding company, Domecq International, in Luxembourg, to manage its widespread interests—one of which is a joint investment with Seagrams in a large Rioja firm. In spite of the clamor for the product—and of the improvement in quality in certain sherry-style rivals in other countries—the Consejo Regulador, the official body which controls Sherry and its closely guarded Denominación de Origen, will not allow its stocks to be diminished by more than 40% in any year. The purpose is to prevent quantity from swamping quality. In one respect, the wine-makers of Jerez are fortunate: they still can increase the acreage of their vines. There are about 18,500 hectares of vineyards (46,500 acres) officially planted, which produce nearly 1.5 million hectoliters (40 million U.S. gallons, 33 million imp.) of the famous wine.

Yet the fascination of Sherry and the mystery of its ageing have not changed, and the *bodegas*, as much as the *feria*, draw visitors to Jerez. Sherry is an anglicized term taken from the name of the city, which has changed over the centuries from the Latin Xeres to the Moorish Sherrisch, and hence to the Spanish Jerez. Vines have grown in the region ever since the Phoenicians founded the town, over a thousand years before Christ. The Greeks came and then the Romans, who ruled the city for four hundred years. It was from the later invaders, the Vandals, that the whole province took the name Andalusia. Then, in 711, the Moors arrived. Until the reconquest of Jerez, about 1264, it lay on the border between the warring Christian and Moslem kingdoms and so was known as Jerez de la Frontera. Much later—in the nineteenth century—the export of Sherry wine reached its peak, and the town enjoyed great good fortune. Toward the end of the century, however, Sherry was declining in popularity, and in the 1890s phylloxera reached Andalusia. The vine disease (which at that period destroyed most of the vineyards of Europe) and the change in fashion menaced the prosperity of Jerez, and for some years exports were sadly reduced. Fortunately, the trade was to revive.

Sherry is known neither by vintage nor by vineyard. Vintage identity is lost in the *solera* system, by which a fine old Sherry is used to discipline a raw young one.

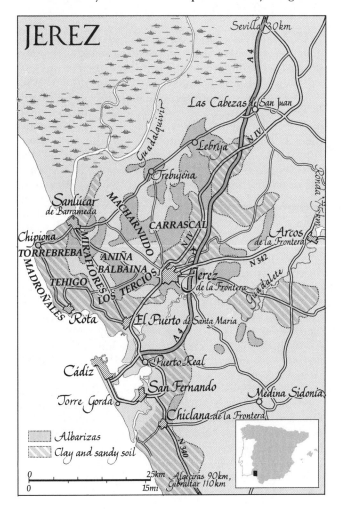

Vineyard names do not exist for two reasons: (1) nearly all Sherry is blended from several different *pagos* (areas), and (2) the important *pagos* are divided into many different vineyards and, therefore, between many owners, so that no one has the exclusive right to the name.

Nevertheless, place of origin is important. Sixty per cent of the stocks of any firm may be purchased from the Zona de Jerez Superior (Zone of Superior Sherry), or "the triangle," as it is called—an irregular triangle lying inside the points of the three important towns, Jerez de la Frontera, Sanlúcar de Barrameda, and Puerto de Santa María. This zone contains the finest soil, named *albariza*. The vineyards are composed of the white chalk soil which nourishes the vine with its lime content and protects it from summer heat by forming a baked crust beneath which moisture is retained. The famous *pagos* of Macharnudo, Carrascal, Añina, Balbaina, and Los Tercios—and Miraflores, Martin Miguel, and Charruado in the east, producing the finest Manzanilla—are inside the triangle. Secondary soils are the *barro* and the *arena*. The former contains some chalk, with a considerable admixture of clay and sand; the latter is sandy, containing alumina and silica. These soils are found in other parts of the Sherry-producing zone, in which the Superior Zone produces the best wine. All Sherries are produced in the Sherry zone, which covers the towns of Jerez de la Frontera, Puerto de Santa María, and Sanlúcar de Barrameda, and it is in these towns that wines from other towns have to be aged in order to bear the Sherry name, the most important of these being Trebujena, Chipiona, Rota, Puerto Real, and Chiclana de la Frontera (all in the province of Cádiz).

VINEYARDS, VINES, AND VINTAGING

There is a saying in Jerez—*Niñas y viñas son malas de guardar*—which might be translated: "It's hard to keep watch over vineyards and young girls."

This is another way of saying that the Palomino, the grape which gives 90% of Sherry, is one of the few great wine grapes in the world which is also delicious to eat. A result is the curious *bien-te-veo* (which means "I can see you"), a small hut or lookout set up on stilts in the vineyards so that an overseer could in the past watch out for whoever might steal the grapes.

There are other varieties of grape in Jerez (Pedro Ximénez, Moscatel in insignificant amounts), but the Palomino is predominant. An apparent abundance of varieties may confuse the amateur, because Palomino is known in the area by no less than seven other names. Listán is the most common of these and is in wide use in the Sanlúcar Manzanilla vineyards. Tempranillo and Palomino de Jerez are also encountered. Whatever it is called, the vine produces thick clusters of pale, fat grapes, hanging like swarms of bees and

465

ripening as much from the reflection of heat off the hard shield of the *albariza* as from the direct sunshine. Pruning removes all but a single branch of the vine, supported in a forked stick against the weight of fruit to come. The production of the vine is limited in order to extend its life—which is one-third shorter (giving it a total of about forty years) than it was before the post-phylloxera replanting onto grafted American roots. The effort to preserve the vines is based on the high cost of replanting. The vineyards themselves are patched here and there in rolling country otherwise given over to sunflower and sugar-beet; but from the main roads and the railways they cannot be seen at all. The whitewashed houses up the narrow dirt tracks that lead from the vineyards are attached, like unimportant outbuildings, to the great sheds within which the vintaging is carried out. In the spring, the plants are treated against disease, and formerly mules used to plod along the rows, their panniers burdened with earthen Arab urns stained brilliant blue by copper sulfate. At harvest time, the grapes are carried in the wooden or plastic boxes and dumped in gleaming heaps on esparto grass mats which resemble large round trays. In an hour or two the whole yard of the wine shed is given over to this sunning, which lasts until the sunshine has brought the sugar-content of the grapes into proper balance as bees and wasps drone over what appear to be mounds of molten honey.

Until quite recently, one could see the harvest as it had been carried out for centuries and the grapes trodden in the *lagares* (wide wooden troughs) by men wearing a special kind of nailed boot. Today, a token treading may be performed as a ritual and a tourist attraction; but in general, the old custom has given way to automatic pressing.

The first fermentation of Sherry, lasting three days to a week, was extremely violent. The barrel bungs foamed over like the mouths of newly opened Champagne bottles. After this, there was a slow fermentation of about two months, during which time the bung stoppers were left open so that the wine was in free contact with the air. At the end, the young wine was cleared of particles and was totally dry—i.e., every bit of fermentable sugar had been converted into alcohol. In December or January the wine is tested for quality (with the nose, not by tasting) and for the type it may finally become. A curious attribute of Sherry is that, without human intervention, it will soon show signs of assuming the character of either a light, dry Fino or a fuller, darker Oloroso. The sign is the pale scum of microscopic yeasty flowers which develops on a Fino and is known as the *flor*. A wine destined to be an Oloroso has little or no *flor*—which can be destroyed by injecting a dose of wine spirits. When a new wine has had its first, tentative classification, it is racked (drawn off the lees into a cask) and tested for alcoholic content, and if this is below strength, will be slightly fortified with wine spirits—a potential Fino or Amon-

tillado up to about 15.5%, an Oloroso to about 18% of alcohol by volume. This addition of brandy definitely separates the one style of Sherry from the other.

After a short rest, the wine is tested again and the cask marked with chalk. One downward stroke *(raya)* means that the wine is good for a Fino or Amontillado, with a clean bouquet and sufficient body; two strokes, that the wine is good for an Oloroso; three, there is some slight flaw; and two strokes with a cross-bar (grid) means that the wine is only fit for burning—i.e., distilling into brandy. For anywhere up to one year, the wine remains in the *añada* casks *(año* means "year") in the spacious, airy *bodega*, through which the air is allowed to circulate. The Sherry is always under the surveillance of the cellarmaster *(capataz)*, and the examination marks chalked on the wood grow more precise: Y *(palma,* a delicate Fino); Y– *(palma cortada,* a fuller Fino); /–*(raya,* an Oloroso style); //–*(dos rayas,* originally selected for a Fino but, having lost its *flor,* now an Oloroso). When it progresses beyond the *añada* stage, the wine enters the *criadera,* or nursery, which is the first stage in the *solera* system.

IN THE SHERRY BODEGAS

The wine is stored in dim, cool sanctuaries at ground level, all facing southeast to the sea. These are the *bodegas* of the great wine firms, to which visitors are welcome. Nothing is asked of the guest but a love for Sherry or the willingness to learn. He will be invited to taste a vast range of wines, and the guide, or perhaps the owner himself, will take up and wield deftly the willowy *venencia,* or sherry dipper—a narrow silver cup at the end of a flexible whalebone spine. The guest is given a hint of the deep mystery of the *flor* as the *venencia* is plunged into the wine. The white scum of *flor* must be penetrated by a stabbing thrust, the bullet-like cup plunging through the creamy layer to reach the wine; the cup disappears into the barrel bung, and with a sudden motion that causes a distinct *pock* of sound, the whalebone wand is flicked sharply down. Pouring the wine, once it has been brought out in the silver *venencia* cup, is an art that looks simple—and is not. The expert grips the flexible shaft between his thumb and forefinger and, holding a glass with his free hand, he lets a long stream of wine cascade through the air and into the glass. The amateur tries it—and with unerring accuracy the Sherry goes up his sleeve.

The white *flor* magically increases at the budding of the vine in spring and at its ripening in the autumn. At first thin and flaky, like the snow in a glass paperweight, *flor* in time looks like a skin of old cream. After its period of flowering, which may continue for years, it dies and settles to the bottom of the wine.

Air turns all wine acid. Sherry—and the wines of the Jura in France—thrive, however, on air. Deprived of it,

they do not produce their characteristic taste. The towering vaulted *bodegas* of Jerez are open to the passage of the air on which the *flor* feeds. Two different microscopic organisms feed on air (technically, they are a bacterium, *Acetobacter*, which turns wine into vinegar, and a yeast of the group responsible for fermentations). In normal (non-Sherry) situations, the *Acetobacter* will appear, and for this reason these wines deteriorate when they come in contact with the air. Somehow, in the region around Jerez (and in Jura), at a concentration of alcohol from 11.5% to 15.5% and at a temperature of 58° to 68°F. (14° to 20°C.), it is the fermenting yeast which succeeds, transforming the wine into that dry, light, crisp condition called Fino in Sherry. The Spaniards believe that the *Saccharomyces* is the yeast that forms a *flor* veil on the surface, consuming whatever sugar is left in the wine after fermentation. Today, Finos are carefully bottled under nitrogen, and steel caps have been substituted for corks to prevent oxidation.

SOLERA

The most interesting thing about Sherry (apart from the mysterious *flor*) is the peculiar system by which it is kept at its best. A very old, very fine Sherry has the power to educate and improve a younger one. Because of this, the old wines are kept in the oldest barrels of what the growers call a *solera*. This is a series of casks graduated by age. A series (or scale) is made up of identical butts. The oldest class in a *solera* is the one called the *solera*. The next oldest is the first *criadera*, the next the second *criadera*, and so on. When the wine is drawn from the *solera*, it is drawn by less than one-third from each butt. Then starts a progressive system by which the *solera* is refilled by the first *criadera* and that in turn by the second *criadera*, etc. The magic result of this system is that the oldest casks remain eternally the same in quality. A cask of 1888, for instance, may retain hardly a spoonful of its original vintage; but each replacement poured back into it over the years will have been educated to be 1888, and replacements still to come will be schooled to the same standard. By this system, it is possible not only to preserve the same quality and character of wine over the years, but also, by constantly refreshing the Fino types with younger wine, to keep these from losing their freshness.

TYPES OF SHERRY

All Sherries stem either from the Fino Amontillado or the Oloroso type. Fino Amontillado is Sherry on which *flor* has developed fully. Oloroso is a wine which has not shown a disposition to have much or any *flor* and the small or nearly nonexistent "flowering" of

which has been suppressed by the addition of a stronger dose of fortifying wine brandy than that given a Fino. No one can influence this first basic decision taken by the wine itself, and no one knows why one cask wants to become Fino while a barrel of what appears to be the same wine, from the same harvest and vineyard, wants to become Oloroso. There is nothing to do but watch and wait, and when the wine has made up its mind, treat it accordingly.

Fino

This is a very pale, light gold wine; the lightest in color of the Sherries. The nose of the wine is pronounced and characteristic—like the scent released by a freshly picked apple. There is a hint of almond too. Ideally, Fino should never be bottled—for when it is drunk from the wood it has always been only in beneficial contact with the air. Less fortified than Oloroso, Fino is more alive. Once bottled, it may keep up to two years—depending on weather and cellaring conditions—but it will not improve at all and will eventually lose its freshness. Because of its delicate constitution, Fino used to be exported at higher alcoholic strength to help it travel (18–20%, instead of the normal 16–17%), and this diminished the bouquet. But this is no longer done.

There is no way of knowing just how old a bottle of Fino is when purchased, since the Sherry (which is always bottled just before shipping) is not dated, although some shippers feel that labels should bear the date of bottling. Under the circumstances, Fino should be bought shortly before it is to be drunk, and from a supplier who can be trusted not to have kept it too long on the shelf. Once opened, Fino is inclined to fade away; and for this reason, the practice in Jerez is rather to buy the wine in half-bottles.

Manzanilla

Manzanilla is both a Sherry Fino—the lightest of Finos—and a separate and individual wine in its own right. This comes about because it is produced in *soleras*, develops *flor*, and comes from the Palomino grape grown on the same kind of chalky, limy soil which produces Fino; but it does these things about 23 kilometers (14 miles) from Jerez, around the seacoast town of Sanlúcar de Barrameda. The vintage is rather earlier here, before the grapes are quite ripe; nor are they usually laid out in the sun to develop extra sugar. The sea also makes a difference, giving the special tang or bitterness, especially in the aftertaste, which distinguishes Manzanilla. This is the palest of the Finos, a fresh, incredibly light, tart wine—usually sold from the barrel in Spain. It is an unchallenged favorite of many Spanish people, and at any bar, along with the inevitable *tapas*—onions, olives, shrimps speared on toothpicks—one could hear calls for Manzanilla.

A peculiar proof of the relationship between Manzanilla and Fino wines of Jerez is that if young Manzanilla is taken to a *bodega* in Jerez for storing, it becomes Jerez Fino; whereas, if a young Jerez Fino is taken to Sanlúcar de Barrameda and kept in the Manzanilla *bodegas*, it will not become Manzanilla. This mysterious behavior is explained by the influence of the sea air. Blowing through the Sanlúcar *bodegas*, it creates Manzanilla, with its own unmistakable, salt-sharp tang.

In the small, whitewashed town of Sanlúcar de Barrameda, Manzanillas are classified into three types according to age: (1) Manzanilla Fino (2) Manzanilla Pasada (3) Manzanilla Olorosa. In fact, Manzanillas are graded in exactly the same way as Sherries are in Jerez. There are some 3,000 hectares (7,500 acres) in vines which produce approximately 200,000 hectoliters (5,300,000 U.S. gallons, 4,400,000 imp.).

Palma

A name often used for a distinguished, delicate Fino in Spain, Palma has recently come into use in export as a brand name. Palmas may be graded 1, 2, 3, or 4, the higher numbers usually indicating greater age; but different *bodegas* apply different meanings to the grades.

Amontillado

A darker-colored Sherry, from one to three degrees stronger in alcohol than a Fino. It averages 18% of alcohol by volume, though with age it may reach 20% and 21%. A Fino which is kept in cask and not refreshed from time to time by younger wine may become an Amontillado. Since there is a great demand for Amontillado, the practice is to watch for a darkening of the *flor* and an increasing nuttiness in the taste of Finos. If this is found, the cask is marked to indicate that it should not be refreshed: in one *bodega* where English influence predominates, the simple word *no* is chalked on the barrelhead.

Amontillados as sold are unfortunately not always pure Amontillado. Many of those seen abroad are sweetened mixtures. They may have Fino or other wines blended in, although there must be some Amontillado or the characteristic nuttiness of flavor will disappear. Generally speaking, the nuttier the taste, the truer the Amontillado. These wines should be dry, clean, and nutty both to the nose and palate. There are some Amontillado-Finos which lie on the borderline. It should be remembered that Sherry types shade into each other; the demarcations are somewhat arbitrary and necessitated by commercial considerations. In one of the largest Jerez *bodegas*, special visitors are sometimes shown a scale of thirty-four glasses in which are Sherries ranging in color from straw to mahogany, in alcohol from 15.2% to 21%, and in taste from light and fresh to pungent. Every one of these will be dry. No Sherry is sweet in its natural state.

Oloroso

A more full-bodied wine than Amontillado. As its name implies, the wine is strong in bouquet—nutty and pungent in the finest bottles. But its most distinctive characteristic is *gordura*, a rich vinosity and opulence that can literally be translated as "fatness." Oloroso leaves a lingering sensation of richness on the palate which produces an illusion of sweetness. In fact, while there are many sweetened Olorosos sold as such—or as Amoroso, Cream, and so on—the natural Oloroso, inside Spain, is dry.

It was not until about a century and a half ago that a taste began to develop with the public for the lighter Sherry derived from the *flor*. Previously, Oloroso was the only style shipped, and the *flor*, which must have existed as it does today, would have been dosed out of existence with wine spirits. The consequence of the taste for Fino was the division of the wines according to whether or not they showed a marked tendency to develop *flor*.

In a true Oloroso, the nose of the wine must be absolutely clean. The average alcoholic strength will be 18% to 20% of the volume, although with age 21% and 22% may be reached. The Olorosos are beautifully golden, the gold darkening with the years and indicating the wine's age in the barrel. Having more body than Finos, Olorosos will survive better in the bottle but, like other Sherries, they do not improve in glass.

Palo Cortado

This is a rare type: an Oloroso with the characteristics of the Fino group. In different *bodegas* Palo Cortado tends to mean different things. At one of the most important firms, a Palo Cortado is an Oloroso with an Amontillado nose. A true Palo Cortado is a vintage wine, very rare in Sherry, and something which simply "happens"—it cannot be achieved by blending. It is admitted, however, that the real thing must be matured for at least twenty years and is commercially not practicable, and that many wines of the style actually on the market are *like* Palo Cortado.

Raya

Very common in Jerez, this designation will not be found abroad. It means a lesser and coarser Oloroso.

Amoroso

A sweetened Oloroso, of a dark color. The style was created for the English taste and is unknown in Spain. (Although in Spain Sherry is taken dry, it is the practice to add sweetener before shipping for many export styles. The best of such sweeteners is Pedro Ximénez, or P.X.)

The full-bodied Amoroso, known as East India, gets its name from the practice in the days of sailing vessels of sending casks of Sherry aboard ship to the East

Indies and back. The airing of the wine and the constant rolling at sea was considered beneficial, and the saying was that "the seasick wines of Jerez are worth double." Brown Sherry is a very dark, sweet Amoroso, likely to be cheaper than East India. Sherries are sometimes darkened by the addition of *color* (a blend of fresh and concentrated grape must) to produce styles demanded in certain markets. Brown Sherry was usually a blend of old Oloroso, P.X., and a touch of *color*.

Cream Sherry

A heavily sweetened Oloroso. It was developed in Bristol, England, and is now extremely popular in the United States also. Some Cream Sherries are bottled in Bristol from Oloroso sent in cask from Jerez; and Creams are now produced in Jerez also to meet the growing demand—although Bristol Cream and Bristol Milk are of course bottled in Bristol.

In England, dark, sweet Sherries may be served, not as aperitifs, but as alternatives to Port at the end of a meal.

Tio Pepe—La Ina

These are not types but brand names for dry Sherry, just as Dry Sack and Double Century are brand names for medium Sherry.

Most Sherry wine is served at a room temperature; but a dry Amontillado should be slightly cooled, whilst Finos and Manzanillas should be chilled.

Sherry butt (Bota)

This storage butt contains 600 liters. The shipping butt contains 500 liters. For buying purposes, the butt is reckoned as holding 516 liters, allowing 16 liters for evaporation, clarification, etc.

See Sherry.

Shiraz

A city in southwest Iran, near the Persian Gulf, which gave its name to the best-known Persian wines. Before the Mohammedan prohibition, wine was freely drunk in Persia; and viticulture persists on a small scale in the mountainous regions. Shiraz is mentioned by Marco Polo, and classical writings carry fabulous accounts of it, in one case telling how the vine was trained by pulleys and weights to grow up one side of the house and down the other.

See Iran.

Shot berries

The formation of grape clusters of varying size; this failure of the vine normally follows *coulure*, or dropping of the flower, in late spring and early summer.

See Chapter Eight, p. 31.

Sicily

Red and white wines.
Region: Italian island.

Sicily, divided from the toe of Italy by the Straits of Messina, is the largest and most romantic of the Mediterranean islands. It has beautiful beaches, the volcanic Mount Etna, and stretches of wild maquis. Oranges, lemons, and vines grow there; and in the nearly three thousand years of occupation, men have left classical ruins, baroque towns and palaces, sun-baked villages, and a few scabrous slums. Summers are hot and the vines prolific: Sicily's contribution to the total wine production of Italy is 9 million hectoliters a year (208 million U.S. gallons, 198 million imp.). Sicily accounts for close to a quarter of all Italian wine exports. Much of the red wines are exported to France for blending.

Fortified wines such as Marsala predominated in Sicily's production, and grape plantings for Marsala, the Grillo grape, covered much of western part of the Island. Since 1960, Sicily has become a large producer of dry red and white table wines. Vineyards have been replanted with Trebbiano, Catarratto and Inzolia for whites; and Sangiovese and Nero Mascalise for dry reds.

TYPES OF WINE

Marsala (D.O.C.)—an aperitif and dessert wine. Marsala, once very popular, is a blended wine made from grape juice syrup (must), from aromatic white wine, and from *passito* of dried grapes, fermented with brandy. The Vergine type is usually made by the *solera* system.

Corvo di Casteldaccia. The best-known Sicilian red and especially white wines. The famous brand Duca di Salaparuta at Casteldaccia is now owned by the government.

Etna (D.O.C.). Red, white, and rosé wines made from grapes grown on the cool, sunny slopes of the cone-shaped mountain. All are high in alcohol—the red is made from Nerello and Mascalese and the white from Carricante and Catarratto. The best comes from Milo, and there is also a rosé, a dark pink, inclining to ruby.

Mamertino. None of the Sicilian wines is really dry, but this golden white wine from the slopes around Messina is semi-sweet and alcoholic, with an aromatic bouquet.

Malvasia delle Lipari (D.O.C.). A sweet yellow wine (perhaps the best Italian wine of its type) from sun-dried grapes, produced on the islands of Salina, Stromboli, and Lipari—part of the province of Messina. *Passito* and *liquoroso* types are made with the dried fruit.

Moscato di Pantelleria (D.O.C.). An amber-colored, perfumed dessert wine from the island of Pantelleria.

Château Sigalas-Rabaud

Faro (D.O.C.). A red wine produced in the neighborhood of Messina; quite a good table wine, usually not too high in alcohol, but sometimes reaches 14%.

Alcamo (D.O.C.). This wine, also known as Bianco d'Alcamo, is made from Catarratto and some Trebbiano grapes grown in northwestern Sicily, between Palermo and Trapani. It is dry, fresh, fruity, fragrant, with a pale straw-yellow color.

Cerasuolo di Vittoria (D.O.C.). A cherry-colored wine of particularly high alcoholic content, suitable for very long ageing, with a bouquet of pomegranates and jasmine. An excellent table wine.

Moscato di Noto (D.O.C.). Produced in the province of Siracusa, this is a pale yellow-colored wine with a deep scent of honey, made in small quantity near the area of production of Moscato di Siracusa.

Château Sigalas-Rabaud

Bordeaux white wine.
District: Sauternes, France.
Commune: Bommes.

The property belongs to the Marquis and Marquise de Lambert. The Marquise is a member of the de Sigalas family, one of whose ancestors fought with La Fayette in the Revolutionary War. *(See* Château Rabaud-Promis *for the origins of the estate.)*

Characteristics. Better than its neighbor, very distinguished. One of the best Sauternes in good years.

Vineyard area: 14 hectares (35 acres).

Average production: 35 *tonneaux* (3,000 cases).

Silent spirit (Cologne spirit or neutral spirit)

British distillers' term for rectified spirit, colorless, odorless, and tasteless, used in making gin and other spirituous drinks.

Siller wine

A style of red wine made in central and southeastern Europe from red and white grapes mixed together before vinification begins. The fermenting juices are racked off the skins after a few days so that only a part of the coloring and the tannin present in the skins passes into the must, thereby making the rest of the winemaker's work easier and the wine drinkable much more quickly. Though the technique may seem at first just that of making a rosé, a typical eastern European Siller is far deeper in color than the average French rosé.

A variation, the Schillerwein of Württemberg in Germany, is usually made from red and white grapes grown together in the same vineyard plot. In Styria, the same wine is called Schilscherwein.

See Schiller wine.

Silvestro

Italian liqueur into which go a number of different herbs, dominated by mint. It is said to have been invented by Fra San Silvestro.

Singlings

Brandy after the first distillation and before redistillation.

Sipon

Slovenian grape variety which may be found on the labels of Ljutomer (or Lutomer) white wines—e.g., Lutomer Sipon. The word is pronounced sheepon and is sometimes spelled Chipon.

See Yugoslavia.

Sirah

Red wine grape.
See Syrah; Petite-Sirah.

Château Siran

Bordeaux red wine.
District: Haut-Médoc, France.
Commune: Labarde-Margaux.

The name is said to go back to 1428, when a certain Guilhem de Siran swore allegiance to the Abbot of Saint Croix in the church of Macau.

The property was originally known as Saint-Siran. In 1809 the Comtesse de Toulouse-Lautrec-Moufa, grandmother of the painter, inherited the estate. Alain Miailhe, former proprietor of the adjoining Château Dauzac and present owner of Château Siran, has completely rebuilt the vatrooms and *chais*.

Characteristics. The wine deserves a better rank than Cru Bourgeois. In the author's personal classification, Château Siran is ranked higher than some Crus Classés. Made quite carefully, Siran has the finesse and character of a superior wine.

Vineyard area: 30 hectares (75 acres).

Average production: 120 *tonneaux* (11,000 cases).

Sizzano (D.O.C.)

Red wine from the Italian Piedmont (*q.v.*).

Skhou

Distilled koumiss (*q.v.*).

Sling

A mixed ice drink in a long glass. The ingredients are spirits (usually gin), cordials, and fruit juice.

Slivovitz

Slivovitz (pronounced shleevovitsa) is the most common name for Serbian and Bosnian plum brandy from Yugoslavia. Sometimes Slivovica, or Slivovitza, or Sljivovica (Sljiva means plum in Serbo-Croatian), it is made from Pořegača or Madjarka blue plums in the second largest plum-growing area in the world. Slivovitz is the national drink in Bosnian and Serbian Yugoslavia, where it is called rakija. The spirit is doubledistilled; and in export, in Western Europe, Britain, the United States, Australia, and other countries, it is sold at 70° proof and 87° proof, in tall bottles or in round, flat bottles, the shape of the traditional Yugoslav wooden flask. Famous since the Middle Ages, it comes from the fruit of trees never less than twenty years old and is fermented three months in 75-hectoliter (2,000-U.S.-gallon, 1,665-imp.) casks. Distilled twice, it matures in the wood in 19-hectoliter (500-U.S.-gallon, 416-imp.) casks; when it is one year old, hand-selected fresh plums are added. The brandy is then bottled and should be given about five more years. Variants of slivovitz are made in other Balkan countries, but Yugoslavia is the most important producer.

Sloe gin

A cordial made from the small, bitter, black plumlike fruit of the blackthorn, steeped in gin (*q.v.*).

Smash

A long, iced drink made with spirits, sugar, and mint.

Château Smith-Haut-Lafitte

Bordeaux red wine.
District: Graves, France.
Commune: Martillac.

The magnificent château stands untenanted in the midst of beech woods. The red wine, classed one of the Firsts of Graves in 1953, is a monopoly of the Louis Eschenauer firm of Bordeaux. White wine has been made since 1968 entirely from Sauvignon Blanc grapes.

Characteristics. A red wine with less character than most of the Graves in the first class, but rewarding when it is allowed to mature fully. The white is clean and pleasant.

Vineyard area: red—45 hectares (112.5 acres); white—5 hectares (12.5 acres).

Average production: red—180 *tonneaux* (17,000 cases); white—20 *tonneaux* (1,900 cases).

Soave (D.O.C.)

Italian white wine grown around Verona. It is dry, with an agreeable bouquet and a smooth texture.
See Veneto.

Sochu

Chinese spirit distilled from saké.

Soft

A wine which is not firm, not hard, and not rough. Wine of certain grape varieties matures rapidly and quickly achieves softness; in other cases, age is the determining factor. Once softnes is attained, it is unlikely that a wine will keep long.

Solera system

Method by which Sherry wine, Málaga wine, and some Spanish brandies are produced.
See Sherry.

Som

Most Rumanian wine is made from the Riesling, Leanyka, and Furmint (known in Rumania as Som).

Somlói Furmint

A white wine from Somló, near Lake Balaton.
See Hungary.

Sommelier

French term for wine waiter.

Sonnenglanz

Important vineyard at Beblenheim, Alsace, France.
See Alsace.

Sonoma

Californian wine region, north of San Francisco, which provides some excellent table and sparkling wines.
See United States: California.

Sorbino

Finnish cherry liqueur.

Sour

A wine which has nearly turned to vinegar and is not fit to drink. The opposite of a sweet wine is a dry wine, not a sour one.

An American mixed drink made with fruit juice (usually lemon), spirits, and ice—i.e., whiskey sour, brandy sour, etc.

South Africa

South Africa, with its dry, hot climate and its viticultural tradition of three centuries, is a wine-producing country, but unfortunately not yet a wine-drinking one, although, happily, the trend toward the civilized habit of taking a glass of wine with a meal becomes more general every day. The great improvement in the quality of sherry-type and table wines is no doubt contributing largely to the slow change for the better in drinking tendencies. Not so many years ago, the so-called sherries were extremely harsh, and the table wines rough and indistinguishable; but this is no longer the case. The sherry is closest to that produced by Jerez de la Frontera. There has, moreover, been a tremendous improvement in the presentation—that is, the labeling—of the better table wines, even in the last few years.

How long it will take to turn South Africans into beverage wine-drinkers, as distinct from those who drink to celebrate, is difficult to say; but the outlook is now hopeful. Ninety per cent of the production is consumed locally. Now that the cheap rough wine of early days is on its way out, growers are making table wines which are, in some cases, attaining a higher average quality than some of their European counterparts. The *vins ordinaires* are some of the best in the world. It is significant that the consumption of table wines in South Africa has, according to a reliable estimate, trebled since 1945 and is now 9.8 liters per capita annually. South African restaurants offer fine values and good selections of the local table wines.

The southwestern Cape is one of the most reliable wine-growing districts in the world. The climate is seldom erratic, and heavy rain just before the grape-picking is a rarity, so that there is scarcely ever a poor vintage. Depending on the area, the picking season, or vintage, begins in February or March, and when a farm has several grape varieties it may go on for as long as two months.

WINE HISTORY

In 1955 the South African wine industry celebrated its tercentenary. It was at the end of the year 1654 that the first cuttings from Holland arrived at the Cape, and probably they were short (three-inch-long) slips of young vines from the Rhineland. The following year another consignment was sent out from Holland, and they were probably all Muscat, Green Grape (Groendruif), Muscatel, and the Steen grape known as Steendruif in Afrikaans.

On February 2, 1659, wine was pressed for the first time at the Cape, and Johan van Riebeeck wrote in his diary: "Today, praised be the Lord, wine was made for the first time from Cape grapes."

Credit should be given to the Co-operative Wine Growers' Association of South Africa for a chronological history of events since, in 1679, Simon van der Stel became governor of the Cape of Good Hope, established his farm at Groot Constantia, and set an example to the colonists by making fine wines. Significant dates follow: *1688* French Huguenots arrived and settled in the Franschoek valley; they extended the vineyards and improved the quality of Cape wines. *1711* South African wines were becoming known, and an early traveler in his writings spoke of the "world-famed Constantia wines," which were then being made at Wynberg. These were sweet wines. *1805* The English took possession of the Cape and, because of the Napoleonic Wars, encouraged the export of South African wines to Great Britain. *1811* The first offcial wine-taster was appointed, by Sir John Cradock, to keep an eye on the quality of the wine exported. *1826* Export trade to Britain flourished and wine growers and merchants invested considerable capital in the industry. *1861* With the enactment of preferential tariffs by the Gladstone government, the export trade in Britain boomed. *1885* Phylloxera ravaged Cape vineyards, and wine-growers faced complete ruin. To combat the disease, they grafted their vines onto disease-resistant American root-stocks. The vines flourished, but soon the industry was faced with an even greater danger—overproduction. *1917* Overproduction meant ridiculously low prices for wine, and the growers decided to form a central organization to look after their interests. This led to the founding in 1918 of the Co-operative Wine Growers' Association of South Africa Ltd., today better known as the K.W.V. *1924* Parliament passed Act 5 of 1924, the Wine and Spirit Control Act. The K.W.V., under its constitution, annually fixes the minimum price to be paid for distilling wine; this Act made the transactions of non-members subject to the same provisions as those of members and changed the face and character of the South African wine industry. *1926* The export trade with Britain and Holland was resumed. *1931* The South African Wine Farmers' Association (London) Ltd. was established in the United Kingdom, with the K.W.V. holding a half interest. The purpose of this company was to effect distribution and maintain continuity of supplies, uniformity of quality, and stability of prices. *1940* The Wine and Spirit Control Amendment Act, No. 23 of 1940, was passed, and provided for the fixing of the price for good wine sold by producers; it also empowered the K.W.V. to limit the production of wine alcohol in the Cape. *1950* K.W.V. acquired full control of the South African Wine Farmers' Association (London) Ltd. *1979* The government prohibited simultaneous control over beer and wine interests and interests in spirits.

WINE REGIONS

As an important form of agriculture, viticulture is limited to the southwestern districts of the Cape, be-

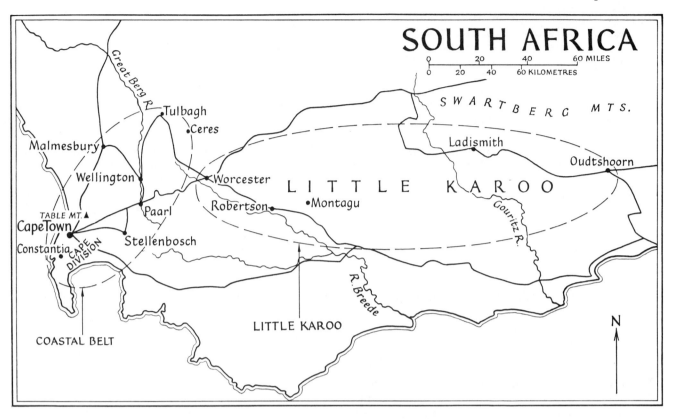

tween latitudes 33° and 34°S. Vines for wine-making, table use, and dried-fruit production are grown along the Orange River and other irrigation projects of the Northern Cape. Table grapes are grown in the High-veld regions of the Transvaal.

The viticultural area may be divided into two distinct regions, the Coastal Belt and the Little Karoo. The former stretches from the coast to the first mountain range, and the districts of Stellenbosch, Paarl, Malmesbury, Durbanville, and the Constantia Valley lie in this area. The latter extends from beyond the Drakenstein range to the Swartberg Mountains and embraces the districts of Worcester, Robertson, Montagu, Oudtshoorn, and Ladismith.

The Cape Division (in which lie the wine farms to the southeast of the Table Mountain range that runs across the Cape Peninsula) is the oldest wine-growing area in the country. Since the legislation in 1973 on South Africa's "Wines of Origin" (details on p. 475), both Cape and Caledon districts come under Stellenbosch. The Stellenbosch vineyards are about 45 minutes by car north of Capetown, and Stellenbosch itself is a handsome old town with great flower gardens and trees. The university there works closely with the S.A. Wine Institute, a department of the Ministry of Agriculture.

The Coastal Belt vines are grown mainly on lower mountain slopes and rolling hills, close to the cooling effect of the sea. The soil varies from sandy to heavy loam. The yield is 3 to 6 tons (3.36 to 6.72 short tons) per acre, from which dry white and red wines are produced, as are good sherry- and port-types. Due to the slight variation in climatic conditions, there is very little variation in the quality of these wines from year to year.

In the Little Karoo, across the mountains in the Breed River region, where the rainfall is less and where the vines are grown under irrigation, the yield is 6 to 10 tons (6.72 to 11.2 short tons) per acre. The soil here is deep, rich, and alluvial. The area is known for its fine sherries, sweet fortified wines, and brandies. Since the 1970s some good table wines, especially from the Colombar grape, are being made.

The seasons in South Africa are not as in Europe. Spring lasts from September to November, summer from December to February, autumn from March to May, and winter from June to August. The grapes reach full ripeness between February and April, and the harvesting begins before the onset of autumn.

GRAPE VARIETIES

South Africa is dominated by the *cultivar*, or grape variety, Steen (Chenin Blanc), which makes up some 30% of all grapes grown for wine. It is grown in all regions and is extremely versatile, being made into dry white wines, semi-sweet wines, botrytis wines, and sparkling wines. The best sherries are made from it, as are white port and even brandy.

The next most popular and widely grown sherry grape is the Palamino grape, known locally as Fransdruif. It makes up 13% of the total crop, but is losing popularity. Cinsaut makes up 10% of the total crop, and the Muscat Alexandrie, or Hanepoot, 7%.

The better-known noble varieties, Cabernet Sauvignon and Cabernet Franc, SA Riesling and Rhine Riesling, Chardonnay, Sauvignon Blanc, Gewürztraminer, Sylvaner, and others produce quality wines.

In the reds, there are a range of port varieties, Shiraz, Pinot Noir, and very small quantities of Carignan, Merlot, Zinfandel, and Grenache.

Pinotage, a locally developed cross between the Pinot Noir and the Hermitage, ranks with Cabernet Sauvignon, each accounting for 2.5% of the wine grape crop.

TYPES OF WINE

Today South Africa makes a wide range of wines from the grape varieties outlined above. White wines constitute 85% of the market, red wines less than 10%. Rosés and sparkling wines make up the balance.

The Constantia wines, already mentioned as being exported in the late eighteenth and early nineteenth centuries, were dessert wines, and these are still of good quality. They include port-type wines—Tawny, Ruby, White, and Vintage—produced from Hermitage and Portuguese variety grapes grown at Paarl, Stellenbosch, and adjoining areas, and made in the Portuguese manner; and Muscadel wines, produced from Muscadel grapes grown at Robertson, Montagu, Bonnievale, and the Nuy district of Worcester. The trend is to varietally labeled wines.

Sherry-type production in South Africa started about fifty years ago, and only as recently as 1942 were these wines produced by the *solera* system, the traditional method of Sherry manufacture in Spain. It is interesting to note the resemblance geographically and climatically between Paarl, center of the South African sherry industry, and the Sherry-producing areas of Andalusia in Spain. Jerez de la Frontera has a latitude of 34°41′N. and Paarl is situated at 33°45′S.

Both light-bodied and full-bodied red natural wines are produced at the Cape—the light from Cabernet, Cinsault, and Shiraz grapes grown in the Constantia Valley, and in the districts of Stellenbosch and Somerset West nearest to the coast; the fuller wines from Cinsault, Shiraz, Pinotage and Gamay grapes grown at Paarl, Stellenbosch, and Durbanville. More Bordeaux style wines are being produced. Rosés have been produced at the Cape for some years now and are gaining in popularity. Reds are aged from one and a half to three years in vats or small cooperage.

Dry and semi-sweet white table wines, which must contain less than 3% sugar, are made from Cape Riesling, Chenin Blanc, Gewürztraminer, Colombard, and Clairette Blanche grapes grown at Paarl, Stellenbosch, and Tulbagh. White wines make up 85% of the production. A bit watery, they are better than similar

wines from Chile. Some very good botrytis wines have been made since the early 1970s.

Sparkling wines are made from Riesling, Sauvignon Blanc, and some Chenin Blanc grapes by natural fermentation, and also by artificial impregnation of the wine with carbon dioxide.

There is some difficulty in giving the total vintage return for South Africa, a figure that has to be compiled from the returns of growers which include both alcoholic products and non-alcoholic products such as table grapes and grapes for the making of raisins. They do not, however, include returns from the main sultana-producing areas. Based on the returns of growers as supplied by the Co-operative Wine Growers' Association, the wine production for the year 1983, district by district, was as follows:

District	Hectoliters
Olifants River	1,000,000
Malmesbury	750,000
Montagu	400,000
Orange River	700,000
Paarl	1,400,000
Robertson	1,400,000
Stellenbosch	1,300,000
Worcester	2,000,000
Total	8,950,000

SPIRITS

Liqueurs with an alcoholic content of 60° to 78° proof spirit, or 30% to 39% by volume, are made in ever-increasing variety, based upon European counterparts; but the legendary liqueur named by early Cape settlers, Van der Hum, is typically South African. It was produced in days gone by in the Old Cape homes with a flavoring made from *naartjie* (tangerine) peel, and is now made on a commercial scale.

Brandy was first made in the Cape in the year 1672. It is now distilled and matured under strict government supervision. The alcoholic content is 75° proof spirit, or 43% by volume. The grapes from which distilling wines are produced are the Palomino, Colombar, and Chenin Blanc varieties grown in the areas around Worcester, Montagu, and Robertson. Only the best-quality distilling wines are allowed to be used for distillation into brandy, and these must be approved by the Government Brandy Board. All types of South African brandy must contain a minimum of 30% brandy distilled in a pot-still, matured for a minimum period of three years in casks of imported oak approved by a government commissioner. If certified by the Government Brandy Board to be pure wine brandy, it qualifies for an excise duty rebate of 54.3 cents per liter absolute alcohol, and provision has been made for higher rebates for matured brandies. The best-known brands are Klipdrift, Oude Meester, Viceroy, Limousin, Richelieu, Marreu, and Bols.

STRUCTURE OF THE WINE INDUSTRY

At the producer's level, the wine industry is highly organized, largely as a result of the monopolistic powers of the Co-operative Growers' Association of South Africa—the K.W.V. already referred to. This was founded in 1918, its main object being: "To so direct, control and regulate the sale and disposal by its members of their produce, being that of the grape, as shall secure or tend to secure for them a continuously adequate return for such produce."

Early opposition from wine-growers who preferred to withhold support from this cooperative was overcome in 1924, when Parliament passed the Wine and Spirit Control Act in terms of which the transactions of non-members were made subject to the same conditions and obligations as were imposed by the Constitution of the K.W.V. Since that time, no person may sell, acquire, or utilize wine in the Cape province for distilling or conversion into spirits except through or with the consent of the Association; nor may any wine-grower sell or distill otherwise dispose of brandy or spirits distilled from his own wine except through and with the consent of the K.W.V.

Under its constitution, the Association annually fixes a minimum price for distilling wine, declares the surplus (i.e., that portion of the vintage which it considers cannot be absorbed by the local market) and indicates what portion of a member's vintage must be held by him and delivered as a surplus, free of charge, to the Association. If the member cannot deliver the specified surplus, owing to his having sold his entire crop, then he must contribute cash instead. Cooperation is compulsory. The K.W.V. is debarred from selling its products for use in Africa south of the equator except to distilling cooperative societies, and to the wholesale trade. In the South African wine industry a clear distinction is made between what is called good wine and distilling wine. The former is intended for consumption as wine, while the latter is intended for distillation into brandy or wine spirits.

The Surplus Declaration by the Association under its constitution for the year 1986 was 40% of the total crop. The K.W.V. has vast cellars and distilleries situated in Paarl, Stellenbosch, Robertson, Montagu, and Worcester, with a total storage capacity of 2.3 million hectoliters. Membership in the Association increased from 4,444 in 1959 to over 6,000 in 1986—evidence of successful organization under the cooperative system. Uncontrolled surpluses before 1918 resulted in wine-growers being barely able to obtain a penny per bottle for their best wines.

In the year 1985, South African exports of wine and brandy amounted to 108,000 hectoliters and 24,000 hectoliters respectively, while the total wine production amounted to 8.3 million hectoliters. Wines and spirits are mainly exported by the KWV and the four biggest wholesale wine-producing companies. These products are exported on a regular basis to more than 30 countries of the world and must satisfy strict analyt-ical and organoleptical standards before they can be exported. The Stellenbosch Farm Wineries is the leader of a group of producing wholesalers; Distillers Corporation, Gilbeys Distillers and Vintners, Douglas Green, and Union Wine are some of the better-known, larger components of this group. These companies buy or make their own bulk wine, which they then blend, mature, bottle, store, and eventually distribute to retail outlets. Because of their extensive research facilities, they are an important force in the development of the latest viticultural and oenological techniques.

South Africa's wine trade is based no longer on preferential tariffs but on quality. Cape wines have to pass a government quality control before they may be exported, and the excise control of brandy in the Republic is among the strictest in the world. All brandies shipped from South Africa carry with them certificates of age, method of maturation, and distillation.

WINES OF ORIGIN LEGISLATION

Whereas the wine-growing countries of Europe have recognized for some time the importance of place of origin in the pedigree and identification of wines, South Africa was, until September 1973, without any system approximating the French Appellation d'Origine Contrôlée. But after investigation by a government committee under Dr. J. A. van Zyl, this system was adopted in South Africa and given the force of law with the W.O. (Wines of Origin) seal—the truth on the label. The seal is awarded by the South African Wine and Spirits Board as its guarantee that "what is stated on the label will also be found in the bottle, insofar as it refers to place of origin, vine variety, and vintage year—or any combination of the three." The system works from vineyard to bottle through the usual complicated system of production records, sampling, testing, certification procedure, and a reasonable system of policing.

The W.O. seal now has to be applied to the capsule on bottled wines which bears the year of vintage or any one of the prescribed list of names of designated areas for the production of Wines of Origin, or of vine cultivars (varieties) approved by the Wine and Spirits Board. By the end of 1973, about fourteen areas had been defined formally in terms of the legislation as areas for Wines of Origin, and fourteen estates were approved for the production of "Estate Wines of Origin."

The geographic areas approved for Wines of Origin included Overberg, Paarl, Piketberg, Robertson, Stellenbosch (including Caledon and Cape), Tulbagh, Worcester, Swartland, Swellendam, Constantia, Durbanville, Olifants River, the Little Karoo, and an area known as Boberg (including Tulbagh). The Boberg designation is limited to liqueur wines such as "sherries" and "ports." The best wines come from Malmesbury, Paarl, Stellenbosch, Tulbagh, Worcester, Constantia, and Durbanville, the last-named being noted for reds.

Fine wines of greatly improved quality are now being produced on many farms, including Backsberg, Boschendal, Welgemeend, Fairview, Landskroon, and Nederburg at Paarl; Groot Constantia in the Cape Town area; Kanonkop, Vergenoegd, Rustenburg, Bertram's Middelvlei, Neethlingshof, Overgaauw, Simonsig, Spier, Uiterwyk, Meerlust, Le Bonheur, Vergenoegd—all at Stellenbosch; and Alto, Theuniskraal, and Twee Jongegzellen at Tulbagh. Other particularly good properties are De Wetshof L'Ormarins, and Hamilton Russel Vineyards.

Unfortified wines designated as Wines of Origin must be derived solely from the indicated origin; fortified wines must be at least 80% of the indicated origin.

An estate wine must comply with certain quality standards defined by the Board and must be produced or manufactured entirely in a cellar on the estate, from grapes grown on the estate. A distinction has been drawn between estate wines produced, manufactured, and bottled on a particular estate, and wine produced or manufactured on the estate but bottled elsewhere.

No wine may be sold or exported under the name of any wine *cultivar* allowed for the making of wine, unless 75% was produced or manufactured from vines of such a *cultivar*, and the wine is characteristic of the variety.

Provision is made for "Wines of Origin Superior" (or W.O.S.), a rare distinction for a superior-quality wine.

Since the introduction of the Wine of Origin Certification, consumer awareness of the differences between wines of different origins, vintages and varietals has expanded drastically and resulted in a greater price differentiation between the wines developed. This has stimulated producers to concentrate on the planting of varietals capable of producing higher quality wines such as Weisser Riesling, Sauvignon Blanc, Chardonnay, Gewurztraminer, Pinot Noir and Cabernet Sauvignon.

The Stellenbosch Research Institute should be commended for its influence in promoting wise control laws governing quality.

The official record and control system facilitates control in detail of the production and handling of wine from the time of pressing until the wine is bottled, labeled, certified, and ready for marketing. This has obliged wineries to acquire additional equipment to deal with small batches of wine separately in all its stages. Not only do varieties have to be processed separately but vintages must be kept apart, and this is expected to add considerably to the cost of the end product.

Southwest France

Apart from the great region of Bordeaux, there are several more wine-growing provinces in this part of France, stretching from the Dordogne to the Pyrenees. Many good wines of these areas have been raised from V.D.Q.S. to Appellations Contrôlées and most will be found under individual headings: Béarn, Bergerac, Cahors, Côtes de Duras, Fronton and Côtes du Frontonnais (Haute-Garonne), red, white and rosé; Côtes de Montravel, Côtes de Saussignac, Buzet, Gaillac, Jurançon, Madiran, Monbazillac, Pacherenc de Vic Bilh, Pécharmant, Villaudric (Haute-Garonne), etc.

A second group of lesser wines, agreeable to drink in their own part of the country, is listed under the Vins Délimités de Qualité Supérieure. These are: Côtes du Marmandais (Lot-et-Garonne), red and white; Lavilledieu (Tarn-et-Garonne), red and white.
See V.D.Q.S.

Spain

Spain has the largest acreage of vineyard in Europe but not the highest yield; Italy and France make more wine. Nearly 30 million hectoliters (789.5 million U.S. gallons, 658 million imp.) are harvested every year from 1,720,000 hectares of vineyards (4,300,000 acres)—more than one-fifth of all the European vineyard land. Here, as elsewhere, the current expansion of viticulture and the gradual modernization of wine-making methods have been very marked in recent years. The country, with its extreme contrasts in climate, landscape, and soil, produces wines of all types: from delicate Fino Sherries to rich dessert wines, from frail wines of old vintage to strong hearty reds, to the delightful whites of Alella and the thin green wines of the northwest. From the central plain comes a great gush of ordinary wine *(vino corriente)* used for carafe wine and for blending both at home and abroad.

The greater part of the country is a vast tableland *(meseta)*, with outbreaks of jagged mountain ranges and snow-covered peaks. Its climate is harsh and Continental with dry, torrid summers and biting winters. Seen from the air, Spain is like a brown relief map wrinkled into dry creeks and valleys, with sudden gleams of water. For the traveler by road or train, however, the monotony is broken: after an expanse of arid grass come umbrella pines, cork oaks, a sweet-smelling scrub of rosemary and lavender, or a patchwork of olive groves. Arriving at one of the great rivers, he is in a landscape of cornfields and poplar trees. Once through the Sierra Morena, into the province of Córdoba, the sharp air softens. In the spring, all Andalusia is green; figs, oranges, and olives grow in season. The winters are mild here, and around the Mediterranean coast the weather is tempered by the sea, and the narrow strip of land bordering the shore is planted like a garden with fruit, olives, and vines—the last growing prolifically near the sea or on the sheltered slopes of some of the mountain valleys. The most productive areas are in La Mancha with New Castile, in Catalonia, and the Levante along the east coast. The best wines come not from these areas but from the Sherry region in Andalusia, from the Rioja vineyards in Logroño, Alava, and Navarre, and from the Penedés district in Catalonia.

HISTORY

The vineyards of Andalusia are very old. In about 1100 B.C. the Phoenicians founded Gadir (Cádiz) and planted vines, presumably brought from the East. Then came Greeks, Carthaginians, and Romans, spreading both the vines and the science of viticulture through Spain. Wine was supplied to Rome, and Cicero praised the growths of Tarragona and Catalonia. When Rome fell, the barbarians invaded—Vandals, leaving their name to Andalusia, were followed by Goths. They must have trampled down the vineyards, but the vine persisted; and when the Arabs landed, in 711, they protected and increased the grapevines for the sake of the fruit. Gradually, the wine-drinking Christian kings won back the land until, in 1492, the last Moorish kingdom of Granada was retaken.

Early in the fourteenth century, Spanish wines were coming to England. By the time of Spain's ascendancy, when the Emperor Charles V was ruling the Netherlands from Spain, Sack (Sherry), Tent (Alicante), and Canary wines were familiar drinks in northern Europe.

At the beginning of this century, Spain, less affected by the phylloxera epidemic than were many European countries, was doing a flourishing export trade. But the French laws against the entry of foreign wines in the early 1930s and the crisis of overproduction, to which importations from Algeria into France contributed, hit Spain hard. Then came the Spanish Civil War. Neglected vines developed phylloxera; whole vineyards, especially those near Madrid and Toledo, were destroyed. Wine became scarce, and the price doubled. The Second World War made conditions worse, and in the 1940s there were outbreaks of mildew and a prolonged series of droughts to contend with. Not until 1952–53 did wine production really improve and prices begin to drop. Since 1959, the vineyard area has been spreading, mainly in New Castile.

The natural consequence has been an increase in export figures. In 1970, they were higher than in the six previous years; in 1976, this total rose again, by 90%, to 6,000,000 hectoliters (158,700,000 U.S. gallons, 132,000,000 imp.). This increase applies to all wines except the lighter, unfermented types with the Denominación de Origen. Spain's leading customers are the United Kingdom, Switzerland, the Netherlands, West Germany, Sweden, and Hungary—in that order. One imagines, from popular pictures of drinkers aiming the wine accurately into their mouths from spouted glass *porrones*, that the Spanish consume much of their own wine. In fact, their consumption is moderate: just under 92 liters a head in 1970, falling to 65 in 1979. The dark *bodega* with its wooden casks and stone floor is still frequented. But many people have taken to the big supermarkets, where they have a greater choice of bottled wines from farther afield than the neighboring villages. Many of these bottles are produced by the new agricultural cooperatives; but it is also possible to find on the shelves such finer products as the good wines of Rioja.

WINE LAWS

Spain is following the trend toward greater control of the complete wine-making process, from planting to bottling and labeling, although, in most districts, there is still a long way to go. Jerez is the shining exception, Rioja second best. The program for establishing an efficient system of place-names (Denominación de Origen or D.O.), with high standards and quality controls, is well in hand, and the following appellations are now functioning:

Andalusia. Jerez-Xeres-Sherry. Condado de Huelva. Málaga. Montilla-Moriles.

Rioja. Rioja.

La Mancha and New Castile. Almansa. La Mancha. Mentrida. Valdepeñas.

Levante. Jumilla. Utiel-Requena. Valencia. Alicante. Yecla.

Old Castile. Rueda. Ribera del Duero.

Catalonia. Alella. Penedés. Priorato. Tarragona. Ampurdán Costa Brava.

Aragon. Cariñena. Campo de Borja.

Navarre. Navarra.

Galicia. Ribeiro. Valdeorras.

Inside Spain, Rioja dominates every first-class wine list—with the result that some of the sound Valdepeñas and other respectable wines are apt to be ignored. Customers have come to think of Rioja as being the only wine fit to accompany a good meal. In general, the white wines are not up to the standard of the red ones, although there are naturally exceptions—Alella, and certain Penedès, for example.

In spite of the wide variety of Spanish wines, individual characteristics are too often ironed out by the vintner's steady hand. Not only are crops from various vineyards vatted together within one area, but there is a good deal of blending across the country. The average goal is plateau, not peak—although this does not apply to the best of Rioja, to the sweet wines of Málaga, or to the fine wines of Montilla-Moriles. While it is encouraging, the new Spanish wine law is in no way as comprehensive as the French—or in a different way, the West German. The positive effects have been noticed from 1975 on, yet even now unscrupulous practices continue, since virtually no strong powers of enforcement are written into the law.

See separate entries for Málaga; Montilla-Moriles; Rioja; Sherry.

OTHER WINE REGIONS

Central Spain: La Mancha and New Castile

In La Mancha, a sea of short-pruned vines, miles of them, breaks the monotony of the plain. In the sun-roasted soil, vines are planted three meters apart, the occasional olive trees which grow among them casting a little shade. The land of Don Quixote has changed less than many parts of Spain. There is light industry now, and some modern improvements in farming; but mud-walled farmyards survive, as well as bell chimneys and outdoor ovens. It is a red-earth region of chalk or slatey soil, of wheat, windmills, and wine.

In the bitter winters, vines have to struggle—which has an invigorating effect on the wine; the grapes ripen well under the scorching summer sun; and after the harvest, wine flows, both red and white, into the carafes of Madrid's cafés, and over the borders to France. There is also a good deal of distillation. Long barrel-ageing is little practiced here. People

like their wines young, brisk, bright, and fresh. The bulk is ordinary (*vino corriente*), some of it labeled, inaccurately, as Valdepeñas for the region's most distinguished wine.

La Mancha, merging with New Castile (which is centered around Madrid) divides into two areas, Upper and Lower: La Mancha Alta and Baja. The first includes the provinces of Albacete and Cuenca; the second, and larger, embraces Toledo and Cuidad Real. In the east, La Mancha borders on Valencia and Alicante; in the west, it touches Estremadura where most of the conquistadores came from; and southwards, it stretches as far as the Sierra Morena. What the Spanish writer José de Castillo has described as the heart of the red wine country is the area where the four districts of La Mancha, Levante, Murcia, and Albacete meet. Here they drink the "valiant" alcoholic reds. However, a fine Cabernet Sauvignon is produced by the Marqués de Griñon in Malpica de Tajo.

Valdepeñas, best and best known of Manchega wines, is produced in the south of the region, 220

478

kilometers (136 miles) south of Madrid on the road to Granada. The town of Valdepeñas, with its innumerable *bodegas*, is dedicated to wine. In this part of the country, *pellejos* are still to be seen—wine-skins made from the whole hide of a pig. Slightly macabre though this appears, it makes a good, airtight container in which the wine keeps well. Some of this wine is still made in *tinajas*, the huge, bulbous terra-cotta jars molded from the clay and ocher-colored soil. The process is simple and traditional; the fermented red wine remains in the *tinaja*, deposits soon sink to the bottom, and the cleared wine is left where it is to mature until the following spring, when it will be pumped into barrels and sold. White and rosé *(rosado)* wines, however, are racked into another amphora after the first fermentation, in order to separate them from the skins. In Toboso and Virranobledo, towns where the legends of Dulcinea and Don Quixote are remembered, *tinajas* are made, many of them to be ornamental rather than useful, as the slow change to oak casks and even glass-lined fermenting vats gets under way.

The reds *(tintos)* have not the deep, blackish color of much of the Spanish wine; they are a clear ruby. A good red Valdepeñas should be smooth and well-balanced, with something of a northern character, though heavier. The name, protected by the Denominación de Origen, is still too often taken in vain. White wines of Valdepeñas are either a pale, greenish shade, or else a deep golden yellow.

The other Manchego wines granted the Denominación de Origen are La Mancha in Albacete, making whites and *claretes* (light reds); Manchuela, stretching from Albacete to Cuenca and the verge of Valencia, producing robust, *tintos*, *claretes*, and *rosados;* Almansa, near the coastal area of Alicante, its strong wines (both *claretes* and blackish *tintos)* sometimes reaching 17° of alcohol; and Mentrida, near Toledo, producing strong, dry, rather ordinary reds.

Leading grapevines planted in La Mancha are: reds—Cencibel, Tinto Basto, Garnacha, Aragón, and Castellana, with some other varieties; whites—principally Airén and Jaén, with Pardillo and Cirial. Cencibel mixed with Airén produces the good *claretes* of Valdepeñas, favored by the chalk and slatey soils. Acreage and production figures are as follows in 1971:

Almansa. (D.O.) 15,000 hectares (37,500 acres) producing 180,000 hectoliters (4.87 million U.S. gallons, 3.96 million imp.) of white and red wine.

Mancha. (D.O.) 200,000 hectares (500,000 acres) producing 2,900,000 hectoliters (76.9 million U.S. gallons, 63.8 million imp.) of red and white wine.

Manchuela. 60,000 hectares (150,000 acres) producing 1 million hectoliters (26.5 million U.S. gallons, 22 million imp.) of red and white wine.

Valdepeñas. (D.O.) 30,000 hectares (75,000 acres) producing 340,000 hectoliters (9 million U.S. gallons, 7.5 million imp.) of red and white wine.

Mentrida. (D.O.) 21,000 hectares (53,000 acres) producing 300,000 hectoliters (7.9 million U.S. gallons, 6.6 million imp.) of red and white wine.

The Levante and Alicante

On Spain's east coast, the fertile strip of irrigated land which borders the Mediterranean between Alicante and Benicarlo—the sunny Costa Blanca, with its *huerta*, the gardenland irrigated by the Arabs, where palms, figs, cotton, oranges, and rice-fields grow—forms only a part of this wine region and has the outlets of two busy ports, Alicante and Valencia. One of the driest districts of Spain, mild and fine in winter, it is a prolific producer of grapes, second only to La Mancha. Behind it is the more rugged zone of Cheste, where the climate is Continental; and this is backed by the steep, bleak mountain slopes of Utiel-Requena. The growths of these three Denominaciones de Origen (Valencia, Alicante, Utiel-Requena) appear to be vinous expressions of the terrain. It is a region of simple wines for quick drinking: more sweet than dry, more red than white; and they wash down the native paella, the fish and prawns, and the game, all plentiful here. Wine is big business, and everywhere new cooperatives with modern equipment are replacing small, individual cellars.

Valencia

Formerly famous for its sweet wines, Valencia now makes dry and sweet *tintos*, *blancos*, and *claretes*, as well as amber-colored *mistelas*, from Muscatel and Malvasia, Planta Nova, Garnacha, Merseguera, Bobal, and other grapes. There is also a popular aperitif, scented with herbs and blended from old *soleras*. The sweetish, bright red wines of Valencia are robust and heady, with anything from 12° to 16° of alcohol. One of the most palatable is Fondillón, for which demand far exceeds the small supply. These reds, and the *rosados*, are taken with meals; at about two years of age, they have the character of vintage wines.

Cheste (not a Denominación de Origen)

In this central zone, vines grow around the towns of Chivas and Turia. Most of the wine is white—dry, sweet, or semi-sweet, either pale in color or deep gold. Merseguera and Planta Nova are leading grapes; 7,500 hectares (18,750 acres) are in vineyard.

Utiel-Requena

In the mountainous area where Valencia touches Castile, the wines—mostly red—are at once weaker, coarse, and more vivid in color than those of the plain. *Tintos*, *claretes*, and *rosados*, all range between 10° to 13° of alcohol; 50,000 hectares (125,000 acres) are planted in vines. This is a Denominación de Origen.

Jumilla

Another Denominación de Origen under Levante is actually in northern Murcia, where the hinterland is poor, though long ago the province was rich in mines. But toward the sea, this, too, has its *huerta*. These vineyards, sloping down to a long river valley, push their way into Valencia. The red wines are pleasantly ordinary, with a trace of sweetness, much of it from the Monastrel grape. Yecla is another flourishing wine town in the same district. Jumilla has 50,000 hectares (125,000 acres) of vineyards.

Yecla

Now raised to the Denominación de Origen, Yecla lies in the same area as Jumilla, in the district of the Levante, bordering on northern Murcia. About 26,-000 hectares (65,000 acres) of vineyard are planted mainly in Monastrel, which gives red wines. Like Jumilla, it is a town of *bodegas*, where the grapes from the adjoining vineyards are made into dark and white wines.

Catalonia

As in the Levante, this region divides into the fertile, sunny land edging the coast of the Costa Brava, and the higher, rockier terrain inland. Vineyards were planted here in Graeco-Roman times; the wines were celebrated in the Middle Ages; and present-day production, both in bulk wines and in better growths rating the Denominación de Origen, is high. Torres in Penedès makes wines of excellent value.

Tarragona

Encircling Priorato, a small area with its own Denominación, Tarragona is traditionally associated abroad with a coarse, strong, sweet red. This conception is out of date, since there is now a far greater variety in the vines, and in the wines—heavy and light, sweet and dry, in both whites and reds. Reus is the important center for Tarragona.

Ampurdán-Costa Brava

Lately awarded the Denominación de Origen, these vineyards of northern Catalonia are planted in the province of Gerona, inland and near the French border. Quite pleasant white and *rosado* wines are made from 6,800 hectares (17,000 acres) of land planted in Cariñena and Garnacha grapes. In the district is the Castello de Perelada—with its wine library and museum—which produces reds, whites and rosés, as well as the famous sparkling wine. After Perelada, the best-known labels are those of the Barón de Terrades.

Alella

The vineyards, about 12 kilometers (20 miles) north of Barcelona, dating back to Roman times, cover the slopes of a steep massif, one vineyard facing the sea, the other inland. The vines, grown in granitic soil around the town of Alella and several neighboring villages, combine well: those with a northern outlook are high in acidity, counteracting the low acidity of the south-facing grapes. A terrain of some 600 hectares (1,500 acres), planted principally in Xarel-Lo, Picpoule, Macabeo, Pansa Blanca, and Red Sumoll grapes, produces white, *rosado*, and red wine. There is also a golden dessert type called Lacre Violeta. The wines of this small region are made in the traditional way (usually kept in oak for three years before bottling) and preserve their natural qualities. Most praised is the soft, fruity Marqués de Alella. The whites are light, with a very agreeable bouquet.

Priorato

Set against the backcloth of the Sierra de Montsant and the ruins of the old priory of the holy mountain, the vineyards are stepped in terraces down to the red-earth valley of the River Ciurana. On the rocky, high ground, grapes and olives grow together, for oil as well as wine is important. Slate in the volcanic soil and the ticklish breezes of the mistral (known locally as *seré*) induce a rich harvest and wines strong in alcohol. In the surrounding villages, almost everybody works among the vines. The market towns are Gandesa and Falset; the wines they sell, both dry and sweet, are good but very strong and vividly red. Some of the common wines reach from 19° to 24° of alcohol. The whites are brilliantly clear, with a fruity scent. The highest vine patch in the district is the Conca del Barbara, climbing to the crest of a hill and making vigorous reds and spirited whites with a distinctive bouquet. Important among the red wine grapes of Priorato are Cariñena and Garnacha. The whites come from Macabeo and Pedro Ximénez.

This district has requested its elevation to a Denominación de Origen. The grapes Macabeo, Parellada, Pansa, Sumoll Tinto, and Bobal are planted in 7,000 hectares (17,500 acres) of vineyards.

Penedès

One of two classified names in the district of Barcelona. This, too, divides into a coastal strip (Baja), a central zone, and mountain vineyards (Alta) which are among the highest in Spain. Throughout the area, most of the soil is the excellent chalky *albariza*. Vineyards of the plain, around Sitges and Vilafranca del Penedès, produce strong, dark wines; one of the principal grapes is Malvasia. From the high ground comes a charming light dry white, from Parellada, Macabeo, and Chardonnay vines. One of the largest firms exporting Spanish wines is owned by the Torres family and has an assortment of very good red wines which have won international prizes, some made with Cabernet Sauvignon, and white wines with an excellent reputation both in Spain and abroad. The Torres winery is at Vilafranca del Penedès.

El Penedès Central specializes in the best sparkling wines of the country. Codorníu and Freixenet are world-famous brands. Only cellars where wine is so made, by the *méthode champenoise*, are allowed the name *cavas*. Jean Leon produces a good Cabernet Sauvignon.

Gandesa Terralta (see Priorato above)

Often mentioned with Priorato; now a candidate for its own Denominación. The bright red, alcoholic wines and the transparent white are obtained from 11,500 hectares (28,500 acres) of vineyard planted primarily in Garnacha, Macabeo, and Cariñena.

Aragón (Kingdom of)

The old Kingdom of Aragón has a reputation for its wines. The sun-baked vineyards, sheltered by the Sierra de la Muela and watered by the River Ebro, make wines of all shades and styles—in particular the Cariñena and Campo de Borja, which both have the Denominación de Origen. Coming, as do the *corrientes*, in reds and whites, sweet and dry, these are wines of distinctive character which attain a high degree of alcohol, although some of them, light in body, provide pleasant, if heady, table wine, taken usually when young. Favored grapes are Garnacha, Cariñena, and Bobal.

Navarre

The Denominación Navarra covers five districts: Montaña, Valdizarbe, Ribera Alta, Ribera Baja, and Tierra Estella. With 22,500 hectares (56,500 acres) this is romantic country, stretching from the woods and mountain streams of the Pyrenees to the fiestas of Pamplona, enclosing rich farmland and old monasteries, and touching down to Logroño—where some of the wines are allowed the Denominación Rioja. In the north, they make tart, prickly *vinos verdes*. Those southern vineyards that do not merge with Logroño are planted either near Pamplona (where the *corrientes* are not unlike those of the French side of the mountains) or, more importantly, in the valleys of the Ebro and Ribera, where the wine is stronger and sometimes rather sharp. Leading grapes are Tempranillo, Graciano, Garracha, and Vivra.

Galicia

On the Atlantic coast, Spain has the greenness and moisture of the whole of that seaboard, where the temperate climate produces large crops of grapes and wine. Inland, vines are pruned low, in the Castilian manner; but nearer the sea, they climb up posts and along wires arranged to protect them from the wet earth—a system known as *parrales*. The region has two Denominaciones: Valdeorras and Ribeiro. Valdeorras, with 6,500 hectares (11,200 acres) in the sheltered valley of the Sil, sticks to the old plan of vineyard plots; the Monterrey Valley, cutting through the south of Orense toward Portugal, has less rainfall than the rest of the region: the vine-covered slopes produce pleasant reds, from Alicante, Albarello, and other grapes, and whites from the Jerez vine. The white wines of Orense province are often stronger and more perfumed than the reds. Ribeiro wines are partly in Orense, partly in Avia—the latter highly regarded in their own country. The reds are successful but, again, weaker than the whites. Traditions of wine-making were handed down by the monasteries. Albariño, Treixadura, Palomino, and Godello are among the grapes used. On this Atlantic shore, near Portugal, wines are often as light, sharp, fresh, and prickly as the Vinhos Verdes of the Minho area. In the Pontevedra district, vines are cultivated on *parrales* in the areas Condado, Albarino, and Rosal.

Condado de Huelva

Huelva borders with Portugal in the extreme south of Spain, with the River Guadalquivir threading between it and the province of Cádiz. This land of vines and *camargue*, of horses, bulls, and grapes, produces wines which have a great reputation in their own country. The Denominación Condado de Huelva embraces the district Condado de Niebla, where vines grow near the river. The vineyard area of 19,000 hectares (47,-000 hectares) produces about 650,000 hectoliters (17,160,000 U.S. gallons, 14,300,000 imp.) of wine. Famous names here are *Condado palido* (pale) and the Oloroso styles are called *Condado viejo* (old). Condado wines are made by the solera system.

Extremadura

The long, narrow province of green forests, deep valleys, and plentiful game bordering Portugal, has no Denominación de Origen but a good deal of wine, most of it pleasant, strong, and brilliant to the eye. Caceres makes full-bodied whites and "valiant" reds. The Almendralejo area also has a good production of average wines to drink with the porks and savory stews and solid gazpachos of the region.

León and Castile. Rueda. Ribera del Duero.

The up-and-coming Denominación de Origen are both Rueda for white and Ribera del Duero for reds. The fine whites of Rueda, from the Verdejo grape, are aromatic. The best are Marqués de Griñon and Marqués de Riscal. What is most interesting about the neighborhood is that, in Valbuena de Ducro, near Valladolid, is the small vineyard of Vega Sicilia (only 100 hectares—250 acres) planted 50% in Tempranillo, 25% in Cabernet Sauvignon, and the balance in Malbec and Merlot. The grapes were brought from Bordeaux by the original landowner, Don Eloy Lecanda, after the phylloxera had destroyed his vines. The wine, made in the Bordeaux style, is aged in oak casks and has considerable fame. It is never less than five years old when bottled; Vega Sicilia and the wine of the neighboring vineyard of Pesquera are considered to be among the best red wines of Spain.

Basque Provinces

Vizcaya and Guipzcoa, in the areas of Bilbao and San Sebastián, are of little interest in wine history, although the thin local Chacolí and cider are drunk with some pleasure by the inhabitants and visiting tourists.

The Islands

The Canaries. Canary Sack and Palma Sack (the latter from Las Palmas, port of Gran Canaria) made the Spanish islands off Africa famous in the Elizabethan Age. The color was named for the bird, the bird for the islands—and the islands were once overrun by dogs *(canes).* The coincidence provided many puns in old plays ("Never in your life . . . unless you see canary, put me down"—*Twelfth Night).*

The importance of Canary wine in the world diminished with the oïdium plague of over a century ago, although some 60,000 hectoliters (1.59 million U.S. gallons, 1.32 million imp.) of *corriente* are still produced for local consumption, most of it white, a little *clarete.* A great variety of grapes is grown. Some of the wines do very well: among them the white Vidueno, the dry white of Palma, the Muscatels, and the Tacorontes or Mountain Wines.

The Balearics. All of these islands grow grapes in small vineyard plots and make wine, mostly in the traditional way. In Majorca, the area of Benisalem produces dark, heavy reds, while Felanitx has lighter rather than flat wines. In Ibiza and Formentor, where the wine is stronger, some modern cooperatives are being established.

Spanish earth

Silicate of aluminum—used in fining or clearing wines.

Sparkling Burgundy

Red, rosé, or white Burgundy wine rendered sparkling either in huge vats or in bottle, according to the champagne method. Since the region's fine wines are never used in its production, sparkling Burgundy, always white, is almost without exception undistinguished.
See Burgundy.

Sparkling wines

Wines made effervescent by the presence of carbon dioxide in the bottle. The best of these wines are made by the champagne method of secondary fermentation in bottles *(see* Champagne). The others are made either by the bulk process—fermenting the wine in big tanks and bottling under pressure *(see* Charmat); or by the less commendable method of adding carbon dioxide in much the same way as it is pumped into gassy fruit drinks *(see* Carbonated wines).

Spätburgunder

German descendant of the Pinot Noir grape, brought there from Burgundy. It comprises 4.5% of the German vineyard area.
See Germany.

Spätlesen

Late-harvested grapes. Richer, fuller wines.
See Germany.

Spätrot (grape)

See Zierfandler.

Spent liquor

The leftover residue after distillation.

Spirits

Potable alcoholic liquids obtained through distillation—e.g., brandy, whisky, gin, vodka.
See Chapter Ten, p. 55.

Spiritus Vini Gallici

"Spirit of French wine"—British pharmaceutical term for brandy.

Spritzer

German term for Rhine wine and soda, one-third wine to two-thirds soda—i.e., the Byronic Hock and seltzer. It is a cool and refreshing summer drink when taken in a tall glass with plenty of ice. Any sound wine can be used, but white or rosé are the favorites.

Spritzig

German term for the light prickle caused by an excess of carbon dioxide.

Spruce beer

This black beer, sometimes called Danzig spruce beer, is fermented at Danzig from young shoots and sap of the spruce tree.

Spumante

Italian term for sparkling wine, of which the most celebrated example is Asti Spumante (D.O.C.).

Stalky

Hardness in wine from the tannin in the stalks. Usually the stalk is separated from the grapes and pressed independently for the juice it yields. It is also used in the distillation of marc or grappa.
See Grappa; Marc.

Stein wines

Steinweine are the green-gold, "stone" wines of Franconia in Germany, and of Styria, Austria. In the famous oval, flat Franconian flask they are of such special character that they are generally destined for the connoisseur.
See Franconia; Austria; Bocksbeutel.

Steinberger

In the finest years of the German Rhines this is one of the best Rheingaus. The entire Steinberg belongs to the Staatsweingut which now make most of their wines in their headquarters and modernized winery at Eltville. The vineyard lies not far from Wiesbaden, beyond the ancient Cistercian dramatic monastery Kloster Eberbach, 3 kilometers north of Hattenheim. Cistercian monks planted the hillside vineyard over 700 years ago. Like Clos de Vougeot in Burgundy, it is a single parcel, enclosed by a huge stone wall.
See Rheingau.

Steinhaeger

A Westphalian (German) gin resembling Hollands.
See Hollands; Geneva.

Stellenbosch

Wine district in the Cape province.
See South Africa.

Stemming

In the making of wine, grapes are usually separated from their stalks before fermentation by a machine known in France as an *égrappoir* or *foulograppe*. Agreement with this practice, first adopted in the fine red wine regions of Burgundy and Bordeaux, is not unanimous, but there are strong arguments in its favor. In the case of red wines, separation increases the degree of alcohol by about 0.5 as a result of changes which take place between the must and the stalk. It makes the wine less astringent and gets rid of foreign substances. The wine will be clearer, suppler, and ready sooner than those which have absorbed extra alcohols and tannins from the stems; and the process saves labor, since the marc which remains after pressing will be less bulky if there are no stalks in it.

The *égrappoir* has not been used much in making white wines, but today it is often employed before the pressing of finer wines.

Still wines

Non-sparkling table or beverage wines. U.S. law stipulates that still wines must contain less than 14% of alcohol. The term is sometimes used for the non-sparkling wines of Champagne.

Stinger

An iced drink made with brandy and crème de menthe and flavored with a twist of lemon.

Stock

A cutting or entire vine onto which a section of another vine called a scion is grafted. The stock grows to provide the healthy and disease-resistant roots of the vine, and the scion matures and grows the fruit.

Stoup

An obsolete term for a drinking vessel, cup, flagon, or tankard—and also for a draught of wine.

Stout

A strong black, heavy, British beer.
See Beer.

Stravecchio

Italian term for very old wine.

Straw wines

Wines from grapes that have been picked at maturity and dried on straw mats in the sun or suspended in lofts before vinification. A notable example is the *vin de paille* from the Jura Mountains in France.

Strega

An Italian liqueur, sweet and yellow in color.

Stück

German Pfalz and Rheinhessen cask of 1,200 liters (317 U.S. gallons, 264 imp.), or 1,550 bottles. The usual Rheingau measure is the *Halbstück* or half *Stück*, containing 775 bottles.

Stuck wine

One which stopped fermenting before all the sugar had been converted to alcohol.

Sturdy

A self-explanatory wine-tasting term, less flattering than robust.

Styria

Wine region of Austria; not a large producer. White and rosé wines are made here; Graz, the capital, has, like Vienna, its *heurige*, or May wines; and another interesting growth is the pale gold Steinwein.
See Austria.

Château Suau

Bordeaux white wine.
District: Sauternes, France.
Commune: Barsac.

The wine is well made but little known.
Vineyard area: 7 hectares (17 acres).
Average production: 17 *tonneaux* (1,500 cases).

Château Suduiraut

Bordeaux white wine.
District: Sauternes, France.
Commune: Preignac.

Once famous and classed as a First Growth (*Premier Cru*) in 1855, the vineyard almost disappeared from existence in the first part of this century. It has been reconstituted, and in the last decade has produced good wines. Formerly known as Cru du Roy, the vineyard adjoins Château d'Yquem along one strip and is now owned by the daughter of M. Fonquernie.
Characteristics. A rather soft Sauternes—the wines have a lightness and balance which give them longevity.
Vineyard area: 60 hectares (150 acres).
Average production: 110 *tonneaux* (10,000 cases).

Sugar wine

"Wine" made by adding sugar and water to grape husks and allowing the mixture to ferment.

Sugaring

A "sugared" wine is one whose grapes received additional sugar before fermentation. Sugaring is usually done to compensate for under-ripeness in the grapes. Permitted sugaring during fermentation is in France called *chaptalisation*.

Sulfur dioxide

The use of sulfur to sterilize wine is almost as old as wine itself: in the *Iliad*, Achilles fumigates his cup with sulfur before pouring a libation to Zeus. In modern wine-making, sulfur dioxide (SO_2) is sprayed on newly picked grapes to stop premature fermentation, is added to newly fermenting wine, put into barrels in which wine will be stored, and is given in discreet doses to wine to keep it healthy. Used in moderation, it imparts no taste or aroma; but if overused it is apt to produce both—a fairly frequent fault with mediocre sweet and semi-sweet white wines where massive doses are added to ensure that the unfermented sugar will not be attacked by yeasts after the wine is bottled.

The action of the sulfur is to kill unwanted yeasts. Those microbes and bacteria which are harmful to wine are the first affected, but *Saccharomyces* yeasts are only attacked if a considerable quantity of sulfur is present. The traditional method of releasing sulfur dioxide, which is a gas, is by burning sulfur wicks; but compressed liquid SO_2 is also available, and tablets of potassium metabisulfite ($K_2S_2O_5$) when dissolved in wine give sulfur dioxide, water, and unimportant quantities of cream of tartar, one of wine's normal constituents.

Sulfurization

The purpose of dosing must or wine with sulfur dioxide (SO_2) or sulfurous acid (H_2SO_3) is to slow down fermentation where necessary, to kill unwanted microorganisms, and to aid in the production of a sound wine. It is very important that sulfurization should not be overdone, a fault which leads, in carelessly made wines, to an unpleasant smell, and even a taste, of sulfur. The amount of sulfurous anhydride which will become bound will increase slightly with increasing sugar content, pH and temperature. The pH determines the amount of SO_2 in the active form (H_2SO_3). As the pH goes up, more SO_2 must be added to have an equivalent amount in the active form. The quantity which may be used is regulated by law, the maximum varying in each wine-making country, since the necessity for sulfurization depends to some extent upon the climate. Yeasts are most resistant to SO_2 when they are most active (which happens in the tumultuous fermentations which take place in very hot weather), and at such times an unusually high dose may be permissible—as it is also when there is some disorder in the wine or must. Where fermentation is slow (as when there have been heavy rains at the beginning of the harvest, or in a cold climate), less than 100 milligrams of sulfur dioxide per liter will be sufficient to sterilize the wine-making processes. Where the temperature of the atmosphere is 68°F. (10°C.) or over, the dose may be as high as 150 milligrams per liter. Sulfurous anhydride added to red wine grapes or

PURIFYING ACTION OF SULFUROUS ANHYDRIDE

Sulfurous acid per liter (in grams)	Volatile acidity (sulfuric acid in grams)	Condition at tasting	MICROSCOPIC EXAMINATION	
			Liquid	Deposit
trace	16.10	Sour and affected by *casse*	Bacteria of *tourne* and *aigre*	Yeast and bacteria
0.050	0.76	Yellow, brown, fairly clear, slight musty taste	Some bacteria	Fairly pure yeast
0.100	0.52	Slightly roseate, sparkling (*droit de goût*)	Free from bacteria	Pure yeast
0.150	0.47	bright pink,		
0.200	0.45	sparkling		
0.250	0.36	(*droit de goût*)		

to the must of white wine in carefully calculated doses helps to destroy biological disorders, while leaving the true alcoholic yeasts free to develop.

The above table shows how SO_2 acts as a purifier, how it kills the bacteria, and how it acts as a preventative of brown *casse* by destroying oxidases. Wines which have been treated with sulfur dioxide are apt to be better balanced and richer in certain elements than are those which have not been so treated. The alcoholic content may rise, the volatile acidity level may drop. This increase is the result of a purer fermentation and hence a better utilization of the sugar. The use of sulfur dioxide does not cause a permanent fading in color. In red wine, loss of color will be temporary, and the wine will regain its hue when action ceases. Under the right conditions, the final color will not only be improved but will be free of any brown or yellowish cast. When the time comes to rack the wine, it will be found that the quantity of SO_2 present will decrease with each racking.

See Sulfur Dioxide; and Chapter Nine, p. 40.

Süssdruck

Swiss light red or rosé made from Pinot Noir.

Suze

Popular yellow, bitter, gentian-based French aperitif. A brand name which belongs to Pernod-Ricard.

Sweden

Sweden's climate provides cold comfort for grapevines, and wines must be—and are—imported from elsewhere. Like her Scandinavian neighbors, Sweden manufactures various spirits, consumes most of what she distills, and imports even more. These imports and all other aspects of the wine and spirits trade are in the hands of the State Monopoly, the Aktiebolaget Vin & Spritcentralen.

The liquor industry was nationalized in 1917, in order to keep the country from "going dry." In the years leading up to that date, Swedish distillers—175,000 of them—were producing about 1 million hectoliters (26.5 million U.S. gallons, 22 million imp.) of spirits per year, and the scant population of 3 million was soaking it up with alarming results. The situation was nearly critical when the legislature began to search for a solution. Temperance advocates were pressuring the lawmakers, and only as a result of the foresight and ability of Dr. Ivan Bratt was the State Monopoly introduced as a compromise to control the sale of spirits on a rationed basis. The control was lifted in 1955.

Present sales of wine (imported) and spirits amount to about 1.5 million hectoliters (39.6 million U.S. gallons, 32.9 million imp.) yearly, but Sweden's population has nearly tripled since nationalization of the industry in 1917, so it is obvious that the drive to slow liquor consumption has had some success. In the past few years, more wine than liquor has been sold for the first time. Much of the wine comes from the extensive supplies the Monopoly has bought over the years. Still, the single most popular drink is the national spirit, aquavit, followed by Swedish punch (*q.v.*), a rice and sugar-cane liqueur. On the shelves of the three hundred or so Monopoly shops may be found more than 850 different wines and spirits.

Imported into Sweden annually are about 800,000 hectoliters (22,440,000 U.S. gallons, 18,700,000 imp.) of wine—well over half of it table wines, the rest fortified wines such as vermouth, Sherry, and Port. Eighty-five percent of this wine is bottled in Sweden. The Monopoly imports wine in huge tankers which dock right at the quay next to the bottling plant in Stockholm. Everyday wines from Portugal, Spain, Algeria, and France are the most popular; they sell at reasonable prices, since the state organization as the largest single purchaser of wine and spirits in the world saves money with bulk shipments. The great wines of France are represented in the stores, and the previously poor selection from Bordeaux has recently improved. Most of the wines are of vintages before the tremendous inflation of French wine prices, so some of these bottles are good values. The Swedish monopoly Spritcentralen distills, sells and ships the vodka called "Absolut," which enjoys a tremendous success in the United States.

Swedish punch

A spicy cordial based on rum. It is sometimes drunk in a small glass as a liqueur, sometimes mixed with hot water to make a punch.

Sweet

Large sugar content makes wines sweet. Sweetness may be added by sugaring or liqueuring, or by artificially halting fermentation before all sugar has been converted to alcohol. The great natural sweet wines are made from overripe grapes, in which the sugar has concentrated. These include the Sauternes and Barsacs of Bordeaux and the great Rhine and Mosel wines designated Auslese, Beerenauslese, or Trockenbeerenauslese (i.e., selected berries, individually picked, and overripe, dried almost to a raisin condition). Many other wine regions throughout the world, among them Anjou, Italy, and California, also produce sweet wines.

Sweet aperitif fortified and Roussillon wines of France

The sun-drenched Mediterranean coastline of France, particularly the corner next to the Spanish border, has long proved its suitability for growing those grape varieties that produce wines as sweet as they are potent. These wines, which are of little interest in countries where port and sherry are available, are known in France as *vins doux naturels* and *vins de liqueur*, or sweet natural wines and fortified wines. In both cases, the wines are strengthened by the addition of pure alcohol or brandy—a process known as "fortifying." The term "sweet natural wine" is apt to be confusing, since it could apply equally to these fortified wines and to sweet but unfortified wines like those made in the Sauternes district of Bordeaux. The difference between a *vin de liqueur* and a *vin doux naturel* is slight, and the terms are often used imprecisely and synonymously. The main difference is that in a *vin de liqueur* the fortifying spirit is added before any fermentation can take place, and the result is thus simply grape juice and spirits. As such, it is in the class of a high grade *mistelle*, except that the latter is used as a base for aperitifs and the former comes from better grapes and is designed to be drunk as it is. The *vin doux naturel* must be at least 90% from one grape variety, or be a blend of the varieties Muscat, Grenache, Maccabéo, or Malvoisie grapes, and the fortifying alcohol (5% to 10% of the volume to be treated) is added in the course of fermentation—not to prevent, but to arrest it. Both systems revolve around the fact that the sugar will not ferment after the wine has reached a certain strength; and both allow the wine to retain its sweetness, while providing it with a high alcoholic content. The legal alcoholic limits are 14% minimum and 21.5% maximum; and most of these wines are sold at about 18%. (These limits do not apply to the *vin de liqueur* made in the region of Cognac and known as Pineau des Charentes, where they are changed to 16% and 22%.)

The sweet wines are made in small and widely scattered areas, ranging from Roussillon in the extreme southwest corner on the Mediterranean, eastward to Frontignan, Lunel, Mireval, and Saint-Jean-de-Minervious, and across the Rhône to Rasteau and Beaumes-de-Venise. Somehow the vines in these areas have managed to survive, in spite of the fact that they have been trampled on by armies—Romans, Arabs, French, and Spanish are among the many that have either crossed the sea or settled in it—and in spite of the phylloxera epidemic. Modern economy seems to be succeeding where ancient armies and insects failed, however, and the present production of these wines is less than 600,000 hectoliters (15.9 million U.S. gallons, 13.2 million imp.) per year—a mere drop in the barrel.

AREAS PRODUCING STILL AND FORTIFIED WINES

Roussillon (Côtes du Roussillon)

Grand Roussillon is the former name for the wine region in southern France consisting of the districts of Banyuls, Maury, Rivesaltes, the Côtes d'Agly, and the Côte du Roussillon in the departments of Pyrénées-Orientales and Aude. The region was granted the Appellation d'Origine Contrôlée of Côtes du Roussillon in 1977. The vines grown in this area, chiefly the Muscat, Grenache, Maccabéo (or Maccabeu), and Malvoisie, produce a variety of wines, including red, white, and rosé. This does not apply to the reds and rosés of the Côtes du Roussillon or Côtes du Roussillon Villages, which are certainly among southern France's best wines in quality and value. The better wines are produced on hillside vineyards with a slate soil. A program of replanting the cheaper, large-producing vines with better varieties—all to the credit of Côtes du Roussillon producers—got underway in the early '80s. Even Cabernet Sauvignon has been spottily planted.

The credit for the introduction of wines into the Roussillon is given to the army of Hannibal, which passed through in 217 B.C. According to local legend, Hannibal left here his sick, tired, and straggling soldiers, who found the climate enough like their native Carthage in North Africa to settle down and plant vines. The vines were pulled up when the Arabs, with their Moslem prohibition against alcohol, moved in, but were replanted after the area had been reconquered. Hot and dry, mountainous and peppered with rocks, the land of Côtes du Roussillon is an arid, unwelcoming place, but vines often thrive in the most unlikely soil. Most of the holdings are small and so is production, and one sees everywhere that friend of the small grower, the cooperative cellar. Here the member-growers bring their grapes in the autumn, and here the wine is made. This system saves each grower the expense of buying individual presses and all the other equipment needed for making wine.

Banyuls

The wines of Banyuls in the extreme southeast corner of Roussillon are generally considered to be the best that the province has to offer. A desolate rocky land cut by steep ravines and baked by the hot sun that throws its early morning beams on the steep vine-covered slopes, Banyuls is known for its sweet heavy fortified wines, although it produces other wines as well. A natural red wine and a rosé, both called Grenache after the informing grape variety, have won some renown in their home country, but are rarely found elsewhere in France and are almost never exported. At harvest time (late in the autumn) the grapes are brought down the steep slopes on muleback, and about four-fifths of the production—total production averages 50,000 hectoliters (1,320,000 U.S. gallons, 1,100,000 imp.) each year—is taken to the nine cooperative cellars to be made into wine. The 2,800 hectares (7,000 acres) of vineyard are tended by some 1,600 growers and their workers.

Côtes du Roussillon (Appellation Contrôlée)

Adjoining Banyuls and lying slightly to the east and north of it is what is perhaps the most romantic section of the region. The history of the Côtes du Roussillon can still be read today from the many ruins on its steep slopes—monasteries and hermitages as well as the fallen estates of the Knights Templars who, after the Crusades, established one of their headquarters in this area. However, as Roussillon's importance in international politics declined, so also did the reputation of its vineyards. What were once the favorite wines of kings were reduced to a small quantity, most of which were consumed locally. The *rancio* of Haut-Roussillon was more or less abandoned to make way for some very good red Roussillon wines.

However, developments in the late 1960s and the 1970s have revitalized this wine-producing region, which was granted an Appellation d'Origine Contrôlée for red and white wines in 1977. Red and rosé wines from the better Côtes du Roussillon villages may qualify for the Côtes du Roussillon Villages appellation as well. In all, the Côtes du Roussillon, plus the "Villages," produce about 350,000 hectoliters (9.3 million U.S. gallons, 7.7 million imp.) of wine per year.

Rivesaltes (Appellation Contrôlée)

Farther away from the Spanish border, and lying next to the Côtes du Roussillon, is the area known as Rivesaltes. Here the sun-baked alluvial soil also produces wines that were better known in the past than they are today, and more honored. The famous wines of Rivesaltes have always come from the Muscat grape, made under the name "Muscat de Rivesaltes" and amounting to about 100,000 hectoliters (2,640,000 U.S. gallons, 2,200,000 imp.) per year. The simple appellation Rivesaltes may contain other grape varieties. In the past half-century or so the growers have been slowly neglecting the Muscat and replanting more and more in Grenache and Malvoisie. The reason for this is that the wine from the Muscat grape is one that must be tended with great care and the yield is very low. But the sweet, amber wine of the Malvoisie still thrives in Rivesaltes and is much appreciated by the inhabitants. Yearly production of "Rivesaltes" is about 230,000 hectoliters (5,992,000 U.S. gallons, 5,060,000 imp.) per year, most of it made at the many cooperatives scattered throughout the region.

Côtes d'Agly

The harsh, gray, rocky soil of this large area, in the northeast of Roussillon, is cut by the upper arm of the River Agly, before it runs down through Rivesaltes. The land is also watered now and then by streams which run swiftly after the infrequent downpours and then dry up for the rest of the year. The most extensively grown vines are those of the Grenache variety. None of the wines used to be considered to equal those of the other sections of Roussillon, but recently they have improved.

Maury (Appellation Contrôlée)

The small area of Maury, in the northeast corner of Roussillon, has had the unfortunate destiny to be in a militarily strategic position and has thus been almost totally destroyed time after time. But whenever the new wave of conquerors settled down or left, the peasant growers would again replant their vines in the unpromising stony soil. The vines grow at the foot of Queribus, the last of the Catharian castles. Mostly planted in vines of the Grenache Noir variety, the wines are sweet, and the red ones are extremely dark in color. This darkness fades with age, and the wines of Maury take on the brownish tinge and a slightly maderised, or *rancio*, taste and may be sold as Maury Rancio. Maury accounts for an average of 50,000 hectoliters (1,320,000 U.S. gallons, 1,100,000 imp.) per year. Its 1,400 hectares (3,500 acres) are tended by about 530 growers and virtually all of the production is vinified in the three cooperative cellars.

Frontignan (Appellation Contrôlée)

Once again the origins of the vines here are lost in the mists of time, but growers in the Frontignan area—facing the Mediterranean Sea, some distance west of the delta of the River Rhône—say that the famous Muscat wines of Frontignan date from Roman times, or that the vines were brought back from the

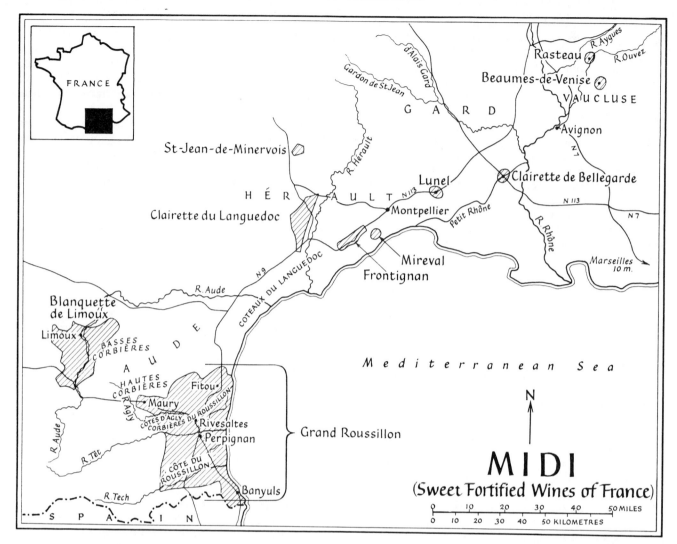

Crusades, or that they were planted to celebrate a royal marriage in 1204. It is widely believed that returning Crusaders did bring back grapevines from the Near East and so altered the course of viticulture in these regions and in the Pyrenees. At the present time, 20,000 hectoliters (530,000 U.S. gallons, 440,000 imp.) of wine are grown annually by some 350 growers on 350 hectares (875 acres) of land around the ancient city of Frontignan in the department of Hérault; 75% of the wine is made at one cooperative cellar.

The Muscat de Frontignan, so called because only the vine of that name is allowed, is made according to one of three methods. The first is for natural wine not enriched by any addition of alcohol, and it is the same as the process for any other natural wine, except for one stage, known as *passerillage*. This originated in Spain and was designed to increase sugar content: the stalks of the grapes are pinched just above the clusters, just before the grapes are picked in the late autumn. This cuts off the passage of sap between the grapes and the vine. The grapes are then allowed to ripen thoroughly in the hot Mediterranean sun, and, since no sap can get to them, they dry out, leaving the

grapes extra-rich in natural sugar. This system allows the wine to attain the legal minimum of 15% alcohol.

The other two types of wine, *vin doux naturel* and *vin de liqueur*, are the more common, and the difference between the processes of production has already been explained. Both systems allow this powerful wine to retain at least a part of its natural sugar, and in both cases the wine must have an alcoholic content of at least 15%.

In an attempt to preserve the integrity of the wine, it has been decreed that all genuine Muscat de Frontignan must be sold in bottles bearing a special seal, which is given by a group of experts only after they have tasted a sample of the wine and approved its quality.

In the area adjacent to Frontignan a lesser-known Muscat is produced, called Muscat de Mireval.

Saint-Jean-de-Minervois (Muscat de)

A tiny pocket in the department of Hérault in southern France, Saint-Jean-de-Minervois makes *vin doux naturel* and *vin de liqueur* following the same customs

488

and regulations as its neighbor, Frontignan. Production here is rarely as high as 2,000 hectoliters (52,800 U.S. gallons, 43,800 imp.) per year, however.

Lunel (Muscat de Lunel)

Like the Muscat wines of Frontignan, those of Lunel are made into *vin doux naturel* and *vin de liqueur*; no unfortified wines are produced here. Another district whose importance is more historical than contemporary, Lunel growers make some 3,300 hectoliters (87,-120 U.S. gallons, 66,000 imp.) of wine a year.

Beaumes-de-Venise (Muscat de)

On the eastern side of the Rhône in the department of Vaucluse, Beaumes-de-Venise makes an excellent *vin doux naturel* and *vin de liqueur* exclusively from the Muscat grape, as does Frontignan. The area produces only 3,000 hectoliters (79,500 U.S. gallons, 66,000 imp.) of wine per year.

Rasteau (Appellation Contrôlée)

Slightly to the north of the region of Beaumes-de-Venise is the delimited area known as Rasteau. This enjoys the peculiar advantage of being able to grow and sell fortified wines, made in the same way as those entitled to any of the Roussillon appellations; and of also making other wines in the same manner as those wines entitled to the name Côtes du Rhône. The result is that the production varies from no fortified wines in one year to almost 3,000 hectoliters (79,500 U.S. gallons, 66,000 imp.) in another. The deciding factor is the weather—and which type of wine it happens to favor. The fortified wines of Rasteau must come at least 90% from the Grenache grape and the others from any vine allowed in the making of Côtes du Rhône. The 130 growers take virtually all of the harvest to the one cooperative cellar.

Pineau des Charentes

At some time toward the end of the sixteenth century, a worker in one of the cellars in the Cognac region of France made the mistake of putting some newly made wine into a barrel already containing a small amount of Cognac. The result of this error has come to be known as Pineau des Charentes. First produced in very small quantities, the output was increased after the First World War and the wine was put onto the commercial market.

Pineau des Charentes must be made by producers of Cognac in the two French departments of Charente and Charente-Maritime and only from their own grapes. The new wine is taken and, within twenty-four hours, a little Cognac, a year or two old, is added to it. The color may be either rosé or white; the rosé variety comes from the Cabernet Sauvignon, Cabernet Franc, Malbec, and Merlot Rouge grapes; the white from the Saint-Émilion, Folle Blanche, Colombard, Blanc Ramé, Jurançon Blanc, Montils, Sémillon, Sauvignon, or Merlot Blanc grapes. It can only be sold after receiving the seal of approval of a committee of tasters which has wide powers. These include the right to approve, to disapprove, to demand further ageing or blending with the same product from another part of the area and to specify the quantities to be used. This last rule was added to improve the quality of some wine from a seaside area that may, when unblended, have a slightly salty taste. Pineau des Charentes, a popular aperitif in France, must contain from 16.5% to 22% of alcohol. Over 20,000 hectoliters (660,000 U.S. gallons, 550,000 imp.) are made each year.

Switzerland

Switzerland is largely a wine-drinking, wine-growing country; and as it is divided into three parts—French-speaking, Italian-speaking, German-speaking—so the vineyards tend to follow, with vines of French, Italian, or German types. There are, however, a few notable exceptions: Johannisberg is grown from the green Sylvaner grape in the French canton of the Valais, and the Bordeaux Merlot has been imported, very successfully, into the Ticino. So the striking general characteristic of Swiss wines is their infinite diversity—the vast difference, for instance, between the sunny Dézaley that grows on the slopes above Lake Geneva and the Vispertermin wines harvested up in the mountains of the Valais, not far from the Matterhorn and 1,100 meters (3,600 feet) above sea level. Hillside vineyards are steeply terraced, existing only by the hard labor of their owner; most of the vineyards are divided into small parcels whose proprietors now tend to join cooperatives and share equipment. In some regions, the wine is vinified by the brokers or cooperatives; in others, it is bottled directly on the property. Every November, there is a big auction of the year's vintage.

The total area of vineyards in Switzerland is 14,000 hectares (35,000 acres). Only three cantons out of the twenty-three plant no vines, but the most important wine-production is in the French parts—Vaud, Valais, Geneva, and Neuchâtel. Vines flourish on the shores of the lakes of Geneva and Neuchâtel, along the right bank of the Upper Rhône, and in the Italian Ticino or Tessin. Cultivation is sparser in east and central Switzerland, and here, as well as in the Ticino and around Geneva, most of the wines are drunk locally. The country produces about 1 million hectoliters (26.5 million U.S. gallons, 22 million imp.) of wine per year. The idea that Swiss wines do not travel is changing; they are seen in the windows of wine merchants in England and in other countries. It is generally agreed that these wines can be very agreeable but a bit short—i.e., not lasting on the palate. Compared to French wines, they are not cheap.

489

FRENCH-SPEAKING SWITZERLAND

La Suisse Romande is a pleasant, sunny country of orchards, castles, and hills sloping down to lake shores.

Vaud

For twenty-five years before Valais surpassed it, Vaud was the largest wine-producing canton in the country. The production comes from the vineyards east and west of Lausanne. This wine region divides into three sections—Lavaux and Chablais to the east of the city, La Côte to the west and the Northern Vaud.

Lavaux

The region stretches for 16 kilometers (10 miles), from Lausanne to Montreux, with Vevey almost exactly in the center (*see* Vevey Festival). It faces south over the lake, getting the best exposure to the sun and protected from extremes of temperature. It is said that wines were made here in Roman times, and this is probably true. It is certain that the Bishop of Lausanne, who was active *c.* 1137, took a serious interest in the cultivation of the vine, commanded the Cistercian monks to tend the grapes and thus established them as the first important growers in the area—which begins at Lutry and ends at Pully. To the traveler, this is one of the most charming wine districts in Switzerland. The Castle of Chillon broods over the lake; the vineyards climb up from the shore in a progression of steep terraces; vines grow in every crevice of the rocks, and the grapes ripen in the double heat of the sun and of the sunshine reflected from the water. But the proprietors lead a hard life; machines cannot be taken up the steep inclines, harvesters have to climb precipitous paths with their *hottes* full of fruit, and when the soil is washed down the slopes by the rain, they must carry it up again on their backs.

Principal vineyards: Dézaley, which produces a golden, still growth, described by many of the Swiss as their finest wine; Saint-Saphorin, Rivaz, Epessés, Riex, Villette, Lutry, Cully. Around Lausanne are the Clos des Abbayes and the Clos des Moines, owned by the city and auctioned each December.

Grape variety: Principally, the Chasselas, which adapts itself well to the soil and climate, producing very dry robust white wines quite different from those grown in France.

La Côte

The pastoral charm of these vineyards on the western shore of Lake Geneva is unspoiled, in a country of orchards, fields, and of vines planted mainly on the upper slopes above the farmland. The wine road passes some charming villages—Féchy, Mont-sur-Rolle, Vinzel, Luins. Others of the lively, pleasant wines grown in this district are Bougy, Begnins, Bur-

sins, and Perroy. Chasselas, Gamay, and Pinot Noir grapes produce some agreeable wines.

Chablais Vaud

These rather heady, smooth white wines are produced in the district of Aigle, on the foothills of the Alps. The growths of Bex, Ollon, Yvorne, Villeneuve, and Aigle have race, acidity, tang, and the true gunflint flavor.

Northern Vaud

In this little area, which stretches as far as Concise near the northern end of Lake Neuchâtel, grow the white and red wines of Orbe, Grandson, Bonvillars, and Concise. A few miles to the east, divided between the cantons of Fribourg and Vaud, the *pétillant* white wines of Vully are planted along the shore of Lake Morat. Some red wines, little known but quite drinkable, are also produced.

Neuchâtel; Lake Bienne

This is the most northerly part of French-speaking Switzerland. The wine region begins a little way up the lake, at Vaumarcus, and continues in an uninterrupted plantation as far as Le Landeron, at the opening of the neighboring Lake Bienne—a less important group of vineyards extends along the farther shores of this lake, their best growths the lively wines of Schafis and Twann. The Neuchâtel white wines, grown in a chalky soil, are light and sprightly. For over a century, the houses of Mauler and Bouvier have been practicing French methods of secondary fermentation in bottle. The red wine made solely from Pinot Noir grapes is considered one of the best Swiss wines. Oeil de Perdrix, also made from the Pinot Noir and short-vatted, is a rosé with a special charm. The town of Neuchâtel, capital of the canton, stands at the northeast corner of the lake. Looking down at it from the hills, you see the formidable castle, and the church of "La Collegiale." Vines surround the town. Neuchâtel was one of the most widely exported wines of Switzerland.

Principal vineyards: Auvernier, Cormondrèche, Cortaillod, Cressier, St.-Blaise—the wines are sold sometimes under the label of a *clos* or village, oftener as Neuchâtel.

Grape varieties: Chasselas and Pinot Noir. Pinot Gris and Chardonnay produce some good wines.

Valais

This is the *vieux pays*—the old land—on the banks of the Rhône as it flows, from its source, between Italy and France. The river is bordered by fruit trees and, on its right bank, vineyards climb the mountainside. On the lower slopes, the sheltered terraces bask in the sun. Higher up, you may catch a glimpse of peasants perched at a dizzy height above the water, breaking up

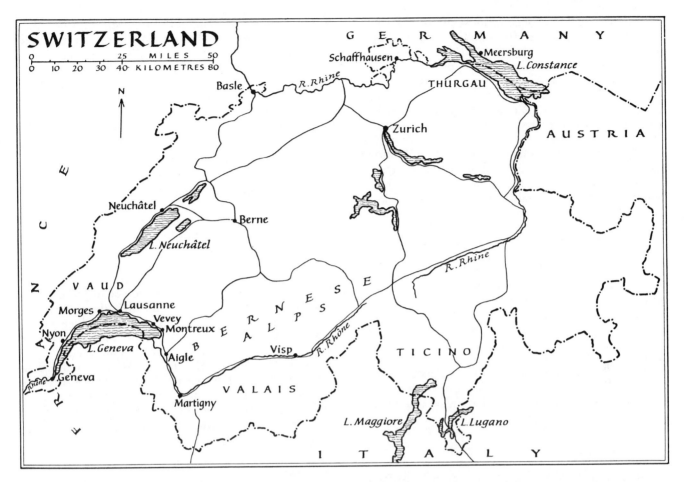

the soil by hand or tying vines to the tall stakes. Here, where the autumns are long, mild, and mellow, vines have been in cultivation since Roman days, and old traditions persist. In spring, the peasants of Anniviers will come down from their mountains, with fife and drum, to enjoy a fête day between their long, hard spells in the vineyards. When the harvest is over and the new wine made, 8-gallon barrels are dragged up to these settlements above the clouds and stored in the cellars, for the wine to mature in its larchwood casks for ten or fifteen years. This is known as the Vin du Glacier, usually a rather hard white wine.

Between Loèche and Martigny, some 5,500 hectares (15,000 acres) are planted in vine, divided among about 20,000 proprietors—about one-third in red, the rest in white. Old vines and young ones march up the slopes and straggle into the gullies. Little aqueducts, or *bisses*, cut into the dry land, bring their glacier water, and walls separate the terraced vineyards. Most Valais wines take their names from the grape, not the place.

Principal growths and grape varieties: Despite appearances, the vine structure of the Valais vineyards is varied. Four grape varieties predominate: Fendant, the regional name for Chasselas; Sylvaner, which confusingly makes a wine called Johannisberg; Gamay, which is blended with Pinot Noir to create the wine of Dôle; and Pinot Noir. The first two produce white wines, the second two produce reds. There are also a number of other vines well known locally: Amigne, Arvine, Hermitage, Pinot Gris (Malvoisie), Paien, and Muscat. These are all white wine grapes, with the exception of Pinot Gris, which can produce a salmon-colored wine. Fendant, or Chasselas, is a lively thirst-quenching wine. It combines good fruit and acidity, and can be quite fine. The wine is dry without being hard. The best Fendants are a touch sweet and round. Fendants usually measure between 10.5 and 11.8% alcohol. The Chasselas vine may have been imported originally by mercenaries returning home from France—since the land was too poor to support all the inhabitants, many hired themselves out as soldiers abroad and later returned with money, honors, and vine plants. A general who fought for Louis XV is actually believed to have brought in the Fendant, with one of the king's gardeners to supervise its planting.

Dôle is produced from a blend of Pinot Noir and French Gamay. The grapes are vatted, vinified, and pressed together. In the blend, it is important that the Pinot Noir predominate. Dôle is a powerful, perfumed red wine, which some connoisseurs consider to be the best of all the Swiss vintages. It is a noble, generous wine of a fine ruby color. The Pinot plant was imported in 1848, and Dôle was first produced about 1851. Although more than half of the planting is Pinot Noir, it should be pointed out that only a small portion is actually sold under such a label.

Johannisberg is the second most important white wine of the Valais, some 10 to 15% of the total production. It is made from Sylvaner, also called Rhine in the Valais. It is the only vintage that goes well with the local asparagus; and in years when the grapes are harvested late, it achieves a *pointe de douceur* and makes an agreeable dessert wine. Riesling, from the Rhine vine, is a pleasant little wine, as is white Hermitage. Colonel Dénéréaz brought in the white grape about one hundred years ago; and quite recently, Dr. Wuilloud managed to acclimatize, in his domaine at Diolly, the red Syrah of Hermitage. The Pinot Gris, gathered late, makes, in the Valais, Malvoisie, a sweet soft dessert wine with a lingering aroma. Arvine, Amigne, and Rèze are the old vines of the Valais. Amigne may have been the *Vitis aminea* of the Romans and Muscat, which also grows here, their *Vitis apiana*. It is certain that Rèze was current at the beginning of the fourteenth century. Arvine is a noble, spirited wine, and Amigne is pleasantly perfumed. The Rèze has almost, but not quite, disappeared. Fendant is the wine that flows most plentifully. The red *vin de pays*, or Vieux Rouge du Valais, is gradually vanishing, and is well worth tasting before it is too late.

The last of the appellations in the Valais is Goron, which is, in fact, a declassified Dôle. Gamay and Pinot Noir lacking in sufficient alcohol are used to produce this popular carafe wine.

Geneva

The vineyards of this smallest canton in Switzerland, planted in a horseshoe around the city of Geneva, produce charming, light wines that are little known abroad. They are mostly rather dry and slightly *pétillants*, with a fine bouquet.

Principal vineyards: Best-known are the growths of the district of Mandement, on the western shore of the lake. The wine that bears this name is light and dry, with a trace of hazelnut in the bouquet. Villages which give their names to Geneva wines are Peissy, Russin, and Satigny—in a small region, the largest Swiss wine parish. Here stands the Priory of Satigny, dating from A.D. 50. In the year 912, the Prior gained possession of the vineyards.

Grape varieties: Chasselas for white wines with a number of "specialty" vines, such as Aligoté, Chardonnay, and Pinot Gris. Lately there have also been plantings in Pinot and Gamay, since the soil reveals distinct potentialities for red wines.

ITALIAN-SPEAKING SWITZERLAND

In the Ticino, the sun shines, the lakes are blue, the stalls in the arcaded streets of the towns are piled with ripe fruit and, although wine-making is not a major occupation, the vineyards bear well, both red and white wines. The native Nostrano, from Bondola and

other grapes, are inclined to be harsh, yet, when they are drunk cool in the shade of an arbor—as Keats liked to drink claret—they have a distinctive, agreeable flavor. In the past few years, the Bordeaux Merlot has been planted here: it gives a soft, fruity red wine, sold under the official label Viti, and promises well for the future of Ticino wine-growing.

GERMAN-SPEAKING SWITZERLAND

The principal wine-making cantons in German-speaking Switzerland are, from the largest in area to the smallest: Zurich, Schaffhausen, Argovia, the Grisons, Thurgovia, Saint-Gallen, and Basle.

Zürich

The leading district in the wine-making of German Switzerland is not so favored in soil and climate as are the warmer western cantons, yet it produces some pleasant wines. Klevner (a strain of Pinot Noir) is now being planted and production has improved.

Principal vineyards: Herrliberg, Meilen, and Erlenbach produce rather sweet red wines. There are white wines, grown mainly along the shores of the lake of Zürich, and some red ones come from Weinland.

Grape varieties: Klevner, Rieling × Sylvaner, Rauschling, and Müller-Thurgau.

Schaffhausen

In this northern canton the most important district is Pettgau. There is a splendidly situated vineyard here, and a fresh and very agreeable wine is made from Klevner. A good deal is also made at Stein-am-Rhein. From Stein come the Blaurock and the Kefersteiner; and a good wine, from Pinot Gris, is made near the town of Schaffhausen.

Other cantons

Argovia, the Grisons, Thurgovia, Saint-Gallen, and Basle have a slightly less favorable climate than the southern part of the country. The wines are agreeable, rather light but fruity, and mainly consumed within the regions where they are produced.

Sylvaner

A productive white grape grown in Alsace, Austria, Switzerland, and Germany. The wines it gives are light and pleasant. It is also called Österreicher or Franken in German-speaking countries.

See Alsace; Austria; Germany; Switzerland.

Synthetic wine

A concoction of concentrated fruit-must, yeast, and water.

Syrah (Sirah)

The grape grown in the Rhône Valley for red Hermitage—it is said to have been brought back, either from the Middle East by Crusaders or to have come from Syracuse with the earlier legions of Probus. In any case, the grapes will flourish in warmer climates, and they have been transplanted to other parts of the world, such as Switzerland, California, Australia, and South Africa.

Syria and Lebanon

In ancient times vines flourished on the shores of the eastern Mediterranean, and this was probably the earliest wine-making region of the world. Damascus was a great center, mentioned in the Bible, and the wines of Helbon and the famous Chalybon were exported all over the then known continents. (*See* Chapter One.).

Nowadays, vineyards are found mainly in the mountainous country away from the coast. In Syria, apart from the district of Latakia, vines grow in the hilly regions of Aleppo, Homs, and Damascus—roughly 105,000 hectares (some 262,500 acres) in all. In Lebanon, despite the war, the acreage is increasing beyond 19,000 hectares (47,500 acres). Three-quarters of the vineyards is planted in the valley of Bekaa. Serge Hochar makes some Cabernet Sauvignons at his 140-hectare (155-acre) Château Musar. In both countries, the bulk of the harvest is intended for table grapes, dried raisins, and grape juice, leaving an inferior quantity of grapes to be pressed for wine. Arak also is made. Spirit-making is generally in the hands of Christians, and it is they who produce and use the wines—ordinary table wines with 9% to 10% of alcohol, from French grape varieties. A little sparkling wine is made as well.

During the Second World War, French troops stationed in Syria naturally demanded wine, and production increased and the wine-making processes improved.

Szekszárdi Kadarka

One of the best of the full-bodied red wines of southern Hungary.
See Hungary.

Szemelt

Hungarian wine term for *auslese*.
See Auslese; Germany.

T

Table wine

In one sense, this is the ordinary wine commonly drunk at table. The term is being used more and more to describe still natural wines, differentiating them from sparkling and fortified wines, as well as from wines with a place-name. U.S. federal law specifies that the term "table wine" applies only to wines having less than 14% of alcohol per volume.

Tafia (taffea)

The early French West Indian Negro word for rum, and therefore one of the first names in general for the spirit. Today tafia is a second-quality spirit made from impure molasses or cane leftovers, while rum proper is made from the first-grade molasses or cane sugar.
See Rum; Egypt.

Taglio

Italian term for blended wine.

Tahbilk

A vineyard in Victoria making mostly white, and a few red, table wines, all sold under the name of the informing grape variety.
See Australia.

Château Talbot

Bordeaux red wine.
District: Haut-Médoc, France.
Commune: Saint-Julien.

Classified a Fourth Growth *(Quatrième Cru)* in 1855, Talbot commands equal prices with some of the Second Growths *(Seconds Crus)*. The wine is made mainly from the Cabernet Sauvignon and Petit-Verdot vines and takes its name from the English Lord Shrewsbury who was killed in 1453 in the region at the end of the Hundred Years' War; but it is uncertain whether Talbot himself ever owned the property. M. Jean Cordier, the minority owner, sold the majority shares of his properties to the "Le Hénin" group in 1983. The *chai* of Château Talbot is impressive, modern, neat, clean, and has become a model for the Médoc.

Considering its good wine, and the many less good wines with a better classification, Château Talbot can be said today to be definitely underclassified.
Vineyard area: 100 hectares (250 acres).
Average production: 400 *tonneaux* (35,000 cases).

Tannat

Important grapevine in Madiran, in the southwest of France. This is considered to be the same as the Harriague, extensively used in Uruguayan viticulture.

Tannin

An important component of wine, drawn from grape skins, pips, and stems and dissolved in the liquid during fermentation. It is an essential constituent of wine, giving character and long-lasting quality. It also combines with the aldehydes to precipitate a deposit. Tannin is an astringent substance found also in tree bark and some nuts; it has certain antiseptic qualities.
See Chapter Nine, p. 40.

Tarragona

One of the dozen or so official wine place-names in Spain.
See Spain.

Tarragona Port

A thick, heavy, red wine, made near Tarragona south of Barcelona in Spain, which incorrectly professes to be Port wine. True Port wine comes only from specially delimited vineyards on the Douro in Portugal. This imitation port from Tarragona has been excluded by law from Britain since 1916. It is forbidden to be sold under that name in the United States and some other countries.

Clos de Tart

Burgundy red wine.
District: Côte de Nuits, France.
Commune: Morey-Saint-Denis.
Official Classification: Great Growth (Grand Cru).

The Clos de Tart received its present name in 1141 when the vineyard called Climat de la Forge was sold to the Bernardines de l'Abbaye de Notre-Dame de Tart, a feminine offshoot of the Cistercian order. A bull of Pope Lucius III confirmed the sale in 1184 and the vineyard has been the Clos de Tart ever since. The sisters cultivated the vineyard—expanding it slightly in 1240—until the French Revolution, when it was seized and sold by the state. Unlike most Burgundian vineyards, the Clos de Tart has been kept intact through the changes it has undergone since the Revolution, and today it is entirely in the hands of the shipping firm of J. Mommessin, whose headquarters are in Mâcon.

Clos de Tart lies just north of the village of Morey, to the right of the vineyard road as you go south, and between Bonnes Mares and the Clos des Lambrays. Its 7.5 hectares (17.8 acres) are entirely enclosed within an ancient wall which borders the road along the mid-section of the hill. The wine is often known as a "ladies' wine," but this is in deference to the distaff side of the Cistercians, for it is sturdy and big. To its Morey characteristic of robustness is added a special delicacy and subtlety, and it ages with great grace. The vineyard has been rated a Great Growth *(Grand Cru)* by the French wine authorities, the highest rank a Burgundian vineyard can receive; and while it may not have all the fiery strength of neighboring Clos des Lambrays—ranked only as *Premier Cru* (First Growth)—it sometimes merits the considerable renown it has received.

Production in an average-quantity year is 275 hectoliters (7,285 U.S. gallons, 6,050 imp.), or the equivalent of about 3,000 cases.

Tartar

This important by-product of wine comprises the greater part of the crystalling deposit left in wine casks and vats. In a relatively pure state, this is cream of tartar; but where there has been contact with lime, some neutral tartrate of calcium will be present also. Remedies against precipitation of tartars in the wine are antitartrates (such as citrate of sodium) and freezing.

Tartaric acid

The most important of the fixed acids found in wine, and one particularly associated with the grape rather than other fruits. COOH·CHOH·CHOH·COOH.
See Chapter Nine, p. 40.

Tartrates

Salts of tartaric acid; a component of wine.
See Chapter Nine, p. 40.

Tastevin

A small silver cup for tasting wine used principally in Burgundy but also in the Midi. It is flat, with raised indentations to reflect the color of the wine.

Tasting

Determining the quality and characteristics of wine simply by tasting and smelling it. A blind tasting is one in which the origin or identity of the wines is not previously disclosed to the tasters.

Tatachilla

Large vineyard in McLaren Vale, South Australia; its wines are sold in England as Keystone burgundy. *See* Australia.

Taupette

Slang in the Cognac region for *preuve*, the little glass tube let down into the Cognac barrel on a chain in order to obtain some of the liquor to test or "prove" it.

Taurasi (D.O.C.)

Strong red wine from the Campania *(q.v.)*.

Tavel (Appellation Contrôlée)

Rosé wine.
District: Rhône Valley, France.

Vintage years mean less along the Rhône than in other fine vineyard regions of France, and probably least of all at Tavel. The reason is that Tavel makes only rosé, and rosé owes far more to soil and grape variety than to weather. The ratio between alcohol and acidity will vary slightly over the years, but the skill of the *vigneron* in making wines from properly matured grapes—picking early in hot years, late in cool ones—does much to regulate it. Furthermore, vintage differences seldom mean a great deal until the wine has attained some age. By its very nature, rosé is a wine to be drunk in its first blush of youth—vintage years can therefore be overlooked (except to check the year marked on the bottle to tell whether or not the wine is still young and fresh; a one-year minimum, five-year maximum is a good rule).

As rosés go, Tavel is full-bodied and sturdy. It is also unquestionably the world's best-known pink wine. Legally, it must contain 11% of alcohol, but usually it reaches 12% or more. The dominant grape in its make-up is Grenache, but several others are also allowed in varying amounts. Grenache must not account for more than 60% of the wine, and there must be at least 15% Cinsault.

The vines grow in a varied soil made up predominantly of cretaceous marl and chalk. The permitted growing area, roughly 750 hectares (1,875 acres), includes almost the entire commune of Tavel—about 8 kilometers (5 miles) from Châteauneuf-du-Pape and the same distance from Avignon, on the right bank of the Rhône—and a tiny section of neighboring Roquemaure. Almost 25,000 hectoliters (662,500 U.S. gallons, 550,000 imp.) of wine are produced annually, and they are shipped not only throughout France but all over the world. Sixty per cent of the total volume is made by the cooperative Les Vignerons de Tavel.

Tawny Port

Port wine matured in wood for anything from four to ten years and blended before it is bottled. Not as heavy and splendid as a great Vintage Port, it will, however, have more finesse and, at its best, great elegance. Tawny Port should not be laid down but instead drunk soon after it is bottled.

See Port.

Tent

Spanish red wine from Alicante. The term was once common in England.

Tequila

Of the three drinks fermented from the juice of the Mexican century plant—tequila (distilled), mescal (distilled), and pulque—tequila is the most civilized. Colorless, tossed down in Mexican style after a lick of salt from the back of the hand, it is like liquid fire in the throat. Popular in the U.S.

See Pulque.

Terlaner (D.O.C.)

White wine of South Tyrol.
See Trentino-Alto Adige.

Château de Tertre

Bordeaux red wine.
District: Haut-Médoc, France.
Commune: Arsac-Margaux.

For some years, the château on the country lane running between Arsac and Margaux was abandoned. It has now been replanted by a Belgian group under the supervision of Philippe Gasqueton of Château Calon-Ségur. Along with the other wines made in Arsac, it has since 1955 enjoyed the right to the place-name Margaux. A Fifth Growth (*Cinquième Cru*) of the 1855 Classification, Château du Tertre is an indication that the old ranking does not always hold true.

Characteristics. The quality of wine slipped almost out of sight, but in 1966 it made a small recovery and has continued to improve, especially in the eighties.

Vineyard area: 50 hectares (125 acres).
Average production: 200 *tonneaux* (18,000 cases).

Thermometer

No vat-house or *chai* should be without a thermometer, and one is also invaluable in a cellar or any room where wine is stored. A *maître de chai* who constantly takes the temperature of the fermenting must will, in very hot weather, probably be able to moderate fermentation where it is excessive and so save the wine—hence, in an unusually hot summer, one vineyard will produce a better wine than another in the same district. A thermometer must be used too in conjunction with such instruments as mustimeters and alcoholmeters, in registering the degree of alcohol. Most countries of the world—whether as a matter of long standing or, as in some more recent cases, because of Common Market agreements—use the Celsius system of figuring temperature in centigrades. The chief exception to the use of Celsius is now the United States, although this is beginning to change.

The variations in their scales are as follows: Centigrade, or Celsius, shows the freezing-point of water as 0° and its boiling-point as 100°; Réaumur shows 0° as the freezing-point of water and its boiling point as 80°; Fahrenheit shows 32° as the freezing-point of water and its boiling-point as 212°.

To ascertain the temperature of a liquid the thermometer should be kept in the liquid for some minutes; the thermometer is quick to respond and the division on the scale at which the mercury stops indicates the temperature of the liquid. Tables showing the respective scales of the three thermometers are given in Appendix E, p. 718, but below are shown the calculations necessary to convert from one scale to another.

To convert Centigrade into Réaumur, multiply the Centigrade temperature by $\frac{4}{5}$. To convert Réaumur into Centigrade, multiply by $\frac{5}{4}$.

To convert Centigrade into Fahrenheit, multiply the Centigrade temperature by 1.8 and add 32. To convert Fahrenheit into Centigrade subtract 32 from the Fahrenheit temperature and divide by 1.8.

To convert Fahrenheit into Réaumur, subract 32 from the Fahrenheit temperature and multiply by $\frac{4}{9}$. To convert Réaumur into Fahrenheit multiply the Réaumur temperature by $\frac{9}{4}$ and add 32.

See Chapter Nine.

Thief

A *pipette*, or tube, for withdrawing wine or liquor from a cask or other container; usually made of glass, sometimes of silver.

Thin

A watery or poor wine, one that lacks alcohol, flavor, and body.

Three-Star; Five-Star, etc.

A designation used in Cognacs and Armagnacs and frequently believed to indicate an exact age of three, five, or some other number of years. Actually, Three-Star is a type, and while it may average roughly an age of five years in Armagnacs, and somewhat younger in Cognacs, it does not necessarily do so. The system was probably devised because of the ease of drawing a star symbol—at the time the use of stars arose in Cognac, the trick of drawing a star without lifting pen from paper was in vogue—and subsequently it became famous. While a Three-Star brandy need not be of any given age, it will always be younger than a V.S.O.P., X.O., or Reserve, and will be less expensive. Star styles and other designations are considered fully under Cognac (*q.v.*).

Tía María

A proprietary West Indian liqueur based on rum and flavored with Jamaican spices and coffee.

Tinta

A grapevine family—Tinta Cão, Tinta Francisca, etc.—used in making Port. Some of these Tintas have now been planted also in California.

Tintara

Vineyard in McLaren Vale, South Australia. *See* Australia.

Tinto

In Spain, a *vino tinto* is a red wine.

Tirage

French term for the act of drawing wine from barrels.

Tischwein

German term for common wine, or *vin ordinaire*. Not to be confused with *Tafelwein*, or table wine.

Toddy

A hot drink made with spirits, sugar, lemon slices, cloves, and hot water. In certain tropical countries, it is also a cold drink, made from the liquor of the fermented sap of palm trees.

Tokaier

See Rülander.

Tokaji

One of the label words for Tokay, followed by an indication of the type of Tokay—e.g., Tokaji Édes Szamorodni.
See Tokay.

Tokay (Tokaj)

Down into the Hungarian river town of Tokaj, the two streams Bodrog and Tisza rush from the Carpathian Mountains; they converge and flow to the Danube and thence into the Black Sea.

Nobody knows how long vines have grown on the volcanic soil in the fork of the rives; they were already there when the Magyar (Hungarian) tribes arrived a thousand years ago. In the corner of Hungary near Slovakia and the Ukraine, the wine was famous at least by the time of the Crusades. The eighteenth-century writer Szirmay de Szirma said that the real fame of Tokay arrived with the discovery of the *aszú* method only half a century before his time. Modern writers, however, date the discovery earlier. The real magic of Tokay Aszú was likely first realized in the middle of the seventeenth century by one Máté Laczkó, private secretary at the court of Lady Zsuzsánna Lóránttffy, widow of György Rákóczi I, Prince of Transylvania. The prince owned extensive Tokay vineyards on Mount Oremus at Sárospatak. This was the beginning of the Aszú Tokay we know today.

There are people in Hungary who will say that the steely wines of great breeding from Lake Balaton are the best in the country, but the world will not agree. Tokay, the most concentrated of all, seems to capture more than any other the romance of wine. Even Champagne cannot quite approach this golden aristocrat, once guarded by an entire troop of Cossacks for the table of Catherine the Great. The most superb Trockenbeerenauslese Rhine or Mosel, or a Château d'Yquem of the greatest year, will lack at least one of the elements that ennoble Tokay. Voltaire said of it: "This wine invigorates every fiber of the brain and brings forth an enchanting sparkle of wit and good cheer from the depths of the soul."

The Tokajhegyalja wine district in northeastern Hungary borders on Czechoslovakia and the Soviet Ukraine. There are some 6,500 hectares (16,250 acres) of vineyards which annually produce about 200,000 hectoliters (5.3 million U.S. gallons, 4.4 million imp.) of various Tokays.

Twenty-eight villages in this defined district have the right to the name for their wines—Tokaji, as it appears on the labels, "wine from Tokaj," the *i* indicating place of origin. All are grown on a volcanic soil with feldspar, porcelain clay, and porphyry in it, a fundamental contribution to the character of the wine. The topsoil is decayed lava and loess. All of the towns with the right to the name are in the southern foothills—Hegyalja means "foothill"—of the Eperjes-Tokaj range, protected to the north by the high Carpathian Mountains. The most important villages are Tállya, Tarcal, Tokaj, Olaszliszka, Erdőbénye, Tolcsva, Mád, Satorajaujhely, and the cultural and political center of the district, Sárospatak. A small part of the producing area is in Czechoslovakia.

As with any great wine, the geographical location and soil are only two of the factors contributing to its originality. There are also the climate, grape, and the methods of winemaking to consider. In Tokaj the summers are hot and dry; the autumns are especially long, so that in good years there is plenty of sunshine to overripen the grapes. Only three grape varieties are permitted: Furmint, Hárslevelű, and Sárgamuskotály.

The Furmint is by far the most important as it is most conducive to overripening and noble rot. Walloon wine-growers brought it to the region in the thirteenth century after a Tartar invasion.

The process by which the more concentrated grades are made has a good deal in common with the method used for Sauternes or the German Trockenbeerenauslesen wines, but in some ways it is unique. The Tokay-Furmint grape, a dull yellow fruit with a thick skin, becomes overripe in the warm rays of the autumn sun, and the parasitic fungus *Botrytis cinerea (q.v.)* begins under the right conditions to reduce the natural acids and concentrate the grape sugar. The Magyars called the grapes that had been blessed in this way *aszú,* which means "dried out," describing the weeping array of water from the fruit. In the days of the Habsburgs, when the wines were particularly popular, they were called *Ausbruch,* the German translation of the Hungarian term.

As in Sauternes or on the Rhineland slopes and Mosel terraces, a late-gathered, dried-berry wine will be made. In France and Germany the essential process is to pick over the vineyard repeatedly, selecting only the overripe or dried-up berries each time. In Hungary, the Furmint grape cluster too ripens unevenly, some berries being ready days before others. But the method devised for Tokay is different. In picking over a Tokay vineyard, the dried grapes are separated from the others and put into containers, the Hungarian name for which is *puttony.*

THE GREAT NAMES IN TOKAY

The berries that have been thus selected are vinified alone or mixed with other grapes and juice, each combination producing one of the famous Tokay wines. It is at this point in the wine-making process that the aszú method begins to differ from the techniques found in the Sauternes region of France or the Rheingau of Germany.

Tokaji Eszencia

Made exclusively from dried-up berries, this is the most treasured of essences used in the making of Tokay wine. The overripe berries and those in a state of noble rot are gathered one by one and are stored in vats until the end of the harvest. Only the weight of the piled-up fruit forces the syrup from the grapes. This immensely rich liquid is slowly fermented for years in the small casks called *gönci.* There is nothing else on earth remotely like this very heart of Tokay, and many stories of its magical life-giving and restorative powers have been told. Tokaji Eszencia made in the classic manner has not been available outside of Hungary for many years. The state cellars make very little of the fabulous wine, and when a bottle of Eszencia of a recent vintage does appear, it is most likely

a blend of standard Aszú wine with a very small part of the essence.

Tokaji Aszú

The Aszú grapes, having yielded their small tribute of Eszencia, are trodden into a paste so that the pips remain whole and unbruised. The skins, on the other hand, almost dissolve. While this process goes on, the grapes not affected by the fungus are harvested and pressed in the usual way. Into this must some of the green and sappy stalks are stirred for a few hours of maceration. A blend of the must and the Aszú dough is then made and macerated in open vats for a few days. The solid pump is filtered out, and the enriched must is poured into the *gönci* casks for the slow and final part of fermentation lasting four to seven years. This slow ageing at 8 to 12°C gives it the fine and distinctive Tokay bouquet. So, as with certain Sherries and Château Chalon wine of Arbois in France, the special bouquet of the wine is due to controlled oxidation. Tokay cellars have a unique mold, characterized by the *Cladosporium cellare,* which forms a black, almost cottony film on the cellar walls. By micro-condensation, it absorbs the ethers, volatile aldehydes, volatile acids, and alcohol vapors caused by wine evaporation that are in the air.

The character of a Tokaji Aszú will be indicated by the *puttonyos* content stated on the neck label. The buckets, or *puttonyos,* of raisin-dry, concentrated grapemash added to the fermentation of the pick-of-the-vineyard run are shown on each bottle of the vatting. Thus, the neck label on every bottle will state: 3 Puttonos, 4 Puttonos, or 5 Puttonos, etc. The more Aszú berries that have been put in, the more concentrated the wine will be. A wine labeled five or six *puttonyos* is one made almost entirely from the aszú mash, with little of the standard grape must added. The nature of the vintage depends on the stage of ripening of the vineyard on the day of picking.

Alcoholic content and other characteristics of course vary with the *puttonyos* content, but alcohol is generally between 13% and 14% by volume. The Furmint grape does not achieve the proper condition for making Aszú below an altitude of 100 meters (350 feet), and all the best wine is made on the slope vineyards ranging between an altitude of 125 and 250 meters (420 and 820 feet). It has been estimated that the Aszú berry proportion of the entire Tokay crop averages about one part in three thousand, although in many years no Aszú can be made at all.

Tokaji Szamorodni

Szamorodni is a Slavonic, not a Magyar word, evidence of the interest that the Russians and Poles have often had in Tokay wines. The word means "such as it was grown" and refers to wine made from grapes from which the Aszú berries have not been selected. Therefore, when the conditions of the vintage favor

the full development of the *Botrytis cinerea*, few of the bunches are left untouched for Tokaji Szamorodni. Conversely, in a year when little Aszú can be made, there is much of this wine. The vinification resembles that of Aszú, since the fermentation is in two stages: firstly the grapes are crushed and macerated for a few hours, oxidizing them, and then they are pressed and fermented. Finally they are aged for two to four years, just long enough, as the Hungarians say, "to wash the sweetness out of the Aszú berries"; then the second in the *gönci* barrels kept in the typical low rock cellars. On the other hand, considerable help has been given to British and American buyers by labeling export bottles of Szamorodni as either dry or sweet; the indications are given in English both on the body and neck label. Szamorodni Sweet will, of course, be from the pickings which included more Aszú berries and can have a tremendous nose. The designation Tokaji Édes Szamorodni also indicates that the Szamorodni is sweet.

Tokaji Aszú and Tokaji Szamorodni are sold only in white bottles of about a pint or half-liter, with long throats, shaped not unlike Indian clubs. The other varieties of Tokay wine are sold in the tall, slender Rhine-style bottle usual for Hungarian wines. By law, these bottles bear the government export mark.

Tokaji Máslás

After an Aszú or Szamorodni has been racked, plain Tokay wine is poured into the little 120-liter or 150-liter barrel and for several months is left to stand on the lees. The result is Tokaji Máslás.

Tokaji Forditás

Tokaji Forditás is made by performing a second time the making of Aszú. The used pulp after the Aszú has been made is revived by the addition of fresh must, and a second fermentation is obtained.

OTHER TOKAY TERMS

Tokaji Aszú-eszencia: very excellent Aszú wine.
Tokaji Édes: sweet Tokay.
Tokaji Száraz: dry Tokay.
Monimpex: the state export monopoly.
Magyar Állami Pincegazdaság: Hungarian state cellars.

Tokay d'Alsace

Formerly, an alternative name for the Pinot Gris grape. However, Common Market regulations now prohibit the use of the word "Tokay."

Tom and Jerry

A drink made of eggs, hot milk or sugar, brandy, and rum.

Tom Collins

An iced drink made of gin and sugar mixed with lime and lemon juice and filled up with soda-water.

Tonneau

In France (1) Any large barrel. (2) The standard wine measure in Bordeaux. Although no container of this size actually exists, a Bordeaux *tonneau* is equal to four *barriques*, or barrels, and contains 900 liters, equivalent to 237 U.S. gallons or 198 imp. gallons. As of 1977 one *tonneau* no longer equals 96 cases of twelve 73-centiliter bottles each, but 100 cases of twelve 75-centiliter bottles each.

Toro

Red wine of Zamora.
See Spain.

Torgiano (D.O.C.)

Good red or white wine from Umbria *(q.v.)* in Italy.

Toul (V.D.Q.S.)

See Côtes de Toul; Lorraine.

Touraine and Coteaux de Touraine (A.O.C.)

White, red, and rosé wines.
District: Loire Valley, France.

The large district spreads over both banks of the Loire around Tours and is famous both as "the garden of France" and the "château country" of such magnificent palaces as Blois, Amboise, Chenonceaux, and Azay-le-Rideau. It is celebrated also as the region where the inhabitants speak the purest and clearest French of all. Over 250,000 hectoliters (6,625,000 U.S. gallons, 5,500,000 imp.) of wines are made annually in the Touraine, some fairly ordinary but a few in the front rank of French wines.

Tours is on the Loire's left bank, an old city not without charm. The best vineyards are across the river and slightly to the north, but you will hardly realize that Indre-et-Loire and Loir-et-Cher (the departments in which Touraine lies) is wine country until you leave the valley. The winding river road threads its way beneath high cliffs, and roadside advertisements inform you that wines may be obtained, but a vine is a rare sight indeed. Most of the vineyards are on the other side of the bluffs which rise steeply from the river, planted on the back sides. These slopes are important, for tunneling back into them are long cellars whose limestone walls maintain a constant temperature and humidity, where the wines age under excellent conditions. There is hardly a house without its deep cellar running back into the hill on which it stands, and hardly a cellar where the wines are not quietly sleep-

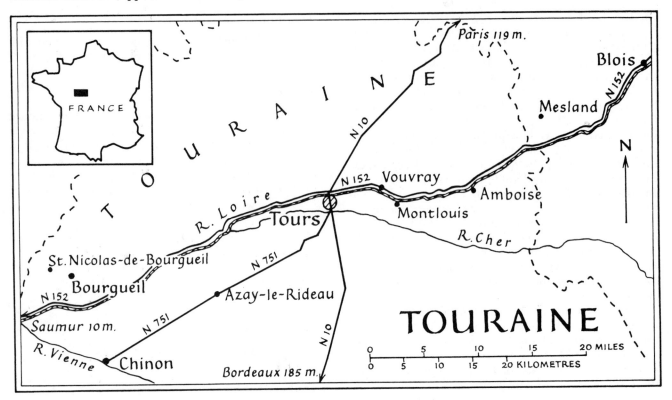

ing, waiting for the "monent of truth" when the cork is pulled and the wine turned gently into the clear glasses.

To most people, Touraine wines mean Vouvray, yet the district produces red and rosé wines as well as white. Touraine white is the finest. Still and sparkling wine, red, rosé, and white, stem from this rich and fertile section of the valley and some have the great vigor the others lack. Many, in certain vintages, are too low in alcohol—in general, the measure of a wine's stamina—to travel, but are decidedly pleasant when sipped in the shadow of a soaring castle wall overlooking the river.

A lot of the Touraine soil is too heavy with clay and too moist to be suitable for wine; but as you climb the slopes you find a coarse-grained limestone topped with a chalky clay, a formation known as *aubuis*, which Loire growers say is ideal for the Chenin Blanc vine, the most widespread variety here; and Vouvray is the best example of the wines it produces. In other localities, the soil is flintier and has less limestone; and Cabernet Franc and lesser amounts of Gamay, Cot, Pinot Noir and Pinot Gris, and a minute amount of Groslot are planted for rosé wines. This is the type of soil prevalent in Chinon.

Wine is named either from district or from one of the more specific sub-districts. The general name is Touraine—Touraine Mousseux (Appellation Contrôlée), if sparkling—applied to wines from the specified area and which have been harvested in no more than 45 hectoliters per hectare (468 U.S. gallons, 390 imp. per acre). Wines with more specific names meet more stringent standards. The Touraine sub-districts

(see under individual headings) are: Bourgueil, Saint-Nicolas-de-Bourgueil, Chinon, Montlouis, Touraine-Amboise, Touraine-Azay-le-Rideau, Touraine-Mesland, Vouvray.

Touraine-Amboise (Appellation Contrôlée)

Loire Valley, red, white, and rosé wines.
District: Touraine, France.

A minor subdivision of the Touraine, making a small quantity of wine generally slightly better than that simply called Touraine but not in the class of the more famous Touraine sub-districts. Red and rosé wines come from Cabernet Franc, Cot, and Gamay grapes; white from Chenin Blanc. Red wines must have 9.5% of alcohol, rosé 10%, and white 10.5%.

See Touraine.

Touraine-Azay-le-Rideau (Appellation Contrôlée)

Loire Valley red, white, and rosé wines.
District: Touraine, France.

Azay-le-Rideau, with its magnificent château, was given the right in 1953 to sell its dry wines under its own name, one that applies equally to the output of the seven surrounding communes. The white wines must be made from Chenin Blanc grapes, must have at least 10% of alcohol, and are good but not exceptional Touraine wines. The red and rosé wines are made mostly from the Groslot grape.

See Touraine.

Touraine-Mesland (Appellation Contrôlée)

Loire Valley red, white, and rosé wines.
District: Touraine, France.

A minor subdivision of the Touraine given its own controlled place-name in 1955. Red and rosé wines come mainly from Gamay grapes; white from Chenin Blanc and Sauvignon. Rosé and red wines must have 10.5% alcohol, red only 10%.
See Touraine.

Touriga

Leading red grape in the Dão region of Portugal. It is also used in making Port.

Tourne

A disorder of wine, in which it becomes gassy and disagreeable to nose and taste, hazes, and loses color.
See Chapter Nine, p. 40.

Traben-Trarbach

White-wine villages on opposite banks of the German Mosel, each possessing some good vineyards.
See Mosel-Saar-Ruwer.

Traminer

Now known commonly as the Gewürztraminer, the Traminer appears frequently on the labels of the German wines derived from this grape. This grape is also planted in the South Tyrol.
See Alsace; Germany; Gewürztraminer.

Trappistine

A very pale yellow-green, herb-flavored, Armagnac-based liqueur made at the Abbaye de Grâce de Dieu in the French department of Doubs.

Trebbiano

The Italian name for Ugni Blanc, one of the most widespread white wine grapes from Italy, especially in Latium and Tuscany. This vine, Saint-Émilion des Charentes, also flourishes in France.
See Saint-Émilion.

Trebbiano di Abruzzo and Trebbiano di Romagna

Italian white wines (D.O.C.s).
See Abruzzi; Emilia Romagna.

Trentino-Alto-Adige (South Tyrol)

White and red wines.
District: Trentino-Alto-Adige. (Known also as Sud Tyrol.)

The Alto Adige is one of Italy's finest growing areas for dry white wines, but at present the potential is only realized in isolated instances. Soil, climate, and vines in this northeast alpine corner are capable of producing inexpensive wines to rival those of Austria or Alsace; but the 5,800 growers have been the inhibiting factor, generally preferring to stick to the traditional methods of making light traditional red wines between the light wines of Germany and the fuller reds found farther south in Italy. Fortunately, modern cooperatives, especially in Trentino, are investing in modern technology and the wines have improved accordingly.

Before 1919 the Alto Adige was part of the Austrian Tyrol. The Treaty of Saint-Germain, at the end of the First World War, transferred it to Italy; but the inhabitants remain Germanic, and Austria continues to drink the wines. What the Austrians do not import goes mostly to Switzerland and Germany, and this division of the spoils predates the coming of the Italians by a considerable time. Just under 85% percent of the 3.8 million hectoliters (100 million U.S. gallons, 83 million imp.) made annually are red; but good though some of them may be, they are sometimes outclassed by the best of the whites. It is a general rule that the finer whites are from the northern Alto Adige section, the reds from Trentino—extending south around the city of Trento to the sunny shores of Lake Garda.

GRAPEVINES

The vines cultivated in Trentino-Alto-Adige are a cosmopolitan group. The Austrian influence is reflected in Rieslings and Traminers, the French in Pinots, Cabernets, and Merlots; and the Italians have introduced—among others—Schiave, Lambrusco, Deroldego, and Garganega (known locally as Terlano). Riesling is the most interesting vine. When cultivated on the chilly slopes, it gives grapes capable of fermenting into marvelous wine. Much the same can be said of Traminer, although it is a general rule that Riesling will always produce the finer fruit under the same conditions. Schiave is common in the northern part of the region, producing sound, sometimes thoroughly delightful red wines; and Merlot seems to be on the increase. The Italian discovery of the Merlot is an important event in modern viniculture, for the result is a wine in the hearty Italian manner but one with the rough edges considerably smoothed.

In Trentino, one of the most widespread vines is the indigenous Deroldego (or sometimes Teroldico), producing largely red wines of ordinary quality. Lambruscos and Merlots are abundant also, but the grapes of these and other vines are usually crushed together or blended after crushing to give a wine with more balance than any one seems able to produce alone.

BEST WINES

Riesling del Trentino (D.O.C.)

Potentially the queen of the Alto Adige, but today too often aged in cask too long. Some exceptions must be allowed, as many good Rieslings are impressive enough to be shipped to Germany. While the wines will never have all the breed of the finest German Rieslings, they could conceivably stand with anything below this level.

Santa Magdalener (D.O.C.) (Santa Maddalena)

Alto Adige red wine, sometimes referred to—even today—as Sankt Magdalener. It is made from Schiave grapes grown on slopes near Bolzano. Santa Magdalener is a clean, smooth, pleasant wine giving a slight aroma of almonds and is probably the finest red wine of the area, deeper in color and with more flavor than Caldaro.

Teroldego Rotaliano (D.O.C.)

This wine from Trentino is either ruby-red or rosé; both are full-bodied, pungent, and sturdy. The good red may tend toward fullness, with a trace of tannic bitterness. Barone des Cles is a good producer.

Traminer Aromatico del Trentino (D.O.C.)

The dry white Gewürztraminer wine is imbued with the typical spicy perfume. The best in Italy comes from the Alto Adige, and although it is not outstanding, it may well be an excellent, reasonably priced bargain.

Caldaro (Lago di Caldaro D.O.C.)

Pleasant garnet-red wine with a trace of almond in the bouquet; from Schiave and occasionally some Pinot and Lagrein grapes grown around Lake Caldaro (formerly the Kaltersee) not far south of Bolzano. It is light and enjoyable but gains little with age. The best is called Classico Superiore.

Vino Santo del Trentino (D.O.C.)

Sweet dessert wine from white Pinot grapes which are dried before vinification. The wine is similar to Tuscan Vino Santo but without all the latter's excellence.

LESSER WINES

Cabernet del Trentino (D.O.C)

Made of Cabernet Franc and Cabernet Sauvignon, the wine is dry, full, and slightly tannic but is certainly not one of the best products of these good grapes. The bouquet is reminiscent of grass.

Valdadige

Red wine from Schiave, Lambrusco, Pinot, and Deroldego grapes grown on the banks of the lower Adige in the Trentino section of the region. White wine is also produced along the river, which is long and passes through a wide variety of soils, rendering the wines variable in the same measure. It is the common red wine of the area.

Colline di Caldaro

Red wine from Schiave and Pinot Noir, grown along slopes in the general vicinity of Lake Caldaro.

Pinot Bianco (Weissburgunder and Chardonnay) (D.O.C.)

Many very good results have been obtained with Pinot Grigio, making these Trentino white wines excellent quality potentials.

Lagarino Rosato (D.O.C.)

Good pink wine from Lagrein grapes. Before 1919 it was called Lagreinkretzer.

Marzemino del Trentino (D.O.C.)

A dry, ruby-red, well-balanced wine with a somewhat bitter taste. The best when young is Bossi-Fedrigotti.

Meranese di Collina (D.O.C.)

Light, red wine from Schiave grapes grown along the hills near Merano, north of Bolzano.

Merlot del Trentino (D.O.C.)

These Bordeaux grapes make a sound dry red wine that is pleasant enough but certainly not outstanding.

Moscato del Trentino (D.O.C.)

Neither so heavy nor so sweet as most Muscat wines and thus an interesting change for Muscat-lovers. A fortified Moscato Liquoroso is also produced.

Pinot Nero del Trentino (D.O.C.)

The Pinot Noir grapevine—sometimes called by its old Austrian name, Blauburgunder—is cultivated in scattered sections of the region. Its wine is bright red, sometimes even pink, and is pleasantly bitter.

Lagrein del Trentino (D.O.C.)

A red wine from the Lagrein grapes, very fruity and dry, usually with about 12% of alcohol.

Sorni (D.O.C.)

Red wine from Merlot, Deroldego, and subvarieties of Schiave grapes. The town of Sorni is slightly north of Trento. The white may be called Scelto.

Sylvaner

A small dry white wine, but perfectly adequate in carafe at or near its source. Bressanone (formerly Brixen) is its headquarters.

Terlaner (D.O.C.)

A well-known and quite presentable greenish-white wine of the Alto Adige. Terlano is the local name for the Garganega vine, but the wine is more often a blend of Terlano, Riesling, and Pinot Noir.

Termeno d'Avio

Unspectacular rosé wine from southern Trentino. It is made from Lambrusco, Merlot, Deroldego, and Marzemino grapes.

Trier

Ancient wine city of the German Mosel. There is a famous museum here, and fair white wines are produced.
See Mosel-Saar-Ruwer.

Trinidad rum

See Rum, Trinidad.

Triple sec

Triple sec white Curaçao was originally the name used by the makers of Cointreau, but so many other firms started using the designation that the originators ceased putting it on their labels and called their liqueur simply Cointreau. Triple sec is now used by a number of manufacturers in various countries of the Curaçao type.
See Curaçao.

Trittenheim

Wine town of the German Mosel. Among the good vineyards are Apotheke and Altärchen.
See Mosel-Saar-Ruwer.

Trockenbeerenauslese

Literally "dried-berry-selected" in the block-building German language, this elephantine word describes the process whereby the finest sweet wine of the Rhine and Mosel and some of the most elegant wines in the world are obtained. The grapes are allowed to dry and shrivel on the vine until the ultimate in concentrated sugar-sweetness is achieved; the berries are then individually selected, in this state of super-maturity, by the pickers. Increasing labor costs in a prosperous postwar Germany are rapidly pricing this exquisite type of wine out of the market. Trockenbeerenauslese is the German equivalent of the Sauternes-style wine of France, with the difference that in the warmer southwestern France it is still possible to produce a naturally sweet wine by individual selection of grapes at a price which, though very high, is still not prohibitive.

Château Trotanoy

Bordeaux red wine.
District and Commune: Pomerol, France.

Jean-Pierre Moueix makes this especially rich and flavorful wine from old vines on a clay and gravel soil.
Vineyard area: 9 hectares (22 acres).
Average production: 30 *tonneaux* (2,500 cases).

Château Trottevieille

Bordeaux red wine.
District and Commune: Saint-Émilion, France.

Always one of the leading Saint-Émilions, it was rated a Premier Grand Cru when the vineyards were officially classified in 1955. Trottevieille sells well abroad, particularly in Belgium. The property belongs to M. Casteja, the son-in-law of the late Marcel Borie, who also owned Château Batailley, a classified vineyard in the Médoc.
Characteristics. A carefully made wine with body and bouquet and a fine color.
Vineyard area: 10 hectares (25 acres).
Average production: 50 *tonneaux* (4,800 cases).

Tuica

A plum spirit made in Rumania. It varies in color from greenish to yellow. It is sometimes taken hot with sugar and peppers.

Tun

A wine cask containing 954 liters (252 U.S. gallons, 210 imp.). A tun filled with water or wine weighs approximately one ton avoirdupois.

Tunisia

The vine was established, especially in the vicinity of Carthage, in Punic and Roman times. Afterward, under the rule of the Moslems, wine-making was forbidden for more than a thousand years. The modern history of wine in Tunisia, now an independent country, began when it came under French control.

Viniculture along French lines was developed in the Cape Bon region (on the peninsula enclosing the Gulf of Tunis on the east); around Tunis itself, and in the Medjerdah and Oued Miliane valleys. Wines were made in quantity, a peak of nearly 1,200,000 hectoliters (31,680,000 U.S. gallons, 26,375,000 imp.) annually being maintained in the 1930s. Phylloxera, the deadly vine louse which had ruined Europe's vineyards in the 1880s, reached Tunisia in 1936. In ten years the vineyard area dropped by half and wine production by nearly two-thirds.

Replanted on grafted, phylloxera-immune American vine-stocks (as were the post-epidemic vineyards of Europe), the Tunisian vine plantation now covers some 38,000 hectares (95,000 acres), not all of which is yet in full production. Quantity stands at about 600,000 hectoliters (15.8 million U.S. gallons, 13.2 million imp.). The earlier peak production is now common, although when the vineyards were first reconstituted, an attempt was made to obtain quality at the expense of quantity.

Tunisia produces red, white, and rosé natural wines, fortified Muscat wines, and *eaux-de-vie*. All wine-growing is confined to a narrow area near the coast, forming a crescent around and behind Tunis but at some distance from the town. The leading districts are Grombalia and the section formed by the triangle Tunis-Mateur-Bordj-Toum, producing quantitatively more than 90% of the total. Growths *(Crus)* are not particularly important in the present state of Tunisian viticulture; however, names of some repute include Carthage, Tébourba, Mornag, Muscat de Kelibia, Côteaux d'Utique, Khanguet, and Sidi-Sâad. Fortified wines are Byrsa and Rancio.

The traditional grape varieties in Tunisia have always been, for the red, Carignan, Alicante-Bouschet, and Cinsault; for white wines, Clairette, Beldi, Merséguera and Pédroximénès; and for the rosé, Alicante-Grenache. The wines have characteristically shown a tendency to maderize—particularly the reds, which are based on Alicante-Bouschet and which mature too

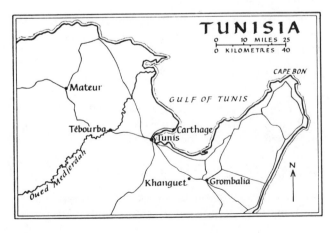

rapidly in the climate, showing a feeble color and then quickly developing the onion-skin hue and a bitterish taste. In an attempt to correct this, Pedro Ximénez vines from Spain, Sémillon and Sauvignon from France, and Merseguera from Italy have been introduced for the white wines; and for the red wines, the Nocera, Pinot Noir, Mourvedre, and Cabernet varieties. The rosés, based on Alicante-Grenache, have proved the most successful of the types, making one of the best rosés of North Africa, provided that they are bottled as soon as they fall clear and are drunk young. Otherwise they will maderize.

A series of controls established between 1942 and 1957 acted as incentives to make wines of quality by guaranteeing that such wines would be identified and therefore command premium prices.

In 1942 the classification Vin Supérieur de Tunisie was established. It includes no restriction as to place of origin within Tunisia nor limitation as to grape varieties. Wines submitted by growers for the classification are analyzed chemically to establish their purity and are then tasted blind by a committee of experts chosen by the Commission of Classification. Vins Supérieurs de Tunisie are sold in bottle. The bottle dressing carries a numbered insignia showing that it belongs to a classed lot, and the vintage must be indicated. The wines must be at least one year old. (The technique parallels almost exactly the one set up in 1955 in Bordeaux for wines to be exported to the U.S.)

In 1947, the Appellation Contrôlée Vin Muscat de Tunisie was established. In place of origin, wines are not restricted except to Tunisia, but they must be of the Alexandrian Muscat, Muscat de Frontignan, or Muscat de Terracina grape varieties. The wines are fortified by one of two means: tasteless, rectified spirit may be added before fermentation has begun, thus preventing fermentation and retaining the entire sugar content of the must as sugar; or the fermenting must may be stopped by the addition of either spirits of wine or completely rectified spirit, resulting in a wine of a minimum of 17% of alcohol and of 70 grams of sugar per liter. The wines made by the first method should properly be called mistelles, since they are actually grape juice with added alcohol, never having undergone fermentation. It is illegal to mix the two types. The better quality results from the use of wine spirits rather than of completely rectified spirit.

In 1957, a place-name system that defined the different wine-producing regions was established. This system also created a hierarchy of wines, broken down as Vins de Consommation Courante (V.C.C.), Vins Supérieurs (V.S.), Vins de Qualité Supérieure (V.D.Q.S.) and Appellation d'Origine Contrôlée (A.O.C.).

Turkey

At the turn of the century, Turkish wines were seen in some quantity in Western Europe. But exports ceased with the First World War, and by the late twenties that war and the Turco-Greek conflict which followed had almost put an end to wine-making. The prolific, grape-producing regions of Thrace and the Aegean had been devastated, and most of the non-Islamic population had disappeared. The land was left to cultivators who liked eating grapes, were forbidden by their religion to drink wine, and were often persuaded that to sell their grapes to wine-making plants was sinful. It was the task of the new republic to revive the country's viniculture.

When, in 1927, the state-monopoly wine industries were started, total production had fallen to some 20,-000 hectoliters (about 528,000 U.S. gallons, 440,000 imp.) a year. Since the middle thirties, however, it has been expanding gradually, and the state has been making a serious effort to raise quality as well as quantity without putting up prices: in order to win customers, Turkey must sell more cheaply than the established wine-producing countries. Up-to-date machinery has been installed in the government plants, employees have been trained in modern techniques of viticulture and viniculture, and the decree of 1928 that the Moslem faith was no longer the official religion has helped to overcome the scruples of some of the growers.

In comparison with the West, Turkey now seems to be a latecomer in wine production; yet the vine flourished in this region long before Greek colonists planted the first vineyards in Gaul. The earliest vines of all are believed to have grown wild in Anatolia and around the shores of the Caspian Sea; and in Mesopotamia the Sumerians are said to have been making wine as long ago as the third millennium B.C. This long start was lost in the Middle Ages when the Turks themselves (ardent converts to Islam) began their conquests, which culminated in the fall of Constantinople in 1453. Grapes went on growing, but most of them were (and are) kept for the table, or made into vinegar or the *miel de raisin* which many of the peasants use instead of sugar. In the early years of the Ottoman Empire there was a must tax on the production of wine in the vineyards of non-Moslems. In 1564 a new tax was levied on all alcoholic drinks—but this proved so difficult to enforce that it was afterward repealed. By the late nineteenth century, although indigenous wine-drinkers were still rare, something like 3.5 million hectoliters (924 million U.S. gallons, 77 imp.) of wine was produced, largely for export.

The types of wine made in Turkey are dry, semi-dry, sweet, fortified, and sparkling. The grapes for the sweet wine are late-picked; the fortified wines are sweet Muscatels; the sparkling wines are carbonated. The best growths come from central and southeastern Anatolia; others of very good to medium quality are produced in the Thracian and Aegean regions. Thrace and Marmara, the Aegean, Middle Anatolia, the Mediterranean, and Southeastern Anatolia are the only wine-producing regions. Officially approved grape varieties are listed on page 506.

METHODS OF WINE-MAKING

Turkish growers rarely make their own wine, although a few do so in places such as Bozcaada and Mürefte. They usually sell their grapes to the townsmen who operate the plants. These fall into two categories: on the one hand, the government-controlled monopolies established in 1927 and the Atatürk Farm Administration; on the other, private enterprises. The state wineries are operated with modern industrial machinery by technically qualified personnel; the private concern, often housed in a shop or shed, may be quite seedy and makeshift, the machinery is usually rather primitive and the makers are unlikely to be trained viniculters. Some of these men make trouble with the peasants by offering for their grapes—already very cheap—a price which is absurdly low.

In pressing the fruit, both hand-operated and hydraulic basket presses are used—the latter in the big plants. The pomace is first pressed by hydraulic processes, afterward by hand presses; only in making wines of better quality is the must of the second pressing processed independently. In well-run plants, the juice ferments in concrete tanks in rooms where the temperature is kept low and is transferred after about a week to more concrete tanks for ageing. Most of the wines are rather light and are aged only from eight to twelve months; a few bigger wines will be left for two to three years. Since most Turkish wines are low in acidity, it is necessary to add sufficient sulfur dioxide—the quantity is controlled by the regulations drawn up in 1954—and to rack the wine earlier than is usual. The first racking generally takes place fifteen to twenty-one days after ageing begins, and then sulfur is added; the second racking comes in four to six months; the third, six months later. Those wines which are allowed longer ageing are afterward racked only once a year. The wine is fined before bottling, mainly with gelatin—blue finings are not permitted—and is always filtered. Most plants blend their wines to achieve consistency of style and sell it in bottle—but some is marketed in cask. The product of the state monopolies is generally cheaper than wine made by private firms.

PRODUCTION

In spite of the efforts of the state, output is still small. The habit of wine-drinking is being urged on the people, and as the old religion loses its hold the custom is indeed growing. Yet most Turks would rather eat their grapes—and these grow luxuriantly over most of the country and are cheaper to buy than most other fruits. Annual domestic consumption of wine is reckoned at barely half a liter per head. In 1950 Turkey came fourth among the countries listed by the Office International du Vin for vineyard acreage—but wine production was by no means proportionate.

Tuscany

Region	White Wine Grapes	White Wine Vineyards
Thrace and Marmara	Clairette, Chardonnay, Yapincik Riesling, Sémillon Beylerce Vasilaki	Tekirdag Tekirdag-Canakkale Bilecik Canakkale-Balikesir
Aegean	Sémillon Bornava Misketi	Manisa-Izmir Manisa
Middle Anatolia	Emir Hasandede	Nevsehir-Kayseri-Nigde Ankara
Mediterranean	Dökülgen	Hatay
South & East Anatolia	Dökülgen, Morozkaraso, Rumi Kabarcik	Gaziantep Gaziantep-Urfa

Region	Red Wine Grapes	Red Wine Vineyards
Thrace and Marmara	Pinot Noir, Gamay, Karalâhana, Cinsaut Adakarasi Papazkarasi Kuntra	Tekirdag Balikesir Edirne-Kiklareli Canakkale
Aegean	Carignan, Grenache, Merlot, Alicante-Bouschet Calkarasi Cabernet Sauvignon	Izmir Denizli Manisa-Izmir
Middle Anatolia	Kalecik Karasi Papazkarasi Dimrit	Ankara Eskisehir-Nevsehir Nevsehir-Kayseri
Mediterranean	Sergi Karasi Burdur Dimitiri	Adana-Hatay Isparta-icel-Burdur
South & East Anatolia	Horozkarasi, Sergi Karasi, Oküzkarasi Okuzgozu, Bogazkere	Gaziantep Gaziantep-kilis

About only 3% of the grapes were being diverted to this end. The situation improves slowly: today the Turks keep track of the grape areas and there are some 670,000 hectares, much of which is not only devoted to wine-making but also to table grapes. Production is probably about 340,000 hectoliters (8.9 million U.S. gallons, 7.4 million imp.), though it may vary widely from year to year.

The principal objective of the state wine industry is, naturally, to increase its export trade; 40,000 or so hectoliters (1,060,000 U.S. gallons, 880,000 imp.) are perhaps exported every year. Sweden, purchasing 50% of the exports, is the principal buyer of Turkish wines, followed by Switzerland and West Germany. Before these figures can substantially be improved, the government department concerned is well aware that certain reforms must be made, primarily in standards of viniculture and the selection of grape varieties. In order to encourage halfhearted growers, regulations were at first only leniently enforced; now peasants must be made to learn modern methods of tending their vines and private manufactureres obliged to model themselves on the state monopolies. Moreover, Turkey is growing too many varieties of grapes, and although permissible vines for each region have been listed, standardization has not yet been enforced. Then, phylloxera, which reached Turkey toward the end of the last century, still lingers in some districts: cultivators have not yet mastered as thoroughly as have the *vignerons* of Western Europe the art of grafting their vines onto disease-resistant American root-stocks. Finally, the government is hoping to find domestic substitutes for the corks and wooden staves (for barrels) which are so expensive to import. With so many improvements planned, one may expect that Turkish wine will soon become familiar abroad.

Tuscany

Red and white wines.
District: Central Italy.

Tuscany is the home of Chianti, so famous that it was sometimes mistakenly assumed to be synonymous with Italian wine. It is perhaps superfluous to add that though several oceans of this renowned wine used to spring from elsewhere in Italy (and the world), all true Chianti comes only from Tuscany. And some of it is excellent.

CHIANTI D.O.C.G.

The Chianti Classico district comprises about 70,-000 hectares (175,000 acres) between Florence and Siena and is as steep, rocky, and unpromising a vineyard area as any. Leave Florence by the busy main road and the Porta Romana, pass the quiet, well-tended, American military cemetery, then turn off to the left and find yourself virtually in another world. The hills are bleak, low-lying but steep, peppered with vines, cypresses, and harsh rocks. The road is no longer a highway but a winding, narrow lane where few cars may be seen, only an occasional cart or horse ambling slowly along in the summer heat. Weatherbeaten signposts point the way to the historic but Romana, pass the quiet, well-tended, American military cemetery, then turn off to the left and find yourself virtually in another world. The hills are bleak, low-lying but steep, peppered with vines, cypresses, and harsh rocks. The road is no longer a highway but a winding, narrow lane where few cars may be seen, only an occasional ox cart or horse ambling slowly along in the summer heat. Weatherbeaten signposts point the way to the historic but dusty and deserted-looking centers: Greve, Radda, Castellina, and Gaiole.

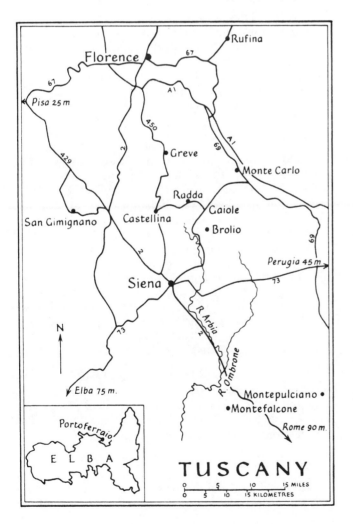

From the tops of the higher hills frown massive fortresses; this is the area which once served as a buffer state between Florence and Siena. The castles were built by the Florentines to stop raiders from Siena; and in 1376 the châtelains combined to form the Chianti League to deal with attackers and hold them off long enough for Florence to arm. The conflicts of bygone times are the province of the historian, but the student of wine can also profit from a glance at this background: it is one of the claims of the area—now known as the Chianti Classico district—to have sole right to the name Chianti. Historically, the Chianti Classico growers say no one else within or without Tuscany is entitled to the name. They reinforce their historical argument by pointing out that geologically the district differs from surrounding areas. The ancient clay-schist soil, the layers of covering flint and limestone, and the thin top of pebbly sand are not duplicated elsewhere. Since soil is an essential—perhaps the most essential—factor in deciding the characteristics of any wine, it follows that nothing grown outside the Chianti Classico district is really Chianti. Logic to the contrary, most Chianti is grown outside.

Perhaps the name is too famous. Perhaps the gay round-bottomed flask—the ubiquitous *fiasco*, now dropped—drew too much attention to it. The fact remains that some 8,000 growers in half a dozen surrounding areas, attracted by the sweet smell of success, began selling their wine as Chianti—admittedly qualifying it by some other term, but calling it Chianti nonetheless. Each area has rightly formed its own *consorzio* to protect the name it has appropriated, and each proclaims, with good reason, its right to go on using that name.

It must be admitted that some of the subsidiary Chiantis are wonderful wines. Chianti Rufina (not Ruffino, which is a trademark) is often considered to be a better balanced wine than the Classico variety, but some of the other offerings are not in the same class. Fortunately, despite the confusion and proliferation of names, real Chianti is available and easily recognizable: the authenticity of any bottle, or *fiasco*, may be verified by checking to see if it has the seal of the Chianti Classico *consorzio* (Consorzio per la Difesa del Vino Tipico di Chianti) portraying a black cockerel on a gold background with a surrounding red circle bearing the name of the organization. The following good wines are allowed the Appellation d'Origine or D.O.C.G.: Chianti Colli Aretini, Chianti Colli Fiorentini, Chianti Colli Senesi, Chianti Colli Pisane, Chianti Montalbano, Chianti Rufina. Chianti Classico, Chianti Ruffina and Colli Fiorentini are obliged to indicate their zone of production on their labels.

Contrary to popular conception, Chianti is apt now to come in a normal tall bottle rather than a *fiasco*—in general, the finest ones are run off in regular bottles, the better to age them. (The straw wrapping of a *fiasco* has been discontinued for reasons of cost—they had a tendency to rot; and furthermore, this expensive style of bottle could not be laid down easily: the cork will not remain in contact with the wine.)

Few Chianti firms put their wine in a *fiasco*, while others confound confusion by using both styles for both qualities. It is an interesting sidelight on the *fiasco* that today it is not as cheap in comparison with a bottle as it was fifty years ago. At that time it was possible to blow the round-bottomed flasks and hire women to weave straw around them for practically nothing. Today labor is more expensive and mass-produced bottles cost less per unit, even if they lack the customer appeal of a *fiasco*. The bulbous *fiasco* is now a thing of the past.

True Chianti, even after years of ageing, is never a very subtle wine. A great part of its charm lies in the heady strength, the sturdy vigor, and slight trace of bitterness—even harshness—which is so characteristic. In the better wines, this bitterness disappears to some extent and the wine mellows and softens; but it never goes entirely away. Some young Chianti may have a prickly, *frizzante*, semi-sparkling bite, caused by adding the fermenting juice of late-maturing grapes to the wine after it is made, and this heightens the refreshing characteristics and adds to its gaiety. This practice, called *governo*, increases the amount of glycerin in the wine, making it more round and supple. Only in the very rarest cases will Chianti be a great wine, but it can almost invariably be counted on to be pleasant.

The wine is traditionally made from five types of grapes used in a set formula. Sangiovese (70% to 90%) is said to impart body and alcoholic content; Canaiolo (50% to 10%) gives bouquet and tempers the hardness; and Trebbiano and Malvasia (50% to 10% combined)—both white grapes—lighten the intensity of the color. Finally, Colorino (about 5%) helps in giving true Chianti its usually bright ruby-red color.

Some large firms have unfortunately set a somewhat low standard of quality in the wines they export. As in most of Italy, the really outstanding wines are made in small quantities, and one is apt to find them only in some Italian hotels or restaurants where the proprietors are willing to pay the price for quality. In such a case it is a pleasure to drink Chianti—which is too often just an ordinary wine in a Chianti bottle.

VIN SANTO (D.O.C. for specific areas only)

The name, it is said, means "wine for the Saints." Fortunately, some is reserved for sinners too, but it is doubtful if it will ever be enough. The real Vin Santo is a semi-sweet golden wine made by farmers in Tuscany—in fact throughout Italy—but never in any quantity. Some firms in and around Florence are beginning to put small amounts on the market, but as yet good ones are rarely sent for export.

Vin Santo is a pleasant dessert wine, albeit one that is not as sweet as most others in this category. It is vinified (in Tuscany, at any rate) from carefully dried Trebbiano and Malvasia grapes—which are dried by suspending them from hooks along the rafters of a loft or attic. The drying takes several months, and at the end about two-thirds of the juice has gone, leaving the rest comparatively rich in sugar. This juice is then pressed and put in small barrels of never more than about 6 hectoliters (150 U.S. gallons, 125 imp.) capacity, which are filled about three-quarters full, then closed and left in a warm place for four years. Heat, as a rule, is death to wine, but in this case a special maderization is wanted; the wine changes in color from white to deep amber and takes on a nutty, almost Sherry-like taste and aroma. At the end of its ageing, it is filtered and is then ready to drink. The grapes are selected more for taste than sugar content and the wine is distinctive—sweet, but the sweetness masked and balanced by its austere, elevated alcoholic content.

OTHER WINES OF TUSCANY

Aleatico di Portoferraio

Sweet red dessert wine from the capital of Elba, the island that was not quite big enough to contain Napoleon. Its Aleatico (made from grapes of that name) is a full, warm, rich wine and one that can be excellent. Its fame, however, seems to be outrunning it, and there are grounds for suspicion today that not all the wine so labeled is what it claims to be.

Elba (D.O.C.)

Two types are produced, a red and a white. The white is a light straw-colored wine made from Trebbiano-Toscano grapes, known locally as Procanico, grown on the Isle of Elba. Italian wine enthusiasts like to compare this to Chablis, but they should not be taken too seriously. The red is deep, dry, ruby wine with a slightly aromatic taste; it comes mostly from Sangiovese, with some Procanico and Canaiolo. The D.O.C. Elba can be applied to white and red naturally sparkling wines. Descriptions that recall Napoleonic times are allowed on the wine labels, provided they had been in use for ten years before July 1967.

Bianco Vergine delle Valdichiana (D.O.C.)

"Virgin white," partly on account of its color, partly since only free-run grape juice is used, not juice extracted in the press. About 11% of alcohol, dry, and pleasantly fresh, in consequence of an acidity slightly higher than is customary in Italy.

Brolio (A Trademark of Ricasoli)

An excellent Chianti Classico named after the huge medieval fortress where the wine is always made by

Barone Ricasoli. The best is never put in *fiasco* and will not always have the name Chianti on the label.

Brunello di Montalcino (D.O.C.G.)

The focus of Italian superior wines is on a beautiful, small, walled town called Montalcino, just south of Siena. The most respected, best-known—and over-priced—winery is Biondi-Santi's "Il Greppo." The Biondi-Santi Brunello, made exclusively from a mutation of the Sangiovese grape, has achieved Italy's highest rating, D.O.C.G. The excessive high price of Biondi-Santi has become a world conversation piece. The wine is hard, very closed in, tannic, and may require decades to mature pleasurably. The 12 hectares of vineyard, planted on the hillsides, produce three different wines: the "Riserva," made on an average every eight years from vines older than 25 years and at least 5 years old; a category called "Annata"; and a third called "Greppo," a *Vino da Tavola*, made from vines under ten years old. Franco Biondi-Santi is the present owner. In contrast to the classic style of Biondi-Santi, Altesino is the champion of the modern, lighter style. This property, now a restored fifteenth-century villa, was purchased in 1970 by a Milanese tycoon, Giulio Consonno, but the winery is run by Claudio Basla and Antonio Cassisi. The D.O.C.G. classification for Brunello makes it mandatory to keep the wines from the Sangiovese grape for four years in casks, which diminishes both freshness and fruit. There is a tendency for a new, lighter, and less expensive style, which, in 1984, was given a D.O.C. rating under the name "Rosso di Montalcino" which requires one year's ageing in wood but must be entirely from the Sangiovese Grosso grape. This tendency towards lightness is also furthered by Angelo Solci, who is Italy's leading exponent of barrique ageing. Other Brunellos are Fattoria dei Barbi; Emilio Costanti; Caparzo; Camigliano; Il Poggione; Argiano; Col d'Orcia, Case Basse, Santa Restituta Grieppone, Capanna, Baricci and Val di Suga. The name of Montalcino is going to be greatly promoted by an investment, claimed to be close to $100,000,000, in a winery in Sant'Angelo Scalo, inaugurated at the end of 1984 by John and Harry Mariani, owners of the American import company Villa Banfi, importers of the best-selling brand Lambrusco. Some 6,000 hectares of different grape varieties have already been planted and more is planned. The wines from this converted Poggio alle Mura's castle, renamed Castello Banfi, and the surrounding vineyards will be Brunello, Chardonnay, Cabernet Sauvignon, and Moscadello. The operation is headed by Ezio Rivella.

Carmagnano (D.O.C.)

An excellent red with some rosés and a fine Vino Santo producer.

Castello di Ama

A Chianti Classico Estate. South of Gaiole, north of Siena, Castello di Ana is becoming a model of excellence, making wines exclusively from 45 hectares of its own vineyards as in the classified growths of the Médoc with equipment which could well be an example for many top Châteaux of Bordeaux.

Lacrima d'Arno (Trademark)

Literally "tear of the Arno River," the wine is a pleasant dry white wine made mostly from the Pinot grape.

Meleto and Castello di Rampolla

Are good Chianti Classicos.

Montecarlo (D.O.C.)

Good red and white wines, delicate and dry, made primarily from Trebbiano and Sangiovese grapes.

Moscadello di Montalcino (D.O.C.)

Tuscan sparkling Muscat wine, but generally closer to *frizzante* (semi-sparkling) than *spumante* (sparkling). It is produced in small quantities by a cooperative cellar.

Vernaccia di San Gimignano (D.O.C.)

White wine from Vernaccia grapes usually vinified to be dry, more rarely sweet. The better-known dry variety is a light amber color with a small bouquet and a slightly bitter aftertaste, and the sweet is still much used as an altar wine—its original purpose.

Vino Nobile di Montepulciano (D.O.C.G.)

A red wine that achieved some literary fame in the eighteenth century when the poet Francesco Redi apostrophized it in his *Bacchus in Tuscany* as *Montepulciano d'ogni vini è il Re* (Montepulciano, of all wines it is king). Perhaps in deference to contemporary republican Italy, the "king" has become something of a commoner. Some 20,000 hectares, or roughly 220,000 cases, are produced annually. Made mostly from the Sangiovese grape by the noble families of Montepulciano, a town 48 kilometers (30 miles) south of Siena, this wine was already exported at the beginning of the fourteenth century. The Italian government recognized its quality by awarding it D.O.C.G. status in 1981. Many excellent wines of Tuscany are not D.O.C.: Tignanello of Antinori from Sangiovese and at least 10% Cabernet Sauvignon and Sassicaia from Cabernet Sauvignon are models of excellent wines that suffer discrimination since the D.O.C. require the exclusive use of the traditional Sangiovese grapes.

U

Ugni Blanc

Widespread vine giving grapes for dry white wine. It is cultivated in southern France—in the region of Cognac (where it is called Saint-Émilion) and elsewhere; also in California and throughout Italy where, under the name Trebbiano, it contributes to most of the better Italian dry white wines.

See Trebbiano; Saint-Émilion.

Ullage

Air space in a bottle or cask between the top and the level of the wine. In bottled wine it is usually brought about by a faulty cork or by overexposure to heat, and the wine should be approached with caution if not suspicion—it may well be bad.

See Ouillage.

Umbria

White and red wines
District: Central Italy

Umbria is halfway between Florence and Rome, crossed by the autostrada del Sole. This region mixes art, Etruscan antiquity and wine and is favored by warm, dry summers and cool, damp winters. Its 12,-000 hectares (30,000 acres) of vineyards produce approximately 1,000,000 hectoliters (26,418,000 U.S. gallons, 21,998,000 imp.) of wine, 50% of which is produced by co-operatives.

The best-known wine of the region is the white *Orvieto* (D.O.C) one of Italy's most consistently delightful wines, some of it semi-sweet, most of it dry. Formerly sweet and often oxidized, its wine-making methods have now transformed Orvieto to a crisp, rather dry, straw-colored white wine, mainly made from the Trebbiano Toscano grapes, averaging 50–60%, with some Verdello, Grechetto, Drupeggio and Malvasia making up the balance. *Orvieto Classico* amounts to approximately one-third of the 90,000 hectoliters (2,376,000 U.S. gallons, 1,980,000 imp.) production. Orvieto is aged in deep cellars dug into tufa rock cliffs.

Colli del Trasimeno (D.O.C.) is the name of white and red wines produced in an area surrounding Lake Trasimeno, near Perugia. The white from Trebbiano, Malvasia, Verdicchio and Grechetto, has a straw-yellow color and a well-balanced taste; the red is from Sangiovese, Ciliegiolo and Gamay and is rather dry and slightly tannic, with a fine scent of violets.

Colli Perugini (D.O.C.) produces red, rosé and white wines on the 1,100 hectares (2,750 acres) planted in Sangiovese and Merlot for red and rosé and Trebbiano Toscano and Grechetto for white.

Sagrantino di Montefalco (D.O.C.) red wine comes from the small area of 155 hectares (387 acres) producing approximately 10,000 hectoliters (264,180 U.S. gallons, 219,980 imp.). The wine is dark and rich-colored, and both sweet or *passito* wines and dry reds are to be found.

Colli Altotiberini: The northern most wine of the region, produced on the foothills of the Apennines. This D.O.C. comes from some 350 hectares (875 acres) producing approximately 25,000 hectoliters (660,450 U.S. gallons, 549,950 imp.) of red and white wine. Trebbiano is the white variety. The reds are produced from the traditional Sangiovese as well as from Merlots.

Torgiano (D.O.C.) wines are red and white. This is a small zone southeast across the Tiber from Perugia. 100,000 hectoliters of the full-bodied red is made with Sangiovese, Cenaiolo and Montepulciano; the white is made from Trebbiano Toscano, Malvasia and Grechetto. Both come from south of Perugia, adjacent to the medieval Turris Janis—the tower of Janus, the two-faced Roman god of doors.

Lungarotti is one of the better Umbrian shippers and sells much of his best under the Rubesco trademark. The Riserva is one of Italy's best red wines.

United Kingdom

Vines are grown in England and wine made commercially—still on a limited scale, although cultivation has developed considerably in the past ten years. Some 480 hectares (1,200 acres) were under vine in 1986, and over 270 growers were selling their wine. The late Jack Ward and his partner Ian Howie of the Merrydown Company established a cooperative with very up-to-date machinery, to which about 30 proprietors send their grapes for pressing; others have their own wine sheds. There are also a fair number of private vineyards, as there once were, cultivated as a hobby, on country estates in the eighteenth and nineteenth centuries. The last of these estates was at Castle Coch, Glamorgan, the property of the Marquess of Bute, which was abandoned during the First World War.

In Norman and early medieval times, the English produced much of their own wine. According to the Venerable Bede, vineyards already existed in his time (*c.* A.D. 730); and one of the laws of Alfred the Great (849–901) decreed that growers should be compensated for damage to their vines. After the Norman Conquest, wine-making naturally spread, especially in the monasteries; vineyards were recorded in the west and south of England; in Wales, Essex, and Suffolk; and later as far north as Lincolnshire and York. But in the mid-fourteenth century, cultivation declined (though it did not cease altogether), mainly because so much wine was coming in from the Continent—especially from Plantagenet possessions in Gascony—that it was easier to import than to grow.

After the Second World War a new interest in wine-making developed, and vineyards were planted in Lincolnshire, East Anglia, southern England, and a few in Wales. Among growers successfully producing and selling English wine have been Mr. and Mrs. Goddard at Barton Manor and the late Sir Guy Salisbury-Jones, who pioneered the vineyard revival at Hambledon, Hampshire. Other well-known names are Mr. Nigel Godden, Pilton Manor, Somerset; Lady Montagu at Beaulieu; Mr. and Mrs. J. G. Barrett, Felsted, Essex; Major Colin Gillespie of Wooton, Somerset, and Mr. Kenneth Barlow, at Adgestone Vineyard on the Isle of Wight. In 1967 the English Vineyards Association was founded for the encouragement of viticulture.

Particularly encouraging to present-day growers in what was once considered an unfavorable climate is the progress of new and more adaptable vine species. A little poor red wine is made from Pinot Noir; but here, as in Germany, the climate is more suitable for white wines. Müller-Thurgau is the grape most widely used. There is still some Seyve-Villard, but this is losing ground, and people are beginning to plant more Seyval Blanc, Triomphe d'Alsace, Chardonnay, Pinot Blanc, with some Huxelrebe, Reichensteiner, Madeleine Angevine, Schonburger, Ortega, Kerner and other German varieties. Many of the vines are trained by the *guyot* method; some by the *gobelet*. Most seasons see a reasonably satisfactory harvest of English wines. Among the more notable vineyards, most of which are in the southern counties and in East Anglia, are Lamberhurst in Kent, owned by Kenneth McAlpine; Richard Barnes Biddenden and Carr Taylor in Sussex. Gay Biddlecombe markets her St. Georges wines also from Sussex. Away from the southeast are: Tom Day of the Three Choirs Vineyard in Gloucestershire and Richard Bache from Astley in the Severn Valley.

The term British wine, as distinct from English wine, is used for certain strong, cheap, fortified mixtures of imported grape concentrate fermented in Britain, resulting in recognizable but uninspiring sweetish wines.

See also English wine; Whisky, Scotch.

United States

The United States has become one of the leading wine-producing countries of the world, ranking sixth in quantity. The American wine industry is 400 years old and despite the setback it suffered from National Prohibition, which ended in 1933, 44 of the 50 states are producing wine in some capacity. California alone is now producing more wine than Bordeaux and Burgundy together.

WINE HISTORY

The Vikings are said to have made the first trip from Europe to the New World. What they saw, apparently, was vines, for they named the new country Vineland. The first wines were reputed to have been made in 1562 by the French Huguenots from Scuppernong grapes near Jacksonville, Florida, although some say the first were made on Parris Island, S.C., in 1570, from *Vitis aestivalis*. Early settlers were inspired by the prospect of making wine in their new territory. The Jamestown colonists in Jamestown, Virginia, made wine about 1609, and Pilgrims from the *Mayflower* probably drank their own homemade wine at the first Thanksgiving in 1623.

The first wines were produced from wild grapes, and were drastically different from the wines the settlers had been weaned on in Europe. European vines were imported by many, including Thomas Jefferson and Lord Baltimore, but they died speedily from diseases, insects, and inclement weather. The first grape that met with some success both in the vineyard and in the wineglass was the Alexander, an accidental cross between a native American and a European vine. It was named for its discoverer, John Alexander, the gardener of William Penn.

In 1600, Franciscan monks brought wine-making for sacramental purposes from Mexico to New Mexico, and eventually to California. Before long, wine was being made in more than a dozen other states.

The first known commercial winery, the Pennsylvania Vine Co., Ltd., of Spring Mill, Pa., opened in 1793 near Philadelphia, and made wine from the Alexander grape. However, it is probable that wine was produced commercially before the advent of the Pennsylvania Vine Co. Through the decades commercial wine-making was centered in Ohio, Missouri, and New York.

In California, growers began importing quality *vinifera* grapevines from Europe, and with the transcontinental railroad, California became a major factor in eastern markets. As the waves of European immigrants arrived, the market for wine grew rapidly, as did the number of wineries.

By the 1860s phylloxera, a burrowing plant louse fatal to the vine, began to spread through the vineyards of California as well as Europe, and breeders on both continents began feverish work to develop resistant species before the vineyards could be decimated. In 1880 the University of California at Davis established its viticulture and oenology department, in part to solve the phylloxera problem. By 1900 the technique of grafting *vinifera* vines to resistant root stocks was perfected, and American wines started winning medals in European competitions.

But a far more dangerous scourge was threatening American wine-making. Gradually the Prohibitionist movement was spreading from state to state, and by 1920, when the U.S. Congress passed the Volstead Act and the 18th Amendment prohibiting the manufacture and consumption of alcoholic beverages nationally, more than 30 states had already passed local Prohibition.

About 100 wineries managed to survive the 13 years of the "Noble Experiment" by making "sacramental wines," "medicinal wines," juice, and concentrate.

Although Prohibition decimated the American wine industry, it was a boon for vineyardists, as juice, concentrate, and fresh grapes for home wine-making increased grape prices considerably. It probably also established the peculiar American tradition of "the quick shot," a furtive drink of high-alcoholic beverages consumed with illicit pleasure behind closed doors.

The 18th Amendment was repealed on December 5, 1933, and more than 1,000 wineries sprang up in the next year. Americans toasted Repeal with the latest vintage, scarcely three months old, and the taste of this hastily produced toast probably turned many Americans against wine for life.

For the next three decades, wine remained mainly the domain of the snob and the wino. Snobs wrote about the rules for wine-drinking, and winos drank cheap high-alcohol "ports" and muscatels for effect rather than taste.

Nonetheless, it was in this period that the seeds of the American wine boom were sown. New viticultural areas were discovered in California, as vines found their way into virtually every valley.

In 1935 a Baltimore newspaper editor and home wine-maker, Philip Wagner, imported French-American hybrids, and began persuading vine-growers throughout the East to rip out their *labruscas* and plant his hybrids.

During World War II, some American soldiers stationed in Europe were exposed to the civilized practice of drinking wine with meals. They returned home having acquired the wine-drinking custom and gave a boost to American wineries.

At the beginning of the war, Frank Schoonmaker, an importer, began spreading the gospel east of the Rockies. Schoonmaker and I were responsible for encouraging the practice of naming American wines after the county and the grape variety from which they were made. "Varietal" labeling has since become the predominant method of naming American wines.

In the 1950s both the University of California at Davis and Cornell University began graduating viticulturalists, chemists, and wine-makers with state-of-the-art technical training.

In 1957 Charles Fournier and Konstantin Frank produced their first wines from *vinifera* grapes at Gold Seal Winery in the New York Finger Lakes region, and over the next few years proved conclusively that *vinifera* could grow and make good wine in New York and other eastern states if carefully matched to site, soil, and root stock.

With the jet age came transcontinental flight, and Americans traveling to Europe were exposed to wine with food.

RECENT DEVELOPMENTS

In 1968, table wine, for the first time since Prohibition, became more popular in the U.S. than the high-alcohol "ports," "sherries," and muscatels, signaling the onset of the wine boom.

Over the next decade, more than a dozen states passed "Farm Winery" laws encouraging grape farmers to make wine from locally grown grapes, and the number of wineries in the U.S. grew from about 400 in 1968 to about 1,000 in 1983.

In 1976, America celebrated its bicentennial, and amid the patriotic resurgence came news from Paris of a tasting staged by a prominent wine merchant at which California Chardonnays and Cabernet Sauvignons had been pitted against French white Burgundies and red Bordeaux; with French experts doing the balloting, the California entries had won, though barely. All of a sudden, California wines became the vogue in the U.S., and by 1980 American consumption of wine had, for the first time, surpassed that of whiskey.

The American wine boom is by now an established fact. The burgeoning American interest in drinking and discussing fine local wines has led to a dramatic growth in the domestic wine industry. Adult per capita consumption, 3.3 gallons in 1982, has grown steadily. This increase in wine-making has affected all levels of the market, from the simplest jug wines to the finest varietals. Fine-quality wines were given a particular boost by the increase in prices among fine French wines in 1973 and 1974. Before the value of the dollar soared in 1982, and French and other imported wines were offered in the United States at less attractive prices, American consumers increasingly turned their backs on European wines, and began to investigate and boost their own top varietals.

A diverse group of individualists from all walks of life, drawn by visions of profit in some cases, but in many instances by the romance of wine, greatly contributed to the formation of many of the new wineries established in the seventies. Doctors, architects, engineers, industrialists, airline pilots, advertising executives, as individuals and as groups of investors, cleared land, planted vines, built vat rooms, and began to make wine. Their energy and dedication, along with American wine-drinkers' great curiosity and receptivity to new wines, spearheaded a general overall improvement in American wines. The largest wineries, such as Gallo, Almadén, and Paul Masson, which had previously specialized in brand-name jug wines and generics, placed more and more emphasis on varietals in their product lines. In 1976 Coca-Cola of Atlanta bought several wineries, but less than ten years later sold them to Seagrams, which, in turn, sold most of them shortly afterwards to Vintners International.

The American wine industry is still feeling the effect of this sudden infusion of new blood and new talent as well as the investments of Europeans in California, New Mexico, Texas, and Virginia. It will be a while before the long-range results are clear.

The diversity of background, training, and temperament of the new wine-makers has led to a period of experimentation in wine-making and vine-tending methods. The decade of the seventies will be remembered as the period of great American oenological creativity, when new and often daring attempts were made to match grape varieties (and their clones and hybrids) with the vicissitudes of climate and soil that had never before been exploited for vine-growing and wine-making.

Some of the results were highly fruitful, and the full benefits will take years to assess. Clones were selected and developed out of an urgent need to find slower-ripening vines in the California heat. Others were found to ripen rapidly in the cold New York climate. Highly sophisticated methods for controlling fermentation came into use. In other instances, these advanced techniques proved to be blind alleys—nothing more than tinkering for its own sake, producing rather eccentric wines of limited appeal: late-harvest Chardonnays and Zinfandels, and inky, concentrated, 100% Cabernet Sauvignons.

With the dramatic increase in demand for wine, there arose a certain tendency for growers and wineries in California to plant varietals in unsuitable soils without the patient experimentation needed to obtain the best match of grape variety, soil, general temperature zone, and specific microclimate. In the East, there was timidity and fear about planting fine wine varieties whose yields and hardiness were less than ideal.

These mistakes and excesses are insignificant when compared with the pioneering strides the American wine industry made in the 1970s and 1980s. In efforts to understand and master practices in viticulture and oenology, certain winery owners and their wine-makers explored and exploited these techniques to their fullest extent, occasionally to the detriment of the wines being made.

Once the techniques were mastered, wine-makers moved ahead to explore other advances in oenology. Cool, slow fermentation temperatures became cooler than ever; carbonic maceration (a fermentation technique; q.v.) was employed more intensively and on more grape varieties than was beneficial to the wine concerned; a vogue for the late-harvest wines and botrytised wines (see Botrytis cinerea) resulted in wines that were more curious than palatable; overly long barrel-ageing occasionally left wines excessively woody and unbalanced.

The coming years will show that these excesses have been minor, the small price paid by a nation and a people in a hurry to produce the best wines possible. Problems susceptible to straightforward technological solutions have been the easiest to solve. For this reason, white wines (by nature less complex and more dependent on enlightened vat-room technique than red wines), and particularly the Chardonnays, have reached a relatively higher level of quality than that achieved so far by most of the reds.

The problems that face wine-making in America will be solved only by patient experimentation in the future. A chronic problem among the finest red and white wines is that the California climate is too sunny and clement, ripening grapes too quickly for them to attain the complex secondary aromatic elements that distinguish the great wines from the merely good. More often than not, sugar levels in the grapes push the alcohol level in the wines beyond 13 and 14%, which is too much for the proper balance if freshness and finesse are to be achieved. Only trial and error in the selection of varietal clones and different microclimates within the proper temperature zones will solve this problem.

Most of the other states are plagued by hobbyists and farmers turned wine-makers with little experience or skill, trying to produce wines in difficult climates, soils, and markets. Beyond perfecting vineyard practices and wine-making techniques lies the equally important and all-too-often-underplayed task of properly marketing the vast amount of new American wines. In the early 1980s, as European prices declined and the U.S. dollar became stronger, American wines found themselves overpriced. As the novelty of the wine revolution continues to wear off and a more competitive market becomes a reality, bankruptcies and mergers are becoming more common, most notably perhaps among the newer wineries. Those wineries with solid financial backing and aggressive, well-planned marketing and pricing programs are the ones most likely to weather economic hardships and increased competition both domestically and from overseas.

Label Laws

As this new generation of American wine enthusiasts comes of age, the other remaining task is to standardize and codify American wine laws, and to name American wines only by American names. The BATF (Bureau of Alcohol, Tobacco and Firearms), a division of the United States Treasury Department, is only in the beginning stages of developing a label-and-appellation system suited to American business conditions and viticultural climates. Once this has been accomplished, American wines will have declared themselves a full-fledged force in the world of wine.

For the past 30 years, most U.S. table wines have

been named after the grape from which the majority of the wine was made. If 51% of the wine was made from Chardonnay, the wine could be called Chardonnay. Other than state and county boundary names, there were no controlled appellations.

In the 1970s the BATF began the process of upgrading these outdated laws. A new set of laws was passed in 1978, and took effect on January 1, 1983. The new label laws state that in order to bear a varietal name, the wine must now contain at least 75% of the named varietal, with the exception of *labrusca* varieties because their flavor is so strong that its character is obvious if only present in 51% of the wine.

The term "estate bottled" has been legally defined for the first time to mean that the wine was made by the winery owning or controlling the vineyards.

"Viticultural areas" are being established as appellations with similar geographic and climatic conditions, as defined by the BATF. Wines labeled with the name of an approved viticultural area must be made from grapes that are at least 85% from that area. Numerous viticultural areas have already been defined, including Napa Valley and Finger Lakes, and more are on the way.

On January 9, 1987, regulations concerning sulfites in wine took effect. Wines containing more than 10 parts per million (ppm) of sulfite must have "Contains Sulfites" or a similar statement on the label in a conspicuous typeface. If they wish, wineries may state the exact content in parts per million and may also list the specific agent, e.g. potassium bisulfite. This information protects the consumer allergic to sulfites.

The new labeling regulations are a giant step forward, but leave plenty of room for improvement. Under the new laws, it is possible for wine labeled Chardonnay to be blended with 25% Thompson Seedless, Concord, or other common cheap grapes. The viticultural area definitions are broad. For example, Napa Valley includes grapes grown in nearby Pope Valley, and on the mountains surrounding the valley. In addition, the BATF has not defined important label terms such as "made" or "produced." A winery can now buy wine that has been grown, crushed, fermented, and aged at another winery, blend and bottle the wine in their own facilities, and state on the label that they "made" or "produced" the wine.

Unfortunately, it is still legal for American wineries to name their blends after European place names, although the trend among small wineries is to abandon this practice. The continued production of innocuous wines named "chablis," "sauternes," "champagne," "burgundy," "rhine," "sherry," "port," and "madeira" is deplorable.

These new laws are now being challenged in the courts, and it is to be hoped that within a short time, the loopholes will be repaired and the U.S. will adopt meaningful laws that protect producers as well as consumers.

WINE GRAPES OF THE UNITED STATES

Wines in the U.S. are produced from four species for the most part: *Vitis vinifera, Vitis labrusca,* "French-American" hybrids, and *Vitis muscadinae.* States west of the Rocky Mountains, including California, employ *Vitis vinifera* and *vinifera-vinifera* crosses almost exclusively. Most states east of the Rockies also grow *vinifera,* but the most populous grape species is by far *Vitis labrusca.* In the South *Vitis muscadinae* are widespread.

(1) Vitis vinifera

Most of the *Vitis vinifera* varieties grown in the U.S. are clones directly descended from the European vineyards, and are basically the same varieties used throughout Europe. *Vitis viniferas* are the species responsible for the greatest wines of the U.S. and, for that matter, the world. Most *viniferas* in the U.S. are grafted onto phylloxera-resistant rootstocks, such as SO4, Rupestris St. George, and 5BB.

Leading Red Wine Grapes

Cabernet Sauvignon. Of the large number of red wine grape varieties, very few have been recommended for planting in California. Of those that have passed rigorous tests, the Cabernet Sauvignon is still the most valuable: it is the best adapted to the cooler parts of the coastal valleys and usually ripens about mid-season; it matures more slowly than the same variety in the Bordeaux region and produces a fuller, heavier wine. In California, the Cabernet frequently lacks bouquet and finesse but has produced, in limited quantities, some remarkably great wines which can compare with some of the better red wines anywhere in the world. The Cabernet Sauvignon from northern California has outproduced in terms of quality some of the best red wines of Italy, Spain, and Portugal and attains an even fuller wine than those made from the same variety in Chile. In the suitable coastal regions it gives a wine of pronounced varietal flavor and bouquet, high acidity, and good color, holding its own with some of the better Bordeaux. Cabernet Sauvignon attains its highest quality after ageing; but only recently have most Californian growers come to realize that their table wines improve with bottle age—and so more matured Cabernet Sauvignons are now appearing on the market. As the price goes up, the value goes down. As stated before, as of 1983 varietal wines can bear the name of a grape on the label provided that the wine is made a minimum 75% of that particular variety. Producers of better varietal wines use a greater percentage of the specified grape, usually 65% to 100% and, as in France, the rest of a blend is a combination of complementary grapes such as Merlot, Malbec, or Cabernet Franc. A 100% Cabernet Sauvignon wine would be an oddity in Bordeaux; and

75%—such as at Château Mouton-Rothschild—is considered very high.

Cabernet Sauvignon is showing promise in Washington, Oregon, Arkansas, Long Island, and Maryland.

Pinot Noir. The outstanding red grape of Burgundy and major grape in the making of Champagne. In California, the Pinot Noir has the reputation of being a difficult varietal. It ripens early and is not always easy in fermentation and ageing. Though some very good wines have been made, they have not yet threatened the supremacy of the better Burgundies. Research on clonal variants better adapted to California conditions has brought some improvement. On the whole, they tend to be lightish, little suited to long ageing. The better California Pinot Noirs come from the cooler climates of southern Napa, Sonoma, Monterey, Mendocino, and Lake counties.

Pinot Noir has shown perhaps its greatest promise in the Willamette Valley of Oregon.

Gamay and Gamay Beaujolais. The first, confusingly, is either the true Gamay of the Beaujolais region of France or Valdeguie; when grown in the Napa Valley it goes by the name of Napa Gamay. The Gamay Beaujolais is not a true Gamay, but a clonal variant of the Pinot Noir, which may in fact be sold as a Pinot Noir if the winery so chooses. The U.S. government is working to identify these grapes and clear up the name confusion. Though made from genetically distinct grapes, wines sold as Gamay (or Napa Gamay) and Gamay Beaujolais will be similarly light, fruity wines, successfully trading on the Beaujolais image of being short-vatted and easy drinking. They are generally low in tannin and high in grape-y aroma. In the parts of the Napa Valley where the late-ripening variety of the Gamay (the Napa Gamay) is produced, it differs from the Gamay Beaujolais in flavor and aroma. The Napa Gamay is also known by its French name, Gamay Noir.

Grenache. The Grenache is a good producer, strong and resistant to disease—a much-sought-after variety. The grape, which is successful in the making of Tavel rosé in the Rhône Valley, is often used for rosés in California also, because of its pinkish color. The Grenache Rosé from the Almadén Vineyards in the Santa Clara Valley was the first and most popular of its kind.

Barbera. In Italy, Barbera at its best is sometimes likened to the Nebbiolo and ages almost as well; in California, it is a high-acid variety of only average vigor and production. Blending is not recommended, but with ageing and special care Barbera may yet yield a wine comparable with some of those in Piedmont. It does best in the coastal valley of California and the intermediate Central Valley region, where it produces a full-bodied, honest wine.

Zinfandel. This is the most widely planted good red-grape variety in California; its exact origin is unknown, although evidence is building to support a theory that it is the same grape as Italy's Primativo grape. It is not grown extensively in any other country or state. It is subject to mildew, and any excessive humidity or irrigation may lead to rotting; generally it is harvested early and finds a growing place in practically all the regions of California, although the best dry wines of this variety are made in the cooler areas. Zinfandel, a very productive variety, produces some pleasant, straightforward wines, and its multiple appeal of bouquet, good color, and wholesome aroma and flavor account for its popularity. A well-made Zinfandel from a good winery is superior to many of the Cabernet Sauvignons found on the market today. This grape variety needs greater recognition and respect than it now has outside California. A red, a white, and a rosé wine can be made from the Zinfandel. This varietal is taking its well-deserved place as the pride of California.

Ruby Cabernet. This is a new hybrid developed by Dr. Olmo of the California Agricultural Experimental Station in Davis. It is a good producer with color and a high acid content, and is found primarily in California.

Grignolino. This grape is one of the several Californian varieties which are native to Piedmont in Italy. It produces a highly characteristic wine ranging from orange-pink to orange-red in color, and it is sometimes bottled as a natural rosé. Grignolino has a unique aroma and an exceptionally high acid content and should be aged several years. There are now only 52 acres in the state of California.

Less Important Red Wine Grapes

Some of the other red wine varieties that produce heavily but are not fine grapes are Alicante-Bouschet, Carignane, Petite-Sirah, and Rubired. The Alicante-Bouschet is a large producer of common wine; unfortunately, too much is still grown in California and finds its way into the so-called burgundies, clarets, and chiantis of the middle and southern regions. Carignane, which is not bad in a good soil, is heavily produced in the warmer regions and often used in blending. Petite-Sirah, a superior variety, is favored in Napa as well as in Sonoma, Monterey, Kern, and San Joaquin counties.

Leading White Wine Grapes

Chardonnay. This is not a large producer generally; it is the grape of French Chablis and other white Burgundies—among them, Meursault and Montrachet. The Chardonnay has all the virtues needed to produce good wine. It ripens well, particularly in the cooler regions, and attains an excellent balance of sugar and acid. Because it adapts itself so well in the cooler parts of Napa, San Benito, Sonoma, Mendocino, and Monterey, it makes the finest white wines of California. The cultivation of the Chardonnay is not an easy task, but the results seem to be worth the trouble. It produced a blander wine in California by not having the richness it has in France. This grape variety has produced the best white wines in the United States, and one hopes that in the eighties it will become more of a food wine, lighter in alcoholic strength, less intense in extracts, and a little more fruity and subtle. Some of the big Chardonnays of California are very fine indeed, but just like the Montrachets, they cannot be drunk every day. The Chardonnays at 14% or over in alcohol by volume will serve to create impact and admiration, but the cooler areas for new Chardonnay plantings will be the trend of the 1980s.

In New York, Pennsylvania, Ohio, Michigan, Virginia, Maryland, Washington, Oregon, and Idaho, Chardonnay also produces superior wines as winemakers in each area experiment with different styles.

Sauvignon Blanc. This is the principal grape variety used in the production of the white Graves of France, and is often called Fumé Blanc throughout California. It is used extensively in France for Pouilly-Fumé and Sancerre. In California, this variety thrives particularly well in the coastal regions. As in the French Sauternes, the Sauvignon Blanc is sometimes blended with Sémillon—plus Muscadelle of Bordelais—to produce a California-type "sauterne." The variety is finding its way alone into bottles from small wineries as good-quality dry wine.

It has also been successful on Long Island, in Maryland, and in Arkansas.

The Sauvignon Blanc should not be confused with the Sauvignon Vert.

Sémillon. This is another variety best suited to the California North coastal region. During the late seventies, *botrytis* vinification suddenly became a winemaker's fad. (This applies, with the possible exception of Phelps and Chateau St. Jean, to Riesling and Gewürztraminer grapes as well.) The expensive and laborious process is not justified when the wines are compared to fine Barsacs, Sauternes, and Anjous of France, and Trockenbeerenauslesen wines of Germany. (This is an excellent reason why wines made with Sémillon from California should not be called sauternes. Sémillon is one of the world's finest grapes and is quite capable of making an original dry or sweet wine in California.)

Pinot Blanc. Evidence is growing that what is called "Pinot Blanc" in California may actually be the Melon grape of Muscadet. It has a good quality, and is a strong, disease-resistant grape with a distinction of its own. Its productivity is rather higher than that of the Pinot Chardonnay, but it rarely exceeds 3 short tons (2.68 long tons) per acre. The Pinot Blanc has often been confused with the Chardonnay, but experts consider the Chardonnay an entirely different variety and not a true Pinot at all. Tests have shown that the Pinot Blanc is beginning to do well in the slightly warmer regions as well as in the cooler districts.

Chenin Blanc. The Chenin Blanc produces and adapts well to regions varying from slightly cool to warm. In France this variety, known as Pineau de la Loire as well as Chenin Blanc, produces delightful white wines of which Vouvray and Saumur are the most familiar. It is above average in quality but lacks the distinction of Pinot Blanc. Chenin Blanc is versatile, since it sometimes produces a fresh, light, fruity wine, slightly sparkling, and at other times it is apt to make a much sweeter wine, according to the whim of the vintner. The Chenin Blanc, as it is commonly called in California, has become quite popular in the past few years. It is now one of the most widely planted better white wine grapes.

Riesling. The Riesling, or White Riesling, or Johannisberg Riesling, is responsible for the outstanding reputation of all the famous wines of the Rhine and Mosel valleys as well as most of the fine Alsatian wines. It performs at its best under relatively cool conditions, which California's somewhat Mediterranean climate cannot quite give. The Riesling is one of the finest grape varieties in the world and produces throughout Europe (except in the Mediterranean region) a wine of excellent quality. The cooler parts of California produce a wine above average but lacking the balance and delicacy of the Riesling wines of Europe. In the North Coast region of California, it is a large producer and ripens late in the season.

America's best Rieslings are currently being produced in the cooler climates of New York, Virginia, Ohio, Pennsylvania, Michigan, Washington, and Oregon. There they produce wines with the applelike crispness often found in German Rieslings. New York's Seneca Lake seems especially promising.

Sylvaner. In California this variety is also known as the Franken Riesling. In the valleys of the Rhine and the Mosel, and in Alsace, it is grown only where the Riesling does not produce well. Its wine is generally of good character and balance and above average in California where it does better than the Riesling (Johannisberg Riesling) when planted in a slightly cool to warm district. Sylvaner is a delicate, early-maturing grape with a certain distinction of character and a good balance of sugar and acid. Light and dry, the wine is usually drunk when it is quite young.

Gewürztraminer. The "Red" Traminer is often favorably compared to the very best Rieslings when grown in the better parts of Alsace and the Jura Mountains in France. In the cooler parts of California it produces a wine with a distinctive strong, spicy aroma and character. It is also called the Red Traminer because of the red blush of the ripening grape. The Krug Winery of St. Helena in Napa Valley produces a small quantity of good Traminer wine. It has an unmistakable bouquet and spiciness. Stony Hill, Château St. Jean, and Hacienda also make good-quality Gewürztraminers. Gewürztraminer produces excellent results near Paso Robles and San Luis Obispo.

In Washington and New York, Gewürztraminer tends to produce more delicate and balanced wines, but its prospects in New York have been diminished by its winter tenderness.

Less Important White Wine Grapes

Some of the other dry white wine grape varieties, some of which are widely produced but lacking in distinction, are the French Colombard, Folle Blanche, Burger, Sauvignon Vert, and Green Hungarian.

The Burger is extensively planted in California, chiefly for its high production and a supposedly neutral character which allows it to "stretch" other wines of superior quality. The Sauvignon Vert, another coarse, heavy grape, is occasionally substituted in blending for the Sauvignon Blanc. The Sauvignon Vert is sometimes called Colombard in Europe, which should not be confused with the French Colombard, a vigorous, highly productive grape of high acid content used for blending in the Chablis-type and Rhine-type of Californian wines. Sauvignon Vert, French Colombard, Burger, and Folle Blanche are favorably grown in the warmer inland valley regions.

Crosses

About 30,000 acres (12,150 hectares) are now planted in crosses, and these grapes represent an important aspect of future wine production in California and eastern U.S. In accepting the American Oenologists' Society Award of Merit in 1973, Dr. Olmo of the Davis school declared: "There is great need for California to make wines that are uniquely Californian in origin. We cannot hope to duplicate the famous wines of other countries merely because we have imported their varieties and use their winemaking methods. Our soils and our climatic areas are not the same. But we can and should produce wines that are as good as those produced elsewhere—by the creation of new varieties that will give a product of high quality with genuine distinctness of type. The first step is to eliminate some of the defects of varieties that we already have. In the future we should not have to rely on varieties that were selected by the French, or the Germans, or the Italians, and have been found by centuries of experience to be suitable in certain regions. Their regions are not ours, and rather than imitate their types, the time will come to build our industry on varieties developed in and bred for California localities."

Two of the more important crosses developed at the University of California at Davis have been the white wine grape Emerald Riesling and the red Ruby Cabernet. At least three other promising crosses have been successfully grown—Rubired, Royalty, and the newest, a wine grape named Carnelian. The Ruby Cabernet is a cross between Cabernet Sauvignon and the tremendously productive Carignane. It produces well and tolerates warmer climates. The grape has some of the characteristics of Cabernet Sauvignon, although the wine will never achieve its status or distinction. The Emerald Riesling, a cross between the White or Johannisberg Riesling and the Muscadelle de Bordelais, yields a white table wine with some of the Riesling characteristics. Another hope for future sound

wines is Professor Olmo's newest hybrid, the Carnelian. This cross of the Cabernet Sauvignon, Carignane, and Grenache produced a grape which gives high yields, makes reasonable wine, and grows well in warmer regions. Carnelian may yield as many as 11 tons to the acre (about 180 hectoliters per hectare). Wines produced from it have been medium-red in color, and light in body with good balance; they can be enjoyed young but mature well. Rubired and Royalty resulted from the need for grapes with good color and acidity and the ability to resist powdery mildew. A nineteenth-century cross called Alicante Gazin was crossed with the Port grape Tinta Cão; the result was the Rubired. Rubired crossed with a little-known plant called Trousseau produced Royalty. Both were introduced in 1964. Of all the California crosses, Emerald Riesling and Ruby Cabernet are the most successful.

(2) Vitis labrusca

The wild grapes found by the Vikings when they named the new world Vineland were probably *Vitis riparia, Vitis rupestris,* and *Vitis labrusca.* Of the three, *labruscas* made the most satisfactory wines when the European *Vitis vinifera* varieties failed to grow because of an unfavorable mixture of phylloxera, viruses, molds, mildews, and inappropriate climates. The *labruscas*, also called "native" or "American" varieties, are generally winter-hardy, long-lived vines that bear great quantities of large thick-skinned grapes in loose bunches. The wines are intensely flavorful and easily identified by the distinctive flavor that is derived from several unique flavor components, especially methyl anthranilate. This taste is commonly called "foxy," a term whose origin is still debated, but was probably derived from the Fox grape, a popular early *labrusca.* Because the taste of these grapes is so intense, most *labruscas* are picked early, before too much flavor develops. Because of their low sugar and high acidity, most *labruscas* are ameliorated (diluted with water), blended with hybrids or California wine, or heavily sweetened to make them palatable.

Labruscas such as Concord and Niagara are used widely to make unfermented grape juice, jellies, soft drinks, and candies in North America, and are rarely found in Europe except in some parts of Italy. Scientists have found several ways to strip some of the foxy flavor from some *labruscas,* but in most cases some of the "jelly" flavor persists.

Labruscas still account for the vast majority of the acreage east of the Rocky Mountains, although the French-American hybrids and *viniferas* are steadily gaining in utilization by wineries. The varieties that tend to make the best wines are Delaware, Dutchess, Isabella, and Niagara, all *labrusca* crosses.

Catawba

A red grape that is usually used in making simple, sweet white, pink, red, and sparkling wines. For years

Catawba was the foundation of eastern sparkling wines, but is fading from prominence as the move to upgrade continues.

Concord

The most widely planted red grape of the eastern U.S. Actually blue-black in color, Concord is hardy, productive, and adaptable to a variety of soils and climates. It is thick-skinned and produces red, white, and rosé wines that are simple, sweet, and strong, with a pronounced foxy aroma and taste. Its use in table wine has diminished considerably in recent years, although it is still a staple in eastern "ports" and "sherries."

Delaware

A dependable native American grape that produces both still and sparkling white wines which are soft and pleasant, and display a foxy quality not as pronounced as Concord or Catawba. Named after the Delaware River, beside which the grape was discovered.

Diamond (Moore's Diamond)

One of the better-producing native varieties, it makes a sound, simple, dry white wine with only a slight foxy taste.

Diana

This early American hybrid was an attempt to improve the Catawba grape. Somewhat inconsistent in production, it nevertheless makes a simple, sound white wine with a distinct foxy flavor.

Dutchess

A late-ripening and somewhat disease-sensitive American hybrid developed in Dutchess County, New York, during the mid-nineteenth century. It gives light, fruity, dry white wines that are not extremely foxy.

Elvira

Vigorous, winter-hardy, and disease-resistant American hybrid grape developed in the late nineteenth century in Missouri. It is picked early and used mostly for blending.

Isabella

An old, winter-sensitive, red-black native American grape used mostly in blending for sparkling wines and for rosé.

Ives

Hardy and vigorous if grown in the proper setting, this tough-skinned grape is often used for its dark color, and yields a strong foxy red wine. A shy bearer, it is not being planted much anymore.

Niagara

Niagara is used for table grapes and to produce a wide range of fruity, intensely foxy white wines, among the best balanced and most popular *labruscas*. The recent trend, admirably, has been to lighter, less sweet Niagaras, and sparkling Niagaras. Acreage has increased dramatically, partly due to its popularity as a juice grape.

Noah

An American hybrid first recorded in Illinois, this hardy, green grape produces a white wine that is sometimes used to blend in sparkling wines. Helpful after the phylloxera disaster, new plantings of the Noah are prohibited in France, but it still is found in other European countries. There are only five U.S. wineries making varietal Noah, and one plans to discontinue the wine soon.

(3) French-American hybrids

Always seeking to improve the raw material of winemaking and develop varieties suited to specific climates and soils, grape breeders have been crossing species and varieties for about two centuries. The need for hybrids became acute with the phylloxera epidemic in the late decades of the 19th century. French and American breeders began crossing between *vinifera* and native American species and seeking a hybrid that makes wine as good as the former from vines resistant to pests and as hardy as the latter. At first the hybrids were designated by numbers, but in recent years they have been given names that are in wide use. The hybrids are often called "direct producers" because they do not have to be grafted onto phylloxera-resistant root stocks. Even so, some growers still prefer to graft these vines to roots especially suited to their soil and climate.

The white hybrids tend to be better than the reds, and some, such as Seyval Blanc, Vignoles, Vidal Blanc, Cayuga White produce wines as good as *viniferas* when properly made.

Chemically, red hybrids have a slightly different pigment structure than *viniferas*, and taste distinctly different from the popular *viniferas*. They do not, however, taste foxy, unless they are blended with *labruscas* or aged in vats that have held *labrusca*. Most red hybrids make their best wine when picked at low sugars, chaptalized, and blended for complexity. The best seem to be Baco Noir, Chancellor, and Léon Millot, although they are still no competition to *vinifera* yet.

The most famous of the hybridizers were Baco, Kuhlmann, Seibel, Seyve, Villard, Ravat, and Couderc. Most French-American hybrids are found east of the Rocky Mountains.

Aurore (Aurora, Seibel 5279)

Widely planted in New York, Aurore is a vigorous, productive hybrid that ripens early and is suitable for short-season areas. It usually produces a semi-dry, fairly neutral-tasting white wine, with good sparkling wine capabilities.

Baco Noir (Baco 1)

The first hybrid widely planted in the U.S., it is a hardy, early-ripening and disease-resistant grape that is good for areas with short growing seasons. High in sugar and acid, Baco Noir produces a complex, medium-bodied red wine with an herbaceous taste and good ageing potential. With age, it browns slightly and develops a smoky aroma reminiscent of light Rhône wines.

Cascade (Seibel 13-053)

A winter-hardy, early ripener that is sensitive to some diseases and whose berries are especially attractive to birds. The blue-black grapes yield fairly large clusters, but due to the lighter color and somewhat neutral taste of the wine, it is often used for rosé or in blending. It is slowly being removed from many vineyards.

Cayuga White (GW 3)

Developed by the New York State Agricultural Experiment Station in Geneva, and released in 1974, it is a vigorous, productive, and promising variety that is gaining in popularity. Cayuga White produces a dry, crisp white wine ranging from good to excellent in quality. It can be fermented totally dry or slightly sweet, and is often reminiscent of Chenin Blanc or Müller-Thurgau.

Chancellor (Chancellor Noir, Seibel 7053)

Originating in the Rhône Valley, it is extensively planted in France as well as the eastern U.S. A heavy producer, it makes a versatile, medium bodied, fairly neutral red wine. It also has good potential as a "port" producer.

Chelois (Seibel 10-878)

Extensively grown in the East, it is moderately winter hardy and produces early-ripening fruit. It does well in cool climates with short growing seasons, and makes a sound, fairly complex, medium-bodied red wine with some ageing potential.

de Chaunac (Seibel 9549)

Successful and widely grown commercial hybrid developed by Seibel and named after Canadian oenologist Adhemar de Chaunac. Hardy, disease-resistant, and a prolific producer, it makes a medium to dark colored wine with a distinct bouquet.

Foch (Maréchal Foch)

Originating in Alsace, it is an early-ripening, fairly winter-hardy variety that grows well in short season areas. Characteristics include small berries on small clusters, and the wine produced is full bodied, with a deep purple color.

Léon Millot

Another of the red hybrid varieties that is a vigorous grower and does well in short season areas. It is related to the Foch, and matures fairly early.

Ravat Blanc (Ravat 6)

This Chardonnay cross is an early-ripening, disease-sensitive and difficult cultivar. Because of its problems, and along with the fact that it is a small producer, Ravat Blanc is not widely grown. In recent years some Vignoles, another Ravat hybrid, have been accidentally labeled Ravat or Ravat Blanc.

Rosette (Seibel 1000)

An old French-American hybrid, very vigorous and winter hardy, but a small and spotty producer. Rosette lacks pigment, so it is often used to make a rosé.

Rougeon (Seibel 5898)

Comparatively new hybrid that is winter hardy and a vigorous grower, but somewhat of a spotty producer. Distinctive in flavor, Rougeon is often used in blending because of its deep color.

Seyval Blanc (Seyval or Seyve-Villard 5-276)

One of the best French-American hybrids, this popular and adaptable grape is a descendant of the Chardonnay. It matures early in tight mildew-susceptible bunches and tends to overbear, necessitating cluster thinning in early summer. Seyval Blanc produces a good quality white wine that ranges in style from semi-dry and fresh, similar to some German wines, to complex and oaky, similar to some Loire whites and white Burgundies. This variety is planted in more eastern states than any other.

Verdelet (Seibel 9110)

Not the most winter-hardy, and with a tendency to overproduce, Verdelet must be thinned to produce its best fruit. Grown primarily in Canada's Niagara Peninsula and in the Finger Lakes, Verdelet makes sound, neutral semi-dry and dessert wines. It is not yet widely planted.

Vidal Blanc (Vidal 256)

A descendant of the Italian Trebbiano grape (also known as St. Emilion or Ugni Blanc), it is a winter-hardy and widely planted hybrid that ripens late. Fruit set can be spotty, but the grape produces a good to very good quality white wine that, like Seyval Blanc, ranges from "German" style, when made in stainless steel fermenters, to "French" style, when aged in oak, although it tends to be "spicier." Found primarily in Michigan and New York.

Vignoles (Ravat 51)

A very promising Pinot Noir hybrid that is moderately early in development and a fairly small producer. Ravat 51 can make a dry, crisp, spicy white wine, that is reminiscent of mild Gewürztraminer, with higher acid. It is also used in sparkling blends and has produced some superb sweet late harvest wines. In recent years several wines made from Vignoles have been accidentally labeled Ravat or Ravat Blanc.

Villard Blanc (Seyve-Villard 12-375)

A white hybrid that is vigorous, productive, and popular in France as well as in parts of the eastern U.S. Large clusters ripen late, producing a fruity wine with some dessert capability. It also can be grown in warmer climates such as the Southwest and Virginia.

Muscadinia

There are three known species within the subgenus *muscadinae*, the most important and widely planted in the U.S. being the *Vitis rotundifolia*. Planted in about ten southeastern states, its heaviest concentrations are in Mississippi, Alabama, Georgia, and the Carolinas, and it is not grown commercially anywhere else in the world. It is a vigorous, late-ripening, disease- and insect-resistant species that is best suited to hot climates. One vine alone can cover up to an acre, with roots sometimes up to two feet in diameter. The fruit is large and varies in color, depending on the variety, and it grows in clusters like cherries instead of in bunches. The mature grapes are extremely fragrant in the vineyards, and are harvested similarly to cherries and olives, by spreading tarps between the rows and shaking the vines. The wines produced are generally known as Muscadine or Scuppernong, the latter

derived from an old Algonquin Indian name. Some varietal names are Carlos, Creek, Hunt, Magnolia, Noble, and Southern Fox. These varieties produce a range of intensely flavorful, distinctive sweet wines, red, white or rosé, that taste peculiar to most wine drinkers. Several cross-breeding experiments are under way in an effort to produce vines that will thrive in hot climates and produce better-tasting wines.

APERITIFS

Aperitifs, or appetizer wines, are technically classed as dessert wines because of their alcoholic content but are classified separately because they are drunk before instead of after meals. The two main aperitifs in the U.S., as elsewhere, are sherry and vermouth. American sherry should, of course, not be confused with the real Sherry, which can come only from the region of Jerez de la Frontera in Spain.

American "Sherry"

The sherry-type wine has the characteristic nutty flavor obtained through processes of ageing and warm temperatures. In California many different regions are used to make these wines. The best-quality grape for the purpose is the Palomino or Napa Golden Chasselas (not a real Chasselas). Authentic Spanish Sherry is made almost entirely from the Palomino. This grape has become a varietal in California and is used for the best sherries, although many growers continue with such varieties as the Flame Tokay, Mission, Thompson Seedless, and Feher Szagos, which produce lesser wines of the type.

In New York, the other major sherry-producing state, this wine is sometimes made from whatever white grapes are on hand, and even red grapes such as Concord. While most are scrupulous, a few producers have the curious habit of taking their spoiled wine, fortifying it with alcohol and sugar, and calling it sherry.

Three styles of sherry-type wines are produced in the U.S.: a dry aperitif with a sugar content of from 0% to 2.5%; medium dry sherry, with 2.5% to 4% of sugar; and a sweet cream sherry with over 4%. All these wines range from not less than 17% of alcohol to about 20%.

Most American sherry is made by heating the fortified wine in wood, concrete, or steel tanks from two to six months, at temperatures varying from 120° to 140°F. (49° to 60°C.). It is then stored in small oak barrels, to be aged for six months—or longer, in the case of better-quality wines.

Scarcely any sherry is made by the Spanish "flor" method, although some is produced for blending purposes by a newly developed method known as the "submerged flor" technique. One exception is the Llords and Elwood winery near San Jose, where an authentic outdoor solera system is used to make a "flor" sherry.

American Vermouth

There are two kinds of vermouth—the dry French type (pale amber) and the sweet Italian type (dark amber). The first step in the making of American vermouth is to select and age neutral white wines. These are then flavored with herbs and other aromatic substances (usually imported) which are introduced into the wine—or an infusion of aromatic herbs is added to the basic fortified wine and the mixture is aged in barrel. Vermouth producers all have their secret formulas containing sometimes as many as fifty different herbs, roots, seeds, barks, flowers, dried fruit, wormwood, etc. Vermouth ranges from 15% to 20% in alcoholic content—a very light type has recently become popular.

DESSERT WINES

American dessert wines have an alcoholic content of not less than 14% and range from medium-sweet to sweet. There are four distinct American dessert wines—"port," "white port," muscatel, and "tokay." There are a few bearing such varietal names as Muscat de Frontignan and Tinta port varieties which are usually of better quality. Most of America's dessert wines are made from grapes grown in California's hot interior valleys.

American "Port"

This is made from many grapes—but rarely from those which go into genuine Port. Carignane, Petite-Sirah, Trousseau, Grenache, Valdepeñas, and Zinfandel are most commonly used in Californian ports; while Alicante-Bouschet, Alicante Gazin, and Salvador are added, for the dark color they contribute in blending. Eastern ports are often made from a hodge-podge of grapes, utilizing anything left over. American port is usually deep red in color, fruity, and heavy-bodied. It ranges from 8% to 14% natural grape sugar content and is usually sweeter and darker in color than the Ports from Portugal. There is also a lighter-colored, lighter-bodied wine known as tawny port.

American ports, like other dessert wines, thrive best in the warmer regions. The better quality wines are made with Tinta Madeira, Tinta Cão, and Touriga (choice Portuguese grape varieties). A great deal of credit must go to the Ficklin Vineyards of Madera in Madera County, which is producing the best port-type wine in California, using the methods employed in Portugal (see Port).

The best eastern ports are made from Chancellor grapes, and can be as good as any from California.

White "Port"

This variety is made from such grapes as the Thompson Seedless, or any of the standard, light-colored wine grapes. It is sweet and straw-colored.

American Muscatel

This is a dessert wine made from Muscat grapes (which are used also for a light Muscat white table wine). Muscatels, which have an unmistakable aroma and flavor, are, on the whole, a drug on the market and are only rarely agreeable wines. They range in color from golden and dark amber to red, and in sweetness from 10% to 15% natural grape sugar content. These muscatels are sometimes sold as cheap substitutes for whiskey, especially in monopoly state stores.

The better varieties of grapes are used in the making of Muscats as table wines, which can be considered as finer wines. The white grapes used are the Muscat de Frontignan (sometimes called Muscat Canelli in California) and Malvasia Bianca, while the red grapes are Malvasia and Aleatico.

Most Muscatels are made from the Muscat of Alexandria (also a table grape) and have a golden color, but there are at least seven other Muscat grape varieties used in California. In the Central and San Joaquin valleys, the Black Muscat or Muscat Hamburg is grown. Californian Muscat varieties find their proper home in the warm climate of the San Joaquin Valley region, where the grapes attain a high sugar content.

Californian "Tokay"

This is made by blending other dessert wines, such as port, angelica, and sherry, and bears no relationship to Hungarian Tokay wines, nor is it necessarily made from the Flame Tokay, a table grape planted extensively in the Lodi area. This tokay ranges from 7% to 10% natural grape sugar content, and has a slightly nutty flavor reminiscent of Sherry. The color of Californian tokay is amber-pink; it is a wine of less than average quality and is the lowest in production of the better-known dessert wines.

Angelica is an original Californian wine and is not one for Californians to be proud of. This white dessert wine, very sweet and straw-colored and blended with brandy, is more of a cordial than a wine. The Mission grape and the cheaper Grenache—the Spanish variety—go into the making of the highly fruity Angelica. "Winos" of the post-Repeal Era popularized Angelica, which is rarely seen today.

Aleatico wine has the spicy, fruity flavor of the Aleatico grape and resembles the red muscatels. There is also an Aleatico table wine, inferior and rarely to be found.

"Malaga" in the U.S. is just a name referring to a cordial wine of no particular distinction, and quite unconnected with the Málaga of Spain.

Berry wines in the U.S. have the distinct taste of the

berries used and include such sweet, fruity wines as blackberry, raspberry, etc. The Sacramento Valley area near Elk Grove is a noted berry-wine-producing region.

Other dessert wines include Californian grenache, (made from the Grenache grape in the San Joaquin Valley); "marsala," rarely found on the market and having nothing in common with the Marsala from Sicily; and "madeira," which is usually a poor imitation of genuine Madeira.

Special natural wines are not strictly a dessert wine type, but they seem to have grown from the recent boom in the berry wine industry. Dr. Maynard Amerine gives a kindly description of the origin of these wines: "The idea of flavored wines dates back in time to the Greek and Roman civilizations. In these periods they resulted from attempts to mask bad odors and tastes. This then led naturally to the practice of adding desirable flavors, allowing the wine to serve as the 'vehicle' for the added flavor, just as spices and perfumes perform useful roles. The addition of botanicals to wine for medicinal and even mystical reasons also made such flavored wines popular in older civilizations; after distillation was discovered, fortified wines and brandy became a favored base for flavored wines and liqueurs."

The American "special" wines are made from a base of wine. The additions may include herbs, spices, fruit juices, aromatics, essences, and other natural flavorings. However, no further alcohol or wine spirits are added. Such concoctions are not wines.

SPARKLING WINES

These may be red, pink, or white, and their alcoholic content ranges from 10% to 14% by volume. The most popular sparkling types in the U.S. are "champagne" and "sparkling burgundy." Although no wines outside France have any right to the title of Champagne, some of the American sparkling wines are made by the true champagne method in which secondary fermentation takes place in the bottle. When this happens, the wine is allowed to bear the label of bottle-fermented champagne, provided the word American or the name of the state is added, with a statement that it is a sparkling wine made by the champagne method in California, the state of New York, etc. The alternative method is the Charmat process, in which secondary fermentation takes place in bulk in huge glass-lined vats.

In France, however, only bottle-fermented sparkling wine is allowed to be authentic Champagne (*q.v.*) and only if it has been made in the Champagne region.

Californian "champagnes" are produced throughout the state, but the finest come from the cooler regions—the counties of Sonoma, Santa Clara, Napa, Mendocino, and Alameda. Sweeter types come from the Cucamonga district in southern California and the interior valleys; bulk-process types are made in both these regions, as well as in the inland valley. Bottle-fermented types are mostly found in the areas which produce good table wines: the Almadén Vineyards of Los Gatos, F. Korbel & Bros. of Guerneville, Weibel Champagne Vineyards of Mission San José, Hanns Kornell, Schramsberg, Beaulieu Vineyards, and Domaine Chandon (owned by the Moët-Hennessy group) are probably the best champagne producers in California. Piper-Heidsieck and Sonoma Vineyards formed a joint venture in 1980, and produce the very good Piper-Sonoma sparkling wines. Freixenet, the Spanish sparkling wine producers, and Louis Roederer, the French Champagne house, also have projects in progress in California.

Pinot Noir and Pinot Chardonnay, the grapes that go into the making of French Champagnes, yield the best quality; other good grapes for Californian champagnes are the Pinot Blanc, Sémillon, Sauvignon Blanc, White Riesling, and Folle Blanche. Some of the inferior grape varieties are the Sauvignon Vert, Burger, French Colombard, and Green Hungarian. Californian champagnes range from dry to sweet and are dosed with sugar in the usual way. Real *brut* champagne used to be rare in California, but not any longer.

Pink champagnes from California may be either bottle-fermented or bulk-processed (the government requires labels to designate bulk-process champagnes as well as the bottle-fermented types).

Of the sparkling wines, Sparkling "burgundy," after champagne the most popular in the country, is red wine made sparkling by either of the two methods used for champagnes. It is usually semi-sweet or sweet, and produced from Pinot Noir, Carignane, Mondeuse, and Petite-Sirah. Of the sparkling wines, mosel- and sauternes-types are treated by the champagne method and are made from the table wines bearing the same names. Sparkling Muscats are made from light Muscat wines, usually Muscat Canelli (Muscat de Frontignan): they tend to be very sweet and are sometimes sold under the Italian name "Moscato Spumante." Another wine is made from the Malvasia Bianca, which produces a sweet Muscat-flavored sparkling wine.

Carbonated wines are made to sparkle by artificial carbonation and, by law in California and many other states, must be designated as such. Sometimes known as effervescent wines, they are mass-produced and much cheaper than the relatively better quality and naturally fermented sparkling wines.

New York and eastern "champagnes" are made from a variety of grapes. Hybrids and *vinifera* are being used more frequently, but *labruscas* are still used extensively. Most useful of the *labruscas* are Delaware and Catawba. Aurora is also used by many. Bully Hill and Wagner in the Finger Lakes make good sparkling Seyval Blanc in the *méthode champenoise*, Glenora is experimenting with Chardonnay, Gold Seal uses Chardonnay in its Blanc de Blanc, and Herman Wiemer is using Riesling. Several other producers in the East are beginning or extending sparkling wine experiments. Taylor, Great Western, and Gold Seal are major producers of bulk processed and bottle-fermented transfer-method champagnes.

Sparkling burgundies and pink champagnes are also made from a wide variety of grapes. Recently several wineries have produced "spumante"-type wines from Muscats and *labruscas* that have met with consumer approval.

United States: Alabama

Although native grapes were domestically grown in Alabama as early as 1840, eventually yielding more than 400,000 gallons in 1880, Prohibition killed wine production. In 1978 farm winery licenses were made available.

Perdido Vineyards. The first winery to take advantage of the new laws was Perdido Vineyards in Perdido, bonded in 1979. All of Perdido's 50 acres are planted to various muscadine varieties, most notably the Carlos, Noble, and Magnolia. Co-owners Jim and Marianne Eddins produce nine different wines, and recent output has been approximately 13,000 cases annually. One of their featured wines that has generated considerable interest lately is Rosé Cou Rouge (Red Neck Rosé).

United States: Arizona

The Arizona deserts are too hot for wine-grape growing. However, cooler regions in the southeastern mountains show promise for *vinifera* grape growing. Sonoita was established as a viticultural area in 1984 by the B.A.T.F.

R.W. Webb Winery in Tucson is the state's first bonded winery. Established in 1980, it now has 20 acres (8 hectares) planted to six varieties of *vinifera* grapes, with a production output of 3,300 cases in 1982. According to Webb, the climatic conditions above 4,000 feet in elevation are ideal for *vinifera,* and there is increasing vineyard activity in a number of areas in the southeastern counties.

United States: Arkansas

However unlikely it may seem, Arkansas produces nearly 163,000 cases of wine annually. Most of the vineyards are in Franklin County, Johnson County, and in the northwest corner of the state around Tontitown. There are some 5,000 acres (2,025 hectares) of vines.

Four of the important wineries—there are eight in the state overall—are at the small town of Altus: Wiederkehr, Post, Sax, and Mount Bethel. The Altus area accounts for nearly all of the wine produced in the state.

Wiederkehr Wine Cellars. In the early 1800s, Johan Andreas Wiederkehr made wine in Switzerland. In 1880, he settled in the backwoods of the Ozark Mountain foothills along the Arkansas River near Altus, planted grapes, and opened the Wiederkehr Wine Cellars. Alcuin Weiderkehr, who studied viticulture and oenology at the University of California at Davis and as an exchange student in Bordeaux, began planting *vinifera* and making European-style wine in Arkansas. Today the 575-acre (230 hectares) winery, known as the *Arkansas Mountain Vineyards* produces more than 625,000 cases a year. Wiederkehr wines have won more medals than any winery outside of California, and most of the wines are sold in Arkansas.

United States: California

In California, climate, soil, and other conditions conducive to the production of good wine are equal to those in most of the great vine-growing regions of the world. California has grown in quantity and quality to become one of the leading wine producing areas in the world. The great handicap in the production of fine wines came from the enormous acreage of poor and mediocre grape varieties in the many districts.

Plantings of the finer vines were the minority until the late seventies, while such red-wine grapes as Carignane and Alicante-Bouschet, and white-wine grapes like French Colombard, and Thompson Seedless, all of which usually produce only ordinary wines, were the majority. Varietal wines of *Vitis vinifera* species were rationed owing to their scarcity. The tables have turned and these varietals are now produced in abundant quantities and in many cases very well vinified. For the most part, the cooler regions in north California—Napa, Sonoma, Livermore Valley, Santa Cruz, Santa Clara, Mendocino, northern Monterey—yield table wines, some of excellent distinction and flavor, and the warmer regions give dessert wines. It was unfortunate that for many years until 1965, 60% of California wines were of the sweet, fortified variety, rather than the table wine type. Since then, table wines have far outsold the so-called ports and sherries and now constitute more than 80% of all the wines produced in the state.

Today 67% of all the wine sold in the U.S. comes from California. The production of all California wine in 1985 totalled about 158 million cases, roughly the same amount produced by all the Appellation Contrôlée wines of France in an abundant year. (Of course, the Appellation Contrôlée wines comprise only the best one-sixth of all French production.) In 1985 sales of California table wines reached 110 million cases, 67% of the whole. Sales of fortified wines declined steadily in the early 1980's to only an 8% share of the market. Sparkling wines produced totalled 11.3 million cases, roughly 7% of the whole; 15 years earlier, "champagnes" represented only about 2% of the production. In the 1980s growth has been steady in the"blush" segment of table wine production. Wine Coolers, the fruit-juice-and-wine concoctions that are packaged and marketed much the same as beer, rose from nowhere in 1980 to an amazing 15% market share in 1985.

WINE HISTORY

The history of California goes back to Cortez, the Spanish conqueror of Mexico who, in 1524, ordained that wine-making should become one of the industries of the New World. The vines were probably of Spanish origin, although it is not certain that cuttings or seeds were brought from Spain. In time, the new wines were competing with the wines of Spain, and the Spanish, like the Emperor Domitian before them, ordered that the colonial vineyards be uprooted. Wine-growing continued, however, and for many years the wine industry in Mexico and Baja California was carefully concealed from Spanish officials. A Jesuit priest, Father Juan Ugarte, planted what were probably the first wine grapes to be grown on the West Coast in about 1697 at Mission San Francisco Xavier in Baja California. This was a European variety, the only one to be planted by the Fathers, and it was named, appropriately enough, Mission—and still has that name today. While the Spanish missions were being established and spreading slowly northward, the Mission grapes made their appearance in the vineyards of Alta California. The Franciscans, led by Padre Junípero Serra, brought them into what is now California, planting them at Mission San Diego de Alcalá soon after its establishment in 1769. The vines prospered and the harvest was said to have been better than any known before in the New World. Padre Serra's Franciscan missionaries constructed twenty-one missions, most of them with vineyards, from San Diego to Sonoma, the northernmost point of the Camino Real, or King's Highway—a great thoroughfare today—but the missions were largely confined to southern California. Descendants of the vines they cultivated are still living. San Gabriel Arcangel Mission near Los Angeles was chosen as the site for their largest winery, and the mission still preserves the little adobe building where the Indians trampled the juice from the grapes. Today visitors still come to see the gnarled remains of the mission's old Trinity vine, which was planted more than a century ago.

Between 1770 and 1830, when the missions were flourishing, wine was produced according to the needs of the Fathers. In the 1830s the Mexican government secularized the missions and these vineyards were mostly abandoned; but it had now been established that wine and brandy could be produced in the state.

New Vineyard Owners

The downfall of the missions and the resulting ruin of the vineyards and wine presses roughly marks the beginning of the modern industry. Before 1830, pri-

vate holdings of vineyards were rare. As early as 1824, however, Joseph Chapman, one of the first Americans to settle in Los Angeles, planted four thousand vines. He was followed by Jean-Louis Vignes, a Frenchman from Bordeaux, who started his commercial venture in wine-making approximately where the Los Angeles Union Station now stands, and by 1833 his successful wine and brandy were acclaimed throughout the state. As others followed him, viniculture expanded and within a generation became the principal industry of the Los Angeles district. Vignes was one of the first to advocate the planting of noble grape varieties. In the early 1830s, he imported cuttings of choice European vines which were delicately packed and shipped from France to Boston and then around Cape Horn to California. The long journey did not damage the vines; they were planted and some bore fruit and were used in Californian wines. Another of the newcomers to Los Angeles who built up, also in the 1830s, an extensive business in grapes and wines was William Wolfskill, a Kentucky trapper. By 1858, two years before his death, Wolfskill had increased his holding to 145 acres (about 58 hectares) with 55,000 vines, and he had a wine cellar with a capacity of 60,000 to 100,000 U.S. gallons (2,300 to 3,800 hectoliters, 50,000 to 83,000 imp. gallons).

Along with Vignes and Wolfskill, the names of Charles Kohler and John Frohling are important in this pioneering record. These two partners of German descent purchased a vineyard of 3,000 vines near Los Angeles, and at the same time they opened a wine shop in a San Francisco basement, the first of its kind, starting with 500 U.S. gallons (416 imp.) in the cellars; by 1862, they had 500,000 U.S. gallons (416,340 imp.) of wine and 20,000 U.S. gallons (16,650 imp.) of brandy in storage vaults.

The Mission grape was introduced into the earliest commercial vineyards by Chapman, Vignes, and other pioneers who planted it first in southern, then in northern California. The vine was a rough, prolific producer, lacking character and ill-suited to the production of table wines; yet for more than eighty years it dominated Californian viticulture.

During the 1850s, each wine district was known by the kinds of wines it manufactured. Port-type came from Los Angeles; hock, "sauterne," and claret from Sonoma and Napa; "sherry" came from Sonoma and El Dorado counties. One contemporary writer on wine said: "But we shall not probably make our best wines till we cease to strive for foreign imitations and strike out boldly for the manufacture of new kinds of wine, which will bring out the excellence with which nature has no doubt enriched the grape in this peculiar climate." This is a point on which California vintners are still being attacked.

European Plantings Increased by Colonel Haraszthy

The great transition from the use of the Mission grape to fine European varieties was brought about by a new settler in California twelve years or so after Jean-Louis Vignes's success with foreign cuttings from France. The extraordinary newcomer on the scene was Ágoston Haraszthy, a Hungarian nobleman, who has since been recognized as the father of Californian viticulture. The first considerable importation of foreign vines began early in 1851, when Colonel Haraszthy introduced a hundred cuttings and six choice rooted vines which he planted in San Diego. Among these was the famous Zinfandel, which was later to be used in the making of a very popular dry red wine. At first, growers clung to the Mission grape and were slow to buy the new variety, believing that the colonel was only speculating on the cuttings, but by 1878 extensive acreages were planted with Zinfandel. Colonel Haraszthy, convinced that the finest foreign grapes could grow in California, experimented with his cuttings to determine the regions of the state best suited to the different kinds. He also believed that, to get the best and quickest results, many types should be introduced.

In 1861, he was assigned by Governor John G. Downey to conduct a viticultural expedition in Europe to gather all varieties that might prove satisfactory. During an extensive three-month sojourn, Haraszthy and his son Árpád visited parts of France, Germany, Switzerland, Italy, and Spain. They selected some 100,000 cuttings from 300 varieties and all were shipped to California in the course of one year. Some of these were planted in his Buena Vista vineyard at Sonoma, but the majority were sold to growers from all parts of the state. In 1863, Haraszthy organized the Buena Vista Vinicultural Society, to which he conveyed his 6,000-acre (2,400-hectare) farm in Sonoma Valley with its 400 acres (160 hectares) in vines; it was his gift of a wide assortment of grapes and his continual research that stimulated the great modern expansion of the industry. Most of the superior varieties of imported vines during this period were planted around San Francisco Bay, which was one of the areas to benefit enormously from Haraszthy's practical demonstration that superior wine can come from non-irrigated grapes.

The great plunge into the wine industry attracted the inexperienced farmers and seekers after immediate profits, indifferent to the choice of vine varieties, soil, or location. The realization of Haraszthy's ideal was postponed and even today it has not been fully achieved. In the 1860s, Los Angeles, Anaheim, and Sonoma stood out as the three major wine and grape districts, possessing more vineyards than any others.

It was the discovery of gold which originally brought the prosperity of the liquid gold—the wine—to California. The wine market prospered in proportion to the gold discovered, and wine from Los Angeles was a luxury even to the Forty-niners. When the gold rush was over, wine prices dropped drastically and the state legislature was forced to keep viticulture alive by exempting new vineyards from taxes. In 1870, the future looked brighter: the new European grape

varieties, Haraszthy's success, and the beneficial legislation of the state and national government led to expansion and national recognition. Unfortunately, the national economic crisis between 1875 and 1877 caused the wine industry to slump. The depression did, however, frighten away amateurs and speculators, and by 1878 those who continued in the industry were producing better wines from finer grape varieties. They survived not only the depression but the phylloxera pest as well.

The Coming of Phylloxera

The phylloxera had appeared in California before 1870; but in 1876 it became a real plague, which went on for at least three years, ravaging vineyards in Sonoma, Napa, Yolo, El Dorado, and Placer counties, as it had been devastating most of the vineyards of Europe. The French were the first to succeed in combating the disease, by grafting their *vinifera* vines onto phylloxera-resistant native American vines; soon Californian growers did the same.

The Beginning of Legislation

Valuable aid in stamping out phylloxera came from the California State Board of Viticultural Commissioners. This organization was formed in 1880 and did much to stabilize the industry. The commission helped growers to find the best climates and soils for each grape variety and gave vital assistance in the control of vine maladies. An elaborate experimental grape-growing station under the College of Agriculture of the University of California also contributed to the progress of the industry. The college has continued the research and teaching of viticulture and oenology to this day; in recent times it was for many years under the capable guidance of Professors Emeritus A. H. Winkler, Maynard A. Amerine, and Harold Berg, and now under Professor A. Dinsmoor Webb, all of them noted researchers who have earned the respect of oenologists and viticulturists throughout the world. The commission sponsored state control laws which established California's earliest standards of quality in wine.

Between 1880 and 1895 viticultural ideas, conditions, and policies within the state were transformed. Tariff, taxation, and the fight for wine control laws were important matters to every grower and vintner in California. Before the turn of the century, the wines were taking prizes in international exhibitions, and California was competing with Europe for world markets.

Between 1900 and 1915 there was a further increase both in cultivation and in sales—but movements toward total abstinence were growing, and when the Prohibition law was passed, viticulture in California suffered a severe blow, and many of the new wineries stopped functioning. Production dropped from about

50 million U.S. gallons (1.9 million hectoliters, 42 million imp. gallons) of wine in 1912 to approximately 27 million U.S. gallons (1 million hectoliters, 22 million imp. gallons) in 1919. But Prohibition was not altogether disastrous: the law still allowed wine to be used for medicinal and sacramental purposes, thus enabling a part of the commercial wine industry to remain. When Prohibition was finally acknowledged a failure, and the Volstead Act was repealed in December 1933, those growers who had not given up were able to resume full-scale production almost immediately. For a time, the demand for wine far exceeded the supply, prices were exaggerated, and inferior wines were sold. Not until 1938 could the market be said to have settled down.

In 1934, standards of quality were laid down for Californian wines by the California Department of Public Health and the Federal Government. Federal regulations safeguarded the controls which ruled that all the wine, wherever sold, must meet Californian requirements.

Perhaps the most important step in the whole industry of Californian wines has been the effort of the vintners to improve varietal plantings and to produce good varietal wines—named after the grape variety (Cabernet Sauvignon, Chardonnay, etc.) from which they are produced. Unfortunately, the attempt to eliminate the Mission grape in the cooler regions and cut down the percentage of Alicante-Bouschet has not been entirely successful. The industry has never completely recovered from Prohibition. At that time the demand was for tough-skinned, very productive grapes which could be shipped to eastern markets. A vine of such high quality as the Cabernet Sauvignon, producing scarcely more than 3 to 6 tons to the acre (about 50 to 100 hectoliters per hectare), was overlooked in favor of Carignane and Alicante-Bouschet, which would yield as much as 15 short tons to the acre (almost 250 hectoliters per hectare). These impaired the quality of post-Repeal wines and are still largely the cause of much legitimate criticism. Even today, in some years 40% to 50% of the grapes used for wine in California are varieties suited only for use as raisins or table grapes.

In general, however, the story since Repeal has been one of improvement, as there have been numerous plantings of fine varietals which can produce the best white and red table wines. Producers who became known in the 1940s and 1950s included Louis M. Martini, the dean of Napa Valley wine-growers; Herman Wente; John Daniel, Jr., of Inglenook; Madame de Latour of Beaulieu Vineyards; and Chaffee Hall of Hallcrest. Peter Mondavi of Charles Krug, and Robert Mondavi; Martin Ray, who at one time owned Paul Masson Vineyards; and Louis Benoist, the former owner of Almadén, all brought skill and ingenuity to winegrowing in California. They likewise did much to maintain the quality of American wines, in spite of the pressure of "mass production." And the late Frank Schoonmaker, a New York wine merchant who, with the help of the author, introduced fine American wines east of the Rockies, is another among those who have fought for quality over quantity in the United States.

There are some 676 bonded wineries in California, but aside from a few dozen very large wineries, the greater percentage tend to produce and sell rather limited quantities of varietal wines, a laudable trend. It is a continually changing scene, especially in recent years, with the constant appearance of new wineries and wines. Some vineyards have become too commercialized, sacrificing quality for quantity. Paul Masson and Cresta Blanca, which formerly produced excellent wines, are examples of this, although they are now making a notable effort to achieve a higher standard. Only a few select wineries insist that Californian wines should be called by original Californian names; for this reason, the late Paul Rossigneux (president of Napa and Sonoma Wine Company), Robert Mondavi, and the late Carl Wente have always been respected for their uncompromisingly high standards.

Today Californian growers are faced with the task of getting the industry to the point at which it can compete on equal terms with the European market—and this can only be done with varietal wines, not with imitations. Sherry comes from Spain, Port from Portugal, Burgundy, Chablis, and Sauternes from France, and to name a Californian wine for one of these is to admit its inferiority. Good grapes, aided by suitable soil and climate, will produce good wines. The planting of fine varietals in Californian soil certainly should result in wine worthy of being judged on its own merit.

RECENT DEVELOPMENTS

In California today grapes and wine have produced a billion-dollar industry. Plantings of grapes increased by more than 150% from 1970 to 1980. New grape-growing regions have been prepared to take the place of those areas lost to the spreading cities of the most populous state in the nation. The time may come when one-sixth of the vast acreage devoted to agriculture in the state will be vineyards. But today the total land area planted in grapes is approximately 730,000 acres (292,000 hectares), of which roughly half, or 365,000 acres, is planted exclusively in wine grapes. The development of winery facilities has also been great: millions of dollars are spent annually for new buildings, equipment, and research.

The expansion of the industry has not affected the range of size of the wineries in California; the very largest still exist side by side with the many small ones. The several producing great volume make more than 65% of California wines. Slightly smaller than these giants are three or four companies which also market a wide selection of wines across the country. The wineries which have become famous in the past ten years are primarily medium-sized with products of average price but above-average quality. It is from these producers and some of the small wineries that the very good California wines come. Though the range of varietal table wines produced by the state's wineries now can be bought in most metropolitan centers around the country, some of the best wines remain known—and indeed available—only in California.

Since the mid-1960s the California wine boom has attracted large corporations, huge food and beverage companies, and financial institutions. The investors include Heublein, Inc., which purchased United Vintners (Inglenook, Italian Swiss Colony, Lejon, and Beaulieu); National Distillers, which bought Almadén Vineyards in 1967 and resold it, to Heublein, Inc., in 1987; and Seagrams, which has expanded its Paul Masson property and, in 1983, acquired The Wine Spectrum (Sterling Vineyards, The Monterey Vineyard, Taylor California Cellars, and Taylor Wine Company) from Coca-Cola of Atlanta. Seagrams resold some of its wineries to Vintners International in 1987. In 1973, Moët-Hennessy, a French Champagne and Cognac conglomerate, founded Domaine Chandon Vineyards. The company acquired 800 acres (320 hectares) of vineyard land in Napa and Sonoma counties and by 1975 was producing sparkling wines by the traditional *méthode champenoise.* Before the vineyards came into production Domaine Chandon bought grapes from local growers. The Simi Winery in Sonoma is another acquisition. Piper Heidsieck, another French Champagne producer, established a joint venture with Sonoma Vineyards in 1980. Nestlé International has owned Beringer since 1972. Several German companies have acquired California properties as well. These include the Peter Eckes Co., which bought Franciscan Vineyards in 1979, and the A. Racke Co., producers of Kupferberg sparkling wines, which bought Buena Vista Vineyards in 1979. Freixenet, the largest seller of Spanish sparkling wine in the United States today, began its 100,000-case Gloria Ferrer project in Sonoma County in 1983. The French Champagne House of Louis Roederer acquired 400 acres (160 hectares) in Mendocino's Anderson Valley in 1982. Distillers Company Ltd., the world's largest Scotch distilling group, now owned by Guinness Brewers, acquired Concannon Vineyards in 1983.

Plantings

In 1969, after several years of decline, the number of new acres planted only in wine grapes began a steady rise. In 1972, 48,000 acres (19,000 hectares) were planted, more than for the entire period 1965–1970. With even greater acreage added in 1973 and 1974, there were more than 322,000 acres (129,000 hectares) of vineyards by the beginning of 1975. By 1986, 340,000 acres of wine grapes (136,000 hectares) were under cultivation, making the total vineyard area of California nearly a third larger than that of Bordeaux and Burgundy combined.

More significant than the fantastic increase in the sheer acreage of the vineyards is the trend for planting better wine grapes. For example, in 1959 the noble Cabernet Sauvignon grape of Bordeaux covered only 630 acres (250 hectares); by 1981 this figure had increased to 30,000 acres (11,000 hectares). Chardonnay and Pinot Noir plantings have grown proportionately. Yet in spite of these gains, and those made by good but less famous wine grapes, the lamentable Thompson Seedless table grape makes more Californian wine than any other variety.

Much of the planting of both great and good wine stocks has been carried out in the newly developed areas of the state. San Benito, Monterey, San Luis Obispo, Lake, Mendocino, Amador, and Santa Barbara counties are some of the places into which vineyards have spread or have been expanded. Almadén Vineyards pioneered grape-growing in the San Benito area, including Paicines and Cienega. Paul Masson, Mirassou, and Wente Bros. started most of the Monterey vineyards in the 1960s. In San Luis Obispo vineyards have spread over 5,600 acres (2,240 hectares) in less than ten years. Wines are produced there from Cabernet Sauvignon, Zinfandel, Sauvignon Blanc, Chardonnay, Merlot, Pinot Blanc, and Gewürztraminer. Most of the vines grow near Paso Robles and the town of San Luis Obispo. Farther south in the state, close to Riverside and Temecula, these same good varieties, plus Johannisberg Riesling and Chenin Blanc, thrive in a climate cooled by ocean breezes. Another southern California venture has begun in Kern County, 100 miles (160 kilometers) north of the city of Los Angeles. Both here and in the southern Salinas Valley in Monterey, many modern sprinkler and irrigation techniques are practiced. And at the opposite end of the state, beyond the famous North Coast vineyards, Zinfandel vines have been planted on the foothills near Mount Lassen.

Research

For almost a century, new plantings and the other aspects of wine-making in the state have been closely guided by the University of California. Its specialists have advised vintners in Australia, New Zealand, Spain, Portugal, Italy, Yugoslavia, Argentina, Brazil, Chile, South Africa, and even Japan. Students come to the branch campus at Davis, 70 miles (110 kilometers) northeast of San Francisco, to study viticulture and oenology or to do graduate work and research. Many of the projects are funded by California wine companies. The close liaison with local producers began in 1875, when the newly established university appointed E. W. Hilgard as Professor of Agriculture. Five years later the legislature decided to create a department for instruction in "the arts and sciences pertaining to viticulture, the theory and practice of fermentation, distillation, and rectification, and the management of cellars . . . to be illustrated by practical experiments."

Three internationally known scientists of the university have played major roles in improving Californian wines over the past three decades: H. P. Olmo, a plant pathologist and geneticist; Professor Maynard A. Amerine, a world-traveling oenologist, researcher, and writer; and Harold W. Berg, a consultant in wine problems whose advice has aided the wine-growers of many countries. Much of Dr. Olmo's work is readily seen in California vineyards, for he has spent forty years breeding new cross strains which will produce sound wine in many parts of the state. Dr. Amerine, respected around the world, has been the president of the American Society of Oenologists, has won awards from many foreign wine organizations, has written several fine books on wine and wine-making, and, most important, has done much to improve the quality of California wines. Professor Berg, recently retired chairman of the wine faculty, has done valuable research in grape processing, wine stabilization, and ageing.

One of the achievements of the men at Davis was the classification of the California viticultural districts into five temperature zones. In the 1930s Professors A. J. Winkler and Maynard Amerine studied the relation between climate and the quality of wine produced from different grape varieties in the various regions of California. They found that temperature is one of the most important climatic factors affecting the successful cultivation of wine grapes and that the summation of daily degree readings is of significant value for predicting the best varieties to be grown in any district. Their heat summation concept developed from the total of mean daily temperatures above 50°F. (10°C.) for the days from April 1 through October 31. 50°F. is the temperature above which most vine-shoot growth occurs; the time period corresponds to the vine-growing season. Thus, a day with an average temperature of 65°F. is given a heat summation value of 15 "degree-days." Five climate regions were then defined according to the totals for the season:

Region I—less than 2,500 degree-days
Region II—2,501 to 3,000 degree-days
Region III—3,001 to 3,500 degree-days
Region IV—3,501 to 4,000 degree-days
Region V—more than 4,000 degree-days

Knowing the temperature region of his vineyard, a grape-grower can make a general prediction as to which vines will prove most successful. Where the total is less than 1,800 degree-days, most grape varieties will not ripen sufficiently to produce wine with the legal minimum degree of alcohol. In warmer districts the grapes mature quickly and yield huge crops, but the acidity, color, and aroma are too low to make good dry table wines. Dessert or fortified wine requiring much natural grape sugar and common·table wines are made in these hot sections of the state. In the cooler vineyards, where a vine can bear only a limited crop, the fruit can ripen slowly, retain its high acidity, and concentrate those elements of color and aroma which make fine table wines.

The premium wine districts of California fall in Regions I, II, and III, while Regions IV and V produce mostly table grapes or the bulk and dessert—fortified—wines already mentioned. These zones are abstract temperature regions and do not necessarily define continuous or similar geographical areas. In the long and flat Central Valley both the northern and southern ends are Region V, yet the middle section is Region IV. In the foothills and coastal valleys distinct microclimates are created by the mountains. Locations with different temperature ratings may be miles apart, or separated only by a few hundred feet on the same hillside. Most of the Napa Valley, for example, is Region III, with a few scattered sections rated I and II. But the nearby Peachland section of Sonoma County is nearly all Region I.

Heat summation data are a useful tool for giving viticulturalists a rough idea of the vines which may be grown successfully in untried parts of the state. The concept can also help determine the approximate rate at which the fruit will ripen. Talk of the five temperature zones has become a part of everyday life in California wine districts. But since such information is only one simple expression of a single factor affecting vineyard climate, too much importance should not be placed on it. And though important, climate is still only one of the variables in the production of fine wine. Some growers in new areas cite a Region I, II, or III rating as synonymous with high grape quality. Such a thermal classification is perhaps a necessary, but certainly not a sufficient, condition for producing good wine grapes. The experience gained through trial and error—in a company with modern techniques—will in the end establish the spots where good wines can be made.

Technological Advances

Mechanical grape harvesting in California plays a more important part in the industry than in any other fine wine district in the world. The practice is most common in the great flat valleys and basins of the interior, where mainly bulk wines are made; but machine picking is used in most parts of the coastal counties, where the best California wines originate. The giant harvesters are of two types: one uses suction to pull the fruit, along with most of the leaves, from the vine, while the other shakes the plant and catches the falling grapes. Where harvesting is done by machine, oenologists think it vital that the grapes be crushed as soon as possible after picking. In more than one vineyard operation, the machines include apparatus for crushing and stemming the grapes in the field. Most have spotlights for work at night.

Another machine, though smaller than those that harvest the fruit, has been developed to perform another time-consuming human chore. To speed up production of sparkling wines at Korbel and other *méthode champenoise* champagne cellars, a new device gently shakes many bottles at once to dislodge the tartrate sediment in the bottle neck for removal. Taittinger and others in the Champagne district in France have converted to this method.

California viticulturalists have improved their techniques of irrigation and have invented new ones for using water in frost protection. The most common device used previously to counter the disastrous spring frosts—which can destroy 75% of the crop—was the old-fashioned smudge pot. It has been replaced in many vineyards by sprinklers which spray the vines during the early morning hours, when the cold takes its heaviest toll. The water on the tender leaves and shoots will freeze at 32°F. and in the process give off a modicum of heat that protects them. In addition, the mist in their air prevents the air temperature from falling too low. Since such systems need at least 50 gallons per minute for each acre to be protected, storage ponds and reservoirs have been dammed to guarantee the supply. But as the call is raised to leave the streams and valleys of many counties in a natural state, it has often been difficult for growers to find the water for frost protection programs.

Just as water for frost protection is not needed in every part of California, neither is it required for irrigation all across the state. In the North Coast districts, where annual rainfall is 30 to 40 inches, many vines are not irrigated, while others may have one deep soaking during the hottest part of the summer. For these plantations irrigation and frost control is often supplied by one sprinkler system. Other parts of the state have climates not so fortunate as some of the areas north of San Francisco. In the San Joaquin Valley, for instance, as much as three acre-feet (43,560 cubic feet) of water are needed each season to ensure good wine grape crops. In those places where it is required, the method of irrigation will vary. The new "drip" plan from Israel waters the plants with a light trickle of water from ground-level pipes. And those same sprinkler systems popular for frost control and irrigation in cooler parts of the state are also employed in the hot climates, where the fine mists help to keep temperatures down when the scorching sun may burn the grapes.

Since supplies of water for any purpose may be more expensive in the future, it is fortunate that not all of the new measures for warding off the spring and even autumn cold rely on it. Wind-machines are one such development. Ground-level models simply circulate the air over the vines to keep the temperature from dropping. Those mounted on towers mix the cool lower-level air with warmer air from above. Another new device is a sophisticated combination of the wind-machine and the smudge pot. Its propane heater first warms the air, then its blowers distribute the hot gas through the vine rows in a series of inflatable plastic ducts.

GRAPE VARIETIES

With the demand for good table wines increasing, more good varieties of *Vitis vinifera* are being planted in California than at any previous time. Unfortunately, however, some growers seeking fast profits from the high prices paid for the very best grapes are planting Cabernet Sauvignon, Pinot Noir, or other fine varieties in districts with climates much too hot for these vines to produce properly.

The largest single expansion of varietal plantings has occurred in Monterey, the lower end of the North Coast wine region. In the hot interior valleys such as the San Joaquin, there have also been improvements in the quality of the grapes. The attempt is being made to reduce the acreage of Thompson Seedless and other table grapes used regrettably for wine, in favor of sound *vinifera* or cross varieties.

The warmest parts of the state will never produce great wine from the classic European varieties, but with carefully selected vines—especially some of the crosses bred by the researchers at Davis—the average quality of much of the bulk wine can be raised.

As good wine grapes became more available, many California wines took on the name of the grape from which they were made.

A few of the red-wine grape varieties successfully planted in California are the Cabernet Sauvignon (sometimes referred to simply as Cabernet but not to be confused with the Cabernet Franc), Pinot Noir, Gamay Beaujolais, Grenache, Barbera, and Zinfandel. Some of the recommended white grape varieties are the Chardonnay, Sauvignon Blanc, Sémillon, Chenin Blanc, Pinot Blanc, White or Johannisberg Riesling, Sylvaner or Franken Riesling (sometimes called Riesling), Gewürztraminer and Traminer (also called the Red Traminer).

VINE-GROWING REGIONS

There are six natural vine-growing regions in California—the North Coast, the Sacramento Valley, the Central Valley, the San Joaquin Valley, the South Coast, and San Luis Obispo. Each has its well-known districts, and almost every grape and type of wine is produced in one or more of these.

These districts are gradually gaining the official recognition they deserve, in the form of BATF (Bureau of Alcohol, Tobacco and Firearms)-designated appellations. As the number of wineries and total wine productions continue to rise, the need for these standard-setting appellation laws becomes more obvious and urgent.

On the following pages is a listing of California's more prominent wineries. Efforts have been made, in quoting production figures, to estimate the amounts the wineries will produce by the 1990s.

North Coast

The North Coast region is north and south of San Francisco Bay in the many valleys which lie parallel to the coastal ranges and is generally characterized by warm summers and moderate annual rainfalls. The best dry table wines, both red and white, are grown here. The principal districts are Napa, Sonoma, Mendocino, Livermore, Santa Clara, San Benito, Santa Cruz, and Monterey.

(1) Napa

This is undoubtedly the most famous red wine district in California, with approximately 150 bonded wineries and some of the finest vineyards in the country. Napa is the Indian word for "plenty," and the valley abounds in rich, fertile land, while the hillsides are planted in fine grapes. There are approximately 30,000 acres (12,000 hectares) of vineyard, and in 1986, 80,000 tons of grapes were harvested. The average yield per acre was about 3 tons, or 50 hectoliters per hectare. This average is low, since much of the acreage was not bearing. The value of the crop exceeded $20 million, compared with $15 million for the Sonoma harvest.

More than half of the production is in red wine. The Cabernet Sauvignon is the royal grape of Napa, producing better than the Pinot Noir. The Cabernet, the same variety used in the great red Bordeaux, is very slow to mature in the Napa region and the wine is sometimes left in casks to age for as long as four years.

The cooler parts of the valley produce some of the best Cabernet Sauvignon wine in America. Since 1970, more than 3,800 acres (1,520 hectares) of this one variety have been added to the valley vineyards. With 6,600 acres (2,640 hectares) of Cabernet, Napa surpasses both Sonoma and Monterey in plantations of this varietal.

Napa is divided into the Upper Valley and the Lower Valley. The center of the Upper Napa Valley is the dignified town of St. Helena, but the district stretches 7 miles (11.3 kilometers) north toward Calistoga and in the south it goes as far as Rutherford and Oakville. The Lower Valley covers the area around the city of Napa, an hour's drive from San Francisco, and takes in the northwestern part of a wide valley bottom running up to the Sonoma County border. The soil in the southernmost part of Napa County is heavy and this region is the coolest, owing to its proximity to San Francisco Bay. The Upper Valley has a gravelly soil, and the mountains influence both the climate and the exposure.

It is a general opinion in Napa that if more grapes were planted on the slopes, better wine would be made—three-quarters of the vines are planted on the flats; and this is one of the few districts where the growers admit that they have good and bad years, so that some will be regarded as vintage years and others not. Another sign of progress in the valley has been the establishment of many group cooperatives; and since 1942 there has been a Vintner's Association to deal with recurrent problems.

Some of the most important vineyards are those of Beaulieu, Beringer, Robert Mondavi, Christian Brothers, Inglenook, Charles Krug, Louis Martini, Freemark Abbey, Sterling Vineyards, Schramsberg, Joseph Heitz, Chappellet, Cuvaison, Clos du Val, Trefethen, and Domaine Chandon, to name a few.

The Lower Napa Valley and Solano County are relatively small producers but the area has recently expanded into neighboring Chiles Valley. The Carneros area of the valley has recently proven to be a prime location and has become the "new" Pinot Noir and Chardonnay area. The cooling breezes from the Bay make Carneros particularly desirable for these varietals with the hope that the wines from this area will not suffer from excessive alcohol content.

Acacia Winery. Specializing in Pinot Noir and Chardonnay wines, this Carneros-district winery came into existence in 1979. A group of partners owned the winery until 1986, when it was acquired by the Chalone Group. Acacia sits high on a hill with a stupendous view of San Pablo Bay. Grapes from 50 acres (20 hectares) of vines in Carneros and local purchases are used to make about 30,000 cases annually. Larry Brooks is the wine-maker.

Beaulieu Vineyard. Georges de Latour founded this beautiful estate and the vineyards in 1900. He imported many cuttings from his native France and found the ideal site for them near Rutherford, where the gravelly soil holds the annual rains without need of irrigation. Beaulieu has maintained a continuous operation right from its beginning: the winery made sacramental wines during Prohibition, and when Repeal followed, Beaulieu enjoyed a success it had never had before with a wide distribution of wines throughout the United States.

There are now eight vineyards with about 1,000 acres (400 hectares) in active production, all of them in the center of Napa Valley, except for about 150 acres in the Carneros region, the southernmost part of the valley, where the bay breezes temper the climate. The principal varieties grown are the Pinot Noir, Chardonnay, Cabernet Sauvignon and Sauvignon Blanc. The Muscat de Frontignan variety, a fortified dessert wine, has been made in limited quantities since 1922, using a modified *solera* method. In 1969, the vineyard was sold to the Heublein Corporation.

One of the great wine-makers of the Napa Valley, André Tchelistcheff, began working under Joseph Ponti in 1937 at Beaulieu. He eventually became the official wine-maker until his retirement in 1973. Tchelistcheff started the tradition of making a Pinot Noir wine, and despite his relative successes with the Beaulieu Pinot Noirs, particularly those from the Carneros region, they are no substitute for the Côte d'Or Burgundies. Tchelistcheff's influence on California's quality wines is an important milestone in California wine history.

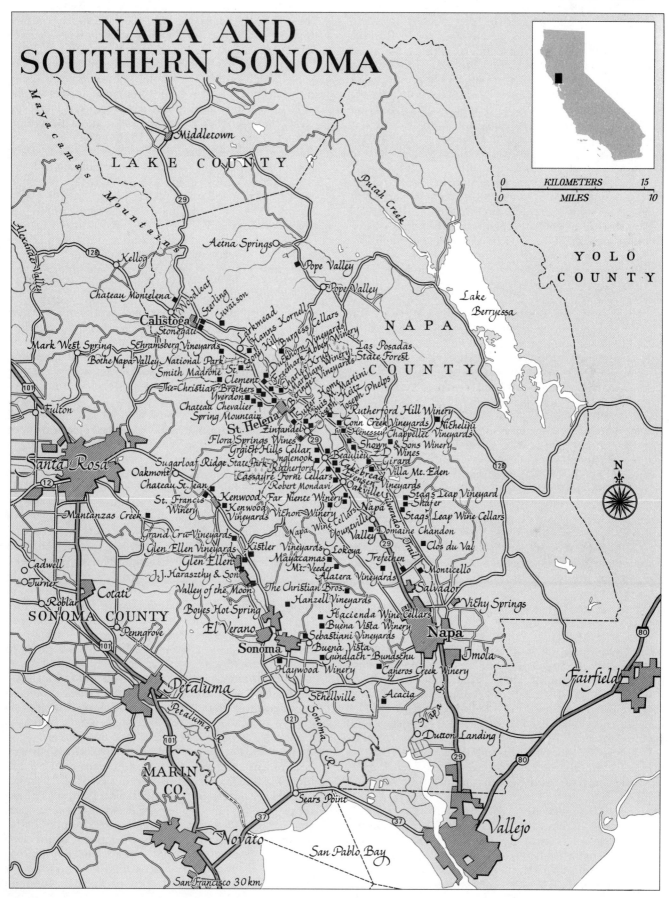

NAPA AND SOUTHERN SONOMA

KILOMETERS
0   15
0   10
MILES

Mayacamas Mountains

Alexander Valley

Middletown

LAKE COUNTY

Putah Creek

YOLO COUNTY

Aetna Springs

Pope Valley

Pope Valley

Lake Berryessa

Kellog

Chateau Montelena

Woodleaf
Sterling
Guvaison

Calistoga
Stonegate
Larkmead
Hanns Kornell
Burgess Cellars

NAPA COUNTY

Mark West Spring
Schramsberg Vineyards
Bothe Napa Valley National Park
Smith Madrone
The Christian Brothers
Yverdon
Chateau Chevalier
Spring Mountain

Long Hill
Duckhorn Vineyards
Freemark Abbey Winery
Charles Krug
Markham Vineyards
St. Clement
Bringer Vineyards
Louis M. Martini
Sutter Home
Jos. Heitz
Joseph Phelps

Las Posadas
State Forest

Fulton

St. Helena
Zinfandel
Flora Springs Wines
Grgich Hills Cellar
Inglenook
Sugarloaf Ridge State Park
Oakmont
Chateau St. Jean
St. Francis Winery
Kenwood
Kenwood Vineyards

Rutherford Hill Winery
Conn Creek Vineyards
Nichelini
Hennessey
Chappellet Vineyards
Shown & Sons Winery
Z.D. Wines
Beaulieu
Girard
Villa Mt. Eden

Santa Rosa

Rutherford
Cassayre Forni Cellars
Robert Mondavi
Far Niente Winery
Vichon Winery

Oakebread
Evensen Vineyards
Oakville
Napa
Stags Leap Vineyard
Shafer
Stags' Leap Wine Cellars

Mantanzas Creek

Grand Cru Vineyards
Glen Ellen Vineyards
Glen Ellen
J.J. Haraszthy & Son
Valley of the Moon
Boyes Hot Spring
El Verano

Kistler Vineyards
Mayacamas
Mt. Veeder
Alatera Vineyards
The Christian Bros.
Hanzell Vineyards

Napa Wine Cellars
Mountville
Napa Valley
Domaine Chandon
Clos du Val
Trefethen
Monticello

Cadwell
Turner
Roblar
Cotati
SONOMA COUNTY
Penngrove

Salvador
Vichy Springs

Sonoma
Hacienda Wine Cellars
Buena Vista Winery
Sebastiani Vineyards
Buena Vista
Gundlach-Bundschu
Haywood Winery

Napa
Imola

Caneros Creek Winery

N

Petaluma

Schellville
Acacia

Fairfield

Petaluma

Sonoma
R.

Dutton Landing

Napa R.

MARIN CO.

Sears Point

San Pablo Bay

Novato

Vallejo

San Francisco 30 km

For the past thirty-five years, the wines of Beaulieu, particularly the Georges de Latour Private Reserve Cabernet Sauvignon, have been among the finest wines produced in the United States.

Beringer Brothers. Two German brothers, Frederick and Jacob Beringer, assured the success of this well-known winery, founded in 1876 at St. Helena. Their original spacious "Rheinhaus" is just north of the city limits. After many years of operation by the Beringer family, the vineyard and winery were sold in 1970 to Nestlé International.

The beautiful tunnels excavated in the limestone hills behind the old winery have been preserved. A new winery has been built directly across Highway 29 from the Rhine House to handle the Beringer-owned vineyards of 2,700 acres (1,080 hectares) of Napa Valley and Knight's Valley (Sonoma County).

Beringer is one of the most picturesque wineries in the Napa Valley and attracts thousands of visitors every year.

Until 1986, the Bordeaux oenologist Patrick Léon was Beringer's consultant and he was succeeded by the Médoc oenologist Mr. Boissenot, who in turn was followed by Mr. Mondavi, formerly of Château Latour.

Other Nestlé wine properties are: Souverain in Sonoma, Napa Ridge, and Los Hermanos in Napa Valley. Nestlé is also a shareholder in the Maison Deutz and C & B Vintage Cellars.

Burgess Cellars. Formerly Souverain Cellars, built in 1943 by J. Leland Stewart, Burgess Cellars is located at about 1,000 feet (300 meters) elevation on the western slopes of Howell Mountain, northeast of St. Helena. Since 1972, when they bought these 22 acres (9 hectares), former corporate pilot Tom Burgess and his wife, Linda, one-time New Yorkers, have made several wines and now specialize in Chardonnay, Zinfandel, and Cabernet Sauvignon. Bill Sorenson is the wine-maker behind the 30,000-case annual production. The Burgess Chardonnay is fermented in oak barrels.

Cain Cellars. A 540-acre (216-hectare) ranch near the top of Spring Mountain bought by Jerry and Joyce Cain in 1980. To date, the Cains make two white and three red wines plus an unusual estate-bottled Malbec.

Cakebread Cellars. While still maintaining his commercial photography, auto repair, and agricultural businesses, Jack Cakebread, along with his wife, Dolores, and his three sons, added wine-making to his many careers in 1973. Forty acres (16 hectares) of vines surrounding the St. Helena winery (designed by Cakebread), plus grapes from local vineyards, provide enough fruit for an annual 40,000 cases. Chardonnay, Sauvignon Blanc and Cabernet Sauvignon, wines are made.

Carneros Creek Winery. Balfour Gibson (previously part owner of San Francisco's Connoisseur Wine Imports), his wife, Anita, and Francis and Kathleen Mahoney form the four-person wine-making team at their 22-acre (8-hectare) Carneros Creek Winery, established in 1973. They are concentrating on growing Pinot Noir. Purchased grapes are used to make Chardonnay, and Cabernet Sauvignon. Relatively close to San Pablo Bay, beneath the slopes of Miliken Peak, Carneros Creek is one of the southernmost wineryies in the Napa Valley. The cooler temperatures and fog in this area enable the grapes to mature longer on the vine; hence the Chardonnay can be picked later, ensuring a good balance between sugar and acidity. Carneros Creek produces about 15,000 cases a year.

Caymus Vineyards. Located on Conn Creek Road in Rutherford, Caymus Vineyards is the domain of longtime Napa Valley grape-grower Charles Wagner, whose German relatives produce wine in the Alsace region. Wagner made his first Cabernet Sauvignon and Pinot Noir in 1972. With the assistance of his son Chuck, nine wines are sold under the Caymus and secondary Liberty School labels, including a first-rate Cabernet Sauvignon and a good Sauvignon Blanc. The 72 acres (30 hectares) of vines yield an average of 50,000 cases annually.

Chappellet Vineyards. One of the most beautiful wineries constructed in the North Coast area is Chappellet, situated on Pritchard Hill, 1,400 feet (424 meters) above the floor of the Napa Valley. It was planned and built by Donn Chappellet, a southern Californian who made a success in the automatic food-vending business. The hillside land he purchased in 1967 (110 acres or 44 hectares) is now planted in Chardonnay, Cabernet Sauvignon, Chenin Blanc, and Johannisberg Riesling. Merlot is also grown and is used primarily in blending with the Cabernet.

The handsome pyramid-shaped winery, built into the side of a hill among oak trees, blends beautifully into the terrain. Its gleaming stainless steel fermenting vats contrast with the new wooden cooperage and the matte metal roof. The oenologist is Cathy Corison.

Chateau Bouchaine. This winery was founded in 1980 on the premise that the Burgundian ideals of elegance, balance, and depth of fruit can be applied to American vine-growing and wine-making. With that in mind, Bouchaine specializes in Chardonnay and Pinot Noir. Grapes for the wines are all purchased from Napa County growers, with the exception of the fruit from the 30-acre (12-hectare) vineyard contiguous to the Carneros-district winery. The redwood structure, a pre-Prohibition winery, was gutted and modernized in time for Chateau Bouchaine's first crush. Projected production is 25,000 cases a year. Jerry Luper, formerly of Chateau Montelena and Freemark Abbey, is a partner in the business and the wine-maker.

Château Chevalier. In 1969, a stockbroker and his wife bought this abandoned winery and restored it, retaining the name given it by its founder George Chevalier in 1891. Brothers John and Gil Nickel (owners of another Napa Valley winery, Far Niente, *(q.v.)*, purchased the property in 1984 and completely replanted the 60-acre (24-hectare) vineyard to produce Cabernet Sauvignon, Chardonnay and Pinot Noir. The magnificent Victorian-style mansion and winery is located on the steep hill sides of Spring Mountain outside St. Helena. Production remains at about 10,-000 cases under the new ownership.

Chateau Montelena. Ever since this winery's 1973 Chardonnay surpassed four top French white Burgundies and five other California Chardonnays in a blind tasting held by a panel of experts in Paris in 1976, its wines have continued to live up to their reputation. Alfred Tubbs, a wealthy San Franciscan whaling man, built the handsome stone winery in 1882. Owned by retired attorney James L. Barrett, businessman Lee Paschich, and real estate developer Ernest Hahn since 1968, Chateau Montelena produces four wines. Bo Barrett, son of one of the owners, is the wine-maker. One hundred acres (40 hectares) of grapes contribute to the 25,000 cases of wine made a year. The Chardonnays are consistently good. Located on the foothills of Mount St. Helena at the northern end of Calistoga, Chateau Montelena features the 5-acre (2-hectare) man-made Jade Lake.

The Christian Brothers. The Christian Brothers, a religious order founded by St. Jean Baptiste de la Salle in France in the seventeenth century, came to California in 1868 and began what is now the largest vineyard operation in the Napa Valley. The Brothers own more than 1,300 acres (520 hectares) of vineyards on Mont La Salle on the edge of the Napa Valley and along Redwood Road in the Mayacamas range. One of their several winemaking facilities is the old "Greystone" ageing cellar just north of St. Helena near Charles Krug and Beringer. Christian Brothers makes vintage-dated varietal wines, table wines, sparkling wines and dessert wines in addition to their brandy, of which they sell more than any other distiller in the United States. Fromm & Sichel, now called The Christian Brothers Sales Co., are the exclusive distributors. Profits from the brandy- and wine-making go to the thirteen schools supported by the Brothers.

Cellarmaster Brother Timothy, one of the industry's more colorful figures, has travelled the country with his collection of antique wine accessories and illustrations.

Chimney Rock Wine Cellars. Formerly an 18-hole golf-course, this 75-acre (30-hectare) vineyard was bought in 1980 by Sheldon 'Hack' Wilson and his wife Stella. Now producing about 20,000 cases, the Wilsons make a Chardonnay, Sauvignon Blanc and Cabernet Sauvignon.

Clos du Val. Deserving admiration is frenchman Bernard Portet, who in 1972 produced his first wines, Cabernet Sauvignon and Zinfandel. Chardonnay and Merlot were added later. Clos du Val has about 300 acres (120 hectares) of vineyards in the Stag's Leap and Carneros districts, and eventually will produce 50,000 cases annually. Excellent Médoc-like vinification.

Conn Creek Winery. Formerly off Highway 29 between St. Helena and Calistoga, Conn Creek moved to Silverado near Rutherford in 1979. It was founded in 1974 by Bill and Kathy Collins. Between 1981 and 1984, the DeWavrin-Woltner family were partial owners, and in mid-1986, a majority of the winery was sold to the U.S. Tobacco Company. The Collins retain ownership interests, and Bill Collins acts as president of the winery. Conn Creek makes a total of about 25,000 cases yearly of Cabernet Sauvignon, Chardonnay and Merlot. Most of the grapes used come from the Collins' own vineyards.

Cuvaison Winery This small winery is north of St. Helena along the Silverado Trail, which runs parallel to "wine" Highway 29. In 1970 two wine-lovers, Thomas Cottrell and Thomas Parkhill, established Cuvaison with the intention of making a limited number of 100% varietal, vintage-dated table wines. In 1973 a controlling interest was purchased by Oakleigh Thorne of New York, who in turn sold Cuvaison in 1979 to a Swiss businessman, Alexander Schmidheiny. Cabernet Sauvignon, Zinfandel, Merlot and Chardonnay wines are produced. Cuvaison has 300 acres (120 hectares) of vineyards in the Carneros district and hopes to be making 40,000 cases of estate-bottled wines by the late eighties.

Diamond Creek Vineyards. Situated high up on Diamond Mountain, due west of Sterling Vineyards and minutes from Schramsberg and Calistoga, this secluded 20-acre (8-hectare) vineyard was founded in 1968 and makes three Cabernet Sauvignon wines, based on three different soil types, from 88% Cabernet Sauvignon grapes, 8% Merlot, and 4% Cabernet Franc. Originally from Los Angeles, Al Brounstein formerly a whole sale distributor of propriety drugs, and his wife, Boots, are the proprietors; they aim to make tannic concentrated wines that require a long aging period. Their 2,500 cases production consists of 3 Cabernet Sauvignons: Volcanic Hills, Gravelly Meadows, and Red Rock Terrace.

Domaine Chandon. In 1976 Domaine Chandon, owned by the French Moët-Hennessy combine, launched its first wines in the California market. Their major product is a sparkling wine, one that is not labeled Champagne, since Moët adheres to the view that Champagne itself can come only from the Champagne district of France. About 30% of the grapes are supplied by their own 1,500 acres (600 hectares) located from Yountville down to Carneros. Other grapes are purchased, some from the Trefethen vineyards. Production is about 500,000 cases annually.

Domaine Mumm. In the early 1980's, Seagram & Sons formed a joint venture with G.H. Mumm, the French champagne house. Their first release, Domaine Mumm Cuvée Napa, was launched in early 1986. Guy Devaux, originally from Champagne, presides over the operation together with Michel Budin, director of production at Mumm in France. Domaine Mumm was constructed at the foot of Sterling Winery, Seagram's Napa Valley property *(q.v.).*

Duckhorn Winery. Operated by Dan and Margaret Duckhorn, this winery's first wines were made in 1978 at the Silverado Trail location, north of St. Helena. About 15,000 cases of wine (Cabernet Sauvignon, Merlot and Sauvignon Blanc) are made a year from estate-grown and locally-purchased grapes. Tom Rinaldi is the winemaker.

Far Niente Winery. Proprietor and wine-maker Gil Nickel, produced Far Niente's first Chardonnay in 1979. His renovated stone winery, just south of Oakville, was originally built in 1885. The 1982 production of 11,000 cases will increase to 28,000. About 70% of the grapes come from its own vineyard, but when all of its young vines mature, Far Niente will produce estate-grown wines. In addition to its big, full Chardonnay, Far Niente makes a Cabernet Sauvignon.

Flora Springs Winery. Owned and operated by the Komes and Garvey families, Flora Springs produced its first wine from the 1978 harvest. The renovation of the stone winery, built in 1888, was completed in 1983. The winery is on St. Helena's Zinfandel Lane. Primarily growers, the Komes sell about 80% of the fruit grown on their 325-acre (130-hectare) vineyard; the remaining 20% makes the winery's annual 20,000-case production. Cabernet Sauvignon, Sauvignon Blanc, and Chardonnay are produced, with Ken Deis doing the wine-making.

Franciscan Vineyards. This winery was sold by founders Raymond Duncan and Justin Meyer in 1979 to the German beverage firm of Peter Eckes & Company, the world's largest producer of brandy, (including the Maria Krön label). Chilean-born Agustin Huneeus is president of the winery. Franciscan grows all its own grapes for its annual 95,000-case production on 500 acres (200 hectares) of vines (half of which are in Sonoma County's Alexander Valley). The wine-making facility is on the wine highway 6 miles (9.5 kilometers) south of St. Helena at Rutherford. The first grapes were harvested in 1973 and the first wines marketed in 1974. Fransiscan's most successful wines are under the Estancia label.

Freemark Abbey Winery. Seven partners reorganized this winery, which is located a short distance north of St. Helena, the premier wine town of the Napa Valley. Freemark Abbey's modern and well-equipped wine-making facilities are in the lower levels of a handsome old brownstone building built in the late nineteenth century and in two newer adjoining buildings. The upper section of the large structure is a store devoted to candles, cookware, and specialized merchandise. Freemark Abbey has 130 acres (52 hectares) of vines in the Napa Valley, and only varietal table wines such as Chardonnay and Cabernet are produced. An "Edelwein" is made from botrytised Johannisberg Riesling grapes and a Cabernet Sauvignon is also made. Production averages 30,000 cases annually. The partners have experimented extensively with aging their wines in oak cooperage, and use only French oak barrels. Some of the owners of Freemark Abbey are involved in the ownership of Rutherford Hill Winery (*q.v.*) as of 1976.

Grgich Hills Cellar. Formerly wine-maker at Chateau Montelena, Mike Grgich, who worked with André Tchelistcheff, joined forces in 1977 with Austin Hills, of the Hills Brothers coffee family, to establish this

winery near the intersection of Highway 29 and Rutherford Road. Mike Grgich made the 1973 Chateau Montelena Chardonnay, which surpassed four French white Burgundies in a 1976 Paris tasting. Now he makes wines from grapes grown on Hills' three properties, one in cooler southern Napa, one in Yountville and the other near Rutherford. Total acreage of vines is 220 (88 hectares). Annual production is around 30,000 cases. Emphasis is on Fumé Blanc and Chardonnay; a Zinfandel was introduced in 1979, and a Cabernet was released in 1984.

Heitz Wine Cellars. With only 125 acres (50 hectares) of home vineyards at his winery, Joseph Heitz looks to other growers in the Napa Valley for many of the grapes to be used in his good, expensive, varietal table wines. Heitz, a former professor of oenology, with a reputation as a master wine-blender, began his own operations in the early 1960s. He first bought the tiny property of Leon Brendel in St. Helena and then purchased an old stone winery with vineyards on Taplin Road, a few miles east of the town. Within a decade, his wines had become so successful that Heitz expanded his facilities. Production is 40,000 cases annually. Heitz makes a wide variety of wines: Chardonnay, Cabernet, Pinot Noir, Zinfandel, and Grignolino, plus "Champagne" and "Port."

Inglenook-Napa Valley Vineyards. This winery is just off Highway 29—called the Napa Valley Wine Road—at the crossroads town of Rutherford. The nearby vineyards were founded in 1879 by Captain Gustave F. Niebaum, on the slopes of Mount St. John. He kept up the vineyards until his death in 1908. His great-nephew, the late John Daniel Jr., became the general manager in 1937. Daniel directed its operation through Prohibition, and after Repeal successfully carried on the family tradition of growing fine grapes on the 225-acre (90-hectare) Rutherford Ranch vineyard which was replanted under the present management. Daniel's heirs are still active in the Napa Valley wine business today. (*See* Moueix-Daniel.) In 1964 the Inglenook organization was sold to United Vintners, which in turn became part of Heublein in 1969. Film director Francis Ford Coppola, of *Godfather* fame, purchased the Niebaum mansion in 1975, and established his own vineyard and winery, the Niebaum-Coppola Estates (*q.v.*). In 1983, Heublein sold most of its wine interests to Allied Grape Growers, but retained Inglenook-Napa Valley in Rutherford and Inglenook-Navalle in Madera (*q.v.*). John Richburg is the present wine-maker, only the first in Inglenook's history of over a century.

Though the production of generic wines was begun by the new owners, they have continued to make some of the fine vintage varietal wines which originally brought fame to the property. The great days of Inglenook started in the 1880s and continued through the late 1930s, when the company became the first California winery to restrict its output to varietals. Bottles of Cabernet Sauvignon and "Cask Selection" wines from these vintages are rare and fetch very high prices at auctions. At present, Inglenook makes white wines and reds, including the rare Charbono.

Keenan Winery. The 45 acres (18 hectares) of steep, terraced vineyards on the slopes of Spring Mountain, originally built by Peter Conradi in 1904, are planted with Chardonnay, Cabernet Sauvignon, Cabernet Franc and Merlot varieties. The first Keenan wines were produced in 1977. Proprietor Robert Keenan, a former San Francisco insurance executive, is limiting production of his wines, which are made in the traditional French method of small cooperage, to a maximum of 10,000 cases a year. Keenan makes a consistently good Chardonnay. All of Keenan's wines are estate-grown.

Hanns Kornell Champagne Cellars. The Hanns Kornell cellars are located 5 miles (8 kilometers) north of St. Helena and east of Highway 29. German-born and -trained Kornell is one of the few remaining independent "champagne" producers in California, even though his winery on Larkmead Lane has been turning out sparkling wine for more than thirty years. The winery itself dates from the late nineteenth century. Kornell took it over after moving from Sonoma, where he established his first winery in 1952. There are no vineyards, for Kornell buys still wine and then develops his sparkling cuvées. He has an inventory of more than 4 million individually processed bottles resting in his cellars. "Sehr Trocken" wine is in the style of the German Sekt and is vintage-dated. A Blanc de Blanc was released in 1983 and is also vintage-dated. Kornell's daughter, Paula, is marketing director, and his son Peter is being groomed to take over as winemaker.

Charles Krug Winery. Established in 1861, this is the oldest operating winery in Napa Valley. The old winery building, trimmed in brown and gold, is north of St. Helena along Highway 29, framed by nearby mountains. In the mid-sixties, after a long simmering family feud, brother Robert Mondavi left Krug to start his own winery (*q.v.*). Krug is now owned and operated by C. Mondavi and Sons, under the leadership of Peter Mondavi and his two sons Marc, and Peter Jr.

Charles Krug, one of the great names in California wine history, was a worthy pupil of Colonel Haraszthy in Sonoma. In 1858 he made the first commercial wine in Napa County, using a small cider press. He built his first winery and planted his first vines on the present St. Helena site in 1861, and soon his wines were famous throughout America and in Europe. During his lifetime he trained C. H. Wente, Jacob Beringer, C. J. Wetmore, and many other leading Californian winemakers, and was a prominent figure in California wine circles until his death in 1892.

Since 1943, when the Mondavis acquired the Krug winery buildings and vineyards, the size, scope, and efficiency of the cellars have increased. They are among the best equipped and most efficient in California. The family has also pioneered wine-making innovations and techniques. Krug Chenin Blanc was the first varietal made from that grape in California.

The premium wines of C. Mondavi & Sons come under two labels: Charles Krug varietal wines (400,000 cases annually) and C. K. Mondavi table wines (1 million cases annually). Vineyards in St. Helena, Yountville, and Carneros cover 1,200 acres (480 hectares).

Llords & Elwood Winery. Founded in 1955 in the San José area by late wine retailer Mike Elwood, Llords & Elwood is now located in Yountville and run by his family. The winery produces a solera-method sherry and several other wines. Production averages 15,000 cases a year.

Long Vineyards. Robert Long's grapes, grown on 15 acres (6 hectares) of vines on the steep slopes of Pritchard Hill in St. Helena, have provided neighboring wineries with some exceptional wines (Mount Veeder's Chardonnays are one example). As of 1977, Long has been making small quantities (no more than 2,000 cases annually) under the Long Vineyards label. Chardonnay, Johannisberg Riesling, and Cabernet wines are produced. Long's former wife, Zelma, oenologist at Simi in Sonoma, is the wine-making consultant.

Louis M. Martini Winery. Founder Louis M. Martini was born in Pietra Ligure, Italy, in 1887 and came to the United States at the turn of the century. For many years his dream had been to produce excellent wines, and when Prohibition was repealed in 1933, he built a large winery at St. Helena, some 65 miles (104 kilometers) north of San Francisco. Over the next ten years he acquired three important, well-situated vineyards and planted them with fine grape varieties. In 1941, Frank Schoonmaker (who deserves the gratitude of all California premium producers) and I started selling American wines under American names. It was then that Louis Martini wines, among others, were for the first time offered east of the Rockies.

The family vineyards today consist of 1,720 acres (690 hectares) in Carneros, the mountains near Sonoma, Healdsburg, St. Helena, Lake County, and Pope Valley.

The late Louis Martini at age 86 was the dean of Napa Valley grape-growers and certainly one of the most important figures in the California industry. His son, Louis P. Martini, is chairman of the company. The third generation, Mike, Carolyn, and Patricia, are all engaged in running the family business. Martini wines have a national reputation for quality and fair price.

Mayacamas Vineyards. The beautiful terraced Mayacamas vineyards are high on the crests of the Mayacamas Mountains, up the tortuous, steep Lokoya Road and 2,000 feet (600 meters) above sea level. They are about 9 miles (14 kilometers) from Route 29. The original owner, Jack F. M. Taylor, began to make wine there in 1945. He and his wife, Mary, were among the first new producers of good wine in Napa after the Second World War. Their output included seventeen red and white table wines, and a remarkable Zinfandel Rosé.

In 1968 Robert Travers and his wife, together with a few partners, bought the small, artisan-like winery and the vineyards from the Taylors. The quality has remained high, but wisely, the selection of wines has been cut back to vintage-dated varietals: Chardonnay, Cabernet Sauvignon, and some other wines. There are 50 acres (20 hectares) of vines. About 5,000 cases are made a year.

Robert Mondavi Winery. One of the leaders of the premium wine industry in California today is quality-minded Robert Mondavi. He and his sons Michael and Timothy and daughter Marcia produce some of the best varietal wines in the United States. Years of work as a partner in the Charles Krug Winery gave Mondavi the experience needed to launch a new operation of his own in 1966. The winery, northwest of the historic town of Yountville, is one of the most efficient and handsome in the state. Mondavi's philosophy is similar to that of the other conscientious North Coast vintners: "There is a place for a relatively small winery to produce, in a limited quantity, wines that will have the complexity and character to be found in the great growths of the world."

The Mondavi vineyards cover 1,100 acres (440 hectares). Once the winery had had its first harvest and began to grow, a share of the business was bought by the Rainier Brewing Company of Seattle, Washington. As of 1978, the winery is once again wholly family-owned.

Robert Mondavi was one of the first in California to experiment with barrels for aging made from different types of oak. In 1979, Mondavi and Baron Philippe de Rothschild, proprietor of Château Mouton-Rothschild and other *Grands Crus* in Pauillac, formed a joint venture, with "Opus One" the proprietary name. A 140-acre (56-hectare) vineyard provides grapes for the Mondavi-Rothschild wine. Plans are in the making for a separate winery, slated for construction in Oakville.

The Spanish-style Mondavi Winery, with handsome paneling and spacious patios, is used by groups for luncheons and wine tastings. The Mondavis also sponsor musical events and Great Chef programs.

Moueix-Daniel. Christian Moueix, son of the co-owner of Château Pétrus of Pomerol and of many other fine vineyards in the Saint-Émilion area, has entered into a joint venture with the heirs of John Daniel. They own a 120-acre (50-hectare) vineyard in west Yountville in Napa. These associates produce "Dominus," a Cabernet-based red.

Half of the vineyard, whose fruit is sold, is planted in white and the other half in old vines of Cabernet Sauvignon, Cabernet Franc, and Merlot.

The plan is to build a winery at this estate. In the meantime, under Christian Moueix's supervision, the grapes are being vinified at the new Rombauer Winery (*q.v.*) on the Silverado Trail.

Mount Veeder Winery. Miami real estate investor Henry Matheson and his wife Lisille bought this small winery and vineyard in 1982. The original owners began planting grapes in 1968; at present, Mount Veeder's 25-acre (10-hectare) vineyard, about 1,000 to 1,400 feet (300 to 425 meters) high in the Mayacamas Mountains, is planted almost entirely in red Bordeaux varietals (Cabernet Sauvignon, Cabernet Franc, Merlot, Malbec and Petit Verdot). The annual 5,000-case production consists of only Cabernet and Chardonnay, both from estate-grown grapes.

Newton Vineyard. Landscaped with formal English gardens and built onto the hillside of Spring Mountain, the Newton Vineyard is the property of partners Peter and Su-Hua Newton longtime Napa residents. Sixty acres (24 hectares) of hillside vines provide some of the grapes for Newton's Cabernet Sauvignon, Merlot, Chardonnay, and Sauvignon Blanc wines; additional grapes are purchased. John Kongsgaard is the wine-maker for the annual 20,000-case production.

Niebaum-Coppola Estates. Francis Ford Coppola, the film director, entered into the wine business in 1975 with the purchase of the Niebaum estate, one-time home of millionaire sea captain and Inglenook founder, Gustav Niebaum. Located in Rutherford, Niebaum-Coppola Estates consists of 85 acres (34 hectares) of vines yielding an annual 4,000 cases. Stephen Beresini oversees the wine-making and winery management. Emphasis is on achieving a premium Cabernet Sauvignon by blending three varietals from estate-grown grapes. A proprietary blend, Rubicon, was first released in 1985.

Robert Pecota Winery. Constructed in 1978, this Calistoga winery offers three wines. Forty acres (16 hectares) of vines adjacent to the winery provide grapes for about 20,000 cases a year. Cabernet Sauvignon, Sauvignon Blanc, and a small amount of Muscat Blanc, a light dessert wine are produced.

Robert Pepi Winery. The Pepi family designed their winery to specialize in the production of a Graves-style Sauvignon Blanc. The wine is aged in upright oak tanks for 6 to 8 months to develop complexity without extracting too much oak. The Pepis have owned their 70-acre (28-hectare) vineyard in Oakville since 1966, while still in the fur business, and sold their grapes until the winery was completed in 1981. They produce about 20,000 cases annually of mostly Sauvignon Blanc, with small amounts of Semillon, Cabernet Sauvignon and Chardonnay.

Joseph Phelps Vineyards. After building two neighboring wineries, Joseph Phelps, president of a Colorado-based construction company, decided to establish his own vineyards on this former ranch on the Silverado Trail, not far from St. Helena, next door to Heitz Wine Cellars. Since 1973, he has been producing eight wines, known for their elegance and balance. These include a Sauvignon Blanc from grapes grown on his 225 acres (90 hectares) and from grapes purchased locally. Walter Schug, the original wine-maker, was trained in Geisenheim, Germany, his successor Craig Williams took the reins in 1983. Production is about 70,000 cases a year. Phelps has planted some experimental Syrah vines (as opposed to Petite Sirah) that are imported from France's Rhone Valley. He also makes some excellent botrytised or late-harvest Rieslings, and Scheurebe, a dessert wine. Phelps also produces a moderately priced wine grown from vineyards adjacent to the winery.

Pine Ridge Winery. Housed in a renovated pre-Prohibition winery in the Stag's Leap appellation, Pine Ridge makes four wines, Merlot, Cabernet Sauvignon, Chardonnay and Chenin Blanc. Partners Gary Andrus (also the winemaker and manager) and J.B. Haralson recently expanded the winery (which was founded in 1978) to a 40,000 case production. The owners grow five varietals on 210 acres (84 hectares) of vineyards and hope one day to have a completely estate-grown operation.

Raymond Vineyards and Cellars. When the Nestlé Company bought Beringer Winery in 1970, the Raymond family (active father Roy Senior and sons Roy Junior and Walter), all part owners of Beringer, purchased and planted 90 acres (36 hectares) south of St. Helena, with plans to establish their own winery. In 1974, the Raymonds' first wines, a Cabernet Sauvignon and a Zinfandel, were crushed. The family-run operation turns out about 80,000 cases annually. The wines are made from eight different grape varieties and are all vintage-dated—a lower priced secondary line called "La Belle". The quality varies, but the wines are generally good. The Raymonds grow most of their own grapes. Walter Raymond is the wine-maker.

Remy-Martin/Schramsberg. In September 1982, Jack and Jamie Davies, owners of Schramsberg Vineyards, embarked on a joint venture with Remy-Martin, one of Cognac's leading producers. As pioneers in this field, the partners' goal is to produce a unique American brandy of the same calibre as the French originals. Sparing no expense, a handsome facility with eight alambic pot stills and two barrel houses (with a capacity for 7000 Limousin oak barrels) was constructed in Napa's Carneros district. The first release, RMS California Brandy, debuted in 1985.

Rombauer Vineyards. Although about 75% of the wines made at this Silverado Trail facility are custom-crushed for about a dozen other assorted vintners (including Moueix Dominus (q.v.), Koerner and Joan Rombauer have been making small amounts of Chardonnay and Cabernet Sauvignon under their own label since 1982. Rombauer, an airline pilot and descendant of one of the authors of *The Joy of Cooking,* oversees the entire operation including his own 10,000-case production; Bob Levy is the winemaker.

Round Hill Cellars. Ernie and Virginia Van Asperen (of the "Ernie's Liquors" retail chain) founded Round Hill in 1976, patterning their wine-making philosophy after the French *négociants'* system. By purchasing local grapes and bulk wine, then vinifying, blending, bottling and aging the wines at the Round Hill facility on St. Helena's Lodi Lane, a wide selection of reasonably priced wines is produced without worry about a single vine. Charles Abela, a former marine mechanic who worked for Ernie for many years, bought Round Hill in 1977 and is president of the winery. About 20,000 cases of wine are produced from purchased grapes and additional 180,000 cases are cellared and sold under three labels (Rutherford Ranch, Round Hill Vineyards, and Round Hill Cellars), annually.

Rutherford Winery. Sharing the same road and hillside as the Napa Valley's famed restaurant and lodge, Auberge de Soleil, the impressive Rutherford Hill Winery resembles a huge hay barn of earlier years. It was founded in 1976 by a group of partners who are also involved in the Freemark Abbey Winery in St. Helena (*q.v.*). Rutherford Hill currently produces 120,000 cases of five varieties. The grapes come from partner-owned vineyards in the Napa Valley. In 1985, the winery completed construction of extensive mined wine-ageing caves with a 6,500-barrel capacity.

Saint Clement Vineyards. Dr. William Casey, a San Francisco ophthalmologist, and his wife, Alexandria, both wine enthusiasts and gourmets, purchased their winery and restored Victorian mansion on the lower slopes of Spring Mountain in St. Helena in 1975 from Mike Robbins. Small quantities of Cabernet Sauvignon, Sauvignon Blanc, and very good Chardonnay wines have been sold under the Saint Clement label since 1975. His three wines are from 100% Napa Valley grapes. Production is about 10,000 cases annually.

Schramsberg Vineyards. Established by a German pioneer, Jacob Schram, the old winery had fallen upon hard times when Jack Davies, an energetic man from Los Angeles, bought the abandoned building and vineyards in 1965. He brought a group of partners into the venture, but it is Davies and his wife who live at Schramsberg and produce its famous sparkling wines. Schramsberg makes only sparkling wines. Former President Nixon took Schramsberg wine to China on his 1972 visit. Davies had replanted the 40 acres (16 hectares) of home vineyard with Pinot Noir and Chardonnay grapes, from which he makes Blanc de Blancs and Blanc de Noir wines. In 1985, the Davieses acquired an adjoining vineyard, bringing the estate to about 60 acres (24 hectares). Production is about 50,000 cases annually.

The winery is on a winding road off Highway 29, between St. Helena and Calistoga. The building dates from the middle of the nineteenth century and has been designated a state landmark.

In September 1982, Schramsberg and Remy-Martin/Far East embarked on a joint brandy-making venture. From California-grown grapes, brandy is made in their Carneros distillery (completed in 1983) following traditional methods. A production of 15,000 cases is projected for 1985.

Shafer Vineyard. Leaving the educational-publication industry behind in Illinois, the Shafers came to California, formed a family partnership, replanted some hillside vineyards in 1973, and founded their winery in 1979. Located in Napa's eastern foothills (in the Stag's Leap district), the Shafers will use all their own grapes (from 65 acres or 26 hectares) to make 14,000 cases of Chardonnay, Cabernet Sauvignon and Merlot. Doug Shafer is the wine-maker.

Charles F. Shaw Winery. Charles F. Shaw has produced a "Méthode Beaujolais" Napa Gamay since 1979 from his St. Helena location.. He is the only American producer of Gamay to bud clones imported from the town of Fleurie in Beaujolais. With the addition of Ric Forman in 1983 as wine-maker, the winery expanded its production to include a Fumé Blanc and a Chardonnay, made in Forman's unique style. Production reached a maximum of 25,000 cases. Shaw owns 50 acres (20 hectares) of vines.

Shown & Sons. Eighteen-year Napa resident Richard Shown purchased this Rutherford property (near Stag's Leap) in the early seventies. He replaced walnut trees with vines and grows all the grapes on 80 acres (32 hectares) needed for his 16,000 annual cases of Cabernet Sauvignon, Zinfandel, Chenin Blanc, Johannisberg Riesling, and Chardonnay. The winery was built new in 1977 and sits on the Silverado Trail across from the driveway up to the Auberge du Soleil restaurant and the Rutherford Hill Winery. Jim Vahl and Gary Gouvea work together to make the wines.

Silverado Vineyards. 1981 marked the first crush at this new Spanish Colonial-style winery on the Silverado Trail, outside Yountville. Mrs. Walter Disney, widow of the famed animated cartoonist, and her daughter and son-in-law, Diane and Ron Miller, own the winery, which features a huge stained glass panel of Mickey Mouse in the cellar. All the grapes from 180 acres (72 hectares) of vineyards (located near the winery in the Stag's Leap area) go into the production of Silverado Vineyards' three wines (Chardonnay, Sauvignon Blanc, Merlot and Cabernet Sauvignon). Wine-maker John Stuart will be producing 50,000 cases annually by the late eighties.

Silver Oak Wine Cellars. Owners Raymond Duncan, creative Denver oilman-turned-viticulturist, and Justin Meyer, also the wine-maker, owned Franciscan Winery and Vineyards until 1979 when they sold it to the German firm of Peter Eckes Co. At Silver Oak, they make only a good Cabernet Sauvignon wine that is aged three years in oak casks and two years in bottles before being sold. Their cellars are located 3 miles (5 kilometers) southeast of Rutherford on Oakville Cross Road. About 15,000 cases are sold annually under the Silver Oak Cellars label; most of their grapes are purchased from growers in Sonoma County's Alexander Valley and in Napa.

Smith-Madrone Vineyards & Winery. The Smith brothers, Stuart and Charles, began planting vines at this Spring Mountain location in 1971. They crushed their first vintage in 1977 and made some good wines in their handmade winery, which features underground cellars and a sod roof. The output of Smith-Madrone will remain under 6,000 cases a year. Thirty-eight acres (15 hectares) provide most of the grapes for Smith-Madrone's Cabernet Sauvignon, Chardonnay, Pinot Noir, and Riesling wines.

Spring Mountain Vineyards. In 1976, Michael Robbins sold his vineyard and winery one mile north of St. Helena on Highway 29 (now the property of St. Clement Vineyards) and relocated on the site of an 1885 vineyard, with an original 90-foot cave and tunnel still intact, farther up the hillside on Spring Mountain Road. A former engineer from Des Moines, Robbins has been making wines in Napa since 1968. His 140 acres (56 hectares) in Rutherford and Napa provide grapes for Cabernet Sauvignon, Chardonnay and Sauvignon Blanc wines, first crushed in the new winery in 1976. An additional 22 acres (9 hectares) of Cabernet Sauvignon are grown on the winery property. The Chardonnays have won numerous awards and critical acclaim. Average annual production is 25,000 cases. A secondary label is Spring Mountain's Falcon Crest, named for the popular television show filmed at the winery.

Stags Leap Winery. Former residents of Los Angeles, Carl and Joanne Doumani, along with several partners, founded their winery in 1970, located on the Silverado Trail about a mile south of Yountville Cross Road. The Doumanis converted the abandoned, run-down Stag's Leap Manor (a former hotel) on their property into a home, and the neighboring stone winery was restored. They produce about 10,000 cases of wine annually from grapes grown on their 100 acres (40 hectares) of vines. Their Napa Valley Petite Sirah is notably rich and intense without being too tannic. Other wines made are Cabernet Sauvignon, Merlot, and Chenin Blanc.

Stag's Leap Wine Cellars (not to be confused with the previous entry). Warren Winiarski surprised everyone when his 1973 Cabernet Sauvignon won first prize in a Parisian blind tasting in 1976. Consequently, his wines, known for their classic proportions and elegance, and for being characteristic of their grape varieties, are much in demand. Stag's Leap Wine Cellars, a family-run operation whose first wines appeared in 1972, is located on the Silverado Trail a mile south of the Yountville Cross Road. In addition to the Cabernet Sauvignon, accounting for roughly half of the yearly 30,000-case production, Winiarski also makes a Merlot and Chardonnay. The name "Stag's Leap" has been the subject of lawsuits between competing wineries and was recently made into a generic place name covering at least seven wineries.

Steltzner Vineyard. Richard Steltzner has been growing grapes on his 100 acre (40 hectares) property since the late 1960s, when he and his family moved to the Napa Valley from San Francisco. Planted in the heart of the Stag's Leap appellation, Steltzner's Cabernet Sauvignon grapes have been the base of many of the finest examples of that varietal produced in California. Steltzner started wine production in 1977 at their wineries and built a small facility of his own in 1983 near his vineyards. Production will one day reach 10,000 cases, consisting primarily of Cabernet Sauvignon with a small amount of Chardonnay.

Sterling Vineyards. Sterling Vineyards, along with The Monterey Vineyard, Taylor California Cellars, and New York State's Taylor Wine Company, was owned by Coca-Cola of Atlanta from 1977 to 1983; together, these wineries formed a subsidiary of Coca-Cola known as The Wine Spectrum. In 1983 The Wine Spectrum was acquired by Jos. E. Seagram & Sons. Sterling, a medium-sized and modern winery, bonded in 1969, is situated 4 miles (6.5 kilometers) north of St. Helena. The 500 acres (200 hectares) of vineyards were cleared in the late 1960s and at present Chardonnay, Cabernet Sauvignon, Sauvignon Blanc, and Merlot wines are made. All the wines are estate-bottled, coming from Sterling's own vineyards.

The winery is located high above the valley and is reached by an aerial tramway, making it a favorite attraction for the many tourists to the Napa Valley.

Stonegate Winery. James Spaulding, Professor Emeritus of Journalism at the University of California at Berkeley, and Barbara Spaulding, owners of Stonegate, planted some vines on the steep slopes west of Calistoga in 1969. Stonegate, located just off Highway 29 on Dunaweal Lane (the road to Sterling Vineyards), was bonded in 1973, when the Spauldings produced their first wines. From grapes grown on their own 35 acres (14 hectares) and from purchased grapes, Stonegate makes several wines, including Sauvignon Blanc, Chardonnay, Merlot, and Cabernet Sauvignon, at the rate of about 15,000 cases annually. David Spaulding is wine-maker.

Stony Hill Vineyard. Situated on a private road north of St. Helena, Stony Hill is small and secluded. The winery produces four wines: Chardonnay, White Riesling, Gewürztraminer, and Sémillon de Soleil. The late Frederick McCrea started the operation in 1984 by planting a 40-acre (16-hectare) vineyard; in 1952, the winery was built on the site of the family's summer home. The small-scale winery makes some of the best white wines in California, but unfortunately the very small supply is sold only by mailing list. Eleanor McCrea has run the winery since her husband's death in 1977; Mike Chelini is the winemaker.

Sutter Home Winery. Driving north into the heart of the North Coast wine country, one can find Sutter Home just south of St. Helena. The Trinchero family founded the winery in 1946. Sutter Home was the first winery to popularize the White Zinfandel (the first was made in 1977) and now produces about 2 million cases annually from Central valley grapes. An additional 60,000 cases of other varietals (including an Amador County Zinfandel) are made. All grapes are purchased.

Trefethen Vineyards. A family operation since 1968, owned by Gene Trefethen and run by son John and daughter-in-law Janet, Trefethen Vineyards has established an excellent reputation for its wines in a short period of time. The four varietals they produce, Chardonnay, Cabernet Sauvignon, White Riesling, and Pinot Noir, are full of finesse and elegance. Their very clean, fruity Chardonnay could well be the pride of Napa after winning "Gault-Millau's" Wine Olympics in Paris; and the Cabernet Sauvignon has also won its share of international honors. Trefethen has 600 acres (240 hectares) of vines from which to select grapes for

its 60,000 cases of wine a year. The remaining grapes, approximately half of the vineyard's production, are sold to other premium Napa Valley wineries. In addition, Trefethen makes excellent inexpensive generic red and white wines under the Eshcol label.

Vichon Winery. Acquired by the Robert Mondavi family in 1985, this winery was founded in 1980 by a group of partners that included a dozen well-known restaurateurs from across the country. The built-in market provided by the owners proved to be excellent showcases for the more subtle, food-oriented styles of Vichon's three wines. Vichon produces Chardonnay, Cabernet Sauvignon and a proprietary wine called Chevrignon (a blend of Semillon and Sauvignon Blanc). Annual case production is 40,000 from purchased grapes.

Villa Mount Eden. Bought in 1970 by San Francisco financier James McWilliams and his wife, Anne, of the Bank of America Giannini family, Villa Mount Eden is a peaceful site where the Oakville Cross Road meets the Silverado Trail. The wines are good, made from estate-grown grapes (from 87 acres, or 35 hectares, of vines); field-crushing and cold-fermenting practices account for the fruitiness of the wines. Mike McGrath was made wine-maker in 1983. In addition to the first wines, Chardonnay and Cabernet Sauvignon first made in 1974, Villa Mount Eden also makes a dry Chenin Blanc and Merlot. About 18,000 cases are made a year.

In August 1986, the U.S. Tobacco Company purchased the winery, which continues to operate independently.

Vose Winery. Hamilton Vose left Chicago and the paper business in 1970 to clear land and plant 120 acres (48 hectares) of vineyards on Mount Veeder's slopes. Joined by wife Lourdes, Vose built their winery, nestled in the pine trees of a small valley, in 1977. It has the capacity to handle up to 25,000 cases annually. Several reds and whites, including a white Zinfandel from Amador County grapes, are produced by wine-maker Celia Welch.

ZD Wines. Founded in Sonoma County in 1969, engineers Gino Zepponi and Norman de Leuze moved their 12,000-case operation to the Napa Valley in 1979. After Zepponi's untimely accidental death in 1985, de Leuze took over full ownership. ZD buys grapes from Santa Barbara, Napa, and Sonoma counties. Chardonnays and big, powerful Pinot Noirs are ZD's best wines to date.

William Hill Winery. In the southern end of Napa Valley on the slopes of Atlas Peak and Mount Veeder. They have something over 600 acres (240 hectares) planted in vineyards.

(2) Sonoma

This district, which lies directly north of San Francisco, yields some excellent table wines and sparkling wines which rank with the very best in the state. Sonoma is one of the three top wine-producing counties in California, with an average total of 31,000 acres (12,400 hectares) planted in vines, and, with about 130, it is second only to Napa in number of bonded wineries. The wines of Sonoma County come from the Sonoma Valley, Santa Rosa, and the Russian River Valley, as well as from a few good, select microclimates such as Alexander Valley and the Dry Creek area. Alexander Valley was established as a viticultural area place name in 1984 by the Bureau of Alcohol, Tobacco and Firearms.

The Sonoma Valley runs parallel to the Napa Valley, separated from it by the high peaks of the Mayacamas Mountains; this is the original "Valley of the Moon" of Jack London. In north Sonoma County, Simi and Sonoma Vineyards, the latter now known as Rodney Strong Vineyards, have gained good reputations.

Santa Rosa is named for the Santa Rosa Creek which empties its waters into the Russian River, and is the site of the Fountaingrove Vineyard, founded in 1873. It is now a cattle ranch, and real estate development complex.

A number of the area's wineries are in the Russian River Valley. The most important of these is Korbel & Bros. "champagne" company, with vineyards on the hillsides along the river. The average yield for all the Sonoma region vineyards is about 2.5 tons an acre, a little more than 40 hectoliters a hectare. The average is low because of the many nonbearing acres included.

Alexander Valley Vineyards. In 1963, Harry Wetzel, Jr., an executive with the Garrett Corporation in Los Angeles, and Russel Green, Jr., bought this acreage in the Alexander Valley, site of settler Cyrus Alexander's adobe house and gravesite, and an 1868 schoolhouse. While gradually restoring the Victorian mansion on the property, Wetzel planted the former grazing lands in vines and sold the grapes to neighboring wineries in the sixties and early seventies. Meanwhile, his son, Hank Wetzel III, and daughter, Katie Wetzel, completed their educations at Davis and became winemaker and sales manager, respectively, for the family corporation established in 1975. That same year, the first Alexander Valley Vineyards wines were produced. Currently, eight estate-bottled wines are made from eight grape varieties grown on 240 acres (98 hectares) and production will eventually reach 50,000 cases annually.

Balverne Winery. Two-hundred and fifty acres (100 hectares) of vines are planted on this beautiful 700-acre (280-hectare) estate located in the Chalk Hill appellation. The emphasis is on Chardonnay and Cabernet Sauvignon, with an average annual production of 20,000 cases. Balverne is owned by a group of limited partners, who began this venture in 1972. In 1980, the winery was built in the hills outside of Windsor.

Bellerose Vineyard. In 1980, after experimenting with a vineyard in Mendocino County for a number of years, Charles and Nancy Richard bought 52 acres (21 hectares) in the Dry Creek Valley. Their winery, on the site of an abandoned winery that dates back to 1877,

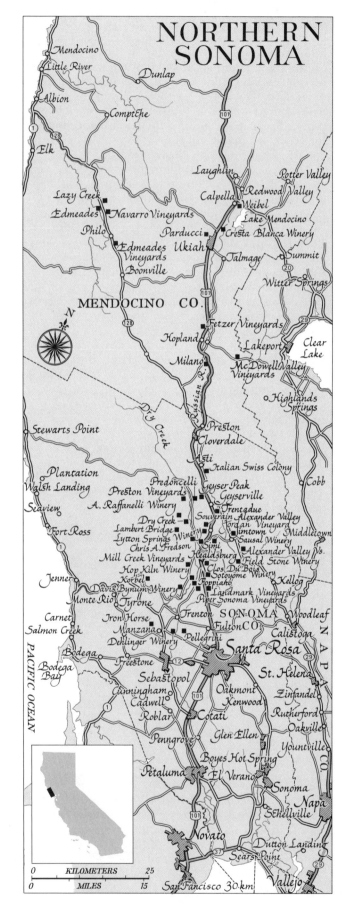

NORTHERN SONOMA

540

was completed for the crush of 1980. Vineyards are planted to Cabernet Sauvignon, Merlot, Cabernet Franc, Petit Verdot, and Malbec from which the Richards make an elegant Bordeaux-style blend called Cuvée Bellerose. Production is limited to 6,000 cases. A Merlot and Sauvignon Blanc are also made.

Belvedere Winery. William Hambrecht, a San Francisco investment banker and Peter Friedman, who has been in the California wine business since the 1960's when he founded Tiburon Vintners with Rodney Strong (see Rodney Strong Vineyards), established Belvedere outside of Healdsburg in 1981. Belvedere makes about 100,000 cases under a negociant system called the Discovery Series, and about 35,000 cases of 4 different vineyard-selected wines, called the Grapemaker Series. An estate-bottled Chardonnay is also produced.

Buena Vista Winery & Vineyards. Situated a mile east from the historic town plaza of Sonoma, and 45 miles (72 kilometers) north of San Francisco, are these historic vineyards originally planted by the great Californian viticulturist Colonel Agoston Haraszthy, who wrote the classic *Report on Grapes and Wines of California* and advised growers from many parts of California on the cultivation of their vines. After his death in 1869, his winery was carried on by his sons Attila and Arpád. The phylloxera plague destroyed many of the European vines at Buena Vista, and the final catastrophe came with the earthquake of 1906, when the winery and storage caves collapsed in ruins. Thereafter, viniculture at this famous vineyard remained at a standstill until 1943, when the two winery buildings were restored and more acreage was bought by Frank Bartholomew, the president of United Press International (*see* Hacienda Wine Cellars, below). The Young's Market company of Los Angeles bought Buena Vista in 1968 and purchased a 700-acre (330-hectare) tract in the Carneros district, that fine region for the varietal wine grape which straddles the border between Sonoma and Napa. Here a new winery was built in 1976.

In 1979, Buena Vista was purchased by A. Racke, the German producers of Kupferberg sparkling wines. Jill Davis is the wine-maker, and about 100,000 cases of wine are produced annually.

Carmenet Winery. Founded in 1980 by members of The Chalone Group, Carmenet was brought under this parent company's wing in 1983, joining the family of Chalone, Edna Valley and later (1986) Acacia Wineries. Carmenet makes a Cabernet Sauvignon-based "Estate Red" and two Sauvignon Blanc-Semillon blends. The winery is north of the town of Sonoma in the Mayacamas Mountains. Production will eventually peak at 27,000 cases.

Chalk Hill Winery. Fred Furth, an internationally prominent attorney and his wife Donna, also an attorney, founded this operation in 1974. That year vineyard plantings, covering 150 acres (60 hectares) in the Chalk Hill appellation (bordered by the Russian River and the Alexander Valley) were begun. The first

wines, made at other facilities under the Donna Maria label, were released in 1979. In 1980, the present winery, an energy-efficient underground structure, was completed and in 1985, the Donna Maria name was changed to Chalk Hill Winery. Chalk Hill specializes in Chardonnay, Cabernet Sauvignon and Sauvignon Blanc and occasionally makes a late harvest Semillon dessert wine. Lawrence Wara is the winemaker behind the 25,000-case production.

Davis Bynum Winery. Davis Bynum began making small amounts of wine in the Bay area in 1965, gradually increasing his yearly production until 1973, when the present winery, a converted hop kiln, was completed. The winery is in the Russian River Valley, 8 miles southwest of Healdsburg. Local grape-growers, who are shareholders in Bynum's corporation, supply about 60% of the grapes needed for the winery's annual 20,000 cases. The principal wines are Chardonnay, Fumé Blanc, Cabernet Sauvignon, Pinot Noir, and Zinfandel.

Chateau St. Jean. Located near Kenwood northwest of the town of Sonoma and southeast of Santa Rosa, beautiful grounds surround the French Mediterranean-style mansion of Chateau St. Jean, which was founded in 1973 by three valley grape-growers. Six grape varieties are planted on 70 acres (28 hectares) and yield 10% of the 180,000-case annual production. Chateau St. Jean specializes in white wines, primarily Chardonnay. Dick Arrowood, St. Jean's energetic wine-master, has succeeded in producing six Chardonnays of the same vintage, three Rieslings varying in flavor, and even more in certain vintages, all from different vineyards, which are usually identified on the labels. Botrytised wines (from Riesling, Gewürztraminer and Sauvignon Blanc-Semillon blends) account for 2% of total production. His best efforts to date, however, have been with Chardonnay and Riesling grapes purchased from the Robert Young Vineyard. Chateau Sr. Jean also makes sparkling wine at a separate Sonoma County facility. In 1984 Suntory Ltd of Japan, who also own Château Lagrange in the Médoc, purchased the vineyard. Arrowood remains as winemaster and has also embarked on his own winery venture, Arrowood Winery, whose first releases are slated for 1988.

Clos du Bois. Clos du Bois wines, made from quality grapes grown on about 700 acres (280 hectares) in both the Dry Creek and Alexander valleys, was founded by Frank Woods in 1974. The wines are innovatively marketed by Woods, whose expertise is also reflected in the successful River Oaks Vineyards operation, which produces larger quantities of fairly priced wines from grapes grown on plots adjacent to those of Clos du Bois. About 100,000 cases are released annually under the Clos du Bois label. Clos du Bois makes several award-winning wines, including some vineyard-designated Chardonnays and Cabernet Sauvignons.

Dehlinger Winery. Klaus Dehlinger, a Berkeley radiologist, and son Tom, who used to be wine-maker at

Hanzell Vineyards, established the Dehlinger Winery in 1976. Tom Dehlinger is now the sole owner of the winery. Growing some grapes on 32 acres (13 hectares) and buying the rest from other Sonoma vineyards, Dehlinger has limited his production to three varietals best suited to the winery's relatively cool region: Cabernet Sauvignon, Chardonnay and Pinot Noir. Located at the intersection of Guerneville and Vine Hill roads in the hills of Sebastopol, this winery produces an average of 6,000 cases a year. Particularly noteworthy are the Chardonnay and Cabernet Sauvignon.

De Loach Vineyards. Former grape-grower and president of the Sonoma County Co-op, Cecil De Loach and his wife, Christine, began their own winery in 1975. They produce about 45,000 cases annually out of their Forestville winery, which was completed in 1979. With 175 acres (70 hectares) of their own vineyard, De Loach grows all the grapes used in their Zinfandel, Pinot Noir, and Gewürztraminer wines. Small amounts of grapes are purchased from other Sonoma County growers to supplement their Sauvignon Blanc, Chardonnay, white Zinfandel and Cabernet Sauvignon.

Domaine Michel. Geneva-based banker Jean-Jacques Michel and his wife Marie-Paule, a psychoanalyst, along with some American partners, masterminded this beautiful Spanish-style winery in the Dry Creek Valley in 1985 after crushing earlier vintages elsewhere. Production will peak at 25,000 cases, a combined total for 4 different varietals.

Donna Maria Winery. See Chalk Hill Winery, previous page.

Dry Creek Vineyard. A few miles northwest of Healdsburg, Dry Creek Vineyard was founded by David Stare in 1972. Ever since a 1970 visit to the Médoc, Stare has pursued vine-growing and wine-making instead of civil engineering. Stare's efforts have resulted in a wide range of good wines, including a very fine Chardonnay and Fumé Blanc. Stare grows about 30% of his own grapes on 45 acres (18 hectares) and makes about 60,000 cases of crisp and elegantly styled wines a year.

Estate William Baccala. William Baccala purchased the Stephen Zellerbach Winery in March of 1986. His winery was previously located in Mendocino County. There are 70 acres (28 hectares) of Cabernet and Merlot grapes at this new location; Chardonnay and Sauvignon Blanc grapes are purchased from neighboring vineyards. Mr. Baccala will continue with both the brands. The building, with 14 cupolas, is designed to efficiently use the region's cool night air for ventilation and refrigeration. Kerry Kamskey makes the annual 35,000 cases of Cabernet Sauvignon, Merlot, Chardonnay and Sauvignon Blanc.

Field Stone Winery. Known for its original and innovative wine-making techniques that one time involved the use of a mechanical harvester and mobile press developed by the winery's late founder, Wallace Johnson, Field Stone also has the distinction of being the first underground winery built in this century. At one time mayor of Berkeley, Johnson owned the property surrounding Field Stone, Redwood Ranch, for many years, and in 1965 began growing grapes as well as raising cattle. Johnson sold his grapes to other Napa and Sonoma vineyards, and in 1976, with the help of his inventions, made his own wines under the Field Stone label. John and Katrina Staten have managed the property since 1979. Field Stone makes eight estate-bottled wines. Production from the 140-acre (56-hectare) vineyard is expected to reach a maximum of 25,000 cases.

Fisher Winery. Fred J. Fisher, a former management consultant, entered the wine business in 1973, with the establishment of what has become 75 acres (30 hectares) of vines in the Mayacamas Mountains and in the Napa Valley. William Turnbull, a noted architect, designed the winery, which was constructed from Douglas fir and redwood cleared from Fisher's land in 1979. Located about 1,200 feet above sea level, on an isolated hillside between Santa Rosa and St. Helena, Fisher produces about 7,000 cases a year of Chardonnay and Cabernet Sauvignon.

Foppiano Winery. Founded by Italian immigrant John Foppiano in 1896, this vineyard, south of Healdsburg between the Old Redwood Highway and the Russian River, is now run by the third and fourth generations, Louis J. and Louis M. Foppiano. Good medium-priced wines are still produced by Foppiano, and the full-flavored varietals have shown excellent progress. Grapes grown from Foppiano's 200 acres (80 hectares), plus locally purchased produce, yield an average of 200,000 cases a year, much of which is under the Riverside Farm label.

Geyser Peak Winery. In 1982, the polo-playing Trione family acquired this winery from the Stroh Brewery in Detroit. Located on a hill just north of Geyserville, Geyser Peak produces 14 varietals, including vintage dated wines, and two sparkling wines called "Opulence." About 500,000 cases are made annually. The Triones own 1,050 acres (420 hectares) of vineyards in three different Sonoma County appellations.

Glen Ellen Winery. The Benziger family had been wine marketers based in New York for over 110 years when they purchased a hidden valley winery west of the town of Glen Ellen in 1980. The entire family is involved in the production of their 4 table wines and several premiums. Glen Ellen encompasses about 100 acres (40 hectares) of wines. Production is about 70,000 cases.

Gloria Ferrer. Frexinet, the largest seller of sparkling wine in the United States, came to the Carneros region of southern Sonoma County from Spain to open the company's sixth sparkling wine facility in 1986. The winery is named after owner Jose Ferrar's wife. Grapes from 250 acres (100 hectares) of vineyards surrounding the winery provide the bulk of the fruit for the projected 100,000 case production. The first release, a Brut from Pinot Noir grapes, was made at another winery while the spectacular $11 million Ferrer facility was under construction (completed in 1986). Extensive caves and tunnels, and a dramatic setting overlooking the San Pablo Bay promise to make Ferrer a popular spot with wine country tourists. Eileen Crane, trained at the University of California at Davis and Domaine Chandon, is the winemaker.

Grand Cru Vineyards. In 1970, Robert Magnani and Allen Ferrara founded Grand Cru Vineyards in Sonoma's Valley of the Moon, near Glen Ellen. Walter and Bettina Dreyer bought the winery in 1981. Built on the site of an 1896 winery, Grand Cru produces some interesting wines, under winemaker Robert Magnani's direction. The 60,000-case winery specializes in dry Chenin Blanc, Sauvignon Blanc, Cabernet Sauvignon and Gewurztraminer.

Gundlach-Bundschu Winery. After four generations, the Bundschu family has set out to re-establish the wine-making reputation earned by two of the original 1858 founders, Jacob Gundlach and Charles Bundschu. Although the 1906 earthquake and fire wiped out their prosperous wine business, the Rhinefarm vineyard, at that time the site for Julius Dresel's grafting experiments, continued to produce grapes for commercial purposes. About 90% of the production of the 350-acre (140-hectare) vineyard, an expansion of the original Rhinefarm, is retained to make about 45,000 cases annually. Wine-maker Lance Cutler is behind the nine-varietal production.

Hacienda Winery. After selling the Buena Vista Winery in 1968, former newspaper editor Frank H. Bartholomew founded Hacienda Winery in 1973, right in the heart of the Valley of the Moon, two and a half miles from the center of Sonoma. By 1977, A. Crawford Cooley, formerly in the electronics industry and manager of his family's Oat Valley vineyard, and winemaker Steve MacRostie were managing Hacienda, with Bartholomew as consultant. Hacienda consists of 110 acres (44 hectares) of vineyards that supply about one third of the grapes needed for about 25,000 cases annually. Hacienda makes six different varietals, most notably a Chardonnay.

Hanzell Vineyards. When James D. Zellerbach retired as U. S. Ambassador to Italy in the 1950s, he came to Sonoma wanting to make wines as good as the fine European ones he had come to know. He modeled his wines, vineyards, and the winery itself on a French original. The building and plantation attempted to resemble those of the Clos Vougeot, and the wines were made from only Burgundy grapes. In his close attention to every French detail, Mr. Zellerbach discovered that much of the complexity of European wines derives from the ageing in barrels made from oak common only to parts of Europe. He was the first to import French barrels, but today the practice is widespread. "Hanzell" is a combination of the ambassador's last name and his wife's first name, Hannah.

After Mr. Zellerbach's death, the property was bought by Douglas Day, whose widow, Mary, continued to make the same small number of fine wines until her death. The property now belongs to Countess Barbara de Brye. Bob Sessions is the wine-maker. Production is about 2,500 cases of Pinot Noir and Chardonnay from Hanzell's 30 acres (12 hectares) near the winery in the Sonoma Valley.

Hop Kiln Winery. As its name indicates, this winery is housed in a remnant of Sonoma County's once-active hop-growing industry, now preserved as a state historical landmark. Owner Dr. Martin Griffin began making wines here in 1975, after 14 years of grape-growing and home wine-making. Part of the yield of 65 acres (25 hectares) of Russian River vineyards is used to produce about 8,000 cases a year of several wines, including a Zinfandel and Petite Sirah from vines planted in 1880.

Iron Horse Vineyards. Owned by attorney Barry Sterling and his wife, Audrey, who decided to enter the wine business after living in France for several years. This property is located in the Sebastopol foothills in the Green Valley appellation. The maritime influence and cool breezes from the Petaluma Gap south of Santa Rosa create ideal growing conditions for Iron Horse's 110 acres (44 hectares) of Chardonnay and Pinot Noir. The winery also owns 35 acres (14 hectares) in the Alexander Valley. Iron Horse grows all their own grapes for their projected 40,000-case production. Three vintage sparkling wines account for half of the production. Reagan toasted Gorbachev in Geneva in November of 1985 with Iron Horse sparkling wine. Forrest Tancer, a partner, is the winemaker.

Italian Swiss Colony. This sprawling winery in the gently rolling hills of Asti was acquired by Allied Grape Growers, an agricultural cooperative in 1983.

The original Italian Swiss Colony was founded in 1881 as an agricultural haven for displaced citizens of those two nations. Even before the turn of the century, it counted more than 1,500 acres (600 hectares) of vineyards. Andrea Sbaboro started the company and built the winery in 1887, but his first wines were failures. A young Italian pharmacist from San Francisco, Pietro Rossi, came to Asti and brought wine-making skills he had learned in Europe. Soon the wines were a success. The present generation of Rossis is still active in the company. Pietro's grandson, Edmund A. Rossi Jr., is Colony's wine-maker today.

When Louis Petri ran Italian Swiss Colony from the 1940s through the 1960s, the winery organization became one of the largest in the world. Colony, once part of the R. J. Reynolds Industries' wine operation, Heublein, became the property of Allied Grape Growers in 1983, along with several of Heublein's other labels (Petri, Lejon, Jacques Bonet, G & D and Annie Greensprings). Before that acquisition, Heublein Wines (the majority owners of Allied's wine subsidiary, United Vintners, since 1969) was the second largest California wine producer after E. & J. Gallo.

Jordan Vineyard and Winery. Tom Jordan, Jr., formerly a Denver-based oilman who moved his business to Santa Rosa, bought this beautiful property in 1972, and with his wife, Sally, has created from scratch a

French-style wine-producing château in the Alexander Valley. The winery, the home, the vineyards, the wine—every aspect of the Jordans' establishment is modeled after the traditional Bordeaux châteaux. A well-balanced and elegant Cabernet Sauvignon, first released in 1979, is the fruit of their efforts; it is produced at the rate of 45,000 cases annually. In 1979 Chardonnay production began and reached 25,000 cases by 1982. The Jordans' 270 acres (108 hectares) are planted primarily in Cabernet Sauvignon, and Chardonnay. A small amount of Merlot is grown for blending purposes. A top winery.

Kenwood Vineyards. Quality, not quantity, is the goal at Kenwood Vineyards, formerly the bulk-wine-producing Julius Pagani Winery and now the property of the Lee family. Six partners (John Sheela is president) have been responsible for this turnaround since 1970, when they bought the property, located in the Sugarloaf Ridge foothills in Kenwood. Offering eight wines from grapes grown at their 20-acre (8-hectare) vineyard, others purchased locally, the Kenwood team plans to produce about 100,000 cases a year.

Kistler Cellars. This winery made a dazzling debut with some vineyard-designated Chardonnays from their 1979 crush. Small amounts of Cabernet Sauvignon and Pinot Noir are also made. Owned by the Kistler family, the winery is situated 2,000 feet up on the western slope of the Mayacamas Mountains, near the town of Kenwood. About half of the grapes for the 8,000-case production are purchased, although the Kistlers do have a 40-acre (16-hectare) vineyard that provides for part of their production. Steve Kistler is the wine-maker.

F. Korbel & Bros., Inc. The Korbel winery and vineyards are located in one of the most picturesque sections of California, alongside the winding Russian River at Guerneville. The Korbel brothers came from the small town of Behine in Czechoslovakia to settle here, where they made their first champagnes in the nineties. After the Second World War they dropped their table wines and devoted their skill exclusively to the production of *méthode champenoise* champagnes. Early in 1954, Anton and Leo Korbel sold the winery to the Heck family. Adolf Heck, originally from St. Louis, was formerly president of Italian Swiss Colony of Asti, California (*q.v.*). His brother Paul held the position of production manager. Adolf became the president and champagne-master of Korbel and upon Mr. Heck's death in 1984, Robert Stashak took over that title, having trained under Heck for twelve years.

Many of the grapes for Korbel's wines come from the 700 acres (280 hectares) of varietal vineyards in the northwestern section of the county. Some of the important varieties used at the ranch for the production of sparkling wine are Pinot Noir and Chardonnay. The winery produces Korbel Rose, Brut, Extra Dry, Sec, Blanc de Blancs, Blanc de Noirs and Natural sparkling wines. About 70% of the production consists of sparkling wines; brandy accounts for the remaining 30%. Very small amounts of still wine are made annually, too. Today, Korbel is the largest producer of *méthode champenoise* sparkling wines in the United States.

Frank Schoonmaker and the author introduced Korbel east of the Rockies in 1942. Since 1966, the Jack Daniels Distilling Company has owned Korbel and distributed the wines.

La Crema Vinera. Begun in Petaluma in 1979. La Crema Vinera produces Chardonnays and Pinot Noirs from Sonoma, Napa, Monterey and Santa Barbara counties. All grapes needed for the 30,000-case production are purchased.

Lambert Bridge. Gerard Lambert, of the St. Louis pharmaceutical firm family, bought this Dry Creek Valley property in 1969 and named it after the nearby landmark that coincidentally bore his name. Specializing in Chardonnay, Cabernet Sauvignon and Merlot, Lambert's wines are made by Ed Killian and managed by Dave Rafanelli (whose father runs the neighboring A. Rafanelli Winery, *q.v.*). The wines debuted in 1975. Although 80 acres (32 hectares) of vines are cultivated, Lambert uses his best-quality Chardonnay, Cabernet, and Merlot grapes from 45 acres for his own wines and sells three other varieties from the remaining 35 acres (14 hectares). Production will peak at 30,000 cases.

Landmark Vineyards. Landmark, which started out as a ranch in the 19th century and became a prune farm in the 1900s, has been transformed into a vineyard by its new owners, the Mabry family, who bought the property in 1975. An elegant arcade of tall cypresses leads the way to the Spanish-style hacienda and winery located in Windsor, not far from the highway exit. The Mabrys have cultivated vines on 80 acres (32 hectares) of vineyards in the Alexander and Sonoma valleys since 1972, and now grow an additional 60 acres (25 hectares) adjacent to the winery. They make about 25,000 cases of estate-grown Chardonnay annually.

Lyeth Winery. Chip Lyeth, Jr., son of a successful Denver banker, came to the Alexander Valley in 1973 and began farming what is now a 100-acre (40-hectare) vineyard. The winery, an English manor-style structure, was built north of Greyserville in 1982. Lyeth makes just two wines, a Cabernet-based red and a Sauvignon Blanc-Semillon blend.

Lytton Springs Winery. Grapes grown on these hillside vineyards near Healdsburg have been sold to many wineries since 1970; in fact, the famed Zinfandels made by the Ridge Vineyards in Cupertino, south of San Francisco Bay, were made largely from the fruit of Lytton Springs' 80-year-old vines. Since the completion of the winery in 1977, one of California's best Zinfandels has been made under the Lytton Springs Winery label. Owner Richard Sherwin produces about 10,000 cases annually from his 50 acres (20 hectares) of Zinfandel grapes and from those he purchases outside.

Martini & Prati Wines, Inc. Seven miles (11 kilometers) northwest of Santa Rosa on Laguna Road stands one of the oldest and largest wineries of Sonoma.

From its 62 acres (25 hectares) of vine, Martini & Prati make generic wines, fruit wines, vermouth, and several varietals. Frank Vannucci is manager. Most of these are shipped in bulk to bottlers in other parts of the country. The winery owns the Fountaingrove label, a 65,000 annual case operation with national distribution.

Matanzas Creek Winery. Sandra MacIver, daughter of Edgar Stern, co-owner of San Francisco's magnificent Stanford Court Hotel, began growing grapes in the Bennett Valley in 1971. Located in two different microclimates between Glen Ellen and Santa Rosa, Matanzas Creek's 45 acres (18 hectares) are planted in three different grape varieties, whose fruit is fermented and vinified in a magnificently renovated dairy barn. The Chardonnay is outstanding and accounts for about half of the production, which will peak at 20,000 cases.

Mill Creek Vineyards. The Kreck family started out in the 1950s as ranchers and cattle raisers in the Alexander Valley. Starting in 1965, the Krecks planted vines, and they now have 65 acres (26 hectares). They bought their present property, near Dry Creek in Healdsburg, in 1969. At first, grapes were sold commercially; now, since the 1976 completion of the Mill Creek winery, about 15,000 cases of seven different wines are produced annually.

Pat Paulsen Vineyards. Entertainer Pat and his wife Jane Paulsen have been growing grapes since 1971 when they planted their Cabernet Sauvignon along the Russian River in the Alexander Valley. Sauvignon Blanc and Chardonnay vineyards were added in 1975 and 1978. Currently, the growing 25,000-case winery, established in 1980, produces a dry Muscat Canelli, and some proprietary table wines in addition to the estate-bottled wines. Jamie Meves is the winemaker.

J. Pedroncelli Winery. This family-owned winery makes a selection of good varietal wines. Pedroncelli is located a mile northwest of Geyserville on Canyon Road. Founder John Pedroncelli, Sr. chose the site in 1927 because the land and climate reminded him of his native Italy.

Today there are about 125 acres (50 hectares) of vineyard supplying some of the grapes for the average annual 125,000-case production. Other grapes are purchased from growers in the nearby Dry Creek and Alexander Valleys. Pedroncelli made the first, and one of the best, Zinfandel rosés in California.

Piper-Sonoma. This winery is the result of a Franco-American collaboration, that of the Champagne firm of Piper-Heidsieck, and its New York-based exclusive importers, Renfield Importers (bought by Schenley Industries in 1985). Piper-Sonoma's cellars, adjacent to Sonoma Vineyards, were completed in 1980 in time for their first crush; in 1982, the visitors' center was opened with the release of the winery's Brut sparkling wine. A Blanc de Noirs is also made. Yield will eventually reach 100,000 cases of sparkling wine, produced mostly from purchased Sonoma County grapes. Rod Strong, wine-master at R. Strong Vineyards (formerly Sonoma Vineyards), holds that position at Piper-Sonoma as well.

Preston Vineyards. Louis Preston and his wife, Susan, established their Dry Creek vineyard in 1975, making wines in the converted prune dehydrator that is surrounded by their 125 acres (50 hectares). The Prestons' selected vines produce about 25,000 cases a year. Preston devotes his wine-making expertise, from vine to bottle, primarily to the production of Zinfandel, Sauvignon Blanc, Cabernet Sauvignon and their proprietary "Cuvée de Fumé." All Preston wines are estate-bottled.

A. Rafanelli Winery. Most of Americo Rafanelli's 35 acres (14 hectares) of Dry Creek vineyards produce grapes that are sold to other wineries, but the cream of the crop is reserved for his Zinfandel, Gamay Beaujolais and Cabernet Sauvignon wines. Having learned wine-making from his father, who made wines in Healdsburg in the forties, Americo makes full-bodied, old-style California wines that are not filtered or processed. His wines are produced at the rate of about 6,000 cases a year.

Sausal Winery. The 8,000-case estate-bottled winery was a bulk facility from 1973 to 1979. Owned and operated by the Demostene family, the winery is on the eastern banks of the Russian River in the Alexander Valley, adjacent to an 80-acre (32-hectare) vineyard. Sausal's first varietal, a 1974 Zinfandel, appeared on the market in 1979. Principal wines are Zinfandel, Cabernet Sauvignon, Chardonnay, and Sausal Blanc, a dry white blend of Chardonnay and French Colombard.

Sam Sebastiani Winery. Due to differences in wine-making and marketing philosophies with his family, Sam Sebastiani went solo in 1986. From premium vineyards in Napa and Sonoma Counties, Sam makes Sauvignon Blanc, Cabernet Sauvignon and Chardonnay at other facilities while his Italian villa-style winery is under construction.

Sebastiani Vineyards. The town plaza of Sonoma, where the State Bear Flag was briefly raised in the 1840s to mark the capital of California, sits in the midst of quite a few buildings that have the same name: Sebastiani. The reason for this is the Sebastiani Winery and vineyards, founded by Samuel Sebastiani in 1904. He had saved enough money in the eight years since his arrival from Italy to come to Sonoma and make wines. Soon the original bulk-wine business was profitable, and buildings with the family name started appearing around the town.

In the late fifties, the winery gave up making anonymous bulk wines and started to produce better ones under the family label. Their successors have been good, and include Cabernet Sauvignon, Zinfandel, Chardonnay, and a surprisingly good Barbera. When August Sebastiani died in 1980, his son Sam presided until 1986 when his brother Don took the reins as the result of a family disagreement. Sam has gone on to run his own winery (see previous entry).

There are about 700 acres (280 hectares) of vineyards.

Simi Winery, Inc. This winery, with an historic stone cellar, is north of Healdsburg. It was built in 1890 by the Simi brothers, two early San Francisco wine merchants. Russell Green, Jr. bought the winery in 1970, rebuilt it and started to make good varietal wines from grapes grown on vineyards he had owned since 1958. The British beverage firm of Scottish & Newcastle briefly owned Simi from 1974 until 1976, when Schieffelin & Company, the New York–based beverage importing firm, established Simi as its subsidiary. Management and operation of the winery are totally independent of Schieffelin, which was purchased in 1981 by Moët-Hennessy of France. Owning 170 acres (70 hectares) of vines in the Alexander Valley, Simi purchases most of the grapes needed for their average annual 145,000 cases from Sonoma, Mendocino, and Napa counties. Zelma Long is winemaker.

Sonoma-Cutrer Vineyards. Sonoma-Cutrer specializes in Chardonnay from their three vineyards: Les Pierres, Cutrer and Russian River Ranches.

The 450 acres (180 hectares) of vineyards, which are located in the Russian River Valley and Carneros regions, were planted in 1972 by former fighter pilot Brice Cutrer Jones. Sonoma Cutrer supplied grapes to other wineries until 1981, when Jones built a winery west of Windsor designed to produce only Chardonnay. The state-of-the-art winery features a unique grape-selecting table at the crush station and a chilling tunnel that culls the must en route from the vineyard to the presses and fermentations tanks. William Bonetti, one of California's foremost Chardonnay experts, is the wine maker. In addition, Sonoma-Cutrer has several championship croquet courses next to the winery which are the site of a number of annual tournaments.

Sonoma Vineyards. See Rodney Strong Vineyards (below).

Souverain. Built in 1972 and originally bought by the Pillsbury Company of Minneapolis, Souverain was owned by a large group of grape-growers for more than ten years until 1986 when it was purchased by Wine World, Nestlé International's Wine Division (which also encompasses the Beringer Winery and Los Hermanos labels). Known as Chateau Souverain under its new ownership, the winery's production has been greatly reduced to 40,000 cases annually with emphasis on better quality varietals from several Sonoma County appellations. Souverain's dramatic architecture, reminiscent of the Hop Kilns that once prevailed in the area, includes a beautiful restaurant.

Rodney Strong Vineyards. Mr. Strong began selling generic and varietal wines under the Tiburon Vintners label in the San Fransisco Bay area. His business grew and became one of the largest capacity wine and grape enterprises in northern California. In 1976, Strong founded a public company, Sonoma Vineyards, in Windsor (off of Highway 101 near Santa Rosa) and put his winemaking talents to work as winemaster. Ren-

field Importers of New York purchased the Company in 1985 and changed the name to Rodney Strong Vineyards. Renfield and Piper-Heidseick of Champagne are partners in Piper-Sonoma (*q.v.*), the neighboring sparkling wine facility. About 50% of the grapes used in Strong's wines come from 1,250 acres (500 hectares) of vines. Production amounts to just under 400,000 cases. Renfield was purchased by Schenley Industries in 1985.

Joseph Swan Vineyards. From his 10 acres (4 hectares) 10 miles (16 kilometers) northwest of Santa Rosa, which are planted mostly in Pinot Noir and Chardonnay grapes, former Western Airlines pilot Joe Swan has been making some very good wines since 1969. His estate-bottled Pinot Noir is styled after some of the Côte d'Or Burgundies, but Swan is primarily known for his fine and concentrated Zinfandel. Maximum production is 1,500 cases a year, most of which is sold to a private mailing list of customers.

Stephen Zellerbach Vineyard. See Baccala Winery at the beginning of this section.

Mark West Winery. Family-owned and operated by airline pilot Bob Ellis and his wife, Joan, this winery is located in Forestville along the Russian River. Bob manages the vineyard, and Joan makes the wine. They began producing Chardonnay, Gewürztraminer, and Pinot Noir in 1976 in their winery, a converted dairy. The Ellises also make a Blanc de Noirs sparkling wine and Zinfandel. The present production is 30,000 cases. Sixty acres (29 hectares) of vines provide about 90% of the grapes needed for Mark West's production.

William Wheeler Winery. Leaving a career in international finance, Bill and his wife Ingrid Wheeler bought 175 acres (70 hectares) in the Dry Creek Valley in 1970, where they grow some of the fruit for their half-dozen wines. Production is about 15,000 cases a year. The Wheelers have their wine-ageing facility and tasting room right off of the Healdsburg town square.

Woodbury Winery. This port-style wine producer is located in Marin County, south of Sonoma. Woodbury, established in 1979, aims to produce 5,000 cases maximum a year. Proprietors Russell (the winemaker) and Linda Woodbury are specializing in vintage wines from top-quality North Coast grapes, primarily blending Petite Sirah, Cabernet Sauvignon, Zinfandel, and Pinot Noir. Woodbury also makes a small amount of pot-distilled brandy from St.-Émilion grapes.

(3) Mendocino

Growers in this district have recently begun to cultivate finer wine grapes, and vineyard area has increased from 1,200 to about 11,000 acres (4,400 hectares) and is still growing. Hillsides once thought impossible to irrigate for frost control are now being watered from farm ponds filled by the run-off from the mountain rains. Cabernet Sauvignon and Gamay Beaujolais are the major grapes planted, but the potential is in Chardonnay and Pinot Noir. Mendocino may have great potential as a fine-wine district, but until the beginning of the seventies it was somewhat ignored. Certain vineyards, especially those in the cooler microclimate, will indeed produce some of the best wine from northern California.

Growers in this cooler district seeking greater recognition are located in the Anderson Valley and in the interior of the county, which includes Redwood Valley. In 1982, the Louis Roederer Champagne firm of France bought 400 acres (160 hectares) in the Anderson Valley, a purchase that will draw more attention to Mendocino County. There are 16 bonded wineries in the county today.

Cresta Blanca Winery. Charles Wetmore, an early and innovative vintner, established Cresta Blanca in 1882. He had traveled in Europe for the state Viticultural Committee and brought back cuttings of fine vines from France. Only seven years after the estate was founded, Cresta Blanca wines won medals at the 1889 Paris Exhibition. After some poor vintages under Schenley ownership, the winery was bought by the Guild Wine Company in 1971. In the early 1970s, the winery was moved from its original Livermore location to Mendocino County, near Ukiah. From mostly locally grown grapes, Cresta Blanca makes a wide variety of wines, including some dessert and sparkling ones. Mendocino County estate-bottled varietals entered the market in 1983. Production averages at 15,000 cases.

Edmeades Vineyards. Deron Edmeades inherited this cool and wet 100-acre (40-hectare) property, as well as the determination to successfully cultivate it, from his father, Dr. Donald Edmeades, in 1972. Young Edmeades's efforts, along with those of wine-maker Tex Sawyer, have finally begun to pay off; their Cabernet Sauvignon, Zinfandel, Chardonnay, and Gewürztraminer are quite satisfactory. Produce from the Anderson Valley vineyard is supplemented with purchased grapes, yielding an average of 24,000 cases of wine a year.

Fetzer Vineyards. In the secluded Redwood Valley lies the 700-acre (280-hectare) vineyard and winery founded by the late Bernard Fetzer. Strictly a family enterprise, with 10 of the 11 Fetzer offspring involved in the winery (John is president). Fetzer Vineyards makes a selection of varietal wines from its Home Vineyard and from two 300-acre (120-hectare) vineyards in Hopland. In addition, about 70% of the grapes needed to make its average annual 900,000 cases are purchased from Lake, Mendocino, Sonoma and Monterey counties.

Husch Winery. Founded in 1971 by Tony and Gretchen Husch, this property was purchased by the H.A. Oswald family, longtime grape-growers of the Ukiah Valley, in 1979. From a combination of fruit from their Ukiah ranch and about 25 acres (10 hectares) of Anderson Valley grapes, Husch makes about 15,000 cases annually. Six varietals are produced.

McDowell Valley Vineyards. Owners Rich and Karen Keehn purchased 360 acres (164 hectares) in the McDowell Valley in 1970 and completed their solar-integrated winery in 1979. This state-of-the-art facility overlooks the McDowell Valley, where vines have been planted since the 1890s. The eight wines are produced from vines averaging about 35 years of age. The B.A.T.F. recognised McDowell Valley appellation is known for its lower peak temperatures and cooler summer nights than surrounding areas, thus providing a longer growing season. The winery goal is to make wines with balance, finesse, and complexity to complement a range of cuisines. About 75,000 cases of estate-bottled wines are produced annually.

Milano Winery. A renovated hop kiln in Hopland, in southeastern Mendocino County, is the site for the Milano Winery. It is owned and operated by winemaster James Milone, who makes his wines from both purchased hillside grapes and those from his own vineyards. A peak production of about 16,000 cases a year was reached in 1982. Milano specializes in Chardonnay.

Navarro Winery. Perched on one of the Anderson Valley's many rolling hills, on Highway 128 near Philo, the Navarro Winery was founded by Ted and Deborah Bennett. Bennett, who left the electronics industry to start the winery in 1974, is co-wine-maker with Tom Lane. The Gewürztraminer, Chardonnay, and Pinot Noir wines come from Navarro's 50-acre (20-hectare) vineyard, while the Cabernet Sauvignon and Riesling are purchased from local growers. Average annual production is 12,000 cases.

Parducci Winery. Immediately after Repeal, Adolf Parducci established this winery just north of Ukiah. His sons John and the late George operated the winery before their families took over. One of the better-known and more innovative North Coast wineries, Parducci makes most of its wines from vineyards in Mendocino and Lake counties. Fruit from Parducci's own 300 acres (120 hectares) and purchased grapes are used to make the average 300,000 annual cases. Since 1969 Cabernet Sauvignons vinified from grapes grown on scattered plots have been produced in an effort to try out new wine-growing districts. A wide selection of varietals is made; the medium-priced Chenin Blanc is consistently good.

Roederer (U.S.). Wholly owned by Champagne's Louis Roederer of France, this winery had its first crush in 1986. Located 4 miles northwest of Philo, Roederer grows 400 acres (160 hectares) of Chardonnay and Pinot Noir in the surrounding Anderson Valley. Anticipated full production is 100,000 cases.

Weibel Winery. The Weibel family, known for their sparkling wines made at their Mission San Jose location (*q.v.*, under Livermore Valley), bought 450 acres (180 hectares) of land in the Redwood Valley in 1969. By the fall of 1972, their newly constructed winery was ready for its first crush. At the Mendocino location, Weibel makes a full line of varietal table wines, which account for about 40% of the total production of 1 million cases a year. The wines are crushed and vinified in Redwood Valley, then bottled downstate at the family's sparkling wine cellars. Third-generation Weibels are currently in management.

(4) Lake

Lake County, bordered by the Mayacamas Mountains on the east and the Mendocino National Forest on the north, was part of the Napa Valley when its wine-making history began in the 1870s. By the turn of the century, there were 5,000 acres (2,000 hectares) of vineyards and a few dozen wineries. Among the most notable Lake County wine-making pioneers were Seramus C. Hastings, first Chief Justice of the California Supreme Court and founder of the Hastings Law School, and Lillie Langtry, the British actress.

Unlike the adjacent counties of Napa, Sonoma, and Mendocino, the railroad never reached Lake County, making the trek to market costly and difficult. The high transportation costs, coupled with periods of depressed wine prices, closed many Lake County wineries even before Prohibition dealt the final blow.

For more than fifty years, vineyards gave way to orchards of Bartlett pears and groves of walnut trees, until only 300 acres (120 hectares) of vines remained in 1965. With the wine boom of the late sixties and seventies, the Lake County wine industry slowly began making a comeback. There now are six wineries and more than 3,000 acres (1,200 hectares) of vineyards, including the vineyards of the Turner Brothers Winery (the county's largest grower, with 560 acres or 224 hectares), whose owners process Lake County grapes at their Woodbridge, California, facility.

Lake County has always been known to produce fine red grape varieties, but recently white wines, such as Sauvignon Blanc and Riesling, have attracted much attention at tastings.

Guenoc Winery. This showcase winery (originally built by Lillie Langtry) overlooks the Guenoc Valley, which is the first single-proprietor appellation in the United States. Owned by the Magoon family from Hawaii, the operation is directed by Orville Magoon. Winemaking is directed by Robert Broman, and Bill Pickering manages the 270-acre (108-hectare) vineyard. Present production of 50,000 cases will double. Petite Sirah, Cabernet, Zinfandel, Chardonnay, Chenin Blanc, and Sauvignon Blanc are produced.

Kendall-Jackson Winery. Formerly known as Château du Lac, this 140,000-case winery is co-owned by Jane Kendall and attorney Jess Jackson. About 90 acres (36 hectares) of vines contribute to the production of 5 varietals, with other grapes purchased from all over the state. The first wines were made in 1980.

Konocti Winery. A small 26-member cooperative was organized in 1974, and produced wine under the Konocti label at other wineries until 1979. That year, the co-op built its present facility and hired Bill Pease as wine-maker. Under his direction, and with André Tchelistcheff as consultant, the wines have steadily improved, winning a variety of awards and remaining reasonably priced at the same time. The 1985 production was 40,000 cases.

Lower Lake Winery. Owned and operated by the Stuermer family, with son Daniel, a Ph.D. chemist, as wine-maker, Lower Lake made their first wine, a Cabernet Sauvignon, in 1977. That same year, they built the first Lake County Winery since Prohibition. They now produce 8,500 cases a year of Fumé Blanc and Cabernet Sauvignon. All grapes are bought from Lake County grape-growers.

(5) Livermore

This is a district noted for its production of many fine wines. Alameda County's Livermore Valley is known throughout the country for its good Sauternes-type, as well as for other outstanding white wines. The valley was named after pioneer Robert Livermore who, as early as 1848, had a vineyard near the town that bears his name.

The Livermore Valley (more of a basin than a valley) comprises two important wine-growing areas—the vineyards surrounding the town of Livermore, and the neighboring sector of Pleasanton. In 1887, Charles A. Wetmore said of the valley: "Here every condition known to be essential for the production of the highest grades of wines and brandies, approximating the noblest French types, exists." With cuttings he brought directly from the vineyards of Margaux and Château d'Yquem in Bordeaux, Wetmore founded in 1882 the concern which won renown as Cresta Blanca, now reopened in Mendocino. Today, the two outstanding wineries of Livermore Valley are Concannon Vineyard and Wente Bros.

The soil of most of the vineyards in this section is made up largely of coarse, arid-looking stones like that of the Châteauneuf-du-Pape vineyards of the Rhône Valley and the gravel of some of those in Graves and the Médoc. This soil is, in California, particularly adapted to the production of full-bodied white wines ranging from very dry to sweet. Recent attempts to make the wines lighter have been successful, and early bottling has done much to improve these wines which only in 1968 were considered by many to be very heavy. Because of the climate and the nature of the soil, it is doubtful if the Pinot Noir will ever be successfully cultivated in Livermore. In the past decade, however, some good red wines have come from the valley, including a Concannon vintage Cabernet Sauvignon and Wente Gamay Beaujolais from Monterey County.

In 1982, the Livermore Valley was designated as an appellation by the B.A.T.F.

Southwest of Livermore and very close to the tip of San Francisco Bay are the wine-growing centers of Mission San José and Irvington, extending almost to Santa Clara County. In this southern Alameda district the red wines are almost as successful as the white; and sparkling wines, aperitifs, and dessert wines are all produced here too. Alameda's vineyards have decreased in size to only about 2,000 acres (800 hectares). However, Almadén purchased 260 acres (104 hectares) in Pleasanton and planted the vineyards in ten sound grape varieties. South of Pleasanton, the Sunol Valley is now flourishing in vine.

The wine boom of the 1970s had little effect on the Livermore Valley region of Alameda County. Wente Brothers and Concannon (sold to Augustin Huneus, former president of Paul Masson, in 1980) remain the leaders in wine production. Urban sprawl, a serious threat to agriculture in the valley, is being controlled by stricter zoning regulations. Increasing numbers of home wine-makers, especially in the East Bay area, are opening small businesses; this trend could develop into an important new phase in Alameda's wine trade.

Concannon Vineyard. Located outside the city of Livermore in Alameda County, Concannon Vineyard has been producing premium wines since 1883, when founder James Concannon brought cuttings of Sauvignon Blanc and Sémillon from Bordeaux to the Livermore Valley. The winery was originally founded to provide sacramental wines for the church, but now Concannon makes a full line of varietal wines. In 1889, James Concannon was instrumental in convincing Mexico's president to establish viticulture on a commercial basis in that country.

For decades, the Livermore Valley was known only for its white wines, but the Concannon family, along with their long-time neighbors, the Wentes, helped to improve the quality and reputation of the red wines. Concannon's most notable innovation was the making of a varietal Petite Sirah, highlighting that grape, previously used only in blending into their generic "Burgundy" wine. It was first released in 1964.

Today, Dr. Sergio Traverso makes Concannon's average annual production of 110,000 cases, consisting of four whites, two reds, one rosé, and two generic wines. Two hundred and twenty acres (88 hectares) of vines provide some of the fruit for Concannon's wines.

In 1983, Distillers Company Ltd. of England (which produces over 50% of the scotch consumed in the world) bought the winery. Jim Concannon remains as its president.

Weibel Vineyards. A company specializing in champagne-type wines. Rudolph Weibel had worked with wines in Switzerland and with Champagnes in France since 1906 and afterward settled in San Francisco in the wine importing business. Weibel began producing wine in 1939 and together with his son, Frederick, founded the Weibel Champagne Vineyards in 1945 at Mission San José in southern Alameda County. The property was once owned by Josiah and Leland Stanford, and wine was sold under the label of Stanford.

In addition to Weibel's Brut sparkling wine (made entirely from Chardonnay grapes), the winery puts out an entire line of vintage-dated, appellation-designated varietal table wines. An estate-bottled Pinot Noir and Chardonnay are made from the 90-acre (36-hectare) vineyard at the Mission San José location; all the other wines bear Mendocino County appellations and are made at Weibel's Redwood Valley facility (*q.v.*). Three solera-type sherries and a port wine are also made.

Total production of all the Weibel wines comes close to a million cases a year, Weibel is the largest private label sparkling wine producer in the U.S. today.

Wente Brothers. An old-established property in the Livermore Valley producing good varietal wines—in particular, some of the finest Graves-type and Sauternes-type in America. The late Carl Wente, the founder, came to the U.S. from Germany in 1880 and owed his early training in Californian wines to Charles Krug of Napa Valley. Wente put his experience into practice when he purchased, in the latter part of 1883, a few vineyards in the Livermore Valley. The firm has long specialized in top-quality table wines—thanks partly to the excellent soil. The winery, built on the site of the original structure, and vineyards are located on Tesla Road outside Livermore. Research has proven that Wente Brothers is the oldest continuously operating family-owned winery in the United States.

Carl Wente enlarged his property, and his two sons, the late Herman and Ernest, added to it the valuable El Mocho Vineyards. On the El Mocho property, Louis Mel, the former owner, planted cuttings of Sémillon, Sauvignon Blanc, and Muscadelle du Bordelais from the famous Sauternes vineyard of Château d'Yquem. Today, these fine properties are in the capable hands of the Wente family, and their Château Wente sauterne is recognized for its quality.

At the present time the estate has 1,500 acres (600 hectares) of vineyard, of which 80% is planted in such choice white varieties. About 700,000 cases are made a year.

Most of the Wente wines are labeled with varietal names rather than the misused place-names borrowed from Europe. Because of the increasing urbanization of the Livermore Valley, the former head of the winery, Karl L. Wente, continued the expansion in Monterey begun by his father, Ernest. Today, the fourth generation, Eric, Philip, and Carolyn, manage the vineyards. Some of the best Wente wines come from this 800-acre (320-hectare) Monterey vineyard planted in Chardonnay and Pinot Noir for the production of their sparkling wine. Frank Schoonmaker and the author selected Wente Brothers as one of America's better wineries in 1941, in order to start selling American wines under American names east of the Rockies, which was unheard of at that time.

(6) Santa Clara–Santa Cruz–San Benito

Following in the footsteps of the founding wineries in this section of the California coast—Paul Masson, Almadén, Mirassou—a number of new wineries were either formed or re-formed during the 1960s and 1970s.

The district centralizes most of its wine-growing in Santa Clara County, where there are some fifty

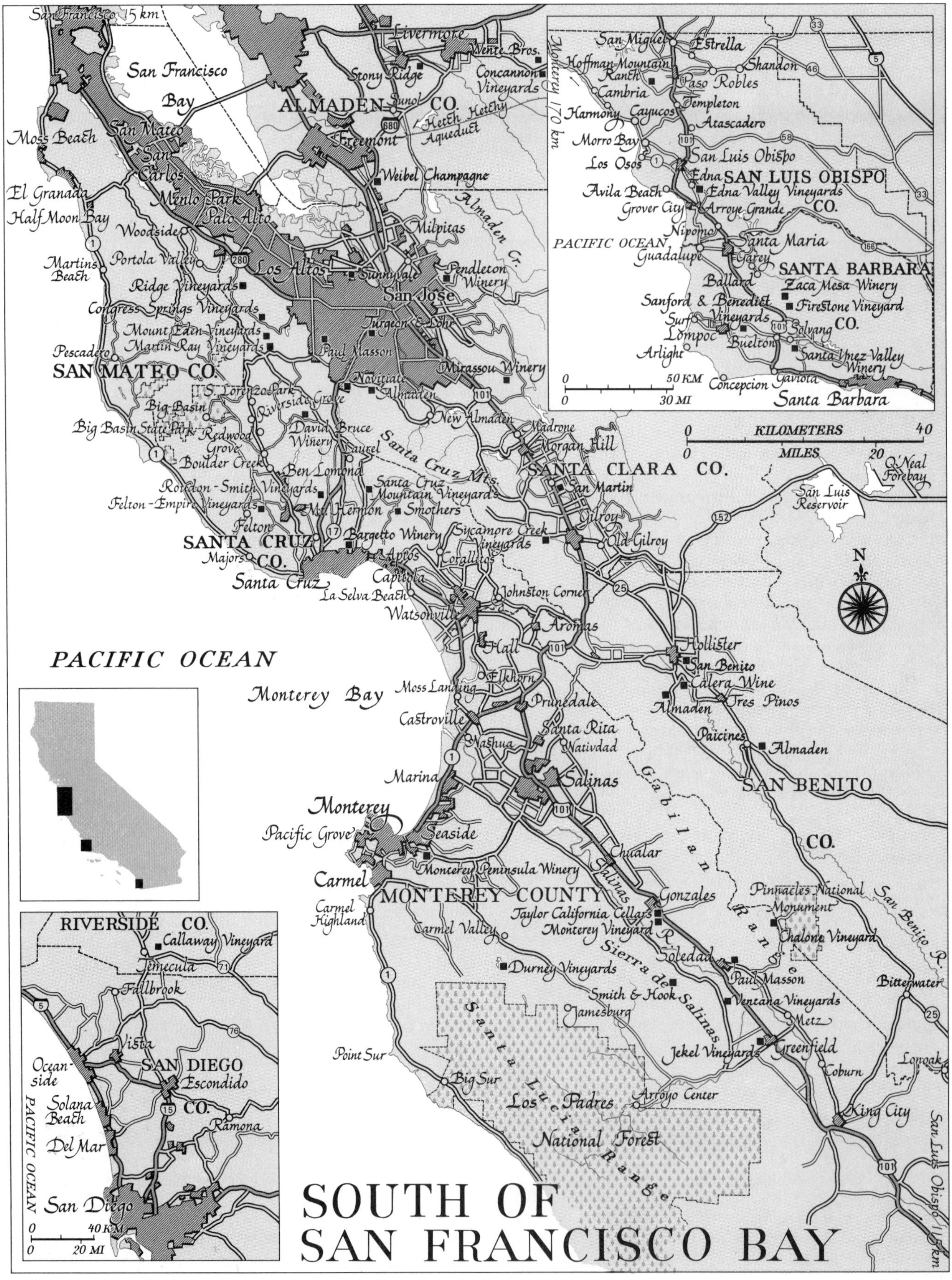
SOUTH OF SAN FRANCISCO BAY
San Francisco 15 km
San Francisco Bay
Livermore
Wente Bros.
Concannon Vineyards
Stony Ridge
ALMADEN CO.
Sunol
Hetch Hetchy Aqueduct
Fremont
Weibel Champagne
Almaden Cr.
Milpitas
Moss Beach
San Mateo
San Carlos
Menlo Park
Palo Alto
El Granada
Half Moon Bay
Woodside
Martins Beach
Portola Valley
Los Altos
Sunnyvale
Pendleton Winery
San Jose
Ridge Vineyards
Congress Springs Vineyards
Mount Eden Vineyards
Martin Ray Vineyards
Turgeon & Lohr
Paul Masson
Pescadero
SAN MATEO CO.
Novitiate
Almaden
Mirassou Winery
S. Lorenzo Park
Riverside Grove
Big Basin
Big Basin State Park
Redwood Grove
David Bruce Winery
Laurel
New Almaden
Madrone
Morgan Hill
Boulder Creek
Ben Lomond
Santa Cruz Mts.
SANTA CLARA CO.
San Martin
Roudon-Smith Vineyards
Felton-Empire Vineyards
Felton
Mt. Hermon
Santa Cruz Mountain Vineyards
Smothers
Gilroy
Old Gilroy
SANTA CRUZ CO.
Majors
Bargetto Winery
Aptos
Sycamore Creek Vineyards
Corralitos
Santa Cruz
Capitola
La Selva Beach
Johnston Corner
Watsonville
Aromas
San Luis Reservoir
O'Neal Forebay
KILOMETERS
MILES
N
PACIFIC OCEAN
Monterey Bay
Hall
Elkhorn
Moss Landing
Castroville
Prunedale
Santa Rita
Nashua
Natividad
Salinas
Hollister
San Benito
Calera Wine
Almaden
Tres Pinos
Paicines
Almaden
SAN BENITO CO.
Gabilan Range
Marina
Monterey
Pacific Grove
Seaside
Carmel
Monterey Peninsula Winery
MONTEREY COUNTY
Chualar
Gonzales
Carmel Highland
Taylor California Cellars
Monterey Vineyard
Salinas R.
Carmel Valley
Pinnacles National Monument
Chalone Vineyard
San Benito R.
Soledad
Sierra de Salinas
Durney Vineyards
Paul Masson
Smith & Hook
Ventana Vineyards
Bitterwater
Jamesburg
Metz
Santa Lucia Range
Point Sur
Jekel Vineyards
Greenfield
Coburn
Lonoak
Big Sur
Los Padres National Forest
Arroyo Center
King City
San Luis Obispo 115 km
San Miguel
Estrella
Hoffman Mountain Ranch
Shandon
Paso Robles
Cambria
Templeton
Monterey 170 km
Harmony
Cayucos
Atascadero
Morro Bay
San Luis Obispo
Los Osos
Edna
SAN LUIS OBISPO CO.
Avila Beach
Edna Valley Vineyards
Grover City
Arroyo Grande
Nipomo
PACIFIC OCEAN
Santa Maria
Guadalupe
Garey
SANTA BARBARA CO.
Ballard
Zaca Mesa Winery
Sanford & Benedict Vineyards
Firestone Vineyard
Surf
Lompoc
Solvang
Buellton
Arlight
Santa Ynez Valley Winery
50 KM
30 MI
Concepcion
Gaviota
Santa Barbara
RIVERSIDE CO.
Callaway Vineyard
Temecula
Fallbrook
Vista
Oceanside
SAN DIEGO CO.
Escondido
Solana Beach
Ramona
Del Mar
PACIFIC OCEAN
San Diego
40 KM
20 MI

bonded wineries. This county consists of three vineyard areas, totalling about 1,400 acres (560 hectares). West of the Santa Clara Valley and at the foothills of the Santa Cruz Mountains lies Los Gatos, and a little to the northwest and higher up the mountain slopes, Saratoga. This Los Gatos-Saratoga area produces some of the finest table wines and sparkling "champagnes" of California. The principal vineyards are those of Almadén, Mount Eden, Ridge, Mirassou, and Paul Masson.

The second area of Santa Clara lies to the east of San Jose and the vineyards of the Evergreen area stretch onto the slopes of Mount Hamilton. Although this district does not produce heavily, the wines are generally superior. The hundred-year-old home winery and vineyards of the Mirassou family are here.

The third area is in the southern part of Santa Clara County near the towns of Madrone, San Martin, and Gilroy. One of the largest in this area is San Martin, and there are 42 wineries making good average wine and catering to the local trade. Santa Clara County is one of the world's greatest fruit-growing districts, and its viticultural past goes back to the days of the Spanish padres who planted the valley's first domestic grapes.

Santa Cruz County is separated from Santa Clara only by the bordering Santa Cruz Mountains. There are nineteen bonded wineries, and the vineyards produce good sound grapes. In the past fifteen years, this county has become more important because of its good varietal vineyards. The push to explore new vineyard areas was particularly felt in Santa Cruz County, which underwent an expansion in vineyard space in the 1970s. It is gaining greater recognition, even though there are only about 100 acres (40 hectares) of grapevines; most of these are at higher and cooler elevations. The good quality achieved by vineyards in the Santa Cruz Mountains, especially Ridge and Martin Ray, inspired people to make further attempts to cultivate vines in this hilly dry region.

San Benito County lies south of Santa Clara and Santa Cruz, and its output of table wines is improving and increasing. Largely because of Almadén, San Benito counts 4,500 acres (1,800 hectares) of varietal grapes, plus six bonded wine cellars. In 1982, San Benito's 2,300-acre (920-hectare) Lime Kiln Valley was approved as an official viticultural area by the B.A.T.F. In addition, part of the simultaneously-designated 8,650-acre (3,460-hectare) Chalone appellation lies in San Benito County.

It is now generally recognized that the Santa Cruz hill vineyards divide into two sectors. The Santa Clara Valley side slopes, the so-called Chaine d'Or, are cooled by temperate ocean and bay breezes. This microclimate (Regions I and II) has made the Chardonnay and Pinot Noir among the preferred grapes. The slopes with a northeastern exposure are a bit warmer and are preferred by growers for the planting of Pinot Noir, Chardonnay, Cabernet Sauvignon, and Pinot Blanc. The soils are light, serpentine-based and have a gravelly shale crust, which keeps the vines well drained.

The following wineries in Santa Clara, San Benito, and Santa Cruz counties represent the changes that have occurred and continue to occur in this area.

Almadén Vineyards. Almadén Vineyards, now part of the city of San José, still stands on its original site. The winery was named after the quicksilver mining town of Almadén, California State Historical Landmark No. 505 which is 7 miles south of the winery. "In 1852 Charles Le Franc made the first commercial planting of fine European wine grapes in Santa Clara County and founded Almadén Vineyards." Whether Le Franc or Étienne Thée, his French compatriot from Bordeaux, was the original founder, is open to debate, but it was undeniably Charles Le Franc who planted choice European grape varieties at the foot of the Santa Cruz Mountains, where the heat of the constant Californian sun is tempered by cool evening breezes from the Pacific. The rocky soil is not fertile enough for large yields, but the hillsides of Almadén offer grapes of special quality.

Almadén wines are almost all varietal wines, bearing the grape name on the label. The Chardonnay is a good American white wine; and the local Cabernet Sauvignon is a red wine of distinction.

Louis Benoist, a San Francisco businessman, bought the vineyards in 1941 and increased the acreage in varietals by securing, under the recommendation of soil experts, two vineyard tracts totaling 300 acres (120 hectares). In 1956 the 3,500-acre (1,400-hectare) Rancho Paicines, was purchased by Almadén Vineyards, and grapes were planted in hillside land—among them Pinot Noir, Cabernet Sauvignon, Johannisberg Riesling, Gewürztraminer, and Chardonnay. The property, classified as a mountain vineyard with elevation ranging from 700 to 1,200 feet (200 to 300 meters), includes several soil types, particularly adapted to the cultivation of fine varietal wine grapes. Still other new vineyards are in Monterey. All in all, with 6,000 acres (2,400 hectares), Almadén owns more vineyards than any other United States' winery. National Distillers bought Almadén in 1967; today it is one of the largest producers in the country. In 1986 Almadén was purchased by the Heublein Co. which in turn was sold to International Distillers and Vintners Co. (I.D.V.) of the U.K., which is owned by another British firm, Grand Metropolitan P.L.C.

Bargetto Winery. A family enterprise since 1933, the Bargetto Winery makes some good wines at the rate of about 40,000 cases a year. Bargetto owns no vineyards; most of their grapes are purchased from select Central Coast, North Coast and Santa Cruz Mountain growers. The winery is located about three miles north of the town in Soquel in the cool coastal Santa Cruz Mountain foothills. The Bargettos make 4 varietals and some fruit wines.

Bonny Doon Vineyard. Started in 1979 by the Grahms, this winery in the Santa Cruz Mountains had its first crush in 1983. Specializing in a Rhone-style red wine with purchased grapes and their own 30 acres (12 hectares), production will peak at 15,000 cases annually.

David Bruce Winery. Located along Bear Creek Road in the peninsula town of Los Gatos, David Bruce's winery includes a small cellar and a 30-acre (12-hectare) hillside vineyard. Owner David Bruce, a retired physician, has been producing big, full wines in California since 1964. In the late seventies, Bruce decided to specialize in Pinot Noir and Chardonnay; his vineyard was grafted over from several varietals to just those two. About 30,000 cases are made a year from estate-grown and purchased grapes. Keith D. Hohlfeldt is the wine-maker.

Calera Wine Company. High up on the slopes of the Gavilan Mountains of San Benito County near Hollister, 24 acres (10 hectares) of Pinot Noir bear grapes that have earned Calera a reputation as one of California's premier producers of this varietal. Calera's first Chardonnay, from purchased Santa Barbara grapes, was made in 1982. Total production is limited to 8,000 cases a year. The winery, which uses a gravity flow design, was founded, and is owned and operated, by the Jensen family. Stephen Doerner is the wine-maker.

Congress Springs Winery. This French-style villa, built on a hilltop and surrounded by redwoods in the Santa Cruz Mountains, is owned and operated by the Eriksons and the Gehrs. The winery was built at the turn of the century by the Pourroys, two French brothers. The seventy-year-old Zinfandel vineyard they planted is still producing. Of the nine varietals Congress Springs makes, the Chardonnay, Pinot Noir, and Pinot Blanc seem particularly suited to its dry-farmed mountainside vineyards. Congress Springs owns 12 acres (5 hectares) of vines and leases 30 acres (12 hectares) more in the Santa Cruz Mountains for its 15,000-case production. Grapes are also purchased from the Santa Clara Valley.

Felton-Empire Vineyards. Known as Hallcrest Vineyards under the former owner, attorney Chaffee Hall. The wines from this 7-acre (2.8-hectare) vineyard in Felton, north of Santa Cruz in Santa Cruz County, are considered the best in the area. After Mr. Hall's death in 1969, his choice Riesling and Cabernet grapes went to the Concannon Winery in Livermore. Then, in 1976, oenologist Leo McCloskey and some partners joined forces, leased the property, renamed it Felton-Empire Vineyards, and within a year presented a complete range of white wines (with a specialty in White Riesling) that have lived up to and surpassed the Hallcrest reputation. Particularly successful is a fully botrytised Riesling, hinting at a German Rheingau Auslese wine, which should be pleasing to those seeking sweet wines. Felton-Empire produces about 20,000 cases a year, and has established itself as California's "Riesling château." It is the Santa Cruz Mountains appellation's second largest winery, Ridge being the largest.

Gemello Winery. In the town of Mountain View, north of San Jose in Santa Clara County, Gemello Winery was established in 1934 by a Piedmontese family. Mario Gemello, son of the founder, retired in 1978 and turned over the management and wine-making to his niece, Sandy Obester, and her husband Paul. Gemello has no vineyards of its own, buying grapes from other regions, including the Alexander Valley in Sonoma County. The Gemello reputation was built on full-bodied red wines, which were often too heavy with wood. Now, Gemello specializes in a lighter-style Cabernet Sauvignon and a White Zinfandel. Production has dropped from 20,000 cases to about 2,000 cases annually.

Kathryn Kennedy Winery. Although tiny (less than 1,000 cases per year), this vineyard and winery is blessed with a prime location for Cabernet Sauvignon vines. Owner Kathryn Kennedy planted 7⅕ acres (3 hectares) of only Cabernet Sauvignon in 1973 near her home on the lower slopes of the hills outside of Saratoga. Together with her son and winemaker Marty Mathis, Kennedy oversees the production of their estate-grown big full-bodied Cabernet, which was first made in 1979.

Obester Winery. Located in a refurbished hay barn just minutes from the Pacific Ocean in Half Moon Bay, this winery was established in 1977. The micro-climate here proves to be too cool for grape-growing but provides an ideal cellar temperature for the 10,000 cases produced annually. Owners Paul and Sandy Obester, who also own the Gemello Winery *(q.v.)*, buy most of their grapes from Mendocino county's Anderson valley. Son Doug is involved in the winemaking.

Paul Masson Vineyards. Begun in Santa Clara in the 1880s, the Paul Masson operations were for many years confined to that region. Only in the late 1960s did the large company move into Monterey, where the soil and climate encourage good varietal wines. Paul Masson wines and "champagnes" are bottled in Gonzales, near Monterey.

The winery is named for a Burgundian who came around the Horn to San Francisco in 1878. Masson carried an introduction to a fellow Frenchman, Charles Le Franc, and soon the two were making a popular "champagne." Masson became Le Franc's partner and his son-in-law, and when Le Franc died in 1892, his successor. In 1905 Masson built a hillside "château" and winery in the midst of his Santa Cruz mountain vineyards. Martin Ray took charge in 1936 but later established his own winery. Since 1942 Paul Masson has been owned by the Seagram distillers, who acquired several other properties, including Taylor California Cellars in 1983.

Masson produces a staggering selection of 43 different wines, including varietal wines, fortified wines, "champagnes," brandies, "proprietary" blends and generics.

Mirassou Vineyards. The vineyards of Mirassou are in the Evergreen district 5 miles (8 kilometers) east of San Jose and 75 miles (125 kilometers) south near Soledad in Monterey. Mirassou wines are made at Evergreen, where they may be sampled in their tasting room. The winery also hosts festivals, concerts, and catered meals throughout the year.

The Mirassou wine business started in Gold Rush days. When the daughter of Pierre Pellier, himself a wine-grower, married Pierre Mirassou, the winery began to prosper. In the 1960s a fifth generation took over the company and started to sell the wines under the family name, instead of in bulk as had been done before. Within a few years wines from Mirassou were known throughout the state. Today, Mirassou makes about 350,000 cases a year of varietal, generic, and sparkling wines.

Mount Eden Vineyards. Established in 1971 by the controversial pioneering vintner Martin Ray, Mount Eden Vineyards is situated high on the slopes of Table Mountain above the town of Saratoga in Santa Clara County. Ray claimed his were the only fine American wines and priced them accordingly. Outrageously expensive for the times (the 1950s), this created quite an uproar in the California wine community. Nevertheless, his exceptional Pinot Noir was one of the best wines made in the state. Since his death in 1976, a group of investors has managed the 36-acre (14-hectare) Mount Eden, whose hard-to-find, good-quality wines are treasured by connoisseurs. About 3,000 cases of Pinot Noir, Chardonnay and Cabernet Sauvignon are produced annually. Jeffrey Patterson is the wine-maker. Frank Schoonmaker and the author discovered Martin Ray and sold his good wines in 1941.

Martin Ray Vineyards. This Saratoga establishment was founded by the late innovator, Martin Ray. Kenton Brooks is the president of the winery corporation that owns the winery; Ray's son, the late Peter Martin Ray, a Stanford professor, was a major shareholder. Paul Wofford is the wine-maker. Output is about 4,000 cases a year of Chardonnay, Merlot, Cabernet Sauvignon, Pinot Noir, and a small amount of hand-made sparkling wine. Grapes from the winery's small vineyard (part of the Santa Cruz Mountains appellation) supplement purchases of Napa and Sonoma County grapes.

Ridge Vineyards. Ridge was founded in 1959 by a group of Stanford Research Institute Scientists, and has produced the classic Monte Bello Cabernet for over a quarter-century. Located in the Santa Cruz Mountains, the estate vineyards and 100-year-old Monte Bello winery overlook San Francisco and the Bay. In the 1960's the wines were made by David Bennion, and since 1970 by Paul Draper. The 40,000-case production includes Cabernets, and especially the excellent Zinfandels from Geyserville, Lytton Springs, York Creek, Howell Mountain and Paso Robles. In 1987 this vineyard was sold to the Japanese Otsuka Pharmaceutical Co.

Roudon-Smith Vineyards. Two electronics engineers, Robert Roudon and Jim Smith, began making wine in 1972. Their present winery was completed in 1978. Purchased grapes from Santa Cruz, as well as from Sonoma, Mendocino, and San Luis Obispo counties,

account for the major bulk of the 10,000-case annual production. Roudon-Smith features Cabernet Sauvignon, Zinfandel, Petite Sirah, Pinot Noir, and Chardonnay wines. The reds have met with some success.

San Martin Winery. A producer of fine varietal wines from throughout California. In addition to premium varietals, San Martin makes three low-alcohol (10%) wines, (Chenin Blanc, Johannisberg Riesling, and Gamay Beaujolais) which are made in the German style and are known as "soft wines." San Martin also makes an elegant Zinfandel from Amador County grapes. Most grapes for the 250,000-case production are purchased. San Martin is part of the Somerset Wine Company which is now owned by Distillers Co. Ltd. of the U.K.

Santa Cruz Mountain Vineyards. Former restaurant and construction company owner Ken Burnap began Santa Cruz Mountain Vineyards with the 1975 vintage of Pinot Noir from his 12-acre (5-hectare) vineyard. The property has been continuously planted in vines since 1863, when it was owned by the Jarvis Brothers Winery, one of the first in the state. The winery is located in the hills outside Santa Cruz, where the ocean dictates the microclimate. In addition to Pinot Noir, Cabernet Sauvignon grapes are purchased from a nearby vineyard, Bates Ranch. The winery was designed for gravity-flow handling in order to make wine without ever having to go through a pump or machine. There is no compromise in time or money for this 3,000-case operation. The winery has consistently won gold medals in the Orange County Fair.

Smith & Hook Winery. A fifteen-member limited partnership, operated by the McFarland Corporation, began in 1972 with the purchase of two adjacent ranches on the western slope of the Santa Lucia Mountains. In 1974, they planted 255 acres (100 hectares) of Cabernet Sauvignon along with small amounts of Cabernet Franc and Merlot for blending, and in 1979 they converted an existing horse barn into a winery. The first vintage was crushed in 1979 at another facility, but by the 1980 crush, the winery was completed. Smith & Hook makes estate-grown Cabernet Sauvignon at the rate of about 10,000 cases a year.

Sycamore Creek Vineyards. Terry and Mary Kaye Parks both left the teaching profession to revive vine-growing and wine-making on the site of the pre-Prohibition Marchetti Winery in 1976. Located in the Uvas Valley outside of Morgan Hill in Santa Clara County, Sycamore Creek has 13 acres (5 hectares) of vines (some of which are over seventy years old), which provide about a quarter the fruit needed for the 5,000 cases made annually. About seven wines are produced annually.

(7) Monterey

This district south of San Francisco was becoming the largest varietal wine-growing region in California.

After a great burst of vineyard planting in the early 1970s, it was only a decade later that the Monterey region has settled down. From a high of 34,000 acres (13,600 hectares) planted in 1978, the vineyard area dropped to 30,000 acres (12,000 hectares) by 1985. Unsuitable plantings were pulled out and a greater effort to match proper grape varieties with the diverse soils and microclimates was made.

The principal vineyards in the Monterey district are in the Salinas Valley and foothills around Soledad and in the region of the Pinnacles National Monument. The valley runs from Monterey Bay 130 miles (210 kilometers) southeast into San Luis Obispo County. The soil is decomposed granite. The rich benchlands surrounding the floor of the Salinas Valley are seldom bothered by frost. They have abundant water from underground sources, including the great underground Salinas River.

It is now generally recognized that Monterey falls into two distinct growing zones. Upper Monterey, the northwest section of the county, is characterized by light soils and cool microclimates (officially Regions I and II) best suited to cultivating Riesling, Gewürztraminer, and Pinot Noir vines. The southeastern part of the county has slightly heavier soils and warmer temperatures (Region III), and some Monterey growers claim it is better suited to Cabernet Sauvignon, Zinfandel, Merlot, and Sauvignon Blanc. In 1982, one specific district, Chalone, was officially recognized as an appellation by the B.A.T.F. Chalone, which lies partially in San Benito County, covers 8,650 acres or 3,460 hectares.

Most of the great planting of vines in Monterey was done by large wineries based outside the county, or by those already established in the region. Mirassou and Paul Masson, when faced with the spreading towns of Santa Clara County, took the word of the university experts and in the early 1960s planted vines in the new district. In addition, as a result of the burst of activity in Monterey in the seventies, several new wineries appeared on the scene. A listing of the older established wineries, and those of the new generation that deserve recognition, follows.

Chalone Vineyard. High in the Gavilán Mountains on the eastern edge of Salinas Valley is Chalone Vineyard. Founded by Richard Graff and Philip Woodward, the Chalone Group is a publicly-held company that also owns Acacia, Carmenet and Edna Valley wineries (all listed separately). The Chardonnay, Pinot Noir, Chenin Blanc, and Pinot Blanc are well-made regional wines, all of which are from fruit grown on the winery's 150 acres (60 hectares). About 20,000 cases are produced a year.

Durney Vineyards. This family-owned wine estate in the beautiful Carmel Valley produces one hundred and twenty acres (48 hectares) of non-irrigated Cabernet Sauvignon, Chenin Blanc, Johannisberg Riesling, Gamay Beaujolais and Chardonnay wines at the 15,000-case winery. These 100% varietal wines have been steadily improving, resulting in some top award-winning wines.

Jekel Vineyards. This family venture begun in 1972 is owned by Bill and Pat Jekel. From their 140-acre (56-hectare) vineyard in the Arroyo Seco appellation of the western Salinas Valley, the Jekels have succeeded in making some very good Chardonnays, Rieslings and Cabernet Sauvignons. All wines are made from the produce of the Jekel Vineyards surrounding the 60,000-case-capacity winery.

J. Lohr Winery. Home-businessman Jerry Lohr switched tracks in 1972 and entered the wine business. From 500 acres (200 hectares) of vineyards in Monterey, the Sacramento Delta region, and Napa, Lohr grows about 75% of the fruit needed to make 250,000 cases annually. Although 12 varietals are produced at the San José Winery, Lohr has matched up specific varietals with the specific conditions in each of his vineyard areas, trying to grow the best possible fruit in each given area.

Monterey Peninsula Winery. Fans of "pure" wines, neither filtered nor clarified, are the most likely devotees of this winery's products. Each bottle bears the name of the plot of land from which it originates. Dentists-turned-wine-makers Deryck Nuckton and Roy Thomas have been purchasing grapes and making wines since 1974. Some inky, intense wines have been made from Zinfandel, Cabernet Sauvignon, and Barbera, as well as Chardonnay grapes. All grapes are purchased, primarily from Monterey County, some from Amador County. Peter Watson-Graft makes the annual 15,000 cases at the winery which is in the town of Sand City.

The Monterey Vineyard. This vineyard is one of the most northerly in the Monterey region, with a 200,000-case capacity winery at Gonzales. Monterey was once part of The Wine Spectrum, a former subsidiary of Coca-Cola of Atlanta that included Sterling Vineyards, Taylor California Cellars, and New York State's Taylor Wine Company. It was acquired by Jos. E. Seagram & Sons in 1983. Wine-master Cary Goff is responsible for production. All of the grapes for the winery's generic, varietal, and special bottlings are purchased in Monterey County.

Taylor California Cellars. Located in Gonzales, Taylor flanks its sister winery, The Monterey Vineyard. Both wineries were part of The Wine Spectrum, which was a subsidiary of Coca-Cola of Atlanta until Jos. E. Seagram & Sons acquired them in 1983. Taylor California Cellars was completed in 1982; the 34-million-dollar facility is headquarters for the fastest-growing brand in the history of the wine industry. Taylor makes nine generics and seven varietals, the majority from purchased wines that are blended and bottled at the Gonzales facility. Production is about 8 million cases annually.

Ventana Vineyards Winery. This converted dairy, built around the turn of the century and now run by Douglas Meador, began with the 1978 vintage of Chardonnay, Chenin Blanc, Sauvignon Blanc and white Riesling. The grapes for the 40,000 case production come from the Meador's 300-acre (120-hectare) vineyards. Chardonnay is the flagship of Ventana's line.

Sacramento Valley

This region extends from the northern part of San Joaquin County up as far as Oroville in Butte County and comprises Sacramento, Placer, Yolo, Amador, Butte, and northern San Joaquin counties. The Sacramento Valley is merely an extension of one great inland valley region marking the heart of Californian agriculture, but with its variations in soil, contour, and climate it is one of four important subdivisions. This region is somewhat affected by the moderating influence of San Francisco Bay, and consequently the summers become slowly hotter and the winters cooler. Some parts of the valley, particularly where the winter frosts are negligible and the summers mild, may eventually prove to be the home of better wines. Much of the land to the north is broken and irregular and entirely unsuitable to the planting of wine grapes. Butte County shows some promise, and wine grapes are grown there in increasing numbers. The whole valley produced few good grapes for many years, but a total of 3,000 acres (1,200 hectares) is now planted.

Most of the region's vineyards are found in the northern section of San Joaquin County and in Sacramento County. The majority go in for mass production, and ordinary table wines and dessert wines abound. If any of the wineries located in the Sacramento, Central, and San Joaquin valleys intend to make better wines, they must go to far-distant counties outside of these hot valleys to obtain quality grapes.

The major district of the Sacramento Valley region is the Lodi-Sacramento, which dominates the better part of the region's wine-growing area. From the state capital of Sacramento southward to the town of Elk Grove, table and dessert wines are bulk-produced and types of "burgundies" and "ports" are made from inferior as well as from good grape varieties grown elsewhere. At Elk Grove in Sacramento County many fruit, dessert, and berry wines are produced, as well as aperitifs and table wines.

In northern San Joaquin County, the lively little city of Lodi is noted for its wineries given over to dessert wines, although table wines are also produced. However, the Lodi area, which branches out in all directions from the city, produces substantial amounts of table wine. Most is vinified from Zinfandel and Tokay grapes. San Joaquin County counts nearly 38,000 acres (15,200 hectares) of wine grapes and has one of the highest per-acre yields in the state. As might be expected, the wines are some of the least good that California can produce. There are twenty-one bonded wineries and fourteen distilleries. San Joaquin makes a great deal of brandy.

Three counties surrounding Sacramento on the north and east have been singled out as among California's most prized sectors for the growing of Zinfandel grapes. Amador County in particular has experienced great development in this regard. Its Shenandoah Valley and Fiddletown vineyards are especially prized for their cool nights, warm days, and red volcanic soil. These attributes are shared to a greater or lesser degree by various sites throughout the three counties, allowing a wide range of Zinfandel styles to be made, from the pleasantly light and flowery to the long-vatted and slow-to-mature. The potential of other varietals is also being explored.

Barengo-Lost Hills Winery. Known for years as Acampo Winery and Distilleries, this property was once owned by the Mondavis of Charles Krug. Dino Barengo bought it in 1944 and changed the name to Barengo Vineyards twenty years later. In 1973, he sold the company to Marvin Adler of Los Angeles, and remained as part of the management. In 1976 Ira Kirkorian and his son Kent, grape growers in the San Joaquin region, acquired Barengo. In 1981, Barengo was sold once again, this time to Herb Benham, Jr., the owner of a large farming corporation in Kern County. The Lost Hills Vineyards marketing group was incorporated with Barengo at the same time. Barengo produced the first Ruby Cabernet wine in the San Joaquin County region and is known for its German-style "May Wine," and "port." The winery is on Highway 99, 3 miles (4.8 kilometers) north of Lodi. Wine production is about 300,000 cases annually, most from Barengo-grown grapes.

D'Agostini Winery. Swiss immigrant Adam Uhlinger founded D'Agostini Winery in 1856, making it the oldest wine establishment in Amador County and now a state historical landmark. Enrico D'Agostini bought the property, 8 miles (13 kilometers) northeast of Plymouth, in 1911. His four sons ran the family business until 1984 when Sacramento wine merchant Armagan Ozdiker bought the winery. The grapes from 125 acres (51 hectares) and purchased grapes produce about 35,000 cases of wine a year.

Franzia Brothers Winery. Franzia Brothers annually makes more than 25 million gallons of wine at its winery situated along Highway 120, about two hours from San Francisco. In 1973, 60% of the company shares were purchased by the Coca-Cola Bottling Company of New York City, leaving the remaining shares with the Franzia family. In 1981, members of the management team privately invested in the winery, purchasing it from Coca-Cola. There are nearly 3,500 acres (1,400 hectares) of vineyards. These were begun in 1906, the year of the San Francisco earthquake; the first Franzia winery was built in 1915. Today Franzia sells improved table, generic, varietal, and sparkling wines under different labels. In terms of quality and market share, Franzia competes with Inglenook, Almadén and Paul Masson.

Guild Wineries. In 1934, Lawrence Marshall organized the Guild cooperative. Alta, Garrett, and Cribari & Sons became part of the group in the 1960s, as did the Schenley wine interests including the Roma, Cresta Blanca and Cook's Champagne brands. Today, Guild comprises eight wineries with headquarters in Lodi which is also the central bottling and blending facility. Guild is owned by nearly 500 growers. In addition to their major brands, Guild makes several different brandies and "Silverado California Vodka."

Monteviña Wines. Three miles from Plymouth in the Shenandoah Valley, Monteviña Wines was opened in 1973 and is owned by retired banker Walter Field. Most of the grapes grown on Monteviña's 90 acres (36 hectares) of vines are retained to make an average of 30,000 cases annually. Located in Amador County, Monteviña makes particularly successful Zinfandels, which grow well in the dry and intense heat of the region, and good Sauvignon Blancs. White Zinfandel and small amounts of Barbera, Cabernet Sauvignon, and Sémillon are also produced.

Oak Ridge Vineyards. Located in the eastern section of Lodi, this is a cooperative which makes and bottles many table and dessert wines, brandies and vermouths under seven different labels. A 50,000-gallon redwood barrel has been converted into a tasting room. The cooperative puts out about 350,000 cases a year.

Stevenot Winery. Located in the Sierra Foothills, south-east of Sacramento, this winery was founded in 1974 by Barden Stevenot whose ancestors settled in the area during the Gold Rush days. The core of Stevenot's ten wines comes from 30 acres (12 hectares) of estate grapes, supplemented by purchases from other foothill vineyards. More than 50,000 cases are made annually.

Central Valley

The major district in the Central Valley, known as the Escalon-Modesto, contains some of the largest distributing Californian wineries. Escalon and Manteca are south of Stockton in the southern part of San Joaquin County, and the vineyards mostly lie in an east-west direction between these two small cities. The Central Valley region covers the southern San Joaquin and Stanislaus counties and takes in northern Merced County in the vicinity of Livingston. It is a large producer of table grapes—Flame Tokay, Thompson Seedless and Sultanina—and unfortunately too many of them are used in the making of average wines. However, good Zinfandel plantings are increasing. The important wineries in Stanislaus County are in Modesto and Salida.

The largest winery in the world, the E. & J. Gallo Company, is in Modesto. The Central Valley produces enormous quantities of mediocre to good wines—mostly dessert wines and a few ordinary table and sparkling wines made from grape varieties that are considered heavy producers and even from table grape varieties producing a substandard quality. Approximately 500,000 short tons (445,000 long tons) of grapes are crushed yearly in this region. The area has a marked resemblance to the lesser areas of southern France and to a lesser degree Algeria, not only in climate but in wines produced. More wine grapes are being planted in the Central Valley. Today, of the 90,000 acres (36,000 hectares) in vines, two-thirds are planted with grapes that yield fairly decent wines.

E. & J. Gallo Winery. Ernest and Julio Gallo are two of the best-known names in the American wine business. Gallo sells more than any other United States winery, making it the leader in this country and throughout the world. It is estimated that Gallo harvests 20% of the Napa Valley crop, 40% of Sonoma's crop and 40% of the Central Coast crop to produce their table wines. Gallo crushes at three facilities (Fresno, Sonoma County, Livingston) and bottles a total of 150,000 cases a day at their Modesto headquarters. Gallo exports to the Caribbean, Canada, the United Kingdom, and several European countries.

In the age of conglomerates, corporate takeovers, and bankruptcies, Gallo has remained family-owned over the years, with Ernest heading the marketing and sales, and Julio directing wine-making and production. Several members of the next generation are actively involved in the operation of the winery today.

A combination of astute merchandising and a product that suits the average American taste has made Gallo wines recognized everywhere. There is obviously expertise involved in producing inexpensive but sound wines on such a huge scale. The company experiments with new wines and its staff of Ph.D.s trained in chemistry, oenology, and microbiology is the largest in California.

Jug table wines make up the majority of Gallo's production, but in the mid-1970s, a line of cork-finished varietals, under the "Wine Cellars of Ernest & Julio Gallo" label, was developed. Eight varietals, including Cabernet Sauvignon, Chardonnay, and Sauvignon Blanc, are made. An underground aging facility, with Yugoslavian and French oak barrels, was built to accommodate the new line.

San Joaquin Valley

The region forms the southern branch of the great inland valley. It is the warmest area, a typical valley climate, with a lack of moderating sea breezes. The annual rainfall is negligible and irrigation is necessary; daytime temperatures in July and August average from 80°F to over 100°F (27°C–34°C). The San Joaquin is a great raisin area, and it produces sweet fortified wines of better than average quality. Dry table wines are also made, but they lack quality, mainly on account of the poor balance between sugar and acid in the grape varieties grown.

The principal district of the region is the Fresno-San Joaquin Valley, comprising five counties. From north to south they are: Madera (lying south of Merced County), Fresno, Kings, Tulare, and Kern counties.

Madera County vineyards surround the city of Madera, the most important in quantity being Papagni (*q.v.*).

Fresno County, with the city of Fresno as its center, has twenty-one bonded wineries, many of them producing wines misnamed port, sherry, sauternes, etc.—handicaps to a promising industry. The wines of the inland valley regions may be improved by the planting of better varieties. Around Fresno there are many towns with large wineries—Fowler, Selma, Reedley, Parlier, and Sanger.

Kings County's vineyards are near Hanford, while Tulare has its centers in Tulare and Cutler.

Kern County's large acreage of vineyards stretches from Delano to Arvin, outside the city of Bakersfield. There are ten wineries in Kern, and although they do not produce directly to the public, they play a considerable role in supplying wine to major firms in other areas. Approximately 1.5 million short tons (1.34 million long tons) of grapes are crushed annually in the San Joaquin Valley. More than half of the 90,000 acres (36,000 hectares) of wine grapes have been planted in the last ten years.

JFJ Bronco Winery. Previous owners of the Franzia Winery, the two Franzia brothers and a cousin, Fred T., John and Joseph S., founded Bronco Winery in 1973, a huge 60-million-gallon-capacity winery, where they crush, receive, blend, finish, and bottle. The winery has become a major producer of table wines and some sparkling wines. Bronco is located 6 miles (10 kilometers) south of Modesto.

California Growers Winery. Arpaxat Setrakian, an Armenian, founded this winery at the small town of Cutler, southeast of Fresno, in 1936. He had been for many years a leader in the raisin industry. The Setrakian family continues to own and operate the winery, making generic and varietal wines at the rate of about 20 million gallons annually.

Ficklin Vineyards. Californian winery specializing in good port-type wine made from the choicest Portuguese grapes. Four of the finest varieties are used: Tinta Cão, Tinta Madeira, Souzão, and Touriga. Exceptional care goes into the making of Ficklin port, and with the help of the Davis Oenological Station, they are producing matured wines somewhat comparable with those of Portugal.

David Ficklin and Walter Ficklin, Jr., founded the winery in 1946 as wine-maker and vineyardist, respectively. In 1983, David's son, Peter, took over as wine-maker, and Walter's son, Steven, took over as vineyardist.

The small winery is in the heart of San Joaquin Valley, near the town of Madera, 22 miles (about 35 kilometers) north of Fresno.

Giumarra Vineyards. "Papa Joe" Giumarra, a Sicilian immigrant, founded this huge 15,000-acre (6,000-hectare) vineyard, of which 8,000 acres (3,200 hectares) are now planted in grapes, in the early 1900s. The winery was incorporated in 1946 and today remains solely family-owned and -operated, with the third generation in charge. Defying the near-tropical climatic conditions of the Central Valley, generally believed to be unsuitable for the growing of noble grape varieties, Giumarra succeeds in cultivating ten varietal grapes and vinifying them well, resulting in some good wines. In 1986 Giumarra began importing grapes from the Central Coast appellation to make an oak-aged Char-

donnay and three other white wines. The average annual production at Giumarra is over 1½ million cases. Located 10 miles east of Bakersfield, Giumarra also grows plums, potatoes, and other crops.

La Mont Winery. In 1978, John La Batt Ltd., the Canadian brewery, bought the rights to the California Wine Association's labels and took over wine-making at the cooperative located in DiGiorgio, 18 miles east of Bakersfield in Kern County, forming the La Mont Winery. Until then, the Association was the sole survivor of what was once almost a wine monopoly in the state: the "Eleven Cellars" group of cooperatives. Before Prohibition, the Association owned more than 60 wineries, including the Perelli-Minetti Winery (founded by the late Antonio Perelli-Minetti, longtime wine-maker at Italian Swiss Colony). Lamont makes a full line of varietals, dessert, and generic wines sold under many of the fine old names of the California wine business, all that remains from the period when the Association was an important force in the state's wine industry. In 1986, Anheuser Busch, the brewers bought La Mont..

Papagni Vineyards. Located in the heart of the Central Valley, 9 miles (15 kilometers) south of Madera, Angelo Papagni's winery has been producing wines since 1973. Papagni's father, Demetrio, an immigrant from Bari in southwestern Italy, grew grapes in the region for many years. John Daddino is the wine-maker behind the approximately 80,000 cases a year made under the Angelo Papagni and Papagni Vineyards labels. Around 2,000 acres (800 hectares) of vines are under cultivation. The Papagni wines have done surprisingly well in some local and European blind tastings. Varietal wines include Chardonnay, Sauvignon Blanc, Barbera, Zinfandel, Muscat (both still and sparkling), and Alicante-Bouschet. Two "sherries," dry and cream, are also made. The Chardonnay and Alicante-Bouschet are almost textbook-defying in quality, especially considering the region where they are grown.

Quady Winery. Andrew Quady, formerly an engineer at the United Vintners winery in Madera, is best known for his exotic dessert wines, made from the Orange Muscat and Black Muscat grapes,. About 6,000 cases are made annually at Quady's handsome winery in Madera.

South Coast Mountains

This region is a combination of three districts—Los Angeles County, San Diego, and Cucamonga-Ontario districts. Los Angeles and San Diego counties, lying in the southern coastal valley region, are cooled by sea breezes, while the inland district of Cucamonga-Ontario—synonymous with San Bernardino County—is an extension of the desert area, and its summers are comparable with those of the San Joaquin Valley. This warmer area is less suitable for the production of good table wines, although quite good fortified wines are made.

In the Escondido district in San Diego County, an area which once devoted most of its wine-growing to muscatels, new vineyards are producing some better-quality wines.

The most famous district in southern California is around Cucamonga. Light wines which are produced in large quantities here should be consumed early because the warm climate is not conducive to the production of full-bodied, lasting growths. Red table wine made from grape varieties which go into so-called chiantis, clarets, and burgundies is a specialty. There are a few vineyards in this area which make a fair Grignolino Rosé. Wines of all natures are produced in the Cucamonga-Ontario district, ranging from red table wines and sparkling "champagne"-types to aperitifs and dessert wines. Quality in this sun-parched region depends on the grower's integrity and his willingness to substitute quality for quantity. Grapes grown in the warmer parts of the hot desert region—such as the Coachella and Imperial valleys—are not suitable for wine and not used for such, although this area does well with its early-maturing table grapes.

Southern California is of little importance in the overall production of wine in the state. Less than 5% of the total is made in the area. There are, however, over thirty wineries, six of them belonging to Brookside Vineyards. Some parts of San Diego and Santa Barbara counties are having a revival of grape and wine production. Santa Barbara leads the area with over 9,000 acres (3,600 hectares) of wine grapes; San Bernardino counts about 3,500 acres (1,400 hectares); and San Diego has about 130 acres (52 hectares).

All the South Coast Mountain region vineyards are planted in ungrafted *vinifera* vines. This is contrary to the practice in the rest of California (with the exception of half of Monterey County).

Brookside Vineyard Company. Brookside has done much to bring wine-growing back to the southern part of the state. The company was started by two immigrants, Théophile Vaché and Marius Biane, with vineyards planted in the 1850s in Redlands. At 150 years old, Brookside is southern California's oldest winery, and also its largest. Owned by a group of San Francisco investors, who bought the winery from Beatrice Foods of Chicago in 1982, Brookside operates several retail outlets in southern California. Under the Brookside and Vaché labels, a wide selection of generic and varietal wines are produced. A 350-acre (140-hectare) vineyard in Temecula provides grapes for the varietals, while grapes and wine are purchased for Brookside's generics.

Callaway Vineyard and Winery. Endowed with good humidity, mild heat, and a long growing season, Callaway's 320 acres (128 hectares) on a hill near Temecula, in Rancho California, north of San Diego, are in what has turned out to be an unexpectedly good vine-growing microclimate. Few people recognized it as such when Ely Callaway, former president of the Burlington Mills textile firm, first planted grapes there

in 1969. Under the direction of Dwayne Helmuth, Callaway makes only wines. Callaway's production is about 100,000 cases annually, making it Southern California's largest premium winery. About 65% of the grapes used in making Callaway's Fumé Blanc, Sauvignon Blanc, dry Chenin Blanc, Chardonnay, White Riesling Vin Blanc and Sweet Nancy dessert wine are purchased. Hiram Walker, the Canadian distillers, bought Callaway in 1981. In turn in 1986 they were taken over by Guinness, the Irish brewers.

Mount Palomar Winery. Founded by Los Angeles radio-station owner John Poole in 1969, Mount Palomar is located 5 miles (8 kilometers) east of Temecula in Rancho California. Poole's son Peter is president of the winery and Joe Cherpin, whose family ran the Cherpin Winery in Fontana, is wine-maker. The vineyards cover 110 acres (44 hectares), yielding roughly 18,000 cases of 6 varietals a year.

San Pasqual Vineyards. Retired Judge Charles Froehlich and attorney Milton Friedman began planting grapes 20 miles (32 kilometers) northeast of San Diego in 1973. Presently 20 acres (8 hectares) are planted in vines and an average of 25,000 cases are made yearly. David Pearson is wine-maker. San Pasqual's specialties are Sauvignon Blanc and Chardonnay. Some of the grapes are supplied by the winery's own vineyards.

(8) San Luis Obispo–Santa Barbara–Santa Ynez

Although they have known wine-making for over a century, San Luis Obispo and Santa Barbara counties have experienced a renaissance of expanded varietal plantings and establishment of new wineries. Located 250 miles (415 kilometers) south of San Francisco, and about 100 miles (165 kilometers) north of Los Angeles, these two counties have grown from three or four wineries in the late 1960s to over forty today.

South of Monterey, at the source of the Salinas River, San Luis Obispo County is today regaining its former reputation as an important vine-growing region. Endowed with a favorable cool microclimate, its wine-producing future looks promising.

The principal growing areas in San Luis Obispo County center around Shandon to the north, the Edna Valley to the south, and Paso Robles and Templeton to the west. There are 25 bonded wineries and about 5,000 acres (2,000 hectares) of vineyards in the county. Vineyard plantings now total over 9,000 acres (3,600 hectares) in Santa Barbara County. The Santa Ynez and Santa Maria valleys are the county's major vine-growing regions.

Much of the new acreage in both counties is taken up by fine varietals such as Chardonnay, Cabernet Sauvignon, Zinfandel, and Riesling. Pinot Noir vines have been surprisingly successfully cultivated in certain pockets of these counties. The best areas of each county are those cooled by ocean breezes, which temper the effect of the warm daytime temperatures and allow the grapes to retain the high acidity levels necessary and too often lacking in southern California wines.

Arciero Winery. Arciero is a spectacular $13 million winery on 700 acres (280 hectares) near Paso Robles. Originaly from Italy, the Arciero brothers, Frank and Philip entered the cement and real estate development business in southern California in the booming 1960s and decided to try their hand in the wine business in 1984 when they bought this property. Production capacity is 500,000 cases of several moderately-priced varietals. 300 acres (120 hectares) of vineyards are planted around the winery.

Corbett Canyon Winery. Formerly known as the Lawrence Winery, this property was founded in 1979 by James Lawrence. The winery was sold in 1980 to Glenmore Distilleries of Louisville, Kentucky, who changed the name to Corbett Canyon in 1984. Production remains at about 150,000 cases from purchased grapes in San Luis Obispo and Santa Barbara counties. Four varietals are produced. Three different sparkling wines, made under the Shadow Creek label, are also produced on the premises, at the rate of about 25,000 cases annually.

Edna Valley Vineyard. This winery is the result of a joint venture between Paragon Vineyards and Chalone Incorporated *(q.v)*. It is located southeast of San Luis Obispo on Highway 227. While the present winery was under construction, the first wines (Pinot Noir and Chardonnay) were made at Chalone. Case production is 40,000.

Estrella River Winery. Six miles east of Paso Robles, bounded by the Gavilan Mountains to the east and the Santa Lucia Mountains to the west, 700 acres (280 hectares) of rolling hills provide the family-run Estrella River Winery with about half of the grapes needed for its 100,000 annual cases. President Cliff Giacobine operates Estrella River. Tom Myers serves as wine-maker. Their first crush took place in 1977 at their spectacular new winery. Altogether, nine varieties are grown and made into satisfactory table wines. Estrella River boasts the largest single planting (32 acres or 13 hectares) of the Syrah grape in the U.S.

The Firestone Vineyard. Kate and Brooks Firestone, and Brooks's father, Leonard, of the famous tire family, have a majority share of this Santa Ynez Valley operation, with the minority share held by Suntory Ltd., a Japanese distillery. Their 300 acres (122 hectares), planted in seven different grape varieties, have been producing nearly 75,000 cases a year since 1975. The Riesling and a good Cabernet Sauvignon are among the more notable of the Firestone wines. Located 5 miles (8½ kilometers) north of Los Olivos, near Santa Barbara, the Firestone Vineyard enjoys a unique microclimate cooled by ocean fogs. In 1986 they purchased J. Carey Cellars.

HMR Estate Winery. Dr. Stanley Hoffman, a cardiologist from Beverly Hills, planted his vineyards at the foot of the Santa Lucia Mountains, 6½ miles (10 kilometers) west of Paso Robles, in 1965. The Hoffman family moved from the city to their ranch and made their first wines in 1975. In 1982, the Hoffmans sold the winery to a group of thirty limited partners who in turn put it on the market in 1986. Guided by the great oenologist Andre Tchelistcheff, HMR makes six wines at the rate of about 30,000 cases a year. Chris Johnson is the wine-maker. About 60% of the grapes needed are purchased from the Central Coast region; the rest come from HMR's 58 acres (27 hectares) of vineyards planted in chalky soil.

Sanford & Benedict Vineyards. Michael Benedict, wine-maker and biology professor at the University of California—Santa Barbara—issued his first wines with former partner Richard Sanford in 1976 (see next entry). One hundred and ten acres (44 hectares) planted in 1972 yield about 10,000 cases a year under the Sanford & Benedict label.

Sanford Winery. Former telecommunications executive Richard Sanford and his wife Thekla have been involved in winemaking in the Santa Barbara area since the 1960s (see previous entry). They established their own winery in 1981 on the rolling Santa Ynez hills five miles west of Buellton. All grapes are purchased for the 30,000-case production. 100 acres (40 acres) of vineyard will provide some of the fruit for Sanford's six varietals in the future. Chardonnay is a specialty. Adobe brick, known for its insulative qualities, has been used in the winery's construction.

Santa Ynez Valley Winery. Boyd Bettencourt and the Davidge family formed this winery corporation in 1976. Two vineyards in the cool Santa Ynez Valley provide most of the grapes needed for the winery's 12,000 annual cases. One vineyard (110 acres or 44 hectares) was planted in 1969 by the Bettencourt and Davidge families making it the oldest in the Santa Ynez Valley. Michael Brown is the wine-maker in their renovated dairy barn. Santa Ynez specializes in varietal white wines, and also makes two reds and some dessert wines.

Tepusquet Vineyards. Although there is no Tepusquet Winery, and there are no plans for one in the future, this substantial (1,250 acres or 500 hectares) vineyard in the Santa Maria appellation supplies grapes to some neighboring and many north coast wineries. An additional 450 acres (180 hectares) of vineyards are located near Paso Robles. About 100,000 cases of wine are made and bottled at other facilities (usually San Martin Winery) and sold under the Tepusquet label, which first appeared in 1982. The vineyards, started in 1971, are owned by brothers Louis and George Lucas, who grew table grapes for many years in the Delano area, and a third partner, Al Gagnon.

York Mountain Winery. Far off the beaten wine track, York Mountain is 9 miles west of the town of Templeton, halfway between Los Angeles and San Francisco. The vineyards are on the eastern slopes of the Santa Lucia Mountains in San Luis Obispo County. In 1882 Andrew York and his three sons built a small stone winery where family members operated until the early 1970s, when it was sold to Max Goldman, an oenologist who has been in the wine business for more than fifty years. His son, Steve Goldman, is the wine-maker behind the average annual 5,000-case production. Six varietals and two generics are produced; some of the grapes are grown on 8 acres (3 hectares) near the winery.

Zaca Mesa Winery. Not far from Los Olivos in the Santa Ynez Valley, Zaca Mesa is owned by former Atlantic Richfield executive Marshall Ream. His Zaca Mesa winery specializes in three white and three red varietals. With 235 acres (94 hectares) on the Santa Ynez estate and 120 acres (45 hectares) in the neighboring Santa Maria Valley, Zaca Mesa supplies most of its own grapes. Ken Brown is the wine-maker behind the 90,000-case production. Zaca Mesa hosts musical concerts and other cultural activities at the winery.

United States: Colorado

Winters in the Rocky Mountains and its foothills are generally too rough for vine-growing, but near Grand Junction, in Palisade, Colorado, a group of wine enthusiasts has successfully cultivated 60 acres (24 hectares) of Riesling, Chardonnay, and Gewürztraminer vines since 1973. Supplemented with California grapes, the group's *Colorado Mountain Vineyards* has produced about 5,000 cases a year since 1978, when the winery opened. The newly planted 22 acres (9 hectares) of *Pikes Peak Vineyards Ltd.* are of Cabernet Sauvignon, Merlot, Riesling, Chardonnay and Sauvignon Blanc, near Colorado Springs.

At least one other winery is planned, near Colorado Springs.

United States: Connecticut

Encouraged by revised farm winery and licensing laws that came into effect in 1978, a number of wine-growers in Connecticut have transformed their backyard vineyards into commercial enterprises. As a result, the 1990s will most likely see an expansion of the state's grape-growing and wine-making industry, once a part of colonial life.

Wineries, most of them still in the early and experimental stages, are scattered all over the state. In the mid-1980s, one can look to those wineries specializing in French-American hybrids for quality wines. Setting a good example is *Haight Vineyard,* located in Litchfield in the northwestern corner of the state. 45 acres (18 hectares) of Chardonnay, Riesling, and Foch grapes have yielded about 3,000 cases a year. The Chardonnay and Riesling are good wines.

Crosswoods Winery, Clarke Vineyards, and *Stonecrop Vineyards* are all in the coastal town of Stonington, where the maritime influence allows for the successful cultivation of hybrids and some white *vinifera* types. *Hamlet Hill Vineyard* in Pomfret, *Hopkins Vineyard* in New Preston, and *St. Hillary Winery* in North Grosvenor are establishments that show promise as good producers. In Fairfield County the Digrazias have 50 acres (20 hectares) of hybrids.

United States: Delaware

Richard Becker owns and operates Delaware's only winery, the *Northminster Winery* in Wilmington. He makes one dry, white wine from locally grown hybrids and *vinifera* juice imported from California.

United States: Florida

The production of Florida's 700 acres (283 hectares) of Muscadine grapes and 140 acres (57 hectares) of bunch grapes is primarily for the fresh fruit market, primarily pick-your-own markets. There are, however, now four promising wineries in the state. Vineyards are located in Pensacola and Tallahassee in the Panhandle as well as in south Florida. Most are located in the northern and north-central parts of the state, where occasional frosts make citrus-growing hazardous. Growth is spurred on by an active research program at the University of Florida's labs in Leesburg, and by scientists Dr. Lorenz Stover, Dr. John Mortensen, and Dr. Robert Bates. Stover is responsible for the development of the Stover grape, a hybrid that has survived for 25 years in his vineyard, and that produces a light, dry, simple white wine. Another hybrid, Conquistador, is being introduced for dry red wines.

Florida vineyards suffer from its semitropical climate. Without freezing weather, vines do not have the benefit of long dormancy, and pests grow unchecked. Pierce's disease, rust, mildew, rot, insects, and hurricanes are among the enemies. Unlimited sun and water, as well as sandy and limestone soils are among the plusses. Still, it is unlikely that grapes harvested in July will ever produce impressive wines.

Alaqua. A small winery belonging to Foster and Rebecca Burgess. 10 acres (4 hectares) of Muscadine, all of which is fermented into wine.

Lafayette Vineyards. Tallahassee in Leon County grow 38 acres (15 hectares) of Muscadine, Florida Bunch and a little *vinifera,* which is not encouraging.

Midulla Vineyards produces most of the wine from bunch grapes in the state, primarily from its 60 acres (24 hectares) of vineyards in Pasco County, about an hour northwest of the Tampa winery, and eight miles west of the Gulf of Mexico. Midulla hopes to expand to 300 acres (121 hectares) in the near future. Midulla also produces orange and other fruit wines.

St. Carlos Winery. A small winery, St. Carlos opened in 1986 near Jacksonville. They have no vineyards and purchase their grapes from Lafayette Vineyards. Produce about 6,000 gallons annually.

United States: Georgia

Richard Vine, a scientist of the regional viticultural and oenological research center at Mississippi State University, believes the hills and mountains in northern Georgia have good wine-growing potential.

B & B Rosser Winery near Athens, specializes in *vinifera,* and was founded in 1979.

Château Elan, northeast of Atlanta near Gainesville, opened in 1983. Started and managed by the late Ed Friedrich, a California wine-maker (previously with Paul Masson and San Martín) and Donald Panoz, a pharmaceutical businessman, Château Elan specializes in *vinifera* made mostly from newly planted Riesling and Chardonnay grapes grown on its own 220-acre (88-hectare) vineyard.

The Monarch Wine Co. of Georgia produces large quantities of wines, primarily sweetened, most notably Shapiro's Kosher Wines.

Other Georgia wineries make Muscadine, and Concord. *Halersham Vineyards* with 40 acres (16 hectares) shows promise.

United States: Hawaii

Bonded in 1977, the *Tedeschi Vineyard and Winery* on Maui is the joint venture of C. Pardee Erdman, Jr. and Emil Tedeschi, a native of California's Napa Valley. Twenty acres (8 hectares) of Carnelian grapes will be made into wines in the 1980s when the vines reach maturity. In the meantime, Tedeschi has made a light, dry pineapple "wine" known as "Maui Blanc." A Hawaiian grape sparkling wine was released in 1983.

United States: Idaho

Despite several encouraging experimental successes sponsored by the University of Idaho in the early 1970s, wine-growing only began to gain momentum in this state in the early 1980s. For the most part, Idaho's winters are too cold for viticulture, but the Sunny Slope near Boise in the southwestern corner of the state and the Clearwater River Valley near Lewiston have proved to be suitable growing areas for *vinifera* varietals.

Sainte Chapelle Winery, in the Sunny Slope area near Caldwell, is the only Idaho wine establishment of any commercial importance to date. Nearly 420 acres (170 hectares) of varietal vines thrive in these vineyards owned by Richard Symms (who planted them in 1971), and partner Jim Mertz. Sainte Chapelle is about a half-hour's drive from Boise at an elevation of 2,500 feet (800 meters). The winery, named after the Gothic chapel in Paris, crushed its first grapes in 1976, and since that time has turned out some very good wines whose quality can be compared to the best in America. The Chardonnays and Rieslings have been particularly successful. Sainte Chapelle wines are produced at the rate of about 65,000 cases annually, and more than 50% of the grapes come from neighboring Washington State.

Perhaps Sainte Chapelle's most valuable contribution is the proof it offers that quality wines can be successfully and profitably made in this state.

Other good wineries in Idaho include Weston Winery, Louis Facelli Winery, Pucci Winery, Brundage Cellars, Camas Winery and Rose Creek Vineyards.

United States: Illinois

The Mogen David Corporation once made Illinois the third largest wine state by bottling 2 million cases of sweet kosher wine from grapes grown in other states. In 1980 Mogen David moved to New York, and Illinois has assumed its proper statistical place as a minor producer.

Gem City Vineland Co. Nauvoo, a town on the Mississippi River near the western border of the state, has vineyards dating back to 1851, when a group of Swiss and Liechtenstein immigrants settled there. At the Nauvoo State Historic Site and Park Vineyard, two of the original acres of *labrusca* vines survive, although their produce is not made into wine. Also in Nauvoo, the Gem City Vineland Company dates back to 1857 and makes *labrusca* wines. At present, the local cheese is better known than the wines.

The Lynfred Winery in Roselle, owned and operated by Lynn and Fred Koehler, produces red and white wines from hybrids and fruits.

Thompson Winery. In Monee, 40 miles (64 kilometers) outside of Chicago, the Thompson Winery, owned by nutritionist John Thompson, is known for its white sparkling wines made according to the *méthode champenoise.* Founded in 1964, production was once about 5,000 cases, but the elements and herbicide-drifts have made matters difficult for Thompson, driving production down to about 2,000 cases. Once 30 acres (12 hectares) were devoted to vines, but acreage is down to about 5 acres (2 hectares).

United States: Indiana

It takes courage to produce the little wine that is already in production. The Hoosier State has neither the image, the micro-climate, nor the consumers to sustain extensive production of *viniferas* which could otherwise encourage additional wine growing for the vinous pioneers who have had a tough time in retaining their wine-state identity. Many settlers of this State came from England, Scotland and Ireland, not countries famed for a tradition of wine production, not that much time was left for vinous activity after successful plantings of corn, soya beans and tomatoes.

A new state law, passed in Indiana in 1971, lifted most of the restraints left over from Prohibition and enabled many wine-growing hobbyists to go commercial. Consequently, Indiana is enjoying a renaissance of its once colorful and prosperous wine past. Between 1800 and 1830, Indiana was among America's foremost wine-growing areas.

Easley Winery in Indianapolis makes several wines from grapes grown in their vineyard near Cape Sandy along the Ohio River.

St. Wendel Cellars. In the southwest, where the Wabash and Ohio rivers converge, lies St. Wendel Cellars, founded in 1975. It produces hybrid blends at the rate of about 10,000 cases a year. A dry red, "Directors

Choice," is its best red, and its "Criterion," a white from Vidal Blanc, is also fairly good.

The Huber Orchard Winery is located in Clark County, about 15 miles (24 kilometers) north of Jeffersonville, and is one of Indiana's three largest wineries. Twenty acres (8 hectares) of hybrid and native vines bear grapes used in making a wide selection of wines.

Oliver Wine Co. Bill Oliver, a law professor at the University of Indiana in Bloomington, and Ben Sparks, a former naval aviator, can be given much credit for pushing the new laws through the state legislature. Oliver's vineyards, consisting of 40 acres (16 hectares) of French hybrids planted on plots in Bloomington, yield more than 10,000 cases of wine a year. He started the plantations in 1966.

Possum Trot Vineyards is also in the central part of the state, south of Indianapolis in Brown County. Ben and Lee Sparks planted their first vine in 1967 and since then have been promoting wine-growing in the Midwest, organizing an annual Indiana Grape Wine symposium. The Sparkses have a tiny 2½-acre (1 hectare) vineyard and turn out very small amounts of French-American hybrids annually.

Swiss Valley Vineyards. Along the Ohio River, Indiana's southern border, several wineries opened up in the 1970s. The town of Vevay was named by the Swiss immigrant Jean Dufour, who founded it in the early 1800s. Hampered by frosts and diseases that destroyed his Kentucky vineyards, Dufour successfully grew a *labrusca* hybrid in Vevay until his death in 1826. More than 100 years later, wine-making in this area has been revived by the Meyer family. The Meyers make tiny amounts of French hybrid wines, sold under their Swiss Valley label, from their 3 acres (1¼ hectares) of vines.

United States: Iowa

Iowa is yet another state that had a thriving wine industry in the 19th century, only to see it extirpated by Prohibition. After Repeal in 1933, the state attempted to re-establish its vineyards, only to be confronted by another setback. About 10 years ago, the spraying of 2,4-D pesticide on corn and bean fields inadvertently damaged the native American grape crop. Fortunately, new vineyards are being planted to replace the devastated vines, especially around Davenport and elsewhere in eastern Iowa.

Christina Wine Cellars is located in McGregor in northeastern Iowa. Owned and operated by Robert Lawlor and his daughter Christina, the winery makes German-style whites from Seyval Blanc and Vidal Blanc, fruit wines, and has a second winery up the Mississippi River in La Crosse, Wisconsin.

Ehrle Brothers. Most wine-making in the state is done by the Amana colonies near Cedar Rapids, originally founded as a German religious group's socialist utopia. Ehrle Brothers, established in 1934, is the oldest winery, and produces a wide range of hybrids, *labruscas*

and fruit wines, about 90% of which is sold to the busy tourist trade. Other Amana wineries are *Ackerman, Colony Village, Sandstone* the *Grape Vine Winery* and the *Private Stock Winery.*

United States: Kentucky

As in so many of its neighbors, Kentucky's 19th-century wine business was a victim of Prohibition. Finally, in 1976, fully revised state laws came into effect, although many counties still remain legally dry by choice.

The Colcord Winery. Located in Paris in Bourbon County, about 60 miles (96 kilometers) east of Louisville and 60 miles (96 kilometers) south of Cincinnati, Ohio, is the first and the only bonded winery in the state. Owner Carlton Colcord has made wines since 1977. Prior to that time, he sold the yield from his 37 acres (15 hectares) of French-American hybrids to wineries in Indiana and Ohio. Annual production of Colcord Winery is currently about 2,900 cases, and Colcord's Kentucky Red and Kentucky White wines are made from blends of hybrids and *labruscas*.

United States: Louisiana

Altar wines were made in the mid-18th century in Louisiana, followed by muscadines and fruit wines until Prohibition. Although there are no commercial vineyards or grape wineries in the state today, Sid's Winery in Port Sulphur, 40 miles (64 kilometers) southeast of New Orleans, is the last remaining producer of "orange wine," made from fermented orange juice brought in from Florida. The only work with grapes is being conducted at the Hammond Research Station in Hammond, Louisiana. Affiliated with Louisiana State University in Baton Rouge, researchers are experimenting with crosses of *vinifera* and various species that are resistant to Pierce's disease. It will be some time before wine-grape growing will come to have any significance in Louisiana.

United States: Maryland

Lord Baltimore tried to establish a large *vinifera* vineyard in Maryland in the mid-1600s, but was unsuccessful. Therefore most wines made in the state came from wild grapes, until 1756 when Col. Benjamin Tasker, Jr. planted two acres (0.8 hectare) of Alexander grapes. By 1828 a Maryland Society for Promoting the Culture of the Vine had come into existence, and about that time Major John Adlum of Georgetown began identifying and planting the wild varieties he found. His most important discovery was found near Clarksburg. It had apparently been brought from North Carolina in 1802, from near the Catawba River, so Adlum named it the Catawba. The Catawba was to become the most important wine grape of the East for many decades.

In 1945, Philip and Jocelyn Wagner licensed Maryland's first winery, *Boordy Vineyards,* near Riderwood. Philip Wagner was an editor at the *Baltimore Sun,* and both were lovers of wine. Rightly, however, they did not love *labrusca* wines. In the early 1930s they ordered several hybrids from France and planted an experimental vineyard, the first hybrid vineyard in the U.S. Their homemade wines were significantly better than commercial eastern wines, and before long other amateur and professional wine-makers were asking the Wagners for cuttings. Before long they were in the nursery business, and by 1945 they opened their winery.

The Wagners made about 4,000–7,000 cases a year, and they became legendary in the fine restaurants of the East Coast. Philip Wagner eventually became editor of the Sun papers, and then retired in 1964 to devote full time to the winery. In 1980 the Wagners sold the winery to a local grower who had sold them grapes for 15 years, and retired from the winery business. They still grow grapes for sale to *Boordy,* and they continue to sell vines, write, and lecture on wine.

In the past few years, several new wineries have opened in Maryland. There are now about nine wineries in the state. There are numerous microclimates, but for purposes of discussion, the state can be divided into two regions, Chesapeake Bay and western Maryland.

Several small vineyards grow near the shores of the Chesapeake Bay and the climate is greatly affected by the maritime influence. As one travels west of Baltimore, the maritime influence diminishes.

Soils vary widely across the state, and in the western part there are numerous valleys and slopes suitable for viticulture. The climate is generally warm enough for reds, and frost is only a minor problem. Humidity is a major problem, and growers must follow a rigid spraying schedule to prevent mildew and rot. Growers also live in fear of errant hurricanes that occasionally slide up the coast.

Boordy Winery. Rob Deford is the grower who bought the Boordy Winery in 1980. He immediately went to the University of California at Davis for a year for a crash course on wine-making. Deford moved the winery to Hydes, a northern suburb of Baltimore. Deford buys only Maryland fruit, and gets his grapes from both sides of Chesapeake Bay as well as from northern and western Maryland.

Berrywine Plantations. The Aellen family grows about six acres (2½ hectares) of French-American hybrids in Mount Airy.

Byrd Vineyards. Bret and Sharon Byrd were real estate brokers when they fell in love with a 49-acre (20-hectare) tract near Meyersville in the Catoctin Valley, nestled between the Catoctin and Appalachian Mountains. They thought it would be an ideal site for a subdivision, especially since this picturesque valley was only about an hour's drive northwest of both Washington and Baltimore. They built their own house first as a model home, fell in love with the unspoiled beauty of the valley, and decided against subdividing. Instead they decided to turn to agriculture, and eventually settled on grapes. "We were so naive," says Bret, "we decided to plant the best vines for wine. We didn't know you weren't supposed to be able to grow *vinifera* in our climate." Well, it turned out that not only would *vinifera* grow, but judging by the wine produced so far at Byrd Vineyards, the microclimate they have chosen may even be superior for wine production. Founded in 1976, Byrd Vineyards now has about 30 acres (12 hectares) of vines, 24 (10 hectares) devoted to *vinifera* including Cabernet Sauvignon, Merlot, Cabernet Franc, Chardonnay, Riesling, Gewürztraminer and Sauvignon Blanc. The remaining 6 acres (2.5 hectares) are primarily Seyval Blanc and Vidal. The soil is called Greenstone, and is primarily volcanic with a lot of sand and quartz. Production is about 5,000 cases and growing. The climate is continental, not maritime, and the high humidity makes rots and mildews a special problem. The winters are mild, with the exception of 1982 when the temperature fell to −13°F (−25°C) and killed most of the buds, sparing the vines. Byrd has entered his wines in numerous tastings and competitions, and he wins awards and praise at a rapid rate, even in competition against California wines. Among their best wines are the Cabernet Sauvignon, Chardonnay, Sauvignon Blanc, Gewürztraminer, and Vidal Blanc.

Montbray Wine Cellars is the winery and unofficial experiment station of Hamilton Mowbray. It is located near the Pennsylvania border in Silver Run, about 40 miles (64 kilometers) northwest of Baltimore. There, without the benefit of the maritime influence, Mowbray has been growing grapes since 1957, and making wine since 1966. His vineyards are in the slate and schist Silver Run valley in the Piedmont Mountains, on the same latitude as Napa Valley. Of his 30 acres (12 hectares), 13 (5.25 hectares) are *vinifera,* and the remainder are almost entirely devoted to Seyval Blanc. Mowbray was the first to successfully grow *vinifera* in the state. In addition to marketing about 3,000 cases annually, Mowbray is deeply involved in research. In 1974 he made America's first Riesling "Ice Wine." Dr. William Krul and Mowbray were the first to successfully propagate whole vines from single-cell tissue cultures grown in test tubes. They began by grinding cells from a Seyval Blanc into a slurry, and placing them in a nutrient medium. The cells then formed numerous embryos that contained identical genetic material. Mowbray now has 5 acres (2 hectares) of clones growing from his test-tube tissue culture. Krul and Mowbray hope that their technique, when combined with the genetic engineering techniques of implanting specific genes, will enable scientists to develop new vines that will be disease resistant, nematode proof, winter hardier, or even better tasting. Until that day, Mowbray is doing just fine, making some of the best Seyvals and *viniferas* in the East.

United States: Massachusetts

Ziem Vineyards. About 80 miles northwest of Washington, D.C., in the limestone soils of Downsville, Robert and Ruth Ziem (pronounced zeem) planted 5 acres (2 hectares) of assorted hybrids in anticipation of Mr. Ziem's retirement from the Navy Department. Ziem Winery produces about 4,000 cases of table wine.

United States: Massachusetts

Massachusetts bears the dubious distinction of developing the Concord grape and introducing it to America's wine industry. Ephraim Bull and others conducted their horticultural experiments in the 1840s, and home wine-makers have grown Concord in Massachusetts since that time. Interest in cultivating *vinifera* and hybrids is now on the rise, with three small wineries upon the scene. In total, the state has between 100 and 150 acres (40–60 hectares) of grapes, about half *vinifera,* much of it near New Bedford, about 20 miles (32 kilometers) southeast of Providence, Rhode Island, and a few even farther south on Martha's Vineyard.

Chicama Vineyards, located on Martha's Vineyard, was the state's first bonded winery. In 1971 California transplants George and Cathy Mathiesen began planting 35 acres (14 hectares) of *vinifera* grapes, and today produce almost 5,000 cases. Cabernet Sauvignon, Merlot, and Pinot Noir are the most promising grapes on this foggy island. The Mathiesens are also experimenting with a new California hybrid called Freedom.

Commonwealth Winery in historic Plymouth was founded by David Tower in 1978. Commonwealth doesn't own any vineyards but buys grapes from growers in the New Bedford area, as well as from Long Island and New Hampshire. The winery produces 10,000 cases of grape wine and 5,000 cases of cranberry-apple "wine." Their Vidal Blanc and Cayuga White are pleasant drinks.

The Nashoba Valley Winery opened in Somerville in 1978. Nashoba Valley produces fruit wines made strictly from New England–grown fruits.

Plymouth Colony Winery: founded in 1983. 6 acres (2 hectares) planted in Riesling and Seyval Blanc.

United States: Michigan

Although Michigan's vine-growing history is short, mainly revolving around grape juice and jam production, its future looks bright. A great deal of expansion is under way, and *labrusca* vineyards are being replaced with better hybrid and *vinifera* varieties. The southwestern area around Paw Paw, the Traverse area in the northern "Lower Peninsula," and the shore of Lake Erie account for most of the grapes. Riesling, Chardonnay, Vidal Blanc and Seyval Blanc vines grown in these areas have yielded some good wines. More small wineries are opening up each year (18 are currently in operation) and if proper care is taken in matching appropriate soils, microclimates, and vines, Michigan may offer even better wines.

(1) Lake Michigan Shores

The majority of Michigan's vineyards and wineries are located in the southwestern corner of the state in Allegan, Berrien, and Van Buren counties, about halfway between Chicago and Detroit. There are now seven wineries within this region. The proposed viticultural area designation for this area is Lake Michigan Shores.

Berrien Vintners: located in Harbert, 40 miles (64 kilometers) west of Paw Paw, William Lett Rutledge started the Molly Pitcher Winery in 1934, named after a famous Revolutionary heroine. When Cecil Pond took over the operation in 1975, he changed the name to Lakeside Vineyard. In early 1983, former Tabor Hill Vineyards owner and Michigan wine pioneer Leonard Olson purchased the winery, and he has reduced the line of labrusca and fruit wines from 47 to seven. In 1985 Olson sold Lakeside to the Kenico Financial Group of Chicago and the name of the vineyard was then changed to Berrien. Olson has remained their wine-maker and has supervised the cultivation of French-American hybrid and *vinifera* wines. Riesling and Chardonnay are produced from grapes purchased from independent contractors. Olson is a talented wine-maker, and much can be hoped for from Berrien Vintners. Annual production is expected to increase to a couple of hundred thousand cases annually.

Fenn Valley Vineyards. This winery was established in 1973 by William Welsch and his family at Fennville, 30 miles (48 kilometers) southwest of Grand Rapids. The Fenn Valley region has officially been granted "viticultural area" status by the U.S. government, and has 50 acres (20¼ hectares) of mostly French-American hybrids and some Riesling, Chardonnay, and Gewürztraminer. The winery produces 30 different wines, including a late-harvest Vignoles, with an annual production of 10,000 cases.

Frontenac Vineyards. Frontenac began in 1933 as a family-owned winery, but today is a corporation headed by John Wieferman. They own no actual vineyards, but produce and import a range of 35 different wines, with an annual production of 150,000 cases from their Paw Paw facility.

Lemon Creek Vineyards & Winery: the Lemon family owns some 40 acres (16 hectares) of vineyards, mainly planted in Riesling, Baco Noir and Vidal. (The are the largest growers of Vidal in Michigan.)

St. Julian Wine Company. Michigan's oldest winery, St. Julian actually had its beginnings in 1921 in Windsor, Ontario, as the Meconi Wine Cellars. After repeal of Prohibition, founder Mariano Meconi moved operations across the river to Detroit, changing the name to the Italian Wine Company. Five years later, he relocated again to the winery's current location in Paw Paw, and changed the name to St. Julian. The winery is now owned and operated by Paul and David Braganini, Meconi's son-in-law and grandson, respectively.

St. Julian produces 40 different wines, with an annual production of 145,000 cases. It contracts with independent grape growers, making wines from mostly French-American hybrids and some *viniferas*. In 1982, St. Julian won a state agricultural development award for its pioneering viticultural efforts. St. Julian has a second winery and tasting room in Frankenmuth. The sparkling wines of this winery are its most interesting products.

Tabor Hill Bronte Wineries: Tabor Hill was founded in 1968 by Leonard Olson and Carl Banholzer who opened up for business in July 1972. The winery soon established its name by producing fine table wines, some of which were made from the first *vinifera* grapes to be grown in Michigan. In 1979 Tabor Hill was sold to David Upton. Located in Berrien County, the grapes from Tabor Hills' 15 acres (6 ha.) of French-American hybrids, Rieslings and Chardonnays go into 15 different wines, comprising a production of 10,000 cases.

In 1985 *Bronte Champagne & Wines,* located in Hartford, just west of Paw Paw, were taken over by Tabor Hill. The original vineyards, now owned by Tabor Hill, were first planted by German prisoners of war during the early 1940s. In 1953 Bronte planted and produced the first commercially marketed French-American hybrid wine in the United States, a Baco Noir.

Tabor Hill Bronte contracts with independent growers of mostly French-American hybrids and *vinifera* and offers 15 different still wines plus 4 sparkling wines with a production of 15,000 cases. Tabor Hill, having taken over Bronte, certainly does not require the great amount of different wines which they are producing.

Warner Vineyards. Warner Vineyards in Paw Paw is the largest winery in Michigan, with a 1.25-million-case capacity. Established in 1939 by John Turner, it was first named Michigan Wineries. The name was changed to Warner Vineyards in 1973, and the winery remains under the direction of James J. Warner, Turner's grandson. Warner Vineyards has 225 acres (91 hectares) of vines, 50 (20¼ hectares) of which are planted to French-American hybrids and some *vinifera*. Fully 80% of their production goes into making grape juice and jam, but Warner also produces a staggering 57 different wines under four labels. Warner has dropped all *labrusca* grapes from its line.

(2) Grand Traverse Bay Region

In the northwestern corner of the lower peninsula of Michigan, activity in the Grand Traverse Bay and Traverse Peninsula areas illustrates the changing face of Michigan's wine industry. Regulated by nearby Lake Michigan, the temperate winters and cool summers form a microclimate suitable to French-Ameri-

can hybrids, as well as Riesling, Chardonnay, and other *vinifera* vines. In January of 1983, this region received official designation as a viticultural area. It is also recognized as the sour cherry capital of the U.S. There are five wineries in the region.

Boskydel Vineyard. Established in 1976 by Bernard Rink and family, Boskydel Vineyard is located at Lake Leelanau, just west of Grand Traverse Bay. It has 24 acres (9¾ hectares) of French-American hybrids, notably Vignoles and de Chaunac, and one acre (1/2 hectare) of Riesling. Boskydel offers seven different wines, with an annual production of 4,000 cases.

Chateau Grand Travers. Located on the narrow, steep, and sandy Old Mission Peninsula that splits Grand Traverse Bay, Chateau Grand Travers was established in 1975 by Edward O'Keefe. It is the state's only 100% *vinifera* winery, with 45 acres (18 hectares) of Chardonnay, Riesling, and Merlot, and another five acres (2 hectares) planted to various other varieties. Chateau Grand Travers offers 20 different wines, including a "beerenauslese eiswein," and annual production of 15,000 cases. The microclimate of this peninsula is one of the most promising in the U.S. Riesling and Chardonnays from this winery are encouraging.

Good Harbor Vineyards. Owned and operated by brothers Bruce and Chris Simpson, Good Harbor was started in 1980, and is located at Lake Leelanau near Grand Traverse Bay. The winery has 18 acres (7¼ hectares) of Seyval Blanc and Vignoles, with one-half acre (1 hectare) each of Chardonnay and Riesling. Good Harbor offers 10 wines, including three fruit wines, and its annual production is 5,000 cases.

Leelanau Wine Cellars. Charles Kalchik and Michael Jacobson started this winery in 1975, located in Omena, just east of Grand Traverse Bay. It has 22 acres (9 hectares) planted to French-American hybrids, primarily Vignoles and de Chaunac, and four additional acres (1½ hectares) of Cabernet Sauvignon, Merlot, Chardonnay, and Pinot Noir of its 2,000 acres (810 hectares) of orchards. Leelanau offers 15 different wines, including four fruit "wines," with an annual production of 12,000 cases. Baco Noir and Seyval Blanc have been Leelanau's strong suits.

L. Mawby Winery. Lawrence Mawby started his winery in 1978. Located in Suttons Bay between the West Arm of Grand Traverse Bay and Lake Leelanau, Mawby has nine acres of French-American hybrids and one mixed acre of Pinot Noir and Chardonnay. Desiring to maintain a small size, Mawby offers only three wines, with an annual production of 600 cases.

(3) Southeastern Region

Three additional winery operations are located in the southeastern section of the Lower Peninsula near Detroit and Lake Erie.

Fink Winery. Established in 1976, the Fink Winery is located 35 miles (56 kilometers) southwest of Detroit in Dundee. It is owned and operated by Carl and Gary Fink, and has 15 acres (6 hectares) of Concord,

Cayuga, Chambourcin, Seyval Blanc, and Riesling, with plans to gradually plant a total of 120 acres (48.6 hectares). Fink offers 11 different wines, including four fruit "wines," and an annual production of 2,500 cases.

Milan Wineries. Located in Detroit, Milan Wineries was established in 1944, and is presided over by Charles Milan. It offers 12 different generic and fortified wines, with an annual production of 45,000 cases.

Seven Lakes Vineyard. Established in 1982, Seven Lakes Vineyard is located at Fenton in Oakland County, 60 miles northwest of Detroit. Owned and operated by Harry Guest and son Chris, Seven Lakes has 25 acres (10 hectares) of various French-American hybrids and some *vinifera,* and a capacity of 4,166 cases.

United States: Minnesota

Despite the infamously cold winters common in Minnesota, two wineries and perhaps twenty producing vineyards do exist in the state. Sturdy French-American hybrids, handled with care, can give some decent grapes. About 100 acres (40 hectares) of vineyards are planted.

Alexis Bailly Vineyard is the domain of David Bailly and his daughter and wine-maker Nan. Bailly's ancestors settled in the town of Hastings in 1834, and he revived the family's prominence locally by returning and planting a vineyard in 1973 (now totaling more than 13 acres or 5 hectares) and making hybrid wines in a log winery surrounded by vines. Surprisingly, the winery makes primarily reds, and the Léon Millot and Foch Nouveau are two highlights.

Northern Vineyards. Established in 1983, Northern Vineyards is located in Stillwater, Washington County, 20 miles east of Minneapolis St. Paul. So far, 20 acres have been planted with French hybrids and production runs at 5,000 cases annually. The winery itself stands in the historic Staples Mill area.

United States: Mississippi

Mississippi's wine history traces a typically southern pattern. Its 19th-century roots were destroyed by Prohibition. Repeal of Prohibition didn't come until 1966. It was accompanied by stiff winery taxes, and delayed the wine boom experienced by other states. These taxes were eventually reduced, primarily through the efforts of the then state senator William G. Burgin, Jr. and Dr. Louis Wise, vice-president of Mississippi State University.

In Mississippi, as in many Southern states, most of the grapes are *muscadines. Muscadines* are not as susceptible as bunch grapes to Pierce's disease, an ailment that can be fatal to the vine, caused by a bacterium and carried by a humidity-loving leaf hopper. Pierce's disease is most common in warm climates where there is not enough cold weather to interrupt the disease's cycle.

At Mississippi State University, there is a large state-of-the-art viticultural research center that serves the regional needs of the South. M.S.U. "Cellarmaster" Richard P. Vine believes the best climate for bunch grapes is in the northern third of the state, in the mountains. These regions, he says, can produce large quantities of inexpensive, good-quality Sauvignon Blanc, Chenin Blanc, Riesling, Gewürztraminer, Sémillon, and Chardonnay. He also predicts that unfermented juice production in the southern part of the state will increase rapidly. The Bureau of Alcohol, Tobacco and Firearms has established the Mississippi Delta viticultural area, located in Mississippi, Tennessee, and Louisiana. Approximately 6,000 square miles and about 250 acres of vineyard. Yields can be as high as 14 tons an acre (210 hectoliters/hectare).

Today there are four wineries in the state, with two more on the way.

Almarla Vineyards, in Matherville in southeastern Mississippi, covers 40 acres (16 hectares). This winery opened in 1979, and although planted strictly to *Muscadines,* proprietor Dr. Alex Mathers, a retired chemist for the U.S. government's Bureau of Alcohol, Tobacco and Firearms, is testing hybrids on a small scale.

Claiborne Vineyards, in 1984 Claiborne Barnwell founded Claiborne Vineyards in Indianola, Sunflower County, at the heart of the Mississippi Delta region. Mr. Barnwell shows great enthusiasm and takes full responsibility for the cultivation of five acres (2 hectares) of vineyard, largely consisting of French hybrids, Cabernet Sauvignon, Chardonnay and Sauvignon Blanc, some of which are still a little on the young side to use in wine-making. Mr. S. Barnwell, Claiborne's son, is optimistic that his 2,000-gallon annual production will increase over the next few years.

The Old South Winery in Natchez, in the pine-forest region, has a 4,200-case capacity and 15 acres (6 hectares) of *muscadines.* Veterinarian Dr. Scott Galbreath is the proprietor, and one of the winery's featured products is a red wine named "Miss Scarlet."

The Winery Rushing in Merigold, in the Delta region, is owned by the Rushing family, the first Mississippians to take advantage of the state's new laws. They own 30 acres (12 hectares) of Muscadines. Since 1977, their average annual production has been 15,000 cases; recently they have opened a restaurant on the premises.

United States: Missouri

As recently as 100 years ago, Missouri's wine business was a flourishing affair. Viticulturists from Missouri sent shiploads of phylloxera-resistant root stocks to Europe. St. Louis was hailed as the oenological research center of the Midwest. But with Prohibition all of this vinous prosperity slowly faded away, and it wasn't until the 1960s that Missouri's wine industry began to regain some of its former vigor. Today there are nearly 30 listed wineries in Missouri.

In 1980, the Bureau of Alcohol, Tobacco and Firearms granted America's first "appellation" to the tiny Missouri River community of Augusta, once a booming wine town. This distinction marks the beginning of a new wine-making era for Missouri, and if proper caution is exercised in planting appropriate grape varieties, the state may have a good chance of recapturing some part of its 19th-century reputation for quality.

Montelle Vineyards and Mount Pleasant Vineyards are the first two wineries to bear the Augusta appellation, which means that their wines are made from at least 85% Augusta grapes.

Bias Vineyard & Winery. Husband and wife team, James and Norma Bias cultivate seven acres of French hybrids in Berger, Franklin County.

Montelle Vineyards was founded by Clayton Byers and Robert Slifer in 1969. Grapes grown on Augusta's hillsides are used to make an exorbitant 40 versions of French and American hybrid and *vinifera* wines. The 1973 vintage was Montelle's first; the whites were better than the reds.

Mount Pleasant Vineyards is owned by Lucian and Eva Dressel, leaders in Missouri's wine revival. Since 1968 they have made French-American hybrid and native American table wines, growing grapes on about 50 acres (20 hectares) and putting out about 10,000 cases annually.

Ozark Vineyards, a French-American hybrid producer since 1976, is located in Cuba.

Three wineries are clustered around St. James, a town in Missouri's Ozark Plateau. *St. James Winery* makes some of its approximately 20,000 cases partly from 22 acres (9 hectares) of native grapes, French-American hybrids, and *vinifera* vines. Jim and Pat Hofherr opened the St. James Winery in 1970. The *Rosati Winery,* associated with the *Ashby Vineyards,* makes 11 different wines, most of them Concord-based. The third and newest winery in the St. James area, *Heinrichhaus,* opened in 1979.

The *Peaceful Bend Vineyards* in Steelville, not far from St. James, bottled its first wines, French-American hybrids, in 1972. Dr. Arneson, owner and wine-maker, is capable of making good wines.

The town of Hermann, once said to have exported more wines than any other American town, now features two wineries. The Held family's *Stone Hill Wine Company* has 60 acres (24 hectares) of primarily native grapes, and produces fruit and berry "wines" as well as some mediocre generics, and sparkling wines. There is a historic cellar and a restaurant on the premises. Total production is around 9,000 cases. Jim Dierberg's *Hermannhof Winery* opened in 1979. Not far from Hermann is *Green Valley Vineyards,* Nicolas Lamb's property.

Kruger's Winery, in Nelson, is run by Harold Kruger, who has been carrying on his German family's wine-making traditions since the early 1970's. *Bowman Wine*

Cellars in Weston, and *Carver Wine Cellars* in Rolla are additional Missouri wine-producers.

In the city of St. Louis *Bardenheier Wine Cellars* is run by descendants of the original 1873 founders. They have recently added Missouri-grown wines to their line of California blends.

Other establishments include *Eckert's Sunny Slope, Edelweiss, Ferrigno Vineyards,* a tiny *Midi Vineyards* in Lone Jack, *Moore-Dupont* with its 150 acres (60 hectares) of *vinefera* and hybrids, and *McCormick Distilling* in Kansas City.

United States: Montana

To date, only one adventurous soul has challenged Montana's cold stormy winters with wine-grape-growing. Dr. Jay Winship has harvested a few tiny amounts of grapes, and may open a winery in the future.

United States: New Hampshire

The Canepa family pioneered vine-growing in New Hampshire in 1969, initially blending the produce of their hardy French-American hybrids with California wines. Their *White Mountain Vineyards* in Laconia was sold in 1982 to real estate investor John Vereen and remains the only bonded winery in the state. Their 3½-acre (1½ hectares) *labrusca* and French-American hybrid vineyard is supplemented with large grape purchases, enabling the winery to produce 48,000 cases. Their Lakes Region Red is a good country wine.

United States: New Jersey

Despite the fact that the Welch's Grape Juice Company, a major juice and jam producer in at least six states, was founded in New Jersey in 1870 by the Prohibitionist dentist Dr. Thomas Welch, this state has managed to maintain a respectable wine-making tradition over the years.

There are now 11 wineries and about 300 acres (120 hectares) under cultivation in the state. Four are located on the sandy loam flatlands that were once ocean bottom near the coast in the shadow of Atlantic City. In addition to the benefits of the maritime influence from the Atlantic, these wineries benefit from the tourism generated by the Atlantic City Boardwalk and casinos.

The rest of the wineries are along the Delaware River on the state's western border, two in the shadow of Philadelphia and five others in the hills of Hunterdon County in the state's northwest.

The temperate climate along the Atlantic is good for wine grapes, although, as in the other Atlantic growing regions, rain, Atlantic storms, and humidity cause their share of problems. In addition, the Atlantic City region is being pressured by urban sprawl, with land values in excess of $25,000 an acre ($62,500 a hectare) and high property taxes.

Bernard D'Arcy Wines. Founded by John Gross in 1934, the winery's true name is Gross' Highland Winery, but the brand name used by the winery is Bernard D'Arcy, after Gross' antecedents Bernard J. and Bernard F. "Skip" D'Arcy, father and son, respectively. Gross was a second-generation wine-maker from Germany who settled in Absecon in 1912 and paid his bills by bootlegging. Gross' Highland has 35 acres (14 hectares) of vine under cultivation, about half in hybrids and *vinifera,* and about half in *labrusca.* The 33,000-case production is partly New Jersey grapes and partly grapes from other states, among them New York and, occasionally, California. Fully 99% of all the D'Arcy wines are sold directly to the consumer at the winery's three retail outlets in the area. Among D'Arcy's best wines is their inexpensive Ronay Blanc, made primarily from Sauvignon Blanc, and small amounts of Vidal Blanc and Villard Blanc.

Renault Winery. In Egg Harbor is the matriarch of New Jersey's wineries, Renault Winery, being both the oldest and the largest. Established in 1864 by Louis Nicholas Renault of Reims, France, the winery has 120 acres (48½ hectares) of *labrusca,* French-American hybrids, and a small amount of *vinifera.* Its 208,000-case capacity is filled by purchasing grapes from other states. By producing a 22% alcohol "Wine Tonic" that was sold nationally in drugstores, Renault managed to stay alive during Prohibition, and now sells two dozen wines. Renault's wine-glass museum, restaurant, and award-winning tours attract many of the tourists from nearby Atlantic City.

Tewksbury Wine Cellars. Located in Tewksbury near Lebanon, about 50 miles from Newark and 65 miles from Manhattan, is Tewksbury Wine Cellars. Veterinarian Dr. Daniel Vernon and his wife Lynn have planted 20 acres (8 hectares) on a limestone belt. About 90% of the acreage is in *vinifera,* about half devoted to Chardonnay. The winery was bonded in 1980. Other wineries include *Amwell Valley Vineyard, Bucks Country Vineyards, Four Sisters Winery* and the *Kings Road Vineyard.*

In the Atlantic City area are two other wineries, *Tomasello Winery* and *Balic Winery. Antuzzi's Winery* is situated in Delran, on the Delaware River, northeast of Philadelphia, and in Hunterdon County three new farm wineries have opened recently: *Alba Winery, Delvista Vineyards,* and *Fennelly Farm Vineyard. Jacob Lee Winery,* near Philadelphia, is now owned by Bucks County Vineyards of New Hope, Pennsylvania. *Laird & Co.,* famous for its "Apple Jack," a brandy, also makes some specialty wines.

United States: New Mexico

One of the duties of the Franciscan missionaries who settled in New Mexico in the early 1600s was, of course, the making of sacramental wines. By 1880, although only a U.S. territory, New Mexico was the nation's fifth-largest wine-producer. Wine-growing dropped, but continued, until Prohibition, peaked in 1945 and then declined steadily until only recently. New Mexican vines, especially the hardier French-American hybrids, benefit from the cool nights and warm, dry growing season. Drastic contrasts in day and nighttime temperatures, water shortages, and soil high in alkali content complicate vine cultivation in this state. Small wineries began to emerge in the late 1970s; however, the 1980s have seen a rapid resurgence of grape and wine production.

Near Las Cruces, in southern New Mexico's Messilla Valley, 50 acres (20 hectares) of vineyard are cultivated by Clarence Cooper, a university physics professor. Cooper's *La Vina Winery* has a new neighbor, *Binns Winery,* owned by the Binns brothers. Another brother team, the Hinkles, grows grapes and makes wines 150 miles to the east, on the edge of the plains at Roswell. Their *Vina Madre Winery* features 40 acres (16 hectares) of *vinifera* grapes.

In central New Mexico, along the Rio Grande, Richard Chiavario's establishment, *Chiavario Vineyards,* in Los Chavez and the Winchells' *West Wind Winery* west of Bernalillo are both producing wine. Just south of Belen lie *Rio Valley Cellars.* Founded in 1983 by Don Spiers and associates, 150 acres (60 hectares) have been planted with French hybrids. Production runs at 14,000 cases.

In Cerrillos, near the old mining town of Santa Fe, Len Rosingana makes wine at his 4 acre (1.6 hectare) *Santa Fe Vineyards.*

The vineyards of northern New Mexico are nestled in and around the Jemez Mountains, in some of the state's most spectacular scenery. The Johnson brothers have combined pottery- , apple-cider- and wine-making at their *La Chiripada Winery,* a popular tourist stop.

In 1983 in Deming, in southwestern New Mexico, 600 acres of vineyard was planted and a winery built by the Vuignier family of Switzerland, helped by Swiss backers. Courageously, the *St. Clair Winery* planted solely *vinifera*: Chardonnay, Sauvignon Blanc, Cabernet Sauvignon, Merlot and Pinot Noir. One hopes that their salesmanship will live up to their optimism at the largest vineyard and winery of the State. Production, currently at 60,000 cases, is expected to increase to 300,000 cases by 1990.

In the mountains of the state's southwest corner, near the cities of Lordsburg and Silver City, a whole new area is being tested for grape production, using water conservation measures such as drip irrigation.

United States: New York

New York makes more wine than any state except California. In 1985 production was 27.3 million U.S. gallons, about 6% of the U.S. total. In 1980, the most recent year for which acreage figures are available, there were 41,000 acres (16,592 hectares) of vineyards, 19,000 of which produced grapes for wine. The remainder are used to produce juice, jelly, and other products. In 1986 about 75,000 tons of grapes were utilized for wine in New York. Of that total, 50% were *labrusca* (used primarily for wine coolers), 40% were hybrids, and 10% were *vinifera*.

WINE HISTORY

New York was one of the first states to plant grapes, in the mid-17th century, on Long Island and Manhattan.

The first commercial winery, Brotherhood Winery, opened in the Hudson River region in 1839. Brotherhood and Thomas Vineyards of California were both founded in the same year, and are the oldest in the U.S.

For decades, New York wines were best known as sweet, grapey "jelly jar" wines made primarily from Concord. Change came slowly to the New York wine industry. In 1952, the late Charles Fournier, the French-born and -trained wine-maker of Gold Seal Winery, hired a Russian immigrant, Konstantin Frank, to plant an experimental *vinifera* vineyard. The two experimented together, and then separately after Frank started his own winery. They proved that with careful selection of soil, site, rootstock and clone, *vinifera*, especially Chardonnay and Riesling, not only could survive, but could make world-class wines.

In the 1950s the State Agricultural Experiment Station in Geneva began experimenting with new hybrids and hybrids brought from Europe and from Philip Wagner in Maryland. Commercially, they were championed in the late 1960s by Mark Miller of Benmarl Winery and Walter S. Taylor of Bully Hill Winery.

After Prohibition, the New York wine industry grew slowly to a total of 39 wineries in 1976. That year, in an effort to encourage this important agribusiness, the state passed a Farm Winery Act that made it easier to open wineries. There are now about 80 wineries in the state.

By the time the Farm Winery Act came along, enough research had been done to identify a number of likely candidates to replace Concord as the backbone of the New York wine industry. When the law was passed, new wineries emphasizing these *viniferas* and hybrids sprang up like vines. The improvement has been astonishing, and the potential for improvement is perhaps even greater than in California.

In New York's cool climate, so far crisp, tart white varieties have been the state's strongest suit, but serious work is being done to improve the reds. Sparkling wines are enjoying a renaissance, with several wineries experimenting with the *méthode champenoise*. Port- and sherry-type wines have traditionally been important to New York wineries, but this segment is shrinking quickly with reduced demand. Significant gallonage in the wine cooler market (27 million U.S. gallons in 1986) has kept New York's production figures high. Three major wine coolers are produced in New York; Sun Country, Seagram, and Calvin Cooler.

The weather causes some problems, however. The growing season often requires chaptalizing, or sugaring, the unfermented juice in order to make stable wines. Rain in the autumn often hampers harvesting, produces rot, and thins the wine. Harsh winters kill buds, canes, roots, and even vines, and make vines susceptible to crown gall. Early thaws can cause vines to push buds prematurely, and make them susceptible to late frosts. In sum, growing grapes in New York is not for the faint-hearted. But wine quality makes it all worthwhile.

So far, the best red varieties are Merlot, Cabernet Sauvignon and Pinot Noir (primarily on Long Island), Baco Noir, Chancellor and Chelois.

The best white varieties have been Riesling, Chardonnay, and Gewürztraminer, Seyval Blanc, Vignoles, Vidal Blanc, and Cayuga White. Perhaps because of the cool climate and the slatey soils, Riesling has shown great potential. In New York, Riesling develops the appley, strawberry-like flavors characteristic of good German Rieslings, with more crispness and liveliness than even the California Rieslings.

VINE-GROWING REGIONS

Most of New York's vines are found in four regions: the Finger Lakes district, the Hudson River Region, along the shore of Lake Erie, and on the eastern tip of Long Island.

(1) Finger Lakes

This series of long, deep lakes was carved into the slaty soil by glaciers. Most of the appellation's 14,000 acres (5,600 hectares) of vines are on the shores of Seneca Lake, Keuka Lake, Canandaigua Lake, and Cayuga Lake. New York's harsh winters are tempered by the spring-fed lakes, and the steep slopes provide excellent air and water drainage. In spring, the cool lakes retard budding until most frost danger has passed, and during the fall, the warm water helps warm the surrounding vineyards as the fruit ripens.

Keuka Lake has been the center of New York's wine industry since the Civil War. In the 1960s, however, Fournier and Gold Seal began experiments on nearby Seneca Lake, and found that because it was lower in elevation, larger, and deeper, it offered a more suitable microclimate for *vinifera;* and in the last decade, it has become the most important of the Finger Lakes for premium wine varieties. Cayuga Lake also looks promising, and in the last three years several vineyards have sprung up on its western shore.

Bully Hill Vineyards. Founded in 1969 by Walter S. Taylor, an heir to the family that founded Taylor Wine Co., Bully Hill was one of the first to champion the hybrids. Taylor has called the hybrids "the greatest innovation since the wine bottle." With the help of his then wine-maker, Hermann J. Wiemer, Bully Hill be-

FINGER LAKES REGION

came known as one of the best wineries in New York in the early 1970s. Taylor has steadfastly refused to plant *viniferas,* however, and in recent years several newer wineries have surpassed him in quality, even with hybrids. The disparaging invective he aims at his competition, and a decline in the quality of his product, have left the continued popularity of his winery open to question.

Canandaigua Wine Company. The third-largest winery in the U.S. with an annual production of about 15,-000,000 cases, Canandaigua's home base is in the Finger Lakes. In 1986 Canandaigua purchased two other New York wineries, Widmer Wine Cellars and Monarch Wine Company. Their major brands include four with annual sales of more than a million cases: Rich-

ard's Wild Irish Rose, J. Roget Champagne, Manischewitz Kosher Wine, and Sun Country Cooler. The company was founded in 1945 by Marvin Sands and is now a public company traded on the American Stock Exchange. The winery has a tasting facility at Sonnenberg Gardens in Canandaigua and offers tours at Widmer Wine Cellars in Naples. In addition to five premises in New York State, Canandaigua also has facilities in California, South Carolina and Virginia. Rumor has it that the Canandaigua Wine Company is negotiating to purchase four sizeable wineries. If this ever becomes a reality, it could put Canandaigua second to Gallo in size and perhaps the largest vineyard company in the world.

Casa Larga Vineyards. Andrew Colaruotolo is a contractor specializing in condominiums. His grandfather and father owned a Casa Larga Vineyard in Gaeta, Italy, and ever since he came to the U.S., Colaruotolo has yearned to return to the family business, if only on weekends. In 1978, with the help of his wife, Ann, and his son John, Colaruotolo opened his winery in Fairport, a suburb of Rochester. Their 15 acres (6 hectares) of vineyard are not really in the Finger Lakes, although the government-drawn boundaries entitle them to the appellation. Lake Ontario, which is visible from the winery, is the dominating factor in Casa Larga's weather. Cold Canadian air is warmed by the lake, and produces severe snow and ice storms, but Casa Larga manages to produce *vinifera* as well as hybrids, a total of about 4,200 cases. The Riesling, Chardonnay, and Gewürztraminer are especially good.

Finger Lakes Wine Cellars Art and Joyce Hunt's family farm, located on the northwest tip of Keuka Lake, is the site of Finger Lakes Wine Cellars, founded in 1981. The Hunts make Chardonnay, Riesling, Seyval, Cayuga and Ravat. Production is expanding rapidly and out-of-state markets may spur plans for a new facility.

Frontenac Point Vineyard. Carol Doolittle worked for the New York Department of Agriculture and was responsible for the development of the first New York State Fair Commercial Wine Competition. Jim Doolittle studied agricultural economics and viticulture at Cornell University, and he also worked for the N.Y. Department of Agriculture. A vineyard and winery had always been their dream. In 1982 they opened Frontenac Point near a point of land of the same name on the west shore of Cayuga Lake. Their 24 acres (10 hectares) are planted primarily with *vinifera*, and the winemaking style is modeled on the French, from barrel fermentation through ageing. They currently produce 2,000 cases per year and expect to reach 4,000 by 1988. Emphasis is on red wines.

Glenora Wine Cellars. Named after a beautiful waterfall not far from the winery, Glenora is owned by four local growers. It was built on a slope on the west side of Seneca Lake near Watkins Glen after the passage of the Farm Winery Act in 1976. Glenora has produced some of the best wines east of the Rockies. In 1982, Glenora decided to specialize in white wines, and has wisely trimmed its product line to emphasize white wines and quality. Glenora's Rieslings have breed and are crisp and lively with a German style. Its Chardonnays are also light, crisp, and fresh, because the winery prefers to emphasize fruit and deemphasize the flavor of oak barrels. Other specialties include a Cayuga White that is reminiscent of a Müller-Thurgau, and Seyval Blancs that claim to be similar to Loire Valley whites. Winemaker/Manager Ray Spencer spends his evenings perfecting his Blanc de Blancs sparkling wine at his own *Barrington Champagne Company.*

Gold Seal Winery. Gold Seal was once one of the state's oldest and proudest labels. Founded in 1865 as the Urbana Wine Co. in Hammondsport on the west shore of Keuka Lake, the winery has gone through a

succession of owners, as well as a succession of winemaking styles and philosophies. It built its reputation on sparkling wines, on a so-called "Sauterne" and a sweet Catawba. In 1950 Gold Seal gained nationwide attention when it won a gold medal at the Sacramento State Fair Wine Competition in California with its Blanc de Blanc Champagne. The following year the competition was limited only to California wineries.

In 1952, Gold Seal became the first winery in the East to successfully experiment with *viniferas* when the late Charles Fournier, formerly of Veuve Clicquot, a prestigious French Champagne house, hired a Russian immigrant, Konstantin Frank. (On Frank, *see* "Vinifera Wine Cellars," below.)

Jos. E. Seagram & Sons bought Gold Seal in 1979 and in 1984 its operations were moved to the Taylor Winery, also a Seagram company. In 1987, Seagrams sold Gold Seal, Great Western, and Taylor to Vintners International.

Great Western Winery. Great Western was founded by Charles Davenport Champlin in 1860 as the Hammondsport and Pleasant Valley Wine Company and is the oldest winery in the Finger Lakes Region. Acquired in 1961 by the Taylor Wine Co., it is now a part of the Seagram Wine Company. Since 1981 Great Western has offered a line of premium varietal wines from hybrid and *vinifera* grapes. Also well known for its "champagne," Great Western began in 1985 to offer a *méthode champenoise* sparkling wine. *See* "Taylor Wine Co.," below.

Hazlitt's 1852 Vineyard. Jerry Hazlitt is a fifth-generation grape grower on the family farm in Hector, New York. His 6,000-gallon production is sold primarily at the winery. Chardonnay and Riesling are notable.

Heron Hill Winery. John Ingle, Jr., was a grapegrower in Naples, N.Y., tired of dealing with the large wineries. Peter Johnstone was an advertising copy writer in New York City who yearned to return to nature. Together they planted 42 acres (17 hectares), primarily in *vinifera*, and opened their doors in 1977 after the passage of the Farm Winery Act. They promptly won four gold medals with their first wines, the 1977 vintage, at the New York State Fair Commercial Wine Competition. In fact, Heron Hill and Glenora each won four golds at that competition, more than all the other New York wineries combined.

Johnstone and Ingle have learned the hard way the importance of microclimate selection. Several unusually harsh winters have damaged their estate vineyards severely.

Heron Hill produces about 8,500 cases, primarily whites of good quality under the Heron Hill and Otter Springs labels, and its Rieslings, Ravats, and Seyvals are good.

Knapp Vineyards. Doug and Suzanna Knapp escalated from viticulture to wine production in 1982 after years of perfecting their skills in the vineyard. The winery is on the east shore of Cayuga Lake and utilizes a small but premium portion of the vineyard production.

Lucas Vineyards. Bill Lucas is a tugboat captain for

Mobil Oil in New York Harbor, and he works one week on water and one week on soil. The soil is a six-hour drive from the water, near Interlaken. He and his wife, Ruth, started planting vines in 1974 and now have 23 acres (9.2 hectares) yielding about 1,500 cases. Ruth stays with the vineyard all year long, and handles their small line of *vinifera* and hybrid wines. Their Cayuga White is light and refreshing, slightly sweet, and reminiscent of a lesser German wine.

McGregor Vineyards. Bob and Marge McGregor began planting their 23 acres (9.2 hectares) of vineyards, primarily with *vinifera*, in 1973. Bob kept his job as a senior engineer at Kodak, and they worked in the vineyards, near Wayne on the east shore of Keuka Lake, on weekends. For several years they sold their grapes to other wineries but in 1980 McGregor Vineyards began producing its own wine. It is best known for small lots of late harvest Riesling and Gewurztraminer, and for Pinot Noir. The McGregors continue to experiment in the vineyard, and have even planted a few hardy Russian *viniferas*. Production will soon expand to 8,000 cases.

Plane's Cayuga Vineyard. Robert Plane is director of the New York State Agricultural Experiment Station in Geneva, New York. He is also president emeritus of Clarkson University and a former provost of Cornell University. His wife, Mary, formerly a university personnel administrator, now actively manages the vineyard and winery operations on their farm on the east shore of Cayuga Lake.

The farm was originally purchased as a summer residence. As their interest in wine and home wine-making grew, they began doing soil and climate studies of the farm and discovered to their delight that it was suitable for growing grapes. They planted Chardonnay, Riesling, and several other varieties in 1982, and sold their grapes to other wineries. When Glenora's "Plane Vineyard" Chardonnay began winning medals and rave reviews, the Planes got serious about starting a winery. Bob took several months off, went to Napa Valley, and worked in the Robert Mondavi Winery while Mary studied viticulture in both the Finger Lakes and Napa Valley.

They renovated a 50-year-old barn on their property and converted it into a winery, and in 1982 released their first wines. Their Chardonnay, Chancellor and Cayuga are consistently good and they have high hopes for a recent planting of Pinot Noir.

Poplar Ridge Vineyards. David Bagley has worked for Brotherhood Winery, Bully Hill, Wagner Vineyards, Lucas Vineyards in New York, and consulted with several other wineries in the East. He now makes wine from his 20 acres (8 hectares) of assorted varieties of *vinifera* and hybrids in Valois, in the best section of the east shore of Seneca Lake. Production is about 4,500 cases of tart, light country wines.

Rolling Vineyards. Ed Grow made his living doing landscaping and snowplowing. Recently he selected 60 prime acres (24 hectares) of Seneca Lake vineyards and planted a long list of *vinifera* and hybrid varieties. With his wife, Jo Anne, Grow opened Rolling Vineyards in 1981 with about 2,000 cases.

Taylor Wine Co. Taylor is located just south of Hammondsport in Pleasant Valley at the southern tip of Keuka Lake. Together with Great Western and Gold Seal Vineyards, it comprises the largest winery complex in New York State. Founded in 1880 by Walter Taylor, a barrel-maker, the company was owned by Coca-Cola of Atlanta from 1976 to 1983 when it was purchased by Joseph E. Seagram & Sons, along with the Coca-Cola Company's three California wineries; they are now all part of Seagram. Among Taylor's wines is a "sherry" called Empire Cream. The company continues to produce more than 30 wines and champagnes, primarily from *labrusca* and hybrid grapes.

Vinifera Wine Cellars. Few individuals have had such a far-reaching influence on wine-making in the U.S. as Konstantin Frank of Vinifera Wine Cellars. Born in 1899 in Russia, Frank was a leading grape and wine scientist in his native Ukraine, and later in Bavaria and Austria. In 1951, at age 52, he moved to New York Ciy, where he began by washing dishes for a living. When he had saved enough money, he bought a one-way ticket to the New York State Agricultural Experiment Station in Geneva, where he was given a hoe and pointed toward a blueberry patch. One summer day in 1952, while sweeping the floors in the hall, Frank buttonholed Charles Fournier, the wine-maker at Gold Seal. He challenged Fournier to plant *vinifera*, arguing that if *vinifera* could grow in the Ukraine, then surely *vinifera* could grow in New York.

Fournier hired Frank, and the two began trial plantings, experimenting with different root stocks and locations, but Frank's individualism and inability to work within the corporate structure eventually got him fired.

With Fournier's help, Frank located a vineyard site not far from Gold Seal, and in 1965 opened his own winery, Vinifera Wine Cellars.

Throughout the 1960s and 1970s, Frank continued his experiments, and garnered praise from around the world. When Frank died in 1985, the winery, which had suffered from neglect in his declining years, was quickly reorganized by his son Willibald and son-in-law Walter Volz. Winemaker Eric Fry was hired, new equipment was purchased, and the label got a facelift. The vineyards are being consolidated to emphasize the best varieties and remove marginal ones. After its brief eclipse during Frank's final illness, Vinifera Wine Cellars seems to be once again in the forefront of the New York wine industry, with the second generation in charge and a talented third generation waiting in the wings.

Among Frank's best wines are his Chardonnays and Gewürztraminers.

Wagner Vineyards. Bill Wagner farms 130 acres of choice lakeside vineyard on the east shore of Seneca

Lake, an area considered by many to be among the best vineyard properties in the Finger Lakes region of New York.

After selling all his grapes to large New York wineries for decades, Wagner saw his extra effort in the vineyard blended into anonymity with lesser grapes, and he decided to open his own winery. He designed and built a striking octagonal winery in 1976 and 1977. In 1978 he had his first crush, and today he produces almost 20,000 cases of 20 different wines. His best are a complex, oaky Chardonnay, Riesling, Seyval Blanc, and Gewurztraminer.

Wickham Vineyards. The Wickham family has been growing wine grapes for over a century and they currently have 140 acres (57 hectares) in cultivation on the east shore of Seneca Lake. In 1981 they opened a winery. Chardonnay, Riesling and Cayuga are among their best wines.

Widmer's Wine Cellars. Widmer is another historic New York label that has changed ownership many times. Founded in 1888 at the southern tip of Canandaigua Lake by John Jacob Widmer, a Swiss immigrant, Widmer's was a family winery until 1961. In recent years, Widmer's concentrated primarily on wines made from Niagara grapes, producing intensely flavorful, grapey white wines. In 1986 it was purchased by Canandaigua Wine Company which plans to produce Manischewitz wines there.

Hermann J. Wiemer Vineyards. Wiemer was born in Germany and weaned on Riesling in Bernkastel. In 1969 he was brought to the Finger Lakes by Walter S. Taylor, who was opening the new Bully Hill Winery. After working with hybrids for 10 years, Wiemer became disenchanted with their performance in the vineyard and on the dinner table at a time when next-door-neighbor Konstantin Frank was proving that *vinifera* not only could thrive in the East but could make good wines. In the late '70s, Wiemer bought 140 choice acres (56 hectares) on the west side of Seneca Lake, near Dundee. In his spare time he tended to the 22 acres (8.8 hectares) of young vines he planted. In 1979 he made 900 cases of his first Chardonnay and Riesling, and was quickly noticed by the media. Before long, Wiemer was getting more attention from the press and local merchants than his publicity-hungry boss. While visiting his family in Germany in 1980, he received a telegram from Taylor: he had been fired.

Now Wiemer is a disciple of the Frank doctrine that hybrids are inferior wine grapes. "Eastern wineries have to upgrade," he says, "but the potential is here." Wiemer's Rieslings and Chardonnays are light, delicate, and well-made wines.

(2) Hudson River Region

The oldest continuous wine-producing region in the U.S.—the first vineyards were planted near New Paltz, just 45 miles (72 kilometers) from New York City, in 1677, by French Huguenots. Although the region gets little moderating effect from the river itself, the steep palisaded valley is a conduit of maritime air and weather generated by the Atlantic. Not all the 1,000-plus acres (400-plus hectares) of vineyards are on the river slopes, however, and some are to be found scattered all the way to the Connecticut border. The vineyard soils are complex, with patches of shale, slate, schist, and limestone. Most of the 15 or so wineries have opened since the Farm Winery Act of 1976, but interest in *vinifera* has been subdued. Hybrids do well in the region, and the reds are slightly better than in the Finger Lakes.

Benmarl Wine Co. Mark Miller was a successful illustrator in New York City, listing among his customers some of the largest magazines and ad agencies. He and his wife, Dene, avid wine lovers, purchased an old vineyard in Marlboro in 1957. They ripped out the old vines and replaced them with *viniferas* and hybrids, species that at that time were untested and unrecommended. After a stint of painting in France for a few years, the Millers returned to their Benmarl (Gaelic for "slatey soil"!) in 1969.

Miller produces about 10,000 cases. Most of the wines are hybrids, and some have been excellent, especially when aged. Benmarl's wines are totally dry, and most have more than a kiss of oak. Miller's Baco Noir wines have been among the East's best reds, and when aged, they develop the complexity and some of the flavors of old Italian or even Rhône wines. The whites, especially the Seyval Blanc and the Chardonnay, are more European in style than most American wineries.

Brotherhood Winery. The oldest continuing, continually operating winery in the U.S. Brotherhood was founded in Washingtonville, about 50 miles (80 kilometers) from Manhattan, by a French shoemaker, Jean Jaques, in 1839. Originally called Blooming Cove, Jaques' first wines were sold to the local church, of which he was an elder. The name was later changed by another owner. Brotherhood is now owned by Eloise Farrell, and managed by her daughter Anne. In recent years, the winery has sold all its vineyards and buys the fruit necessary to make its 100,000 cases from the Finger Lakes and elsewhere in the state.

Most of the wines are thick and sweet, and as a result have attracted little attention to the winery from wine buyers, which is a pity, because the traditionally produced ports are as fair as any in the U.S. for the price. Very fair vintage ports were made from the Chancellor grape in 1976 and 1978.

Cagnasso Winery. Owner of one of the smallest wineries in the state, Joe Cagnasso is primarily a consultant to other wineries, although some of the varietal hybrids he produces under his own label are often better than his clients'. Cagnasso, an Italian immigrant, founded the winery in 1977 in Marlboro and produces only a very small quantity of wine.

Cascade Mountain Vineyards. Cascade Mountain is nestled in Amenia among the Berkshire foothills near the

Connecticut border in an area thought to be too cold for grapes. But former novelist William Wetmore and his family built their rustic winery virtually by hand starting in 1973, and have proved the experts wrong. Wetmore's puckish humor is evident in the names he chooses for his pleasant table wines: Le Hamburger Red, A Little White Wine, and Pardonnez Moi, a dry white wine for social emergencies.

Clinton Vineyards. Founded in 1977 by a former artist and designer, Ben Feder, Clinton Vineyards specializes in the Seyval grape, making a Seyval Blanc table wine, and a *méthode champenoise* Sparkling Seyval. The table wine is a very good white, reminiscent of Loire Valley whites or dry California Chenin Blanc. Feder also makes a small amount of Riesling.

Cottage Vineyards. A prim little vineyard across the highway from Benmarl is the avocation of Allan W. MacKinnon, an administrator for Merrill Lynch in Manhattan, and his wife, Nola. Cottage Vineyards was bonded in 1981 and produces 500 cases a year of Seyval Blanc and a red blend.

Hudson Valley Winery. A historic compound of old stone buildings perched high above the west shore of the Hudson River in Highland. Hudson Valley Winery produced its first wines in 1907 under the guidance of financier Alexander Bolognesi. Herbert Feinberg, formerly of importer Monsieur Henri, has owned it since 1972, and unfortunately continues to make several of the same wines from *labruscas* as did the founder. In addition, several hybrids are being produced, but the winery's strong suit is tourism. Feinberg sponsors tastings of wines from all over the world, special dinners, cross-country ski weekends, harvest festivals, free vine days, concerts, and other innovative activities that attract thousands of tourists from miles around.

Royal-Kedem Winery. Kedem makes only kosher wines, but proudly states that "Kosher wine needn't be sweet, just special!" Indeed, although Kedem makes its share of sweet kosher wines, it also produces a large line of dry wines made from French-American hybrids and *labruscas,* more than 40 different types, for a total of 1.3 million cases. Although most of the wine is made from New York grapes, Kedem also produces California Zinfandel and California Chenin Blanc, a honey wine, and fruit wines. The winery was founded in 1946 on Manhattan's Lower East Side by five refugee partners. In 1948, Eugene Herzog, a Czechoslovakian-trained wine-maker, whose family had been making wine for eight generations, joined Kedem as a truck driver. Business was bad, and in lieu of pay Herzog was offered a partnership. By 1954 he had bought his partners out, and in 1968 the winery was moved to Milton on the Hudson River. Today the wine is made in Milton, and bottled in Brooklyn by Eugene's family: Herman is president, Philip is vice-president, Ernest is wine-maker, and David is sales manager.

Walker Valley Vineyards. Located about 20 miles west of Newburgh in the foothills of the Catskill and the Shawangunk Mountains, Walker Valley Vineyards has quickly grown to a 3,300-case winery. Owner Gary Dross, a physical education teacher, grows grapes and produces wine from hybrids and *vinifera,* including Chardonnay, Riesling, Pinot Noir, and Seyval. His success has required a doubling of the winery size and Dross plans to open a cafe at the winery in 1987. One of his best wines is his so-called Nouveau.

West Park Vineyards Louis Fiore, proprietor of West Park Vineyards, was out to prove a point in 1981 when he planted only Chardonnay at his vineyard site across the Hudson from the Culinary Institute of America. *Vinifera* grapes were considered risky in the Hudson Valley, but Fiore wanted to do it right or not at all. He is assisted by general manager Nelda Bennett, who studied in Germany, and marketing consultant Kevin Zraly, best known as the wine director of the Windows on the World restaurant in the World Trade Center in New York City. West Park produces only Chardonnay. 1986 production was 2,200 cases and Fiore plans to limit production to 5,000 cases.

Windsor Vineyards. Formerly the Great River Winery in Marlboro, Windsor is owned and operated by Sonoma (now Rodney Strong) Vineyards of California. Some table and sparkling wines are made there, but most of the wine sold is from California. *See* Sonoma Vineyards, under "California."

(3) Lake Erie

On the south shore of Lake Erie, running from about 100 miles (160 kilometers) east of Cleveland almost all the way to Buffalo, there is pretty much of an unbroken narrow belt of vineyards, from 2 to 15 miles wide, wedged between an escarpment and the lake on gravelly loam and glacial alluvial till. Here the vines are dominated by the lake effect, and while frosts may burn vineyards and orchards on the south side of the ridge line, between it and the lake the vines are well protected. The Lake Erie Region appellation crosses three state lines, New York, Pennsylvania, and Ohio, and includes 25,000 acres and eight wineries in New York.

The first vineyards were planted in the region in 1818 by Deacon Elijah Fay near Brocton, N.Y., in Chautauqua County, not far from the Pennsylvania border. In 1859 his son, Joseph, and two partners opened the first winery. Acreage expanded rapidly, with Concord, Catawba, and Delaware the dominant varieties.

In 1897, Thomas and Charles Welch, prohibitionist dentists, moved their grape juice business, then called "unfermented wine," from New Jersey to Westfield, N.Y., to take advantage of the surplus of Concord fruit. Their business grew rapidly, and the Welch brothers almost singlehandedly established the Concord flavor as the "true" grape flavor of America. Later, the two kosher wine giants, Mogen David and Manischewitz, began making wine from Lake Erie fruit. Today most of the grapes in the region still go to juice, jelly and kosher wine. Hybrids account for the greater part of the wine grapes used by the new small wineries, with a modest but growing number of *vinifera* vineyards appearing.

Johnson Estate Winery. A former torpedo bomber pilot with two Distinguished Flying Crosses, Johnson graduated from Cornell University in 1946 with a bachelor's degree in agriculture. After a series of globetrotting jobs managing agricultural estates from Kenya to Australia, Johnson returned in 1961 to his family's turn-of-the-century vineyard, began replacing Concords with hybrids, and opened a winery. The 200-acre (80 hectare) estate overlooks Lake Erie at the closest approach of the Alleghany Plateau to the lake, a position which offers a favorable microclimate. His most famous wine is a botrytised sweet Delaware called Liebestropfchen ("little love drops"), developed by wine-maker William Gulvin.

Merritt Estate. Thirty-five miles southwest of Buffalo in Forrestville, the smokestacks have given way to the gentle rolling vineyards that have been in the Merritt family since the turn of the century. It was not until the 1976 Farm Winery Act that a descendant of a German immigrant family, William T. Merritt, and his family began making wine from their ancestors' 100 acres (40 hectares) of vines. Today Merritt makes primarily hybrid wines, and a Niagara that is flavorful and refreshing, without the syrupy sweetness typical of many *labruscas*.

Mogen David. Near Westfield this large producer of kosher wine, primarily from Concord and other *labruscas*, has a large plant and hundreds of acres. To many American Jews, this sweet jelly taste is the traditional flavor of the Sabbath and Passover, but in reality their ancestors in Europe never tasted Concord, a native American variety. European kosher wines are traditionally dry *vinifera* products.

Woodbury Vineyards. Gary Woodbury, his brother Bob and sister-in-law Page, were the first, in 1969, to plant vinifera grapes in the Dunkirk area of the Lake Erie Viticultural District. Initial success with Riesling and Chardonnay led them to build a 12,000 case winery and hire Canadian Andrew Dabrowski as wine-maker. Today Woodbury is involved in a 100-acre (40 hectare) *vinifera* research project, managed by Markus Riedlin, a native of Germany and graduate of the school of viticulture and enology at Geisenheim. Chardonnay, Riesling, Gewurztraminer and Seyval are their best wines.

(4) Long Island

Drive east from Manhattan about three hours and on both the north and south forks of Long Island you will find one of the most promising viticultural areas in the U.S. Surrounded by water, Long Island has temperate winters, frost poses no problem, there are 210 days of sunshine, and the vines thrive in the sandy soil. A handful of new wineries have sprung from the former potato farms, and more are sure to come.

The area seems to show good promise with Chardonnay, Sauvignon Blanc, Merlot, Pinot Noir, and Cabernet Sauvignon. With the increasing number of vintners, Long Island wineries should show rapid gains in discovering the styles of wine appropriate to their distinctive climate.

The wineries of Long Island have a marketing advantage in that the Long Island population as well as the summer resort visitors have easy access to the vineyards. With well-promoted curiosity, local pride and a certain amount of chauvinism can help in selling a part of the production, especially if Long Island wineries were to decrease their prices.

Bridgehampton Winery. Currently the South Fork's only winery, Bridgehampton began in the 1982 vintage with Chardonnay and Riesling. Today production also includes Sauvignon Blanc, Pinot Noir and Merlot. The Chardonnay is elegant and stylish.

Hargrave Vineyard. The first Long Island winery to open was Hargrave Vineyard. It was founded by Alex and Louisa Hargrave in 1973. He held a degree in East Asian Studies from Princeton University and she was a student at Smith College. In the late '60s they began talking about getting back to the land. Their love of wine and food hatched the winery concept, and so in 1971 and 1972 they drove across the country, looking for the perfect location to grow grapes. When they heard about experiments on Long Island, they investigated and decided the soil, climate, and market access were more to their liking than those of California or any other state they had visited. They bought 55 acres (22 hectares) in Cutchogue on Long Island's North Fork and planted Pinot Noir, Cabernet Sauvignon, Merlot, Chardonnay, Sauvignon Blanc and Johannisberg Riesling. Their Chardonnay, Sauvignon Blanc and Cabernet Sauvignon are particularly fine. The pioneering work of the Hargraves has laid a solid foundation for newer arrivals to build upon.

Lenz Vineyards. Peter and Patricia Lenz ran a restaurant in the Hamptons before starting their winery on the North Fork of Long Island in 1978. The first crush was in 1983 and Gewürztraminer has been notable. Lenz produces both a varietal Merlot and a Proprietor's Reserve blend of Merlot, Cabernet Sauvignon and Cabernet Franc.

Pindar Vineyards. With 175 acres (71 hectares) of grapes and an annual production in 1986 of 35,000 cases, Pindar is by far the largest winery on Long Island. They produce Cabernet Sauvignon, Merlot, Pinot Noir, Chardonnay, Riesling and Gewürztraminer. A sparkling wine made from Chardonnay and Pinot Noir is scheduled for 1987 release.

United States: North Carolina

Wines made from Scuppernong grapes, which can withstand the heat of the South, dominate North Carolina's wine scene. Before Prohibition, Paul Garrett developed his Scuppernong empire in his home state of North Carolina and eventually expanded into other parts of the South. His *Virginia Dare* brand, of doubtful quality, became especially well known immediately after Repeal. The winery is now owned by Canandaigua Winery of New York State.

The Biltmore Estate Winery in Asheville specializes in *vinifera* wines. The current 220-acre (88-hectare) vineyard will be expanded to 500 acres (200 hectares). Eventually, Biltmore's French wine-maker, Philippe Jourdain, hopes to produce 100,000 cases annually.

Today, a few other wineries making Scuppernong wines primarily are also in operation.

United States: Ohio

When pioneering Cincinnati wine-maker Nicholas Longworth gave Henry Wadsworth Longfellow some of his Catawba wine in the 1850s, its taste moved the poet to pen his famous "Ode to Catawba Wine," in which he states "Catawba wine has a taste more divine, more dulcet, delicious, and dreamy."

More than a century later, *labrusca* is still king in Ohio, with Concord and Catawba accounting for 89% of Ohio's harvest. With acreage at about 3,000 (1,215 hectares) and declining slowly, only 27% of the crop is used for wine production, the rest going into juice, jelly, or for table use.

At least 95% of the grapes are grown in the Lake Erie Region viticultural area that stretches in a narrow belt along the south shore of the Great Lake from near Sandusky through Erie, Pennsylvania, into New York and virtually all the way to Buffalo, New York. A subregion of the Lake Erie Region is the Lake Erie Islands, a cluster of nine small islands not far from the Sandusky shore. A small amount of vines can also be found in Warren County in the state's southwest corner, between Dayton and Cincinnati.

Interestingly, Cincinnati, deep in the heartland of America, was once the center of the American wine industry. In 1823 Longworth planted vines on a hill overlooking the Ohio River, and founded an industry that by 1860 produced twice as much wine as California, and about a third of all the wines in the U.S. Eventually, black rot, powdery mildew, and other diseases and pests stifled the industry.

Despite the slight declining trend in acreage, the number of wineries, as in other states, has grown steadily. There are now more than 40 wineries, most making indifferent country wine from *labruscas* and hybrids.

Chalet Debonne. The Debevc family of Madison, 45 miles from Cleveland, had been growing grapes since before Prohibition, and making wine for personal use all along. Then, in 1971, after Tony, Jr. graduated from Ohio State University, Tony, Sr. and the family opened their winery. In addition to the winery, the Debevcs have built a chalet that attracts both locals and tourists for sausage, cheese and crackers, and homemade bread to accompany the wines. Chalet Debonne produces mostly *labruscas* and hybrids, with a few *viniferas*. Vidal Blanc is this winery's best wine.

Château Lagniappe. Lagniappe is a Cajun word that means "a little bit more." It is the 13th roll in the baker's dozen. It is also an apt description for the activities of proprietor Dr. Thomas Wykoff in Cleveland Heights. First there is Au Provence, an award-winning 34-seat restaurant. Then there is the *Cedar Hill Wine Co.*, which operates a storefront wine shop next door to the restaurant. Then there is Château Lagniappe, the winery in the cellar beneath them both. Wykoff is also head surgeon of the ear, nose, and throat department of Cleveland's St. Luke's Hospital.

In 1974 Wykoff made his first commercial wine, 625 cases, and five months later he opened his restaurant. Today 80 percent of the 2,000-case production is sold in Au Provence's intimate and romantic dining room. Lagniappe wines are among the best made in the East, even though Wykoff buys all his grapes from vineyard owners, mostly on Lake Erie or in the Finger Lakes Region in New York. Chardonnay, Seyval Blanc, and Vidal Blanc are "specialties of the house."

Grand River Vineyards. Bill Worthy was an investment banker with Cleveland Trust when he began planting near Madison in the Lake Erie Region. For several years his grapes were in demand by other wineries, and in 1978 he opened his own winery. His Seyval Blanc is among the East's best.

Markko Vineyards. Arnulf Esterer was an engineer at Union Carbide and a wine buff. In 1966 he was visiting friends in the Finger Lakes in New York when he heard of Konstantin Frank. He visited Frank's new winery, and immediately became a disciple. In 1968 he began planting cuttings of *vinifera* near Conneaut, just a few miles from Lake Erie and the Pennsylvania border, and in 1972 built the winery. Esterer was the first in Ohio to plant *vinifera* and, courageously, that is all he still grows. His production is exclusively Chardonnay, Riesling, and Cabernet Sauvignon. He has also managed to achieve a distinctive style of wine—rich, oaky, and flavorful, if sometimes overwhelming.

Meier's Wine Cellars. Although the winery's principal location is in Silverton, a suburb of Cincinnati in southwestern Ohio, most of its vineyards are on Isle St. George, the largest island of a small archipelago in Lake Erie near Sandusky. This handful of "Wine Islands," as they are known, is planted primarily with *labrusca*, but more and more to hybrids and *vinifera*. Isle St. George holds about 350 acres (140 hectares) of Meier's best vineyards, about 25% of which are *vinifera*. Lake Erie is shallow in the area of the Wine Islands, and it freezes solid in winter and thaws late in spring, protecting the vines against spring frosts. In fall, the lake is warmer than the mainland, and harvest on the Wine Islands is several weeks delayed, giving the area one of the longest growing seasons in the northeast. Founded in 1895, Meier's, now owned by Paramount Distillers of Cleveland, produces about one million cases, the most famous of which is their Number 44 Creme Sherry. It has also purchased Mantey Winery west of Sandusky, and the historic Lonz Winery on Middle Bass Island.

Meier's has also recently purchased the picturesque *Mon Ami Cellars* on nearby Catawba Island (actually a peninsula), with vaulted limestone caves and a good restaurant.

Most of the remaining Ohio wineries specialize in a mixture of *labrusca* wines, grape juice, wines from fruits, and sweet "ports" and "sherries" of minor consequence. A few worth mentioning, because they have shown potential, are *Heritage Vineyards* in West Milton, *Klingshirn Winery* in Avon Lake, and *Moyer Vineyards* in Manchester.

United States: Oklahoma

The Pete Schwartz Winery in Okarche is the only bonded winery in the state. In operation since 1970, the winery buys Concord grapes from Arkansas.

Cimarron Cellars in Caney is the only commercial vineyard in the state. Proprietor Dwayne Pool grows 40 acres of hybrid and *vinifera* grapes, and sells his entire crop to La Buena Vida Vineyards in Springtown, Texas.

United States: Oregon

"Wine"-making is not new to Oregon. The state was producing about 7,000 cases a year at the turn of the century, much of it from fruit other than grapes. There were several dozen wineries at the time of Prohibition, and dozens more opened upon Repeal. Only two of the post-Repeal wineries are left, however, and of the 40 or so newer wineries, more than half have opened since 1977.

Most of the vineyards are near the coast, between the Coast Range on the west and the Cascade Mountains on the east. There are two distinct viticultural areas: in the north on the Willamette River near Portland, and in the south along the Umpqua and Rouge rivers near Roseburg. The growing season is cool, almost too cool, with cold winters, and rain that has an unfortunate habit of arriving early while the grapes are still being picked. This makes picking a muddy affair, and wet grapes make thin wine, if they don't burst first and attract mold. Birds and deer are also major problems.

The effort, however, is well worthwhile. As Oregon growers experiment to match vine and soil, they have already shown a proclivity for the finicky Pinot Noir, as well as Gewürztraminer, Chardonnay, Riesling, and botrytised Riesling. Some of America's finest examples of Pinot Noir come from Oregon.

Refreshingly well-written state labeling laws forbid the use of European place names on wine labels, so Oregon makes no "chablis," "burgundy," "rhine," etc. Johannisberg Riesling in Oregon is known as White Riesling or simply Riesling. The law also requires that the wine must contain a minimum of 90% of the grape variety named on the label, fully 15% more than the federal laws require. The exception is for Cabernet Sauvignon, with a 75% minimum, because this variety usually benefits from more liberal blending, as in Bordeaux.

(1) The Willamette Valley

Most of Oregon's wineries and vineyards are in the Willamette Valley, a viticultural area within 40 miles of Portland, and they find a ready market in this urbane little city. The 5,200-square-mile region is enclosed by natural boundaries: the Columbia River on the north, the Coast Range Mountains on the west, the Calapooya Mountains on the south, and the Cascade Mountains to the east.

Amity Vineyards. Myron Redford's winery in Amity has already established a reputation for its Gewürztraminer, its Pinot Noir, and its carbonic maceration Pinot Noir Nouveau. Amity grows 12 acres (4.8 hectares) of Pinot Noir, Chardonnay, Gewürztraminer, and Riesling. Redford first began considering a winery in 1970 after overhearing a conversation at the University of Washington in which Lloyd Woodburne was describing his efforts to establish Associated Vintners in Washington. He went to work for Woodburne part-time, and in 1974 he moved to Oregon, purchased the land, and began his winery.

Arterberry Winery. Fred Arterberry, Jr., is producing *méthode champenoise* sparkling wine in Oregon, and a good one at that. This tiny winery produces only about 1,000 cases of *vinifera* wines, including 250 cases of Red Hills Vineyards sparkling wine. A 1977 graduate of the University of California at Davis, Arterberry remembers that in his last year at Davis he heard John Wright of Napa Valley's Domaine Chandon describe the new venture's grape requirements at a technical conference. He then realized that everything Wright was looking for was available in Oregon except the fame and tourism of Napa Valley. Arterberry has worked part-time for other local wineries, including Eyrie Vineyards, Knudsen Erath, and Sokol Blosser, and still works part-time at other wineries while his sparkling venture matures.

Château Benoit. Founded in 1979 by Dr. Fred Benoit and his wife, Mary, this winery near McMinnville has 50 acres (20 hectares) of Riesling, Chardonnay, Pinot Noir, and Müller-Thurgau. Its best-known wine is a Sauvignon Blanc made from grapes grown in Washington by Sagemoor Farms. Benoit produces about 8,000 cases, and keeps the Benoit family so busy that Fred has had to retire from his medical practice.

Eyrie Vineyards. David and Diana Lett were the first to plant *vinifera* vines in the Willamette Valley since Prohibition. The area is now the heart of Oregon's burgeoning wine industry. David, a graduate of the University of California at Davis, while touring Europe and working with Souverain's Leland Stewart, developed his theory of "marginal climate grape growing." The theory is one that Europeans have known empirically for centuries: "Any grape variety produces its best fruit when it is grown in a climate that is marginal to the maturation of the fruit." In 1965 he packed up his theory and moved to Oregon, and in 1966 the vineyard was planted and named after an eyrie of red-tailed hawks that watches over their 20 acres (8 hectares) in the Red Hills area near Dundee. Eyrie's Pinot Noir is the state's best known, although Lett is also successful with Chardonnay, Pinot Gris, Pinot Munier, and Muscat Ottonel. The Pinot Noir has Burgundy-like structure and flavor, with depth, complexity, and ageability.

Knudsen-Erath Winery. Richard Erath was an electronics engineer at Tektronix in Beaverton and a home wine-maker from California. In 1967 he smuggled 600 pounds of grapes from Oregon into California and made some wine for personal consumption. He was so impressed with the results that in 1969 he planted 4 acres (1½ hectares) near Newberg; in 1972 he moved to Oregon and produced his first 350 cases of commercial wine. Today he and his partner, Calvert Knudsen, a lumber executive, own 111 acres (45 hectares) of vineyards, among the largest vineyard holdings in the state. The vineyards are one-third each Pinot Noir, Chardonnay, and White Riesling. Erath also purchases Gewürztraminer, Pinot Gris, Merlot, and Sauvignon Blanc, and produces a total of about 30,000 cases in an average year. The Pinot Noir, Chardonnay, and Riesling are especially good.

Oak Knoll Winery. Ronald Vuylsteke (pronounced Vulstick) was an engineer at Tektronix at the same time Richard Erath of nearby Knudsen Erath worked for the Beaverton firm. The two would talk wine over lunch. On the side he taught home-wine-making, and on May 18, 1970, he bonded his family winery. With help from his wife, Marjorie, and scions Ron Jr., John, Steve, Doug, and Sara, his winery in Hillsboro grew rapidly. Oak Knoll owns no vineyards, and Vuylsteke has had the opportunity to work with perhaps a wider range of grapes and microclimates than any other Oregon producer. He takes his Pinot Noir seriously, and speaks at length about the two "Pommard" clones grown in the area, as well as the importance of malo-lactic strains and types of oak. Now Oak Knoll produces about 9,000 cases of *vinifera* wines and about 11,000 cases of fruit "wines." On May 18, 1980, during its tenth-anniversary "Bacchus Goes Bluegrass" Festival, Mother Nature joined the thousands at the celebration by exploding nearby Mount St. Helens.

Shafer Vineyard Cellars. David and Linda Shafer just wanted to grow grapes when, in 1973, they planted their 20 acres (8 hectares) of Pinot Noir, Riesling, and Chardonnay near Forest Grove. But eventually a combination of the desire to see their product through to the finish, and what they freely admit was naïveté, created a winery in 1981. Production is about 6,000 cases annually and growing steadily.

Sokol Blosser Winery. William Blosser came under the spell of fine wine while living in France in 1963 and 1964. When he returned home to Oregon in 1966, he started paying attention to the local wines and studying viticulture. In 1971 he began planting a vineyard, and by 1977 launched his winery with the help of Susan Sokol, now Susan Blosser. Located in the Red Hills area near Dundee, Sokol Blosser has 45 acres (18 hectares) of vineyard, one-third each Pinot Noir,

Chardonnay, and Riesling. The winery produces about 20,000 cases, and the Pinot Noir and Sauvignon Blanc (from purchased grapes) are especially good.

There are several other promising wineries in the Willamette Valley around Portland, among the best being *Adelsheim* in Newburg, *Ponzi* in Beaverton and *Tualatin* in Forest Grove. Others include the strange-tasting *Cote des Colombes*, *Elk Cove Vineyards*, *Glen Creek* and *Hidden Springs*.

Several others have located farther south along the Willamette River near Eugene: *Alpine Winery* in Monroe, *Forgeron Vineyard* in Elmira, and *Hinman Vineyards* in Eugene.

(2) The Umpqua Valley Region

The first of the modern generation of wineries in Oregon, *Hillcrest Winery* was started in this southwestern Oregon valley near Roseburg, where the climate is somewhat warmer and drier than in the Willamette Valley.

Bjelland Vineyards was founded in 1968 by Paul and Mary Bjelland just southeast of Roseburg. In addition to producing good wines, Bjelland is largely responsible for organizing the Oregon Winegrowers Association and the Oregon Wine Festival.

Hillcrest Winery. Richard Sommer deserves the title of "Father of Wine's Rebirth in Oregon." An agronomist from the University of California at Davis, he was looking for a cooler climate to plant his vines. In 1961 he planted his first vines in the Umpqua Valley and in 1963 bonded his winery. In 1975 Hillcrest moved to a new facility near Roseburg and now produces 10,000 cases a year. Sommer has a passion for Riesling that shows in his wine, and he has devoted 20 of his 30-acre vineyard (8 of his 12 hectares) to this cool-climate grape.

(3) The Hood River Region

In the north-central part of the state, where the Hood River converges with the Columbia, in the shadow of Mt. Hood, are two other interesting wineries, *Hood River Vineyards* and *Mt. Hood Winery.*

United States: Pennsylvania

Pennsylvania became the home of the first commercial winery in the U.S. in 1793, when a Frenchman, Pierre Legaux, founded the Pennsylvania Vine Company at Spring Mill on the Schuylkill River near Philadelphia. It later failed in the early 1800s, and wine-making in Pennsylvania became limited to a handful of small wineries until 1963, when Melvin Gordon opened the Conestoga Vineyards winery near Valley Forge. A major reason for the long drought was the Pennsylvania Liquor Control Board, one of the nation's most restrictive and backward state control systems. In 1968, when the state passed a farm winery bill making it easier to sell Pennsylvania-grown and

-produced wine, a limited wine boom resulted. Penn State University established an active research program, and today there are over 55 wineries in the state. Most of the wineries are concentrated in two areas. One is in Pennsylvania Dutch country, in the southeastern corner of the state, from near Philadelphia to a section along the Susquehannah River, near Harrisburg. The other region is in the northeast corner in the Lake Erie Region viticultural area around Erie. The latter is also the home of Welch's huge juice plant, in the town of North East, so it is no coincidence that Concord is still king in Pennsylvania.

(1) Lake Erie Region

This viticultural area has been officially designated by the U.S. government as a controlled appellation "viticultural area," and extends in a narrow strip from near Sandusky, Ohio, to near Buffalo, N.Y. The northwest corner of Pennsylvania has an "ear" that wedges between Ohio and New York into the region which is heavily planted with grapes. The center of the grape industry in the Region is North East, a town that is dominated by the huge Welch's juice plant. Concord accounts for the vast majority of the grapes in the Region, but a few wineries have been successful with the better French-American hybrids and with *vinifera*.

Heritage Wine Cellars. Located in North East, Heritage Wine Cellars was bonded in 1978 by the Bostwick family. It has 300 acres (65 hectares) of *labrusca* and French-American hybrids, and produces 12,500 cases of 27 different wines.

Mazza Vineyards. Bonded in 1972, Robert Mazza's winery is located in North East. Mazza has two acres of *labrusca* and French-American hybrids, with the bulk of his grapes purchased from independent growers. He produces 6,500 cases of 17 different wines. Mazza's Rieslings and Vidal Blancs have been among the East's best.

Penn Shore Vineyards. Located near North East, Penn-Shore was established in 1969. All of its French-American hybrid and *labrusca* grapes are purchased from independent growers. Penn-Shore offers 19 different wines, with an annual production of 18,000 cases.

Presque Isle Wine Cellars. Situated in North East, Doug and Marlene Moorhead's winery opened in 1969. They purchase *labrusca, vinifera,* and French-American hybrids from independent contractors and produce about 1,000 cases of 12 different wines. Fully 80% of their sales are grapes, juice, supplies, and equipment for home wine-makers. The Moorheads are highly regarded by commercial wine-makers for their expertise.

(2) Southeastern Pennsylvania

Although most of the state's grapes come from the Lake Erie Region, the greater number of wineries is located in the southeastern section of Pennsylvania surrounding Harrisburg, Lancaster, and Philadelphia. Lancaster, Bucks, and York counties have several wineries each, while Adams, Cumberland, Merks, Chester, Delaware, Montgomery, and Northampton counties have one or two in each. The majority of the state's population and the tourist industry is concentrated in this area, and because the climate and topography seem suitable to growing French-American hybrids and *vinifera*, more vineyards are being planted. So far, the only designated viticultural area is the Lancaster Valley Region, near the town of Lancaster and near the Susquehanna River.

Adams County Winery. Located in historic Gettysburg, 30 miles (48 kilometers) south of Harrisburg, Adams County Winery was established in 1975. Proprietors Ronald and Ruth Cooper have 7 acres (2.8 hectares) of French-American hybrids, notably Vidal and Seyval Blanc, and some *vinifera*. Adams County Winery offers 25 different wines with a production of 2,500 cases.

Bucks Country Vineyards. Bonded in 1973, Bucks Country is located in New Hope just north of Philadelphia on the Delaware River. It has 47 acres (19 hectares) of various French-American hybrids, and depends on independent growers for the grapes necessary to produce 30,000 cases of 18 different wines.

Chaddsford Winery is located in Chadds Ford in Delaware County, 10 miles (16 kilometers) north of Wilmington, Delaware, and was opened in June 1983 by Eric and Lee Miller. No strangers to the wine business, Lee has written extensively on eastern wines, and Eric is the son of Mark Miller, eastern wine pioneer and proprietor of Benmarl Wine Co., in Marlboro, New York. With no vineyards of its own, Chaddsford currently contracts with independent growers. It offers a Chardonnay and various French-American hybrid blends, with an annual production of 30,000 gallons.

Conestoga Vineyards was the first farm winery in Pennsylvania, established in 1963 at Birchrunville, near Valley Forge, by Melvin Gordon. In 1983 the winery moved to Lancaster. Conestoga has 4 acres (1½ hectares) of French-American hybrids, notably Vidal Blanc, and is also conducting experiments in growing various *vinifera* varieties. It produces 2,000 cases of 20 different wines.

Mt. Hope Winery is situated on an estate crowned by a palatial Victorian mansion near Manheim in Lancaster County. Established in 1980, Mt. Hope was once affiliated with the Mazza Vineyards in Erie County, although the two are now separate operations. It has 10 acres (4 hectares) of mostly French-American hybrids and some *vinifera*, with an additional 50 acres (20 hectares) under contract, mostly in Adams County. Mt. Hope produces 20,000 cases under 20 different labels.

Naylor Wine Cellars was established in 1978 by Robert and Audrey Naylor, and is located near Stewartstown, 35 miles (56 kilometers) north of Baltimore, Maryland. It consists of 24 acres (10 hectares) of various French-American hybrid, *labrusca,* and *vinifera* grapes.

Naylor sells 10,000 cases of 25 different wines. Naylor's Baco Noir is a good example of the grape.

Nissley Vineyards. In 1971 Richard Nissley was building bridges for a living. When he retired, he turned his wine-making hobby into a business, and a tobacco barn into a winery. The winery, near Bainbridge in the Lancaster Valley Region, about 60 miles (96 kilometers) from Philadelphia, was bonded in 1976, and today has grown to 32 acres (13 hectares) of mixed varieties, and produces about 20,000 cases. All of Nissley's whites are well made.

Tucquan Vineyard and Winery is the oldest vineyard in Lancaster County, planted in 1968 by Tom and Lucinda Hampton. Tucquan Winery came on line in 1978. Located in Holtwood on the Susquehanna River, it holds about 10 acres (4 hectares) of French-American hybrids and some *labrusca.* Tucquan produces 2,100 cases all told, of seven different wines.

There are several other small wineries experimenting with French-American hybrids and *vinifera* in southeast Pennsylvania. Some of the more promising are *Allegro Vineyards* in Brogue, *Blue Ridge Winery* in Carlisle, *Brandywine Vineyards* in Kemblesville, *Buckingham Valley Vineyard* in Buckingham, *Calvaresi Winery* in Reading, *Country Creek Vineyard* in Telford, *Franklin Hill Vineyards* in Bangor, *Lancaster County Winery* in Lancaster, *The Little Vineyard* in Quakertown, *Neri Wine Cellar* in Langhorne, *Stephen Bahn Winery* in Brogue, *Quarry Hill Winery* in Shippenburg, and *York Springs Winery* in the town of the same name.

(3) Other Wineries

There is an effort towards wine-growing and wine-making around Pittsburgh, and in the center of the state near Penn State University. These include *Buffalo Valley Winery* in Lewisburg, *Whispering Wine Cellars* in Wampum, *Hillcrest Winery* in Greensburg, *Kolln Winery* in Bellefonte, *Lapic Winery* in New Brighton, and *Nittany Valley Winery* in State College in the shadow of Penn State University.

United States: Rhode Island

A handful of small wineries have sprung up in this tiny state where the best vineyards are virtually surrounded by water, and thus protected from the harsh winters.

Diamond Hill Winery is in the very northeast corner of the state near Woonsocket. There the climate is more continental, and winters more harsh than downstate. Diamond Hill planted about five acres (2 hectares) of Pinot Noir in 1976, produced small quantities in 1979 and 1980, and were wiped out by the winter of 1980–81. Owners Peter and Clair Berntson, and Andy and Jean Berntson are undaunted, and have replanted the entire vineyard, but now they train them so one cane and the graft can be buried in the winter.

Prudence Island Vineyards is buried underground on Prudence Island in the middle of Narragansett Bay.

Bill and Natalie Bacon and their sons Bill, Jr. and Nathanael manage the tiny winery and tend to their 16 acres (6.5 hectares) of vineyard planted entirely with *vinifera.* They produce only about 850 cases, and the Gewürztraminer, Chardonnay, and Gewürztraminer and Riesling blend are their best.

Sakonnet Vineyards. Jim and Lolly Mitchell's Sakonnet Vineyards are perched on a hill on a slender peninsula overlooking the wide mouth of the Sakonnet River and the America's Cup sailing course. Their 45 acres (18 hectares) is the largest single vineyard in New England. Production is 10,000 cases of *viniferas* and hybrids. The decomposed slate soil and 220 frost-free days yield a Chardonnay that is crisp and elegant. Their Vidal Blanc and their America's Cup White (a blend of Vidal Blanc and Seyval Blanc) are delightful drinks in the Loire style. Riesling and Pinot Noir have also shown promise at Sakonnet.

South County Vineyards in Slocum has offered tiny amounts of *vinifera* since 1974, mostly from purchased grapes.

United States: South Carolina

South Carolina was one of the first states to develop grape-growing and wine-making when, in 1764, a colony of French Huguenot emigrants was allowed by the British to establish vineyards and wine-making facilities along the upper Savannah River. Prohibition had a devastating effect on the wine industry, but today the state is enjoying a resurgence of its wine-grape production.

Truluck Vineyards Winery. In Lake City, about halfway between Columbia and Myrtle Beach, Truluck Winery is owned and operated by Dr. James Truluck, a dentist, and his son Jay. Located on a former tobacco farm, with approximately 53 acres of vineyards, the winery offers 20 different wines, almost entirely French-American hybrids, most notably Vidal Blanc, Verdelet, and Cayuga. With an eye toward the future, Truluck also carries on extensive experiments with about 250 varieties of *vinifera* and other species. Annual output is about 8,000 cases, and the winery sponsors several wine festivals during the year.

Two other operations worth mentioning are the *Foxwood Wine Cellars* in Woodruff that makes sweet wines from Concord and Scuppernong grapes, and *Tenner Brothers* in Patrick, a sizable grower of *muscadines,* owned by the Canandaigua Wine Co. of New York.

United States: Tennessee

An estimated 150 acres (61 hectares) of vines are under cultivation in Tennessee, with more acreage planned for the future, mostly east and south of Nashville. There are only three licensed wineries in the state, with several more planning to open soon.

Highland Mountain Winery. In Jamestown, about 50 miles (80 kilometers) northwest of Knoxville, the

Highland Winery produces about ten wines from 9 acres of various *labrusca* varieties. Unfortunately, its five-year-old plantings of *vinifera* were recently lost to damaging frost. It supplements its vineyard output by purchasing muscadines planted in and around Chattanooga.

Smoky Mountain Winery is in Gatlinburg, about 10 miles (16 kilometers) southeast of Knoxville. Bonded in 1981, it buys hybrids, *labruscas, muscadines,* and other fruits from independent growers, and annual output is 2,500 cases with plans to expand. Located in one of the South's most famous tourist areas, it has no trouble selling its wines.

The Tiegs Winery in Lenoir City, about 10 miles (16 kilometers) southwest of Knoxville, owned by Peter and Terry Tiegs, was licensed in 1979, shortly after the state revised its winery laws. It has four acres of Vidal and Seyval Blanc planted, with two more acres planned for the future. Output is small, about 800 cases annually, and, although the winery is located in a "dry" county, Tiegs has no problem selling them.

United States: Texas

Franciscan missionaries came to Texas in the mid-1600s, equipped with European vine-stocks to make their sacramental wines. Unable to survive the harsh weather and many insects, the European plants were replaced with native vines, and Texas enjoyed a wine-growing spurt until Prohibition. Since Repeal, there has been renewed interest in wine-growing in this vast state, and if the industry continues to develop as quickly and successfully as it did in the 1970s, Texas stands a good chance of becoming the nation's number two grape and wine producer, after California. There are more than 18 wineries in Texas, six of which were founded in 1982.

Through many viticultural studies and experiments, the land-rich and well-endowed University of Texas has been a major source of information, inspiration, and encouragement to potential Texan grape-growers, who have responded by planting vines on their cattle ranches and irrigated plateaus. The university itself established a commercial grape industry in 1980 and had close to 1,000 acres (400 hectares) of *vinifera* vines at their Escondido Vineyard Development in west Texas. Ste. Genevieve, despite its financial difficulties, has become the largest winery and has taken over the 1,000 acres planted by the university. University officials predict that 15,000 to 60,000 acres (6,000 to 24,000 hectares) of their total of two million acres (810,000 hectares) will support grapes one day.

Not surprisingly, water is the major stumbling block in developing west Texas viticulture. However, drip irrigation systems, some of which desalinate water as they are applied, have proved to work well in this semi-arid area of the state. In the late spring, water in the form of hail can have a devastating effect and wipe out an entire crop, as it did in Bakersfield in 1979. But overall, cooler temperatures, high pH soils, and lower humidity provide favorable growing conditions, especially for *vinifera* vines. Chenin Blanc, French Colombard, Sauvignon Blanc, Sémillon, Emerald Riesling, and White Riesling are the most successful whites; Ruby Cabernet, Barbera, Zinfandel, and Petite Sirah are the reds that perform the best.

South of the university's vineyards is the *Wimberley Valley Winery.* Gretchen Glasscock, an oil heiress, founded this winery which has a high-altitude, 40-acre (16-hectare) vineyard planted in a microclimate similar to that of California's coastal valleys. It is now known as the *Blue Mountain Vineyards,* specializing in *vinifera.*

In the Lubbock area, *Llano Estacado* and *Pheasant Ridge* are two promising wineries. Llano Estacado was started by two Texas Technological University professors, who have experimented with more than 100 grape varieties, concentrating on *viniferas.* Now owned by 40, shareholders, its 1980 crop was destroyed by a springtime hailstorm, but it has nonetheless become Texas' second largest winery, with a projected annual case production of 40,000. Pheasant Ridge Winery is vineyard technician Bobby Cox's venture, with 30 acres (12 hectares) of vines planted on his family's farm. Its first varietals were made in 1982.

Three wineries of note are gathered around the Dallas/Fort Worth area. Ron Weatherington ventured into wine-making by planting 8 acres (3 hectares) outside Fort Worth and naming it *Sanchez Creek Vineyard.* Over the years, he has converted his vines to Rhône varieties, and specializes in a Rhône-style red blend. Very small amounts are made by Dean Hart, son of the founder. In 1983 the winery was sold to Ron Weatherington.

La Buena Vida, also outside Fort Worth, is owned by Bobby Smith and son Steve. They work primarily with French-American hybrids and specialty wines. Capacity of their winery is 16,000 cases.

Chateau Montgolfier, owned by orthopedic surgeon Henry McDonald, is another promising Dallas area winery.

In the central hilly part of the state, in Austin's outlying regions, several wineries have appeared. *Fall Creek Vineyards,* in Tow, belongs to lawyer-cattle rancher-oilman Ed Auler, who picked up grape-growing in 1974. Auler favors *vinifera* grapes on his 30-acre (12-hectare) vineyard and can make up to 10,000 cases in his spectacular winery.

The Val Verde Winery, 300 miles (480 kilometers) south of Lubbock, has been run by the Qualia family for three generations. The Qualias have begun replacing their South Carolinian vines with *vinifera* and French-American hybrids suitable to the hot, moist microclimate of Del Rio, with the hope of producing some decent wines.

Dallas businessman Robert Oberhellman established *Oberhellmann Vineyards,* where he grows *vinifera* grapes at high elevations, in this hilly area. His neighbors, Dale and Penny Bettis, started their *Cypress Valley Winery* in a similar microclimate.

United States: Utah

Others in the Austin and San Antonio region are the French-owned *Moyer Texas Champagne Co., Guadalupe Valley Winery, Messina Hof Wine Cellars;* and *Texas Vineyards* north of Dallas.

United States: Utah

Although wine was produced in the mid-to-late 19th century in southern Utah under the instruction of Brigham Young and the Mormon Church, involvement gradually dissipated owing to the Church's eventual disapproval of drinking and the increasing superiority of the wines coming from neighboring California.

The Summum Winery in Salt Lake City is the only bonded winery in the state today, established in 1980 and operated as a non-profit corporation by the Church of Summum. It purchases pre-crushed *vinifera* grape juice from Napa Valley, California, and its 25,000-case production goes into various blended sacramental wines. There are no commercial vineyards in the state.

United States: Virginia

Wine-growing has its place in Virginia's colorful history: the first settlers in Roanoke cultivated native vines, George Washington and Thomas Jefferson both grew grapes on their Virginia plantations, and Virginian wines won medals in Vienna and Paris in the late 1800s. The industry faded with Prohibition, and in recent years has been revived. Today, about 50% of Virginia's 800 acres (320 hectares) of vines are *vinifera*, the remainder being primarily French-American hybrids. More than 30 wineries exist in the state, most in four separate areas. The Shenandoah Valley is the first approved viticultural area.

(1) The Middleburg Area

The Middleburg area has been the center for new developments in the state's wine-growing industry. A half-dozen wineries are scattered in and around the city, located in the northern part of the state.

Meredyth Vineyards, within the city's boundaries, is north Virginia's largest commercial vineyard and was started in the early 1970s. Archie Smith, Jr., owner of Meredyth, grows 45 acres (18 hectares) of French-American hybrids and *vinifera,* and makes eight wines.

Piedmont Vineyards, another Middleburg winery, has 30 acres (12 hectares) of primarily Chardonnay and Sémillon vines.

Farfelu Vineyards' vines were planted in 1967; now 35 acres (14 hectares) of *vinifera* and hybrids produce fruit. Charles Raney and his family own the winery, located in Flint Hill. Nearby, in Hume, *Oasis Vineyards* has primarily *vinifera* vines covering 40 acres (16 hectares). The wines were first crushed in 1980 at the newly completed winery.

Naked Mountain has a tiny 5-acre (2-hectare) *vinifera* vineyard, whose Chardonnay was first made into wines in 1981 at the Markham location.

(2) Shenandoah Valley

Tri-Mountain Winery, northwest of Middleburg, is named for the three mountains that form the Shenandoah Valley. The first vintage for Tri-Mountain was 1981; about 25 acres (10 hectares) of Concord, hybrid, and *vinifera* vines are grown.

Shenandoah Vineyards, further south in the same valley, has 40 acres (16 hectares) of vines, equally divided between *vinifera* and hybrids. The Randels, owners of the winery, have been making seven wines since 1977.

(3) The Charlottesville Area

Barboursville Vineyards, with 50 acres (20 hectares) of various *vinifera,* first made wine in 1978. Zonin Gambellara, an Italian producer-bottler-shipper of table wines headquartered in Venice, bought the Barboursville operation in the 1970s. The winery, a former plantation, is a Virginia historic landmark.

Rapidan River Vineyards is located between Charlottesville and Middleburg, comprises 55 acres (22 hectares) of vines, owned by Norman Martin and Jean Leducq of France, and specializes in German-style wines.

Montdomaine Cellars, completed in 1983, makes Chardonnay, Merlot, and Cabernet Sauvignon from its 30 acres (12 hectares) of vines located south of Charlottesville. Production is projected for 6,000 cases annually.

Chermont Winery, in Albemarle County, with 10 acres (4 hectares) of *vinifera* vines. Founded in 1981.

Oakencroft Vineyards, in Charlottesville, is owned by Felicia Rogan. 17 acres (7 hectares) of Seyval, Chardonnay, and Merlot are planted; the first crush was in 1983.

Blenheim Wine Cellars, also in Charlottesville, has 11 acres (4½ hectares) of *vinifera.* Founded in 1982.

Bacchanal Vineyards, west of Charlottesville, was completed in 1982 and makes eight *vinifera* wines from 6 acres (2½ hectares) of vines.

Rose Bower Vineyard and Winery, established in Hampton-Sydney in 1974, has 6 acres (2½ hectares) of hybrids and *viniferas,* and makes six wines.

Prince Michel Vineyards. Founded in 1983 by Norman Martin and Jean Leducq (who also own Rapidan River Vineyards), this syndicated winery comprises 115 acres (45 hectares) of *vinifera* grapes. As the vines age, Virginia's largest estate-bottled vineyard should produce laudable wines. 60 miles from Monticello.

(4) Roanoke River

The north fork of the Roanoke River, in the southeastern part of the state, was proposed as a viticultural area in 1983.

MJC Vineyard, in the Pearis Mountains in that area, makes several wines from its 15 acres (6 hectares).

Chateau Morrisette, in the Rocky Knob viticultural area atop the Blue Ridge Parkway, features 17 acres (7 hectares) of hybrids and some *vinifera.* Its wines were first released in 1983.

(5) Other Wineries

Ingleside Plantation is located near the Potomac in eastern Virginia. The approximately 30 acres (12 hectares) of *vinifera* and hybrids produce fruit for a dozen different wines.

Many other wineries are scattered all over the state, and as long as the new generation of wine-growers concentrates its efforts on cultivating the most suitable French-American hybrids and *vinifera* vines on the most suitable soils, Virginia can look forward to earning a reputation as a quality wine-producer in the 1980s.

United States: Washington

Washington now produces more grapes than any state with the exception of California, and lists about 60 wineries, with 8 having started in 1975. *Vinifera* currently covers 12,000 acres (4,800 hectares).

Washington has long been an important source of Concord grapes for juice, jelly, and wine, but it was not until 1967 that a real breakthrough came. California's most prominent wine-maker, André Tchelistcheff, went to Washington that year and tasted a homemade Gewürztraminer from the cellar of Washington State University Professor Philip Church. Tchelistcheff called it the finest white wine made from Gewürztraminer in the U.S. Since the day Tchelistcheff pronounced Washington's potential, more growers have been pulling out their Concords and replacing them with *viniferas.* Today Washington's burgeoning vineyards are supplying grapes not only to its own wineries but also to wineries in California, Oregon, Idaho, Michigan, and Canada. The resulting wines can compete with California, and, for that matter, with any in the world. Especially promising have been Gewürztraminer, Riesling, Chardonnay, Sauvignon Blanc, Sémillon, Cabernet Sauvignon, Pinot Noir, and Merlot.

Columbia Valley is the general B.A.T.F. appellation covering vineyards in either the Yakima Valley or the Walla Walla Valley. Washington is endowed with an almost ideal combination of climate and soil. The warm days and cool nights combine to produce well-balanced grapes—flavorful, sweet, and high in acid. The area lies just north of latitude 46 degrees, the same latitude that cuts across the Bordeaux and Burgundy regions. In the light, sandy soils of Yakima Valley, phylloxera cannot survive, so the expense of grafting is obviated. As rain is almost nonexistent and irrigation is cheap and plentiful, farmers can apply water in the precise amount at the precise time.

Growers do have their problems in Washington, however. The winters can be harsh, with occasionally a whole month below freezing, and, if the snow cover is light, this extreme cold can freeze roots. Another hazard is the proximity of the vineyards to active volcanoes. After the first eruption of Mount St. Helens, Yakima vineyards were covered with ash, and the vine leaves could not collect sunshine. The ash had to be shaken and blown off the leaves. Still another hazard is man-made: Grapes are a minor crop in Yakima, surrounded by grain. In order to control weeds, grain farmers often use the chemical 2,4-D, which can kill vines. Substitute sprays, more agreeable spraying schedules, and legislation are being considered.

Columbia Winery, formerly *Associated Vintners,* was formed in 1962 by ten wine-loving faculty members at the University of Washington. Originally located in Kirkland, it later expanded and moved to Redmond, and then again to its present site in Bellevue, not far from Seattle. AV, as it prefers to be called, purchases all of its *vinifera* grapes from independent growers, and currently offers nine different wines, with an annual production of 35,000 cases. Its Chardonnay is one of the best produced in the state, and under wine-master/partner David Lake, an English master of wine, has expanded to a series of individual vineyards of Cabernet Sauvignons of outstanding quality.

E. B. Foote Winery. This Seattle-based winery was founded in 1978 and is owned and operated by Eugene B. Foote and family. Purchasing all of its various *vinifera* grapes from independent growers, Foote offers four white and two red wines, with a production of about 2,000 cases a year that it hopes to double in the near future.

Hinzerling Vineyards is located at Prosser in the Yakima Valley, and had its first releases of Cabernet Sauvignon, Gewürztraminer, Chardonnay, and Riesling in 1976. It has 25 acres (10 hectares) of *vinifera,* and also buys grapes from independent growers to produce nine different wines. Wine-maker Mike Wallace hopes eventually to reach 12,000 cases annually.

Kiona Vineyards Winery is located near Benton City in the Yakima Valley, just west of Richland. Founded in 1979, it has 32 acres (13 hectares) of various *vinifera* grapes, including the German Limberger variety that produces a soft red wine. Kiona, which means "brown hills," offers seven different wines, with an annual production of 5,000 cases.

T. W. Langguth Winery. The well-known Mosel-based German wine firm has established an important new vineyard and winery for production of Riesling which today has exhibited a remarkable Mosel-like style.

Manfred Vierthaler. Founded in 1976, this winery is located at Shelton in western Washington, 30 miles west of Tacoma. It contracts for most of its *vinifera* grapes to produce 15 different wines, primarily German-style whites, with a production average of 15,000 cases a year. Vierthaler also has two restaurants at the winery.

Mont Elise Vineyards. Formerly named Bingen Wine

Cellars, Mont Elise was founded in 1975 by Charles V. Henderson, and is located in Bingen, 65 miles east of Portland, Oregon. It contracts with independent growers for its Chenin Blanc, but the remainder of its wine is produced from 35 acres (14 hectares) of various *vinifera*. Mont Elise offers six different wines, comprising an annual production of 4,000 cases.

Neuharth Winery was founded in 1979 by Eugene Neuharth, and is located northwest of Seattle in Sequim near the Strait of Juan de Fuca and Puget Sound. Although Neuharth purchased Chenin Blanc and Zinfandel from California when it started, it now buys all of its *vinifera* grapes from independent Washington growers. Neuharth offers Dungeness Red, White, and Rosé, named after the famous crabbing area nearby.

Preston Wine Cellars. The largest family-owned winery in Washington, Preston was founded in 1976. It now has 181 acres (73 hectares) of various *vinifera* varieties. Located at Pasco in the proposed Columbia River Basin viticultural area, Preston offers 13 different wines, including a good Chardonnay. Current annual production is 60,000 cases.

Sagemoor Farms. One of the largest suppliers of grapes in the Pacific Northwest area is a large vineyard partnership without a winery. Sagemoor Farms owns 466 acres (189 hectares) of *vinifera* just north of Pasco on the Columbia River. Sagemoor grows ten premium varietals, with large concentrations of Cabernet Sauvignon, Chardonnay, and Johannisberg Riesling. Sagemoor has sold grapes that have found their way into prizewinning wines in Washington, Oregon, Idaho, New York, Michigan, California, Pennsylvania, and British Columbia, and because the vineyard's reputation is growing, the Sagemoor vineyard designation is proudly printed on the producer's label.

Chateau Ste. Michelle. The National Wine Company (Nawico) and the Pommerelle Company began separately in 1934 to produce fruit juice and *labrusca* wines. They merged in 1954, forming the American Wine Growers. *Vinifera* grapes were first planted in Washington in the 1950s, and it took considerable time before growers felt confident enough to plant them in large quantities.

In 1967, with the aid of consultant André Tchelistcheff, American Wine Growers picked its first crop of *vinifera*. They were sold under the name Chateau Ste. Michelle, a name chosen on a whim. In 1974, the company was sold to United States Tobacco Company who built a magnificent château at Woodinville, outside Seattle, to house Chateau Ste. Michelle's winery and main offices. Near Grandview in the Yakima Valley, Ste. Michelle maintains the original Nawico vineyard, now producing red grapes only. The primary white grape vineyard is in Paterson, in Colombia Valley, with a new winery and tasting room named River Ridge. All of Chateau Ste. Michelle's 3,000 acres (1,200 hectares) of *vinifera* are east of the Cascade Mountains. The company currently offers 11 different wines from nine varieties, with an annual production of 300,000 cases. The only Washington winery with national distribution, Chateau Ste. Michelle is now selling approximately 500,000 cases.

Many other wineries are within 100 miles of Seattle in western Washington. Some of the best are *Bainbridge Island Winery* in Bainbridge Island, *Haviland Vintners* in Lynnwood, *Hoodsport Winery* in Hoodsport, *Lost Mountain Winery* in Sequim, *Mt. Baker Vineyards* in Everson, *Mt. Rainier Vintners* in Puyallup, *Quilceda Creek Vintners* in Snohomish, *Snohomish Valley Winery* in Marysville, *Snogualmie Winery* in Snogualmie, *Paul Thomas Winery* in Bellevue, and *Daquila Wines* in Seattle.

Other notable wineries in the Yakima Valley and along the Columbia River are *Champs de Brionne Winery* in Quincy, *Salishan Vineyards* in La Center, *Langguth Winery* in Mattawa, *Quail Run Vintners* in Zillah, *Tucker Cellars* in Sunnyside, *Lowden Schoolhouse Winery* and *Woodward Canyon Winery* in Lowden, and *Hogue Cellars, Pontin del Roza* and *Yakima River Winery*, in Prosser.

In the far eastern part of the state in the Spokane area are *Arbor Crest, Latah Creek Wine Cellars*, and *Washington Cellars. Worden's Washington Winery* was started in 1980 by Jack Worden. Located in Spokane in eastern Washington, Worden's purchases all of its *vinifera* from the Pasco area near the Columbia River. With an emphasis on white, Worden's offers seven different wines, including three styles of Riesling. Annual production: about 10,000 cases.

United States: West Virginia

There are only two main wineries in West Virginia. *The Fisher Ridge Wine Company* in Liberty, 7 miles (11 kilometers) northwest of Charleston, is the first winery in West Virginia in more than 100 years. Established in 1979, Fisher Ridge has 7 acres (3 hectares) of primarily French-American hybrids and a few *viniferas*, with an annual production of 700 cases.

West-Whitehill Winery is located at Keyser in the mountainous eastern panhandle, 80 miles (128 kilometers) southeast of Pittsburgh, Pa. Bonded in July, 1981, West-Whitehill produces French-American hybrid wines from 8 acres (3 hectares) of vines.

United States: Wisconsin

Most of the winery activity in Wisconsin is limited to apple, cherry, cranberry, and other fruit wine production, with many of the 10 or so operating wineries buying bulk fruit juice from other states, as well as using local fruit. Of this group, the *Christina Wine Cellars* in La Crosse, which also owns a winery in McGregor, Iowa, and the *Stone Mill Winery* in Cedarburg, also make various grape wines.

Wollersheim Winery is the most important winery and vineyard in the state and is located near Madison in Prairie du Lac. The land that the winery is on was once owned by Agoston Haraszthy, the Hungarian "Count" who was instrumental in founding the California wine industry. He planted vineyards and dug a cave nearby. However, he was drawn to California by the Gold Rush of 1849 before a winery could be built. Haraszthy sold the land to the Kehl family from Nierstein, Germany, who founded the Kehl Weinburg in 1856. The Kehl vineyards were destroyed in the record winter freeze of 1899, and were never replanted. In 1972, the land was bought and the winery revived by Robert Wollersheim and his family. On a bluff overlooking the Wisconsin River, Wollersheim possesses 22 acres (8.8 hectares) of French hybrids, notably Foch and Seyval Blanc, and some Riesling. The first vintage took place in 1976, and current annual production is about 7,500 cases, with plans to expand in the future.

The Baco Noir is light but complex, and among the best examples of this grape.

St. Croix Winery. Prescott Pierce County. 15 acres (6 hectares) of hybrid grapes.

Upper Moselle

See Mosel-Saar-Ruwer.

Uruguay

The smallest of the South American countries achieves a vinous importance incommensurate with its size by producing some 800,000 hectoliters (21.15 million U.S. gallons, 17.60 million imp.) of wine annually; but the Uruguayan is a wine-drinking man and little of it is exported. Small amounts sometimes trickle into neighboring Brazil, but, in general, if you want to drink Uruguayan wines you must go to Uruguay.

Red, white, and rosé wines are made. The pink is considerably deeper in color than is usual, verging more toward Spanish *clarete* than French rosé. Vermouth is also produced, and some fortified and sparkling wines. Contrary to the general rule, fortified wines are often sold as port and sparkling wines as champagne, but in other respects, Uruguayans tend to prefer wines with local names; or wines named from the dominant or informing grape used. The most widespread vine is Harriague, and it is reasonably established that this is the Tannat of Madiran in the French Pyrenees. Vidiella, of obscure origin, and Cabernet from the Bordeaux region of France are also fairly widely planted; and when wine from the two is blended together the result is well balanced and agreeable. Some Barbera and Nebbiolo—imported from Italy and keeping their original names—are also to be found. White wines are made, notably from Sémillon and Pinot Blanc grapes. 50% of the production is in Frutilla and some hybrids and the American Isabella vine are planted, but the increased production of these varieties is accompanied—as it always is—by a marked decrease in quality.

Uruguayan viticulture was established in the 1890s near Montevideo and today extends over the low hills and plains of the departments of Montevideo, Cane-

lones, San José, and Maldonado (along the River Plate), Soriano and Paysandú (next to Argentina), and Florida (in central Uruguay). The country is actually an extension of the Brazilian plain, and the gently rolling, volcanic hills—*cuchillas*—never rise above 600 meters (2,000 feet). Climate is temperate and mild—maintaining an average high of 71°F. (22°C.) in th summer months of January and February, and an average low of 50°F. (10°C.) in the winter month of July—and rainfall is sufficient but not excessive. The vineyards cover about 16,000 hectares (40,000 acres).

SPIRITS

The Uruguayans distill quantities of brandy—most of which is miscalled cognac—and some grappa, distilled from pomace after the grapes have been pressed. Caña—a type of rum—is popular, as is amara (or amargo), an aperitif. Anisette, gin, and guindado (fermented cherries reinforced with alcohol) are also fairly common. A popular Vino Seco is made by adding a large quantity of white wine to red, then enriching the mixture with wine alcohol and letting the whole maderize in the sun, a process which sounds somewhat distressing to conservative amateurs of wine. All wines and spirits are controlled by the state, and various schools at the University of Uruguay are attempting to improve knowledge, and thus wines, by sending students to study abroad, particularly in Italy and France.

Ürziger Würzgarten

White wine.
Middle Mosel, Germany.

The best wine-producing vineyard of Ürzig produces a spicy and fruity wine, from volcanic and slate soil of such steepness that vintaging becomes a death-defying mountain sport.

See Mosel-Saar-Ruwer.

Usquebaugh

The anglicized form of *uisgebeatha*, original Celtic name for whisky.

U.S.S.R.

See Russia.

Utiel-Requena

A Spanish Denominación de Origen located south of Barcelona and west of Valencia. The 50,000 hectares (125,000 acres) of Tempranillo, Garnacha, and Bobal produce a creditable strong red and some lighter rosé wines.

V

Vacqueyras (Appellation Contrôlée)

One of the best communes of the Côtes du Rhône, producing white, red, and rosé wines.

See Rhône.

Vaduzer

Red wine of Liechtenstein.

Two-thirds of the wine which is grown in the little principality on the Swiss-Austrian border is called Vaduzer, after Vaduz, the capital. The remaining third is produced in Schaan, Triesen and Balzers and known as Schaaner, Triesner and Balzner.

Vineyards were probably established in Liechtenstein by Roman invaders and later by monks in the first centuries of the Christian era. At this time the country was not Liechtenstein but a part of the Roman Empire (and later of Germany). In 1699 and 1712, the Princes of Liechtenstein purchased the Rhine plains and towering mountains, over which they have ruled ever since. All the vines were cultivated by monks until 150 years ago, when the vineyards were secularized. Today, some 800 hectoliters (20,000 U.S. gallons, 17,-000 imp.) are made annually.

Vaduzer is a light wine, bordering on a rosé. It is made exclusively from the Blauburgunder grape, although in earlier times white Elbling was the dominating grape there. Riesling-Sylvaner was tried too; but both varieties were abandoned. The small growers have a cooperative, and a single domain, Bockwingert, comprises about half the vineyard area in Vaduz. The most interesting estate is the Abtwingert, the vineyard of the Rotes Haus.

In 1525, this Red House already belonged to the Benedictines of the order of Saint Johann in Toggenberg. It was probably a hundred or more years old then. A visit to the massive Gothic wine press still in operation in the cellars shows why the Rotes Haus is classed second to the castle of the Prince of Liechtenstein among the sights of the principality. In the middle of the nineteenth century, Alois Rheinberger—the Rheinbergers are the present owners—took the methods of Vaduzer wine-making to Illinois and planted the well-known vineyard of Masberg Mansion at Nauvoo.

Valdadige (Etschtaler) (D.O.C.)

Fair white and red wines grown on the banks of the River Adige, from Merano to Verona in the Veneto.

See Trentino-Alto Adige.

Valais

The dramatic alpine vineyard region on either narrow bank of the upper Rhône River east of Geneva in Switzerland (*q.v.*).

Valderorras

A small hillside district, with a less humid microclimate than in the rest of Galicia in northwestern Spain, has become known as the Denominación de Origen Valdeorras. Its 5,000 hectares (12,500 acres) produce white and red wine of rather average quality. The Godello grape makes the whites and the reds which come from Mencia and the Alicante.

Valdepeñas (Denominación de Origen)

Favorite wine of the cafés of Madrid, grown in vineyards south of the capital in La Mancha. Strong red wines and dry white wines. Until the great popularity of Rioja, this was the best-known Spanish nonfortified wine. Some 30,000 hectares (75,000 acres) produce these heavy, rather common and neutral wines.

See Spain.

Valencia

Dark red wines called Clariano are made from the Monastrell variety in the southern part of this Denominación de Origen zone.

White heavy wines with a tendency to oxidation are produced in and around Valentino. They are drunk as cheap aperitifs or as dessert wines. The grape varieties are the Pedro Ximénez and the Muscatel.

Some ordinary white wines come from Cheste.

Valgella (D.O.C.)

Red wines of Valtellina, Italy, made from the Nebbiolo grape.

See Lombardy.

Valle d'Aosta

Most vineyards grow on terraces in Italy's smallest wine region. The two best-known wines are Donnaz and Enfer d'Arvier, from the terraced mountainsides of the volcano.

See page 387.

Valpantena

A wine, which is part of Valpolicella. The largest owner is the firm of Bertani.
See Veneto.

Valpolicella (D.O.C.)

The best wines of Veneto, in Italy—ruby red, fragrant and fruity, with a delicate bouquet and a rich texture.
See Veneto.

Valtellina (D.O.C.)

Name of a series of red Italian wines made from Nebbiolo grapes.
See Lombardy.

Van der Hum

A South African liqueur of which the principal ingredient is the peel of the *naartjie*, a type of South African orange. The subsidiary ingredients vary according to the producer, with each one having his own closely guarded formula. The liqueur is tawny in color and has a strong taste of orange. Van der Hum means "what's his name"; a variation, known as Brandy-Hum, is made by diluting Van der Hum to half quantity with brandy, thus reducing the sweetness.
See South Africa.

Varietal wine

American term for wine made wholly or predominantly from the grape variety named on the label, such as California Pinot Noir, New York State Riesling, etc. The rule was established in an attempt to break away from meaningless generic names such as Californian burgundy and is now followed by most of the best wine-makers. Originally, a varietal wine had to be legally at least 51% from the grape variety named, but the minimum content requirement is now 75%. The day when American producers cease entirely to use misappropriated and misapplied European place-names and adopt varietal names for wines that are strictly American will be a bright day indeed for American wine-lovers.

Vat

A container for wine, varying in size; the name is derived from the Dutch word for 100 liters (1 hectoliter—or 26.4 U.S. gallons, 22 imp.). It is the usual translation for the French *cuve*—a vessel of oak, stainless steel, or cement (sometimes lined with glass) in which wines are fermented and blended.

V.D.P.V. (Verband Deutscher Prädikatswein-Versteigerer)

The most important association of wine-growers in Germany. In German, a *Versteigerer* is an auctioneer, and the name of the organization reflects that time when many of the important individual estates held auctions for the sales of the wines. Today only a small number of the vineyard owners of Germany belong, but many of the very best producers do. As a group, their purpose is to maintain the quality of and promote the cause of fine German wines. Quite often the label of the member estate will include the emblem of the association: a black eagle with grapes on its breast surrounded by the letters V.D.P.V. Until the passage of the 1971 West German Wine Law, the name was Verband Deutscher Naturwein-Versteigerer, but the new title was adopted to conform to the ruling abolishing the use of the word *Natur* with regard to wine.
See Germany.

V.D.Q.S.

These letters stand for Vins Délimités de Qualité Supérieure, or delimited wines of superior quality. They are found on wines from certain sections of France—wines which are considered good enough to be quality-controlled, but not of the caliber of the wines of Appellation d'Origine Contrôlée. In effect, they make up a secondary classification of the better wines of France.

Although the classification only dates back to 1949, it includes a number of wines, some of them extremely good. Many of the better—but none of the best—wines of France are included, and previously all the best wines of Algeria. In the decrees covering the various V.D.Q.S. wines, the growing area, the vines permitted, and the minimum limits of alcohol are always stipulated. In most cases, the wines must be tasted by a committee of experts set up for that purpose and only after approval has been given have they the right to the name. V.D.Q.S. wines carry these initials as well as the name of the place of origin on their labels, and in the case of estate-bottled wines, the name of the grower will also be included. They are likely to be good buys, if they can be found, and provided most of the price goes for the wine and not for duties and transportation, for they are sound and do not carry the high price that may go with a greater reputation.

V.D.Q.S. Place-Name Wines

Cabardès
Chateaumeillant
Cheverny
Côte Roannaise
Coteaux d'Ancenis (followed by the name of grape variety)
Coteaux de Pierrevert
Coteaux du Giennois
Coteaux du Giennois–Cosnes-sur-Loire
Coteaux Varois
Coteaux du Vendomois
Côtes d'Auvergne
Côtes d'Auvergne (followed by the place-name)
Côtes de Gien
Côtes de Gien-Cosnes-sur-Loire
Côtes de la Malepère
Côtes de Saint-Mont
Côtes de Toul
Côtes du Brulhois
Côtes du Cabardès et de l'Orbiel
Côtes du Forez
Côtes du Luberon
Côtes du Marmandais
Côtes du Vivarais
Côtes du Vivarais (followed by the vintage-name)
Fiefs Vendéens
Gros Plant *or* Gros Plant du Pays Nantais

Haut Comtat
Mousseux du Bugey
Pétillant du Bugey
Roussette du Bugey
Roussette du Bugey (followed by the vintage-name)
Saint-Pourçain
Sauvignon de Saint-Bris
Tursan
Valençay
Vin du Bugey
Vin du Bugey mousseux
Vin du Bugey pétillant
Vin du Bugey (followed by the vintage-name)
Vin du Bugey Cerdon mousseux
Vin du Bugey Cerdon pétillant
Vins d'Entraygues et du Fel
Vins d'Estaing
Vins de Lavilledieu
Vins de Marcillac
Vins de Moselle
Vins de l'Orléanais
Vins du Haut-Poitou
Vins du Thouarsais

Some V.D.Q.S. wines are treated in this book either under their own proper names or under regional headings.

Vega Sicilia

This bodega produces red wines which are the pride of Spain; 100 hectares (250 acres) of Cabernet Sauvignon, Malbec, Tinto Aragones, and Garnacha are planted on a plateau at an altitude of some 800 metres. The bodega is just outside the small town of Valbuena de Duero in the province of Valladolid. These excellent full-bodied red wines, after having spent sometimes more than ten years in barrel, are rationed in tiny quantities to a small list of customers at very high prices.

Velvety

Used of a wine which, through ageing, has reached sufficient maturity to conserve body, yet produces a sensation of great smoothness.

Vendange

French term for the grape harvesting; also the vintage season.

Venencia

In Spain, especially Jerez de la Frontera, a bullet-shaped silver cup on a pliable whalebone handle usually about two and a half feet long. This is used for taking samples from Sherry casks.

Veneto (Venetia)

Red and white wines.
District: Northeast Italy.

The wines of Veneto are about the most charming and consistently good in Italy, although rarely if ever could one of them be classified as great. The region around Venice and Verona produces some 8.5 million hectoliters (225 million U.S. gallons, 187 million imp.) per year and is considered third in importance among Italian wine districts. Soave is dry, white, and—as the name implies—distinctly suave, while Valpolicella, Valpantena, and Bardolino perform graceful variations on a theme, the dominant notes of which are dry, red, and light. The typically Italian pungency and harshness seem to be absent from these wines, which come from the vineyards around Verona, city of Romeo and Juliet. Wander round Verona's Roman amphitheater or listen to the opera on a summer evening; amble through the ancient streets or into one of the medieval courtyards—and the Veronese wines, pleasant to drink anywhere, here seem perfectly delicious. It is true that wines always taste best in their own district; but these, fortunately, are able to travel—and seem to carry a bit of Verona with them.

THE BEST WINES OF VENETO

Valpolicella, Recioto della Valpolicella and Amarone (all D.O.C.)

These are unquestionably the best. They are ruby-red, of medium alcoholic content (perhaps 12% to

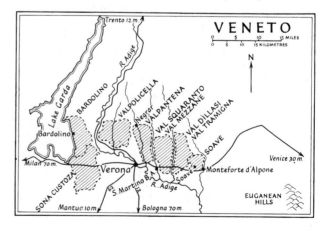

13%), have a delicate bouquet and a rich, mouth-filling texture. Every now and then a bottle will emerge with a slight trace of residual sugar, which will start working in the bottle, giving the wine a *frizzante* or prickling taste that is by no means unpleasant. As is the case with other Veronese wines, the best bottles can be expected to come from the smaller houses—because of the unfortunate predilection many firms have for labeling wines according to demand rather than supply.

The principal grapevines cultivated in the vineyards of the 19 communes producing Valpolicella are Corvina, Rondinella, Rossignola, Negrara, Molinara, Corvinon and Pelara.

Valpantena, the name of a valley within the district, is a good example of the local wine, and its labels will carry the valley name following the name *Valpolicella.* Recioto della Valpolicella (D.O.C.) is produced in five communes from partly dried, selected grapes—the result is a particularly good sort of Veneto wine which should be consumed within two years. The name derives from the word *recia*, which means "ear" in the local dialect, and it is from the "ear" or uppermost part of the grape bunch that the ripest fruit is selected to make this wine. Recioto may be dry, semi-sweet, or sweet and sparkling. The dry wine is called Amarone (D.O.C.).

Bardolino (D.O.C.)

This is grown in the place of that name, and in the neighboring wine territories on the southeastern shore of Lake Garda: a dry wine, clear ruby-red in color. When very young, it has a beguiling charm, which it tends to lose after a short time. The "new look" in Italian viniculture is very much in evidence here, for Bardolino is now being fermented a considerably shorter time than is traditional, resulting in a wine which is lighter, fresher, cleaner, and distinctly more pleasant than it would otherwise be, with an alcoholic content of 10.5% to 13%. It is made from a variety of grapes, with Corvina, Molinara, Rondinella, and Negrara in the lead.

Bianco di Custoza (D.O.C.)

This white, dry wine borders on Lake Garda.

Soave, Recioto di Soave and Soave Classico (all D.O.C.)

Like its red counterparts, Soave is not great but usually good. It has, at its best, a light straw color with greenish highlights, and a dry, very slightly acid taste. It comes from the main variety of Garganega grapevine. The 6,000 hectares (15,000 acres), of which 2,000 hectares (5,000 acres) are Soave Classico, are found around the towns of Soave and Monteforte d'Alpone, about 25 kilometers (15 miles) east of Verona. Care should be taken when buying the wine because its increasing popularity has not been accom-

panied by a comparable increase in output. A Recioto di Soave Spumante (sparkling) is very occasionally seen, but it has little to offer and its export future is dubious.

Prosecco di Conegliano–Valdobbiadene (D.O.C.)

A pleasant wine made from Prosecco grapes in the province of Treviso, some 48 kilometers (30 miles) due north of Venice, it is known either as Prosecco di Conegliano or Prosecco di Valdobbiadene. By any name the wine is delicately dry and very fruity, and sparkling and semi-sparkling types are also made.

MINOR WINES OF VENETO

Colli Euganei (D.O.C.)

Small red and white wines from the Euganean Hills in the province of Padua, 45 kilometers (28 miles) southeast of Soave.

Breganze (D.O.C.)

Red and white wines made 25 km from Vicenza. White Breganze is of Tocai, Pinot, and Vespaido grapes; the red, of Merlot and Cabernet. When only one grape variety is used, the D.O.C. name may be followed by the name of that variety; thus, Breganze Cabernet, etc.

Cabernet di Lison-Pramaggiore (D.O.C.)

Not far from Venice, this full-bodied red table wine is made from Cabernet Blanc and some Merlot grapes. It is dry, and with a bouquet almost recalling the scent of sweet grass. When aged for more than three years, the wine may be called Riserva.

Gambellara and Recioto di Gambellara Spumante (D.O.C.)

Gambellara is a light, dry white wine resembling Soave, although Soave is higher in alcohol. Garganega and some Trebbiano grapes go into the wine, which is made not far east of the town of Soave. Recioto di Gambellara Spumante is a sweet sparkling wine made in the same manner as the other similar wines of the region.

Merlot di Lison-Pramaggiore (D.O.C.)

A rather dry but full red table wine made near Venice from Merlot and Cabernet grapes.

Colli Berici (D.O.C.)

South of Vicenza, the Berici Hills produce light red and white wines. Red wines are made principally from

Venezuela

Cabernet Franc and Merlot; white wines from Tocai, Pinot Blanc, Garganega, and Sauvignon Blanc. Lesser wines from the same vines are made in the River Piave district (D.O.C.)

Venezuela

Venezuela has no vineyards. The country does produce spirits, but not many of them and only in small quantities.

The leading spirit is probably cocui (sometimes cocuy) from the agave cocui plant, the equivalent of the Mexican tequila/mescal spirits. It varies in proof from 80° to 100°, depending upon the still used and the purity desired, and it is drunk neat rather than complemented with lime and salt, as tequila is. The taste of cocui is a special one, somewhat similar to that of tequila but slightly harsher.

Rums—and some excellent ones are made—are popular, as are *aguardientes*; beer is on the increase and a few liqueurs are produced in the vicinity of Caracas. In addition to these, a beverage fermented from corn and called *chicha* is popular with the Indians. *Chicha* is coarse, acid, unusually high in alcohol and altogether far too rough to be widely appreciated. About 35,000 hectoliters (927,000 U.S. gallons, 770,000 imp.) of wine is imported annually.

Vente sur souches

French term for advance sale of wines made before the harvest, "on the vinestock." When the agreement is based on a certain degree of alcohol in the wine, the price can be fixed under a reserve for an increase or decrease of this price, according to whether the wine, when it is made, has an unexpectedly higher or lower degree of alcohol. Every contract for a *vente sur souches* must include a declaration that the consenting parties are aware of this rule (art. 320–332, Code du Vin). Any infraction of the law is subject to indirect taxation and to a fine (art. 1760, Code du Vin). Sometimes up to the sixties there have been advance sales of Classified Growths of Bordeaux. The quotations have then been given in *tonneaux*, or tons.

Véraison

French term for the maturing of the grape, when it changes from green to a reddish hue or to a translucent greenish-white.
See Chapter Eight, p. 31.

Verdelet

Not the most winter-hardy French-American hybrid, and possessed of a tendency to overproduce, Verdelet (Seibel 9110) must be thinned to produce its best fruit. Grown primarily in Canada's Niagara Peninsula and in the Finger Lakes district of New York

Verdelet makes sound, neutral, semi-dry and dessert wines. It is not yet widely planted.

Verdelho

A leading grape variety used in Portugal in making White Port and grown elsewhere—in Australia, for example.
Also the designation of a sweet, soft Madeira wine.

Verdicchio dei Castelli di Jesi (D.O.C.)

Light, dry or semi-sweet, white Italian wine.
See The Marches.

Verdot

The grape, also known as Petit Verdot, is used plentifully in the ordinary red wines of Bordeaux and sparingly in the better Médocs.

Vergennes

American grapevine whose fruit yields a pleasant, light, dry wine. Originally from Vermont, the vine is most widely cultivated in New York State.

Verjus

In French, grapes resulting from a late or second flowering of the vine. Such grapes do not mature and they retain a high acid content; they are used by the winemaker in very hot summers when the ripe grapes are deficient in acid.

Vermentino

This grape produces a good white wine in Liguria, the Italian Riviera, and is grown also in Corsica.

Vermentino Ligure

Thin, light, white Italian wines, sometimes slightly sparkling.
See Liguria.

Vermouth

Vermouth is not a wine. It is wine-based, but it undergoes so many additions and manipulations that it ceases to be recognizable as the product of the vine. It is, however, a popular and excellent aperitif and is indispensable in some cocktails—principally, of course, in the Dry Martini.

The name is thought to derive from either the German *Wermut* or the Anglo-Saxon *wermod*, both meaning "wormwood." Vermouth was certainly being made in Italy in the seventeenth century, and now it is produced all over the world; the two main types are "French" and "Italian." Vermouth is also made in California and many wine-producing countries.

Vermouth-making is a complicated but not a great art. It requires wine, sugar syrup or mistelle (unfermented grape juice fortified with brandy), alcohol, assorted herbs and plants, a pasteurizer, refrigerating vats, vast filters, and a table of ingredients, weights, and measures. When these essentials are collected, the process becomes a production-line affair.

The essential matter is the wine, usually white and fairly insipid. The transformations in taste will be such that the use of distinctive or fine wine would be a needless expense; and much Italian vermouth is based on the product of the southern Italian plains, that of France on the output of the Midi. Next in importance are the herbs and flavorings. These will include wormwood, hyssop, quinine, coriander, juniper, cloves, camomile, orange-peel, and sometimes even rose petals, but the exact ingredients and their proportions are jealously guarded by each manufacturer. The wine may be aged as much as two years or it may not be aged; but the first step will be the addition of sugar syrup, or mistelle. After this come alcohol and flavorings.

The flavoring herbs which give vermouth its character are macerated and steeped in alcohol. They are sometimes heated, so that the flavor may pass into the spirit in the same manner as in an infusion of tea. When the alcohol is sufficiently flavored, it is added to the sweetened wine and the whole mixture agitated to blend it together. Even in the most modern plants, wooden paddles are generally used for blending, so that any extraneous tastes may be kept out of the eventual vermouth. Tannin is added, then gelatin to clarify it; and, finally, the mixture is pasteurized. After pasteurization, it is refrigerated, falling sometimes as low as 14°F. (−10°C.) for a period of two weeks or so. During this time any tartrates in the wine form crystals and drop to the bottom of the vats, and from there the vermouth is put through a huge Seitz filter to remove any last impurities and tartrate particles that might remain. After this rigorous treatment, the vermouth is stored for a few months, bottled, and shipped. It can now be reasonably expected to survive in tropical heat or arctic cold; but manufacturers say that prolonged periods of excessive temperature will turn even this hardy creature, oxidizing it and giving it a musty and unpleasant taste. Such an occurrence, however, takes considerable heat.

French vermouths are generally held to be dry, Italian sweet. This is to some extent true, but both types are made in each country, although the very sweet are all Italian. The very dry French Chambéry is allowed the Appellation d'Origine. This is a special type, lighter than those from Sète in southern France. Chambéry is made from lighter wines, many coming from surrounding alpine hillsides—the herbs are not the same as those used by the manufacturers of the heavier vermouths. Another popular dry type is Noilly-Prat. The Italian Cinzano may be red or white, sweet or fairly dry—as also may Martini and Gancia.

Vernaccia

White-wine grape used in Italy for wines of The Marches, Sardinia, etc.

Vernaccia di Oristano (D.O.C)

One of the best-known wines of Sardinia (*q.v.*).

Verveine du Vélay

French liqueur made in Puy, central France, on a brandy base, flavored with herbs. There are two varieties, one yellow and one green; the green is the stronger.

Verzenay

Village near Reims producing a First-Growth Champagne.
See Champagne.

Verzy

Commune of the mountain of Reims district producing a First-Growth Champagne.
See Champagne.

Vevey Festival

The world's most important wine festival, given since the seventeenth century, in the town of Vevey, Switzerland, a development of the activities of the medieval Wine-Growers Guild. The official name is Fête des Vignerons. The fête has taken place in this century in 1905, 1927, and 1955. The 1955 festival, which took five years to prepare, was one of Europe's biggest tourist events that year. The performances, sometimes by as many as 3,300 participants including 950 children, celebrated the wine before daily audiences of 15,000 for two weeks.
See Switzerland.

Vidal

J. L. Vidal was an agronomist and grape hybridizer who worked in Charente, France.

Vidal Blanc

Vidal Blanc (Vidal 256), a descendant of the Italian Trebbiano grape (also known as St. Emilion or Ugni Blanc), is a winterhardy and widely planted French-American hybrid that ripens late. Fruit set can be spotty, but the grape produces a good-to-very-good-quality wine that, like Seyval Blanc, ranges from "German" style when made in stainless steel fermenters, to "French" style when aged in oak, although it then tends to be spicier. Found primarily in the eastern U.S., especially Michigan and New York.

La Vieille Cure

This French liqueur was made at Cenons near Bordeaux until 1986 according to a formula which included various brandies and fifty-two different herbs. It was golden in color and somewhat similar to Benedictine.

Vieux-Château-Certan

Bordeaux red wine.
District and Commune: Pomerol, France.

The heirs of the Theinpont brothers, Belgian wine merchants, make this subtle, velvety, full-bodied wine.
Vineyard area: 14 hectares (35 acres).
Average production: 75 *tonneaux* (7,000 cases).

Vigne

In France, an individual grapevine, but in winegrowers' parlance, a small parcel of a vineyard.

Château Vignelaure

Château Vignelaure, a domaine in southern France, is situated in Rians, some 30 kilometers from Aix-en-Provence, just outside the limits of the Côtes de Provence appellation. Consequently, it is entitled to the appellation contrôlée of Coteaux d'Aix-en-Provence even though it is superior to most red Côtes de Provence wines.

Georges Brunet is the former proprietor of Château La Lagune in the Haut Médoc which he sold in the 1960s to move to sunnier climes.

Château Vignelaure comprises 55 hectares planted with 60% Cabernet Sauvignon, 30% Syrah, and 10% Grenache which produce full-bodied wines. Unfortunately, despite the wines' slow maturing nature, the estate does not have much stock of the older vintages.

Vigneron

French term for a wine-maker and wine-grower; a skilled vineyard worker.

Vignoble

French term for vineyard.

Vignoles

A very promising French-American hybrid grape that is moderately early in development and a fairly small producer. Vignoles (Ravat 51), a Pinot Noir Cross, can make a dry, spicy, crisp white wine that is reminiscent of a mild Gewürztraminer, with higher acid. It is also used in sparkling blends and has produced some superb sweet late-harvest wines. In recent years several wines made from Vignoles have been accidentally labeled Ravat or Ravat Blanc in the eastern U.S.

Vila Nova de Gaia

A village lying opposite the city of Oporto, on the River Douro in northern Portugal. Most of the Port lodges, or warehouses, are in Vila Nova de Gaia and all Port wine which is legally Port is shipped from Oporto.
See Port.

Villafranca del Penedès (Catalonia)

Wines from the province of Barcelona. The best types are dry.
See Spain.

Villard Blanc

Villard Blanc (Seyve-Villard 12.375) is a white French-American hybrid grape that is vigorous, productive, and popular in France as well as in parts of the eastern U.S. Large clusters ripen late, producing a fruity wine with some dessert capability. It can also be grown in warmer climates such as the southwestern U.S. and Virginia.

Vin

French term for wine.

Vin blanc

French for white wine.

Vin bourru

French term for wine still on the original lees, or just drawn from the barrel. It is a term of praise when applied to such wines as Beaujolais, which are to be drunk young.

Vin de coule

French term for wine before the first pressing.

Vin de cuvée

Term used in Champagne for wine of first pressing.

Vin doux naturel

In France, sweet wine which has been fortified with brandy, added to stop fermentation and ensure both a high alcoholic content and a residue of unfermented sugar. The yeasts cease their activity when approximately 16% of alcohol is present. Most of the French *vins doux naturels* come from the Roussillon region on the Mediterranean near the Spanish border; the bulk of the rest, from Frontignan nearer the mouth of the Rhône. This may be red or white and contains from 14% to 17½% of alcohol by volume (although the great bulk is sold at 18%) and has little attraction for wine-drinkers where Sherry and Port—to which it bears some small resemblance—are available.

See also Vin de Liqueur; Sweet fortified wines of France.

Vin fin

A much-abused French term meaning "wine of quality." The inference is that the wine so called is superior. This is sometimes true—as in the case of Vins Fins de la Côte de Nuits—but is much too loosely used when it appears on a label with a commercial trade name.

Vin de garde

A great French wine with high alcoholic content and much tannin. Worth laying down until maturity has subdued all early excesses.

Vin du Glacier

Hard white wine of Valais, so named because after the harvest it is stored in high alpine villages.
See Switzerland.

Vin de goutte

French wine before the wine is pressed.

Vin gris

Pink wine frequently attributed to Alsace but really pertaining to nearby Lorraine.
See Lorraine; Alsace.

Vin d'honneur

French for wine of honor. Since, from earliest times, wine has been poured in libation to the gods and has graced the tables of kings, it was natural that men should serve it to those they wished to honor. Even today, *vins d'honneur* are offered on certain occasions. Historic wine ceremonies recalled by Mssrs Renouil and Traversay in their *Dictionnaire du vin* are:
Vin de bourgeoisie—offered in the Middle Ages to the mayor and any citizen who was made burgher of a town.
Vin de coucher (nuptial wine)—offered before they retired by newly married couples to the guests who had honored their wedding feast.
Vin de l'étrier (stirrup cup)—offered to a parting guest.
Vin de curé—offered to the priest after baptism.
Vin de veille (night-cap)—courtiers used to place this

beside the king's bed in case he should want a drink during the night.
Vin du clerc—offered by defendants to the clerk of the tribunal after a verdict in their favor.

Vin jaune

Yellow wine of the Jura region in France. This is made from late-picked grapes and kept for an unusually long time; when it is in the barrel it forms a white film, known in Sherry-making as *flor*.
See Jura.

Vin de liqueur

This French term has two meanings: (1) a very sweet wine, such as a rich Sauternes; (2) wine of approximately 18% of alcohol caused by the addition of brandy and added to Champagne prior to shipment.

Vin de marc

Wines made in France from a pressing of the residues with added water and sugar.

Vin mousseux

Sparkling wine.

Vin ordinaire

The French term for common wine.

Vin de paille

"Straw wine," made in the Jura region of France, and elsewhere. It derives its name from the time-honored process of drying the grapes on beds of straw before pressing, as well as from the color of the wine.
See Jura.

Vin de presse

In France, wine made from the pressing of the residues after the regular wine has been made. Taken by itself, it is very tannic and harsh.

Vin de primeur

In French, young wine. Often used as a synonym for Vin bourru (*q.v.*).

Vin de queue

French term for inferior wine made from the pressing of the stalks.

Vin rosé

French term for pink wine, made from red grapes by fermenting the juice on the skins (which give the

Vin rouge

color) a shorter time than is taken for red wine. Rosé should never be a mixture of red and white wines—although it sometimes is; it should be served quite cool.

Vin rouge

French for red wine.

Vin Santo (D.O.C. for certain areas in Tuscany)

See Tuscany.

Vin de tête

In Sauternes, wine from the first crushing; the best, Château d'Yquem, 1921, had a crème de tête.

Vinage

French term for adding alcohol to wine to raise its strength. In some districts, and for cheap wines, a moderate addition of alcohol improves the product; but the practice can only be condemned in the case of fine wines.

Vinasse

Residual liquor. In French, the residue of wines and fermented liquors after distillation, also a derogatory term for ordinary wine.

Vine

Woody-stemmed climbing plant of the *Ampelidaceae* family, which includes Virginia creeper and other varieties as well as the grape-producing *Vitis* (with its sub-genera Euvites and *Muscadiniae*), which alone is of importance to the wine-maker.
See Chapter Eight, p. 31.

Vine species

For classification of the species of genus *Vitis, see* Chapter Eight, p. 31.

Vinello (vinettino)

Forms of the diminutive applied to the Italian word for wine to express contempt for a wine's poorness or thinness. Therefore, a little, thin wine.

Vineyard

An area planted in grapevines.

Vinho liquoroso

Portuguese for fortified wine.

Vinho do rodo

Portuguese for sparkling wine.

Vinho trasfugado

Portuguese term for Madeira, after it has been racked, or drawn off its lees.

Vinhos Verdes

Light and crackling or slightly sparkling, these "green" and slightly acid wines from the north of Portugal, just below Spanish Galicia, are extremely popular in their homeland and make charming hot-weather drinks.
See Portugal.

Viniculture

The series of varied operations included in the making and maturing of wine.
Oenology usually refers to the more scientific aspects of wine production and study, while viniculture relates to the more practical considerations.

Vinifera

Species of genus *Vitis* (sub-genus Euvites) which embraces those native European vines responsible for the greatest wines of the world. *Vitis vinifera* has been transplanted to Australia, South Africa, the United States, and South America.
See Chapter Eight, p. 31.

Vinification

Wine-making.

Vino da arrosto

Italian term for wine of breed.

Vino de color

In Spain, concentrated grape juice for coloring and sweetening wines.

Vino corriente

Spanish term for common wine.

Vino dulce

In Spain, very sweet wine for blending.

Vino espumoso

Spanish for sparkling wine.

Vino de pasto

Spanish for table wine. It is also a type of Sherry of no great distinction.

Vino Santo

Sweet white dessert wine made in Greece and in the Venetian region of Italy, where the golden wine comes from white grapes left to dry on the plant or on mats.

Vino tierno

Spanish term for heavy, sweet wine, used in blending.

Vino de la tierra

Spanish term for *vin de pays*, or ordinary wine of the region.

Vino tinto

Spanish term for red wine.

Vinosity

The essential quality or heart of the wine, a strong personality achieved by the accentuation of the best characteristics of the particular type. The term is often used to suggest high alcoholic content, an error arising from the failure to realize that alcohol is only one among the ingredients contributing to the character of the wine.

Vinprom

The State Enterprise for handling wine-growing and the wine trade in Bulgaria (*q.v.*).

Vins Délimités de Qualité Supérieure

See V.D.Q.S.

Vins de la Moselle

One of the two controlled place-names in the Lorraine area in France. The growths are classed Vins Délimités de Qualité Supérieure. Some are rosés, some white.
See also Luxembourg.

Vins Natures de la Champagne

See Champagne.

Vins de pays

A controlled class of wines made in various regions in France. In the hierarchy of French wines, they are technically a step above the least distinguished category, *vins de consommation courante*. But their level of quality is far below that of most V.D.Q.S. wines. *Vins de pays* are grown and made in specific lesser areas with certain grape variations and methods of production, which are specified by the Ministry of Agriculture and controlled by local growers associations. Typically, they will bear the name of the *pays* in which they were grown, as in Vins du Pays des Vals d'Agly in the Pyrénées Orientales, or Vins du Pays de Haut Rive, in the Aude. Their quality can vary from the pleasant-if-unexceptional to downright poor. The greatest producer of *vins de pays* in France is the Languedoc-Roussillon region, with over forty different areas.

These regional wines often have a low alcoholic content and so are sometimes not fit to travel; yet, drunk young and in the region where they are made, they may be very pleasant. For example, a restaurant in the Savoie recommends a Roussette d'Apremont, the *vin de pays*. This small white wine is taken by at least 70% of the customers—and they are quite right. The same may be said of many of the small wines of Anjou and the Jura (particularly around the region of Arbois), although the same wines would be disappointing if they had to undergo ageing and shipment.

Vins de Savoie or Roussette de Savoie (A.O.C.)

White, red, and sparkling wines.
District: Southeast France.

Wines made throughout the French foothills of the Alps in the Savoie, Haute-Savoie, Ain, and Isère departments. Nearly all of the 70,000 hectoliters (1,855,000 U.S. gallons, 1,540,000 imp.) produced each year is white wine made from the Altesse, Jacquère, or Roussette grapes. Mondeuse-Noir and Gamay, are used for the small quantity of red wine. Principal wines are Abymes, Apremont, Arbin, Ayse, Charpignat, Chautagne, Chignin, Chignin-Bergeron, Cruet and Montmelia.

Vintage and vintage charts

The vintage is the *vendange*, or gathering, of the grapes, and hence the wine from grapes of a specific harvest, the date of which will be shown on the label.

Champagne and Port have given the word *vintage* a special connotation, namely, "a very good year." The lesser years are blended to give a non-vintage wine, and it is only in the great years that a vintage is stated on the label. Bordeaux, Burgundies, Rhine wines—any wine from a good vineyard—will bear a vintage date on the label irrespective of whether the year was good or poor.

The vintages of different years are rated on a scale (usually from 1 to 20); the system is a useful one in countries of temperate climate where in spite of careful viticulture, variations in the weather may so affect the harvest that one year's yield may be excellent, the next only average, and the third quite poor. But these ratings, printed on charts and circulated among con-

Vintage port

sumers, may lead to a certain amount of confusion, because they do not tell enough.

Charts are based on the fact that wine-makers can judge, roughly, at the time of the harvest how good the wine is going to be. The statisticians then come along and summarize the consensus of opinion into ratings. But these estimates of its quality apply to the wine at its peak, which may be in five years' time, or in fifteen. The charts stated that 1961, for instance, was a great year; but not that a slow-maturing red wine, such as Bordeaux, would not reach perfection for some twenty years because an excess of tannin makes it slow to mature, and so a great deal of this wine was drunk prematurely.

For the same reason, of two young wines, the pleasanter to drink now may very well be the one which has received the lower vintage mark, simply because it is not going to last so long, and will therefore have developed better in its first two or three years than the wine of the greater vintage.

Moreover, there are endless exceptions to vintage ratings. Several poor red wines were made in Burgundy in the great year of 1976, but the chart cannot tell you this. On the other hand, there is always a vineyard which comes up with something magnificent, even in the worst years. These wines will be good bargains, because they cannot be so highly priced as an equal wine of a "good" year. On the whole, red wines from leading vineyards in the finest districts seldom fall below a certain standard, even in a poor summer.

In countries where the summers are consistently long and hot, the weather will not seriously affect the differences in quality among wines, and vintage ratings are, therefore, of little importance.

Vintage port

Along the River Douro in Portugal, where the only true Port wine is made, not every year is considered worthy of being called a vintage year. The last quarter of a century has seen some half a dozen great vintages, but a vintage may be declared by an individual Port wine-maker for his wine, and so the practice is not uniform. Vintage Port, selected from the best years, is always the wine of a single year, which will be indicated. Any Vintage Port should be aged in bottle for at least a decade; it goes on improving in glass for many, many years.

See Port.

Vintage wines

Of a particular vintage year, which is marked on the label.

Virginia

Wine-producing region in the United States. The vineyards, few but good, are situated principally in

Albemarle and Clarke counties, with Charlottesville at the center.

See United States.

Viticulteur

A French vine-grower, usually one with his own vineyard. A *vigneron* is almost the same, but more often is the name of a sharecropper.

Viticultural ecology

The study of the relationship of the vine and the climate and soil in which it grows, and the quality of wine which its fruit produces.

Viticulture

The science and art of grape-growing.

Vitis vinifera

The species of vine from which most of the wine in the world is made. For a fuller account of this and other types of vine *(Vitis)*—for example, *Vitis labrusca, Vitis riparia, Vitis coignetiae*—see Chapter Eight, p. 31.

Vitiviniculture

The study and practice which encompasses all grape-growing and wine-making activities.

Vodka

Vodka, once the traditional Russian drink, taken neat and tossed off quickly before, during, and after meals, is now an international drink consumed and indeed made over most of the Western world. (It still shows at its best with caviar.) The neutrality of the spirit has made it popular; many people who like to drink do not really care for the taste of alcohol. The lack of smell is another virtue. The fashion for vodka-drinking in the West started in California and soon spread over America and then Europe. Some people like to dilute it with mineral water or tomato juice, others to take neat vodka and follow it with a chaser. And it is, of course, a remarkably good base for Martinis and other cocktails.

Vodka, which was native to Poland, Latvia, Lithuania, and Estonia, as well as Russia, was popularly assumed to be a spirit made from potatoes. Like gin, it is distilled from grain at very high proof, rectified into a spirit with neither the taste nor the aroma of the materials used. It remains unflavored—although some individual vodkas are infused with herbs and aged for more than three years—sometimes in barrels that have contained wine.

Different vodkas range from about 65° proof to more powerful types at 98° proof.

Volatile acidity

In wine, the state caused by the presence of acetic acid (the acid of vinegar), which is produced by aerobic spoilage bacteria and is the principal cause of vinegary wine. Such acidity commonly occurs when first-year ageing casks are left incompletely filled; as the wine evaporates, the casks must be "topped up" every two weeks or so.

See Chapter Nine.

Volnay (Appellation Contrôlée)

Burgundy red wine.
District: Côte de Beaune, France.

The Volnays are rather delicate wines for Burgundy, quick to mature, with less depth of color than the Beaunes and Pommards and greater elegance. They are suave, rounded, well balanced, with a particularly fine bouquet. The commune lies south of Pomerol, on rather high ground. Some of the vineyards are more exposed than others, and as a measure against the disasters of frost and hail, they are much parceled out. The total area is about 213 hectares (527 acres); the average yield, approximately 8,000 hectoliters (212,000 U.S. gallons, 176,000 imp.).

In the Middle Ages, Volnay had a light, *oeil de perdrix* color which was much relished and the wine was popular. The dukes of Burgundy made presents of Beaune and Volnay to kings and to the papal court at Avignon. Louis XI, who kept his prisoners in cages, defeated the Burgundian dukes, annexed their land, and got possession also of the vines of which they were so proud. Volnay seems to have been a special favorite; the entire harvest of 1477 was taken, by his orders, to his château at Plessis-les-Tours.

Volnay is only a jump away from Meursault, and the white wines must be sold as Meursault. There is an old jingle which runs:

> *Entre Pommard et Meursault*
> *C'est toujours Volnay le plus haut.*

Topographically, this is indisputable. Set between two hills, the village dominates its vineyards and is itself dominated by the church—most of the vineyard paths lead down, the village streets climb up, to the church. Caillerets, the highest of the vineyards, close to the cemetery, is also the best. Up the slopes, you can see across the great Burgundian valley, sometimes as far as the snow-capped Jura peaks. Just south of Volnay, off to the right and up a lane, is the small village of Monthélie. Its wines, lesser and less known than the Volnays, are also less expensive.

Another local jingle was:

> *Qui n'a pas de vignes en Caillerets*
> *Ne sait ce que vaut le Vollenay.*

which means that no *vigneron* can really know what Volnay means unless he owns a strip of vines in Caillerets, *les cailles du roi*. The Volnay vineyards are as follows:

FIRST GREAT GROWTHS (*Premiers Grands Crus*)

Vineyard	Hectares	Acres
Les Caillerets	2.7	6.7
Les Caillerets-dessus	14.7	36.6
Clos des Ducs	2.4	6
Les Brouillards	6.5	16.2
Les Mitans	4	9.9
L'Ormeau	4.3	10.7
Les Angles	3.5	8.7
Les Pointes d'Angles	1.5	3.7
Les Fremiets	6.5	16.2
Les Champans	11.3	28.2
Les Chevrets	6	14.9
Le Clos des Chênes	16.9	42.1
La Barre	2	4.9
La Bousse d'Or	1.9	4.8

Vöslau

One of the regions near Baden producing red wines and Roten Sekt (red sparkling wine).

See Austria.

Vosne-Romanée (Appellation Contrôlée)

Burgundy red wine.
District: Côte de Nuits, France.

No vineyards have ever been praised so highly and so consistently as the best of Vosne-Romanée. In good years the wines are unquestionably magnificent and are among the most expensive in the world.

The five greatest vineyards of Vosne are minuscule, even by Burgundian standards. Their combined area is barely 26 hectares (65 acres) and the annual output is only slightly more than 525 hectoliters (14,000 U.S. gallons, 11,600 imp.), the equivalent of less than 6,000 cases. Demand for the largest of them—Romanée Saint-Vivant—is so insistent that the grower could never hope to approach it, and wines from La Romanée and Romanée-Conti are so rare that drinking one of them must always be an event.

Romanée-Conti is the great wine of the commune in spite of the small size of the vineyard—just 1.8 hectares (4.5 acres). The pre-war vintages—hardly more than a memory now—were the most magnificent, for replanting and the large number of young vines in the vineyard have, since the fifties, brought the quality slightly down from its former height. While the Romanée-Conti is the "central jewel in the necklace of Burgundian wines," La Romané, La Tâche, Richebourg, and Romanée Saint-Vivant are worthy companions for it. *(See under separate headings.)*

The great unifying factor in the wines of Vosne is their velvety softness and finesse. All of the wines of the commune share these characteristics, and in addition they are light and delicate and beautifully balanced; they are feminine wines, not assertive, and they age most gracefully. This is true not only of the greatest vineyards, but also of those classed just slightly below—such as Grande Rue, Gaudichots, Beaumonts, and Malconsorts, all of which produce wonderful wines.

The vineyards which produce the wines that go to market with the words Vosne-Romanée on the label are mostly in that commune, but some are in adjoining Flagey-Échezeaux. Wines from Flagey's two greatest vineyards—Grands-Échezeaux and Échezeaux—may carry their own names or may be declassed into First Growth of Vosne-Romanée (Vosne-Romanée *Premier Cru*). Since the names are not well known and rather difficult for the non-Gallic tongue to pronounce, growers often use the lesser name for these wines despite the general rule that the more specific the name the better the wine and therefore the higher the price. These two vineyards alone increase the Vosne-Romanée vineyard area by 72 hectares (180 acres) and there are 51 more acres in Flagey, producing wines that carry the name Vosne-Romanée, geography to the contrary. Vineyard acreage actually within Vosne amounts to about 172 hectares (425 acres), and the combined amount of wine made in an average year for quantity amounts to 6,500 hectoliters (172,500 U.S. gallons, 143,000 imp.). The classified vineyards of Vosne are:

In Vosne-Romanée

GREAT GROWTHS (*Grands Crus*)

Vineyard	Hectares	Acres
La Romanée-Conti	1.8	4.5
La Tâche	6	14.9
Les Richebourg	8	19.8
La Romanée	.83	2
La Romanée Saint-Vivant	8.5	21.3

FIRST GROWTHS (*Premiers Crus*)

Vineyard	Hectares	Acres
Les Gaudichots	5.8	14.3
Les Malconsorts	5.9	14.7
La Grande Rue	1.3	3.3
Les Beaux-Monts	2.4	6
Les Suchots	13.1	32.4
Clos des Réas	2.1	5.3
Aux Brûlées	3.8	9.6
Aux Petits-Monts	3.7	9.2
Aux Reignots	1.7	4.2
La Chaume	7.4	17.9

In Flagey-Échezeaux

GREAT GROWTHS (*Grands Crus*)

Vineyard	Hectares	Acres
Grands-Échezeaux	9.2	23
Échezeaux	30	75

Vougeot (Appellation Contrôlée)

Burgundy red and white wines.
District: Côte de Nuits, France.

Stand on the vineyard road on the bluff to the south of Chambolle-Musigny and you can see the land pitch sharply down in front of you, revealing on the plateau below the famous castle of the Clos de Vougeot (*q.v.*) surrounded by vineyards, the whole enclosed by a weather-beaten stone wall.

Excepting the Clos—the largest single vineyard in Burgundy and one of the most famous in the world—there is not a great deal to Vougeot. A tiny settlement nestles to one side of the low wall with its small arched entries, and outside this wall lie several vineyards whose wines are sold—if they conform to the proper minimum standards—as Vougeot, followed by the name of the vineyard.

Commune and Clos take their name from the River Vouge, a tiny stream that comes bubbling down the hill separating Vougeot from Chambolle-Musigny. The settlement is an ancient one and its vineyards have been in continuous cultivation for centuries, for when the Cistercians arrived at the beginning of the twelfth century these were among the lands given to them by local squires. The monks pieced together the vineyard which lies within the walls of the Clos, built the château, and made the name famous; and they left their stamp on the other vineyards of the area as well. No single group in history has done so much for the cause of fine wines as the Cistercians, and their crowning achievements are the Clos de Vougeot and Kloster Eberbach in the Rheingau. The vineyards outside the walls are Les Petits-Vougeots and Les Cras (both planted in Pinot Noir and producing red wines) and La Vigne-Blanche, or Clos Blanc de Vougeot (planted in Chardonnay and Pinot Blanc and giving white wine). The Clos Blanc is owned entirely by the Dijon shipping firm of Héritiers Guyot.

The Clos is, of course, the great wine of the commune. The others, however, are pleasant and often entrancing. Red Vougeot is generally full-bodied, filling the mouth, yet it always has an assertive bouquet all its own. The white is dry, sometimes quite fruity, and very much like one of the white wines from Aloxe-Corton on the Côte de Beaune, without having all the great breed of the finest from Aloxe.

Within the walls of the Clos are 50 hectares (124 acres) of vines, but outside are only some 12 hectares (30 acres). From these twelve, approximately 360 hectoliters, (10,000 U.S. gallons, 8,000 imp.) of red wine and 45 hectoliters (1,200 U.S. gallons, 1,000 imp.) of white are produced in an average year for quantity.

GREAT GROWTH (*Grand Cru*)

Vineyard	Hectares	Acres
Clos de Vougeot	50	124

FIRST GROWTHS (*Premiers Crus*)

Vineyard	Hectares	Acres
Clos Blanc de Vougeot	1.8	4.6
Les Petits-Vougeots	5.8	14.4
Les Cras	4.2	10.6

Clos de Vougeot (Appellation Contrôlée)

Burgundy red wine.
District: Côte de Nuits, France.
Commune: Vougeot.
Official Classification: Great Growth (Grand Cru).

The 50 hectares (124 acres) of the Clos de Vougeot (or Clos Vougeot) are so famous that the vineyard is practically a national asset of France; it was a tradition for passing regiments of the French army to salute the vines. Started in the twelfth century by Cistercian monks, on the slopes above their monastery, it remained in the hands of the clergy until the French Revolution, when the state confiscated church property. The monks did not plant the entire vineyard—some of it they accepted as a gift from early Burgundians with names such as Hugues le Blanc, Eudes-le-Vert, and Wallo Gile—but they consolidated the holding and built a wall around it.

In the sixteenth century the vineyard was so big that it was felt that a château and a house for the wine-press should be added to the buildings inside the wall. The drawing-up of the plans for this building was entrusted to a young and zealous monk, and he went to work with fervor but made the mistake of signing the completed blueprint with his own name. The abbot informed him that he had committed the deadly sin of pride and ordered that the plans should be given to other monks to complete. These new hands botched them hopelessly. Legend has it that the original architect, following the strict code of the Middle Ages, repented his sin and died of chagrin, and the Clos was built complete with all its structural faults as a monument to his sinful pride and fall from grace.

Since its foundation, the building has undergone repeated additions and renovations. The last—although this is almost a continuous process—was at the hands of the Confrérie des Chevaliers du Tastevin de Bourgogne, the society which makes sure that the rest of the world does not forget the wines of Burgundy. The members of the order, who are mostly shippers, growers, and visiting dignitaries interested in wines, meet every month or so in the great dining room of the château, and the halls which once resounded with the plainsong of the Church now reverberate with the noise and tumult of the Chevaliers singing the songs—and the praises—of Burgundy. The great dining hall can seat five hundred people, and the towering stone pillars are decorated with coats of arms, with baskets which once were used to carry in the grapes, and with the dates of the most famous vintage years, dating back to 1108.

Since the vineyard was confiscated, after the Revolution, it has seldom been under one ownership—the last proprietor lived in the nineteenth century, and his grave lies beside the terraced drive leading up to the forbidding gates of the château. Since his death the ownership has become more and more diverse and today there are about a hundred people with holdings within the walls.

Each one of the owners has his own plot. His vines will be of varying ages, and age has a direct effect on quality. The vines will be tended as each owner desires, the grapes will be picked when he feels that it is time, and wine-making procedures will vary according to his talent, conscience, and ability. Once made, the wines will be sold to different people, some in barrel to shippers and some bottled by the growers. Apart from all else, the vineyard itself is divided into three different sections and the wines will vary accordingly. As a result, drawing a common set of taste characteristics which are distinctly Clos de Vougeot is extremely difficult. If such a summation had to be made, it would be fair to say that in a good year a characteristic Clos de Vougeot is relatively full-bodied and with a big nose, which does not have all the austere majesty of a Chambertin nor the delicate grace of a Musigny or a Romanée-Saint-Vivant but inclines toward the latter. In any case, it is a mouth-filling wine, and the aftertastes are glorious and lingering.

Average yearly production for the whole 50 hectares (124 acres) is about 2,000 hectoliters (53,000 U.S. gallons, 44,000 imp.).

Of the three sections of the Clos set up by the early monks, that just behind the château, leading up to the wall, is traditionally the best part, with the middle section just behind it; and the bottom, close to the Route Nationale (national highway), distinctly inferior. The difference is partly in the pitch of the slope—very flat at the bottom, becoming steeper toward the château—and partly in the soil. Chalky clay, reddish-brown in color and rich in pebbles, makes up the top parts; and the bottom, more brown than red, has more humus and fewer pebbles. The land at the bottom is prone to hold moisture, and only in dry years do the vines produce comparably with those planted higher up.

At one time the vineyard was divided into plots, and despite the divided ownership many of these still retain their traditional identity. In the uppermost part are Musigny de Clos de Vougeot (closest to Chambolle-Musigny), Garenne, Plante Chamel, Plante Abbé, Montiottes Hautes, Chioures, Quartier de Marci Haut, Grand Maupertuis, and Petit Maupertuis. The middle is made up of Dix Journaux, Baudes Bas, and Baudes Saint-Martin; and the bottom, where the wine is generally inferior but commands nevertheless the same high price, has Montiottes Bas, Quatorze Journaux, and the bottom portions of Baudes Bas and Baudes Saint-Martin.

Some white wine is made in the little commune of Vougeot. This is not entitled to the name Clos de Vougeot but is sold as Clos Blanc de Vougeot.

Vouvray (Appellation Contrôlée)

Loire Valley dry white wine; still, semi-sparkling, or sparkling.
District: Touraine, France.

Vouvray is the famous wine of Touraine, the peaceful, parklike Loire Valley region in the heart of the château country. The vineyards climb the slopes, upstream and across the river from Tours, once the center of the courtly life of the Valois. The best vineyards are the ones above the cliffs, where the cellars have been dug out of the hillsides. There are only 700 growers in Vouvray, and the wine is produced by eight communes—Chançay, Noizay, Parçay-Meslay, Reugny, Rochecorbon, Sainte-Radegonde, Vernou, and Vouvray itself—and even in lesser years it is a light, delightful wine, excellent to drink with the local blood sausage and *rillettes* (little pots of pork *pâté*) on the terrace of the restaurant of Pont de Cisse, which looks out over the sloping vineyards.

These vineyards date from the eighth century, and they have been in continuous production, except for a few years at the end of the last century, when they were devastated by phylloxera. The vines were reconstituted with grafts from sturdy phylloxera-resistant American root-stocks, and the first harvest from the new plants was gathered about 1900. In 1936 it was laid down that the bearing portions of the vine must be Chenin Blanc or Arbois, and no other grapes are legally permitted.

The vines thrive in a clay and limestone *aubuis* soil on the chalky hills of the district, which also provide cellars in which the wines mature. The casks are stored in caves cut into the cliff—caves in which people also lead a troglodyte existence. Driving along the riverbank toward Vouvray, you can see houses which often are merely façades, with rooms dug back into the hillside. The high-vaulted, deep caverns make splendid cellars; in Marc Bredif's, there is a vast circular tasting room, with an old grindstone set in the middle as a table, and niches cut out of the chalky walls for the bottles.

The wines are characteristically soft and dry, but with a tendency toward sweetness which may become pronounced in a year when the sun has been strong or the picking late; the extra sunshine generates more grape sugar, which ferments into a higher alcoholic content. The sweet wines keep longer than their drier counterparts and usually travel better; but both types are found abroad. Although Vouvray rarely suffers a poor vintage, the wines are apt to have an acid finish when there has been insufficient sun. Once or twice in a decade, there is a great vintage year, and then the sweet, sunny wines are produced in abundance. Yet most Vouvrays, whether still, sparkling, or *pétillants*,

are dry, although the driest usually conserves a trace of sugar; unlike Sauternes, most of the dry Vouvrays produced from the Chenin grape are short-lived and their chief characteristic is a fruity freshness, although, in the few rich years, exceptions can be found. Some of the dry wines are made *mousseux* (sparkling) or *pétillants* (semi-sparkling or crackling); and to many drinkers *pétillant* is synonymous with Vouvray, although a much greater quantity of still table wine is produced.

Vouvray labels rarely carry vineyard names, because wines are generally blended by local firms and sold under their names, although the town or commune of origin is sometimes included. The better bottles, of course, carry the vintage year, the best of which are 1947, 1949, 1955, 1957, 1959, 1961, 1964, 1966, 1967, 1969, 1970, 1971, 1973, 1976, 1978, and 1985. Most of the older vintages, belonging to the occasional great years, are unobtainable today.

Vouvray sparkling wine must be bottle fermented and made by the champagne process (*see* Champagne). On an average, 60,000 hectoliters (1.59 million U.S. gallons, 1.32 million imp.) of wine are produced annually in this region.

Vrac

Wine sold *en vrac* includes the price of the wine bottle and cork, and may or may not include the capsule and label, but never the price of the case.

V.S.O.

Of Cognacs, this means Very Special Old.

V.S.O.P.

Very Special Old Pale. This designation used in Cognacs and Armagnacs indicates a brandy in type—but not in actual vintage in the sense of wines—about twelve years old. Market demand being greater in Cognacs, the V.S.O.P.s are sold more quickly, and are now on an average younger than V.S.O.P. Armagnacs. Age in brandy is fully discussed under Cognac (*q.v.*).

V.V.S.O.P.

Of Cognacs, Very Very Special Old Pale.

W

Wachau

Important wine zone in Lower Austria. Among the wines from this district are Kremser and Dürnsteiner. *See* Austria.

Wachenheim

Good wine town of the German Palatinate. The best vineyards are Gerümpel, Rechbächel, Goldbächel and Luginsland.
See Palatinate.

Wacholder

German beverage resembling gin.

Wachstum

In German, this means the same as Kreszenz *(q.v.)*.

Waldmeister

German name for woodruff, a wild herb which is essential in May wine—a popular wine punch made in Germany from a young wine base.

Walluf

Oldest wine-producing town in the Rheingau. *See* Rheingau; Germany.

Walporzheim

Region of the German Ahr Valley producing red wine.
See Ahr.

Wash

Whisky after fermentation and before distillation.

Washington

Wine-growing state in the U.S., one of the regions outside California where the *Vitis vinifera* flourishes.
See United States.

Wassail

English traditional custom of preparing a special punch for Christmas Eve. The name comes from the Anglo-Saxon *wes hál*, "be in good health."

Wawern

German white wine of the Saar region.
See Mosel-Saar-Ruwer.

Wedderburn

Pot-distilled and slow-fermented, this heaviest style of West Indian rum used to be identified with Jamaica, in contrast to the lighter rums of Puerto Rico and Cuba. Today the different centers make rums of both types. Jamaica is producing an increasing quantity of the lighter style in addition to Wedderburn and Plummer.
See Rum, West Indies; Rum, Jamaican.

Weeper

British term for leaker *(q.v.)*.

Wehlener Sonnenuhr

German wine experts are unanimous in naming Wehlener Sonnenuhr as the best Mosel wine, in spite of the fact that Bernkasteler Doctor is better known. No other Mosel has greater elegance or finesse than Sonnenuhr at its best. J. J. Prüm is the greatest growers name in this wine.
See Mosel-Saar-Ruwer.

Wein

German term for wine.

Weinbauer

German term for wine-grower.

Weinberg

German term for a hillside vineyard.

Weingut

German term for wine estate.

Weinviertel

Important valley and region north of the Danube.
See Austria.

Weissbier

German name for a sour beer popular in Berlin.

Weissburgunder

Weissburgunder

The chief grape variety cultivated in Styria, Austria.

Welschriesling

The chief grape variety cultivated in Burgenland, Austria.

Whiskey, American

American whiskey and the American people grew up together. The pioneer needed a drink as sturdy as himself, as rugged as the land he grappled with; something to cure snakebite, ward off disease, something to enjoy when he returned from the lonely plains and forests to the honkytonk saloons. Young whiskey, rough and "green," helped to sustain the men who conquered the young American continent and still holds undisputed sway over the tastes of their descendants. Sixteen bottles a year pour down the throat of the average American adult; altogether more than 60 million cases of whiskey, ranging from well-matured, often magnificent spirit to harsher "spirit blends," are consumed. Even "moonshine" and "bootleg" can be found. One out of every four drinks of hard liquor consumed in the United States is bootleg—the untamed spirit of the plains still prevails.

Whiskey was originally spelled whisky and was made in the mists and moors of Scotland. Probably at the same time it was whiskey among the peat bogs and lake country of Ireland. Today it is spelled whiskey in the United States and in Ireland. It is made in various parts of the world, but the largest single producer is the United States. American whiskeys differ from their European counterparts not only in taste and aroma but in general nature. They are not regional in character; Scotch whisky is inimitably Scotch, Irish whiskey the unique product of Ireland, but American whiskeys are classed by type, not origin. Bourbon, rye, or other styles can be made anywhere in America, and as long as they meet the government's specifications and pay their taxes, they have the government's blessing.

WHISKEY'S RISE TO POPULARITY

The Founding Fathers of the American republic were not whiskey-drinkers. The pilgrims of the North and the Virginia gentlemen of the South had tastes which turned toward beer and wine, rum and applejack. Whiskey had to await the settlement of Pennsylvania by Scotch-Irish immigrants and the great surge of Westering; and its original production owed much—as is the case with applejack—to poor roads and lack of communication. The settlers had brought over with them the secrets of distilling, and the land was fertile—perfect for grain, the base of whiskey. But transport was another problem. The roads that ex-

isted were poor, and in rainy seasons impassable, and if the farmer failed to get his crop to market he was ruined. But if he let the grain ferment, distilled it either at his own home in small pot stills or in those of a neighbor, the problem was solved. With the grain turned into whiskey, he had a less bulky cargo and a lighter one—a product that was easier to sell. In Pennsylvania and over in Kentucky, distilling was built up at the small farms into an important industry. The rum-makers of New York tried to have the spirit banned from the state, but in spite of their efforts whiskey won the competition and replaced rum as the common drink. The industry grew and prospered until a famous commotion forced it to move farther west.

In 1791 the government of President Washington was having financial difficulties. To raise money, it established an excise tax on whiskey—and the makers protested. The violence of the Whiskey Rebellion, or insurrection, has been greatly exaggerated, although the President felt called upon to send troops of the militia to ensure the maintaining of peace and order—and the proper collection of excise taxes. The farmers grumbled, declared the government was meddling in their private affairs, and moved west, to southern Indiana and Illinois, deeper into Kentucky and farther west in Pennsylvania. Hostile Indians were easier to face than friendly tax collectors. What the farmers looked for—and found—in these areas was pure, clear, distiller's water, with little organic material but rich in sulfate of lime and earthy carbonates; the kind of water found over veins of chalk or limestone. In the eastern United States, a deep base of limestone runs through western Pennsylvania, through Kentucky, Indiana, and southern Illinois, then ducks underground and reappears in Maryland. Today 80% of America's licensed distillers are to be found in these five states, where American distilling came of age.

From these early beginnings, whiskey became a business—and big business at that. In 1911 the nation produced over 100 million U.S. gallons (83 million imp.), a figure which was not to be exceeded until 1935. Between these dates fell the Dark Age of American spirits, when distilleries were closed and padlocked, and bootlegger and smuggler reigned. On November 16, 1920, the Volstead Act became the Eighteenth Amendment to the Constitution of the United States, thus proclaiming Prohibition; and not until December 5, 1933, was the politician ready to admit officially that the noble experiment was in reality a dismal failure. It took the distillers a little while to dust their equipment and get back into production, but by 1935 they were in full swing. Since Repeal—excepting the years of the Second World War—the industry has followed a strong albeit slightly erratic course. Peak production was in 1951, when the amount distilled was over 205 million U.S. gallons (170,600,000 imp.). Since then the industry has stabilized, producing approximately 100 million U.S. gallons (83 million imp.) annually and withdrawing about the same amount from the warehouses where the spirit ages.

WHISKEY-MAKING

Whiskey is made from grain. Any grain may be used, but in America the important ones are corn (maize) and rye with some millet, sorghum, and barley. The grain is "mashed" (diluted with water and cooked in huge pressure cookers) then left to ferment into "beer" or "distiller's beer." Sweet mash whiskey is made by adding selected yeasts to start the fermentation; sour mash by triggering it with some leftover "spent beer" or "draff"—the residue of a previous fermentation. Both "beer" and "draff" are then pumped into huge patent stills for distillation and rectification. By American law, all whiskey must be distilled at less than 190° proof U.S. (166° British), or about 95% alcohol. Above that figure, the spirit loses all the characteristics or congeners of the grain used and becomes merely neutral or "silent" spirit. Most whiskey is distilled from 140° to 160° proof, and some as low as 125°, notably some of the better Bourbons and ryes. After distillation, it is diluted and aged (the Bourbon in new, charred oak barrels), is diluted again—to between 80° and 100° proof—and bottled.

The origin of the charred barrel for ageing whiskey is unknown. According to one legend, it began in the West Indies in the making of rum. A fire in a warehouse charred some of the barrels which were used as they were, and the spirit was so improved by the experience that it became general practice to use charred barrels for rum, and later for whiskey. Another story attributes the origin to Kentucky: here the practice of steaming barrel staves to make them bend more easily was overdone and the wood charred; but it is hard to believe that a Kentuckian would be so careless in a matter so important as whiskey. Whatever the origin, the practice improves and softens the taste of the spirit and imparts body and color to it.

WHISKEY TYPES

American whiskey types are fairly rigidly defined by law. Some definitions have little interest for the consumer, since the types concerned are never on sale and serve merely as the base from which others are developed. The more important are:

Bourbon Whiskey

Originally the corn whiskey made in Bourbon County, Kentucky; now any whiskey distilled at no more than 160° proof, stemming from a mash of at least 51% corn, and aged for not less than two years in new charred oak barrels—most stays in the barrels for four years. It may be made by the sour mash process, and most bottles will be Straight Bourbon.

Corn Whiskey

Different from Bourbon, corn whiskey must be made from a mash of at least 80% corn, and may be aged in used or uncharred barrels.

Rye Whiskey

The mash must contain at least 51% rye, distillation must be no higher proof than 160°, and ageing accomplished in new charred oak barrels. Some Straight Rye and Blended Straight Rye are found, but not to the same extent as in Bourbon.

Other definitions include:

Whiskey

The most general name of all, never found alone on bottles. A label which carries any other term—Straight, Blended, Bourbon, etc.—must, of course, fulfill the requirements for whiskey as well as for the other terms it carries. According to the government, whiskey is "an alcoholic distillate from a fermented mash of grain distilled at less than 190° proof in such a manner that the distillate will have the taste, aroma, and characteristics generally attributed to whiskey, and withdrawn from the cistern room of the distillery at not more than 110° proof and not less than 80° proof and is further reduced before bottling to not less than 80° proof." Since no ageing period is specified, a bottle simply labeled whiskey would be reasonably raw and undrinkable.

Straight Whiskey

Whiskey distilled at no more than 160° proof and aged at least two years in new charred oak barrels. Straight whiskeys found on the market are usually Straight Bourbon or Straight Rye; they comprise about 27% of total whiskey sales.

See Whiskey, Light.

Blended Straight Whiskey

A blend of two or more straight whiskeys. This type makes up only about 1% of whiskey sales, but serves as a base for one of several blended whiskeys.

Blended Whiskey

A blend made of at least 20% 100°-proof straight whiskey, either with other whiskey or neutral spirit or both, bottled at no less than 80° proof. About 25% of all whiskeys sold are blended. The advantage is that they are lighter and less expensive than straights, and the leeway of 80% (which can be made up of any combination of whiskeys or plain spirit) allows the distiller to make a consistent standard whiskey, one that will not vary from year to year. It also permits the making of some very poor excuses for whiskey. One to which a large proportion of neutral spirit is added is known as a spirit blend and offers little to the civilized palate. The secret of a blended whiskey at any distillery is in the art of a master blender, who can distinguish what characteristics are needed to produce the replica of the firm's previous whiskey, determine the amounts of each component, and ensure that all the ingredients blend or "marry" properly. A small amount of Sherry—up to 2.5%—may be added as a blending agent.

Bottled-in-Bond Whiskey

The words do not necessarily guarantee a superior whiskey, but in fact this is what is usually indicated. The term is allowed only for straight whiskeys, at least four years old, bottled at 100° proof, the product of a single distillery by the same distiller and from a single season or year. The whiskey is aged in government-controlled warehouses (although control is fiscal, not qualitative) and taxes are paid on withdrawal.

Whiskey, Bourbon

Early in the colonial history of America, a Baptist minister, Elijah Craig, established a still in Georgetown, Kentucky, and began producing whiskey from a base of corn. The still is said to have been one of the first in Kentucky and customers in neighboring towns christened his product Bourbon County Whiskey, from the county of origin. It was considerably later that Kentucky became the unchallenged headquarters of the American whiskey industry.

Kentucky today has more than half of the nation's licensed distilleries and remains the major source for Bourbon, but the whiskey has long since jumped the county lines. By American regulation the name applied to any whiskey distilled from a fermented mash of grain containing at least 51% corn (the other grains vary, but a good balance is achieved with corn, rye, and malt) distilled at not more than 160° proof (in practice somewhere between 125° and 140° is more common) and aged in new charred oak barrels. Whiskey aged two years in wood and unblended is Straight Bourbon Whiskey; blended only with other Straight Bourbons, it is Blended Straight Bourbon, or Bourbon—A Blend of Straights.

Blended Bourbon is a mixture of Bourbon and other spirit, either whiskey or grain neutral spirit. A Straight Bourbon is usually a heavy, dry, mellow and full-bodied spirit, while a blended one will be lighter, from the addition of neutral spirit. In the United States, Straight Bourbon and Blended Straight Bourbon are the largest selling whiskeys, with some 80 million U.S. gallons (67 million imp.) or approximately 30 million cases sold annually, mostly in the South and West.

When the ground corn has been weighed and prepared for mashing, it is mixed with limestone water and steamed. The other ingredients (rye and barley malt) are then added. The yeast, sour wine in character, takes about five days to grow; this, with the mash, is pumped through coolers into the fermenters at a temperature of about 70°F. (21°C.) and left for the necessary period, while the yeast is being nourished by maltose sugars—and so the whiskey is made. Part of the mixture produced while the temperature rises is called new beer, and in distillation this has to be separated from the whiskey by heating—alcohol has a lower boiling point than new beer, therefore the whiskey forms vapors, which are condensed for further distillation. The new whiskey passes into a cistern where the proof is reduced, and is then poured into barrels to mature in a government bonded warehouse. Every six months characteristics are tested and graded. When it is ready for bottling, it is checked against standard samples of its brand, regauged for tax payment, and then bottled.

Whiskey, Corn

Whiskey distilled from a mash of fermented grain containing at least 80% corn. It is aged, if at all, in used containers, but usually gets little ageing, since the demand for it is in rural areas where fiery, young "corn likker" sets standards of taste. Corn whiskey, unaged, is raw, colorless, and—to say the least—unsubtle. It differs from Bourbon in many respects; legally, in that Bourbon must be from a mash 51% of which is corn, and must be aged in new, charred cooperage.

See also Whiskey, American.

Whiskey, Irish

"Of all wine, Irish wine is the best" was the ingenuous statement of Peter the Great of Russia; and it simply confirmed what generations of Irish had always believed. Just how many generations is a disputed point, for some maintain that the making of whiskey goes back at least a thousand years; others put it at a mere five hundred or so. Unquestionably, long before either whiskey or brandy was commercially renumerative, the Gael—both Irish and Scot—was distilling his fermented barley malt for his own pleasure. The Irish claim that brandy—a comparative newcomer—came about thanks to Irish missionaries taking the secret of distillation into France. How else, they ask, can you explain the similarities in the methods of distilling and the coincidence of *uisge beatha* and *eau-de-vie*, both of which mean "water of life?"

Until a century ago, Scotch whisky was for Scotsmen and Irish was the stuff which enjoyed popular favor. Then the Scots learned how to blend their brews and still keep them inimitably Scotch and made them known with brilliant salesmanship. After a period of doubt as to whether these blends could in fact be legally called whisky, these doubts were resolved by a Royal Commission and the world clamored for them. The world is still there, and the Irish, in spite of improving prospects and faithful adherents all over the globe, are having some trouble in finding an expansion of the markets for their austerely dry pot-still, unblended spirit of distinctive flavor. A further burden on the Irish distiller is high taxation, so that the Irishman cannot afford a fair share of his natural drink, and the moonshiner is attempting to provide a beverage made without the benefit of the excise officials. The popular name for this beverage is poteen—illegal whiskey named from the little—and easily dismantled—pot still in which it is made. Back in the bogs and around the lakes, poteen-making is popular and profitable, and the police rarely catch up with a bootlegger before he has packed up and moved on. If, in his hurry, he were to leave some behind him, the lucky finder would be saved more than one pound ($2.40) a bottle.

In spite of taxes, the Irishman loves his whiskey. Even horses, they say, hardly know how to leave the stuff alone. It happened some time ago, but they still talk about it in Dublin. Back in a small agricultural town a farmer, after a long night journey, stopped to water his horse at the local trough. The horse drank deep, and when his thirst was quenched, he moved away from the trough, staggered slightly and collapsed—dead drunk. The trough was found to be full of fine old whiskey, pure and ready to drink. Rejoicing was general until someone called the police who, in turn, called in the local excise people. Their inquiries showed that a nearby distillery was using convenient local waterpipes to drain its whiskey out of an excise-free warehouse for bottling, but someone had got it on the wrong circuit. The fine was large, and horses are staying sober in that part of Ireland now.

The excise officials are not always so fortunate. In spite of their efforts, poteen-making persists in certain areas, and in those parts, it is said that no self-respecting cattle or sheep dealer would consider doing business with a man who didn't offer him a small *deoch* to ward off early morning chill in the winter animal fairs. This may or may not have an effect upon the price, depending presumably upon the quality of poteen offered.

The making of quality Irish whiskey, such as Old Bushmills', follows much the same principles as the making of Scotch. (*For full details of the distilling process, see* Whisky, Scotch.) There are, however, some important differences in procedure. The popular and prestige Irish whiskeys are pure pot-still, containing no grain whiskeys as in the average Scotch. Also, they are three times distilled against twice in Scotland. Next, the mash is all of Irish grain—mostly barley, malted and unmalted, with a little wheat, oats, and rye. The malted barley is not, as it is in Scotland, dried directly over peat, so it lacks the "smoky" or "peaty" taste so common in Scotch. The wash, or whiskey before distil-

lation, is placed in great stills, much larger than the Scottish type, sometimes capable of holding up to 750 hectoliters (20,000 U.S. gallons, 16,600 imp.); and distilling is done to bring out the whiskey at about 50° over proof (roughly 86% alcohol by volume or 172° by American standards) instead of 20° over proof (70% or 140° American) preferred by the Scot. As in all pot-still spirits, the middle section of the distillate is the only part drawn off, and the "heads" and "tails" are held over to be redistilled. The Irish calculate that a mere 10% of the wash comes over as whiskey, and much of this will evaporate as the spirit ages.

An Irishman, writing of his native whiskey, says it takes seven days of a man's time to make whiskey and seven years of its own. The man may spend a greater or lesser amount of time making the preparations, but the whiskey will not really be worth the name unless it gets the full time, although by Irish law it is mature at five. Some is aged for ten years, and the very best for twelve or fifteen—always in the wood; for once out of the cask whiskey will age no more.

Scotch whisky is a blend of heavy malt whisky with grain whisky, which changes the character of both ingredients and produces what the world knows as Scotch. On the other hand, Irish whiskey blends, in the mash, the ingredients of malt and grain and, after pot-still distillation, the addition of grain whiskey or grain spirit has no syllogistic effect but merely weakens the flavor. Irish whiskey will have caramel added—to give it the proper color—and water, so that it will be within reasonable limits. Most is sold at 30° under proof in Britain and Ireland (80° proof American), but this is subject to minor variations. Furthermore, most of the whiskey is the traditional pot-still whiskey. Irishmen have been pushing Irish punch (Irish whiskey, lemon peel, sugar, and boiling water) and Irish coffee (Irish whiskey, coffee, and sugar with a layer of cream floating over the top) in promoting their product—and there are now several blended whiskeys on the market. While they have been criticized for not adapting their ideas earlier to the changing world taste, their critics are perhaps unaware of the true nature of the product. There can be no doubt that a characteristic pot-still Irish whiskey properly aged is a magnificent spirit.

Whiskey, Light

As Scotch and Canadian whiskies became more popular in the United States in the early 1970s, American distillers grew eager to produce a lighter whiskey, but one could not be made due to the U.S. federal laws controlling the alcoholic strength at which American-made whiskeys were distilled. The regulations stipulated that American whiskeys—such as Bourbon and rye—must be distilled at less than 160° proof, or below an alcoholic content of 80%. And the lower the percent of alcohol at production, the more whiskey flavor is retained by the spirits. To make "light whiskey," then, the American companies had to be able to distill their spirit at more than 160° proof. As the proof rises toward 200°, the whiskey becomes a grain alcohol spirit with no taste, like vodka.

Federal laws held another obstacle to the new liquor; that all American-made whiskeys (except corn) should be aged in new, charred oak barrels.

In 1967, the necessary changes in the laws were effected, and Light Whiskey was defined as a "grain distillate produced in the United States on or after January 26, 1968 at a proof of over 160° and less than 190° and stored in used charred or uncharred new oak barrels." Further, "if Light Whiskey is mixed with less than 20% of straight whiskey on a proof gallon basis, the mixture is designated Blended Light Whiskey or Light Whiskey—A Blend." The products have not been all that successful.

Whiskey, rye

Most American rye whiskey is made in the states of Pennsylvania and Maryland and is consumed generally in that region. Straight rye accounts for less than 23,000 hectoliters (500,000 U.S. gallons, 332,000 imp.) of whiskey per year, and many consumers switched from it during and after the war, when several well-known brands changed from making straight to making blended whiskey.

According to government regulations, rye must be distilled from a mash of fermented grain containing at least 51% rye, at a proof not to exceed 160°, and must be aged in new charred oak barrels. Straight Rye has at least two years' barrel-age and is unblended; Blended Straight Rye—as the name implies—is a blend of two or more Straight Ryes. Bottles labeled simply Blended Rye will have neutral spirit or sometimes other whiskeys added, resulting in a lighter, less distinctive, less expensive spirit. Ryes are generally heavier and slightly more austere than Bourbons, with some affinity to Irish whiskey, although they are made in patent instead of Irish-style pot stills.

Whisky, Canadian

The most distinctive characteristic of Canadian whisky, generally speaking, is its lightness of body. All Canadian whisky, Canadian rye whisky, must, by law, be produced from cereal grain only. The combination of grains used, their treatment, and the special and rigid control exercised by the distiller during the entire production process, set Canadian whisky apart from any other grain distillate.

Canadian whisky is well known outside its own country, and its good reputation has been built up over 130 years by one company, over 100 years by each of four others, and by several distillers not so long established who are yet maintaining the traditions of their elders.

This is how Canadian whisky is made:

The Grain

No amount of ageing will make good whisky out of an inferior batch of grain. Therefore, when the grain is moved to the distillery, none is accepted until it has been throroughly tested and approved by the distiller's chemist. When the grain, which consists of corn and rye and barley malt, has been milled into a fine meal or coarse flour, it is fed into a large cooker containing a fixed amount of water. This mash is heated with live steam in order to get the starch into solution, and when this has been accomplished barley malt is added to convert the starch into grain sugar. This step, saccharification, produces the grain sugar which is later fermented into alcohol by the introduction of yeast.

The Yeast

The culture and development of the yeast is a full-length story in itself. Each distillery carefully develops in test-tube bottles an isolated, pampered culture. One of the most critical points of control is the development of the living yeast cells. Since these *are* alive, sterile techniques and extreme caution are employed to prevent contamination.

Fermentation

The mash which has been saccharified is pumped from the cookers through large cooling coils into fermentation vats or tanks, which are then inoculated with the living yeast cells. The cells convert the sugar in the mash into alcohol and carbon dioxide, and this process takes about three to four days.

Distillation

When fermentation is complete the fermented mash is pumped into a continuous-operation, temperature-controlled, multiple-column patent still, usually cylindrical in shape and several stories high. This complex modern equipment allows many variations in the distilling procedure and consequently many variations in the final product. Thus the distiller is able to control the concentration of those components which contribute the flavor to the whisky.

Ageing

The next major step is the ageing of the whisky. Canadian distillers have found nothing that can do the job of mellowing and maturing their product better than nature itself. The unmatured whisky from the still is reduced to bareling strength and put into wood casks or barrels which may be charred on the inside, and this young whisky now faces a four-, six-, eight-, or twelve-year wait, in temperature-controlled warehouses. During the ageing process, a number of slow chemical reactions occur, the more volatile components of the whisky evaporate and the wood brings out a mellowing process. Certain wood sugars and tannin are extracted from the wood, and it is these extracts which give the whisky its golden coloring. When sufficiently aged, various batches of whisky are "married"—an art in itself. The resulting product is tasted and tested for quality, and when approved the whisky is filtered many times, bottled, labeled, and ready for the market.

Canadian whisky for consumption in Canada is bottled at 70° proof (Sikes) or 39.9% of absolute alcohol by volume. Canadian whisky bottled in Canada for export is usually bottled at the proof strength permitted or used in the country of destination. It is exported to 154 different countries and territories throughout the world.

The Canadian distiller is subject to more government supervision and control than any other manufacturer or privately-owned enterprise in the nation. Some two hundred excise officers are stationed in Canadian distilleries, and their control extends from the receipt of grain at the distillery all through the production process, bottling, and shipment, and terminates with the payment of excise duty.

There is no government interference, however, with the distilling techniques employed by individual distillers. Each has complete control over the quality and character of his products.

The label on a bottle of Canadian whisky, which states distilled, aged, blended, bottled under Canadian government supervision is no idle boast, it is a statement of fact.

Whisky, malt

This is Scotch whisky made in Scotland entirely from malted barley (with yeast and water), to be distinguished from grain whiskies in which some maize (corn), wheat, oats, or rye will be used.

Malt whisky is distilled in pot stills, grain whisky in patent stills. For this reason, grain whisky distilleries can turn out many times more than the 81 malt whisky distilleries in the same length of time.

There are four types of Scotch malt whisky: Highland, Islay, Lowland, and Campbeltown. The first is produced widely throughout the Highlands. Many distilleries are in the vicinity of the River Spey. This is considered the best. Islay, in the Inner Hebrides and the peninsula of Kintyre, is usually stronger-flavored. The comparatively few distilleries in the south making Lowland Malt Whisky produce it generally for blending. West Highland Malts are also often referred to as Islay. There are eight distilleries on the island of Islay producing Islay malts with the characteristic "smokiness" which has made them famous. They are Ardbeg, Bowmore, Bruichladdich, Bunnahabhain, Caol Ila, Lagavulin, Laphroaig, and Campbell. MacAllan Malt Whisky is matured exclusively in sherry casks. Of all the types of whisky, it is the single malts which are increasing fastest in sales.

See Whisky, Scotch.

Whisky, Scotch

Scotch whisky is imitated everywhere. At one time the Japanese made it in a town they renamed Aberdeen for the benefit of their bottle labels. The Germans, thorough if not successful, imported the actual water from Speyside in Scotland, but they did not get Scotch, which was, and remains, inimitable.

Just why it is that Scotch can be made only in Scotland is one of the mysteries—akin to the unanalyzable combination of known ingredients that is the true virtue of great wines. Supposedly, Scotch is merely the product of barley, yeast, Scottish water, and Scottish air, and a distilling process which holds no mystery at all.

The barley, it appears, can come from anywhere. It has been imported from as far away as Australia and California, or grown at home in Scotland and England. The foreign barley used to be considered the better, because it was drier—an important factor—but now, most of it is domestically grown. What makes Scotch "Scotch" is another matter. Blending—these days—has something to do with it. Until a century ago, Scotch was for Scotsmen, a straight, high-proof beverage. Blending began, and it is this trick which has carried the fame of the drink around the world—only in Scotland is unblended "singles" Scotch whisky to be found in any quantity. The secret of the blending lies in the fact that all the components are Scottish, with Scotch malt whisky as the irreplaceable base. To produce their unique malt whiskies, the Scottish distillers themselves rely on techniques which are more like magic than science. It is an authentic story that the actual physical shape of the pot still can have something to do with the whisky distilled in it; and one distiller, having built a new still and never being able to recapture the lost beauty of his spirit, was compelled to have his worn-out still recopied—including the patches.

The whisky runs through quite a history—and several identities—before it becomes the Scotch we know. Arrived at the distiller, barley is screened to get rid of extraneous seeds, etc. Following, generally, a period of storage, there is the steeping: the barley is plunged into water in large vats and left for a predetermined saturation period. Then it goes to the broad cement floors where the maltmen spread and tend it. In two or three days it germinates; rootlets spring forth, and when, four or five days later, these wither and the grain becomes modified, the maltmen consider that the barley is "malted."

The malt is conveyed to the kiln floor, where it lies on sheets of perforated metal until thoroughly dried by warm air from peat fires burning below. Toward the end of this process, when it is considered that the green malt has absorbed so much of the peaty flavor that it will retain it till liquor meets palate, coke or anthracite is added to bring the temperature to 160°F. (71°C.). Devised to let the controlled heat pass off, the kiln roofs are cowled with "pagoda tops," the air escaping under the ruffled eaves aided today by extractor fans which lend a strange Chinese grace to the sturdy, blunt, Scottish stone buildings.

After its trial by fire, the malt is allowed to rest for about two months, then it is screened and the withered rootlets, or malt culms, are strained off to become useful cattle food. The malt itself is ground or crushed in a roller mill of appropriate design.

The ground malt is then poured into the mash tun, a great claw-armed, circular tub with a sprocket rod splashing endlessly around, stirring the crushed malt through the seething water. Four waters, each hotter than the one before, are used in this extracting of the solubles from the malt. This solution is called wort— pronounced wurt. The first two waters, which have been saved from an earlier extraction, are known as the sparge. The infused waters passing off from the tun stream through the cooling machine, which cools them down by 72% to 75°F. (24°C.), an appropriate temperature for adding yeast. After this, they are lodged in the fermenting vats, usually called the backs. The third and fourth washings of waters become the new sparge, to be saved and used as first and second waters in a later extraction. The residue after the wort is drawn is the draff, or cattle food.

Yeast is added to the wort in the backs—fermenting vats sometimes of larch or pine, but today often of steel—and fermentation begins. The active element of the yeast changes the sugary wort into alcohol and carbon dioxide; the carbon dioxide escapes into the air and the alcohol remains at about a gallon of proof spirit per 10 gallons of wort. Once again the name of this product we are following through its conversion from barley to whisky changes. What was once malt, and then wort, is now wash.

The wash flows into the copper pot stills—dully-gleaming affairs which in the great distilleries can dwarf the size of a man—and is distilled. It passes through a phase after the first distillation when it carried still another name, "low wines" (because it has not yet reached the height of full strength); but during redistillation the clear and stronger fractions are collected in the spirit receiver vat and are now classified as whisky. This new whisky will be about 16° over proof or about 58% alcohol by volume and will require to be reduced a little by pure spring water. At around 11° over proof or 55.5% alcohol by volume, it enters the cask. The distiller will have expected to get a range of from 2.5 to 3 gallons from his bushel of barley, but he will lose something of both strength and volume while his whisky lies for the maturation period in cask. In a damp climate he will lose more strength and in a dry one more volume. It is something to think about that each year 11 million liters (3 million U.S.

gallons, 2.5 million imp.) of Scotch whisky evaporate into the soft Scottish air.

The cask itself is the final contribution to the beauty of the whisky. This improves greatly with age—in barrel, not in bottle—and it matures usually in casks made from American oak. The casks must be oak. When wine-steeped casks are not obtainable, the distiller will have to add a little caramel or burnt-sugar coloring to give his whisky the tawny tinge the public expects.

Whisky casks are known as butts if they hold more than 364 liters (96 U.S. gallons, 80 imp.); as hogsheads if they hold from 205 to 364 liters (54 to 96 U.S. gallons, 45 to 80 imp.); barrels if they hold 160 to 205 liters (42 to 54 U.S. gallons, 35 to 45 imp.); and as quarters if their capacity is less than 136 liters (36 U.S. gallons, 30 imp.) Octaves hold between 41 and 68 liters (11 and 18 U.S. gallons, 9 and 15 imp.). The butts are of three different types, varying in shape: puncheons, pipes, and one called simply a butt.

The blenders are the great artists of the whisky trade, and it is fascinating to see these men at work, going more by sense of smell than taste, their nostrils dilating sensitively in the tall, narrow, tulip-shaped, noseing glasses with their short two-finger-wide stems. When a blender has made his selections, the ingredients are mixed together by paddle stirrers in colossal vats, then left to "marry." The proportions will be about 40% malt whisky and 60% grain whisky, though occasionally these will be approximately reversed. It is the blending which creates the infinite scale of whiskies; it is not uncommon for a blend to be made up from as many as fifty types. Most experts agree that the best Scotch blends usually consist of about half Highland and Lowland malts, a little Islay or Campbeltown, and the remainder, unmalted grain whisky. On the whole, the Highland malts are light in body and full-flavored; the Lowland malts are also light, but less distinctly smoky; while the Campbeltowns and Islays are noted for heavy body and plenty of smoke.

Before bottling, whisky is reduced by the addition of soft water from the Scottish lochs—and it is filtered.

The shortage of Scotch in the 1940s was mainly the result of the wartime ban on distilling and the limited ration of barley allowed the industry in the first years after the war (the quota of barley 1945–50 covered one year's distillation), combining with the long period necessary for ageing. Another factor has been the great increase in world sales, especially in the United States. At the present time, when supplies are fortunately adequate, Americans are drinking 13 million—or more—cases a year of this most popular of all the grain spirits—which has now become the most fashionable aperitif and nightcap drink in France and other European countries. The present trend shows an increase in the consumption of single malts.

The rise in excise on Scotch whisky has been astronomical. A hundred years ago it was 10s. ($1.40) a proof gallon. The two great upward leaps were after the two world wars—to £1 10s. ($4.20) after the First; and to £11 11s. 11d. ($32.47) after the Second. It is now some $66 U.S. the proof gallon.

White Port

Port wine (Oporto, Portugal) made from white grapes. Generally, it inclines to be a little sweeter than red Port and finds its great market in France; but there is a growing tendency also to manufacture a dry White Port which is served as an aperitif in Portugal and is beginning to be known and appreciated abroad.

See Port.

Wienerwald-Steinfeld

A good vineyard region in Austria, embracing Gumpoldskirchen and Baden.

See Austria.

Wiltingen

A town in the Saar Valley, southwest of Trier. The 290 hectares (725 acres) of surrounding vineyards produce excellent white wines of which the best-known is Scharzhofberg.

See Mosel-Saar-Ruwer.

Wine

The word should apply only to the naturally fermented juice of the grape, although it is extended too often to "wines" made from vegetables, berries, and other fruits. The term is abused especially in reference to drinks made from cherries. True wine produced from grapes can be divided into three main types:

(1) Still beverage, or table wines to accompany a meal. These divide again into red, white, and rosé (according to the grapes used and the length of time the skins have been left to ferment with the juice); and into dry or sweet wines, depending on whether all the grape sugar has been allowed to ferment into alcohol, or whether some residual sugar has been left.

(2) Sparkling wines, of which Champagne, made by the process of secondary fermentation in bottle, is the finest example.

(3) Fortified wines, such as Port, Sherry, and Madeira, to which brandy has been added.

The different wine-growing countries make, from a variety of grapes, numerous wines in each category— every one of importance is to be found under its own heading.

For an analysis of the nature of wine and an account of how it is made, *see* Chapter Nine, p. 40.

Wine Cooler

A low-alcohol wine mixed with fruit juices and sparkling water (under 8%); the most rapidly growing wine product in the U.S.A.

Wine counterfeiters and grape thieves

Throughout history the growers of the grape have not dealt lightly with those who pilfered or tampered with their products. In Germany, grape thieves were led through the villages with their hands held up before them and locked in a fiddle-shaped wooden vise. This was equipped with a bell which clanged above their heads, so that all the villagers might turn out to mock them. Alternatively, the thief might be forced to ride backward through the town on a donkey, the stolen goods in his hands, the legend emblazoned on his back and breast: "He stole grapes!" It was in Germany also that wine counterfeiters and wine adulterators were severely punished during the Middle Ages, being sentenced to death for falsifying the honest product of the grape.

Wine fountains

For hundreds of years the wine fountains, from which wine flowed in place of water, brightened the scene at harvest and other festivals in many countries. Old German chronicles tell of the wine fountain of Urach (claiming to be the oldest in Germany with its date of 1474), where the wine flowed for three days and nights in alternating jets of red and white, to celebrate a royal wedding. Wine fountains were known to the Egyptians, the Greeks, and the Romans. Today the custom has been revived and the wine fountains flow at many European harvest festivals.

Wine gallon

A gallon of 128 U.S. (160 British) fluid ounces of wine or spirits irrespective of proof or alcoholic strength; also known as bulk gallon.

See Proof gallon.

Wine societies

Different wine-making districts of France have each their own society or *confrérie*, part medieval relic, part sales promotion. Growers and shippers take part, dressed in the historic costumes with which they have been invested at a long ceremony of inauguration, followed by a feast. Among the more famous of these associations are the Commanderie du Bontemps du Médoc et de Graves (*q.v.*), La Connétablie de Guyenne, La Jurade de Saint-Émilion, Les Chevaliers du Tastevin at Nuits-Saint-Georges, Les Compagnons du Beaujolais, La Commanderie de Champagne de l'Ordre des Coteaux, La Confrérie des Chevaliers de la Chantepleure de Vouvray, and La Confrérie Saint-Étienne in Alsace. Others are La Confrérie des Compagnons de la Capucine at Toul, Les Compagnons Hauts-Normands du Gouste-Vin, La Conseil des Echansons de France in Paris, La Commanderie des Vins et Spiriteux de France (also in Paris), the Nouvel Ordre Hospitalier, Curieux et Courtois des Chevaliers de Saint-Bacchus in Paris, the Ordre Bachiques et Epicurien du Gay Savoir et Bien Mangier et Bien Boire, Les Compagnons du Pintou in Auvergne, La Confrérie Vineuse des Piliers Chablisiens, La Confrérie des Trois Ceps in the Yonne, Le Cousinerie de Bourgogne, La Confrérie des Vignerons de Saint-Vincent in Macon, La Confrérie du Gosier-Sec de Clochemerle in the Beaujolais, La Confrérie des Chevaliers de la Syrah et Roussette for the Rhône Valley, l'Ordre Illustre des Chevaliers de Meduse in the Côtes de Provence, La Confrérie des Echansons de Vidauban, La Confrérie des Comtes de Nice et de Provence, l'Echansonnerie des Papes at Châteauneuf-du-Pape, Le Commanderie de Tavel, l'Ordre de la Boisson de la Stricte Observance des Costières du Gard, Antica Confraria de Saint-Andu de la Galiniera for the Hérault, le Consulat de Septimanie of the Coteaux du Languedoc, l'Illustre Cour des Seigneurs de la Corbière, La Commende Majeure de Roussillon pour Garder le Devoir et le Droit de la Vigne et du Vin, l'Ordre de la Dive Bouteille in Gaillac, La Confrérie du Vin de Cahors, La Viguerie Royale du Jurançon, La Viguerie du Madiran, La Commanderie des Chevaliers de Tursan, Le Grand Conseil de Bordeaux, l'Académie du Vin de Bordeaux, Les Compagnons de Bordeaux, le Club des Amis du Vin de Bordeaux, La Commanderie du Bontemps de Sauternes et Barsac, La Commanderie de Bontemps de Sainte-Croix-du-Mont, La Connétablie de Guyenne, Les Compagnons du Loupiac, La Confrérie des Hospitaliers de Pomerol, Les Gentilhommes de Fronsac, le Consultat de la Vinée de Bergerac, Le Principauté de Franc-Pineau in Charentes, l'Ordre des Chevaliers Bretvins, La Confrérie des Chevaliers du Sacavin in Anjou, La Confrérie des Vignerons de la Canette in Bouille-Loretz (Deux-Sèvres), La Confrérie des Vin Gousiers d'Anjou, La Commanderie du Taste-Saumur, La Confrérie des Hume-Piot du Loudonois, La Confrérie Vineuse de Tiré-Douzils in Poitou, Les Entonneurs Rabelaisiens in Chinon, La Confrérie des Fripe-Douzils in Bourgueil, La Confrérie des Chevaliers des Cuers du Baril in the Touraine, La Coterie des Closiers de Montlouis, La Commanderie des Grands Vins d'Amboise, La Confrérie des Compagnons de Grandgousier, La Confrérie des Baillis de Pouilly-sur-Loire, le Collège des Chanoines de Tannay, Les Chevaliers de Sancerre, La Compagnie des Vignerons d'Honneur, La Compagnie d'Honneur des Sorciers et Birettes for Anjou, La Confrérie de Chevaliers du Cep in Verdigny, l'Ordre des Chevaliers du Paissiau, La Maîtrise des Echansons in Reuilly, Le Cercle des Chevaliers du Cep in Châteauroux, l'Ordre des Vins Palais in Saint-Pourcain, La Confrérie des Compa-

gnons du Bousset d'Auvergne, La Confrérie de Saint-Verny, La Confrérie de Bacchus et d'Icare in Lyon, La Compagnie du Sarto for the Savoie, La Commanderie des Nobles Vins du Jura et Gruyère de Comte, and La Pairie des Vins d'Arbois. There are societies, also, in honor of the great French brandies: La Confrérie des Alambics Charentais at Cognac; and La Compagnie des Mousquetaires d'Armagnac at Condom.

In Switzerland there is the Confrérie des Vignolants de Neuchâtel, l'Ordre de la Channe, and La Confrérie de Guillon. Belgium has the Gilde de Saint-Vincent de Belgique and the Confrérie des Chevaliers Rabelaisiens de Belgique. In Italy the societies are the Confraternità della Cheer, the Cavaliers d'Asti et de Montferrato, and the Confraternità d'la Tripa. The United States too has at least one group: the Universal Order of the Knights of the Vine of California.

Winery

The American name for an establishment where wine is made.

Winkel

Town with several good vineyards, on the bank of the Rhine.
See Rheingau.

Wintrich

Good white wine district of the German Middle Mosel.
See Mosel-Saar-Ruwer.

Winzer

German term for wine-grower. Winzerverein on a label indicates that the wine has been produced by a cooperative.

Wood

The cask. Wine is "in the wood" when it is in the cask.

Woody

This can indicate two conditions in a wine or spirit, usually curable: (1) a smell from wholesome oak when the liquor has been too long in the oak; (2) a taint from defective wood.

Worcester

Wine district of the Cape province.
See South Africa.

Wort

The extract from malt which is fermented to make malt whisky. The word is pronounced "wurt."
See Whisky, Scotch.

Württemberg

German State of Baden-Württemberg
Vineyard area: approx. 9,600 hectares (23,800 acres)
51% red wines; 49% white wines

Location: The Württemberg region is the valley of the River Neckar, flowing north and then northwest from above Stuttgart to its confluence with the Rhine at Mannheim and the valleys of the six smaller rivers that enter it.

After numerous setbacks, Württemberg wines began to improve in quality during the last century, and by means of the replanting of the vineyards with Riesling and other noble vines. The expansion of city and industrial areas, have reduced the total vine plantation considerably. The area is a meeting point for the warmth coming from the sea zones and for the Continental land-mass cold. This causes sudden and violent changes of weather.

The vineyards are scattered through the valleys of the Neckar River and its tributaries. Stuttgart and Hellbronn are major cities in the region, but with regard to wine Weinsberg is important as the site of the oldest oenological school and experimental station in Germany. It is also the largest wine estate in the region. The region is divided into five districts (Bereiche), two of which are very small: Bereich Württembergischer Bodensee and Bereich Oberer Neckar. The traditional heart of the region lies within Bereich Remstal-Stuttgart, Bereich Württembergisches Unterland and Bereich Kocher-Jagst-Tauber.

Grape Varieties: Riesling (24%); Trollinger, a fair red grape found almost exclusively here (23%); Müllerrebe, also called Schwarzriesling—Pinot Meunier (13%); Müller-Thurgau (10%); Kerner, crossing of Trollinger and Riesling developed in Weinsberg (9%); Limberger (6%).

The most popular product of the Württemberg wine-growers is the light pink, aromatic Schillerwein. Though rosé in color, it is not vinified in the manner of many of the other rosé wines made in Europe. To make the Schillerwein, red and white grapes are mixed before crushing, and the whole fermented together. "Schillern" refers to a play in colors. The wine is well known and much demanded in the production region. Soil types range from loess, clay, loam and red marl to shell limestone (Neckar Valley). In general, the soils are deep and rich and yield wines that claim to be robust.

Here, as in neighboring Baden, the cooperatives are of major importance in the production of wine because most of the growers are part-time or hobby vintners with less than half a hectare (1 acre) of vineyards or, "vine gardens," as they are called here. Of the region's 16,500 growers, only 11% produce their own wine. The majority contribute their grapes to the cooperatives. Annual production, based on a ten-year average: 900,000 hectoliters. Local consumption is high; thus, little Württemberg wine is seen outside the region, let alone abroad.

In addition to the wines of the Zentralkellerei in Möglingen (Central Cellars) and smaller cooperatives, the following producers offer good quality: Schlosskellerei Affaltrach; Weingut Graf Adelman; Gräfl von Bentzel-Sturmfeder'sches Weingut; Schlossgut Hohoenbeilstein; Fürst zu Hohenlohe-Öhringen'sche Schlosskellerei; Von Stapf'sches Weingut; Württembergische Hofkammerkellerei; and the Staatl. Lehr- und Versuchsanstalt in Weinsberg.

See Appendix B, p. 699.

Würzburg

Center of the German Steinwein of Franconia *(q.v.)*.

Wynberg

First district in Cape province to produce wine.
See South Africa.

X

Xérès

French for Sherry *(q.v.)*. Xeres was the name given by the ancient Romans to the Sherry city of Jerez.

X.O.

The oldest style of Cognac found on the general market. The designation is used mainly by the Cognac firm of Hennessy. While, except in the exceedinlgly rare vintage brandies, age designations in brandy indicate a style rather than an exact number of years, X.O.s often claim, and frequently have, about forty years of barrel-age. (Brandies, like other spirits, do not age in bottle.) Age in brandy is fully discussed under Cognac *(q.v.)*.

Xynisteri

One of the dominating grapes in Commandaria, the famous dessert wine of Cyprus. The other is the Mavron.

Y

Yakima Valley

Wine region in Washington State, one of the rare districts outside California where European grapevines have flourished.
See United States.

Yalumba

Famous vineyard in Eden Valley, South Australia, from which comes a dry white wine called Carte d'Or.
See Australia.

Yam wine

Beverage fermented from yam roots in Africa and South America.

Yamanashi

One of the main vine-growing districts of Japan (*q.v.*).

Yawa

West African palm wine.

Yayin

Biblical term for wine, evidently related to *vinum, Wein,* etc.

Yeasts

Natural, microscopic, unicellular organisms found on the skins of grapes, and responsible for alcoholic fermentation. One of these, *Saccharomyces cereviseae,* is the true wine-maker which gives the wine its character and its main constitution. As the last grams of sugar are fermented out, this yeast disappears and dies. A lesser variety, *Saccharomyces bayanus,* important in the white wines of Bordeaux, as well as in the Pomerols and Saint-Émilions, is more resistant to alcohol than *S. cereviseae* and increases as fermentation advances. *Saccharomyces acidifaciens,* yet another variety of fermenting yeast, is often found to be a cause of trouble in white wines. In many modern wineries yeast selections or cultures are chosen with great care.

Undesirable yeasts may also be found in ripe grapes. These can be destroyed by sulfuring of the must and by adding cultured yeasts.
See Chapter Nine, p. 40.

Yecla

From the province of Murcia, Spain, a new and rather ordinary Denominación has been created. Yecla has 27,000 hectares (67,000 acres) producing red, white, and pink wines.

Yeso

In Spain, gypsum-rich dust used for "plastering" (*q.v.*).

Château d'Yquem

Bordeaux white wine.
District and Commune: Sauternes, France.

Château d'Yquem is the greatest natural sweet white wine, the only wine which can always, without fear of argument, be claimed to be the best of its kind—although a few Trockenbeerenauslesen of Germany may in great years be compared with it. This was recognized in ratings of Bordeaux in the eighteenth century; and in 1855, when Sauternes and Médoc were classified on the basis of their known excellence and sales, d'Yquem was the only wine classed a First Great Growth *(Premier Grand Cru)*.

Distinguished even among the finest of the other Sauternes by an extra suavity and full richness and vinous luscious depth, and a more beautiful gold in color, d'Yquem is the result partly of the highest possible wine-making standards, partly of the magnificent exposure of the terrain on a hill commanding the whole Sauternes district, and also of something almost magical which must be in the soil itself. In every great wine zone there are one or two plots which somehow manage, year in and year out, to produce wines better even than those of vineyards touching their borders. There is no more remarkable example of this than Château d'Yquem.

The property, which had produced wine for at least two or three centuries, came into the family of the Marquis de Lur-Saluces by marriage in 1885. It is owned and directed today by Count Alexandre de Lur-Saluces, an heir of Marquis Bertrand de Lur-Saluces, who was a great campaigner for all French wines and was the head of both the French wine promotional organization and the Association of the Classified Growths of Bordeaux. More than a century and a half ago Thomas Jefferson had already written: "Sauterne. This is the best white wine of France and the best of it is made by Monsieur de Lur-Saluces." Add an *s* to Sauterne, and place the word "sweet" in front of white wine to avoid controversy about the excellence of some dry whites, and the statement is true today.

Yugoslavia

Château d'Yquem is and always has been expensive. Today, it is generally sold to Bordeaux shippers bottled—that is to say, at the château with no charges added for casing, etc.—at about 600 francs (approximately £60 or $100) per bottle. It achieved what was probably the highest price paid for any wine in the last century when the brother of the Emperor of Russia bought four barrels of the 1847 vintage for 20,000 francs (about £3,646 or $10,200 now). Costly as it is, the high price of the wine is justified not only by market demand, but by two special factors. About 1847, Château d'Yquem, first of all the Sauternes vineyards, introduced the practice of using only hyper-rich, half-rotted grapes attacked by the so-called noble rot *(pourriture noble)*. This process—requiring the vineyard to be picked over many times, because the bunches reached the desired maturity at different intervals—has made the production of all Sauternes expensive and is now the practice in all Sauternes vineyards. Château d'Yquem, in addition to this, sells under its own name only the best; the wine of poor years or from lesser sections in mediocre years is sold to the trade simply as Sauternes, at a financial loss. In 1954, for example, the vineyard declared 336 barrels of fine wine and 172 barrels of district Sauternes; and in 1955, 480 barrels with 100 barrels of Sauternes. "All the wines of Château d'Yquem are château bottled. But the vineyard gives its name only to wines very rigorously selected . . ."—Marquis Bertrand de Lur-Saluces. Until 1876, different segments of the pressing were sold separately in differing grades, but since that date the harvest has been equalized by the vatting together of the pick of different days. The wine is aged for three years in new wooden barrels, or *barriques*. The wine has an extremely long life, and bottles of a hundred years and older can still be found in excellent condition, if they have been properly kept. Although this great sweet wine is properly appreciated, the present fashion for dry wines is so irresistible that Château d'Yquem is now making some fair dry white wine called Y (Y Grec).

The castle itself, a turreted and walled château-fort on its high hill, is one of the landmarks of southwestern France; and one of the most charming evenings to be spent in Europe is at the annual concert given in the great courtyard by some internationally known string quartet as part of the May Bordeaux Music Festival. The floodlit château gleams like a fairy-tale castle, its battlements and towers visible over miles of the dark Sauternes countryside.

Hail is the great enemy of the vineyard, and in 1951, 1952, and 1973 the crop was wiped out. No d'Yquem was produced in 1964, 1972 or 1974.

Characteristics. Full-bodied and luscious, with superb finesse, this expensive wine is well worth the price. It ages exceedingly well, for maderization acquired through ageing becomes an asset and is not offensive. The great sweetness offsets any overlay of excessive oxidation.

Vineyard area: 100 hectares (250 acres).
Average production: 60 *tonneaux* (5,500 cases of d'Yquem, some 2,000 cases of Y—both quantities vary greatly).

Yugoslavia

Yugoslavia, the state of the Southern Slavs, which now embraces the Croatian and Slovene provinces of the Austro-Hungarian Empire, Serbia, Montenegro, Macedonia, Bosnia, and Herzegovina, has the eighth largest vineyard area in Europe.

In few places does wine better fulfill the truism that it never tastes as good as where it is grown. In Macedonia and Montenegro, almost self-contained and inaccessible parts of the world which have kept their native characteristics even today, the wines, when you drink them there, are enhanced by the local costumes, the hardy romance of the surroundings, and sometimes by the very vessels in which they are kept. The carved, round, wooden brandy- and wine-flasks, ornate canteens with their leather bindings and carrying straps of braid, are among the most attractive in the world. It is not necessary to visit the rugged regions to experience the charm of Yugoslav wines. Many thousands of tourists taste the red wines of Dalmatia in the white, walled city of Dubrovnik. A very different experience from drinking such full, red, alcoholic (13% to 14%) southern wines as Dingač (pronounced Dingach) or Bol in their place of origin is that of drinking the white wines of Slovenia in the alpine north.

At the present time, Dalmatian wines are probably not at their potential best, and the wines of Slovenia are more fully realized. Slovenian white wines, Serbian white, red, and rosé, some of the wines of Istria, and lately the dry white wines and red wines of Macedonia are frequently to be met with in Great Britain and the United States. The countries to which Yugoslavia chiefly exports her wines are Germany, both East and West, Czechoslovakia, Poland, and Britain.

HISTORY

Wine is of very ancient origin in Yugoslavia, as it is in all the Mediterranean and Balkan countries. Some historians say it came from Thrace, up through the Macedonian mountains and into what is now Yugoslavia, about four thousand years ago. It is certainly true that the Dalmatian and Istrian wines flourished under the Greeks, and Slovenian wines under the Romans. Slovenia and the Danube Plain (Croatia) are full of Roman remains, decorated very often with wine and grape motifs; the several languages of Yugoslavia have common words for various aspects of vine care and wine-making, taken direct from the Latin; and the museums in towns as far apart as Dubrovnik in Dalmatia and Ptuj in Slovenia, not 80 kilometers (50 miles)

614

south of the Austrian border, have many Greek and Roman wine amphorae and implements dug up in the environs.

Here as in other countries of Europe, wine culture was carried on by the feudal lords and the great monasteries in the Middle Ages. We hear of the wines of Ohrid, far in the south, and of Albania, being in great favor in Europe at the time of the Crusades.

It must be remembered, however, that for centuries part of Yugoslavia was overrun by the Turks. Sarajevo, in the center of the country, is even today the most Turkish city west of Istanbul. The needle-minarets of its seventy or eighty mosques remind us of the Moslem influence; and the Moslem is forbidden to drink wine. Thus where the Turk dominated, viticulture was abandoned until these regions were liberated from Moslem influence—a slow process of emancipation lasting from 1804 until 1912.

On the other hand, parts of what is now Yugoslavia belonged to Austria. Ljutomer, for instance, was for centuries in Styria and thus was Austrian. The consequence was that northern Yugoslav wines and methods of viticulture are typically Austrian. Even today, confusion is caused by the fact that certain of these wines gained a world reputation under German names, which are now being replaced by Yugoslav appellations. Ljutomer, one of Yugoslavia's most famous wines, named after the town near which it grows in the northernmost tip pressed into Austria and Hungary, first became known as Luttenberger, its Austrian name, and was frequently supposed to be a wine from Austria. It is seldom realized that Luttenberger and Ljutomer are different names for the same wine.

VINES AND STATISTICS

Yugoslavia has something over 240,000 hectares (600,000 acres) of vineyards and makes each year roughly 7.4 million hectoliters of table wine (195.5 million U.S. gallons, 162.7 million imp.). The quantity produced is approximately the same as the amounts made each year in the neighboring countries of Greece, Rumania, and Hungary. Yugoslavia's average consumption is some 13 liters per head annually, 1½ times the U.S. rate. The export trade has grown in recent years; now about 1,100,000 hectoliters (29 million U.S. gallons, 24.2 million imp.) are shipped abroad. Very little wine is imported.

The vines grown are numerous and varied. Particularly in the north of the country, where the Austrian influence was most felt, there are imported vines such as Riesling, Traminer, Sylvaner, Merlot, Muscat, Pinot Blanc, and Sauvignon. However, a number of native vines are also used—as are hybrids, many of which were planted at the time of the phylloxera crisis which hit Yugoslavia about the turn of the century.

WINE-GROWING DISTRICTS

Yugoslavia was created just after the First World War out of six separate Slavonic-speaking states: Serbia, Croatia, Slovenia, Bosnia-Herzegovina, Montenegro, and the northern part of Macedonia. While they make up a harmonious whole, each state still clings to its ancient habits and customs, and the wines grown in each are different from the others. The proportional amounts of wine by state are as follows: Serbia 45%; Croatia 35%; Slovenia 9%; Macedonia 9%; Bosnia-Herzegovina 2%; Montenegro negligible.

Serbia

With about 80,000 hectares (200,000 acres) Serbia is the great bulk-wine producing section of Yugoslavia and until recently most of its wines were more likely to be served in their place of origin than found abroad. They are named after the general district from which they come. Most Serbian wines are made from the Prokupac vine, commonly known as the "national vine of Serbia" (though it is slowly giving way to imported Gamay and Cabernet). Among the best-known names are:

Župa (pronounced Zhoopa). Here, in the center of Serbia, the warm, sun-bathed hills produce a vast amount of red wine which is full, heavy, and rich, but not particularly noted for its breed or distinction. A pink, or rosé, wine is also made, and both types stem from the Prokupac vine. The vineyards are extensive, with the city of Aleksandrovac the central wine town.

Krajina (pronounced Krayina). Centered around the city of Negotin, this district lies on the borders of Rumania and Bulgaria. The wines are almost entirely red, made from a blend of the Prokupac, Skadarka, and Začinak wines. They were once fairly well known in France, where they were sent at the time of the worst of the phylloxera crisis at the end of the last century. A white wine named Bagrina of Krajina, after the vine, is also made.

Vlasotinci (pronounced Vlasotinsi). From the south of Serbia. Most of the wines are pink and are made from the Prokupac and Plovdina vines.

Venčac-Oplenac (pronounced Ventchats-Oplenats). Up the Morava River from Župa, this region is the heart of the part of Serbia called Šumadija (Shumadiya), where the insurrection against Turkish rule started at the beginning of the last century. Wines are grown—the main headquarters being the city of Topola—mainly from the Prokupac, Pinot Noir, Gamay, and most recently Chardonnay vines; both red and rosé wines are made. The rosé of Oplenac is well known.

Smederevo. An enormous region lying on the rolling hills on the south side of the Danube near the Rumanian border. A good white wine is produced here from the Smerdervka and Wälschriesling grapes.

Vojvodina (25,000 hectares—62,500 acres—of vine-

Yugoslavia: Wine-Growing Districts map. Labels include: ITALY, HUNGARY, RUMANIA, SLOVENIA, Ljutomer, Varaždin, Zagreb, CROATIA, SLAVONIA, R. Drava, Erdut, Kutjevo, Slavonski Brod, Vukovar, Ilok, FRUŠKA GORA, R. Danube, Belgrade, Medjice, R. Sava, ISTRIAN PEN, Pljeŝiveca, BOSNIA, HERZEGOVINA, Smederevo, Venčac-Oplenac, Topola, Aleksandrovac, SERBIA, Negotin, KRAJINA, Žadar, DALMATIA, Šibenik, Kastel, Split, BRELA, HVAR, Sveta Nedelja, VIS, Pitovska Plaza, KORČULA, Dingač, Postup, LASTOVO, Sarajevo, MONTENEGRO, Medjice, KOSMET, KOSOVO I METOHIJA, R. Morava, Vlasotinci, ALBANIA, MACEDONIA, BULGARIA, GREECE. N (compass). YUGOSLAVIA. Scale: 0 20 100 MILES 200 / 0 20 100 200 KILOMETRES 300.

yards). An autonomous province of Serbia, east of Croatian Slavonia and bordering on Hungary and Rumania. The region is an important agricultural center, growing grapes for wine as well as for the table, and many of the big new plantations have replaced the older native varieties with better Western strains. There are three districts: Fruška Gora is a gentle wooded mountain between the Sava and the Danube, where there are vast vineyards and giant modern wineries. They grow Wälschriesling, Sémillon, Traminer, White Pinot, and Sauvignon Blanc. The best areas are Erdevik, Vrdnik, and Sremski Karlovici, which in the last century—when this was part of Hungary—made a red wine called Carlowitz (Karlovice Rothwein), popular in Great Britain, Austria, and the Netherlands. Sound white wines are produced there now, comparable to the high quality of those from the Maribor area of Slovenia. This was formerly a good district for red wines, growing Skadarka and other native grape varieties. The policy of the government is now to replant

the white wine-producing vines, and to replace the native red varieties with the Burgundian Gamay and Pinot Noir, since the emphasis is not on red wine production. Bermet was a local vermouth, formerly made at Sremski Karlovici.

The second of the Vojvodinian districts, Suvotička Peščare, between the Danube and the Tisza rivers, is reclaimed sand land, an extension of the Hungarian Alföld—the Great Plain. Planting has been somewhat improved here and now includes Austrian Grüner Veltliner, Wälschriesling, the Hungarian Ezerjó and Muscat Ottonel, plus a good local variety called Kevedinka for white wines. Kadarka, Blaufränkisch, and Pinot Noir produce the red wines. No high-quality wines are made here, and it will be interesting to see how this region with its new plantings, some of them necessarily experimental, will develop.

The third and the largest of the Vojvodinian regions is the small part of the Banat that is not Rumanian. Bits of it are deep, sandy land unsuitable for cultivation, but two-thirds of the vineyard area of Vojvodina is in this area, although the majority of the grapes grown are for the table rather than for wine. The Banat has its own peculiar climate; it is in the extreme southeastern corner of the Pannonian Plain, where the foothills rise to become the Transylvanian Alps. Vršac is in the foothills and is still a center of wine production; some of the wine is said to be of good quality. It is primarily a white wine area and the same vines are grown as in Fruška Gora, but with the addition of a local Riesling-type called Banatski Rizling Kreaca. The small amount of red wine also comes from Merlot, Cabernet Sauvignon, Gamay, and Pinot Noir grapes.

Kosmet. Another autonomous province of Serbia, bordering on Albania and Macedonia. The ancient Greeks first grew vines here on the foothills of the mountains. The modern vineyards were only replanted in the sixties, decades after the phylloxera devastation at the end of the last century, using Cabernet Sauvignon, Cabernet Franc, Gamay, and Pinot Noir. These red wines are rather pleasant and popular in several Western European countries. A little white wine is made from Žilavka and Wälschriesling. The Kosmet region joins with Macedonia to form one great wine district. There are 150,000 hectares (375,000 acres) of vines in Serbia, Kosmet, and Macedonia combined.

Croatia

The wines of Croatia (about 40,000 hectares, or 100,000 acres) can most conveniently be divided into two major types: those which are grown in the inland section stretching from the broad Danubian plain to the mountains above Zagreb, between the Drava and Sava rivers; and those which come from the Adriatic coast, including the wines of the once Italian portion of the Istrian Peninsula and of the fabulous Dalmatian coast.

The inland vine-growing districts include the valleys of the Danube, Drava, and Sava rivers and extend to the alpine slopes which lead into Slovenia, adjoining the famous wine district of Ljutomer, perhaps the best in Yugoslavia. The flatter vineyards produce wines more like those in Serbia, however; most of them are light, slightly acid but agreeable wines with no particular breed but without pretense. The wines most frequently encountered include those from Pljesivica (pronounced Plyeshivitsa), Vinica (Vinitsa), Varaždin (Varajdeen), and Medjugorica (Mejugoritsa).

In the northeast part of Croatia, the Austrian influence begins to make itself felt. Traminers and Rieslings, Sauvignons and Sémillons make their appearance in the vineyards and these white wines, when they are well made, are numbered among the best of the country, having a richness in alcohol, a trace of unfermented sugar and a perfume that may be expected in wines from such vines. The important vine-growing

towns are Kutjevo (pronounced Kutyevo), Erdut, Ilok, Vukovar, Belji, Djakoro, and Slavonski Brod.

Along the coast are the vineyards of Istria and Dalmatia. The most famous vineyards in this region are on the islands of Vis, Hvar, Brač, and Korčula, and the Istrian Peninsula. Hills recede inland from the broken coastline and the land is covered with huge rocks. The hills themselves are shaved bare by the constant Adriatic wind, the *borra*. Yet in spite of this, vines grow and produce wines of the Mediterranean style—typically big, full, and deep red, with lots of tannin and very little acid. Often the Dalmatians cut them with water before drinking—in much the manner of the French with the heady wines of Algeria. White wines are also made.

The vines are various. There appear to be some not known as named varieties elsewhere. This would seem to indicate a very early introduction of the vine into the region. In fact, some Yugoslavian viticulturists believe that one type of vine is native to Yugoslavia.

Among the least "Dalmatian" of the wines grown are those of Polja (pronounced Polya), which form a bridge between the wines of the inland vineyards and those grown along the coast. Lighter and lighter-colored than most Dalmatian wines, the white wines of Imotski and Promina are the most typical.

Most of the red Dalmatian wines (red wines lead white by a ratio of about two to one) are grown from the Mali Plavac vine, a native Yugoslav variety. The best are cultivated around the regions of Bol, Pitovske Plaže (pronounced Pitovsky Plaza), Sveta Nedelja (Sveta Nedelya), Vis, Brela, Lastovo, Postup, and Dingač (Dingach). The wines are often sold with the name of the vine and the place of origin (Plavac of Vis, wine from the Plavac grown around Vis). Sometimes they carry only the place-name.

Some pink, or rosé wines grown along the coast go under the name of Opol, and the best are found around the villages of Vis, Šibenik, and Kaštel.

The better white wines of Dalmatia resemble the reds in that they are heavy, deep in color, and are distinctly mouth-filling wines. The best-known come from the Grk (pronounced Gerk), Pošip (Poship), Bogdanuša (Bogdanoosha), Vugava, and Maraština (Marashtina) vines. Grk is pale-yellow and dry, with an odd aftertaste all its own, and is grown mostly on the island of Korčula, as is Pošip, and near the city of Split. The other vines are most sucessfully cultivated on the islands of Hvar and of Vis near Šibenik and Žadar respectively.

A curious type of sweet wine called Prošek (pronounced Proshek) is made from semi-dry grapes, or by use of concentrated wine and grape juice, or by cooking the must; this is mostly for the Dalmatian palate.

The wines of the Istrian Peninsula are grown more in the Italian manner than the Yugoslavian. Various other plants are found in the same plots of land growing alongside the vines, which are often trellised or draped over trees. Teran accounts for a small part of the production here and extends into the Slovenian part of the Istrian Peninsula, where it is better known. One of the better-known wines is the Malvazÿa, grown from the vine called Malvasia in Italy, Malvoisie in France, and Monemvasia in its native Greece. It makes some of the more agreeable wines of Yugoslavia. Also grown are Cabernets, the vine of France's Bordeaux region, Merlots, and some members of the Pinot family imported from Burgundy.

Slovenia (Ljutomer)

The whole wine region of Slovenia is influenced by the nearness of the Adriatic on the west and the enormous Danube plain on the east, moderating the alpine climate and providing fairly mild, moist winters and temperate summers. The Atlantic winds, blowing through "the Viennese Gate," an Alpine mountain pass, help to maintain the temperate climate. The towering mountains of the Julian Alps break up into limestone *karst* toward the Adriatic, and this is the characteristic stony vineyard soil. Twenty thousand hectares (50,000 acres) are in vines.

The region can be broken down into three parts: the Adriatic shore, the basin of the River Douro, and the basin of the River Sava. The most important is the basin of the Drava, with the famous Ljutomer. Important growths here include Ormož (pronounced Ormoj), Pohorje (Pohorye), Kozjak (Kozyak), Slovenske, Gorice (Goritze), and Gornie Radgona (Gornye Radgona).

The Ljutomer white table wines are readily available in England, the United States, and other markets. Often spelled Lutomer, the wines are identified by the regional name followed by the informing grape variety: i.e., Lutomer Riesling, Lutomer Sylvaner, Lutomer Sauvignon, Lutomer Traminer, Lutomer Sipon (pronounced Sheepon). The Sauvignons and Rieslings are dry, the Sylvaner has a slight sweet tendency, the Traminer is fairly sweet—with, of course, the spiciness always characterizing the wines of that grape variety. The color varies in the wines from a full gold to one tinged with green; while German—and sometimes French, according to the grape variety—in style, the wines are never as subtle and delicate as the comparable German and French wines; they are less highly developed and individual. On the other hand, they can have a very full bouquet and distinctive taste that may be just a little excessive. The Riesling often achieves 14% to 15% of alcohol, and most of the others are only a little less strong. Sipon—also sometimes spelled Chipon—is a native grape variety. The wine is either dry or sweet, depending upon how it has been vinified, and tends to keep a light freshness even when aged a considerable time. Barbera, Merlot, and Cabernet Sauvignon grapes are currently used to produce most of the wines in this region.

The other two wine sections of Slovenia are of lesser importance. The best-known wine of the River Sava is the pink Cviček (pronounced Tsveechek), a light, fresh rosé that is much sought after by local Yugoslavs

during the heat of the summer. The most important of the Adriatic wines is the red Kraški Teran (Krashki Tayran) from the northern part of Istria, a wine with a wide and ancient reputation for having curative powers, perhaps because of its richness in lactic acid, in iron, and in tannin. But it is an acquired taste.

Macedonia

Red, white, pink, and a certain amount of dessert wines are grown in Macedonia. Macedonia (about 30,000 hectares, or 75,000 acres) is now one of Yugoslavia's important wine regions. The Turkish invasion was responsible for practically doing away with the vineyards for a considerable period, and these were never reconstituted after the phylloxera epidemic. However, the Yugoslav government has made a great and successful effort to rebuild the vineyards since the end of the Second World War; and a large amount of wine intermediate in character between the Mediterreanean and the more northerly type is grown. The Vranac (pronounced Vranats) vines are important for red wines, Žilavartea and Smederevka for white. Districts growing wines today include Tikveš (pronounced Tikvesh), Demir Kapija (Demeer Kapiya), and such towns as Tetovo, Ohrid, Bitola, Štip, Djeudyjelÿa, and others. Yugoslav wine experts are watching the progress of Macedonian wine with satisfaction.

OTHER YUGOSLAV WINES

Bosnia-Herzegovina and Montenegro, with a total of 7,500 hectares (18,750 acres), are the smallest of the wine-producers of Yugoslavia, together accounting for hardly more than 2% of the wines produced. Montenegrin wines are almost entirely confined to those grown from the Vranac vine. Of the wines of Bosnia-Herzegovina two are better known: Žilavka and Blatina. The best is white Žilavka, and particularly the Žilavka grown around the city of Mostar, a big, rich, alcoholic (13% to 14%) wine with a profound perfume. It is generally made by vinifying grapes from the native Yugoslav Žilavka vine with about 30% of other varieties. Today, vine cultivation is increasing in Herzegovina and Montenegro.

VINTAGES

According to the Institute of Viniculture in Maribor there were only two outstanding vintages in the 1800s, those of 1834 and 1890. In general, vintage is of small importance in Yugoslavia, owing to the fact that most of the wine is blended. While it is true that export is restricted to a few authorized exporters and there are some large domaines and cooperatives, the actual grape-growing is, astonishingly, still 95% in the hands of the peasant-growers—each at present limited by law to owning a maximum of about 10 hectares (25 acres). The fortunes of the Yugoslav grower have been varied and in certain years up to two-thirds of the crop was destroyed by vine disease in certain parts of Serbia and elsewhere; while in Istria, and along the Adriatic, in the best wine areas the production was above average. But in recent years his lot has generally improved, and with it so has the quality of the wine. As more Yugoslavian wine goes to Western consumers, the fa-vorable and encouraging trend has been to make fewer blended ones and more varietal wines—wines labeled and sold featuring the grape variety rather than the name of the district.

SPIRITS

See Maraschino; Slivovitz.

Z

Zagarolo

White wine from near Rome.
See Latium.

Zamora

Spanish province, north of Salamanca. Here the thick, dark Toro vines are grown; and, at Quintanella de Abajo, the Vaga Sicilia.
See Spain.

Zeller Schwarze Katz

The "Black Cat" wine of Zell on the German Mosel is a good deal more famous than it deserves to be. This is due to the name and the publicity, but the wine is basically a light, refreshing wine for everyday consumption.
See Mosel-Saar-Ruwer.

Zeltinger Sonnenuhr

A lovely feminine Mosel, frequently the best in the district of Zeltingen, where wines run a wide gamut of variety for Mosels.
See Mosel-Saar-Ruwer.

Zierfandler

Grape variety cultivated in Austria. It is also known as Spätrot.

Zikhron Yaacov

Important center of Israel's wine industry.
See Israel.

Zilavka

Native Yugoslav grape from which a white wine of this name is grown near Mostar in Bosnia-Herzegovina: it is big, rich, and alcoholic, with a distinctive perfume.
See Yugoslavia.

Zimbabwe

In 1965, when Rhodesia declared independence, importation of wine was forbidden and a few farmers started vineyards and wineries now amounting to approximately 1,000 hectares (2,500 acres) producing approximately 180,000 cases, mainly white. The main grape varieties are Colombard, Chenin Blanc and Sauvignon Blanc.

Zinfandel

One of the more popular and best red wine grapes in California, where it produces good, sound wines. The grape may be the Primitivo from Italy. Some Zinfandel vines have been transformed into white grapevines.
See United States: California.

Zubrówka (Zubrovka)

A type of Polish vodka much appreciated abroad. Pale green in color, it is flavored with a wild grass that is a favorite food of the *zubra*, or Polish bison, which figures on the label. In each bottle of genuine Zubrówka a blade of the grass is enclosed.
See Poland.

Zupa

Prolific region for red and pink wines in the Serbian part of Yugoslavia *(q.v.)*.

Zwack

A proprietary brand of liqueurs formerly made in Hungary and now produced in Austria and Italy. Zwack liqueurs, and especially the apricot brandy known as Barack Pálinka, were one of the most popular brands in the U.S. before the Second World War.

Zwicker

On an Alsatian bottle label, the term indicates the blending of noble and common wines. Alsatian wines bearing trade-names are usually Zwickers.

Zymase

The complex of enzymes found in yeasts which ferments alcohol and carbon dioxide gas from sugars.

Zymotechnology

The technology of fermentation, and more particularly yeast fermentations.

Appendixes

Bordeaux Wines

I THE OFFICIAL CLASSIFICATION OF THE GREAT GROWTHS OF THE GIRONDE: CLASSIFICATION OF 1855

The official production is given in tons *(tonneaux)*, the Bordeaux standard measure, consisting of 4 barrels. A *tonneau* averages around 96 cases when it is bottled.

The following figures of production are approximate, varying from year to year, and an estimate has been attempted by deducting the ullage, or evaporation, which is usually of 15%.

HAUT-MÉDOC WINES

FIRST GROWTHS *(Premiers Crus)*

	Commune	Hectares	Tonneaux	Average Production Cases (12 bottles)
Château Lafite-Rothschild	Pauillac	88	250	22,000
Château Latour	Pauillac	60	250	22,000
Château Mouton-Rothschild*	Pauillac	70	250	22,000
Château Margaux	Margaux	75	250	23,000
Château Haut-Brion**	Pessac. Graves	40	140	13,000

*Decreed a First Growth in 1973.

**This wine, although a Graves, is universally recognized and classified as one of the five First Growths of the Médoc.

SECOND GROWTHS *(Deuxièmes Crus)*

Château Rausan-Ségla	Margaux	23	140	11,000
Château Rauzan-Gassies	Margaux	29	120	11,000
Château Léoville-Las-Cases	St.-Julien	80	260	25,000
Château Léoville-Barton	St.-Julien	45	180	18,000
Château Léoville-Poyferré	St.-Julien	60	220	22,000
Château Durfort-Vivens	Margaux	31	90	8,000
Château Lascombes	Margaux	110	375	35,000
Château Gruaud-Larose	St.-Julien	76	250	22,000
Château Brane-Cantenac	Cantenac-Margaux	115	375	35,000
Château Pichon-Longueville-Baron	Pauillac	30	120	11,000
Château Pichon-Longueville-Comtesse-de-Lalande	Pauillac	72	280	25,000
Château Ducru-Beaucaillou	St.-Julien	50	220	20,000
Château Cos-d'Estournel	St.-Estèphe	60	275	25,000
Château Montrose	St.-Estèphe	70	320	30,000

THIRD GROWTHS *(Troisièmes Crus)*

Château Giscours	Labarde-Margaux	78	350	33,000
Château Kirwan	Cantenac-Margaux	30	120	10,000
Château d'Issan	Cantenac-Margaux	35	130	11,000
Château Lagrange	St.-Julien	110	500	40,000
Château Langoa	St.-Julien	15	60	6,000

	Commune	Hectares	Tonneaux	Average Production Cases (12 bottles)
Château Malescot-Saint-Exupéry	Margaux	32	140	12,000
Château Cantenac-Brown	Cantenac-Margaux	42	150	13,000
Château Palmer	Cantenac-Margaux	40	140	12,000
Château La Lagune	Ludon	70	280	24,000
Château Desmirail	Margaux	0	0	0
Château Calon-Ségur	St.-Estèphe	50	200	20,000
Château Ferrière	Margaux	—	10	900
Château Marquis-d'Alesme-Becker	Margaux	15	75	7,000
Château Boyd-Cantenac	Cantenac-Margaux	18	80	7,000

FOURTH GROWTHS (Quatrièmes Crus)

	Commune	Hectares	Tonneaux	Average Production Cases (12 bottles)
Château Saint-Pierre	St.-Julien	17	60	5,000
Château Branaire	St.-Julien	49	200	19,000
Château Talbot	St.-Julien	100	400	35,000
Château Duhart-Milon-Rothschild	Pauillac	58	230	20,000
Château Pouget	Cantenac-Margaux	12	50	4,000
Château La Tour-Carnet	St.-Laurent	30	120	11,000
Château Lafon-Rochet	St.-Estèphe	45	130	11,000
Château Beychevelle	St.-Julien	70	280	26,000
Château Prieuré-Lichine	Cantenac-Margaux	68	260	20,000
Château Marquis-de-Terme	Margaux	38	150	14,000

FIFTH GROWTHS (Cinquièmes Crus)

	Commune	Hectares	Tonneaux	Average Production Cases (12 bottles)
Château Pontet-Canet	Pauillac	76	400	40,000
Château Batailley	Pauillac	55	220	20,000
Château Grand-Puy-Lacoste	Pauillac	45	180	17,000
Château Grand-Puy-Ducasse	Pauillac	36	140	14,000
Château Haut-Batailley	Pauillac	22	60	6,000
Château Lynch-Bages	Pauillac	76	300	28,000
Château Lynch-Moussas	Pauillac	40	175	17,000
Château Dauzac	Labarde-Margaux	55	220	20,000
Château Mouton-Baronne-Phillippe (formerly known as Mouton Baron Phillippe)	Pauillac	45	180	16,000
Château du Tertre	Arsac-Margaux	50	200	18,000
Château Haut-Bages-Libéral	Pauillac	23	100	8,000
Château Pédesclaux	Pauillac	30	130	8,000
Château Belgrave	St.-Laurent	35	100	9,000
Château Camensac	St.-Laurent	62	260	25,000
Château Cos Labory	St.-Estèphe	15	60	5,000
Château Clerc-Milon-Rothschild	Pauillac	25	125	9,000
Château Croizet-Bages	Pauillac	25	100	8,000
Château Cantemerle	Macau	55	280	25,000

EXCEPTIONAL GROWTHS (Crus Exceptionnels)

	Commune		Commune
Château Villegeorge	Avensan	Château la Couronne	Pauillac
Château Angludet	Cantenac-Margaux	Château Moulin-Riche	St.-Julien
Château Chasse-Spleen	Moulis	Château Bel-Air-Marquis d'Aligre	Soussans-Margaux
Château Poujeaux-Theil	Moulis		

See author's suggested revised classification on pp. 127–129.

II THE CRUS BOURGEOIS AND CRUS ARTISANS OF THE MÉDOC

The following figures of production are approximate and indicate average annual output, as given by the communes and taken from their Déclarations de Récoltes records.

MINOR GROWTHS OF THE HAUT-MÉDOC

	Commune	Hectares	Acres	Tonneaux
Château d'Agassac	Ludon	33	83	80
Château Andron-Blanquet	St.-Estèphe	15	37.5	75
Château Aney	Cussac	22	55	100
Château Angludet	Cantenac-Margaux	30	75	120
Château Anthonic	Moulis	18	45	50
Château d'Arches	Ludon	4	10	17
Château d'Arcins	Arcins	82	200	330
Château Arnauld	Arcins	18	45	80
Château d'Arsac	Arsac	16	40	90
Château Balac	St.-Laurent	11	27	50
Château Barateau	St.-Laurent	7	17.3	31
Château Barreyres	Arcins	100	250	400
Château Beaumont	Cussac	57	220	350
Château Beauséjour	St.-Estèphe	15	38	75
Château Beau-Site	St.-Estèphe	25	62	135
Château Beau-Site-Haut-Vignoble	St.-Estèphe	19	47	80
Château Bel Air	St.-Estèphe	4	10	25
Château Bel Air	Cussac	35	40	160
Château Bel-Air Lagrave	Moulis	12	30	46
Château Bel-Air-Marquis d'Aligre	Soussans-Margaux	17	42	50
Château Belgrave	Listrac	9	22	33
Château Belle Rose	Pauillac	6	15	30
Château Bellevue	Cussac	1	2.5	3
Château Bel Orme-Tronquoy de Lalande	St.-Seurin-de-Cadourne	25	62	130
Cru Bergeron	Moulis	6	15	30
Château Bernones	Cussac	16	40	90
Cru Bibian Darriet	Listrac	2	5	9
Château Biston Brillette	Moulis	19	48	75
Château Bois du Monteil	Cantenac	5	13	30
Château Bonneau	St.-Seurin-de-Cadourne	5	12.5	9
Château Bonneau-Livran	St.-Seurin-de-Cadourne	7	18	40
Château Bouqueyran	Moulis	9	22	35
Château Bournac	St.-Estèphe	3	10	8
Château Brame-les-Tours	St.-Estèphe	6	15	30
Château Branas	Moulis	3	7.5	12
Château du Breuil	Cissac	25	63	100
Château Brillette	Moulis	27	67	40
Château de Cach	St.-Laurent	14	35	80
Château Cambon	Blanquefort	5	12.5	20
Château Cambon La Pelouse	Macau	60	150	240
Château Canteloup et Commanderie	St.-Estèphe	15	37.5	50
Château Capdelong	St.-Julien	5	13	30
Château Cap du Haut	Moulis	7	17.3	35
Château Capbern-Gasqueton	St.-Estèphe	36	89	75
Château Capléon-Veyrin	Listrac	5	12.5	23
Château Caronne Sainte-Gemme	St.-Laurent	42	105	200
Château du Cartillon	Lamarque	28	70	150
Château Chambert-Marbuzet	St.-Estèphe	7	18	40
Château Charmail	St.-Seurin-de-Cadourne	20	50	100
Château Charmant	Margaux	6	15	20
Château Chasse-Spleen	Moulis	66	264	210
Château Cissac	Cissac	45	113	220
Château Citran	Avensan	92	230	368

	Commune	Hectares	Acres	Tonneaux
Château Clarke	Listrac	131	327.5	500
Château Colombier-Monpelou	Pauillac	14	35	90
Château de Côme	St.-Estèphe	7	17	40
Château Constand Lesquireu	Vertheuil	61	153	350
Château Corconnac	St.-Laurent	7	17	35
Domaine de Coudot	Cussac	6	15	35
Château Coufran	St.-Seurin-de-Cadourne	60	150	300
Château Coutelin-Merville	St.-Estèphe	16	40	90
Château Deyrem-Valentin	Soussans-Margaux	7	17.3	30
Château Dillon	Blanquefort	38	95	150
Château Doyac	St.-Seurin-de-Cadourne	12	30	70
Château Duplessis Fabre	Moulis	9	22	45
Château Duplessis Hauchecorne	Moulis	16	40	70
Château Dutruch Grand Poujeaux	Moulis	30	75	120
Château Fonbadet	Pauillac	15	38	100
Château Fonréaud	Listrac	50	125	300
Château Fontesteau	St.-Sauveur	12	30	50
Château Fort de Vauban	Cussac	7	17	35
Château Fourcas-Dupré	Listrac	40	100	220
Château Fourcas-Hosten	Listrac	45	113	280
Château Gaudin	Pauillac	10	25	60
Château Glana	St.-Julien	42	105	220
Château Gloria	St.-Julien	50	125	200
Château Gobineau	Listrac	8	20	12
Château Grand Canyon	Pauillac	6	15	30
Château Grand Clapeau Olivier	Blanquefort	11	27.5	35
Château Grand Duroc Milon	Pauillac	5	13	25
Château Grand Moulin	St.-Seurin-de-Cadourne	18	45	100
Château Grandis	St.-Seurin-de-Cadourne	5	12	24
Château Grave La Cour	St.-Estèphe	6	15	40
Château des Graviers	Arsac	7	18	45
Château Gressier Grand Poujeaux	Moulis	20	50	100
Château Hanteillan	Cissac	70	175	350
Château Haut-Bages-Monpelou	Pauillac	10	25	60
Château Haut-Brega	St.-Seurin-de-Cadourne	7	17	40
Château Haut-Breton Larigaudière	Soussans-Margaux	5	13	30
Château Haut-Carmail	St.-Seurin-de-Cadourne	5	12	25
Château Haut-Laborde	St.-Sauveur	20	50	100
Château Haut-Logat	Lissac	9	22	45
Château Haut-Madrac	St.-Sauveur	20	50	120
Château Haut-Marbuzet	St.-Estèphe	40	100	200
Château Haut-Pauillac	Pauillac	5	13	30
Château Haut-Tayac	Soussans-Margaux	6	15	25
Château Hennebelle	Lamarque	4	10	14
Château Houissant	St.-Estèphe	20	50	100
Château Hourtin Ducasse	St.-Sauveur	30	75	150
Château du Junca	St.-Sauveur	8	20	50
Château La Bécade	Listrac	22	55	115
Château La-Bécasse	Pauillac	4	10	20
Château La Bridane	St.-Julien	17	43	90
Château La Closerie-Grand-Poujeaux	Moulis	7	17.5	23
Château La Couronne	Pauillac	3	7.5	20
Château La Dame Blanche (the white wine of Château du Taillan, which has only the Appellation Bordeaux Blanc Supérieur)	Le Taillan	5	13	20
Château La Fleur Milon	Pauillac	13	32	50
Château La Galiane	Soussans-Margaux	4	10	16
Château la Grave	St.-Sauveur	8	20	45
Château La Gurgue	Margaux	10	25	35

	Commune	Hectares	Acres	Tonneaux
Château La Haye	St.-Estèphe	6	15	20
Château La Hontete	St.-Seurin-de-Cadourne	8	20	45
Château La Houringue	Macau	27	68	150
Château La Mouline	Moulis	45	112	200
Château La Mothe	St.-Seurin-de-Cadourne	18	45	100
Château de la Ronceray	St.-Estèphe	5	13	30
Château La Rose Brana	St.-Estèphe	11	28	60
Domaine La Rose Maucaillou	Soussans-Margaux	6	15	35
Coopérative de la Rose Pauillac	Pauillac	110	275	500
Château La Rousselière	St.-Estèphe	8	20	45
Château La Tour du Haut Moulin	Cussac	24	60	100
Château La Tour-de-Mons	Soussans-Margaux	30	70	120
Château La Tour Pibran	Pauillac	7	17	25
Château La Tour du Roc	Arcins	9	22	30
Château La Tour des Ternes	St.-Estèphe	12	30	13
Château Labégorce	Margaux	30	74	130
Château Labégorce-Zédé	Soussans-Margaux	21	52.5	100
Château Lachesnaye	Cussac	20	50	100
Château Ladouys	St.-Estèphe	4	10	10
Château Laffitte-Carcasset	St.-Estèphe	23	63	135
Château Lafon	Listrac	12	30	55
Château Lagorce	Moulis	3	7.5	7
Château Lagravette-Peyredon	Listrac	5	12.5	10
Château Lalande	Listrac	12	30	55
Château Lalande-Borie	St.-Julien	18	45	100
Château Lamarque	Larmarque	47	117	250
Château Lamothe-Bergeron	Cussac	60	150	300
Château Lamothe-Cissac	Cissac	47	118	250
Château Landat	Cissac	30	75	150
Château Lanessan	Cussac	40	100	220
Château Larose Trintaudon	St.-Laurent	172	430	750
Cru Larragay	Listrac	2	5	6
Château Larrivaux	Cissac	21	53	100
Cru Lauga	Cussac	3	7.5	4
Château Lavillotte	St.-Estèphe	12	30	70
Château Le Boscq	St.-Estèphe	13	32.5	65
Château le Bourdieu	Vertheuil	32	80	180
Château Le Crock	St.-Estèphe	32	80	180
Château Le Fournas Bernadotte	St.-Sauveur	20	50	120
Château Le Meynieu	Vertheuil	15	38	80
Château Le Roc	St.-Estèphe	1	2.5	5
Château Le Souley-Ste.-Croix	Vertheuil	18	45	100
Château Lemone-Lafon-Rochet	Ludon	6	15	15
Château l'Ermitage	Listrac	5	13	30
Château Les Barraillots	Margaux	5	13	30
Château Les Ormes-de-Pez	St.-Estèphe	30	75	150
Cru Lescourt	Listrac	2	5	5
Château Lestage	Listrac	52	130	280
Château Lestage	St.-Seurin-de-Cadourne	1	2.5	5
Château Lestage Darquier	Moulis	4	10	8
Château Lestage Darquier Grand Poujeaux	Moulis	5	12.5	20
Château Lestage Simon	St.-Seurin-de-Cadourne	32	80	150
Château Leyssac	St.-Estèphe	12	30	70
Château L'Hôpital	St.-Estèphe	5	12.5	30
Château Lieujean	St.-Sauveur	12	30	70
Château Ligondras	Arsac-Margaux	7	18	35
Château Liouner	Listrac	13	33	70
Château Liversan	St.-Sauveur	45	112	180
Domaine du Lucrabey	Cissac	5	12.5	7

	Commune	Hectares	Acres	Tonneaux
Château Mac-Carthy	St.-Estèphe	4	10	12
Château MacCarthy Moula	St.-Estèphe	6	15	12
Château de Magnol	Blanquefort	17	42	90
Château Malescasse	Lamarque	32	80	100
Château Malleret	Le Pian	60	150	280
Château Malmaison	Moulis	4	10	5
Château Marbuzet	St.-Estèphe	7	18	40
Château Marque	St.-Seurin-de-Cadourne	1	2.5	6
Château Marsac-Seguineau	Soussans-Margaux	7	17	30
Château Martinens	Cantenac-Margaux	30	75	120
Clos du Mas	Listrac	5	12.5	9
Château Maucaillou	Moulis	45	112	230
Château Maucamps	Macau	15	38	70
Château Mauvesin	Moulis	7	18	35
Château Médrac	Moulis	1	12.5	2
Château Meyney	St.-Estèphe	50	125	300
Château Monbrison	Arsac-Margaux	14	35	70
Château Mongravey	Arsac-Margaux	5	13	30
Château Montbrun	Cantenac-Margaux	9	22	40
Château Morin	St.-Estèphe	10	25	60
Château Moulin-à-Vent	Moulis	20	49	90
Château du Moulin du Bourg	Listrac	7	17	35
Château Moulin de Laborde	Listrac	16	40	90
Château Moulin Rose	Lamarque	3	7.5	9
Château Moulin de la Rose	St.-Julien	4	10	14
Château du Moulin Rouge	Cussac	15	48	80
Château Moulis	Moulis	12	30	50
Château Nexon-Lemoyne	Ludon	16	40	75
Château Pabeau	St.-Seurin-de-Cadourne	10	25	33
Château Padarnac	Pauillac	5	13	30
Château Paveil de Luze	Soussans-Margaux	24	60	120
Château Pey La Rose	Pauillac	6	15	30
Château de Peyrabon	St.-Laurent	29	72	100
Château Peyrabon	Pauillac	5	13	30
Château Peyrabon	St.-Sauveur	53	133	350
Château Peyredon	Listrac	3	7.5	9
Château de Pez	St.-Estèphe	25	62.5	100
Château Phélan-Ségur	St.-Estèphe	55	138	300
Château Pibran	Pauillac	7	17.5	30
Château Picard (see Château Beauséjour)	St.-Estèphe	12	30	60
Château Pichon	Parempuyre	23	58	130
Château Pierre Bibian	Listrac	14	35	60
Château Plantey	Pauillac	27	68	160
Château Pomeys	Moulis	7	17	25
Château Pomys	St.-Estèphe	7	18	45
Château Pontac-Lynch	Cantenac-Margaux	9	23	60
Château Pontet-Chappez	Arsac-Margaux	4	10	20
Château Pontoise-Cabarrus	St.-Seurin-de-Cadourne	24	63	125
Château Poujeaux	Moulis	50	125	280
Château Puy Castera	Cissac	25	63	120
Château Ramage La Batisse	St. Sauveur	54	135	300
Château du Raux	Cussac	15	48	70
Château Renouil Franquet	Moulis	4	10	8
Château du Retout	Cussac	25	63	120
Château Reverdi	Listrac	4	10	18
Château Reysson	Vertheuil	52	130	300
Château Robert Franquet	Moulis	8	20	30
Château Rose Ste.-Croix	Listrac	6	15	16
Château Ruat	Moulis	11	28	35

	Commune	Hectares	Acres	Tonneaux
Château St. Ahon	Blanquefort	27	67	150
Château St.-Estèphe	St.-Estèphe	10	25	30
Château St.-Marc	Soussans-Margaux	7	18	40
Château St.-Martin	Listrac	2	5	8
Château St.-Paul	St.-Seurin-de-Cadourne	19	47	100
Château St.-Sauveur	St.-Sauveur	12	30	60
Château Saransot-Dupré	Listrac	10	25	40
Château Ségur	Parempuyre	30	75	140
Château Sémeillan-Mazeau	Listrac	12	30	50
Château Sénéjac	Le Pian	16	40	70
Château Senilhac	St.-Seurin-de-Cadourne	14	35	65
Château Siran	Labarde-Margaux	30	75	120
Château Sociando-Mallet	St.-Seurin-de-Cadourne	30	75	150
Château Soudars	St.-Seurin-de-Cadourne	15	48	70
Château du Taillan (The white wine is called Château La Dame Blanche)	Le Taillan	20	50	80
Château Tayac	Soussans-Margaux	34	85	200
Château Terrey-Gros-Caillou	St.-Julien	14	35	80
Château Teynac	St.-Julien	5	13	19
Château Tour Granins	Moulis	9	22	50
Château Tour Marbuzet	St.-Estèphe	8	20	45
Château Tour du Mirail	Cissac	18	45	100
Château Tour St.-Joseph	Cissac	10	25	60
Château Tronquoy-Lalande	St.-Estèphe	13	32.5	60
Château Verdignan	St.-Seurin-de-Cadourne	48	118	200
Château Vieux Braneyre	Cissac	10	25	60
Château Vieux Coutelin	St.-Estèphe	7	18	45
Château Villegeorge	Avensan	9	22	40

MINOR GROWTHS OF THE MÉDOC (OR BAS-MÉDOC)

	Commune	Hectares	Acres	Tonneaux
Domaine des Anguilleys (Château Vieux Robin)	Bégadan	8	20	45
Clos Beau Rivage de By	Bégadan	5	12.5	25
Château Bégadanet	Bégadan	4	10	12
Cru Bel-Air Mareil	Ordonnac-et-Potensac	3	7.5	12
Château Bellerive	Valeyrac	9	22.5	50
Château Bellevue	Valeyrac	15	37	70
Château des Bertins	Bégadan	25	62	125
Château Blaignan	Blaignan	62	155	300
Château Bois de Roc	St.-Yzans	25	62	125
Château Brie Caillou	St.-Germain-d'Esteuil	18	45	100
Château des Brousteras	St.-Yzans	17	42	100
Domaine de By	Bégadan	31	77	145
Château Carcanieux-les-Graves	Queyrac	20	40	100
Château Castéra	St.-Germain-d'Esteuil	50	125	260
Cave Coopérative "Belle Vue"	Ordonnac-et-Potensac	130	322	700
Cave Coopérative "St.-Jean"	Bégadan	500	1,250	2,300
Château Chantelys	Prignac	6	15	30
Château des Combes	Bégadan	4	10	20
Domaine de la Croix	Ordonnac	16	40	80
Coopérative ("La Chatellenie")	Vertheuil	—	—	300
Coopérative de Prignac, Château Bensse	Prignac	200	494	950
Coopérative de Queyrac, Château St.-Roch	Queyrac	56	138	300
Coopérative de St.-Yzans, Cave St.-Brice	St.-Yzans	140	346	1,000

	Commune	Hectares	Acres	Tonneaux
Cru des Deux-Moulins	St.-Christoly	13	32.5	48
Château Gallais-Bellevue (*see* Château Potensac)				
Château Greysac (Château Bertins)	Bégadan	52	125	250
Château Grivière	Blaignan	15	37	80
Château Haut-Blaignan	Blaignan	7	17	42
Château Haut Canteloup	St.-Christoly	18	45	100
Château Haut Maurac	St.-Yzans	25	62	120
Château Hauterive	St.-Germain-d'Esteuil	75	187	350
Cru Hontane (*see* Château Côtes de Blaignan)				
Château Hourbanon	Prignac	6	15	32
Château La Cardonne	Blaignan	55	133	300
Château La Clare	Bégadan	18	45	90
Château La Croix du Breuil	Louquéques	15	37	80
Château La France	Blaignan	6	15	30
Château La Gorce	Blaignan	37	92	180
Château La Gorre	Bégadan	7	17	40
Château Landon	Bégadan	25	62	150
Château La Ribeau	St.-Yzans	18	45	100
Château La Rivière	Blaignac	12	30	60
Château La Rose Garamay (*see* Château Livran)				
Château La Tour-Blanche	St.-Christoly	26	64	150
Château La Tour de By	Bégadan	60	148	300
Château La Tour Haut-Caussan (now Château Haut-Cassan)	Blaignan	11	27.5	60
Château La Tour-St.-Bonnet	St.-Christoly	40	99	215
Château La Tour Seran	St.-Christoly	18	45	100
Château Laujac	Bégadan	25	62	150
Château La Valière	St.-Christoly	18	45	100
Château Le Boscq	St.-Christoly	25	62	125
Château Le Tréhon	Bégadan	16	40	100
Clos Les Moines	Couquéques	18	45	110
Château Les Ormes-Sorbet	Couquéques	25	62	120
Château Les Tourelles	Blaignan	31	77	125
Château Les Tuileries	St.-Yzans	15	37	80
Château L'Hermitage	Couquéques	6	15	15
Château Livran, Château La Rose Garamay	St.-Germain-d'Esteuil	40	100	200
Château Loudenne	St.-Yzans	28	68	150
Château Lugagnac	Vertheuil			
Clos Mandillot	St.-Christoly			
Château Monthil	Bégadan	25	62	100
Clos du Moulin	St.-Christoly	8	20	40
Château Panigon	Civrac	31	77	150
Château Patache d'Aux	Bégadan	42	105	350
Château Pay-de-Lalo	St.-Germain-d'Esteuil	2	5	7
Château Peymartin	Ordonnac	15	37	80
Château Plagnac	Bégadan	32	70	150
Château Potensac, Château Gallais-Bellevue	Ordonnac-et-Potensac	40	100	200
Château Preuillac	Lesparre	35	87	150
Château Reysson	Vertheuil	34	85	65
Château Roquegrave	Valeyrac	25	62	100
Château St.-Bonnet	St.-Christoly	40	100	300
Château St.-Christoly	St.-Christoly	18	45	100
Château St. Christophe	St.-Christoly	18	45	100
Château St.-Germain	St.-Germain-d'Esteuil	2	5	8
Cru St.-Louis	Conquéques	3	7.5	11
Château St.-Saturnin	Bégadan	25	62	120
Château Sigognac	St.-Yzans	56	140	250
Château Vernous	Lesparre	22	55	100
Cru de Vieux-Château Landon	Bégadan	27	67	110
Château Vieux Robin, Domaine des Anguilleys	Bégadan	15	37	100

III SAINT ÉMILION: 1986 OFFICIAL CLASSIFICATION

In 1985 the best Saint-Émilion wines were again for the third time classified as First Great Growths and Great Growths.
On the 27th May 1986 this classification became law and the vineyards that were dropped will have the right to use their form of classification on the 1985 labels only and those which have been elevated will be able to show their new status as of the 1986 vintage.

FIRST GREAT GROWTHS (St.-Émilion—Premiers Grands Crus Classés)

		Hectares	Acres	Tonneaux	Approximate Cases
A)	Château Ausone	7	17.5	35	2,800
	Château Cheval Blanc	35	88	160	14,000
B)	Château Beauséjour-Bécot*	16.6	41	85	6,800
	Château Beauséjour-Duffau-Lagarosse	7	17	25	2,000
	Château Bélair	13	33	50	4,000
	Château Canon	18	45	75	6,500
	Château Figeac	34	85	180	15,000
	Clos Fourtet	18	45	70	6,700
	Château La Gaffelière	22	55	90	8,500
	Château La Magdelaine	11	27	40	3,500
	Château Pavie	35	88	200	16,000
	Château Trottevieille	10	25	50	4,000

GREAT GROWTHS (St.-Émilion—Grands Crus Classés)

	Hectares	Acres	Tonneaux
Château l'Angélus	28	70	112
Château l'Arrosée	9	22.5	35
Château Balestard-la-Tonnelle	8	20	40
Château Beauséjour-Bécot*	16.6	41	85
Château Bellevue	6	15	24
Château Bergat	4	10	20
Château Berliquet	9	22.5	60
Château Cadet-Bon	3	7.5	20
Château Cadet-Piola	7	17.5	30
Château Canon-la-Gaffelière	22.5	45	125
Château Cap-de-Mourlin (Jacques Capdemourlin)	15.5	38.5	90
Château Chapelle Madeleine	1	2.5	1
Château-Le-Châtelet	5	12.5	30
Château Chauvin	12	30	60
Château Corbin	12	25	60
Château Corbin-Michotte	7	17.5	35
Château Couvent-des-Jacobins	8	20	40
Château Croque-Michotte	10	25	50
Château Curé-Bon-La Madeleine	5	12.5	20
Château Dassault	26	65	130
Château Faurie-de-Souchard	8.5	21	45
Château Fonplégade	17	42.5	100
Château Fonroque	18	45	60
Château Franc-Mayne	6.5	16	35
Château Grand-Barrail-Lamarzelle-Figeac	23.5	58	150
Château Grand-Corbin	13.5	33	65
Château Grand-Corbin-Despagne	25.5	63	160
Château Grand-Mayne	17.5	44	70
Château Grand-Pontet	14	32.5	60
Château Guadet-St.-Julien	5.5	13	25
Château Haut-Corbin	7	18	35
Clos des Jacobins	8	20	45
Château La Clotte	1	2.5	5

*Château Beauséjour-Becot properly belongs among the First Great Growths, but was unjustly demoted to a Great Growth in the 1986 classification.

Saint-Émilion: Principal Growths

	Hectares	Acres	Tonneaux
Château La Clusière	3	7.5	12
Château La Dominique	17	42.5	70
Clos La Madeleine	1	2.5	4
Château Lamarzelle	5.5	12	35
Château La Tour-Figeac	16	40	100
Château La Tour-du-Pin-Figeac	7	17.5	45
Château La Tour-du-Pin-Figeac-Moueix	8.5	21	65
Château Laniote	5	12.5	25
Château Larcis-Ducasse	11	25	60
Château Larmande	16	40	65
Château Laroze	28	70	100
Château La Serre	7	17.5	40
Château Le Prieuré	4.5	11	25
Château Matras	16	40	60
Château Mauvezin	5	12.5	30
Château Moulin du Cadet	5	12.5	30
Clos de l'Oratoire	6	15	35
Château Pavie-Decesse	8.5	21	40
Château Pavie-Macquin	12	30	50
Château Pavillon-Cadet	1	2.5	5
Château Petit-Faurie-de-Soutard	9	22.5	50
Château Ripeau	14	35	70
Château St.-Georges-Côte-Pavie	6	15	21
Clos St.-Martin	2.5	6	10
Château Sansonnet	6.5	16	30
Château Soutard	22	55	120
Château Tertre-Daugay	8	20	45
Château Trimoulet	16	40	70
Château Troplong-Mondot	25	62.5	150
Château Villemaurine	6.5	16	35
Château Yon-Figeac	21	52.5	120

PRINCIPAL GROWTHS INCLUDING GRANDS CRUS OF SAINT-EMILION

	Hectares	Acres	Tonneaux
Domaine Allée-de-Lescours	4	10	11
Clos d'Armens	2	5	7
Château d'Arthus	5	12.5	13
Clos d'Arthus	12	30	23
Château Badette	8	20	23
Domaine de Badon-Patarbet	2	5	12
Château Barbey	2	5	9
Château Barbeyron	4	10	13
Château Barde-Haut	12	30	43
Château Bardoulet	2	5	7
Domaine de Bardoulet	3	7.5	15
Château du Basque	8	20	35
Château Béard	5	12.5	22
Château Béard La Chapelle	20	50	100
Château Beau-Mazerat (see Château Grand-Mayne)			
Château Beausite	4	10	15
Château Bel-Horizon	2	5	5
Château Belair-Sarthou	5	12.5	19
Château Belle-Assise	16	40	100
Château Bellefont Belcier Guillier	11	27.7	42
Château Bellegrave	11	27	55
Château Belles-Plantes	3	7.5	9
Château Bellevue-Figeac	8	20	45
Cru Bellevue-Mondotte	2	5	7

	Hectares	Acres	Tonneaux
Clos Bellevue-Puyblanquet	3	7.5	7
Château Bellisle-Mondotte	26	65	120
Clos Bernachot	2	5	8
Clos Berthoneau (see Château Du Roy)			
Château Bézineau	7	17.5	40
Cru Bibey	6	15	18
Château Bicasse-Lartigue	3	7.5	11
Château Bigaroux	31	77.5	150
Château Billerand	8	20	27
Cru Biquet	4	10	19
Château Bois-Grouley	5	12	25
Château Bois-Redon-Grand-Corbin	4	10	16
Château Bord-Fonrazade	4	10	14
Château Bord-Lartigue	2	5	11
Château Boulerne	9	22.5	32
Château Bouquey	6	15	30
Domaine du Bourg	2	5	13
Château Boutisse	16	40	77
Château Brisson	4	10	13
Château Brisson, Château Destieux	9	22.5	30
Château Brun	6	15	20
Clos Brun	3	7.5	13
Clos du Calvaire	2	5	7
Château le Calvaire	12	30	60
Château Cantenac	12	30	60
Clos Cantenac	2	5	10
Château Canterane	10	25	50
Château Caperot (see Château Monbousquet)			
Clos Caperot	3	7.5	10
Château Capet	15	38	70
Château Capet-Guiller	15	37	80
Château Cardinal Villemaurine	12	30	60
Château Carteau-Bas-Daugay	6	15	30
Château Carteau-Côtes Daugay	8	20	40
Château Carteau-Pin-de-Fleurs	3	7.5	16
Château Cassevert (see Château Grand-Mayne)			
Château Castelot	10	25	43
Domaine de la Cateau	3	7.5	11
Château de Cauze	31	78	125
Château Cauzin	4	10	23
Clos de la Cavaille-Lescours	1	2.5	7
Cave Coopérative, Royal St.-Émilion, Côtes Rocheuses	814	2,035	5,709
Château Champion	5	12.5	16
Château Chante-Alouette	6	15	23
Clos Chante-l'Alouette, Domaine Haut-Patarabet	4	10	24
Château Chantecaille	3	7.5	17
Château Chantegrive	5	12.5	20
Domaine de la Chapelle	3	7.5	15
Château Chatelet (see Château Larques)			
Château Cheval-Brun	5	12.5	14
Château Cheval-Noir	4	10	11
Château du Clocher	3	7.5	13
Domaine de la Clotte	5	12.5	15
Château du Comte	3	7.5	5
Clos Cormey	7	17.5	29
Château Cormeil-Figeac	20	50	100
Château Côte-Migon-la-Gaffelière	1	2.5	6
Château Côte de la Mouleyre	8	20	40
Château Côte de Rol-Valentin	3	7.3	9

Saint-Émilion: Principal Growths

	Hectares	Acres	Tonneaux
Château Côtes-Bernateau	12	30	70
Cru Côtes-Pressac	2	5	8
Cru Côtes-Roland	2	5	9
Clos Côtes-Roland-de-Pressac	2	5	9
Château Côtes-Veyrac	2	7.5	19
Château Coudert	3	7.5	12
Château Coudert-Pelletan	9	22.5	36
Château Croix de Figeac	3	7.5	12
Domaine de la Croix-Mazerat	2	5	5
Château Croix-du-Merle	3	7.5	8
Château Croix-Peyblanquet	4	10	9
Château de la Croix-Simard	1	2.5	7
Château Croix-Villemaurine	1	2.5	5
Clos Daupin	2	5	10
Château des Demoiselles	1	2.5	5
Domaine des Dépendances Cru Jaugueblanc	6	15	30
Domaine Despagne	7	17.5	15
Château Despagnet	3	7.5	13
Château Destieu	4	10	15
Château Destieux	9	22.5	30
Château Destieux	7	17.5	25
Château Destieux (*see* Château Brisson)			
Château Destieux-Berger	13	32	60
Château Destieux-Verac	11	27.5	36
Château l'Étoile-Pourret (*see* Château La Grâce-Dieu)			
Domaine des Escardos	7	17.5	12
Château Fagouet-Jean-Voisin	6	15	35
Château Faleyrens	5	12.5	12
Château Faugère	13	32	60
Château de Ferrand	30	75	148
Château Ferrandat	28	70	130
Cru Ferrandat	1	2.5	9
Château Pont-de-Figeac, Château Grangeneuve	25	62.5	79
Petit Clos Figeac	3	7.5	15
Château Fleurus	1	2.5	8
Château Flouquet	25	63	120
Château Fombrauge	50	125	200
Château Fond-Razade	4	10	8
Château Fond-de-Rol	1	2.5	5
Château Fonrazade	9	22	50
Clos Fonrazade	4	10	25
Clos Fontelle	1	2.5	5
Château Fougères	9	22.5	45
Château Fougueyrat, Château La Tour-Laroze, Cru Le Châtelet	19	47.5	87
Château de Fouquet	6	15	5
Château Fourney	39	97	160
Château Fourney (*see* Château Vieux-Guinot)			
Château Franc (*see* Château Franc-Patarabet)			
Château Franc-Beau-Mazerat	3	7.5	11
Château Franc-Cantenac	3	7	15
Château Franc-Cormey	2	5	4
Château Franc-Cros	4	10	14
Château Franc-Laporte	9	22.5	50
Clos Franc-Larmande	3	7.5	9
Château Franc-Mazerat	2	5	8
Château Franc-Patarabet, Château Franc	6	15	30
Château Franc Peilhan	3	7.5	9
Château Franc-Petit-Figeac	3	7.5	22
Château Franc Pipeau	3	7.5	17

	Hectares	Acres	Tonneaux
Château Franc Pourret	11	27.5	49
Château Franc-la-Rose	4	10	20
Château Franc-Rozier	3	7.5	15
Domaine de la Gaffelière	10	25	50
Château Gaillard	20	50	100
Château Gaillard-de-Gorce	8	20	40
Château Gastebourse (see Château Pontet Clauzure)			
Château Gaubert, Clos des Moines	10	25	55
Clos Gerbaud	1	2.5	7
Château Godeau	3	7.5	8
Clos Gontey	2	5	13
Château Grand-Berc	10	25	55
Château Grand-Bigaroux	9	22	50
Château Grand-Caillou-Noir	3	7.5	16
Château Grand-Corbin-Manuel	8	20	40
Château Grand-Faurie	1	2.5	5
Domaine du Grand-Faurie	4	10	17
Château Grand-Gontey	4	10	16
Clos Grand-Gontey	4	10	17
Domaine du Grand-Gontey	2	5	9
Château Grand Jacques	11	27.5	46
Château Grand-Mazerat (see Château Grand-Mayne)	17	42.5	85
Château Grand-Mirande	6	15	32
Château Grand Nauve	13	32	60
Château Grand-Peilhan-Blanc	7	17.5	34
Château Grand Pey-de-Lescours	31	77	150
Château Grand-Rivallon	3	7.5	9
Château Grangeneuve (see Château Figeac)			
Château Grangey	5	12.5	22
Château des Graves	4	10	24
Cru des Graves	2	5	6
Château Graves-d'Armens	6	15	35
Château Graves d'Arthus	5	12.5	21
Château des Graves-de-Mondou	4	10	14
Château Gravet	12	30	60
Château Gravet-Renaissance	15	37	70
Clos Gravet	11	27.5	51
Clos du Gros	1	2.5	6
Château Gros-Caillou	17	42	100
Clos des Gros-Chênes	5	12.5	27
Cru Grotte-d'Arcis	3	7.5	14
Château Guadet-Franc-Grâce-Dieu	8	20	40
Château Gueyrot	6	15	27
Château Guillemot	7	17.5	17
Château Guinot	4	10	16
Clos Guinot	6	15	40
Domaine du Haut-Badon	3	7.5	8
Domaine de Haut-Barbey	2	5	7
Château Haut-Barbeyron	4	10	5
Château Haut-Benitey	5	12.5	13
Château Haut-Berthonneau	1	2.5	7
Clos Haut-Bibey	2	5	11
Château Haut-Brisson	13	32	65
Clos Haut-Cabanne	1	2.5	6
Château Haut-Cadet	13	32.5	36
Château Haut-Fonrazade, Cru La Tour-Fonrazade	11	27.5	43
Château Haut-Grâce-Dieu (see Château Peyrelongue)			
Château Haut-Grand-Faurie	4	10	21
Cru Haut-Grand-Faurie	1	2.5	5

Saint-Émilion: Principal Growths

	Hectares	Acres	Tonneaux
Château Haut-Gueyrot	9	22	50
Château Haut-Jauge Blanc	1	2.5	5
Château Haut-Jean-Faure, Clos La Fleur-Figeac, Clos La Bourrue, Château Tauzinat-l'Hermitage	7	17.5	49
Château Haut-Jeanguillot	4	10	17
Château Haut-Lartigue	3	7.5	15
Château Haut-Lavallade	10	25	50
Château Haut-Mauvinon	8	20	28
Château Haut-Mazerat, Vieux Château Mazerat	8	20	35
Château Haut-Panet-Pineuilh	2	5	9
Château Haut-Peyroutas	11	27	60
Château Haut-Pontet	5	12.5	25
Château Haut-Pourret	5	12.5	30
Château Haut-Rabion	5	12.5	17
Château Haut-Renaissance	22	55	100
Domaine Haut-Trimoulet	5	12.5	20
Château Haut-Robin	4	10	14
Château Haut-Rocher	8	20	40
Château Haut-Segottes	7	17.5	42
Château Haut-Simard	20	50	150
Château Haut-Touran	3	7.5	8
Château Haut-Troquart-La Grâce Dieu	4	10	19
Domaine Haut-Vachon	4	10	18
Château Haut-Veyrac	7	17.5	30
Château Haute-Nauve	8	20	40
Domaine Haute-Rouchonne	8	20	40
Château Hautes-Graves-d'Arthus	9	22.5	47
Château l'Hermitage-Mazerat	4	10	17
Château Jacques Blanc	17	42.5	100
Clos Jacquemeau	1	2.5	5
Château Jacqueminot	4	10	15
Château Jacques Noir	4	10	20
Château Jaubert-Peyblanquet	5	12.5	11
Château Jaugueblanc	5	12.5	21
Clos Jaumard	2	5	8
Château Jean Blanc	6	15	33
Clos Jean Guillot	7	17	35
Cru Jeanguillot	2	5	8
Château de Jean-Marie	4	10	20
Château Jean-Marie-Cheval-Brun	2	5	8
Château Jean-Voisin	12	30	60
Château Jean-Voisin-Carbonneyre	15	37	60
Grand Domaine Jean-Voisin	2	5	7
Château Joly	6	15	27
Cru Jubilé	2	5	9
Château Jupille et Château Carillon	22	55	100
Château Justice	3	7.5	15
Château La Barde	3	7.5	6
Clos Labarde	15	37	70
Château La Barthe	9	22	50
Domaine La Beillonne	2	5	14
Château La Bouygue	3	7.5	17
Château La Chapelle	4	10	20
Château La Chapelle-Lescours	16	40	90
Château La Clotte-Grande-Côte	4	10	11
Château La Côte-Daugay	1	2.5	6
Clos La Croix	9	22.5	49
Château La Croix-Chantecaille	6	15	32
Clos La Croix-Figeac	3	7.5	18

	Hectares	Acres	Tonneaux
Château La Croizille	4	10	9
Château La Fagnouse	5	12.5	37
Château La Fleur	5	12.5	28
Château La Fleur-Cadet	4	10	14
Clos La Fleur-Figeac (*see* Château Haut-Jean-Faure)			
Château La Fleur-Pourret	6	15	30
Château La Fortine	2	5	6
Château La Garelle	9	22.5	50
Cru La Garelle	1	2.5	8
Clos La Glaye	4	10	17
Château La Gomerie	5	12	25
Château La Grâce-Dieu-les-Menuts	13	32	70
Château La Grange de Lescure	21	52	100
Château La Mauléone (*see* Château Pontet Clauzure)			
Château La Mélissière	13	32	70
Château La Mouleyre	7	17.5	19
Château La Nauve	9	22.5	31
Château La Rose-Côtes-Rol	4	10	19
Château La Rose-Rol	4	10	19
Château La Rouchonne	9	22	50
Château La Sablière	6	15	28
Château La Sablonnerie	10	25	35
Château La Tour	7	17.5	27
Château La Tour-Baladoz	7	17	40
Château La Tour-Bertonneau	2	5	8
Château La Tour-des-Combes	12	30	60
Château La Tour-Cravignac	3	7.5	16
Château La Tour-Fonrazade	8	20	40
Château La Tour-Puyblanquet	6	14	21
Château La Tour-St.-Émilion	4	10	18
Château La Tour-St. Pierre	11	275	55
Château La Tour-Vachon	4	10	21
Clos Labrit	3	7.5	19
Château Lagaborite	2	5	8
Château La Grave-Figeac	3	7.5	17
Château Lapelletrie	9	22.5	54
Château Lapeyre	13	32	65
Château Larcis-Bergey	1	2.5	8
Château Lardon-Jacqueminot	15	37.5	74
Château Larmande	21	52	100
Château Laroque	44	110	200
Domaine Laroque, Château Nardon	3	7.5	19
Clos Larose	2	5	10
Château Larques, Château Chatelet	19	47.5	36
Château Lartigue	6	15	35
Clos Lartigue	1	2.5	5
Cru Lartigue	3	7.5	11
Clos Lartigues	2	5	8
Château Lassègue	20	50	100
Château Latour Blanche	1	2.5	4
Château Latour-Pourret	6	15	16
Château Lavallade	17	42	100
Château Lavergne	2	5	15
Clos Lavergne	9	22.5	46
Château Le Basque	18	45	47
Château Le Bon-Pasteur	3	7.5	9
Clos Le Bregnet	5	12.5	22
Château Le Castelot	5	12.5	21
Château Le Cauze	20	50	130

Saint-Émilion: Principal Growths

	Hectares	Acres	Tonneaux
Cru Le Châtelet (*see* Château Fougueyrat)			
Château Le Freyche	4	10	13
Clos Le Freyche	4	10	9
Château Le Grand-Barrail	3	7.5	11
Château Le Grand-Faurie	4	10	17
Château Le Gueyrot	4	10	15
Château Le Jurat	9	22	39
Château Le Loup	6	15	5
Château Le Merle	6	15	12
Château Le Peillan	13	32.5	20
Château Le Poteau	4	10	17
Château Le Rocher	3	7.5	10
Château Le Sable-Villebout	13	32	70
Château Le Tertre	4	10	13
Château Le Thibaut	9	22.5	33
Château Le Thibaut-Bordas	3	7.5	13
Cru Le Vignot	1	2.5	7
Château Les Bazilliques	6	15	30
Château Haut-Sarpe, Clos du Vieux, Château Les Grandes-Plantes-Haut Béard	10	25	50
Clos Les Graves	4	10	12
Château Les Jouans	12	30	90
Château Les Moulins	4	10	19
Château Les Moureaux	4	10	23
Château Les Roquettes-Mondottes	3	7.5	10
Château Les Templiers	8	20	40
Château Les Tuilleries	3	7.5	18
Château Les Vieilles-Nauves	2	5	7
Château Les-Vieilles-Souches-La-Marzelle	4	10	18
Château Lescours	32	80	160
Château Lespinasse	16	40	80
Domaine de Liamet	2	5	8
Château de Lisse	25	62.5	100
Domaine du Logis-de-Moureaux	1	2.5	6
Domaine de Longat	3	7.5	6
Château de Long-Champ	4	10	26
Château Magnan-la-Gaffelière	2	5	10
Clos du Maine	2	5	10
Château Malineau	4	10	14
Château Mangot	20	50	66
Château Marrin	19	47	100
Château Maurillon	1	2.5	7
Château Mayne-Vieux	5	12.5	17
Château Melun	14	35	75
Château Menichot	5	12.5	18
Clos des Menuts	22	55	100
Domaine des Menuts	1	2.5	5
Château du Merle	6	15	18
Château Meylet-la-Gomerie	2	5	10
Château Millery-Lapelletrie	2	5	10
Château Milon	25	63	100
Château Milon-Feuillat	3	7.5	10
Château Mitrotte	1	2.5	6
Château des Moines	4	10	21
Château des Moines	4	10	23
Château Monbousquet, Château Caperot	31	77.5	144
Château Mondotte-Bellisle	6	15	16
Château Mondou	4	10	16
Clos Mondou	2	5	9

	Hectares	Acres	Tonneaux
Château Monlot-Capet	8	20	37
Clos Monplaisir	2	5	8
Château Montbelair	18	45	100
Château Montlabert	10	25	40
Domaine de Montlabert	2	5	10
Château Montremblant	5	12.5	25
Château Morillon	2	5	8
Château de la Mouleyre	5	12.5	19
Château Moulin-Bellegrave	11	27	60
Château Moulin de Cantelaube	3	7.5	6
Château Moulin-de-Pierrefitte	3	7.5	14
Château Moulin-St.-Georges	11	27.5	48
Château Moulin-St.-Georges, Château Pindefleurs	13	32.5	65
Cru Mourens	2	5	7
Château Myosotis	3	7.5	10
Cru Napoléon	2	5	7
Château Nardon (see Domaine Laroque)			
Clos de Naudin	2	5	6
Château de Neuville	1	2.5	7
Château Pailhas	12	30	51
Clos Pailhas	3	7.5	8
Clos du Palais-Cardinal	5	12.5	6
Château Panet	22	55	80
Château Paradis	15	37	80
Château Paradis, Château Patarabet	19	47.5	64
Château Parans	7	17.5	35
Clos Pasquette	3	7.5	15
Domaine de Pasquette	5	12.5	26
Château Patarabet	7	17	45
Château Patarabet (see Château Paradis)			
Clos Patarabet	1	2.5	5
Cru Patarabet	1	2.5	4
Domaine Patarabet-la-Gaffelière	2	5	8
Clos Patarabet-Lartigue	2	5	9
Château Patris	5	12.5	29
Château Patris	9	22	50
Château Pavillon-Figeac	4	10	9
Château Peillan-St.-Clair	6	15	18
Château Pelletan	5	12.5	16
Château Pérey	2	5	10
Domaine de Pérey	2	5	10
Domaine Petit-Basque	2	5	6
Château Petit-Bigaroux	5	12.5	15
Château Petit-Bois de la-Garelle	3	7.5	14
Château Petit Bord	1	2.5	4
Domaine du Petit Clos	4	10	18
Château Petit-Cormey	6	15	25
Château Petit-Faurie	4	10	25
Château Petit-Faurie-Trocard	4	10	21
Clos Petit-Figeac, Clos Pourret	3	7.5	16
Château Petit-Fombrauge	2	5	6
Cru Petit-Gontey	2	5	9
Château du Petit-Gontey	3	7.5	9
Château Petit-Gravet	5	12.5	10
Domaine du Petit-Gueyrot	2	5	12
Château Petit-Mangot	16	40	70
Château Petit-Val	5	12.5	27
Château Peygenestou	2	5	10
Château Peymouton	3	7.5	10

Saint-Émilion: Principal Growths

	Hectares	Acres	Tonneaux
Château Peyreau	18	45	75
Château Peyrelongue, Château Haut-Grâce-Dieu	11	27.5	52
Château Peyrouquet	24	60	120
Château Peyroutas	14	35	70
Clos Pezat	1	2.5	6
Château Picon-Gravignac	4	10	12
Château Pidoux	2	5	10
Clos Piganeau	1	2.5	8
Château Pindefleurs (*see* Château Moulin-St.-Georges)	9	22	50
Château Piney	9	22	50
Cru Piney	1	2.5	4
Château Pipeau	24	60	70
Château Pipeau-Menichot	10	25	50
Château Plaisance	9	15	50
Cru Plaisance	4	10	20
Cru Plateau-Jappeloup	3	7.5	6
Château Pointe-Bouquey	9	22	50
Château du Pont de Bouquey	3	7.5	11
Château Pont-de-Mouquet	12	30	40
Château Pontet	4	10	17
Domaine du Pontet	3	7.5	12
Château Pontet Clauzure, Château La Mauléone, Château Gastebourse	8	20	43
Clos Pourret (*see* Clos Petit-Figeac)			
Château Pressac	24	60	90
Clos Pressac	7	17.5	32
Château Puyblanquet-Carille	18	45	100
Château Quentin	27	67.5	80
Château Quercy	4	10	22
Château Queyron	16	40	90
Château Queyron-Pindefleurs	12	30	70
Château Rabat	3	7.5	10
Château Rabion	5	12.5	19
Domaine Rabion-Pailhas	4	10	14
Château Régent	4	10	20
Château Reine-Blanche	5	12.5	16
Château les Religieuses	2	5	9
Château Renaissance	5	12.5	24
Château de Rey	4	10	19
Château Reynard	4	10	14
Château Rivallon	8	20	24
Domaine de Rivière	5	12.5	21
Château Robin	9	22	50
Château Robin-des-Moines	5	12.5	7
Château Roc	4	10	20
Clos du Roc	3	7.5	8
Château Roc-St.-Michel	4	10	18
Château Rochebelle	3	7.5	7
Château du Rocher	18	45	90
Château Rocher-Bellevue-Figeac	4	10	20
Château de Rol	5	12.5	24
Côtes de Rol	4	10	26
Domaine de Rol	3	7.5	13
Château Rol-de-Fombrauge	8	20	40
Clos Rol-de-Fombrauge	5	12.5	23
Cru Rol-de-Fombrauge	4	10	15
Château aux Roquettes	2	5	7
Domaine de la Rose	2	5	12
Château Roucheyron	6	15	28
Clos Roucheyron	1	2.5	5

Saint-Émilion: Principal Growths

	Hectares	Acres	Tonneaux
Domaine du Rouy	2	5	9
Château du Roy, Clos Berthoneau	3	7.5	20
Royal St.-Émilion (*see* Cave Coopérative)			
Château Roylland	3	7.5	15
Château Rozier	17	42	90
Château Rozier-Béard	6	15	22
Clos du Sable	2	5	5
Château St.-Christophe	7	17.5	29
Clos St.-Émilion	8	20	44
Domaine St.-Jean-de-Béard	4	10	11
Clos St.-Julien	3	7.5	9
Château St.-Lô	8	20	38
Château St.-Martial	7	17.5	35
Château St.-Pey	19	47	100
Château St.-Pierre	4	10	11
Château St.-Roch	3	7.5	9
Château St.-Valéry	3	7.5	13
Château de Sarenceau	5	12.5	26
Château de Sarpe	6	15	12
Clos de Sarpe	3	7.5	10
Clos des Sarrazins	6	15	14
Château Saupiquet	1	2.5	9
Domaine Saupiquet	2	5	8
Domaine de Sème	4	10	20
Château Sicard	41	102.5	200
Château Simard	25	62	120
Clos Simard	3	7.5	13
Château Soutard-Cadet	3	7.5	11
Château Tarreyre	2	5	11
Château Tauzinat	3	7.5	5
Domaine Tauzinat	3	7.5	10
Château Teyssier	18	45	100
Château Toinet-Fombrauge	8	20	36
Château Tonneret	2	5	10
Château Tour des Combes	15	38	70
Château du Touran	4	10	25
Château Tour St. Christophe	45	113	225
Château Touzinat	7	17.5	40
Château Trapaud	11	27.5	94
Château Trapeau	8	20	47
Domaine de Trapeau	3	7.5	20
Château Trianon	5	12.5	21
Clos Trimoulet	4	10	21
Château Troquart (*see* Château Ripeau)			
Château Truquet	4	10	18
Château Vachon	3	7.5	16
Château du Val-d'Or	20	50	100
Clos Valentin	4	10	21
Clos Verdet-Monbousquet	5	12.5	11
Clos Vert-Bois	4	10	10
Château Veyrac	13	32	65
Château Vieille-Cloche	4	10	20
Château Vieille-Tour-La-Rose	3	7.5	16
Clos du Vieux (*see* Château Les Eyguires)			
Château Vieux-Castel-Robin	4	10	17
Château Vieux-Ceps, Château Badon	6	15	28
Vieux-Château-Chauvin	4	10	18
Vieux-Château-Fortin	5	12.5	16
Château Vieux Garouilh	12	30	60

Saint-Émilion: Lesser Growths

	Hectares	Acres	Tonneaux
Château Vieux-Guinot, Château Fourney	13	32	80
Château Vieux-Larmande	4	10	11
Vieux Châteaux Logis	15	37	60
Vieux-Domaine-Menuts	3	7.5	13
Château Vieux-Moulin-du-Cadet	3	7.5	16
Vieux-Château-Peymouton	9	22.5	37
Vieux-Château-Peyrou	1	2.5	7
Clos Vieux-Pontet	2	5	6
Château Vieux-Pourret	4	10	19

LESSER GROWTHS OF SAINT-ÉMILION AND SURROUNDING VILLAGES

	Commune	Hectares	Acres	Tonneaux
Château Ambois	St.-Georges-St.-Émilion	1	2.5	4
Domaine d'Arriailh	Montagne-St.-Émilion	4	10	6
Château Austerlitz	Sables-St.-Émilion	5	12.5	18
Château Barbe-Blanche	Montagne-St.-Émilion	15	37.5	90
Château Barraud	Montagne-St.-Émilion	4	10	21
Domaine de Barraud	Montagne-St.-Émilion	4	10	11
Château Bayard	Montagne-St.-Émilion	11	27.5	50
Clos Bayard	Montagne-St.-Émilion	5	12.5	22
Domaine de Bayard	Montagne-St.-Émilion	8	20	19
Clos Beaufort-Mazerat	St.-Émilion	2	5	9
Château Beauséjour	Montagne-St.-Émilion	14	35	60
Château Beauséjour	Puisseguin-St.-Émilion	14	35	80
Château Beausite	Montagne-St.-Émilion	3	7.5	10
Château Bélair	Montagne-St.-Émilion	8	20	50
Château Bel-Air	Puisseguin-St.-Émilion	11	27.5	60
Château Bel-Air-Lussac	Montagne-St.-Émilion	19	47.5	105
Château Bellevue	Montagne-St.-Émilion	7	17.5	30
Château de Bellevue	Montagne-St.-Émilion	11	27.5	60
Château Béouran	St.-Émilion	1	2.5	7
Cru Berlière	Montagne-St.-Émilion	4	10	15
Château Berlière	Montagne-St.-Émilion	3	7.5	25
Château Berliquet	St.-Émilion	7	17.5	19
Château Bertineau-Goby	Montagne-St.-Émilion	9	22.5	28
Château Binet	Montagne-St.-Émilion	9	22.5	19
Château Bonneau	Montagne-St.-Émilion	9	22.5	35
Domaine de Bonneau	Montagne-St.-Émilion	4	10	12
Château Branne	Montagne-St.-Émilion	6	15	35
Château Calon	Montagne-St.-Émilion	35	87.5	120
Château Calon-Montagne	St.-Georges-St.-Émilion	3	7.5	11
Château Calon-St.-Georges	St.-Georges-St.-Émilion	3	7.5	25
Château Cap-d'Or	St.-Georges-St.-Émilion	5	12.5	70
Château de Cassat	Puisseguin-St.-Émilion	13	32.5	65
Cave Coopérative des Côtes-de-Castillon	St.-Étienne-de-Lisse	3	7.5	14
Cave Vinicole de Puisseguin	Puisseguin-St.-Émilion	570	1,408	3,200
Domaine du Chatain	Montagne-St.-Émilion	3	7.5	10
Château Chêne-Vert	Montagne-St.-Émilion	7	17.5	30
Château Chêne-Vieux	Puisseguin-St.-Émilion	8	20	50
Domaine de la Clotte	Montagne-St.-Émilion	5	12.5	14
Coopérative de Montagne	Montagne-St.-Émilion	145	358	706
Clos des Corbières	Montagne-St.-Émilion	2	5	8
Château Corbin	Montagne-St.-Émilion	18	45	150
Domaine de Corniaud	Montagne-St.-Émilion	5	12.5	15
Domaine de Corniaud-Lussac	Montagne-St.-Émilion	3	7.5	10
Château Côte de Bonde	Montagne-St.-Émilion	7	17.5	55
Château Côtes-du-Fayan	Puisseguin-St.-Émilion	8	20	20
Château Coucy	Montagne-St.-Émilion	18	45	85

	Commune	Hectares	Acres	Tonneaux
Château du Courlat	Montagne-St.-Émilion	12	30	60
Domaine Croix-de-Grézard	Montagne-St.-Émilion	2	5	9
Château Croix-de-Justice	Puisseguin-St.-Émilion	16	40	70
Château Cruzeau	Sables-St.-Émilion	3	7.5	14
Château Daviau-La-Chapelle	Montagne-St.-Émilion	5	12.5	30
Château Divon	St.-Georges-St.-Émilion	4	10	19
Clos l'Église	Montagne-St.-Émilion	4	10	17
Clos de l'Église	Montagne-St.-Émilion	13	32.5	46
Clos de l'Église (*see* Château St.-Georges)				
Château Faizeau	Montagne-St.-Émilion	10	25	45
Château Fongaban (*see* Château Mouchet)				
Château Fontmurée	Montagne-St.-Émilion	1	2.5	3
Château de Font-Murée	Montagne-St.-Émilion	10	25	39
Domaine Franc-Baudron	Montagne-St.-Émilion	6	15	20
Château Froquard	St.-Georges-St.-Émilion	3	7.5	15
Château Gaudet-Plaisance	Montagne-St.-Émilion	4	10	30
Château Gaillard	Sables-St.-Émilion	4	10	16
Château Garderose	Sables-St.-Émilion	5	12.5	20
Château Gay-Moulins et Chateau des Moines	Montagne-St.-Émilion	18	45	80
Clos Gilet	Montagne-St.-Émilion	3	7.5	13
Château Gironde	Puisseguin-St.-Émilion	4	10	5
Domaine du Gourdins	Sables-St.-Émilion	1	2.5	6
Domaine des Grands-Champs	Montagne-St.-Émilion	4	10	10
Domaine des Grands-Pairs	Montagne-St.-Émilion	2	5	8
Domaine de Grimon	St.-Georges-St.-Émilion	5	12.5	20
Château Gueyrosse	Sables-St.-Émilion	4	10	15
Château Guibeau	Puisseguin-St.-Émilion	41	102.5	200
Château Guillon	St.-Georges-St.-Émilion	13	32.5	40
Domaine Haut-Caillate	St.-Georges-St.-Émilion	2	5	10
Château Haut-Chéreau	Montagne-St.-Émilion	2	5	5
Domaine Haut-Corbière	Sables-St.-Émilion	2	5	11
Château Haute-Bastienne	Montagne-St.-Émilion	1	2.5	8
Château Haute-Faucherie	Montagne-St.-Émilion	8	20	35
Château Haut-Goujon	Montagne-St.-Émilion	3	7.5	5
Domaine Haut-Guillennay	Sables-St.-Émilion	2	5	10
Château Haut-Guitard	Montagne-St.-Émilion	4	10	46
Château Haut-Langlade	Montagne-St.-Émilion	4	10	14
Château Haut-Larose	Montagne-St.-Émilion	5	12.5	30
Clos Haut-Listrac	Puisseguin-St.-Émilion	4	10	14
Domaine de Haut-Marchand	Montagne-St.-Émilion	4	10	6
Clos Haut-Montaiguillon	St.-Georges-St.-Émilion	5	12.5	24
Château Haut-Musset	Montagne-St.-Émilion	5	12.5	45
Château Haut-Piquat	Montagne-St.-Émilion	16	40	80
Château Haut-Plaisance	Montagne-St.-Émilion	7	17.5	25
Château Haut-Poitou	Montagne-St.-Émilion	2	5	9
Château Haut-Pourteau	Montagne-St.-Émilion	2	5	8
Château Haut-St.-Georges	St.-Georges-St.-Émilion	2	5	15
Château Haut-Sarpe	St.-Christophe-des-Bardes	9	22.5	50
Château Haut-Troquard	St.-Georges-St.-Émilion	3	7.5	16
Clos Haut-Troquard	St.-Georges-St.-Émilion	1	2.5	6
Château l'Hermitage	Montagne-St.-Émilion	6	15	50
Château Jura-Plaisance	Montagne-St.-Émilion	8	20	30
Château-La-Bastienne	Montagne-St.-Émilion	17	42.5	80
Château La Cabanne	Puisseguin-St.-Émilion	4	10	20
Château La Chapelle	Montagne-St.-Émilion	2	5	15
Château La Clotte	Puisseguin-St.-Émilion	2	5	4
Château La Couronne	Montagne-St.-Émilion	4	10	50
Château La Croix-de-la-Bastienne	Montagne-St.-Émilion	2	5	12
Cru La Croix-Blanche	Montagne-St.-Émilion	2	5	7

	Commune	*Hectares*	*Acres*	*Tonneaux*
Château La Croix-de-Blanchon	*Montagne-St.-Émilion*	5	12.5	40
Château La Faucherie	*Montagne-St.-Émilion*	3	7.5	6
Château La Fleur-Perruchon	*Montagne-St.-Émilion*	5	12.5	35
Château La Fleur-St.-Georges (*see* Château St.-Georges)				
Château La Grande-Clotte	*Montagne-St.-Émilion*	5	12.5	40
Château La Grenière	*Montagne-St.-Émilion*	12	30	80
Château La Mayne	*Sables-St.-Émilion*	3	7.5	8
Château La Paillette	*Sables-St.-Émilion*	3	7.5	10
Château La Papeterie	*Montagne-St.-Émilion*	2	5	4
Château La Perrière	*Montagne-St.-Émilion*	5	12.5	35
Château La Picherie	*St.-Georges-St.-Émilion*	12	30	55
Château La Plante	*Sables-St.-Émilion*	1	2.5	5
Clos La Rose	*Puisseguin-St.-Émilion*	7	17.5	30
Château La Roseraie-du-Mont	*Puisseguin-St.-Émilion*	4	10	9
Château La Tête-du-Cerf	*Montagne-St.-Émilion*	6	15	15
Château La Tour-Ballet	*Montagne-St.-Émilion*	1	2.5	5
Château La Tour-Blanche	*Montagne-St.-Émilion*	3	7.5	19
Château La Tour de Gillet	*Montagne-St.-Émilion*	6	15	50
Château La Tour-de-Grenet	*Montagne-St.-Émilion*	24	60	175
Château La Tour-Guillotin	*Puisseguin-St.-Émilion*	15	37.5	75
Château La Tour-Paquillon	*Montagne-St.-Émilion*	8	20	35
Château La Tour-St.-Georges (*see* Château St.-Georges)				
Château La Tour-de-Ségur	*Montagne-St.-Émilion*	12	30	70
Château La Vaisinerie	*Puisseguin-St.-Émilion*	8	20	27
Clos La Vallée-du-Roi	*Montagne-St.-Émilion*	3	7.5	8
Domaine de Lamaçonne	*Montagne-St.-Émilion*	3	7.5	12
Château Langlade	*Montagne-St.-Émilion*	6	15	30
Domaine de Laplaigne	*Puisseguin-St.-Émilion*	7	17.5	31
Château Larue	*Montagne-St.-Émilion*	4	10	13
Château Latour	*Montagne-St.-Émilion*	5	12.5	21
Château Latour-Musset	*Montagne-St.-Émilion*	10	25	35
Château Latour-de-Ségur	*Montagne-St.-Émilion*	8	20	45
Château Le Chay	*Puisseguin-St.-Émilion*	13	32.5	58
Cru Le Franc-Rival	*Montagne-St.-Émilion*	2	5	9
Château Le Gravier-Gueyrosse	*Sables-St.-Émilion*	3	7.5	12
Château Le Mayne	*Puisseguin-St.-Émilion*	10	25	45
Clos Le Pas-St.-Georges	*St.-Georges-St.-Émilion*	6	15	31
Château le Pont-de-Pierre	*Montagne-St.-Émilion*	3	7.5	15
Château Le Puy-St.-Georges (*see* Château St.-Georges)				
Château Le Roc-de-Troquard	*St.-Georges-St.-Émilion*	3	7.5	10
Château Le-Tertre-de-Perruchon	*Montagne-St.-Émilion*	3	7.5	7
Château Lenoir	*Sables-St.-Émilion*	4	10	13
Château Léonard	*Puisseguin-St.-Émilion*	9	22.5	30
Château Lépine	*Sables-St.-Émilion*	2	5	7
Château Les Bardes	*Montagne-St.-Émilion*	3	7.5	13
Château Les Carrières	*Montagne-St.-Émilion*	2	5	20
Château Les Côtes-de-Gardat	*Montagne-St.-Émilion*	5	12.5	24
Château Les Eyguires	*St.-Christophe-des-Bardes*			
Domaine Les Genêts	*Montagne-St.-Émilion*	3	7.5	9
Château Les Grandes-Vignes	*Montagne-St.-Émilion*	2	5	10
Château Les Jacquets	*St.-Georges-St.-Émilion*	5	12.5	22
Château Les Laurets	*Puisseguin-St.-Émilion*	60	150	250
Château Les Renardières	*St.-Georges-St.-Émilion*	4	10	14
Château Les Tuileries-Laporte-Bayard	*Montagne-St.-Émilion*	45	112.5	225
Château Les Vieux-Rocs	*Montagne-St.-Émilion*	6	15	20
Château Lestage	*Montagne-St.-Émilion*	8	20	50
Château L'Ormeau-Vieux	*Puisseguin-St.-Émilion*	7	17.5	23
Château Lucas et Château Rouzaud	*Montagne-St.-Émilion*	16	40	110
Château de Lussac	*Montagne-St.-Émilion*	20	50	140

	Commune	Hectares	Acres	Tonneaux
Château du Lyonnat	Montagne-St.-Émilion	35	87.5	200
Château Lyon-Perruchon	Montagne-St.-Émilion	4	10	11
Château Macureau	Montagne-St.-Émilion	6	15	26
Clos des Magrines	Puisseguin-St.-Émilion	3	7.5	6
Château Maison-Blanche	Montagne-St.-Émilion	30	75	150
Château de Maisonneuve	Montagne-St.-Émilion	7	17.5	20
Clos Maisonneuve	Montagne-St.-Émilion	2	5	8
Domaine de Maisonneuve, Château St.-Georges-Macquin	St.-Georges-St.-Émilion	17	42.5	54
Château Martinet	Sables-St.-Émilion	12	30	56
Clos Maurice	St.-Sulpice-de-Faleyrens	1	2.5	6
Château Meynard	Sables-St.-Émilion	6	15	11
Château Montaiguillon	Montagne-St.-Émilion	23	57.5	130
Château Montaiguillon	St.-Georges-St.-Émilion	3	7.5	16
Château Montesquieu	Puisseguin-St.-Émilion	14	35	63
Clos Montesquieu	Montagne-St.-Émilion	3	7.5	12
Château Mouchet, Château Fongaban	Puisseguin-St.-Émilion	10	25	35
Château Mouchique	Puisseguin-St.-Émilion	4	10	17
Château du Moulin	Puisseguin-St.-Émilion	6	15	30
Château Moulin-du-Jura	Montagne-St.-Émilion	3	7.5	10
Château de Musset	Montagne-St.-Émilion	7	17.5	40
Château Naguet-La-Grande	Montagne-St.-Émilion	5	12.5	12
Château Négrit	Montagne-St.-Émilion	12	30	60
Château Pavillon-Fougailles	St.-Émilion	1	2.5	5
Château Petit-Clos du Roy	Montagne-St.-Émilion	8	20	50
Château Petit-Refuge	Montagne-St.-Émilion	2	5	15
Château Peyrou	St.-Étienne-de-Lisse	5	12.5	24
Château Piron	Montagne-St.-Émilion	6	15	25
Château Plaisance	Montagne-St.-Émilion	20	50	100
Clos Plaisance	Montagne-St.-Émilion	9	22.5	28
Clos Plince	Sables-St.-Émilion	1	2.5	6
Château du Puy	Montagne-St.-Émilion	6	15	35
Château Puy-Bonnet	Montagne-St.-Émilion	5	12.5	30
Château Puynormond	Montagne-St.-Émilion	7	17.5	50
Domaine du Puynormond	Montagne-St.-Émilion	5	12.5	21
Château Quinault	Sables-St.-Émilion	12	30	58
Domaine de Rambaud	Montagne-St.-Émilion	3	7.5	6
Clos des Religieuses	Puisseguin-St.-Émilion	8	20	20
Château Rigaud	Puisseguin-St.-Émilion	3	7.5	15
Château Roc-de-Puynormond	Montagne-St.-Émilion	6	15	10
Château Rocher-Corbin	Montagne-St.-Émilion	9	22.5	68
Château des Rochers (see Château Bonneau)				
Domaine des Rocs	Montagne-St.-Émilion	8	20	40
Château Rocs-Marchand	Montagne-St.-Émilion	9	22.5	9
Château Roudier	Montagne-St.-Émilion	30	75	150
Château Roudier	St.-Georges-St.-Émilion	3	7.5	17
Domaine du Roudier	Montagne-St.-Émilion	10	25	50
Château des Roziers	Montagne-St.-Émilion	4	10	14
Château Sablons	Montagne-St.-Émilion	5	12.5	20
Château St.-Georges, Château La Tour-St.-Georges, Château Le Puy-St.-Georges, Château La Fleur-St.-Georges, Clos de l'Église	St.-Georges-St.-Émilion	35	87	250
Château St.-Georges-Macquin (see Domaine de Maisonneuve)				
Château St.-Jacques-Calon	Montagne-St.-Émilion	6	15	45
Château St.-Louis	St.-Georges-St.-Émilion	8	20	35
Château St.-Michel	Montagne St. Émilion	2	5	9
Château St.-Paul	Montagne-St.-Émilion	5	12.5	23
Château Samion	St.-Georges-St.-Émilion	4	10	20
Château Soleil	Puisseguin-St.-Émilion	15	37.5	60
Château Taureau	Montagne-St.-Émilion	13	32.5	80

Pomerol: Principal Growths

	Commune	Hectares	Acres	Tonneaux
Château Teillac	*Puisseguin-St.-Émilion*	20	50	100
Château Terrien	*Montagne-St.-Émilion*	7	17.5	35
Château Tetre-de-la-Mouleyre	*Montagne-St.-Émilion*	2	5	8
Clos Teynac-Rival	*Montagne-St.-Émilion*	3	7.5	14
Château Teyssier	*Puisseguin-St.-Émilion*	20	50	100
Château des Tours	*Montagne-St.-Émilion*	70	175	300
Château Vieux-Bonneau	*Montagne-St.-Émilion*	8	20	60
Vieux-Château-Calon	*Montagne-St.-Émilion*	5	12.5	35
Vieux-Château-Goujon	*Montagne-St.-Émilion*	2	5	10
Château Vieux-Guillou	*St.-Georges-St.-Émilion*	4	10	17
Vieux-Château-La-Beysse	*Puisseguin-St.-Émilion*	4	10	6
Château Vieux-Logis-de-Cazelon	*Montagne-St.-Émilion*	2	5	8
Château Vieux Montaiguillon	*St.-Georges-St.-Émilion*	3	7.5	13
Château Vieux-Mouchet	*Montagne-St.-Émilion*	1	2.5	6
Domaine du Vieux-Moulin-de-Calon	*Montagne-St.-Émilion*	1	2.5	6
Vieux-Château-Négrit	*Montagne-St.-Émilion*	5	25	40
Vieux-Château-Palon	*Montagne-St.-Émilion*	5	12.5	17

IV POMEROL

The wines of Pomerol are not officially classified. Château Pétrus is recognized as being the outstanding Great Growth, followed by other wines italicized below, which are considered superior in their class.

The following figures of production are approximate, and indicate average annual output, as given by the communes and taken from their Déclarations de Récoltes records.

PRINCIPAL GROWTHS

	Hectares	Acres	Approximate Cases
Clos des Amandiers	2	5	1000
Clos Barrail-du-Milieu, Clos du Pellerin	2	5	500
Château Beauchêne	4	10	4,000
Château Beauregard	13	32	5,000
Château Beauséjour-de-Bonalque	2	5	500
Château Beau-Soleil	3	7.5	2,000
Château Bel-Air, Vieux-Château-Boënot	13	32	5,000
Château Belle Brise	2	5	700
Château Bellegrave	6	15	2,000
Château Bellevue-Montviel	85	13	2,000
Château Boënot, Château Trintin	4	10	4,000
Château Bonalgue	3	7.5	900
Château Le Bon-Pasteur	6	15	2,000
Château Bourgneuf-Vayron	9	22.5	3,000
Château de Bourgueneuf	5	13	2,000
Château Brun-Mazeyres	3	7.5	2,000
Château de Cantereau	3	7	1,000
Château du Casse	2	5	700
Château du Castel	2	5	800
Château Certan-Giraud	7	17.5	3,000
Château Certan-Marzelle	4	10	2,000
Château Certan-de-May	4	10	2,000
Château Chêne-Liège	2	5	900
Château Clinet	6	15	2,000
Clos du Clocher, Château Monregard-Lacroix	5	12.5	3,000
Château Clos Bel-Air	2	5	900
Domaine des Clones	2	5	500
Château du Couvent	2	5	700
Château Deltour	2	5	700
Château Domaine de l Église	7	17	3,000

	Hectares	Acres	Approximate Cases
Château Elisée	2	5	700
Château Enclos Haut-Mazeyras	7	17	3,000
Château Fagnard	2	5	800
Château Ferrand	11	27.5	4,000
Château Ferron	2	5	700
Château Feytit-Clinet	6	15	2,000
Château Feytit-Guillot	1	2.5	500
Château Franc-Maillet	4	10	2,000
Château Gazin	25	62	7,000
Château Gombaude-Guilhot	6	15	3,000
Château Gouprie	3	7.5	2,000
Cru Grand-Mazeyres	2	5	500
Château Grand-Moulinet	1	2.5	500
Clos des Grands Sillons-Gabachot	3	7.5	2,000
Château Grange Neuve	4	10	2,000
Château Grate-Cap	9.5	24	4,000
Domaine des Graves de Maillet	1	2.5	400
Château Graves-Guillot	2	5	700
Château Guillot	5	12	2,000
Château Guillot-Trochaud	3	7.5	1,000
Château Haut-Cloquet	2	5	1,000
Cru Haut-Groupey	2	5	500
Château Haut-Maillet	5	12.5	2,000
Clos Haut-Mazeyres	9	22.5	2,000
Château de Haut-Pignon	2	5	500
Domaine de Haut-Trochaud	1	2.5	500
Domaine des Jacobins	1	2.5	500
Château la Bassonnerie	4	10	2,000
Château La Cabanne	12	30	3,000
Château La Chichonne	2	5	500
Clos Lacombe	2	5	500
Château La Commanderie	5	12.5	2,000
Château La Conseillante	11	27.5	4,000
Château La Croix	17	42	5,000
Château La Croix-de-Gay	11	27.5	4,000
Château La Croix des Templiers	3	7.5	900
Château La Croix du Casse	9	23.5	4,000
Château La Croix-St.-Georges	4	10	2,000
Château La Croix-Taillefer	2	5	600
Château Lafleur	4	10	1,000
Domaine de Lafleur	4	10	2,000
Château Lafleur-Gazin	7	17	2,000
Château La Fleur du Mayne	3	7.5	900
Château Lafleur-Pétrus	9	22	3,000
Château La Fleur-des-Rouzes	7	17	2,000
Château Lafleur du Roy	3	7.5	2,000
Château La Fleur-Treyssac	1	3	400
Château La Ganne	5	12.5	2,000
Château Lagrange	8	20	3,000
Château Lagrave-Trigant de Boisset	8	20	3,000
Château La Loubière	2	5	700
Château La Patache	2	5	500
Château La Pointe	20	50	7,000
Domaine La Pointe, Clos Bel-Air	4	10	800
Château La Renaissance	5	12.5	2,000
Clos La Rose	3	7.5	2,000
Château La Rose-Figeac	5	13	2,000
Clos La Soulatte	2	5	500

Pomerol: Principal Growths

	Hectares	Acres	Approximate Cases
Château Latour-Pomerol	9	22	4,000
Château La Truffe	2	5	700
Domaine de la Vieille École	2	3	400
Clos de la Vieille Église	2	5	500
Château La Violette	4	10	900
Château Le Bon Pasteur	7	18	2,000
Château Le Caillou	5	12.5	3,000
Château Le Carillon	4	10	2,000
Château Le Gay	8	20	2,000
Clos l'Église	5	12.5	2,000
Domaine de l'Église	7	17.5	3,000
Château de l'Église-Clinet	4	10	2,000
Château l'Enclos	10.5	26	4,000
Château Le Pin	1	3	500
Château Les Bordes	2	5	2,000
Clos Les Grands-Champs, Château Guillot	5	12.5	2,000
Château Les Grands-Sillons	2	5	1,000
Château Les Hautes-Rouzes	2	5	800
Clos Les Rouzes-Clinet	2	5	900
Château L'Évangile	13	32.5	3,000
Château Margot	1	2.5	500
Château Marzy	7	17.5	4,000
Château Mayne	3	7.5	900
Château du Mayne	2	5	900
Château Mazeyres	10	25	4,000
Clos Mazeyres, Château Beauchêne	6	15	2,000
Château Moulinet	17	42.5	7,000
Château Nénin	20	50	7,000
Château la Nouvelle-Église	2	5	500
Clos du Pèlerin			
Château du Petit-Moulinet	3	7.5	1,000
Château Petit Plince	3	7.5	900
Château Petit-Village	9	22.5	4,000
Château Pétrus	12	30	4,000
Château Pignon-Larroucaud	2	5	300
Château Plince	7	17.5	3,000
Clos Plince	1	2.5	300
Château Plincette	1	2.5	400
Château La Providence	3	7.5	600
Château Ratouin	3	7.5	700
Domaine des Ramparts	4	10	1,000
Clos René	16	40	6,000
Domaine de René	3	7.5	700
Château Rêve-d'Or	5	12.5	2,000
Château Robert	4	10	1,000
Château Rocher-Beauregard	2	5	700
Château Rouget	13	32.5	6,000
Clos du Roy	3	7.5	1,000
Château St.-André	2	5	1,000
Château Sainte-Marie	4	10	2,000
Château Saint-Pierre	3	7.5	2,000
Château de Sales	47.5	119	12,000
Château Tailhas	9	22.5	800
Château Taillefer, Clos Beauregard, Château Toulifaut, Clos Toulifaut,	21	52.5	9,000
Château des Templiers	3	7.5	2,000
Château Thibéaud-Maillet	2	5	2,000
Domaine Tour du Roy	1	2.5	400

	Hectares	Acres	Approximate Cases
Château Tristan	1	2.5	400
Château Tropchaud l'Église	3	7.5	1,000
Château Trotanoy	9	22.5	3,000
Château de Valois	6	15	3,000
Vieux-Château-Boënot (see Château Bel-Air)	3	7.5	2,000
Vieux-Château-Bourgneuf	5	12.5	2,000
Vieux-Château-Certan	14	35	7,000
Vieux-Château-Cloquet	2	5	600
Vieux Château Hautes Graves Beaulieu	1	2.5	500
Château Vieux-Maillet	4.5	11.25	500
Château Vieux Taillefer	2	5	500
Château Vieux Tressac	2	5	700
Château Vrai-Croix-de-Gay	6	20	2,000

APPELLATION LALANDE DE POMEROL

COMMUNE DE LALANDE DE POMEROL

Clos des Arnaud
Château de Bel Air
Château Bourseau
Petit Clos de Brouard
Château de la Commanderie
Château les Cruzelles
Clos de l'Église
Clos l'Étoile
Domaine de Grand Moine
Château Grand Ormeau
Clos Haut Cavujon

Château Laborde
Château des Moines
Château Templiers
Clos de Moines
Château de Musset
Château Perron
Château Perron
Sabloire du Grand Moine
Château de Viaud
Domaine de Viaud
Clos de la Vieille Forge

COMMUNE DE NÉAC

Domaine du Bourg
Château Canon Chaigneau
Clos du Casrel
Château Chatain
Clos du Chatain
Domaine du Chatain
Château les Chaumes
Château Chevrol Bel Air
Château Drouilleau Belles Graves
Château Fougeailles
Château Gachet
Château Garraud
Domaine des Grands Bois Chagneau

Domaine du Grand Ormeau
Château Haut Ballet
Château Haut Chaigneau
Château Lafaurie
Château Lavinot la Chapelle
Château Les Grandes Versaines
Château Moncets
Château Moulin à Vent
Château Siaurac
Domaine de Surget
Château de Teysson
Château Tournefeuille

V FRONSAC

The following figures of production are approximate, and indicate average annual output, as given by the communes and taken from their Déclarations de Récoltes records.

PRINCIPAL GROWTHS

	Commune	Hectares	Acres	Tonneaux
Château d'Alem	Saillans	13	33	70
Château Arnauton	Fronsac	24	60	100
Au Tertre	Fronsac	4	10	20

	Commune	Hectares	Acres	Tonneaux
Château Beauséjour	Saillans	8	20	40
Château Bélair	Saillans	6	15	40
Château Bourdieu-La-Valade	Fronsac	10	25	50
Château Capet	Fronsac	4	10	20
Château du Carillon	Saillans	8	30	40
Château de Carles	Saillans	16	40	70
Château Chadène	St.-Aignan	10	25	50
Château du Faure-Haut-Normand	Saillans	13	32.5	27
Château de Fronsac	Fronsac	7	18	30
Château Gagnard-et La Croix Bertrand	Fronsac	11	27.5	20
Château Hauchat	St.-Aignan	6	15	25
Château Jeandeman	St.-Aignan	23	57.5	100
Domaine Labory	Saillans	6	15	10
Domaine du La Brand	Saillans	5	12.5	12
Château La Croix	Fronsac	20	50	100
Château La Croix Gandineau	Fronsac	5	12.5	12
Château La Croix-Laroque	Fronsac	5	13	25
Château La Dauphine	Fronsac	6	15	14
Château La Grave	Fronsac	3	7.5	7
Château La Laguë	Fronsac	8	20	50
Château Lalande-Maussé	Saillans	8	20	45
Château Lambert	St.-Aignan	3	7.5	15
Château La Rivière	La Rivière	40	100	160
Château La Tour-Beau-Site	Fronsac	10	25	50 ·
Château La Valade (Roux)	Fronsac	12	30	50
Château La Vieille Curé	Saillans	14	35	32
Château Le Bosquet	St.-Aignan	7	18	35
Château Les Abories de Meyney	La-Rivière	3	8	15
Château Les Roches-de-Ferrand	St.-Aignan	12	30	60
Château Les Trois-Croix	Fronsac	12	30	60
Château Magondeau	Saillans	15	37.5	60
Domaine de Manieu	La Rivière	6	15	20
Château Mayne-Vieille	Galgon	22	55	100
Château Meyney	St.-Aignan	8	20	35
Château de Montahut	Fronsac	7	18	35
Château Moulin des Tonnelles	St.-Aignan	9	23	50
Château Moulin-Haut-Laroque	Saillans	12	30	50
Château Moulin-Haut-Villars	Saillans	4	10	20
Château Musseau-Bellevue	St.-Aignan	6	15	30
Domaine Normand	Saillans	6	15	30
Château Puyguilhem	Saillans	10	25	40
Château Peychez	Fronsac	4	10	8
Château Pipeau	La Rivière	5	13	25
Château Plainpoint	St.-Aignan	12	30	45
Château Pontus	Fronsac	8	20	40
Château Renard	La Rivière	10	25	40
Château Richelieu	Fronsac	13	33	60
Château Roc St.-Bernard	Saillans	4	10	12
Château Rouet	La Rivière	10	25	50
Château Saint-Cric-Les-Tonnelles	St.-Aignan	10	25	50
Château du Tasta	St.-Aignan	12	30	45
Château Tessendey	Saillans	5	13	25
Château Les Tonnelles	St.-Aignan	12	30	50
Château Tour-Picot	La Rivière	5	13	25
Château Vieille-Croix	Saillans	10	25	40
Château Vieux Moulin	Fronsac	8	20	35
Château Vieux-Vincent	St.-Aignan	10	25	50
Château Villars	Saillans	24	60	100

	Commune	Hectares	Acres	Tonneaux
Château St. Vincent	St.-Aignan	7	17.5	30
Château Vincent	St.-Aignan	10	25	50

VI CANON FRONSAC

The following figures of production are approximate, and indicate average annual output as given by the communes and taken from their *Déclarations de Récoltes* records.

PRINCIPAL GROWTHS

	Commune	Hectares	Acres	Tonneaux
Château Barrabaque	Fronsac	7	17.5	14
Château Belloy	Fronsac	5	12.5	10
Château Bodet	Fronsac	10	25	38
Château Caillou	Fronsac	3	7.5	9
Château Canon	Fronsac	2	5	10
Château de Canon	St.-Michel	10	25	30
Château Cassagne-Haut-Canon	St.-Michel	8	20	40
Château Combes-Canon	St.-Michel	2	5	7
Château Comte	Fronsac	3	8	10
Château Coustolle et Bourdieu-Lavalade	Fronsac	20	50	100
Château du Gaby	Fronsac	10	25	50
Château du Gazin	St.-Michel	6	15	25
Château Grand Renouil	St.-Michel	6	15	11
Château Haut-Ballet	St.-Michel	5	13	20
Château Haut-Gros-Bonnet	Fronsac	8	20	40
Château Haut-Lariveau	St.-Michel	3	8	10
Château Haut-Mazeris	St.-Michel	6	15	16
Château Haut-Panet	Fronsac	4	10	20
Château Junayme	Fronsac	16	40	75
Château La Chapelle-Lariveau	St.-Michel	5	12.5	16
Château La Duchesse	Fronsac	3	8	15
Château La Fleur-Canon	St.-Michel	4	18	30
Château La Marche-Canon	Fronsac	6	15	30
Château Larchevêque	Fronsac	5	12.5	10
Château Lariveau	St.-Michel	7	17.5	18
Château Mausse	St.-Michel	10	25	50
Château Mazeris	St.-Michel	14	35	50
Château Mazeris Bellevue	St.-Michel	12	30	50
Château Moulin-Pey-Labrie	Fronsac	8	20	40
Château Panet	Fronsac	4	10	8
Château du Pavillon-Gros-Bonnet	Fronsac	3	8	15
Château Perron	Fronsac	3	7.5	4
Château Pey-Labrie	Fronsac	8	20	40
Château Pichelèbre	Fronsac	12	30	60
Château Queyran-de-Haut	St.-Michel	3	8	10
Domaine de Roullet	Fronsac	3	7.5	5
Château Roullet	Fronsac	3	7.5	7
Château de Toumalin	Fronsac	8	20	40
Château de Toumalin et Château Bourdieu-Panet	Fronsac	6	15	30
Château Vrai Canon Bouché	Fronsac	12	30	55
Château Vrai Canon Boyer	St.-Michel	7	17.5	22

VII GRAVES: 1959 OFFICIAL CLASSIFICATION

The vineyards of the Graves district were officially classified in 1953 and in 1959. Château Haut-Brion, the greatest of all Graves, is also officially classified with the great Médocs.

The following figures of production are approximate, and indicate average annual output as given by the communes and taken from their Déclarations de Récoltes records.

CLASSIFIED RED WINES OF GRAVES

	Commune	Tonneaux	Approximate Cases
Château Haut-Brion	Pessac	130	12,000
Château Bouscaut	Cadaujac	120	10,000
Château Carbonnieux	Léognan	130	12,000
Domaine de Chevalier	Léognan	50	5,000
Château Fieuzal	Léognan	100	9,000
Château Haut-Bailly	Léognan	100	9,000
Château La Mission-Haut-Brion	Talence	70	6,000
Château La Tour-Haut-Brion	Talence	20	1,500
Château La Tour-Martillac (Kressmann La Tour)	Martillac	90	8,000
Château Malartic-Lagravière	Léognan	60	5,000
Château Olivier	Léognan	90	8,000
Château Pape-Clément	Pessac	120	11,000
Château Smith-Haut-Lafitte	Martillac	180	17,000

CLASSIFIED WHITE WINES OF GRAVES

	Commune	Tonneaux	Approximate Cases
Château Bouscaut	Cadaujac	400	4,000
Château Carbonnieux	Léognan	150	14,000
Domaine de Chevalier	Léognan	10	950
Château Couhins	Villenave-d'Ornon	5	400
Château La Tour-Martillac (Kressmann La Tour)	Martillac	20	2,000
Château Laville-Haut-Brion	Talence	20	2,000
Château Malartic-Lagravière	Léognan	10	900
Château Olivier	Léognan	65	6,000
Château Haut-Brion	Pessac	14	1,000

OTHER PRINCIPAL GROWTHS

wh = WHITE; r = RED

	Commune		Hectares	Acres	Tonneaux
Château André-Lamothe	Portets	wh	2	5	11
		r	4	10	15
Domaine Andron	St.-Selve	wh	3	7.5	5
Clos d'Armajan	Budos	wh	4	10	15
Château d'Arricaud	Landiras	wh	20	50	80
		r	4	18	30
Château des Arrocs	Langon	wh	3	7.5	10

	Commune		Hectares	Acres	Tonneaux
Domaine Arzac	St.-Selve	wh	2	5	5
Clos l'Avocat	Cérons	wh	3	7.5	10
Château Bardins	Cadaujac	wh			17
			17	43	
		r			2
Château Baret	Villenave-d'Ornon	wh			45
			13	33	
		r			35
Domaine du Barque	St.-Selve	r	6	15	20
Cru Barrouet	Pujols	wh	3	7.5	7
Domaine du Basque	Pujols	wh	3	7.5	12
Château Batsères	Landiras	wh	4	10	15
		r	4	10	15
Château Beauchêne	Beautiran	wh	3	7.5	7
		r	2	5	5
Domaine du Beau-Site	Portets	wh	0.3	0.8	2
		r	3	7.5	9
Château Bel-Air	Portets	wh	2	5	6
		r	3	8	10
Château Bel-Air	St.-Morillon	wh	3	10	10
Château Bellefontaine	St.-Pierre-de-Mons	wh	3	7.5	7
Domaine Bellevue	Toulenne	wh	1	2.5	7
Château Belon	St.-Morillon	wh	3	7.5	6
		r	4	10	30
Domaine de Bequin	Portets	wh	5	12.5	11
		r	9	23	35
Château Bernard-Raymond	Portets	wh	3	7.5	13
		r	2	5	11
Château Bichon Cassignols	La Brède	wh			11
			5	12.5	
		r			10
Domaine de Biot	Arbanats	wh	2	5	5
		r	2	5	4
Domaine de la Blancherie	La Brède	wh	10	25	30
Château Boiresse	Ayguemortes	wh	4	10	15
		r	5	13	20
Château de Bonat	St.-Selve	wh	5	12.5	25
		r	13	33	50
Clos de la Bonneterie	Portets	wh	2	5	6
		r	2	5	4
Clos de la Borderie	Portets	wh	3	7.5	9
		r	2	5	8
Domaine du Boscq	St.-Morillon	wh	2	5	5
Château Boyrein	Roaillan	wh	6	15	16
		r	15	38	60
		wh	3	7.5	7
Domaine de Brochon	Arbanats	r	2	5	3
		wh	2	5	4
Château Brondelles	Langon	wh	7	17.5	19
Château Bruhaut	St.-Pierre-de-Mons	wh	14	35	55
Domaine de Bruilleau	St.-Médard-d'Eyrans	wh	2	5	4
Château deBudos	Budos	r	9	22.5	31
		wh	4	10	11
Clos Cabannes	St.-Pierre-de-Mons	wh	3	8	12
Clos Cabanne	St.-Pierre-de-Mons	r	2	5	10
		wh	3	7.5	40
Château Cabannieux	Portets	r	15	7.5	70
		wh	4	10	10

Graves: Principal Growths

	Commune		Hectares	Acres	Tonneaux
Domaine de Calens	*Beautiran*	r	6	17.5	5
Cru Camegaye	*Landiras*	wh	2	5	9
Clos Cantalot	*St.-Pierre-de-Mons*	wh	7	17.5	22
Cru de Cap-de-Hé	*Pujols*	wh	2	5	10
Château Carmes-Haut-Brion	*Pessac*	r	2	5	8
Domaine Carros	*St.-Selve*	wh	2	5	9
Domaine de Casseuil	*Langon*	wh	4	10	20
		r	3	8	10
Domaine Castelnaud	*St.-Pierre-de-Mons*	wh	2	5	5
Château Catalas	*Pujols*	wh	6	15	17
Château Cazebonne	*St.-Pierre-de-Mons*	wh	7	17.5	25
		r	6	15	25
Clos Chantegrive	*Podensac*	wh	10	25	50
		r	5	12.5	25
Cru Chante l'Oiseau	*La Brède*	wh	9	23	40
Château Chaviran	*Martillac*	r	4	10	16
Château Cherchy	*Pujols*	wh	4	10	20
Cru Cherchy	*Pujols*	wh	2	5	9
Château Chicane	*Toulenne*	r	6	15	25
Domaine du Ciron	*Pujols*	wh	5	12.5	19
Château de Clare	*Landiras*	wh	3	7.5	20
		r	5	13	20
Cru du Couet	*St.-Pierre-de-Mons*	wh	2	5	5
Domaine de Courbon	*Toulenne*	wh	4	10	25
Domaine du Courreau	*St.-Médard-d'Eyrans*	wh	3	7.5	5
		r			3
Domaine du Courreau	*St.-Morillon*	wh	3	7.5	11
Château Crabitey	*Portets*	wh	2	5	4
		r	16	40	60
Domaine de la Croix	*Langon*	wh	4	10	18
		r	2	5	8
Château de Cruzeau	*St.-Médard-d'Eyrans*	wh	11	28	50
		r	36	90	160
Clos Darrouban	*Portets*	wh	2	5	3
		r			3
Domaine de Darrouban	*Portets*	wh	3	7.5	15
		r	2	5	3
Château Despagne	*St.-Pierre-de-Mons*	wh	4	10	14
Château Doms et Clos du Monastère	*Portets*	wh	7	18	20
		r	18	45	70
Domaine du Druc	*Landiras*	wh	2	5	6
Domaine de Durse, Domaine de Papoula	*Portets*	wh	2	5	7
		r	1	2.5	7
Domaine Étienne	*St.-Morillon*	wh	2	5	6
Domaine de Faye	*Portets*	wh	1	2.5	6
		r	2	5	7
Château Fernon	*Langon*	wh	40	100	120
		r	4	10	15
Château Ferran	*Martillac*	wh	6	15	11
		r	5	13	20
Château Ferrande	*Castres*	wh	10	25	40
		r	32	75	180
Château Fieuzal	*Léognan*	wh	1.4	3.5	15
		r	22	55	80
Château Foncla	*Castres*	wh	3	7.5	10

	Commune		*Hectares*	*Acres*	*Tonneaux*
Château Foncroise	*St.-Selve*	wh			
			7	17.5	10
		r			
Château des Fougères	*La Brède*	wh	2	5	5
Clos des Fougères	*Virelade*	wh	4	10	11
		wh	4	10	15
Château de France	*Léognan*	r	26	65	100
Domaine des Gaillardas	*St.-Selve*	wh	4	10	10
Cru Galand	*Cérons*	wh	1	2.5	4
Clos du Gars	*La Brède*	wh	2	5	10
Château Gazin	*Léognan*	wh			
			13	33	50
		r			
Clos de Gensac	*Pujols*	wh	4	10	25
Domaine de la Girafe	*Portets*	wh	5	12.5	22
		r	4	10	15
Cru de Gonthier	*Portets*	wh	1	2.5	5
		r	2	5	7
Château Gorre	*Martillac*	wh	1	2.5	1
		r	2	5	3
Château du Grand-Abord	*Portets*	wh	5	12.5	18
		r	18	45	60
Château Grand Chemin	*Cérons*	wh	2	5	8
		wh	3	8	10
Domaine Grandmaison	*Léognan*	r	11	28	55
Château des Graves	*Portets*	wh	3	7.5	6
		r	6	15	25
Domaine de Gravettes	*St.-Morillon*	wh	4	10	15
		r	5	13	20
Château Graveyron	*Portets*	wh	6	15	18
		r	4	10	10
Château de la Gravière	*Toulenne*	wh	7	17.5	25
Château des Gravières	*Portets*	wh	3	7.5	12
		r	19	48	120
Clos des Gravières	*Portets*	wh	2	5	15
		r	1	2.5	5
Domaine des Gravières	*Portets*	r	2	5	6
Domaine de Guérin	*Castres*	r	4	10	6
Château Guillaumot	*La Brède*	wh	2	5	10
Château des Guillemins	*Langon*	wh	8	20	28
Domaine de Guirauton	*St.-Morillon*	wh + r	6	15	12
Domaine des Guizats	*Pujols*	wh	2	5	8
Hannetot Grand Maison	*Léognan*	r	5	12.5	15
Château Haut-Bergey	*Léognan*	r	13.5	34	70
Château du Haut-Blanc	*Pujols*	wh	3	8	10
Domaine du Haut-Blanc	*Pujols*	wh	4	10	12
Domaine Haut-Callens	*Beautiran*	r	3	7.5	12
Domaine du Haut Courneau	*Portets*	wh	17	42.5	30
		r	5	12.5	60
Cru Haut-Gravette	*St.-Morillon*	wh	3	7.5	6
Château Haut-Madère	*Villenave-d'Ornon*	r	2	5	3
Château Haut-Nouchet	*Martillac*	wh			20
			7	18	30
		r			
Cru Hautes Plantes	*Landiras*	wh	3	7.5	8
Château Haut-Reys	*La-Brède*	wh	3	7.5	15
Château Jamnets	*St.-Pierre-de-Mons*	wh			5
			2	5	
		r			4

Graves: Principal Growths

	Commune		Hectares	Acres	Tonneaux
Clos Jamnet	La Brède	wh	4	10	15
Cru Janot-Bayle	Budos	r	8	20	16
Domaine du Jau	St.-Morillon	wh	3	7.5	5
Château Les Jaubertes	St. Pardon de Conques	wh	6	15	35
		r	7	18	30
Clos Jean Dubos	Pujols	wh	2	5	10
Château Jean-Gervais, Clos Puyjalon	Portets	wh	13	33	50
		r	22	55	45
Château Jean de Maye	Portets	wh	4	10	15
		r	3	8	11
Clos de l'Abbaye-de-Larame	Mazères	wh	6	15	12
		wh	6	15	30
Château La Garde	Martillac	r	41	102	200
Château Langueloup	Portels	wh + r	2	5	6
Cru La Hounade	Pujols	wh	2	5	9
Château La Louvière	Léognan	wh	10	25	50
		r	37	93	170
Clos de La Magine	St.-Pierre-de-Mons	wh	6	15	14
		r	5	13	20
Cru La Mainionce	Pujols	wh	3	7.5	13
Cru Lamédecine	St.-Pierre-de-Mons	wh	2	5	5
Cru de Lamoigon	Pujols	wh	3	7.5	5
Château Lamothe-Bouscat	Cadaujac	r	4	10	15
Clos Lamothe	Portets	wh	3	7.5	9
		r	8	20	25
Château Lamouroux	Cérons	wh	8	20	37
Château Laouilley	Roaillan	wh	3	7.5	3
Domaine La Payrère	St.-Selve	wh	5	12.5	8
		r			2
Domaine de Larnavey	St.-Selve	r	2	5	8
Château Larrivet-Haut-Brion	Léognan	r	14	35	80
		wh	1	3	5
Cru Larroucat	Pujols	wh	2	5	8
Cru La Salle	Martillac	wh	3	7.5	8
Domaine La Solitude	Martillac	wh	5	13	25
		r	19	48	40
Château Lassalle	La Brède	wh	6	15	26
Cru La Terce	Budos	r	2	5	3
Château La Tour-Léognan	Léognan	wh	3	8	15
		r	7	18	30
Château La Tour Bicheau	Portets	wh	4	7.5	12
		r	6	12.5	25
Château La Tour-de-Boyrein	Langon	wh	13	32.5	40
		r	4	10	20
Château La Tourte	Toulenne	wh	6	15	16
		r	4	8	10
Cru Le Bourut	Pujols	wh	2	5	9
Cru de l'Église	Virelade	wh	2	5	5
Château Léhoult	Langon	wh	4	10	8
		r	3	8	10
Château Le Mayne	Preignac	wh	2	22.5	30
Château Le Pape	Léognan	r	5	13	15
Cru Les Graves	Toulenne	wh	4	10	12
Château Lespault	Martillac	wh	4	10	3
		r	0.5	1.2	2
Château de l'Espérance	La Brède	wh	4	10	10
		r	8	20	25
Cru Lestage	Landiras	wh	4	10	9

	Commune		Hectares	Acres	Tonneaux
Domaine Lestang	St.-Selve	wh + r	5	12.5	5
Château Le Thil	Léognan	r	3	7.5	4
		wh	9	23	35
Cru de l'Hermitage	Budos	r	4	10	15
Clos de l'Hôpital	Castres	r	7	18	35
Château de l'Hospital	Portets	wh }			
			8	20	5
		r }			
Château Liché	St.-Pardon-de-Conques	wh	3	8	10
		r	3	8	10
Château Limbourg	Villenave-d'Ornon	wh }			5
			10	25	
		r }			6
Château Liot-Moros	Pujols	wh	5	12.5	15
Cru Liot	Budos	wh	3	7.5	4
Château Lognac	Castres	r	15	38	30
Domaine de Louisot	Virelade	wh	4	10	13
Clos Louloumet	Toulenne	wh	3	7.5	8
Cru de Lubat	St.-Pierre-de-Mons	wh	8	20	14
		r	4	10	15
Château des Lucques	Portets	wh	2	5	11
		r	8	20	50
Domaine des Lucques	Portets	wh	2	5	10
		r	12	30	60
Château Ludeman-La Côte	Langon	wh	7	17.5	20
		r	3	9	10
Château Lusseau	Ayguemortes	r	4	10	10
Château Madélis	Portets	wh	2	5	6
		r	13	33	10
Château Madran	Pessac	r	3	7.5	4
Château Magence	St.-Pierre-de-Mons	wh	15	38	60
		r	11	28	45
Château Magneau	La Brède	wh + r	5	12.5	11
Château Maillard	Mazères	wh	5	12.5	13
		r	38	95	150
Clos de la Maison Blanche	Budos	wh	2	5	5
Château Malleprat	Martillac	wh	3	7.5	5
		r	4	10	5
Domaine de Maron	Landiras	r	2	5	9
Cru Massiot	Martillac	wh	2	5	6
		wh	8	20	30
Château de Mauves	Podensac	r	12	30	50
Château de May	Portets	wh	3	7.5	10
		r	2	5	5
Domaine du Mayne	Langon	wh	3	7.5	8
Château Mayne-d'Inbert	Podensac	wh	10	25	50
		r	5	12.5	25
Château Millet	Portets	wh	20	50	90
		r	45	113	250
Château Mirabel	Pujols	wh	3	7.5	14
Château du Mirail	Portets	wh	5	12.5	16
		r	23	58	60
Château Moderis	Virelade	wh + r	5	12.5	10
Château de Mongenan	Portets	wh	2	5	5
		r	5	13	15
Clos de Mons	La Brède	wh + r	3	7.5	8
Cru Morange	Virelade	wh + r	2	5	7
Clos du Moulin-à-Vent	St.-Pierre-de-Mons	wh	5	12.5	18

Graves: Principal Growths

	Commune		Hectares	Acres	Tonneaux
Cru du Moulin-à-Vent	Landiras	wh	3	7.5	10
Château Mouteou	Portets	wh	2	5	6
		r	1	2.5	4
		wh	2	5	10
Château Moutin	Portets	r	2	5	10
Château Mouyet	Budos	r	2	5	11
Cru Nodoy	Virelade	wh + r	5	12.5	20
Clos de Nouchet	Castres	r	3	7.5	10
Château de Nouguey	Langon	wh	2	5	6
Clos Le Pape	La Brède	wh	6	15	25
Domaine de Papoula (see Domaine de Durse)					
Cru Patiras	Toulenne	wh	2	5	4
Château Le Pavillon-de-Boyrein	Roaillan	r	25	63	110
Château Peydebayle	St.-Pierre-de-Mons	wh	2	5	5
		r	2	5	10
Château Péran	Langon	wh	3	8	10
		r	3	8	10
Cru Pérran	Landiras	wh	3	7.5	12
Domaine Perin de Naudine	Castres	r	5	12.5	15
Château Perron	Roaillan	wh	14	35	37
Château Pesilla	Landiras	wh	4	10	16
Château Pessan	Portets	wh	2	5	10
		r	8	20	40
Château Péyran	Landiras	wh	4	10	11
Château des Peyrères	Landiras	wh	4	10	14
Cru Pezeau	Beautiran	r	3	7.5	10
Château Pingoy	Portets	wh	1	3	5
		r	7	18	15
Château Picque-Caillou	Mérignac	wh	18	45	75
Château Piron	St.-Morillon	wh	15	37.5	50
		r	5	13	20
Château de Places	Arbanats	wh	1	2.5	4
		r	6	15	25
Château des Places	Arbanats	wh	2	5	9
		r	6	15	25
Château Plantat	St.-Morillon	wh	3	8	10
		r	6	15	10
Domaine des Plantes	Landiras	wh	6	15	25
		r	4	10	15
Domaine des Plantes	Landiras	wh	4	10	11
Domaine du Plantey	Castres	wh			2
			2	5	
		r			7
		wh	3	8	10
Château Pommarède	Castres	r	3	7.5	10
Château Pommarède-de-Haut	Castres	wh	1	3	5
		r	5	13	20
Château Pontac-Monplaisir	Villenave-d'Ornon	wh	6	15	30
		r	8	20	45
Le Pontet	St.-Médard-d'Eyrans	r	5	12.5	20
Cru de Portail	Landiras	wh	2	5	7
Château de Portets	Portets	wh	4	10	25
		r	11	20	45
Cru de la Poste	Virelade	wh	4	10	6
Château Poumey	Gradignan	r	4	10	7
Clos Puyjalon (see Château Jean-Gervais)					
Château Queyrats, Clos d'Uza, Château St. Pierre	St.-Pierre-de-Mons	wh	34	85	77
Château Rahoul	Portets	wh	3	7.5	15
		r	15	37.5	50

	Commune		Hectares	Acres	Tonneaux
Château de Respide	Langon	wh ⎫			55
		⎬	65	163	
		r ⎭			40
Château Respide	St.-Pierre-de-Mons	wh	4	10	5
Château Respide	Toulenne	wh	7	18	20
		r	2	5	10
Château La Rocaille	Virelade	wh + r	9	22.5	13
Château Rochemorin	Martillac	wh	6	15	24
		r	36	95	160
Domaine Roland	Langon	wh	3	7.5	6
Château Roquetaillade-la-Grange	Mazères	wh + r	38	95	130
		r	10	25	40
Château Roquetaillade-Roquetaillade	Mazères	wh	3	7.5	9
Château Roubinet	Pujols	wh	8	20	32
Cru Roudet	Pujols	wh	2	5	10
Château de Rouillac	Canéjean	r	5	12.5	20
Cru Sadout	Virelade	wh + r	6	15	19
Château Saige-Fort-Manoir	Pessac	r	5	12.5	11
Château St.-Gérôme	Ayguemortes	wh	4	10	7
		r	5	13	10
Clos St.-Hilaire	Portets	wh	3	7.5	12
		r	3	7.5	8
Clos St.-Jean	Pujols	wh	8	20	23
Château St.-Pierre (*see* Château Queyrats)					
Château St.-Robert	Pujols	wh	12	30	50
		r	16	40	65
Domaine du Sapeur	Portets	wh ⎫			9
		⎬	4	10	
		r ⎭			10
Cru Sarraguey	Virelade	wh + r	5	12.5	20
Domaine des Sarrots	St.-Pierre-de-Mons	wh	2	5	5
Clos Sentouary	St.-Pierre-de-Mons	wh	2	5	5
Domaine de Terrefort	Landiras	wh	6	6	25
		r	12	30	50
Domaine de Teycheney	Virelade	wh	2	5	4
Domaine de Teychon	Arbanats	wh	4	10	16
		r	7	18	30
Château Toumilon	St.-Pierre-de-Mons	wh	5	12.5	9
		r	6	15	25
Clos Toumilon	St.-Pierre-de-Mons	wh	2	5	4
		r	2	5	10
Château Tourteau-Cholet	Arbanats	wh	13	32.5	40
		r	21	52	40
Clos de la Tuilerie	Portets	wh	3	7.5	10
		r	2	5	10
Cru La Tuilerie	Landiras	wh	2	5	7
Château des Tuileries	Virelade	wh	3	7.5	14
		r	2	5	10
Château Le Tuquet	Beautiran	wh ⎫			100
		⎬	26	65	
		r ⎭			20
Château Tustoc	Toulenne	wh	8	20	26
Clos d'Uza (*see* Château Queyrats)					
Domaine des Vergnes	Portets	wh	2	5	4
		r	1	2.5	4
Clos Viaut	St.-Pardon-de-Conques	wh	2	5	4
		r	7	18	30
Clos Viaut	St.-Pierre-de-Mons	wh	2	5	5
Cru Videau	Pujols	wh	6	15	25

	Commune		Hectares	Acres	Tonneaux
Château La Vieille-France	Portets	wh ⎤			25
		⎬	16	40	
		r ⎦			15
Château de Virelade	Virelade	wh	3	7.5	9
		r	29	73	15

VIII SAUTERNES AND BARSAC

As in the Médoc, the Sauternes vineyards were officially classified in 1855. This classification is known as the Official Classification of the Great Growths of the Gironde.

The total production from these vineyards represents approximately 25 per cent of the total Sauternes production, amounting roughly to 350,000 cases per year.

The following figures of production are approximate, and indicate average annual output, as given by the communes and taken from their Déclarations de Récoltes records.

FIRST GREAT GROWTH

	Tonneaux	Cases
Château d'Yquem	60	5,500

FIRST GROWTHS

Château Guiraud	90	8,000
Château La Tour-Blanche	50	4,000
Château Lafaurie-Peyraguey	50	4,000
Château de Rayne-Vigneau	150	11,000
Château Sigalas-Rabaud	35	3,000
Château Rabaud-Promis	65	5,000
Clos Haut-Peyraguey	25	2,000
Château Coutet	75	6,500
Château Climens	65	6,000
Château Suduiraut	70	6,000
Château Rieussec	100	8,500

SECOND GROWTHS

Château d'Arche	50	4,000
Château Filhot	100	10,000
Château Lamothe	25	2,000
Château Myrat (no longer producing wine)	—	—
Château Doisy-Védrines	35	6,000
Château Doisy-Daëne	30	2,000
Château Suau	15	1,000
Château Broustet	30	3,000
Château Caillou	40	4,000
Château Nairac	40	3,000
Château de Malle	40	4,000
Château Romer	5	1,000
Château Romer-du-Hayot	60	3,000

MINOR GROWTHS

	Commune	Hectares	Acres	Tonneaux
Château d'Arche-Lafaurie	Sauternes	19	47.5	48
Château d'Arche-Pugnau, Château Peyraguey-le-Rousset	Preignac	15	37.5	32
Château d'Arches, Château Lamothe	Sauternes	15	37.5	40
Château d'Arche-Vimeney	Sauternes	5	12.5	11

	Commune	Hectares	Acres	Tonneaux
Château d'Argilas le Pape	*Preignac*	2	5	4
Château d'Armajan-les-Ormes	*Preignac*	1	2.5	2
Cru d'Arrançon	*Preignac*	5	12.5	10
Cru Arrançon-Boutoc	*Preignac*	3	7.5	9
Château des Arrieux	*Preignac*	5	12.5	15
Château Augey	*Bommes*	10	25	26
Cru Baboye	*Fargues*	2	5	5
Château Barbier	*Fargues*	6	15	16
Cru de Barboye	*Bommes*	2	5	4
Château Barjuneau	*Sauternes*	6	15	15
Domaine Barjuneau-Chauvin	*Sauternes*	4	10	10
Clos Barreau	*Fargues*	1	2.5	4
Château Barrette	*Sauternes*	5	12.5	14
Cru Barrette	*Fargues*	1	2.5	2
Cru Bas-Peyraguey	*Preignac*	2	5	4
Château Bastor-Lamontagne	*Preignac*	38	95	90
Cru Bataille	*Bommes*	4	10	10
Château Batsalle	*Fargues*	4	10	9
Cru Batsalle	*Fargues*	1	2.5	3
Château Baulac-Dodigeos	*Barsac*	5	12.5	12
Cru Beylieu	*Fargues*	7	17.5	13
Château Béchereau	*Bommes*	8	20	25
Cru Bel-Air	*Preignac*	2	5	4
Château Bergeron	*Bommes*	8	20	20
Cru Bergeron	*Preignac*	4	10	11
Château Bernisse	*Barsac*	3	7.5	8
Cru Bignon	*Bommes*	1	2.5	3
Cru Bordessoulles	*Preignac*	3	7.5	7
Château Bousclas	*Barsac*	3	7.5	8
Cru Bousclas	*Barsac*	4	10	12
Cru Boutoc	*Preignac*	5	12.5	10
Cru Boutoc	*Sauternes*	2	5	5
Château Bouyot	*Barsac*	6	15	15
Cru Bouyréou	*Preignac*	1	2.5	2
Château Brassens-Guitteronde	*Barsac*	5	12.5	14
Château Briatte	*Preignac*	8	20	20
Cru Camelong	*Bommes*	1	2.5	2
Château Cameron et Raymond-Louis	*Bommes*	9	22.5	35
Château Camperos	*Barsac*	3	7.5	10
Château Cantegril	*Barsac*	14	35	38
Cru Caplane	*Bommes*	2	5	5
Cru Caplane	*Sauternes*	3	7.5	10
Domaine de Caplane	*Sauternes*	5	12.5	25
Cru Carbonnieu	*Bommes*	10	25	30
Château de Carles	*Barsac*	6	15	16
Cru du Carrefour	*Sauternes*	1	2.5	2
Cru de la Cave	*Preignac*	2	5	5
Cru du Chalet	*Barsac*	2	5	5
Cru du Chalet	*Preignac*	1	2.5	3
Domaine de la Chapelle	*Preignac*	2	5	4
Château de la Chartreuse	*Preignac*	5	12.5	10
Cru Chauvin	*Sauternes*	2	5	4
Cru Claveries	*Fargues*	1	2.5	2
Château Closiot	*Barsac*	5	12.5	11
Château Commarque	*Sauternes*	4	10	10
Cru Commarque	*Bommes*	1	2.5	3
Cru Commarque	*Sauternes*	6	15	11
Château Commet-Magey	*Preignac*	4	10	8
Cru Commet-Magey-Briatte	*Preignac*	4	10	11

	Commune	*Hectares*	*Acres*	*Tonneaux*
Domaine Cosse	*Fargues*	6	15	12
Domaine de Couite	*Preignac*	3	7.5	8
Cru Coussères	*Fargues*	1	2.5	2
Château Coustet	*Barsac*	6	15	21
Cru Coustet	*Barsac*	1	2.5	2
Domaine du Coy	*Sauternes*	3	7.5	8
Château de Coye	*Sauternes*	1	2.5	3
Cru Druenn	*Bommes*	2	5	4
Château Ducasse	*Barsac*	5	12.5	12
Cru Ducasse	*Fargues*	2	5	5
Château Dudon	*Barsac*	8	20	20
Domaine Duperneau	*Bommes*	3	7.5	9
Clos d'Espagnet (*see* Château Esterlin)				
Château Esterlin, Clos d'Espagnet	*Sauternes*	3	7.5	7
Château de Fargues	*Fargues*	12	30	7
Château Farluret	*Barsac*	4	10	11
Cru Fillau	*Fargues*	4	10	10
Château Fleury, Château Terre-Noble	*Barsac*	2	5	4
Clos Fontaine	*Fargues*	9	22.5	25
Château Fontebride	*Preignac*	2	5	7
Domaine de la Forêt	*Preignac*	21	52.5	61
Cru Gavach	*Fargues*	3	7.5	7
Château Gilette, Domaine des Justices, Château Les Rochers, Château Les Remparts, Château Lamothe	*Preignac*	14	35	30
Clos Girautin	*Barsac*	1	2.5	3
Château Grand-Carretey	*Barsac*	1	2.5	2
Cru Grand-Carretey	*Barsac*	6	15	16
Cru Grand-Jauga	*Barsac*	2	5	6
Château Grand-Mayne-Qui-Né-Marc	*Barsac*	1	2.5	3
Cru Gravaillas	*Preignac*	2	5	4
Château Gravas	*Barsac*	8	20	20
Château Grillon	*Barsac*	6	15	18
Domaine Guilhem-du-Rey	*Preignac*	7	17.5	22
Château Guimbalet	*Preignac*	1	2.5	4
Château Guitteronde	*Barsac*	9	22.5	22
Château Guitteronde-Sarraute	*Barsac*	4	10	10
Château du Haire	*Preignac*	4	10	9
Cru du Haire	*Preignac*	6	15	18
Château Hallet	*Barsac*	10	25	24
Château Haut-Bergeron	*Preignac*	4	10	13
Château Haut-Bommes	*Bommes*	7	17.5	14
Château Haut-Claverie	*Fargues*	9	22.5	20
Château Haut-Fontebride	*Preignac*	6	15	20
Cru Haut-Lagueritte	*Bommes*	2	5	4
Château Haut-Mayne	*Fargues*	2	5	5
Cru Haut-Piquant	*Sauternes*	1	2.5	3
Cru du Hère	*Preignac*	2	5	2
Château Hourmalas (*see* Château St.-Marc)				
Cru Hourmalas	*Barsac*	2	5	6
Château Jany	*Barsac*	2	5	6
Cru Jauguet	*Barsac*	5	12.5	14
Château Jean-Galan	*Bommes*	6	15	15
Château Jean-Laive	*Barsac*	4	10	11
Clos de Jeanlaive	*Barsac*	5	12.5	11
Cru Jeannonier	*Bommes*	3	7.5	4
Domaine Jean-Robert	*Preignac*	1	2.5	3
Domaine du Juge	*Preignac*	4	10	10
Cru Junka	*Preignac*	3	7.5	4
Château Les Justices	*Preignac*	3	7.5	6

	Commune	Hectares	Acres	Tonneaux
Domaine des Justices (*see* Château Gilette)				
Cru La Bernisse	*Barsac*	3	7.5	7
Château La Bouade	*Barsac*	12	30	31
Clos La Bouade	*Barsac*	3	7.5	8
Domaine de Labouade-Rambaud	*Barsac*	1	2.5	3
Cru Labouchette	*Preignac*	2	5	5
Château La Brouillère	*Bommes*	4	10	9
Cru Labrousse	*Barsac*	2	5	5
Château La Chapelle-St.-Aubin	*Bommes*	3	7.5	6
Château La Clotte	*Barsac*	5	12.5	12
Cru Lacoste	*Barsac*	2	5	4
Cru La Côte	*Fargues*	5	12.5	9
Château Lafon, Château Le Mayne	*Sauternes*	6	15	19
Château Lafon-Laroze	*Sauternes*	3	7.5	5
Cru Lagardan	*Bommes*	3	7.5	10
Domaine de Lagauche	*Bommes*	2	5	4
Cru l'Agnet	*Bommes*	2	5	3
Château Lagravette	*Bommes*	2	5	5
Château La Gravière	*Preignac*	2	5	5
Cru Lahonade-Peyraguey	*Bommes*	2	5	6
Château Lahouilley	*Barsac*	3	7.5	9
Château La Hourcade	*Preignac*	4	10	13
Cru Lalot	*Preignac*	3	7.5	8
Cru La Maringue	*Bommes*	1	2.5	2
Château Lamothe (*see* Château d'Arches)				
Château Lamothe (*see* Château Gilette)				
Cru Lamothe	*Sauternes*	6	15	14
Château Lamourette	*Bommes*	7	17.5	20
Cru Lanère	*Sauternes*	11	27.5	21
Château Lange	*Bommes*	5	12.5	12
Cru Lanusquet	*Fargues*	2	5	5
Clos Lapachère	*Barsac*	4	10	10
Château Lapelou	*Barsac*	6	15	16
Château Lapinesse	*Barsac*	16	40	44
Cru Lapinesse	*Barsac*	7	17.5	19
Cru La Pinesse	*Barsac*	2	5	5
Domaine de Laraude	*Sauternes*	2	5	5
Château Laribotte	*Preignac*	11	27.5	25
Château l'Arieste	*Preignac*	18	45	40
Clos l'Arieste	*Preignac*	3	7.5	8
Château La Tour	*Barsac*	2	5	4
Château Latrezotte	*Barsac*	7	17.5	20
Cru l'Aubépin	*Bommes*	10	25	26
Cru l'Aubépine	*Bommes*	2	5	4
Cru l'Aubépins	*Sauternes*	3	7.5	6
Château Lauvignac	*Preignac*	3	7.5	6
Château Laville	*Preignac*	15	35	35
Château Le Coustet	*Barsac*	5	12.5	10
Cru Le Haut Bommes	*Bommes*	0.5	1.2	2
Château Le Hère	*Bommes*	6	15	10
Château du Mayne	*Preignac*	9	22.5	25
Château Le Mayne (*see* Château Lafon)				
Château Le Mouret	*Fargues*	6	15	6
Cru Le Pageot	*Bommes*	2	5	4
Château l'Ermitage	*Preignac*	7	17.5	13
Château Le Roc	*Preignac*	1	2.5	3
Château Larose-Monteil	*Preignac*	8	20	20
Cru Le Rousseau	*Bommes*	2	5	3
Château Le Sahuc	*Preignac*	3	7.5	9

663

	Commune	Hectares	Acres	Tonneaux
Cru Les Cailloux	*Bommes*	2	5	4
Cru Les Gravilles	*Barsac*	1	2.5	2
Château Le Sourd Béteille	*Bordeaux*	3	7.5	10
Château Les Plantes	*Barsac*	5	12.5	14
Château Les Remparts (*see* Château Gilette)				
Château Les Rochers	*Preignac*	7	17.5	18
Château Les Rochers (*see* Château Gilette)				
Cru Les Rochers	*Preignac*	2	5	4
Cru Les Tuileries	*Fargues*	1	2.5	3
Cru Le Tachon	*Bommes*	2	5	4
Château Leyret	*Preignac*	2	5	4
Château Liot	*Barsac*	11	27.5	29
Château de Luzies	*Barsac*	3	7.5	9
Cru Mahon	*Bommes*	3	7.5	10
Cru Mahon	*Preignac*	2	5	6
Cru de Mahon	*Preignac*	2	5	3
Clos des Maraings	*Preignac*	3	7.5	6
Château Masereau	*Barsac*	7	17.5	15
Château Mathalin	*Barsac*	11	27.5	35
Domaine de Mathalin	*Barsac*	1	2.5	3
Château Mauras	*Bommes*	13	32.5	36
Cru Mauras	*Bommes*	13	32.5	30
Cru Mauvin	*Preignac*	6	15	16
Château du Mayne	*Barsac*	7	17.5	17
Château du Mayne	*Preignac*	2	5	5
Château Mayne-Bert (*see* Château Camperos)				
Clos Mayne-Lamouroux	*Barsac*	2	5	5
Cru Menate	*Barsac*	1	2.5	2
Château Menota, Château Menota-Labat	*Barsac*	17	42.5	54
Château Menota-Labat (*see* Château Menota)				
Château Mercier	*Barsac*	2	5	4
Clos Mercier	*Barsac*	3	7.5	8
Cru Mercier	*Barsac*	1	2.5	4
Clos de Miaille	*Barsac*	1	2.5	2
Cru Miaille	*Barsac*	1	2.5	3
Cru Miselle	*Preignac*	3	7.5	7
Château du Mont	*Preignac*	4	10	11
Château Montalivet (*see* Château Camperos)				
Château Monteau	*Preignac*	9	22.5	21
Cru Monteil	*Bommes*	3	7.5	7
Cru Monteil	*Preignac*	1	2.5	2
Domaine de Monteil	*Preignac*	7	17.5	19
Cru Montjoie	*Preignac*	2	5	4
Château Montjou (*see* Château Terre Noble)				
Cru Mothes	*Fargues*	2	5	5
Clos du Moulin Neuf	*Preignac*	1	2.5	2
Château Mounic	*Fargues*	1	2.5	2
Domaine de Mounic	*Fargues*	1	2.5	2
Château Moura	*Barsac*	1	2.5	4
Cru Mouret	*Fargues*	3	7.5	7
Clos de Moynet	*Preignac*	2	5	4
Cru Mussotte	*Fargues*	1	2.5	3
Clos de Nauton	*Fargues*	4	10	7
Château Padouen	*Barsac*	10	25	20
Château Pageot	*Sauternes*	5	12.5	12
Cru du Pajot	*Bommes*	4	10	7
Château Paloumat	*Fargues*	2	5	2
Château Le Pape	*Preignac*	3	7.5	12
Clos du Pape	*Fargues*	5	12.5	11

	Commune	Hectares	Acres	Tonneaux
Château Partarieu	Fargues	18	45	40
Cru Passérieux	Barsac	3	7.5	7
Château Pébayle	Barsac	5	12.5	15
Château Peillon-Claverie	Fargues	12	30	35
Château Pechon-Terre-Noble	Barsac	3	7.5	9
Château Pernaud	Barsac	17	42.5	35
Cru de Perret	Bommes	2	5	6
Château Perroy-Jean-Blanc	Bommes	7	17.5	17
Cru Petit-Grillon	Barsac	2	5	5
Cru Peyraguey	Preignac	2	5	5
Château Peyraguey-le-Rousset (see Cru d'Arche-Pugnau)				
Château de Peyre	Fargues	1	2.5	3
Clos Peyret	Preignac	1	2.5	3
Château Peyron	Fargues	4	10	17
Château Piada, Clos du Roy	Barsac	11	27.5	29
Cru Pian	Barsac	2	5	7
Château Piaut	Barsac	9	22.5	22
Château du Pick	Preignac	19	47.5	50
Clos de Pierrefeu	Preignac	4	10	10
Cru Pilote	Fargues	6	15	20
Cru du Piquey	Bommes	1	2.5	2
Cru de Pistoulet-Peyraguey	Bommes	2	5	4
Cru du Placey	Barsac	1	2.5	3
Cru Planton	Barsac	1	2.5	3
Château Pleytegeat	Preignac	12	30	51
Cru Pouteau	Fargues	6	15	20
Cru Pouton	Preignac	2	5	6
Clos des Princes	Barsac	2	5	6
Château Prost	Barsac	8	20	21
Château Pugneau	Preignac	3	7.5	8
Cru Puydomine	Bommes	2	5	4
Château Raspide	Barsac	5	12.5	16
Château Raymond-Lafon	Sauternes	15	37.5	35
Château des Remparts	Preignac	1	2.5	4
Cru Richard Barbe	Bommes	2	5	5
Cru Ripaille	Preignac	4	10	10
Château du Roc	Barsac	2	5	5
Clos des Rocs	Preignac	1	2.5	3
Château de Rolland	Barsac	14	35	39
Domaine de la Roudette	Sauternes	2	5	6
Château Roumieu	Barsac	18	45	46
Château Roumieu-Lacoste	Barsac	5	12.5	14
Château Rouquette	Preignac	6	15	17
Cru Rousset-Peyraguey	Preignac	5	12.5	15
Clos du Roy (see Château Piada)				
Château Sahuc	Preignac	2	5	5
Château Sahuc-Latour	Preignac	9	22.5	25
Château St.-Amand	Preignac	16	40	40
Château St.-Marc, Château Hourmalas	Barsac	6	15	14
Château St.-Michel	Barsac	1	2.5	3
Cru St.-Michel	Barsac	1	2.5	3
Clos St.-Robert	Barsac	1	2.5	3
Cru St.-Sardeau	Fargues	2	5	6
Cru Saubade-Terrefort	Sauternes	2	5	3
Château Simon	Barsac	4	10	12
Château Simon-Carretey	Barsac	4	10	7
Château Solon	Preignac	4	10	13
Cru Soula	Fargues	4	10	9
Château Suau	Barsac	5	12.5	14

Cérons: Principal Growths

	Commune	Hectares	Acres	Tonneaux
Domaine Tchit	Fargues	1	2.5	3
Cru Terrefort	Bommes	4	10	11
Domaine de Terrefort	Bommes	10	25	35
Château Terre Noble, Château Montjou	Barsac	9	22.5	24
Château Terre-Noble (*see* Château Fleury)				
Cru des Terres Rouges	Barsac	2	5	4
Château Thibaut	Fargues	10	25	30
Cru Thibaut	Fargues	4	10	12
Château de Touilla	Fargues	3	7.5	4
Château Trillon	Sauternes	20	50	50
Cru Trinquine	Preignac	2	5	4
Cru Tucan	Barsac	2	5	3
Château Tucau	Barsac	3	7.5	9
Château Valmont-Mayne	Barsac	2	5	4
Château Veyres	Preignac	10	25	30
Cru Vigne-Vieille	Barsac	3	7.5	8
Château Villefranche	Barsac	6	15	13
Château Violet	Preignac	11	27.5	30
Cru du Violet	Preignac	3	7.5	20
Cru du Violet-et-Lamothe	Preignac	5	12.5	12
Château Voigny	Preignac	6	15	18

IX CÉRONS

The following figures of production are approximate, and indicate average annual output, as given by the communes and taken from their Déclarations de Récoltes records.

PRINCIPAL GROWTHS

	Commune	Hectares	Acres	Tonneaux
Château d'Anice	Podensac	12	30	50
Château Archambeau	Illats	4	10	34
Clos Avocat	Cérons	4	10	8
Clos de l'Avocat	Cérons	3	7.5	9
Château Balestey	Cérons	10	25	20
Clos de Barial	Illats	9	22.5	22
Clos du Barrail	Cérons	8	20	19
Château Beaulac	Illats	3	7.5	7
Château Beaulieu	Cérons	6	15	30
Cru Bel-Air	Illats	3	7.5	12
Clos de Bos-Lancon	Illats	4	10	12
Cru de Bouley	Illats	4	10	8
Domaine de Bourdac	Illats	7	17.5	40
Clos Bourgelet	Cérons	7	17.5	15
Cru de Boutec	Illats	5	12.5	20
Cru de Braze	Illats	7	17.5	18
Cru Brouillaou	Podensac	11	27.5	28
Cru de Cabiro	Illats	3	7.5	11
Château Cages	Illats	5	12.5	17
Domaine du Caillou	Cérons	5	12.5	10
Domaine Caillou Rouley	Podensac	8	20	15
Château Cantau	Illats	4	10	9
Clos Cantemerle	Cérons	3	7.5	7
Château de Cérons	Cérons	15	37.5	28
Château Chantegrive	Podensac	30	75	120
Domaine de la Citadelle	Illats	4	10	14
Cru Cleyrac	Cérons	5	12.5	15
Cru des Deux Moulins	Illats	4	10	8

	Commune	Hectares	Acres	Tonneaux
Château Ferbos	Cérons	10	25	40
Domaine du Freyron	Cérons	3	7.5	5
Domaine de Gardennes	Illats	3	7.5	6
Château Grand Chemin	Cérons	4	10	8
Château des Grand-Chênes	Cérons	3	7.5	6
Grand Enclos du Château de Cérons	Cérons	11	27.5	30
Château Hauret	Illats	4	10	9
Cru Haut-Buhan	Illats	7	17.5	18
Château du Haut-Gravier	Illats	11	27.5	22
Château La Hontasse (P. Banos)	Illats	3	7.5	6
Cru Haut La Hontasse (R. Banos, J. Banos)	Illats	5	12.5	15
Château Haut-Mayne	Cérons	5	12.5	10
Cru de Haut-Mayne	Cérons	3	7.5	6
Château Haut-Rat	Illats	16	40	40
Château Huradin, Domaine du Salut	Cérons	8	20	30
Clos du Jaugua	Illats	4	10	8
Domaine de Jaussans	Illats	8	20	20
Château LaLanette Ferbos	Cérons	5	12.5	22
Château Lamouroux	Cérons	10	25	22
Château Lanette	Cérons	5	12.5	12
Château Laroche	Illats	14	35	45
Cru Larrouquey	Cérons	7	17.5	18
Château Larrouquey	Cérons	5	12.5	12
Château La Salette	Cérons	5	12.5	12
Domaine Le Cossu	Podensac	5	12.5	11
Château Le Huzet	Illats	7	17.5	18
Cru Le Tinan	Illats	3	7.5	6
Cru de Lionne	Illats	7	17.5	18
Cru Madérot (Édouard Sterlin)	Podensac	9	22.5	18
Cru Majans	Cérons	3	7.5	6
Cru Marc	Illats	5	12.5	16
Château des Mauves	Podensac	7	17.5	16
Château Mayne d'Anice	Podensac	4	10	9
Cru Maynine	Illats	3	7.5	10
Domaine de Menaut Larrouquey	Cérons	12	30	32
Cru de Menjon	Illats	3	7.5	9
Cru du Moulin-à-Vent (Baron)	Illats	2	5	6
Cru Moulin-à-Vent (Biarnes)	Illats	16	40	50
Château Moulins-à-Vent	Cérons	4	10	12
Clos des Moulins-à-Vent	Cérons	5	12.5	14
Cru des Moulins-à-Vent (Lafond)	Cérons	3	7.5	6
Cru des Moulins-à-Vent (Lapujade, Despujols)	Cérons	9	22.5	14
Domaine des Moulins-à-Vent	Illats	9	22.5	21
Château Moulin de Marc	Cérons	7	18	35
Château de Navarro	Illats	13	33	80
Cru du Noulin	Cérons	3	7.5	6
Cru des Parrajots	Illats	3	7.5	8
Cru du Perliques	Illats	3	7.5	8
Château du Peyrat	Cérons	14	35	45
Cru Peyroutene	Cérons	4	10	9
Cru Pinaud	Cérons	4	10	10
Domaine de Prouzet	Illats	7	17.5	13
Château du Roc	Cérons	5	12.5	8
Clos des Roches	Illats	2	5	6
Cru St.-Roch	Illats	2	5	5
Domaine du Salut (see Château Huradin)				
Château du Seuil	Cérons	3	7.5	13
Château Sylvain	Cérons	11	27.5	28

	Commune	Hectares	Acres	Tonneaux
Château Thomé-Brousterot	*Illats*	8	20	18
Château Uferic	*Cérons*	6	15	14
Cru Voltaire	*Cérons*	4	10	7

X LOUPIAC

The following figures of production are approximate, and indicate average annual output, as given by the communes and taken from their Déclarations de Récoltes records.

PRINCIPAL GROWTHS

	Hectares	Acres	Tonneaux
Château Barbe Morin	5	12.5	16
Cru Barberousse	4	10	15
Château Bel-Air	5	12.5	16
Château Bertranon	2	5	5
Château Bouchoc	2	5	4
Château Caudiet	10	25	35
Domaine du Chay	12	30	30
Château Chichoye	2	5	7
Clos de Ciron	4	10	9
Château Clos Jean	14	35	45
Château Couloumet	5	12.5	12
Château du Cros	4	10	20
Château Dauphine Rondillon	15	37.5	55
Château de l'Ermitage	2	5	7
Château La Nève	9	22.5	40
Château Le Tarey	5	12.5	13
Château Le Pavillon	4	10	14
Château Loupiac-Gaudiet	2	5	10
Château de Malendure	3	7.5	6
Cru Marges Dusseau	4	10	17
Château Mazarin	2	5	10
Côtes de Mossac	2	5	7
Château Moulin Neuf	10	25	40
Cru du Moulin Vieux	5	12.5	18
Château du Noble	7	17.5	15
Château Peyruchet	12	30	34
Cru du Plainier	5	12.5	14
Château Pontac	10	25	36
Château Ricaud	15	37	60
Domaine de Roby	5	12.5	20
Château Rondillon	12	30	40
Cru de Rouquette	8	20	18
Cru de la Sablière	4	10	13
Cru St.-Romain	4	10	11
Château Terrefort	8	20	34
Clos de Terrefort	3	7.5	6
Cru de Terrefort	4	10	16
Cru de Terrefort Pierre Noire	3	7.5	11
Château Turon Lanère (Dalas)	3	7.5	10
Château Turon Lanère (David)	5	12.5	18
Château du Vieux-Moulin	9	22.5	40

XI SAINTE-CROIX-DU-MONT

The following figures of production are approximate, and indicate average annual output, as given by the communes and taken from their Déclarations de Récoltes records.

PRINCIPAL GROWTHS

	Hectares	*Acres*	*Tonneaux*
Cru Abraham	4	10	15
Cru Baret-les-Arrivaux	3	7.5	12
Château Bel-Air	3	8	15
Clos Belle-Vue	4	10	17
Château de Bertranon	5	15	20
Château Bouchoc	3	7.5	10
Domaine du Bougan	3	7.5	6
Domaine du Bugat	3	7.5	14
Cru du Canet	3	7.5	6
Château des Coulinats	3	7.5	13
Château Coulac	3	8	15
Domaine de Coullander	1	2.5	5
Château du Crabitan	5	12.5	21
Domaine Damanieu	3	7.5	12
Domaine de l'Escaley	2	5	9
Domaine du Gaël	2	5	10
Cru de Gaillardet	1	2.5	4
Château Gensonne	2	5	5
Cru de Guerisson	3	7.5	7
Château Haut de Baritault	5	12.5	15
Cru Haut-Larrivat	3	7.5	12
Cru Haut-Medouc	3	7.5	15
Domaine de l'If	3	7.5	15
Château Jean-Lamat	4	10	16
Château Laborie	6	15	24
Château La Caussade	5	12.5	20
Domaine de Lacoste	2	5	9
Cru de La Côte Doré	2	5	8
Château Lafuë	4	10	15
Château La Grave	6	15	17
Cru La Grave	2	5	6
Château La Gravière	11	27.5	51
Château La Graville	4	10	10
Château Lamarque	15	37.5	25
Château La Mouleyre	4	10	8
Clos La Mouleyre	4	10	16
Cru La Mouleyre	3	7.5	12
Château La Peyrère	5	12.5	26
Clos l'Arabey	2	5	7
Château La Rame	16	40	65
Cru La Rame	6	15	27
Clos Larrivat	3	7.5	13
Château Laurette	15	37.5	66
Château du Grand Peyrot	5	12.5	11
Clos Le Haut-Crabitan	2	5	8
Château Le Pin	3	7.5	13
Château l'Escaley	5	12.5	23
Clos Les Arrivaux	3	7.5	11
Cru Les Arroucats	2	5	7
Domaine Les Marcottes	4	10	20
Cru Le Tarey	5	12.5	23
Château Loubens	10	25	34

Côtes de Bourg or Bourg

	Hectares	Acres	Tonneaux
Domaine de Louqsor	1	2.5	5
Château Lousteau Vieil	7	17.5	33
Château des Mailles	6	15	24
Cru Medouc	4	10	8
Clos du Medouc	2	5	7
Cru Medouc La Grave	2	5	8
Château Megnien	3	7.5	13
Château du Mont	7	17.5	30
Cru de Montagne	5	12.5	19
Domaine des Noyers	7	17.5	25
Clos du Palmiers	3	7.5	12
Domaine de Pampelune	3	7.5	15
Domaine de Parenteau	4	10	19
Château du Pavillon	11	27	40
Cru Peillot	2	5	9
Cru du Pin	2	5	6
Château de la Princesse	2	5	9
Château Roustit	9	22.5	40
Château de Tastes	6	15	18
Château Terfort	3	7.5	11
Cru du Terrefort	2	5	9
Château Vertheuil	10	25	25
Domaine du Vignots	2	5	7

XII CÔTES DE BOURG OR BOURG

The following is a list of some of the more important of the many hundreds of wine châteaux in the region.

Name	Commune	Name	Commune
Château de Barbe	*Villeneuve*	Château de Haut-Castenet	*Bourg*
Château Barrieux	*Samonac*	Château Haut-Launay	*Teuillac*
Château Bégot	*Lansac*	Château Haut-Rousset	*St.-Ciers-de-Canesse*
Domaine de Bel-Air	*St.-Seurin-de-Bourg*	Château La Barde	*Tauriac*
Château Bélair-Coubet	*St.-Ciers-de-Canesse*	Château La Croix de Millorit	*Bayon*
Château de Bousquet	*Bourg*	Château La Croix-Davids	*Lansac*
Château Brulesécaille	*Tauriac*	Château Lagrange	*Bourg*
Château de Bujan	*Gauriac*	Château La Grolet	*St.-Ciers-de-Canesse*
Château Camponac	*Bourg-sur-Gironde*	Château Lalibarde	*Bourg*
Château Caruel	*Bourg*	Domaine de Lalibarde	*Bourg*
Château Castel La Rose	*Villeneuve*	Château Lamothe	*Lansac*
Château du Castenet	*Samonac*	Château Laroche	*Tauriac*
Domaine de Christoly	*Prignac-Marcamps*	Château La Tour-Seguy	*St.-Ciers-de-Canesse*
Château Civrac	*Lansac*	Château Laurensanne	*St.-Seurin-Bourg*
Château Colbert	*Comps*	Clos Lemoine de Leudonat	*Gauriac*
Château Coubert	*Villeneuve*	Château Le Sablard	*Lansac*
Château Croûte-Courpon	*Bourg*	Château Les Haumes	*St.-Ciers-de-Canesse*
Château Donis	*Lansac*	Château de Lidonne	*Bourg-sur-Gironde*
Château Eyquem	*Bayon*	Château Macay	*Samonac*
Château Falfas	*Bayon*	Château de Marquisat	*Lansac*
Château Grand-Jour	*Prignac-Marcamps*	Château Mendoce	*Villeneuve*
Château Grand Launay	*Teuillac*	Château Mercier	*St.-Trojan*
Château de la Grave	*Bourg*	Château Nodot	*Bayon*
Château Gravettes-Samonac	*Samonac*	Domaine de Noriou-Lalibarde	*Bourg*
Château de Grissac	*Prignac-Marcamps*	Château Peychaud	*Teuillac*
Château Groleau	*Mombrier et Teuillac*	Château de Peyror	*Gauriac*
Château Gros-Moulin	*Bourg*	Château Plaisance	*Villeneuve*
Château de Guerry	*Tauriac*	Château Poyanne	*Gauriac*
Château Guionne	*Lansac*	Château Réty	*Tauriac*
Château Guiraud	*St.-Ciers-de-Canesse*	Château Rousselle	*St.-Ciers-de-Canesse*

Name	Commune	Name	Commune
Château Rousset	Samonac	Château de Thau	Gauriac
Château Sauman	Villeneuve-de-Blaye	Château Tour de Tourteau	Samonac
Château Tayac	St.-Seurin-de-Bourg		

XIII BLAYE

Following are a few of the more important wine properties.

Name	Commune	Name	Commune
Château Barbet	Cars	Château La Hargue	Plassac
Château Bellevue	Cars	Château Lamothe	St.-Paul
Château Berthenon	St.-Paul	Château La Perotte	Eyrons
Château Chaillou	St.-Paul	Château Lassale	St.-Genès
Château Breuil	St.-Martin-Caussade	Château La Taure Ste.-Luce	Blaye
Château Cantemerle	St.-Genès	Château La Tour Gayet	St.-Androny
Château Cazeaux	St.-Paul	Château Le Cone Moreau	Blaye
Domaine du Chai	Fours	Château Le Cone Sebilleau	Blaye
Château Charron	St.-Martin	Château Le Cone Taillasson	Blaye
Château Chasselauds	Cartelègue	Château Le Menaudat	St.-Androny
Château Clos d'Amières	Cartelègue	Château Les Alberts	Mazion
Château Crusquet de Lagarcie	Cars	Château Les Bavolliers	St.-Christ-de-Blaye
Château Crusquet Sabourin	Cars	Château Lescadre	Cadres
Château Dupeyrat	St.-Paul	Château Les Chaumes	Fours
Château Gadeau	Plassac	Château Les Moines	Blaye
Château Gigault	Mazion	Château Les Pts Arnauds	Cars
Château Gontier	Blaye	Château Les Ricards	Cars
Château Gontier	Blaye-Plassac	Château Le Virou	St.-Girons
Domaine de Graulet	Plassac	Château Mayence	Mazion
Château Guillonnet	Anglade	Château Mazerolles	Cars
Château Haut-Cabat	Anglade	Château Monconseil	Plassac
Château Haut-Sociondo	Cars	Moulin de la Pitance	St.-Girons
Château La Bertonnière	Plassac	Château Pardaillan	Cars
Château La Brousse	St. Martin-Caussade	Château Perrein	Mazion
Château La Cabane	St. Martin-Caussade	Château Peyrebrune	Cartelègue
Château La Cave	Blaye	Château Pinet	Berson
Château La Cure	Cars	Château Pinet La Roquete	Berson
Château Lafont	Cartelègue	Château Puy Beney	Mazion
Château La Garde	St.-Seurin-Cursac	Château Puy Beney Lafitte	Mazion
Château La Garde Roland	St.-Seurin-Cursac	Château Rebouquet	Berson
Château La Girouette	Fours	Château Ricadet	Cartelègue
Château Lagrange	Blaye	Château Segonzac	St.-Genès-de-Blaye

NOTE. In addition to all the châteaux listed in this Appendix there are approximately 1,500 others in the communes of Bordeaux which do not have separate listings.

German Wines

The *Bestimmtes Anbaugebiet* is a designated region carrying the official name of each of the eleven German wine-producing areas. Each of these largest regions is divided into one or more sub-regions, or districts, called a *Bereich.* Within the *Bereich* are found the separate villages and the vineyards associated with them. These towns or communes may be variously called *Weinbauort, Gemeinde,* or *Gemarkung.* As for the vineyards themselves, an individual plot is called an *Einzellage;* but all of the *Einzellagen* are officially grouped into sections of vineyards named *Grosslagen. See* Germany.

I ANBAUGEBIET (region): AHR

BEREICH (sub-region): WALPORZHEIM/AHRTAL
GROSSLAGE (SECTION OF VINEYARDS): KLOSTERBERG

Weinbauort (village)	*Einzellage (vineyard)*	*Weinbauort (village)*	*Einzellage (vineyard)*
Ahrweiler	Daubhaus	Marienthal *(cont.)*	Rosenberg
	Forstberg		Stiftsberg
	Riegelfeld		Trotzenberg
	Rosenthal	Mayschoss	Burgberg
	Silberberg		Laacherberg
	Ursulinengarten		Lochmühlerley
Altenahr	Eck		Mönchberg
	Übigberg		Schieferley
Bachem	Karlskopf		Silberberg
	Sonnenschein	Neuenahr	Kirchtürmchen
	Steinkaul		Schieferley
Dernau	Burggarten		Sonnenberg
	Goldkaul	Pützfeld	Übigberg
	Hardtberg	Rech	Blume
	Pfarrwingert		Hardtberg
	Schieferlay		Herrenberg
Ehlingen	Kapellenberg	Reimerzhoven	Eck
Heimersheim	Burggarten	Walporzheim	Alte Lay
	Landskrone		Domlay
Heppingen	Berg and Burggarten		Gärkammer
Kreuzberg	Übigberg		Himmelchen
Lohrsdorf	Landskrone		Kräuterberg
Marienthal	Jesuitengarten		Pfaffenberg
	Klostergarten		

II ANBAUGEBIET (region): BADEN

BEREICH (sub-region): BADISCHE BERGSTRASSE/KRAICHGAU
GROSSLAGE (SECTION OF VINEYARDS): HOHENBERG

Weinbauort (village)	*Einzellage (vineyard)*	*Weinbauort (village)*	*Einzellage (vineyard)*
Berghausen	Sonnenberg	Dietlingen	Keulebuckel
Bilfingen	Klepberg		Klepberg

Weinbauort (village)	Einzellage (vineyard)
Durlach	Turmberg
Dürrn	Eichelberg
Ellmendingen	Keulebuckel
Eisingen	Klepberg
	Steig
Ersingen	Klepberg
Grötzingen	Lichtenberg
	Turmberg
Hohenwettersbach	Rosengarten
Jöhlingen	Hasensprung
Söllingen	Rotenbusch
Weingarten	Katzenberg
	Petersberg
Wöschbach	Steinwengert

GROSSLAGE (SECTION OF VINEYARDS): MANNABERG

Weinbauort (village)	Einzellage (vineyard)
Bruchsal	Klosterberg
Dielheim	Rosenberg
	Teufelskopf
Heidelberg	Burg
	Dachsbuckel
	Dormenacker
	Herrenberg
Heidelsheim	Altenberg
Helmsheim	Burgwingert
Horrenberg	Osterberg
Leimen	Herrenberg
	Kreuzweg
Malsch	Ölbaum
	Rotsteig
Malschenberg	Ölbaum
Mingolsheim-Langenbrücken	Goldberg
Mühlhausen	Heiligenstein
Nussloch	Wilhelmsberg
Obergrombach	Burgwingert
Oberöwisheim,	
Unteröwisheim	Kirchberg
Östringen	Hummelberg
	Rosenkranzweg
	Ulrichsberg
Rauenberg	Burggraf
Rettigheim	Ölbaum
Rotenberg	Schlossberg
Stettfeld	Himmelreich
Tairnbach	Rosenberg
Ubstadt	Weinhecke
Untergrombach	Michaelsberg
	Weinhecke
Wiesloch	Bergwäldle
	Hägenich
	Spitzenberg
Zeutern	Himmelreich

GROSSLAGE (SECTION OF VINEYARDS): STIFTSBERG

Weinbauort (village)	Einzellage (vineyard)
Bahnbrücken, Gochsheim,	
Oberacker	Lerchenberg
Bauerbach	Lerchenberg
Berwangen	Vogelsang
Binau	Herzogsberg
Diedesheim	Herzogsberg

Weinbauort (village)	Einzellage (vineyard)
Eberbach	Schollerbuckel
Eichelberg	Kapellenberg
Eichtersheim	Sonnenberg and
	Kletterberg
Elsenz	Spiegelberg
Eppingen	Lerchenberg
Eschelbach	Sonnenberg
Flehingen	Lerchenberg
Gemmingen	Vogelsang
Hassmersheim	Kirchweinberg
Heinsheim	Burg Ehrenberg
Herbolzheim	Berg
Hilsbach	Eichelberg
Kürnbach	Lerchenberg
Landshausen and Menzingen	Spiegelberg
Menzingen, Münzesheim	
and Neuenbürg	Silberberg
Michelfeld	Himmelberg
	Sonnenberg
Mühlbach	Lerchenberg
Neckarmühlbach	Hohberg
Neckarzimmern	Götzhalde
	Kirchweinberg
	Wallmauer
Neudenau	Berg
Odenheim	Königsbecher
Rohrbach a. G.	Lerchenberg
Steinsfurt	Steinsberg
Sulzfeld	Burg Ravensburger,
	Dicker Franz
	Burg Ravensburger,
	Husarenkappe
	Burg Ravensburger
	Löchle
	Lerchenberg
Tiefenbach	Schellenbrunnen
	Spiegelberg
Waldangelloch	Sonnenberg
Weiler	Goldberg
	Steinsberg
Zaisenhausen	Lerchenberg

GROSSLAGE (SECTION OF VINEYARDS): RITTERSBERG

Weinbauort (village)	Einzellage (vineyard)
Dossenheim	Ölberg
Grossachsen	Sandrocken
Heidelberg	Heiligenberg
	Sonnenseite ob der Bruck
Hemsbach	Herrnwingert
Hohensachsen	Stephansberg
Laudenbach	Sonnenberg
Leutershausen	Kahlberg
	Staudenberg
Lützelsachsen	Stephansberg
Schriesheim	Kuhberg
	Madonnenberg
	Schlossberg
	Staudenberg
Sulzbach	Herrnwingert
Weinheim	Hubberg
	Wüstberg

673

Baden: Badisches Frankenland

BEREICH (sub-region):
BADISCHES FRANKENLAND

GROSSLAGE (SECTION OF VINEYARDS): TAUBERKLINGE

Weinbauort (village)	Einzellage (vineyard)
Beckstein	Kirchberg
	Nonnenberg
Dertingen	Mandelberg
	Sonnenberg
Gerlachsheim	
Grossrinderfeld	Beilberg
Höhefeld	Kemelrain
Impfingen	Silberquell
Kembach	Sonnenberg
Klepsau	Heiligenberg
Königheim	Kirchberg
Königshofen	Kirchberg
	Turmberg
	Walterstal
Krautheim	Heiligenberg
Külsheim	Hoher Herrgott
Lauda	Altenberg
	Frankenberg
	Nonnenberg
Lindelbach	Ebenrain
Marbach	Frankenberg
Oberlauda	Altenberg
	Steinklinge
Oberschüpf	Altenberg
	Herrenberg
Reicholzheim	First
	Kemelrain
	Satzenberg
Sachsenflur	Kailberg
Tauberbischofsheim	Edelberg
Uissigheim	Stahlberg
Unterschüpf	Mühlberg
Werbach	Beilberg
	Hirschberg
Wertheim	Schlossberg

BEREICH (sub-region): BODENSEE

GROSSLAGE (SECTION OF VINEYARDS): SONNENUFER

Weinbauort (village)	Einzellage (vineyard)
Bermatingen	Leopoldsberg
Bodman	Königsweingarten
Hagnau	Burgstall
Hilzingen	Elisabethenberg
Immenstaad	Burgstall
Kippenhausen	Burgstall
Kirchberg	Schlossberg
Konstanz	Sonnenhalde
Markdorf	Burgstall
	Sängerhalde
Meersburg	Bengel
	Chorherrnhalde
	Fohrenberg
	Haltnau
	Jungfernstieg
	Lerchenberg
	Rieschen
	Sängerhalde

Weinbauort (village)	Einzellage (vineyard)
Oberuhldingen	Kirchhalde
Reichenau	Hochwart
Singen	Elisabethenberg
	Olgaberg
Stetten	Fohrenberg
	Lerchenberg
	Sängerhalde
Überlingen	Felsengarten

Not yet assigned a *Grosslage* (section of vineyards):

Weinbauort (village)	Einzellage (vineyard)
Erzingen	Kapellenberg
Gallingen	Ritterhalde
	Schloss Rheinburg
Hohentengen	Ölberg
Nack	Steinler
Rechberg	Kapellenberg

BEREICH (sub-region): MARKGRÄFLERLAND

GROSSLAGE (SECTION OF VINEYARDS): VOGTEI RÖTTELN

Weinbauort (village)	Einzellage (vineyard)
Bamlach	Kapellenberg
Binzen	Sonnhohle
Blansingen	Wolfer
Efringen-Kirchen	Kirchberg
	Oelberg
	Sonnhohle
	Steingässle
Egringen	Sonnhohle
Eimeldingen	Sonnhohle
Feuerbach	Steingässle
Fischingen	Sonnhohle
Grenzach	Hornfelsen
Haltingen	Stiege
Herten	Steinacker
Hertingen	Sonnhohle
Holzen	Steingässle
Huttingen	Kirchberg
Istein	Kirchberg
Kleinkems	Wolfer
Lörrach	Sonnenbrunnen
Ötlingen	Sonnhohle
	Stiege
Rheinweiler	Kapellenberg
Riedlingen	Steingässle
Rümmingen	Sonnhohle
Schallbach	Sonnhohle
Tannenkirch	Steingässle
Weil am Rhein	Schlipf
	Stiege
Welmlingen	Steingässle
Wintersweiler	Steingässle
Wollbach	Steingässle

GROSSLAGE (SECTION OF VINEYARDS): BURG NEUENFELS

Weinbauort (village)	Einzellage (vineyard)
Auggen	Letten
	Schäf
Bad Bellingen	Sonnenstück
Badenweiler	Römerberg

674

Weinbauort (village)	Einzellage (vineyard)
Ballrechten-Dottingen	Altenberg
	Castellberg
Britzingen	Altenberg
	Rosenberg
	Sonnhohle
Dattingen	Altenberg
	Rosenberg
	Sonnhohle
Feldberg	Paradies
Hügelheim	Gottesacker
	Höllberg
	Schlossgarten
Laufen	Altenberg
Liel	Sonnenstück
Lipburg	Kirchberg
Mauchen	Frauenberg
	Sonnenstück
Müllheim	Pfaffenstück
	Reggenhag
	Sonnhalde
Niedereggenen	Röthen
	Sonnenstück
Neiderweiler	Römerberg
Obereggenen	Röthen
Schliengen	Sonnenstück
Steinenstadt	Schäf
	Sonnenstück
Sulzburg	Altenberg
Zunzingen	Rosenberg

GROSSLAGE (SECTION OF VINEYARDS): LORETTOBERG

Weinbauort (village)	Einzellage (vineyard)
Bad Krotzingen	Steingrüble
Biengen	Maltesergarten
Bollschweil	Steinberg
Buggingen	Höllberg
	Maltesergarten
Ebringen	Sommerberg
Ehrenstetten	Oelberg
	Rosenberg
Eschbach	Maltesergarten
Freiburg	Jesuitenschloss
	Steinler
Grunern	Altenberg
	Schlossberg
Heitersheim	Maltesergarten
	Sonnhohle
Kirchhofen	Batzenberg
	Höllhagen
	Kirchberg
Mengen	Alemannenbuck
Merzhausen	Jesuitenschloss
Norsingen	Batzenberg
Pfaffenweiler	Batzenberg
	Oberdürrenberg
Schallstadt	Batzenberg
Scherzingen	Batzenberg
Schlatt	Maltesergarten
	Steingrüble
Seefeld	Maltesergarten
Staufen im Bresgau	Schlossberg

Weinbauort (village)	Einzellage (vineyard)
Tunsel	Maltesergarten
Wettelbrunn	Maltesergarten
Wittnau	Kapuzinerbuck
Wolfenweiler	Batzenberg
	Dürrenberg

BEREICH (sub-region): KAISERSTUHL-TUNIBERG

GROSSLAGE (SECTION OF VINEYARDS): ATTILAFELSEN

Weinbauort (village)	Einzellage (vineyard)
Gottenheim	Kirchberg
Merdingen	Bühl
Munzingen	Kapellenberg
Niederrimsingen	Rotgrund
Oberrimsingen	Franziskaner
Opfingen	Sonnenberg
Tiengen	Rebtal
Waltershofen	Steinmauer

GROSSLAGE (SECTION OF VINEYARDS): VULKANFELSEN

Weinbauort (village)	Einzellage (vineyard)
Achkarren	Castellberg
	Schlossberg
Amoltern	Steinhalde
Bahlingen	Silberberg
Bickensohl	Herrenstück
	Steinfelsen
Bischoffingen	Enselberg
	Rosenkranz
	Steinbuck
Bötzingen	Eckberg
	Lasenberg
Breisach a. Rh.	Augustinerberg
	Eckartsberg
Burkheim	Feuerberg
	Schlossgarten
Endingen	Engelsberg
	Steingrube
	Tannacker
Eichstetten	Herrenbuck
	Lerchenberg
Ihringen	Castellberg
	Fohrenberg
	Kreuzhalde
	Schlossberg
	Steinfelsen
	Winklerberg
Ihringen (Ortsteil Blankenhornsberg)	Doktorgarten
Jechtingen	Eichert
	Enselberg
	Gestühl
	Hochberg
	Steingrube
Kiechlinsbergen	Ölberg
	Teufelsburg
Königschaffhausen	Hasenberg
	Steingrüble
Leiselheim	Gestühl
Neuershausen	Steingrube
Nimburg	Steingrube

675

Baden: Breisgau

Weinbauort (village)	Einzellage (vineyard)	Weinbauort (village)	Einzellage (vineyard)
Oberbergen	Bassgeige	Münchweiler	Kirchberg
	Pulverbuck	Oberschopfheim	Kronenbühl
Oberrotweil	Eichberg	Oberweier	Kronenbühl
	Henkenberg	Schmieheim	Kirchberg
	Käsleberg	Sulz	Haselstaude
	Kirchberg	Wallburg	Kirchberg
	Schlossberg		
Riegel	St. Michaelsberg		
Sasbach	Limburg		
	Lützelberg		
	Rote Halde		
	Scheibenbuck		
Schelingen	Kirchberg		
Wasenweiler	Kreuzhalde		
	Lotberg		

BEREICH (sub-region): BREISGAU

GROSSLAGE (SECTION OF VINEYARDS): BURG ZÄHRINGEN

Weinbauort (village)	Einzellage (vineyard)
Buchholz	Sonnhalde
Denzlingen	Eichberg
	Sonnhalde
Freiburg	Schlossberg
Glottertal	Eichberg
	Roter Bur
Heuweiler	Eichberg
Hochburg	Halde
Lehen	Bergle
Sexau	Sonnhalde
Wildtal	Sonnenberg

GROSSLAGE (SECTION OF VINEYARDS): BURG LICHTENECK

Weinbauort (village)	Einzellage (vineyard)
Altdorf	Kaiserberg
Bleichheim	Kaiserberg
Bombach	Sommerhalde
Broggingen	Kaiserberg
Ettenheim	Kaiserberg
Hecklingen	Schlossberg
Heimbach	Bienenberg
Herbolzheim	Kaiserberg
Kenzingen	Hummelberg
	Roter Berg
Köndringen	Alte Burg
Malterdingen	Bienenberg
Mundingen	Alte Burg
Nordweil	Herrenberg
Ringsheim	Kaiserberg
Tutschfelden	Kaiserberg
Wagenstadt	Hummelberg

GROSSLAGE (SECTION OF VINEYARDS): SCHUTTERLINDENBERG

Weinbauort (village)	Einzellage (vineyard)
Friesenheim	Kronenbühl
Heiligenzell	Kronenbühl
Hugsweier	Kronenbühl
Kippenheim	Haselstaude
Lahr	Herrentisch
	Kronenbühl
Mahlberg	Haselstaude
Mietersheim	Kronenbühl

BEREICH (sub-region): ORTENAU

GROSSLAGE (SECTION OF VINEYARDS): FÜRSTENECK

Weinbauort (village)	Einzellage (vineyard)
Berghaupten	Kinzigtäler
Bermersbach	Kinzigtäler
Bottenau	Renchtäler
Diersburg	Kinzigtäler
	Schlossberg
Durbach	Bienengarten
	Josephsberg
	Kapellenberg
	Kasselberg
	Kochberg
	Ölberg
	Plauelrain
	Schlossberg
	Schloss Grohl
	Steinberg
Erlach	Renchtäler
Fessenbach	Bergle
	Franzensberger
Gengenbach	Kinzigtäler
	Nollenköpfle
Haslach	Renchtäler
Hofweier	Kinzigtäler
Lautenbach	Renchtäler
Nesselried	Renchtäler
	Schlossberg
Niederschopfheim	Kinzigtäler
Nussbach	Renchtäler
Oberkirch	Renchtäler
Ödsbach	Renchtäler
Ohlsbach	Kinzigtäler
Ortenberg	Andreasberg
	Franzensberger
	Freudental
	Schlossberg
Rammersweier	Kreuzberg
Reichenbach	Amselberg
	Kinzigtäler
Ringelbach	Renchtäler
Stadelhofen	Renchtäler
Tiergarten	Renchtäler
Ulm	Renchtäler
Zell-Weierbach	Abtsberg
Zunsweier	Kinzigtäler

GROSSLAGE (SECTION OF VINEYARDS): SCHLOSS RODECK

Weinbauort (village)	Einzellage (vineyard)
Altschweier	Sternenberg
Baden-Baden	Eckberg
	Sätzler
Bühlertal	Engelsfelsen
	Klotzberg

Weinbauort (village)	Einzellage (vineyard)	Weinbauort (village)	Einzellage (vineyard)
Eisental	Betschgräbler	Obertsrot	Grafensprung
	Sommerhalde	Ottersweier	Althof
Kappelrodeck	Hex vom Dasenstein		Wolfhag
Lauf	Alter Gott	Renchen	Kreuzberg
	Gut Alsenhof	Sasbachwalden	Alter Gott
Mösbach	Kreuzberg		Klostergut Schelzberg
Neusatz	Burg Windeck	Sinzheim	Frühmessler
	Kastanienhalde		Klostergut Fremersberger
	Sternenberg		Feigenwäldchen
	Wolfhag		Sätzler
Neuweier	Altenberg		Sonnenberg
	Gänsberg	Steinbach	Stich den Buben
	Heiligenstein		Yburgberg
	Mauerberg	Varnhalt	Klosterbergfelsen
	Schlossberg		Sonnenberg
Oberachern	Alter Gott		Steingrübler
	Bienenberg	Waldulm	Kreuzberg
Obersasbach	Alter Gott		Pfarrberg
	Eichwäldele	Weisenbach	Kestelberg

III   ANBAUGEBIET (region): HESSISCHE BERGSTRASSE

BEREICH (sub-region): STARKENBURG

GROSSLAGE (SECTION OF VINEYARDS): SCHLOSSBERG

Weinbauort (village)	Einzellage (vineyard)
Heppenheim (including Erbach and Hambach)	Centgericht
	Eckweg
	Guldenzoll
	Maiberg
	Steinkopf
	Stemmler

GROSSLAGE (SECTION OF VINEYARDS): ROTT

Weinbauort (village)	Einzellage (vineyard)
Alsbach	Schöntal
Bensheim-Auerbach	Fürstenlager
	Höllberg
Bensheim-Schönberg	Herrnwingert
Zwingenberg	Alte Burg
	Steingeröll

Not yet assigned a *Grosslage* (section of vineyards):

Seeheim	Mundklingen

GROSSLAGE (SECTION OF VINEYARDS): WOLFSMAGEN

Weinbauort (village)	Einzellage (vineyard)
Bensheim (including Zell and Gronau)	Hemsberg
	Kalkgasse
	Kirchberg
	Paulus
	Streichling

BEREICH (sub-region): UMSTADT

Not yet assigned a *Grosslage* (section of vineyards)

Weinbauort (village)	Einzellage (vineyard)
Dietzenbach	Wingertsberg
Gross Umstadt	Herrnberg
	Steingerück
Klein-Umstadt	Stachelberg
Rossdorf	Rossberg

IV   ANBAUGEBIET (region): FRANKEN

BEREICH (sub-region): MAINVIERECK

GROSSLAGE (SECTION OF VINEYARDS): REUSCHBERG

Weinbauort (village)	Einzellage (vineyard)
Hörstein	Abtsberg

Not yet assigned a *Grosslage* (section of vineyards)

Wasserlos	Schlossberg
	Luhmännchen
Michelbach	Steinberg
	Apostelgarten
Aschaffenburg	Pompejaner
Obernau	Sanderberg
Rottenberg	Gräfenstein

GROSSLAGE (SECTION OF VINEYARDS): HEILIGENTHAL

Weinbauort (village)	Einzellage (vineyard)
Grossostheim	Reischklingeberg
	Harstell
Wenigumstadt	Residual vineyards

Not yet assigned a *Grosslage* (section of vineyards):

Weinbauort (village)	Einzellage (vineyard)
Bürgstadt	Centgrafenberg
	Mainhölle
Dorfprozelten	Predigtstuhl
Engelsberg	Klostergarten

677

Franken: Steigerwald

Weinbauort (village)	Einzellage (vineyard)
Erlenbach a. Main	Hochberg
Grossheubach	Bischofsberg
Grosswallstadt	Lützeltalerberg
Klingenberg	Hochberg
	Schlossberg
Kreuzwertheim	Kaffelstein
Miltenberg	Steingrübler
Rück	Jesuitenberg
	Johannisberg
	Schalk

GROSSLAGE (SECTION OF VINEYARDS): KIRCHBERG

Weinbauort (village)	Einzellage (vineyard)
Astheim	Karthäuser
Escherndorf	Berg
	Fürstenberg
	Lump
Fahr	Residual vineyards
Hallburg	Rosenberg
	Kreuzberg
Hergolshausen	Mainleite
Köhler	Residual vineyards
Krautheim	Sonnenleite
Neuses am Berg	Glatzen
Neusetz	Residual vineyards
Nordheim	Kreuzberg
	Vögelein
Obereisenheim	Höll
Obervolkach	Landsknecht
Sommerach	Katzenkopf
	Rosenberg
Stammheim	Eselsberg
Untereisenheim	Sonnenberg
	Berg
	Höll
Volkach	Ratsherr
Wipfeld	Zehntgraf
Zeilitzheim	Heiligenberg

GROSSLAGE (SECTION OF VINEYARDS): BURG

Weinbauort (village)	Einzellage (vineyard)
Hammelburg	Heroldsberg
	Trautlestal
Rimbach	Landsknecht
Ramsthal	St. Klausen
Saaleck	Schlossberg
Wirmsthal	Scheinberg

GROSSLAGE (SECTION OF VINEYARDS): ROSSTAL

Weinbauort (village)	Einzellage (vineyard)
Arnstein	Residual vineyards
Eussenheim	First
Gambach	Kalbenstein
Gössenheim	Homburg
Himmelstadt	Kelter
Karlburg	Residual vineyards
Karlstadt	Im Stein
Laudenbach	Residual vineyards
Mühlbach	Residual vineyards
Retzstadt	Langenberg
Stetten	Stein

GROSSLAGE (SECTION OF VINEYARDS): HONIGBERG

Weinbauort (village)	Einzellage (vineyard)
Dettelbach	Berg-Rondell
	Sonnenleite

GROSSLAGE (SECTION OF VINEYARDS): HOFRAT

Weinbauort (village)	Einzellage (vineyard)
Alberstshofen	Herrgottsweg
Buchbrunn	Heisser Stein
Kitzingen	Eselsberg
	Wilhelmsberg
Mainstockheim	Hofstück
Marktbreit	Sonnenberg
Marktsteft	Sonnenberg
Repperndorf	Kaiser Karl
Segnitz	Pfaffensteig
	Zobelsberg
Sulzfeld	Cyriakusberg
	Maustal

GROSSLAGE (SECTION OF VINEYARDS): EWIG LEBEN

Weinbauort (village)	Einzellage (vineyard)
Randersacker	Marsberg
	Pfülben
	Sonnenstuhl
	Teufelskeller
Theilheim	Altenberg

GROSSLAGE (SECTION OF VINEYARDS): RAVENSBURG

Weinbauort (village)	Einzellage (vineyard)
Erlabrunn	Weinsteig
Güntersleben	Sommerstuhl
Oberleinach	Weinsteig & Himmelberg
Retzbach	Benediktusberg
Thüngersheim	Johannisberg
	Scharlachberg
Unterleinach	Himmelberg
Veitshöchheim	Wölflein
Zellingen	Sonnleite

Not yet assigned a Grosslage (section of vineyards):

Weinbauort (village)	Einzellage (vineyard)
Böttigheim	Wurmberg
Rimpar	Kobersberg
Veitshöchheim	Sonnenschein
Würzburg	Abtsleite
	Innere Leiste
	Pfaffenberg
	Schlossberg
	Stein
	Stein/Harfe

BEREICH (sub-region): STEIGERWALD

GROSSLAGE (SECTION OF VINEYARDS): SCHILD

Weinbauort (village)	Einzellage (vineyard)
Abtswind	Altenberg
Greuth	Bastel

GROSSLAGE (SECTION OF VINEYARDS): HERRENBERG

Weinbauort (village)	Einzellage (vineyard)
Castell	Bausch
	Feuerbach
	Hohnart
	Kirchberg
	Kugelspiel
	Reitsteig
	Schlossberg
	Trautberg

GROSSLAGE (SECTION OF VINEYARDS): KAPELLENBERG

Weinbauort (village)	Einzellage (vineyard)
Oberschwappach	Sommertal
Sand am Main	Kronberg
Schmachtenberg	Eulengrund
Steinbach	Nonnenberg
Ziegelanger	Ölschnabel

Not yet assigned a *Grosslage* (section of vineyards):

Altmannsdorf	Sonnenwinkel
Bamberg	Alter Graben
Dingolshausen	Köhler
Donnersdorf	Falkenberg
Eltmann	Schlossleite
Gerolzhofen	Arlesgarten
Handthal	Stollberg
Kammerforst	Teufel
Königsberg in Bayern	
Orsteil Unfinden	Kinnleitenberg
Krum	Himmelreich
Michelau	Vollburg
Mönchstockheim	Köhler
Oberschwarzach	Herrenberg
Prichenstadt	Krone
Sand am Main	Himmelsbülh
Weiher	Weinberg
Zell am Ebersberg	Schlossberg
Zeil am Main	Mönshang

GROSSLAGE (SECTION OF VINEYARDS): SCHLOSSBERG

Weinbauort (village)	Einzellage (vineyard)
Grosslangheim	Kiliansberg
Kleinlangheim	Wutschenberg

Weinbauort (village)	Einzellage (vineyard)
Rödelsee	Küchenmeister
	Schwanleite
Sickershausen	Storchenbrünnle
Wiesenbronn	Wachhügel
	Geissberg

GROSSLAGE (SECTION OF VINEYARDS): BURGWEG

Weinbauort (village)	Einzellage (vineyard)
Iphofen	Julius-Echter-Berg
	Kalb
	Kronsberg
Markt Einersheim	Vogelsang
Possenheim	Residual vineyards

GROSSLAGE (SECTION OF VINEYARDS): SCHLOSSTÜCK

Weinbauort (village)	Einzellage (vineyard)
Bullenheim	Paradies
Ergersheim	Altenberg
Frankenberg	Herrschaftsberg
Hüttenheim	Tannenberg
Ingolstadt	Rotenberg
Ippesheim	Herrschaftsberg
Seinsheim	Hohenbühl
Weimersheim	Roter Berg

Not yet assigned a *Grosslage* (section of vineyards):

Weinbauort (village)	Einzellage (vineyard)
Dietersheim	Burg Hoheneck
Iphofen	Domherr
Ipsheim	Burg Hoheneck
Martinsheim	Langenstein
Neudorf	Hüssberg
	Mönchsbuck
	Sonnenberg
	Wonne
Tiefenstockheim	Stiefel
Reusch	Hohenlandsberg
Weigenheim	Hohenlandsberg

BEREICH (sub-region): BAYER, BODENSEE

Weinbauort (village)	Einzellage (vineyard)
Nonnenhorn	Seehalde
	Sonnenbüchel

V ANBAUGEBIET (region): MITTELRHEIN

BEREICH (sub-region): BACHARACH

GROSSLAGE (SECTION OF VINEYARDS): SCHLOSS REICHENSTEIN

Weinbauort (village)	Einzellage (vineyard)
Niederheimbach	Froher Weingarten
	Reifersley
	Schloss Hohneck
	Soonecker
	Schlossberg
Oberheimbach	Klosterberg
	Römerberg
	Sonne
	Wahrheit
Trechtingshausen	Morgenbachtaler

GROSSLAGE (SECTION OF VINEYARDS): SCHLOSS STAHLECK

Weinbauort (village)	Einzellage (vineyard)
Bacharach	Hahn
	Insel Heylesern Wert
	Kloster Fürstental
	Mathias Weingarten
	Posten
	Wolfshöhle
Bacharach/Steeg	Hambusch
	Lennenborn
	St. Jost
	Schloss Stahlberg

Mittelrhein: Rheinburgengau

Weinbauort (village)	Einzellage (vineyard)
Manubach	Heilgarten
	Langgarten
	Mönchwingert
	St. Oswald
Oberdiebach	Bischofshub
	Fürstenberg
	Kräuterberg
Rheindiebach	Fürstenberg
	Rheinberg

BEREICH (sub-region): RHEINBURGENGAU

GROSSLAGE (SECTION OF VINEYARDS): BURG HAMMERSTEIN

Weinbauort (village)	Einzellage (vineyard)
Bad Hönningen	Schlossberg
Dattenberg	Gertrudenberg
Hammerstein	Hölle
	In den Layfelsen
	Schlossberg
Kasbach	Stehlerberg
Lcubsdorf	Weisses Kreuz
Leutesdorf	Forstberg
	Gartenlay
	Rosenberg
Linz	Rheinhöller
Rheinbrohl	Monte Jup
	Römerberg
Unkel	Berg
	Sonnenberg

GROSSLAGE (SECTION OF VINEYARDS): BURG RHEINFELS

Weinbauort (village)	Einzellage (vineyard)
St. Goar	Ameisenberg
	Frohwingert
	Kuhstall
	Rosenberg

GROSSLAGE (SECTION OF VINEYARDS): GEDEONSECK

Weinbauort (village)	Einzellage (vineyard)
Boppard	Elfenlay
	Engelstein
	Fässerlay
	Feuerlay
	Mandelstein
	Ohlenberg
	Weingrube
Brey	Hämmchen
Rhens	König Wenzel
	Sonnenlay
Spay	Engelstein

GROSSLAGE (SECTION OF VINEYARDS): HERRENBERG

Weinbauort (village)	Einzellage (vineyard)
Dörscheid	Kupferflöz
	Wolfsnack
Kaub	Backofen
	Blüchertal
	Burg Gutenfels
	Pfalzgrafenstein

Weinbauort (village)	Einzellage (vineyard)
Kaub (cont.)	Rauschelay
	Rosstein

GROSSLAGE (SECTION OF VINEYARDS): LORELEYFELSEN

Weinbauort (village)	Einzellage (vineyard)
Bornich	Rothenack
Kamp-Bornhofen-Kestert	Liebenstein-Sterrenberg
	Pilgerpfad
Nochern	Brünnchen
Patersberg	Teufelstein
St. Goarshausen	Burg Katz
	Burg Maus
	Hessern
	Loreley-Edel

GROSSLAGE (SECTION OF VINEYARDS): MARKSBURG

Weinbauort (village)	Einzellage (vineyard)
Braubach	Marmorberg
	Mühlberg
	Koppelstein
Filsen	Pfarrgarten
Koblenz-Ehrenbreitstein	Kreuzberg
Lahnstein	Koppelstein
Osterspai	Liebeneck-Sonnenlay
Urbar	Rheinnieder
Vallendar	Rheinnieder
Koblenz	Schnorbach Brückstück

GROSSLAGE (SECTION OF VINEYARDS): LAHNTAL

Weinbauort (village)	Einzellage (vineyard)
Bad Ems	Hasenberg
Dausenau	Hasenberg
Fachbach	Sites not chosen
Nassau	Schlossberg
Obernhof	Goetheberg
Weinähr	Giebelhöll

GROSSLAGE (SECTION OF VINEYARDS): SCHLOSS SCHÖNBURG

Weinbauort (village)	Einzellage (vineyard)
Damscheid	Frankenhell
	Goldemund
	Sonnenstock
Dellhofen	Römerkrug
	St. Wernerberg
Langscheid	Hundert
Niederburg	Bienenberg
	Rheingoldberg
Oberwesel	Bernstein
	Bienenberg
	Goldemund
Oberwesel	Ölsberg
	Römerkrug
	St. Martinsberg
	Sieben Jungfrauen
Perscheid	Rosental
Urbar	Beulsberg

Not yet assigned a Grosslage (section of vineyards):

Weinbauort (village)	Einzellage (vineyard)
Hirzenach	Probsteiberg

VI ANBAUGEBIET (region): MOSEL-SAAR-RUWER

BEREICH (sub-region): BERNKASTEL

GROSSLAGE (SECTION OF VINEYARDS): BADSTUBE

Weinbauort (village)	Einzellage (vineyard)
Bernkastel-Kues	Bratenhöfchen
	Doctor
	Graben
	Lay
	Matheisbildchen

GROSSLAGE (SECTION OF VINEYARDS): BEERENLAY

Weinbauort (village)	Einzellage (vineyard)
Lieser	Niederberg-Helden
	Rosenlay
	Süssenberg

GROSSLAGE (SECTION OF VINEYARDS): KURFÜRSTLAY

Weinbauort (village)	Einzellage (vineyard)
Andel	Schlossberg
Bernkastel-Kues	Johannisbrünnchen
	Kardinalsberg
	Rosenberg
	Schlossberg
	Stephanus-Rosengärtchen
	Weissenstein
Brauneberg	Juffer
	Juffer-Sonnenuhr
	Kammer
	Klostergarten
	Mandelgraben
Burgen	Hasenläufer
	Kirchberg
	Römerberg
Kesten	Herrenberg
	Paulinsberg
	Paulinshofberger
Lieser	Niederberg-Helden
	Rosenlay
	Schlossberg
	Süssenberg
Maring-Noviand	Honigberg
	Kirchberg
	Klosterberg
	Römerpfad
	Sonnenuhr
Mülheim	Amtsgarten
	Elisenberg
	Helenenkloster
	Sonnenlay
Osann-Monzel	Kätzchen
	Kirchlay
	Paulinslay
	Rosengarten
Veldenz	Carlsberg
	Elisenberg
	Grafschafter Sonnenberg
	Kirchberg
	Mühlberg
Wintrich	Grosser Herrgott
	Ohligsberg

Weinbauort (village)	Einzellage (vineyard)
Wintrich (cont.)	Sonnseite
	Stefanslay

GROSSLAGE (SECTION OF VINEYARDS): MICHELSBERG

Weinbauort (village)	Einzellage (vineyard)
Hetzerath	Brauneberg
Minheim	Burglay
	Günterslay
	Kapellchen
	Rosenberg
Neumagen-Dhron	Engelgrube
	Goldtröpfchen
	Grosser Hengelberg
	Haschen
	Hofberger
	Laudamusberg
	Nusswingert
	Rosengärtchen
	Roterd
	Sonnenuhr
Piesport	Domherr
	Falkenberg
	Gärtchen
	Goldtröpfchen
	Grafenberg
	Günterslay
	Hofberger
	Kreuzwingert
	Schubertslay
	Treppchen
Rivenich	Brauneberg
	Geisberg
	Niederberg
	Rosenberg
Sehlem	Rotlay
Trittenheim	Altärchen
	Apotheke
	Felsenkopf
	Leiterchen

GROSSLAGE (SECTION OF VINEYARDS): MÜNZLAY

Weinbauort (village)	Einzellage (vineyard)
Graach	Abtsberg
	Domprobst
	Himmelreich
	Josephshöfer
Wehlen	Abtei
	Hofberg
	Klosterberg
	Klosterhofgut
	Nonnenberg
	Rosenberg
	Sonnenuhr
Zeltingen-Rachtig	Deutschherrenberg
	Himmelreich

Weinbauort (village)	Einzellage (vineyard)	Weinbauort (village)	Einzellage (vineyard)
Zeltingen-Rachtig (cont.)	Schlossberg	Burg (cont.)	Thomasberg
	Sonnenuhr		Wendelstück
		Dreis	Johannisberg
		Enkirch	Batterieberg

GROSSLAGE (SECTION OF VINEYARDS): NACKTARSCH

Weinbauort (village)	Einzellage (vineyard)		
Kröv	Burglay		Edelberg
	Herrenberg		Ellergrub
	Kirchlay		Herrenberg
	Letterlay		Monteneubel
	Paradies		Steffensberg
	Steffensberg		Weinkammer
			Zeppwingert

GROSSLAGE (SECTION OF VINEYARDS): PROBSTBERG

Weinbauort (village)	Einzellage (vineyard)		
		Erden	Busslay
Fell	Maximiner Burgberg		Herrenberg
Kenn	Held		Prälat
	Maximiner Hofgarten		Treppchen
Longuich	Herrenberg	Flussbach	Reichelberg
	Hirschlay	Hupperath	Klosterweg
	Maximer Herrenberg	Kinheim	Hubertuslay
Mehring	Vineyards on the right		Rosenberg
	side of the Mosel	Lösnich	Burgberg
Riol	Römerberg		Försterlay
Schweich	Annaberg	Platten	Klosterberg
	Burgmauer		Rotlay
	Herrenberg	Traben-Trarbach	Burgweg

GROSSLAGE (SECTION OF VINEYARDS): SANKT MICHAEL

Weinbauort (village)	Einzellage (vineyard)		
			Gaispfad
Bekond	Brauneberg		Hühnerberg
	Schlossberg		Königsberg
Detzem	Maximiner Klosterlay		Kräuterhaus
	Würzgarten		Kreuzberg
Ensch	Mühlenberg		Schlossberg
	St. Martin		Taubenhaus
	Sonnenlay		Ungsberg
Klüsserath	Bruderschaft		Würzgarten
	Königsberg		Zollturm
Köwerich	Held		
	Laurentiuslay	Traben-Trarbach (Ortsteil Starkenburg)	Rosengarten
Leiwen	Klostergarten	Traben-Trarbach (Ortsteil Wolf)	Auf der Heide
	Laurentiuslay		Goldgrube
Longen	Zellerberg		Klosterberg
Lörsch	Zellerberg		Schatzgarten
Mehring	Blattenberg		Sonnenlay
	Goldkupp	Ürzig	Würzgarten
	Zellerberg		Goldwingert
Pölich	Held	Wittlich	Bottchen
	Südlay		Felsentreppchen
Schleich	Klosterberg		Klosterweg
	Sonnenberg		Kupp
Thörnich	Enggass		Lay
	Ritsch		Portnersberg
			Rosenberg

GROSSLAGE (SECTION OF VINEYARDS): SCHWARZLAY

GROSSLAGE (SECTION OF VINEYARDS): VOM HEISSEN STEIN

Weinbauort (village)	Einzellage (vineyard)	Weinbauort (village)	Einzellage (vineyard)
Bausendorf	Herzlay	Briedel	Herzchen
	Hubertuslay		Nonnengarten
Bengel	Klosterberg		Schäferlay
Burg	Falklay		Schelm
	Hahnenschrittchen		Weisserberg
	Schlossberg	Pünderich	Goldlay
			Marienburg

Weinbauort (village)	Einzellage (vineyard)
Pünderich (cont.)	Nonnengarten
	Rosenberg
Reil	Falklay
	Goldlay
	Moullay-Hofberg
	Sorentberg

BEREICH (sub-region): OBERMOSEL
GROSSLAGE (SECTION OF VINEYARDS): GIPFEL

Weinbauort (village)	Einzellage (vineyard)
Biltzingen	Sites not chosen
Fellerich	Schleidberg
Fisch	Sites not chosen
Helfant-Esingen	Kapellenberg
Kirf	Sites not chosen
Köllig	Rochusfels
Kreuzweiler	Schloss Thorner Kupp
Merzkirchen	Sites not chosen
Meurich	Sites not chosen
Nittel	Blümchen
	Hubertusberg
	Leiterchen
	Rochusfels
Oberbillig	Hirtengarten
	Römerberg
Onsdorf	Hubertusberg
Palzem	Carlsfelsen
	Lay
Porz	Sites not chosen
Rehlingen	Kapellenberg
Soest	Sites not chosen
Temmels	Münsterstatt
	St. Georgshof
Wasserliesch	Albachtaler
	Reinig auf der Burg
Wehr	Rosenberg
Wellen	Altenberg
Wincheringen	Burg Warsberg
	Fuchsloch

GROSSLAGE (SECTION OF VINEYARDS): KÖNIGSBERG

Weinbauort (village)	Einzellage (vineyard)
Edingen	Sites not chosen
Godendorf	Sites not chosen
Grewenich	Sites not chosen
Igel	Dullgärten
Langsur	Brüderberg
Liersberg	Pilgerberg
Mesenich	Held
Metzdorf	Sites not chosen
Ralingen	Sites not chosen
Wintersdorf	Sites not chosen

BEREICH (sub-region): SAAR-RUWER
GROSSLAGE (SECTION OF VINEYARDS): RÖMERLAY

Weinbauort (village)	Einzellage (vineyard)
Franzenheim	Johannisberg
Hockweiler	Sites not chosen
Kasel	Dominikanerberg
	Herrenberg
	Hitzlay

Weinbauort (village)	Einzellage (vineyard)
Kasel (cont.)	Kehrnagel
	Nieschen
	Paulinsberg
	Timpert
Korlingen	Laykaul
Mertesdorf	Herrenberg
	Johannisberg
Mertesdorf (Ortsteil Maximin Grünhaus)	Abtsberg
	Bruderberg
	Herrenberg
Morscheid	Dominikanerberg
	Heiligenhäuschen
Riveris	Heiligenhäuschen
	Kuhnchen
Sommerau	Schlossberg
Trier	Altenberg
	Andreasberg
	Augenscheiner
	Benediktinerberg
	Burgberg
	Deutschherrenberg
	Deutschherrenköpfchen
	Domherrenberg
	Hammerstein
	Herrenberg
	Jesuitenwingert
	Karthäuserhofberg Burgberg
	Karthäuserhofberg Kronenberg
	Karthäuserhofberg Orthsberg
	Karthäuserhofberg Sang
	Karthäuserhofberg Stirn
	Kupp
	Kurfürstenhofberg
	Leikaul
	Marienholz
	Maximiner Rotlei
	St. Martiner Hofberg
	St. Martiner Klosterberg
	St. Matheiser
	St. Maximiner Kreuzberg
	St. Petrusberg
	Sonnenberg
	Thiergarten Felsköpfchen
	Thiergarten Unterm Kreuz
Waldrach	Doktorberg
	Ehrenberg
	Heiligenhäuschen
	Hubertusberg
	Jesuitengarten
	Jungfernberg
	Krone
	Kurfürstenberg
	Laurentiusberg
	Meisenberg
	Sonnenberg

GROSSLAGE (SECTION OF VINEYARDS): SCHARZBERG

Weinbauort (village)	Einzellage (vineyard)
Ayl	Herrenberger
	Kupp
	Scheidterberger
Falkenstein	Herrenberg
	Hofberg
Filzen	Altenberg
	Herrenberg
	Pulchen
	Steinberger
	Unterberg
	Urbelt
Hamm	Altenberg
	Liebfrauenberg
Irsch	Sonnenberg
Kanzem	Altenberg
	Hörecker
	Ritterpfad
	Schlossberg
	Sonnenberg
Kastel-Staadt	König Johann Berg
	Maximin Staadt
Kommlingen	Auf der Wiltingerkupp
Könen	Fels
	Kirchberg
Konz	Euchariusberg
	Klosterberg
	Sprung
Krettnach	Altenberg
	Euchariusberg
Niedermennig	Euchariusberg
	Herrenberg
	Sonnenberg
Oberemmel	Agritiusberg
	Altenberg
	Hütte
	Karlsberg
	Raul
	Rosenberg
Ockfen	Bockstein
	Geisberg
	Heppenstein
	Herrenberg
	Kupp
	Neuwies
	Zickelgarten
Pellingen	Herrgottsrock
	Jesuitengarten
Saarburg	Antoniusbrunnen
	Bergschlösschen
	Fuchs
	Klosterberg
	Kupp
	Laurentiusberg
	Rausch
	Schlossberg
	Stirn
Schoden	Geisberg
	Herrenberg
	Saarfeilser Marienberg
Serrig	Antoniusberg
	Helligenborn

Weinbauort (village)	Einzellage (vineyard)
Serrig (cont.)	Herrenberg
	Hoeppslei
	König Johann Berg
	Kupp
	Schloss Saarsteiner
	Schloss Saarfelser
	Schlossberg
	Vogelsang
	Würtzberg
Wawern	Goldberg
	Herrenberger
	Jesuitenberg
	Ritterpfad
Wiltingen	Braune Kupp
	Braunfels
	Gottesfuss
	Hölle
	Klosterberg
	Kupp
	Rosenberg
	Sandberg
	Schlagengraben
	Schlossberg

BEREICH (sub-region): ZELL/MOSEL

GROSSLAGE (SECTION OF VINEYARDS): GOLDBÄUMCHEN

Weinbauort (village)	Einzellage (vineyard)
Briedern	Rüberberger Domherrenberg
Bruttig-Fankel	Götterlay
Cochem	Bischofstuhl
	Hochlay
	Klostergarten
	Sonnenberg
Ellenz-Poltersdorf	Altarberg
	Kurfürst
	Rüberberger Domherrenberg
Ernst	Feuerberg
	Kirchlay
Klotten	Brauneberg
	Burg Coreidelsteiner
	Rosenberg
	Sonnengold
Moselkern	Kirchberg
	Rosenberg
	Übereltzer
Müden	Funkenberg
	Grosslay
	Leckmauer
	St. Castorhöhle
	Sonnenring
Pommern	Goldberg
	Rosenberg
	Sonnenuhr
	Zeisel
Senheim	Römerberg
	Rüberberger Domherrenberg
Treis-Karden	Dechantsberg
	Juffermauer
	Münsterberg

GROSSLAGE (SECTION OF VINEYARDS): GRAFSCHAFT

Weinbauort (village)	Einzellage (vineyard)
Alf	Arrasburg-Schlossberg
	Burggraf
	Herrenberg
	Hölle
	Kapellenberg
	Katzenkopf
	Kronenberg
Beuren	Pelzerberger
Bremm	Calmont
	Frauenberg
	Laurentiusberg
	Schlemmertröpfchen
Bullay	Brautrock
	Graf Beyssel-Herrenberg
	Kirchweingarten
	Kroneberg
	Sonneck
Ediger-Eller	Bienenlay
	Calmont
	Elzogberg
	Engelströpfchen
	Feuerberg
	Hasensprung
	Höll
	Kapplay
	Osterlämmchen
	Pfaffenberg
	Pfirsichgarten
	Schützenlay
Neef	Frauenberg
	Petersberg
	Rosenberg
Nehren	Römerberg
St. Aldegund	Himmelreich
	Klosterkammer
	Palmberg-Terrassen
Zell-Merl	Sites not chosen

GROSSLAGE (SECTION OF VINEYARDS): ROSENHANG

Weinbauort (village)	Einzellage (vineyard)
Beilstein	Schlossberg
Bremm	Abtei
	Kloster Stuben
Briedern	Herrenberg
	Kapellenberg
	Römergarten
	Servatiusberg
Bruttig-Fankel	Kapellenberg
	Layenberg
	Martinsborn
	Pfarrgarten
	Rathausberg
	Rosenberg
Cochem	Arzlay
	Nikolausberg
	Rosenberg
Ediger-Eller, Ortsteil Eller	Stubener Klostersegen
Ellenz-Poltersdorf	Silberberg
	Woogberg

Weinbauort (village)	Einzellage (vineyard)
Mesenich	Abteiberg
	Deuslay
	Goldgrübchen
Senheim	Bienengarten
	Rosenberg
	Vogteiberg
	Wahrsager
Treis-Karden	Greth
	Kapellenberg
	Treppchen
Valwig	Herrenberg
	Palmberg
	Schwarzenberg

GROSSLAGE (SECTION OF VINEYARDS): SCHWARZE KATZ

Weinbauort (village)	Einzellage (vineyard)
Zell	Burglay-Felsen
	Domherrenberg
	Geisberg
	Kreuzlay
	Nussberg
	Petersborn-Kabertchen
	Pommerell
Zell-Kaimt	Marienburger
	Römerquelle
	Rosenborn
Zell-Merl	Adler
	Fettgarten
	Klosterberg
	Königslay-Terrassen
	Stefansberg
	Sonneck

GROSSLAGE (SECTION OF VINEYARDS): WEINHEX

Weinbauort (village)	Einzellage (vineyard)
Alken	Bleidenberg
	Burgberg
	Hunnenstein
Burgen	Bischofstein
Dieblich	Heilgraben
Güls	Bienengarten
	Im Röttgen
	Königsfels
	Marienberg
Hatzenport	Burg Bischofsteiner
	Kirchberg
	Stolzenberg
Kattenes	Fahrberg
	Steinchen
Kobern-Gondorf	Fahrberg
	Fuchshöhle
	Gäns
	Kehrberg
	Schlossberg
	Uhlen
	Weissenberg
Lay	Hubertsborn, Hamm
Lehmen	Ausoniusstein
	Klosterberg

685

Weinbauort (village)	Einzellage (vineyard)	Weinbauort (village)	Einzellage (vineyard)
Lehmen (cont.)	Lay	Oberfell	Brauneberg
	Würzlay		Goldlay
Löf	Goldblume		Rosenberg
	Sonnenring	Winningen	Brückstück
Moselweiss	Hamm		Domgarten
Moselsürsch	Fahrberg		Hamm
Niederfell	Fächern		Im Röttgen
	Goldlay		Uhlen
	Kahllay		

VII   ANBAUGEBIET (region): NAHE

BEREICH (sub-region): KREUZNACH

GROSSLAGE (SECTION OF VINEYARDS): KRONENBERG   GROSSLAGE (SECTION OF VINEYARDS): PFARRGARTEN

Weinbauort (village)	Einzellage (vineyard)	Weinbauort (village)	Einzellage (vineyard)
Bad Kreuznach	Berg	Dalberg	Ritterhölle
	Brückes		Schlossberg
	Forst		Sonnenberg
	Galgenberg	Gutenberg	Felseneck
	Gutental		Römerberg
	Hinkelstein		St. Ruppertsberg
	Hungrier Wolf		Schlossberg
	Kahlenberg		Schloss Gutenburg
	Kapellenpfad		Sonnenlauf
	Kauzenberg-Orionberg	Hergenfeld	Herrschaftsgarten
	Kauzenberg-Rosenhügel		Mönchberg
	Kauzenberg-In Den		Sonnenberg
	Mauern	Schöneberg	Schäfersley
	Krötenpfuhl		Sonnenberg
	Mollenbrunnen	Sommerloch	Birkenberg
	Mönchberg		Ratsgrund
	Narrenkappe		Sonnenberg
	Osterhöll		Steinrossel
	Rosenberg	Spabrücken	Höll
	St Martin	Wallhausen	Backöfchen
	Steinberg		Felseneck
	Tilgesbrunnen		Hasensprung
	Vogelsang		Höllenpfad
Orsteil Bosenheim	Galgenberg		Hörnchen
	Hirtenhain		Johannisberg
	Höllenbrand		Johannisweg
	Paradies		Kirschheck
Orsteil Ippesheim	Himmelgarten		Laurentiusberg
	Junker		Mühlenberg
Orsteil Planig	Höllenbrand		Pastorenberg
	Katzenhölle		Sonnenweg
	Nonnengarten		
	Römerhalde		

GROSSLAGE (SECTION OF VINEYARDS): SCHLOSSKAPELLE

Weinbauort (village)	Einzellage (vineyard)	Weinbauort (village)	Einzellage (vineyard)
Orsteil Winzenheim	Berg	Bingen-Bingerbrück	Abtei Ruppertsberg
	Honigberg		Hildegardisbrünnchen
	In den siebzehn		Klostergarten
	Morgen		Römerberg
	Rosenheck	Burg Layen	Hölle
Bretzenheim	Felsenköpfchen		Johannisberg
	Hofgut		Rothenberg
	Pastorei		Schlossberg
	Schlossgarten	Dorsheim	Burgberg
	Vogelsang		Goldloch
Hargesheim	Mollenbrunnen		Honigberg
	Straussberg		

Weinbauort *(village)*	Einzellage *(vineyard)*	Weinbauort *(village)*	Einzellage *(vineyard)*
Dorsheim *(cont.)*	Jungbrunnen	Langenlonsheim *(cont.)*	Löhrer Berg
	Klosterpfad		Rothenberg
	Laurenziweg		St. Antoniusweg
	Nixenberg		Steinchen
	Pittermännchen		
	Trollberg		
Eckenroth	Felsenberg		
	Hölle		
Genheim	Rossel		

BEREICH (sub-region): SCHLOSS BÖCKELHEIM

GROSSLAGE (SECTION OF VINEYARDS): BURGWEG

Weinbauort *(village)*	Einzellage *(vineyard)*
Altenbamberg	Kehrenberg
	Laurentiusberg
	Rotenberg
	Schlossberg
	Treuenfels
Bad Münster a. St.-Ebernburg	Erzgrupe
	Felseneck
	Feuerberg
	Götzenfels
	Höll
	Köhler-Köpfchen
	Königsgarten
	Luisengarten
	Rotenfelser im Winkel
	Schlossberg
	Steigerdell
	Stephansberg
Duchroth	Felsenberg
	Feuerberg
	Kaiserberg
	Königsfels
	Rothenberg
	Vogelschlag
Niederhausen an der Nahe	Felsensteyer
	Hermannshöhle
	Kertz
	Klamm
	Pfaffenstein
	Pfingstweide
	Rosenberg
	Rosenheck
	Steinberg
	Steinwingert
	Stollenberg
	Herrmannsberg
Norheim	Dellchen
	Götzenfels
	Kafels
	Kirschheck
	Klosterberg
	Oberberg
	Onkelchen
	Sonnenberg
Oberhausen an der Nahe	Felsenberg
	Kieselberg
	Leistenberg
	Rotenberg
Schlossböckelheim	Felsenberg
	Heimberg
	In den Felsen
	Königsfels
	Kupfergrube
	Mühlberg

Main table (left region):

Weinbauort *(village)*	Einzellage *(vineyard)*
Guldental	Apostelberg
	Hipperich
	Hölle
	Honigberg
	Rosenteich
	St. Martin
	Sonnenberg
	Teufelsküche
Laubenheim	Fuchsen
	Hörnchen
	Junker
	Karthäuser
	Krone
	St. Remigiusberg
	Vogelsang
Münster-Sarmsheim	Dautenpflänzer
	Kapellenberg
	Königsschloss
	Liebehöll
	Pittersberg
	Rheinberg
	Römerberg
	Steinkopf
	Trollberg
Rümmelsheim	Hölle
	Johannisberg
	Rothenberg
	Schlossberg
	Steinköpfchen
Schweppenhausen	Schlossgarten
	Steyerberg
Waldlaubersheim	Altenburg
	Bingerweg
	Domberg
	Lieseberg
	Otterberg
Weiler	Abtei Ruppertsberg
	Klostergarten
	Römerberg
Windesheim	Preiselberg
	Fels
	Hausgiebel
	Hölle
	Römerberg
	Rosenberg
	Saukopf
	Schäfchen
	Sonnenmorgen

GROSSLAGE (SECTION OF VINEYARDS): SONNENBORN

Weinbauort *(village)*	Einzellage *(vineyard)*
Langenlonsheim	Bergborn
	Königsschild
	Lauerweg

Nahe: Schloss Böckelheim

Weinbauort (village)	Einzellage (vineyard)
Traisen	Bastei
	Kickelskopf
	Nonnengarten
	Rotenfels
Waldböckelheim	Drachenbrunnen
	Hamm
	Kirchberg
	Königsfels
	Kronenfels
	Marienpforter Klosterberg
	Muckerhölle
	Mühlberg
	Römerberg

GROSSLAGE (SECTION OF VINEYARDS): PARADIESGARTEN

Weinbauort (village)	Einzellage (vineyard)
Alsenz	Elkersberg
	Falkenberg
	Hölle
	Pfaffenpfad
Auen	Kaulenberg
	Römerstich
Bayerfeld-Steckweiler	Adelsberg
	Aspenberg
	Mittelberg
	Schloss Stolzenberg
Boos	Herrenberg
	Kastell
Desloch	Hengstberg
	Vor der Hölle
Feilbingert	Bocksberg
	Feuerberg
	Höchstes Kreuz
	Kahlenberg
	Königsgarten
Gaugrehweiler	Graukatz
Hochstätten	Liebesbrunnen
Kalkofen	Graukatz
Kirschroth	Lump
	Wildgrafenberg
Lauschied	Edelberg
Lettweiler	Inkelhöll
	Rheingasse
Mannweiler-Cölln	Rosenberg
	Schloss Randeck
	Seidenberg
	Weissenstein
Martinstein	Schlossberg
Meddersheim	Altenberg
	Edelberg
	Liebfrauenberg
	Präsent
	Rheingrafenberg
Meisenheim	Obere Heimbach
Merxheim	Hunolsteiner
	Römerberg
	Vogelsang
Monzingen	Frühlingsplätzchen
	Halenberg
	Rosenberg

Weinbauort (village)	Einzellage (vineyard)
Münsterappel	Graukatz
Niederhausen an der Nahe	Graukatz
Niedermoschel	Geissenkopf
	Hahnhölle
	Layenberg
	Silberberg
Nussbaum	Höllenberg
	Rotfeld
	Sonnenberg
Oberhausen an der Nahe	Graukatz
Obermoschel	Geissenkopf
	Langhölle
	Schlossberg
	Silberberg
	Sonnenplätzchen
Oberndorf	Aspenberg
	Beutelstein
	Feuersteinrossel
	Weissenstein
Oberstreit	Auf dem Zimmerberg
Odernheim	Kloster-Disibodenberg
	Hessweg
	Kapellenberg
	Langenberg
	Montfort
	Weinsack
Raumbach	Schlossberg
	Schwalbennest
Rehborn	Hahn
	Herrenberg
	Schikanenbuckel
Sobernheim	Domberg
	Marbach
Sobernheim-Steinhardt	Johannesberg
	Spitalberg
Staudernheim	Goldgrube
	Herrenberg
Unkenbach	Römerpfad
	Würzhölle
Waldböckelheim	Johannesberg
	Kastell
Weiler bei Monzingen	Heiligenberg
	Herrenzehntel
Winterborn	Graukatz

GROSSLAGE (SECTION OF VINEYARDS): ROSENGARTEN

Weinbauort (village)	Einzellage (vineyard)
Bockenau	Geisberg
	Im Felseneck
	Im Neuberg
	Stromberg
Braunweiler	Hellenpfad
	Michaeliskapelle
	Schlossberg
	Wetterkreuz
Burgsponheim	Höllenpfad
	Pfaffenberg
	Schlossberg
Hüffelsheim	Gutenhölle
	Mönchberg
	Steyer
Mandel	Alte Römerstrasse
	Becherbrunnen

Weinbauort (village)	Einzellage (vineyard)	Weinbauort (village)	Einzellage (vineyard)
Mandel (cont.)	Dellchen	St. Katharinen	Fels
	Palmengarten		Klostergarten
	Schlossberg		Steinkreuz
Roxheim	Berg	Sponheim	Abtei
	Birkenberg		Grafenberg
	Höllenpfad		Klostergarten
	Hüttenberg		Mühlberg
	Mühlenberg		Schlossberg
	Sonnenberg	Weinsheim	Katergrube
Rüdesheim	Goldgrube		Kellerberg
	Wiesberg		Steinkaut

VIII   ANBAUGEBIET (region): RHEINGAU

BEREICH (sub-region): JOHANNISBERG

GROSSLAGE (SECTION OF VINEYARDS): BURGWEG

Weinbauort (village)	Einzellage (vineyard)
Lorch	Bodenstal-Steinberg
	Kapellenberg
	Krone
	Pfaffenwies
	Schlossberg
Lorchhausen	Rosenberg
	Seligmacher

GROSSLAGE (SECTION OF VINEYARDS): STEIL

Weinbauort (village)	Einzellage (vineyard)
Assmannshausen	Frankenthal
	Hollenberg
	Hinterkirch
Aulhausen	Berg Kaisersteinfels
Geisenheim	Fuchsberg
	Klaus
	Klauserweg
	Kilzberg
	Mäuerchen
	Mönchspfad
	Rothenberg
	Schlossgarten
Rüdesheim	Berg Roseneck
	Berg Rottland
	Berg Schlossberg
	Bischofsberg
	Drachenstein
	Kirchenpfad
	Klosterberg
	Klosterlay
	Magdalenenkreuz
	Rosengarten

GROSSLAGE (SECTION OF VINEYARDS): ERNTEBRINGER

Weinbauort (village)	Einzellage (vineyard)
Johannisberg	Goldatzel
	Hansenberg
	Hölle
	Klaus
	Mittelhölle
	Schwarzenstein
	Schloss
	Johannisberg
	Vogelsang

GROSSLAGE (SECTION OF VINEYARDS): GOTTESTHAL

Weinbauort (village)	Einzellage (vineyard)
Oestrich	Doosberg
	Klosterberg
	Lenchen
	Schloss
	Reichhartshausen

GROSSLAGE (SECTION OF VINEYARDS): MEHRHOLZCHEN

Weinbauort (village)	Einzellage (vineyard)
Erbach	Hohenrain
	Honigberg
	Marcobrunn
	Michelmark
	Rheinhell
	Schlossberg
	Siegelsberg
	Steinmorgen
Hallgarten	Hendelberg
	Jungfer
	Schönhell
	Würzgarten

GROSSLAGE (SECTION OF VINEYARDS): HONIGBERG

Weinbauort (village)	Einzellage (vineyard)
Mittelheim	Edelmann
	Goldberg
	St. Nikolaus
Winkel	Bienengarten
	Dachsberg
	Gutenberg
	Hasensprung
	Jesuitengarten
	Klaus
	Schlossberg
	Schloss Vollrads

GROSSLAGE (SECTION OF VINEYARDS): DEUTELSBERG

Weinbauort (village)	Einzellage (vineyard)
Hattenheim	Engelmannsberg
	Hassel
	Heiligenberg
	Mannberg
	Nussbrunen
	Pfaffenberg
	Rheingarten
	Schützenhaus

689

Weinbauort (village)	Einzellage (vineyard)
Hattenheim (cont.)	Wisselbrunnen
	Steinberg

GROSSLAGE (SECTION OF VINEYARDS): HEILIGENSTOCK

Weinbauort (village)	Einzellage (vineyard)
Kiedrich	Gräfenberg
	Klosterberg
	Sandgrub
	Wasseros

GROSSLAGE (SECTION OF VINEYARDS): STEINMACHER

Weinbauort (village)	Einzellage (vineyard)
Dotzheim	Judenkirch
Eltville	Langenstück
	Rheinberg
	Sandgrub
	Sonnenberg
	Taubenberg
Frauenstein	Herrnberg
	Homberg
	Marschall
Martinsthal	Langenberg
	Rödchen
	Wildsau
Niederwalluf	Berg-Bildstock
	Oberberg
	Walkenberg
Oberwalluf	Langenstück
	Vitusberg
Rauenthal	Baiken
	Gehrn
	Langenstück
	Nonnenberg

Weinbauort (village)	Einzellage (vineyard)
Rauenthal (cont.)	Rothenberg
	Wülfen
Schierstein	Dachsberg
	Hölle
Wiesbaden	Neroberg

GROSSLAGE (SECTION OF VINEYARDS): DAUBHAUS

Weinbauort (village)	Einzellage (vineyard)
Boddiger	Berg
Flörsheim	Herrnberg
	St. Anna Kapelle
Frankfurt	Lohrberger Hang
Hocheim	Berg
	Domdechaney
	Herrnberg
	Hofmeister
	Hölle
	Kirchenstück
	Königin
	Viktoriaberg
	Reichesthal
	Sommerheil
Hocheim	Stein
	Stielweg
Mainz-Kostheim	Berg
	Reichensthal
	Steig
	Weiss Erd
Wicker	König Wilhelmsberg
	Mönchsgewann
	Nonnberg
	Stein

IX ANBAUGEBIET (region): RHEINHESSEN

BEREICH (sub-region): BINGEN

GROSSLAGE (SECTION OF VINEYARDS): ABTEY

Weinbauort (village)	Einzellage (vineyard)
Appenheim	Daubhaus
	Drosselborn
	Eselspfad
	Hundertgulden
Gau-Algesheim	Goldberg
	Johannisberg
	Rothenberg
	St. Laurenzikapelle
	Steinert
Nieder-Hilbersheim	Honigberg
	Steinacker
Ober-Hilbersheim	Mönchpforte
Partenheim	Sankt Georgen
	Steinberg
Sankt Johann	Geyersberg
	Klostergarten
	Steinberg
Sprendlingen	Hölle
	Honigberg
	Klostergarten
	Sonnenberg
	Wissberg

Weinbauort (village)	Einzellage (vineyard)
Wolfsheim	Götzenborn
	Osterberg
	Sankt Kathrin

GROSSLAGE (SECTION OF VINEYARDS): ADELBERG

Weinbauort (village)	Einzellage (vineyard)
Armsheim	Geiersberg
	Goldstückchen
	Leckerberg
Bermersheim v. d. H.	Hildegardisberg
	Klostergarten
Bornheim	Hähnchen
	Hütte-Terrassen
	Kirchenstück
	Schönberg
Ensheim	Kachelberg
	Bingerberg
Erbes-Büdesheim	Geisterberg
	Vogelsang
Flonheim	Bingerberg
	Klostergarten
	La Roche

Weinbauort (village)	Einzellage (vineyard)
Flonheim (cont.)	Pfaffenberg
	Rotenpfad
Lonsheim	Mandelberg
	Schönberg
Nack	Ahrenberg
Nieder-Weisen	Wingertsberg
Sulzheim	Greifenberg
	Honigberg
	Schildberg
Wendelsheim	Heiligenpfad
	Steigerberg
Wörrstadt	Kachelberg
	Rheingrafenberg

GROSSLAGE (SECTION OF VINEYARDS): KAISERPFALZ

Weinbauort (village)	Einzellage (vineyard)
Bubenheim	Honigberg
	Kallenberg
Engelstadt	Adelpfad
	Römerberg
Gross-Winternheim	Bockstein
	Burberg
	Heilighäuschen
	Höllenweg
	Horn
	Kirchenstück
	Klosterbruder
	Lottenstück
	Pares
	Rabenkopf
	Rheinhöhe
	Rotes Kreuz
	Schlossberg
	Sonnenberg
	Sonnenhang
	Steinacker
	Täuscherspfad
Heidesheim	Geissberg
	Höllenberg
	Steinacker
Ingelheim	Schloss Westerhaus
Jugenheim	Goldberg
	Hasensprung
	Heiligenhäuschen
	St. Georgenberg
Schwabenheim	Klostergarten
	Sonnenberg
	Schlossberg
Wackernheim	Rabenkopf
	Schwalben
	Steinberg

GROSSLAGE (SECTION OF VINEYARDS): KURFÜRSTENSTÜCK

Weinbauort (village)	Einzellage (vineyard)
Gau-Bickelheim	Bockshaut
	Kapelle
	Saukopf
Gau-Weinheim	Geyersberg
	Kaisergarten
	Wissberg

Weinbauort (village)	Einzellage (vineyard)
Gumbsheim	Schlosshölle
Vendersheim	Goldberg
	Sonnenberg
Wallertheim	Heil
	Vogelsang

GROSSLAGE (SECTION OF VINEYARDS): RHEINGRAFENSTEIN

Weinbauort (village)	Einzellage (vineyard)
Eckelsheim	Eselstreiber
	Kirchberg
	Sonnenköpfchen
Frei-Laubersheim	Alte Römerstraase
	Fels
	Kirchberg
	Reichskeller
	Rheingrafenberg
Fürfeld	Eichelberg
	Kapellenberg
	Steige
Hackenheim	Galgenberg
	Gewürzgarten
	Kirchberg
	Klostergarten
	Sonnenberg
Neu-Bamberg	Eichelberg
	Heerkretz
	Kirschwingert
	Kletterberg
Pleitersheim	Sternberg
Siefersheim	Goldenes Horn
	Heerkretz
	Höllberg
	Martinsberg
Stein-Bockenheim	Sonnenberg
Tiefenthal	Graukatz
Volxheim	Alte Römerstrasse
	Liebfrau
	Mönchberg
Wöllstein	Äffchen
	Haarberg-Katzensteg
	Hölle
	Ölberg
Wonsheim	Hölle
	Martinsberg
	Sonnenberg

GROSSLAGE (SECTION OF VINEYARDS): SANKT ROCHUSKAPELLE

Weinbauort (village)	Einzellage (vineyard)
Aspisheim	Johannisberg
	Sonnenberg
Badenheim	Galgenberg
	Römerberg
Biebelsheim	Honigberg
	Kieselberg
Bingen	Bubenstück
	Kapellenberg
	Kirchberg
	Osterberg
	Palmenstein
	Pfarrgarten

Weinbauort (village)	Einzellage (vineyard)
Bingen (cont.)	Rosengarten
	Scharlachberg
	Schelmenstück
	Schlossberg-Schwätzerchen
	Schwarzenberg
Dromersheim	Honigberg
	Klosterweg
	Mainzerweg
Gensingen	Goldberg
Grolsheim	Ölberg
Horrweiler	Gewürzgärtchen
	Goldberg
Ockenheim	Hockenmühle
	Klosterweg
	Kreuz
	Laberstall
	St. Jakobsberg
	Schönhölle
Pfaffen-Schwabenheim	Hölle
	Mandelbaum
	Sonnenberg
Sponsheim-Bingen	Palmenstein
Welgesheim	Kirchgärtchen
Zotzenheim	Johannisberg
	Klostergarten

BEREICH (sub-region): NIERSTEIN

GROSSLAGE (SECTION OF VINEYARDS): AUFLANGEN

Weinbauort (village)	Einzellage (vineyard)
Nierstein	Bergkirche
	Glöck
	Heiligenbaum
	Kranzberg
	Ölberg
	Orbel
	Schloss Schwabsburg
	Zehnmorgen

GROSSLAGE (SECTION OF VINEYARDS): DOMHERR

Weinbauort (village)	Einzellage (vineyard)
Budenheim	Sites not chosen
Essenheim	Römerberg
	Teufelspfad
Gabsheim	Dornpfad
	Kirchberg
	Rosengarten
Klein-Winternheim	Geiershöll
	Herrgottshaus
	Villenkeller
Mainz-Finthen	Sites not chosen
Mainz-Drais	Sites not chosen
Ober-Olm	Kapellenberg
Saulheim	Haubenberg
	Heiligenhaus
	Hölle
	Pfaffengarten
	Probstey
	Schlossberg

Weinbauort (village)	Einzellage (vineyard)
Schornsheim	Mönchspfad
	Ritterberg
	Sonnenhang
Stadecken-Elsheim	Blume
	Bockstein
	Lenchen
	Spitzberg
	Tempelchen
Udenheim	Goldberg
	Kirchberg
	Sonnenberg

GROSSLAGE (SECTION OF VINEYARDS): GÜLDENMORGEN

Weinbauort (village)	Einzellage (vineyard)
Dienheim	Falkenberg
	Herrenberg
	Höhlchen
	Kreuz
	Siliusbrunnen
	Tafelstein
Oppenheim	Daubhaus
	Gutleuthaus
	Herrenberg
	Kreuz
	Sackträger
	Schützenhütte
	Zuckerberg

GROSSLAGE (SECTION OF VINEYARDS): GUTES DOMTAL

Weinbauort (village)	Einzellage (vineyard)
Dalheim	Altdörr
	Kranzberg
	Steinberg
Dexheim	Doktor
Friesenheim	Altdörr
	Bergpfad
	Knopf
Hahnheim	Knopf
	Moosberg
Köngernheim	Goldgrube
Lörzweiler	Königstuhl
Mommenheim	Kloppenberg
	Osterberg
	Silbergrube
Nackenheim	Schmittskapellchen
Nieder-Olm	Goldberg
	Klosterberg
	Sonnenberg
Nierstein	Pfaffenkappe
Selzen	Gottesgarten
	Osterberg
	Rheinpforte
Sörgenloch	Moosberg
Undenheim	Goldberg
Weinolsheim	Hohberg
	Kehr
Zornheim	Dachgewann
	Guldenmorgen
	Mönchbäumchen
	Pilgerweg
	Vogelsang

GROSSLAGE (SECTION OF VINEYARDS): KRÖTENBRUNNEN

Weinbauort (village)	Einzellage (vineyard)
Alsheim	Goldberg
Dienheim	Herrengarten
	Paterhof
	Schloss
Dolgesheim	Kreuzberg
	Schützenhütte
Eich	Goldberg
Eimsheim	Hexelberg
	Römerschanze
	Sonnenhang
Gimbsheim	Liebfrauenthal
	Sonnenweg
Guntersblum	Eiserne Hand
	Sankt Julianenbrunnen
	Sonnenberg
	Sonnenhang
	Steinberg
Hillesheim	Altenberg
	Sonnheil
Ludwigshöhe	Honigberg
Mettenheim	Goldberg
Oppenheim	Herrengarten
	Paterhof
	Schloss
	Schlossberg
Ülversheim	Aulenberg
	Schloss
Wintersheim	Frauengarten

GROSSLAGE (SECTION OF VINEYARDS): PETERSBERG

Weinbauort (village)	Einzellage (vineyard)
Albig	Homberg
	Hundskopf
Alzey	Schloss Hammerstein
Bechtolsheim	Homberg
	Klosterberg
	Sonnenberg
	Wingertstor
Biebelnheim	Pilgerstein
	Rosenberg
Framersheim	Hornberg
	Kreuzweg
	Zechberg
Gau-Heppenheim	Pfarrgarten
	Schlossberg
Gau-Odernheim	Fuchsloch
	Herrgottspfad
	Ölberg
	Vogelsang
Spiesheim	Osterberg

GROSSLAGE (SECTION OF VINEYARDS): REHBACH

Weinbauort (village)	Einzellage (vineyard)
Nierstein	Brudersberg
	Goldene Luft
	Hipping
	Pettenthal

GROSSLAGE (SECTION OF VINEYARDS): RHEINBLICK

Weinbauort (village)	Einzellage (vineyard)
Alsheim	Fischerpfad
	Frühmesse
	Römerberg
	Sonnenberg
Dorn-Dürkheim	Hasensprung
	Römerberg
Mettenheim	Michelsberg
	Schlossberg

GROSSLAGE (SECTION OF VINEYARDS): SANKT ALBAN

Weinbauort (village)	Einzellage (vineyard)
Bodenheim	Burgweg
	Ebersberg
	Heitersbrünnchen
	Hoch
	Kapelle
	Kreuzberg
	Leidhecke
	Mönchspfad
	Reichsritterstift
	Silberberg
	Westrum
Gau-Bischofsheim	Glockenberg
	Herrnberg
	Kellersberg
	Pfaffenweg
Harxheim	Börnchen
	Lieth
	Schlossberg
Lörzweiler	Hohberg
	Ölgild
Mainz	Edelmann
	Hüttberg
	Johannisberg
	Kirchenstück
	Klosterberg
	Sand
	Weinkeller

GROSSLAGE (SECTION OF VINEYARDS): SPIEGELBERG

Weinbauort (village)	Einzellage (vineyard)
Nackenheim	Engelsberg
	Rothenberg
Nierstein	Bildstock
	Brückchen
	Ebersberg
	Findling
	Hölle
	Kirchplatte
	Klostergarten
	Paterberg
	Rosenberg
	Schloss Hohenrechen

GROSSLAGE (SECTION OF VINEYARDS): VOGELSGÄRTEN

Weinbauort (village)	Einzellage (vineyard)
Guntersblum	Authental
	Bornpfad
	Himmelthal

Weinbauort (village)	Einzellage (vineyard)
Guntersblum (cont.)	Kreuzkapelle
	Steig-Terrassen
Ludwigshöhe	Teufelskopf

BEREICH (sub-region): WONNEGAU

GROSSLAGE (SECTION OF VINEYARDS): BERGKLOSTER

Weinbauort (village)	Einzellage (vineyard)
Bermersheim	Hasenlauf
Eppelsheim	Felsen
Esselborn	Goldberg
Flomborn	Feuerberg
	Goldberg
Gundersheim	Höllenbrand
	Königstuhl
Gundheim	Hungerbiene
	Mandelbrunnen
	Sonnenberg
Hangen-Weisheim	Sommerwende
Westhofen	Aulerde
	Benn
	Brunnenhäuschen
	Kirchspiel
	Morstein
	Rotenstein
	Steingrube

GROSSLAGE (SECTION OF VINEYARDS): BURG RODENSTEIN

Weinbauort (village)	Einzellage (vineyard)
Bermersheim	Seilgarten
Flörsheim-Dalsheim	Bürgel
	Frauenberg
	Goldberg
	Hubacker
	Sauloch
	Steig
Mörstadt	Katzenbuckel
	Nonnengarten
Ober-Flörsheim	Blücherpfad
	Deutschherrenberg

GROSSLAGE (SECTION OF VINEYARDS): DOMBLICK

Weinbauort (village)	Einzellage (vineyard)
Hohen-Sülzen	Kirchenstück
	Sonnenberg
Mölsheim	Silberberg
	Zellerweg am schw. Herrgott
Monsheim	Rosengarten
	Silberberg
Offstein	Engelsberg
	Schlossgarten
Wachenheim	Horn
	Rotenberg

GROSSLAGE (SECTION OF VINEYARDS): GOTTESHILFE

Weinbauort (village)	Einzellage (vineyard)
Bechtheim	Geyersberg
	Rosengarten
	Stein

Weinbauort (village)	Einzellage (vineyard)
Osthofen	Goldberg
	Hasenbiss
	Leckzapfen
	Neuberg

GROSSLAGE (SECTION OF VINEYARDS): LIEBFRAUENMORGEN

Weinbauort (village)	Einzellage (vineyard)
Worms	Affenberg
	Am Heiligen Häuschen
	Bildstock
	Burgweg
	Goldapfel
	Goldberg
	Goldpfad
	Hochberg
	Kapellenstück
	Klausenberg
	Kreuzblick
	Lerchelsberg
	Liebfrauenstift-Kirchenstück
	Nonnenwingert
	Remeyerhof
	Rheinberg
	Römersteg
	Sankt Annaberg
	St. Cyriakusstift
	St. Georgenberg
	Schneckenberg

GROSSLAGE (SECTION OF VINEYARDS): PILGERPFAD

Weinbauort (village)	Einzellage (vineyard)
Bechtheim	Hasensprung
	Heiligkreuz
Dittelsheim-Hessloch	Edle Weingärten
	Geiersberg
	Kloppberg
	Leckerberg
	Liebfrauenberg
	Mönchhube
	Mondschein
	Pfaffenmütze
Frettenheim	Heil
Monzernheim	Goldberg
	Steinböhl
Osthofen	Kirchberg
	Klosterberg
	Liebenberg
	Rheinberg

GROSSLAGE (SECTION OF VINEYARDS): SYBILLENSTEIN

Weinbauort (village)	Einzellage (vineyard)
Alzey	Kapellenberg
	Pfaffenhalde
	Römerberg
	Rotenfels
	Wartberg
Bechenheim	Fröhlich

Weinbauort (village)	Einzellage (vineyard)	Weinbauort (village)	Einzellage (vineyard)
Dautenheim	Himmelacker	Wahlheim	Schelmen
Freimersheim	Frankenstein	Weinheim	Heiliger Blutberg
	Rotenfels		Hölle
Heimersheim	Sonnenberg		Kapellenberg
Mauchenheim	Sioner Klosterberg		Kirchenstück
Offenheim	Mandelberg		Mandelberg

X ANBAUGEBIET (region): RHEINPFALZ (PALATINATE)

BEREICH (sub-region): SÜDLICHE WEINSTRASSE

GROSSLAGE (SECTION OF VINEYARDS): BISCHOFSKREUZ

Weinbauort (village)	Einzellage (vineyard)	Weinbauort (village)	Einzellage (vineyard)
Böchingen	Rosenkranz	Gleiszellen-Gleishorbach	Frühmess
Burrweiler	Altenforst		Kirchberg
	St. Annaberg	Göcklingen	Herrenpfad[6]
	Schäwer	Hergersweiler	Narrenberg[5]
	Schlossgarten	Heuchelheim-Klingen	Herrenpfad[6]
Dammheim	Höhe	Kapellen-Drusweiler	Rosengarten
Flemlingen	Herrenbuckel	Klingenmünster	Maria Magdalena
	Vogelsprung	Niederhorbach	Silberberg
	Zechpeter	Oberhausen	Frohnwingert
Gleisweiler	Hölle	Pleisweiler-Oberhofen	Schlossberg
Knöringen	Hohenrain	Rohrbach	Mandelpfad[3]
Nussdorf	Herrenberg	Steinweiler	Rosenberg[4]
	Kaiserberg	Winden	Narrenberg[5]
	Kirchenstück		
Roschbach	Rosenkränzel		
	Simonsgarten		
Walsheim	Forstweg		
	Silberberg		

GROSSLAGE (SECTION OF VINEYARDS): KÖNIGSGARTEN

Weinbauort (village)	Einzellage (vineyard)
Albersweiler	Kirchberg
	Latt
Arzheim	Rosenberg
	Seligmacher[7]
Birkweiler	Rosenberg[8]
	Kastanienbusch
	Mandelberg
Frankweiler	Biengarten
	Kalkgrube
Godramstein	Klostergarten
	Münzberg
Landau	Altes Löhl
Ranschbach	Seligmacher[7]
Siebeldingen	Im Sonnenschein
	Mönchspfad
	Rosenberg[8]

GROSSLAGE (SECTION OF VINEYARDS): GUTTENBERG

Weinbauort (village)	Einzellage (vineyard)
Bad Bergzabern	Wonneberg[1]
Dierbach	Kirchhöh
Dörrenbach	Wonneberg[1]
Freckenfeld	Gräfenberg
Kandel	Galgenberg
Kapsweyher	Lerchenberg
Minfeld	Herrenberg
Niederotterbach	Eselsbuckel
Oberotterbach	Sonnenberg[2]
Schweigen-Rechtenbach	Sonnenberg[2]
Schweighofen	Sonnenberg[2]
	Wolfsberg
Steinfeld	Herrenwingert
Vollmersweiler	Krapfenberg

GROSSLAGE (SECTION OF VINEYARDS): MANDELHÖHE

Weinbauort (village)	Einzellage (vineyard)
Kirrweiler	Mandelberg
	Oberschloss
	Römerweg
Maikammer	Heiligenberg
	Immengarten
	Kirchenstück
Maikammer-Alsterweiler	Kapellenberg

GROSSLAGE (SECTION OF VINEYARDS): KLOSTER LIEBFRAUENBERG

Weinbauort (village)	Einzellage (vineyard)
Bad Bergzabern	Altenberg
Barbelroth	Kirchberg
Billigheim-Ingenheim	Mandelpfad[3]
	Pfaffenberg
	Rosenberg[4]
	Sauschwänzel
	Steingebiss
	Venusbuckel

GROSSLAGE (SECTION OF VINEYARDS): ORDENSGUT

Weinbauort (village)	Einzellage (vineyard)
Edesheim	Forst
	Mandelhang

NOTE: Numbers following a vineyard name indicate that the plot is divided between two (or more) villages.

Weinbauort (village)	Einzellage (vineyard)
Edesheim (cont.)	Rosengarten
	Schloss
Hainfeld	Kapelle
	Kirchenstück
	Letten
Rhodt	Klosterpfad
	Rosengarten
	Schlossberg
Weyher	Heide
	Michelsberg

GROSSLAGE (SECTION OF VINEYARDS): HERRLICH

Weinbauort (village)	Einzellage (vineyard)
Eschbach	Hasen
Göcklingen	Kaiserberg
Herxheim bei Landau	Engelsberg
Herxheimweyher	Am Gaisberg
Ilbesheim	Rittersberg
	Sonnenberg[9]
Impflingen	Abtsberg
Insheim	Schäfergarten[10]
Leinsweiler	Sonnenberg[9]
Mörzheim	Pfaffenberg
Rohrbach	Schäfergarten[10]
Wollmesheim	Mütterle

GROSSLAGE (SECTION OF VINEYARDS): SCHLOSS LUDWIGSHÖHE

Weinbauort (village)	Einzellage (vineyard)
Edenkoben	Bergel
	Blücherhöhe
	Heidegarten
	Heilig Kreuz
	Kastaniengarten
	Kirchberg
	Klostergarten
	Mühlberg
	Schwarzer Letten
St. Martin	Baron
	Kirchberg
	Zitadelle

GROSSLAGE (SECTION OF VINEYARDS): TRAPPENBERG

Weinbauort (village)	Einzellage (vineyard)
Altdorf	Gottesacker
	Hochgericht
Bellheim	Gollenberg[11]
Böbingen	Ortelberg
Bornheim	Neuberg
Essingen	Osterberg
	Rossberg
	Sonnenberg
Freimersheim	Bildberg
Gross-u. Kleinfischlingen	Kirchberg
Hochstadt	Roterberg
Knittelsheim	Gollenberg[11]
Lustadt	Klostergarten[12]
Ottersheim	Kahlenberg
Römerberg	Alter Berg
	Narrenberg
	Schlittberg

Weinbauort (village)	Einzellage (vineyard)
Schwegenheim	Bründelsberg
Venningen	Doktor
Weingarten	Schlossberg
Zeiskam	Klostergarten[12]

BEREICH (sub-region): MITTELHAARDT-DEUTSCHE WEINSTRASSE

GROSSLAGE (SECTION OF VINEYARDS): FEUERBERG

Weinbauort (village)	Einzellage (vineyard)
Bad Dürkheim	Nonnengarten
	Steinberg
Bobenheim am Berg	Kieselberg
	Ohligpfad
Ellerstadt	Bubeneck
	Dickkopp
	Sonnenberg
Gönnheim	Martinshöhe
Kallstadt	Annaberg
	Kreidkeller
Weisenheim am Berg	Vogelsang

GROSSLAGE (SECTION OF VINEYARDS): GRAFENSTÜCK

Weinbauort (village)	Einzellage (vineyard)
Bockenheim	Burggarten
	Goldgrube
	Hassmannsberg
	Heiligenkirche
	Klosterschaffnerei
	Schlossberg
	Sonnenberg[14]
	Vogelsang[13]
Kindenheim	Burgweg
	Katzenstein
	Sonnenberg[14]
	Vogelsang[13]
Obrigheim	Benn
	Hochgericht
	Mandelpfad
	Rosengarten
	Schloss
	Sonnenberg[14]

GROSSLAGE (SECTION OF VINEYARDS): HOCHMESS

Weinbauort (village)	Einzellage (vineyard)
Bad Dürkheim	Hochbenn
	Michelsberg[15]
	Rittergarten
	Spielberg
Ungstein	Michelsberg[15]

GROSSLAGE (SECTION OF VINEYARDS): HÖLLENPFAD

Weinbauort (village)	Einzellage (vineyard)
Battenberg	Schlossberg
Grünstadt	Bergel
	Goldberg
	Honigsack
	Hütt
	Klostergarten

Weinbauort (village)	Einzellage (vineyard)
Grünstadt (cont.)	Röth
	St. Stephan
	Schloss
Kleinkarlbach	Frauenländchen
	Herrenberg
	Herrgottsacker
	Kieselberg
	Senn
Mertesheim	St. Martinskreuz
Neuleiningen	Feuermännchen
	Schlossberg
	Sonnenberg

GROSSLAGE (SECTION OF VINEYARDS): HOFSTÜCK

Weinbauort (village)	Einzellage (vineyard)
Deidesheim	Nonnenstück
Ellerstadt	Kirchenstück
Friedelsheim	Gerümpel
	Rosengarten
Gönnheim	Klostergarten
	Mandelgarten
	Sonnenberg
Hochdorf-Assenheim	Fuchsloch[16]
Meckenheim	Neuberg
	Spielberg
Niederkirchen	Klostergarten
	Osterbrunnen
	Schlossberg
Rödersheim-Gronau	Fuchsloch[16]
Ruppertsberg	Gaisböhl
	Hoheburg
	Linsenbusch
	Nussbien
	Reiterpfad
	Spiess

GROSSLAGE (SECTION OF VINEYARDS): HONIGSÄCKEL

Weinbauort (village)	Einzellage (vineyard)
Ungstein	Herrenberg
	Nussriegel
	Weilberg

GROSSLAGE (SECTION OF VINEYARDS): KOBNERT

Weinbauort (village)	Einzellage (vineyard)
Dackenheim	Kapellgarten
	Liebesbrunnen
	Mandelröth
Freinsheim	Musikantenbuckel
	Oschelskopf
	Schwarzes Kreuz
Herxheim am Berg	Himmelreich
	Honigsack
	Kirchenstück
Leistadt	Herzfeld
	Kalkofen
	Kirchenstück
Weisenheim am Berg	Mandelgarten
	Sonnenberg

GROSSLAGE (SECTION OF VINEYARDS): MARIENGARTEN

Weinbauort (village)	Einzellage (vineyard)
Deidesheim	Grainhübel
	Herrgottsacker
	Hohenmorgen
	Kalkofen
	Kieselberg
	Langenmorgen
	Leinhöhle
	Mäushöhle
	Paradiesgarten
Forst	Elster
	Freundstück
	Jesuitengarten
	Kirchenstück
	Musenhang
	Pechstein
	Ungeheuer
Wachenheim	Altenburg
	Belz
	Böhlig
	Gerümpel
	Goldbächel
	Rechbächel

GROSSLAGE (SECTION OF VINEYARDS): MEERSPINNE

Weinbauort (village)	Einzellage (vineyard)
Gimmeldingen	Biengarten
	Kapellenberg
	Mandelgarten
	Schlössel
Haardt	Bürgergarten
	Herrenletten
	Herzog
	Mandelring
Königsbach	Idig
	Jesuitengarten
	Ölberg
	Reiterpfad
Mussbach	Bischofsweg
	Eselshaut
	Glockenzehnt
	Johannitergarten
	Kurfürst
	Spiegel
Neustadt an der Weinstrasse	Mönchgarten

GROSSLAGE (SECTION OF VINEYARDS): PFAFFENGRUND

Weinbauort (village)	Einzellage (vineyard)
Diedesfeld	Berg
Duttweiler	Kalkberg
	Kreuzberg
	Mandelberg
Geinsheim	Gässel
Hambach an der Weinstrasse	Kroatenpfad
	Langenstein
	Lerchenböhl

GROSSLAGE (SECTION OF VINEYARDS): REBSTÖCKEL

Weinbauort (village)	Einzellage (vineyard)
Diedesfeld	Johanniskirchel
	Ölgässel
	Paradies
Hambach	Feuer
	Kaiserstuhl
	Kirchberg
	Schlossberg
Neustadt an der Weinstrasse	Erkenbrecht
	Grain

GROSSLAGE (SECTION OF VINEYARDS): ROSENBÜHL

Weinbauort (village)	Einzellage (vineyard)
Erpolzheim	Goldberg
	Kieselberg
Freinsheim	Goldberg[17]
Lambsheim	Burgweg[18]
Weisenheim/Sand	Altenberg
	Burgweg[18]
	Goldberg[17]
	Hahnen
	Halde
	Hasenzeile

GROSSLAGE (SECTION OF VINEYARDS): SCHENKENBÖHL

Weinbauort (village)	Einzellage (vineyard)
Bad Dürkheim	Abtsfronhof
	Fronhof
	Fuchsmantel[19]
Wachenheim	Fuchsmantel[19]
	Königswingert
	Mandelgarten
	Odinstal
	Schlossberg

GROSSLAGE (SECTION OF VINEYARDS): SCHNEPFENFLUG VOM ZELLERTAL

Weinbauort (village)	Einzellage (vineyard)
Albisheim	Heiligenborn
Bolanden	Schlossberg
Bubenheim	Hahnenkamm
Einselthum	Kreuzberg[20]
	Klosterstüch[21]
Gauersheim	Goldloch
Harxheim	Herrgottsblick
Immesheim	Sonnenstück
Kerzenheim	Esper
Kirchheimbolanden	Schlossgarten
Morschheim	Im Heubusch
Niefernheim	Königsweg[22]
	Kreuzberg[20]
Ottersheim/Zellerthal	Bräunersberg

Weinbauort (village)	Einzellage (vineyard)
Rittersheim	Am hohen Stein
Rüssingen	Breinsberg
Stetten	Heilighäuschen
Zell	Klosterstück[21]
	Königsweg[22]
	Kreuzberg[20]
	Schwarzer Herrgott

GROSSLAGE (SECTION OF VINEYARDS): SCHNEPFENFLUG AN DER WEINSTRASSE

Weinbauort (village)	Einzellage (vineyard)
Deidesheim	Letten
Forst	Stift
	Süsskopf
	Bischofsgarten[23]
Friedelsheim	Bischofsgarten[23]
	Kreuz
	Schlossgarten
Wachenheim	Bischofsgarten[23]
	Luginsland

GROSSLAGE (SECTION OF VINEYARDS): SCHWARZERDE

Weinbauort (village)	Einzellage (vineyard)
Bissersheim	Goldberg
	Held
	Orlenberg
	Steig
Dirmstein	Herrgottsacker
	Jesuitenhofgarten
	Mandelpfad
Gerolsheim	Klosterweg
	Lerchenspiel
Grosskarlbach	Burgweg
	Osterberg
Grossniedesheim	Schafberg
Hessheim	Lange Els
Heuchelheim/Frankenthal	Steinkopf
Kallstadt	Kronenberg
	Steinaker
	Saumagen
Kirchheim	Geisskopf
	Kreuz
	Römerstrasse
	Steinacker
Kleinniedesheim	Schlossgarten
	Vorderberg
Laumersheim	Kirschgarten
	Mandelberg
	Kappelenberg
Obersülzen	Schnepp
Ungstein	Osterberg
	Bettelhaus

XI ANBAUGEBIET (region): WÜRTTEMBERG

BEREICH (sub-region): REMSTAL-STUTTGART

GROSSLAGE (SECTION OF VINEYARDS): HOHENNEUFFEN

Weinbauort (village)	Einzellage (vineyard)	Weinbauort (village)	Einzellage (vineyard)
Beuren	Schlossteige	Kappishäusern	Schlossteige
Frickenhausen	Schlossteige	Kohlberg	Schlossteige

Weinbauort (village)	Einzellage (vineyard)
Linsenhofen	Schlossteige
Metzingen	Hofsteige
	Schlossteige
Neuffen	Schlossteige
Weilheim	Schlossteige

GROSSLAGE (SECTION OF VINEYARDS): WEINSTEIGE

Weinbauort (village)	Einzellage (vineyard)
Esslingen	Ailenberg
	Burg
	Kirchberg
	Lerchenberg
	Schenkenberg
Fellbach	Gips
	Goldberg
	Herzogenberg
	Hinterer Berg
	Lämmler
	Mönchberg
	Wetzstein
Gerlingen	Bopser
Stuttgart	Kriegsberg
	Mönchberg
(Ortsteil Gaisburg)	Abelsberg
(Ortsteil Untertürkheim)	Gips
(Ortsteil Uhlbach)	Götzenberg
(Ortsteil Obertürkheim)	Ailenberg
(Ortsteil Untertürkheim)	Altenberg
(Ortsteile Bad Cannstatt, Feuerbach, Münster, Wangen, Zuffenhausen)	Berg
(Ortsteil Bad Cannstatt)	Halde
(Ortsteile Bad Cannstatt, Untertürkheim)	Herzogenberg
(Orteil Obertürkheim)	Kirchberg
(Ortsteile Hedelfingen, Rohracker)	Lenzenberg
(Ortsteile Bad Cannstatt, Untertürkheim)	Mönchberg
(Ortsteil Degerloch)	Scharrenberg
(Ortsteile Rotenberg, Uhlbach, Untertürkheim)	Schlossberg
(Ortsteil Uhlbach)	Steingrube
(Ortsteile Bad Cannstatt, Mühlhausen, Münster)	Steinhalde
(Ortsteil Untertürkheim)	Wetzstein
(Ortsteile Bad Cannstatt, Hofen, Mühlhausen, Münster)	Zuckerle

GROSSLAGE (SECTION OF VINEYARDS): SONNENBÜHL

Weinbauort (village)	Einzellage (vineyard)
Kernen	
Orsteil Rommelshaussen	Mönchberg
Orsteil Stetten	Mönchberg
Weinstadt	
Orsteil Beutelsbach	Burghalde
Orsteil Endersbach	Hintere Klinge
Orsteil Schnait	Burghalde
Orsteil Strümpfelbach	Altenberg

GROSSLAGE (SECTION OF VINEYARDS): KOPF

Weinbauort (village)	Einzellage (vineyard)
Beinstein	Grossmulde
Breuningsweiler	Holzenberg
Bürg	Schlossberg
Grossheppach	Wanne
Grunbach	Berghalde
Hanweiler	Berg
Kleinheppach	Greiner
Korb	Berg
	Hörnle
	Sommerhalde
Neustadt	Söhrenberg
Schorndorf	Grafenberg
Waiblingen	Hörnle
Winnenden	Berg
	Holzenberg
	Rossberg
Winterbach	Hungerberg

GROSSLAGE (SECTION OF VINEYARDS): WARTBÜHL

Weinbauort (village)	Einzellage (vineyard)
Aichelberg	Luginsland
Baach	Himmelreich
Beutelsbach	Altenberg
	Käppele
	Sonnenberg
Breuningsweiler	Haselstein
Endersbach	Happenhalde
	Wetzstein
Geradstetten	Lichtenberg
	Sonnenberg
Grossheppach	Steingrüble
	Zügernberg
Grunbach	Klingle
Hanweiler	Maien
Hebsack	Lichtenberg
Hertmannsweiler	Himmelreich
Kleinheppach	Sonnenberg
	Steingrüble
Korb	Steingrüble
Rommelshausen	Häder
Schnait i. R.	Altenberg
	Sonnenberg
Stetten i. R.	Brotwasser
	Häder
	Puvermächer
Strümpfelbach	Gastenklinge
	Nonnenberg
Waiblingen	Steingrüble
Winnenden	Haselstein

BEREICH (sub-region): WÜRTTEMBERGISCH UNTERLAND

GROSSLAGE (SECTION OF VINEYARDS): SCHALKSTEIN

Weinbauort (village)	Einzellage (vineyard)
Allmersbach a. W.	Alter Berg
Affalterbach	Neckarhälde
Asperg	Berg
Beihingen	Neckarhälde
Benningen	Neckarhälde

Weinbauort (village)	Einzellage (vineyard)
Besigheim	Felsengarten
	Wurmberg
Bietigheim	Wurmberg
	Felsengarten
Bissingen	Felsengarten
Erdmannhausen	Felsengarten
Gemmrigheim	Neckarhälde
	Wurmberg
Grossingersheim	Schlossberg
Hessigheim	Felsengarten
	Käsberg
	Wurmberg
Höpfigheim	Königsberg
Kirchberg	Kelterberg
Kleinaspach	Kelterberg
Kleiningersheim	Schlossberg
Löchgau	Felsengarten
Ludwigsburg (Ortsteil Hoheneck)	Neckarhälde
Marbach	Neckarhälde
Markgröningen	Berg
	Sankt Johännser
Mundelsheim	Käsberg
	Mühlbächer
	Rozenberg
Murr	Neckarhälde
Neckarweihingen	Neckarhälde
Poppenweiler	Neckarhälde
Rielinghausen	Kelterberg
Rietenau	Güldenkern
Steinheim/Murr	Burgberg
Walheim	Felsengarten
	Wurmberg

GROSSLAGE (SECTION OF VINEYARDS): STROMBERG

Weinbauort (village)	Einzellage (vineyard)
Bönnigheim	Kirchberg
	Sonnenberg
Diefenbach	König
Ensingen	Schanzreiter
Erligheim	Lerchenberg
Freudenstein	Reichshalde
Freudental	Kirchberg
Gründelbach	Steinbachhof
	Wachtkopf
Häfnerhaslach	Heiligenberg
Hofen	Lerchenberg
Hohenhaslach	Kirchberg
	Klosterberg
Hohenstein	Kirchberg
Horrheim	Klosterberg
Illingen	Forstgrube
	Halde
	Schanzreiter
Kirchheim	Kirchberg
Kleinsachsenheim	Kirchberg
Knittlingen	Reichshalde
Lienzingen	Eichelberg
Maulbronn	Eilfingerberg Klosterstück
	Reichshalde
Mühlhausen	Halde

Weinbauort (village)	Einzellage (vineyard)
Obererdingen	Kupferhalde
Ochsenbach	Liebenberg
Ötisheim	Sauberg
Riet	Kirchberg
Rosswag	Forstgrube
	Halde
	Lichtenberg
Schützingen	Heiligenberg
Spielberg	Liebenberg
Sternenfels	König
Vaihingen	Halde

GROSSLAGE (SECTION OF VINEYARDS): HEUCHELBERG

Weinbauort (village)	Einzellage (vineyard)
Brackenheim	Dachsberg
	Mönchsberg
	Schlossberg
	Wolfsaugen
	Zweifelberg
(Ortsteil Botenheim)	Ochsenberg
Cleebronn	Michaelsberg
Dürrenzimmern	Mönchsberg
Eibensbach	Michaelsberg
Frauenzimmern	Kaiserberg
	Michaelsberg
Güglingen	Kaiserberg
	Michaelsberg
Haberschlacht	Dachsberg
Hausen/Z.	Jupiterberg
Heilbronn (Ortsteil Klingenberg)	Schlossberg
	Sonntagsberg
Kleingartach	Grafenberg
Leingarten	Grafenberg
	Leiersberg
	Vogelsang
Massenbachhausen	Krähenberg
Meimsheim	Katzenöhrle
Neipperg	Grafenberg
	Steingrube
	Schlossberg
Niederhofen	Grafenberg
Nordhausen	Sonntagsberg
Nordheim	Grafenberg
	Gräfenberg
	Ruthe
	Sonntagsberg
Pfaffenhofen	Hohenberg
Schwaigern	Grafenberg
	Ruthe
	Sonnenberg
Stetten a. H.	Sonnenberg
Stockheim	Altenberg
Weiler/Z.	Hohenberg
Zaberfeld	Hohenberg

GROSSLAGE (SECTION OF VINEYARDS): WUNNENSTEIN

Weinbauort (village)	Einzellage (vineyard)
Beilstein	Schlosswengert
	Steinberg
	Wartberg
Gronau	Forstberg

Weinbauort (village)	Einzellage (vineyard)
Grossbottwar	Harzberg
	Lichtenberg
Hof und Lembach	Harzberg
	Lichtenberg
Ilsfeld	Lichtenberg
Kleinbottwar	Götzenberg
	Lichtenberg
	Oberer Berg
	Süssmund
Ludwigsburg (Ortsteil Hoheneck)	Oberer Berg
Oberstenfeld	Forstberg
	Harzberg
	Lichtenberg
Steinheim	Lichtenberg
Winzerhausen	Harzberg
	Lichtenberg

GROSSLAGE (SECTION OF VINEYARDS): SCHOZACHTAL

Weinbauort (village)	Einzellage (vineyard)
Abstatt	Burgberg
	Burg Wildeck
	Sommerberg
Auenstein	Burgberg
	Schlossberg
Ilsfeld	Rappen
Löwenstein	Sommerberg
Unterheinriet	Sommerberg

GROSSLAGE (SECTION OF VINEYARDS): KIRCHENWEINBERG

Weinbauort (village)	Einzellage (vineyard)
Flein	Altenberg
	Eselsberg
	Sonnenberg
Heilbronn	Altenberg
	Sonnenberg
Ilsfeld (Ortsteil Schozach)	Roter Berg
	Schelmenklinge
Lauffen	Jungfer
	Katzenbeisser
	Riedersbückele
Neckarwestheim	Herrlesberg
Talheim	Hohe Eiche
	Schlossberg
	Sonnenberg
Untergruppenbach	Schlossberg

GROSSLAGE (SECTION OF VINEYARDS): STAUFENBERG

Weinbauort (village)	Einzellage (vineyard)
Brettach	Berg
Duttenberg	Schön
Erlenbach	Kayberg

GROSSLAGE (SECTION OF VINEYARDS): SALZBERG

Weinbauort (village)	Einzellage (vineyard)
Affaltrach	Dieblesberg
Eberstadt	Eberfürst
	Sommerhalde
Eichelberg	Hundsberg
Ellhofen	Wildenberg
	Steinacker
Eschenau	Paradies

Weinbauort (village)	Einzellage (vineyard)
Grantschen	Wildenberg
Lehrensteinsfeld	Steinacker
Löwenstein	Altenberg
	Wohlfahrtsberg
Löwenstein (Ortsteil Hösslinsülz)	Dieblesberg
Sülzbach	Altenberg
Weiler	Hundsberg
	Schlierbach
Weinsberg	Wildenberg
Wimmental	Altenberg
Willsbach	Dieblesberg

GROSSLAGE (SECTION OF VINEYARDS): LINDELBERG

Weinbauort (village)	Einzellage (vineyard)
Adolzfurt	Schneckenhof
Bretzfeld	Goldberg
Dimbach	Himmelreich
Geddelsbach	Schneckenhof
Harsberg	Dachsteiger
Heuholz	Dachsteiger
Kesselfeld	Schwobajörgle
Langenbeutingen	Himmelreich
Michelbach a. W.	Dachsteiger
	Margarete
Maienfels	Schneckenhof
Obersöllbach	Margarete
Pfedelbach	Goldberg
Siebeneich	Himmelreich
Schwabbach	Himmelreich
Unterheimbach	Schneckenhof
Untersteinbach	Dachsteiger
Verrenberg	Goldberg
	Verrenberg
Waldbach	Himmelreich
Windischenbach	Goldberg

BEREICH (sub-region): KOCHER-JAGST-TAUBER

GROSSLAGE (SECTION OF VINEYARDS): KOCHERBERG

Weinbauort (village)	Einzellage (vineyard)
Belsenberg	Heiligkreuz
Bieringen	Schlüsselberg
Criesbach	Burgstall
	Hoher Berg
Dörzbach	Altenberg
Ernsbach	Flatterberg
Forchtenberg	Flatterberg
Ingelfingen	Hoher Berg
Künzelsau	Hoher Berg
Möckmühl	Ammerlanden
	Hofberg
Niedernhall	Altenberg
	Burgstall
	Engweg
	Hoher Berg
Siglingen	Hofberg
Weissbach	Altenberg
	Engweg
Widdern	Hofberg

Württemberg: Kocher-Jagst-Tauber

GROSSLAGE (SECTION OF VINEYARDS): TAUBERBERG

Weinbauort (village)	Einzellage (vineyard)
Elpersheim	Mönchsberg
	Probstberg
Wermutshausen	Schafsteige

Not yet assigned a *Grosslage* (section of vineyards):

Weinbauort (village)	Einzellage (vineyard)
Kressbronn am Bodensee	Berghalde
Tübingen (Ortsteile	
Hirschau, Unterjesingen)	Sonnenhalden

Weinbauort (village)	Einzellage (vineyard)
Haagen	Schafsteige
Laudenbach	Schafsteige
Markelsheim	Mönchsberg
	Probstberg
Niederstetten	Schafsteige
Oberstetten	Schafsteige
Reinsbronn	Röde
Vorbachzimmern	Schafsteige
Weikersheim	Hardt
	Karlsberg
	Schmecker

APPENDIX C

Containers and Measures

I BOTTLE SIZES

Wine	Bottles	Metric capacity	U.S. ounces	British ounces	U.S. EQUIVALENT Gal.	Qt.	Pt.	Oz.	BRITISH EQUIVALENT Gal.	Qt.	Pt.	Oz.
ALSACE	½ bottle	36.00 cl.	12.17	12.67				12				13
	bottle	72.00 cl.	24.34	25.34			1	8			1	5
ANJOU	½ bottle	37.50 cl.	12.68	13.20				13				13
	bottle	75.00 cl.	25.36	26.40			1	9			1	6
BEAUJOLAIS	½ bottle	37.50 cl.	12.68	13.20				13				13
'Pot'	⅔ bottle	50.00 cl.	16.90	17.60			1	1				18
	bottle	75.00 cl.	25.36	26.40			1	9			1	6
BORDEAUX												
Fillette	½ bottle	37.50 cl.	12.68	13.20				13				13
	bottle	75.00 cl.	25.36	26.40			1	9			1	6
Magnum	2 bottles	1.50 l.	50.71	52.79		1	1	3		1	–	13
*Marie-Jeanne	3 bottles (approx.)	2.50 l.	84.53	88.00		2	1	4		2	1	8
Double Magnum	4 bottles	3.00 l.	101.42	105.59		3	–	5		2	1	6
Jeroboam	6 bottles	4.50 l.	152.16	158.40	1	–	1	8		3	1	18
Imperial	8 bottles	6.00 l.	202.85	211.18	1	2	–	11	1	1	–	11
BURGUNDY	½ bottle	37.50 cl.	12.68	13.20				13				13
	bottle	75.00 cl.	25.36	26.40			1	9			1	6
Magnum	2 bottles	1.50 l.	50.71	52.79		1	1	3		1	–	13
CHAMPAGNE												
Split	¼ bottle	20.00 cl.	6.76	7.04				7				7
Half Bottle	½ bottle	37.5 cl.	13.52	14.08				14				14
Bottle	bottle	75 cl.	27.05	28.16			1	11			1	8
Magnum	2 bottles	1.60 l.	54.09	56.31			1	6			1	–	16
Jeroboam	4 bottles	3.20 l.	108.19	112.63		3	–	12		2	1	13
*Rehoboam	6 bottles	4.80 l.	162.28	168.94	1	1	–	2	1	–	–	9
*Methuselah	8 bottles	6.40 l.	216.37	225.25	1	2	1	8	1	1	1	5
*Salmanazar	12 bottles	9.60 l.	324.46	337.88	2	2	–	4	2	–	–	18
*Balthazar	16 bottles	12.80 l.	432.74	450.51	3	1	1	1	2	3	–	10
*Nebuchadnezzar	20 bottles	16.00 l.	540.93	563.14	4	–	1	13	3	2	–	3
MOSELLE	½ bottle	35.00 cl.	11.83	12.32				12				12
	bottle	70.00 cl.	23.67	24.63			1	8			1	5
PORT												
Quart	bottle	75.75 cl.	25.61	26.66			1	10			1	7
Magnum	2 bottles	1.51 l.	51.20	53.15		1	1	3		1	–	13
Tappit Hen	3 bottles	2.27 l.	76.84	79.89		2	–	13		2	–	–
Jeroboam	4 bottles	3.03 l.	102.45	106.64		3	–	6		2	1	7
RHINE	½ bottle	35.00 cl.	11.83	12.32				12				12
	bottle	70.00 cl.	23.67	24.63			1	8			1	5

*No longer used.

703

Containers and Measures

Wine	Bottles	*Metric capacity*	*U.S. ounces*	*British ounces*	Gal.	Qt.	Pt.	Oz.	Gal.	Qt.	Pt.	Oz.
					U.S. EQUIVALENT				BRITISH EQUIVALENT			
SHERRY												
Pint	½ bottle	37.86 cl.	12.80	13.32				13				13
Quart	bottle	75.75 cl.	25.61	26.66			1	10			1	7
U.S.												
Tenth	½ bottle	37.86 cl.	12.80	13.32				13				13
Fifth	bottle	75.72 cl.	25.60	26.65			1	10			1	7
Magnum	2 bottles	1.51 l.	51.20	53.15		1	1	3		1	–	13

NOTE: Basic metric capacities, and in some cases ounces, upon which most figures in this table are based, are those fixed by law. Actual contents will almost always vary because of differences in corking space.

II COOPERAGE

	Cask or barrel	*Description*	*Metric capacity liters*	*U.S. equivalent U.S. gallons*	*British equivalent imp. gallons*
FRANCE					
Alsace	Foudre	As in Germany, a huge barrel for sales and storage purposes	1,000 liters or any other size. No standard size is adhered to	264.2	220.0
	Aume	Used principally for shipping. Same size as Burgundy *feuillette*		30.1	25.1
Beaujolais	Pièce		216	57.1	47.5
	Feuillette	One-half *piece*	108	28.5	23.7
	Quartaut	One-quarter *piece*	54	14.3	11.9
Bordeaux	Barrique	*Hogshead*—so-called. Most common Bordeaux cask. Yields 25 cases of 12 bottles each	225	59.4	49.5
	Tonneau	A measure equivalent to 4 *barriques*. No actual barrel this size. Château production and price quotations stated in *tonneaux*. Yields 100 cases of 12 bottles each	900	237.8	197.9
	Demi-Barrique or Feuillette	One-half *barrique*	112	29.6	24.6
	Quartaut	One-quarter *barrique*	56	14.8	12.3
Burgundy	Pièce	Regular Burgundy barrel. When bottled, yields 24-25 cases of 12 bottles each	228	60.2	50.1
	Queue	Old French measure consisting of 2 *pièces*. No actual cask this size. Sales by Hospices de Beaune made in terms of *queues*	456	120.5	100.3
	Feuillette	One-half *piece*	114	30.1	25.1
	Quartaut	One-quarter *piece*	57	15.1	12.6
Chablis	Feuillette	Standard Chablis barrel. Larger than *feuillette* of Côte d'Or	132	34.9	29.0
Champagne		Regular Champagne cask. Also called a *pièce*	205	54.2	45.1
			108	28.5	23.7
Loire Valley Anjou / Layon / Saumur	Piece	Capacity variable	220	58.1	48.4
Vouvray	Piece	Capacity same as Bordeaux *hogshead*	225	59.4	49.5
Mâconnais	Piece	Nearly the same size as the Beaujolais *piece*	215	56.8	47.3
The Midi and Algeria	Demi-Muid	Storage barrel	600–700 (approx.)	171.7 (approx.)	143.0 (approx.)
Rhône Valley	Piece	Standard barrel in the area of Châteauneuf-du-Pape. Slightly smaller than *piece* of Côte d'Or	225	59.4	49.5

	Cask or barrel	Description	Metric capacity liters	U.S. equivalent U.S. gallons	British equivalent imp. gallons
GERMANY *Rhine and Mosel*	Ohm	An old Hock or Rhine measure which is now obsolete and is no longer used	150	39.6	33.0
	Doppelohm	Double *ohm* equal to a quarter *stück*	300	79.2	66.0
	Fuder (Mosel)	Large storage cask	1,000	264.2	219.9
	Stück (Rhine)	Huge storage cask	1,200	317.0	264.0
	Doppelstück (Rhine)	Double *stück*	2,400	634.0	527.8
	Halbstück (Rhine)	One-half *stück*	600	158.4	132.0
	Viertelstück (Rhine)	One-quarter *stück*	300	79.2	66.0
AUSTRALIA AND SOUTH AFRICA	Hogshead		295.3	78.0	64.9
LISBON	Pipe		531.4	140.4	117.0
MADEIRA	Pipe	Standard Madeira shipping cask. Yields on average 44½ cases of 12 bottles each	418.0	110.4	92.0
	Hogshead	One-half Madeira *pipe*	209.0	55.2	46.0
MARSALA	Pipe	Slightly larger than Madeira *pipe*. Yields 45 cases of 12 bottles each	422.6	111.6	93.0
	Hogshead	Same size as Madeira *hogshead*	209.0	55.2	46.0
PORT	Pipe	Standard Port cask. Average yield is 56 dozen reputed quarts	522.5	138.0	115.0
	Hogshead		259.0	68.4	57.0
	Quarter Cask	One-quarter standard	127.2	33.6	28.0
SHERRY	Butt	Standard Sherry cask. Yields, when bottled, 52 cases of 12 bottles each	490.7	129.6	108.0
	Hogshead	One-half *butt*, yields 26 cases of 12 bottles each	245.4	64.8	54.0
	Quarter Cask	One-quarter standard, or one-half *hogshead*	122.7	32.4	27.0
	Octave	One-eighth standard	61.4	16.2	13.5
TARRAGONA	Pipe	Same capacity as *pipe* of Port	350	92.5	77.0
	Hogshead		400	105.8	88.1
COGNAC	Hogshead	Most commonly used brandy cask	545.2	144.0	120.0
ARMAGNAC	Hogshead		272.6	72.0	60.0
RUM	Puncheon	Size varies considerably	422.6–518.0	111.6–136.8	92.9–113.9
	Hogshead	Equally variable in size	245.4–272.6	64.8–72.0	54.0–59.9
WHISKY—SCOTCH	Butt	Standard distillery cask. Sometimes a rum *puncheon*, made from oak, cut down to the *butt* length of stave and gallonage	491.0 (approx.)	129.7 (approx.)	108.0 (approx.)
	Puncheon	Capacity varies between 95 and 120 imp. gallons	431.9–545.5	114.1–144.1	95.0–120.0
WHISKEY—U.S.	Barrel	Standard new barrel for either Rye or Bourbon whiskey as required by law	181.7	48.0	40.0
WHISKY—CANADIAN	Barrel	Capacity variable. Usually exceeds slightly the standard U.S. 48-gallon barrel	181.7 (approx.)	48.0 (approx.)	40.0 (approx.)

	Cask or barrel	Description	Metric capacity liters	U.S. equivalent U.S. gallons	British equivalent imp. gallons
SPIRITS (*Aged*) U.S.	Barrel	Used cooperage: same U.S. barrel and size as for whiskey	181.7	48.0	40.0
	Hogshead	Cask holding between 45 and 80 imp. gals.		54.0-96.0	45.0-80.0
	Barrel	Cask holding between 35 and 45 imp. gals.		42.0-54.0	35.0-45.0
	Quarter	Cask holding between 15 and 30 imp. gals.		18.0-36.0	15.0-30.0
	Octave	Cask holding between 9 and 15 imp. gals.		10.8-18.0	9.0-15.0

CASE

			Metric capacity liters	U.S. equivalent U.S. gallons	British equivalent imp. gallons
Bordeaux and Burgundy			8.52	2.25	1.87
Champagne			9.23	2.4375	2.0304

Comparative Table of Spirit Strength

Sikes (British) U.P. (Under proof)	American	Gay-Lussac and Tralles	Sikes (British) U.P. (Under proof)	American	Gay-Lussac and Tralles
60.0°	45.7°	22.9°	39.6°	69.0°	34.5°
59.8	46.0	23.0	39.0	69.7	34.9
59.0	46.9	23.4	38.8	70.0	35.0
58.9	47.0	23.5	38.0	70.9	35.4
58.0	48.0	24.0	37.9	71.0	35.5
57.1	49.0	24.5	37.0	72.0	36.0
57.0	49.1	24.6	36.1	73.0	36.5
56.3	50.0	25.0	36.0	73.1	36.6
56.0	50.3	25.1	35.3	74.0	37.0
55.4	51.0	25.5	35.0	74.3	37.1
55.0	51.4	25.7	34.4	75.0	37.5
54.5	52.0	26.0	34.0	75.4	37.7
54.0	52.6	26.3	33.5	76.0	38.0
53.6	53.0	26.5	33.0	76.6	38.3
53.0	53.7	26.9	32.6	77.0	38.5
52.8	54.0	27.0	32.0	77.7	38.9
52.0	54.9	27.4	31.8	78.0	39.0
51.9	55.0	27.5	31.0	78.9	39.4
51.0	56.0	28.0	30.9	79.0	39.5
50.1	57.0	28.5	30.0	80.0	40.0
50.0	57.1	28.6	29.1	81.0	40.5
49.3	58.0	29.0	29.0	81.1	40.6
49.0	58.3	29.1	28.3	82.0	41.0
48.4	59.0	29.5	28.0	82.3	41.1
48.0	59.4	29.7	27.4	83.0	41.5
47.5	60.0	30.0	27.0	83.4	41.7
47.0	60.6	30.3	26.5	84.0	42.0
46.6	61.0	30.5	26.0	84.6	42.3
46.0	61.7	30.9	25.6	85.0	42.5
45.8	62.0	31.0	25.0	85.7	42.9
45.0	62.9	31.4	24.8	86.0	43.0
44.9	63.0	31.5	24.0	86.9	43.4
44.0	64.0	32.0	23.9	87.0	43.5
43.1	65.0	32.5	23.0	88.0	44.0
43.0	65.1	32.6	22.1	89.0	44.5
42.3	66.0	33.0	22.0	89.1	44.6
42.0	66.3	33.1	21.3	90.0	45.0
41.4	67.0	33.5	21.0	90.3	45.1
41.0	67.4	33.7	20.4	91.0	45.5
40.5	68.0	34.0	20.0	91.4	45.7
40.0	68.6	34.3			

Comparative Table of Spirit Strength

Sikes (British)	American	Gay-Lussac and Tralles	Sikes (British)	American	Gay-Lussac and Tralles
19.5°	92.0°	46.0°	8.5°	124.0°	62.0°
19.0	92.6	46.3	9.0	124.6	62.3
18.6	93.0	46.5	9.4	125.0	62.5
18.0	93.7	46.9	10.0	125.7	62.9
17.8	94.0	47.0	10.3	126.0	63.0
17.0	94.9	47.4	11.0	126.9	63.4
16.9	95.0	47.5	11.1	127.0	63.5
16.0	96.0	48.0	12.0	128.0	64.0
15.1	97.0	48.5	12.9	129.0	64.5
15.0	97.1	48.6	13.0	129.1	64.6
14.3	98.0	49.0	13.8	130.0	65.0
14.0	98.3	49.1	14.0	130.3	65.1
13.4	99.0	49.5	14.6	131.0	65.5
13.0	99.4	49.7	15.0	131.4	65.7
12.5	Proof	50.0	15.5	132.0	66.0
12.0	100.6	50.3	16.0	132.6	66.3
11.6	101.0	50.5	16.4	133.0	66.5
11.0	101.7	50.9	17.0	133.7	66.9
10.8	102.0	51.0	17.3	134.0	67.0
10.0	102.9	51.4	18.0	134.9	67.4
9.9	103.0	51.5	18.1	135.0	67.5
9.0	104.0	52.0	19.0	136.0	68.0
8.1	105.0	52.5	19.9	137.0	68.5
8.0	105.1	52.6	20.0	137.1	68.6
7.3	106.0	53.0	20.8	138.0	69.0
7.0	106.3	53.1	21.0	138.3	69.1
6.4	107.0	53.5	21.6	139.0	69.5
6.0	107.4	53.7	22.0	139.4	69.7
5.5	108.0	54.0	22.5	140.0	70.0
5.0	108.6	54.3	23.0	140.6	70.3
4.6	109.0	54.5	23.4	141.0	70.5
4.0	109.7	54.9	24.0	141.7	70.9
3.8	110.0	55.0	24.3	142.0	71.0
3.0	110.9	55.4	25.0	142.9	71.4
2.9	111.0	55.5	25.1	143.0	71.5
2.0	112.0	56.0	26.0	144.0	72.0
1.1	113.0	56.5	26.9	145.0	72.5
1.0	113.1	56.6	27.0	145.1	72.6
0.3	114.0	57.0	27.8	146.0	73.0
Proof	114.29	57.14	28.0	146.3	73.1
O.P.			28.6	147.0	73.5
(Over proof)			29.0	147.4	73.7
0.6	115.0	57.5	29.5	148.0	74.0
1.0	115.4	57.7	30.0	148.6	74.3
1.5	116.0	58.0	30.4	149.0	74.5
2.0	116.6	58.3	31.0	149.7	74.9
2.4	117.0	58.5	31.3	150.0	75.0
3.0	117.7	58.9	32.0	150.9	75.4
3.3	118.0	59.0	32.1	151.0	75.5
4.0	118.9	59.4	33.0	152.0	76.0
4.1	119.0	59.5	33.9	153.0	76.5
5.0	120.0	60.0	34.0	153.1	76.6
5.9	121.0	60.5	34.8	154.0	77.0
6.0	121.1	60.6	35.0	154.3	77.1
6.8	122.0	61.0	35.6	155.0	77.5
7.0	122.3	61.1	36.0	155.4	77.7
7.6	123.0	61.5	36.5	156.0	78.0
8.0	123.4	61.7			

Sikes (British)	American	Gay-Lussac and Tralles	Sikes (British)	American	Gay-Lussac and Tralles
37.0°	156.6°	78.3°	56.6°	179.0°	89.5°
37.4	157.0	78.5	57.0	179.4	89.7
38.0	157.7	78.9	57.5	180.0	90.0
38.3	158.0	79.0	58.0	180.6	90.3
39.0	158.9	79.4	58.4	181.0	90.5
39.1	159.0	79.5	50.9	181.7	90.9
40.0	160.0	80.0	59.3	182.0	91.0
40.9	161.0	80.5	60.0	182.9	91.4
41.0	161.1	80.6	60.1	183.0	91.5
41.8	162.0	81.0	61.0	184.0	92.0
42.0	162.3	81.1	61.9	185.0	92.5
42.6	163.0	81.5	62.0	185.1	92.6
43.0	163.4	81.7	62.8	186.0	93.0
43.5	164.0	82.0	63.0	186.3	93.1
44.0	164.6	82.3	63.6	187.0	93.5
44.4	165.0	82.5	64.0	187.4	93.7
45.0	165.7	82.9	64.5	188.0	94.0
45.3	166.0	83.0	65.0	188.6	94.3
46.0	166.9	83.4	65.4	189.0	94.5
46.1	167.0	83.5	66.0	189.7	94.9
47.0	168.0	84.0	66.3	190.0	95.0
47.9	169.0	84.5	67.0	190.9	95.4
48.0	169.1	84.6	67.1	191.0	95.5
48.8	170.0	85.0	68.0	192.0	96.0
49.0	170.3	85.1	68.9	193.0	96.5
49.6	171.0	85.5	69.0	193.1	96.6
50.0	171.4	85.7	69.8	194.0	97.0
50.5	172.0	86.0	70.0	194.3	97.1
51.0	172.6	86.3	70.6	195.0	97.5
51.4	173.0	86.5	71.0	195.4	97.7
52.0	173.7	86.9	71.5	196.0	98.0
52.3	174.0	87.0	72.0	196.6	98.3
53.0	174.9	87.4	72.4	197.0	98.5
53.1	175.0	87.5	73.0	197.7	98.9
54.0	176.0	88.0	73.3	198.0	99.0
54.9	177.0	88.5	74.0	198.9	99.4
55.0	177.1	88.6	74.1	199.0	99.5
55.8	178.0	89.0	75.0	200.0	100.0
56.0	178.3	89.1			

The equivalent density table for grape musts expressed in Oechsle, Baumé, Balling/Brix; alcoholic content will be found in the entry "Mustimeter or saccharometer," on pages 339 to 341.

APPENDIX E

Conversion Tables

I MEASUREMENT OF LENGTH

Centimeters	Inches	Ft.	Ins.	Meters	Ft.	Yds.	Ft.	Ins.	Yds.	Kilometers	Miles
1	0.394		2/5	1	3.281	1		3 2/5	1.094	1	0.621
2	0.787		4/5	2	6.562	2		6 7/10	2.187	2	1.243
3	1.181		1 1/5	3	9.843	3		10 1/10	3.281	3	1.864
4	1.575		1 3/5	4	13.123	4	1	1 1/2	4.374	4	2.486
5	1.969		2	5	16.404	5	1	4 4/5	5.468	5	3.107
6	2.362		2 2/5	6	19.685	6	1	8 1/5	6.562	6	3.728
7	2.756		2 4/5	7	22.966	7	1	11 3/5	7.655	7	4.350
8	3.150		3 1/5	8	26.247	8	2	3	8.749	8	4.971
9	3.543		3 1/2	9	29.528	9	2	6 3/10	9.843	9	5.592
10	3.937		3 9/10	10	32.808	10	2	9 7/10	10.936	10	6.214
20	7.874		7 9/10	20	65.617	21	2	7 2/5	21.872	20	12.427
30	11.811		11 4/5	30	98.425	32	2	5 1/10	32.808	30	18.641
40	15.748	1	3 7/10	40	131.234	43	2	2 4/5	43.745	40	24.855
50	19.685	1	7 7/10	50	164.042	54	2	1/2	54.681	50	31.069
60	23.622	1	11 3/5	60	196.850	65	1	10 1/5	65.617	60	37.282
70	27.559	2	3 3/5	70	229.659	76	1	7 9/10	76.553	70	43.496
80	31.496	2	7 1/2	80	262.467	87	1	5 3/5	87.489	80	49.710
90	35.433	2	11 2/5	90	295.276	98	1	3 3/10	98.425	90	55.923
100 = 1 meter	39.370	3	3 2/5	100	328.084	109	1	1	109.361	100	62.137

10 millimeters = 1 centimeter	10 decimeters = 1 meter	10 dekameters = 1 hectometer
10 centimeters = 1 decimeter	10 meters = 1 dekameter	10 hectometers = 1 kilometer

MEASUREMENT OF LENGTH (continued)

Inches	Centimeters	Feet	Meters	Yards	Meters	Miles	Kilometers
1	2.540	1	0.305	1	0.914	1	1.609
2	5.080	2	0.610	2	1.829	2	3.219
3	7.620	3 = 1 yard	0.914	3	2.743	3	4.828
4	10.160	4	1.219	4	3.658	4	6.437
5	12.700	5	1.524	5	4.572	5	8.047
6	15.240	6	1.829	6	5.486	6	9.656
7	17.780	7	2.134	7	6.401	7	11.265
8	20.320	8	2.438	8	7.315	8	12.875
9	22.860	9	2.743	9	8.230	9	14.484
10	25.400	10	3.048	10	9.144	10	16.093
11	27.940	20	6.096	20	18.288	20	32.187
12 = 1 foot	30.480	30	9.144	30	27.432	30	40.280
20	50.800	40	12.192	40	36.576	40	64.374
30	76.200	50	15.240	50	45.720	50	80.467
40	101.600	60	18.288	60	54.864	60	96.561
50	127.000	70	21.336	70	64.008	70	112.654
60	152.400	80	24.384	80	73.152	80	128.748
70	177.800	90	27.432	90	82.296	90	144.841
80	203.200	100	30.480	100	91.440	100	160.934
90	228.600						
100	254.000						

12 inches (in.) = 1 foot (ft.)	3 feet = 1 yard (yd.)	1,760 yards = 1 mile

II SQUARE MEASURE

Square centimeters	Square inches	Square meters	Square feet	Hectares	Acres	Square kilometers	Square miles
1	0.155	1	10.764	1	2.471	1	0.368
2	0.310	2	21.528	2	4.942	2	0.722
3	0.465	3	32.292	3	7.413	3	1.158
4	0.620	4	43.056	4	9.884	4	1.544
5	0.775	5	53.820	5	12.355	5	1.931
6	0.930	6	64.583	6	14.826	6	2.317
7	1.085	7	75.347	7	17.297	7	2.703
8	1.240	8	86.111	8	19.768	8	3.089
9	1.395	9	96.875	9	22.239	9	3.475
10	1.550	10	107.639	10	24.711	10	3.861
20	3.100	20	215.278	20	49.421	20	7.722
30	4.650	30	322.917	30	74.132	30	11.583
40	6.200	40	430.556	40	98.842	40	15.444
50	7.750	50	538.196	50	123.553	50	19.305
60	9.300	60	645.835	60	148.263	60	23.166
70	10.850	70	753.474	70	172.974	70	27.027
80	12.400	80	861.113	80	197.684	80	30.888
90	13.950	90	968.752	90	222.395	90	34.749
100	15.500	100	1,076.391	100 = 1 square kilometer	247.105	100	38.610

10,000 square centimeters = 1 square meter   10,000 square meters = 1 hectare   100 hectares = 1 square kilometer

II SQUARE MEASURE (continued)

Square inches	Square centimeters	Square feet	Square meters	Acres	Hectares	Square miles	Square kilometers
1	6.452	1	0.093	1	0.405	1	2.590
2	12.903	2	0.186	2	0.809	2	5.180
3	19.355	3	0.279	3	1.214	3	7.770
4	25.806	4	0.372	4	1.619	4	10.360
5	32.258	5	0.465	5	2.023	5	12.950
6	38.710	6	0.557	6	2.428	6	15.540
7	45.161	7	0.650	7	2.833	7	18.130
8	51.613	8	0.743	8	3.238	8	20.720
9	58.064	9 = 1 sq. yd.	0.836	9	3.642	9	23.310
10	64.516	10	0.929	10	4.047	10	25.900
20	129.032	20	1.858	20	8.094	20	51.800
30	193.548	30	2.787	30	12.141	30	77.700
40	258.064	40	3.716	40	16.187	40	103.600
50	322.580	50	4.645	50	20.234	50	129.499
60	387.096	60	5.574	60	24.281	60	155.399
70	451.612	70	6.503	70	28.328	70	181.299
80	516.128	80	7.432	80	32.375	80	207.199
90	580.644	90	8.361	90	36.422	90	233.099
100	645.160	100	9.290	100	40.469	100	258.999

144 square inches = 1 square foot   4,840 square yards = 1 acre
9 square feet = 1 square yard   640 acres = 1 square mile

III CUBIC MEASURE

Cubic centimeters	Cubic inches	Cubic decimeters	Cubic feet	Cubic meters	Cubic yards
1	0.061	1	0.035	1	1.308
2	0.122	2	0.071	2	2.616
3	0.183	3	0.106	3	3.924
4	0.244	4	0.141	4	5.232
5	0.305	5	0.177	5	6.540
6	0.366	6	0.212	6	7.848
7	0.427	7	0.247	7	9.156
8	0.488	8	0.283	8	10.464
9	0.549	9	0.318	9	11.772
10	0.610	10	0.353	10	13.080
20	1.220	20	0.706	20	26.159
30	1.831	30	1.059	30	39.239
40	2.441	40	1.413	40	52.318
50	3.051	50	1.766	50	65.398
60	3.661	60	2.119	60	78.477
70	4.272	70	2.472	70	91.557
80	4.882	80	2.825	80	104.636
90	5.492	90	3.178	90	117.716
100	6.102	100	3.531	100	130.795

1,000 cubic centimeters = 1 cubic decimeter
1,000 cubic decimeters = 1 cubic meter = 1 stere

III CUBIC MEASURE (continued)

Cubic inches	Cubic centimeters	Cubic feet	Cubic decimeters	Cubic yards	Cubic meters
1	16.387	1	28.317	1	0.765
2	32.774	2	56.633	2	1.529
3	49.161	3	84.951	3	2.294
4	65.548	4	113.267	4	3.058
5	81.935	5	141.584	5	3.823
6	98.322	6	169.901	6	4.587
7	114.709	7	198.218	7	5.352
8	131.097	8	226.535	8	6.116
9	147.484	9	254.852	9	6.881
10	163.871	10	283.168	10	7.646
20	327.741	20	566.337	20	15.291
30	491.612	30	849.505	30	22.937
40	655.483	40	1,132.674	40	30.582
50	819.353	50	1,415.842	50	38.228
60	983.224	60	1,699.011	60	45.873
70	1,147.094	70	1,982.179	70	53.519
80	1,310.965	80	2,265.348	80	61.164
90	1,474.836	90	2,548.516	90	68.810
100	1,638.706	100	2,831.685	100	76.455

1,728 cubic inches = 1 cubic foot
27 cubic feet = 1 cubic yard

IV   WEIGHTS

Grams	Avoirdupois ounces	Lb.	Oz.	Kilograms	Avoirdupois pounds	Cwts.	Qtrs.	Sts.	Lb.	Oz.
1	0.035		–	1	2.205				2	3
2	0.071		–	2	4.409				4	7
3	0.106		–	3	6.614				6	10
4	0.141		–	4	8.818				8	13
5	0.176		–	5	11.023				11	–
6	0.212		–	6	13.228				13	4
7	0.247		–	7	15.432			1	1	7
8	0.282		–	8	17.637			1	3	10
9	0.317		–	9	19.842			1	5	13
10	0.353		–	10	22.046			1	8	1
20	0.705		–	20	44.092		1	1	2	1
30	1.058		1	30	66.139		2	–	10	2
40	1.411		1½	40	88.185		3	–	4	3
50	1.764		1¾	50	110.231		3	1	12	4
60	2.116		2	60	132.277	1	–	1	6	4
70	2.469		2½	70	154.324	1	1	1	–	5
80	2.822		2¾	80	176.370	1	2	–	8	6
90	3.175		3¼	90	198.416	1	3	–	2	7
100	3.527		3½	100	220.463	1	3	1	10	7
150	5.291		5¼	150	330.69	2	3	1	8	11
200	7.055		7	200	440.92	3	3	1	6	15
250	8.818		8¾	250	551.16	4	3	1	5	3
300	10.592		10½	300	661.39	5	3	1	3	6
350	12.346		12½	350	771.62	6	3	1	1	10
400	14.110		14	400	881.85	7	3	–	13	14
450	15.873		15¾	450	992.08	8	3	–	12	1
500	17.637	1	1¾	500	1,102.31	9	3	–	10	5
550	19.401	1	3½	550	1,212.54	10	3	–	8	9
600	21.164	1	5¼	600	1,322.77	11	3	–	6	12
650	22.928	1	7	650	1,433.00	12	3	–	4	–
700	24.691	1	8¾	700	1,543.24	13	3	–	3	4
750	26.455	1	10½	750	1,653.47	14	3	–	1	7
800	28.219	1	12¼	800	1,763.70	15	2	1	13	11
850	29.983	1	14	850	1,873.93	16	2	1	11	15
900	31.746	1	15¾	900	1,984.16	17	2	1	10	2
950	33.510	2	1½	950	2,094.39	18	2	1	8	6
1,000 = 1 kilogram	35.274	2	3¼	1,000 = 1 ton (metric)	2,204.63	19	2	1	6	10

IV WEIGHTS (*continued*)

Metric tons	Long or gross tons	Tons	Cwts.	Qtrs.	Sts.	Lb.	Oz.
1	0.984	–	19	2	1	6	9¾
2	1.968	1	19	1	–	13	3½
3	2.953	2	19	–	–	5	13¼
4	3.937	3	18	2	1	12	7
5	4.921	4	18	1	1	5	¾
6	5.905	5	18	–	–	11	10¼
7	6.889	6	17	3	–	4	4
8	7.874	7	17	1	1	11	1½
9	8.858	8	17	–	1	3	11¼
10	9.842	9	16	3	–	10	4¾
20	19.684	19	13	2	1	6	6¼
30	29.526	29	10	2	–	2	11
40	39.368	39	7	1	–	12	15¾
50	49.210	49	4	–	1	9	1¼
60	59.052	59	1	–	–	5	6
70	68.895	68	17	3	1	1	11
80	78.737	78	14	2	1	11	12¼
90	88.579	88	11	2	–	8	1
100	98.421	98	8	1	1	4	6

IV WEIGHTS (*continued*)

Avoirdupois ounces	Grams	Avoirdupois pounds	Kilograms	Long or gross tons	Metric tons
1	28.350	1	0.454	1	1.016
2	56.699	2	0.907	2	2.032
3	85.049	3	1.361	3	3.048
4	113.398	4	1.814	4	4.064
5	141.748	5	2.268	5	5.080
6	170.097	6	2.722	6	6.096
7	198.447	7	3.175	7	7.112
8	226.796	8	3.629	8	8.128
9	255.146	9	4.082	9	9.144
10	283.495	10	4.536	10	10.161
16 = 1 pound	453.592	14 = 1 stone	6.350	20	20.321
20	566.990	20	9.072	30	30.481
30	850.486	28 = 1 quarter	12.701	40	40.642
40	1,133.981	30	13.608	50	50.802
50	1,417.476	40	18.144	60	60.963
60	1,700.971	50	22.680	70	71.123
70	1,984.467	60	27.216	80	81.284
80	2,267.962	70	31.751	90	91.444
90	2,551.457	80	36.287	100	101.605
100	2,834.952	90	40.823		
		100	45.359		
		112 = 1 hundredweight	50.802		

16 ounces (oz.)	= 1 pound (lb.)
14 pounds	= 1 stone (st.)
28 pounds	= 1 quarter (qtr.)
112 pounds	= 1 hundredweight (cwt.)
20 hundredweight	= 2,240 lb. = 1 ton (long)
2,000 pounds	= 1 ton (short)

V CAPACITY

Centiliters	Ounces (U.S.)	U.S. equivalent			Ounces (British)	British equivalent	
		Qts.	Pts.	Oz.		Pts.	Oz.
20	6.763			6¾	7.039		7
25	8.454			6½	8.799		8¾
30	10.144			10¼	10.599		10½
35	11.835			11¾	12.319		12¼
36	12.173			12¼	12.671		12¾
37.5	12.681			12¾	13.199		13¼
40	13.526			13½	14.078		14
45	15.217			15¼	15.838		15¾
50	16.907		1	1	17.598		17½
55	18.598		1	2½	19.358		19¼
60	20.289		1	4¼	21.118	1	1
65	21.980		1	6	22.877	1	2¾
70	23.670		1	7¾	24.637	1	4¾
75	25.361		1	9¼	26.397	1	6½
80	27.052		1	11	28.175	1	8¼
85	28.742		1	12¾	29.917	1	10
90	30.433		1	14½	31.676	1	11¾
95	32.124	1	–	–	33.436	1	13½
100 = 1 liter	33.814	1	–	1¾	35.196	1	15¼

100 centiliters = 1 liter

V CAPACITY (continued)

Liters	Pints (U.S.)	Gallons (U.S.)	U.S. equivalent				Pints (British)	Gallons (British)	British equivalent			
			Gals.	Qts.	Pts.	Oz.			Gals.	Qts.	Pts.	Oz.
1	2.113	0.264		1	–	1¾	1.760	0.220			1	15¼
2	4.227	0.528		2	–	3½	3.520	0.440		1	1	10½
3	6.340	0.793		3	–	5½	5.279	0.660		2	1	5½
4	8.454	1.057	1	–	–	7¼	7.039	0.880		3	1	¾
5	10.567	1.321	1	1	–	9	8.799	1.100	1	–	–	16
6	12.681	1.585	1	2	–	11	10.559	1.320	1	1	–	11¼
7	14.794	1.849	1	3	–	12¾	12.319	1.540	1	2	–	6½
8	16.908	2.113	2	–	–	14½	14.078	1.760	1	3	–	1½
9	19.021	2.378	2	1	1	¼	15.838	1.980	1	3	1	16¾
10	21.134	2.642	2	2	1	2¼	17.598	2.200	2	–	1	12
11	23.248	2.906	2	3	1	4	19.358	2.420	2	1	1	7¼
12	25.361	3.170	3	–	1	5¾	21.118	2.640	2	2	1	2½
13	27.475	3.434	3	1	1	7½	22.877	2.860	2	3	–	17½
14	29.588	3.699	3	2	1	9½	24.637	3.080	3	–	–	12¾
15	31.702	3.963	3	3	1	11¼	26.397	3.300	3	1	–	8
16	33.815	4.227	4	–	1	13	28.157	3.520	3	2	–	3¼
17	35.928	4.491	4	1	1	14¾	29.917	3.740	3	2	1	18½
18	38.042	4.755	4	3	–	¾	31.676	3.960	3	3	1	13½
19	40.155	5.019	5	–	–	2½	33.436	4.180	4	–	1	8¾
20	42.269	5.284	5	1	–	4¼	35.196	4.400	4	1	1	3¾
30	63.403	7.925	7	3	1	6½	52.794	6.599	6	2	–	15¾
40	84.538	10.567	10	2	–	8½	70.392	8.799	8	3	–	7¾
50	105.672	13.209	13	–	1	10¾	87.990	10.999	10	3	1	19¾
60	126.806	15.851	15	3	–	13	105.588	13.199	13	–	1	11¾
70	147.941	18.493	18	1	1	15	123.186	15.398	15	1	1	3¾
80	169.075	21.134	21	–	1	1¼	140.784	17.598	17	2	–	15¾
90	190.210	23.776	23	3	–	3¼	158.382	19.798	19	3	–	7¾
100 = 1 hectoliter	211.344	26.418	26	1	1	5½	175.980	21.998	21	3	1	19¾

V CAPACITY (continued)

Centiliters	Fluid ounces (U.S.)	U.S. equivalent			Fluid ounces (British)	Liters	Pints (U.S.)	U.S. equivalent				Pints (British)
		Qts.	Pts.	Oz.				Gals.	Qts.	Pts.	Oz.	
17.047	5.765			5¾	6	0.568	1.201			1	3¼	1
19.889	6.725			6¾	7	1.136	2.402		1	-	6½	2 = 1 qt.
22.730	7.686			7¾	8	1.705	3.603		1	1	9¾	3
25.571	8.647			8¾	9	2.273	4.804		2	-	12¾	4 = 2 qts.
28.412	9.608			9½	10	2.841	6.005		3	-	—	5
31.253	10.568			10½	11	3.409	7.206		3	1	3¼	6 = 3 qts.
34.095	11.529			11½	12	3.978	8.407	1	-	-	6½	7
36.936	12.490			12½	13	4.546	9.608	1	-	1	9¾	8 = 1 gal.
39.777	13.451			13½	14	5.114	10.809	1	1	-	13	9
42.618	14.411			14½	15	5.682	12.010	1	2	-	¼	10
45.460	15.372			15¼	16	11.365	24.019	3	-	-	¼	20
48.301	16.333	1		¼	17	17.047	36.029	4	2	-	½	30
51.142	17.294	1		1¼	18	22.730	48.038	6	-	-	½	40
53.983	18.254	1		2¼	19	28.412	60.048	7	2	-	¾	50
56.824	19.215	1		3¼	20 = 1 pt.	34.095	72.057	9	-	-	1	60
85.237	28.823	1		12¾	30	39.777	84.067	10	2	-	1 .	70
113.649	38.430	1	-	6½	40 = 1 qt.	45.460	96.076	12	-	-	1¼	80 = 10 gals.
142.061	48.038	1	1	—	50	51.142	108.086	13	2	-	1½	90
170.473	57.646	1	1	9¾	60	56.825	120.095	15	-	-	1½	100
198.885	67.253	2	-	3¼	70							
227.298	76.861	2	-	12¾	80 = 2 qts.							
255.710	86.469	2	1	6½	90							
284.122	96.076	3	-	—	100							

Centiliters	Fluid ounces (U.S.)	Fluid ounces (British)	British equivalent			Liters	Pints (U.S.)	Pints (British)	British equivalent			
			Qts.	Pts.	Oz.				Gals.	Qts.	Pts.	Oz.
17.744	6	6.245			6¼	0.473	1	0.833				16¾
20.701	7	7.286			7¼	0.946	2 = 1 qt.	1.665			1	13¼
23.658	8	8.327			8¼	1.419	3	2.498		1	-	10
26.615	9	9.368			9¼	1.893	4 = 2 qts.	3.331		1	1	6½
29.573	10	10.408			10½	2.366	5	4.163		2	-	3¼
32.530	11	11.449			11½	2.839	6 = 3 qts.	4.996		2	1	-
35.487	12	12.490			12½	3.312	7	5.829		2	1	16½
38.445	13	13.531			13½	3.785	8 = 1 gal.	6.661		3	-	13¼
41.402	14	14.572			14½	4.258	9	7.494		3	1	10
44.359	15	15.613			15½	4.732	10	8.327	1	-	-	6½
47.316	16 = 1 pt.	16.653			16¾	9.463	20	16.653	2	-	-	13
50.274	17	17.694			17¾	14.195	30	24.980	3	-	-	19½
53.231	18	18.735			18¾	18.927	40	33.307	4	-	1	6¼
56.188	19	19.776			19¾	23.658	50	41.634	5	-	1	12¾
59.145	20	20.817		1	¾	28.390	60	49.960	6	-	1	19¼
88.718	30	31.225		1	11¼	33.121	70	58.287	7	1	-	5¾
118.291	40	41.634	1	-	1¾	37.853	80 = 10 gals.	66.614	8	1	-	12¼
147.864	50	52.042	1	-	12	42.585	90	74.940	9	1	-	18¾
177.436	60	62.450	1	1	2½	47.316	100	83.267	10	1	1	5¼
207.009	70	72.859	1	1	12¾							
236.582	80	83.267	2	-	3¼							
266.154	90	93.676	2	-	13¾							
295.727	100	104.084	2	1	4							

V CAPACITY (*continued*)

Liters	Gallons (U.S.)	American equivalent				Gallons (British Imperial)
		Gals.	Qts.	Pts.	Oz.	
4.546	1.201	1	–	1	9¾	1
9.092	2.402	2	1	1	3½	2
13.638	3.603	3	2	–	13¼	3
18.184	4.804	4	3	–	7	4
22.730	6.005	6	–	–	¾	5
27.276	7.206	7	–	1	10¼	6
31.822	8.407	8	1	1	4	7
36.368	9.608	9	2	–	13¾	8
40.914	10.809	10	3	–	7½	9
45.460	12.010	12	–	–	1¼	10
90.919	24.019	24	–	–	2½	20
136.379	36.029	36	–	–	3¾	30
181.838	48.038	48	–	–	4¾	40
227.298	60.048	60	–	–	6¼	50
272.758	72.057	72	–	–	7¼	60
318.217	84.067	84	–	–	8½	70
363.677	96.076	96	–	–	9¾	80
409.136	108.086	108	–	–	11	90
454.596	120.095	120	–	–	12¼	100

Liters	Gallons (U.S.)	Gallons (Imperial)	British equivalent			
			Gals.	Qts.	Pts.	Oz.
3.785	1	0.833		3	–	13¼
7.571	2	1.665	1	2	1	6½
11.356	3	2.498	2	3	–	19¾
15.141	4	3.331	3	1	–	13
18.927	5	4.163	4	–	1	6
22.712	6	4.996	4	3	1	19¼
26.497	7	5.829	5	3	–	12¾
30.282	8	6.661	6	2	1	5¾
34.068	9	7.494	7	1	1	19
37.853	10	8.327	8	1	–	12¼
75.706	20	16.653	16	2	1	4½
113.559	30	24.980	24	3	1	16¾
151.412	40	33.307	33	1	–	9
189.265	50	41.634	41	2	1	1½
227.118	60	49.960	49	3	1	13½
264.971	70	58.287	58	1	–	6
302.824	80	66.614	66	2	–	18¼
340.678	90	74.940	74	3	1	10½
378.531	100	83.267	83	1	–	2¾

VI   TEMPERATURE

Centigrade degrees	Fahrenheit degrees		Centigrade degrees	Fahrenheit degrees
100.0	212.0		40.0	104.0
97.2	207.0		38.9	102.0
95.0	203.0		36.1	97.0
94.4	202.0		35.0	95.0
91.7	197.0		33.3	92.0
90.0	194.0		30.5	87.0
88.9	192.0		30.0	86.0
86.1	187.0		27.8	82.0
85.0	185.0		25.0	77.0
83.3	182.0		22.2	72.0
80.5	177.0		20.0	68.0
80.0	176.0		19.4	67.0
77.8	172.0		16.7	62.0
75.0	167.0		15.0	59.0
72.2	162.0		13.9	57.0
70.0	158.0		11.1	52.0
69.4	157.0		10.0	50.0
66.7	152.0		8.3	47.0
65.0	149.0		5.5	42.0
63.9	147.0		5.0	41.0
61.1	142.0		2.8	37.0
60.0	140.0		0.0	32.0
58.3	137.0		—2.8	27.0
55.5	132.0		—5.0	23.0
55.0	131.0		—5.5	22.0
52.8	127.0		—8.3	17.0
50.0	122.0		—10.0	14.0
47.2	117.0		—11.1	12.0
45.0	113.0		—13.9	7.0
44.4	112.0		—15.0	5.0
41.7	107.0			

APPENDIX F

Vintage Chart

No vintage chart is a sure guide to the wines rated, for great wines cannot be standardized. Wines are a product of inconstant nature and fallible man. There will be enough enjoyable bottles in any one district in any off year to make exceptions invalidating anything so dogmatic as a vintage chart. Often overlooked, nevertheless a major factor in the purchase of wines, is the proper selection of wines that are sufficiently mature for present-day consumption. Very great years are often slow in maturing, hence your consideration of whether the wines will be consumed immediately or laid away for future consumption should be a determining factor in your selections.

EXPLANATION OF RATINGS

20, 19—exceptionally great	14, 13, 12—very good	7, 6—low average
18, 17—very great	11, 10—good	5, 4—poor
16, 15—great	9, 8—fair	3, 2, 1—very poor

N.B.: Many dry white wines as well as many reds may be too old for present-day consumption. All such wines are indicated by *italic figures*. All white Bordeaux older than 1964 which are not Sauternes, Barsac, or Ste. Croix-du-Mont should be considered as possibly being maderized.

Vintage	Red Bordeaux	White Bordeaux	Red Burgundy (Côte d'Or)	White Burgundy	Red Burgundy (Beaujolais)	Rhône	Loire	Alsace	Champagne
1926	15	*14*	12	*12*	*11*	*12*	*11*	*12*	*12*
1927	*2*	*6*	*2*	*2*	*3*	*7*	*5*	*3*	*3*
1928	19.5	17	17	16	*17*	16	*15*	*15*	19
1929	19	19	19	*19*	*19*	19	*16*	*17*	18
1930	0	*0*	*4*	*4*	*4*	*9*	*6*	*4*	*4*
1931	*3*	*2*	*4*	*4*	*3*	*10*	*7*	*5*	*6*
1932	*1*	*1*	*3*	*4*	*5*	*11*	*7*	*5*	*6*
1933	10	*6*	*17*	*16*	*17*	*14*	*14*	*12*	*15*
1934	17	15	17	*16*	*17*	*16*	*15*	*16*	*15*
1935	*5*	*6*	*12*	*13*	*12*	*9*	*12*	*14*	*11*
1936	*8*	*8*	*8*	*6*	*9*	*14*	*9*	*10*	*10*
1937	15	18	15	*15*	*13*	*14*	*14*	*17*	*14*
1938	9	*8*	*14*	*13*	*10*	*13*	*9*	*10*	*12*
1939	*5*	*6*	*3*	*3*	*8*	*10*	*8*	*4*	*8*
1940	8	*9*	*9*	*9*	*8*	*9*	*8*	*11*	*8*
1941	*2*	*1*	*4*	*4*	*5*	*9*	*7*	*8*	*12*
1942	12	15	*12*	*15*	*14*	*15*	*11*	*13*	*15*
1943	14	15	*14*	*15*	*12*	*15*	*16*	*15*	*13*
1944	*11*	*9*	*4*	*5*	*7*	*9*	*7*	*5*	*9*
1945	19	19	19	*14*	*17*	*17*	*18*	*17*	*17*
1946	*8*	*7*	*12*	*9*	*10*	*15*	*10*	*10*	*11*
1947	19	18	18	*17*	*17*	16	*19*	*17*	*19*
1948	15	16	13	*10*	*10*	*8*	*10*	*12*	*14*
1949	18	18	19	*16*	*17*	17	*16*	*17*	*17*
1950	14	15	*12*	*18*	*12*	*15*	*10*	*8*	*9*
1951	*9*	*6*	*8*	*8*	*7*	*9*	*7*	*9*	*7*
1952	15	15	16	*16*	*16*	*17*	*14*	*15*	*17*
1953	19	16	15	*14*	*18*	*13*	*17*	*17*	*17*

Vintage Chart

Vintage	Red Bordeaux	White Bordeaux	Red Burgundy (Côte d'Or)	White Burgundy	Red Burgundy (Beaujolais)	Rhône	Loire	Alsace	Champagne
1954	12	9	10	11	10	16	10	11	10
1955	18	17	17	18	17	16	16	17	18
1956	12	10	10	14	9	14	12	13	12
1957	14	13	13	15	15	17	13	14	13
1958	11	13	13	17	13	16	15	16	12
1959	17	16	18	16	16	16	17	19	18
1960	13	13	8	14	10	16	14	13	14
1961	20	19	19	18	19	18	17	17	18
1962	17	16/18	15	16	16	15	16	15	16
1963	8	6	9	11	9	7	9	11	7
1964	16	10/13	16	15	17	15	15	15	16
1965	11	10	10	11	11	15	10	10	6
1966	18	19	15	16	16	17	15	14	18
1967	15	13/19	13	15	14	16	14	14	15
1968	9	7	11	6	11	10	10	11	9
1969	13	13	18.5	16	15	17	15	14	14
1970	18	17	14	16	14	15	15	14	16
1971	17	10/17	16	16	16	16	18	17	17
1972	13	11	14	11	12	12	10	12	12
1973	15.5	13	14	16	13	15	13	13	15
1974	15	13/7	14	15	13	13	14	13	13.5
1975	18.5	13/19	11	14	11	15	13	15	14
1976	17.5	15	17	15.5	19	16	16	19.5	14.5
1977	15	16/13	13	14	12	15	13	13.5	15
1978	18.5	16	18	17	17	17	16	16	16.5
1979	19	15	15.5	17	14	15	14	14	14
1980	16.5	16/18	13.5	16	12	14	13	13	13
1981	17.5	18	15	15	17	13	15	17	14
1982	19	16	16	17	13	17	15	15	16
1983	19	19.5	17	15	18	18	14	19	14
1984	15.5	16/18	16	17	15	13	15	15	13
1985	19	17	17	16	19	16	16.5	18.5	16
1986	19.5	18	16	17	18	15.5	16	16	13

NOTE: Figures for subsequent years will be obtainable on application to the publishers.

Select Bibliography

Aaron, Sam, and Beard, James. *How to Eat Better for Less Money*. New York: 1970.

Aaron, Sam, and Fadiman, Clifton. *The Joys of Wine*. New York: 1975.

Abel, Dominick. *Guide to the Wines of the United States*. New York: 1979.

Adams, Leon D. *The Wines of America*. 3d ed., rev. New York: 1985.

Allen, H. Warner. *Claret*. London: 1924.
  A Contemplation of Wine. London: 1951.
  A History of Wine. London: 1961.
  Natural Red Wines. London: 1951.
  Rum. London: 1931.
  Sherry and Port. London: 1954.
  White Wines and Cognac. 1952.
  The Wines of Portugal. London: 1963.

Ambrosi, Hans. *Wo grosse Weine Wachsen*. Munich: 1973.
  Deutscher Wein-Atlas. Bielefeld: 1973.
  Welt-Atlas des Weines. Bielefeld: 1983.

Ambrosi, Hans, and Becker, Dr. Helmut. *Der Deutsche Wein*. Munich: 1979.

Amerine, Maynard A., Berg, Harold W., and Cruess, William V. *The Technology of Wine Making*. 3d ed. Westport: 1972.

Amerine, Maynard A., and Joslyn, Maynard A. *Commercial Production of Table Wines*. Berkeley: 1940.
  Dessert Appetizers and Related Flavored Wines. Berkeley: 1964.
  Table Wines: The Technology of Their Production. Rev. ed. Berkeley, Los Angeles and London: 1970.

Amerine, Maynard A., and Roessler, Edward B. *Wines: Their Sensory Evaluation*. San Francisco: 1976.

Amerine, Maynard A., and Singleton, Vernon L. *Wine: An Introduction for Americans*. Berkeley and Los Angeles: 1978.

Anderson, Burton. *Vino: The Wines and Winemakers of Italy*. Boston: 1980.
  The Pocket Guide to Italian Wines. Rev. ed. New York: 1984.
  Guide to Italian Wines. New York: 1985.

Asher, Gerald. *On Wine*. New York: 1982.

Balzer, Robert Lawrence. *The Pleasures of Wine*. New York: 1964.
  Wines of California. New York: 1978.

Barbadillo, Manuel. *El vino de la alegría*. Jerez de la Frontera: 1951.

Barry, (Sir) Edward. *Wines of the Ancients*. London: 1775.

Barty-King, Hugh, and Massel, Anton. *Rum, Yesterday and Today*. London: 1983.

Benvegnin, Lucien Capt. Émile, and Piquet, Gustave. *Traité de vinification*. Lausanne: 1951.

Berry, Charles W. *In Search of Wine*. London: 1935.

Bert, Pierre, *In vino veritas*. Paris: 1975.

Bertall,—. *La Vigne: voyage autour des vins de France*. Paris: 1878.

Bespaloff, Alexis. *Signet Book of Wine*. New York: 1980.
  Guide to Inexpensive Wines. New York: 1973.
  The Fireside Book of Wine. New York: 1984.

Bijur, George. *Wines with Long Noses*. London: 1951.

Bode, Charles G. *Wines of Italy*. London and New York: 1956.

Bourke, Arthur. *Winecraft: The Encyclopedia of Wines and Spirits*. London: 1935.

Bradford, Sarah. *The Englishman's Wine*. London: 1969.

Bradley, Robin. *The Small Wineries of Australia*. Melbourne: 1982.

Bréjoux, Pierre. *Les Vins de Loire*. Paris: 1974.
  Les Vins de Bourgogne. Paris.

Broadbent, Michael. *The Great Vintage Wine Book*. London and New York: 1980.
  Wine Tasting. 5th ed. London and New York: 1979.
  Complete Guide to Wine Tasting and Wine Cellars. London and New York: 1984.
  The Complete Winetaster and Cellarman. London: 1982, 1984.
  Pocket Guide to Wine Tasting. London: 1982.

Brunel, Gaston. *Guide des Vignobles et des Caves du Rhône*. France: 1980.

Brunet, R. *Dictionnaire d'oenologie et de viticulture*. Paris: 1946.

Bürklin, Albert; Schultz, F. R.; von Bassermann-Jordan; von Diersburg, Roeder; and Weingarth, Otto, eds. *Verband deutscher Naturwein versteigerer*. 1953.

Butler, Frank Hedges. *Wine and the Wine Lands of the World*. London: 1926.

Capus, Joseph. *L'Évolution de la législation sur les appellations d'origine et la genèse des appellations contrôlées*. Paris: 1947.

Cardinali, Bartolomeo. *Vini d'Italia*. Bologna: 1978.

Carling, T. E. *The Complete Book of Drink*. London: 1951.
  Wine Lore. London: 1974.

Carosso, Vincent P. *The California Wine Industry, 1830–1895*. Berkeley and Los Angeles: 1951.

Carter, Youngman. *Drinking Bordeaux*. New York and London: 1966.

Carvelho, Benot de, and Correia, Lopes. *Vinhos de Nosso Pais*. Lisbon: 1978.

Casabianca, A. *Guida storica del Chianti*. Florence: 1957.

Cassagnac, Paul de. *French Wines*. Translated by Guy Knowles. London: 1930.

Chappaz, Georges. *Le Vignoble et le vin de Champagne*. Paris: 1951.

Chidgey, Graham. *Guide to the Wines of Burgundy*. London: 1977.

Christie's Wine Publications. *Christie's Wine Companion*. London: 1981.

Chroman, Nathan. *The Treasury of American Wine*. New York: 1973.

Churchill, Creighton. *The World of Wines*. New York: 1964.

Ciais, Afrien; Quittanson, Charles; and Vanhoutte, René. *La Protection des appellations d'origine des vins et eaux-de-vie et le commerce des vins*. Montpellier: 1949.

Club des Gourmets. *Guia Practica de Los Vinos de España*. Madrid: 1983.

Corato, Ricardo di. *Vini d'Italia*. Milan: 1978.

Cornelssen, F. A. *Das Buch vom deutschen Wein*. Mainz: 1954.

Croft-Cooke, Rupert. *Madeira*. London: 1961.
  Port. London: 1957.
  Sherry. London: 1955; New York: 1956.

Crosby, Everett. *The Vintage Years*. New York: 1973.

Select Bibliography

Dallas, Philip. *Italian Wines*. London: 1974.
De Bosdari, C. *Wines of the Cape*. 3d ed. Cape Town; Amsterdam: 1967.
DeGroot, Roy A. *The Wines of California*. New York: 1982.
De Kerdéland, Jean. *Historique des vins de France*. Paris: 1964.
Delamain, Robert. *Histoire de Cognac*. Paris: 1935.
Del Castillo, José, and Hallett, David R. *The Wines of Spain*. Bilbao: 1972.
Desgraves, Louis. *Bordeaux au cours des siècles*. Bordeaux: 1954.
Dettori, Renato G. *Italian Wines and Liqueurs*. Rome: 1953.
Dion, Roger. *Histoire de la vigne et du vin de France*. Paris: 1959.
Doléris, J. A. *Les Vignobles et vins de Béarn*. Pau: 1935.
Dopson, Betty, and Topolos, Michael. *Napa Valley Wine Tour*. St. Helena, Cal.: 1978.
Doutrelant, Pierre-Marie. *Les bons vins et les autres*. Paris: 1976.
Dovaz, Michel. *Le Livre du vin*. Paris: 1976.
Duijiker, Hubrecht. *The Great Wine Châteaux of Bordeaux*. Amsterdam: 1975.
Dumay, Raymond. *Guide du vin*. Paris: 1968.
Les vins de Loire et les vins du Jura. Paris: 1979.

Ediciones Castell. *Los Vinos de España*. Spain: 1983.
Editions Dussaut. *Les Grands Vins de Bordeaux*. Bordeaux: 1984.
Engel, Ferdinand. *Wirtschaftssicherung des österreichischen Weinbaus*. Vienna: 1946.
Enjalbert, Henri. *Histoire de la vigne et du vin*. Paris: 1975.
La Seignerie et le vignoble du Château Latour. Bordeaux: 1974.
Les Grands Vins de Saint-Émilion, Pomerol, Fronsac. Paris: 1983.
Ensrud, Barbara. *The Pocket Guide to Wine*. New York: 1980.
Wine with Food. New York: 1984.
Esteves Gonçalves, Francisco. *Portugal, a Wine Country*. Lisbon: 1984.
Evans, Len. *The Australia and New Zealand Complete Book of Wine*. Sydney: 1973.
Eyland, J. M. *Ma Muse en vendanges*. Montpellier: 1960.

Faes, H., ed. *Lexique viti-vinicole international: français, italien, espagnol, allemand*. Paris: 1940.
Faith, Nicholas. *The Winemasters*. London: 1978.
Château Margaux. London: 1980.
Victorian Vineyard, Château Loudenne and the Gilbeys. London: 1983.
Fegan, Patrick W. *Vineyards and Wineries of America*. Brattleboro, Vermont: 1982.
Féret, Claude. *Bordeaux et ses vins*. 13th ed. Bordeaux: 1982.
Ferré, Louis. *Traité d'oenologie bourguignonne*. Paris: 1958.
Finigan Robert. *Essentials of Wine*. New York: 1987.
Fisher, M. I. *Liqueurs: Dictionary and Survey*. London: 1959.
Foillard, David. *Le Pays de Beaujolais*. Villefranche: 1929.
Forbes, Patrick. *Champagne: The Wine, the Land and the People*. New York: 1968.
Francisque, Michel. *Histoire du commerce et de la navigation à Bordeaux*. Bordeaux: n.d.
Fried, Eunice. *Burgundy: The Country, the Wine, the People*. New York: 1987.
Frolov-Begreev, Anton M. *Ampelografia U.S.S.R.* 7 Vols. Moscow: 1946–62.

George, Rosemary. *Chablis*. London: 1984.
Guía de Los Vinos y Bodegas de España. Folio. Barcelona: 1984.
Ginestet, Bernard. *La Bouillie Bordelaise*. Paris: 1975. Côtes de Bourg, Graves, Haut Médoc, Margaux, Pauillac, Pomerol, St.-Estèphe, St.-Julien: 1984

Gold, Alec, ed. *Wines and Spirits of the World*. Coulsdon: 1972.
Goldschmidt, Eduard, ed. *Deutschlands Wienbauorte und Weinbergslagen*. 6th ed. Mainz: 1951.
González Gordon, Manuel M. *Sherry: The Noble Wine*. London: 1972.
Got, Armand. *Monbazillac*. Bordeaux: 1947.
Grossman, Harold J. *Grossman's Guide to Wines, Spirits and Beers*. Rev. ed. New York: 1980.
Gunyon, R. E. H. *The Wines of Central and Southeastern Europe*. New York: 1971.
György, Paul. *The Fine Wines of Germany and All the World's Wine Lore*. Berlin: 1965.

Halász, Zoltán. *Hungarian Wines Through the Ages*. Budapest: 1962.
Hallgarten, S. F. *Rhineland, Wineland*. London: 1951.
Alsace and Its Wine Gardens. Rev. ed. London: 1965.
Alsace, Wine Gardens, Cellars and Cuisine. London: 1978.
German Wines. London: 1976.
Hallgarten, S. F. and F. L. *The Wines and Wine Gardens of Austria*. London: 1979.
Halliday, James, and Jarratt, Ray. *The Wines and History of the Hunter Valley*. Sydney: 1979.
Hanson, Anthony. *Burgundy*. London: 1982.
Harrison, Godfrey. *Bristol Cream*. London: 1955.
Hazan, Victor. *Italian Wine*. New York: 1982.
Healey, Maurice. *Stay Me with Flagons*. London: 1963.
Hedrick, Ulysses P. *The Grapes of New York*. Albany: 1908.
Grapes and Wines from Home Vineyards. New York: 1945.
Heinen, Winifred. *Rheinpfalz: Gesamtwerk Deutscher Wein*. Essen: 1980.
Mosel, Saar, Ruwer: Gesamt Deutscher Wein. Essen: 1978.
Henderson, Alexander L. *The History of Ancient and Modern Wines*. London: 1824.
Higounet, Charles. *Histoire de l'Aquitaine*. Toulouse: 1973.
Hinkle, Richard Paul. *Central Coast Wine Book*. St. Helena, Cal.: 1980.
Hornickel, Ernst. *The Great Wines of Europe*. London: 1965.
Hyams, Edward. *Dionysos, A Social History of the Wine Vine*. London: 1965.

Ibar, Leandro. *El Libro del Vino*. Barcelona: 1982.
Isnard, Hildebert. *La Vigne en Algérie*. 2 Vols. Gap: 1951–54.
The Italian National Wine Committee and the Italian Foreign Trade Institute. *Discovering Italian Wines*. U.S.A.: 1975.

Jacquelin, Louis, and Poulain, René. *The Wines and Vineyards of France*. Translated by T. A. Layton. London and New York: 1962.
Jacques-Petit, F. *Les Appellations des vins et eaux-de-vie de France*. Angers: 1957.
James, Walter. *Wine in Australia*. Rev. ed. Melbourne: 1963.
A Word Book of Wine. London: 1961.
Jeffs, Julian. *Sherry*. London: 1961.
The Wines of Europe. London: 1971.
Johnson, Frank E. *The Professional Wine Reference*. New York: 1978.
Johnson, Hugh. *Wine*. London: 1966.
World Atlas of Wine. London: 1977; New York: 1979; 1985.
Pocket Encyclopedia of Wine. Rev. ed. London and New York: 1985.
The Atlas of German Wines. London: 1986.
Jones, Idwal. *Vines in the Sun*. New York: 1949.
Jung, Hermann. *Wein in der Kunst*. Munich: 1961.

Kaufman, William. *Champagne*. New York: 1973.
   The Traveler's Guide to the Vineyards of North America. New York: 1980.
   Pocket Encyclopedia of California Wines. San Francisco: 1982.
Keller, D. Josef, ed. *Pfalzwein Almanach*. Neustadt: 1953.
Kittel, J. B., and Breider, Hans. *Das Buch vom Frankenweine*. Würzburg: 1958.
Kraemer, Ado. *Im Lande des Bocksbeutels*. 3d ed. Würzburg: 1961.
Krug, Henri and Rémi. *L'Art du Champagne*. Paris: 1979.

Laffer, H. E. *The Wine Industry of Australia*. Adelaide: 1949.
Lafforgue, Germain. *Le Vignoble girondin*. Paris: 1947.
Lafon, René; Lafon, Jean; and Couillaud, Pierre. *Le Cognac: sa distillation*. 4th ed. Paris: 1964.
Langenbach, Alfred. *German Wines and Vines*. London: 1962.
   The Wines of Germany. London: 1951.
Larmat, Louis, ed. *Atlas de la France vinicole*. Paris: 1949.
   Vignobles et routes du vin. Paris: 1979.
   Les vins de Bourgogne. Paris: 1953.
   Les vins des Côtes du Rhone. Paris: 1943.
Latimer, Patricia. *Sonoma & Mendocino Wine Book*. St. Helena, Cal.: 1979.
Layton. T. A. *Wines of Italy*. London: 1961.
   Lebensfreude aus Rheinhessen. Mainz: 1954.
Léon-Gauthier, Pierre. *Les Clos de Bourgogne*. Beaune: 1931.
Leonhardt, George. *Das Weinbuch; Werden des Weines von der Reb bis zum Glase*. 2d ed. Leipzig: 1963.
Lichine, Alexis. *Alexis Lichine's Guide to the Wines and Vineyards of France*. Rev. ed. New York: 1979, 1982, 1984, 1986.
   Wines of France. Rev. ed. New York: 1951/1970.
Lucia, Salvatore P. *Wine as Food and Medicine*. New York and Toronto: 1954.
   A History of Wine as Therapy. Philadelphia and Montreal: 1963.
Lutz, H. F. *Viticulture and Brewing in the Ancient Orient*. Leipzig and New York: 1922.

Magistocchi, Gaudencio. *Tratado de enología adaptado a la república Argentina*. Buenos Aires: 1955.
Malvezin, F. *Histoire de la vigne et du vin en Aquitaine*. Bordeaux: 1919.
Marchou, Gaston. *Bordeaux sur la règne de la vigne*. Bordeaux: 1947.
   Le Vin de Bordeaux cet inconnu. Montpellier: 1973.
Marrison, L. W. *Wines and Spirits*. London: 1957.
Massee, William E. *Wines and Spirits, a Complete Buying Guide*. New York: 1961.
Mayne, Robert, and others. *The Great Australian Wine Book*. New South Wales: 1985.
Meinhard, Heinrich. *German Wines*. London: 1971.
Melville, John. *Guide to California Wines*. 2d ed. San Carlos, Cal.: 1960.
Mendelsohn, Oscar A. *The Earnest Drinker*. London: 1950.
   The Dictionary of Drink and Drinking. London: 1965.
Moore, Rodrigo Alvarado. *Chile, Tierra del Vino*. Santiago: 1985.
Morris, Dennis. *The French Vineyards*. London: 1958.
Mouillefert, P. *Les Vignobles et les vins de France et de l'étranger*. Paris: 1891.
Muir, Augustus, ed. *How to Choose and Enjoy Wine*. London: 1953.
Müller, Karl. *Weinbau-Lexikon für Winzer, Weinhändler, Küfer und Gastwirte*. Berlin: 1930.

Nelson, James. *Great Cheap Wines, A Poor Person's Guide*. San Francisco: 1977.

Office International de la Vigne et du Vin. *Lexique de la vigne et du vin: Français, Italiano, Español, Deutsch, Portugues, English, Ruskii*. Paris: 1963.
Olken, Charles E., Singer, Earl G., and Roby, Norman S. *The Connoisseurs' Handbook of California Wines*. New York: 1982.
Olney, Richard. *Yquem*. Switzerland: 1985.
Orizet, Louis. *Le livre du vin*. Paris: 1968.
   Vignobles et vins d'Aquitaine. Bordeaux: 1970.

Pacottet, Paul, and Guittonneau, L. *Vins de Champagne et vins mousseux*. Paris: 1930.
Parker, Robert, Jr. *Bordeaux*, New York: 1986.
Pellucci, Emanuele. *Brunello di Montalcino*. Fiesoli: 1981.
Penin, José. *Manual de Vinos Españoles*. Madrid: 1981.
   Manual de los Vinos de Rioja. Madrid: 1982.
Penning-Rowsell, Edmund. *The Wines of Bordeaux*. Rev. ed. London: 1979.
Peppercorn, David. *Bordeaux*. London: 1982.
   Pocket Guide to the Wines of Bordeaux. London: 1986.
Peppercorn, David, and Cooper, Brian. *Drinking Wine*. London and New York: 1979.
Perold, A. I. *A Treatise on Viticulture*. London: 1927.
Pestel, H. *Les vins et eaux-de-Vie à appellations d'origine contrôlées en France*. Mâcon: 1959.
Peynaud, Émile. *Le goût du vin*. Paris: 1980.
   Oenologie pratique, connaissance et travail du vin. Paris: 1971 and 1981.
Pijassou, René. *Le Médoc*. Paris: 1980.
Ponsot, Maurice. *Vins, alcools et spiritueux de France*. 3d ed. Paris: 1949.
Postgate, Raymond. *An Alphabet of Choosing and Serving Wine*. London: 1955.
   The Plain Man's Guide to Wine. London: 1951.
   Portuguese Wine. London: 1969.
Poupon, Pierre, and Forgeot, Pierre. *Les Vins de Bourgogne*. Rev. ed. Paris: 1977.
   Quelques Aspects du problème viti-vinicole luxembourgeois. A pamphlet. Luxembourg: 1956.
Price, Pamela V., and Seldon, Philip, eds. *The Great Wine Châteaux of Bordeaux*. New York: 1975.

Rainbird, George. *Sherry and the Wines of Spain*. London: 1966.
Ray, Cyril. *The Wines of Italy*. Rev. ed. London and New York: 1979.
   Lafite. New York: 1969.
   Complete Imbibers. London: 1952–64.
   Mouton-Rothschild. Rev. ed. London: 1980.
   Robert Mondavi of the Napa Valley. California: 1984.
Read, Jan. *The Wines of Spain and Portugal*. London: 1977.
   Guide to the Wines of Spain and Portugal. London: 1978.
   The Wines of Portugal. London: 1982.
   The Wines of Spain. London: 1982.
   Pocket Guide to Spanish Wines. London: 1983.
Redding, Cyrus. *A History and Description of Modern Wines*. London: 1833.
   French Wines and Vineyards. London: 1860.
Rendu, Victor. *Ampélographie française*. Paris: 1857.
Renouil, Yves, and de Traversay, Paul. *Dictionnaire du vin*. Bordeaux: 1962.
   La Revue du Vin de France. Paris.
Ribéreau-Gayon, Jean, and Peynaud, Émile. *Traité d'oenologie*. 2 Vols. Paris: 1960.
   Sciences et techniques de la vigne. 2 Vols. Paris: 1971.
Robb, J. Marshall. *Scotch Whisky*. London, Edinburgh, and New York: 1950.

Rodier, Camille. *Le Vin de Bourgogne*. 3d ed. Dijon: 1948.
    Wine Lore. Dijon: 1931.
Roncarati, Bruno. *D.O.C. The New Image for Italian Wines.*
    London: 1971.
    Viva Vino, DOC Wines of Italy. London: 1976.
Roudie, Philippe. *Le Vignoble bordelais*. Toulouse: 1973.
Roupnel, Gaston. *La Bourgogne*. Paris: 1946.
Rozet, Georges. *La Bourgogne, tastevin au main*. Paris: 1949.
Rudd, Hugh R. *Hocks and Moselles*. Constable's Wine Library;
    London: 1935.

Saintsbury, George. *Notes on a Cellar-Book*. London: 1920,
    1963; New York: 1933.
Samalens, Jean and Georges. *Armagnac*. London: 1980.
Sandeman, Sons & Company, Ltd., George G. *Port and
    Sherry*. London: 1955.
Saunders, Peter. *A Guide to New Zealand Wine*. Auckland:
    1982.
Schoenman, Theodore, ed. *Father of California Wine: Agoston
    Haraszthy*. Santa Barbara, Cal.: 1979.
Schoonmaker, Frank. *Encyclopedia of Wine*. Rev. ed. New
    York: 1980.
    The Wines of Germany. Rev. ed. New York: 1966.
Schoonmaker, Frank, and Marvel, Tom. *American Wines*. New
    York: 1941.
    The Complete Wine Book. New York: 1934; London: 1935.
Scott, J. M. *Vineyards of France*. London: 1950.
Seely, James, *Great Bordeaux Wines*, London: 1986.
Seltman, Charles. *Wine in the Ancient World*. London: 1957.
Shand, P. Morton. *A Book of French Wines*. London: 1960.
    A Book of Other Wines than French. London: 1929.
Sichel, Peter. *Frank Schoonmaker's Classic: The Wines of Ger-
    many*. New York: 1980.
Sichel, Peter, and Ley, Judy. *Which Wine?* New York: 1977.
Simon, André L. *Champagne*. London and New York: 1962.
    The Commonsense of Wine. London: 1966.
    Concise Encyclopaedia of Gastronomy, Section VIII. London:
    1946.
    A Dictionary of Wines, Spirits, and Liqueurs. London: 1958.
    Know Your Wines. London: 1956.
    A Wine Primer. London: 1946.
    The Wines of the World. London: 1949.
Simon, André L., and Hallgarten, S. F. *The Great Wines of
    Germany*. London and New York: 1963.
Simon & Schuster. *Pocket Guide to Italian Wines*. London:
    1982.
Spurrier, Stephen. *French Fine Wines*. London: 1984.
Stein, Gottfried. *Reise durch die deutschen Weingärten*. Munich:
    1957.
Street, Julian L. *Wines*. 3d ed. New York: 1961.
Sutcliffe, Serena. *André Simon's Wines of the World*. 2d ed.
    London, New York: 1981.
    Pocket Guide to the Wines of Burgundy. New York: 1986.

Thompson, Robert, ed. *California Wine*. Menlo Park: 1973.
Thorpy, Frank T. *Wine in New Zealand*. Auckland: 1971.
Thudichum, John L. W., and Dupré, August. *A Treatise on the
    Origin, Nature and Varieties of Wine*. London and New
    York: 1872.
    Time-Life Foods of the World: Wines and Spirits. New York:
    1968.
Todd, W. J. *Port*. London: 1926.
    Tokay-Hegyalia. Pest: 1867.
Torres, Miguel A. *Wines and Vineyards of Spain*. San Francisco:
    1982.
    Vino Español, un incierto futuro. Barcelona: 1978.
    Los Vinos de España. Barcelona: 1983.
Tovey, Charles. *Wine and Wine Countries*. London: 1862.
Tucker, T. G. *Life in Ancient Athens*. London: 1912.

Union Générale de syndicats pour la Défense des Grands
    Vins de Bourgogne. *Décrets définissant les vins à appellation
    d'origine contrôlée de la région de Bourgogne*. Nuits-Saint-
    Georges: 1944.

Valente-Perfeito, J. C. *Let's Talk about Port*. Oporto: 1948.
Veronelli, Luigi. *I Vini d'Italia*. London: 1964.
Viala, Pierre, and Vermorel, Victor. *Traité général de viticul-
    ture*. 7 Vols. Paris: 1901–1910.

Wagner, Philip M. *American Wines and Wine-Making*. New
    York: 1956.
    A Wine-Grower's Guide. Rev. ed. New York: 1965.
Wasserman, Sheldon. *The Wines of Italy—A Consumer's Guide*.
    New York: 1976.
    The Wines of the Côtes du Rhône. New York: 1977.
Waugh, Alec. *In Praise of Wine*. London: 1959.
Waugh, Harry. *Harry Waugh's Wine Diary*. 9 Vols. London:
    1975–1981.
Weeks, C. C. *Modern Science and Alcoholic Beverages*. Manches-
    ter: 1921.
Weiss, Harry B. *The History of Applejack or Apple Brandy in
    New Jersey from Colonial Times to the Present*. Trenton:
    1954.
Wilkinson, P. W. *First Steps in Ampelography*. Sydney: 1900.
    Nomenclature of Australian Wines. Sydney: 1919.
Wilson, Rev. A. M. *Wines of the Bible*. London: 1877.
    A Brief Discourse on Wines. London: 1861.
Wine and Spirit Trade Record. *Clarets and Sauternes*. London:
    1920.
Winkler, Albert J. *General Viticulture*.
Winroth, Jon. *Wine as You Like it*. Neuilly, France: 1981.

Yoxall, Harry W. *The Wines of Burgundy*. London and New
    York: 1979.

Zraly, Kevin. *Complete Wine Course*. New York: 1985.

Acknowledgments

Joachim Cálem, Oporto.

Colin Campbell, of Cognac.

Inspector Canal, of the Institut National des Appellations d'Origine des Vins et Eaux-de-Vie, Armagnac.

Dorothy Cann, French Culinary Institute, New York.

R. E. Dejean de Castillo, Argentine Embassy, London.

Lucio Caputo, Italian Wine and Food Institute, New York.

Manuel Casanueva, Chilean Embassy, Paris.

Mario Castagna, Italian Trade Commission, New York.

Dr. J. Cavadias, of the Royal Greek Embassy, Paris, Delegate to the Office International du Vin.

André Cazes, Mayor of Pauillac.

Jean-Michel Cazes, Château Lynch-Bages, Pauillac.

Mlle Chabert, former President of the Cave Coopérative, Fleurie.

C. Chaillot, I.N.A.O., Paris.

The late Georges S. Chappaz, of the Institut National des Appellations d'Origine des Vins et Eaux-de-Vie, Paris.

Pierre Chauveau, of Cognac.

Chérif Chikhi, Algerian Embassy, Washington, D.C.

Santiago Coello, Consejo Regulador, Rioja.

Jim Connell, Healdsburg, California.

Aldo Contemo, Monteforte d'Alba, Piedmont.

H. K. H. Cook, Australian Government Trade Commission, New York.

Henri Coquillaud, Director, Bureau National Interprofessionel du Cognac.

Darryl Corti, of Sacramento, California.

Philippe Cottin, of Pauillac.

Pierre Couillaud, of the Viticultural Station, Cognac.

Dr. P. Csepregi, Budapest.

F. Jiménez Cuende, of Madrid.

The late Prof. Dalmasso, of the University of Turin, and Vice-President of the International Wine Office.

Paul Damiens, Technical Adviser of the I.N.A.O.

N. Danilatos, Wine Institute, Ministry of Agriculture, Athens.

Virgilio Augusto Dantas, of Lisbon.

J. Dargent, of the Comité Interprofessionel du Vin de Champagne, Épernay.

C. V. Dayns, New Zealand House, London.

Jean Delamain, of Jarnac.

Jean Delmas, of Château Haut-Brion.

Marie-José Deshayes, O.I.V., Paris.

G. Despagne, President of Syndicat Viticole de Montagne St. Emilion.

Leonard A. T. Dennis, of London.

Deutsche Weinsiegel-Gesellschaft, Frankfurt.

Jorge D. Dias, Casa de Portugal, London.

Eduardo A. Diaz Peralta, Mendoza, Argentina.

Mauricio González Diez, of Jerez.

J. Dolezal, Pilsner Urquell Co. Ltd., London.

Beltrán Domecq, formerly of Williams & Humbert, Jerez de la Frontera.

José Ignacio Domecq, of Pedro Domecq, Jerez de la Frontera.

Manuel Domecq, of Pedro Domecq, Jerez de la Frontera.

Matthew W. Downer, Public and Trade Relations Department, Brown-Forman Distillers Corporation, Louisville, Kentucky.

Georges Duboeuf, of Romanèche-Thorins.

Jean Ducamin, Secretary General, Union des Coopératives de Bas-Armagnac, Réans.

Nico van Duyvenbode, Ottawa.

Clay Easterly, Tennessee Viticultural and Oenological Society.

M. Eltaief, Tunis.

The late Jakob Graf zu Eltz, of Eltville.

Mogador Empson, of London.

Neil Empson, Milano, Italy.

André Enders, Director of C.I.V.C., Épernay.

The late René Engel, of Vosne-Romanée.

Barbara Ensrud, New York.

M. Espinosa, Embassy of Mexico, Paris.

David Estrada, of Los Gatos, California.

H. B. Estrada, President, Bacardi Imports, Inc., New York.

R. L. Exshaw, of John Jameson and Son, Ltd., Dublin.

Carlos Falco, Marques de Griñon, Madrid.

Richard Figiel, *Eastern Grape Growers & Winery News,* Watkins Glen, New York.

Robert C. Finigan, Editor, *Finigan's Private Guide to Wines.* New York.

R. W. Finlayson, President, Toronto Wine and Food Society.

Don A. Fisher, Distilled Spirits Institute, New York.

Sir Guy Fison, London.

Peter Fleck, of Zuider-Paarl, South Africa.

G. S. Foulds, Australian Wine Centre, London.

Georges Fouquier, of Bordeaux.

M. Franchini-Netto, Brazilian Embassy, London.

H. A. S. Fraser, Association of Canadian Distillers, Montreal.

M. Friedas, Office International de la Vigne et du Vin, Paris.

The late Ed Friedrich, Chateau Elan, Braselton, Georgia.

Conte Gelasio Gaetani Lovatelli, of Montalcino.

Angelo Gaja, Barbaresco, Piedmont.

James Gallander, Ohio Research and Development Center.

Edoardo Gancia, Director of Gancia and Company, Canelli.

José Ramón García de Angulo, President of the Consejo Regulador, Jerez.

Jean Gardere, Rhum Barbancourt, Haiti.

Jean-Paul Gardère, of Château Latour.

Fernando Garcia-Delgado, Consejo Regulador, Jerez dela Frontera.

Prof. Pier G. Garoglio, of the Istituto di Industrie Agrarie, University of Florence.

William Garrett, Editor, *National Geographic,* Washington.

Anna Gariazzo, Milano, Italy.

Dr. E. Ercole Garrone, Director of the Consorzio, Asti.

Philippe Gasqueton, manager, Château Calon-Ségur, Saint-Estèphe.

German Agricultural Society (D.L.G.), Frankfurt.

Ing. C. Gavaneanu, Rumanian Embassy, Paris.

Bernard Ginestet, of Margaux.

Pierre Ginestet, former co-proprietor of Château Margaux, Margaux.

Jean Godet, of La Rochelle.

Pierre Goffre-Viaud, Controller of the I.N.A.O.

Craig Goldwyn, International Wine Review, Ithaca, N.Y.

Manuel González Gordon, of Jerez.

The late Henri Gouges, President of the Burgundy Growers Association, Nuits-Saint-Georges.

G. Maxwell A. Graham, of Oporto.

John A. Grant, of Dumbarton, Scotland.

A. O. Grass, Canadian Wine Institute, Ontario.

The late Count Matuschka V. Greiffenclau, of Schloss Voll-

Acknowledgments

A work of this scope could not have become a reality without the knowledgeable and willing assistance of persons, institutions, and associations identified in many ways with the wines and spirits of the world.

First, I want to thank my assistants for their continued helpfulness: in particular, the Hon. Julian Grenfell, Peter C. Handler, Philip I. Togni, Anthony Wood, Harold Jurgenson, Paul Zuckerman, Parker R. Reis, Katie Philson, Martin Sinkoff, Professor Lucio P. Ruotola, Susanne McEvoy, Catherine Currie, Jane Kettlewell, and Elizabeth Lafargue.

To those listed below and to all the other unnamed people who furnished indispensable data and information through pamphlets and brochures I am deeply grateful.

Introductory Chapters

Dr. Maynard A. Amerine, Department of Viticulture and Enology, University of California, Davis, California.

The late James A. Beard, of New York, author of *The Fireside Cookbook* and *Fish Cookery.*

Dr. Herbert L. Gould, of New York.

Dr. Charles P. Mathé, of San Francisco, Chairman of Board of Governors, The Society of Medical Friends of Wine.

Prof. E. Peynaud, formerly of the Station Oenologique de Bordeaux.

The late Senator Professor Georges Portmann, of Bordeaux.

General

Sam Aaron, of Sherry-Lehmann, New York.

Leon Adams, of Sausalito.

Mr. Agostini, I.N.A.O., Paris.

Agricultural Ministry, Vienna.

Rafael Aguilar, Spanish Embassy Commercial Office.

José Duarte Amaral, President, Junta Nacional do Vinho, Lisbon.

Dr. Hans Ambrosi, Eltville, West Germany.

E. T. Andersen, of Vineland Station, Ontario.

Abdelâziz Arifi, Morocco.

Patricia Armstrong, Edinburgh.

Richard L. Arrowood, of Sonoma, California.

Luigi Artusio, of the Stabilimento Fontanafredda.

Gerald Asher, San Francisco.

Prof. Dr. Á. Ásvány, Budapest.

Australian Wine Board.

Raul Azparren, President, Camara de Comercio del Estado Lara, Barquisimeto.

Jeff Baker, of Davis, California.

Fernando Augusto Bandeira, of the Casa do Douro, Regua.

Manuel Barbadillo, of Sanlúcar de Barrameda.

Catherine Bardy, French Embassy, New York.

Mr. & Mrs. J. G. Barrett, of Felsted, Essex.

Hayim S. Bar-Shai, of Jerusalem.

Joseph Bartolo, Embassy of Malta, Paris.

Dr. Friedrich von Bassermann-Jordan, of Deidesheim.

Joseph Baum, of New York.

Ed Beard, of St. Helena, California.

Comte Hubert de Beaumont, formerly of Château Pauillac.

The late Right Honourable Joseph Bech, former Prin ister, Grand Duchy of Luxembourg.

Richard O. Beeker, Northminster Winery, Wilm Delaware.

Ambassador Jean Beliard, of Paris.

Lennart Berenmark, of the Company Aktiebolaget Vi tcentralen, Stockholm.

Paul Bergweiler, of Bernkastel-Kues.

Cavalier Guglielmo Bertani, of Verona.

Alexis Bespaloff, of New York.

G. Biehler, of Málaga.

Jochen G. Bielefeld, Deutsche Wein-Information, M

Max Bilan, Union of Chambers of Commerce and In Ankara.

H. Blechner, Austrian Embassy, London.

Tansuğ Bleda, Turkish Delegation to the O.E.C.D.,

Anthony Dias Blue, San Francisco.

R. E. Boillot, of Volnay.

D. I. Bonarjee, High Commission of India, London.

G.L. Bond, English Vineyards Association Ltd., Lon

André Bonin, Fédération Internationale des Confréri chiques, Paris.

E. Bonvin, Swiss Growers' Association, London.

The late Sr. Bosch, President, Compañía Ron Bacardi Santiago de Cuba.

P. J. Botha, of Zuider-Paarl, South Africa.

Julian Boyd, of Princeton, New Jersey.

Antonio S. Braga, Portuguese Trade Commission, York.

Pierre Bréjoux, formerly of the I.N.A.O., Paris.

J. Michael Broadbent, M.W. London.

Toni Bromser, Diplom Weinbauinspektor, Staatswe lerei, of Kloster-Eberbach.

The late Ambassador David Bruce, of New York Cit Peking, China.

Bernard Brun, Bureau Balaresque, Bordeaux.

Michael Buller, New York.

The late Dr. A. Bürklin-Wolf, of Wachenheim, Vice-I dent of the German Wine Association.

W. D. Burnet, Distillers' Co. Ltd., Edinburgh.

W. Bret Byrd, Byrd Vineyards, Myersville, Maryland.

rads, former President of the German Wine Growers' Association.

The late Franz Greis, of Bernkastel-Kues.

The late Lord Grenfell, of London.

Louis Gros and Sons, of Vosne-Romanée.

The late Lester Gruber, of Detroit.

Herman Guntrum, of Weingut Louis Guntrum, Nierstein.

R. E. H. Gunyon, of Sandwich, Kent.

Carl Haessler, Pennsylvania State University, North East, Pennsylvania.

Susan Hall, Powys, Wales.

Bernard Haramboure, of Pauillac.

A. J. Hasslacher, M.C., Madeira Association, London.

J. Hastings-Trew, formerly of the Cyprus Viticultural Board, London.

Thomas Heeter, of Château Nairac, in Sauternes.

C. P. Hegwood, Jr., Mississippi State University.

Maurice Hennessy, of Cognac.

Dr. Eva Herpay, Budapest.

Bernard Hine, of Jarnac.

The late François Hine, of Jarnac.

Robert Hine, of Jarnac.

P. Höhl, of the Section de la Viticulture et de l'Économie vinicole, Division de l'Agriculture, Berne.

J. H. Hopkins, John Jameson & Son, Ltd., Dublin.

G. W. B. Hostetter, of Niagara Falls, Ontario.

Gordon S. Howell, Jr., Michigan State University, East Lansing.

Jean Hugel, of Riquewihr, Alsace.

Dot. Augusto Ippoliti, of Florence.

Dr. Lorenzetto B. R. Luigi Ispettore, of the Consorzio of Chianti, Florence.

Carlos García Izquierdo, Instituto Nacional de Denominaciones de Origen, Madrid.

Michel Jaboulet-Vercherre, of Pommard.

Julius L. Jacobs, of San Francisco.

Pierre Janneau, of Condom.

Japan Winery Association, Tokyo.

Douglas Jooste, Deputy Chairman, J. Sedgwick & Co. Ltd., Cape Town, S. Africa.

Prue Judd, British Embassy, Paris.

Peter Jurgens, former President, Almadén Vineyards, San Francisco.

The Honorable Kenneth Keating, U.S. Embassy, Tel Aviv.

The late Alfred A. Knopf, of New York.

Charles K. Knox, Minnesota Grape Growers Association, St. Paul.

C. Kok, Stellenbosch, South Africa.

Professor Kosinsky, Professor of Viticulture, University of Agriculture, Budapest.

E. Kovalčícová, of Bratislava, Czechoslovakia.

Paul C. Kovi.

Edouard Kressmann, of Bordeaux.

The late René Kuehn, of Ammerschwihr.

Henry Lacoste.

John W. Laird, of New York.

Cathy Laloubère, of Bordeaux.

Douglas Lamb, of Sydney, Australia.

René Lambert, Bordeaux.

Harry Lanser, Connecticut Grape Growers Association.

Don Antonio Larrea, Chief of the Viticultural Station at Haro, Rioja.

R. de Treville Lawrence, Sr., The Plains, Virginia.

Daniel Lawton, of Bordeaux.

Hugues Lawton, of Bordeaux.

Jerome J. Lehrer, Swiss Wine Bureau, New York.

The late Baron LeRoy de Boiseaumarié, of Châteauneuf-du-Pape, President of the Institut National des Appellations d'Origine des Vins et Eaux-de-Vie.

Raymond LeSauvage, Bordeaux.

Henri Levèque, wine-broker, Podensac, Gironde.

Juan Lewis, Research Assistant, Beverage Testing Institute, Ithaca, New York.

José Joaquim da Costa Lima, former Director of the Port Wine Institute, Oporto.

O. Lindo, J. Wray & Nephew, Ltd., Kingston, Jamaica.

Brett T. Lineham, New Zealand Trade Commission, New York City.

The late Madame Edmond Loubat, of Château Pétrus, Pomerol.

Mr. Luciano, Italian Embassy, Paris.

Jean-Pierre Lucquiaud.

Mlle Gesa Lundemann, of Madrid.

Comte Alexandre de Lur-Saluces, of Château d'Yquem, Sauternes.

Alexander McNally, of New York and Connecticut.

M. Maby.

John Marshall, Minnesota Grape Growers Association, Lake City.

Michel Firino Martell, of Cognac.

Henri Martin, former President, Comité Interprofessionel des Vins de Bordeaux, and Mayor of Saint-Julien.

Gil Pires Martins, Vice-President, Junta Nacional do Vinho, Lisbon.

Camilo Martins de Oliveira, National Director, Portuguese Trade Commission, New York.

J. P. Mas, of the I.N.A.O. in Bordeaux and Angers.

Diana Masieri, of New York City.

Egon Mauer, manager of the Langwerth von Simmern Estate, Eltville.

Fred May, of London.

Roberto Mazzi, Negrar, Veneto.

Abel Médard, Director, Comité Interprofessionel du Vin de Champagne, Épernay.

D. Homen de Mello, of Lisbon.

E. Menia, O.N.C.V., Algiers.

Pierre Meslier, régisseur of Château d'Yquem, Sauternes.

Prince P. von Metternich, of Schloss Johannisberg.

Dr. Franz Werner Michel, Deutsches Weininstitut, Mainz.

Mark Miller, Benmarl Wine Co., Marlboro, New York.

Wallace Milroy, London.

J. William Moffett, Association of American Vintners, Watkins Glen, New York.

Robert Mondavi, of Napa, California.

The late Duc Pierre de Montesquiou-Fezensac, Château de Marsan, Auch.

Renato Mora, Chilean Consulate, New York.

John Mortenson, University of Florida, Leesburg, Florida.

Christian Moueix, of Libourne.

Jean-Pierre Moueix, of Libourne.

Margaret Mountford, Australian Wine and Brandy Corporation, Adelaide.

Hamilton Narby, Château Guiraud, Sauternes.

Dr. Antonio Niederbacher, of the Unione Italiana Vini, Milan.

Robert Niederman, Ica, Peru.

Acknowledgments

Milos Nikolic, Yugoslav Information Center, New York.
Peter Nomikos, Santorini and London.

Dr. Giorgio Odero, proprietor, Frecciarosso Vineyards, Casteggio.
President de Oliveira, of the Junta Nacional do Vinho, Lisbon.
Julio Saro Diez Ordonez, Instituto Nacional de Denominaciones de Origen, Madrid.

Raymond-Julien Pagès, President, Fédération d'Auvergne des Vins et Spiritueux, Clermont-Ferrand.
José de Paiva, Trade Commission of Portugal, Paris.
H. F. M. Palmer, Secretary, Australian Wine Board, Adelaide.
M. Paran, Israeli Embassy, London.
Andrés de Blas Pardilla, of Madrid.
Anne-Marie Pargade, of Bordeaux.
Colin Parnel, Publisher, *Decanter* magazine.
Frank R. Passanante, Australian Trade Commission, New York.
David Peppercorn, M.W. London.
Pierre Perromat, President of the I.N.A.O., Paris.
Scott Phillips, Wiederkehr Wine Cellars, Arkansas.
Sp. Phylaktis, Cyprus High Commission, London.
Jacques Pomerleau, Canadian Embassy, Paris.
Dr. Robert Pool, New York State Agricultural Station, Geneva, New York.
Bruno Prats, President of the Committee of Classified Growths and owner of Château Cos d'Estournel, Saint-Estèphe.
Frank Prial, New York.
Jimmie Pridmore, Clemson University, York, South Carolina.
R. Protin, Director, Office International du Vin, Paris.
Manfred Prüm, of Wehlen.
The late Sebastian Prüm, of the Johann Josef Prüm Estate, Wehlen.

Charles Quittanson, former Inspector of Fraud, Institut National des Appellations d'Origine des Vins et Eaux-de-Vie, Dijon.

Renato Ratti, La Morra, Piedmont.
Jean de Premio Real, of Mexico City.
Axel du Réau, C.I.V.C., Épernay.
H. Parks Redwine, Atlanta, Georgia.
Joachim Ress, of Winkel.
Theodor Rettinger, and son, of Wachenheim.
Peter Reynier, of J. B. Reynier, London.
Bettino Ricasoli, of Florence.
Marie-Christina Rizzardi, Bardolino, Veneto.
Bertrand de Rivoyre, Ambares and Bordeaux.
J. Bernard Robb, of the Virginia Alcoholic Beverage Control Board, Richmond, Virginia.
Gaspar Roca, Puerto Rico.
Felicia Rogan, Oakencroft Winery, Charlottesville, Virginia.
Dr. Bruno Roncarati, of London.
Jaroslav Rosa, Czechoslovakia.
Baron Philippe de Rothschild.
P. Rouvinet, Federal Agricultural Office, Bern, Switzerland.
Professor Lucio P. Ruotola, of Stanford University.

Brian St. Pierre, Wine Institute, San Francisco.
Tadashi Sakuda, Suntory, Ltd., Osaka.
Francisco Salamero, of Rioja.

The late Maj. General Guy Salisbury-Jones, Hambledon, Hampshire, England.
The late Joseph Salzmann, of Kaysersberg.
Jean Samalens, of Laujuzan.
Catrine Sandison, London.
Manuel Santolalla Lacalle, Consejo Regulador, Montilla-Moriles.
Étienne Sauzet, of Puligny-Montrachet.
Noël Sauzet, of Jarnac.
Jerry Schever, Remich, Luxembourg.
D. V. Schiazzano, Italian Chamber of Commerce, London.
Elizabeth Schumann, of Bordeaux and London.
Elizabeth Schwartz, International Wine Review, Ithaca, N.Y.
Guy Schyler, of Château Lafite, Pauillac.
M. D. L. Scott, Vice-President, Public Relations Division, Heublein, Inc., Hartford, Connecticut.
R. I. C. Scott-Hayward, Johannesburg.
Tom Seabrook, W. & J. Seabrook, Melbourne.
James E. Seewald, Colorado Mountain Vineyards, Palisade.
Maurice Seignour, President of the Côtes du Rhône Brokers Association, Vacqueyras.
Philip Seldon, *Vintage* Magazine, New York.
The late Allan H. Sichel, Bordeaux and London.
Peter Allan Sichel, of Cantenac.
Peter M. F. Sichel, of New York City.
Freiherr Langwerth von Simmern, of Eltville.
Werner Sitzmann, of Málaga.
S. Sklar, of London.
Archie Smith, Meredyth Vineyards, Middleburg, Virginia.
Evangelos Spanidis, Greek Embassy, Paris.
Prof. Dr. Steinberg, Director, Viticultural School and Research Station, Geisenheim.
Jane Stockwood, of London.
Eric Stonyer, New Zealand Embassy, Paris.
Serena Sutcliffe, M.W. London.
James Symington, Oporto.
Ing. Miroslav Synak, Bratislava, Czechoslovakia.

Claude Taittinger, of Reims.
Pierre Tari, Union des Grands Crus, Bordeaux.
André Tchelistcheff, of Napa, California.
Dmitri Tchelistcheff, Bodegas de Santo Tomás, Ensenada.
Jacques Théo, Bordeaux; former President of C.I.V.B., Bordeaux.
H. Gregory Thomas, former Grand Master, Commanderie de Bordeaux, New York.
Dr. K. S. Tiwari, Directorate General of Technical Development, New Delhi.
Georgi Toromanov, Sofia, Bulgaria.
Miguel Torres, Barcelona, Spain.
Byron G. Tosi, of New York.
Louis Trapet, of Gevrey-Chambertin.
John and Janet Trefethen, of Rutherford, California.

H. Vella, of Pauillac.
Jean Vermorel, of Vaux-en-Beaujolais.
George Vierra, of Napa, California.

Philip Wagner, proprietor, Boordy Vineyard, Riderwood, Maryland.
Robert Wakeman, Research Assistant, Beverage Testing Institute, Ithaca, New York.
D. D. Ward, Managing Director, Mount Gay Distilleries Ltd., Barbados.
Jack L. Ward, Horam Manor, Sussex.

728

Elizabeth Watts, Australian Wine and Brandy Corporation, Sydney.

Harry H. Waugh, former Director, John Harvey and Sons, Ltd., Bristol and London, and director of Château Latour, Pauillac.

Hildegard Weber, Deutsches Weininstitut, Mainz.

The late H. Seymour Weller, Château Haut-Brion, Pessac.

Jan Wells, of San Francisco.

Odile Weltert, of New York and Lyon.

The late William Widmer, Widmer's Wine Cellars, Naples, New York.

Al Wiederkehr, Wiederkehr Wine Cellars, Altus, Arkansas.

Warren Winiarski, of Napa, California.

Prof. Albert J. Winkler, of the College of Agriculture, University of California, Davis, California.

Tom Young, Stonecrop Vineyards, Stonington, Connecticut.

V. Zanko, of the Poduzeče Industrijskih Vinarija, Zagreb.

Bruce Zoecklein, Oenologist, University of Missouri, Columbia.

Diego Zorrilla de San Martin, Ministre, Uruguayan Embassy, Paris.

Index

In place names beginning with the word Château, abbreviated Ch., the abbreviation is disregarded in alphabetizing; thus Ch. Margaux will be found under Margaux. Alphabetization is word by word; a short word precedes a longer one beginning with the same letters. Prepositions and conjunctions within a name are not alphabetized. For example, entries appear in this order: Clos du Roi, Clos Saint-Pierre, Clos du Verger, Clos de Vougeot, Closeau. When an item has its own entry in the alphabetical text the page number for this entry precedes all other page references.

ABBREVIATIONS:

Fr. = French	Ch., Chx = Château, Châteaux
Germ. = German	comm. = commune
Gk = Greek	dept. = department
Hung. = Hungarian	dist. = district
Ital. = Italian	prov. = province
Portug. = Portuguese	vd = vineyard
Sp. = Spanish	

Index

Index

734

Index

Index

Index

Index

Eudemis, grape moth, 231, 39
Eugenia, ancient Roman grape, 185
Eumelan, American grape, 231
Eussenheim, Franconia, 678
Euvites, sub-genus, 31, 72
Euxinograd, Bulgaria, 135
Ch. l'Évangile, Pomerol, 231, 127, 390
Evans and Tate, vd W. Australia, 93
Evelita, Portugal, 401
Evelyn, John, 268
Evenos, comm. Provence, 407
Ewig Leben, Grosslage, Franconia, 678
excise tax, 231
excoriose, vine disease, 231, 38
exports of wine, by countries, table, 231
Extra, brandy type, 85
extra sec (Fr.), extra dry, 231, 170
Extremadura, W. Spain, 481
Eylaud, Max, studies of alcohol, 28
Eyrie Vineyards, Oregon, 577–78
Ezerjó, Hung. grape and wine, 231, 274, 275; in Yugoslavia, 516

F

Faberrebe, hybrid grape, 423
Facelli, Louis, Winery, Idaho, 561
Fachbach, Mittelrhein, 680
Faconnières, Les, vd Côte de Nuits, 343
Factory House (Feitoria Inglesa), Oporto, 232, 397
Fagon, physician to Louis XIV, 137, 404
Fahr, Franconia, 678
Fahrenheit temperature, conversion to Centigrade and Réaumur, 496, table, 718
faible (Fr.), weak brandy in Cognac manufacture, 195
Faisca, Portugal, 402
Falanghino, Ital. grape, 147
Falernian, ancient Roman wine, 147, 186, 187, 188, 232
Falerno, Campania, 232, 147, 285
Falernum, W. Indian flavoring syrup, 232
Falkenberg, vd Bernkastel, 348
Falkenberg, vd Rheinhessen, 426
Falkenstein, Lower Austria, 95
Fall Creek Vineyards, Texas, 581
Falset, Catalonia, 480
fan leaf (infectious degeneration, *court noué*), vine disease, 232, 38, 213, 341; phylloxera related to, 38, 383
Far Niente Winery, Napa, California, 534
Fara (D.O.C.), Piedmont, 232, 387
Faranah, grape, in Algeria, 63
Farfelu Vineyard, Virginia, 582
Fargues, comm. Sauternes, 459, 460, 461
Faro, Sicily, 285, 470
Fass (Germ.), cask, 232
Fassle (Germ.), drinking vessel, 232
fat wines, 232
fatty degeneration *(graisse)*, disorder of wine, 53, 257
Faugères, Hérault, 210
Ch. Faurie-de-Souchard, Saint-Émilion, 631
Faverolles, Champagne, 165
Faye d'Anjou, comm. Anjou, 232, 74
Féchy, Vaud, 490
Feder, Ben, owner of Clinton Vineyards, 574
federweisser (feather white), Germ. term for new wine, 232
fehér bór (Hung.), white wine, 232
Fehér Szagos, grape, in California, 520
Feilbingert, Nahe, 688
feints, leavings in whisky distillation, 232
Feldbach, Styria, 95
Feldberg, Baden, 674
Fell, Bernkastel, 681
Fellbach, Württemberg, 699
Fellerich, Obermosel, 682
Felsenberg, Nahe, 363
Felseneck, vd Nahe, 363
Felton-Empire Vineyards, Santa Cruz County, California, 552
Fen Chiu, Chinese grain spirit, 181
Fendant, Valais, 232
Fendant (variety of Chasselas grape), 232, 99, 173, 491
Fenn Valley Vineyards, Michigan, 564
fennel as flavoring for spirits, 81, 255
Fennelly Farm Vineyard, New Jersey, 568
Fer, grape, in Bergerac, 113
Fèrebrianges, Champagne, 165
fermé (Fr.), firm or stubborn wine, 232
fermentation, 232–33, 40, 41–43, 45, 51; of beer, 111; mannitic, 324, 50, 53; secondary

(malolactic), 324, 43, 45, 46, 50, 104, 169, 183; stopping, 44, 484–85; *see also* sulfur dioxide
Fernan Nuñez, Montilla, 340
Fernão Pires, Portug. grape, 400
Fernet Branca, Ital. bitters, 233, 115
Ferrara, Allen, founder of Grand Cru Vineyards, 543
Ferrer, Gloria, winery, Sonoma, California, 542–43
ferric phosphate, precipitate of, in casse, 54
ferric tannate, precipitate of, in casse, 54
Ch. Ferrière, Haut-Médoc, 232, 128, 326, 333, 624
Ferrigno Vineyards, Missouri, 567
ferrocyanide, *see* potassium ferrocyanide
Festigny, Champagne, 165
Fetească Albă, grape, in Czechoslovakia, 219; in Rumania, 444, 445
Fetească Neagră, Rumanian grape, 445
Fetească Regale, grape, in Czechoslovakia, 219
Fetească de Tîrnave, Rumania, 445
Fetzer Vineyards, Mendocino County, California, 547
Feuerbach, Baden, 674
Feuerberg, Grosslage, Palatinate, 375, 661–2
feuillettes, Burgundian half-barrels, 143, 155
Fèves, Les, vd Côte de Beaune, 109, 203, 208
Fez, Morocco, 343
Fiano, Ital. grape, 232, 147, 148
Fiano di Avellino (D.O.C.), Campania, 148
fiasco, Ital. wine flask, 232, 176, 507–8
Fichots, Les, vd Côte de Beaune, 382
Ficklin Vineyards, Madera County, California, 521, 557
Fiddletown vds., Sacramento Valley, 555
Fiefs Vendéens, V.D.Q.S., 588
Field, Walter, owner of Monteviña Vineyards, 556
Field Stone Winery, Sonoma, California, 542
field-budding, 34
Fiètres, Les, vd Côte de Beaune, 65
Ch. de Fieuzal, Graves, 232, 128, 261, 652
Ch. Figeac, Saint-Émilion, 232, 88, 127, 453, 631
Ch. Filhot, Sauternes, 232, 213, 461, 660
fillette (Fr.), half-bottle, 234, 124
film yeast, see *flor*
Filsen, Mittelrhein, 680
Filsen, Saar-Ruwer, 351, 683
Fine Champagne, blend of Grande and Petite Champagne brandies, 234, 193
Fine Maison, restaurant house-specialty brandy, 193
finesse (Fr.), breed of wine, 234, 133
Finger Lakes, dist. New York, 234, 129, 221, 569–73
Finger Lakes Wine Cellars, New York, 571
fining of wine *(collage),* 234, 44, 46, 183
finish (aftertaste) of wine, 234
Fink Winery, Michigan, 565–66
Fino, dry Sherry with *flor,* 234, 340, 464, 466, 467, 468, 469
Finos de Mesa (Sp.), fine table wines, 434
Fins Bois, dist. Cognac, 234, 190, 192, 193
Fior d'Alpi (Edelweiss), Ital. flower-flavored liqueur, 234, 227
Fiorano, wine, Latium, 301
Firestone Vineyard, The, Santa Barbara, California, 559
firkin, beer barrel, 234
Fisch, Obermosel, 682
Fischerpfad, vd Rheinhessen, 424
Fischingen, Baden, 674
Fisher Ridge Wine Company, W. Virginia, 584
Fisher Winery, Sonoma, California, 542
Fitou (Appellation Contrôlée), dist. S. France, 234
Fitz-Ritter, wine estate, Palatinate, 375
fixed acidity, 235, 50, 60
Fixey, comm. Côte de Nuits, 136
Fixin (Appellation Contrôlée), comm. Côte de Nuits, 235, 136, 141, 203, 205, 206, 207, 208, 560
Flagey-Échezeaux, comm. Côte de Nuits, 235, 205, 208, 226, 259, 598
flagon, bottle, 235
Flame Tokay, American table grape, 520, 556
flat wine, 235
Flehingen, Baden, 673
Flein, Württemberg, 701
Flemlingen, Palatinate, 695
fleur (Mycoderma), film of micro-organisms, 53
Ch. La Fleur-Pourret, Saint-Émilion, 128
Fleurie (Appellation Contrôlée), Beaujolais, 235, 103, 104, 105, 107, 142, 289
Fleury-la-Rivière, Champagne, 165

fliers, particles in wine, 235
Flip, mixed drink, 235
Floc, aperitif, 236, 87
Floc, 223
Flomborn, Rheinhessen, 694
Flonheim, Rheinhessen, 691
flor (flowers of wine), film of micro-organisms, 236, 53, 217, 289, 340; on Sherry, 53, 236, 466–67, 468; "submerged flor" technique in California, 520–21
Flor Fino, Cyprus, 217
Flora Springs Winery, Napa, California, 534
floraison (Fr.), flowering of vines, 236, 36
Florence, wine of, 4, 5
Florida, state U.S.A., 560
Florida Bunch, grape, 560
Flörsheim, Rheingau, 690
Flörsheim-Dalsheim, Rheinhessen, 694
flowers of wine, see *flor*
flowery wine, 236
fluid ounce, 236
Flussbach, Bernkastel, 682
flûte (Fr.), bottle, 236
Foch, American hybrid grape, 519, 560, 566, 585; in Canada, 149
Foggia, prov. S. Italy, 80
Föhn wind, 99
Folatières, Les, vd Côte de Beaune, 409
Folha de Figo (Fig Leaf), grape, in Brazil, 132
Folle (Fuella), grape, in Provence, 407
Folle Blanche, grape, 236; in Armagnac, 86; in California, 517, 522; in Cognac, 194, 489; hybrid with Noah, *see* Baco 22A; in Nantes, 356
Fondillón, Valencia, 479
Ch. Fonplégade, Saint-Émilion, 631
Fonquernie, M., daughter of, owner of Ch. Suduiraut, 484
Ch. Fonréaud, Haut-Médoc, 307, 626
Ch. Fonroque, Saint-Émilion, 631
Fontaine Denis Nuisy, Champagne, 165
Fontenay, comm. Chablis, 155, 157
Fonteny, Le, vd Côte de Nuits, 254
Fontès, comm. Languedoc, 210
food: wine as, 27–28; wine with, 10–12
Foote, E.B., Winery, Washington, 583
Foppiano Winery, Sonoma, California, 542
Forastera, Ital. grape, 148
Forbidden Fruit, American shaddock liqueur, 236
Forchtenberg, Württemberg, 702
foreshots, in whisky-making, 236
Forêts, Les, vd chablis, 157
Forgeron Vineyard, Oregon, 578
Forrester family, owners of Bôa Vista, Alto Douro, 116
Forst, Palatinate, 373, 374, 375, 377, 698
Förster, Emil, wine estate, Rheinhessen, 427
Forster Jesuitengarten, vd Palatinate, 236
Forster Kirchenstück, vd Palatinate, 236
Fort-de-France, Martinique, rum center, 441
Ch. Fortia, vd Rhône Valley, 174
fortified wines, 236, 12, 44, 45; ageing, 46; Australian, 90; in California, 520–2, 523, 528, 535, 556; Chilean, 177; Madeira, 319–21; sweet, of France, 486–89, map, 488; Tunisian, 504; Turkish, 505; in Uruguay, 586; *see also* Port; Sherry
forzato (Ital.), wine from overripe grapes, 236
Fosse, La, vd Chalonnais, 159
Fouchère, vd Côte de Nuits, 254
foudre (Fr.), *Fuder* (Germ.), large cask, 236, 244
foulograppe (Fr.), grape stemmer, 483
Fountaingrove Vineyard, Sonoma dist., California, 540
fountains of wine, 609
Four Sisters Winery, New Jersey, 568
Ch. Fourcas-Dupré, Haut-Médoc, 128, 236, 307, 626
Ch. Fourcas-Hosten, Haut-Médoc, 236–37, 128, 307, 626
Fourcaud-Laussac, M., owner of Ch. Cheval-Blanc, 175
Fourchaume, vd Chablis, 157
Fournier, Charles, New York State sparkling wines, 512, 569, 571, 572, 573
Fournières, Les, vd Côte de Beaune, 66
Fourtet (Clos Fourtet), Saint-Émilion, 237, 127, 453, 631
Fousselottes, Les, vd Côte de Nuits, 161
fox-grape, *Vitis labrusca,* eastern American species, 237, 37, 40, 149, 180, 517, 569
Foxwood Wine Cellars, South Carolina, 580
foxy taste of wine, 237, 197, 276, 278, 517

Index

Index

Index

Index

Index

Nordhausen, Württemberg, 701
Nordheim, Franconia, 243, 678
Nordheim, Württemberg, 701
Nordweil, Baden, 676
Norheim, Nahe, 367, 363, 687
Norsingen, Baden, 675
Norte, Argentina, 84
North Carolina, state U.S.A., 575–76
North Coast region, California, 530–56
Northern Vineyards, Minnesota, 566
Northland, New Zealand, 366
Northminster Winery, Delaware, 560
Norton, American grape, 367
Norway, 367; aquavit, 81–82, 367
Norwegian punch, 410
nose, bouquet of wine, 367
Nostrano, Ticino, 492
Notre-Dame du Raisin, Brouilly, pilgrimage to, 108
Novocherkassk, Russia, 447
Noyau (crème de noyau), liqueur, 367, 214
nu (Fr.), price of wine without container, 368
Nuckton, Deryck, owner of Monterey Peninsula Winery, 554
Nuits-Prémeaux, comm. Côte de Nuits, 208; *see also* Prémeaux
Nuits-Saint-Georges (Appellation Contrôlée), comm. Côte de Nuits, 368–9, 141, 203, 205, 206–7, 208; marc of, 324, 368
Numa Pompilius, wine regulations, 185
Nuragus di Cagliari (D.O.C.), Sardinia, 458
Nussbach, Baden, 676
Nussbaum, Nahe, 688
Nussbien, vd Palatinate, 375, 377, 445
Nussbrunnen, vd Rheingau, 419
Nussdorf, Palatinate, 695
Nussdorf, nr. Vienna, 94, 96
Nussloch, Baden, 673
Nussriegel, vd Palatinate, 375
nylon powder for fining white wine, 46

O

oak for barrels, 370, 364; Limousin, 56, 86, 123–24, 131, 190, 195; for whisky, 603, 608
Oak Knoll Winery, Oregon, 578
Oak Ridge Vineyards, Sacramento Valley, California, 556
Oakencroft Vineyards, Virginia, 582
Oasis Vineyards, Virginia, 582
oast house, 370
Ober-Flörsheim, Rheinhessen, 694
Ober-Hilbersheim, Rheinhessen, 691
Ober-Olm, Rheinhessen, 692
Oberberg, vd Rheingau, 421
Oberbergen, Baden, 675
Oberbillig, Obermosel, 683
Oberdiebach, Mittelrhein, 680
Oberdingen, Württemberg, 690
Obereggenen, Baden, 675
Obereisenheim, Franconia, 678
Oberemmel, Saar-Ruwer, 351, 370, 684
Oberfell, Zell-Mosel, 686
Oberhausen, Palatinate, 696
Oberhausen an der Nahe, Nahe, 687, 688
Oberheimbach, Mittelrhein, 679
Oberhellman Vineyards, Texas, 581
Oberkirch, Baden, 676
Oberlauda, Baden, 674
Oberlin Wine Institute, Colmar, 68
Obermoschel, Nahe, 693
Obermosel, Bereich, Mosel-Saar-Ruwer, 250, 344, 350; towns and vds, list, 682–3
Obernai, Alsace, 68
Oberndorf, Nahe, 688
Obernhof, Mittelrhein, 680
Oberreihen, dist. Germany, 251
Oberrimsingen, Baden, 675
Oberrotterbach, Palatinate, 695
Oberrotweil, Baden, 676, 99
Obersasbach, Baden, 677
Oberschopfheim, Baden, 676
Oberschüpf, Baden, 674
Oberschwarzach, Franconia, 679
Obersöllbach, Württemberg, 702
Oberstenfeld, Württemberg, 701
Oberstetten, Württemberg, 702
Oberstreit, Nahe, 688
Obersülzen, Palatinate, 699
Obertsrot, Baden, 677
Oberuhldingen, Baden, 674
Obervolkach, Franconia, 678
Oberwalluf, Rheingau, 393, 690
Oberweier, Baden, 676

Oberwessel, Mittelrhein, 338, 680
Obester Winery, San Mateo County, California, 552
Obrigheim, Palatinate, 697
obscuration, in alcoholic strength of brandy, 370
Occidente, Argentina, 84
Ochagavia, Silvestre, founder of Chilean viniculture, 179
Ockenheim, Rheinhessen, 428, 692
Ockfen, Saar-Ruwer, 350, 351, 684
Ockfener Bockstein, Saar-Ruwer, 370
octave, small cask, 370, 608
Ödakra Taffel Aquavit, Swedish, 81
Odenas, Beaujolais-Villages, 105, 108
Odenheim, Baden, 673
Odernheim, Nahe, 688
Odessa, 447; Technical Wine Institute, 446
Odinstal, vd Palatinate, 377
Odobeşti, vd Rumania, 444, 445
odors, wine contaminated by, 54
Ödsbach, Baden, 676
Odysseus, 2, 184, 187
Oechslé degrees, 370; alcoholic content and specific gravity, Baumé equivalents, table, 82
Oedheim, Württemberg, 702
oeil de perdrix (Fr.), pinkish tint in white wines, 370, 490, 597
oenology, science of wine, 370, 594
Oesterreichischer (Sylvaner, Franken Riesling), grape, 370; *see also* Sylvaner
Oestrich (Östrich), Rheingau, 689
Oetinger, Freiherr von, wine estate, Rheingau, 418
Oeuilly, Champagne, 165
off-license, English, 370
Offenau, Württemberg, 702
Offenburg, Baden, 686
Offenheim, Rheinhessen, 695
Office International du Vin, 6, 505
Oger, Champagne, 165
Oggau, Burgenland, 370, 94, 95, 135
Ohio, state U.S.A., 576–7, 221
Ohligsberg, vd Bernkastel, 330
Ohlsbach, Baden, 676
Ohrid, Macedonia, 615, 618
oïdium, powdery mildew, 371, 6, 38, 129, 403; in Beaujolais, 108; in Bordeaux, 259; in Canary Islands, 482; in Japan, 287; in Madeira, 319, 320; in New Zealand, 365; in Spain, 435
Oiry, Champagne, 165
Okanagan Valley, British Columbia, 148, 149, 150
Okayama, dist. Japan, 287
O'Keefe, Edward, owner of Ch. Grand Travers, 565
Oklahoma, state U.S.A., 577
okolehao (oke), Hawaiian spirit, 371
Oktemberian, Armenia, 447
Öküz Gözü, Turkish grape, 510
Olaszrisling, Hung. grape, 274, 275
Ölberg, vd Rheinhessen, 427
Old South Winery, Mississippi, 566
Old Tom gin, 371, 255
oldest bottled wine, 371
Oleron's disease (bacterial blight of vines), 371, 38
Oliena, Sardinia, 458
Olifants River, S. Africa, 475
Oliver, Bill, vd. owner, 562
Oliver Wine Co., Indiana, 562
Ch. Olivier, Graves, 371, 260, 652
Olizy-Violaine, Champagne, 164
Ollioules, comm. Provence, 407
Ollon, Vaud, 490
Olmo, Dr. H. P., of University of California College of Agriculture, 515, 517, 528
Oloroso, Sherry without *flor*, 371, 133, 340, 464, 466
Olson, Leonard, Michigan wine pioneer, 564, 565
Oltrepò Pavese (D.O.C.), Lombardy, 371, 312
Olympus, Cypriot wine, 217
Omar Khayyám, 228, 278
Ondenc, grapes, 113, 245
Onsdorf, Obermosel, 683
Ontario, prov. Canada, 148–49
oölite, limestone clay, 202
Opfingen, Baden, 675
Ophthalmo, Cypriot grape, 217
Opimian, Roman vintage wine of 121 B.C., 371, 186, 188
Opol, Dalmatia, 617
Oporto, Hungarian grape, 274, 275
Oporto, Portugal, 371, 393; Factory House, 232, 397; Port shipped from, 4
Oppenheim, Rheinhessen, 371, 423, 428, 692, 693
Optima, hybrid grape, 376
Oran, dept. Algeria, 64

orange, bitter, as flavoring for aquavit, 80
orange bitters, 371, 115
orange brandy, 371
orange gin, 256
orange liqueurs, 215, 258, 334, 442
Orange Muscat, grape, 557
orange peel as flavoring for gin, 255
Orange River, S. Africa, 473, 474
orange wine: Brazil, 371; Louisiana, 562
Orbe, Vaud, 490
Orbel, vd Rheinhessen, 427
Ordensgut, Grosslage, Palatinate, 376, 696
Ordinaire, Dr., inventor of absinthe, 59
ordinaire (Fr.), everyday wine, 371
Oregon, state U.S.A., 371, 577–78
Orgeat, flavoring syrup, 371
Orianda (Sémillon Oreanda), Crimea, 447, 449
Originalabfüllung, Originalabzug (Germ.), estate-bottled or pure, unsweetened wine, 372, 230, 462
Orlando, vd New South Wales, 91
Orlando, wine producer S. Australia, 90, 92
Orme, En l', vd Côte de Beaune, 109
Ormeau, L', vd Côte de Beaune, 597
Ormes, Champagne, 163
Ch. Les Ormes-de-Pez, Haut-Médoc, 128, 627
Ormož, Slovenia, 618
Orta Vova (D.O.C.), Apulia, 80
Ortega, Ger. grape, 511
Ortenau, Bereich, Baden, 99–100, 676–7
Ortenberg, Baden, 100, 676
Orthsberg, vd Saar-Ruwer, 351, 353
Ortiz Garza, Nazario, Mexican wine- and brandy-maker, 336
Orveaux, En, vd Côte de Nuits, 226
Orvieto (D.O.C.), Umbria, 372, 286, 510
Osaka, dist. Japan, 372, 287
Osann-Monzel, Bernkastel, 681
Osey (Aussey), Rhenish wine in England, 3, 4, 66
Osiris, Daniel, donor of Ch. La Tour-Blanche to French State, 296
Osler, Sir William, on wine, 30
Osterberg, vds Rheinhessen: (Bingen), 424; (Selzen), 424
Osterspai, Mittelrhein, 680
Osthofen, Rheinhessen, 428, 692
Östrich (Oestrich), Rheingau, 428, 689
Östringen, Baden, 673
Ostuni (D.O.C.), Apulia, 80
Othello, Cypriot wine, 217
Ötisheim, Württemberg, 701
Ötlingen, Baden, 674
Otsuka Pharmaceutical Co., owners of Ridge Vineyards, 553
Ottersheim, Palatinate, 696
Ottersheim/Zellertal, Palatinate, 698
Ottersweier, Baden, 677
Otto I, Holy Roman Emperor, 94
Ottonel, Hung. grape, 274; *see also* Muscat Ottonel
Oudart, Frère Jean, work with Champagne, 163
Oudtshoorn, S. Africa, 472
ouillage (Fr.), ullage, topping of wine to compensate for evaporation, 372, 43
Ouras grape, 245
ouvrée (Fr.), old Burgundian land measure, 372
ouzo, Gk and Cypriot spirit, 372, 218, 228, 264
Överste Brännvin, Swedish, 81
oxhoft, Scandinavian liquid measure, 372
oxidation, 372, 43–4, 45, 46, 498; *see also* maderization of wine
Oyes, Champagne, 165
Ozark Vineyards, Missouri, 567

P

Paarl, S. Africa, 373, 473–76
Pacherenc du Vic Bilh (Appellation Contrôlée), Pyrenees, 373, 322
Padthaway, dist. S. Austalia, 93
Pagney-derrière-Barine, comm. Lorraine, 313
pai chiu, Chinese grain spirits, 181
Paien, grape, 491
Paigny-les-Reims, Champagne, 165
País, Chilean grape, 373, 177, 179
Palacio da Brejoeira, Portugal, 399
Palatinate (Pfalz, Rheinpfalz), S. Germany, 373–76, 24, 247, 250, 251, 253; map, 374
Palestine, ancient wines of, 2, 280
Palette (Appellation Contrôlée), Provence, 376, 408
Pallas, M., Fr. wine expert in Crimea, 447
Pallet, Le, comm. Loire Valley, 356

Index

Index

Index

Index

Index

Index